Technological Economics

Shoubo Xu

Technological Economics

北京交通大学出版社
http://www.bjtup.com.cn

Springer

Shoubo Xu
Beijing Jiaotong University
Beijing, China

ISBN 978-981-15-8581-4 ISBN 978-981-15-8582-1 (eBook)
https://doi.org/10.1007/978-981-15-8582-1

Jointly published with Beijing Jiaotong University Press
The print edition is not for sale in Chinese mainland. Customers from Chinese mainland please order the print book from: Beijing Jiaotong University Press.

This Springer imprint is published by the registered company Springer Nature Singapore Pte Ltd.
The registered company address is: 152 Beach Road, #21-01/04 Gateway East, Singapore 189721, Singapore

Preface

Between December 1962 and April 1963, based on the request from the Party Central Committee headed by Mao Zedong regarding establishing a new discipline that would combine technology and economics together, the Party Central Committee Leadership for Science assigned the author of this book three tasks: investigating the relevant domestic and international progress made on the subject, coining a new subject to be called "technological economics", and drafting the outline of developing technological economy in China. As an important emerging scientific research field, technological economics was initiated in 1962 and was officially launched in the Ten-Year National Scientific and Technological Development Plan (1963–1972),[1] which was approved by the Party Central Committee and the State Council in 1963. The newly-named field of technological economics was listed in the development plan and became one of the seven main science and technology research fields, together with subjects such as natural resource study, industrial science and technology, agricultural science and technology, medical science and technology, science of technology, and basic science. For the first time, technological economics was listed together with other main research fields in the history of Chinese science and technology development, even in the history of science and technology development in the world, with profound significance. However, unlike in other main research fields mentioned above, the theories and research methods in technological economics were still awaiting development; thus, the new field could not be named as the science and technology of technological economics, or the science of technological economics. Therefore, the term "technological economics" was used and adopted.

Exploring theories and research methods in technological economics was the most important task in the aforementioned development plan regarding technological economy. Because no one else took on this task, the author of this book

[1]The Ten-Year National Scientific and Technological Development Plan (1963–1972) [EB/OL]. Available at http://www.most.gov.cn/ztzl/gjzcqgy/zcqgylshg/t20050831_24439.htm.

worked individually from 1963 to 1965 and finished the research report on Methodology in Technological Economics Study.[2] This report consists of six sections, namely the introduction, an economic evaluation criteria for technological problem-solving, comparison principles in technological economics, computational methods in technological economics, an example solution using technological economics, and using mathematical methods in technological economics research. It has 26 chapters and about 240,000 words. The main portion of the report was published in 1964 in the Chinese Science Bulletin, a journal of the Chinese Academy of Sciences, with the title Purpose, Task, and Methods in Technological Economics Research. This paper comprehensively and systematically proposed the core of technological economics, including the definition of technological economics, the basic principles of the contradictory but unified development relationship between technology and economy, the purposes and meaning of technological economic research, three important tasks and 12 aspects of technological economic research, two research methods and five research steps in technological economic studies, the integrative and interdisciplinary characteristics of technological economics, and the relationship between technological economics and other related sub-disciplines, such as agricultural technological economics, industrial technological economics, technological economics in the construction industry, and technological economics in transportation industry. It was well received by party leaders and experts.

In 1965, the expert panel on comprehensively utilizing combustible minerals from the State Scientific and Technological Commission[3] recommended publishing the research report On Methodology in Technological Economics Study. However, due to the burst of the Great Cultural Revolution in 1966, this report was not published as a book. Instead, it was criticized publicly. The author of this book, unfortunately, was named as a "reactionary academic authority" and was criticized.

After the Third Plenary Session of the 11th Central Committee of the Communist Party of China in 1978, technological economics as a discipline was reborn. Accordingly, the author named the research report of On Methodology in Technological Economics as *Introduction to Technological Economics* and it was published by Shanghai Science and Technology Press in 1980 with its original content, five sections, 26 chapters, and about 240,000 words. It has attracted attentions from scholars in China as well as scholars across the world. For example, after reviewing this book, Eric Dark, a Swedish scholar, noted that "neither the name of technological economics nor its research methods appeared in the economics studies existed in the Soviet Union" in his article entitled Chinese Technological Economics[4] which was published in the September Issue, 1981, in

[2]Actually it is the prototype of Introduction to Technological Economics published in 1980.

[3]The author was the youngest member in the expert panel of comprehensively utilizing combustible minerals of the State Scientific and Technological Commission. The leader was Hou Xianglin, a member of Chinese Academy of Sciences.

[4]Eric Dark, Chinese Technological Economics, Translation Series for Quantitative and Technological Economics, 1983, (1): pp. 36–42 (Translation of Asian Survey, September Issue, 1981).

an American journal entitled *Asian Survey*. He made the following comments: "In Soviet Union's economics studies, the discipline that is the closest to technological economics is Industrial Sector Economics"; "Technological economics is somewhat closer to the cost-benefit analysis in western economics studies"; and "It is very interesting to study the concepts in the discipline of technological economics." This feedback proved that the discipline of technological economics established by a Chinese scholar was not only well known in China, but also internationally known. In 1980, *Introduction to Technological Economics* as the first book on technological economics was published for the first time in the world. The technological economic principles and methods introduced in this book reflected the characteristics of planned socialist economy which was established by the first generation party leadership headed by Mao Zedong, which focused on hard technological economics and macro-technological economics.

By implementing the reform and opening up policy, the second generation Party Central Committee headed by Deng Xiaoping initiated the new era of socialist market economy. As the Founding Executive Director of the Chinese Society for Technological Economics and the Founding Director of the Institute of Technological Economics of the Chinese Academy of Social Sciences, the author of this book delivered numerous lectures and presentations on technological economics at diverse forums and classes hosted by the central government and provincial governments, as well as at Tsinghua University, Beijing College of Chemical Industry,[5] and the Graduate School of Chinese Academy of Social Sciences.[6] The audiences included government employees, professors, graduate students, college students, engineers, and managers.

In 1984, entrusted by China Association for Science and Technology (CAST), the author finished the book *Technological Economics*, which has two volumes, 24 chapters, and 450,000 words and was published by the CAST Lecturer Group and China Society of Science and Technology Policy Studies. This is the second edition of the technological economics monograph. Compared with the first edition, the second one offered new content, such as the ten characteristics of technological economics, the six-force theory, evaluation principles for greater, faster, better, and more economical results, comprehensive evaluation principles and their quantitative computational methods, new methods for defining economic effect coefficients, setting reasonable prices for imported and exported goods, methods for setting proper tax rates and interest rates, and many examples of new applications. In addition, the second edition absorbed new overseas research achievements, such as serial decision-making and probability analysis methods, and it reviewed the use of feasible study and value engineering adopted in western economy. The second edition was selected as the teaching material for continuing education for scientific and technological management cadres.

---

[5]Teacher Training Session for Technological Economics Program in higher education institutions in China.

[6]Technological Economics was chosen as the textbook.

It was officially proposed at the Third Plenary Session of the 12th Central Committee of Communist Party of China in 1984 that the Chinese economic system was a socialist planned commodity economy, which emphasized not only macro-control, but also micro-invigoration. In other words, this economic system focused on both macro- and micro-economic results. Directed by this newly launched principle and policy, the author updated and revised the second edition. In 1986, the third edition was published by Jiangsu People's Publishing House. This edition had eight sections, 35 chapters, and 600,000 words. It expanded the content in the second edition by adding the theories, research methodologies, and applications of micro-technological economics. The first and second editions of this book mainly covered macro-technological economics, which fitted a socialist planned economy. The third edition covered integrative technological economics, which included both macro-technological and micro-technological economics and fitted a socialist planned commodity economy. This was a major breakthrough and a significant movement put forward by the reform of the Chinese economic system. Soon after the third edition was published, it became the textbook for the major of Technological Economics in higher education institutions across China.

In 1988, in order to better meet the diverse needs from the society in China, especially the demands from engineers and technicians as well as from college students majoring in science and engineering, the author revised the third edition and compressed the content according to feedback from readers. Published again by Jiangsu People's Publishing House, the fourth edition had four sections and 19 chapters, reduced from eight sections and 35 chapters in the third edition. The words reduced from 600,000 to 400,000, accordingly. However, the fourth edition made improvements to the scope and depth of the book as well as to the practicability of its content. It consisted of four sections: Introduction to Technological Economics, Theories of Technological Economics, Research Methods of Technological Economics, and Applications of Technological Economics. More specifically, Introduction to Technological Economics roundly elaborated the six characteristics of theory and research methods in a technological economics study: (1) guided by the economic theories of Marxism and Mao Zedong Thought; (2) based on the economic law of socialism and law of value; (3) aiming at achieving greater, faster, better, and more economical results in building socialism; (4) adopting both qualitative and quantitative methods; (5) considering the practice of Chinese Socialist Modernization Construction; and (6) aiming at correctly understanding and handling the relationships of unity and contradiction, and the developments and changes between technology and economy. This section creatively extended the concept of technology and proposed a new concept, generalized technology, which included soft technology and hard technology. In addition, this section discussed the objects of study of newly proposed generalized technology. In the Principles of Technological Economics section, the author originally proposed six principles in technological economics: (1) the principle of effect in technological economics; (2) the standardization principle in technological economics; (3) the comparative principle in technological economics; (4) the optimization principle in technological economics; (5) forecasting and decision-making in technological economics; and (6) information and control in technological economics. Specifically, the author elaborated the principle of effect in technological economics and further proposed seven sub-principles, namely, the contradictory and unification principle in technological economics, the principle of economic effect indicators, the principle of economic increment, the principle of time effect, the principle of supply and demand effect, the principle of systems, and the principal of six forces substitution. In order to make it more readable, the author adjusted the order of the methods introduced in Section Three by moving the methods for computing each single index, specifically the method for computing time factor, to the beginning and by placing comprehensive computing methods at the end. This section combined the strength of economic analysis methods in the East and the West and added new content to the methods for computing time factors, the methods for technological economic assessment, and the methods for comprehensively assessing technologies. Considering that the number of application cases had been limited in the third edition, the author added application cases regarding micro-technological economic theories and methods in the fourth section, including some daily life cases. Therefore, the fourth edition could meet not only the requirements from governmental officials, consulting firms, banks, financial institutions for policy-making, planning, macro-economic control, capital investment, feasibility studies, and project appraisal, but also requirements from engineers, technicians, and business management practitioners who conduct engineering design, product development, operations management. Furthermore, the fourth edition could serve as a good reference for readers from the third industry in the fields of scientific research, culture, education, and healthcare, as well as for ordinary families. The unique characteristic of the fourth edition was that it combined and unified macro-technological economics and micro-technological economics in theories, methods, and applications. As such, it was selected as the textbook for a required course in the national Continuing Education Program for Engineers approved by the Central Radio and TV University. It has been printed several times and has helped more than 100,000 people pass the exam in Beijing. The fourth edition has played a key role in training engineers and technicians.

Since 1988, China has made tremendous progress in economic and societal development under the leadership of the Central Committee of the Communist Party of China, headed by Deng Xiaoping, Jiang Zemin, and Hu Jintao, respectively. Especially after the 14th National Congress of the Communist Party of China in 1992 that clarified the goal of establishing a socialist market economy system in China, the economy in China has been developing even more rapidly. For nearly 20 years, the author worked at the Technological Economy Research Institute of the State Development and Planning Commission (SDPC), and at Beijing Jiao Tong University, respectively. During this period, the author conducted a series of important studies about the soft technological economy and the hard technological economy for the state, for local governments, and for firms and obtained more than 200 findings. This number was greater than the total that the author had obtained before 1988. Thus, the author thought that it was necessary to add these 200-plus findings to the latest book of this book. Meanwhile, the author enriched and improved the theories and methods in technological economics according to the requirements of the socialist market economy system. This book made technological economics have more of the characteristics of Chinese Economics in the East, more original content, and more practical results of implementation. It will help researchers and scholars, both in China and overseas, to better understand the history and achievements of technological economics which was born in China and has contributed to the development of Chinese economy and society and the great rejuvenation of the Chinese nation.

More than 60 years have passed since the new China was founded. Almost 50 years have passed since Technological Economics was approved by the Party Central Committee and the State Council to be listed in the Ten-Year National Scientific and Technological Development Plan (1963–1972). The author, who began to study the theories, methods, and applications of technological economics in 1963, has continued the study for more than 50 years. Although 50 years is only a short period in the development of the Chinese nation, it is the majority of a person's life. The author was criticized heavily during the Great Cultural Revolution because of establishing and developing this new inter-discipline. Chinese technological economics has experienced unusual development path. The author once noted: "Establishing a discipline is hard, but it is harder to make people accept it. Be persistent and dauntless, because all difficulties will be overcome one day. This is the law for invention, discovery, and innovation."[7]

The characteristics of this book include the movement from a technological economics study focusing on macro-technological economics theories and methods and the problem-solving for hard technological economy issues before the reform and opening up, to the focus shifting to micro-technological economy theories and methods and the problem-solving of both hard and soft technological economy issues after the reform and opening up, and finally to fixing hard and soft technological economy issues by combining macro- and micro-technological economy theories and methods. That is the focus of the technological economics study today: technological economics with unique Chinese characteristics. The book is abundant in content and works to combine theory and practice. Many cases in this edition are significant technological economy issues in China that are currently awaiting solutions. The research results in this edition have attracted much attention from leaders in the Party Central Committee and are adopted in practice. Great economic benefits and social benefits have been achieved, due to this adoption.

It must be pointed out that although the materials and data in the previous editions are out of date, they still serve to support an elaboration of theories and methods. Therefore, the latest book retains them, unchanged. On one hand, these materials and data help readers know better about the history of technological economics. On the other hand, time-sensitive materials and data are changing all the time. Any update at present time will be out of date soon. Thus, there is no need to update these materials and data.

[7]Xu Shoubo: Epigraph for the 45th anniversary of Science Times (published in Science Times on November 24, 2003).

In order to adopt and unify terms and notations in technological economics, the technical terms in technological economics originally born in China were adopted. Chinese Pinyin is used as well.

According to the scientific outlook on development, the book still needs improvement, although it has included more new innovative materials and enhancements as compared with previous editions. The author hopes to continue revising and improving the book in his remaining years. There is no end to studying. So keep studying and never stop. There is no end to researching either. So continue making innovations and never stop.[8]

The author wants to express his thankfulness to the chief editor Lv Ping and editor Li Xue from Economic Science Press, and Xu Lida, Hou Hanping, Huang Zongyuan, and Guo Lihua from Beijing Jiao Tong University. Without their help and support, this book would not be available.

Beijing, China
September, 2011

Shoubo Xu

[8]Xu Shoubo: Epigraph for graduates of Beijing Jiao Tong University in 2009 (on the graduates' album of Beijing JiaoTong University in 2009).

Contents

About the Author

Shoubo Xu (1931–), Shaoxing, Zhejiang province, graduated from power engineering department of Nanjing Institute of Technology in 1955. In 1960, he received his Ph.D. in technology and science from the Energy Institute of the former Academy of Sciences of USSR. He was elected as an academician of the Chinese Academy of Engineering in 2001. He is a professor and doctoral supervisor at the School of Economics and Management, Beijing Jiaotong University. He serves as the founding director of China Center for Economic Research, the Institute of Logistics, and Comprehensive Energy Research Institute at Beijing Jiaotong University.

For more than 50 years, he has been specialized in scientific research and teaching at the Chinese Academy of Sciences, the Chinese Academy of Social Sciences, the China National Development and Reform Commission, and the Ministry of Education.

He has made 449 theoretical and application achievements, including technological economics, comprehensive energy engineering, logistics, and management, in four disciplines, with more than 50 awards, including nine scientific and technological progress awards (one for each country and one third for the country, one for the provincial and ministerial level, four for the second prize, and twice for the third prize).

He served as the national science and technology economy and management modernization of the expert group members, the first secretary-general, Chinese technical and economic research institute, Chinese academy of social sciences institute of technology economy (now number of economy and technology research institute) first, graduate school of Chinese academy of social sciences, director of technology economics (now number economic predecessor of the department of economics and technology) of the first department, the state planning commission technical and economic research institute (now the national development and reform commission, the industry economy and technology research institute) director.

He served as the national science and technology commission combustible comprehensive utilization of mineral expert group members, the technical and economic research center under the state council energy group, national energy commission, head of the advisory, the department of energy senior advisory committee and the state council NengYuanBan research advisory bureau, the first deputy executive director of the energy institute—the first Beijing energy society, the first vice President of Chinese society for the study of the energy base, ZongKaoHui comprehensive energy, Chinese academy of science (now the national development and reform commission energy research institute), head of the first. He was the first vice President of China logistics research association and the first director of logistics technical economics committee of China logistics association.

The Technical Economics (fifth edition, Beijing: economic science press, 2011.8) written by Shoubo Xu academician won the third session of the Chinese government published book award nomination. This award is not only affirmed Shoubo Xu academician "technical economics" original subject status and contribution, at the same time for "technical economics" in the new era better promote social and economic development is of great significance.

Part I
Introduction to Technological Economics

This section describes the most significant research result achieved by the author during his early study on technological economics. As the most important part of this book, this section is the foundation for the following sections. There are six chapters in this section. The first chapter elaborates the origin and development of technological economics according to the author's personal experience. The second chapter covers the objects of technological economics study. The purpose and meaning of technological economics study is discussed in the third chapter. The fourth chapter points out the tasks and contents of technological economics study. In the fifth chapter, methods and procedure of technological economics study are introduced. Finally, the sixth chapter outlines the sub-disciplines of technological economics and the relationship between technological economics and other disciplines.

Chapter 1
Origin and Development of Technological Economics

1.1 Introduction

Did technological economics originate in China? Or did it originate in another country or other countries? How, when, and why did it form? What is its development process? How does it play on the economic and social development of China? The answers are not well known by young people in China or by scholars across the world. As such, based on his personal experience, the author elaborates how technological economics formed and developed as an inter-discipline under the leadership of Yu Guangyuan, a famous economist in the Party Central Committee Leadership for Science during early 1960s. This chapter consists of four parts: the background of technological economy plan, the history of technological economics, the development of technological economics, and the development prospects of technological economics.

1.2 Background of Technological Economy Plan

Before the start of the introduction to the origin of technological economics, the background of the technological economy plan must be explained. It is an objective fact that the technological economy's plan was made before technological economics formed.

It is well known that the former Soviet Union assisted China in establishing 156 key projects during the first five year plan (1952–1957) after new China was founded in 1949. China achieved great economic development at the end of the first five year plan. However, in the second five year plan (1958–1962), because of a number of reasons such as the Great Leap Forward, the Mass Movement of Making Iron, mass movements, natural disasters, and the breakup between China and the former Soviet Union, the Chinese economy decreased greatly. In December 1962, the Party Central Committee requested that a long term national economy plan and a long term

S. Xu, *Technological Economics*,
https://doi.org/10.1007/978-981-15-8582-1_1

science and technology plan for 1963–1972 be made. As such, the Party Central Committee Leadership for Science decided to make the second ten year (1963–1972) long-term national science and technology development plan independently, relying on Chinese experts. according to the first twelve year (1956–1967) long-term national science and technology development plan developed with the help of experts from the former Soviet Union. Yu Guangyuan, a well-known economist in the Party Central Committee Leadership for Science, proposed that technology development and related policy making should focus on economic effects and that technology should be integrated with economy. He assigned the author to conduct research and to find out if there was any discipline that focused on combining technology studies and economy studies. After careful study, the author found that there was a discipline called "power economics" inside the power department at the Moscow Institute of Engineering Economy in the former Soviet Union. This discipline was also called Industrial Sector Economics, but a discipline called "engineering economics" did not exist. In the literature of Industrial Sector Economics and investment effect studies, terms such as "technological economics index" and "technological economics analysis" existed, but there was no discipline called "technological economics" at that time. Meanwhile, the Chinese almost knew nothing about the situation in western world at that time. Few examples about combining technology and economy, such as how to determine the economic section of power leads, could be found in the engineering or technology literature in China. Accordingly, the author reported the situation to Yu Guangyuan and suggested that the new field that integrated technology and economy be named "technological economics", based on the requirement of the Party Central Committee Leadership for Science. Later, the suggestion was accepted after peer review among experts. Next, under the leadership of the State Science and Technology Commission (SSTC), from January to April in 1963 at Beijing Friendship Hotel, the author drafted the seventh chapter of this book, entitled Technological Economics in the Ten-Year National Scientific and Technological Development Plan (1963–1972). In December 1963, the outline was approved by the Party Central Committee and the State Council. It was listed as one of the seven main science and technology research fields in the Ten-Year National Scientific and Technological Development Plan (1963–1972).[1] But, unlike other main research fields such as industrial science and technology, agricultural science and technology, medical science and technology, the science of technology, and basic science, the theories and research methods in technological economics were still awaiting development; thus, the new field could not be named as "the science and technology of technological economics" or "the science of technological economics". As such, the term "technological economics" was used and adopted.

In conclusion, the technological economy plan in China was made at a most difficult time for Chinese social and economic development. It was the urgent requirement of the social and economic development in China. This is the background on

[1]The seven research fields include natural resource study, industrial science and technology, agricultural science and technology, medical science and technology, the science of technology, and basic science. More details are at the website of Ministry of Science and Technology of China.

which the technological economy plan in China was made. The following is the seventh chapter, titled Technological Economics in the Ten-Year National Scientific and Technological Development Plan (1963–1972), approved by the Party Central Committee and the State Council.

Chapter 7 Technological Economics

All production technologies must have technological advantages and economic rationality. Only after meeting these requirements can they be popularized and applied widely. Therefore, all results of production technology research must be analyzed from the perspectives of technology and economy before they are popularized in practice and then become the foundation for making state level technology measures, technology policies, and national economy development plans. The calculating, analyzing, and comparing the economic effects of each technology, in other words, conducting technology economic studies, is a significant component of scientific and technological work. It is also an important step in promoting science and technology to serve socialist construction greater, faster, better, and more economically.

The study of technological economics does not cost much money, but it can save a huge amount of manpower and resources in science and technology research, production, and construction. China is in the period of agricultural and industrial technological reform, so it is urgent to develop new technologies and to upgrade technological equipment. As such, enhancing the study of technological economics becomes extremely important.

The study of technological economics must be carried out widely. In scientific and technological work, various technological economic problems occur frequently. Scientific and technological workers should be encouraged to learn and to apply the methods of technological economics research. They also should be encouraged to conduct research on technological economics when they are working on their tasks.

The study of technological economics needs professionals to complete it. With the rapid development of science and technology and an increased connection between internal and external production segments, many comprehensive and complicated problems regarding technological economics appear. In order to resolve these problems, accumulating various technological economic data systematically and frequently, as well as studying and evaluating the theories and methods for economic effects of various technologies, are required. Due to the development of operational research and computers, more professionals who know technological economics and also have strong background in mathematic are needed. Therefore, professional study institutes are needed in order to train professional talent, to build professional research teams, and to establish research centers for technological economics, while a mass technological economics study is widely advocated.

More attention should be paid to comprehensive technological economics research on the allocation of productive forces. The unified socialism plan economy system in China requires allocating industrial and agricultural productive forces reasonably and establishing a transportation network, a power transmission network, and a communication network efficiently. Schemes for allocating productive forces must be supported by science and technology based on natural conditions, natural resources, and social and economic conditions. These schemes should be further studied from the perspective of technological economics. Such studies provide support for making the development plans of the national economy and for determining economic divisions.

In the next decade, special attention should be paid to the following issues regarding technological economics:

I. Technological economic research on utilizing land reasonably. This is indispensable for land utilization compartmentalization and for agricultural compartmentalization. Economic effects analysis and comparison must be performed based on natural area compartments, and it must take into consideration the research on agrometeorology, crop allocation, farming systems, and plans for farmland construction. A planting area for each crop is then proposed. Meanwhile, economic effects analysis must be conducted by considering different land types (grassland, mountainous region, and mudflat), climate, hydrologic conditions, and transportation conditions for developing agriculture, forestry, animal husbandry, by work, and fishery. Plans should be compared from the perspective of technological economics. Such research can provide systemic supports for exploiting the lands and the water areas in China.

II. Technological economic analysis on the comprehensive operations of agriculture, forestry, animal husbandry, by work, and fishery. The potential and economic effects of comprehensive operations of agriculture, forestry, animal husbandry, by work, and fishery must be determined, especially the combination of agriculture and animal husbandry, by calculating the consumption and circulation of food, feed, fertilizer, and fuel and by considering the balance of manpower. The proper redistribution of agricultural production in the suburban areas of large and middle size cities must be explored, according to demands for food, vegetables, fruits, livestock, eggs, and milk.

III. Technological economic research on agricultural technology reform. Based on the comprehensive analyses of how to increase the yield of a certain area and of improving labor productivity, research must be conducted on the relative economic effects of different steps in areas where mechanization, electrification, chemicalization, and adequate irrigation are achieved and other technological reform measures are adopted. Such research will provide support for related segments to be able to make plans regarding investments of agricultural technology reform and regarding allocation of agricultural machines and fertilizer. An economic effects analysis should also be conducted to consider changing the design of agricultural machines to meet the requirements of agriculture and changing the procedure of agriculture to meet the requirements of machines. Exploring the proper scale and distribution of tractor stations and the most economic plan for allocating agricultural machines should also be completed. When studying electrification in rural areas, the relative benefits between mains supply and small power plants in different areas should be analyzed. When studying water development and utilization, solutions for technological economic problems in flood control, irrigation, electric power generation, and shipping should be explored. The economic benefits of ground water utilization and underground water utilization should be compared. The proper irrigation scale should be studied. The relative economic effects of mechanical irrigation and drainage and electric irrigation and drainage in different areas should be compared, as well.

IV. Technological economic research on nutrition composition of food. The most economic and most proper nutrition programs for people at different ages and with different occupations according to the demands of calories and protein from human bodies, their present level of productivity, and the characteristics of agriculture in China, should be explored. A study the most proper ratio of agriculture production among staple food grain, minor cereals, beans, oil, meat, and eggs Should be conducted. Food processing should be studied, in order to find solutions for improving its nutritive value and for utilizing it efficiently.

V. Technological economic research on fuel and energy. The proper fuel and energy composition and compartmentization for the national economy, regions, and segments according to the distribution of fuel and energy resources, investment in exploitation and utilization, and production costs in China, should be explored. Electric network compartmentalization, based on the compartmentalization of fuel and energy and on the industry distribution, should be studied. Systematic technological economic research on the proper proportion of gasoline and diesel; comprehensive utilization of combustible minerals, gas, and heat supply in cities; and the choosing between diesel locomotives and electric locomotives in railway transportation must be completed.

VI. Technological economic research on selection of raw materials. In order to make raw material polices on a national scale,, we must emphatically study the following technological economic problems: the relative economization of using combustible minerals such as petroleum, natural gas, and coal to produce nitrogenous fertilizer and basic organic synthesis raw materials; technological and economic problems in selecting alloy elements in alloy steel systems; the economic effects of selection and replacement among agricultural and forestry products and chemical materials in light industries and in the textile industry; the economic effects of replacing wood by other materials in each segment of the national economy; the economic effects of replacing steel by synthesized materials and silicate materials; and the technological economic problems of multipurpose utilization of various kinds of raw materials and resources, especially paragenetic minerals of metal.

VII. Technological economic research on new processes, new equipment, and increasing product variety. A study of the technological economic effects of adopting a new process and new equipment under the current situation in China must be conducted. Especially, the economic benefits and conditions for firms to upgrade their equipment given the low level of equipment possession and the low technology level across many production segments in China should be considered. By doing this, we can provide a direction for investment. The economic benefits of different mechanization and automation levels achieved by production segments for the purpose of providing scientific support for planning the steps for each segment in national economy to realize mechanization and automation and for setting the priority of investment must be considered. The relative economic effects of various standardization and serialization schemes of industrial products should be studied, and special attention should be paid to an analysis of standardization, serialization, and lectotype selection of agricultural machines and electrical products. What specific products can be used in both industry and agriculture and what products must be developed specifically for industry or for agriculture should also be explored.

VIII. Technological economic research on the construction industry. Technological economic problems in the process of realizing industrialization directed by the trend of building industrialization should be studied, along with technological economic problems in architectural design, architectural structure, and building materials.

IX. Technological economic research on integrated transportation. The economic benefits and range of use of railway, roads, airlines, and pipeline transportation in diverse regions and with different length should be studied. The economic benefits of matching programs among transportation modes and provide scientific support for allocating transportation resources and for combined transport should also be considered.

X. Technological economic research on the structure, distribution, and production scale of industries. The connection between industry segments should be studied, and a proper ratio for the development of industry segments according to the requirements of technological progress and the characteristics of materials should be proposed, for the purpose of establishing which industry segments are in urgent need of and require enhancement. Comprehensive development plans for the main industrial centers and newly established industrial bases should be explored. The economic benefits for firms with different scales should be studied, focusing on specialization and alliance under certain technological process conditions and transportation conditions and with different amount of resources under control.

XI. Strengthen study on theories and methods in technological economics. Theories that can support assessing technological economics, including the effect of investment, should be studied, applying new calculating methods based on new technologies to assess economic benefits. Methods for calculating the total consumption of materials and the total consumption of labor in the production of material goods should be explored, along with methods for calculating socially necessary labor in the socialist system. Applications of operational research and computers in technological economic analysis and calculation should be studied.

Source: The Ten-Year National Scientific and Technological Development Plan (1963–1972) [EB/OL] http://www.most.gov.cn/ztzl/gjzcqgy/zcqgylshg/200508/t20050831_24439.htm.

1.3 History of Technological Economics

Chapter 7, Technological Economics in the Ten-Year National Scientific and Technological Development Plan (1963–1972), proposed to study 11 technological economic problems. The first ten relate to the practical technological economic problems in certain segments in national economy. They are technological, practical, and specific. In contrast, the final problem is about theory and method in this technological economic study. It is economic, theoretical, and fundamental. Economist Yu Guangyuan highlighted the importance of theory and method in a technological economic study. All disciplines should have their own theories and methodologies. Without theories and methodologies, a technological economy will not develop as technological economics, and it will not exist as an independent discipline. Therefore, technological economy and technological economics are different. "Technological economy" is the name of the research that was urgently carried out then, whereas "technological economics" refers to the name of a discipline that has theories and methodologies about the study of technological economics.

Nowadays, some people think that technological economics appeared in 1950s and that it was imported from the former Soviet Union. Some think that technological economics emerged after reform and opening-up in the 1980s and that it was imported from the west. Some authors of technological economics textbooks do not mention the origin of technological economics in China. This author thinks that it is quite necessary to note how technological economics appeared and evolved in China by following the spirit of seeking truth from facts. According to the author's firsthand experience, technological economics first appeared in 1963 in a scientific outline. But as a discipline, technological economics does not appear in 1963; rather, it appears in 1965, when the author finished summarizing the 11 tasks about technological economic study in the technological economy plan.

Here are the details about how technological economics came into being: Exploring Theories and Research Method in Technological Economics was the 11th and the most important task in the aforementioned development plan regarding technological economy. In 1963, the SSTC appointed the Institute of Economy under Chinese Academy of Sciences to take on this task. But because this institute specialized in the study of political economics, it could not work on this task. Without any help, the author took this task individually. It cost the author three years (1963–1965) to finish a research report on Methodology in Technological Economics Study.[2] This report first proposed the discipline of technological economics systematically and comprehensively. It consists of six sections, namely the Introduction, Economic

[2]Xu [Xu65].

Evaluation Criteria for Technological Problem Solving, Comparison Principles in Technological Economics, Computational Methods in Technological Economics, and Example Solution Using Technological Economics, and Using Mathematical Methods in Technological Economic Research. It has 26 chapters and about 240,000 words. The main part of the report was published in 1964 in the Chinese Science Bulletin, a journal of the Chinese Academy of Sciences, with the title as *Purpose, Task and Methods in Technological Economics Research.*[3] This paper first proposed the core of technological economics, including the definition of technological economics, the basic principles of the contradictory but unified development relationship between technology and economy, the purpose and meaning of technological economics research, three important tasks and 12 aspects of technological economic research, two research methods and five research steps in technological economic studies, the integrative and interdisciplinary characteristics of technological economics, and the relationship between technological economics and other related sub-disciplines, such as agricultural technological economics, industrial technological economics, technological economics in the construction industry, and technological economics in transportation industry. It was well received by party leaders and experts. In 1965, *On Methodology in Technological Economics Study*, the first research report on technological economics in China, earned general consent among the expert panel on Comprehensively Utilizing Combustible Minerals from the State Scientific and Technological Commission[4] and was recommended to be published as monograph of technological economics.

In 1966, however, due to the burst of the Great Cultural Revolution, this report was not published as a book.

History shows that technological economics was originally established in 1965 in China and that it was well accepted by party leaders and experts.[5] Therefore, technological economics was not imported from the former Soviet Union in 1950s nor from the west in 1980s.

Looking back at the development process of science, it can be seen that the emergence of technological economics in 1965 in China was not a happenstance. There are two trends in the development of modern science and technology. On one hand, divisions between science and technology become more and more refined. As a result, more disciples grow to have their own specialty. On the other hand, cross-permeation and a combination of disciplines happen more often. This causes many inter-disciplines in various sizes. These two trends are the specialty and integration of science and technology. They supplement each other and promote each other.

---

[3]Xu [Xu64].

[4]The author was appointed as a member of expert panel on Comprehensively Utilizing Combustible Minerals from the State Scientific and Technological Commission headed by Hou Xianglin, a member of Chinese Academy of Sciences. The author was the youngest member in the panel.

[5]Although the first edition of Technological Economics was published in 1980 with the title Introduction to Technological Economics, it has the same content with the research report on Methodology in Technological Economics Study published in 1965.

Specialty and integration are objective laws in the development of science and technology and they are independent of man's will. The emergence of technological economics conforms to the development law of modern science and technology. It is not only the result of a specialty development of science and technology, but also the result of the integration of development between science and technology. This is because economics was a discipline originally, but the development of a specialty generates many sub-disciplines in economics. Technological economics is one of them. Technological economics did not emerge from economics solely; rather, it gradually came into being through the crossing and development of natural sciences, technological sciences, and social sciences (see Fig. 1.1).

The system of technological economics consists of two parts: technological economics itself and the sub-disciplines in technological economics. Since technological economics provides basic theories and methods for technological economic studies, it inevitably focuses more on economics. If it focused more on technological sciences, technological economics would not have solid theories and methods. In contrast, each sub-discipline in technological economics must focus on both engineering and technology. Otherwise, it would be hard to tell what technological economic problems within a specific discipline need study. As result, the solutions for these problems are hard to find, as well. The sub-disciplines will be very similar with technological economics and their existence will not make any sense.

1.4 Development of Technological Economics

Technological economics has not developed smoothly in China. It has undergone four phases: the creation and initial development of technological economics, the overall destruction of technological economics, popularization and continued development of technological economics, and the development of applications of technological economics.

1.4.1 Creation and Initial Development of Technological Economics

The creation and initial development phase of technological economics lasted from 1963 until 1966. In this phase, the author studied the theories and methods of technological economics and then established the system of theory and method of technological economics with Chinese characteristics. This system has the following six characteristics: (1) it is guided by the economic theories of Marxism and Mao Zedong thought; (2) it is based on the economic law of socialism and the law of value; (3) it aims at achieving greater, faster, better and more economical results

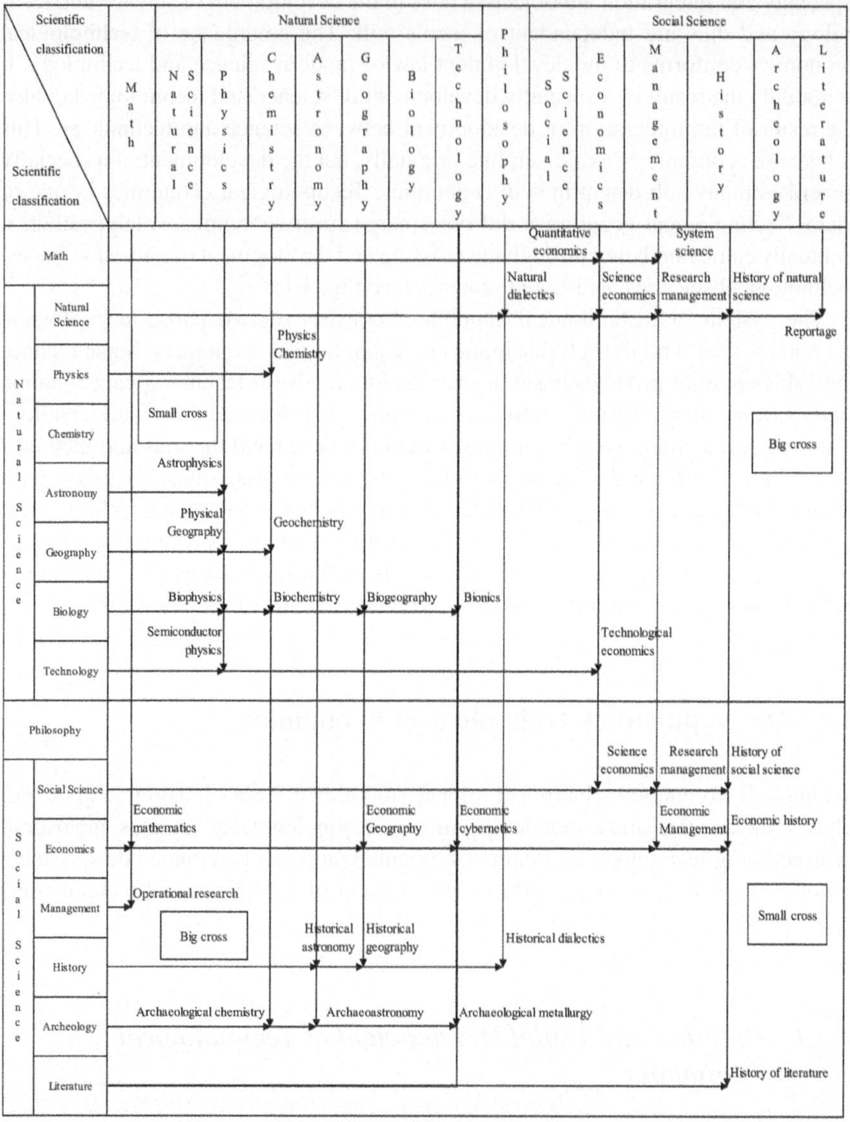

Fig. 1.1 Framework of the development of interdisciplinary science

in building socialism; (4) it adopts both qualitative and quantitative methods; (5) it considers the practice of Chinese Socialist Modernization Construction; and (6) it aims at correctly understanding and handling the relationship between unity and contradiction, and at developing and changing between technologies[6] and economy.

[6]Technology includes technical progress.

The symbolic achievements in this phase are noted in the paper named Purpose, Task, and Methods in Technological Economics Research and the research report on Methodology in Technological Economics Study, which has 240,000 words.

1.4.2 Overall Destruction of Technological Economics

This phase began in 1966 and ended in 1976. In this phase, the newly established system of theory and the method of technological economics was completely overthrown. All institutes that conducted technological economics research were withdrawn. The study of technological economics completely stopped. This phase is a crushing blow for the study of technological economics. This phase lasted 10 years.

1.4.3 Popularization and Continued Development of Technological Economics

Technological economics became popular and continued to develop from 1977 to 1988. After the Third Plenary Session of the 11th Central Committee of the Communist Party of China (CPC), technological economic study came back to life again and experienced its strongest development. The Chinese Society for Technological Economics[7] was established in November 1978. The Institute of Technological Economics of the Chinese Academy of Social Sciences[8] was founded in 1980. Moreover, the Department of Technological Economics[9] was established in the graduate school of the Chinese Academy of Social Sciences and it began to cultivate graduates majoring in technological economics for the first time in China. Later, research associations of technological economics were established in many regions and segments as well. Lectures on technological economics were organized. Research Institutes of Technological Economics were also established inside many segments. Courses about technological economics were provided by many science and engineering universities and could be found at some liberal arts universities as well. Technological Economics became a major available to undergraduates, masters, and doctoral students. In this tide of technological economics, undergraduate to graduate students, students to teachers, enterprises to government agencies, and general cadres to leading cadres were all interested in learning technological economics. Technological economics experienced popularization and quite rapid development during this

[7]The author was the Founding Executive Director of Chinese Society for Technological Economics.

[8]The author was the Founding Director of the Institute of Technological Economics of Chinese Academy of Social Sciences.

[9]The author was the first Chair of department of technological economics in the graduate school of Chinese Academy of Social Sciences.

phase. The book *Technological Economics*, written by the author, was published four times for specific readers—in 1980, 1984, 1986, and 1988 respectively. Meanwhile, the author actively promoted knowledge about technological economics on various media, such as the Manual for Modern Engineers and Science and the Technology Manual for Leading Cadres. This tide of support for technological economics reached its summit when the fourth edition of Technological Economics was selected as the textbook for the National Continuing Education Program for Engineers approved by the Central Radio and TV University in 1988 and when the author offered lectures about technological economics to audiences across China via satellite TV.

1.4.4 Development of Applications of Technological Economics

Applications of technological economics have grown quickly since 1989. The purpose of the popularization of technological economics is to serve Chinese socialist modernization and economic development. In fact, during the time when technological economics was becoming popular, more and more applications of technological economics became available and were widely adopted. Significant social and economic benefits have been achieved due to these applications. However, the Chinese economy development was badly impacted by the riot or the counterrevolutionary riot which occurred in April 1989. The national economic growth decreased continuously for two years and the annual growth rate dropped to 4% or so. Even in 1991, the growth rate was less than 10%. These slow growth rates seriously delayed the realization of the grand strategic objective put forward at the Twelfth National Congress of CPC. This objective set a goal: that the Chinese economy would grow two times stronger in 2000 than it had been in 1980. As such, Deng Xiaoping travelled in the south in 1992 and gave a speech (which has become quite famous). Since then, the Chinese economy has been developing rapidly. In this phase, beyond the many hard technological economic energy problems many soft technological economic problems were waiting for solutions, for example, problems about the growth speed of economy, the transition to a new economic growth mode, the adjustment of industrial structure, equality and efficiency for socialist market economy, the scientific judgment for a macro-economic situation, and the strategies of saving and planning. From 1989 to 2001, the author served as a director of the Technological Economic Research Institute, a national think tank of the State Development and Planning Commission (SDPC). Led by the SDPC, the author organized research on the applications of technological economics and achieved a number of solid results. These findings were adopted by the Party Central Committee and the State Council. Under their leadership, China created a miracle by doubling its energy production and quadrupling its economic aggregate in 1995, five years earlier than planned. An achievement of this stature is unprecedented around the world. In the 21st century, the Chinese economy continues to grow quickly and strongly. The author was transferred to Beijing Jiao Tong University. Beyond conducting research on theories and methodology in technological economics and energy issues, he studied logistics and achieved more than 80 research results. Accordingly, the author has been well received by scholars in China as well as scholars across the world. Now, China is becoming the second largest economic entity in the world. It should be pointed out that the great social and economic successes in China are achieved by the correct leadership of CPC headed by Deng Xiaoping, Jiang Zemin, and Hu Jintao. Also, it should be accepted that these great successes are partly attributed to technological economics.

1.5 Development Prospect of Technological Economics

As mentioned above, the development of technological economics underwent a destructive strike which almost destroyed technological economics. After the reform and the opening-up, the Chinese Society for Technological Economics and the Institute of Technological Economics of the Chinese Academy of Social Sciences were established in succession. Many articles introduced and discussed theories, methods, and applications of technological economics. As such, many overseas experts brought their attention to technological economics and then visited China to better understand technological economics. Some of them even wanted to get the first research book of technological economics in China, named *Introduction to Technological Economics*. Later, a booklet was published in the U.K. to introduce the development of technological economics and related research institutions in China. Some scholars published articles on Asian Survey, a journal in the U.S., to make comments on technological economics in China. Eric Dark, a Swedish scholar, noted that[10]: (1) "neither the name of technological economics nor its research methods appeared in the economics studies existing in the Soviet Union"; (2) "in Soviet Union's economics studies, the discipline that is the closest to technological economics is Industrial Sector Economics"; (3) "Technological economics is somewhat closer to the cost-benefit analysis in western economics studies"; and (4) "It is very interesting to study the concepts in the discipline of technological economics." These comments accepted the research results about technological economics achieved by Chinese scholars and hoped that the study of technological economics in China would have a bright future. More specifically, they hoped that the study of technological economics in China maintained its own characteristics, including the terms, concepts, and methods of organizing this discipline. Scholars from other countries, such as the U.S., Germany, and France, visited China to learn more about technological economics. The author served as their instructor. Meanwhile, other scholars across China made great efforts in the research of technological economics and achieved solid results. They made huge contributions to developing technological economics with distinctly Chinese

[10] Eric [Er81].

characteristics. However, some phenomena that are not good for the development of technological economics exist and they raise concerns. For example, some scholars still choose value engineering and feasibility studies as the focuses of technological economics. They even changed the name "technological economics" to "engineering economics" and want to replace technological economics with engineering economics. In addition, some textbooks do not introduce the origin and development of technological economics. As a result, readers do not know that this discipline was established in China, not imported from abroad. Those scholars who deny the fact that technological economics was established in China are either ignorant or have ulterior motives, some have made public speeches on something that is not true and it has caused terrible effects.

Therefore, the situation regarding the development of technological economics in China is rather severe. There are two prospects for technological economics in China. The first is to improve and complete technological economics by heading in the direction of establishing technological economics with distinctly Chinese characteristics, in order to contribute to the great rejuvenation of the Chinese nation. The other one is fairly dangerous. In this prospect, technological economics might exist in name only or does not exist at all. From the perspective of foreign scholars, existing in name only equals extinction. The author worries that the discipline of technological economics that did not extinct in the Great Cultural Revaluation might perish quietly. Thus, the author continues to tell readers and the younger generation the origin and development of technological economics, based on his personal experience. Meanwhile, the author sets an example by his own action with perseverance for developing technological economics with distinct Chinese characteristics. Next, the author makes comments on the following four questions: (1) Why must the study of technological economics have and keep distinctly Chinese characteristics? (2) What are these distinctly Chinese characteristics and what are its standards? (3) What are the characteristics of the technological economics research that were accepted by scholars abroad at the beginning of the reform and opening-up, and what new characteristics have been added in the past 30 years? and (4) how does technological economics keep distinctly Chinese characteristics?[11]

1.5.1 Why Must the Study of Technological Economics Have Distinct Chinese Characteristics?

Some people may think that there is no issue about Chinese characteristics and foreign characteristics in the study of technological economics because science is transnational. However, the author argues that the outline of Building Socialism with Distinct Chinese Characteristics proposed by Deng Xiaoping can be used as the guideline for every industry. For technological economics, distinct Chinese Characteristics mean more. Why?

[11]Xu [Xu92].

1. **Since technological economics was established and developed based on the demand in China, it is natural that technological economics will have distinctly Chinese characteristics.**

We all know that the early 1960s was a phase of adjustment for China. The experiences of combining of technology and economics in the 1950s coexisted with lessons learned from the Great Leap Forward: complete separation of technology and economics. The mass movement of making iron is an example in which the loss overweighs the gain. It is also a classic bad example of breaking principles of technological economics. Technology and economy must be combined. Economic effects should be taken into account during technological development. This combination requires a discipline that studies both technology and the economy, in particular, a discipline that studies the economic effects of technologies. This is the background on which technological economics originates. It can be seen that technological economics originated in a certain condition in China. Just as its name has distinctly Chinese characteristics, so does its content.

2. **Although technological economics is an inter-discipline that combines technology and economy, its focus is economy, not technology. So it belongs to economics.**

As we know, economics is a social science. Social science in China has distinctly Chinese characteristics. As a branch of Chinese economics, technological economics has distinctly Chinese characteristics. As such, technological economics must conform to the social system of China and must comply with the theories, terms, and concepts proposed by Chinese economists.

3. **Technological economics is not a pure theoretical science, but an application science.**

The most important task for technological economics is to solve technological and economic problems in China. Therefore, the study of technological economics must integrate with the practice of China, must take Chinese characteristics into account, and must be suitable for the reality in China. Accordingly, technological economics must be applicable in China and be further proved to be useful.

4. **All theories come from practice. Theories must be tested by practice. Technological economics cannot be an exception.**

The theories and methods of technological economics must come from practice—and they must be tested by practice as well. It must be pointed out that the practice should be in China, not abroad. Theories and methods in foreign-related disciplines must be tested by practice in China; then, they can be Chinese theories and methods. Thus, the theories and methods of technological economics must be suitable for China and must have distinctly Chinese characteristics.

In conclusion, it is an objective demand for technological economics to have distinctly Chinese characteristics. It is the requirement from building socialism with distinctly Chinese characteristics.

1.5.2 What Are the Distinctly Chinese Characteristics of Technological Economics?

Technological economics must have distinctly Chinese characteristics. What are distinctly Chinese characteristics? Comrade Deng Xiaoping pointed out, "Combining the universal truth of Marxism and the actual situation of China, selecting our own route, and building socialism with distinct Chinese characteristics are the conclusions that we reach from long term historical experience,"[12] As such, all of those contents in technological economics that combine Marxism, Mao Zedong thought, Deng Xiaoping theory, the Hu Jintao scientific development outlook, and the practice of socialism modernization in China can be called distinctly Chinese characteristics. Meanwhile, independence, initiative, and self-reliance, starting from the actual situation of China, researching the situation and problems of China, and not copying theories and methods from abroad are distinctly Chinese characteristics as well. In particular, if theories and methods are from abroa and are not developed by China, or if contents partly absorbed from resources abroad are not tested by practice in China, they have foreign characteristics, not distinct Chinese characteristics. For technological economics, if the cases are mostly from abroad, or if they do not focus on the problems in China, they lack distinct Chinese characteristics.

If the development of technological economics is not independent, does not rely on the Chinese people, does not start from the actual situation of China, and just copies theories and formulas from abroad, technological economics with distinct Chinese characteristics will not be established. Comrade Deng Xiaoping also pointed out, "Do not expect China become dependent on foreign countries!"[13] China should not put its natural science and social science in a subordinate position. Since technological economics is a discipline established by Chinese scholars independently, it, in particular, should not be subordinate. Comrade Deng Xiaoping further pointed out that the Chinese people have national pride. Of course, this does not oppose learning and inferring useful things from foreign technological economics. Learning from the outside is very necessary for developing technological economics in China. Otherwise, mistakes such as self-seclusion will be made.

1.5.3 What Distinct Chinese Characteristics Does Technological Economics Have?

At the beginning of the reform and opening-up, foreign experts pointed out the following three distinct characteristics that technological economics has after reading Introduction to Technological Economics:

---

[12] Deng [De83].

[13] Deng [De83].

1. **The Name "Technological Economics" Has Distinct Chinese Characteristics**

So far there is no such name of a discipline in other countries. Instead, each country has its own name for the discipline that is similar to technological economics, such as "engineering economics" and "cost-benefit analysis" in the U.S., "industrial economics" in Japan, and "economic computing study" in France. Western countries do not have the same name for this discipline although they share the same social system. Therefore, it is not necessary for China to use names from western countries because China has different social system.

2. **The Terms and Concepts in Technological Economics Have Distinct Characteristics**

The unique terms and concepts in technological economics include: technology, technical solution, economic effect, magnitude of social use-value, quantity of social labor consumption, effect, consumption costs, economic effect coefficient of investment, economic effect coefficient of labor, effect coefficient of materials and resources, effect coefficient of materials and resources consumption, calculation period, price correction, comprehensive utilization apportion, time factor, overall social labor productivity, social net income, social national income, additional social net income rate, additional social national income rate, etc.

3. **The Method in Technological Economics Has Distinct Characteristics**

First, technological economics is an independent system as a discipline, because the book Introduction to Technological Economics describes a complete system. More specifically, Sect. 1.1 conducts introduction of technological economics. Section 1.2 elaborates upon the economy evaluation criteria of technical solutions. Section 1.3 explains comparison principles of economy. Section 1.4 covers the calculation methods in technological economics. And finally, Sect. 1.5 provides comparison examples and applications of mathematics methods in the study of technological economics.

Second, technological economics is an inter-discipline between natural science and social science because it focuses on the study of the contradictory relationship between technology and economy and the law for the development of this relationship. Third, technological economics has evaluation criteria and comparison principles. Fourth, technological economics proposes calculation methods for many indices in the technology economy, such as overall social labor productivity, social net income, additional social net income rate, social national income, and additional social national income rate. Fifth, diverse research methods are adopted for technological economics, including the case comparison method, the tabulation method, the graphical method, the mathematic analysis method, and the multiple solution comparison.

During the 1980s, the author contributed to insisting that technological economics bear distinctly Chinese characteristics by studying theories and methods in technological economics and by practice. After the Third Plenary Session of the 11th Central Committee of the CPC, the author of this book delivered numerous lectures and presentations on technological economics at diverse forums and classes hosted by the central government and by provincial governments, as well as at Tsinghua University, Peking University, Beijing College of Chemical Industry, and the Graduate School of Chinese Academy of Social Sciences. After gathering the comments and feedback, the author revised the first edition of Technological Economics. The second edition had two volumes (I and II) and was published by China Association for Science and Technology in 1984. It was later selected as the teaching material for continuing education for scientific and technological management cadres. This updated edition had much new content, including ten characteristics of technological economics in China, the six-force theory, evaluation principles for greater, faster, better and more economical results, comprehensive evaluation principles and their quantitative computational methods, setting reasonable prices for imported and exported goods, new methods for defining economic effect coefficients, methods for setting proper tax rates and interest rates, and many examples of new applications. In addition, this edition absorbed new overseas research achievements, such as serial decision making and probability analysis methods, and reviewed feasible studies and value engineering adopted in the western economy.

With the continuous development of the reform of political and economic systems in China, the Party Central Committee pointed out that the economic system in China was not a planned economy, nor a market economy, but a planned commodity economy, which emphasizes not only macro-control, but also micro-invigoration. In other words, this economic system focused both macro- and micro-economic results. As such, the author made further revision to the second edition. The third edition of Technological Economics was published by Jiangsu People's Publishing House in 1986. It expanded the content in the second edition by adding the theories, research methodologies, and applications of micro-technological economics. The first and second editions of this book mainly covered macro-technological economics, which fitted the socialist planned economy. The third edition covered integrative technological economics, which included both macro-technological and micro-technological economics and fitted the socialist planned commodity economy. This was a major breakthrough in the development of technological economics since it took account of the actual situation of China.

In order to further improve and perfect technological economics, the author made many revisions and added new content to the third edition, based on his research and practice. The fourth edition of Technological Economics was published again by Jiangsu People's Publishing House in 1988. This edition consisted of four sections: Introduction to Technological Economics, Theories of Technological Economics, Research Methods of Technological Economics, and Applications of Technological Economics.

The first section creatively expanded the concept of technology and proposed a new concept, generalized technology, which included soft technology and hard technology. In addition, this section roundly discussed the objects of study of the newly proposed generalized technology. This section argued that the criteria for classifying macro-technological economics and micro-technological economics were the different theories and research methods of technological economics. Macro-technological economics focuses on economic benefits and efficiency in a socialist society and aims to explore objective laws for technological economics. It reflects the overall interest connections in a society. In contrast, micro-technological economics focuses on the benefits of a specific firm and aims to explore local laws for technological economics. It only reflects the interest connections in a certain part. In socialist societies, the theories and methods of macro-technological economics are primary and determine technical solutions, whereas the theories and methods of micro-technological economics can only play their roles in determining technical solutions when they do not contradict those of macro-technological economics. Otherwise, they can only adjust profit allocation.

The second section elaborated principles of technological economics. This section originally proposed six complete principles in technological economics: (1) the principle of effect in technological economics; (2) the standardization principle in technological economics; (3) the comparative principle in technological economics; (4) the optimization principle in technological economics; (5) forecasting and decision making in technological economics; and (6) information and control in technological economics. Specifically, the author elaborated upon the principle of effect of technological economics and further proposed seven sub-principles, namely the contradictory and unification principle in technological economics, the principle of economic effect indicators, the principle of economic increment, the principle of time effect, the principle of supply and demand effect, the principle of systems, and the principle of six forces' substitution. These principles objectively and fully reflected the development law of technological economics in China.

The third section covered the calculation methods in technological economics. Among the eighteen time factor computing formulas, seven were proposed for the first time by the author. When discussing the theoretical principles and calculation methods of shadow price, the author proposed a new method, the decomposition algorithm, for calculating shadow prices. Besides the net income (profit payments and tax turnover) method, the author also used the national net income (net output value) method to assess macro technological economics. Different from those calculation methods adopted in the western countries, this method used annual value to calculate total value. It was more practical. When discussing comprehensive evaluation methods, the author not only introduced the hierarchy analysis method as proposed by Saaty [Sa88],[14] but also proposed his own hierarchy analysis method, which had a lot merits.

The fourth section mainly talked about applications of technological economics. Compared with the third edition, the fourth edition added many more application cases regarding micro-technological economics, including the length of deposit that yields the biggest benefits and whether it is worth buying a refrigerator. In a word, the fourth edition of Technological Economics systematized the principles of technological economics and integrated macro- and micro-technological economics from the positions of theories, methods, and applications.

---

[14] Saaty [Sa88].

The characteristics of the fifth edition of this book reflected the important achievements that the author learned during the fourth development phase of technological economics, especially the innovation that the author made in energy technological economics, logistics technological economics, soft technological economics, and principles and methods of technological economics. This edition reviewed the development of technological economics during the past 50 years in China and looked into the future of technological economics in the 21st century. For the first time, it outlined the route of the development of technological economics in China. It considered the movement from technological economics study focusing on macro-technological economics theories and methods and the problem-solving for hard technological economy issues before reform and opening-up in 1963. It also considered the shift in focus to micro-technological economy theories and methods and the problem-solving of both hard and soft technological economy issues after reform and opening-up in 1977. Finally, it considered the concept of moving to fixing hard and soft technological economy issues by combining macro- and micro-technological economy theories and methods, which has been considered since 1989. Today, the focus of technological economics study is technological economics with uniquely Chinese characteristics. This edition is abundant in content and combines theory and practice together. Many cases in this edition are significant current Chinese technological economy issues that await solutions. The research results in this edition have attracted much attention from leaders in the Party Central Committee and have been adopted in practice. Great economic benefit and social benefits have been achieved due to the adoption. The social and economic development of China in the past 50 years or so proves the theories and methods that the author proposed regarding technological economics and shows that they have powerful vitality.

1.5.4 How to Keep the Distinctly Chinese Characteristics?

It is rather difficult to establish the discipline of technological economics in China, but it is more difficult to keep the distinctly Chinese characteristics of technological economics. To keep the distinctly Chinese characteristics of technological economics, the key approaches include the guidance of the economic theories of Marxism and Mao Zedong Thought, a close connection to the practice in China, proceeding from reality in China, finding the solution for the practical problems regarding economic theories in China, and refining theories and methods for technological economics based on practice in China. It is necessary to learn and refer to the achievements made by related disciplines abroad, but never to copy them. We should have national pride and we should be responsible. We should be proud of bringing the science and culture of our own nation to a great height of development. We must be creative and take our own path. In the era of knowledge economy and under the background of economic globalization, more and more problems regarding technological economics need solutions. As such, technological economics in China has a bright future. In addition, technological economics with distinctly Chinese characteristics might have reference value for other countries, including both developed ones and developing ones.

References

[De83] Deng X. P. (1983). Selected Works of Deng Xiaoping (1975–1982), People Publishing House, 372.

[Er81] Eric Dark, Chinese Technological Economics, Translation Series for Quantitative and Technological Economics, 1983, (1): Page 36–42 (Translation of Asian Survey, September Issue, 1981).

[Sa88] Saaty, T. L. (1988). What is the analytic hierarchy process? (pp. 109–121). Springer Berlin Heidelberg.

[Xu64] Xu, S (1964). Purpose, Task, and Methods in Technological Economics Research, Chinese Science Bulletin, the 7th issue.

[Xu65] Xu, S (1965). On Methodology in Technical Economics Study, A research report of Integrated Survey Commission of Chinese Academy of Sciences.

[Xu92] Xu, S (1992). Theory and Practice of Technological Economics in China, My Opinion on Economics. Own Accounts of 100 Chinese Economists, Nanjing, Jiangsu People's Publishing House, 749–790.

Chapter 2
Objects of the Technological Economics Study

2.1 Introduction

What is technology? What is economy? What is a technological economy? These are the questions encountered by the author when he worked on identifying the 11 tasks about the technological economic study in the Technological Economy Plan. Because these questions were related to the objects of the technological economics study, the author started his research by exploring the answers to these questions. This chapter consists of four topics: the concepts of technology and economy, the objects of the study of technological economics, hard technological economics and the soft technological economics, and macro-technological economics and micro-technological economics.

2.2 Concepts of Technology and Economy

The term "technology" is well-known. However, there are different understandings about technology. The first group believes that technology is the skill of people. In other word, technology is the experience and knowledge accumulated in people's work. Although it has diverse forms, technology can be materialized at the end. For example, the technology of physical work is represented by operative skills, whereas the technology of brainwork is represented by planning, design, and management. Many people hold this view. The second group believes that technology is a generic terms for the instruments of labor, including all kinds of machines and equipment. This view is widely held by economics literature. The reason is that with the development of productive technology in human society (including material production and mental production), instruments of labor are gradually developed as well. The application and invention of instruments of labor are the symbols of the characteristics in human labor. Karl Marx once pointed out: "The criterion for identifying economic development period is not what are produced, but how and by what means products

S. Xu, *Technological Economics*,
https://doi.org/10.1007/978-981-15-8582-1_2

are made".[1] The third group believes that technology is production capability, which has the skills of labor and instruments of labor as its factors, while the fourth group thinks that technology is production capability. Unlike those in the third group, the members of the fourth group think that production capability includes three factors: labor, the instruments of labor, and the objects of labor.

The first two views are very popular. They have been adopted by Modern Chinese Dictionary. Relatively speaking, they are narrow definitions of technology. In contrast, the last two are broader concepts of technology. They were proposed during the 1960s when technological economics had been established. In the author's view, the fourth understanding is the most comprehensive and scientific. So it is widely adopted in technological economics.

In recent years, science has been categorized into hard science and soft science. Similarly, technology has been categorized into hard technology and soft technology, as well. It is commonly thought that natural science is hard science, whereas the social sciences, together with interdisciplinary science (formed between social science and natural science) are the soft sciences. In a similar way, natural technology is hard technology, whereas social technology is soft technology. Natural technology includes various operative skills, abilities, and related capital goods formed on the base of working experience and of the development of natural scientific principles. In contrast, soft technology includes skills and methods regarding organizing and managing society, economy, science, and culture, as well as related capital goods formed on the base of working experience and the principles of natural science and social science. Therefore, technical progress should consist of both hard technical progress and soft technical progress. Hard technical progress includes: (1) adopting new skills, (2) adopting new equipment, (3) adopting new instruments, (4) adopting new technologies, (5) adopting new raw materials, (6) adopting new materials, (7) adopting new energy, (8) adopting new products, (9) adopting new design, and (10) adopting new schemes. Similarly, soft technical progress includes: (1) adopting new systems and mechanisms, (2) adopting new policies and guidelines, (3) adopting new laws and regulations, (4) adopting new strategies, programs, and plans, (5) adopting new culture propaganda, (6) adopting new political and ideological work, (7) adopting new administrative measures, (8) adopting new economic measures, (9) adopting new working methods, and (10) adopting other new schemes. It should be pointed out that this new view of science is relative. It includes the improvement and perfection of existing technology, partially or completely. It does not mean, solely, brand new technologies. It can be seen that the content of hard technology and soft technology fall far outside of the confines of the productive force. If hard technology refers to a productive force, soft technology is built from the content of production's relations and superstructure. As such, the new understanding of technology is general and it includes both hard technology and soft technology. This is the fifth way to consider of technology, which moves further than the fourth one. Technology in technological economics used to refer to the old, broader concept of technology, but now it refers to the new general concept of technology.

[1]Marx [MA53].

"Economy" has several different meanings as well. The first meaning refers to production relations, such as the economic base and the political economy. The other meaning refers to the process of social production and reproduction which includes exchanging, allocation, circulation, and consumption. This meaning can be found in the national economy, in human economic activity, in sectoral economics, and in the domestic economy. The third meaning of "economy" refers to saving. Marx once said: "The real economy, in other words, saving, means saving labor time. That is to say, economy is the minimum production cost. This kind of saving equals to developing productive forces."[2] The use of the term "economy" in technology economics falls into this meaning.

In one word, the concepts of technology and economy in technological economics should be compatible with the objects of a technological economics study, because different concepts will have different study objects. It should be pointed out that the concepts of technology and economy in technological economics mentioned above are determined by the objects of the technological economics study. Next, the author will discuss the objects of the technological economics study.

2.3 Objects of the Technological Economics Study

Each discipline has its own research objects. Technological economics is not an exception. The objects of the study of technological economics are not purely technical matters, because technical sciences study technical matters specifically. Neither are the objects of technological economics study pure economics issues (i.e., the meaning of economy in production relations), because these issues are studied in political economics or industrial sector economics. The objects of the study of technological economics are technological economics issues. Then, what are technological economics issues? Specifically, they are issues about the economic results of technology. In other words, they are issues about the feasibility and economic rationality of technology. In fact, the study of the economic results of technology must focus on feasible technologies, because non-feasible technologies do not have any economic result at all. Studying them does not make any sense. Meanwhile, the study of the economic results of technology should not ignore technological results and other related results, because they are the foundation of the study of the economic results of technology. Therefore, the study of the economic results of technology includes both studying the feasibility of technology and studying technical results. However, this does not mean that technological economics is a discipline that studies only technical results and economic results. Each discipline has its own research focus. For instance, the study of technology sciences focuses on studying technical results, whereas technological economics focuses on studying the economic results of technology. Since

[2]Marx [MA66].

the economic issues of technology are mainly represented by the economic results of technical policies, technical measures, and technical schemes, the objects of a study of technological economics are the economic results of technical policies, technical measures, and technical schemes. Because all science research aims to uncover the rules in objective world, the study of technological economics has the purpose of exploring the objective rules of the technological economy. The research on technological economics issues essentially studies the objective rules of the technological economy. Due to the categorization of the narrow definition of technology and the broader concept of technology, technological economics has the same categories, narrow concept of technological economics, and broader concept of technological economics. The narrow definition of technology usually refers to instruments of labor, so the objects of the narrow concept of the study of technological economics are the economic results of technology, the instruments of labor in particular, in the process of production and work. In contrast, the objects of the broader concept of technological economics study are the economic results of the whole production capability and the whole production process, as well as the economic results of all labors, including material production and nonmaterial production. Mao Zedong pointed out in On Contradiction: "The criterion for categorizing science studies is identifying the unique contradictoriness of objects in science. Therefore, the study that focuses on a specific contradiction in a certain field is the research object of a certain discipline in science".[3] The study of technological economics focuses on the contradiction between technology and economy in production and work. Thus, the object of technological economics study is to explore the unique contradictory relation between technology and economy and the regularity of the development and changing of this relationship.

In sum, the author proposes the following six descriptions of the objects of technological economics study:

(1) Technological economics is a discipline that studies the issues of the technology economy.
(2) Technological economics is a discipline that studies the economic results of technical policies, technical measures, and technical schemes. The author said this in *Introduction to Technological Economics*: "Technological economics is a discipline that calculates, evaluates, and analyzes the economic results of technical schemes, including technical measures, design, and lines." Because calculation, evaluation, and analysis in this description are not the objects of technological economics study, but of research methods, they are removed.
(3) Technological economics is a discipline that studies the laws of saving in the process of production and work.
(4) The narrow concept of technological economics studies the economic results and savings of technology (i.e. the instruments of labor) in the process of production and work.
(5) The broader concept of technological economic studies the economic results of production capability and production. So it is also called "production capability

[3]Selected Works of Mao Zedong (Volume 1), People Publishing House, 1966, p. 284.

economics" or "production economics." In addition, it studies the economic results of labor (including both material and nonmaterial production). Thus, it is called "labor result economics."

(6) Technological economics is a discipline that studies the contradictory relationship between technology and economy and the regularity of the development and changing of this relationship.

The author thinks that the last description makes the greatest sense. The task for technological economics is to correctly understand and handle the dialectic relationship between technology and economy, to explore the rational relationship between technology and economy (namely, the best relationship), and to make technology and economy adapt mutually. Those technologies that are compatible with the economy are called "appropriate technologies" abroad. Appropriate technologies fit national conditions, are compatible with concrete condition, and have good economic results. They can be the most advanced technologies. They can be in-between or lagging ones, as well. One technology is applicable in one country or region, but it might not be applicable in other countries or regions. Hence, it is very necessary to conduct technological economics studies. If a technology is applicable anytime and anywhere and has good economic results, the contradictory relation between technology and economy will not exist. As a result, there is no need to conduct technological economics studies. However, this does not exist. The contradiction between technology and economy is ubiquitous in the practice of social production. It drives lagging technologies to develop into advanced ones. It also drives some advanced technologies to be more advanced. Meanwhile, this contradiction causes technologies with bad economic results to become new ones with good economic results. It also causes technologies with good economic results to become ones with better economic results. In other words, the contradiction between technology and economy continuously promotes the development of technology and economy, as well as the improvement of social productive forces and economic results. The study of technological economics consciously serves the contradiction between technology and economy.

The overseas disciplines that study technological economics have different names, such as "industrial sector economics", "engineering economics", "cost-benefit analysis", "industrial economics", and "economic calculation study". The names reflect their research ranges, theories, and methods. But the objects of study are the same. Thus, no matter how different the names are, the research is the same in essence because they all study the contradictory relationship between technology and economy.

2.4 Hard Technological Economics and Soft Technological Economics

The seventh chapter of the Ten-year National Scientific and Technological Development Plan (1963–1972) noted: "Pay special attention to the study of the eleven aspects of technological economics." Among these eleven aspects, the former ten are all technological economic issues about the productive force, namely hard technological economic issues. None of them is related to the soft technological economics issues, which are about production relations or the building of the superstructure. Thus, technological economics, prior to the reform and opening-up, was hard technological economics.

After the reform and opening-up, due to the further reformation of production relations and the building of the superstructure, the soft technological economic issues attracted more and more attention. Soft technological economics mainly studies the following issues: (1) technological economics issues about mechanism and system, (2) technological economics issues about policies and guidelines, (3) technological economics issues about laws and regulations, (4) technological economics issues about strategy, programs, and plans, (5) technological economics issues about culture and propaganda, (6) technological economics issues about ideological and political work, (7) technological economics issues about administrative measures, (8) technological economics issues about economic measures, (9) technological economics issues about working manners, and (10) other technological economics issues. Facts have shown that the development of soft technological economics plays a key role in promoting the development of hard technologies, the economy, and even the entire society in China. It contributes a lot to the achievements earned after the reform and the opening-up. It can be argued that the requirements from the reform and opening-up drove the study of soft technological economics.

In China, technological economics evolved from hard technological economics, which mainly focused on studying the hard economic issues before the reform and the opening-up, to the soft technological economics that mainly focused on studying the soft economic issues after the reform and opening-up. And then it gradually began to cover both hard and soft economic issues (i.e. comprehensive technological economics). This change is significant progress.

2.5 Macro-Technological Economics and Micro-Technological Economics

Macro-technological economics differs from micro-technological economics not in the type of research questions that it addresses, but in the perspective of the theories and methods adopted by them. The former was from the state level, whereas the latter was from the firm level. Compatible with the socialist economic system and its reform in China, the technological economics established prior to the reform and opening-up was macro technological economics, which was fit for a planned economy. Because the traditional planned economy was the public sector of the economy, independent firms that could carry out production and allocation by themselves did not exist before the reform and opening-up. Firms' production and allocation were all determined by the state. Activities of firms were all for the national interest; the interests of firms were ignored. Sun Zhifang, a well-known economist, once argued that profits were crucial for firms. However, he was criticized for this view in the planned economy era.

After the reform and opening-up, China stepped into a new era of socialist market economy. As the main part of socialist market economy, firms must pursue their own micro-economic benefits. As a result, micro-technological economics grew quickly. It must be pointed out that the theories and methods of both macro-technological economics and micro-technological economics must be adopted when studying technological economics in a socialist society, no matter what the types of the research questions are (hard technological economic issues or soft technological economic issues, macro-technological economic issues or micro-technological economic issues).

The 50-year development process of the technological economy in China proved that the theories and methods of macro-technological economics are premise, whereas those of micro-technological economics are base. Neither of the two can be discounted. Thus, from the perspective of the theories and methods of technological economics, technological economics in China is comprehensive and combines theories and methods in both macro-technological economics and micro-technological economics. This evolution is significant progress as well.

References

[MA53] Marx, K. (1953). Capital (Volume 1), People Publishing House, p 174.

[MA66] Marx, K.(1966). Critique of Political Economy (Draft) (3rd Fascicle), People Publishing House, p 284.

Chapter 3
Purpose and Meaning of the Technological Economics Study

3.1 Introduction

What is the purpose of the study of technological economics? Why should a study of technological economics be conducted? What is the meaning? These questions will be answered in this chapter. Whether from the perspective of the development of science and technology or from the perspective of the development of economy and society, the purpose of technological economics study is very clear. Studying technological economics is necessary.

3.2 Purpose of the Study of Technological Economics

The goal of developing science and technology is to boosting modernization construction. All technologies, including mature ones that have been adopted widely in practice, new ones that have just been applied in practice, and those still under research and testing, need to perform a technological economics study. The study of technological economics is an indispensable and important component in economic construction and in the work of science and technology. It is the important intermediate link that allows science and technology to support production and construction. Generally speaking, all research results that are achieved in science and technologies need to be analyzed by technological economics before they serve as the foundation for technology measurement making, technology policy making, and the planning of the national economy. The study of technology science, together with the study of technological economics, provides technological and economic supports for resolving practical issues in the development of a national economy.

With the development of science and technology, the number of mature technologies picked up by people gets bigger and bigger. Take transportation as an example. Beyond the old transportation technologies, such as carriages, tricycles, and wooden vessels, people have mastered many modern transportation technologies, including

S. Xu, *Technological Economics*,
https://doi.org/10.1007/978-981-15-8582-1_3

steamships, trains, cars, airplanes, pipelines, transmission lines, conveyer belts, high-speed trains, roads, and air cushions. It is important that technological economics consider what transportation schemes should be chosen for the goal of finishing the transportation tasks and achieving the biggest economic results in certain areas and under certain conditions. The scheme that brings the biggest benefit to the national economy depends on the comprehensive analysis and research of the technology economy's performance of each transportation approach by considering location, economic conditions, and traffic volume, and by the evaluating and comparing the economic results of each transportation scheme.

Because of invention and creation, new technologies are continuously adopted in production and construction, such as information technology, biotechnology, nanotechnology, oxygen steelmaking, water cooling generators, fluidization technology and boiling combustion technology in chemical reaction, chipless and less-chip processing technology in machinofacture, coal chemical technology, solar electric power generation, and wind power generation. Compared with the old technologies, do these new ones generate any benefits and or bigger benefits? The answer relies on careful technological economics research and analysis. Only after the economic results of new technologies have been confirmed can they be promoted in practice.

In order to develop science and technology and to improve social productive forces, we need to conduct research and development and to create newer and more advanced technologies. But which technologies under research and development can meet the actual requirements in China and can achieve the expected goals? To find the answer, it's necessary to analyze the technological economic results of each technology development scheme by considering both the experience abroad and the concrete conditions in China.

Therefore, the study of technological economics can assess the economic results of technology measures and schemes, and can analyze and compare their economic values before they are carried out in the practice of social production. Such analysis and comparison will help us select those technologies that are fit for the characteristics of the resources and for the natural conditions in a certain area or a certain country. In addition, they will enable mature technologies to better meet the requirements of actual conditions of a certain area or a certain country. They can also help us make the decision about replacing old technologies with new ones in production and construction. In this way, they can promote the development of technology and can guide the direction of development. These analyses and comparisons can further help us make the judgment about which technologies are worthy of studying and of development. Accordingly, they provide supports for the making of a science and technology research plan and the identification of research direction. Meanwhile, after being implemented in practice, each technology scheme should undergo technological economic analysis as well, so that corresponding measures can be taken to achieve better economic results.

Although the above discussion is mainly about the hard technological economics issues, it is applicable to the soft technological economics issues as well. For example, survey, research, and testing must be conducted before answering related questions, such as when and where new systems and mechanisms, new principles and policies, new laws and regulations, new strategies, new plans, new schemes, new culture and propaganda, new ideological and political work, new administrative measures, and new working manners should be adopted. Assessment and comparison must be conducted on all the soft technological schemes before they can serve as supports for decision making.

3.3 Meaning of Technological Economics Study

Looking back the economic construction process after the new China was founded, it can be seen that either for the state or for firms and villages, the largest economic results could be achieved if attention were paid to technological economics. If not, a state will make mistakes, firms will suffer losses, and villages will fall behind. Profound lessons are available. Each area, each department, and each firm has successful experience and unsuccessful lessons. For China, the first Five-year Plan was successful. However, after the one-size-fits-all policies and guidelines, it became clear that big steel-making, the reversion of coal transportation from north to south and the switch from coal to oil were big mistakes. Since the Third Plenary Session of the 11th Central Committee of the CPC, because attention has been paid to technological economics, great successes have been achieved. However, problems still exist. For instance, the study of technological economics was not conducted beforehand. The study of technological economics was not performed correctly. The study of technological economics was even used as a means for vying over projects and investments. Moreover, wrong theories and methods were applied in the study of technological economics. These problems will cause mistakes in decision-making. Many examples have proven this; therefore, in order to avoid making blind decision and mistakes, the study of technological economics must be enhanced.

Some technological economics issues are very simple. For example, a certain factory has old equipment, which uses up a large amount of resources. The cost of its products is high, so it plans to upgrade its equipment. The result of technological economics calculation shows that this factor can save 20,000 RMB in its production's total cost if it maintains the same volume of production and if all other conditions (e.g. the product quality and the consumption of labor) remain the same. Because the cost of upgrading the equipment is 40,000 RMB, it can be seen that the factory should do the upgrade. The investment on the upgrade will be recovered in two years. For these kinds of technological economics issues, many conditions are known. Only two technological schemes need to be compared. The scope of each scheme is not big. People with a basic knowledge of technology and economy can analyze and calculate the results of such technological economics issues and can easily make a reasonable decision.

However, science and technology have developed quickly since the 20th century. More and more technologies are being understood and used by people. Most of them aim to do the same task. As a result, many technology schemes become available for one single project in the construction of the national economy. In other words, very often more than two schemes need to be analyzed and compared. For example, many modern technologies are available for building a power station, if other conditions are not considered. The power station can be thermal, hydropower, atomic, wind, solar, or geotherm. The thermal power station can be condensing thermal or heat supply thermal. For these two types of thermal power, coal, oil, or natural gas can be selected. By parity of reasoning, many technological schemes are available for building a power station. Furthermore, with the development of science and technology, more and more advanced technologies are being mastered by people. As a result, for each technological scheme, the scope of available parameters becomes wider and wider. Accordingly, the number of available parameters become bigger and bigger. Suppose that the reserves of water resources in a river are two million kilowatts. The old dam construction techniques and water turbine manufacturing technology only allowed people to build a hydropower station with the capability of up to 100,000 kW on this river. But new dam construction techniques and water turbine manufacturing technology make it possible to build a hydropower station with capability of 1,000,000 kW. In this case, the fluctuation range of the technological parameter (installed capability) in this hydropower station development scheme becomes wider. In other words, the number of available technological schemes increases. As we know, the larger the number of available technological schemes is, the more complicated the technological economics issues are. Finding the solutions for these issues is getting harder. This example indicates that the continuous development and progress of science and technology is one of the main reasons that causes modern technological economics issues to become more complicated and difficult. In addition, complicated and difficult modern technological economic issues are impacted by the number of technological economics factors that affect the economic result of each scheme and the change scope of these factors. Generally speaking, technological economic issues at the state level, or those having a broader impact are more complicated and difficult than those having impact in a more local area. The study of technological economics issues whose purpose is general guidance is more complicated and difficult than that for fixing specific technological economics issues. This is because the former has a larger number of variables and their fluctuation range is wide. For instance, it is more complicated and difficult to study the ratio of a planned thermal power station and hydropower station across a country or in a big electrical power system than it is to study the economics of building certain number of thermal power stations and hydropower stations in a specific area. The former study must consider the complicated location factors, such as the distribution of waterpower and fuel resources in this area, the investment, the cost and labor productivity of fuel exploitation in this area, the construction costs of hydropower station and thermal power station in this area, the size of electric load in this area, and the power consumption specifics in this area. Another example is that it is more complicated and difficult to study when it is more reasonable to build a heat supply thermal power station, an issue with general guidance purpose, than to study the building of a specific heat supply thermal power station with all conditions known. This is because the former study needs to assume several variable conditions, such as coal price, thermal load quantity, thermal consumption, the length of the heat supply network, the unit type of the thermal power station, the capacity of thermal power station, and the construction cost of condensing the thermal power station. In the latter study, all of these conditions are known. So the latter study is an easier one to resolve. In addition, there is another reason that makes the study of technological economics problems complicated and difficult in a socialist system. Socialist production is an organic whole, in which each production division connects with each other. The selection of a technological scheme will not only cause changes inside a division, but will also connect with changes in other divisions. The more divisions are involved, the more complicated the issue is. For example, the study of technological schemes of hydropower stations and thermal power stations involves many divisions in the national economy other than the hydroelectric division, such as submerged land and minerals, the migration of residents and industry, the increased irrigated areas of farmlands, the increased fish production, the industrial water supply, the shipping capacity, and the tourist industry. Construction of thermal power stations mainly involves fuel exploitation divisions and transportation divisions. In a socialist system, the calculation of the economic results of the technological schemes of building hydropower stations and thermal power stations should not be limited only to certain divisions. Instead, the whole national economy should be considered. It should not only consider the economic results of hydroelectric division, but it should consider the economic impact caused by the selection of building hydropower stations and thermal power stations on other related divisions, such as agriculture, industry, and transportation. Although the examples provided above are all the hard technological economic issues in energy division, the ideas behind them are applicable to both the hard technological economic issues and the soft ones in other divisions in the national economy.

To sum up, other than simple technological economics issues, a large number of difficult, important, and complicated issues exist in practice. Resolving these issues needs special knowledge, which requires technological economics professionals to perform long-term, systematic studies.

Chapter 4
Tasks and Contents of a Technological Economics Study

4.1 Introduction

What are the tasks of technological economics study? What are the contents of technological economics study? The answers are discussed in this chapter. It should be said that technological economics study exists in economy, in society, and in every field of people's lives. Thus, the tasks of technological economics study are comprehensive, and the contents of technological economics study are varied. More details follow.

4.2 Tasks of Technological Economics Study

The tasks of a technological economics study are understanding and handling the relationship between technology and the economy correctly, exploring the objective laws of technological economics, and identifying the rational relationship between technology and economy, looking toward the best and most coordinative relationship. More specifically, there are three parts to the tasks of a technological economics study.

1. **The main task of a technological economics study is to research the theories and methods of economic evaluation and of the comprehensive evaluation of technological schemes.**

This task has two aspects to its completion. The first is to study the common theories and methods for evaluating technological schemes according to the theories of the socialist political economy. The second is to explore the technological economic principles of technological schemes by combining technologies for producing materials and immaterialities. The studies of these two aspects are synergistic and complementary. With these theories and methods, related departments, such as the planning and design departments, the production department, and the economic management department, can solve practical technological economic issues, based on specific

S. Xu, *Technological Economics*,
https://doi.org/10.1007/978-981-15-8582-1_4

conditions. The practical technological economic issues include the issues of agriculture, industry, construction, communication and transportation, city planning, environmental protection, post and telecommunications, scientific research, education, and administrative management.

2. **It is also an important task for a technological economics study to search for the objective laws of technological development both at home and abroad (including the hard and soft technologies) and the interrelationship and laws of development between technological progress and economic development from the perspective of total analytic demonstration of technological economics.**

The research about technological development at home and abroad can often guide us as we consider the direction and trends of diverse technologies at different development stages. Studying the development laws of technologies abroad is similar with working on intelligence abroad, yet it is a bit different. The former study not only needs to introduce the status of the development of technologies abroad, but also needs to identify the direction and laws of the development of technologies abroad and to further explain why they develop in a specific way, based on the principles of technological economics.

3. **Technological economics should study and resolve practical technological economic issues**

Besides offering related technological economic theories and methods, a technological economics study should provide conclusions and suggestions for resolving practical technological economic issues, especially complicated and comprehensive significant technological economic issues. In this way, the state and related units can get reference and foundation for their practical work.

The technological economics study should be conducted carefully. For example, the high professional sectortasks should be conducted by a specific research institute of technological economics in each department, whereas the highly comprehensive ones should be conducted by comprehensive research institutes. The study of technological economics needs cooperation and coordination among departments, especially the planning and statistics department, the economic management department, the planning and design department, and the production department, as well as the science and technology department.

4.3 Contents of the Technological Economics Study

The aforementioned technological economic issues are the economic issues of production, productive forces, and all labor. Because the area os production and labor contains all of the departments and aspects of social material production and services, from a lateral view, technological economic issues exist in all departments of the social economy, such as agriculture, industry, communication and transportation, post and telecommunications, municipalities, construction, business, foreign trade, tourism, the service industry, environmental protection, education, heath, scientific research, and defense. From a vertical view, they exist in each stage of production and construction, such as experimental study, survey and investigation, planning and design, construction, and production. It can be seen that the contents of a technological economics study are broad. Other than theories and methods, there are many practical issues, including the hard and soft technological issues as well as the macro and micro ones. Roughly speaking, the following issues are included:

(1) The rational exploitation and comprehensive utilization of various resources, including lands, farming, forestry, animal husbandry, side-line production and fishery, mountain areas, timber, conventional energy sources, new energy sources, water resources, seawater resources, metal, nonmetal lean ore, complex paragenic minerals, secondary resources such as waste and used materials, bagasse, spent pulping liquor, coal ash of power stations, and metallurgy residue.
(2) The cultivation and selection of good strains of seeds, including food crops, and commercial crops, as well as livestock variety and the improvement and development of biological species.
(3) The manufacturing and utilization of various industrial raw materials and materials, including the fibrous materials in textile and paper industries, synthesis ammonia, benzene, olefin, acetylene, pesticide, detergent, and the sulfuric acid in chemical industry, as well as the construction materials such as timber, steel, cement, plastic, and glass-fiber reinforced plastics.
(4) The production and supply of energy sources, including the reasonable structure of energy production and consumption, the rational supply of energy sources to departments of the national economy, the selection of energy type and base from departments of the national economy, the rational division of energy sources, the reasonable approaches of energy conservation, the industrial and urban coal gasification and thermalization, the reasonable proportion of hydropower stations and thermal power stations, the development of a dynamical system, the fuel constitution of power machines, the economic load dispatching of the dynamical system, and the selection of new energy sources.
(5) The adoption of new technologies, new processes, new equipment, and new instruments, including new cultivation techniques, plant protection techniques and rearing techniques, new productive technologies and skills including the three highs (high temperature, high humidity, and high pressure) productive technologies for metallurgy blast furnaces; the top-blown converter of oxygen steelmaking; continuous ingot casting techniques; the techniques of vacuum electric smelting and fluidization; the textile technology of electrostatic spinning; the techniques of improving machinery rotation speed and adopting a united process; the overall pressing and high pressure synthesis techniques used in synthesis ammonia production; the chipless and less-chip processing techniques used in machinofacture; the water cooling techniques of the large-scale

turbonator; the new process flow of petroleum refining, storage, and maintenance; the packaging and transportation techniques of various materials; new information technology; agricultural irrigation, electrification, mechanization and chemicalization; mechanization; the automation in national economic departments; the equipment replacement in national economic departments; and industrialized and prefabricated construction.

(6) The generating of various standards and series for engineering goods, construction, engineering design, product quality, and environmental protection.

(7) The production, type selection, and composition of products and equipment, including those for light industries and consumption goods industries, the proportion of various foods, the proportion of wool spinning products and cotton spinning products, the proportion of knit goods and textiles, the proportion of other inter-substituted products, the trial-production and production of new products, and the production of technological devices and the equipment in the national economic department, as well as the selection of technological parameters.

(8) The specialization, coordination and conglomeration of production, including the specialization and coordination of the machine building industry, instrument factories, the conglomeration of steelworking and chemical fertilizer plants, and the conglomeration of petroleum refining and petrochemical operations, as well as the conglomeration of the coal and mining industry, the metallurgical industry, and the chemical industry.

(9) The scale, structure, layout, and reserve of productive forces, including the rational scale and layout of agricultural tractor stations, livestock farms, power stations, chemical plants, metallurgical works, petroleum refineries, coal mines, and light industrial plants; the rational scale of small, medium, and large industries; the rational structure of industries in the national economy, the rational internal structure of agriculture and stock farming, and the optimum reserve of production equipment and products for firms.

(10) The confirmation of construction modes (e.g. new construction, expansion, and heavy repair) and construction duration, including the construction modes of industrial firms, the selection of new construction, expansion and heavy repair, the confirmation of rational construction duration for engineering projects, and the rational organization of production and construction process flow.

(11) The selection and coordination of transportation modes, including railway, road, sea transportation, river transportation, aviation, pipeline transportation, and conveyer belts, the rationalization of freightage, the configuration of railway terminals, and the coordination of various transportation modes and combined transportation, as well as the development of a comprehensive communications and transportation network.

(12) The selection and coordination of information technologies, including post and telecommunication, telegram, telephone, wireless communication, and satellite communication; and the rational scale of a special communication network and a public communication network, as well as the development of a comprehensive Internet.

(13) The selection of safety measures for defense and military safety, including the selection of military technologies, the production and development of weapons, and the selection of combination modes of military and civilian production.
(14) The scale and layout of city construction, including the configurations of urban industry, residences, tourism, services, the business network, and transportation, as well as rational city scale and the layout of industrial cities.
(15) The scale, structure, and layout of scientific research, education, and health agencies, including the scale and configuration of scientific research institutions, the formulation of scientific research plans, the combination of scientific research and production, the application and promotion of achievements in scientific research, the scale and configuration of schools, the selection of modes for talent training, and the selection of medical treatment modes, as well as the production and promotion of both traditional Chinese medicine and western medicine.
(16) The mode selection for environmental pollution prevention, including the optimum selection of integrated approaches for regional pollution prevention, the comprehensive utilization of three types of industrial wastes, and the rational adoption of single prevention technology.
(17) The rational selection of technological conditions and technological parameters in the production run, including the selection of the proportion of raw materials and technical conditions, such as temperature, flow rate, pressure, speed, size, and strength.
(18) The rational circulation of goods and the rational confirmation of import and export commodities.
(19) The rational selection of imported engineering technologies.
(20) The rational allocation and usage of manpower, capital, materials, natural forces, transportation capacities, and time.
(21) The technological economic issues of system and mechanism.
(22) The technological economic issues of policies and guidelines.
(23) The technological economic issues of laws and regulations.
(24) The technological economic issues of strategy, scheme, and planning.
(25) The technological economic issues of culture propaganda.
(26) The technological economic issues of ideological and political work.
(27) The technological economic issues of administrative measures.
(28) The technological economy issues of economic measures.
(29) The technological economic issues of working manners.
(30) Other issues of hard and soft technological economics.

The problems listed above are only the important technological and economic issues that occur in national economic construction. They are not all of the technological and economic issues. It should be said that Economic result issues exist for all technologies. Some of them are big, some are small, some are complicated, some are simple, some are important, and some are unimportant.

Chapter 5
Methods and Procedures of the Technological Economics Study

5.1 Introduction

What are the methods of the technological economics study? What are the procedures of the technological economics study? How can the technological economics study be conducted? What questions should be considered? These questions will be answered in this chapter. We will specially discuss the methods and procedures of technological economics study.

5.2 Methods of Technological Economics Study

There are three methods for conducting the technological economics study:

1. **Investigation**

Although it has been adopted widely in many fields, investigation is especially important for the technological economics study. As we know, the study of technological economics is different from the study of natural science and technology. Generally speaking, the technological economics study does not require special labs. This is because the issues that the technological economics study aims to resolve are practical ones in the development of the national economy. The results of technological economics study on these issues cannot be tested in labs. Meanwhile, the resources and data required by the technological economics study cannot be achieved via experiments in labs, not can they be processed in labs.[1]

However, the technological economics study has its unique labs, namely the practice of the development of the national economy per se and the objects of production and construction (including intermediate experiments and industrial experiments).

[1]Test here refers to those on the purely theoretical side, far away from the practical requirements of national economic construction.

S. Xu, *Technological Economics*,
https://doi.org/10.1007/978-981-15-8582-1_5

For instance, the construction in the chemical industry is the experimental base for the technological economics study on the chemical industry. The construction of the national economy is the experimental base for the technological economics study on the national economy. Thus, the investigations of practical issues in production and construction are similar to the experiments that would be conducted in labs. The investigations in the technological economics study serve the following purposes:

(1) Collecting materials, original data, suggestions, and feedback about technological economics;
(2) Testing theories, methods, and conclusions in technological economics;
(3) Summarizing general laws and experiences of technology development;
(4) Discovering new technological and economic issues in production and construction.

It can be seen that investigation is an essential and important part in any technological economics study. It is also an important method in any technological economics study. Investigation must be adopted throughout the whole process of a technological economics study, from the selection of research topics to the promotion of research results. At the same time, it is necessary to obtain the technological and economic materials and data via technological approaches.

2. **Mathematical Calculation**

Traditional economic science primarily adopts argumentation and analysis as its research approach, whereas the natural science and technological science choose mathematical calculation. The technological economics study enjoys the benefits of the research methods in natural science and technological science by using mathematical calculation to study the relationship between technology and economy, based on the quantitative results. Therefore, mathematical calculation is often applied in any technological economics study. Some mathematical calculations are easy and simply use basic mathematics. But others are complicated, so advanced mathematics, operational research, and the use of a computer are required to resolve them.

3. **Argumentation and Analysis**

The research method adopted for use in social economic science, argument and analysis, is applied in technological economics study as well. Each technological economic issue needs both dialectical and systematical analyses. Argumentation is required for all materials, for calculating data, for consideration factors, and for compiling final results.

It should be pointed out that the abovementioned three methods must be combined together in the study of technological economics. The technological economics study will use a comprehensive method that combines investigation, mathematical calculation, and argumentation and analysis. This comprehensive method is determined by the characteristics of technological economics, which is an inter-discipline between natural science and social science.

5.3 Procedure of Technological Economics Study

Like other scientific research, the technological economics study has its own procedure, which consists of six steps (see Fig. 5.1).

1. **The development of technological schemes**

As we know, many substituted schemes can be adopted to meet the same requirement. But in certain conditions or circumstances, investigations and analyses are required to make the decision about which schemes should be selected. At the step of the development of technological schemes, no possible practical schemes should be missed, because this might cause the final selected scheme to not be the best, when put into practice. Similarly, non-existent or non-practical (or non-practical before the deadline) schemes should be compared with those that can be realized, because this may make the comparison and selection of technological schemes lack foundation. Therefore, when developing technological schemes, we should comprehensively and carefully base our decisions on materials and situations in our hands. For example, when conducting a technological economics study on making certain

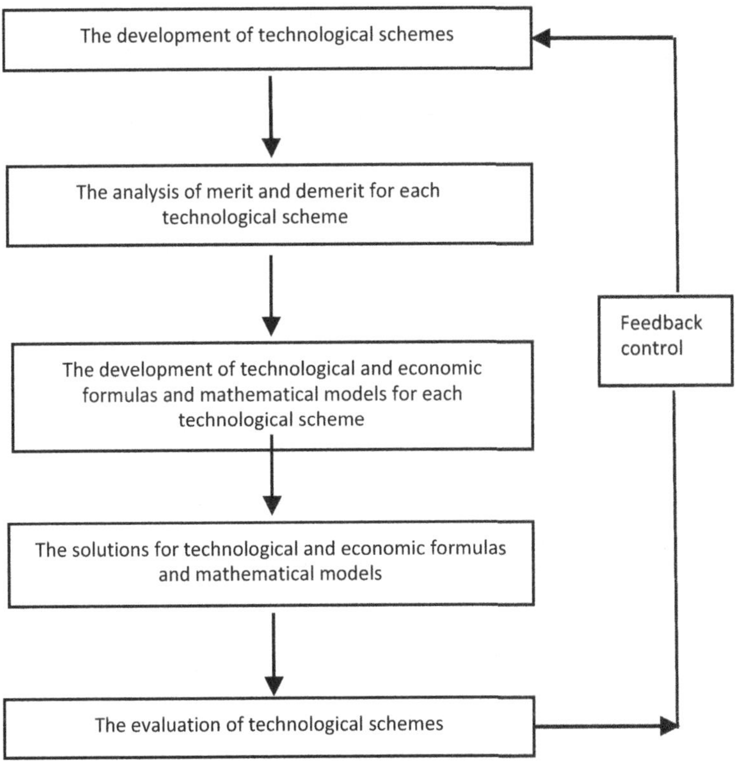

Fig. 5.1 The schema of the technological economic study procedure

types of electric locomotives, beyond listing manufacturing schemes for all types of electric locomotives, we should also provide other possible schemes that meet the same national economic requirements (railway transportation in this case). In other words, we should consider alternative schemes, such as the manufacturing schemes for internal-combustion locomotives. In practice, some possible schemes will be neglected, due to incomplete investigation and lack of consideration. For instance, in the process of evaluating the economic results of urban thermalization schemes, a scheme that combines condensing power stations and scatted small boiler rooms is usually listed. The alternative existing scheme, which combines condensing power stations and regional boiler rooms, is missed. It should be pointed out that the latter scheme might be much more economical than the former one. In some cases, a certain technological scheme is not put onto the list to compare with other ones because the technology does not pass the tests at home and abroad or because the resources required, or other conditions, are missing in China.

2. **The analysis of internal and external pros and cons as well as influencing factors for each technological scheme from the perspective of technological economics**

Each technological scheme has its own merits and demerits. The evaluation of each technological scheme will be more accurate if the analysis of them is complete, thorough, and comprehensive. The analysis of merits and demerits for each technological scheme must start from investigation, considering the entire interest of the national economy and the interrelationship and impacts of the internal and external factors of technological schemes, such as politics, defense, society, culture, technology, economy, environment, and resources. It is not objective to search the merits of one technological scheme and the demerits of another based on subjective will and wish; this approach should be avoided. At the same time, the merits and demerits of technological schemes are related to their internal and external factors. Thus, when comparing and analyzing technological schemes, those factors that have impact on merits and demerits must be identified. For example, when analyzing and evaluating a hydroelectric construction scheme and a thermal power construction scheme, both the benefits of hydroelectric construction, such as the reduction of reserve capacity of the power system; the reduction of house supply; the lack of a need for fuel; and the comprehensive efficiency of electric power and water conservation, and the disadvantages of hydroelectric construction, such as submerging land, salinizing soil, high construction costs, and a long construction period, should be identified. In previous practice, the reduction of reserve capacity of a power system and the reduction of house supply caused by hydroelectric construction were usually neglected. As a result, the economic results of hydroelectric construction were smaller. In contrast, the disadvantages of hydroelectric construction, such as submerging land and salinizing soil, were not paid close enough attention, in some areas. Therefore, the economic results of hydroelectric construction were increased artificially. Similarly, for thermal power construction, the social impacts and economic loss caused by environmental pollution were not taken into consideration for a long time. Moreover, although the construction period of thermal power stations is a short one, that of a coal mine is long. The neglect of this consideration led to the increase in the estimate of the economic results of thermal power construction schemes. Incorrect decisions were made at the end of the consideration. In another example, when analyzing and evaluating the manufacturing schemes for a new model machine, not only their advantages and disadvantages regarding manufacturing, but also the merits and demerits about how they are to be adopted in all departments across the national economy should be assessed. If the advantages and disadvantages regarding manufacturing are taken into account solely, and their utilization is neglected, an incorrect conclusion will be reached when the technological economics study is completed. Thus, a key step in any technological economics study is the analysis of the advantages and disadvantages of technological schemes and their impact factors. They should be examined comprehensively.

3. **The development of functions between economic indicators and parameters for technological schemes, and listing of the corresponding formula and equation of technological economics, also called technological economics mathematical model**

Based on the analysis of the merits and demerits of technological schemes, mathematical formulas and equations can be developed to calculate the economic indicators and to express the functions among parameters for various technological schemes. The equations and formulas calculating the economic indicators and expressing functions among parameters for technological schemes are called technological economic equations and formulas, or the technological economic mathematical model. For instance, there are some technological schemes numbered 1, 2, 3…i. A, B, C…J are the economic indicators for technological schemes. $X_1, X_2, X_3, \ldots X_k$ are the parameters for technological schemes, also called decision variables. $\alpha, \beta, \gamma, \ldots \omega$ are the technological economic parameters that impact economic indicators.[2] According to the properties of technological economic issues and specific conditions, the following economic formulas and equations can be developed:

Form I:

$$A_1 \text{ or } B_1,\ C_1 \ldots J_1 = f_1(\alpha_1, \beta_1, \gamma_1, \ldots, \omega_1)$$

$$A_2 \text{ or } B_2,\ C_2 \ldots J_2 = f_2(\alpha_2, \beta_2, \gamma_2, \ldots, \omega_2)$$

[2] In order to describe issues more clearly, we divide the parameters into two types. One represents technological scheme and is called the parameter of technical scheme, expressed by $X_1, X_2, X_3 \ldots$. For example, in order to choose the economic section of a conductor, conductor section s is the parameter that represents technological scheme, because s represents the different technological schemes. The other parameter does not represent the technical scheme. It is called the parameter of technological economics and is expressed by α, β, γ … For example, the factors influencing the economic sections of a conductor, such as electrovalence, utilization time, and the electrical conductivity of conductor, are this type of parameters, which have a known fixed value at a certain time, location, and condition.

$$A_i \text{ or } iB_i,\ C_i \ldots J_i = f_i(\alpha_i, \beta_i, \gamma_i, \ldots, \omega_i)$$

Form II:

$$A \text{ or } B,\ C \ldots J = f(X, \alpha, \beta, \gamma, \ldots, \omega)$$

Form III:

$$\begin{cases} A_\Sigma \text{or } B_\Sigma, C_\Sigma \ldots J_\Sigma = f(X_1, X_2, \ldots, X_k, \alpha, \beta, \gamma, \ldots, \omega) \\ F_1 = f_1(X_1, X_2, \ldots, X_{k-m}, \alpha, \beta, \gamma, \ldots, \omega) \\ F_1 = f_2(X_1, X_2, \ldots, X_{k-n}, \alpha, \beta, \gamma, \ldots, \omega) \\ \ldots \end{cases}$$

Form I of the technological economic formula is applied widely in practice, such as the selection of factory site and farm; the selection of a fine variety of agriculture; the selection of raw materials, fuel, and power; the selection of crop rotation systems; the selection of reform measures of agricultural technology; and the selection of construction modes. T Form II of the technological economic formula is utilized in the optimal selection of technological parameters, such as the selection of economic insulation thickness of pipeline, the confirmation of economic pressure drop and flow rate of pipelines, and the selection of the economic section of electric conductor. Form III of the technological economic formula is adopted to perform the optimal selection of parameters in many technological schemes, such as the confirmation of reasonable proportion of hydropower and thermal power in complex power systems, the confirmation of the rational sectoral structure of national economy, and the scheduling of communications and transportation.

It is necessary to point out that when developing the technological economic formulas and equations, the main economic indicators and parameters can only be selected correctly based on the actual requirements. The number of economic indicators for technological schemes is large, and so is that of the parameters. It is not practical to consider every economic indicator and parameter or to develop formulas to calculate them, because, on the one hand, this will make work complicated. On the other hand, it is useless for the optimal selection of technological schemes.

4. **The calculating and solving formulas and equations of technological economics**

For calculating and solving the formulas and equations of technological economics, the necessary resources and data, including the indicators of technology, economy, and technological economics, must be loaded into these formulas and equations first, and then calculations can be conducted. Next, after the value of each economic indicator is ready, comparison of technological schemes can be performed. The optimal scheme is selected based on the results of comparison or on the question of whether the optimal economic indicator can be achieved. In the ordinary way, solving formulas and equations of technological economics means finding the maximum or minimum values of economic indicators. The maximum or minimum values are determined by economic standards and indicators. For example, if economic indicators, such as material consumption, investment, cost, value, annual consumption cost, and total consumption cost, are taken as the economic standards and the indicators of the technological scheme, the minimum values, not the maximum values, of economic indicators need to be calculated. In contrast, if economic indicators, such as social labor productivity, net income, and net output value, are taken as economic standards and indicators, the maximum values, not the minimum values of economic indicators need to be calculated.[3] Two approaches are usually adopted to calculate the maximum or minimum values of economic indicators. The first one uses listing and diagram, whereas the other one uses mathematical analysis including higher mathematics, applied mathematics, and operations research, in order to find the optimal scheme. This approach is only valid when the functional relations of the economic indicators and parameters can be completely expressed by the mathematical formulas. However, in practice, the functional relations of economic indicators and parameters cannot be completely expressed by mathematical formulas. In other words, such relations are not regular. Thus, in practice, the first approach is applied much more frequently. When operations research is applied, the technological economic formulas (Form III) will be more complicated, because many equations with constraint conditions are added. Such complicated technological economic formulas are called mathematical technological and economic models in operations research. Economic indicators are the objectives in objective functions. Due to the complications and difficulties of calculating and solving the mathematical models of technological economics, the computer is increasingly used. We will not, however, discuss in detail the applications of mathematical methods in the technological economics study. It should be pointed out that for the purpose of getting the economic optimal technological scheme, the most advanced and correct mathematical calculation methods, along with accurate and reliable resources and data, must be adopted. Resources and data are also called information. The degree of accuracy and the reliability of resources and data greatly affect the economic results of calculation for any technological scheme. Therefore, handling the basic materials and data correctly is an important step in any technological economics study. In some circumstances, the advanced mathematical methods must be adopted, especially in mathematical statistics and probability theory. For instance, the statistics and forecast for requirement of products, the accident rates of machines and equipment, current, temperature, wind speed, percentage of sunshine, and other indicators of technological economics require mathematical statistics and probability theory.

---

[3] Which economic indicators should be adopted in technological schemes will be discussed in detail in the Chap. 2, Theories in Technological Economics and in Chap. 3, Methods in Technological Economics.

5. **The comprehensive evaluation of technological schemes**

The above methods merely evaluate the economic results of technological schemes from the perspective of quantity. However, sometimes the merits and demerits of technological schemes cannot be calculated with formulas in quantity. The merits and demerits of technological schemes in politics, defense, society, culture, environment, ecology, and natural resources should be taken into consideration, as well. In this instance, comprehensive analysis, argumentation, and evaluation are needed to select the optimal technological economic schemes.

6. **Feedback control of technological schemes**

It should also be pointed out that the aforementioned procedure of a technological economic study is a dynamic process. Sometimes feedback control is needed, according to the results of economic and comprehensive assessment. The initial schemes may need to be revised and updated and then the procedure needs to be gone over again. When some important indicators change greatly with the development of technology and economy, the procedure needs to start again from the beginning in order to achieve higher economic results. In a word, each stage of the technological schemes needs to be performing technological and economic work.

It must also be pointed out that the above-mentioned procedure of a technological economic study is a primary one, but it is not the only one. Other procedures can be adopted according to the characteristics of the technological and economic issues.

Chapter 6
Sub-disciplines of Technological Economics and the Relationship Between Technological Economics and Other Disciplines

6.1 Introduction

Is Technological Economics a large discipline or small one? If it is a large one, what are its sub-disciplines? What characteristics does Technological Economics have? Which disciplines have close relationships with Technological Economics? These are questions that will be answered in this chapter. This chapter covers the sub-disciplines of Technological Economics, the characteristics of Technological Economics, and the relationship between Technological Economics and other disciplines.

6.2 Sub-disciplines of Technological Economics

Technological Economics is a large discipline that contains many sub-disciplines (see Fig. 6.1).

These sub-disciplines are categorized by the characteristics of the issues in Technological Economics that they study. In other words, they are categorized according to the the contradictory relationships between technology and economy they study. Technological issues exist in the departments of the national economy and in the stages and aspects of production and construction. Therefore, corresponding sub-disciplines of Technological Economics exist. For example, based on the departments of the national economy, the sub-disciplines of Technological Economics can be categorized into primary industry Technological Economics; secondary industry Technological Economics; tertiary industry Technological Economics; agricultural Technological Economics; industrial Technological Economics; construction Technological Economics; communication and transportation Technological Economics; post and telecommunications Technological Economics; business Technological Economics; culture, education, and public health Technological Economics; science Technological Economics; defense Technological Economics; and public utility Technological Economics. Furthermore, industrial Technological Economics can

S. Xu, *Technological Economics*,
https://doi.org/10.1007/978-981-15-8582-1_6

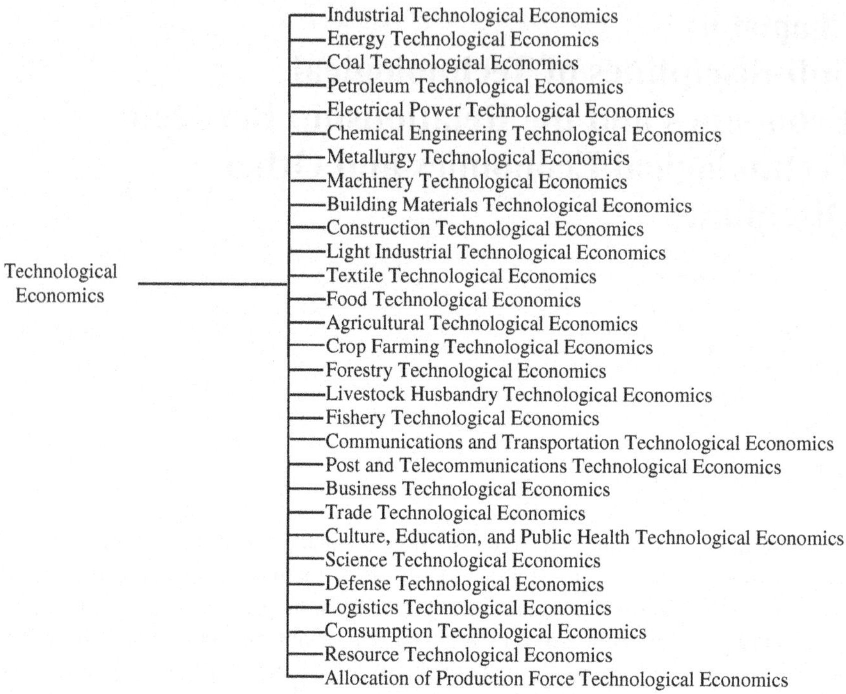

Fig. 6.1 Sub-disciplines of Technological Economics

be dub-categorized into coal Technological Economics, petroleum Technological Economics, electrical power Technological Economics, chemical engineering Technological Economics, metallurgy Technological Economics, machinery Technological Economics, building materials Technological Economics, light industrial Technological Economics, food Technological Economics, and textile Technological Economics. Similarly, agricultural Technological Economics can be further categorized into crop farming Technological Economics, forestry Technological Economics, livestock husbandry Technological Economics, and fishery Technological Economics. By parity of reasoning, other sub-disciplines can be categorized. For example, based on the stage of production and construction, Technological Economics can be categorized into experimental investigation Technological Economics, reconnaissance Technological Economics, planning and design Technological Economics, construction Technological Economics, and production Technological Economics. Some comprehensive and trans-departmental studies on Technological Economics can have their own sub-disciplines, such as energy Technological Economics, transportation Technological Economics, resource Technological Economics, consumption Technological Economics, logistics Technological Economics, environmental Technological Economics, and information Technological Economics. It should be pointed out that among these sub-disciplines, some have been developed for quite a long time, such as energy Technological Economics, also called "comprehensive energy technology" overseas, and transportation Technological Economics, called "comprehensive transportation technology" overseas. Others just emerge and are still in the budding stage.

6.3 Characteristics of Technological Economics and the Relationship Between Technological Economics and Other Disciplines

Technological Economics has many characteristics, so it is closely related to other disciplines (see Fig. 6.2). The characteristics of Technological Economics are listed as below:

1. **Comprehensiveness**

Technological Economics is a comprehensive inter-discipline which combines natural science, technological science and social science, and economics. It does not study pure technological issues, nor pure economic issues. Instead, it studies the

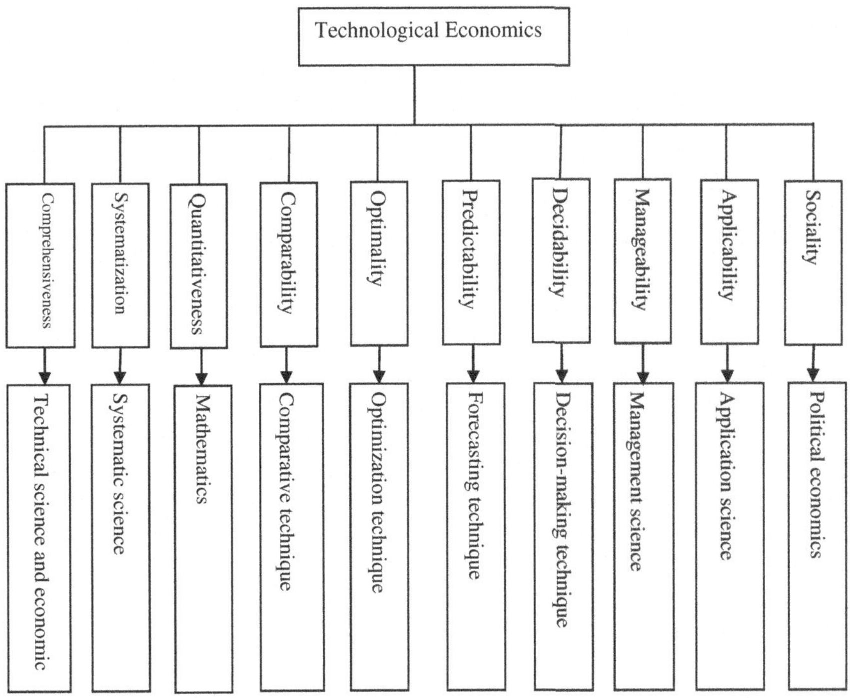

Fig. 6.2 Characteristics of Technological Economics and the Relationships between Technological Economics and other Disciplines

economic issues of technology; in other words, it studies the issues of the relationship between technology and the economy. This is the unique characteristic of Technological Economics and the way in which Technological Economics differs from technological science and economics. Therefore, Technological Economics is very close to technological science (e.g. crop cultivation; farming; irrigation and water conservancy; the feeding of livestock, poultry and fish; grasslands; forestry; agricultural machinery; energy; the chemical industry; metallurgy; machinery; light industry; textile; transportation; post and telecommunications; construction; and environmental protection), and economics (e.g. political economics, sectoral economics, economic statistics, and economic geography). Due to these characteristics, Technological Economics can be placed in both the category of natural science and technological science and in the category of social science and economics. For example, energy Technological Economics is close to power engineering, heat engineering, hydraulic engineering, new energy engineering, political economics, industrial economics, and economic geography. So it is a sub-discipline of energy science and a sub-discipline of economics. Technological Economics researchers must have knowledge across a variety of diverse disciplines. Other than natural science and technology of production, they must know and understand political economics, the allocation of the productive force, and economic accounting. Technological Economics study must comprehensively consider the factors of technology and economy and their relationships. Researchers must not only consider economic issues from the perspective of technology, but must also consider technological issues from the perspective of economics. Technologies are the base, whereas the economy is the target. These two must be studied together. Equal attention should be paid to each. The focus is to explore the economic rationality of technologies.

2. **Systematization**

According to the principles of Marxist philosophy, no technology or economy is isolated. They are part of the whole system of technology and economy in a society. Thus, each technological economic issue should be put into the whole technology and economy system in a society for studying. The relationship and interaction between them and other parts should be explored. The merits or demerits of technological schemes caused by other portions should be analyzed systematically. For instance, when studying the economic issue of energy production, the research should begin with production, transportation, processing, transition, storage, distribution, and the usage of energy. The interrelationship between energy and the national economy should be considered, as well. The views of the system and of systematic analysis are very important in technological economic study. Therefore, Technological Economics is very close to system science. Knowledge of the methods of system science are very necessary for technological economic researchers.

3. **Quantitativeness**

Traditional economics mainly focuses on discussion, argument, and qualitative analysis. In contrast, Technological Economics focuses on quantitative analysis, so it is a kind of quantitative science. Quantitativeness is an important characteristic of Technological Economics. For each technological economic issue, other than qualitative analysis, quantitative analysis is required. Quantitative conclusions are indispensable as well. Thus, Technological Economics is very close to mathematics, including ordinary mathematics, calculus, linear algebra, mathematical statistics, probability theory, operations research, and computer techniques. Mathematics is the foundation of Technological Economics because various mathematics formulas and methods are applied in any Technological Economics study. Technological Economics researchers should be proficient in mathematical methods and calculation tools. It should be pointed out that Technological Economics is essentially different from quantitative economics. The former explores the relationship and the regularity between technology and economic rationality by studying technological schemes, whereas the latter mainly explores the quantitative relationship of the macro economy by studying economic quantitative models.

4. **Comparability**

Comparative principles and methods are important in any Technological Economics study. Comparison produces identification. Therefore, it is necessary to compare two technological schemes so that the solution for a technological economic issue can be found. Due to the development of science and technology, two or more options are frequently available for meeting the requirements of the society and the people. If there is only one technological scheme available, a comparison of Technological Economics is meaningless. However, in the strict sense, the situation that only one technological scheme would be available does not exist, because even though only one feasible technological scheme exists, items to be compared can always be found. This object is not to accept the existing technological scheme. Thus, the comparison between accepting and not accepting the technological scheme can be conducted. In socialist society, the only technological scheme must be used for some specific purposes or needs. Not accepting the scheme is not an option. For instance, a state-run farm is required by the state to produce a certain amount of crops. This scheme must be carried out no matter what the cost will be. It is meaningless to compare this scheme with not using it. In this scenario, it should be considered what schemes are available for producing the required amount of crops, such as total mechanization, semi-mechanization, and total manual work. These three schemes should be compared from the perspective of Technological Economics. Comparability is an important characteristic in Technological Economics. Researchers in this field must know comparative principles and methods.

5. **Optimality**

The purpose of technological and economic study is to select an optimal scheme, the one that is feasible and has economic rationality, by comparing available technological schemes. How to pick the optimal scheme is an important task in Technological Economics. Thus, Technological Economics is related to optimal methods. Researchers in this field must know optimal methods, such as operations research.

6. **Predictability**

Technological and economic study conducts analysis, comparison, calculation, evaluation, and optimization on available technological schemes, one of which will be used in the future. Thus, a technological and economic study has predictability. Among these schemes, some are more practical so they carry certainty. In this case, the predictions about them are more accurate. Others are not so practical and have a smaller certainty. Thus, the predictions about them are not accurate. Scientific prediction methods must be applied in any Technological Economics study, especially when analyzing and processing data and resources with high randomness. From this, it can be seen that Technological Economics is close to forecasting study. Researchers in this field must know prediction techniques.

7. **Decidability**

Technological Economics is close to decision science as well. In a sense, Technological Economics is a method or an approach for decision making. It provides scientific supports for decision makers and helps them find solutions for technological economic issues so that they can make decisions on multiple technological schemes and multiple targets. Therefore, decidability is an important characteristic of Technological Economics. Researchers in this field should also know a great deal about decision making.

8. **Manageability**

Because the Technological Economics study provides services for management organization and personnel, the result of Technological Economics is an important measurement for management, especially economic management. So Technological Economics is close to management science. According to the author's large management science theory, Technological Economics and management should both be placed in the category of big management.[1] It has been proved in practice that the promotion and adoption of the results of a Technological Economics study depend on the scientific management of leaders at different levels.

9. **Applicability**

Technological Economics has a direct relationship with the development of the national economy. It is a kind of applied science. The goals and tasks of a Technological Economics study are clear. The Technological Economics study must take into account the natural resources, technology conditions, and social economic status in a certain country or area. Its data and resources mostly come from the practice of production, not from experiments in labs. Therefore, Technological Economics has high applicability and is close to the national economy.

[1]Xu and Xu [2011].

10. **Sociality**

According to the author's entity theory of Technological Economics, technological economic issues exist in every society. But the goals and methods of a Technological Economics study differ across societies. In the socialist system, the Technological Economics study must follow the basic economic laws and fair efficiency laws. It must start from the benefits of the entire national economy. Partial and sectoral interests must be subordinated to the overall interest of the whole country. Temporary interests must be subordinated to long-term fundamental interests. Thus, the standpoints, viewpoints, and methods of the Technological Economics study are different across different societies. Technological Economics in China is socialist Technological Economics, which is guided by Marxism and Mao Zedong Thought. Of course, useful things abroad should not be excluded. Instead, they should be considered and learned from.

It should be noted that the ten characteristics listed above are the main ones for Technological Economics. Sub-disciplines of economics share the first five characteristics with Technological Economics. These characteristics indicate that Technological Economics is close to many different disciplines. However, it also essentially differs from other disciplines. The essential difference is that Technological Economics specifically studies the contradictory relationship between technology and the economy, whereas other disciplines study other contradictory relationships.

Reference

Xu, S.B. and Xu, L. D. (2011). Human society has only one science – Big management science. Research report at Beijing Jiaotong University

Part II
Theories of Technological Economics

This section describes the core of technological economics. Since he founded technological economics about 50 years ago, the author has developed ten theories of technological economics, including the effect of the technological economy, the evaluation of the technological economy, the comparison in the technological economy, the optimization in the technological economy, the control in the technological economy, the decision-making in the technological economy, the entity in the technological economy, the economic elements in the technological economy, the information in the technological economy, and the comprehensive evaluation of the technological economy. The last four are new theories that have been added in this edition. The details of these ten theories are discussed in this section.

Chapter 7
Theory of the Technological Economy Entity

7.1 Introduction

The seventh chapter, entitled Technological Economics in the Ten-Year National Scientific and Technological Development Plan (1963–1972), was developed because the Party Central Committee headed by Mao Zedong realized the urgency and the necessity of combining technology and the economy. Given that little was known about how to combine technology and the economy, what the regularities of the combination would be, and how to evaluate the combination, a discipline that specifically studied these questions needed to be established. This is the external factor that drove the emergence of technological economics in China. The Theory of Contradictions notes that external causes are the conditions for changes, while internal causes are the basis for changes, and that external causes take effect through internal causes.[1] If external causes exist and internal causes do not, the outline of technological economics would not have been developed in China. What, then, were the internal causes? The theory of technological economy entity was the internal cause that drove the emergence of technological economics in China. The author argues that since the appearance of human society, including primitive society, agricultural society, industrial society, and information society, an economy, an objective indivisible entity that combines technology and economy, has been in existence. This entity is technological economy. The existence of the technological economy is the internal cause that drove the outline of technological economics. The theory of technological economy entity is the most important basic theory in technological economics. This chapter covers this theory and the contradictory, but unified, principle of technological economics.

[1] Mao [MA66].

S. Xu, *Technological Economics*,
https://doi.org/10.1007/978-981-15-8582-1_7

7.2 Opinions of the Theory of Technological Economy Entity

7.2.1 Objective Reality of the Theory of Technological Economy Entity

Technology and the economy have long been isolated and have been treated as two completely different categories. Studies were separated in two categories as well. The author argues that, since the beginning of history, all entities are technological economy entities, that no pure technological entities exist, and that no pure economic ones exist, either. For example, agricultural technologies and the agricultural economy exist in agricultural society. Industrial technologies and the industrial economy exist in industrial society. Information technologies and the information economy exist in information society. Technology and the economy are integrated and are indivisible. They are separated merely for the purpose of meeting the requirements of human cognition, scientific research, and the social division of labor (Table 7.1).

It should be pointed out that the technological economy is an entity existing objectively. It is not a man-made blend of technology and the economy. Thus, the entity of technological economy is not divisible. Those that can be split are not entitative technologies, nor an entitative economy, but entities themselves. For instance, a machine can be disassembled into its parts. A factory can be separated into several workshops. An industrial sector can be divided into industries, enterprises, and units. A national economy can be divided into primary, secondary, and tertiary industries. A country can be divided into provinces, cities, counties, communities, and families. All of these entities, big and small, have technology and economy. The two coexist in one large entity at every moment. They are indivisible. This characteristic is determined by the contradictory but unified relationship between technology and the economy.

Table 7.1 Interrelation between technology and economy

Category		Economy			
		Best	Better	Bad	Development & change
Technology	Most advanced(advanced)	=	⊥	⊥	~
	Advanced(medium)	⊥	=	⊥	~
	Unadvanced(traditionally laggard)	⊥	⊥	=	~
	Development & Change	~	~	~	~

Note Symbol "=" means that technology and the economy are unified and adaptive; "⊥" means that technology and the economy are contradictive and conflicted; "~" means that technology and the economy are developing and changing together

7.2.2 Four Forms of the Entity of the Technological Economy

In human society, all technological economy entities have four forms: their technological form, their economic form, their information form, and their comprehensive form. It should be pointed out that all technological economy entities are in comprehensive form. In order to meet the requirements of scientific research, cognition, and the resolution of practical issues, people usually inspect the technological form, the economic form, and the information form of technological economy entities separately when they check their comprehensive form. For example, similar to technological economy entities in agriculture, industry, and service, logistics is a cross-departmental comprehensive entity of the technological economy. It is the entity logistic if it is inspected from the perspective of the technological form; it is the capital logistic from if it is viewed from the perspective of economic form; it is the information logistic if considered from the perspective of information form; and it is the comprehensive logistic if viewed from the perspective of comprehensive form. Therefore, logistics has four formats, namely entity logistics, capital logistics, information logistics, and comprehensive logistics. This reflects the theory that technological economy entities have four forms. From this, it can be seen that studies on any technological economy entity in human society should consider these four forms.

In modern commodity economy societies, the basic objective entity that exists is commodity. Commodities can be classified into six categories based on their characteristics: manpower, the property force, the material force, the natural force, the transportation force, and the time force. The continuous circle of these six types of commodities – from input, production, and circulation to consumption – drives the development of the economy and the increase of wealth per capita in human societies. Meanwhile, the technology levels and the economic efficiency of these six categories of commodities increase continuously as well. As a result, the technologies and the economy in technological economy entities are improved together. This is the law of how technologies and economy in human societies grow.

7.2.3 Varieties of the Entity of Technological Economy

From the perspective of region, the entities of technological economy exist in every country and in every area (such as province, city, county, and community). From the perspective of sector, the entities of technological economy exist in every sector of the national economy, including the primary industry (agriculture), the secondary industry (industry and construction), the tertiary industry (service industries, such as services for farming, forestry, husbandry, and fishery; geological exploration; water conservancy management; communication; transportation and warehousing; post and telecommunication; wholesale and retail; trade; catering; finance; insurance; real estate; social work; public health; sports; social welfare; education; culture;

arts; radio, film; TV; scientific research; comprehensive technological services; state organs; party organs; and social organizations). In addition, the entities of the technological economy exist in each industry, enterprise, unit, and family. From the perspective of stage, the entities of the technological economy exist in each stage of production and construction, such as investigation and survey, development research, planning and design, construction, and production. From the perspective of comprehensive field, the entities of the technological economy exist in every comprehensive field, including energy, resources, environmental protection, logistic, and information, of national economic construction in all countries and regions.

7.2.4 Scientific Research Properties of the Entity of Technological Economy

People have long studied the different forms of the entities of the technological economy, according to their requirements. As such, different disciplines appeared. Natural science and engineering science study the entities of the technological economy from the perspective of technology forms. Humanity and the social sciences (including economics) study the entities of technological economy from the perspective of economic forms. Information science studies the entities of the technological economy from the perspective of information forms. Technological economy science studies the entities of the technological economy from the perspective of comprehensive form. It can be seen that the perspective of a technological economy science study is different from those of natural science, engineering science, humanity science, social science, and information science. In terms of disciplines, technological economy science consists of technological economics and its sub disciplines, such as agricultural technological economics, industrial technological economics, construction technological economics, services technological economics, energy technological economics, logistics technological economics, environment technological economics, business technological economics, real estate technological economics, information technological economics, education technological economics, and finance technological economics.

7.3 Contradictory Unification Principle for Technological Economy

Technology and the economy are very close among the entities of the technological economy. They are unified and adaptive, contradictive and conflicted, developing and changing together.

7.3.1 *Unified and Adaptive Principle of Technology and Economy*

There are two aspects to the unified and adaptive principle of technology and economy. On one hand, people must work and produce by using certain technologies to develop the economy. Any technology applied in labor and production needs to consume and occupy manpower, capital power, material power, natural power, transportation power, and time. Thus, technology cannot be separated from economy in production and labor. Neither can the economy be separated from technology. They coexist and are a single entity, indivisible. On the other hand, technology and the economy promote and adapt to each other within this entity. The development of technology promotes the economy. Similarly, the development of the economy promotes technology as well.

7.3.2 *Contradictory and Conflicted Principle of Technology and Economy*

Other than the unified and adaptive relationship, technology and the economy are contradictive and conflicted. Their contradictions and conflicts exist in daily life. There are four situations: (1) Technology itself is advanced. But, due to the restrictions of the social economic conditions and the technological conditions, the economic results of technology are not satisfying. So the technology cannot be widely applied in practice, in production. For example, modern technologies, such as new energies for power generation and the complete mechanization and automation in all national economic sectors, are not developed well in China; (2) Technology is unadvanced but has good economic results. Some of these kind of technologies are adopted in practice, such as agricultural manual labor, other manual labor, and bicycles for transportation, because they meet the actual requirements in a certain country or a certain area; (3) Technology is advanced, but under certain circumstances, some technologies are adopted because of good economic results and others are not because of bad economic results. For instance, roads and railways are both advanced transportation methods. But railways are good for long-distance transportations, whereas roads are good for short ones; (4) Some technologies have same good economic results. But in certain conditions, one is better than the other and is adopted in practice. For example, many similar products are available in the market at similar prices. Some were produced by an advanced technology, while others by an unadvanced one. Some have good quality, while others have poor quality. Those products that were produced with advanced technology and with good quality will be accepted widely. But those produced with unadvanced technology and with poor quality will have difficulty in development.

7.3.3 *Developing and Changing Principle of Technology and Economy*

As technology and the economy contradict each other continuously, their relationship will change. The original non-economic technologies will change to economic ones, whereas the original economic technologies will change to non-economic ones. The original laggard technologies will become advanced, whereas the original advanced technologies will become unadvanced. The original unified and adaptive relationship will become contradictive and conflicted, whereas the original contradictory and conflicted relationship will become unified and adaptive. Many examples can prove these changes. Vacuum tubes were an advanced technology. But after the semi-conductor appeared, they became unadvanced. Similarly, black and white television was advanced, but color television made it unadvanced. In a word, the development of science and technology, especially of information technology, drives the economic results of technologies.

It should be pointed out that although the examples listed above are all hard technology ones, these theories work for soft technologies as well. In sum, the relationship between technology and the economy is contradictive and unified and develops dialectically. This is the contradictory but unified principle for the technological economy.

Reference

[MA66] Mao, Z. D. (1966). Theory of Contradictions. Selected Works of Mao Zedong. Beijing, People Publishing House, Page 291.

Chapter 8 Theory of Technological Economy Factors

8.1 Introduction

The author initially proposed four production factors, namely the labor force, investment, materials and resources, for calculating the total social labor consumption and the total social consumption cost in his research report about technological economics *On Methodology in Technological Economics Study*[1] finished in 1963–1965. He argued later, in 1984[2] and 1986,[3] that labor and production should have six conditions or six forces simultaneously. The six conditions include laborers, implements of labor, labor objects, labor environments, labor space, and labor time. The six forces include manpower, capital power (or financial resources), the material force, natural forces, transportation power, and time. In 1988,[4] the author further proposed the six force substitution principle. He argued that the six forces were, essentially, the six production factors. Based on these research results, the author proposed the theory of technological economy elements, one of the fundamental theories in technological economics. The author noted that all technological economy entities are the production entities of the national economy and the social life entities. Both production and life must have their required conditions, which can be called production factors and life elements. Technological economy elements are the generic terms of production factors and life elements. This chapter discusses the theory of production factors and the theory of life elements, in detail.

[1]This research result, *Introduction to Technological Economics*, was published by Shanghai Science and Technology Publishing House in 1980. This monograph of technological economics is the first edition of the book that the author wrote about technological economics. China Association for Science and Technology.

[2]Xu, S. (1984). *Technological Economics* (volumes I & II), China Science and Technology Policy Study, Modern Management Knowledge Lecturer Group of China Association for Science and Technology. This is the second edition of the book that the author wrote about technological economics.

[3]Xu [XU86].

[4]Xu [XU88].

S. Xu, *Technological Economics*,
https://doi.org/10.1007/978-981-15-8582-1_8

8.2 The Theory of Production Factors

The theory of production factors is a basic one in technological economics. It consists of the hierarchical theory of production factors and the six forces theory of production factors.

There is plenty of literature about the intension and the extension of the production factors, but disagreement still exists. This is because people usually define the production factors from diverse perspectives in practice. As a result, there is no uniform definition of production factors available. The second reason is that the definitions of production factors that have been adopted in practice lack theoretical conscientiousness because people usually discuss production factors from diverse perspectives at the practical level. Therefore, it is necessary to conduct systematical research on the basic theories in technological economics, such as the scientific concept of production factors and the levels of the production factors. Following, find a discussion about these two issues, in detail.

The production factor refers to all of the economic resources put into production and the service activities that are found in the textbooks of western economics. According to *Ci Hai* (the Chinese Word Dictionary), the production factor is all of the social resources that can be used in production, including land, labor, and funding (capital). Sometimes, the entrepreneurs' talent is included as well.[5] The *Concise Encyclopedia Britannica* (1986) points out that the production factor is the economic resources used for producing commodities and services.[6] The three definitions above are essentially the same, because they all treat production factors as resources that are put into the effort of production. However, the definition of resource (either economic or social) is too broad. In other words, they can refer to both physical materials and abstract nonmaterial materials. Thus, these definitions are very confusing if people try to follow them in order to understand what "production factor" is. In the *Economy and Management Dictionary*, production factor is defined as the necessary factor or condition that is needed for the production of material resources.[7] Compared with the previous three definitions, this one is the most accurate, and it is not easily misunderstood. But it neglects the nonmaterial things that human societies produce. In fact, the production factor does exist in the field of nonmaterial production.

The author argues that the production factor has both a narrow sense and broad sense.

The narrow sense of the production factor refers to the basic material resources that are necessary for producing commodities and services. It should be pointed out that these resources are necessary, but they are not required to be invested. In addition, these resources are basic materials, not economic or social resources. These two characteristics make this definition different from the existing ones. They are the author's own innovation.

---

[5]Ci Hai [CI89].

[6]*Concise Encyclopedia Britannica* (Volume 7), Encyclopedia of China Publishing House, 1986, Page 162.

[7]Ma and Sun [MS85].

More specifically, the basic material resources needed for producing commodities and services are not always money inputs. Although many inputs require money, such as manpower, raw materials of energy production, factory building, machines, and equipment, some inputs do not require money. For example, sunshine and air are provided by the nature. They are indispensable material resources, both in life and in production, but they cannot be bought with money. Therefore, it is more suitable to call these things necessary resources, rather than inputs.

The term "social and economic resources" has broad meanings. It can refer either to material resources or to abstract non-material resources. Thus, the author argues that the production factors are the material resources in social and economic resources. They include natural resources but they do not cover non-material economic and social materials. Similarly, there are many factors or conditions that impact production, such as the production relations. As such, the author notes that the basic material resources do not include non-material resources. It can be seen that it is more accurate to use the term "basic material resource" than to choose "economic resource" or "social resource."

The broad sense of the term "production factor" refers to the elements that compose production entity (the production system) at different levels in the large production of the national economy. This meaning is an understanding of production factor from the perspective of systematology. The so-called production entity (production system) can be either the entire production system of a country or a specific production department, industry, or unit. The author believes that many scholars refer to this broad sense when they mention the term production factor. However, because the term "production factor" has never received a clear definition, understanding about production factor can be confusing.

In order to elaborate upon the concept of production factor more clearly, the author proposes a specific hierarchy theory of production factors.

8.2.1 The Hierarchy Theory of Production Factors

The hierarchy theory of production factors aims to explore the hierarchical characteristics of production factors. National economic production consists of diverse production factors. According to their effect ranges and levels in social national economic production, the production factors can be categorized into the four hierarchies shown in Fig. 8.1.

The top level in the hierarchy is the sectoral production factor, which has the largest range and the highest level in social national economic production. After new China was founded, the socialist planned economy had been implemented for several decades. During that period, the production sector referred to the material production department, namely agriculture and industry. After reform and the opening-up, China began to transit to a socialist market economy. The meaning of the term "production sector" changed. Besides the primary industry (agriculture) and the secondary industry (industry and construction industry), the non-material production

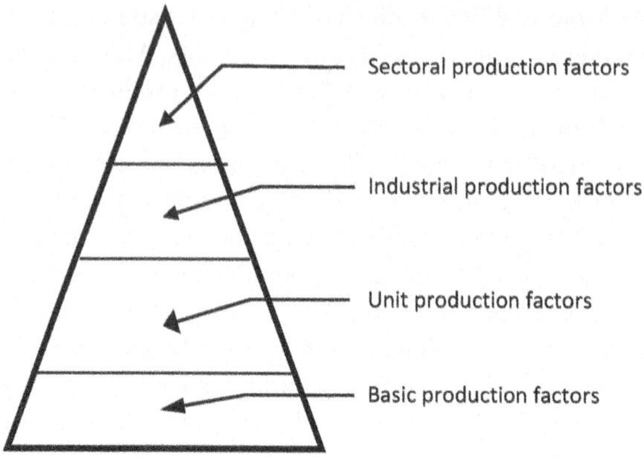

Fig. 8.1 Hierarchies of production factors

sector became an independent production sector called "tertiary industry" (service industry). As a result, the whole of the social national economic production comprised three components: primary industry, secondary industry, and tertiary industry. At the top level in social national economic production, these three production sectors are called "sectoral production sectors."

The second level is the industrial production factor, which has the second biggest range in social national economic production. As we know, each sector consists of many production industries. For example, primary industry contains farming, forestry, livestock husbandry, and fisheries Secondary industry contains four main industries: mining; manufacturing; production and supply for power, gas and water; and construction, along with other small industries. Tertiary industry contains services for farming, forestry, husbandry and fisheries, geological prospecting, water conservancy management, communication, transportation and warehousing, post and telecommunications, wholesale, retail, trade, and catering, financial and insurance, real estate, social services, health and sports, social welfare, education, culture, art, radio, film and television, scientific research, comprehensive technological services, national party organs, social organizations, and other services. These industries are components of the three industry sectors.

The third level is the unit production factor. Industrial production factors consist of many unit factors, which are the basic and the most important production entities, such as enterprise, unit, and family. Each industry has its own unit production factors. Therefore, the whole social national economic production is made up of numerous unit production factors, essentially.

The bottom level is the basic production factor. Each unit production factor must have six independent basic factors (also called six forces) at the same time. That is to say, any unit production factor consists of manpower, capital power,[8] the material force, natural forces, transportation forces, and time. These basic production

[8]Capital power was originally called fund force, which is the form of value superficially. In contrast, the other five production factors are the form of substance. In order to explain that the six production factors are all the form of substance, the author chose capital power to replace fund force.

factors are indispensable for production. If any of them is missing, production will not continue. Thus, the six forces are basic, important, and indispensable production factors. It is well known that a molecule of material is made up of chemical elements, which are the most basic and important components of materials. Basic production factors are similar to chemical elements. As such, the basic production factors can be called production elements as well. Material molecules are made up of chemical elements. For example, water molecules are made up of hydrogen and oxygen. Similarly, unit production factors are made up of basic production factors. For instance, the agriculture unit production factor is made up of the six agriculture production elements, including agricultural manpower, agricultural capital power (e.g. farmland, equipment, and instruments of labor), agricultural material forces (seed, fertilizer, pesticide, water, and electric power), agricultural natural forces (land, natural agricultural resource, light, and heat), transportation forces (logistic and people), and agricultural time (agricultural production time).

Table 8.1 is an example of the hierarchy theory of production factors. It lists farming, forestry, livestock husbandry and fisheries in the primary industry, coal, electric power, steel, and information in the secondary industry, and communication, education, culture, and management in the tertiary industry. This table shows the details of the four hierarchies of production factors. Each of the six forces has its own unique meaning. There is no overlap among them; they play their roles independently in the process of production. In sum, the six forces are the six production elements. This is how the six elements theory of production factors was named.

It should be pointed out that the first, second, and third hierarchies of production are all made up of the independent basic production factors in the fourth hierarchy. They are production entities at different levels, so they are also called "comprehensive production factors." All comprehensive production factors have outputs and products (material products and service). Different from the comprehensive production factors, the fourth level of production factors are six single ones, each of which is considered to be input in the process of production. They are not components of production activities and production entities. Although they do not generate output or products, the production process cannot be realized only with them. The hierarchy theory of production factors indicates that if there are no six forces, there are no unit production factors; if there are no unit production factors, there are no industrial production factors; if there are no industrial production factors, there are no sectoral production factors; if there are no sectoral production factors, there is no social national economic production. As such, the basic production factors (or the six forces) are the most important material basis for social national economic production. They are the base of production factors.

In sum, the sectoral production factors, the industrial production factors, and the unit production factors are comprehensive production factors composed of the six basic production factors. The six basic production factors are single production factors and are different from the other three ones. Only the single production factors are the basic production factors. They can be mentioned in the same breath with traditional production factors initially proposed by western scholars, such as labor, capital, and land. However, the comprehensive production factors cannot.

Table 8.1 An example of the hierarchy theory of production factors

Sectoral production factor		The primary industry			
Industrial production factor		Agriculture	Forestry	Livestock Husbandry	Fishery
Unit production factor		Agricultural enterprise	Forestry enterprise	Livestock Husbandry enterprise	Fishery enterprise
Basic production factor	Manpower	Laborers of agriculture	Laborers of forestry	Laborers of livestock husbandry	Laborers of fishery
	Capital force	Farmland, instruments of labor, and equipment	Forest farm, instruments of labor, and equipment	Animal farm, breeding stock, instruments of labor, and equipment	Fishing boat, catching tools, and equipment
	Material forces	Seed, fertilizer, pesticide, water and electric power	Sprout, fertilizer, pesticide, water, and electric power	Pup, feed, water, and energy	Fish fry, feed, water, and electric power
	Natural forces	Land, natural agricultural resource, light, and heat	Forest land, natural forestry resource, light, and water	Grassland, natural grass resource, light, and heat	Water area and natural fishery resources
	Transportation forces	Agricultural logistics and personnel	Forestry logistics and personnel	Livestock husbandry logistic and personnel	Fishery logistics and personnel
	Time forces	Agricultural production time	Forestry production time	Livestock husbandry production time	Fishery production time
Sectoral production factor		The secondary industry			
Industrial production factor		Coal industry	Electric power industry	Steel industry	Information industry
Unit production factor		Coal enterprise	Electric Power enterprise	Steel enterprise	Information enterprise
Basic production factor	Manpower	Personnel for coal production, technology, and management	Personnel for electricity production, technology, and management	Personnel for steel production, technology, and management	Personnel for information production, technology, and management

(continued)

Table 8.1 (continued)

Sectoral production factor		The primary industry			
Industrial production factor		Agriculture	Forestry	Livestock Husbandry	Fishery
Unit production factor		Agricultural enterprise	Forestry enterprise	Livestock Husbandry enterprise	Fishery enterprise
	Capital forces	Coal mining equipment and facilities	Power plant equipment and facilities	Steel plant equipment and facilities	Information production line, equipment, and facilities
	Material forces	Explosives, pit wood, steel, and electric power	Fuel and motive power	Iron ore, coking coal, thermal coal, and electric power	Information materials, components, and electric power
	Natural forces	Coal resources, land, sunshine, and air	Construction area, water, sunshine, and air	Construction area, water, sunshine, and air	Construction area, water, sunshine, and air
	Transportation forces	Logistics and personnel for coal production	Logistics and personnel for electric power production	Logistics and personnel for steel production	Logistics and personnel for information production
	Time forces	Coal production time	Electric power production time	Steel production time	Information production time
Sectoral production factor		The tertiary industry			
Industrial production factor		Communication	Education	Culture	Management
Unit production factor		Communication enterprise	Education enterprise	Culture enterprise	Management enterprise
Basic production factor	Manpower	Communication service personnel and technicians	Teachers and relevant personnel	Actors and relevant personnel	Managers
	Capital forces	Post office, communication equipment, and facilities	Classroom, teaching equipment, and information products	Performance sites, props, and garments	Office spaces and office equipment
	Material forces	Consumable materials, electric power and energy	Chalk and energy for lighting, heating, and ventilation	Energy for lighting, heating, and ventilation	Consumable office materials and energy

(continued)

Table 8.1 (continued)

Sectoral production factor		The primary industry			
Industrial production factor		Agriculture	Forestry	Livestock Husbandry	Fishery
Unit production factor		Agricultural enterprise	Forestry enterprise	Livestock Husbandry enterprise	Fishery enterprise
	Natural forces	Construction area, sunshine, and air	Construction area, sunshine and, air	Construction area, sunshine, and air	Construction area, sunshine, and air
	Transportation forces	Logistics and personnel for communication service	Logistics and personnel for education service	Logistics and personnel for culture service	Logistics and personnel for management service
	Time forces	Communication service time	Teaching time	Performance time	Management work time

For a long time, guided by the narrow sense of production factors, the production factors have referred to the independent basic material resources, such as labor, capital, and land. However, according to the broad sense of the term "production factors", some people argue that technology, education, information, culture, and management are production factors as well. The key point here is that this argument does not indicate the hierarchies of production factors. For example, education can be an industrial production factor, a unit production factor, or a basic production factor (e.g. talents). According to the narrow sense of production factors, only the specific products of education, culture, technology, and information, such as talents, books, and computers and software, are production elements. They are the six elements of production factors. It is unsuitable and not rigorous to call them production factors without categorizing them into hierarchies. The author argues that the hierarchy theory of production factors has both theoretical and practical significance.

8.2.2 The Six Elements Theory of Production Factors

As a basic theory in technological economics, the six elements theory of production factors explains the basic laws of economic production in human society. Figure 8.2 shows the diagram for the six elements of production factor.

The six elements theory of production factor includes six principles: the principle of the entity value of six forces, the principle of occupation and consumption of six forces, the unified principle of six forces space, the principle of combined action of six forces, the principle of replacement of six forces, and the principle of coordinated development of six forces. They are independent, and each of them explains a law in production. However, interactions exist among them, as shown in Fig. 8.3.

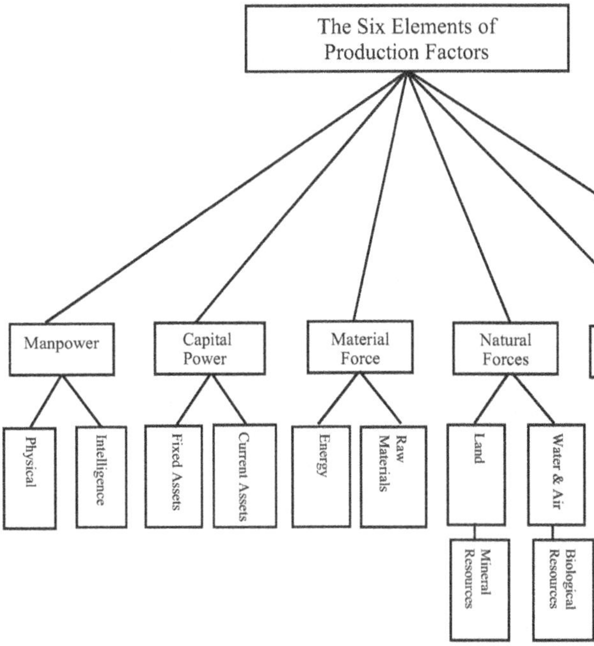

Fig. 8.2 Schematic diagram of six elements of production factor

Fig. 8.3 Relation diagram of the six forces of the production factor

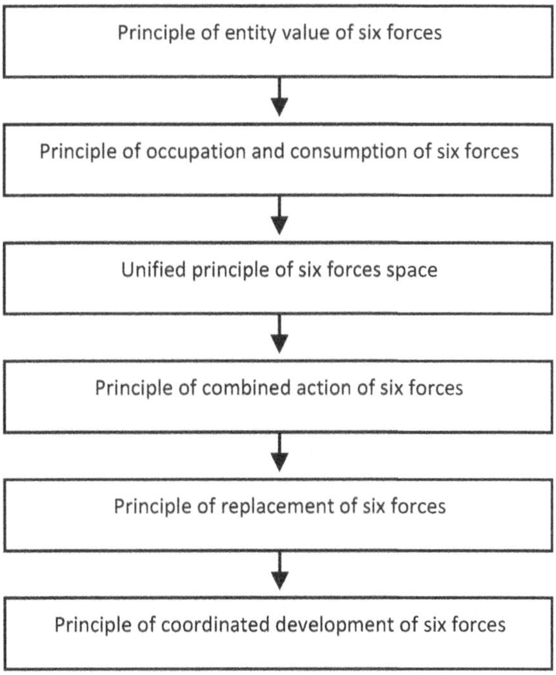

The principle of the entity value of six forces explains the relationship between substantial form and value form of the six basic production factors. In the process of production, the substantial form of the six basic production factors is primary and plays a basic role. The principle of occupation and consumption of six forces illustrates that the six basic production factors, either in substantial form or in value form, have the properties of occupation and consumption in the process of production. These two properties are equally important. The unified principle of six forces space notes that the six basic production factors must be combined with time and location (production site or service site). Basic production factors that are not combined with time and location do not work in the process of production. The principle of the combined action of six forces explains that the six basic production factors must coordinate each other for production after they are combined with time and location. The principle of the replacement of six forces notes that each of the six basic production factors can be substituted but cannot be replaced completely by the other ones. The principle of the coordinated development of six forces notes that production should focus on people and that the six basic production factors should develop in a coordinated manner, continuously improving production efficiency, and promoting the well-being of mankind. It should be pointed out that manpower is primary, and it is the most important among the six basic production factors.

The first five principles cover how to produce and the last one explains the purposes and requirements of production. This is the interrelationship among the six principles. Next, specific details about each of these six principles will be discussed.

1. **Principle of Entity Value of Six Forces**

All six basic production factors are material resources. However, each factor has two forms: the substantial form and the value form in the practice of social commodity economy production.

The substantial form of that production factor is primary, whereas the value form of the production factor is secondary. The latter is the monetary reflection of the price of the former. Those taking effect in the process of production are the substantial forms of production factors, not the value forms.

In commodity economy societies, due to the particularity and the measurable characteristics of money, the value form of the production factor can be used for commodity exchanges, unified measurement, and economic accounting.

After the foundation of the new China, the socialist planned economy focused on the production of material goods. Therefore, much attention was paid to the substantial form of the production factor. But the value form of the production factor did not attract much attention. After reform and the opening-up, China began to enter the period of the socialist market economy. The focus of people's attention changed. Much attention was paid to the value form of the production factor. The substantial form of production factor did not attract much attention. In fact, ensuring substantial supplies is the most important approach to protect production. Especially when the supply of production factors cannot meet the demand, the substantial form of production factor becomes more important. Therefore, the substantial form of production factors should considered first at all times. Equal attention should be paid to the substantial form and the value form of the production factor. Neither of them should be neglected.

This is the principle of the entity value of the six forces, which is the first object law in production. This principle is very important in technological economics. Both the input and output of production require consideration of the material index and the value index simultaneously and the performance of quantitative calculation.

The material index must be adopted to measure the status of supply and demand of the six production elements. Meanwhile, the value index must also be adopted to measure the input and output of the six production elements. Table 8.2 lists the intensions of the substantial form and the value form of the production factor.

Actual intension of substantial and value forms of six production factors is listed in Table 8.2.

Table 8.2 Two forms and two properties of production factors

No.	Production factor	Substantial form	
		Property of production occupation	Property of consumption occupation
1	Manpower	Laborers	Living labor
2	Capital power	Plants, machines, and equipment	Depreciation and abrasion of plants, machines, and equipment
3	Material force	Energy and raw materials	Energy and raw materials
4	Natural forces	Mineral resources, land, sunshine, and air	Mineral resources, land, sunshine, and air
5	Transportation power	Logistics and personnel	Mobile service of production factor
6	Time	Production time	Production time
No.	Production factor	Value form	
		Property of production occupation	Property of consumption occupation
1	Manpower	Current assets such as wages	Cost of labor wages
2	Capital power	Fixed assets, such as plants, machines, and equipment	Depreciation and major repair cost of plants, machines, and equipment
3	Material force	Current assets, such as reserved raw materials of energy	Cost of raw materials of energy
4	Natural forces	Fixed assets, such as mineral resources and land	Cost of natural resources
5	Transportation power	Current assets, such as logistics and personnel	Cost of logistics and personnel
6	Time	Current assets, such as interest	Time cost such as interest

2. **Principle of Occupation and Consumption of Six Forces**

The production factor "occupation" means that some factors are adopted but are not processed during the production process. Production factor consumption refers to those factors that are consumed during the production process, including physical processing and chemical processing. The six basic production factors are both occupied and consumed in the process of production. The production factors that are only occupied or only consumed do not exist in practice. In a normal production process, each production factor plays its own unique role. The production factor "occupation", without the production factor "consumption", will cause waste of production factors. In this case, the normal production process does not exist. The production factors are occupied first and then are consumed in production process. The production factors can be categorized into two groups, the occupation-lead factors and the consumption-lead factors, according to the roles that they play and the priority of occupation and consumption. Capital power is an occupation-led factor, and manpower, the material force, natural forces, transportation power, and time are consumption-led factors. Any production factor has both production occupation and production consumption. Production consumption and production occupation rely on each other. The production consumption and production occupation of each production factor have substantial form and value form. This is the content of the principle of occupation and the consumption of the six forces, the second law in production.

The relationship between the occupation and the consumption of the six forces is explained in detail:

(1) Manpower occupation and consumption. From the perspective of substantial form, "manpower occupation" refers to personnel occupied in the production process. Manpower consumption refers to the labor that occupied personnel do in production, including physical labor and brainwork. From the perspective of the value form, manpower occupation is the current assets, such as wages. Manpower consumption is a labor-related cost, such as salary. So-called "unused personnel" refers to the status in which only manpower occupation exists, but manpower consumption does not. That is not a normal production process. In a normal production process, every laborer should play his or her role. Labor waste should not exist.

(2) Capital power occupation and consumption. From the perspective of substantial form, the term "capital power occupation" refers to the fixed assets and the current assets occupied in the production process, including plants, machines, equipment, facilities, raw materials, and fuel held in stock. "Capital power consumption" refers to the consumption of occupied capital in the production process, such as the aging and abrasion of plants, machines and equipment, and the consumption of stocked raw materials and fuel. From the perspective of value form, "capital power occupation" refers to fixed assets, including plants, machines and equipment. "Capital power consumption" refers to the depreciation and overhaul of plants, machines, and equipment.

(3) Material force occupation and consumption. From the perspective of substantial form, "material force occupation" refers to frequently consumed materials occupied in the production process, including energy and the raw materials in stock. "Material force consumption" refers to those materials that are consumed completely in the production process and cannot be reused. From the perspective of value form, "material force occupation" covers the current assets, such as stocked energy and raw materials. "Material force consumption" means the cost of energy and raw materials.
(4) Natural forces occupation and consumption. From the perspective of substantial form, "natural forces occupation" refers to the natural materials occupied in the production process, including land, mineral resources, rivers, and lakes. "Natural forces consumption" refers to those natural materials that consumed in production process, such as explored minerals, water, and air. From the perspective of value form, "natural forces occupation" means the fixed assets, including materials and land. "Natural forces consumption" means the cost of natural resources.
(5) Transportation power occupation and consumption. From the perspective of substantial form, "transportation power occupation" refers to the logistics and the stream of people occupied in production processes, including railway, road, airport, river, sky, train, car, ship, and plane. "Transportation power consumption" refers to the logistics and the stream of people consumed in the production process. From the perspective of value form, "transportation power occupation" means the logistics and the stream of people occupied. "Transportation power consumption" means the cost of logistics and stream of people.
(6) Time occupation and consumption. From the perspective of substantial form, "time occupation" refers to the time occupied in production process, including the time used for scientific research, technology development, construction, production, marketing, and sales. "Time consumption" refers to the time consumed in production process. From the perspective of value form, time is often used as a tool for quantity calculation and evaluation. "Time occupation" means the current assets, such as capital interest. "Time consumption" means costs related to time, such as interest.

The actual meanings of "occupation" and "consumption" regarding the six production factors are shown in Table 8.2.

3. **Unified Principle of Six Forces Space**

It has been seen that the production process cannot move forward even when the six basic production factors are in place, but they are at different locations without close connection. The production process can only move forward when the six basic production factors at different locations are connected by logistics and by a stream of people. This is what the unified principle of six forces space means. The significance of transportation power is that it can connect production factors at various locations and gather them all at the production site or the service site.

Transportation power plays a vital role in the production process. For example, production stops very often due to the limited coal supply in China. Much of the time, this is caused by limited transportation. Coal in Shanxi province cannot be transported to other places, whereas many factories in the south have to stop running due to the lack of coal.

Thanks to the development of science and technology and the applications of remote control and automation technology, most especially the rapid development of the Internet, personnel can perform production at remote sites far away from where equipment, tools, and facilities are located. For instance, doctors in Beijing can check patients in remote areas via the Internet. Drones can perform tasks automatically. These examples indicate that manpower can now be united with the other five production factors in one space without the support of stream of people. It can rely on the Internet and on remote technology to function in the same space with the other five production factors. However, it should be pointed out that drones, remote control, and automation all need manpower.

It also should be pointed out that the above examples do not violate the unified principle of six forces space because, without the unification of manpower and the other five production factors, no production process can proceed. This is the third law in production.

4. **Principle of Combined Action of Six Forces**

Jean (1803) pointed out that facts prove that produced value depends on the effects and coordination of labor, capital, and natural forces. This view point indicated that the importance of the common effects of multiple production factors attracted scholars' attention, even long ago.

The six elements of the production factor propose six independent basic production factors, namely manpower, capital power, the material force, natural forces, transportation power, and time. Each factor plays specific and unique effect in the production process. Meanwhile, production cannot proceed without coordination among these six factors. No factor can be missed. This is the fourth law in production.

China has suffered a shortage of energy for a long time. The shortage is so serious that many factories have had to stop production. In this case, the missing of the one factor, energy, prevents other factors from playing their roles. Shutdown and stopped production can lead to a huge loss to the national economy. Currently, the shortage in the oil supply is very serious. It is a strategic task to fix the problem of long-term energy shortage.

Countless facts prove that none of the six forces can be missing. If anyone force is missing, production will stop. Those production factors occupied will be left unused. Losses will occur. Therefore, the combined action of six forces is critical.

5. **Principle of Replacement of Six Forces**

In the field of technological economics, the author first proposed the principle of the "mutual replacement of six forces", also called the principle of replacement of six forces for short, which reflects the laws of technological progress and production development. In primitive society, the main production factors were manpower and natural forces. People used hands and feet as labor tools and worked on objects existing in nature to produce daily necessities, such as food, clothing, houses, fuel, and energy. Later, in agricultural society, although technologies, instruments of labor, and the division of labor were all more advanced now, the main production factors were still manpower and land. In industrial society, the industrial revolution (caused by the development of science and technology) made powerful energy, machines, equipment, and vehicles available. Production efficiency was greatly improved and huge material wealth was produced. Manpower was replaced by machines. Natural materials were gradually able to be substituted for manmade ones.

With the progress of science and technology and the development of the economy, more and more technological schemes (including methods and measures) have become available to achieve certain goals. In other words, more and more alternative technological schemes are available. As such, substitutions are available inside each force. For example, petroleum and coal can replace each other inside the material force (energy and raw materials). At present, China is short of petroleum. Coal, which is abundant in China, can be used as a replacement for petroleum. After the energy crisis, many power plants in developed countries switched from petroleum to coal to generate electricity and they have achieved good results. Since reform and the opening-up, China has adopted the same approach and has decreased the demand and consumption of petroleum.

In addition, the six forces can replace each other. For instance, capital power can replace the material force. Plenty of capital can be used for purchasing advanced energy-saving equipment to lower energy consumption. It must be pointed out that each force can only replace part of another force. No force can be completely replaced.

Because all technological schemes consist of six forces, different technological schemes have different amounts and structures of the six forces. When technological schemes change, the amount and the structure of the six forces will change as well. Accordingly, the economic results of production will change. Mutual replacement among six forces is the fifth law in production.

Based on the quantity and structure of the six forces, production can be categorized into six types: the manpower-intensive type (the physical power-intensive type and the intelligence-intensive type), the capital power-intensive type, the material force-intensive type, the natural force (resources)-intensive type, the transportation force-intensive type, and the time-intensive type. With the development of the social economy and the progress of science and technology, the capital power-intensive type and the intelligence-intensive type production will increase, while the material force-intensive type and the natural force-intensive type production will reduce continuously. This is the trend.

6. **Principle of Coordinated Development of Six Forces**

In the long history of national economic production development in human society, the six forces have developed harmoniously. In agricultural society, due to lagging science and technology, the factor of manual work (i.e. capital power and material force) was limited and undeveloped. Production counted on natural production factors (i.e. manpower and natural forces). In industrial society, the development of science and technology promoted the development of the production factor, such as machines, equipment, energy, black metal, nonferrous metal, and industrial chemicals. Social economic production relied more on the production factor and developed quickly. In the era of the information economy and the knowledge economy, social economic production relies even more on the production factor and on advanced science and technologies. The six forces should be utilized more efficiently and reasonably. The role of each force should be played completely. The six forces should achieve sustained and coordinated development to better promote the well-being of mankind. This is the sixth law in production.

The principle of the coordinated development of the six forces includes coordination between the quantity and quality of the six forces and the coordination between the input and output of the production factors of the six forces.

8.3 Theory of Life Factors

So far, there has been a lot of research on the theoretical issues of production factors, both at home and abroad. However, research specifically focusing on life factors is lacking. Literature about life factors is not available. In human society, there are two main behaviors: production and life. In order to study the technological economics issues in production, the author proposes the six elements theory of production factors. Similarly, in order to study technological economics issues in life, the author proposes the six elements theory of life factors.

8.3.1 New Concept of Life Factor

As we know, human lives contain ten aspects: food, clothing, usage, housing, transportation, culture, education, science, health, and sports. According to the State Statistics Bureau, people's consumption behaviors can be divided into eight categories: food; clothing; housing; household equipment, appliances, and service; healthcare, communication and transportation; culture, education and entertainment; and other commodities and services.[9] Either of the above categorizations requires manpower, capital power, material force, natural forces, transportation power, and time. These six elements are independent, and none of them is dispensable for achieving life content and consumption content. Thus, life factors are different from life content and consumption content.

---

[9]Chinese Statistic Summary 2006, China Statistical Publishing House.

However, in real life, clothing, food, usage, and housing are called "life factors" by scholars. Sports and travel are called "the fifth life factor." This view is similar to the one that considers education, information, culture, and management to be production factors. In order to define the concept of "production factor", the author proposed the hierarchy theory of production factors. According to this theory, production factors are categorized into different levels. Sectoral production factors, industrial production factors, and unit production factors are comprehensive production factors composed of the six basic production elements, namely manpower, capital power, material force, the natural forces, and time. These six basic production elements are single production factors, not comprehensive ones. Only single production factors are independent basic production factors, which can be mentioned in the same breath with traditional production factors initially proposed by western scholars, such as labor, capital, and land. But comprehensive production factors cannot. Similarly, life factors can be categorized into single ones and comprehensive ones. Food, clothing, usage, housing, transportation, culture, education, science, health, and sports are life behaviors, not life factors. If life behaviors are called life factors, they are comprehensive life factors, not single ones. A single life factors refer to manpower, capital power, material force, the natural forces, and time. They are completely independent. The basic six life elements comprise the most important material base in human society; they are the foundation of human life factors.

There are three theories about life factors[10]:

(1) Survival theory of life factors. This theory argues that life factors are the basic factors or conditions required by human life. It considers the six basic life factors (manpower; capital power; material force; the natural forces; and time), as the required conditions for human survival and development. This is the reason it was named. This topic belongs to the domains of sociology, medical science, and life science.

As we know, there is a bottom line to the requirements of life factors from human survival and development. This bottom line is determined by the physiological requirements of human beings, not by human desires. If it is not met, human beings cannot survive, nor can they develop.

The life factor "manpower" refers to the manpower of a person and the manpower of other people, such as parents, nurses, and doctors. As a key life factor, manpower is the most important one for human survival and development. Human survival and development rely on manpower. From birth to growing up, and then to aging, people need their own manpower as well as manpower from others.

The life factor "material force" refers to foods, medicine, fuel, electricity, and the other materials needed for daily life. It is important for human beings, because people will die of hunger or cold if the requirements of material force are not met.

The life factor "capital power" means houses, living facilities, living utensils, and living goods required by human life. In primitive society, people used their hands

[10]Without special explanation as a comprehensive life factor, the life factor in this book refers to the single life factor.

and feet as living tools (equal to capital power) for making a living. But in modern society, people cannot survive without capital power beyond their hands and feet.

The life factor "natural forces" refer to the natural resources required by human life, such as air, water, and land. Although some natural forces are valueless, they are very important for human life. For example, if there is not enough air, people could be choked to their deaths. If water is not available, people will die of thirst. If there is no land, people will have no place to live. Even in primitive society, people had caves in which to live.

The life factor "transportation power" means the logistics and the stream of people needed by human life. Without transportation, life factors in other places, such as manpower, the material force, natural forces, and capital power, are not accessible. People will die of starvation, cold, suffocation, and thirst.

The life factor "time" refers to the time resources required by human life. This is an important life factor and the symbol of human life. The time of life for a person is the length that he/she can live. Time coexists with human life. A person's life is limited, and so is life factor time. Suppose the average life span is 75 years. About 1/3 to 1/4 of that time is the growth period. And 1/5 to 1/4 is the retirement period (setting retiring age as 65). Then only about 1/2 of a person's life is his/her working period, about 38 years. After removing the holidays in the working period (about 31%), it becomes clear that a person works for about 1/3 of his/her life span, almost 9,500 days. After removing 2/3 working time on a working day (counted as 8 h a day), a person works about 1/3 of his/her work days. It can be seen that a person only works 1/9 of his/her life span, about 75,000 h.

Figure 8.4 shows the demand and supply of life factors. It indicates the minimum amount of life factors required by human life. If this bottom line is not met, human

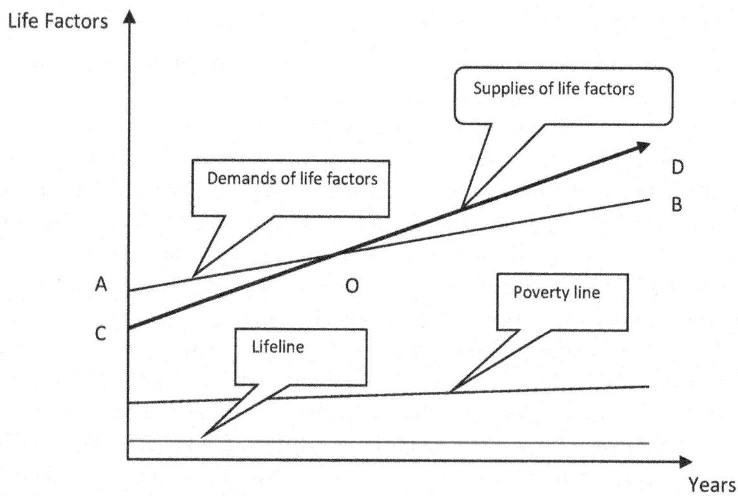

Fig. 8.4 Demands and supplies of life factors

life will not continue, and life will end. The life line in this figure indicates the minimum amount.

When the supply of life factors is just higher than the demands of the lifeline, people live in poverty because the supply is small. This status is indicated by poverty line in Fig. 8.4. The value of the poverty line changes as time goes by. For example, the poverty line for rural residents in 1978 in China was 100 RMB annual net income per capita. In 1985, the line changed to 206 RMB. In 1990, the line increased to 300 RMB. The line continued to change later and rose to 530 RMB, 625 RMB, and 683 RMB in 1995, 2000, and 2005 respectively. Since the the reform and opening-up, the number of rural residents who had annual net income per capita lower than the poverty line in China has been dropping, from 250,000,000 in 1978 to 23,650,000 in 2005.

When the supply of life factors is lower than the demand of people's normal life, indicated by the period when CO < AO in Fig. 8.4, some special measures must be taken. For instance, in the late 1950 s and early 1960 s, when Chinese economy was undergoing hard conditions, the supply of life factors could not meet the demand of people's normal lives. As a result, a coupon-based weight supply was implemented.

With the development of production, the supply of life factors can meet the demand of people's normal lives, as indicated by the period when OD > OB in Fig. 8.4. During this time, the quality and categories of life factors could be adjusted according to the people's diverse demands.

Table 8.3 shows the yearly Chinese household ownership of durable consumer goods per 100 households from 2000 to 2005.

(2) Input theory of life factors. This theory notes that input is required for people to live with purpose. It treats the six independent basic life factors, namely manpower, capital power, material force, natural forces, transportation power, and time, as input for people to live with purpose. Since input exists, output exists as well. It is common that input and output need to be compared. The question of whether input is worth or reasonable is an issue of technological economy in life. It should be studied by technological economics. The author discussed this issue in a specific work.[11]

(3) Wealth theory of life factors. This theory argues that life factors are human beings' wealth. It treats the six independent basic life factors, namely manpower, capital power, material force, natural forces, transportation power, and time, as wealth possessed by human beings.

As mentioned above, manpower is the most important factor. It is the key factor among the six independent basic life factors. Similarly, it is the key production factor and the most important one in the six independent basic production factors. As such, possessing unique dual identities, manpower plays key roles in production and in life in human society.

Humans are the most valuable wealth. All wealth in human society is created by human beings. The appearance, survival, and development of human beings relies

[11] Xu [XU88], page 526–529.

Table 8.3 Yearly Chinese household ownership of durable consumer goods per 100 households

Item	2000		2001		2002		2003		2004		2005	
	Rural	Urban	Rural	Urban	Rural	Urban	Rural	Urban	Rural	Urban	Rural	Urban
Motorcycle	21.9	18.8	24.7	20.4	28.1	22.2	31.8	24.0	36.2	24.8	41.0	25.0
Car	–	0.5	–	0.6	–	0.9	–	1.4	–	2.2	–	3.4
Washing Machine	28.6	90.5	29.9	92.2	31.8	92.9	34.3	94.4	37.3	95.9	40.2	95.5
Refrigerator	12.3	80.1	13.6	81.9	14.8	87.4	15.9	88.7	17.8	90.2	20.1	90.7
Television	101.7	3000	105.2	3000	108.6	3000	110.6	3000	113.0	3000	105.7	3000
Color Television	48.7	116.6	54.4	120.5	60.5	126.4	67.8	130.5	75.1	133.4	84.0	134.8
VHS Player	–	20.1	–	19.9	–	18.4	–	17.9	–	17.6	–	15.5
Video Camera	–	1.3	–	1.6	–	1.9	–	2.5	–	3.2	–	4.3
DVD Player	–	37.5	–	42.6	–	52.6	–	58.7	–	63.3	–	68.1
Audio System	–	22.2	–	23.8	–	25.2	–	26.9	–	28.3	–	28.8
Camera	–	38.4	–	39.8	–	44.1	–	45.4	–	47.0	–	46.9
Computer	0.5	9.7	0.7	13.3	1.1	20.6	1.4	27.8	1.9	33.1	2.1	41.5
Fitness Equipment	–	3.5	–	4.0	–	3.7	–	4.1	–	4.2	–	4.7
Air Conditioner	1.3	30.8	1.7	35.8	2.3	51.1	3.5	61.8	4.7	69.8	6.4	80.7
Water Heater	–	49.1	–	52.0	–	62.4	–	66.6	–	69.4	–	72.7
Ventilator	–	54.1	–	55.5	–	60.7	–	63.6	–	65.6	–	67.9
Microwave Oven	–	17.6	–	22.3	–	30.9	–	37.0	–	41.7	–	47.6
Mobile Phone	4.3	19.5	8.1	34.0	13.7	62.9	23.7	90.1	34.7	111.4	50.2	137.0
Line Phone	26.4	–	34.1	–	40.8	93.7	49.1	95.4	54.5	96.4	58.3	94.4

Data resource China Statistic Summary 2006, China Statistical Publishing House, 2006

on the six independent basic life factors. The six independent basic life factors are the basic requirements and the goals of human beings. When communist society comes true, people can get what they need freely because life factors are abundant. Thus, the amount of wealth in human society is not determined by the number of production factors, nor by the number of intermediate products, but by the number of final products. The number of intermediate products just indicates the consumption of production; it does not reflect the amount of wealth in human society. Different from production factors, life factors are all final products. They are not intermediate ones. Therefore, life factors, themselves, are wealth. Life factors can be possessed by residents or by societies. The more life factors there are, the better it will be.

The author argues that human beings' pure life behavior, the survival theory of life factors, does not create wealth. The input theory of life factors can create some wealth, but not much. Only by following the wealth theory of life factors can human society create more and more wealth via production. In this way, the continuously growing material and cultural demands of human beings can be met. The wealth theory of life factors is a theory about the output of human beings' production. How to achieve a bigger and better output of life factors with a small input of production factors is an issue within the field of social economic production. Obviously, it is an issue studied by technological economics. The authors have discussed this issue in several works.[12]

As wealth, some life factors are consumed. Others are accumulated. The more wealth there is, the more consumption there is. This is also true for accumulation. Those life factors that are not consumed can be used as production factors for expanded reproduction to create more wealth.

8.4 Six Elements Theory of Life Factors

The aforementioned six elements theory of production factors proposed the principle of the entity value of the six forces, the principle of occupation and consumption of the six forces, the unified principle of six forces space, the principle of the combined action of the six forces, the principle of replacement of the six forces, and the principle of the coordinated development of the six forces. The same idea can be applied to life factors.

It should be pointed out that the six elements theory of life factors is a specific application of the six elements theory of production factors in human social life.

As important basic theories in technological economics, the six elements theory of production factors and the six elements theory of life factors can be applied in many fields of production and life. They have important practical and theoretical significance.

[12]Xu [X88], page 429–555.

References

[CI89] Ci Hai, Shanghai Lexicographic Publishing House, 1989, Page 4525.
[MS85] Ma, H. & Sun, S. Q. (1985). *Economy and Management Dictionary*, China Social Science Publishing House, Page 232–233.
[XU86] Xu, S. (1986). *Technological Economics* (Edition 3), Jiangsu People's Publishing House.
[XU88] Xu, S. (1988). *Technological Economics* (Edition 4), Jiangsu People's Publishing House.

Chapter 9
Information Theory of the Technological Economy

9.1 Introduction

The information theory of the technological economy is one of the basic theories in technological economics. The author proposed the information principle of technological economy in the 4th edition of *Technological Economics,* published in 1988. However, the concept and definition of technological economy information was not covered. Before discussing the concept and definition of technological economy information, the concept of "information" should be clarified. There are about 100 concepts and definitions of information. N. Wiener, the founder of control theory, pointed out: "information is information. It is neither material nor energy." Yixin Zhong, a Chinese scholar, studied the definitions of information from diverse perspectives in his book *Principles of Information Science.*[1] From an ontological hierarchy perspective, he defined the information as the status and the mode of status change regarding the movement of things. More specifically, information is the status and the mode of status change regarding the movement of things perceived by subjects. However, the author has his own view about the definition of information. This chapter discusses four questions about the technological economy information, including the concept of technological economy information, the materials of technological economy information, the formats of technological economy information, and the requirements of technological economy information.

[1]Zhong [Z96].

S. Xu, *Technological Economics*,
https://doi.org/10.1007/978-981-15-8582-1_9

9.2 Information Concepts

The author argued that the information reflects the characteristics of things and their moving statuses and modes. In other words, information reflects the development and change in the internal and external characteristics of things. Similar to the aforementioned ontological hierarchy definition, this one focuses on reflection, which means "the perceiving of subjects." The difference between the two is that the author argues that information not only reflects the status of the movement of things and their changing modes, but also the characteristics of things. The author further argues that information does not equal the status of the movement of things and their changing modes. It merely reflects the status and modes. "Things" are objects and phenomena that exist objectively. "Phenomena" are different from objects. They are not objects themselves, but they come from objects. They are what happens to objects.

In sum, "technological economy information" refers to the reflection on the characteristics of things in technological economy and their moving status and modes. It includes both the information about all of the objects in the technological economy and the information about the movement and phenomena of objects. It should be pointed out that the popular statement, which argues that information is substantial property, is not complete because information reflects both the characteristics of objects (substantial entities) and phenomena. A better statement should be that information comprises the common attributes of objects and phenomena. Take business, a technological economy entity, as an example. The information of the business technological economy comprises not only the attributes of commodities (objects), but also the attributes of business activities (phenomena). Therefore, it is both the common attributes of commodities (objects) and business activities (phenomena).

9.3 Information Substance

From the perspective of information science, all technological economy objects can be categorized into two groups. One group can reflect their own characteristics, movement status, and modes. They are called "the technological economy information source substance." Basic information source substance includes six production and life elements, namely manpower, capital power, the material force, natural forces, transportation power, and time. The other group specifically reflects the characteristics of other information source substances and their movement status and modes. This is called the technological economy information carrier. There are three types of information carrier. The first type includes those objects that send and receive technological economy information, such as all producers, servers, consumers, post and telecommunications offices, TV stations, broadcast stations, satellites, computers, transceivers, faxes, telephones, TVs, radios, and cameras. The second type includes those objects that transmit technological economy information, such as manpower delivery, railway, road, waterway, aviation, telephone line, TV cable, optical fiber, light, sound, radio waves, and the Internet. The third type includes those objects that store technological economy information, such as human brains, computer hard drives, floppy disks, CDs, letters, materials, newspapers, magazines, books, pictures, photos, filmstrips, video tapes, records, and cassettes. It should be pointed out that technological economy information carriers have duality. They are not only the carriers of technological economy information, but also the substance of technological economy information sources. For instance, as a carrier of technological economy information, TV receives information about other things. Meanwhile, information reflection about the quality of TV exists as well. Thus, TV is an economy information source substance.

9.4 Information Forms

It is well accepted that information has five forms, namely the five forms that can be perceived directly by the five sense organs of human body. The first form is visual information, such as objects, words, numbers, colors, images, codes, passwords, ciphers, signs, gestures, and flag signals. The second one is auditory information, such as language and sound. The third one is olfactory information, such as odors. The fourth one is gustatory information, such as sourness, sweetness, bitterness, piquancy, and saltiness. The fifth one is haptic information, such as coldness, heat, hardness, and softness perceived by skin or hair via contacting objects.

140 years ago, Marx, in his book *Das Kapital,*[2] pointed out that the materiality of a commodity cannot be felt and that the owner will supplement this insufficiency by using his or her five or more sense organs. In other words, the characteristics of commodities can be perceived via a human's five or more sense organs. This is the information of commodities. Marx noted that humans have five or more sense organs. But no scholar has pointed out what those sense organs (other than the five known ones) are, to date. Although some scholars have proposed the concept of "the sixth sense", there is no clear answer about what indeed the sixth sense is and which human organ can perceive it. The author thought that other than the five sense organs, the sixthe one is the human brain. The sixth sense is perceived by the brain and can be called "the conscious sense." The human brain can perceive conscious information, such as spirit, moods, inspirations, ideas, memories, understanding, and dreams. This information exists in the human body. Conscious information is the most important information. It includes information perceived by humans both directly and indirectly. It also includes perceptual knowledge and rational knowledge. Conscious information is vital for the development of the human economy and for society. Table 9.1 lists the six types of technological economy information.

In conclusion, technological economy information has six types: visual information, auditory information, olfactory information, gustatory information, haptic information, and conscious information. Based on the six sense organs and studied

[2]Marx[M83].

Table 9.1 Six types of technological economy information

Serial number	Type	Sense organ
1	Visual information	Eyes
2	Auditory information	Ears
3	Olfactory information	Nose
4	Gustatory information	Mouth and tongue
5	Haptic information	Body
6	Conscious information	Brain

from the perceptual and rational perspectives, human beings understand and change the objects of the technological economy in human society in order to bring benefits to humankind and to continuously move social technological economy forward. This is an objective law that is independent of man's will.

9.5 Information Requirements

It is well known that without material, data, or information, technological schemes cannot be provided, nor will their advantages and disadvantages or their economic evaluation and comprehensive evaluation be analyzed.. If the evaluation of technological schemes could not provide useful information, technological economics would not serve socialist modernization construction. Thus, information is the base and the goal of the technological economy. The level of the technological economy depends on the abilities of information collection, storage, transmission, processing, and application. Technological economics requires sufficient, accurate, timely, useful, and economic information.

9.5.1 Sufficiency

The technological economy needs diverse information. From the perspective of effect, the eight aspects of information, including politics, defense, society, culture, technology, the economy, environmental ecology, and natural resources, are required. From the perspective of input, information about input, the quota index of consumption, cost, price, tax, and interest is required. Furthermore, information regarding conditions about demand and supply, objective requirements, and standards is required as well. Such information might come from historical summaries, predictions, macro materials, micro materials, domestic sources, foreign sources, official sources, or folk sources. Research on hard and soft technological schemes requires a huge amount of technological economy information. Without sufficient information, work related to the technological economy cannot be conducted. In practice, the situation of insufficient information occurs all the time. This is either because the amount of information collected by investigation and survey is not sufficient, or because the collected information is not stored, searched, or processed in an efficient manner. With the wide application of computers and the development of information networks (specifically the Internet), more and more useful information is provided for the work of the technological economy.

9.5.2 *Accuracy*

Inaccurate information will cause errors and wrong decisions in technological economy work. It is hard to require that all information be accurate. Information that is 80–90% accurate can be considered useful. Accurate information relies on the process through which it is processed. Interference, including that from leaders, physical interference occurring in transmission (i.e. print error), semantic noise jamming (i.e. correct understanding of semanteme of information), and application noise jamming should be suppressed. Evaluations should be conducted before information is used. Useless information should not be adopted.

9.5.3 *Timeliness*

Information must be timely; otherwise, it is useless. In practice, the technological economy evaluation of hard and soft technological schemes or feasibility reports has deadlines. If the information is not provided within a required time period, the evaluation process (and even the final result) will be affected. Some types of information are time-sensitive. They are only valid during a certain time period. If some negative information is provided after an engineering project is completed, it will be useless, even though it is an objective reality. It would become a part of lessons learned from this project.

9.5.4 *Usefulness*

Not all information is useful or valid. There are two standards for judging the value and the effectiveness of information, namely objective standards and subjective standards. All collected information should match the fact. Subjective standards should not be adopted to judge information. The information that matches the facts is useful and it should be adopted. Otherwise, it should be rejected. Only when objective standards are not available can subjective standards be used to judge whether information is useful. But some issues will appear, due to the adoption of subjective standards. For example, a piece of information might match the fact, per se, and is useful. However, it becomes useless if the decision makers do not adopt it. Therefore, the information must be useful and objective standards should be adopted to judge the information.

9.5.5 Economy

Collecting a huge number of materials and data and processing a huge amount of information costs a lot. Sometimes the cost could be enormous. From the perspective of technological economics, it is not correct to collect a large amount of information without considering the cost. However, it is also incorrect not to collect timely, useful, and sufficient information by spending necessary amounts. In fact, this is an issue in the information technological economy.

References

[Z96] Zhong, Y. X. (1996). *Principles of Information Science* [M], Beijing, University of Posts and Telecommunications Press, Page 38.
[M83] Marx, K. (1983). *Das Kapital* (Volume 1) [M], Beijing: People Publishing House, Page 62.

Chapter 10
Effect Theory of the Technological Economy

10.1 Introduction

The effect theory of the technological economy is one of the most important basic theories in technological economics. It is pointed out in Chap. 7 that all entities of the technological economy are entities of national economic production and social life. Production and life conducted by human beings in all entities of technological economy have goals, and each aims for certain results. Due to the differences in the characteristics of activities, the characteristics of the results are different. There are two categories of results. The first one is generated in production activities and can be measured by numbers, such as output, production value, and profits. The other one is not generated in production activities and cannot be measured by numbers. No matter which production activities people conduct and no matter which category the result belongs to, labor is spent. Therefore, all activities are connected with the economy. They are related to the waste and the saving of labor. The issue of saving and wasting labor exists in all activities, no matter what results they have. This issue is the economic result of the technological economy. This chapter discusses the concept of effect, the economic result indicators, and the five principles that affect technological economy, namely the principle of economic increment, the principle of time effect, the principle of supply and demand effect, the principle of system, and the principle of six forces substitution.

10.2 Effect Concepts

Each activity conducted by human beings in social practice has certain purposes, and aims for certain effects. As such, the issues of effect and economic effect exist in all activities conducted by human beings. The issue of effect and the issue of economic effect coexist, but they are not the same. The economic effect is the comparison between the effect and the cost of labor. This is the general concept and definition

S. Xu, *Technological Economics*,
https://doi.org/10.1007/978-981-15-8582-1_10

of "economic effect." There are other definitions of economic effect, such as the comparisons between output and input, between income and spending, between achievement and cost, between benefit and cost, between labor result and labor cost, between satisfied demand and labor cost, between useful effect and labor cost, between useful value and labor cost, and between economic benefit and cost. These statements are the concept of economic effect indeed. Their connotations are the same.

According to the hierarchy theory of the technological economy, economic effect can be categorized into levels of nation, region, section, industry, trade, firm, macro, and micro. Economic effect can also be categorized based on other standards. For example, according to the application, an economic effect can be categorized into absolute economic effect and relative economic effect, direct economic effect and indirect economic effect, rated economic effect and excessive economic effect, objective economic effect and subjective economic effect. Based on the time factor, economic effect can be categorized into static economic effect and dynamic economic effect, near-term economic effect and long-term economic effect.

It should be pointed out that the concept of economic effect mentioned above refers to the comparison between effect and labor cost, not to the ratio between them. Although comparison and ratio are very similar conceptually, they are different. Ratio is only one type of comparison. It is a concept of relative quantity, which expresses the comparison of two in the format of proportion. Difference is a type of comparison as well. It is a concept of absolute value. Ratio and difference, these two types of comparison, are both adopted in practice. Each of them has unique characteristics and applications.

10.3 Principle of Economic Result Indicators

The principle of economic result indicators is also called the principle of division and subtraction. It can be indicated by the following two mathematical expressions:

$$\text{Economic effect}(E_{\div}) = \frac{Effect(X)}{LaborConsump(L)} \tag{10.1}$$

$$\text{Economic effect } (\text{E}_{-}) = \text{Effect (X)} - \text{LaborConsumption(L)} \tag{10.2}$$

The first expression of economic result indicators adopts division, whereas the second one adopts subtraction. A general economic result indicator must meet two requirements. First, it must completely express the concept and definition of economic effect. In other words, an indicator and its concept and definition must be consolidated. Second, this indicator must have strong general meaning. All other indicators should be its derivatives. The above two expressions meet these requirements. So they are general expressions and can be applied universally.

10.3.1 The Relationship Between Division and Subtraction and Their Advantages and Disadvantages

1. The Relationship Between Division and Subtraction

Division and subtraction, in the above each indicate the relationship between the income X and the cost L. Figure 10.1 shows the relationship. It can be seen from Fig. 10.1 that the relationship between X and L is a dot at a given time. The position of this dot shows the status of the economic effect at that time. The diagonal is a line that indicates the time when X and L are equal. That is to say $E_{\div} = 1$ and $E_{-} = 0$. In the area below the diagonal, the cost is larger than the income. That is to say $X < L$, $E_{\div} < 1$ and $E_{-} < 0$. In the area above the diagonal, the income is larger than the cost. That is to say $X > L$, $E_{\div} > 1$ and $E_{-} > 0$. If the position of a point is known in this figure (i.e. point A), the values of $E_{\div}$ and E_{-} will be available. $E_{\div}$ is the slope of a point in this figure and can be expressed as $\frac{AG}{OG}$. The slopes of all points above the diagonal are larger than 1, whereas those of the points below the diagonal are smaller than 1. E_{-} refers to the vertical distance from a point to the diagonal. It can

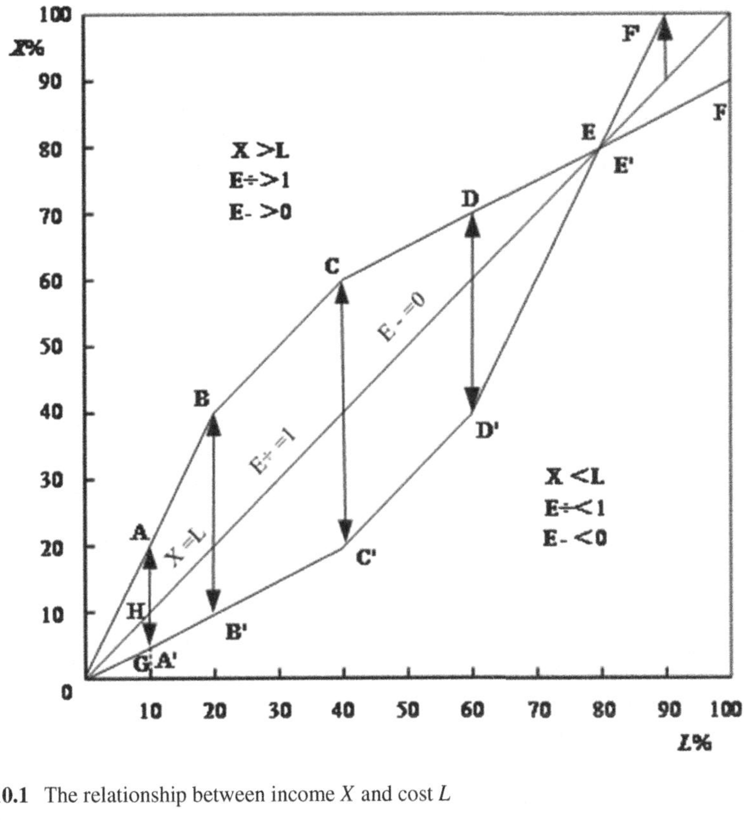

Fig. 10.1 The relationship between income X and cost L

be expressed as $AH = AG - OG$. Points above the diagonal have positive values of E_-, whereas those below the diagonal have negative ones. In this way, Fig. 10.1 clearly indicates the relationship between division and subtraction. That relationship can be expressed as below:

$$E_{\div} = \frac{X}{L} = \frac{E_-}{L} + 1 \tag{10.3}$$

$$E_- = X - L = (E_{\div} - 1)L = (1 - \frac{1}{E_{\div}})X \tag{10.4}$$

Derivation can be conducted between the expressions of division and subtraction. If either of them is known, the other one can be calculated.

2. **Advantages and Disadvantages of Division and Subtraction**

Both division and subtraction have advantages and disadvantages. In general, subtraction is not as good as division because it has the following disadvantages:

First, when economic effect X cannot be calculated in numbers or units of income and the costs are different, subtraction is not applicable, and Expression (10.2) has no economic meaning at all. Only when economic effect X can be calculated in numbers and when the units of income and cost are the same does Expression (10.2) have economic meaning. In other words, subtraction is applicable when all of the indicators are merit ones. As such, subtraction can only be used to calculate economic effects in the fields of material production and life. It cannot be applied to calculate economic effects in the fields of culture, education, or public health. In contrast, division is applicable when the units of income X and cost L are different. For example, income X is known to be the production of 70,000 tons of coal and the labor consumption is known to be 200 people. If subtraction is used to calculated the economic effect, the expression E_- = 70,000 ton coal—200 people does not have any economic meaning at all. In such a case, economic effect $E_{\div}$ = 350 ton coal/person calculated by division indicates life labor productivity.

Second, division is more applicable when used to compare the economic effects of two or more schemes. For instance, there are two schemes. One has an income of 60,000 RMB and costs 20,000 RMB. The other has an income of 30,000 RMB and costs 10,000 RMB. The results of division show that these two schemes have the same economic effect, which is 30,000 RMB with the cost of 10,000 RMB. However, if subtraction is applied in this case, the net income of the first scheme is 40,000 RMB, whereas that of the second one is 20,000 RMB. This difference shows that the first scheme has a larger economic effect than the second one. This example shows that division is more applicable because it compares the two schemes with the same standard, the income produced at a certain amount of cost. However, subtraction does not generate comparability in this case. Only when the numbers of incomes are the same or the numbers of costs are the same can subtraction be applied. For example, if one raises the income of the second scheme to 60,000 RMB, its cost rises to 20,000 RMB. Then subtraction can be applied and generates the same net income (40,000 RMB) for both schemes. This result indicates that the two schemes have the same economic effect. This result is consistent with the result generated by division. From this it can be seen that only when the income or the cost are the same can subtraction generate correct results.

Third, division is more convenient. Expression (10.1) shows that economic effect E is directly proportional to income X and inversely proportional to cost L. The bigger the income X, the higher the economic effect E. The lower the cost L, the higher the economic effect E. For instance, two schemes share the same income X. One scheme has labor consumption L_1 and the other has labor consumption L_2. Because the economic effect E is inversely proportional to the cost L, the smaller one between L_1 and L_2 generates a higher economic effect.

Despite the above disadvantages, subtraction has the following advantages.

First, if schemes share the same number of certain costs, these costs can be neglected when subtraction is applied to calculate the economic effect. The reason is that these costs only affect the absolute economic effect, not the relative economic effect. The result of economic effect comparison is not impacted, even if these costs are neglected. However, this approach does not work for division. These costs cannot be neglected when division is applied because both the absolute economic effect and the relative economic effect will be impacted. The result will be incorrect. For example, two development schemes about an acre of land are available. The income of the first scheme X_1 is 100 and the cost L_1 is 80. The income of the second scheme X_2 is 60 and the cost L_2 is 50. Division generates the economic effect of the first scheme, $E_{\div 1}$ 1.25 and $E_{\div 2}$ 1.2. This result shows that the first scheme is better than the second one. If the same amount of costs (20) in these two schemes is deducted, $E_{\div 1}$ changes to 1.67 and $E_{\div 2}$ rises to 2. The second scheme becomes better than the first one. This result is inconsistent with the first one and is incorrect. The same amount of costs should not be deducted because that leads to a wrong result. But subtraction is applicable in this case. E_{-1} is 20 and E_{-2} is 10. This indicates that the first scheme is better than the second one. After the same amount of costs (20) is deducted, E_{-1} changes to 40 and E_{-2} becomes 30. This result is consistent. In such a case, subtraction is better than division. It should be pointed out that when division is adopted, correct results still can be achieved if the same amount of costs is deducted for schemes with the same incomes.

Second, under certain circumstances, subtraction is more applicable than division. For instance, the comparison of profit, net income, or national income between technological schemes needs the subtraction expression (10.2). For the two schemes, if the first one generates production 0.1 billion RMB with the cost of 60 million RMB and the second one generates the same amount of production with the cost of 80 million RMB, the net incomes for these two schemes can be calculated with Expression (10.2) at 40 million RMB and 20 million RMB for the two schemes respectively. Thus, the first scheme is better than the second one.

The term "economic result" was very commonly used in the past. But after the premier of the State Council called for improvement of economic effects in the government work report in November 1981, the term "economic effect" became popular. What are the differences between these two terms? What is their relationship? Some think that they are the same and are interchangeable. Others argue that they are different. Next, we will discuss these two opinions.

10.3.2 Relations of Economic Efficiency, Economic Effect, and Economic Result

As mentioned above, "economic effect" can be expressed in two forms: division and subtraction. The former generates relative values whereas the latter generates absolute values. The author argues that division generates economic efficiency indicators, and subtraction generates economic benefit indicators. The terms "economic effect", "economic efficiency", and "economic benefit" are related but are not the same. Although economic efficiency and economic benefits are economic effects, they have different meanings. Consequently, their applications are different. In the past, the term "economic effect" was widely used in economic studies. The term "economic efficiency" was seldom used. But in fact, profit rate on funds, rates of profits and taxes on funds (i.e. rates of net profits on funds), and labor productivity are all indicators of economic efficiency. Next, the relationship among economic efficiency, economic benefit, and economic effect is discussed.

In order to clearly understand the concepts of economic effect and economic benefit, it is necessary to identify the meanings of "effect" and "benefit." According to the definitions in several dictionaries at home and abroad, "effect" generally refers to results. Human beings' activities have results, which are effects. Both results and effects can be good or bad. Good results are useful effects, which are called benefits. Accordingly, benefits are good effects, not bad ones. Effects and benefits are both results, but the former refers to all results, whereas the latter refers only to good results.

The purpose of economic construction is to gain more good economic results, not bad ones. The larger the good economic results, the better. There are two types of economic benefits: overall economic benefit (gross economic benefit) and net economic benefit. The indicators of overall economic benefit include total output and total income (for service departments). The indicators of net economic benefit include national income (net output), net income (profit and tax), and profit. They are usually expressed by subtraction and can be calculated by subtracting the cost from the overall economic benefit. When the costs are the same, the overall economic benefit is positively related with the net economic benefit. That is to say, the bigger the overall economic benefit, the bigger the net economic benefit. However, when the costs are not the same, such a correlation does not exist. In such a case, larger overall economic benefit does not always mean a larger net economic benefit. Only net economic benefit brings tangible benefits to countries and people. When the overall economic benefit is not positively related with the net economic benefit, the maximum net economic benefit should be set as the goal. As such, when we talk about improving economic benefit, we refer to the net economic benefit.

Next, we will introduce some indicators of economic benefit that are often used, including output value, net output value, national income, net income, gross national product, added value, and gross domestic product. Among these indicators, output value is an indicator of overall economic benefit. Others are indicators of net economic benefit.

"Output value", or gross output value calculated based on current prices, is the total amount of the value of products based on price at a factory. When the output value or the gross output value is calculated based on fixed prices, the goal is to compare them at different times by removing the false factors in the results caused by rising prices. If the price does not change, the increase of the output value is the increase of production. "Gross national product" (aggregate social product) refers to the sum of the output values of the material production sectors, such as industry, agriculture, the construction industry, freight transportation, business, and the catering industry. The gross output value of industry and agriculture is the sum of the output values of industry and agriculture.

"Net output value" is the newly created value ($V + M$) by laborers in the material production sectors in a certain time. It is the sum of tax, profit, and salary. The sum of the net output values of all of the material production sectors in a society is the national income. In China, material production sectors include industry, agriculture, the construction industry, freight transportation, business, and the catering industry. Culture, education, public health, scientific research, sport, service, finance, banking, passenger transportation, non-business telegram and telephone services are not material production sectors. Net output value and national income are the indicators of net economic benefit. National income can be used for accumulation and consumption. Accumulation includes productive accumulation, such as exploiting mines, building factories, and purchasing productive means, and non-productive accumulation, such as building schools and hospitals, and constructing office buildings. Consumption includes personal consumption (i.e. wage and welfare) and social group consumption (i.e. culture, education, public health, scientific research, and sports).

"Net income" is the balance after the cost is deducted from the income that firms get from selling their products. It is the equivalent of surplus value (M). It is the sum of profit and tax. Profit is the balance after the cost and the tax are deducted from firms' income. It is a portion of newly created wealth (M).

Net output value is an indicator that measures the volume of production activities in a society, according to the old accounting system. Added value is the indicator that measures the volume of production activities in a society according to the new accounting system. It is the newly added value in the production process. More specifically, it is the differential section between the value of a product or service and the intermediate value of its cost. For example, industry added value and industry net output both reflect the products manufactured by industries during a certain period. But they are different. Industry added value does include depreciation, but does not include the labor value paid to other sectors or interest expense. In contrast, industry net output does not include depreciation but does include both the labor value paid to other non-material production sectors and interest expense.

"Gross domestic product" is the indicator that reflects the results of the production activities of all of the resident units in a country or a region. "Resident unit" refers to those that have an economic benefit center in a country. Production activities include those conducted by all of the sectors in all three industries. Its value is the sum of the added value produced by all of the sectors across a country.

"Gross national product" refers to the sum of original income (i.e. laborers' wages, net value of production tax, depreciation of fixed assets, and operation surplus) received by all of the resident units during a certain period in a country or a region. Income received by permanent residents in a country via foreign investment or working overseas (also called factor income achieved oversea) should be calculated as the gross national product of this country. Income received by non-citizens via investment or via working in a country (called overseas payment of factor income) should not be calculated as gross national product of this country. Therefore, the gross national product can be calculated by adding the gross domestic product and the net factor income received by resident units from overseas (i.e. factor income received from overseas minus payment of factor income for noncitizens). More specifically, the gross national product is the sum of the gross domestic product and the net value of remuneration of labor and the return on investment (including bonuses, dividends, and interest) received from overseas, namely gross national product = gross domestic product + net factor income gained from overseas.

Table 10.1 shows the relationship among economic efficiency, economic benefit, and economic effect. Table 10.2 lists the categories of economic effect indicators.

Table 10.1 Relationship among economic efficiency, economic benefit, and economic effect

Serial no.	Economic effect		Economic effect indicators	
			Economic efficiency indicator(relative value)	Net economic benefit indicator(absolute value)
	(1)	(2)	(1)/(2)	(1)–(2)
1	Effect	Labor consumption	Yes	Those with the same units have net economic benefit indicators. Subtraction can be performed between them. Those with different units do not have net economic benefit indicators
2	Labor effect	Labor consumption	Yes	
3	Useful effect	Labor consumption	Yes	
4	Meeting demand	Labor consumption	Yes	
5	Useful value	Labor consumption	Yes	
6	Benefit	Cost	Yes	
7	Economic benefit	Labor consumption	Yes	
8	Income	Expenditure	Yes	
9	Output	Input	Yes	
10	Gain	Spending	Yes	

Table 10.2 Categories of economic effect indicators

Indicators			Economic effect	
			Absolute economic effect	Relative economic effect
Economic effect	Economic efficiency	Absolute economic efficiency	Labor productivity, return on investment, investment-net income ratio, investment-national income ratio, social labor productivity	
		Relative economic efficiency		Rate of return on incremental investment, profit-tax rate of incremental investment, firm additional profit margin, social additional rate of net income, social additional national income ratio, social additional labor productivity
	Net economic benefit	Absolute net economic benefit	Profit, tax, net income, national income, social net income, and social national income	
		Relative net economic benefit		Additional abnormal profit, additional net income, and additional national income

There are two types of indicators for economic effect. One is the indicator for economic efficiency expressed by relative values. The other is the indicator for net economic benefit, expressed by absolute values.

10.4 Principle of Economic Increment

The law of conservation of energy does not apply in social economy development, because the value created by human labor does not equal the labor consumption as a whole. The output is larger than the input. The economic effect of the technological economy always increases. As such, "the principle of economic increment" is also called "the law of non-conservation of economy." In fact, the economic increments caused by different technologies vary. Some are large, while some are small. Some are zero, and some are negative. For either absolute increment or relative increment, the bigger the better. The best scenario is that, other than required increment, there exists the maximum abnormal increment. Technologies with such effect are the best. In practice, the amount of absolute increment and relative increment are closely related with the size of input and additional (marginal) input. There are three types of such relationship, namely increasing effect, decreasing effect, and mixed effect. In most cases, output is directly proportional to input. The more input, the more output, and vice versa. This general law is called "the principle of increasing effect." For increasing effect, the relationship between output and input can be linear or nonlinear (as shown in Fig. 10.2). As a simple format of nonlinear increasing effect, linear increasing effect is easy to apply. However, objects are complicated, so the relationship between output and input is always nonlinear. For example, a firm might begin energy saving by reducing movable property. At this stage, large output effects can be achieved with small input. When the amount of movable property reaches zero, more input is required to achieve certain kind of energy saving effect. But once a technological breakthrough occurs, large effects can be achieved with small input. However, decreasing effects can happen, as well. In other words, larger input might lead to smaller output. This is similar to the law of diminishing returns and is called "the principle of decreasing effect." Decreasing effect can be linear or nonlinear (as shown in Fig. 10.3). It should be pointed out that decreasing effect usually coexists

Fig. 10.2 Increasing effect

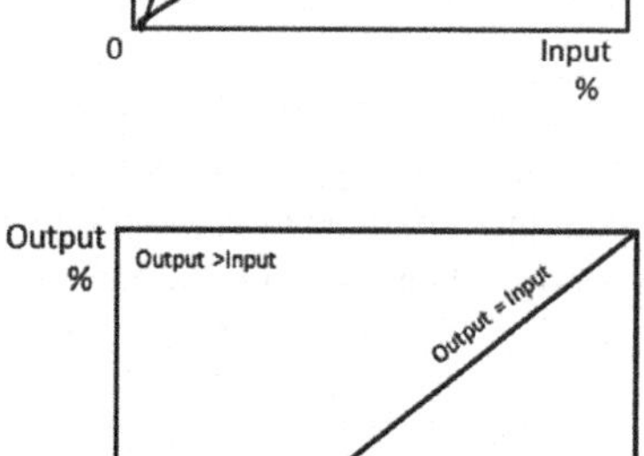

Fig. 10.3 Decreasing effect

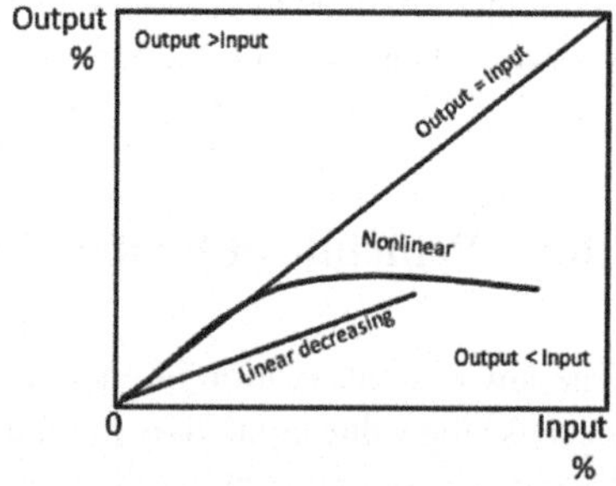

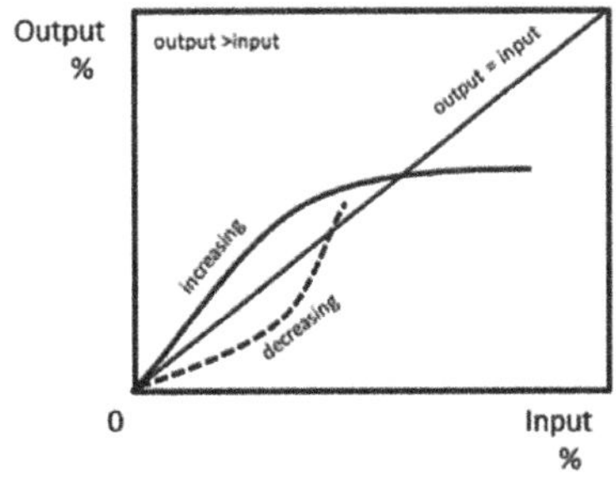

Fig. 10.4 Mixed effect

with increasing effect. For energy saving technologies, small input can generate big effect at the beginning. But after a certain point, a larger input will not yield good output. At the end, the loss might outweigh the gain. This occurs in social expanded reproduction as well. When the amount of investment on infrastructure is kept under a certain size in a country, its economic effect will increase. But once the amount reaches a certain size, its economic effect will decrease (as shown in Fig. 10.4). This is an example of mixed effect. The principles of increasing effect, decreasing effect, and mixed effect are important in the principle of economic increment. It is necessary and useful to understand these three principles well in order to perform technological economic works. The goal is to prevent the occurrence of decreasing effect and to achieve the maximum increasing effect.

According to the requirements of the principle of economic increment, the formulas for accessing economic effect are:

$$E_{\div} = \frac{X}{L} = ZD \text{ (maximum)}, \ (E_{\div} \geq 1) \tag{10.5}$$

$$E_{-} = X - L = ZD \text{ (maximum)}, \ (E_{-} \geq 1) \tag{10.6}$$

That[1] is to say,Q the value created in production activities must be larger than the input of the labor value. An increment must occur. The bigger, the better. For a society, the larger the social economic effect $E_{\div}$ and E_{-} is, the faster the development of the social economy is. If $E_{\div} < 1$ and $E_{-} < 0$, the social economy will not develop.

Economic effect evaluation formulas (10.5 and 10.6) have three types:

(1) Material type $E_{\div} = \frac{X(material)=ZD}{L(material)}$
(2) Value type $E_{-} = \frac{X(value)=ZD}{L(value)}$

$$E\_X(value) - L(value) = ZD$$

(3) Material value type $E_{\div} = \frac{X(material)=ZD}{L(value)}$ or $E_{-} = \frac{X(value)=ZD}{L(material)}$

[1] $E_{\div} \geq 1$ and $E_{-} \geq 0$ are only applicable when X and L are indicators with the same unit. This is the case hereafter.

Table 10.3 The same comparable scale

Serial no.	X_A	X_B	L_A	L_B	E_A	E_B
Case 1	6	6	2	3	3/1	2/1
Case 2	6	4	2	2	3/1	2/1
Case 3	6	2	2	3	3/1	0.67/1

It can be seen from Formulas (10.5) and (10.6) that when labor consumption *L* has the minimum value, labor effect *X* reaches the maximum and so does economic effect *E*. The oft-stated achieving of the maximum labor effect with the minimum labor consumption is a concept of economic effect evaluation indeed, not a concept of economic effect per se. Some economists propose that the economic effect is a concept of comparison. Thus, something comparable is needed. According to the above formulas, when labor consumption *L* is the same, the larger labor effect *X* will generate the larger economic effect. Similarly, when labor effect *X* is the same, the smaller labor consumption *L* will generate the larger economic effect. Table 10.3 lists three cases for two schemes. In the first case, the two schemes have the same economic effect but have different labor consumption. In the second case, the two schemes have the same labor consumption but different economic effect. In the third case, the two schemes have different economic effect and the different labor consumption. Results generated by Formula (10.5) show that the economic effect of Scheme *A* is 3 units of labor effect with 1 unit of labor consumption, in all of the three cases. The economic effect of Scheme *B* is 2, 2, and 0.67 unit(s) of labor effect with 1 unit of labor consumption in the three cases respectively. The results indicate that the Scheme *A* is better than Scheme *B* in all of the three cases, which share the same comparable scale.

It should be pointed out that two methods can be adopted to calculate the economic effect and labor consumption in the aforementioned economic effect evaluation formulas. The first one chooses the sum of economic effect and the sum of labor consumption and generates the absolute economic increment caused by technological schemes. The second one chooses the differences of economic effect and the differences of labor consumption based on comparison and generates the relative economic increment between technological schemes. The former is called "the standard formula of absolute economic effect evaluation" and the latter is called "the standard formula of relative economic effect evaluation."

(1) Standard formula of absolute economic effect evaluation

$$E_{Absolute} = \frac{X}{L} = ZD \quad (E_{Absolute} \geq 1) \tag{10.7}$$

$$E_{Absolute} = \frac{X}{L} = ZD \quad (E_{Absolute} \geq 0) \tag{10.8}$$

$$E_{Absolute} = X - L = ZD \qquad (E_{Absolute} \geq 0) \tag{10.9}$$

(2) Standard formula of relative economic effect evaluation

$$E_{Relative} = \frac{\Delta X}{\Delta L} = ZD \qquad (E_{Relative} \geq 1) \tag{10.10}$$

$$E_{Relative} = \frac{\Delta (X - L)}{\Delta L'} = ZD \qquad (E_{Relative} \geq 0) \tag{10.11}$$

$$E_{Relative} = \Delta (X - L) = ZD \qquad (E_{Relative} \geq 0) \tag{10.12}$$

In the above formulas, L'' is comprehensive input and L' is individual production factor input.

The standard formula of absolute economic effect evaluation can be applied to assess the economic effect of a single technological scheme as well as the relative economic effect of multiple technological schemes. But when it is used for assessing the relative economic effect, the results that it generates are not as accurate as those generated by the standard formula of relative economic effect evaluation. The standard formula of relative economic effect evaluation is applied to calculate the relative economic effect of multiple technological schemes specifically. Absolute economic effect must be assessed first, and then relative economic effect is assessed next. Usually, if a technological scheme does not generate good absolute economic effect, it should not be adopted even though it may generate good relative economic effect.

The relationship among economic increment analysis, macro-analysis, and average analysis is discussed next. Increment analysis is additional analysis. It is also called marginal analysis overseas. It applies increment (additional) indicators to analyze economic effect. In contrast, macro-analysis and average analysis choose the total amount index and the average index respectively to analyze economic effect. Table 10.4 shows that the total output is the sum of each additional indicator (marginal number). If the additional indicator is positive, the total output increases. If additional indicator is negative, the total output decreases. When additional indicator

Table 10.4 Relationship among additional indicator, total, and average

Unit of input	Total output	Average output	Additional (Marginal) output
0	0	0	0
1	100	100	100
2	150	75	50
3	230	77	80
4	430	107	200
5	580	116	150

equals zero, the total output reaches its maximum. Average output is generated by dividing the total output by the amount of input. It does not matter whether the additional indicator is positive or negative. If the additional indicator is larger than the average output, the average output increases. If the additional indicator is smaller than average output, the average output decreases. If the additional indicator equals the average output, the average output remains unchanged. Because "average" and "total" are often used in daily life, people tend to choose average in the reasoning process. For example, if a firm earned an average profit of 1 RMB for each piece of its products, its decision makers will think that a 10,000 piece increase in output will generate a profit of 10,000 RMB. In another example, if the average profit rate of a scheme is 10% per investment unit and the rate of another scheme is 15%, the second scheme will be thought to be better than the first one. In fact, these average-based analyses cannot guarantee the best technological economic effect, because when a product has an average profit of 1 RMB in the past, an increase in output might cause the additional profit of each piece of product to be higher than its average profit. The reason is that the fixed cost of production does not change with the increase of output. Similarly, for the scheme with the average profit rate of 15% per investment unit, it is possible that its additional (marginal) return on investment is smaller than 10% and that its average profit rate of 15% per investment unit is larger than 15%. Thus, other than macro-analysis and average analysis, additional (marginal) analysis is necessary to achieve the largest increment of technological economic effect.

10.5 Principle of Time Effect

Creatures on earth grow and die every day. Materials get damaged, and there is corrosion and degradation. These are all caused by time. For the development of technology and the economy, new technologies constantly emerge. Old ones are continuously improved and upgraded. Inapplicable ones die out. Technological economy indicators and market demands continue to change. Those technologies with low economic effect improve, while those with high economic effect continuously develop. All of these indicate that time is taking its effect.

In the ordinary course of events, the increment of technological economic effect continuously increases as time goes on. As such, time has the effect of economic increment. Different technologies have different such kind of effect. Some have a large effect, while others have a small one. Some even have a negative effect. The same technology may have a different economic increment effect in different time periods. For instance, certain technologies have a good short-term economic increment effect but an unsatisfying long-term effect, whereas some technologies have an unsatisfying short-term economic increment effect but a good long-term effect. Therefore, the evaluation of technological economic effect must take time effect into account. In essence, the principle of time effect is a dynamic principle.

In practice, people pay attention to time in life, but ignore time in the economy. Accordingly, the principle of time effect in technological economic effect is neglected. In the process of the social national economy's expanded reproduction, the principle of time effect is the most important. All expanded reproduction and accumulation of material and capital rely on time. Due to time effect, the technological economic effect of one ton of steel and one RMB this year does not equal the same in the next year. The former is larger than the latter. The total technological economic effect of one RMB in ten years does not equal the sum of the effect of one RMB in one year. The former is larger than the latter, as well.

According to the principle of time effect, for the same amount of technological economic effect, the more recent one must be bigger than the older one. Capital in this year is more useful than the same amount of capital several years later. This is not only because money depreciates, but also because a certain amount of money can be invested into production and can generate new values. New values can, in turn, be invested again, in order to generate more new values. Time effect in this process is the same as it is in atomic nucleus fission. As such, time effect is also called fission effect. If the long-term economic effect is not impacted, it is reasonable that people will value short-term activities and will chase a larger short-term economic effect.

In sum, the principle of time effect means much in technological economics.

10.6 Principle of Supply and Demand Effect

The relation between supply and demand in the national economy has three statuses: balance between supply and demand, underproduce, and oversupply. Balance between supply and demand is a normal status in the market; it is the best situation. But because things develop in a complicated and uneven manner, unevenness between supply and demand occurs all the time. In actual life, limited resources, excessive growth of demand, and poor planning of supply cause underproduction, also called short supply. Redundant resources, sharp decrease in demand, and poor planning of supply cause oversupply, also called excessive supply. Either short supply or excessive supply in manpower, capital power, material force, natural forces, transportation power, or time will cause damage to the technological economic effect. The damage is called "short term/long term effect", or shortage/surplus effect. When short supply in manpower, capital power, material force, natural forces, transportation power, or time occurs, an extra amount of any type of these forces added to a technological scheme will cause a short term effect. In contrast, when excessive supply of any of these six forces occurs, an extra amount of any type of these forces added by a technological scheme will cause a long term effect. For example, the huge population in China leads to an excessive supply of members in the labor force. Redundant labor does not play a role and becomes a burden of national economy. As such, a long term effect occurs. In addition, economic damage caused by overproduction and overstocked products, as well as idleness of equipment, are examples of the long term effect. Generally speaking, short term effect is more serious than long term effect. The reason is that long term effect only causes damage in the value of products. For instance, the loss value of coal caused by a long term effect is not more than coal's sales revenue. The loss caused by a short term effect of coal includes the damages in the entire production process across a society. It is estimated that the size of a short term effect caused by a ton of coal is 20–60 times bigger than that of the long term effect caused by the same amount of coal. When supply equals demand, another kind of supply and demand effect, called "opportunity effect", will play a role. For example, one technological scheme uses capital that is supposed to be used by other technological schemes. In this case, other technological schemes will suffer damages due to missing the opportunity of using this capital. Similarly, if other technological schemes use the capital, this technological scheme will suffer damage due to loss of the opportunity of using the capital. This damage is considered to be opportunity effect. Here is an example: A manager can allocate a certain amount of capital to factory A and get economic benefit of $S_{A.}$ But if the manager allocates the capital to factory B instead, the loss of S_A for factory A is the opportunity cost and the can for factory B is the opportunity effect. When supply equals demand, when a technological scheme uses more production factors, the opportunity effect will occur. In essence, opportunity effect is the same as short term effect. They both reflect the impact caused by a limited and insufficient production factor. But they are different. The short term effect reflects the impact of the unevenness between supply and demand, whereas the opportunity effect reflects the impact of allocation when supply equals demand. The impact of the opportunity effect is smaller than that of the short term effect. The reason is that, when supply equals demand, all production factors contribute to the technological economic effect. In such a case, the contribution of each production factor is a part of, not the entire, technological economic effect. When a technological scheme adopts additional production factors, the technological economic effect caused by the change is just a proportion, not the whole. In contrast, the short term effect impacts the whole technological economic effect. In sum, supply and demand effect includes short term effect, long term effect, and opportunity effect. Among them, the short term effect has the biggest impact on technological economic effect. The opportunity effect has a smaller impact. The impact caused by long term effect is the smallest. In actual life, supply and demand effect affects both input and output. Table 10.5 shows the common nine cases.

(1) The best technological economic effect caused by the long term effect of input and the short term effect of output;

Table 10.5 Supply and demand effect

Category		Output		
		Short term effect	Normal	Long term effect
Input	Long term effect	1	4	7
	Normal	2	5	8
	Short term effect	3	6	9

Note Numbers in the table represent the ranking of technological economic effect

(2) The second best technological economic effect caused by normal input and the short term effect of output;
(3) The third best technological economic effect caused by the short term effect of input and the short term effect of output;
(4) The fourth best technological economic effect caused by the long term effect of input and normal output;
(5) The fifth best technological economic effect caused by normal input and normal output;
(6) The sixth best technological economic effect caused by the short term effect of input and normal output;
(7) The seventh best technological economic effect caused by the long term effect of input and the long term effect of output;
(8) The eighth best technological economic effect caused by normal input and the long term effect of output;
(9) The ninth best technological economic effect caused by the short term effect of input and the long term effect of output.

It can be seen that an important approach for increasing technological economic effect is to overcome long term effect and short term effect and to allocate production factor reasonably.

10.7 Principle of Systems

A society is a large system. All technological schemes are subsystems within this large system. A large system is an organic integrity consisting of subsystems, which are not easily piled up. The sum of the maximum economic effect of each subsystem does not equal the maximum economic effect of a large system. The economic effect of subsystems is impacted by the large system. Subsystems, in turn, affect the economic effect of the large system. The result of the technological economic effect evaluation from the perspective of the large system of the social economy is different from that from the perspective of firms. Large systems take account of the total economic effect in a society that is caused by technologies. The total economic effect includes the direct economic effect of firms as subsystems and the indirect economic effect not caused by firms. There are two parts in indirect economic effect. One is the economic effect of output sections, including both useful output sections and harmful output sections, such as production and allocation sections, circulation sections, final consumption sections, and environment pollution-related victim sections. The other is the economic effect of input sections, such as suppliers of factory building, machines and equipment, raw materials, energy, transportation, and manpower (see Fig. 10.5). Small systems usually only consider the direct economic effect of technologies. Therefore, the economic effect of large systems is more important than that of small ones. When these two are in conflict, the economic effect of

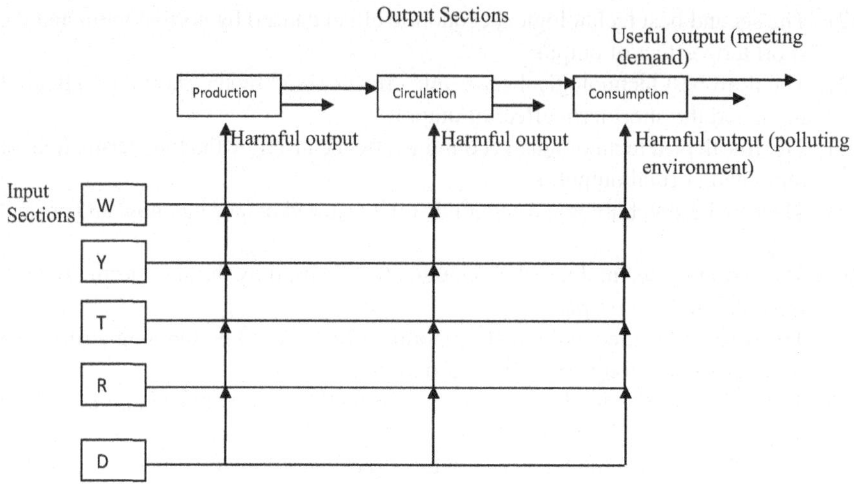

Fig. 10.5 Diagram of Sections in Technological Economy

the large systems take priority. In theory, output sections and input sections have many levels. The relationship among these levels can be direct, one-time indirect, twice indirect, or multiple indirect. It can be argued that all of the sections and industries in a society are related. This argument is called "the principle of system." However, when assessing indirect economic effect, it should not consider all direct and indirect sections in a society. This is because of the difficulty and unnecessariness of conducting this kind of calculation. Therefore, it is reasonable to take account of those sections that have a large impact on economic effect. In other words, these sections are involved and usually have a direct and recurrent relationship. For example, sections that provide raw materials, energy, and transportation to a firm are its direct and recurrent related input sections. Although those sections that provide machine, equipment, factory building, and land have a direct relationship with the firm, this relationship only happens once. It is not recurrent. Thus, these sections have a smaller impact on economic effect than the material, energy, and transportation sections. Sections that have an indirect relation have a much smaller impact on economic effect. Other than particular cases, they are not taken into consideration. Furthermore, sections that allocate, transport, and process the products of a firm are its direct and recurrent related output sections. According to the principle of system, sections that provide raw materials and energy are the most important input-related sections. Those conducting infrastructure construction are the second most important input-related sections. Users are the most important output-related section. The economic effect of users matters greatly. In one word, the economic effect of all technological schemes is reflected by users. For instance, steelworks produce steel. It would seem, then, that steelworks would have a large economic effect. But if the steel is not consumed by users, the steelworks do not have real economic effect at all in a society. Therefore, assessing the economic effect of products from the perspective of users has real meaning. This is the case for the transportation sections as well. The oft-stated "user first" is actually an important principle of economic effect. It is also an important aspect of the principle of system.

10.8 Principle of Six Forces Substitution

The practice of human labor and production proves that any labor or production scheme must have six basic conditions.

(1) Laborers. As an important condition, "laborers" refers to people who undertake work. Laborers include blue collar workers, white collar workers, technicians, and managers.
(2) Labor materials, which are also called "labor methods." The main labor materials are labor tools, such as machines, equipment, and instruments. Other materials, such as labor safety measures, equipment, environmental protection devices, communication devices, and power equipment, are not involved in the labor or production processes directly. But without them, the labor or production processes cannot begin or be finished successfully.
(3) Labor objects. In this section, there are two categories. The first category is natural resources without any human labor applied, such as coal. The second category is material with human labor applied, such as raw materials, materials, fuel, seed, and feed.
(4) Labor environment. Sunshine, air, temperature, humidity, microorganisms, and water are required by laborers and by the labor process. These are also called "environmental resources." Lack of these resources or the bad condition of these resources will affect the labor and production process. For example, a lack of sunshine will affect agriculture badly. Flooding will damages agriculture, as well. Polluted air and water will impact laborers and equipment. Although air does not have a cost, it is necessary for production. Without air, fuel would not burn. Air cooling would not work. To make matters worse, laborers would not survive.
(5) Labor space. The labor and production process needs space. This space can be factory buildings or land. In addition, conditions for labor must be connected with these spaces. Raw materials several hundred kilometers away cannot be processed before they are transported to the space where they are needed. As such, transportation power is needed to bring all of the labor conditions together.
(6) Labor time. All labor processes take time. No labor and production can be done without time, so time is an important condition as well.

Labor and production cannot be conducted if any of the above six conditions is missing. The first three conditions are the three factors for labor and production. They are well known and have been discussed completely in political economics. Although the latter three are very common, they have not been widely studied. In technological economics, studies on all of the six conditions are required in order to explore economic effect of labor and production. Studies on the latter three conditions become more and more important. For instance, clean air was an environmental resource without any cost in the past. But with the development of agriculture and industry, air pollution has become worse. In certain areas, clean air is not free and easy to access any longer. Additional labor is required to get clean air. In a word, all labor and production needs the above list six independent conditions. Six forces (resources) derive from these six conditions, including manpower, capital power, material force, natural forces, transportation power, and time. "Manpower" refers to the diverse laborers who are needed in labor and production process. "Capital power" means all of the kinds of capital that is needed in the labor and production process. Specifically, it refers to investment in fixed assets and current capital. "Material force" means all of the materials needed in the labor and production process, specifically recurrent consumable materials, such as raw materials and energy. "Natural forces" are the natural resources and natural conditions that are needed in the labor and production process. "Transportation power" is the transportation capacity required by the labor and production process. "Time", here, means the time needed by the labor and production process.

The principle of six forces substitution must be taken into account in order to assess the technological economic effect. Due to the advancement of science and technology and the development of the economy, more and more technological schemes are available to achieve certain goals. In other words, more substitutive technological schemes are available. Substitutive technological schemes are not only available inside a force, but also available among forces. For example, roads can replace railways. Nuclear power can replace oil power. Chemical fiber can replace cotton. Plastic can replace steel. Cement can replace wood. Machines can replace manual work. These substitutions are replacements among the six forces, indeed. All technological schemes consist of six forces. What makes them different are the amount and the structure of the six forces. As such, when technological schemes change, the amount and structure of the six forces within them change as well, and vice versa. Substitution of six forces is an objective law. Technological schemes (just as in industries or sections) can be categorized into the following six types, according to the amount and the structure of the six forces inside them.

1. Manpower-intensive type. This type can be further divided into two groups. The first is physical labor intensive and includes agricultural manual labor, manual construction, manual labor, and the service industry. The other is intelligence intensive and includes scientific research, education, culture, and management.
2. Capital power intensive type. This type of technological scheme requires huge investment. Industries in this type include heavy industries that have high degree of mechanization and automation, firms with advanced equipment, hydroelectric power, and nuclear power. This type is technology (equipment) intensive, indeed.
3. Material force intensive type. This type of technological schemes consumes a huge amount of raw materials and energy and includes the chemical industry, metallurgy, machinery, and the textile industry.

4. Natural force (resource) intensive type. This type of technological scheme requires a huge amount of natural resources and includes mining, lumbering, and fisheries.
5. Transportation power intensive type. This type of technological scheme requires a huge capacity for transportation and includes logistic firms and those firms that are far away from raw material and energy areas.
6. Time intensive type. This type of technological scheme includes engineering constructions with a long time period, scientific research, and personnel training.

The above categories are based on one main force (production factor). In practice, two or more forces might jointly be the main force. For instance, manual fisheries belong to both the manpower intensive type and the natural force intensive type. Therefore, it can be called a "manpower and natural resource intensive type." Another example is a hydropower station with a long construction period. This kind of technological scheme can be called a "capital and time intensive type." Other examples can be provided by parity of reasoning. Six forces substitution is the requirement of technology advancement and economy development. It is also an important leverage for improving the technological economic effect. The trend of human history indicates that technological schemes tend to be the intelligence intensive type, the capital intensive type, the material force intensive type, the transportation force intensive type, and the mixed type. More important, technological schemes must take the local conditions into account in order to achieve the best technological economic effect. A good example is that human resource industry development now has priority in China because plenty of manpower is available.

The six principles regarding technological economic effect have been discussed so far. They reflect the object laws of the development of technological economy. They dominate the technological economic effect, anytime/anywhere, across social systems. One of the main tasks in technological economics is to study and understand these principles, to grasp them, and to serve the national economic construction. In addition, these principles can be applied to macro technological economics as well as in micro technological economics.

Chapter 11
Evaluation Theory of the Technological Economy

11.1 Introduction

The evaluation theory of the technological economy is an important basic theory in technological economics. Objective standards are needed, in order to tell whether a technological scheme is economic. In a socialist society, the following three principles must be taken account for either a planned economy or a market economy: (1) Technological schemes must meet the demands of the people and those of national economic development; (2) Technological schemes must have a good economic effect, including both direct effect and indirect effect; (3) The economic effect of technological schemes should be assessed by time. Both the short-term effect and the long-term effect should be taken into consideration. By following the above three principles, the author specifies the principle of evaluating economic effect of technological schemes. Next, the evaluation theory of the technological economy will be discussed, including the principle of the standard for evaluating greater, faster, better, and more economical results; the practical standard for evaluating greater, faster, better, and more economical results; the two applications of the principle of the standard for evaluating greater, faster, better, and more economical and their express formulas; the financial evaluation and economic evaluation; the absolute economic evaluation and relative economic evaluation; and both the static economic evaluation and the dynamic economic evaluation.

11.2 Evaluation Standard Principle of Greater, Faster, Better, and More Economical Results

The three principles for evaluating technological economic effect can further specified as this: achieving the same amount and quality of technological effect at a fast speed and with a minimum labor consumption to meet the demands of people and national economic development in a certain time period or by achieving the greatest

S. Xu, *Technological Economics*,
https://doi.org/10.1007/978-981-15-8582-1_11

and best economic effect at the same speed and with the same amount of labor consumption. This principle is called the principle of the standard for evaluating greater, faster, better, and more economical results. It can be expressed as:

$$E_{\div} = \frac{X\Sigma}{L\Sigma} = ZD \tag{11.1}$$

$$E_{-} = X\Sigma - L\Sigma = ZD \tag{11.2}$$

In the above formulas, X stands for the labor effect of technological schemes, namely output. L stands for the labor consumption of technological schemes, namely input. The footnote symbol $\sum$ stands for the sum of direct and indirect economic effect of technological schemes. It also stands for the sum of the short-term and long-term economic effect of technological schemes.

The following formulas can be used for evaluating economic effect in the production field.

$$E_{\div} = \frac{S\Sigma}{L\Sigma} = ZD \tag{11.3}$$

$$\text{or } E_{-} = S\Sigma - L\Sigma = ZD \tag{11.4}$$

In the above formulas, S stands for the use-value of technological schemes. The other letters have the same meanings as those in Formulas 11.1 and 11.2.

It should be pointed out that the above two groups of formulas are very similar. The reason is that Formulas 11.3 and 11.4 are specific cases that apply Formulas 11.1 and 11.2 within the production field.

Next, the labor consumption $L_{\sum}$ and use-value $S_{\sum}$ will be discussed in details.

11.2.1 Labor Consumption $\mathrm{L}_{\sum}$ *of Technological Schemes*

Occupation and consumption have been discussed in Chap. 8. They are two of the phenomena in production process. When calculating labor consumption, different methods are applied. Several examples are provided next, in order to explain how to calculate the labor consumption of technological schemes. The production of cotton includes the costs for living labor, such as the labor of workers, technicians, and managers in textile mills; and for materialized labor, such as cotton, cotton yarn, fuel, energy, ancillary materials, the wear and tear of machinery, equipment, and factory buildings. The materialized labor consumption actually is the living labor consumption in other production sections.[1] Therefore, it is not enough to examine just

[1]From the perspective of the entire society, materialized labor is the living labor of other sections. They occur one after another. For example, steel produced on a certain day in steelworks is the

the living labor consumption of the economic effect of technological schemes. The materialized labor cost of technological schemes, namely the living labor cost in other production sections, should also be taken into consideration from the perspective of the entire society. However, it is not enough, either, if just the living labor L_v and the materialized labor L_u's direct costs in technological schemes are examined. As we know, production process costs include living labor and materialized labor. In addition, it occupies labors, machinery, factory building, raw materials, materials, fuel, and semi-finished products. In most cases, if a technological scheme occupies large amount of materialized labor, it will use less living labor and materialized labor costs and will occupy less living labor. If a technological scheme occupies a small amount of materialized labor, it will use more living labor and materialized labor and will occupy more living labor. The amount of occupied labor cannot be directly added to or subtracted from the amount of labor consumption. When examining the amount of occupied labor and the amount of labor consumption together, the effect coefficient of the amount of occupied labor and the effect coefficient of the amount of occupied materialized labor can be adopted. The effect coefficient of the amount of occupied labor is the increased amount of the social labor consumption of technological schemes caused by the occupation of one unit of labor force, namely social loss. The effect coefficient of the amount of occupied materialized labor is the increased amount of the social labor consumption of technological schemes caused by the occupation of one unit of materialized labor. The amount of occupied labor and the amount of occupied materialized labor can be converted into the consumption of social labor via their coefficients. In this way, the amount of occupied labor and the amount of occupied materialized labor can be directly added to or subtracted from the consumption of living labor and the consumption of materialized labor.

Labor consumption in a technological scheme should include the consumption of both living labor and materialized labor. It should examine both occupied labor and occupied materialized labor. Such a comprehensive method is usually reasonable. But, under certain circumstances, it does not work well because it merely considers the consumption of living labor and materialized labor and the impact of occupied labor and occupied materialized labor, and it neglects the impact of consumed materials (materialized labor), adopted natural forces, and transportation power on the other sections in a society. Sometimes, the more natural forces and transportation power that is consumed and occupied by a technological scheme, the more its consumption of labor in other sections will be. Thus, the labor consumption of technological schemes must take account of the impact of the consumption and occupation of material, natural forces, and transportation power. Because the consumption and occupation of material, natural forces, and transportation power cannot be calculated directly with labor consumption, the effect coefficients of material, natural forces, and transportation power must be adopted. The effect coefficient of material application

steelworkers' living labor. On the next day, the steel is sent to a machinery factory, as raw material, so that workers there can make machines. The final product (machines) consists of living labor of the machine workers and the living labor of the steelworkers that occurred a day ago. "Living labor" is different from "labor force." The former usually refers to the amount of labor consumed by labors. It is not related with occupation. The latter refers to the labor. It can be occupied.

is the increased amount of labor consumption in other sections caused by one unit of material adopted by technological schemes. The effect coefficient of natural forces is the increased amount of labor consumption in other sections caused by one unit of material adopted by technological schemes. The effect coefficient of transportation power is the increased amount of labor consumption in other sections caused by one unit of material adopted by technological schemes. It should be pointed out that labor consumption mainly focuses on opportunity effect and short-term effect, under the principle of supply and demand. But in actual life, a long term effect occurs. The effects of supply and demand differ in the values of economic effect coefficients.

The content of the labor consumption of technological schemes explained completely. However, the methods listed above do not work well under certain circumstances. The reason is that these methods only examine the changes of social labor consumption caused by the manpower, capital force, material force, natural forces, transportation power, and time that are directly consumed and occupied by technological schemes. The changes in labor consumption in other sections indirectly caused by technological schemes are not taken into consideration. As we know, in the implementation of technological schemes, manpower, capital force, material force, natural forces, transportation power, and time are directly consumed and occupied. Technological schemes also indirectly cause changes in other sections. In order to evaluate the economic effect of technological schemes correctly and comprehensively, the labor consumption directly caused by technological schemes should be considered, but also the changes of labor consumption indirectly caused by technological schemes should be considered. Only by using this comprehensive approach can the objective laws of technological economy that reflect the facts be found.

In sum, the labor consumption (direct and indirect) of technological schemes consists of the following seven parts: the living labor consumption L_v, the materialized labor consumption L_u, the labor consumption caused by labor occupation $l_r R$, the labor consumption caused by materialized labor occupation $l_u U$, the labor consumption caused by material consumption $l_w W$, the labor consumption caused by the consumption and occupation of natural resources $l_d D$, and the labor consumption caused by the consumption of transportation power $l_y Y$. These components can be expressed as:

$$L_{\sum} = L_v + L_u + l_r R + l_u U + l_w W + l_d D + l_y Y$$

To the right of the equation in this formula, the first two are direct labor consumption, which should always be considered. The remaining five are indirect labor consumption in other sections caused by technological schemes. They need to be considered under certain circumstances.

11.3 Use-Value $S_{\sum}$ of Technological Scheme

Economic effect is the comparison between the result of labor and labor consumption. Economic effect of technological schemes is the comparison between the result of the implementation of technological schemes and the labor consumption. For technological schemes in production fields, "useful effect" usually means commodities. Commodities have use-value, which is measured by quantity and quality. In actual life, many technological schemes are comprehensive and they have multiple aspects of use-value. Because of this, just focusing on one aspect of the use-value of technological schemes is not correct. Instead, multiple aspects of use-value of technological schemes should be comprehensively taken into consideration. It should be pointed out that the use-value mentioned above means the amount of use-value directly produced by a technological scheme in a certain section.[2] However, other than the amount of use-value directly produced by a technological scheme in a certain section, the use-value indirectly generated by a technological scheme in other sections should be taken into account as well. For example, when evaluating the use-value of a railway in a newly-developed area, besides the use-value directly produced by the railway (the amount of completed transportation workload), how the railway promotes the development of the national economy in this area, and the additional value indirectly generated by it in other sections should be considered as well. For another example, as a comprehensive technological scheme, a key water control project can produce a direct use-value, such as electricity generation, shipping, irrigation, or tourism, and can cause salinization of the soil around it, as well. The indirect result leads to a decrease in agriculture output. The drop in the use-value in other sections caused by technological schemes should not be neglected.[3]

It can be seen that evaluating the use-value of technological schemes should begin from the interests of the entire society. Both use-value directly generated in a specific section and the amount of use-value indirectly generated in other sections should be considered. The amount of use-value is related to the status between supply and demand. Short-term products produced by technological schemes have larger use-value. Normal ones have a larger use-value as well. But long-term ones are useless; they do not have any use-value.

[2]When comparing technological schemes, we do not conduct comprehensive evaluation on the amount of use-value from diverse aspects. Instead, we assess the amount of use-value of each aspect individually as a matter of convenience. For example, a key water control project can be split into multiple technical schemes, each of which covers an individual use-value. Then corresponding individual use-values are compared. The details of this approach will be discussed in later chapters.

[3]Suppose that salinization of soil causes a decrease in agricultural output as well as in the amount of use-value of other sections (i.e. agriculture section). This is an approach used to evaluate the economic effect of water conservancy exploitation. It usually assumes that the labor consumption spent by the agriculture section keeps unchanged. In the previous example, an opposite approach is adopted. We assume that the amount of agricultural output remains unchanged and that the labor consumption spent by the agricultural section increases. As a matter of convenience, usually the approach in the latter example is adopted.

The above discussion generates the following expressions for the evaluation standard principle of greater, faster, better and more economical results, based on Formulas 11.3 and 11.4.

$$E- = S_{\sum} - L_{\sum} = S_{\sum} - (L_v + L_u + l_r R + l_u U + l_w W + l_d D + l_y Y) = ZD \tag{11.5}$$

$$\text{or } E_{\div} == S_{\sum}/(L_v + L_u + l_r R + l_u U + l_w W + l_d D + l_y Y) = ZD \tag{11.6}$$

In the above expressions, $S\sum$ is the use-value of technological schemes.

$L\sum$ is the labor consumption of technological schemes.
$S\sum$ is the use-value of technological schemes.
$Lv\sum$ is the total living labor consumption of technological schemes.
$L_{u\sum}$ is the total materialized labor consumption of technological schemes.
$l_r R_{\sum}$ is the labor consumption in other sections caused by the total occupied labor of technological schemes.
$l_u U_{\sum}$ is the labor consumption in other sections caused by the total occupied materialized labor of technological schemes.
$l_w W_{\sum}$ is the labor consumption in other sections caused by the total material consumption of technological schemes.
$l_d D_{\sum}$ is the labor consumption in other sections caused by the total natural forces consumption of technological schemes.
$l_y Y_{\sum}$ is the labor consumption in other sections caused by the total transportation power consumption of technological schemes.
l_r *is* the coefficient of occupied labor.
l_u *is* the coefficient of occupied materialized labor.
l_w *is* the coefficient of material consumption.
l_d *is* the coefficient of natural forces consumption.
l_y *is* the coefficient of transportation power consumption.
$R_{\sum}$ *is* the total labor occupied by technological schemes.
$U_{\sum}$ *is* the total materialized labor occupied by technological schemes.
$W_{\sum}$ *is* the total material consumed by technological schemes.
$D_{\sum}$ *is* the total natural forces consumed by technological schemes.
$Y_{\sum}$ *is* the total transportation power consumed by technological schemes.

11.4 Practical Evaluating Standard of Greater, Faster, Better and More Economic Results

11.4.1 The Content of the Practical Standard for Evaluating Greater, Faster, Better, and More Economic Results

The principle and expressions for evaluating socialist economic effect have been discussed. But it is hard to apply the expressions in practice, because the use-value and labor consumption of technological scheme are difficult to accurately calculate and compare. For the purpose of convenient usage and given commodity production, value rules, and currency existing in socialist societies, usually value format of physical quantity and money quantity is adopted. In fact, the value format only approximately reflects the size of the economic effect. In such as case, the practical format of the evaluation standard principle of greater, faster, better, and more economic results can be summarized in these ways: in a certain time period, achieving the most and the best economic effect at the fastest speed and with the minimum amount of manpower, capital force (financial resource), material force, natural forces, and transportation power, in order to meet the demand of people and the development of national economy; or achieving the same quality and quantity of economic effect at the fastest speed and with the minimum amount of manpower, capital force (financial resource), material force, natural forces, and transportation power; or achieving the most and the best economic effect at the same speed and with the same manpower, capital force (financial resource), material force, natural forces, and transportation power.[4]

11.4.2 Formula of the Principle of Standard for Evaluating Greater, Faster, Better and More Economic Results

The principle of the standards for evaluating greater, faster, better, and more economic results can be expressed in two types of formula. One is used for evaluating macroeconomic effect. The other is used for evaluating microeconomic effect.

1. Formulas for Evaluating Macroeconomic Effect

    (1) Social excessive labor productivity I

$$E_{\text{a}} = \frac{\text{Social Total Benefits X}_{\sum}\text{or S}_{\sum}}{\text{Social Total Consumption IZ}_{\sum}} = Max\,(ZD)\,(E_{\text{a}} \geq 1) \quad (11.7)$$

[4]The fast speed can be called "the shortest time."

(2) Social excessive labor productivity II

$$E_b = \frac{\text{Social Total Benefits X}_{\Sigma}\text{or S}_{\Sigma}}{\text{Social Total Consumption IIZu}_{\Sigma}} = Max\,(ZD)\,(E_b \geq 1) \quad (11.8)$$

(3) Social excessive net income

$$E_c = \text{Social Total Benefits } X_{\Sigma} \text{ or } S_{\Sigma} - \text{Social Total Consumption } IZ_{\Sigma} = Max\,(ZD)\,(E_c \geq 0) \quad (11.9)$$

(4) Social excessive national income

$$E_d = \text{Social Total Benefits } X_{\Sigma} \text{ or } S_{\Sigma} - \text{Social Total Consumption } IIZ_{u\Sigma} = Max\,(ZD)\,(E_d \geq 0) \quad (11.10)$$

In the above formulas,

$$X = X^0 \pm \Delta X$$

$$S = S^0 \pm \Delta S$$

$$Z = Z^0 \pm \Delta Z$$

$$Z_u = Z^0 \pm \Delta Z$$

$$S_{\Sigma} = \sum\sum j_z G = \sum\sum (j_{0z} G_0 \pm \Delta \cdot j_z G)$$

$$Z_{\Sigma} = \sum\sum (C + C_R + C_T + C_W + C_D + C_Y)$$

$$Z_{u\Sigma} = \sum\sum (C_U + C_R + C_T + C_W + C_D + C_Y)$$

$$C = C_V + C_U = C^0 \pm \Delta C$$

$$C_U = C_U^0 \pm \Delta \cdot C_U$$

$$C_R = x_r R = x_r R^0 \pm x_r \Delta R$$

$$C_T = x_t T = x_t T^0 \pm x_t \Delta T$$

$$C_W = x_w W = x_w W^0 \pm x_w \Delta W$$

$$C_D = x_d D = x_d D^0 \pm x_d \Delta D$$

$$C_Y = x_y Y = x_y Y^0 \pm x_y \Delta Y$$

$X_{\sum}$ is social total benefits of technological schemes in a certain time period, including political benefits, defense benefits, social benefits, cultural benefits, technological benefits, economic benefits, environmental and ecological benefits, and natural resource benefits. It is expressed in physical form.
$S_{\sum}$ is the money form of total social benefits of technological schemes in a certain time period.
$Z_{\sum}$ is the total social consumption of technological schemes in a certain time period. It is the total socialcost and all expenditure including wages and salaries.
$Z_{u\sum}$ is total social consumption of technological schemes in a certain time period. It is the total social cost and all expenditures excluding wages and salaries.
j_z is the value or reasonable price of one unit of output or one unit of service.
G is the total output or the total completed service produced by technological schemes per year.
C_V is the total expenditure of technological schemes related to labor consumption per year, such as total wages/salaries (including surcharge of wage/salary).

C_U is the total expenditure of technological schemes related to materialized labor consumption per year, such as the costs of depreciation, fuel, power, raw material, material, seed, feed, and fertilizer.

C is the sum of the cost of living labor and materialized labor consumed by technological schemes per year, namely the total cost (not including profit tax and interest).

R is the total amount of labor occupied by technological schemes per year.

T is the total amount of capital occupied by technological schemes per year, including investment in fixed assets and current capital.

W is the total amount of materials consumed by technological schemes per year.

D is the total amount of natural resources consumed by technological schemes per year.

Y is the total amount of transportation power consumed by technological schemes per year.

x_r, the coefficient of labor utilization economic effect with the unit RMB/person∗year, is the change in social consumption or net income (national income) caused by the utilization of one unit of labor.

x_t, the coefficient of capital utilization economic effect with the unit RMB/RMB∗year, is the change in social consumption or net income (national income) caused by the utilization of one unit of capital.

x_w, the coefficient of material utilization economic effect with the unit RMB/ton, is the change in social consumption or net income (national income) caused by the utilization of one unit of material.

x_d, the coefficient of natural resource utilization economic effect, is the change in social consumption or net income (national income) caused by the utilization of one unit of natural resource. For example, its unit can be RMB/mu∗year.

x_y, the coefficient of the transportation power utilization economic effect with the unit RMB/ton, is the change in social consumption or net income (national income) caused by the utilization of one unit of transportation power.

C_R is the cost of labor occupied by technological schemes per year.

C_T is the cost of capital occupied by technological schemes per year.

C_W is the cost of material consumed by technological schemes per year.

C_Y is the cost of transportation power occupied by technological schemes per year.

Letters with the superscript 0 in the above formulas represent the direct economic effect generated by technological schemes. Those with Δ at the left represent the changes of indirect economic effect generated by technological schemes.

Symbol $\sum\sum$ is the simplification of two types of sums. One is the sum of the economic effect generated by each part of a technological scheme. The other is the sum of the economic effect in some specific years generated by a technological scheme.

From the money-format calculation formulas and the indicators for economic effect, it can be seen that E_a is actually the total output (production value or income) of one unit of comprehensive input (total social consumption including wage/salary) in a certain time period. It is social (total) labor productivity.[5] As another form of social (total) labor productivity, E_b is the total output (production value or income) of one unit of comprehensive input (the total social consumption excluding wage and salary). E_c is the social net income indeed. E_d is the social national income (net production value).[6] However, formulas for calculating total social labor productivity, social net income, and social national income (net production value) as described here are different from those commonly used for calculating labor productivity, net income, and national income (net production value). The latter are the simplified format of the former, under certain specific conditions.

The above formulas show that E_a and E_c differ from E_b and E_d in the expenditure on wage and salary (including surcharge of wage/salary). Wage/salary are calculated in E_a and E_c, but are not calculated in E_b and E_d. It should be pointed out that the social net income is the excessive net income from the perspective of a society. Therefore, it can also be called "social excessive net income." The social national income (net production value) refers to the excessive national income from the perspective of a society. It can be called "social excessive national income", as well. Social (total) labor productivity is the excessive total labor productivity from the perspective of a society. It can also be called "social (total) excessive labor productivity." These formulas treat the maximum of economic effect as the best. Here is one basic standard. The values of E_a and E_b are larger or are equal to 1. The values of E_c and E_d are larger or are equal to 0.

2. Formulas for Evaluating Microeconomic Effect

(1) *Firm (total) excessive labor productivity*

$$E_e = \text{Firm Total Benefits} S_{\sum f} / \text{Firm Total Consumption} Z_{\sum f} = Max\,(ZD)\,(E_e \geq 1) \quad (11.11)$$

(2) *Firm excessive profit*

$$E_f = \text{Firm Total Benefits} S_{\sum f} - \text{Firm Total Consumption} Z_{\sum f} = Max\,(ZD)\,(E_f \geq 0) \quad (11.12)$$

In the above formulas,

---

[5]Generally, "labor productivity" refers to the number of products produced by a unit of living labor in a production process in a certain production section. It is actually "living labor productivity." On this point, it is narrowly defined labor productivity, or local labor productivity. "Local labor productivity" is different from the meaning of labor productivity here, which starts from the perspective of the entire society.

[6]The author argues that "national income" has two meanings. The narrow one refers to national income generated by material production sections (i.e. industry, agriculture, construction, commerce, and transportation). The general one refers to national income generated by material production sections and the third industry. The meaning of "national income" chosen for use in this book is the second one.

$$S_f = S_{sale} - S_{tax}$$

$$Z_f = T + C + C_{tax} - C_j - T_l - T_c$$

S_{sale} is the annual sales revenue of a firm.
S_{tax} is the income tax paid by a firm (such as commercial and industrial taxes and adjustment tax).
C_{tax} is the cost tax paid by a firm (such as fuel special tax, capital occupation tax, land tax, and environment tax).
T is the investment of a firm, including the investment in fixed assets and current capital.
C is the cost of a firm, including interest.
C_j is the basic cost of depreciation.
T_l is the amount of collected current capital.
T_c is the amount of the collected salvage value of fixed assets.
$\sum$ is the sum of the values of a firm in its term of service.

All of the letters in the above formulas have the superscript 0 because they refer to direct economic effect. Indirect economic effect is excluded. For the purpose of easy understanding, their superscripts are omitted.

3. Schema of the Principle of the Standard for Evaluating Greater, Faster, Better and More Economic Results

In order to help readers better understand the principle of the standards for evaluating greater, faster, better, and more economical results and its formulas, the author designs the schema (see Fig. 11.1) by choosing macroeconomic effect evaluation as an example. This figure indicates the relations between the six conditions, six forces, and six expenditures in the generalized production process studied in technological economics.

11.5 Two Applications of the Evaluation Standard Principle of Greater, Faster, Better and More Economic Results and Related Formulas

There are two applications of the principle of the standard for evaluating greater, faster, better, and more economic results. The first one is to determine whether technological schemes are economically reasonable by evaluating their economic effect. The second one is to find the technological scheme with the best economic effect by evaluating their economic effect. Two indicators, namely the total indicator and the increment indicator, can be applied to conduct the evaluations. The evaluation of absolute economic effect uses the total indicator, whereas the evaluation of relative

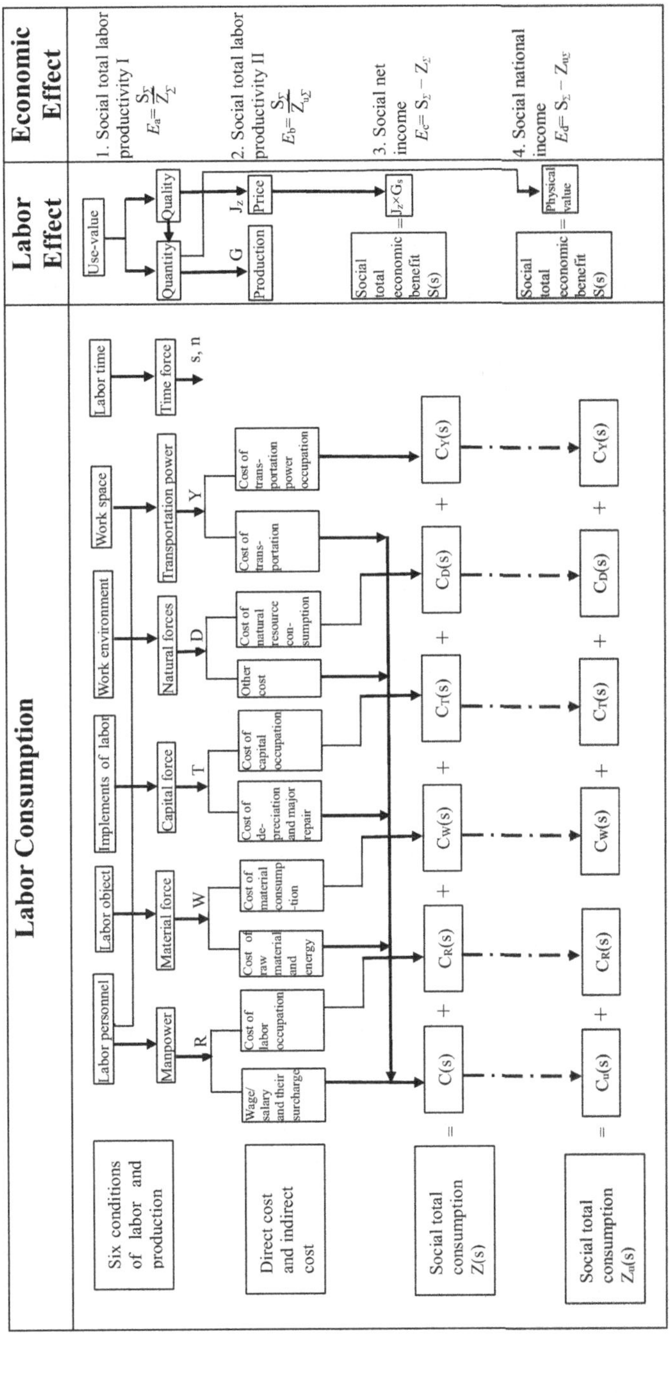

Fig. 11.1 The principle of the standard for evaluating greater, faster, better and more economical results and the formulas of its application

economic effect uses the increment indicator. The formula for evaluating absolute economic effect can be used for assessing one single technological scheme. For multiple technological schemes, formulas for evaluating both absolute economic effect and relative economic effect are needed. The formula for evaluating the absolute economic effect is the same as the one for evaluating greater, faster, better, and more economic results E_a, E_b, E_c, E_d, E_e, and E_f discussed in last part.

11.5.1 Formula for Evaluating Greater, Faster, Better, and More Macroeconomic Results

1. Total Social additional excessive labor productivity I E_{af}

$$E_{af} = \frac{\text{Social Total Additional Benefits } \Delta X_{\Sigma} \text{ or } \Delta S_{\Sigma}}{\text{Social Total Additional Consumption } I\Delta Z_{\Sigma}} = Max\,(ZD) \quad (11.13)$$

2. Social additional excessive (total) labor productivity II Ebf

$$E_{bf} = \frac{\text{Social Total Additional Benefits } \Delta X_{\Sigma} \text{ or } \Delta S_{\Sigma}}{\text{Social Total Additional Consumption } II\Delta Zu_{\Sigma}} = Max\,(ZD) \quad (11.14)$$

3. Social additional excessive net income rate Ecf

$$E_{cf} = \frac{\Delta E_c}{\Delta R};\ \frac{\Delta E_c}{\Delta T};\ \frac{\Delta E_c}{\Delta W};\ \frac{\Delta E_c}{\Delta D};\ \frac{\Delta E_c}{\Delta Y};\ \frac{\Delta E_c}{\Delta N} = Max\,(ZD) \quad (11.15)$$

4. Social additional excessive national income rate E_{df}

$$E_{df} = \frac{\Delta E_d}{\Delta R};\ \frac{\Delta E_d}{\Delta T};\ \frac{\Delta E_d}{\Delta W};\ \frac{\Delta E_d}{\Delta D};\ \frac{\Delta E_d}{\Delta Y};\ \frac{\Delta E_d}{\Delta N} = Max\,(ZD) \quad (11.16)$$

In the above formulas, ΔZ and ΔZ_u are the additional comprehensive input of the technological schemes. ΔX and ΔS are the total additional output achieved by the technological schemes. ΔR, ΔT, ΔW, ΔD, ΔY, and ΔN are the amount of additional input on manpower, capital, material, natural resource, transportation, and time, respectively, used by technological schemes during a certain time period. ΔE_c and ΔE_d are additional net output (additional social net income and additional social national income) achieved by technological schemes in a certain time period due to added manpower, capital, material, natural resources, transportation power, and time. E_{af} and E_{bf} are the total additional output generated by additional comprehensive input of technological schemes. E_{cf} and E_{df} are additional excessive net output achieved by additional individual input of technological schemes.

The above formulas treat the largest calculated value as the best economic effect. Some conditions must be satisfied: E_{af} and E_{bf} must be larger than or equal to 1. For E_{cf} and E_{df}, if the indirect cost (i.e. $x_r R$, $x_t T$, $x_w W$, $x_d D$, $x_y Y$) caused by the denominator is deducted from the numerator (E_{cf} or E_{df}), E_{cf} and E_{df} should be larger than or equal to 0. Otherwise, E_{cf} and E_{df} should be larger than or equal to the standard economic effect coefficients of the denominator (i.e. x_r, x_t, x_w, x_d, x_y) or be larger than or equal to 1 (when the time factor is considered by ΔT in the denominator).

11.5.2 Formula for Evaluating Greater, Faster, Better, and More Microeconomic Results

1. Firm additional excessive (total) labor productivity E_{ef}

$$E_{\text{ef}} = \frac{\text{Firm Additional Benefits } \Delta X_{\sum f} \text{ or } S_{\sum f}}{\text{Firm Total Additional Consumption } \Delta Z_{\sum f}} = Max\,(ZD)\,(E_{\text{ef}} \geq 1) \tag{11.17}$$

2. Firm additional excessive profit rate E_{ff}

$$E_{\text{df}} = \frac{\Delta E_f}{\Delta R}; \frac{\Delta E_f}{\Delta T}; \frac{\Delta E_f}{\Delta W}; \frac{\Delta E_f}{\Delta D}; \frac{\Delta E_f}{\Delta Y}; \frac{\Delta E_f}{\Delta N} = Max\,(ZD)(E_{\text{ff}} \geq 0) \tag{11.16}$$

In these two formulas, E_{ef} is the total additional output generated by the additional comprehensive input of technological schemes.

E_{ff} is the additional net income generated by the additional individual input of technological schemes.
$\frac{\Delta \text{Ef}}{\Delta \text{T}}$ is the additional investment excessive profit rate.
$\frac{\Delta \text{Ef}}{\Delta \text{W}}$ is the additional material excessive profit rate.

Meanings of the other fractions can be determined by parity of reasoning.

The formula for calculating relative economic effect can be used in many ways. As we know, other than the huge number of technological economy issues inside each section, technological economic issues that are trans-sectional and that need comparison exist in practice. For example, when many infrastructure projects are begun at the same time, capital will become limited. As such, the number of projects must be controlled. How to reduce the number of projects depends on the result of calculating their economic effect. Suppose there are 100 projects. Research and investigation must be conducted in order to collect technological economics material and data. Then the calculation of the economic effect can be implemented, based on these data. The economic effect generated by the occupied capital of each technological scheme varies. The net income (national income) generated by a certain amount of capital can change from less than 10% to 200%. Some projects even generate a negative net income (national income). According to the values of economic effect, these projects can be ranked in a list. Those projects that have smaller values should be cancelled first. The list can be modified until the required investment matches the available input. The allocation of manpower usually does not take account of the economic effect. But, in fact, manpower should be allocated and used based on amount of its economic effect. The reason is that each person produces a certain amount economic effect, no matter which industry and position he is in. But the economic effect produced by every person is different. This is caused by subjective as well as objective factors. For instance, technicians whose majors match their position requirements produce more net income than those whose majors do not match their position requirements. People working in overstaffed departments will produce a smaller net income. Thus, when allocating manpower, workers should be ranked based on the amount of average net income (national income) they produce each year. Those who produce a small net income or who cannot support themselves should be sent to places where more net income can be produced. Those whose educational majors do not match their position requirements should be sent to other positions whose requirements match their majors. Meanwhile, new industries where all workers can produce their biggest economic effect should be explored.

These examples indicate that in order to meet diverse demands, manpower, capital force, material force, natural forces, transportation power, and time should be allocated reasonably. Fixing these issues requires a cross-section comparison and the use of formulas for evaluating relative economic effect, such as social additional net income rate and social additional national income rate. Similarly, a firm additional profit rate can be applied to evaluate the microeconomic effect.

11.6 Application Scope of Three Types of Economic Standard Principles Regarding National Income, Net Income, and Profits

Formulas for evaluating economic effect can be categorized into three groups: (1) National income, such as E_b, E_d, E_{bf}, and E_{df}; (2) Net income, such as E_a, E_c, E_{af}, and E_{cf}; (3) Profit, such as E_e, E_f, E_{ef}, and E_{ff}. The first two groups are applied for evaluating the macroeconomic effect. The third one is applied for evaluating the microeconomic effect. In order to understand how important the two evaluation approaches are, we will consider both national income and net income.

National income and net income are two important indicators.[7] They are used for evaluating socialist economic effect. In addition, they are the main goals of socialist

[7]National income is the sum of profit, tax, and wage/salary, namely $V + M$. Net income is the sum of profit and tax, namely M.

economic development. As we know, in the socialist planned economy period, the production of industry and agriculture was adopted as a way to measure economic development in China. Practice proved that there were many drawbacks caused by the adoption of this indicator. Specifically, the production of industry and agriculture is disconnected from the goal of socialist production, the benefits of workers, the improvement of labor productivity, the improvement of economic benefits, the actual economic conditions, and the real speed of the development of the national economy. These drawbacks caused the goal of economic development in China improper for a long time. Many serious mistakes were made due to improper economic development goals. The correct goals for socialist economic development are national income and net income.[8] These two indicators overcome the drawbacks of the production of industry and agriculture. National income and net income are consistent with the goal of socialist production, the benefits of workers, the improvement of labor productivity, and the improvement of economic benefits. They reflect the actual economic conditions and the real speed of the development of the national economy. Thus, the adoption of these two indicators can clarify the goal of socialist production, correctly reflect the real economic condition, combine the goals of the nation and the benefits to the individual, greatly increase enthusiasm for labor, improve labor productivity and economic benefits, and promote the development of the national economy.

When evaluating the macroeconomic effect, which one—national income or net income—should be chosen? Next, the application scope of these two indicators will be discussed in details.

The expenditure on wages andsalaries has a double meaning. On the one hand, similar with other costs spent in production and construction, wage/salary reflects the amount of living labor consumed in production and construction. As such, it is a type of consumption. Therefore, if other conditions do not change, spending on wage/salary should be minimized. However, on the other hand, wage/salary is different from other costs spent in production and construction, because it is workers' income. The larger wage/salary is, the larger workers' income will be, and the larger the national income is. One hopes for a large wage/salary.

Due to the double meaning of wage/salary, two approaches are applied when evaluating technological schemes. The first one treats wage/salary as consumption. The second one treats it as income. In the aforementioned formulas about E_a, E_c, E_{af}, and E_{cf}, wage/salary is treated as consumption, whereas in the formulas about E_b, E_d, E_{bf}, and E_{df}, wage/salary is treated as a portion of the national income.

Next, some cases will be discussed which will further explain the relationship between the two approaches. Specifically, applications about E_c, and E_d and their relationship will be discussed in detail. In the first case, technological schemes *A* and *B* have the same total production and consumption, namely the same social total

---

[8] Recently, the State Statistics Bureau adopted the indicator of gross national product. In fact, it has the same meaning as the general national income. Compared with the latter, the former includes the income of depreciation.

consumption, in given n_j years. But the expenditure on wage/salary C_v of technological scheme *A* is larger than that of *B*. In this case, the two technological schemes have the same value of $E_{c.}$ If E_c is chosen for evaluating the economic effect, the two technological schemes have the same economic effect. However, it should be noticed that technological scheme *A* has a larger expenditure on wage/salary than technological scheme *B* does. In other words, the wage/salary income or the national income of technological scheme *A* is higher than that of technological scheme *B*. Thus, if the net production value (national income) E_d is chosen for evaluating the economic effect, technological scheme *A* has a larger economic effect than technological scheme *B* (see Case *I* in Table 11.1). In the second case, the technological scheme *A* has a larger total consumption than the technological scheme *B* in given n_j years (see Case *II* in Table 11.1). Only their expenditures on wage/salary are different. All of their other consumption is the same. If E_d is chosen for evaluating the economic effect, the two technological schemes have the same economic effect. But if E_c is chosen for evaluating the economic effect, their economic effects are different. The net income of technological scheme *A* is smaller than that of technological scheme *B*. In fact, the amount of difference between their net incomes is exactly the same as that of the difference between their expenditures on wage/salary. That is to say, the extra amount of living labor spent on technological scheme *A* is worthless because no more value is produced. Therefore, the technological scheme *B* has a larger economic effect than the technological scheme *A*. In the third case (see Case *III* in Table 11.1), the total consumption of technological schemes *A* and *B* are different in given n_j years. The technological scheme *A* consumes 600,000RMB and the technological scheme *B* consumes 700,000RMB. The other expenditures of these two technological schemes are different too. Technological scheme *A* consumes 200,000RMB and the technological scheme *B* consumes 300,000RMB. The two technological schemes have the same expenditures on wage/salary: 400,000RMB. These data show that the additional expenditure spent on the technological scheme *B* does not increase wage/salary. If either net income E_c or net production value (national income) E_d is chosen for evaluating the economic effect, technological scheme *A* has a larger economic effect than the technological scheme *B*. According to Table 11.1, the net income E_c of the technological scheme *A is* 100,000RMB more than that of technological scheme *B*. The national income, E_d, of technological scheme *A* is 100,000RMB more than that of technological scheme *B*, as well. In the fourth case (see Case *IV* in Table 11.1), the total consumption of technological schemes *A* and *B* are different in given n_j years. Technological scheme *A* consumes 100,000RMB more than the technological scheme *B*. The expenditure on wage/salary of technological scheme *A* is 400,000RMB more than that of technological scheme *B*. The other consumption of technological scheme *A* is 300,000RMB less than that of technological scheme *B*. If net income E_c is chosen for evaluating the economic effect, technological scheme *A* has a smaller economic effect than the technological scheme *B* because the former has 100, less net income than the latter. But if net production value (national income) E_d is chosen for evaluating the economic effect, technological scheme *A* has a larger economic effect technological scheme *B* because the former has 300,000RMB more net production value (national income) than the latter.

Table 11.1 The standard for evaluating technological economy by considering the double meaning of wage/salary (Unit: 10,000RMB)

Case #	Technological scheme	Total production $\sum_{s=1}^{nj} jzGs$	Total wage/Salary $\sum_{s=1}^{nj} Cvs$	Total cost other than wage/Salary $\sum_{s=1}^{nj}(Zs - Cvs)$	Total cost = Total wage/Salary + Other cost $\sum_{s=1}^{nj} Zs$	Net income = Total production − total cost E_c	Net production value(national income) = Total production-Total cost + Total wage/Salary E_d	The sum of net income and net production value $E_c + E_d$	Result
I	*A* *B*	100 100	40 20	20 40	60 60	40 40	80 60	120 100	Technological Scheme *A* has larger economic effect
II	*A* *B*	100 100	30 20	40 40	70 60	30 40	60 60	90 100	Technological Scheme *B* has larger economic effect
III	*A* *B*	100 100	40 40	20 30	60 70	40 30	80 70	120 100	Technological Scheme *A* has larger economic effect
IV	*A* *B* *C*	100 100 100	50 10 40	30 60 32	80 70 72	20 30 28	70 40 68	90 70 96	Technological Scheme *C* has larger economic effect

In this case, although technological scheme *A* has 100,000RMB less net income than technological scheme *B*, the former has 300,000RMB more net production value (national income) than the latter. In other words, technological scheme *A* produces more national income with less net income. As such, technological scheme *A* has a larger economic effect than technological scheme *B* at the state level.

Here is another case. Technological scheme *A* has 80,000RMB less net income and 20,000RMB more net production value (national income) than technological scheme *C*. If the main goal is national income, technological scheme *A* should be adopted. If net income is the goal, technological scheme *C* should be adopted. Application scope of net income E_c and net production value (national income) E_d can be achieved based on the analysis of these four cases. In the first case, when the technological schemes have the same net income E_c but different net production value (national income) E_d, E_d should be adopted to evaluate the economic effect. In the second case, when technological schemes have the same E_d but different E_c, E_c should be adopted to evaluate the economic effect. In the third case, when a technological scheme has the bigger E_c and a larger E_d, either E_c *or* E_d can be adopted to evaluate the economic effect because the results will be the same. In the fourth case, the technological scheme with bigger E_d has a smaller E_c, whereas the technological scheme with the bigger E_c has a smaller E_d. In such a case, if a country has abundant manpower, and the amount of increased national income is larger than that of decreased net income, the total social income will increase in this country in general, even though its net income decreases. Thus, E_d should be adopted to evaluate the economic effect, especially in certain sections such as the construction industry. For short-term technological scheme in these sections, it is more reasonable to adopt E_b, E_d, E_{bf} *and* E_{df} because redundant labor can be completely utilized.

In the above four cases, the author also applies the comprehensive approach (addition) to calculate the net income and the sum of national income. The results are consistent with those achieved in the above analysis. As such, it is reasonable to adopt comprehensive evaluation approaches that have the indicators of net income and national income to assess the economic effect of technological schemes. Specifically, when conflict results are achieved by using net income and national income as indicators, the comprehensive approaches will generate satisfying results. This is proved by the above four cases.

It should be pointed out that national income and net income are applicable to all sections in the national economy. The concept of "national income" applied in China now only includes value created by the material production sections ($V + M$). Value ($V + M$) created by non-material production sections is not included. Actually, this type of value, such as that created in the third industry, is national income too. The author argues that the national income created by material production sections is the narrowly defined national income. Generalized national income includes value created by both the material production sections and the non-material production sections. "National income" is considered, in this book, to mean the generalized national income. Similarly, "net income" is considered, in this book, to mean the generalized net income.

The drawbacks of applying the production of industry and agriculture to evaluate macroeconomic effect are discussed. These drawbacks also exist when applying the production of industry and agriculture to evaluate microeconomic effect. Firms' economic benefit does not depend on their production, but on their profits. The "ox nose theory" proposed by economist Zhifang Sun argues that profit is the main index used to evaluate firms' economic benefit. Therefore, it is reasonable to apply a profit type index to evaluate the microeconomic effect. Because profit does not reflect the whole newly-created economic benefit, it cannot be adopted as an index for evaluating macroeconomic effect.

11.7 Other Economic Evaluation Standard Principles

Many principles and formulas have been proposed in related literatures around the world at present. These principles and formulas only differ in name, but have the same content. For example, "firm profit tax" is called "net income" or "profit." "Investment" is called "capital." "Net production value" is called "national income." These principles can be categorized into seven groups, according to their content.

1. The maximum of the rate of net output and input. This group includes return on investment, the rate of investment and net income, the investment national income (net production value) rate, the profit rate on cost, the profit rate on wages, the coefficient of the economic effect of investment utilization, the coefficient of the economic effect of manpower utilization, the coefficient of the economic effect of material utilization, the coefficient of the economic effect of transportation power utilization, the coefficient of the economic effect of natural resource utilization, and the internal rate of return.
2. The minimum of the rate of input and net output. This group includes payoff period and recovery period of added investment.
3. The maximum of the rate of output and input. This group includes the rate of capital and production value, the rate of cost and production value, the living labor productivity, and the benefit-cost ratio.
4. The minimum of the rate of input and output. This group includes the minimum of product value and the minimum of norm quota of consumption.
5. The minimum of the difference between output and input (the maximum of net output). This group includes the maximum of profit, the maximum of net income, the maximum of national income, and the maximum of net present value.
6. The maximum of output. This group includes the maximum of production value and the maximum of income.
7. The minimum of input. This group includes the minimum of investment, the minimum of cost, the minimum of labor, the minimum of material consumption, the minimum of transportation power, the minimum of natural resources,

the minimum of required time, the minimum of the total cost in standard pay-off period, the minimum of the annual cost in standard pay-off period, and the minimum of the annual calculated cost.

It should be pointed out that the maximum (or minimum) has a prescribed value in practice. If the calculated value is larger (or smaller) than a prescribed value, a technological scheme is thought to be economically reasonable. The above-listed maximums and minimums all have this characteristic. But they all have drawbacks, as well. For instance, some just consider input but neglect output. Some only consider output but neglect input. Some consider both input and output, but neglect the time factor. Some consider the time factor, but do not consider input comprehensively and neglect the combined input of the six factors. Some do not have scientific names, such as "net present value" and "internal rate of return." Mathematical calculations prove that the principles listed above are derivatives of the twelve formulas for evaluating greater, faster, better, and more economic results. They can only be adopted under certain conditions. The standard for evaluating greater, faster, better, and more economic results has universal meaning.

11.8 Financial Evaluation and Economic Evaluation

"Economic evaluation" is the evaluation of economic effect, indeed. It evaluates the economic effect of manpower, material force, capital force, natural forces, transportation power, and time. "Financial evaluation" is the evaluation of financial cash flow balance. It is the money capital format of evaluation, specially focusing on financial status. It can also be called "local economic evaluation." Economic evaluation assesses objective economic effect, so it should be reasonable evaluation. Thus, unreasonable information or data in current investment, cost, price, tax, and interest should not be adopted. Only those reasonable numerical values should be adopted. Economic evaluation must reflect object requirement. It should be as reasonable as possible. In contrast, financial evaluation usually adopts regulations and data from the current financial system. Even though they are unreasonable, they must be adopted. Therefore, the characteristic of financial evaluation is to reflect real life. If real life is reasonable, so is financial evaluation, and vice versa.

Because economic evaluation is required to be objective and reasonable, it might not be able to be used in real life. Thus, economic evaluation methods are complicated. But financial evaluation focuses on real life. The data it requires are ready-made and easy to get. Therefore, financial evaluation methods are much easier. In socialist conditions, as the standard for evaluating economic effect of technological schemes, economic evaluation plays a vital role in the selection of technological schemes. Financial evaluation, however, does not play any role in technological scheme selection. It cannot be adopted as a standard to evaluate the economic effect of technological schemes. But financial evaluation is very necessary for better managing firms, activating firms' initiative, and generating better benefits allocation between firms and the state after the technological schemes are realized.

11.9 Firm (Micro) Financial Evaluation and Social (Macro) Economic Evaluation

"Firm financial evaluation" here means conducting financial evaluation from the perspective of firms, not evaluating firms' economic effect. It is also called "firm economic evaluation" or "microeconomic evaluation".[9] "Social economic evaluation" refers to conducting economic evaluation from the perspective of a society (including its state and firms). It does not intend to evaluate a society's economic effect. The differences between these concepts are discussed here, for the purpose of preventing confusion. Social economic evaluation is also called "national economic evaluation" or "macroeconomic evaluation." The relationship between firm financial evaluation and social economic evaluation has four cases: (1) both firm financial evaluation and social economic evaluation are good; (2) both firm financial evaluation and social economic evaluation are bad; (3) firm financial evaluation is good, but social economic evaluation is bad; (4) firm financial evaluation is bad, but social economic evaluation is good. It is obvious that the first case is advisable and the second case is not advisable. In the third case, although firm financial evaluation is good, social economic evaluation is bad. Therefore this case is not advisable. In the fourth case, even though firm financial evaluation is bad, social economic evaluation is good. Overall, this case is the most advisable.

11.10 Absolute Economic Evaluation and Relative Economic Evaluation

"Absolute economic evaluation" refers to the evaluation of the economic effect of technological schemes, whereas relative economic evaluation refers to the evaluation of the relative economic effect of multiple technological schemes. Absolute economic evaluation is the base. It can be applied to evaluate either the absolute economic effect of an individual technological scheme or the relative economic effect of multiple technological schemes. In contrast, "relative economic evaluation" can only be applied to evaluate the relative economic effect of multiple technological schemes. If relative economic evaluation is conducted on two cases which mean to adopt or abandon a technological scheme, increment indicators ΔX, ΔS, ΔZ, ΔEc,

[9] It is not proper for some people to call "financial evaluation" "firm economic evaluation." Similarly, the name of "microeconomic evaluation" is not proper either. The reason is that financial evaluation and economic evaluation are different.

ΔT...in relative economic evaluation become total amount indicators X, S, Z, Ec, T...

In such as case, relative economic evaluation changes into absolute economic evaluation. Technological economics issues studied in technological economics usually need comparison. As such, the relative economic evaluation is more important than the absolute economic evaluation. The relationship between absolute economic evaluation and relative economic evaluation has four cases: (1) both absolute economic evaluation and relative economic evaluation are good; (2) both absolute economic evaluation and relative economic evaluation are bad; (3) absolute economic evaluation is good, but relative economic evaluation is bad; (4) absolute economic evaluation is bad, but relative economic evaluation is good. It is easy to reach conclusions for the first and second cases. For the third case, although absolute economic evaluation is good, relative economic evaluation is bad. Overall, the case is not advisable. The result of the fourth case depends upon the circumstances.

11.11 Static Economic Evaluation and Dynamic Economic Evaluation

Static economic evaluation does not consider the time factor, whereas dynamic economic evaluation takes the time factor into account. The principle of the standard for evaluating greater, faster, better, and more economical results, discussed above, takes the time factor into consideration; therefore it is "dynamic economic evaluation." "Static economic evaluation" usually calculates the annual benefits and costs for technological schemes. It does not take into account the benefits and costs in a given time period. Thus, static economic evaluation has many limitations. The relationship between static economic evaluation and dynamic economic evaluation has four cases: (1) both static economic evaluation and dynamic economic evaluation are good; (2) both static economic evaluation and dynamic economic evaluation are bad; (3) static economic evaluation is good, but dynamic economic evaluation is bad; (4) static economic evaluation is bad, but dynamic economic evaluation is good. The first and the fourth cases are advisable. The second and the third cases are not advisable. In sum, dynamic economic evaluation is the primary between these two. Ways to consider the time factor will be discussed in later chapters.

Chapter 12
Comparison Theory of the Technological Economy

12.1 Introduction

Other than evaluating the economic effect of an individual technological scheme based on its cost and the benefit that it will generate, technological economics study needs to conduct comparisons among technological schemes and identify which has the best economic effect. The technological scheme comparison is an important aspect in any technological economics study. The comparison theory of the technological economy is an important theory. It consists of the principle of technological scheme comparison, the principle of demand-meeting comparison, the principle of consumption and cost comparison, the principle of price comparison, and the principle of time comparison.

12.2 Comparison Principle of Technological Schemes

What are the objects in a technological scheme comparison? How does one select alternative technological schemes? What principles should be followed in order to conduct technological scheme comparisons? When are technological schemes comparable? When are they not comparable? How does one change technological schemes that are incomparable into comparable ones? These are the questions that will be answered in this chapter.

1. **Principle for alternative technological scheme selection**

Technological scheme comparison must be conducted to resolve technological economy issues. Alternative technological schemes are required for technological scheme comparisons. How does one select alternative technological schemes? The principles include not missing any possible technological schemes, not considering

S. Xu, *Technological Economics*,
https://doi.org/10.1007/978-981-15-8582-1_12

any excessive technological schemes, and selecting the right one. More specifically, all of the possible alterative technological schemes should be considered. None should be missed. Otherwise, the best technological schemes might be overlooked. In addition, those unworkable ones should not be taken account of. If they are included in a technological scheme comparison, the final result will be negatively impacted. Furthermore, any alternative technological scheme selection must proceed from reality. If wrong alternative technological schemes are selected, the entire technological economy evaluation will generate a useless result. Correctly selecting alternative schemes relies on investigation and study, as well as the use of experts' knowledge.

2. **Principle for comparative technological scheme confirmation**

Technological schemes should compare alternative ones. Meanwhile, comparison between alternative ones should be conducted, as well. All of these schemes can be called comparable schemes. Comparable schemes must be reasonable. In other words, they must have comparability. For example, when comparing solar energy heating and boiler heating, the technological scheme of solar energy heating must take account of boiler heating as backup, due to the changes in solar energy caused by season, climate, day, and night. Therefore, a complete solar energy technological scheme should include both solar water heater and boiler heating. This technological scheme then can be compared with the scheme that uses boiler heating alone. It should be pointed out that many incomplete technological schemes are compared in practice.

3. **Principle for comparability of technological economy**

When performing technological economic effect evaluation, technological schemes must have comparability. In other words, technological schemes without comparability cannot be compared. Comparability of items in the technological economy should be made based on the requirements of a technological economic effect evaluation. In socialist society, a technological economic effect evaluation needs to follow the principle of greater, faster, better, and more economical results, and the other twelve principles and formulas, such as social total labor productivity. The other principles and formulas are their particular cases and transformation. Thus, when considering the principle of comparability and conditions, we should follow the requirements of the principle of greater, faster, better, and more economical results. More specifically, these requirements include demand-meeting, consumption cost, price, and time. Technological scheme comparison can be conducted only when two or more technological schemes have comparability in demand-meeting, consumption and cost, price, and time.

12.3 Principle of Demand–Meeting Comparison

As we know, the goal of technological schemes is to meet certain demands. For instance, the technological scheme of a machine tool aims to meet the demand of machine processing. The technological scheme of agricultural irrigation aims to meet the demand of increasing agricultural output. The technological scheme of construction aims to meet the demand of building houses. The technological scheme of digital education aims to meet the demand of education. All technological schemes are based on meeting certain demands. Since all technological schemes aims for meeting certain demands, two technological schemes must meet the same demands if they are chosen to be compared. Otherwise, they cannot replace each other and then do not have comparability. As such, the principle of demand-meeting is important for any technological scheme comparison.

For technological schemes regarding the national economy production and construction, they meet the demands of the national economy and the social requirements with the indicators of output, labor, variety, quality, and features. When the principle of demand-meeting comparison is conducted, the indictors of technological schemes should have comparability. At first sight, the output (including variety) and quality (including features) of many technological schemes are not comparable, in any case. For example, coal and natural gas are not comparable. Plastic and steel are not comparable. Other examples are too numerous to mention. However, real life comparisons between the aforementioned technological schemes are conducted very often. For example, the production of synthesis ammonia can choose either coal or natural gas as its raw material. Then which, between these two raw materials, is more economical and reasonable for exploitation and transportation? In this case, a comparison between the technological scheme that exploits and uses coal and the one the exploits and uses natural gas is required. Some may ask: are these two technological schemes comparable? The answer is yes. The reason is that although coal and natural gas are different in chemical composition and physical appearance, they play the same role as the raw material for producing synthesis ammonia. Either coal or natural gas can meet the demand of producing synthesis ammonia; therefore, they are comparable. It can be seen that it is very important for technological economy comparison to find the comparability between those technological schemes that look not comparable. If comparability is considered in general terms, many technological schemes are not comparable. However, if we make a concrete analysis of concrete conditions, some technological schemes are comparable under given conditions. It should be pointed out that when technological schemes are comparable, it does not mean they are completely the same.

The principle of demand-meeting comparison consists of two parts: the output and labor service comparison and the quality and feature comparison.

The requirements of output and labor service comparison are these: (1) The net output, net complete work, and net contribution of each technological scheme should be compared. If their gross outputs are equal but their losses vary in the process of production, circulation, and consumption (i.e. the amount that really meets users' demands varies), they are not comparable. (2) Some technological schemes can improve production and output after they are adopted, whereas some cannot. The net production capacity and net output of the latter should be adjusted to be the same as those of the former before comparison can be conducted. (3) Comprehensive utilization schemes should be compared with combined schemes, which can meet the same demands but consist of individual technological schemes. Or comprehensive utilization schemes should be broken down first and then each part should be compared with other corresponding individual technological schemes. For example, the technological scheme of a thermal power station must be compared with a combined scheme, which consists of one condensing power station for generating electricity solely and one boiler room for heat supply. In another example, if coke-oven gas is selected for a technological scheme about city coal gasification construction, it is very hard to find a combined scheme to compare with this scheme because the production of coke-oven gas is a comprehensive utilization scheme which generates coal gas, coke, and tar. As such, only after coke and tar and their costs are removed from the comprehensive utilization scheme can the remained coal gas and its cost be compared with a technological scheme that adopts coal for city coal gasification construction. (4) Technological schemes with different production scales cannot be compared before their net production scales are adjusted to the same size. (5) Besides the direct output and labor service, the indirect change of output and the labor service in other departments caused by technological schemes should be taken into consideration. For instance, if the products of technological schemes *A* and *B* are short-term ones, users' indirect benefits should be considered. In another example, if technological schemes *A* and *B* have the same net direct output, but *A* causes environmental pollution and reduces agricultural output while *B* does not, these two technological schemes are not comparable. The loss of agricultural output and damage caused by technological scheme *A* must be considered first before these two technological schemes can be compared.

The requirements of quality and feature comparison are these: (1) For indicators of quality and feature that are measurable, the comparison should focus on how they meet the final demands. For example, there are two technological schemes that produce 100,000 pieces of 20w fluorescent lamps. One adopts existing technologies and the fluorescent lamps it produces last 3,000 h. The other adopts the latest technologies and its products last only 18,000 h. In this case, the former has a use value of 6 million kw/h, whereas the latter has a use value of 36 million kw/h. Thus, they are not comparable. Instead, a technological scheme that produces 100,000 pieces of 20w fluorescent lamps with the latest technologies should be compared with another technological scheme that produces 600,000 pieces pf 20w fluorescent lamps with existing technologies. (2) For indicators of quality and feature that are not measurable, such as good appearance, comfort, convenience, cleanliness, and deliciousness, grading can be adopted for evaluation. Various schemes can be ranked by scores.

It should be pointed out that a certain type of technological schemes do not fall into the category of production. Their useful effect is not production. When comparing them, the requirement of meeting the same demand must be satisfied.

In practice, some technological schemes that do not meet the requirement of meeting the same demand can be compared. But it is not surprising that incorrect results are achieved. For instance, Datong in Shanxi province has coal that needs to be transported to Beijing. What is the most economic approach for transportation? Three technological schemes are proposed. The first one adopts railway use. The second one gasifies coal in Datong first and then transports coal gas to Beijing. The third one generates electricity with coal in Datong first and then transports electricity to Beijing. The comparison of these three technological schemes is based on the same coal consumption amount (12 million tons). The result indicates that transporting coal is the most economical approach. Transporting electricity is less economical. Transporting coal gas is lest economical. Such a comparison does not meet the requirement of meeting the same demand, though. The three technological schemes deliver different products, although each delivers energy. Coal is the primary energy, whereas electricity and coal gas are the secondary energies. Due to the differences in their quality and their result of use, they meet different demands. Electricity can be used for lamps, electromotors, TV, and radio. But coal and coal gas cannot. Thus, they cannot be substituted by one another and, therefore, cannot be compared. Under certain conditions, coal and coal gas can be compared when they are used for supplying heat. But the comparison should not be based on the same amount of coal consumption (12 million tons, in this case). Instead, the comparison should be based on the same amount of residential consumption (i.e. cooking) or fuel consumption in industries. More specifically, the questions are these: in order to meet the demands of cooking fuel for the two million residents in Beijing, how much coal gas is needed? And how many tons of coal are needed to be transported from Datong? Comparison based on this demand meets the requirement of meeting the same demand. Thus, the conclusion reached from comparing the aforementioned three technological schemes does not reflect object economy rules. By following the principle of demand-meeting comparison, these comparisons should be conducted in terms of transporting energy from Shanxi to Beijing: (1) Compare the technological scheme that builds power plants in Datong and generates electricity first, and then transports that electricity to Beijing, with the technological scheme that transports coal to Beijing via railroad, builds power plants in Beijing, and then generates electricity in Beijing. These two technological schemes should have the same net generated output and net generation for Beijing. (2) Compare the technological scheme that builds gasworks in Datong, generates coal gas first, and then transports coal gas to Beijing via pipeline, with the technological scheme that transports coal to Beijing via railroad, builds gasworks in Beijing, and generates coal gas in Beijing. The two technological schemes should have the same caloric content in coal gas. (3) Compare the technological scheme that transports coal to Beijing via railroad with the technological scheme that builds gasworks in Datong, generates coal gas first, and then transports coal gas to Beijing via pipeline. The two technological schemes should have the same heat energy.

In another example, two transportation schemes are available for transporting 30 million tons of goods from point *A* to point *B*. One scheme covers a distance of 800 km, whereas the other one covers 1000 km. Someone compares the two schemes by using 30 million tons $\times$800 km and 30 million tons $\times$1000 km. The result shows that, with the same freight rate, the second scheme has a bigger freight mileage than the first one. So the second one is more economical and it is better. However, this comparison does not meet the requirement of meeting the same demand, either. The reason is that the requirement of meeting the same demand is not freight mileage, but transporting 30 million tons of goods from point *A* to point *B*, in this case. Accordingly, the transportation scheme with a longer distance is not economical.

12.4 Principle of Consumption and Cost Comparison

In comparing technological schemes, the economic effects that meet the same demands must be compared. Because economic effect includes demand-meeting, the consumption, and cost, comparison of technological schemes must meet requirements regarding consumption and cost. The same calculation principle and approach must be adopted in order to measure consumption and cost. If different calculation principles and approaches are applied to technological schemes, they become incomparable. Thus, the principle of consumption and cost comparison is indispensable in technological scheme comparison.

The principle of consumption and cost comparison requires these steps: (1) Start from the perspectives of system and social total consumption and consider the consumption and cost of the technological schemes themselves and related output departments. For example, in a comparison of energy-saving new products and old products, the production departments of the new products might spend more, but the energy cost of the output department (i.e. users) decreases. If the savings in users' energy cost are not considered, the new product's technological scheme cannot be compared with the old product's technological scheme. (2) Both the direct consumption and cost of technological schemes and the consumption and cost in related departments should be considered. For instance, the technological scheme of thermal power construction must take into account the cost of supporting facilities (i.e. coal and railway transportation). The technological scheme of metallurgy construction must take into account the consumption and cost of exploiting iron mines and transportation. The consumption and cost in related departments must be taken into consideration. (3) All of the direct and indirect costs of technological schemes must be considered. Direct consumption and cost are annual production and operation costs. Indirect consumption and cost refer to the expenditures regarding occupying capital, materials, transportation power, labor, and natural resources caused by using capital, materials, transportation power, labor, and natural resources. For the micro technological economy, it refers to taxes, interests, and insurance expenses. (4) Only after the total consumption and cost of comprehensive utilization schemes are apportioned can the apportioned part be compared with individual technological schemes that meet a specific requirement. (5) All indicators for consumption and cost comparison, either investment indicators or cost indicators, must be comparable. In practice, technological schemes for comparison are very specific. Depreciation can adopt specific indicators. When the indicators are not specific, especially when the alternative technological scheme is an assumed one, average indicators are usually adopted. (6) Generally, consumption and costs that are already spent are not considered. Only new consumption and costs will be considered. For instance, if an idle plant and its equipment are utilized, their consumption and cost should be treated as sunk cost and not counted into consumption and cost unless they can be sold or leased (such as a half-finished building, road, or dam).

12.5 Principle of Price Comparison

The law of value still plays a certain role in the socialist system. Thus, indicators of price are needed when comparing the economic effect of technological schemes (including economic benefits, consumption, and cost). If different and unreasonable indicators of price are adopted to compare technological schemes, incorrect results will be achieved. As such, attention should be paid to the principle of price comparison.

The principle of price comparison requires that: (1) A unified reasonable price or a general reasonable price must be adopted to compute the price of diverse outputs when calculating benefits. The reasonable price for output refers to the total social consumption and cost of a unit of output. A certain value, or the social average value, in the technological schemes is compared. The general reasonable price refers to the sum of the reasonable price for output and the economic effect coefficient of this output, namely the shadow price. For a micro technological economy comparison, all outputs must adopt the unified current price. (2) A unified reasonable price or a general reasonable price must be adopted to compute the price of input of consumption and cost, as well, especially the prices of fuel, energy, raw materials, materials, and transportation in cost, and the prices of equipment, buildings, and land in investment. The reasonable price for input refers to the total social consumption and cost of a unit of output in the production departments that have inputs. It can be a certain value in these production departments, or it can be the social average value. The general reasonable price of input (shadow price) refers to the sum of the reasonable price for input, and the economic effect coefficient of this input. For a micro technological economy comparison, all inputs must adopt the unified current price as well. It is correct that technological scheme *A* adopts the parity price whereas technological scheme *B* adopts the free market price. (3) Prices in corresponding time period should be adopted to compare technological schemes. For instance, the long term price should be adopted when comparing long term technological schemes. The short term price should be adopted when comparing short term technological schemes. If one technological scheme adopts the current price without considering the factors of technological process and the improvement of labor productivity, while the other adopts the long term price with the consideration of technological process and the improvement of labor productivity, these two technological schemes are not comparable because they do not meet the requirement of price comparison.

12.6 Principle of Time Comparison

As we know, the economic effect of technological schemes takes quantity, as well as time, into account. For example, two technological schemes have the same production output, investment, and cost, but the time they require is different. One has an earlier date for full operation, or the investment of one technological scheme is in place earlier. In such as case, the two technological schemes will have different economic effects. The time factor must be taken into consideration when comparing these two technological schemes.

The principle of time comparison requires that: (1) Either the same calculation period should be chosen for comparing technological schemes or the average annual expenditure and benefit should be chosen. It is not correct to choose a five-year calculation period for technological scheme *A* and a ten-year calculation period for technological scheme *B*. (2) The difference in the impacts of technological schemes on the national economy caused by the sequence of input on manpower, material force, capital force, transportation power, and natural forces should be considered. For instance, if the same amount of input is spent at different time, the two inputs become incomparable. The time factor must be considered before comparing them. (3) Time comparison is applicable not only to main projects, but also to supporting ones. For example, in terms of construction period, both the construction period of the main projects and that of the supporting projects should be taken into consideration, because the latter impacts the construction period of the entire technological scheme.

Chapter 13
Optimization Theory of the Technological Economy

13.1 Introduction

It is well known that natural selection exists in nature. In a similar way, selection exists in technological economy, as well. There are numerous diverse technologies in the world, but their economic effects vary. Practice has proven that technologies with a bad economic effect usually die out in the process of technology development. In contrast, those with a good economic effect will survive and develop. This is called the "optimization of technological economy." In daily life, things that lack consideration of the optimization of technological economy occur quite frequently. For example, the growth rate of production might be estimated as 10% for the next year, based on the growth rate of production 8% in this year. The sales volume might be estimated as 150,000 pieces for the next year, based on the sales volume of 100,000 pieces in this year. From the perspective of the technological economy, these estimations lack optimization analysis. Optimization analysis requires a series of technological schemes and then chooses the best one; it doesn't just work on one technological scheme. Practice has proven that the use of technological schemes without optimization analysis usually causes mistakes. Even though they can achieve some economic benefits, the benefits are not at the maximum. Thus, optimization theory plays an important role in technological economics.

13.2 Unlimited Optimization and Limited Optimization

There are two types of optimization in the technological economy: limited optimization and unlimited optimization. As mentioned in previous chapters, all technological schemes consume six forces. If the optimization of technological schemes is based on an unlimited supply of the six forces, the optimization is called an unlimited one. For instance, if a plan to build a factory does not have any limitations regarding the investment and supply of raw material, energy, and water, an optimized technological

S. Xu, *Technological Economics*,
https://doi.org/10.1007/978-981-15-8582-1_13

scheme can be selected among many available schemes. In another example, if two technological schemes have plenty supply of capital, equipment, land, raw material, energy, water, and manpower, the selection between them is unlimited optimization as well. In practice, many selections of technological schemes are unlimited optimization. Especially, unlimited optimization is widely applied in micro technological economy evaluations. For limited optimization, supply of some or all of the six forces is limited. In such a case, optimization is conditional and it is conducted to a limited extent. For a country, a sector, or an area, the amount of the six forces is usually limited. Even in the environment of the reform and the opening-up, the amount of imports and exports is limited. Therefore, the optimization of technological schemes should consider the limited conditions from the perspective of the macro level. Limited optimization is usually applied in macro technological economics. The reason is that the methods of optimum planning in operational research (including linear programming, nonlinear programming, static programming, and dynamic programming) are indeed limited optimization that is applied in practice very often.

13.3 Local Optimization and Global Optimization

Local optimization and global optimization, also called "subsystem optimization" and "large system optimization", are very common in technological economy. As we know, local optimization and global optimization are closely connected. Local optimization is the base of global optimization. Global optimization is coherent with local optimization, but they are conflicted, as well. In terms of amount, they are superimposed as well as non-superimposed. Here are two examples. In the first example, suppose a large system consists of three smaller subsystems, each of which has three technological schemes with a different economic effect (see Table 13.1). According to the table, we can see that the first technological scheme has the optimal economic effect. Therefore, their optimization is coherent and they are superimposed regarding amount. In other words, the economic effect of a large system is the sum of the economic effect of the three subsystems. Examples like this are very common in practice. For instance, value analysis begins from the optimization of parts and then

Table 13.1 The relationship between local optimization and global optimization (I). *Unit* 10,000 RMB

	Subsystem 1	Subsystem 2	Subsystem 3	Large system
Technological scheme 1	*300*	*400*	*500*	*1200*
Technological scheme 2	250	350	500	1100
Technological scheme 3	200	350	450	1000

Note The numbers in this table are the amount of economic effect. The italicized numbers with border are the optimal technological schemes

Table 13.2 The relationship between local optimization and global optimization (II). *Unit* 10,000RMB

	Subsystem 1	Subsystem 2	Subsystem 3	Large system
Technological scheme 1	*300*	350	480	1200
Technological scheme 2	250	*400*	450	1300
Technological scheme 3	250	380	*500*	*1400*

Note The numbers in this table are the amount of economic effect. The italicized numbers with border are the optimal technological schemes

finds the optimization of the economic effect of the final product. The optimization of parts is coherent with that of the final products. In the second example, as shown in Table 13.2, the optimization of each subsystem is in conflict with the optimization of the large system. The amount of their economic effect is not superimposed. For instance, the optimal technological scheme for subsystem 1 is technological scheme 1. The optimal technological scheme for subsystem 2 is technological scheme 2. The optimal technological scheme for subsystem 3 is technological scheme 3. But the optimal technological scheme for the large system does not match these technological schemes. In contrast, it matches the technological scheme 3 for each subsystem. Furthermore, the optimal economic effect of the large system is not the sum of the optimal economic effect of the three subsystems. Such kind of examples are very common in practice too. For instance, a power system consists of two subsystems, a thermal power plant and a hydropower station. The two subsystems have their own technological scheme with optimal economic effect. But after they are integrated into one large system, the two subsystems collaborate well. Hydropower undertakes peak load and thermal power undertakes base load. In addition, they generate networking benefits. Therefore, the economic effect of the large system is larger than the sum of the economic effect of the two subsystems. The optimal technological scheme for the large system is not the optimal technological schemes for the subsystems.

13.4 Static Optimization and Dynamic Optimization

Static optimization and dynamic optimization should be applied in technological scheme selection as well. "Static optimization" means that optimization is conducted without considering any time factor. Usually, static optimization does not generate optimal technological schemes. The reason is that time is an objective factor which impacts the optimization of technological schemes. Dynamic optimization takes time factor into consideration, so it better meets the requirements, in practice. When the results of static optimization and dynamic optimization are not consistent, dynamic optimization should be adopted.

13.5 Single-Target Optimization and Multi-target Optimization

A technological scheme is a system. In practice, both single-target systems and multi-target systems exist. They both need optimization. Optimization for multi-target systems is called "multi-target optimization", whereas optimization for single-target systems is called "single-target optimization". Different approaches are applied in these two types of optimization. A multi-target system is usually split into several single-target ones first, and then optimization is conducted on the single-target ones individually. For one technological economy issue, the results of multi-target optimization and single-target optimization are sometimes consistent and are sometimes conflicted. Because multi-target optimization is more comprehensive, its result is usually adopted when it is conflicted with that of single-target optimization.

13.6 Optimization and Satisfaction

Ideal optimal technological schemes are the goal of technological economy optimization. The real optimal technological schemes rely on finding all of the available technological schemes and their results. However, this is very hard to achieve, due to the complicated actual conditions and any uncompleted and/or inaccurate data, as well as the limitation of time and funds. As such, the optimal technological schemes that we select, in practice, are not the real ones, but are satisfying ones. In other words, some standards are usually designed before the start of optimization. When the selected technological schemes meet these standards, they are satisfying. For example, the coefficient for economic effect of investment is set as 15%. If this coefficient of a technological scheme is equal to or larger than this value, it is satisfying.

Chapter 14
Control Theory of Technological Economy

14.1 Introduction

Technological economics is much like management. According to Robbins (1996), management means leading, planning, organizing, and control.[1] The control theory of technological economy consists of open loop control, closed loop control, macro control, and micro control.

14.2 Open Loop Control and Closed Loop Control

Technological economy evaluation is a type of system engineering. Based on the principles of cybernetics, technological economy evaluation is a combined control system that consists of open loop control and closed loop control. Open loop control relies on feed-forward information, whereas closed loop control depends on feedback information. Chap. 5 covered the six steps in technological economics research. The first five steps adopt open loop control. The last step adopts closed loop control.

In the pre-event stage, when technological schemes have not been implemented, open loop control is usually adopted. The characteristics of open loop control are to develop a diversified prediction based on a large amount of historical and present data, and to calculate the economic effect and the comprehensive effects, according to predictions and the selection of the optimal technical scheme.

The characteristics of closed loop control are to provide feedback to the original technological schemes based on the results of technological economy evaluation, to control, and to adjust the original technological schemes in order to achieve satisfying results. Closed loop control is useful in the pre-event stage, as well. During the implementation of technological schemes and once the technological schemes are

[1] [RO96].

S. Xu, *Technological Economics*,
https://doi.org/10.1007/978-981-15-8582-1_14

completed, adjustment and control are needed because of the changes of object conditions. These processes are called mid-event control and post-event control. Because these two controls rely on feedback information to perform their adjustments, they are closed loop controls.

Many engineering projects have bad mid-event and post-event benefits due to their use of poor pre-event technological economic studies. Adjustment and control must be conducted according to feedback information.

Technological Economics work needs a high quality of pre-control, post-control, open loop control, and closed loop control. Among them, pre-control is the key point of technological and economic work.

14.3 Macro Control and Micro Control

Technological economics control must balance macro control and micro control. In macro control, control indicators are needed to prevent overlapping construction and struggles for investment, raw materials, energy, and land. For example, when evaluating the economic effects of a small tobacco factory, the building of it does not have a good economic effect if the short-term effect of tobacco is considered. For the micro technological economy, good micro control will achieve satisfying micro economic effects.

Reference

[Ro96] Robbins, P. S. (1996). Management. China Renmin University Press.

Chapter 15
Decision Making Theory of Technological Economy

15.1 Introduction

The decision making theory of the technological economy is one of the most important theories in technological economics. Decision making in a technological economy relies on prediction. Other than studying the past and present economic effects of technological schemes, technological economics also studies the economic rationality of future feasible technological schemes. Any research about the future depends on prediction. As such, studying any future technological economy relies on prediction, as well. This chapter covers the principle of prediction and the principle of decision making in a technological economy.

15.2 Principle of Prediction

Prediction in a technological economy is neither technology prediction solely, nor economic prediction solely. It is the technological economics prediction of technologies. In order to predict the economic effect, the correct prediction of the parametric variables of a technological economy is necessary.

Prediction in a technological economy is time-sensitive. Because calculation and the evaluation of the economic effects of technological schemes are based on a certain time period, both short-term and long-term future economic effects should be considered. Accordingly, long-term prediction is more important for a technological economic study than short-term prediction.

From the perspective of the requirement of technological economy, mathematical (quantitative) prediction is very important. For those technological schemes in which mathematical prediction is hard to apply, experience prediction should be adopted. In practice, mathematical prediction and experience prediction are usually mixed together. Mathematical prediction applies some approaches, such as trend extrapolation, exponential smoothing, correlation analysis and regression analysis, and input

S. Xu, *Technological Economics*,
https://doi.org/10.1007/978-981-15-8582-1_15

and output method. Experience prediction often adopts diverse specific investigation methods.

Prediction in a technological economy can be conducted at either the macro level or the micro level. The former is called macro prediction in a technological economy and the latter is called micro prediction in a technological economy. The macro and micro levels here do not mean the ranges of predicted technological economic issues. Instead, they refer to the standpoints and perspectives of prediction. Macro prediction in a technological economy is at the level of national standpoint, whereas micro prediction in a technological economy is at the level of firms. The goals of macro prediction in a technological economy and micro prediction in a technological economy are different. Thus, different parametric variables are adopted.

15.3 Principle of Decision Making

The decisions made in a technological economy can be categorized into one-time decisions, serial decisions, single-target decisions, multi-target decisions, certainty decisions, and uncertainty decisions. Usually, there are two types of technological economics issues. The first type needs only a one-time decision. The other type requires a serial decision. For example, if a factory need to be expanded, that expansion can be conducted in the next year, a year after, or two years after. When should the expansion be conducted so that the biggest economic benefits can be achieved? This issue cannot be answered by a one-time decision. In another example, the upgrade of equipment in a factory can be done in two years, six years, or ten years. When should the upgrade be conducted so that the largest economic benefits can be achieved? The answer requires multiple decision making. Different approaches are applied in one-time decisions and serial decisions. The latter usually adopts a decision tree and network chart methods.

In practice, the goal of a technological scheme evaluation has several levels. Besides the comprehensive economic goal, there are seven other goals on the highest level, including politics, defense, society, culture, technology, environmental ecology, and natural resources. Below these goals, there are other lower-level goals. Decision making about the multiple goals of technological economics issues at the same level is called multi-target decision making, whereas decision making about a single goal of technological economic issues at the same level is called a single-target decision. For example, economic evaluation of a technological scheme is single-target decision. Comprehensive evaluation (economic evaluation of comprehensive effect or comprehensive effect evaluation) is a multi-target decision. When performing a multi-target decision, multiple levels of goals should not be put at the same level. In addition, a multi-target decision should not be applied on any correlated goals in an arbitrary manner. For instance, depreciation, raw material consumption, and labor productivity may seem to be unrelated. In fact, they are components in cost. They can be connected and combined into one single comprehensive goal cost. Accordingly, multi-target decision making is not applicable. Instead, a single-target decision is the better choice. When performing a multi-target decision, the priorities of each goal should be taken into consideration. Some goals have higher priorities than others. Those goals with high priority play a larger role in decision making than those with low priority. Their level of priority depends on the actual situation. For instance, economic goals are more important for economic departments. Although technological goals are important as well, their main role is to serve economic goals. Thus, the technological goals are not as important as the economic ones, in such a case. Those important technological goals will not be adopted if they cause loss. In other words, the level of importance of economic goals plays a key role in decision making.

Some technological economic issues are certain, whereas others are not. Uncertain technological economic issues are the parametric variables that impact decision making in technological economic issues, such as resource reserves, production and sales volume, the supply and demand of products, product price, the supply and demand of raw materials and energy, the price of raw materials and energy, investment, cost, construction period, service period, residual value, the utilization hours of equipment, natural conditions, and social conditions. These parametric variables are affected by a variety of factors including politics, society, science and technology, manpower, material, finance, nature, management, and methods of data collection. They are uncertain and do not have fixed values. Decisions about certain technological economic issues are certain decision making, in which the common decision making approaches of the technological economy can be applied. In contrast, decisions about uncertain technological economic issues are uncertain decision making. For them, special approaches are required, including technological and economic factor analysis, economic critical point analysis, economic safety factor analysis, minimum maximum (or maximum minimum), the expected value method, the analog method, and decision tree analysis.

decision is the better choice. When performing a multi-target decision, the priorities of each goal should be taken into consideration. Some goals have higher priorities than others. Those goals with high priority play a larger role in decision making than those with low priority. Their level of priority depends on the actual situation. For instance, economic goals are more important for economic departments. Although technological goals are important as well, their main role is to serve economic goals. For the technological departments, technological goals are as important as [illegible]. These important technological goals [illegible] the field of [illegible] decision making.

[illegible]

Chapter 16
Comprehensive Evaluation Theory of Technological Economy

16.1 Introduction

The term "comprehensive evaluation theory of the technological economy" is short for "the comprehensive evaluation theory of technological economy's technological scheme." It is one of the base theories in technological economics. The author provides his personal comments regarding the necessity of comprehensive evaluation, comprehensive evaluation theory, and development history, according to his experience. In general, this comprehensive evaluation includes eight criteria: politics, defense, society, culture, technology, the economy, the environment, and resources. Evaluation of technological schemes uses some of these criteria based on the practical situation.[1]

16.2 Necessity of Comprehensive Evaluation

In the 1960s, the author conducted systemically researched theories and methods in technological economics. He first proposed the theory of the technological economy work procedure.[2] Technology selection must first identify several applicable technologies, namely technological schemes, which are a kind of combination based on technologies consisting of six forces[3]: manpower, capital force, material force,

---

[1] [Xs11].

[2] The author first proposed the five steps in technological economics study in his paper the goal and methods of technological economics published in Science Bulletin, 1964, vol. 7. The five steps are illustrated by the schematic diagram of word procedure in technical economy in the second edition of technological economics, published in 1984. But the reverse direction of the line after the fifth step was not named. In the fourth edition, Technological Economics, published in 1988, this line was named as feedback control, the sixth step.

[3] The author first proposed the six force theory in the second edition of technological economics published in 1984.

S. Xu, *Technological Economics*,
https://doi.org/10.1007/978-981-15-8582-1_16

natural forces, transportation power, and time, while aiming for achieving certain goals and meeting certain requirements. Technological schemes can be categorized into hard technological schemes and soft technological schemes.[4] They cover nearly all of the fields of human production and life.

A comprehensive evaluation is a significant step in technological economics. Why was the comprehensive evaluation proposed? What are the theories of comprehensive evaluation? How did the comprehensive evaluation of technological schemes develop in China?

Technological economics was founded in 1963 in China, aiming for making technologies serve the economy more effectively and better promoting the national economy development with greater, faster, better, and more economical results. Accordingly, economic evaluation criteria and technological evaluation criteria are the most important. However, since China is a socialist country led by the Communist Party of China, everything must stem from the fundamental interests of the state and the people. Thus, politics, defense, and society must be considered. Especially before the reform and opening-up, the basic line of taking class struggle as the key link was established, based on the internal and external situations of China. During that period, these three criteria were specifically important. In fact, in the research report of *Methodology of Technological Economy,* a national scientific research task completed from 1963 to 1965, the author pointed out: "in order to resolve the complex issue of technological scheme selection, we must first study the evaluation criteria for technological schemes. Due to the complexity of practical situations and their diverse requirements, different evaluation criteria for technological schemes are needed. For example, from the perspective of technology, technological schemes are required to be safe, reliable, and flexible. From the perspective of the economy, technological schemes are required to achieve the largest benefits with the fastest speed and the minimum cost of manpower, material, and capital. From the perspective of defense, technological schemes are required to meet the requirements of anti-aircraft defense and combat readiness. From the perspective of politics, technological schemes are required to follow the policies, guidelines, and routes of the party and of the country. From the perspective of society, technological schemes are required to meet the requirements of improving labor conditions, living conditions, and environmental health, and conforming to people's living habits. It can be seen that the evaluation criteria of technological schemes should not be single but multiple. It should cover politics, defense, society, technology, and economy."[5] This is the reason why comprehensive evaluation is needed. The practical situation and the requirements that China had at that time led to only five evaluation criteria, instead of the seven. It can be said that the five evaluation criteria were correct until now. In the book *Introduction to Technological Economics,* a publication of the research report of

[4]The author first proposed the concept of new general technology, which includes hard technology and soft technology, in the fourth edition of Technological Economics, published in 1988.

[5][Xs65].

Methodology of Technological Economy, published in 1980,[6] these five criteria were adopted: politics, defense, society, technology, and the economy.

16.3 Theories of Comprehensive Evaluation and Their Development History

In 1984, the author added what he had achieved in his study from 1980 to 1984 to the first edition of *Introduction to Technological Economics,* and the published the second edition, which consists of Volumes I and II.[7] In the second edition, the author extended the five criteria by separating environmental ecology from society criteria and by separating natural resources from economic criteria, given the increasing importance of environmental ecology and natural resources at home and abroad. As such, the original five criteria became seven criteria: politics, defense, society, technology, the economy, environment, and resources. These seven criteria remained unchanged in the third and fourth edition of *Introduction to Technological Economics,* published in 1986 and 1988, respectively.

Since the foundation of People's Republic of China 60 years ago, especially since the reform and opening-up 30 years ago, the development of the economy and society in China have achieved tremendous progress. China's hard power and soft power have both increased greatly. Based on the thorough research on the practice of economic development during the past several decades in China, the author argues that other than the aforementioned seven criteria, cultural criteria should be separated for the following reasons:

(1) According to the requirements of socialist basic economic law in Marxist political economics, people's demands can be categorized into their material demands and their cultural demands. Likewise, human civilization can be classified into material civilization and spiritual civilization. However, the seven criteria do not cover cultural or spiritual evaluation. Putting culture inside societal criteria does not match culture's position.
(2) Since the reform and the opening-up in 1978, economic construction has achieved tremendous progress in China. The policy changes the lagging status of Chinese economy. With the continuous development of economic construction, the importance of culture becomes prominent for the following reasons:

    Since 1978, the Communist Party of China, the party in power, turned its basic line toward focusing on the central task of economic construction. It established Deng Xiaoping's theory of building Socialism with Chinese

---

[6][Xs80].

[7]This edition was published by China Science and Technology Policy Studies and the lecture team of modern management from the China Association for Science and Technology. This book was the text book for the further education of National Science and Technology management staff.

Characteristics as the guiding theory for national economic and social development. Economic development was then boosted. The goal, set in 1980 by the Party's 12th Representative Conference, of quadrupling the gross domestic product (GDP) in 1980 by the year of 2000 was achieved five years early, with double consumption of energy. This is a miracle in the history of world economic development and provides a solid foundation for cultural construction and development. However, along with the large achievements in economic construction, diverse foreign culture and lagging culture strike the minds of Chinese. It is urgent to put cultural construction into an important strategic position. Only in this way can the economy and society be promoted to develop further.

Culture plays a key role in the development of the economy and society. This can be proved by the speeches of Chinese leaders. The fact that China is a large developing country with stable politics proves the importance of culture in economic and social development. For example, after China achieved tremendous progress in its economy from 1981 to 1995, Jiang Zemin presented the important thoughts of three represents in the 16th Representative Conference of the Communist Party of China. He pointed out that when leading people to carry out modernization construction in a large developing country with a lagging economy and culture, our party must focus on development, the primary task for governing and rejuvenating the country. We must insist upon the advancement of our party and make the superiority of the socialist system develop advanced production capability and culture, while realizing the basic benefits to the broad masses of the people, ensuring all-round social progress, and promoting man's development in an all-round way.[8] According to Jiang Zemin's important thoughts of three represents, realizing the basic benefits to the broad masses of the people, ensuring all-round social progress, and promoting man's development in an all-round way are the aims of the party. Developing advance production capability and developing an advancement of culture are the support. The former is a requirement from material, whereas the letter is a requirement from culture. It can be seen that Jiang Zemin's important thoughts of three represents pay much attention to the role of culture and make important innovations. The general-secretary Hu Jintao spoke more specifically and clearly about culture. He pointed out: "in this day and age, culture more and more becomes the important source of national cohesion and creation, the important factor of competition of comprehensive national strength. Enriching cultural life more and more becomes our people's earnest wish. We must hold to the direction of the advancement of socialist culture, set off a new climax in socialist cultural construction, stimulate cultural creation among all people, and improve our country's soft power, so that people's basic cultural rights can be better ensured, social cultural life can be richer and more colorful,

---

[8] [Ji02].

Table 16.1 Development of the evaluation criteria of technological schemes

Stage	Evaluation criteria	Source
After the foundation of the People's Republic of China	Politics (P), defense (D), society (S), technology (T), and economy (E)	Xu, S. (1965). Methodology of Technological Economy[R], research report of Comprehensive Investigation Committee of China Academy of Science
After the reform and opening-up	Politics(P), defense (D), society (S), technology (T), and economy (E), Environment (E_V), and resource (R)	Xu, S. (1982). Trial Method of Program Evaluation in National Economic Construction *(Discussion Draft)* [J], *Quantity and Technological and Economic Communication*, 9
The 21st century	Politics (P), defense (D), society (S), culture (C), technology (T), and economy (E), environment (E_V), and resource (R)	Xu, S. (2011). Research on Comprehensive Evaluation Theory of Technological Program, *Journal of Beijing Jiaotong University (Edition of Social Science)*, 10(1), 36–39

> and people's mental outlook becomes higher-spirited."[9] His presentation insisted upon constructing socialism with Chinese characteristics across all directions. He clearly put cultural construction at the same important level with economic construction, political construction, social construction, and defense and army construction.
>
> It can be seen that in the complex economic and social situation at present, culture is separated and becomes an independent criteria together with the other seven criteria: politics, defense, society, technology, the economy, the environment, and resources. This is not only a creation in the comprehensive evaluation theory of technological schemes, but it also is proven by the tremendous achievement and practice in the world's largest developing country: China. Accordingly, the previous seven criteria change to eight criteria, namely politics, defense, society, culture, technology, economy, the environment, and resources.
>
> In sum, the development of the evaluation criteria of technological schemes experienced three stages (see Table 16.1): Stage One, after the foundation of the People's Republic of China; Stage Two, after the reform and opening-up; and Stage Three, which is occurring in the new century.

The author argues that the evaluation criteria of technological schemes (PDSCTEE$_V$R) are not equally important to states, firms, and individuals. Some criteria are very important; some are not so important; others are not important at all. Their importance depends on the situation in a state and the practical situation. For

[9] [Hu07].

example, for a long time, China has had a huge population. Its economy is lagging. Its GDP per capita is low. Thus, economic criteria is very important to China. In addition, China has suffered foreign invasion for quite a long time, so its national territory and its sovereignty security face threats. Accordingly, defense criteria is very important, as well. What is more, in the areas where the environment and ecology have been seriously damaged, environmental criteria has high importance. Practice has proven that, given the development of modern science and technology, technological schemes that meet the same demand can usually satisfy the requirements from the seven criteria: politics, defense, society, culture, technology, the environment, and natural resource. But economic criteria play a key role in the selection of technological schemes. However, this does not mean that economic criteria are the only criteria for the selection of technological schemes.

It should be pointed out that comprehensive evaluation usually includes eight individual criteria: politics (P), defense (D), society (S), culture (C), technology (T), the economy (E), the environment (EV), and resources (R). These criteria should be selected based on the practical situation and requirements from certain technological schemes. Although they are closely connected, each of these eight criteria has its unique content (see Table 16.2). They cannot replace each other. Therefore, each

Table 16.2 Contents of the evaluation criteria of technological scheme

First-level content	Second-level content
Politics (P)	1. Four fundamental principles; 2. The Party's policies and guidelines; 3. Governmental laws and regulations; 4. Political prestige; 5. International influence
Defense (D)	1. National territorial integrity; 2. National sovereignty safety; 3. Combat preparation; 4. Combat capability; 5. Defense capability; 6. Safeguarding world peace
Society (S)	1. Employment; 2. Labor; 3. Living; 4. Health care; 5. Education; 6. Public security; 7. Social stability
Culture (C)	1. The socialist core value system; 2. Harmonious culture and civilization; 3. Enhancing Chinese culture; 4. Innovation culture; 5. Developing cultural industry; 6. Enriching spiritual and cultural lives; 7. Protecting historical relics
Technology (T)	1. Feasibility; 2. Reliability; 3. Advancement; 4. Applicability; 5. Scientific meaning; 6. Academical level; 7. Intelligence and information
Economy(E)	1. More, faster, better, and more economical results; 2. Most optimum distribution of resources; 3. Combing macro and micro economic results; 4. Combining national economic evaluation and financial evaluation; 5. Combining long-term and short-term benefits; 6. Economic development mode; 7. Economic development strategy; 8. coordinated development of economy
Environment (E_V)	1. Environmental pollution; 2. Ecological balance; 3. Natural disasters
Resource (R)	1. Protecting resources; 2. Utilizing resources; 3. Exploiting resources; 4. expanding resources

Note The third-level contents are omitted in the table

criteria should be evaluated independently.

The evaluation of each single criterion will generate the individual effect (including benefit and efficiency), such as that political effect, the defense effect, the societal effect, the cultural effect, the technology effect, the economic effect, the environmental effect, and the resources effect. The selection of technological schemes should not rely on the size of a certain individual effect, but the size of the comprehensive effect. The goal of any comprehensive evaluation is to examine each technological scheme roundly, to identify the comprehensive effect of each technological scheme, and to select the technological scheme that has the best comprehensive effect.

References

[Hu07] Hu, J. T. (2007). Report on the 16th Representative Conference of the Communist Party of China. Available at https://cpc.people.com.cn/GB/64162/64168/106155/106156/6430009.html.

[Ji02] Jiang, Z. M. (2002). Report on the 16th Representative Conference of the Communist Party of China. Available at https://cpc.people.com.cn/GB/64162/64168/64569/65444/4429125.html.

[Xu65] Xu, S. (1965). The criteria for selecting technological schemes, the 7th chapter in 2nd section of Methodology of Technological Economy[R], research report of Comprehensive Investigation Committee of China Academy of Science.

[Xu80] Xu, S. (1980). Introduction to Technological Economics. Shanghai scientific and technical publishers. This is the first edition of this book.

[Xu11] Xu, S. (2011). Research on Comprehensive Evaluation Theory of Technological Program, Journal of Beijing Jiaotong University (Edition of Social Science), 10(1), 36–39.

Part III
Research Methods of Technological Economics

This part covers the methods of technological economics. It is based on Part I, Introduction to Technological Economics, and Part II, Theories of Technological Economics. Technological economics does not cover only theories. Essentially, it focuses more on applications. Theories rely on research methods, which can be applied to resolve practical problems. On the other hand, research methods must be guided by theories. Therefore, this book highlights theories and research methods equally. This part consists of five parts: (1) Part 1 covers how to establish a technological economy index system; (2) Part 2 covers how to calculate a technological economic index; (3) Part 3 covers how to assess a technological economy; (4) Part 4 introduces how to assess technologies comprehensively; and (5) Part 5 introduces how assessment methods are applied in a technological economy.

Chapter 17
Method for Establishing a Technological Economics Index System

17.1 Introduction

Technological economy indices are needed for assessing the economic benefit or the economic efficiency of technological schemes and for resolving technological economics problems. In practice, there are different categories and levels of technological economics indices, which consist many technological economics index systems. This chapter mainly covers how to establish a technological economics index system. Specifically, the effect and the interactive relationship among the seven groups of technological economics index systems are discussed: (1) the economics index system and the technological index system; (2) the monetary index system and the material index system; (3) the comprehensive index system and the single index system; (4) the quantitative index system and the qualitative index system; (5) the relative quantitative index system and the absolute quantitative index system; (6) the macro index system and the micro index system; and (7) the dynamic index system and the static index system. Based on the discussion, the author proposes a technological economics assessment index system.

17.2 Economics Index System and Technological Index System

In practice, diverse technological and economic index systems are adopted. They focus on either value or substance, relative perspectives or absolute perspectives, quantity or quality. Essentially, these index systems fall into two categories: economic indices and technological indices. Economic indices reflect the economic status of technological schemes, whereas technological indices reflect the technological status of technological schemes. Because a technological economy studies the economic rationality of technological schemes, economics index systems are the main focus, and technological index systems serve economic index systems. Economics indices

S. Xu, *Technological Economics*,
https://doi.org/10.1007/978-981-15-8582-1_17

are applied in a technological economy in three ways. First, they are used for measuring the economic effect of a technological scheme. These indices include social labor productivity, profit, net income, national income, return on investment, profit and tax investment ratio, investment-national income ratio, and payback period, etc. These indices are comprehensive ones, so they are applicable to many technological economic problems. For example, the targets of objective functions in mathematical models for a technological economy adopt these indices. Second, economic indices are used for calculating equations and formulas in a technological economy. These indices include the unit consumption of coal for electricity generation, the investment for unit kilowatt, the coke ratio for iron making, the labor cost per unit for farmland, the amount of anthracite produced with a ton of synthesis ammonia, the consumption of electricity and steam, the metal consumption for machine manufacturing, the cotton yarn consumption for cloth production, the prices of various products, and the price of transportation. These kind of indices have the largest number of formats. Usually, a specific index system is available for a certain technological economics problem. Third, economic indices can be uncertain ones that impact the economic effects of technological economics schemes. For instance, the economic effects of different material-based approaches for producing synthesis ammonia vary with the price of materials (anthracite, coke, or heavy oil). Accordingly, the price index of materials is the economic factor that impacts the economic effects of technological economic schemes.

Different from economic indices, the technological indices of technological schemes are more specialized. Because technological schemes have different technological characteristics, they need different technological indices. For instance, the technological indices for motor manufacturing schemes include the power factor and the speed of rotation. Technological indices for hydropower station construction schemes include the normal high water level, the level of dead water, the service capacity, and the reserve capacity. Technological indices for railway construction scheme contain grade and camber. Technological indices for a chemical plant production scheme contain temperature and pressure. Technological indices are applied in a technological economy in three ways, as well. First, they are used to assess whether the technological schemes are feasible and advanced. In this case, technological indices work as indicators of performance for technological schemes. Second, technological indices can be used as the bases and necessary conditions for calculating economic indices, because the economic indices of technological schemes vary when different technological indices are adopted. Third, in many cases, the technological indices, per se, are parameters that must be achieved in technological economy studies, such as the volume of a hydropower station and the grade of railways. Technological indices become primary parameters and variables in equations and formulas of the technological economy. In practice, some indices, such as efficiency, utilization hour, and the consumption of raw material, fuel, and power, look like economic indices and also like technological indices. According to the requirement, they can be treated as either economic indices or as technological indices. The final technological economic results will not be impacted.

17.3 Monetary Index System and Material Index System

The above-mentioned economic index systems can be grouped into monetary index systems and material index systems. In a socialist market economy, the commodity economy and the value law play an important role. Value (monetary) indices are widely adopted in the production, exchange, circulation, and consumption of products and in the calculation of the consumption of social labor for productions. Value (monetary) indices are calculated based on domestic currency or foreign currencies. In a technological economy, value (monetary) index systems are the primary ones. The biggest benefit of value (monetary) index systems is that diverse material indices (e.g. certain number of tons of steel, coal, cement, or grain) can be easily expressed by value (monetary) indices. In this way, it is very convenient to perform an economics assessment and a calculation of technological schemes. Otherwise, and economics assessment of technological schemes can hardly be performed. Material indices are expressed in materials. They are important economics indices as well. On one hand, they are the base for calculating value (monetary) indices, because all value (monetary) indices rely on material indices, which include the output index of products, the consumption index of fuel and power, the consumption index of raw materials (e.g. seed, fertilizer, and fodder), the consumption index of labor, the index rate of land utilization, and the index rate of other resource utilization. On the other hand, material indices can be applied for calculating material balance and for knowing more about the utilization of materials. It should be pointed out that most of the economics indices mentioned above are based on value (monetary) indices. When value (monetary) indices are adopted for expressing the economic standards of technological schemes, two conditions must be satisfied: (1) the material index of the output of technological schemes must meet the demands of markets and the requirements of plans; (2) all other indices of consumption and of the utilization of the materials of technological schemes must meet the requirements of material balance. Additionally, technological index systems are not generally expressed in the format of value (monetary) indices.

17.4 Comprehensive Index System and Single Index System

Either economics indices or technological indices can be treated in an integrated manner or separately. Comprehensive indices and single ones are relative. For instance, the cost index contains raw materials, fuel and energy, depreciation, wages, and other costs. Therefore, compared with these individual indices, the cost index is a comprehensive one. It is also a comprehensive index for assessing the operation efficiency of technological schemes. However, the cost index becomes a single index compared with the index of the total labor capacity in a society, which measures the total economic effect of technological schemes. In this case, the cost index is a component of the index of the total labor capacity in a society. The uses of comprehensive indices and single indices are different. Single indices reflect the partial technological economics situation of technological schemes or activities. As a component of comprehensive indices, single indices are convenient for calculating and reflecting the technological economics situation of a certain aspect or part. But single indices cannot reflect the economic efficiency of technological schemes in all directions. Moreover, some single indices might be incompatible with other single indices. In contrast, comprehensive indices reflect the overall technological economy situation of technological schemes or activities. The biggest advantage of comprehensive indices is that they can overcome the inconsistences among single indices and can reflect the technological economics characteristics of technological schemes in all directions. Accordingly, comprehensive index systems are the primary ones for assessing the economic effects of technological schemes.

17.5 Quantitative Index System and Qualitative Index System

Quantity indices reflect the quantitative relations among the factors of the technological economy, whereas quality indices reflect the essence, characteristics, and features of products, services, and factor resources. Quantity indices and quality indices are equal important in terms of reflecting the technological economics characteristics of technological schemes. However, from the perspective of technological economics calculation, quantity indices are more important than quality ones because the former can be calculated while the latter cannot. Although they are different, quantity indices and quality indices are closely related. Many quality indices can be converted into quantity ones through certain methods. For example, the quality index of equipment reliability can be measured by service life, depreciation rate, and other quantity indices. The product quality indices of technological schemes (e.g. physical property and chemical property) can be reflected by price to a certain degree. Meanwhile, it should also be pointed out that, in practice, many quality indices cannot be reflected by quantity indices, such as aesthetic property, comfort level, purity, taste, and intensity of labor. Instead, these quality indices can be quantified by fuzzy grading methods.

17.6 Relative Quantitative (Unit) Index System and Absolute Quantitative (Total) Index System

Either absolute quantitative indices or relative quantitative indices can be adopted in a technological economy, based on the practical requirements. Absolute quantitative indices express a technological economy in absolute quantities, whereas relative quantitative indices express a technological economy in relative quantities. Absolute quantitative indices include the numbers of net income; national income; profit;

investment; annual production cost; output of grain; the production of steel and electricity; the numbers of hours that equipment run per year; and the amount of consumption of fuel and raw materials. Relative quantitative indices include the social productivity of labor, the social additional productivity of labor, the social additional net income ratio, the social additional national income ratio, the return on investment, the profit rate on cost, the living labor capacity, the ratio between additional investment and the saving of annual production cost, the ratio between annual production cost and total investment, and the depreciation rate. Relative quantitative indices are usually coefficients, proportions, percentages, and ratios. They are easier to calculate, compared with absolute ones. In addition, they reflect the relative economic relationships between technological schemes. Therefore, relative quantitative indices are adopted more often than absolute ones.

In a calculation and comparison of technological economy, usually the absolute total economic indices are adopted, including total output, total output value, total service income, total net income, total net production value (national income), total investment, total annual production cost, total consumption of raw materials, fuel, and energy, total land occupation, total consumption of building materials, and total labor. Sometimes, for the purpose of easy calculation, relative unit indices are adopted, such as the investment per unit of productive capacity, the unit cost, the fuel and power consumption per unit of product, the raw material consumption per unit of product, the production of unit personnel (i.e. labor capacity), and the unit price, etc. These unit indices are usually averages. Sometimes they can be additional numbers, too. Very often, unit indices are required to calculate total indices. For instance, the total investment for a power station with a capacity of 0.5 million kilowatts can be achieved by multiplying the investment per kilowatt by 0.5 million kilowatts. Unit indices have unique usages. When the output indices of technological schemes are not equal, it is more convenient to choose unit indices instead of total indices. It should be noted that total indices are absolute quantitative indices, but not all absolute quantitative indices are total indices. For example, a factory invests 50,000 RMB for a certain machine. In this case, the investment is an absolute quantitative index, not a total investment index of this factory. Similarly, unit indices are relative quantitative indices, but not all relative quantitative indices are unit indices. For instance, percentage is a relative quantitative index, not a unit index.

17.7 Macro Index System and Micro Index System

Macro indices reflect a technological economy from macroscopic perspectives, whereas micro indices reflect a technological economy from microscopic perspectives. Generally, macroscopic perspectives are on the international, national, or regional levels, while microscopic perspectives are at the firm or enterprise level. Micro indices provide the base for macro indices, while macro indices are the integration of micro indices. Commonly used macro indices include the gross national product, the national income, the gross output of industry and agriculture, the gross social production value, the domestic investment in fixed assets, the domestic working capital, the total domestic profit and tax, the social discount rate, the national bank rate, the state-set tax rate, the state-set price, the national investment-net income ratio, the investment-national income ratio, the national investment effect coefficient, the national energy utilization effect coefficient, the national labor utilization effect coefficient, the national land utilization effect coefficient, the national transportation capacity utilization effect coefficient, etc. Commonly used micro indices focus on firm level factors, such as output, product variety, quality, consumption of raw materials, consumption of fuel and power, depreciation costs, wages and additional cost, workshop expenses, firm management expenses, firm costs, firm fixed assets, circulating funds, return on investment, production value, profit, net production value, occupation of labor, and occupation of land, etc. Macro indices are used for resolving macro technological economic problems, whereas both macro indices and micro indices are needed for resolving micro technological economic problems. Some macro indices, such as the national capital utilization effect coefficient, the national material utilization effect coefficient, the national labor utilization effect coefficient, the national land utilization effect coefficient, the national price, and the national exchange rate, impact micro indices via macro control. For instance, water resources are very limited in many northern areas in China. The rise of water consumption in one firm will greatly impact other firms. Therefore, macro indices, such as the water resource utilization effect coefficient or the shadow price of water should be adopted in these areas. If the existing water price is adopted in a technological economics assessment, the result might be incorrect. In addition, the national investment effect coefficient, or the national capital utilization effect coefficient, is an important macro index. The value of the investment effect of a construction project must be larger than or equal to the national investment effect. Otherwise, the construction will suffer losses.

17.8 Dynamic Index System and Static Index System

Dynamic indices take time into account, whereas static indices do not. Dynamic indices and static indices are widely adopted in technological economics. Relatively speaking, dynamic indices are more reasonable. Therefore, they are adopted in practice more than static indices. An economic index has a dynamic status as well as a static status. For example, the return on investment, the investment-net income ratio, the investment-national income ratio, the investment recovery period, the return on added investment, the added investment-net income ratio, the added investment-national income ratio, and the added investment recovery period have both dynamic status and static status. Dynamic index systems are the primary ones in a technological economy, whereas static index systems are special cases of dynamic index systems. The evaluation standard principle of greater, faster, better, and more economical results in technological economy, such as the social excessive labor productivity E_a and E_b, the social excessive net income E_c, the social excessive national income

E_d, the total social additional labor productivity E_{af} and E_{bf}, the social additional excessive net income rate E_{cf}, the social additional excessive national income rate E_{df}, and the total firm labor productivity E_e, the firm excessive profit E_f, the total firm additional labor productivity E_{ef}, and the firm additional excessive profit rate E_{ff} are dynamic indices. In addition, the overseas internal rate of return and the net present value are dynamic indices, as well.

17.9 Assessment Index System for Technological Economy

The assessment index system for a technological economy is a set of interrelated technological economics index systems with the purpose of conducting a technological economics evaluation. In practice, two systems are commonly used, namely the macro technological economy assessment index system and the micro technological economy assessment index system. These two assessment index systems integrate the aforementioned seven groups of index systems and reflect the requirements of the standard principle of greater, faster, better, and more economical results. Figure 17.1 shows a macro technological economy assessment index system, which consists of four levels of indices. The first level has eight macro economy evaluation indices reflecting the principle of greater, faster, better, and more economic results (E_a, E_b, E_c, E_d, E_{af}, E_{bf}, E_{cf}, E_{df}). The second level consists of two social total benefit indices (X, S) and two total social consumption cost indices (Z, Z_u). X is a substance benefit index and$S$ is a monetary benefit index. The third level consists of the demand satisfaction indices (G, P), the price and value index j_g, the time indices (n_k, n_d, n_f, n_j, θ), and the consumption cost indices (C, C_u, W, Y, R, T, D, x_w, x_y, x_r, x_t, x_d).

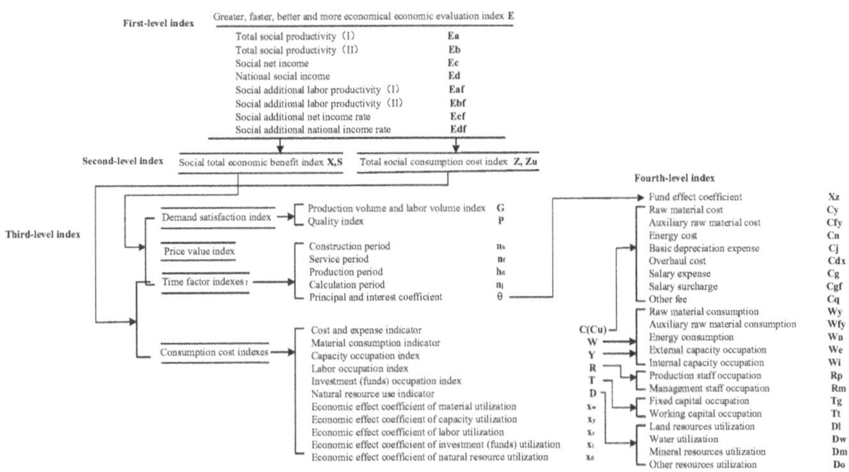

Fig. 17.1 Macroeconomic (national economy) evaluation index system of technical solutions

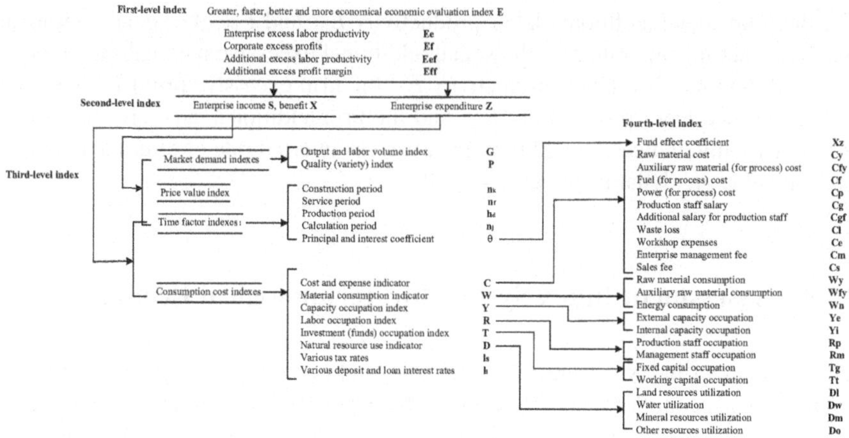

Fig. 17.2 Microeconomic (enterprise finance) evaluation index system of technical solutions

The total number of indices in this level is 20. The fourth level consists of the capital effect coefficient, the cost indices (C_y, C_{fy}, C_n, C_j, C_{dx}, C_g, C_{gf}, C_q), the material consumption indices (W_y, W_{fy}, W_n), the transportation capacity occupation indices (Y_e, Y_i), the labor occupation indices (R_{pp}, R_{mp}), the investment occupation indices (T_g, T_l), and the natural resource utilization indices (D_l, D_w, D_m, D_o). The total number of indices in this level is 22. Altogether, there are 54 indices in the macro technological economy assessment index system. It should be noted that, in reality, the number of indices is larger than 54 because the indices in the first level have many descendent indices, such as profit and tax investment ratios (economic internal rate of return), excess profit and tax investment ratios, and the investment recovery period. Figure 17.2 shows a micro technological economics assessment index system, which consists of four levels of indices, as well. The first level has four micro economy evaluation indices, reflecting the principle of greater, faster, better, and more economic results (E_e, E_f, E_{ef}, E_{ff}). The second level consists of three indices, namely firm income *S*, performance *X*, and firm expenditure *Z*. The third level consists of market demand indices (*G*, *P*), price index j_g, time indices (n_k, n_d, n_f, n_j, θ), and consumption cost indices (*C*, *W*, *Y*, *R*, *T*, *D*, l_s, L_l). The total number of indices in this level is 16. The fourth level consists of the capital effect coefficient, cost indices (C_y, C_{fy}, C_{fuel}, C_g, C_{gf}, C_{waste}, C_{ws}, C_{em}, C_{sale}), material consumption indices (W_y, W_{fy}, W_n), transportation capacity occupation indices (Y_e, Y_i), labor occupation indices (R_{pp}, R_{mp}), investment occupation indices (T_g, T_l), and natural resource utilization indices (D_l, D_w, D_m, D_o). The total number of indices in this level is 24. Altogether, there are 47 indices in the micro technological economy assessment index system. Similarly, if some descendent indices, such as return on investment (financial internal rate of return) and investment recovery period, are included, the total number of indices in a micro technological economy assessment index system will be larger than 47.

Chapter 18
Methods for Computing Technological Economy Indices

18.1 Introduction

The technological economics index system covered in Chap. 17 contains about 50 primary technological economy indices. This chapter discusses the calculation methods for each technological economy index individually. More specifically, these methods are for computing time factor, time indices, reasonable price, standard coefficients of economy indices, tax rate and interest rate, the investment and cost of technological schemes, the output and benefits of technological schemes, cost and benefits using shadow price, and the allocated expense of utilizing technological schemes comprehensively.

18.2 Calculation Method for Time Factor

In the calculation of technological economics, either from the macro perspective or from the micro perspective, the input and output of technological schemes are expressed with a value, namely in the format of capital. Therefore, the time factor of capital is actually the time factor of the input and output of technological schemes.

The time factor is an important component in the process of calculating economic results. It should be considered in two aspects. On the one hand, data is not static. For example, the investment coefficient decreases over the years, due to the deduction of an annual basic depreciation cost. On the other hand, the economic effect of time should be considered, namely compound interest. This chapter discusses how to calculate the time factor of capital.

S. Xu, *Technological Economics*,
https://doi.org/10.1007/978-981-15-8582-1_18

18.2.1 Interest Factor

The interest factor is the sum of 1 and the capital effect coefficient. It is used for calculating the time factor, especially for compound interest. Here is the formula.

$$\theta(\text{interest factor}) = 1 + x_z(\text{capital effect coefficient}) \quad (18.1)$$

The capital effect coefficient refers to the amount of economic benefit generated by a unit of capital during a certain period. It means different things in the macro technological economy and the micro technological economy. The micro technological economy adopts the bank rate/foreign lending rate i directly, as return on investment x_{t1} specified by enterprises in each industry sector. The macro technological economy chooses the capital effect coefficient in two ways. The first way adopts a value that is smaller than the economic effect coefficient of investment utilization. For example, the Soviet Union adopted 0.15 for the economic effect coefficient of investment utilization x_t and 0.1 for the coefficient of capital effect x_z. In the evaluation of investment on construction, x_t was set as 0.12 whereas x_z was set as 0.08. In this case, x_z was about two thirds of x_t. The other way adopts the same value as the economic effect coefficient of investment utilization.[1] Because capital and investment play the same role in socialist societies, the second method is more reasonable. It should be pointed out that time and capital, per se, do not generate an economic effect in the national economy. Instead, it is human labor that generates economic effect. However, when production conditions, including laborers, are met, time and capital generate economic effect through human labor.

18.2.2 Method of Simple Interest

The method of simple interest calculates interest based on principal only; it does not consider any interest generated by interest. Here is its formula.

$$\text{Accumulated account } T_n = (1 + nx_z)T \quad (18.2)$$

T refers to principal. x_zT refers to the effect in each year. n means the number years based on which interest is calculated. Table 18.1 lists the method of simple interest in detail.

The assumption of the method of simple interest is that the amount of effect generated by capital each year, namely the newly-added capital, is not spent in national economic construction. The method of simple interest deals with problems statically. Therefore, it does not follow the objective law of economic development.

[1]The economic effect coefficient of investment utilization is calculated based on pure income, not national income.

Table 18.1 Method of Simple Interest

Time	The amount of effect generated by capital each year	The accumulated effect	The accumulated amount of capital
The beginning of the 1st year (Investment T)			
The end of the 1st year	$x_z T = (\theta - 1)T$	$(\theta - 1)T$	$T_1 = T + (\theta - 1)T$ $= (1 + x_z)T$
The end of the 2nd year	$x_z T = (\theta - 1)T$	$2(\theta - 1)T$	$T_2 = T + 2(\theta - 1)T$ $= (1 + 2x_z)T$
……	……	……	……
The end of the nth year	$x_z T = (\theta - 1)T$	$n(\theta - 1)T$	$T_n = T + n(\theta - 1)T$ $= (1 + nx_z)T$

18.2.3 Method of Compound Interest

The method of compound interest calculates interest based on both principal and corresponding interest. This method meets the requirement of the objective development of the economy. The reason is that if a country invests a million yuan in the development of its national economy and this investment generates a net income of 150,000 yuan in this year, the net income will not be held in the next year. Instead, it will be invested again to generate more net income. This process, which is called socialist extended reproduction, will repeat again and again. Thus, the method of compound interest is more suitable for calculating the time factor. The method of compound interest includes the ordinary compound interest method and the continuous compound interest method.

1. **Ordinary compound interest method**

This method calculates compound interest based on the year. Specifically, it calculates compound interest once a year. This method is suitable for use in the technological economy because the calculation unit in technological economy is also based on the one year unit. Here is the formula for ordinary compound interest method.

$$\text{The accumulated amount } T_n = T\theta^n = T(1 + x_z)^n \qquad (18.3)$$

Table 18.2 provides the derivation steps for the formula for ordinary compound interest method.

2. **Continuous compound interest method**

This method calculates compound interest based on quarter, month, or day. It allows compound interest to be calculated continuously several times or unlimited times in a given year. Here is the formula.

Table 18.2 Ordinary compound interest method

Time	The amount of effect generated by capital each year	The accumulated effect	The accumulated amount of capital
The beginning of the 1st year (Investment T)			
The end of the 1st year	$x_z T = (\theta - 1)T$	$(\theta - 1)T$	$T_1 = T + (\theta - 1)T = T\theta$
The end of the 2nd year	$x_z T_1 = x_z\ [(1 + x_z)\ T]$	$(\theta^2 - 1)T$	$T_2 = T + (\theta^2 - 1)T = T\theta^2$
……	……	……	……
The end of the nth year	$x_z T_{n-1} = x_z\ [(1 + x_z)^{n-1}\ T]$	$(\theta^n - 1)T$	$T_n = T + n(\theta^n - 1)T = T\theta^n$

$$\text{The accumulated amount } T_n = T(1 + x_{z\text{-actual}})^n \tag{18.4}$$

(1) Compound interest is calculated continuously a limited number of times in a given year. The commonly-used month-based compound interest calculation is one application in this category. For example, if the investment is T yuan and the monthly capital effect coefficient is 0.01, the yearly capital effect coefficient is $0.01 \times 12 = 0.12$, which is called the nominal capital effect coefficient. The actual capital effect coefficient should be $(1 + 0.01)^{12} - 1 = 0.127$. It can be seen that the actual capital effect coefficient is larger than the nominal capital effect coefficient. The technological economy should adopt the actual capital effect coefficient. The relationship between these two coefficients can be expressed by the following formulas.

The actual capital effect coefficient

$$x_{z\text{-actural}} = \left(1 + \frac{\text{The nominal capital effect coefficient } x\text{z-actual}}{\text{Compound interest calculated times per year } \alpha}\right)^{\alpha} - 1 \tag{18.5}$$

The nominal capital effect coefficient

$$x_{z\text{-nominal}} = \begin{array}{l}\text{Compund}\\ \text{interest}\\ \text{calculated}\\ \text{times per}\\ \text{year } \alpha\end{array} \times \left[\left(1 + \begin{array}{l}\text{The nominal}\\ \text{capital effect}\\ \text{coefficient } X_{z\text{-actural}}\end{array}\right)^{\frac{1}{\alpha}} - 1\right] \tag{18.6}$$

When $\alpha = 1$, $x_{z\text{-actural}} = x_{z\text{-nominal}}$. When $\alpha > 1$, $x_{z\text{-actural}} > x_{z\text{-nominal}}$.

(2) Compound interest is calculated continuously an unlimited number of times in a given year. If compound interest is calculated based on day, hour, minute, or

second, the relationship between the actual yearly capital effect coefficient and the nominal yearly capital effect coefficient can be expressed as:

$$x_{z\text{-}actural} = e^{xz\text{-}nrminal} - 1 \quad (18.7)$$

The actual capital effect coefficient is larger than the nominal capital effect coefficient when this method is adopted.

At present, the continuous compound interest method is seldom adopted in the technological economy, but this method is helpful for building mathematical models for the technological economy.

18.2.4 Time Factor Calculation Table and Its Method of Use

Time factor is important in conducting an economic evaluation of the technological economy. Calculation of the time factor must adopt a time coefficient, which has attracted much attention in domestic and overseas literature. The author proposed the calculation method and calculation table of seven time coefficients ($x_1 \sim x_6$, x_7) in early 1960s.[2] Later, 11 time coefficients were proposed in domestic and overseas literature[3] (x_1~ x_6, x_9, x_{11}, x_{13}, x_{15}, x_{17}). These two groups of time coefficients share six coefficients (x_1~ x_6). Accordingly, there are 12 time coefficients altogether (x_1~ x_6, x_7, x_9, x_{11}, x_{13}, x_{15}, x_{17}). Recently, the author proposed six practical time coefficients (x_8, x_{10}, x_{12}, x_{14}, x_{16}, x_{18}) based on his new research. As a result, the 18 time coefficients constitute a complete index system. Appendix 2 is a time factor calculation table for easy reference. Next, the time factor indices system is discussed in detail.

1. $\boldsymbol{X_1}$—Time value coefficient X_s

The time value coefficient is also called the final value coefficient, which refers to the final total capital value of a certain amount of capital after considering its compound interest for n years. The total capital value includes the principal and the increased value. Western engineering economics calls the time value coefficient by the names single-payment compound amount factor or single-payment compound factor.

When the time value is adopted for conducting a technological economy calculation, two assumptions are usually made. The first is that the occupied capital is invested at the beginning of a year. Thus, compounding interest is calculated from the year when the capital begins to be spent. The second is that the cost of consumption and the income are calculated at the end of a year. Accordingly, compounding interest calculation starts from the next year. The time value coefficient can be used

---

[2]Xu [Xu65].

[3]Canada [Ca71].

for two purposes: one is to calculate the total value of a certain amount of capital n years from now. The other is to calculate the final value of capitals invested in different years at a certain future time, so that these capitals can be added, deducted, or divided. Here is the formula for the time value coefficient:

$$X_1 = X_s = \theta^n = (1 + X_z)^n \tag{18.8}$$

2. $\boldsymbol{X_2}$—Discount factor X_x

The discount factor refers to the present value of a certain amount capital after n years when compounding interest is considered. Western engineering economics calls the discount factor by the name single-payment present value factor. Technological economy calculation usually converts future capital to the value at the beginning, not the end of a certain year. For example, if capital at the end of 2020 is converted to the present value in 2010, compounding interest should be calculated for 11 years, not 10 years. The discount factor is used for converting future capital in n years to the present value. It is often adopted for converting capitals in different years to their present value in a certain year. In this way, capitals in different years can be calculated. The discount factor is the reciprocal of the time value coefficient. The following is its formula.

$$X_2 = X_z = \frac{1}{X_s} = \frac{1}{\theta^n} = \frac{1}{(1 + X_z)^n} \tag{18.9}$$

3. $\boldsymbol{X_3}$—Accumulated time value coefficient X_{ls}

This coefficient refers to the total spent (or earned) capital value of certain amount of capital spent (or earned) in n years with compound interests considered. It is called the uniform series compound amount factor in western engineering economics. It equals the accumulated time value coefficient in n years. Here is its formula.

$$\begin{aligned} X_3 = X_{ls} &= \sum_{s=1}^{n} \theta^{n-s} = \theta^{n-1} + \theta^{n-2} + \cdots\cdots + \theta^{n-n} \\ &= \theta^{n-1} + \theta^{n-2} + \theta^{n-3} + \cdots\cdots + \theta + 1 = \frac{\theta^n - 1}{\theta - 1} \end{aligned} \tag{18.10}$$

4. $\boldsymbol{X_4}$—Yearly average coefficient of accumulated time value X_{lsp}

This coefficient refers to the value calculated by converting the total capital in n years to the average amount of capital during the n years. Western engineering economics calls it capital storage factor or sinking fund saving factor. The yearly average coefficient of cumulative time value is the reciprocal of the accumulated time value coefficient. Because it is used in different ways, the yearly average coefficient of accumulated time value is called by different names. For example, in technological economics, the yearly average coefficient of accumulated time value is called the fixed assets basic depreciation recovery coefficient X_{gj} for the reason that it considers the fixed assets' basic depreciation rate of time factor. Specifically, it refers to the portion between the yearly recovery total capital and the yearly total capital that needs recovery, when the same amount of capital needs recovery with the consideration of compound interest and when recovery total capital equals the total capital that needs recovery after a certain number of years. Here is its formula.

$$X_4 = X_{lsp} = \frac{1}{X_{ls}} = \frac{1}{\sum_{s=1}^{n} \theta^{n-s}} = \frac{\theta - 1}{\theta^n - 1} \tag{18.11}$$

5. $\boldsymbol{X_5}$—Accumulated discount coefficient X_{lx}

This coefficient refers to the total spent (or earned) present value of capital spent (or earned) in n years, during which a certain amount of capital is spent (or earned) each year, with compound interests considered. It is called uniform series present value factor or equal amount multiple present value factor in western engineering economics. It equals the accumulated discount coefficient of each year in n years. The technological economy begins to calculate compound interest for yearly recurrent expenditure or income from the very beginning of the n year period. Here is its formula.

$$X_5 = X_{lS} = \sum_{S=1}^{n} \frac{1}{\theta^s} = \frac{1}{\theta} + \frac{1}{\theta^2} + \cdots\cdots + \frac{1}{\theta^n} = \frac{\sum_{S=1}^{n} 6^{n-s}}{\theta^n} = \frac{6^n - 1}{(\theta - 1)6^n} \tag{18.12}$$

6. $\boldsymbol{X_6}$—Yearly average coefficient of accumulated present value X_{lxp}

This coefficient is used for converting the total capital at the beginning of an n-year period to the yearly average present value of the n-year period. It is called the capital recovery factor in western engineering economics. The yearly average coefficient of accumulated present value is the reciprocal of the accumulated discount coefficient. This coefficient is also called the investment recovery coefficient X_{th}, which refers to the portion between the yearly recovery capital and the occurred investment in that year, when the compound interest is considered, and when the recovery total capital equals the total occurred investment after a certain number of years. Here is its formula.

$$X_6 = X_{l\times p} = \frac{1}{X_{lx}} = \frac{1}{\sum_{s=1}^{n} \frac{1}{\theta^S}} = \frac{(\theta - 1)\theta^n}{\theta^n - 1} \tag{18.13}$$

It should be pointed out that the investment recovery coefficient includes both the fixed asset basic depreciation recovery coefficient and the investment occupancy economy effect coefficient. It equals the sum of these two coefficients. Therefore,

$$X_6 = X_{th} = \frac{(\theta - 1)\theta^n}{\theta^n - 1} = \frac{(\theta - 1)}{\theta^n - 1} + (\theta - 1) = l_j + x_i \tag{18.14}$$

7. $\boldsymbol{X_7}$—Accumulated equidifferent time value coefficient X_{lcs}

This coefficient refers to the total capital spent (or earned) in an n-year period when equidifferent capital is spent (or earned) in each year, with compound interests considered. It is actually the sum of the accumulated time value coefficient of each of the n years. The accumulated equidifferent time value coefficient is called the arithmetic sequence future value coefficient in western engineering economics. Technological economics does not double-count the cost of fixed asset occupancy. Therefore, the yearly basic depreciation cost is deducted from the cost of fixed asset occupancy. Because of this deduction, the accumulated equidifferent time value coefficient is also called the basic depreciation cost deduction coefficient x_j. Here is its formula.

$$\begin{aligned} X_7 = X_{lcs} &= \sum_{s=1}^{n} (s-1)\theta^{n-s} = \sum_{s=1}^{n-1} s\theta^{n-s-1} \\ &= \theta^{n-2} + 2\theta^{n-3} + 3\theta^{n-4} + \cdots\cdots + (n-1)\theta^{n-n} \\ &= \frac{1}{\theta - 1}(\theta^{n-1} + \theta^{n-2} + \theta^{n-3} + \cdots\cdots + 1 - n) \\ &= \frac{1}{\theta - 1}\left(\frac{\theta^n - 1}{\theta - 1} - n\right) \end{aligned} \tag{18.15}$$

Here is an example of the application of the accumulated equidifferent time value coefficient. If the fixed asset in a technological schema is T_g yuan and the yearly collected basic depreciation cost is $Cj\ (= ljT_g)$, what is the fixed asset occupancy cost (time value) in an n-year period? Here is the answer: (1) The yearly occupancy cost of the fixed asset T_g is $x_t T_g$. After considering the compound interest in the n years, the total fixed asset occupancy cost is $x_t T_g(\theta^n - 1)/(\theta - 1)$. (2) The yearly collected basic depreciation cost is Cj. This means that the yearly occupied fixed asset is decreasing. Accordingly, the fixed asset occupancy cost decreases. For instance, if the collected basic deprecation cost is Cj_1 in the first year, the fixed asset occupancy cost $x_t\ Cj_1$ should be deducted in each year from the second year. After considering the time factor, the total deduction is $x_t Cj_1 \frac{\theta^{n-1}-1}{\theta-1}$. In a similar way, if the collected basic deprecation cost is Cj_2 in the second year, the total deduction of fixed asset occupancy is $x_t\ Cj_2\ (\theta^{n-2} - 1)/(\theta - 1)$, ……and so on. (3) The total fixed asset occupancy cost in the n years should be:

$$\begin{aligned} & x_t T_g \frac{\sigma^n - 1}{\theta - 1} - \left(x_t C_{j1} \frac{\theta^{n-1} - 1}{\theta - 1} + x_t C_{j2} \frac{\theta^{n-2} - 1}{\theta - 1} + \cdots\cdots + x_t C_{jn} \frac{\theta^{n-n} - 1}{\theta - 1}\right) \\ & = x_t T_g \frac{\theta^n - 1}{\theta - 1} - x_t C_j \left(\frac{\theta^{n-1} - 1}{\theta - 1} + \frac{\theta^{n-2} - 1}{\theta - 1} + \cdots\cdots + 1\right) \end{aligned}$$

$$= x_t T g \frac{\theta^n - 1}{\theta - 1} - x_t C_j \sum_{s=1}^{n} \frac{\theta^{n-s} - 1}{\theta - 1} \tag{18.16}$$

In the above equation, $\sum_{s=1}^{n} \frac{\theta^{n-s}-1}{\theta-1}$ is the basic depreciation deduction coefficient (time value), which can be obtained by checking the accumulated equidifferent time value coefficient table.

8. $\boldsymbol{X_8}$—Accumulated equidifferent time value fund coefficient X_{lcsj}

This coefficient is adopted when converting the total capital at the end of an n-year period to the equidifferent capital in each of the n years. It is the reciprocal of the accumulated equidifferent time value coefficient. Here is its formula.

$$X_8 = X_{lcsj} = \frac{1}{X_{lcs}} = \frac{1}{\sum_{s=1}^{n} (s-1)\theta^{n-s}} = \frac{1}{\sum_{s=1}^{n} s\theta^{n-s-1}} = \frac{(\theta - 1)}{\frac{\theta^n - 1}{\theta - 1} - n} \tag{18.17}$$

9. $\boldsymbol{X_9}$—Accumulated equidifferent present value coefficient X_{lcx}

This coefficient refers to the total spent (or earned) present value in an n-year period when equidifferent capital is spent (or earned) in each year with compound interests considered. It is called the arithmetic sequence present value coefficient in western engineering economics. This coefficient is the sum of the accumulated present value of each of the *n* years. Here is its formula.

$$\begin{aligned} X_9 = X_{l\alpha} &= \sum_{s=1}^{n} (s-1)\theta^{-s} = \sum_{s=1}^{n-1} s\theta^{-s-1} \\ &= \theta^{-2} + 2\theta^{-3} + 3\theta^{-4} + \cdots\cdots + (n-1)\theta^{-n} \\ &= \frac{1}{(\theta - 1)\theta^n}\left(\theta^{n-1} + \theta^{n-2} + \theta^{n-3} + \cdots\cdots + 1 - n\right) \\ &= \frac{1}{(\theta - 1)\theta^n}\left(\frac{\theta^n - 1}{\theta - 1} - n\right) \end{aligned} \tag{18.18}$$

10. $\boldsymbol{X_{10}}$—Accumulated equidifferent present value fund coefficient X_{lcxj}

This coefficient is adopted when converting the present value of capital at the beginning of an n-year period to the equidifferent fund in each of the n years. It is the reciprocal of the accumulated equidifferent present value coefficient. Here is its formula.

$$X_{10} = X_{lcxj} = \frac{1}{x_{lcx}} = \frac{1}{\sum_{s=1}^{n} (s-1)^{\theta - s}} = \frac{1}{\sum_{s=1}^{n} s\theta^{-s-1}} = \frac{(\theta - 1)\theta^n}{\frac{\theta^n - 1}{\theta - 1} - n} \tag{18.19}$$

The application of this coefficient can be explained by the following example. Suppose the price a piece of equipment is 2,410,000 yuan. One user has an installment plan of yearly equidifferent increasing payments over 15 years. If the discount rate is 10%, what is the annual payment? Here are the answers: according to the accumulated equidifferent present value fund coefficient table, the accumulated equidifferent present value fund coefficient for the compound amount coefficient 1.1 in 15 years is 0.0249. Accordingly, the equidifferent fund is $2{,}410{,}000 \times 0.0249 = 60{,}000$ yuan. It can be seen from this that the payment for the first year is 0, the second year is 60,000 yuan, the third year is $2 \times 60{,}000 = 1{,}200{,}00$ yuan, and so on. The payment for the 15th year is $14 \times 60{,}000 = 840{,}000$ yuan.

11. X_{11}—Accumulated equidifferent fund yearly average coefficient X_{lcjp}

This coefficient is adopted for converting the accumulated fund calculated by present value or time value to a yearly average when a certain income (or spending) increases with the same differential in each year during an n-year period. It is called a fixed differential converting factor or an equidifferent series factor in western engineering economics. This coefficient is calculated by multiplying the accumulated equidifferent time value (or present value) coefficient and the yearly average coefficient of accumulated time value (or present value). Here is its formula.

$$X_{11} = X_{lcjp} = X_{lcs} \cdot X_{lsp} = X_{lcx} \cdot X_{lxp} = \frac{1}{(\theta - 1)} - \frac{n}{\theta^n - 1} \tag{18.20}$$

Here is an example. Suppose the major repair cost of a large piece of equipment increases ΔC_{dx}. The major repair cost for the first year is C_{dx0}. The second year is $C_{dx0} + \Delta C_{dx}$. The third year is $C_{dx0} + 2\Delta C_{dx}$. ...... The nth year is $C_{dx0} + (n - 1)\Delta C_{dx}$. What is the yearly average major repair cost in the n years? Here are the answers.

(1) Find the accumulated present value of the major repair cost in the n years.

$$C_{dx\Sigma} = \sum_{s=1}^{n} C_{dxs}\frac{1}{\theta^s} = \frac{C_{dx0}}{\theta} + \frac{C_{dx0} + \Delta C_{dx}}{\theta^2} + \frac{C_{dx0} + 2\Delta C_{dx}}{\theta^3} + \cdots\cdots + \frac{C_{dx0} + (n-1)\Delta C_{dx}}{\theta^n}$$
$$= C_{dx0}\left(\frac{\theta^n - 1}{(\theta - 1)\theta^n}\right) + \Delta C_{dx}\left(\frac{1}{\theta^2} + \frac{2}{\theta^3} + \frac{3}{\theta^4} + \cdots\cdots + \frac{n-1}{\theta^n}\right)$$

(2) Convert the accumulated present value of the major repair cost in the n years to the yearly average major repair cost.

$$C_{dx} = C_{dx\Sigma} \times \frac{(\theta - 1)\theta^n}{\theta^n - 1} = C_{dx0} + \Delta C_{dx}\left(\frac{1}{\theta^2} + \frac{2}{\theta^3} + \frac{3}{\theta^4} + \cdots\cdots + \frac{n-1}{\theta^n}\right)\frac{(\theta - 1)\theta^n}{\theta^n - 1}$$
$$= C_{dx0} + \Delta C_{dx}\left(\frac{1}{\theta - 1} - \frac{n}{\theta^n - 1}\right)$$

In the above equation, $\frac{1}{\theta-1} - \frac{n}{\theta^n-1}$ is the accumulated equidifferent fund yearly average coefficient X_{lcjp}, which is also called the yearly basic deprecation average deduction coefficient. It can be seen that the yearly average major repair cost with the time factor considered can be easily calculated by using the accumulated equidifferent fund yearly average coefficient.

12. $\boldsymbol{X_{12}}$—Accumulated equidifferent yearly fund average coefficient X_{lcpj}

This coefficient is adopted for converting the average fund in each year of an n-year period to an equidifferent fund. It is the reciprocal of the accumulated equidifferent fund yearly average coefficient. Here is its formula.

$$X_{12} = X_{lcpi} = \frac{1}{X_{lcjp}} = X_{ls} \cdot X_{lcsi} = X_{lx} \cdot X_{lcxj} = \frac{1}{\frac{1}{(\theta-1)} - \frac{n}{\theta^n-1}} \tag{18.21}$$

13. $\boldsymbol{X_{13}}$—Accumulated geometric time value coefficient X_{lbs}

This coefficient refers to the value of the total spending or earning capital in an n-year period when the geometric amount of capital is spent (or earned) in each year, with compound interests considered. Here is its formula.

(1) If the geometric coefficient β does not equal to the interest factor θ ($\beta \neq \theta$):

$$\begin{aligned} X_{13} = X_{lbs} &= \sum_{s=1}^{n} \beta^{s-1}\theta^{n-s} = \theta^{n-1} + \beta\theta^{n-3} + \cdots\cdots + \beta^{n-1}(n-1)\theta^{n-n} \\ &= \theta^{n-1}\left[1 + \frac{\beta}{\theta} + \left(\frac{\beta}{\theta}\right)^2 + \cdots\cdots + \left(\frac{\beta}{\theta}\right)^{n-1}\right] \\ &= \theta^{n-1}\left[\frac{\left(\frac{\beta}{\theta}\right)^n - 1}{\frac{\beta}{\theta} - 1}\right] \\ &= \frac{\theta^n - \beta^n}{\theta - \beta} \end{aligned} \tag{18.22.1}$$

In the above equation, $\beta = 1+x_c$.

(2) If the geometric coefficient β equals to the interest factor θ ($\beta = \theta$):

$$\begin{aligned} X_{13} = X_{lbs} &= \theta^{n-1} + \beta\theta^{n-2} + \beta^2\theta^{n-3} + \cdots\cdots + \beta^{n-1}\theta^{n-n} \\ &= \theta^{n-1} + \theta^{n-1} + \cdots\cdots + \theta^{n-1} = n\theta^{n-1} \end{aligned} \tag{18.22.2}$$

Here is an example. Suppose the operation period of a technological schema is 15 years and the same amount of energy is saved each year. The profit generated by the saved energy in the first year is 100,000 yuan. The price of energy rises 6% each year. Therefore, the profit generated in each year increases as well. If the interest factor is 1.1, what is the total profit generated by saved energy in 15 years? To answer this question, the geometric coefficient needs to be calculated. In this example, the geometric coefficient β is 1.06, which does not equal the interest factor, 1.1. Thus, the formula 18.22.1 is adopted to calculate the result. According to the accumulated geometric time value coefficient table, $X_{13} = 44.52$. Accordingly, the total profit generated by the saved energy in 15 years is 100,000 × 44.52 = 4,452,000 yuan.

14. $\boldsymbol{X_{14}}$—Accumulated geometric time value fund coefficient X_{lbsj}

This coefficient is adopted for converting the total value of the capital at the end of an n-year period to a geometric fund in each year. It is the reciprocal of the accumulated geometric time value coefficient. Here is its formula.

(1) When $\beta \neq \theta$:

$$X_{14} = X_{lbsj} = \frac{1}{X_{lbs}} = \frac{1}{\sum_{s=1}^{n} \beta^{s-1}\theta^{n-s}} = \frac{\theta - \beta}{\theta^n - \beta^n} \tag{18.23.1}$$

(2) When $\beta = \theta$:

$$X_{14} = X_{lbsi} = \frac{1}{X_{lbs}} = \frac{1}{n}\theta^{l-n} \tag{18.23.2}$$

15. $\boldsymbol{X_{15}}$—Accumulated geometric present value coefficient X_{lbx}

This coefficient refers to the present value of the total spending or earning capital in an n-year period when the geometric amount of capital is spent (or earned) in each year, with compound interests considered. Here is its formula.

(1) When $\beta \neq \theta$:

$$\begin{aligned} X_{15} = X_{lbx} &= \sum_{s=1}^{n} \frac{\beta^{s-1}\theta^{n-s}}{6^n} = \sum\nolimits_{s=1}^{n} \frac{\beta^{s-1}}{6^s} \\ &= \frac{1}{\theta} + \frac{\beta}{\theta^2} + \frac{\beta^2}{\theta^3} + \cdots\cdots + \frac{\beta^{n-1}}{6^n} \\ &= \frac{1}{\theta}\left[1 + \frac{\beta}{\theta} + \left(\frac{\beta}{\theta}\right)^2 + \cdots\cdots + \left(\frac{\beta}{\theta}\right)^{n-1}\right] \end{aligned}$$

$$= \frac{1}{\theta}\left[\frac{\left(\frac{\beta}{\theta}\right)^n - 1}{\frac{\beta}{\theta} - 1}\right] = \frac{1 - \beta^n\theta^{-n}}{\theta - \beta} \tag{18.24.1}$$

(2) When $\beta = \theta$:

$$X_{15} = X_{lbx} = \frac{1}{\theta} + \frac{\beta}{\theta^2} + \frac{\beta^2}{\theta^3} + \cdots\cdots + \frac{\beta^{n-1}}{\theta^n} = \frac{n}{\theta} \tag{18.24.2}$$

Here is an example. Suppose the operation period of a technological schema is 15 years and the same amount of energy is saved each year. The profit generated by the saved energy in the first year is 100,000 yuan. The price of energy is predicted to rise 6% each year. Therefore, the profit generated in each year increases as well. If the interest factor is 1.1, what is the present value of the total profit generated by saved energy in 15 years? To answer this question, one needs to check the accumulated geometric present value coefficient table. When n $= 15, \theta = 1.1$,and $\beta = 1.06$, $X_{15} = X_{lbx} = 10.66$. Therefore, the present value of the total profit generated by saved energy in 15 years is 100,000×10.66 = 1,060,000 yuan.

16. $\boldsymbol{X_{16}}$—Accumulated geometric present value fund coefficient X_{lbxj}

This coefficient is adopted when converting the present value of capital at the beginning of an n-year period to the geometric fund in each of the n years. It is the reciprocal of the accumulated geometric present value coefficient. Here is its formula.

(1) When $\beta \neq \theta$:

$$X_{16} = X_{lbxj} = \frac{1}{X_{lbx}} = \frac{1}{\sum_{s=1}^{n-1} \frac{\beta^{s-1}}{\theta^s}} = \frac{\theta - \beta}{1 - \beta^n\theta^{-n}} \tag{18.25.1}$$

(2) When $\beta = \theta$:

$$X_{16} = X_{lbxj} = \frac{1}{X_{lbx}} = \frac{1}{\frac{1}{\theta} + \frac{\beta}{\theta^2} + \frac{\beta^2}{\theta^3} + \cdots + \frac{\beta^{n-1}}{\theta^n}} = \frac{\theta}{n} \tag{18.25.2}$$

17. $\boldsymbol{X_{17}}$—Accumulated geometric fund yearly average coefficient X_{lbjp}

This coefficient is adopted for converting the accumulated fund calculated by present value or time value to a yearly average when a certain income (or spending) increases with the same geometric proportion in each year during an n-year period. This coefficient is calculated by multiplying the accumulated geometric time value (or present value) coefficient and the yearly average coefficient of accumulated time value (or present value). Here is its formula.

(1) When $\beta \neq \theta$:

$$X_{17} = X_{lbjp} = X_{lbs} \cdot X_{lsp} = X_{lbx} \cdot X_{lxp} = \frac{\theta^n - \beta^n}{\theta - \beta} \cdot \frac{\theta - 1}{\theta^n - 1} \quad (18.26.1)$$

(2) When $\beta = \theta$:

$$X_{17} = X_{lbjp} = X_{lbs} \cdot X_{lsp} = X_{lbx} \cdot X_{lxp} = n\theta^{n-1} \cdot \frac{\theta - 1}{\theta^n - 1} \quad (18.26.2)$$

18. $\mathbf{X_{18}}$—Accumulated geometric yearly fund average coefficient X_{lbpj}

This coefficient is adopted for converting the average fund in each year of an n-year period to a geometric fund. It is the reciprocal of the accumulated geometric fund yearly average coefficient X_{lbj}. Here is its formula.

(1) When $\beta \neq \theta$:

$$X_{18} = X_{lbpj} = \frac{1}{X_{lbjp}} = X_{ls} \cdot X_{lbsi} = X_{lx} \cdot X_{lbxj} = \frac{\theta - \beta}{\theta^n - \beta^n} \cdot \frac{\theta^n - 1}{\theta - 1} \quad (18.27.1)$$

(2) When $\beta = \theta$:

$$X_{18} = X_{lbpi} = \frac{1}{X_{lbjp}} = X_{ls} \cdot X_{lbsi} = X_{lx} \cdot X_{lbxj} = \frac{\theta^{1-n}}{n} \cdot \frac{\theta^n - 1}{\theta - 1} \quad (18.27.2)$$

The aforementioned 18 formulas are widely adopted in practice, especially in technological economy evaluation. The following are some applications.

(1) Calculation method for equal amount recovery M of investment with residue

Suppose the annual interest rate for investment T is i, and the recovery residue of the investment after n years is T_c. What is the recovery profit for each year so that the investment can be recovered in n years?

Set the equal amount recovery profit for each year as M. According to the time factor formulas, the net investment is $T\theta^n - T_c$, with the annual interest rate in the n years considered. The sum of the annual recovery profit is $M\frac{\theta^n - 1}{\theta - 1}$ with the annual interest rate in the n years considered. The net investment should equal the sum of annual recovery profit at the end of the n-year period. Thus,

$$T\theta^n - T_c = M\frac{\theta^n - 1}{\theta - 1}$$

$$M = \frac{(T\theta^n - T_c)(\theta - 1)}{\theta^n - 1} = T\frac{(\theta - 1)\theta^n}{\theta^n - 1} - T_c\frac{\theta - 1}{\theta^n - 1}$$

$$\because \frac{(\theta - 1)\theta^n}{\theta^n - 1} = \frac{\theta - 1}{\theta^n - 1} + (\theta - 1)$$

$$\therefore M = (T - T_c)\frac{(\theta - 1)\theta^n}{\theta^n - 1} + (\theta - 1)T_c \quad (18.28)$$

Here is an application of this coefficient. Suppose a factory invests 1,000,000 yuan and the annual interest rate is 10%. After running for 15 years, the residue of the investment is 200,000 yuan. What is the annual recovery profit with which the factory recovers its investment in 15 years? Load these numbers into the formula 18.28.

$$M = (1,000,000 - 200,000) \times 0.1315 + 0.1 \times 200,000 = 125,000$$

It can be seen that the factory can recover its investment in 15 years with an annual recovery profit of 125,000 yuan.

(2) Calculation method for unequal amount recovery M_s of investment without residue

A firm gets a loan T from a bank with the annual interest i and the length of maturity of n years. The firm repays the principal and interest on the loan once a year. How much should it repay?

First of all, the principal for each repayment is $\frac{T}{n}$.l. Next, the interest for each repayment is

$$\frac{n \cdot l - s + 1}{n \cdot l}T \times \frac{i}{l}$$

Therefore, the principal and interest for each repayment is

$$M_s = \frac{T}{n.l} + \frac{n.l - s + 1}{n.l}T \times \frac{i}{l} \quad (18.29)$$

In this formula, $\frac{i}{l}$ is the interest rate for each repayment, and $\frac{n.l - s + 1}{n.l}$ is the unpaid principal, on which interest needs to be calculated for the s time. For example, the unpaid principal, on which interest needs to calculate for the first time, is T. The unpaid principal, on which interest needs to be calculated for the last time is $\frac{T}{n.l}$. The total principal and interest for the n years is

Table 18.3 Statement of the repayment

Repayment Time	Principal (Unit 10,000 Yuan)	Interest (Unit 10,000 Yuan)	Repayment Amount (Unit 10,000 Yuan)
1st Time (6 months)	10	100 × 0.468 = 4.680	14.680
2nd Time (12 months)	10	90 × 0.468 = 4.212	14.212
3rd Time (18 months)	10	80 × 0.468 = 3.744	13.744
4th Time (24 months)	10	70 × 0.468 = 3.276	13.276
5th Time (30 months)	10	60 × 0.468 = 2.808	12.808
6th Time (36 months)	10	50 × 0.468 = 2.340	12.340
7th Time (42 months)	10	40 × 0.468 = 1.872	11.872
8th Time (48 months)	10	30 × 0.468 = 1.404	11.404
9th Time (54 months)	10	20 × 0.468 = 0.936	10.936
10th Time (60 months)	10	10 × 0.468 = 0.468	10.468
Total	**100**	**25.74**	**125.74**

$$\sum_{s=1}^{n.l} M_s = n.l\frac{T}{n.l} + \sum_{s=1}^{n.l} \frac{n.l - s + 1}{n.l} T \times \frac{i}{l} = T + \frac{nl + 1}{2} T \times \frac{i}{l} \tag{18.30}$$

Here is an application of this coefficient. Suppose a firm gets a 1,000,000 yuan loan from a bank with the annual interest rate of 9.36% and the length of maturity of 5 years. The firm repays the principal and interest on the loan twice a year. Altogether, there are 10 repayments. How much should this firm repay each time?

Based on the formula 18.30, the total principal and interest for the n years is 1,257,400 Yuan. Table 18.3 lists the statement of the repayments.

(3) Calculation method for dynamic investment recovery period n_c

Suppose the annual recovery profit of investment T is M and the interest rate is i. When will the investment be recovered completely? First, set the investment recovery period as n_c years. According to the aforementioned formulas, the investment with the interest rate of the n_c years considered is $T\theta^{nc}$. The total recovery profit in each year with the interest rate of the n_c years considered is $M\frac{\theta^{nc}-1}{\theta-1}$. In the n_c year, the total recovery profit equals to the investment. In other words, n_c year is the dynamic investment recovery period. The following is the derivation of the formula.

$$\because M\frac{\theta^n - 1}{\theta - 1} = T\theta^{nc}$$

After transposition,

$$1 - \frac{1}{\theta^{n_c}} = (\theta - 1)\frac{T}{M}$$

$$1-(\theta-1)\frac{T}{M}=\frac{1}{\theta^{n_c}}=\theta^{nc}$$

$$\log\left(1-\frac{iT}{M}\right)=-nc.\log(1+i)$$

$$n_c=\frac{-\log\left(1-\frac{iT}{M}\right)}{\log(1+i)} \tag{18.31}$$

Here is an example. A firm invests 1,000,000 Yuan. The annual recovery profit is 200,000 Yuan and the annual interest rate is 10%. How many years will the dynamic investment recovery period be? The answer is:

$$n_C=\frac{-\log\left(1-\frac{0.1\times 100}{20}\right)}{\log(1+0.1)}=\frac{0.301}{0.041}=7.3\ \text{years}$$

In this example, the static investment recovery period is 5 years. Thus, for the same example, dynamic investment recovery period is longer than static investment recovery period. Table 18.4 lists all of the formulas for calculating the time factor. Formulas for calculating continuous compound interest are included in the table. Compared with the formulas for calculating ordinary compound interest, they have $e^{\text{xz}-\text{nominal}}$ as the interest factor, instead of θ.

18.3 Defining Time Index

A time index is very important for calculation and evaluation in a macro and a micro technological economy. The comparable principle is discussed in Chap. 12. This chapter covers ways to define some main time indices, including the construction period, the period of service, and the calculation period.

18.3.1 Construction Period

The construction period refers to the duration from the beginning of the design of a project to the time when all construction of the project has been completed and the project is put into operation. The construction period consists of the design period, the construction period, and the break-in period. Generally speaking, the construction period only has input, but no output. However, in order to increase the economic effect of construction, sometimes construction and production are done in a staged manner. Sometimes, a small quality of production is conducted under the condition of not blocking construction. In this case, it is hard to differentiate between the construction period and the period of service. For the purpose of clarifying these

Table 18.4 Formulas for calculating time factors

Number	Name	Symbol	Other names	Ordinary compound interest	Continuous compound interest	Application			
						Known	Finding	Illustration	Formula
X_1	Time value coefficient	X_s	Final value coefficient, single-payment compound amount factor, single-payment complex factor (F/P, I, N)	θ^n	$e^{nx_z\text{-nominal}}$	$\sum_x$	$\sum_s$	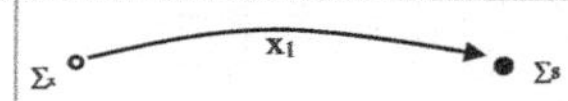	$\sum_s = X_1 \sum_x$
X_2	Discount factor	X_x	single-payment present value factor (P/F, I, N)	$\frac{1}{\theta^n}$	$\frac{1}{e^{nxz\_nominal}}$	$\sum_s$	$\sum_x$	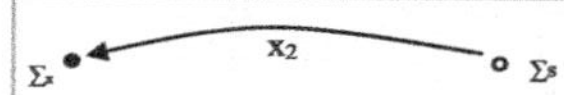	$\sum_x = X_2 \sum_s$
X_3	Accumulated time value coefficient	X_{ls}	Uniform series compound amount factor (F/A, I, N)	$\frac{\theta^n - 1}{\theta - 1}$	$\frac{e^{nxz\_nominal} - 1}{e^{xz\_nominal} - 1}$	P	$\sum_s$	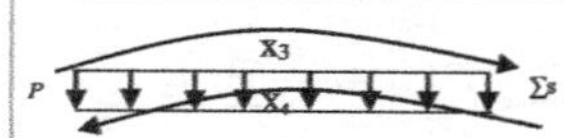	$\sum_s = X_3 P$
X_4	Yearly average coefficient of accumulated time value	X_{lsp}	Capital storage factor, sinking fund saving factor (A/F, I, N), fix asset basic deprecation recovery coefficient	$\frac{\theta - 1}{\theta^n - 1}$	$\frac{e^{xz\_nominal} - 1}{e^{nxz\_nominal} - 1}$	$\sum_s$	P	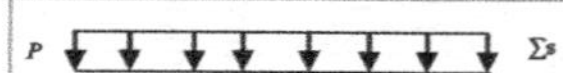	$P = X_4 \sum_s$

(continued)

Table 18.4 (continued)

Number	Name	Symbol	Other names	Ordinary compound interest	Continuous compound interest	Application			
						Known	Finding	Illustration	Formula
X_5	Accumulated discount coefficient	X_{lx}	Uniform series present value factor, equal amount multiple present value factor (P/A, I, N)	$\frac{\theta^n - 1}{(\theta - 1)\theta^n}$	$\frac{e^{nxz\_nominal} - 1}{(e^{xz\_nominal} - 1)e^{nxz\_nominal}}$	P	$\sum_x$	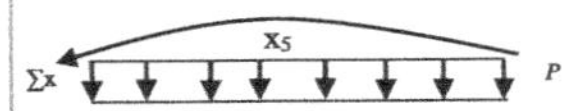	$\sum_x = X_5 P$
X_6	Yearly average coefficient of accumulated present value	X_{lxp}	Capital recovery factor (A/P, I, N)	$\frac{(\theta - 1)\theta^n}{\theta^n - 1}$	$\frac{(e^{xz\_nominal} - 1)e^{nxz\_nominal}}{e^{nxz\_nominal} - 1}$	$\sum_x$	P	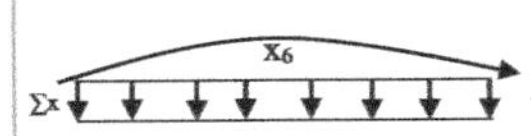	$P = X_6 \sum_x$

(continued)

Table 18.4 (continued)

Number	Name	Symbol	Other names	Ordinary compound interest	Continuous compound interest	Application			
						Known	Finding	Illustration	Formula
X_7	Accumulated equidifferent time value coefficient	X_{lcs}	Arithmetic sequence future value coefficient (F/G, I, N), basic depreciation deduct coefficient	$\frac{\frac{\theta^n-1}{\theta-1}-n}{\theta-1}$	$\frac{\frac{e^{nxz\_nominal}-1}{e^{xz\_nominal}-1}-n}{e^{xz\_nominal}-1}$	J	$\sum_s$	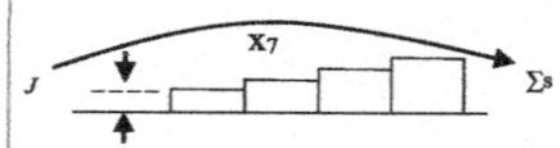	$\sum_s = X_7 J$
X_8	Accumulated equidifferent time value fund coefficient	X_{lcsj}	–	$\frac{\theta-1}{\frac{\theta^n-1}{\theta-1}-n}$	$\frac{e^{xz\_nominal}-1}{\frac{e^{nxz\_nominal}-1}{e^{xz\_nominal}-1}-n}$	$\sum_s$	J	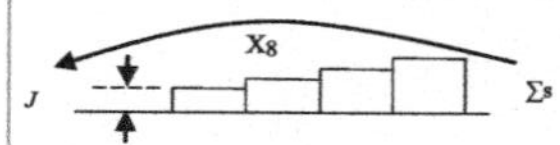	$J = X_8 \sum_s$

(continued)

Table 18.4 (continued)

Number	Name	Symbol	Other names	Ordinary compound interest	Continuous compound interest	Application			
						Known	Finding	Illustration	Formula
X_9	Accumulated equidifferent present value coefficient	X_{lcx}	Arithmetic sequence present value coefficient (P/G, I, N)	$\frac{\frac{\theta^n-1}{\theta-1}-n}{(\theta-1)\theta^n}$	$\frac{\frac{e^{nxz\_nominal}-1}{e^{xz\_nominal}-1}-n}{(e^{xz\_nominal}-1)e^{nxz\_nominal}}$	J	$\sum x$	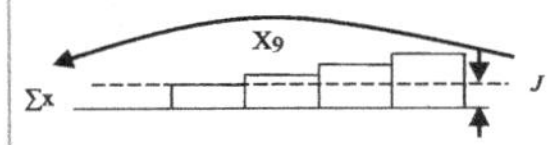	$\sum x = X_9 J$
X_{10}	Accumulated equidifferent present value fund coefficient	X_{lcxj}	–	$\frac{(\theta-1)\theta^n}{\frac{\theta^n-1}{\theta-1}-n}$	$\frac{(e^{xz\_nominal}-1)e^{nxz\_nominal}}{\frac{e^{nxz\_nominal}-1}{e^{xz\_nominal}-1}-n}$	$\sum x$	J	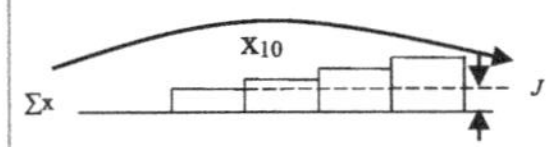	$J = X_{10} \sum x$

(continued)

Table 18.4 (continued)

Number	Name	Symbol	Other names	Ordinary compound interest	Continuous compound interest	Application			
						Known	Finding	Illustration	Formula
X_{11}	Accumulated equidifferent fund yearly average coefficient	X_{lcjp}	Fixed differential converting factor, equidifferent series factor (A/G, I, N), basic depreciation yearly average deduct coefficient	$\frac{1}{\theta-1}-\frac{n}{\theta^n-1}$	$\frac{1}{e^{xz\_nominal}-1}-\frac{n}{e^{nxz\_nominal}-1}$	J	P	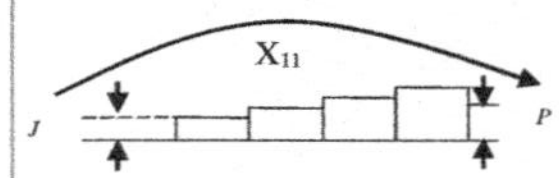	$P = X_{11}$ J
X_{12}	Accumulated equidifferent yearly fund average coefficient	X_{lcpj}	–	$\frac{1}{\frac{1}{\theta-1}-\frac{n}{\theta^n-1}}$	$\frac{1}{\frac{1}{e^{xz\_nominal}-1}-\frac{n}{e^{nxz\_nominal}-1}}$	P	J	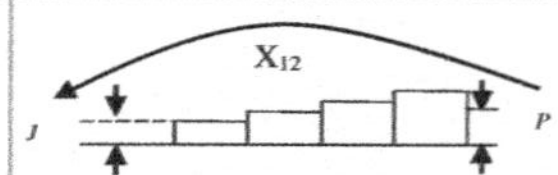	$J = X_{12}$ P

(continued)

Table 18.4 (continued)

Number	Name	Symbol	Other names	Ordinary compound interest	Continuous compound interest	Application			
						Known	Finding	Illustration	Formula
X_{13}	Accumulated geometric time value coefficient	X_{lbs}	Geometric sequence future value coefficient (P/A, I, J, N)	1. $\frac{\theta^n-\beta^n}{\theta-\beta}(\beta \neq \theta)$ 2. $n\theta^{n-1}(\beta = \theta)$	1. $\frac{e^{nxz\_nominal}-e^{nxc}}{e^{xz\_nominal}-e^{xc}}(x_{z\_nominal} \neq x_c)$ 2. $ne^{(n-1)x_{z\_nominal}}(x_{z_{nominal}} = x_c)$	J	$\sum s$	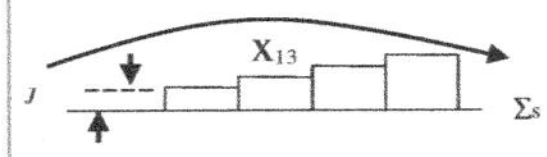	$\sum s = X_{13}J$
X_{14}	Accumulated geometric time value fund coefficient	X_{lbsj}	–	1. $\frac{\theta-\beta}{\theta^n-\beta^n}(\beta \neq \theta)$ 2. $\frac{1}{n}\theta^{1-n}(\beta = \theta)$	1. $\frac{e^{xz\_nominal}-e^{xc}}{e^{nxz\_nominal}-e^{nxc}}(x_{z\_nominal} \neq x_c)$ 2. $\frac{1}{n}e^{(1-n)x_{z\_nominal}}(x_{z_{nominal}} = x_c)$	$\sum s$	J	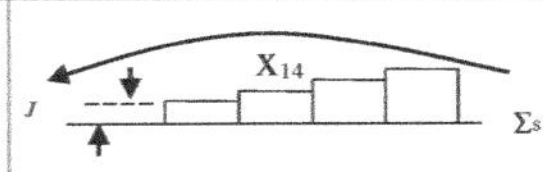	$J = X_{14}\sum s$
X_{15}	Accumulated geometric present value coefficient	X_{lbx}	Geometric sequence present value coefficient (P/A, I, J, N)	1. $\frac{1-\beta^{n-n}}{\theta-\beta}(\beta \neq \theta)$ 2. $\frac{n}{\theta}(\beta = \theta)$	1. $\frac{1-e^{n(xc-xz\_nominal)}}{e^{xz\_nominal}-e^{xc}}(x_{z\_nominal} \neq x_c)$ 2. $\frac{n}{e^{xz\_nominal}}(x_{z_{nominal}} = x_c)$	J	$\sum x$	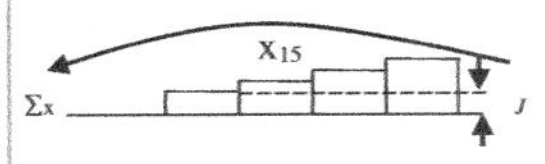	$\sum x = X_{15}J$

(continued)

Table 18.4 (continued)

Number	Name	Symbol	Other names	Ordinary compound interest	Continuous compound interest	Application			
						Known	Finding	Illustration	Formula
X_{16}	Accumulated geometric present value fund coefficient	X_{lbxj}	–	1. $\frac{\theta-\beta}{1-\beta^{n-n}}(\beta \neq \theta)$ 2. $\frac{\theta}{n}(\beta = \theta)$	1. $\frac{e^{xz\_nominal}-e^{xc}}{1-e^{n(xc-xz\_nominal)}}\left(x_{z\_nominal} \neq x_c\right)$ 2. $\frac{e^{xz\_nominal}}{n}\left(x_{z_{nominal}} = x_c\right)$	$\sum x$	J	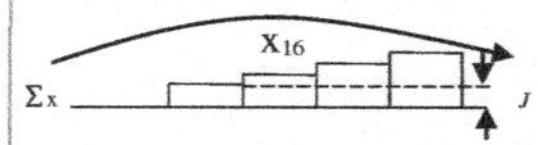	$J = X_{16}\sum x$
X_{17}	Accumulated geometric fund yearly average coefficient	X_{lbjp}	–	1. $\frac{(\theta^n-\beta^n)(\theta-1)}{(\theta-\beta)(\theta^n-1)}$ $(\beta \neq \theta)$ 2. $n\theta^{n-1}\frac{-1}{\theta^n-1}$ $(\beta = \theta)$	1. $\frac{e^{nxz_{nominal}}-e^{nxc}}{e^{xz_{nominal}}-e^{xc}} \cdot \frac{e^{xz_{nominal}}-1}{e^{nxz_{nominal}}-1}$ $\left(x_{z\_nominal} \neq x_c\right)$ 2. $ne^{(n-1)x_{z_{nominal}}} \cdot \frac{e^{xz_{nominal}}-1}{e^{nxz_{nominal}}-1}$ $\left(x_{z_{nominal}} = x_c\right)$	J	P	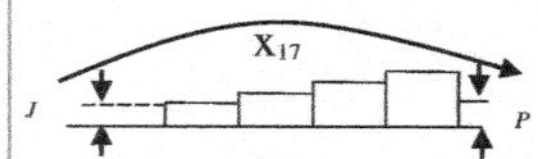	$P = X_{17} J$
X_{18}	Accumulated geometric yearly fund average coefficient	X_{lbpj}	–	1. $\frac{(\theta-\beta)(\theta^n-1)}{(\theta^n-\beta^n)(\theta-1)}$ $(\beta \neq \theta)$ 2. $\frac{\theta^{1-n}(\theta^n-1)}{n(\theta-1)}$ $(\beta = \theta)$	1. $\frac{e^{xz_{nominal}}-e^{xc}}{e^{nxz_{nominal}}-e^{nxc}} \cdot \frac{e^{nxz_{nominal}}-1}{e^{xz_{nominal}}-1}$ $\left(x_{z\_nominal} \neq x_c\right)$ 2. $\frac{e^{(1-n)xz_{nominal}}}{n} \cdot \frac{e^{nxz_{nominal}}-1}{e^{xz_{nominal}}-1}$ $\left(x_{z_{nominal}} = x_c\right)$	P	J	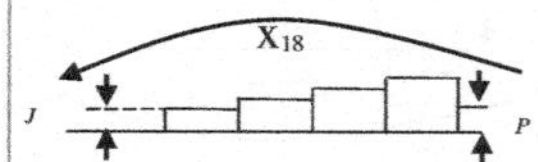	$J = X_{18} P$

two, this book determines that a construction period does not end until a project is completed finished and enters full operation.

The length of a construction period plays a key role in the evaluation of economic effect of technological economic schemes. A short construction period means an earlier full operation date; more created net wealth; lower cost, spending, and investment; and smaller payment for the use of long-term state funds.

The length of a construction period is closely related with a project's size, characteristics, and construction method. Some projects have a short construction period of several months. Others have long construction period of 1–3 years or 3–5 years, or even more than 5 years. Usually, the construction period of energy-related projects is about 10 years (see more details in Table 18.5).

The length of a construction period can be rational or irrational. Under certain conditions, some special measures are needed to shorten a construction period, such as increasing manpower and machines. But these measures will lead to the rise in investment and cost. Careful calculation and study are needed to determine whether it is rational to shorten construction period.

Table 18.5 Construction period of projects (new construction)

Category	Scale	Construction period
Coal mine	10 million tons/year	15–20 years
	2 million tons/year	10 years
Oil and gas field	10 million tons/year	3–5 years
Oil refinery	1 million tons/year	3–5 years
Hydropower station	1 million KW	~15 years
Thermal power station	1 million KW	3–4 years
Nuclear power station	1 million KW	8–10 years
Terrestrial heat power station		5 years
Railway		5–8 years (Newly-built) 3–5 years (Modification)
Port berth		3–5 years
Steel works	Large-scale	5–10 years
Petrochemical works	Large-scale	10–15 years
Machinery factory	Large-scale	3–5 years
Fertilizer plant	Large-scale	5 years
Cement plant	Large-scale	3–5 years
Cotton mill	Large-scale	2–3 years

18.3.2 Period of Service

Period of service is actually production period, which comes after construction period. In this period, technological schemes begin to generate benefit and output. Accordingly, this period is the most important time for technological schemes. There are two situations. In the first one, the designed production capability is achieved when the period of service begins. The time used for achieving the designed production capability is zero. In the other situation, the designed production capability is gradually achieved after several years. In practice, the second situation is more common. Therefore, a period of service usually has a window during which the designed production capability is gradually achieved. Obviously, the shorter the window is, the better the result will be.

There are three types of period service.

(1) Technical service period (or technical life time) refers to the service life that a project or a machine has, from the perspective of technology. A project or a machine cannot function properly beyond its service life.
(2) Economic service period (or economic life time) refers to the service life that a project or a machine has, from the perspective of economic effect. A project or a machine might still function properly after a certain amount of time, but the operation does not have any economic benefit, and should be abandoned. Generally speaking, an economic service period is always shorter than a technical service period. Defining an economic service period is a special technological economic problem.
(3) Period of depreciation (or depreciation life time) refers to the service life that a project or a machine has, from the financial perspective. It is used for calculating the basic depreciation of fixed asset. Usually, avperiod of depreciation shares the same value with avtechnical service period.

18.3.3 Defining Calculation Period

A calculation period is required by the evaluation of economic effect. Usually, it is also called a calculation period of service because it is related to period of service. In technological economic calculation, a calculation period sometimes includes a construction period and a calculation period of service. The calculation period for the economic effect of technological schemes is usually around 15 years (10–20 years) in China, considering the combination of present benefits and long-term benefits, the requirement for developing the national economy, the needs of the national economy, the impact of the development of science, and the accuracy of economic data. Reduction or extension might be needed for some individual technological schemes. A calculation period might be longer or shorter than the actual service period or the same as the service period.

18.4 Calculation Method for Rational Price

Price is the monetary expression of value. Price affects the distribution of benefit to all stakeholders, as well as production and saving. Price is one important aspect in technological economic calculation. When calculating the income of technological schemes, the price of the products generated by the technological schemes should be adopted. When calculating the spending of technological schemes, the price of the inputs of the technological schemes should be adopted. Price directly impacts economic effect. For the micro technological economy, the current price can be chosen for analysis, calculation, and evaluation. For the macro technological economy, current prices that do not reflect values should not be adopted for analysis, calculation, and evaluation. In international business, goods should not be traded at prices based on current rate. Four options are available for resolving this issue: (1) adopting rational prices; (2) adopting total consumption and cost in the relevant sectors; (3) adopting rational prices for import-export commodities; (4) adopting prices and rational rates in international markets.

18.4.1 Adopting Rational Prices

In order to get the maximum economic benefits, rational prices of commodities should be calculated by following these two formulas.

1. **Price formula type one**

$$\begin{aligned}
&\text{Rational price}\, j_g = \text{Value } j_z = c' + v' + m' = \text{Cost } c(\text{excluding interest and tax})\\
&+ \text{standard coefficient of economic result of capital utilization } x_t\\
&\times \text{capital occupation amount } t_z + \text{standard coefficient of economic result of material utilization } x_w\\
&\times \text{material consumption amount } w\\
&+ \text{standard coefficient of economic result of transport capacity utilization } x_y\\
&\times \text{transport capacity occupation amount } y\\
&+ \text{standard coefficient of economic result of labor force utilization } x_r\\
&\times \text{labor force occupation amount } r\\
&+ \text{standard coefficient of economic result of natural resource utilization } x_d\\
&\times \text{natural resource usage amount } d
\end{aligned} \tag{18.32}$$

2. **Price formula type two**

Price formula type two can be achieved by switching the cost c in Formula 18.32 with c_u (excluding interest, tax, and wage).

Price formula type one is good for evaluating the net income in a macro technological economy, whereas price formula type two is good for evaluating the national income in a macro technological economy. Take price formula type one as an example. The c in it is the cost of product per unit, equivalent to $c'+v'$, among which c' is the value of transfer of the materials consumed in the production process and v' is the value generated by laborers. The last five sections in formula 18.32 are the wealth generated by a unit product for society, equivalent to m'. In other words, they are the value generated for society. If only $x_t t_z$ are considered in the last five sections, price formulas become the format of production price, namely rational price = production price.

The other four sections are values created for society and are related with material consumption (W), transport capacity occupation (Y), manpower occupation (R), and natural resource utilization (D). The sections in the price formula reflect the relationship between supply and demand. For example, the coefficient of the economic result of material utilization x_w demonstrates that value comes from scarcity. If materials are not scarce, the standard coefficient of the economic result of material utilization x_w equals zero. The aforementioned price formula is more complete than a production formula. The latter is a particular case of the former, under certain conditions. Because the price formula is derived based on the principle of the best economic effect, it is also called the optimal price formula. Prices calculated by this formula are the optimal prices for commodities. Optimal prices have many advantages compared with present prices and production prices. More specifically, optimal prices allow product manufacturers get fair and equitable profit and tax, to improve the utilization of capital, to reflect the impact of product scarcity and the shortage of transport capacity, and to fully consider the shortage of certain factors, such as the labor force and natural resources. Therefore, calculating optimal prices in macro technological economic calculation and evaluation can avoid reaching incorrect conclusions.

The following are some examples about calculating optimal prices.

According to relevant document, the average investment for a large-scale coal production base in China is about 120 Yuan per ton. The occupied current capital is 13 Yuan per ton. The basic depreciation rate is 3.8%. The basic depreciation cost is 4.6 Yuan per ton. The major repair depreciation rate is 2.2%. The major repair depreciation cost is 2.6 Yuan per ton. Wages, raw materials, energy, and other costs are 13 Yuan per ton. The average production cost is 20 Yuan per ton. The present producer price is 21 Yuan per ton. This price needs to be corrected. According to price formula type one, the optimal price for coal can be calculated by the following steps. Set $x_r = 0$, $x_w = 0$, $x_y = 0$, and $x_d = 0$. Thus, the optimal price formula becomes the production price formula.

$$J_{g\text{-}coal} = c_{coal} + x_t t_{z\text{-}coal} \tag{18.33}$$

(1) Calculate $t_{gz\text{-}coal}$ first. Assume that construction period of a coal mine is 6 years and the average construction investment is 120 Yuan per ton in the 6 years. Thus, the average construction investment is 20 Yuan per ton in each year. Coal mine construction investment per unit can be calculated by following the above formula with time factor considered:

$$t_{gz\text{-}coal} = \frac{t_{g\text{-coal}}}{n_k}\left(\frac{\theta^{n_j+n_k}-1}{\theta^{n_j-1}} + \frac{\theta^{n_j+n_k-1-1}}{\theta^{n_j-1}} + \cdots + \frac{\theta^{n_j+1}-1}{\theta^{n_j-1}}\right)$$

$$= \frac{120}{6}\left(\frac{\theta^{21}-1}{\theta^{15}-1} + \frac{\theta^{20}-1}{\theta^{15}-1} + \frac{\theta^{19}-1}{\theta^{15}-1} + \frac{\theta^{18}-1}{\theta^{15}-1} + \frac{\theta^{17}-1}{\theta^{15}-1} + \frac{\theta^{16}-1}{\theta^{15}-1}\right) = 212 \text{ Yuan per ton}$$

(2) Calculate $t_{j\text{-}coal}$.

$$T_{j\text{-}coal} = \frac{c_{coal}}{e-1} - \frac{c_{coal}n_j}{\theta^{n_j}-1} = \frac{4.6}{0.15} - \frac{4.6 \times 15}{8.14-1} = 21 \text{ Yuan per ton}$$

(3) Therefore

$$t_{z\text{-}coal} = t_{g_z\text{-}coal} + t_{l-\text{coal}} + t_{j\text{-}coal} = 212 + 13 - 21 = 204 \text{ Yuan per ton}$$

(4) The production cost of coal c_{coal} is known and equals 20 Yuan per ton. Set $x_t = 0.15$.
(5) Load c_{coal}, $t_{z\text{-}coal}$, and x_i into the above formula and the optimal price of raw coal in China is

$$J_{g\text{-}coal} = 20 + 0.15 \times 204 = 50 \text{ Yuan per ton}$$

This price is conservative, because the construction period usually lasts about 10 years. In the above example, the construction period is set at 6 years. Following the same calculation method, the optimal price for cleaned coal is 70 Yuan per ton. The assumption for the above calculation steps is that the supply of energy, transport capacity, labor force, and natural resources are adequate, namely that x_w, x_y, x_r, and x_d in the price equation are all equal to zero. However, there has long been a short energy supply in China. Energy is in short supply. Thus, the energy utilization economic effect coefficient should be taken into consideration. The optimal price equation of coal turns into:

$$J_{g\text{-}coal} = C_{coal} + x_t t_{z\text{-}coal} + x_w w_{coal} \tag{18.34}$$

Based on a data analysis, x_w in the above equation can adopt 200 Yuan per ton standard coal or 143 Yuan per ton mine run coal. w can adopt 0.03 as the energy consumption for coal production. The optimal price of mine run coal under the condition of short energy supply can be seen as 54 Yuan per ton by loading the value of $x_w w$ and the value of $J_{g\text{-}coal}$ calculated above into formula 18.34.

Due to the short supply of coal, and considering the short-term effect of coal, the supply price per ton for coal should be the sum of the optimal price of coal production and coal economic effect coefficient, namely,

Table 18.6 Optimal prices of coal, oil, power and rail transport in China

Type Situation	Coal	Oil	Power	Rail transport
1.Considering energy short supply (production price)	50 Yuan/ton (70 Yuan/ton)[a]	90 Yuan/ton[b]	62 Yuan/kW	0.035 Yuan/ton-km
2.Not considering energy short supply (shadow price)	197 Yuan/ton (217 Yuan/ton)	580 Yuan/ton[c]	562 Yuan/kW	–
3.Present price	21 Yuan/ton (44 Yuan/ton)	100 Yuan/ton	66 Yuan/kW	0.010 Yuan/ton-km

Note[a]The number without parenthesis is the price of mine run coal. The number with parenthesis is the price of cleaned coal
[b]Not considering the reasonable price ratio with coal
[c]Considering the reasonable price ratio with coal

$$J_{g\text{-}coal-supply} = J_{g\text{-}coal} + x_{w\text{-}coal} \tag{18.35}$$

The rational price for coal supply can be achieved as 197 Yuan per ton by following the above formula. This price is the same as the shadow price in the western economy.

The optimal prices for other energies and the optimal price for transportation can be calculated in the same way. Table 18.6 lists the optimal prices for coal, oil, power, and rail transport in China.

It can be seen from table above that the optimal prices for coal and transportation deviate quite a bit from the present price. Therefore, the present price should not be adopted in a macro technological economic evaluation. If considering the short supply of energy, the present prices are too low. Special attention should be paid to this. Based on the above analysis, it can be seen that the present prices for light industry products and agricultural products are not rational and that the average price for heavy industry products is rational. The prices for coal and transportation are the most irrational. Thus, adjustment should be made and rational prices should be adopted. The prices for metallurgy, power, chemical industry, building materials, forestry, and other heavy industries are generally rational. When conducting an economic evaluation in the technological economy, those irrational prices should be revised. For rational prices, present prices can be adopted as an approximation.

18.4.2 Adopting the Total Consumption Costs of Relevant Sectors

In order to avoid the error caused by irrational prices of input products, the total consumption costs of relevant sectors, rather than the price, can be adopted in a macro technological economic evaluation. Here is an example. In a technological schema about making synthetic ammonia using coal as raw material, one single factor cannot produce synthetic ammonia from the perspective of the whole national economy. Coal mines, electric power plants, and railroads that support synthetic ammonia must be constructed. Coal mines provide raw material for producing ammonia and fuel for boilers. Electric power plants provide power and railroads transport coal. Therefore, when calculating the social total consumption cost of the schema, the costs of coal mines, electric power plants, and railroads must be included in addition to the total consumption cost of the synthetic ammonia factory. The total costs can be expressed as:

$$\begin{aligned} Z = & \left(C' chemical + x_w W_{chemical} + x_y Y_{chemical} + x_r R_{chenical} + x_t T_{z-chemical} + x_d D_{z-chemical}\right) \\ & + \left(C_{coal} + x_w W_{ceal} + x_y Y_{coal} + x_1 R_{coal} + x_t T_{z\text{-}coal} + x_d D_{z\text{-}coal}\right) \\ & + \left(C_{power} + x_w W_{power} + x_y Y_{power} + x_r R_{power} + x_t T_{z-power} + x_d D_{z-power}\right) \\ & + \left(C_{transport} + x_w W_{transport} + x_y Y_{transport} + x_r R_{transport} + x_t T_{z-transport} + x_d D_{z-transport}\right) \end{aligned} \tag{18.36}$$

The first line in the above formula represents the costs excluding those of coal, power, and transportation. The second line, third line, and fourth line represent the costs of coal, power, and transportation, respectively. In this way, the macro technological economic evaluation canavoid using the price index.

However, this method is, in essence, the same as the one that adopts a rational price; they just have different formats. We will prove this next. As we know, the costs of coal, power, and transportation are usually calculated in this way:

$$C_{coal} = Q_{coal} \times j_{g\text{-}coal} = \text{The amount of coal consumed per year} \times \text{price of coal} \tag{18.37.1}$$

$$C_{power} = Q_{power} \times j_{g\text{-}power} = \text{The amount of power consumed per year} \times \text{price of power} \tag{18.37.2}$$

$$C_{transport} = Q_{ransport} \times j_{g\text{-}ransport} = \text{The amount of coal transported per year} \times \text{price of transportation} \tag{18.37.3}$$

Thus, the cost of coal C_{coal}, the cost of power C_{power}, and the cost of transport $C_{transport}$ should be:

$$C_{coal} = Q_{coal} \times j_{g\text{-}coal} = C_{coal} + x_w W_{coal} + x_y Y_{coal} + x_r R_{coal} + x_t T_{z\text{-}coal} + x_d D_{z\text{-}coal} \tag{18.38.1}$$

$$C_{power} = Q_{power} \times j_{g\text{-}power} = C_{power} + x_w W_{power} + x_y Y_{power} + x_r R_{power} + x_t T_{z-power} + x_d D_{z-power} \tag{18.38.2}$$

$$\begin{aligned} C_{transport} = Q_{ransport} \times j_{g\text{-}ransport} = & C_{transport} + x_w W_{transport} + x_y Y_{transport} + x_r R_{transport} \\ & + x_t T_{z-transport} + x_d D_{z-transport} \end{aligned} \tag{18.38.3}$$

Simplify the formulas and we can get:

$$j_{g\text{-}coal} = c_{coal} + x_w w_{coal} + x_y y_{coal} + x_r r_{coal} + x_t t_{z\text{-}coal} + x_d d_{z\text{-}coal} = z_{coal} \tag{18.39.1}$$

$$j_{g\text{-}power} = c_{power} + x_w w_{power} + x_y y_{power} + x_r r_{power} + x_t t_{z-power} + x_d d_{z-power} = z_{power} \quad (18.39.2)$$

$$j_{g\text{-}ransport} = c_{transport} + x_w w_{transport} + x_y y_{transport} + x_r r_{transport} + x_t T_{z-transport} + x_d D_{z-transport} = z_{transport} \quad (18.39.3)$$

In the above formulas, $c_{coal} = C_{coal}/Q_{coal}$, $w_{coal} = W_{coal}/Q_{coal}$, $y_{coal} = Y_{coal}/Q_{coal}$, $r_{coal} = R_{coal}/Q_{coal}$, $t_{coal} = T_{z\text{-}coal}/Q_{coal}$, $d_{z\text{-}coal} = D_{z\text{-}coal}/Q_{coal}$.

The symbols for power and transport are the same as that for coal.

It can be seen that formulas 18.39.1, 18.39.2, and 18.39.3 are the formulas for rational price. Therefore, adopting the total consumption costs of relevant sectors is actually adopting rational price. But this method is only valid for comparing schemas that have same outputs but different inputs.

18.4.3 Adopting Rational Prices for Imported and Exported Commodities

Foreign trade commodities should adopt rational prices so that macro technological economic evaluation can be correctly conducted.

1. **Rational Price for Imported Commodities**

Suppose that commodity A needs to be imported. First of all, it is necessary to calculate the amount of commodity B that needs to be exported to exchange for commodity A, based on the principle of barter. Next, the total cost for exporting commodity B should be calculated, based on rational price. This cost should equal the spending of importing commodity A. In this way, the rational price for importing commodity A can be determined. Here is the formula.

$$\begin{aligned}&\text{Rational price of imported commodity } j_{import}\\ &= \frac{\textit{Rational domestic price of exported commodity } j_{export} \times \text{amount of exported commodity } G_{export}}{\text{amount of imported commodity } G_{import}}\\ &= \frac{\textit{Rational domestic price of exported commodity } j_{export} \times \text{price of imported commodity } j_{import-im} \text{ in international market}}{\textit{price of exported commodity } j_{export-im} \textit{ in international market}}\\ &\le \text{rational price of the same domestic commodities } j_z \end{aligned} \quad (18.40)$$

From the perspective of a macro technological economy, the rational price of imported commodity j_{import} based on formula 18.40 should be smaller or equal to rational price of the same domestic commodities j_z. Otherwise, there is no need to import this commodity. Such kind of foreign trade is not mutually beneficial.

2. **Rational Price for Exported Commodities**

Suppose that one kind of commodity B needs to be exported. First of all, it is necessary to calculate the amount of commodity A that needs to be imported. Next, the total cost for importing commodity A should be calculated, based on its rational domestic price. This cost should be equal to the earning of exporting commodity B. In this way, the rational price for exporting commodity B can be determined. Here is the formula.

$$\begin{aligned}
&\text{Rational price of exported commodity } j_{export}\\
&= \frac{\textit{Rational domestic price of imported commodity } j_{import} \times \text{amount of imported commodity } G_{import}}{\text{amount of exported commodity } G_{export}}\\
&= \frac{\textit{Rational domestic price of imported commodity } j_{import} \times \text{price of exported commodity } j_{export-im}\text{in international market}}{\textit{price of imported commodity } j_{import-im}\textit{in international market}}\\
&\geq \text{rational domestic price of the exported commodity } j_z
\end{aligned} \tag{18.41}$$

From the perspective of economic evaluation, the rational price of the exported commodity j_{import} determined based on formula 18.41 should be larger than or equal to its rational domestic price. Otherwise, there is no need to export this commodity.

It can be seen that rational prices for imported/exported commodities are related to their amount and their rational domestic prices. It must be pointed out that the rational prices for imported/exported commodities and the price in the international market, as mentioned above, should consider the costs of transportation and the commission charge of foreign trade.

18.4.4 Adopting the Price in International Market and Rational Exchange Rate

In macroeconomic evaluation, if the prices in the international market are adopted for foreign trade commodities, the exchange rate must be rational. When the exchange rate is not rational, adjustments must be taken. The rational exchange rate can be determined by the following methods.

1. **Determining Rational Exchange Rate for Each Commodity**

The rational exchange rate for each commodity can be determined by using the aforementioned rational price of the imported/exported commodities formula. Here are the steps.

$$\begin{aligned}
&\text{Rational price of imported commodity } j_{import}\\
&= \text{Price of imported commodity in international market } j_{import-im} \times \text{rational exchange rate}\\
&= \frac{\textit{Rational domestic price of exported commodity } j_{export} \times \text{amount of exported commodity } G_{export}}{\text{amount of imported commodity } G_{import}}
\end{aligned}$$

$$= \frac{\textit{Rational domestic price of exported commodity } j_{export} \times \text{price of imported commodity } j_{import-im} \text{ in international market}}{\textit{price of exported commodity } j_{export-im} \textit{ in international market}} \quad (18.42)$$

Thus,

$$\begin{aligned} &\text{The rational exchange rate for imported commodity} \\ &= \frac{\textit{Rational domestic price of exported commodity } j_{export} \times \text{amount of exported commodity } G_{export}}{\text{price of imported commodity } j_{import-im} \text{ in international market} \times \text{amount of imported commodity } G_{import}} \\ &= \frac{\textit{Rational domestic price of exported commodity } j_{export}}{\textit{price of exported commodity } j_{export-im} \textit{ in international market}} \text{ Yuan/US Dollar} \end{aligned} \quad (18.43)$$

Or,

$$\begin{aligned} &\text{The rational price for exported commodity (in RMB) } j_{export} \\ &= \text{Price of exported commodity in international market } j_{export-im} \times \text{rational exchange rate} \\ &= \frac{\textit{Rational domestic price of imported commodity } j_{import} \times \text{amount of imported commodity } G_{import}}{\text{amount of exported commodity } G_{export}} \\ &= \frac{\textit{Rational domestic price of imported commodity } j_{import} \times \text{price of exported commodity } j_{export-im} \text{ in international market}}{\textit{price of imported commodity } j_{import-im} \textit{ in international market}} \end{aligned} \quad (18.44)$$

Thus,

$$\begin{aligned} &\text{The rational exchange rate for exported commodity} \\ &= \frac{\textit{Rational domestic price of imported commodity } j_{import} \times \text{amount of imported commodity } G_{import}}{\text{price of exported commodity } j_{export-im} \text{ in international market}} \\ &= \frac{\textit{Rational domestic price of imported commodity } j_{import}}{\textit{price of imported commodity } j_{import-im} \textit{ in international market}} \text{ Yuan/US Dollar} \end{aligned} \quad (18.45)$$

2. **Determining Comprehensive Rational Exchange Rate for All Commodities**

Suppose that there are many commodities for importing and exporting. Then, a comprehensive rational exchange rate is needed. The method for determining the comprehensive rational exchange rate is very similar to the methods introduced above.

The comprehensive rational exchange rate for imported commodities

$$= \frac{\sum j_{export} \times G_{export}}{\sum j_{import-im} \times G_{import}} \text{ Yuan/US Dollar} \quad (18.46)$$

The comprehensive rational exchange rate for exported commodities

$$= \frac{\sum j_{import} \times G_{import}}{\sum j_{export-im} \times G_{export}} \text{ Yuan/US Dollar} \quad (18.47)$$

It can be seen that rational exchange rate is based on rational prices of imported/exported commodities. In fact, they are the same thing.

18.4.5 Rational Price Ratio

1. **External and Internal Price Ratio**

In order to know whether the price of a certain commodity is rational, the price is usually compared with the prices of other commodities. If one sets the price of a certain commodity as 1, the ratio between this price and the prices of other irreplaceable commodities is the price ratio of those irreplaceable commodities. This ratio is also called the external price ratio of this specific commodity. The ratio between the prices of replaceable commodities is called internal price ratio.

2. **Principle and Method for Setting External Price Ratio**

The principle and method for setting the rational external price ratio are the same as those for setting the rational price. First, set the optimal prices for commodities, based on formula 18.32. Second, set the optimal price of a certain commodity as 1. Then, compare the prices of other commodities that are irreplaceable to this commodity with the price to get the rational external price ratio. Therefore, whether the external price ratio is rational or not depends on the base for setting the commodities' optimal price. If their prices are set based on the optimal price formula, the external price ratio is rational. Otherwise, the external price ratio is not rational.

3. **Principle and Method for Setting Internal Price Ratio**

The general principle for setting the internal price ratio is the same as that for setting prices for commodities. Here are the steps. (1) Calculate the optimal price for replaceable commodities by following formula 18.32; (2) Calculate and compare the final effect of using each commodity based on its optimal price (3) Set the commodity with the smallest effect of using it as the base (actually any commodity can be set as the base). Set the optimal price of the base commodity as 1. Compare the prices of replaceable commodities with the price of the base commodity, and the internal price ratio can be achieved. Thus, it is very important to set the prices for the replaceable commodities. Here is an example of setting the prices for the replaceable commodities about energy. Usually the prices for replaceable commodities depend on their quality. For instance, the thermal value is the main index for fuel. The thermal value for ordinary coal is 5,000 kilocalories per kilogram. The thermal value for lower-grade coal is 2,500 kilocalories per kilogram. The thermal value for heavy oil is 10,000 kilocalories per kilogram. The thermal value ratio of these three fuels is 2:1:4. Thus, the prices for replaceable energies can be calculated based on this ratio by following the principle of pricing by quality. For example, if the price for lower-grade coal is 25 Yuan per ton, the prices for ordinary coal and heavy oil should be 50 Yuan per ton and 100 Yuan per ton respectively. This method is easy, but it is not accurate. Wrong results are very likely to be generated because each fuel has diverse components. Some components determine thermal value, while others, such as sulfur, ash, and water, determine other characteristics. All of the components of a fuel impact its economic effect when the fuel is utilized. Here is an example. Two types of washery coal, A and B, have the same heat productivity. The amount of ash in A is 1% less than that in B. Practice shows that if the amount of ash in washery coal drops 1%, the coke ratio and the consumption of limestone will both decrease 2%, whereas the production of pig iron will increase 3%. It can be seen that it is not rational to calculate the price ratio of energy based on heat productivity. Therefore, the prices for replaceable commodities should be calculated by considering the quality of each commodity and the impact generated by its comprehensive economic effect when it is utilized. The following formula can be adopted to calculate the prices for replaceable commodities.

$$j_{g\text{-}replaceable} = j_{g\text{-}replaceable/original} \pm E_{cf\text{-}replaceable} \tag{18.48}$$

In this formula, $j_{g\text{-}replaceable}$ is the price for replaceable commodities based on rational internal price ratio. $j_{g\text{-}replaceable/original}$ is the price for replaceable commodities based on the original optimal price formula. $E_{cf\text{-}replaceable}$ is the increased/decreased economic benefits caused by adopting one ton of the replaceable commodity compared with using one ton of the basic commodity under the condition of meeting the same demand.

$$E_{cf\text{-}replaceable} = \frac{E_{c\text{-}replaceable} - E_{c\text{-}basic}}{W_{replaceable}}$$

In addition, comprehensive grading can be applied to set the rational internal price ratio of commodities. For example, there are two commodities, *A* and *B*, which can replace each other. They have five indices for quality and feature. First, these two commodities are graded individually for each index. Then their total scores are calculated by adding their scores for each index. If the total score for commodity *A* is F_a and the total score for commodity *B* is F_b, the rational internal price ratio for *A* (set commodity *B* as the basic commodity) is:

$$j_a : j_b = F_a : F_b \tag{18.49}$$

18.4.6 Rational Bargain, Reduced Price and Privileged Price

In practice, present bargain, reduced price, and privileged price can be applied in the micro technological economy. However, rational bargain, reduced price, and privileged price should be adopted in macro technological economy.

Bargain is a price that considers short-term effect. A rational bargain must take short-term effect into consideration. Here is its formula:

$$j_{bargain} = j_{rational} + x_{w\text{-}short\text{-}term} \tag{18.50}$$

A present bargain should not higher than a rational bargain.

Reduced price, or privileged price, is a price that considers the long-term effect. The rational reduced price, or the privileged price, must take long-term effect into consideration. Here is the formula:

$$j_{reduced} = j_{rational} + x_{w\text{-}long\text{-}term} \tag{18.51}$$

The rational reduced price can be achieved by the following method. Suppose that there is an overstocked product. The product will be sold out in $n_{overstock}$ years. If the product is on sale at a reduced price now, the actual cash income $j_{reduced}\ \theta^{\ noverstock}$ achieved based on the reduced price with the time factor considered equals the actual cash income j_z achieved based on the original price after $n_{overstock}$ years. That is to say,

$$j_{reduced}q^{noverstock} = j_z \tag{18.52}$$

Thus,

$$\text{Rational reduced price } j_{reduced} = \text{Present original price } j_z \times \text{discount factor}\frac{1}{\theta^{n-overstock}} \tag{18.53}$$

Similarly, when equipment capacity, production, and labor are abundant, prices should drop. The decreased price is called the privileged price. For example, a hydropower station generates more power in a high flow period. The extra water flow will be wasted if it does not generate power. Thus, the privileged price of power should be adopted during high flow period. In a similar way, the privileged price of power should be adopted when the daily load is low for thermal power plants. Here is the principle for setting the privileged price. The privileged price $j_{privileged}$ should be equal to or be higher than the additional cost Δz of the product or of the labor per unit using the abundant capacity. The principle can be expressed by the following formula.

$$\text{Rational privileged price } j_{privileged}1 \geq \text{ Additional cost } \Delta z \text{ of product or labor per unit} \tag{18.54}$$

For instance, a huge volume of coal in Shanxi province is transported outward by cargo trains. When they return back to Shanxi province, those cargo trains are empty. Using the cargo trains to deliver cargos only has a small cost in locomotive energy consumption, loading and unloading cargos, and marshalling, without extra investment from the state. The increased cost Δz is much lower than the rational freight rate. Therefore, the privileged price is lower than the rational freight rate in this case.

It should be pointed out that the present reduced price and the privileged price should be equal to or higher than the rational reduced price and the privileged price.

18.5 Calculation Methods for Standard Economic Effect Coefficients

Standard coefficients of economic results are important parameters in macro technological economic evaluation. They can be used for calculating the indirect cost caused by a single input and the indirect benefit generated by a single output.

18.5.1 Calculation Methods for the Standard Economic Effects Coefficient of Capital Utilization Effect

1. Calculation method for economic effect coefficient of capital utilization

Economic effect coefficient of capital utilization refers to the size of the economic effect on the sectors in the national economy generated by a certain unit of capital. It is related to the supply of capital. There are two methods for calculating the economic effect coefficient of capital utilization. One is average index calculation and the other is increment index calculation.

(1) Average index calculation

(1) Short-term effect

$$x_t = \frac{J_g - C}{T} \tag{18.55.1}$$

$$or\quad x_t = \frac{J_g - C_u}{T}\ \text{Yuan/Yuan}\cdot\text{Year} \tag{18.55.2}$$

(2) Opportunity effect

$$x_t = \frac{E_{ct}}{T} \tag{18.56.1}$$

$$or\quad x_t = \frac{E_{dt}}{T}\ \text{Yuan/Yuan}\cdot\text{Year} \tag{18.56.2}$$

In the above formulas,

$$E_{ct} = J_g - C - x_w W - x_y Y - x_r R - x_d D_z \tag{18.56.3}$$

$$E_{dt} = J_g - C_u - x_w W - x_y Y - x_r R - x_d D_z \tag{18.56.4}$$

(3) Long-term effect

$$x_t = (1 + x_{dx})l_{j-privilege} - (1 + x_{dx})l_j \text{ Yuan/Yuan} \cdot \text{Year} \quad (18.57)$$

In this formula, $(1 + x_{dx})\ l_{j\text{-}privilege}T$ and $(1 + x_{dx})\ l_j\ T$ are privileged basic depreciation and major repair costs and normal basic depreciation and major repair costs.

(2) Increment index calculation

(1) Short-term effect

$$x_t = \frac{\Delta(J_g - c)}{\Delta T}, x_t = \frac{\partial(J_g - c)}{\partial T} \quad (18.58.1)$$

$$or \quad x_t = \frac{\Delta(J_g - c_u)}{\Delta T}, x_t = \frac{\partial(J_g - c_u)}{\partial T} \text{ Yuan/Yuan} \cdot \text{Year} \quad (18.58.2)$$

(2) Opportunity effect

$$x_t = \frac{\Delta E_{ct}}{\Delta T}, \quad x_t = \frac{\partial E_{ct}}{\partial T} \quad (18.59.1)$$

$$or \quad x_t = \frac{\Delta E_{dt}}{\Delta T}, \quad x_t = \frac{\partial E_{dt}}{\partial T} \text{ Yuan/Yuan} \cdot \text{Year} \quad (18.59.2)$$

(3) Long-term effect

$$x_t = \Delta\left[(1 + x_{dx})\left(l_{j-privilege} - l_j\right)\right]T/\Delta T \quad (18.60.1)$$

$$x_t = \partial\left[(1 + x_{dx})\left(l_{j-privilege} - l_j\right)\right]T/\partial T \text{ Yuan/Yuan} \cdot \text{Year} \quad (18.60.2)$$

It should be pointed out that the result generated by average index calculation is the economic effect caused by the total capital, whereas the result generated by increment index calculation is the economic effect caused by the new increased capital.

The economic effect coefficient of capital utilization changes each year. As a result, it is necessary to calculate the average in a certain period. Accordingly, all of the formulas above need to be revised. Here are the revisions for the short-term formulas 18.58.1 and 18.58.2.

$$x_t = \frac{\sum \Delta(J_g - c)}{\sum \Delta T} \tag{18.61.1}$$

$$\text{or} \quad x_t = \frac{\sum \Delta(J_g - c_u)}{\sum \Delta T} \tag{18.61.2}$$

In the above formulas, the denominator represents the total investment in a certain period. The molecule represents the total increased net income (national income) caused by increased investment in the same period. The increased investment includes infrastructure investment on new enterprises, investment on expansion, reconstruction, and technological transformation of existing enterprises, and current capital. However, formulas 18.61.1 and 18.61.2 neglect the time lag issue in investment result. If the investment result is set to begin after a certain number of years, the economic effect coefficient of the capital utilization should be calculated with the following formulas:

$$x_t = \frac{\sum \Delta(J_g - c)}{\sum \Delta T(1 + X_t)^{nk}} \tag{18.62.1}$$

$$\text{or} \quad x_t = \frac{\sum \Delta(J_g - c_u)}{\sum \Delta T(1 + X_t)^{nk}} \tag{18.62.2}$$

The above formulas are derived in this way. Suppose an investment ΔT begins to yield economic returns after its construction period n_k. If the investment is required to yield economic returns in the year when it begins, it must begin n_k years ahead. Accordingly, the investment that yields economic returns at the beginning year is not ΔT any longer. Instead, it should be $\Delta T\,(1 + x_t)^{nk}$. Therefore, the economic effect coefficient of the capital utilization should be calculated with Formula 18.62.1 and 18.62.2.

2. Calculation method for economic effect standard coefficient of capital utilization

The economic effect coefficient of capital utilization varies across regions, sectors, firms, and schemes because of different situations. What economic effect coefficient of capital utilization should be adopted in the macro technological economy as the standard coefficient? Next, three methods for calculating the standard economic effect coefficient of capital utilization based on short-term effect are introduced.

(1) General method

As discussed before, the economic effect coefficient of capital utilization is adopted for the purpose of considering the impact of the capital occupied by technological schemes in the economy when capital is not abundant. Thus, the calculation for the coefficient should first identify whose capital utilization and economic effects are influenced by the capital occupation of technological schemes. For instance, technological scheme *A* occupies more capital than technological scheme *B*. It impacts the investment and economic effect of technological scheme $B\ x_{t\text{-}b}$. Therefore, the standard coefficient x_{tb} should be $x_{t\text{-}b}$. Standard economic effect coefficients of capital utilization in other situations can be achieved by parity of reasoning.

(2) Balance method

Suppose the available capital is $T_{\sum}$. There are i schemes that will utilize the capital. The first scheme needs to occupy capital T_1. The economic effect generated by the occupied capital per unit is x_{t1}. The second scheme needs to occupy capital T_2. The economic effect generated by the occupied capital per unit is x_{t2}…… The i scheme needs to occupy capital T_i. The economic effect generated by the occupied capital per unit is x_{ti}. Set $x_{t1} > x_{t2} > x_{t3......} > x_{ti}$. Then capital $T_{\sum}$ can be allocated, based on the social additional net income rate or the additional national income rate. Figure 18.1 shows that the limited capital can only meet the requirements of the first and the second schemes. No capital will be available for the third scheme or later schemes. In the process of calculating the standard economic effect coefficient of capital utilization x_{tb} for each scheme in the macro technological economy, the following factors should be considered. Because the first and the second schemes occupy capital, no capital is available for the third and the fourth schemes. This causes loss x_{t3} and x_{t4}. The average loss is x_t ($x_t = \frac{x_{t3}T_{3+}x_{t4}T_4}{T_{\sum}}$, suppose $T_{\sum} = T_3 + T_4 = T_1 + T_2$). Thus, this average can be adopted as the standard economic effect coefficient of capital utilization x_{tb}. The standard coefficient can also choose the value of x_{t3} from a conservative perspective. If the third and the fourth schemes use capital $T_{\sum}$, the first and second schemes will not have capital to use. In this condition, the losses are x_{t1} and x_{t2}. Accordingly, the standard economic effect coefficient of capital utilization x_{tb} should choose the value of x_{t2} (when $T_{\sum} \leq T_2$) or the average $x_t = \frac{x_{t1}T_{1+}x_{t2}T_2}{T_{\sum}}$ (when $T_{\sum} = T_1 + T_2$). Standard economic effect coefficients of capital utilization for other schemes can be achieved by parity of reasoning. The standard coefficients achieved by balance method are relatively precise.

(3) National comprehensive balance method

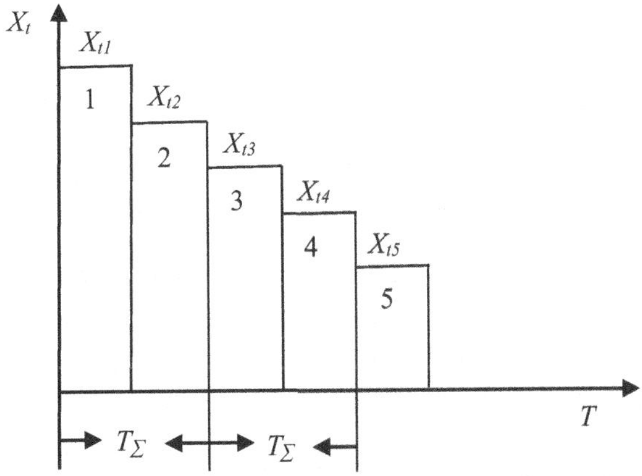

Fig. 18.1 Calculation method for the standard economic effect coefficient of capital utilization

As we know, the national economy is an organic whole in which sectors are closely connected. The capital occupied by a technological scheme is but one part in the whole investment in national economy. The economic impact of a technological scheme affects the whole national economy, not just a certain sector, or other schemes. As such, the standard economic effect coefficient of capital utilization should be calculated from a national comprehensive perspective. Here is the formula.

$$x_{tb} = \frac{\sum_{i=1}^{n} x_{ti} \Delta T_t}{\sum_{i=1}^{n} \Delta T_i} \tag{18.63}$$

In this formula, ΔT_i and x_{ti} are the economic effect coefficients of investment and capital utilization in sector i respectively, and n is the number of sectors in national economy.

The national average economic effect coefficient of capital utilization achieved by using the third method is the best option for calculating the standard coefficient.[4] This coefficient can be adopted for technological economic calculation in each sector in the national economy. Some people argue that different coefficients should be adopted for different sectors, in practice. But the research conducted by the author in the 1960s proves that a standard coefficient must be adopted for all sectors. Otherwise, errors will occur. Here are three reasons. First, capital invested in national economic construction must meet the requirements of developing the national economy in proportion, regardless of the resources, the state, the groups, or individuals. Blind investments for the benefit of a certain sector, firm, or group should be avoided. The impact on the national economy as a whole must be considered. Second, it is necessary to adopt a standard coefficient for motivating sectors and allocating benefits. Third, if the economic effect coefficient of capital utilization in a certain sector is adopted for calculating the economic effect of investment in all sectors, a coefficient similar to the average coefficient of all sectors is adopted, indeed, for the total investment.

3. Calculation method for economic effect standard coefficient of capital utilization in China

China should adopt the standard economic effect coefficient of capital utilization. Because this coefficient is used for comparing the impact on future capital occupation among technological schemes, it should be calculated based on the total amount of planned investment and the increased net income (national income). However, the total amount of planned investment and the increased net income (national income) are influenced by many factors, such as price, production technology, wages, the structure of the production sectors, and the economic situation in a country. It is very hard to get a precise standard coefficient beforehand. Thus, previous statistical data are usually used for calculating the standard coefficient in practice. When selecting previous data, the general years, not those having a specific economic situation, should be chosen. For instance, after analyzing the data from the first five-year

[4]It is also called social discount rate.

Table 18.7 Total investment on economic construction, investment on infrastructure, national net income, and national income during the first five-year plan in China. *Unit* RMB100 million Yuan

Year	Total investment on economic construction	National investment on infrastructure	National net income	National income
1952	76.3	43.6	155.0	653.5
1953	86.5	80.0	196.4	745.0
1954	123.6	90.7	231.8	788.2
1955	137.6	93.0	239.4	838.5
1956	159.1	148.0	275.1	956.8
1957	149.1	138.3	299.1	999.9

Source National Bureau of Statistics: "Great Decade", People's Publishing House, 1959

plan to the fifth five-year plan, the author thinks that data from the first five-year plan had better representativeness. Table 18.7 lists the total investment on economic construction, investment on infrastructure, national net income, and national income during the first five-year plan in China.

The data in Table 18.7 show that the accumulated total investment in the first five-year plan, including investment on infrastructure, technology innovation cost, technology transformation cost, equipment transformation cost, and current capital, is 65.59 billion Yuan. The national investment on infrastructure is 55 billion Yuan. The accumulated increased national net income is 14.41 billion Yuan. The accumulated increased national income is 34.8 billion Yuan. If the time lag for the investment effect is set as three years, the economic effect coefficient of national capital utilization during the first five-year plan can be calculated based on formula 18.62.1 and 18.62.2.

If it is calculated based on the national total investment, $x_t = 0.15$.
If it is calculated based on the national investment on infrastructure, $x_t = 0.16$.

It is more reasonable to calculate the coefficient based on the national total investment because the increment of the national net income or the national income in each year depends not only on the rise of the investment on infrastructure but also on the rise of investment on technology innovation, technology transformation, equipment transformation, and current capital. In other words, the increment relies on the rise of total investment on economic construction. However, the results achieved above are very close. Therefore, 0.15 can be used as the standard economic effect coefficient of national capital utilization. In the above calculation, the construction period is taken as three years. Accordingly, if the data of investment from 1953 to 1957 are chosen, the data of the national net income or the national income from 1956 to 1960 should be selected. But because the income data between 1958 and 1960 are not reliable, the income data of the first five-year plan are chosen instead. Obviously, these data are an approximation. Reevaluation must be done. Right now, some sectors suggest that 0.1 should be chosen as the social discount rate, which might be lower.

Last but not least, the literature that the author reviewed shows that a standard economic effect coefficient of national capital utilization was adopted for calculating the economic effect issued by Soviet Union in 1969 and 1980 and calculation methods (basic principles) for economic effect generated by new technologies, innovation, and rationalization proposals issued by Soviet Union in 1977. The former set the coefficient as 0.12, whereas the latter set the coefficient as 0.15, which is the same as the value that the author achieved in 1960s, based on the situation of China.

18.5.2 Calculation Methods for the Standard Economic Effect Efficient of Material Utilization

1. Calculation method for economic effect coefficient of material utilization

The economic effect coefficient of material utilization refers to the size of economic effect generated by a certain unit of material when production requirements are met. It represents the impact of the material utilized by technological schemes on the sectors in national economy, namely the increased/decreased social consumption cost or the net income (national income). This coefficient is closely related to the condition of supply and demand. Just as with the economic effect coefficient of capital utilization, there are two methods for calculating the economic effect coefficient of material utilization.

(1) Average index calculation

(1) Short-term effect

$$x_w = \frac{J_g - C}{W} \tag{18.64.1}$$

$$or \quad x_w = \frac{J_g - C_u}{W} \text{ Yuan/Ton} \tag{18.64.2}$$

(2) Opportunity effect

$$x_w = \frac{E_{cw}}{W} \tag{18.65.1}$$

$$or \quad x_w = \frac{E_{dw}}{W} \text{ Yuan/Ton} \tag{18.65.2}$$

In the above formulas,

$$E_{cw} = T_g - C - x_t T_z - x_y Y - x_r R - x_d D_z \tag{18.65.3}$$

$$E_{dw} = T_g - C_u - x_t T_z - x_y Y - x_r R - x_d D_z \tag{18.65.4}$$

(3) Long-term effect

$$x_w = \frac{(j_{w\text{-}privilege} - j_w)W}{W} = j_{w\text{-}privilege} - j_w \text{ Yuan/Ton} \tag{18.66}$$

In this formula, $j_{w\text{-}privilege}$ is the privileged price of material and j_w is the rational price of material.

(2) Increment index calculation

(1) Short-term effect

$$x_w = \frac{\Delta(J_g - c)}{\Delta w}, x_w = \frac{\partial(J_g - c)}{\partial w} \tag{18.67.1}$$

$$or \quad x_w = \frac{\Delta(J_g - c_u)}{\Delta w}, x_w = \frac{\partial(J_g - c_u)}{\partial w} \text{ Yuan / Ton} \tag{18.67.2}$$

(2) Opportunity effect

$$x_w = \frac{\Delta E_{cw}}{\Delta w}, \quad x_w = \frac{\partial E_{cw}}{\partial w} \tag{18.68.1}$$

$$or \quad x_w = \frac{\Delta E_{dw}}{\Delta w}, \quad x_w = \frac{\partial E_{dw}}{\partial w} \text{ Yuan/Ton} \tag{18.59.2}$$

(3) Long-term effect

$$x_w = \frac{\Delta(j_w - privilege - j_w)W}{\Delta w} \tag{18.69.1}$$

$$x_w = \frac{\partial(j_w - privilege - j_w)w}{\partial W} \text{ Yuan / Ton} \tag{18.69.2}$$

2. Calculation method for economic effect standard coefficient of material utilization

The economic effect coefficient of material utilization can be calculated with a general method, a balance method, or a national comprehensive balance method. These methods are discussed in details early in this chapter. Which method should be adopted depends on the actual situation.

3. Calculating economic effect standard coefficient of material utilization

There are many materials in a given country. Each of them has an economic effect coefficient of material utilization. In practice, only the coefficients of some main materials are adopted. Next, the economic effect coefficient of energy utilization will be discussed in detail. Every sector in the national economy needs energy. The energy supply does not merely impact some sectors, but it affects the whole national economy. Thus, the national comprehensive balance method is used for calculating the standard economic effect coefficient of energy utilization. Table 18.8 lists the standard economic effect coefficients of energy utilization based on short-term effects from 1953 to 1980 in China.

Some of the coefficients in Table 18.8 are calculated with average index method, while others are calculated with increment index method. Because the consumption of energy by new technological schemes influences the energy supply of new construction projects and existing firms, the results achieved with the increment index method are more reasonable. This is different from the reasonable method for calculating the standard economic effect coefficients of capital utilization. The energy production in China was expected to double in 2000, whereas the economy was expected to quadruple. Therefore, the economic effect generated by energy per ton needed to double by 2000. This requirement must be considered in the calculation of standard coefficients in the macro technological economy. In this era, the

Table 18.8 The standard economic effect coefficients of energy utilization based on short-term effect (1953–1980)

Period (year)	1953–1957	1958–1962	1963–1965	1966–1970	1971–1975	1976–1980
$x_{w\text{-}energy} = \frac{\sum \Delta(J_g - C)}{\sum \Delta W_{energy}}$	304	13	685	186	90	133
$x_{w\text{-}energy} = \frac{\sum (J_g - C)}{\sum W_{energy}}$	339	206	234	228	198	171
$x_{w\text{-}energy} = \frac{\sum \Delta(J_g - C_u)}{\sum \Delta W_{energy}}$	732	/	1856	614	367	582
$x_{w\text{-}energy} = \frac{\sum (J_g - C_u)}{\sum W_{energy}}$	1176	513	649	714	580	532
$x_{w\text{-}power} = \frac{\sum \Delta(J_g - C)}{\sum \Delta W_{power}}$	1.2	0.03	0.74	0.40	0.18	0.19
$x_{w\text{-}power} = \frac{\sum (J_g - C)}{\sum W_{power}}$	1.8	1.03	0.70	0.57	0.47	0.37
$x_{w\text{-}power} = \frac{\sum \Delta(J_g - C_u)}{\sum \Delta W_{power}}$	2.89	Negative	2.0	1.31	0.74	0.83
$x_{w\text{-}power} = \frac{\sum (J_g - C_u)}{\sum W_{power}}$	6.33	2.52	1.94	1.75	1.38	1.15

Note The unit of $x_{w\text{-}energy}$ is Yuan/ton of standard coal. The unit of $x_{w\text{-}power}$ is Yuan/kwh

Table 18.9 Standard economic effect coefficients for heavy oil and natural gas

Serial number	Uses	$x_{w\text{-}heavyoil}$(Yuan/ton)	$x_{w\text{-}naturalga}$(Yuan/ kilostere)
1	Raw chemical materials	150–260	100–200
2	Civilian uses	76	85–170
3	Oil-fired boilers/kilns	30–60	35–94
4	Substitute of tar in metallurgy	50	35–60
5	Small boilers below 2 ton/h and locomotive boilers	9–17	30–38
6	Coal-fired boilers	5–10	10–20
7	Medium-size boilers above 4 ton/h	~5	7
8	Down-draught kilns	~1	3
9	Power plant boilers	2–3	7

Note The standard economic effect coefficients for heavy oil and natural gas are calculated by comparing with coal

standard economic effect coefficients of energy utilization $x_{w\text{-}energy}$ could be set as 200 Yuan per ton of standard coal (based on net income), or 600 Yuan per ton of standard coal (based on national income). The standard economic effect coefficients of power utilization $x_{w\text{-}power}$ can be set as 0.5 Yuan per kwh (based on net income), or 1.5 Yuan per kwh (based on national income). Sometimes, energy supply varies across regions. In this case, the regional standard economic effect coefficients of energy utilization can be adopted. Generally speaking, the standard economic effect coefficients of energy utilization are suggested to be adopted across a country.

Next, let us discuss the calculation of the standard economic effect coefficients for heavy oil and natural gas. Table 18.9 lists the standard economic effect coefficients for heavy oil and natural gas based on the opportunity effect of uses with the method of the social additional net income rate. Heavy oil is suitable for uses 1–4. It is a reasonable option for uses 5–9. For users who have oil-fired boilers or oil-fired kilns, the fourth use is their critical use (which non-Chinese scholars call marginal use). The standard economic effect coefficients for heavy oil and natural gas can be set as 50–70 Yuan per ton of oil and 50–70 Yuan/per kilostere of gas.

18.5.3 Calculation Methods for the Standard Economic Effect Coefficient of Transportation Utilization

The economic effect coefficient of transportation utilization refers to the size of the economic effect generated by a certain unit of transportation when production requirements are met. It represents the impact of the transportation utilized by technological schemes on the sectors in national economy, namely the increased/decreased social consumption cost or the net income (national income). This coefficient is closely related to the condition of transportation supply and demand.

(1) Average index calculation

(1) Short-term effect. Transportation bridges production and consumption. Lack of transport capacity affects production and consumption. On the one hand, firms producing materials suffer the shortage of transportation. On the other hand, firms and or consumers using the materials have limited access to the produced materials.

$$x_y = \frac{J_g - C}{w} = \frac{J_{g\text{-}production} - C_{production}}{Y} + \frac{J_{g\text{-}use} - C_{use}}{Y} = x_{W\text{-}production} + x_w \tag{18.70.1}$$

$$\text{or } x_y = \frac{J_g - C_u}{W} = \frac{J_{g\text{-}production} - C_{u-production}}{Y} + \frac{J_{g\text{-}use} - C_{use}}{Y} = x_{w\text{-}production} + x_w \tag{18.70.2}$$

In the above formulas, $x_{w\text{-}production}$ is the economic effect coefficient of material production. x_w is the economic effect coefficient of material utilization.

(2) Opportunity effect

$$x_y = \frac{E_{cy}}{y} = \frac{E_{cy\text{-}production}}{Y} + \frac{E_{cy\text{-}use}}{Y} = x_{w\text{-}production} + x_w \tag{18.71.1}$$

$$\text{or } x_y = \frac{E_{dy}}{Y} = \frac{E_{dy\text{-}production}}{Y} + \frac{E_{dy\text{-}use}}{Y} = x_{x-production} + x_w \tag{18.71.2}$$

In the above formulas,

$$E_{cy} = J - C - x_t T_z - x_w W - x_r R - x_d D_z \tag{18.71.3}$$

$$E_{dy} = J - C_u - x_t T_z - x_w W - x_r R - x_d D_z \tag{18.71.4}$$

(3) Long-term effect

$$x_y = \frac{(j_{y\text{-}privilege-j_y})Y}{Y} = j_{y\text{-}privilege} - j_y \tag{18.72}$$

In this formula, $j_{y\text{-}privilege}$ is the privileged price of transpiration and j_y is the rational price of transportation.

Table 18.10 The economic effect coefficients of transportation utilization in China(1953–1980)

Period (year)	1953–1957	1958–1962	1963–1965	1966–1970	1971–1975	1976–1980
x_y, Yuan/ton-kilometer (based on net income)	0.18	0.16	0.14	0.14	0.13	0.10
x_y, Yuan/ton-kilometer (based on national income)	0.63	0.39	0.39	0.42	0.37	0.31

(2) Increment index calculation

The three-effect increment index calculation methods for the economic effect coefficient of transportation utilization are the same as those for capital utilization and material utilization.

It can be seen from the above formulas that the economic effect coefficient of transportation utilization x_y is actually the sum of the economic effect coefficients of material production and material utilization. For instance, the economic effect coefficient of transportation utilization x_y for the outward transport in Shanxi province is 178 Yuan/ton, in which $x_{w\text{-}production}$ is 35 Yuan/ton. x_w is 143 Yuan/ton. Sometimes the economic effect coefficients of material production $x_{w\text{-}production}$ are neglected for the purpose of simplicity. As a result, the economic effect coefficient of transportation utilization is equal to the economic effect coefficients of material utilization.

Because the calculation methods for the economic effect coefficients of material utilization were introduced early in this chapter, the calculation methods for the economic effect coefficients of transportation utilization are not discussed repeatedly here. Table 18.10 lists the economic effect coefficients of transportation utilization based on short-term effect.

18.5.4 Calculation Methods for the Standard Economic Effect Coefficient of Labor Utilization

Labor utilization is the use of manpower. Labor utilization generates an economic effect when other production requirements are met. The amount of economic effect generated by one unit of labor is the economic effect coefficient of labor utilization. This coefficient represents the impact of one unit of labor utilized by the technological schemes on the sectors in the national economy, namely the increased/decreased social consumption cost or the net income (national income). It is determined by the labor supply and demand.

(1) Average index calculation

(1) Short-term effect.

$$x_r = \frac{J_g - C}{R} \tag{18.73.1}$$

$$or \quad x_t = \frac{J_g - C_u}{T} \tag{18.73.2}$$

(2) Opportunity effect

$$x_r = \frac{E_{cr}}{W} \tag{18.74.1}$$

$$\text{or} \quad x_r = \frac{E_{dr}}{W} \tag{18.74.2}$$

In the above formulas,

$$E_{cr} = J_g - C - x_t T_z - x_w W - x_y Y - x_d D_z \tag{18.74.3}$$

$$E_{dr} = J_g - C_u - x_t T_z - x_y Y - x_r R - x_d D_z \tag{18.74.4}$$

(3) Long-term effect

$$x_r = \frac{(1 + x_{gf}) v_{long} R - (1 + x_{gf}) v R}{R} = (1 + x_{gf})(v_{long} - v) \tag{18.75}$$

In this formula, v_{long} is the wage of long-term personnel and v is the rational wage. v_{long} of job-waiting youth is zero.

(2) Increment index calculation

The three-effect increment index calculation methods for economic effect coefficient of labor utilization are the same as those for capital utilization and material utilization.

The economic effect coefficient of labor utilization is closely related with the number of laborers, the technology level, the usage of labor, the types of labor, and the natural conditions in labor area. In addition, income varies across regions. The coefficient can be calculated with the general method, the balance method, and the national comprehensive balance method. Tables 18.11, 18.12 and 18.13 list the national economic effect coefficients of labor utilization, the national agricultural economic

Table 18.11 The national economic effect coefficients of labor utilization in China (1953–1980)

Period (year)	1953–1957	1958–1962	1963–1965	1966–1970	1971–1975	1976–1980
x_r, Yuan/person year (based on net income)	110	176	144	156	211	236
x_y, Yuan/person year (based on national income)	384	431	365	480	615	726

Table 18.12 The national agricultural economic effect coefficients of labor utilization in China (1957–1980)

Period (year)	1957	1965	1975	1980
$x_{r\text{-}agriculture}$, Yuan/person year (based on net income)	30	33	47	47
$x_{y\text{-}agriculture}$, Yuan/person year (based on national income)	140 (347)	163 (293)	208 (320)	271 (355)

Note The calculation is based on the data from the national rural collective basic accounting units. The values in parentheses are national agricultural data. The figures in the tables are based on the national rural collective as the basic accounting unit and those in brackets are national agriculture data

Table 18.13 The national non-agricultural economic effect coefficients of labor utilization in China (1953–1980)

Period (year)	1953–1957	1958–1962	1963–1965	1966–1970	1971–1975	1976–1980
$x_{r\text{-}non\text{-}agriculture}$, Yuan/person year (based on net income)	552	530	757	768	947	857
$x_{y\text{-}non\text{-}agriculture}$, Yuan/person year (based on national income)	650	749	1020	1320	1806	1860

effect coefficients of labor utilization, and the national non-agricultural economic effect coefficients of labor utilization, respectively, in China. These coefficients are all calculated based on short-term effect.

The economic effect coefficients listed above are all calculated based on year. If the time base is changed to hour, the coefficients of labor utilization become the coefficients of time utilization. Tables 18.14 and 18.15 list the economic effect coefficient of time utilization per hour regarding all of the labor force in China and the economic effect coefficient of time utilization per hour regarding all non-agricultural workers in China. These coefficients can be used for evaluating the economic benefits of saved time and the costs of wasted time in transportation, post and telecommunications, and other labor service sectors.

Table 18.14 The economic effect coefficient of time utilization per hour about all labor force in China (1953–1980)

Period (year)	1953–1957	1958–1962	1963–1965	1966–1970	1971–1975	1976–1980
x_s, Yuan/person year (based on net income)	0.05	0.07	0.06	0.065	0.09	0.10
x_s, Yuan/person year (based on national income)	0.16	0.18	0.16	0.20	0.26	0.30
x_s, Yuan/person year (based on wage)	0.11	0.11	0.10	0.135	0.17	0.20

Table 18.15 the economic effect coefficient of time utilization per hour about all non-agricultural workers in China (1953–1980)

Period (year)	1953–1957	1958–1962	1963–1965	1966–1970	1971–1975	1976–1980
x_s, Yuan/person year (based on net income)	0.23	0.22	0.32	0.32	0.39	0.36
x_s, Yuan/person year (based on national income)	0.27	0.31	0.43	0.55	0.75	0.78
x_s, Yuan/person year (based on wage)	0.04	0.09	0.11	0.23	0.36	0.42

18.5.5 Calculation Methods for the Standard Economic Effect Coefficient of Natural Resources Utilization

Natural resources include land, rivers, lakes, territorial waters, springs, groundwater, air, living creatures, energy, and minerals. Natural resources were thought to be abundant. Because air, water, and land are everywhere, it was thought that the utilization of natural resources by technological schemes did not impact sectors in national economy. However, things are changing in some areas. For example, because Shanxi province is short of water, any usage of water in Shanxi province will impact other sectors. Eventually, the whole national economy will be affected. More specifically, the usage of water in one province will influence the usage of water in another province. The usage of water in upriver areas will influence the usage of water in downriver areas. Pumping water from deep wells will affect pumping water from shallow wells. Water leakage in coal mining will cause water shortage in surrounding areas. Waste water will pollute clean water. These examples prove the influence of water utilization on national economy. Air utilization has the same problems. Polluted air will damage the development of the national economy as it requires a huge amount of effort and resources to purify the air. Thus, the impact of air utilization on the national economy must be considered. In terms of minerals, the same consideration is required. For instance, although Shanxi province has abundant coal reserves, the impact of mineral utilization on the national economy still exists. When firm *A* exploits coal in a certain area, firm *B* will impact firm A if it exploits the same area. China has a large population, which generates huge pressure on land use. When a technological scheme utilizes land, it affects the whole economy, eventually. Accordingly, the impact of land on the national economy must be taken into consideration. The economic effect coefficient of natural resources utilization is used to measure the impact. If a technological scheme can save and protect natural resources, it has direct and indirect economic benefits. The calculation of indirect economic benefits relies on the economic effect coefficient of natural resources utilization.

The economic effect coefficient of natural resources utilization refers to the amount of economic benefit generated by the usage, per unit, of natural resources. This coefficient represents the impact of one unit of natural resources utilized by technological schemes on the sectors in national economy, namely the increased/decreased social consumption cost or the net income (national income). The calculation methods for the economic effect coefficient of natural resources utilization are the same as those for the economic effect coefficient of capital utilization.

(1) Average index calculation

(1) Short-term effect.

$$x_d = \frac{J_g - C}{D} \tag{18.76.1}$$

$$or \quad x_d = \frac{J_g - C_u}{D} \tag{18.76.2}$$

(2) Opportunity effect

$$x_d = \frac{E_{cd}}{D} \tag{18.77.1}$$

$$\text{or} \quad x_d = \frac{E_{dd}}{D} \tag{18.77.2}$$

In the above formulas,

$$E_{cd} = J_g - C - x_t T_z - x_w W - x_y Y - x_d D_z \tag{18.77.3}$$

$$E_{dd} = J_g - C_u - x_t T_z - x_y Y - x_r R - x_d D_z \quad (18.77.4)$$

(3) Long-term effect

$$x_d = \frac{(j_{d-privilege} - j_d)D}{D} = j_{d-privilege} - jd \quad (18.78)$$

In this formula, $j_{d\text{-}privilege}$ is the privileged price of natural resources and j_d is the rational price of natural resources.

(2) Increment index calculation

The three-effect increment index calculation methods for the economic effect coefficient of natural resources utilization are the same as those for capital utilization and material utilization.

The economic effect standard coefficient of natural resources utilization can be calculated with the general method, the balance method, or the national comprehensive balance method. Tables 18.16 and 18.17 list the coefficients of natural resources utilization calculated based on short-term effect.

The economic effect coefficients of land utilization vary across regions in China. Specific situations in each area should be taken into consideration in the calculation of the coefficients. For instance, the economic effect coefficient of land utilization per mu in Shanghai is higher than the coefficients in other regions. Sometimes, because technological schemes occupy more land, industry, business, and tourism, industries cannot develop due to the limited land supply. Net income and national income in these industries are negatively impacted. In this case, land occupation cost $x_d D$ must

Table 18.16 The economic effect coefficients of agricultural land utilization in China (1957–1980)

Period (year)	1957	1965	1975	1980
$x_{d\text{-}agriculture}$, Yuan/mu year (based on net income)	3.5	5.0	9.2	9.6
$x_{d\text{-}agriculture}$, Yuan/mu year (based on national income)	16 (40)	25 (44)	41 (63)	55 (72)

Table 18.17 The economic effect coefficients of land utilization in China (1953–1980)

Period (year)	1953–1957	1958–1962	1963–1965	1966–1970	1971–1975	1976–1980
$x_{d\text{-}land}$, Yuan/mu year (based on net income)	15	29	26	33	52	64
$x_{d\text{-}land}$, Yuan/mu year (based on national income)	52	72	72	100	150	196

be calculated based on the economic effect coefficients of land utilization in these industries.

18.5.6 The Relationship Among the Economic Effect Coefficients

The economic effect S_c of technological schemes (net income or national income) is the result of the integration of manpower, capital power, material force, transport capacity, and natural force input during a certain time period. Transport capacity is determined by material force. To simplify the formula, transport capacity and material force are both represented by W. We can get the following formula:

$$S_c = f\,(W,\ R,\ T,\ D) = x_w W + x_r R + x_t T + x_d D \tag{18.79}$$

Next, let us discuss some special cases to know better how each factor affects the economic effects. When a certain raw material or energy W is in short supply, technological schemes cannot be carried out due to the lack of raw material or energy. In this case, the economic effect is zero and other factors (R, T, D) do not function. If supply of the raw material or energy W is abundant, technological schemes will generate economic effects S_c. Therefore,

$$x_w = \frac{S_c}{W}$$

In a similar way, we can get $x_r = \frac{S_c}{R}$, $x_t = \frac{S_c}{T}$, $x_d = \frac{S_c}{D}$.

These are the economic effect coefficients of the short-term effect.

Now, let us discuss the roles that the factors play under normal circumstances. The formula 18.79 is a general one, in which x_w, x_r, x_t, and x_d are interconnected and are mutually replaceable. In addition, these coefficients are variables, which can change with many factors, including time. Thus, it is very hard to get the economic effect coefficients of the opportunity effect. Sometimes, the total economic effect S_c of technological schemes is allocated to W, R, T, and D in definite proportions. When the size of S_c is fixed, the value of each economic effect coefficient can change between a minimum (zero) and a maximum $(S_c/W,\ S_c/R,\ S_c/T,\ S_c/D)$. Here is the formula:

$$0 \le x_w \le \frac{S_c}{W},\quad 0 \le x_r \le \frac{S_c}{R},\quad 0 \le x_t \le \frac{S_c}{T},\quad 0 \le x_d \le \frac{S_c}{D}$$

It can be seen that the economic effect coefficients in macro technological calculation are actually some practical values selected in the above ranges.

18.5.7 Other Calculation Methods for Economic Effect Coefficients

Some complicated mathematical methods can be applied to calculate economic effect coefficients based on opportunity effect.

1. Production function method

The production function method can be applied to calculate several economic effect coefficients. The commonly used production function is rgw Cobb-Douglas Production Function. Here is its formula:

$$S_c = f(W, R, T, D) = AW^a R^b T^c D^d \tag{18.80}$$

In this formula, *a, b, c,* and *d* represent the economic effect increase coefficients of material utilization, labor utilization, capital utilization, and natural resources utilization, respectively. *A* is a constant.

$$a = \frac{\frac{\Delta S_C}{S_C}}{\frac{\Delta W}{W}}, \quad b = \frac{\frac{\Delta S_C}{S_C}}{\frac{\Delta R}{R}}, \quad c = \frac{\frac{\Delta S_C}{S_C}}{\frac{\Delta T}{T}}, \quad d = \frac{\frac{\Delta S_C}{S_C}}{\frac{\Delta D}{D}}$$

Based on the data of previous years, regression can be applied to get the values of *a, b, c, d,* and *A*. Next, the economic utilization coefficients under each circumstance with other conditions unchanged can be achieved by conducting partial differential on formula 18.80.

$$x_w = \frac{\partial S_C}{\partial W} = a\frac{S_C}{W} = \frac{\frac{\Delta S_C}{S_C}}{\frac{\Delta W}{W}} \times \frac{S_C}{W} = \frac{\Delta S_C}{\Delta W} \tag{18.81}$$

$$x_r = \frac{\partial S_C}{\partial R} = b\frac{S_C}{R} = \frac{\frac{\Delta S_C}{S_C}}{\frac{\Delta R}{R}} \times \frac{S_C}{R} = \frac{\Delta S_C}{\Delta R} \tag{18.82}$$

$$x_t = \frac{\partial s_c}{\partial T} = c\frac{S_C}{T} = \frac{\frac{\Delta S_C}{S_C}}{\frac{\Delta T}{T}} \times \frac{S_C}{T} = \frac{\Delta S_C}{\Delta T} \tag{18.83}$$

$$x_d = \frac{\partial S_C}{\partial D} = d\frac{S_C}{D} = \frac{\frac{\Delta S_C}{S_C}}{\frac{\Delta D}{D}} \times \frac{S_C}{D} = \frac{\Delta S_C}{\Delta D} \tag{18.84}$$

2. Linear dual programming method

For any linear programming problem in seeking the maximum of an objective function, there is a symmetric linear programming problem in seeking the minimum of an objective function, and vice versa. The original linear programming problem is called the original plan. Its dual linear programming problem is called the dual program.

The economic effect coefficients can be achieved by resolving the dual program. Here is an example.

Suppose that there are eight units of labor and three units of capital. They are occupied by two technological schemes. What will be the outputs of these two technological schemes G_1 and G_2 be when the economic effect is the largest? What are the economic effect coefficients of utilization for each production condition?

(1) The linear programming model based on the information in the problem.

Find Max $S_c = 3.5G_1 + 2.5G_2$

$$\text{The constraint conditions are} \begin{cases} G_1 + G_2 \le 3T \\ 4G_1 + 2G_2 \le 8R \\ G_1, G_2 \ge 0 \end{cases}$$

(2) Find the dual program.

The coefficients for the variables and constants in the original plan are listed below.

	G_1	G_2	
T	1	1	3
R	4	2	8
	3.5	2.5	

Rotate the above Table 90° counter clockwise and a new table can be achieved.

	3	8	
G_1	1	2	2.5
G_2	1	4	3.5
	T	R	

The dual program can be achieved based on the new table.
Find Min $Z = 3x_t + 8x_r$

$$\text{The constraint conditions are} \begin{cases} x_t + 2x_r \ge 2.5 \\ x_t + 4x_r \ge 3.5 \\ x_t, x_r \ge 0 \end{cases}$$

This dual program is symmetrical to the original plan, as shown in Table 18.18.

(3) Solve the original plan and the dual program

The original plan and the dual program can be solved with simplex method. Once either of them is solved, the other one will be solved. The solution for the original plan is that when the economic effect is the largest ($S_c = 8.5$), $G_1 = 1$ and $G_2 = 2$. The solution for the original plan is $x_t = 1.5$ and $x_r = 0.5$.

Table 18.18 The dual program and the original plan

Product / Production conditions value	G_1	G_2	The number of production conditions
x_t	1	1	≤3
x_r	4	2	≤8
Net income per unit of product	≥3.5	≥2.5	Min Z
			MaxS_c

3. Input-output analysis method

The input in the national economy yields both net income and national income. Analyzing input and output can find the impact of the changes of input on output. In other words, economic effect coefficients can be achieved with an input-output analysis method. Just as with the linear dual programming method, the input-output analysis method requires a huge amount of data. Furthermore, the mathematic computation is rather complicated and computers are required to conduct the computation.

In recent years, China began to adopt a production function and a linear plan (including input and output) to calculate economic effect coefficients. Strong achievements has been made.[5] First, by following the homogeneous function, the data from 1962 to 1982 in China was processed as samples, which are loaded in computers. Linear regression can be performed with ordinary least square procedure (i.e., *OLS* program). The regression equation for production function is:

$$S_{c-nation} = 0.00051T^{0.54}R^{1.03}$$

$$\therefore c = 0.54$$

$$x_{\rm tg} = c\frac{S_{\text{c-nation}}}{T} = 0.54\frac{S_{\text{c-nation}}}{T} = 0.24 \text{ Yuan/Yuan} \cdot \text{year}$$

Based on the above equation, the economic effect coefficient of capital utilization $x_{\rm tg}$ from 1978 to 1982 in China can be calculated and the result is 0.24. Run regression based on the relationship between net income and national income from 1953 to 1980 in China and get $\frac{\partial S_{\text{c-netincome}}}{\partial S_{\text{c-nationalincome}}} = 0.34$.Thus, the economic effect coefficient of capital utilization x_{tc} can be achieved.

$$x_{tc} = \frac{\partial S_{\text{c-netincome}}}{\partial S_{\text{c-nationalincome}}} \times x_{tg} = 0.34 \times 0.24 = 0.08 \text{ Yuan/Yuan} \cdot \text{year}$$

[5]Zhu [Zh84].

Next, using linear regression, refer to the national production input and output table in 1979 in China made by the Industry Economy Institute at the Chinese Academy of Social Sciences, and load the data into computer. The economic effect coefficient of capital utilization in 1980 can be achieved.

$$x_{tg} = 0.33 \text{ Yuan/Yuan} \cdot \text{year}, x_{tc} = 0.12 \text{ Yuan/Yuan} \cdot \text{year}$$

Compare these two methods and we can find that the production function method only represents the values of previous status and current status. The values might not be optimal. In contrast, the linear dual programming method generates the optimal values, which are bigger than those generated by production function method. In practice, values can be selected from a range.

$$x_{tg} = 0.24 - 0.33 \text{ Yuan/Yuan} \cdot \text{year}, x_{tc} = 0.08 - 0.12 \text{ Yuan/Yuan} \cdot \text{year}$$

18.6 Calculation Methods for Tax Rate and Interest Rate

18.6.1 Calculation Method of Tax Rate

Five indirect costs are discussed in previous chapters, including the cost of capital occupation C_r, the cost of labor occupation (cost of using labor) C_R, the cost of material consumption C_w, the cost of using natural resources C_D, and the cost of transport occupation C_Y. In addition, five economic effect coefficients are discussed, as well. These parameters are useful in evaluating the national economy precisely. But in fact, they are not connected directly with practice. Therefore, they are easily neglected by firms and sectors when they calculate the micro economic effect. In order to fix this issue, the author argues that other than price, tax should be adopted in calculation. For example, the cost of capital occupation can be replaced by the tax of capital occupation (capital tax). The cost of labor occupation can be replaced by the tax of labor occupation (labor tax). The cost of material consumption can be replaced by the tax of material consumption (material tax). The cost of using natural resources can be replaced by the tax of using natural resources (resource tax or environment tax).The cost of transport occupation can be replaced by the tax of transport occupation (transportation tax). Some of these taxes are under enforcement and others are not. Usually, tax is not considered individually in a macro technological economic calculation, because tax and profit are both net income and they are combined in the calculations. However, tax is a type of cost in a micro technological economic calculation and it should be considered individually. Tax has two categories. The first category includes those taxes related with firms' input. The second category includes those taxes related with firms' output. Taxes in the first category are part of firms' costs, so they can be called cost taxes. The five taxes listed above are all cost taxes. Taxes in the second category are part of firms' income, so they can be called income taxes. Tax can be categorized in other ways. For instance, some taxes are related to firms' total income, such as industrial and commercial taxes, product taxes, value added taxes, sales taxes, agricultural taxes, animal husbandry taxes, salt taxes, local taxes, and tariffs. Some taxes are related with net income, such as income tax. Tax is a tool for adjusting an economy. Reasonable taxes promote the increase of economic benefits, whereas unreasonable taxes damage economic development. Thus, defining a reasonable tax rate is very important. This chapter discussed how to define the tax rate for the five taxes mentioned above. The indirect cost in macro technological economic calculation is caused by technological schemes. Capital, material, labor, transportation, and natural resources occupied by technological schemes could be used for other purposes. Because they are occupied by technological schemes, compensation should be provided. The compensation is called indirect cost, which is collected in the format of tax from the firms' net income. The amount of the collection is related with the tax rate. Tax rates for the five taxes mentioned above cannot be determined optionally. Instead, the tax rates should be determined based on the aforementioned economic effect standard coefficients. The reasonable tax rates for these five taxes are indeed the five standard economic effect coefficients. The practical tax rate for these five taxes should be smaller than or equal to the reasonable tax rates. In order to allocate the economic benefits in firms, sectors, and nations, some practical tax rates (i.e., scarce resource consumption taxes) can be the same as rational tax rates. Some practical tax rates (i.e., the capital occupation tax) should be lower than rational tax rates. In this way, a part of the net income (M) can be held by firms in the form of profit. China began collecting a special oil tax from July 01, 1982. As a kind of material consumption tax, it has two tax rates. One is 40–70 Yuan/ton for crude oil. The other is 70 Yuan/ton for heavy oil. These practical tax rates are close to the value of the economic effect coefficient of heavy oil utilization $x_{w\text{-}oil}$ suggested early in this chapter. Recently, a capital occupation tax is collected in China as well. The annual tax rate for fixed capital occupation is 9.6% and 2.5% for working capital. These tax rates are smaller than the economic effect coefficient of capital utilization x_t suggested early in this chapter. As mentioned before, the economic effect coefficient of land utilization $x_{d\text{-}land}$ varies across regions. Table 18.19 lists the tax rates of land utilization in the Shenzhen Special Zone. Table 18.20 lists the charge scale for environmental pollution (environmental tax rate) in some Chinese cities. At present, taxes for labor utilization and

Table 18.19 Tax rates of land utilization in Shenzhen Special Zone

Use of land	Tax rate (10,000 Yuan/mu year)
1. Commercial	4.67–13.3
2. Tourism and construction	4.0–6.7
3. Commercial residential	2.0–4.0
4. Industrial	0.67–2.0

Source Provisional Regulations on Land Management in Shenzhen Special Economic Zone, 1982 China Economic Yearbook

Table 18.20 Charge scale for environment pollution (environmental tax rate) in some Chinese cities

Cities	Wastewater (Yuan/ton)			Exhaust gas (Yuan/ton)		Waste Residue (Yuan/ton)	
	Heavy metals	Poisonous and Harmful	Paper making, Virus, and Others	Coal burning	Oil burning	Harmless	Harmful
Suzhou	0.20	0.20	0.05	5.0	10.0	/	/
Nanjing	0.20	0.15	0.15	5.0	10.0	1.0	100.0
Xuzhou	0.15	0.10	/	2.0	5.0	1.0	/
Wuxi	/	0.20	0.10	/	/	/	/
Nantong	0.20	0.10	0.05	5.0	10.0	0.30	/

Source Environmental Management, National Environmental Management, Economics and Law Society. Shanxi People's Publishing House, 1981

taxes for transportation utilization are not collected, but they will be collected sooner or later. because these taxes will promote the flow and utilization of personnel and the development of transportation.

Macro technological economic calculation must adopt five economic effect standard coefficients, not practical tax rates. In practice, if practical tax rates are reasonable, then it is appropriate to adopt them. If practical tax rates are quite different from the standard coefficients, they should be adjusted. The methods for adjustment are those for calculating the five economic effect standard coefficients.

18.6.2 Determining Interest Rate

Calculation methods for the economic effect coefficient of capital utilization are discussed early in this chapter. Unlike the macro technological economy, micro technological economy does not adopt the economic effect coefficient of capital utilization to reflect the impacts of capital utilization and time factors. Instead, the methods for calculating the capital occupation tax and interest are adopted. In fact, the interest rate is a type of economic effect coefficient of capital utilization. It just adopts different values. When banks are owned by the state, the capital in banks is owned by the state as well. If firms do not get loans from banks, the capital in banks can be invested in national economic construction. As a result, the economic effect of capital will be achieved. Thus, the impact that the loans that firms borrow from banks have on the national economy is the economic effect coefficient of capital utilization, not the interest rate. Interest rates, whether loan interest rates or saving interest rates, should be smaller than the economic effect coefficient of capital utilization. If interest rates are higher than the economic effect coefficient of capital utilization, it is not profitable for banks to collect savings and to spend on construction. Similarly, it is not profitable for firms to borrow money from banks and spend on construction. Here, we focus on determining the maximum value of interest rate. The exact value of the interest rate is impacted by policies and benefits of diverse stakeholders. It is beyond the scope of the technological economy.

18.7 Calculation Methods for Inputs and Costs of Technological Schemes

The input and costs of technological schemes are not the same, but they are closely related. The input of technological schemes refers to the six resources or forces that are spent on technological schemes. The cost of technological schemes means the direct and indirect consumption that is caused by input and in monetary format. Next, the calculation methods for the input of capital, material, transportation, manpower, and natural forces and for cost are discussed in detail.

18.7.1 Calculation Method for Investment Occupation of Technological Schemes

Investment is a main input in technological schemes, especially in those capital-intensive technological schemes. Calculating the amount of investment can estimate the balance of investment, compare investments, calculate the depreciation cost of fixed assets, and calculate the economic impact of investment on national economic income. The investment (T) of technological schemes is different from the cost (C) of technological schemes. The former is the one time or several times input of technological schemes which occurred before final products were produced or the useful effects were created, and occupied for a long time in the process of production. The latter is the cost of the continuous consumption occurring in the process of production.

The investment of technological schemes includes fixed assets and current capital. The term fixed assets refers to the value of machines, equipment, tools, instruments, livestock, forestry, and so on. Current capital refers to the value of raw materials, materials, fuel, semi-finished products, works-in-process, and wages. In other words, current capital is the funding that are required for firms' stock, production, and sales. Fixed assets and current capital share some common characteristics, but they also have some unique ones. They both are occupied by technological schemes for long periods. Fixed assets can only be recouped when production completely stops or when the fixed assets are scrapped. Similarly, current capital can only be recouped when production or operation completely stops. However, the amount of investment occupation of fixed assets decreases yearly with the payback of the depreciation cost of fixed assets. In contrast, the amount of investment occupation of current capital remains unchanged if other conditions stay the same, because current capital does not need the payback of depreciation costs. The amount of current capital occupation is related to the raw materials, fuel, and spare parts required by production, the amount of wages, production time, and circulation time. The amount of fix assets occupation is related to the amount of investment on infrastructure construction. The capital spent on fixed assets is occupied during the infrastructure construction period before production begins, whereas current capital is not occupied until production begins. Set fixed assets as T_g and current capital as T_l. Here is the investment equation for technological schemes.

$$T = T_g + T_l \tag{18.85}$$

In a technological economy, the current capital coefficient method can be used for estimating the amount of current capital. The current capital coefficient is the ratio between current assets and fixed assets. It varies across sectors and technological schemes (see Tables 18.21 and 18.22). The amount of current capital can also be calculated by the ratio between current assets and production or by finding the actual demand of current capital, item by item. Current capital in firms and sectors can be categorized into a normed current fund and a nonquota current fund. The categories and components of firms' current capital are listed in Fig. 18.2.

The amount of fixed-asset investment of technological schemes (commonly known as capital construction investment) can be calculated with the following methods.

1. Estimating investment index per production capacity unit

This easy and convenient method is widely adopted in practice. The investment index per production capacity unit is related to size of construction, the method of construction, the period of construction, the price of building materials, equipment, geohydrologic conditions, and location. It varies as these conditions change.

2. Estimating investment of subdivisional work

This method adds up the estimation investment of each subdivisional work.

3. Estimating ratio coefficient of investment of subdivisional work

This method estimates the total investment, based on the investment constituent. The investment T_g of fixed assets in technological schemes consists of three parts. The first part is the cost of construction work and cultivation ($T_{g\text{-}construction}$). The second part is the cost of purchasing and installing machines, equipment, pipelines, tools, instruments, and the cost of purchasing livestock and nursery plants ($T_{g\text{-}equipment}$). The third part includes the cost of geological exploration, design, experiment and research, personnel training, and the compensation for the removal of households, machines, and factories ($T_{g\text{-}other}$). Accordingly, fixed assets investment can be calculated by the following formula:

Table 18.21 Capital occupation of state-owned firms in China

Year	All state-owned firms			Industry			Agriculture			Construction			Transportation, post and Telecommunications			Business		
	Fixed assets (%)	Current capital (%)	Coefficient of current capital	Fixed assets (%)	Current capital (%)	Coefficient of current capital	Fixed assets (%)	Current capital (%)	Coefficient of current capital	Fixed assets (%)	Current capital (%)	Coefficient of current capital	Fixed assets (%)	Current capital (%)	Coefficient of current capital	Fixed assets (%)	Current capital (%)	Coefficient of current capital
1952	58.4	41.6	0.71	74.2	25.8	0.35	/	/	/	32.7	67.3	2.06	94.2	5.8	0.06	8.5	91.5	10.8
1957	56.6	43.4	0.77	76.9	23.1	0.30	/	/	/	52.7	47.3	0.90	95.1	4.9	0.05	10.5	89.5	8.5
1962	62.1	37.9	0.61	72.2	27.8	0.39	/	/	/	46.2	53.8	1.16	91.8	8.2	0.09	15.8	84.2	5.3
1965	61.2	38.8	0.63	71.7	28.3	0.39	/	/	/	56.0	44.0	0.79	94.2	5.8	0.06	15.6	84.4	5.4
1970	57.2	42.8	0.75	67.1	32.9	0.49	/	/	/	61.8	38.2	0.62	92.5	7.5	0.08	12.5	87.5	7.0
1975	59.8	40.2	0.67	68.4	31.6	0.46	65.9	34.1	0.52	60.7	39.3	0.65	91.6	8.4	0.09	16.5	83.5	5.1
1980	62.2	37.8	0.61	77.7	22.3	0.29	57.5	42.5	0.74	70.3	29.7	0.42	93.2	6.8	0.07	21.3	78.7	3.7

Note Coefficient of current capital k_l= current capital/fixed assets

Table 18.22 Capital occupation of state-owned industrial firms in China (1980)

Industry	Fixed assets (%)	Current capital (%)	Coefficient of current capital k_l
Metallurgical Industry	80	20	0.25
Electric Power Industry	97	3	0.03
Hydropower	99	1	0.01
Coal Industry	90	10	0.11
Oil Industry	85	15	0.18
Chemical Industry	77	23	0.30
Machinery Industry	66	34	0.52
Building Materials Industry	81	19	0.23
Forest Industry	81	19	0.23
Food Industry	67	33	0.49
Textile, Sewn, and Tannery Industry	64	36	0.56
Papermaking, Culture and	74	26	0.35
Education Industry Other Industrial	76	24	0.32

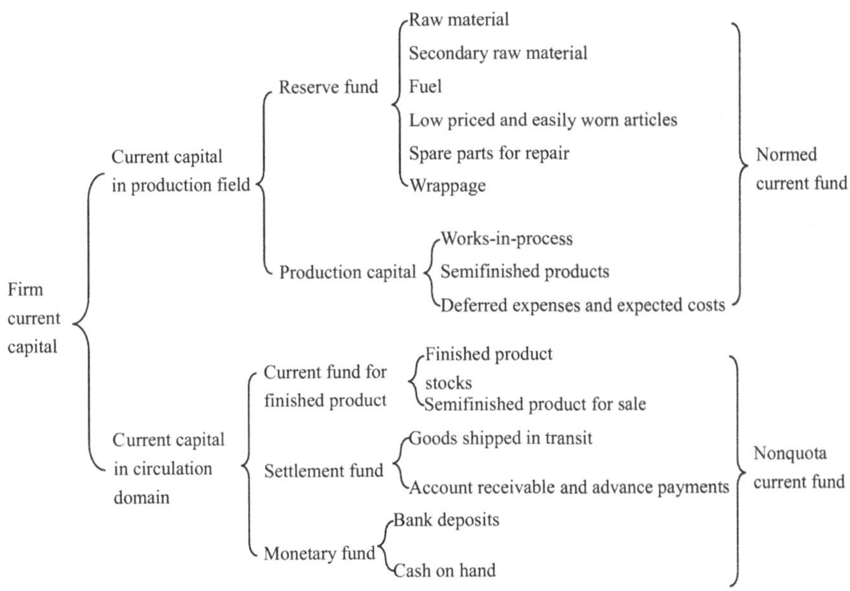

Fig. 18.2 The categories and components of firms' current capital

$$T_g = T_{g\text{-}construction} + T_{g\text{-}equipment} + T_{g\text{-}other} \quad (18.86)$$

The ratio of the three portions in formula 18.86 varies across technological schemes. If one of the main investments in technological schemes is chosen as a benchmark, the total investment can be calculated using the ratio coefficient of each sectional investment. This approach is called the method of construction coefficient in the western world. It is mainly applied in technological schemes in which the investment mainly consists of equipment costs.

Here are examples for each method.

Method one: Total investment can be calculated by following these steps:

(1) $$\begin{aligned} T_{g\text{-}equipment} &= T_{g\text{-}equipment-purchase} + T_{g\text{-}installation} + T_{g\text{-}instrument} + T_{g\text{-}pipeline} + T_{g\text{-}accessary} \\ &= (1 + X_{instrument} + X_{internal-pipeline} + X_{external-pipeline} + X_{accessary})(1 + X_{installation})T_{g\text{-}equipment\text{-}purchase} \end{aligned} \quad (18.87)$$

(2) $$\begin{aligned} T_{g\text{-}construction} &= T_{g\text{-}building} + T_{g\text{-}construction} \\ &= (1 + X_{construction})X_{building}(1 + X_{installation})T_{g\text{-}equipment-purchase} + X_{construction}T_{g\text{-}equipment} \end{aligned} \quad (18.88)$$

(3) $$T_{g\text{-}other} = \left(X_{unexpected} + X_{scale}\right)\left(T_{g\text{-}equipment} + T_{g\text{-}building}\right) \quad (18.89)$$

(4) $T_{g\text{-}equipment\text{-}purchase}$ is already known. $T_{g\text{-}construction}$, $T_{g\text{-}equipment}$, and $T_{g\text{-}other}$ can be calculated by using formula 18.87, 18.88, 18.89 based on the investment ratio coefficients listed in Table 18.23. At last, the total investment can be achieved by using formula 18.86.

Method two:

$$T_g = X_{total} T_{g\text{-}equipment} \quad (18.90)$$

(1) Estimate the total value of equipment $T_{g\text{-}equipment}$ based on experiences.
(2) Calculate by using formula 18.90 based on the total investment coefficients X_{total} for the factories listed in Table 18.24 to achieve the total investment.

The coefficients list in Table 18.23 and Table 18.24 are just for reference. Specific investment ratio coefficients should be adopted in China.

4. Estimating exponent of production scale

This method is called the 0.6 exponent in foreign countries. It is based on the impact of the production scale on investment. Here is its formula.

$$T_g = T_{g0}\left(\frac{G}{G_0}\right)^k \quad (18.91)$$

In this formula, T_g refers to the investment of new factory with a certain scale. T_{g0} refers to the investment of similar factories. G refers to the scale of new factories. G_0 refers to the scale of similar factories. The value of k usually takes 0.6. Here is the range of k's value change.

Table 18.23 Investment ratio coefficients for subdivisional work in firms (data from foreign countries)

Investment ratio coefficients for subdivisional work	Range of values
$X_{installation}$	0.43
$X_{internal\_pipeline}$	Solid factory 0.07–0.10, solid-liquid factory 0.10–0.30, fluid factory 0.30–0.60
$X_{instrument}$	No automatic control 0.03–0.05, partial automatic control 0.05–0.12, complete automatic control 0.12–0.20
$X_{subsidary\text{-}facility}$	Use the existing power supply facilities 0, a little expansion 0–0.05, massive expansion 0.05–0.25, new built 0.25–1.0
$X_{external\_pipeline}$	Short distance 0–0.05, middle distance 0.05–0.15, long distance 0.15–0.25
$X_{building}$	Outdoor 0.10–0.30, outdoor-indoor 0.2–0.60, indoor 0.6–1.0
$X_{construction}$	Simple 0.20–0.35, complex 0.35–0.60
$X_{unexpected}$	Mature and reliable production 0.10–0.20, possibly varied production 0.20–0.30, theoretic prediction 0.30–0.50, ordinary 0.30
X_{scale}	Large industrial factory 0–0.05, small industrial factory 0.05–0.15, experimental run and installation 0.15–0.35

Table 18.24 The total investment coefficients for firms (data from foreign countries)

Type of Factory	Calculating based on the value of delivered equipment	Calculating based on the value of installed equipment
Solid handling and processing (e.g. briquetting coal dust or agricultural lime)	3.10	2.16
Solid—fluid handling and processing (e.g. mineral organic extraction with ore preparation facilities)	3.63	2.56
Fluid handling and processing (e.g. grease fractionation from crude oil with continuous saponification)	4.74	3.30

(1) Expanding the production scale by increasing the size of equipment, $k = 0.6–0.7$.
(2) Expanding the production scale by increasing the amount of equipment in the same size, $k = 0.8–1.0$.
(3) Experimental production factory and industrial factories with high temperature and high pressure, $k = 0.3–0.5$.

The coefficients above do not apply to factories expanding 50 times compared with the original size. Specific values should be adopted in China.

5. Estimating by analyzing firms' scale

This method estimates investment by analyzing the relationship between investment and firms' scale. Here is its formula:

$$T_g = a + bG \tag{18.92}$$

$$T_g = G^b \tag{18.93}$$

$$T_g = a + bG + cG^2 + \cdots\cdots \tag{18.94}$$

In the above formulas, G is firm size and *a*, *b*, *c*...... are constants. The least squares method can be applied, based on the investment data of the same type of firms.

Investment on fixed assets and the original value of fixed assets. As mentioned earlier in this chapter, an investment consists of investment on fixed assets and investment on current capital. Investment on fixed assets is what technological schemes spend on fixed assets. It includes investment on infrastructure and spending on the renovation and reformation of existing fixed assets. Investment on fixed assets does not become the original value of fixed assets completely after technological schemes are completed. Not until the costs of training, construction organization moving, prototype and sample purchase, and the investment on scrapped project are deducted, and the technological schemes are accepted, can an investment on fixed assets become the original value of those fixed assets. The macro technological economy chooses investment on fixed assets, not the original value of fixed assets, to calculate investment, because the costs of training, construction organization moving, prototype and sample purchase, and the investment on scrapped projects are all actual spending. Table 18.25 lists the formation rate of fixed assets in China. In contrast, the micro technological economy chooses the original value of fixed assets, not the investment on fixed assets. Formation of current capital exists as well. For example, tools and instruments purchased in the construction period become current capital after they are handed over to firms.

Rational price of investment and present price. The price affects the estimation of investment. For the macro technological economy, fraudulent investment should be removed and non-disclosure should be added. In a word, investment should be calculated with rational supply price. For instance, railroad construction costs have soared in recent years. Actually, the rise is caused by the compensation for land requisitioned. The high price does not represent the true value of land. Thus, the irrational proportion in railroad construction cost should be cut. However, calculating investment based on the present price is acceptable for the micro technological economy.

Table 18.25 Formation rate of fixed assets across sectors in China (*Unit* %)

Sector	Formation rate of fixed assets	Sector	Formation rate of fixed assets
1. Coal	91.0	23. Papermaking	88.8
2. Crude oil	90.0	24. Daily-use machinery and electrical appliance	85.8
3. Natural gas	90.0	25. Household articles	85.8
4. Gasoline, kerosene	91.9	26. Food industry	89.4
5. Heavy oil, diesel oil, oil refining	91.9	27. Plastic	85.8
6. Electric power	87.0	28. Medicine and medical instruments	86.6
7. Forest industry	83.7	29. Wholesale and retail of grain and oil	96.0
8. Nonmetallic ore	92.7	30. Retail trade	96.0
9. Building materials	78.3	31. Wholesale trade	96.0
10. Chemical mines	96.0	32. Railroad transportation	92.7
11. Fertilizer	85.6	33. Waterway transportation	90.7
12. Agricultural chemicals	98.1	34. Road transit	97.9
13. Chemical engineering	85.7	35. Air transportation	83.7
14. Steel	86.1	36. Pipeline transportation	94.1
15. Nonferrous metal	91.8	37. Loading and unloading	97.0
16. Machinery	90.8	38. Running water	93.6
17. Electric machinery	90.8	39. Public service	91.9
18. Agricultural machinery	91.6	40. Building	87.7
19. Electronics industry	87.4	41. Production of grain, oil, cotton, and food	90.2
20. Railroad industry	87.4	42. Vegetable production	90.2
21. Ship and marine instruments	87.2	43. Other farm and sideline products	90.2
22. Textile industry	84.4		

Datas source Li, Z. and Zhang, J. (1985). Theoretic prices of commodities. Technological Economic Research, 7

Basic price and buildup price. Investment on fixed assets neglecting the time factor in construction period is called the basic price, whereas investment on fixed assets considering the time factor in construction period is called the buildup price. Investment on fixed assets consists of a basic price and a buildup price. The buildup price can be calculated based on the economic effect coefficients of investment in the macro technological economy. In the micro technological economy, the buildup price can be calculated based on the lending rate. The buildup price is the sum of the basic price and the present interest (or rational interest) in the construction period. However, the buildup price cannot be used for calculating basic depreciation costs because basic depreciation costs are the compensation of the original value of the fixed assets, and the interest in buildup price does not represent the original value of the fixed assets. The buildup price is useful for calculating the investment of technological schemes.

Here are the methods for calculating the basic price and the buildup price.

$$T_{g\text{-}basic} = \sum_{s=1}^{nk} T_{gs} \tag{18.95}$$

$$T_{g\text{-}buildup} = \sum_{s=1}^{nk} T_{gs}\theta^{nk-s+1} \tag{18.96}$$

Suppose a project has an annual investment of 10 million Yuan, the construction period is 10 years, and the basic price is 100 million Yuan. If interest factor is 1.1, the buildup price is 174.9 million Yuan. It can be seen from this example that the basic price and the buildup price are quite different. It is not rational to calculate basic depreciation costs with a buildup price. Thus, the macro technological economy does not adopt buildup costs.

18.7.2 Calculation Methods for the Usage Amount of Materials, Transportation, Labor, and Natural Resources by Technological Schemes

The purpose for calculating the usage amount of materials, transportation, labor, and natural resources is to: (1) Estimate their supply and demand conditions; (2) Evaluate and compare their value (the amount of consumption and the amount of occupation); (3) Calculate their direct consumption cost in overall costs, such as the costs of raw material, energy, transportation, wages and surcharges, and natural resources; (4) Calculate their indirect consumption costs in the macro technological economy, such as the costs of material consumption, transportation occupation, labor occupation, and the usage of natural resources. The usage amounts of materials, transportation, labor, and natural resources are calculated with a normed index, such as normed consumption and normed occupation. In the calculation process, technology progress, the supply and demand condition, and the economic benefit should be considered. The direct consumption coefficient and the total consumption coefficient of inputs can be calculated with input-output analysis.

18.7.3 Calculation Methods for the Cost of Technological Schemes

1. Calculation methods for the cost of macro technological economic evaluation

The cost index adopted in macro technological economic evaluation is the social (total) consumption cost index, or the social (total) cost index, in technological schemes. This includes the social consumption cost, both in this department and in other departments as well. The social consumption cost has two parts: the direct consumption cost or direct cost and the indirect consumption cost or indirect cost.

(1) Calculating direct consumption cost

The direct consumption cost (or direct cost) is a basic and a main cost in social consumption cost of technological schemes. It is usually called cost consumption,[6] namely the production cost or the operating cost. The total cost consumption in one year is called the annual production cost or the annual operation cost. The calculation of the cost consumption in the technological economy is usually based on years.

The calculation items and content for cost consumption vary, based on the characteristics of technological schemes. Generally, there are eight types of costs: raw materials C_y, secondary raw materials C_{fy}, energy (fuel and power) C_n, wages C_g, wage surcharges C_{gf}, basic depreciation costs C_j, heavy repaisr C_{dx}, and other costs C_q. Here is the formula for calculating the narrowly defined cost.

$$C_{direct} = C = C_y + C_{fy} + C_n + C_g + C_{gf} + C_j + C_{dx} + C_q \tag{18.97}$$

Sometimes, raw materials, secondary raw materials, and energy are merged into one term, material consumption, for the purpose of simplicity. Wages and wage surcharges are combined. Basic depreciation costs and heavy repair costs are merged as depreciation and heavy repair costs. The other costs include firm administrative expenses and internal transportation costs. Sometimes, new items are added to the formula. No matter how many items are included, the content of cost consumption should be covered.

[6]The cost generally mentioned is a narrowly defined cost, which refers to the direct cost. The generalized cost includes direct costs and indirect costs. Social costs, mentioned earlier, belong to generalized costs.

(1) Calculating the cost of raw material, secondary raw material, and energy (fuel and power)

$$C_y = W_{raw\_material} \times j_{g\_raw\_material} \tag{18.98}$$

$$C_{fy} = W_{secondary\_raw\_material} \times j_{g\_secondary\,raw\_material} \tag{18.99}$$

$$C_n = W_{energy} \times j_{g\_energy} \tag{18.100}$$

In the above formulas, W represents the amount of consumption and j_g represents price (including transportation price). If the arrival prices of raw material, fuel, and power do not match the rational prices, adjustment is required. The arrival prices should be close to rational prices, or prices should be calculated following the approach for calculating cost consumption in related sectors.

(2) Calculating the cost of wages

$$C_g = R \times V \tag{18.101}$$

In this formula, R represents the number of personnel and V represents the annual average salary.

(3) Calculating the cost of wage surcharge

Wage surcharges are calculated based on the percentage of wages. Here is its formula.

$$C_{gf} = x_{gf} \times C_g \tag{18.102}$$

In this formula, x_{gf} represents the supplementary wage coefficient, which falls between 0.15 and 0.20.

(4) Calculation methods for basic depreciation cost

i. Common deprecation method

This method averages the original value of fixed assets, estimated clearing expenses, and residual value based on the projected length of service. It is all called the average method or the linear method. This method is widely applied in China. Here is its formula.

$$C_j = \frac{T_g - T_{residual} + T_{clearing}}{n_f} = l_j \times T_g \tag{18.103}$$

$$l_j = \frac{C_j}{T_g} = \left(1 - \frac{T_{residual} - T_{clearing}}{T_g}\right)\frac{1}{n_f} \tag{18.104}$$

In the above formulas, l_j represents the basic depreciation coefficient and T_g represents the total original amount of fixed assets of technological schemes.

If $T_{residual}$ and $T_{clearing}$ are not considered, the basic depreciation coefficient is the reciprocal of the length of service.

ii. Production or working time depreciation method

This method is based on the original value of fixed assets, estimated clearing expense, and residual value. It first calculates the depreciation cost of production per unit or working time per unit, based on the total production or total working time during the length of service of fixed assets. Then the depreciation cost of production per unit or working time per unit is multiplied by the production or the working time in each year. In this way, the depreciation cost in each year is achieved. This method is appropriate for calculating the depreciation cost for machines and equipment. Here is its formula.

$$C_{js} = \frac{G_s}{\sum_{s=1}^{n_f} G_s}\left(T_{g\text{-}T_{residual}+T_{clearing}}\right) = l_{is} T_g \tag{18.105}$$

$$l_{js} = \frac{G_s}{\sum_{s=1}^{n_f} G_s}\left(1 - \frac{T_{residual} - T_{clearning}}{T_g}\right) \tag{18.106}$$

$$C_{js} = \frac{H_s}{\Sigma_{s=1}^{n_f} H_s}\left(T_g - T_{residual} + T_{clearing}\right) = l_{is} T_g \tag{18.107}$$

$$l_{js} = \frac{H_s}{\sum_{s=1}^{n_f} H_s}\left(1 - \frac{T_{residual} - T_{clearning}}{T_g}\right) \tag{18.108}$$

In the above formulas, $\sum_{s=1}^{n_f} G_s$ represents the total production in the length of service. G_s is the production in each year. $\sum_{s=1}^{n_f} H_s$ represents the total working time in the length of service. H_s is the working time in each year. l_{js} is the basic depreciation rate.

iii. Fixed-rate descending deprecation method

This method chooses the remainder of fixed assets subtracted by the depreciation cost in each year as the base and then applies a fixed deprecation rate. It generates more depreciation cost at the beginning of the length of service. The purpose of this method is to recovery the depreciation cost earlier because the efficiency of new machines are high and technologies keep developing. Here is its formula.

$$C_j = l_j \times T_{g-clearing} \tag{18.109}$$

$$l_j = 1 - \sqrt[n_j]{\frac{T_{residual} - T_{clearning}}{T_g}} \tag{18.110}$$

iv. Time factor deprecation method

This method considers that the depreciation cost collected each year can be invested in production to generate economic benefits until the end of the length of service. The sum of the collected annual depreciation costs and the economic benefits that are generated is just enough to compensate the spending on fixed assets (the sum of the original fixed assets and clearing expense minuses residual value). Here is its formula.

$$C_j = l_j \times T_g \tag{18.111}$$

$$l_j = \left(1 - \frac{T_{residual} - T_{clearning}}{T_g}\right)\frac{\theta - 1}{\theta^n f_{-1}} \tag{18.112}$$

The depreciation cost generated by this method is small. Thus, this method is seldom adopted in practice. However, it is useful for technological economic research.

(5) The cost of heavy repair is calculated based on the percentage of the basic depreciation cost. Here is its formula.

$$C_{dx} = x_{dx} \times C_j \tag{18.113}$$

In this formula, x_{dx} is the coefficient of heavy repair, which is about 0.5. The coefficient varies across sectors.

(6) Calculation methods for the other costs. There are several methods available. One method is to add the costs, item by item. The other method is to calculate based on the percentage of a certain cost (e.g. wages). The former is more accurate, whereas the latter is much easier.

(2) Calculating indirect consumption cost

The calculation of the indirect consumption cost of technological schemes must consider the short-term effect, the opportunity effect, and the long-term effect according to supply and demand conditions. Next, we discuss how to calculate short-term effect, opportunity effect, and long-term effect.

(1) Calculating short-term effect

The short-term effect reflects the impact of the imbalance between supply and demand. The impact can be calculated by multiplying the economic effect coefficients (x_t, x_w, x_y, x_r, and x_d) with the amount of usage of the resources in short supply. The values of these coefficients are the unamortized values achieved with average the index calculation, the increment index calculation, the general method, and the balance method covered earlier in this chapter. For instance, x_t is 0.15 and x_{w_energy} is 200 Yuan/ton standard coal.

(2) Calculating opportunity effect

The opportunity effect reflects the impact of the balance between supply and demand. The values of economic effect coefficients it adopts are the amortized values arrived at by using the production function method and the linear dual programming method. For instance, the value of x_t falls between 0.08 and 0.12.

(3) Calculating long-term effect

The long-term effect reflects the impact of the imbalance between supply and demand and overstocked products. The values of the economic effect coefficients can be achieved by using the long-term effect formulas covered earlier in this chapter. Usually, the values fall between 0 and the negative value of corresponding expense in cost. For instance,

$$x_{w\_long} = 0 \sim -j_w \tag{18.114}$$

$$x_{y\_long} = 0 \sim -j_y \tag{18.115}$$

$$x_{r\_long} = 0 \sim \left(v + x_{gf} v\right) \tag{18.116}$$

$$x_{d\_long} = 0 \sim -j_d \tag{18.117}$$

$$x_{t\_long} = 0 \sim -(1 + x_{dx}) l_j \tag{18.118}$$

In the above formulas, j_w is the rational price of materials. j_y is the rational price of transportation. j_d is the rational price of natural resources. $v + x_{gf}v$ is the wage and surcharge wage. $(1 + x_{dx})l_j$ is the sum of basic depreciation cost and heavy repair rate.

When the economic effect coefficients are ready, the indirect annual consumption cost can be calculated with the following formula.

$$C_{indirect} = C_T + C_W + C_Y + C_R + C_D \tag{18.119}$$

Figure 18.3 is the diagram of components in social consumption cost.

The social consumption cost can be categorized into the annual social consumption cost, the total social consumption cost, the static social consumption cost, and the dynamic social consumption cost. The concept of a social consumption cost, covered above, refers to the annual social consumption cost. The total social consumption cost

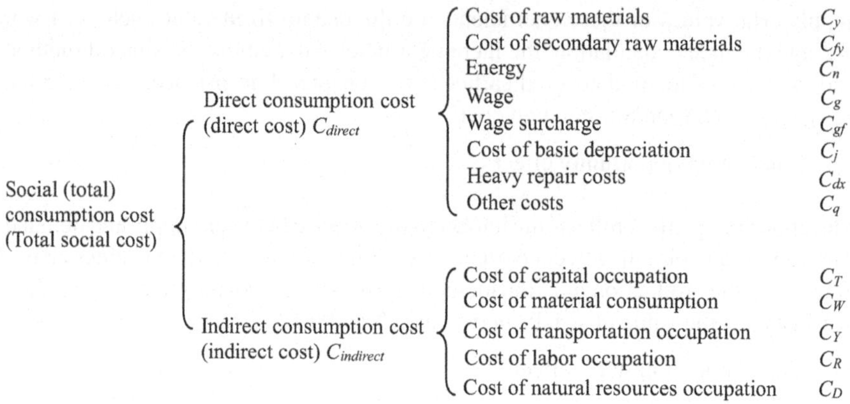

Fig. 18.3 The components of social consumption cost

can be calculated by two methods. One is to add up the annual social consumption cost in each year. The other is to add up the complete costs during a certain period. The static method does not consider the time factor when adding up the costs. In contrast, the dynamic method considers the time factor. The calculation methods will be discussed in the next chapter.

2. **Calculation methods for the cost of micro technological economic evaluation**

The cost index in a micro technological economic evaluation is firms' total consumption cost, also called firm total cost index, which includes both the direct cost and indirect cost. Figure 18.4 is the diagram of the components in a firms' total consumption cost.

The cost for raw materials refers to the expenses for raw materials and on materials that are used for production or are components in the final products.

The cost for secondary materials refers to the expenses for materials that are used for production or for facilitating production but that are not components in the final products.

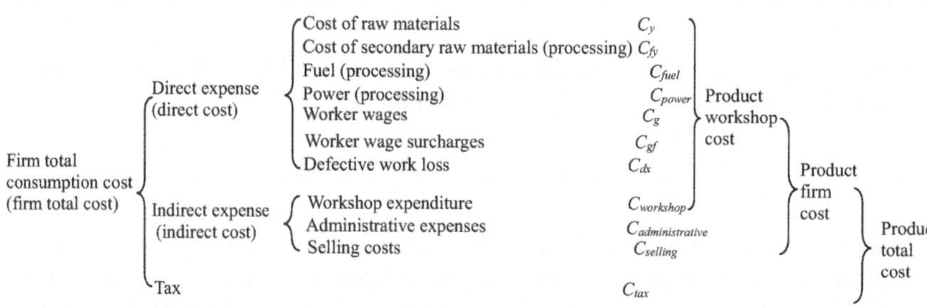

Fig. 18.4 The components in firm total consumption cost

The cost for fuel refers to the expenses for fuel that are used for production and for providing thermal energy for production.

The cost for power refers to the expenses for the power that is used for production.

The cost for worker wages and wage surcharges refers to the wages (basic wages and additional wages) paid for workers who are involved in production and to the surcharges collected based on their total wages and the rates set by the states (13–15%). The surcharges include medical costs (5.5%), the welfare fund (3%), the bonus fund (2.5%), the union fund (2%), and other charges (2%).

Defective work loss refers to the cost generated by defective work in production. It includes the repair cost for defective work and the loss of unrepairable defective work, namely their costs minus their residuals.

The cost of the workshop refers to the expenses for administration that supports production in workshops, operation costs, and the maintenance cost and depreciation cost of machines, equipment, and factory buildings. These expenses cannot be integrated directly into product costs. Administration and operating costs include the salary and surcharges for non-worker personnel in the workshop, labor protection costs, transportation costs, inspection expenses, material consumption costs, water and electricity fees, heating fees, rewards for innovation and rationalization proposals, shutdown losses, and other expenses.

Firm administrative expense refers to the expenses of the operation for organizing and managing production, operation costs, and other costs. It includes salary and surcharges for administration staff, office expenses, scientific research costs, and expenditure taxes.

Selling cost refers to the expenses for the selling of the final products. It includes warehouse administration costs, advertising costs, and expenditures for marketing agencies.

Firms' product cost has the following categories.

(1) Factor cost and project cost. Factor cost is the portion in firms' expenditure that is calculated based on economic characteristics. The direct cost shown in Fig. 18.3 has a factor cost consisted of eight items of expenditure. Project cost is the portion in firms' expenditure that is calculated based on production link and usage. The total project cost shown in Fig. 18.4 is project cost.
(2) Design cost, planned cost, and effective cost. Planned cost is calculated according to design objectives. It is a kind of predictive cost that aims to maximize the rationality and correspond to the act. The effective cost is the cost that actually occurs. It can used for assessing the management of production. The planned cost is made based on the average advance cost that firms have achieved. It is the foundation for making plans. The design cost usually chooses the factor cost for calculation, whereas the planned cost and the effective cost choose the project cost for calculation.

(3) Total cost and unit cost. The total cost is the whole expenditure that is spent for production during a certain period. The allocated total cost based on units in a year is called the unit cost.
(4) Variable cost and fixed cost. The expenditure in cost varying with the amount of production is the variable cost. The portion that does not change with the amount of production is called the fixed cost. Spending on raw materials is variable cost. Depreciation costs and administrative expenses are fixed costs. For the expenditures on fuel, power, and wage, some portions are variable cost and some portions are fixed cost.

Tax

Firms in China pay 30 taxes, which fall into six categories: (1) Circulation tax, such as production tax, value added tax, and sales tax. (2) Income tax, such as the state-owned enterprise income tax, the state-owned enterprise adjustment tax, the collectively-owned enterprise income tax, the foreign enterprise income tax, the Sino-foreign joint venture income tax, and the personal income tax. (3) Specific resource extreme difference income taxes, such as the salt tax and the resource tax. (4) Special taxes, such as the oil burning tax, the building tax, the state-owned enterprise bonus tax, the state-owned enterprise wage adjustment tax, and the city maintenance construction tax. (5) Act taxes, such as the slaughtering tax, the domestic animal trade tax, and the fair trade tax. (6) Property and usage tax, such as the property tax, the operation taxes for vehicles and ships, and the land use tax. Other than these taxes, firms need to pay other taxes, such as customs duties, the import regulatory tax, an agricultural tax, the animal husbandry tax, a deed tax, a national energy transportation tax, and an education surtax.

18.8 Calculation Methods for Outputs and Benefits of Technological Scheme

The technological economy needs to calculate outputs and benefits. Outputs and benefits are similar, but they are different. Output refers to the results of technological schemes, whereas benefit refers to the direct and/or indirect impact brought on by the results. Useful impact is a positive benefit, while harmful impact is a negative benefit. Output and benefit can be calculated with object or value. Sometimes, it is hard to measure them in quality. A calculation for output and benefit can balance the amount of output with objects, balance the amount of output with value, and assess economic effect and efficiency. Next, the calculation methods are discussed.

18.8.1 Calculation Methods for Output of Technological Schemes

1. **Calculation methods for the amount of technological scheme output**

In the field of material production, the amount of technological scheme output is usually calculated with the quantity of product and/or the amount of labor (e.g. volume of transport). In the field of non-material production, the formats of the outputs of the technological scheme vary, such as performing a session, convening ten meetings, examining 100 documents, processing 1000 letters from the masses, publishing 10,000 books and magazines, treating 100,000 patients, or cultivating 1,000,000 students. The output of technological schemes, both in the field of material production and in the field of non-material production, is in materialized format. The outputs of technological schemes in the field of material production can be calculated in a materialized format and with monetary specifications. Scientific prediction of the output of technological schemes is very important in the technological economy.

The prediction of the requirement for product and labor can be performed with the consumption coefficient method, the consumption increment coefficient method, the economic effect coefficient method, and the economic effect increment coefficient method.

(1) The consumption coefficient method (or the requirement coefficient method). This method predicts the requirement of products and labor with the indices of products or labor consumed by one unit amount of kind or monetary specification. The consumption coefficient can be calculated with the consumption quota approach, the correlational analysis approach, extrapolation, and the input-output approach.

   (a) The consumption quota approach (or the requirement quota approach). This approach is easy and is adopted widely. If the amount of kind and monetary specification is known, the requirements of product and labor can be achieved by multiplying the amount with the quota of one unit. For example, if the number of the population is known, multiply this number with the quota of the average per capital dwelling area, and the total amount of requirement for dwelling can be obtained. The key to this approach is to adopt the rational value of the quota per unit. In other words, the quota per unit needs to be predicted. The future quota per unit might be the same as the current value, higher than the current value, or lower than the current value. In order to predict the quota per unit scientifically, possible changes toall factors that impact the quota should be analyzed carefully, one by one.
   (b) The correlational analysis approach (the regression analysis approach). This approach predicts the requirements of product and labor by analyzing the correlation between the requirements and one or more factors. If the predicted requirements correlate only with one factor, simple regression analysis should be adopted. If the predicted requirements correlate with

multiple factors, multiple regression analysis should be adopted. Here is an example. It is known that the requirement for energy N correlates with the economic magnitude net income M. The approximate formula of the correlation can be obtained by using the least square method. Although the approximate formula is a simple regression analysis equation, it has the following several formats:

$$N = a + bM \tag{18.120}$$

$$N = aM^b \tag{18.121}$$

$$N = a + bM + cM^2 + \cdots\cdots \tag{18.122}$$

In the above formulas, the net income M is known. a, b, c ....are coefficients, which can be calculated with the least square method, based on archived data. The details of the calculation are not covered here. Once the equation is obtained, the requirement for energy can be predicted, based on the equation. The correlational analysis approach is actually a kind of unit consumption quota method. But the amount of energy consumption changes in each year, so it should be calculated with this formula:

$$N = n(t)M \tag{18.123}$$

If multiple factors are involved in correlational analysis, the following multiple regression equation should be adopted.

$$G = a + b_1X_1 + b_2X_2 + \cdots\cdots + b_mX_m \tag{18.124}$$

In this formula, G represents the requirements of product and labor that need to be predicted. It is a dependent variable. $X_1, X_2, X_3, \ldots\ldots X_m$ are correlated factors, which are independent variables. a, b_1, b_2, ...b_m are coefficients, which are correlation coefficients or regression coefficients.

The correlational analysis approach has limitations. It is applicable only when the future correlation is similar to the previous correlation.

I. Extrapolation. This approach adopts time series, which predict the future requirement with an unweighted average method or a weighted average method based on archived data in chronological order. A moving average method and exponential smoothing are often applied. Extrapolation is valid for short-term prediction.
II. Input-output approach. This is a complicated approach which requires a huge amount of data and needs computers to perform computation. Its details are not covered here.

(2) The consumption (demand) increment coefficient method. The method predicts the requirement for product and labor, based on the correlation between the incremental speed of the demand for a certain product or labor and the economic growth rate. It is called an elastic coefficient method in foreign countries. Here is its formula.

$$G = \left(1 + d_{product}\right)^{t} G_0 = \left(1 + \beta\alpha_{economy}\right)^{t} G_0 \tag{18.125}$$

In this formula, β is the consumption increment coefficient of the demand for a certain product or unit of labor. The key to this method is to accurately predict the consumption increment coefficient of the demand for a certain product or labor. This coefficient can be calculated by performing an average, either for one year or for multiple years. Here are its formulas:

$$\beta = \frac{d_{product}}{d_{economy}} = \frac{\frac{\Delta G}{G_0}}{\frac{\Delta M}{M_0}} = \frac{\frac{\Delta G}{G_0} - 1}{\frac{\Delta M}{M_0} - 1} \text{ (calculating average in one year)} \tag{18.126}$$

$$\beta = \frac{d_{product}}{d_{economy}} = \frac{\left(\frac{G_t}{G_0}\right)^{\frac{1}{\theta}} - 1}{\left(\frac{M_t}{M_0}\right)^{\frac{1}{\theta}} - 1} \tag{18.127}$$

In the above formulas, $d_{product}$ is the average annual growth rate of the demand for a certain product or labor. $\alpha_{economy}$ is the average annual growth rate of national economy. ΔG is value change of the average annual growth rate of the demand for a certain product or labor. G_0 is the demand for a certain product or labor in a base year. ΔM is value change in the average annual growth rate of the national economy. M_0 is the size of the national economy in a base year. G_t is the demand for a certain product or labor in the t year after the base year. M_t is the size of the national economy in the t year after the base year.

After performing a simple derivation, the following formula can be achieved.

$$\beta = \left[\left(1 + \alpha_{econony}\right)^{t}\sqrt{\frac{\frac{G}{M_t}}{\frac{G_0}{M_0}}} - 1\right]\frac{1}{\alpha_{economy}} \tag{18.128}$$

In this formula, $\frac{G}{M_t}$ is the demand for product or labor from one unit of the amount of national economy (such as the production value, the net income, the national income) in the t year after the base year, namely the unit consumption quota. $\frac{G_0}{M_0}$ is the demand for product or labor from one unit of the amount of the national economy (such as the production value, the net income, the national income) in the base year. It is also a unit consumption quota.

Therefore, once the unit consumption quota has been predicted, the consumption increment coefficient can be calculated with the above formula. It should be pointed out that this process is applicable to the correlational analysis approach and to extrapolation, as well.

(3) The economic effect coefficient method. The economic effect coefficient of a product or labor is the reciprocal of its unit consumption indices. This method is essentially the same as the consumption coefficient method.
(4) The economic effect increment coefficient method. The economic effect increment coefficient of a product or labor is the reciprocal of its consumption increment coefficient. This method is essentially the same as the consumption increment coefficient method.

2. **Calculation methods for the quality of technological scheme output**

The quality of the output of technological schemes greatly impacts their total benefits. High quality brings more benefits. It is very hard to calculate the quality of technological scheme output. In practice, there are four methods available. The first one calculates the quality of technological scheme output with the performance assessment criteria of quality and function, or with ratings to quantify quality. The second method chooses production or the amount of labor to measure quality, or reflects quality in prices. For example, a quality index, such as the defective index, the rate of qualified products, the rate of high-class products, and the service life, can be quantified by this method. The third method quantifies quality based on the size of the economic effect it generates in the consumption process, or reflects quality in prices. For instance, making the rational price ratio for oil and coal is one application of this method. The fourth method reflects quality in prices based on the rating of the quality of output. Overall, these methods calculate the quality of a technological scheme output based on the comparative principle of satisfying needs, from the perspectives of the users.

18.8.2 Calculation Methods for Benefits of Technological Schemes

The outputs of the technological schemes in the field of material production clearly have economic benefits. In contrast, the outputs of technological schemes in the field of non-material production might not have economic benefits. For example, calling a meeting is an output, but not a benefit. Theatrical performances are outputs, but not benefits. In the technological economy, the calculation for benefits is more important than that for output. In practice, there are eight types of benefits, namely political benefits, national defense benefits, social benefits,[7] cultural benefits, technological benefits, economic benefits,[8] environmental and ecological benefits, and natural resources benefits. Although these benefits correlate with each other, each is independent. The eight types of benefits vary across technological schemes. Some technological schemes have all of them, whereas others only have part of them. Some benefits are primary, while others are secondary, in technological schemes. Some benefits are big, while others are small. Some benefits can be quantified, while others can only be qualified. Some benefits exist currently, while others are latent. The calculation for the eight benefits of technological schemes must consider the practical situation. Five methods are available for calculating benefits for technological schemes.

$$Benefit\,(X) = Physical\ \ product\,(G) \times Quality\ \ function\,(P) \tag{18.129}$$

$$Benefit\,(X) = Physical\ \ product\,(G) \times Quality\ \ function\ \ rating\,(F) \tag{18.130}$$

$$Benefit\,(X) = Direct\ \ rating(F) \tag{18.131}$$

$$Benefit\,(S) = Physical\ \ product\,(G) \times Quality\ \ function\ \ rating\ \ price\,(j_g) \tag{18.132}$$

$$Benefit\,(S) = Physical\ \ product\,(G) \times Price\,(j_g) \tag{18.133}$$

Formulas 18.129, 18.130, and 18.131 are often adopted for calculating benefits other than economic benefits.

For the macro technological economy, benefits in the above formulas refer to total social benefits. Therefore, both the direct benefits (or internal benefits) generated by technological schemes and the indirect benefits (or external benefits) generated by technological schemes for a society should be taken into consideration. If the direct benefits are always positive, the indirect benefits might be positive or negative. They might not be the benefits in the same category. Here are the formulas:

$$X = X^0 \pm \Delta X = X_{direct} \pm X_{indirect} \tag{18.134}$$

$$S = S^0 \pm \Delta S = S_{direct} \pm S_{indirect} \tag{18.135}$$

[7] Society has two twofold meanings here. The first refers to the society in sociology. For example, employment, birth and old age, sickness, and death are social issues. The second meaning refers to the entire society. For example, social economic benefits mean benefits for the whole society. Social benefits have the first meaning.

[8] Economic benefits here refer to the benefits in the domain of economy.

Next, let us talk about indirect benefit. Compared with the calculation for direct benefit, the calculation for indirect benefit is more difficult because indirect benefit is invisible. Comprehensive and systematic investigation and analysis are required for calculating indirect benefit. Specifically, it is necessary to analyze the impacts that technological schemes have on circumstances from the perspectives of politics, the national defense, culture, technology, the economy, the environment and ecology, and natural resources. How big is the impact? Do the technological schemes follow the principles and policies of the party? What impact do the technological schemes have on politics, national defense strategies, employment, the development of culture, the development of science and technology, the development of regional economy and the sector economy, improvement of location of production, sectors of input, sectors of output, users, environmental ecology, resource development and protection, and foreign exchange earnings? In a word, indirect benefit can only be qualitatively analyzed and quantitatively calculated via comprehensive and systematical consideration of the external impacts (spread effect) or generated by technological schemes.

Early in this chapter, calculation methods for macro social consumption cost were introduced. Specifically, the impact of supply and demand effect on indirect consumption costs and calculation methods are discussed. Similarly, the impact of the supply and demand effect on indirect economic benefits should be considered when calculating the macro total social benefits. When the output of a technological scheme is short term, the calculation of its indirect economic benefits should adopt the economic effect coefficients of the short-term effect. When the output of a technological scheme is long term, the calculation of its indirect economic benefits should adopt the economic effect coefficients of the long-term effect.

For the micro technological economy, only direct benefits are calculated for technological schemes. Indirect benefits are not calculated. In addition, the present price is adopted for calculating economic benefits. Sometimes, the present price considers a supply and demand situation. For instance, when supply falls short of demand, the bargain price can be adopted for calculation. When supply exceeds demand, only a reduced price or a privileged price can be adopted for calculation.

The benefit of technological schemes can be categorized into the annual benefit, the total benefit, the dynamic benefit, and the static benefit.

18.9 Calculating Costs and Benefits with Shadow Price

Shadow price is a new term that appeared in the late 1950s in foreign countries. It was introduced into China in 1980s. Much foreign literature discusses the shadow price, but often has quite different views about the shadow price. Many introductions to shadow price are available in China, but they are confused. What on earth is the theoretical foundation of shadow price? How to calculate the shadow price? How to apply the shadow price in China? These questions need to be carefully studied.

The new term shadow price appeared in the late 1950s abroad, and was introduced domestically in the 1980s. There is a lot of foreign literature on the shadow price that shows different opinions and a variety of confusing domestic introductions. A thorough study on what the theoretical basis of the shadow price is and how to calculate it is needed. The results then can be applied in the reality of China.

18.9.1 The Theoretical Principles for Shadow Price

There are several theories about shadow price available right now. Some are from foreign countries and some originate in China. Due to the different theoretical principles, these theories provide different concepts and calculation methods about the shadow price (see Table 18.26).

Optimal Allocation of Resources is the first theory initiating shadow price. Jan Tinbergen, a Dutch econometrician who won the Nobel Prize for economics in 1958, originally proposed the idea of shadow price in economic analysis. Kantorovich from the Soviet Union calculates prices with regression and assesses the degree of scarcity for resources. He calls the price calculated with this method the optimal planning price, namely the shadow price. Shadow price, in this traditional sense, is the value generated by the margin when resources are optimally utilized, or the estimation of price when resources yield the maximum output.

The other theoretical principle for the shadow price is the opportunity cost and welfare economics. Opportunity cost refers to the loss of potential gain from other alternatives if a specific kind of resource is allocated to one alternative. The larger the loss, the larger the opportunity cost, and vice versa. In other words, the opportunity cost is the shadow price. In the strict sense, opportunity cost is shadow price for input. For example, a worker gets a wage of *G* Yuan in other factories. If this worker is hired by a technological scheme, the shadow price for the worker's wage is *G* Yuan. Much of the literature proposes the term consumer willing-to-pay price, which reflects the shadow price. Here is another example. A type of product is applied in technological scheme *P*. The price of this product is *A* Yuan when it is applied in other technological schemes. Thus, the opportunity cost for this product in *P* is *A* Yuan. The price that consumers are willing to pay is the shadow price. According welfare economics, shadow price refers to the increment of welfare caused by the change in margin of the available commodities or production factors.[9]

Other than the aforementioned two theory principles, there are two more theory principles. The first one is the opportunity benefit, which corresponds to the opportunity cost (expenditure). The opportunity cost, just as the name implies, can only reflect the loss for input, not the benefit of output. However, in an economic assessment, two shadow prices, one reflecting the loss for input and the other reflecting the benefit of output, are needed. What is the opportunity benefit? The opportunity benefit refers to the loss of potential gain from other alternatives if a product is sold to

[9] Squire and Van der Tak [Sq75].

Table 18.26 Six methods for calculating shadow price

Serial number	1	2	3	4	5	6
Name	Linear programming dualization	*L-M* method (OECD)	*S/V* method	*UNIDO* method	Value-added method	*XSB* method
Theoretical Principles	Optimal Allocation of Resources	Opportunity cost, opportunity benefit, and welfare economics	Opportunity cost, opportunity benefit, and welfare economics	Opportunity cost, opportunity benefit, and welfare economics	Opportunity cost, opportunity benefit, and welfare economics	Total benefit and total expenditure
Price base for shadow price	Domestic market price	International market price	International market price	Domestic market price	Domestic market price	Rational domestic price
Calculation method	Shadow price for input and output = optimal planning price (resource equilibrium price)	Shadow price for input and output available for foreign trade = international market price (port price) × official exchange rate; Shadow price for input and output unavailable for foreign trade = domestic market price × conversion factor × official exchange rate	Shadow price for input and output available for foreign trade = international market price (port price) × official exchange rate; Shadow price for input and output unavailable for foreign trade = domestic market price × conversion factor × official exchange rate	Shadow price for input and output unavailable for foreign trade = domestic market price; Shadow price for input and output available for foreign trade = international market price × shadow exchange rate	Shadow price for input and output unavailable for foreign trade = domestic market price; Shadow price for input and output available for foreign trade = international market price × amended exchange rate	Shadow price for input and output (material, transportation, capital, manpower, and natural resources) = rational price + economic effect coefficients; Shadow price for connected input and output = price in international market × rational exchange rate or rational domestic price + economic effect coefficients

(continued)

Table 18.26 (continued)

Serial number	1	2	3	4	5	6
Advantages	Optimizing resource allocation and achieve the optimal effect	Practical, convenient, good for countries with strong foreign trade	Practical, convenient, good for countries with strong foreign trade	Practical, convenient, good for countries with weak foreign trade; close connection with domestic market price	Practical, convenient. Amended exchange rate reflects the scarcity of foreign exchange	Practical, convenient, fit for the practice in China. Easy to get close rational price and shadow coefficients. Makes domestic prices comparable. Reflects supply and demand.
Disadvantages	Difficulties in practice	Unstable international market price, loose connection with domestic market price	Unstable international market price, loose connection with domestic market price		Does not eliminate the incomparability between foreign-trade products and nonforeign-trade products, and the incomparability of the domestic present price	
Notes	Initiated in 1958	Manual of Industrial Project Analysis In Developing Countries, 1968	Economic analysis of projects, 1975	Guidelines for project evaluation, 1972	Manual for evaluation of industrial projects, 1980	Methods in technological economy, 1965; An introduction to technological economy, 1980

one alternative. The bigger the loss, the bigger the opportunity benefit, and vice versa. In other words, the opportunity benefit is the shadow price for output. For example, a ton of cement is sold to factory *A* at the price of 100 Yuan. If the cement is sold to factory *B* now, its shadow price is 100 Yuan. Although the opportunity benefit has never been covered by domestic and foreign literature, it exists all the time. It can provide the foundation for calculating the shadow prices for output. Although the shadow prices for output can be explained by the opportunity cost (including the consumer willing-to-pay price) indirectly, explaining the shadow prices for output with the opportunity benefit is easier and clearer. The combination of opportunity cost and opportunity benefit can provide a complete theoretialc principle for the shadow price. The second one is the total benefit and total consumption theory, initiated by the author in 1965. According to this theory, the benefits of technological schemes consist of both direct benefits and indirect benefits. The expenditure of technological schemes includes both direct expenditure and indirect expenditure. Calculation for direct benefit and direct expenditure should adopt rational prices. In contrast, calculation for indirect benefit and indirect expenditure should adopt the economic effect coefficients of resource utilization. Mathematical calculation has proven that the sum of rational prices and economic effect coefficients is equal to the shadow prices. Therefore, the theoretical principles for the shadow price consist of the rational price theory and the economic effect coefficient theory.

18.9.2 Shadow Price Calculation Method

1. **Linear programming dualization**

This method calculates the shadow price based on the theory of Optimal Allocation of Resources. The optimal solution for linear programming is the production and the production value when the total benefit is at maximum with limited resources. The optimal solution for the dual problem is the shadow prices of inputs. If the parameters for input and output are close, it is easy to find solution for this linear programming. However, in practice, total social input and output are connected. Their amount is huge. In order to calculate the shadow price, it needs to find the balance of supply and demand with the condition of the maximum total value of many inputs and outputs. Then, all inequality constraints need to be converted into equality constraints under the condition that each commodity is fully utilized. The situation when materials are redundant and the shadow price equals zero does not exist. Last, the shadow price under a balanced condition can be calculated. It is very hard to develop a macro mathematics model to calculate the shadow price with all of the above conditions satisfied. Furthermore, such a model does not agree with objective reality. Thus, the number of the application of this method is very small.

2. *L-M* Method, or *OECD* Method

This method was initiated by welfare economist Ian Little. and professor of economic mathematics James Mirrlees. from University of Oxford in 1968 when they wrote the handbook for the Organization of Economic Cooperation and Development (*OECD*).[10] This method categorizes the input and output of technological schemes into goods available for foreign trade and goods unavailable for foreign trade. For goods available for foreign trade, the calculation for shadow prices adopts the port price in the international market and converts the shadow prices with official exchange rate (OER) into domestic currency. For goods unavailable for foreign trade, the calculation for shadow prices coverts the domestic price into the port price with a conversion factor. The conversion factor can be calculated with a trade data method, a decomposition method, and an input-output method. *L-M* method proposes a universal standard conversion factor (*SCF*) for all goods unavailable for foreign trade.

$$SCF = \frac{M + X}{M(1 + d) + X(1 + S)} \tag{18.136}$$

In this formula, M refers to the total *C.I.F* for imported commodities denominated in foreign currency. X refers to the total *FOB* for exported commodities denominated in foreign currency. $M + X$ refers to the total value of imported and exported commodities calculated with international market price and denominated in foreign currency. d is the import tariff. s is the export subsidy. $M(1 + d) + X\ (1 + s)$ is the total value of imported and exported commodities calculated with the domestic market price and denominated in domestic currency. Accordingly, the formula for calculating a shadow price with *L-M* method is:

$$\begin{aligned}&\text{Shadow price for goods available for foreign trade}\\&= \text{Port price} \times \text{official exchange rate}\end{aligned} \tag{18.137}$$

$$\begin{aligned}&\text{Shadow price for goods unavailable for foreign trade}\\&= \text{Domestic price} \times \text{standard conversion factor} \times \text{official exchange rate}\end{aligned} \tag{18.138}$$

In order to adjust the domestic prices for good unavailable for foreign trade, the cost decomposition method can be adopted to delineate the input into goods available for foreign trade and basic production factors in infrastructure, in two rounds. Then shadow prices can then be further calculated. The advantages of the *L-M* method are easy and practical, especially for countries with strong foreign trade. Only some

[10] Little and Mirrlees [Li68].

small adjustments are needed for small amounts of goods unavailable for foreign trade. *L-M* adopts the international market price.

3. **S/V Method or the S/V/T Method**

In 1975 and in 1979, Lyn Squire. and Herman G. Van der Tak, researchers from the World Bank, proposed new calculation methods for shadow prices, respectively. Their new methods were called the S/V method.[11] Very similar to the *L-M* method, the S/V method adopts prices in international markets by converting domestic prices into international market prices with a conversion factor. The S/V method argues that the goals of resource utilization are to increase national income and to achieve fairness in the allocation of national income. Thus, these two goals are taken into consideration in the S/V method. Shadow prices considering an increment goal only are efficiency prices, whereas shadow prices considering both increment goals and fairness goals are social prices.

4. **UNIDO Method**

This method is initiated by Partha Dasgupta, a professor from London School of Economics, and Stephen Marglin, a professor from Harvard University, for the United Nations Industrial Development Organization (UNIDO).[12] Different from the *L-M* method, the UNIDO method adopts domestic prices. It converts the port prices in the international market for goods available for foreign trade into domestic prices with shadow exchange rate (*SER*), namely

$$\text{Shadow price for goods available for foreign trade} = \text{port price} \times \text{shadow exchange rate} \tag{18.139}$$

$$\text{Shadow price for goods unavailable for foreign trade} = \text{domestic price} \tag{18.140}$$

Here is the formula for calculating shadow exchange rate:

$$SER = \frac{M(1+d) + X(1+S)}{M+X} \cdot OER = \frac{OER}{SCF} \tag{18.141}$$

This method is simple and practical, especially for countries with weak foreign trade. But it is arguable that domestic prices should be adopted in the calculation.

5. **Value-added method**

This method was proposed by UNIDO and the Development Center for Arab states in 1980.[13] Based on the domestic market price, it converts the port price of goods available for foreign trade into a domestic price with an amended exchange rate or a

[11] Squire and Van der Tak [Sq75].

[12] Dasgupta et al. [Da72].

[13] Manual for evaluation of industrial projects, UNIDO, 1980.

tourist exchange rate. The amended exchange rate can be calculated approximately by the following formula:

$$\text{Amended exchange rate}(AER) = OER \cdot \frac{M}{X} \tag{18.142}$$

In this formula, M stands for the foreign exchange spending of a country during a certain period. X stands for the foreign exchange income of a country during a certain period. This method is simple and practical. The amended exchange rate reflects the income and expenses of foreign exchange in a country.

6. **XSB Method**

This method was proposed by the author based on the theories of total benefit and total expenditure.[14] According to the Six Forces Theory of technological economic effect, the total social consumption cost includes both direct cost and indirect cost[15,16] Here is its calculation formula (based on net income evaluation methods).

$$Z = C_{direct} + C_{indirect} = C + x_w W + x_r R + x_t T + x_y Y + x_d D \tag{18.143}$$

The cost C in the above formula can be broken down into eight items, namely raw material cost C_y, secondary raw material cost C_{fy}, energy cost C_n, wage C_g, wage surcharge C_{gf}, basic depreciation cost C_j, heavy repair cost C_{dx}, and other cost C_q. The calculation formulas for each item are as following:

Raw material cost C_y= rational price of raw material $j_{w\text{-}raw}$ × consumption of raw material W_{raw}

Secondary raw material cost C_{fy}= rational price of secondary raw material $j_{w\text{-}secondary}$ × consumption of secondary raw material $W_{secondary}$

Energy cost C_n= rational price of energy $j_{w\text{-}energy}$ × consumption of energy W_{energy}

Wage C_g= rational wage rate v × quantity of labor force R

Wage surcharge $C_{gf} = x_{gf} \times C_g = x_{gf} \times v \times R$

Basic depreciation cost C_j= basis depreciation rate l_j × investment of fixed assets T_g

Heavy repair cost $C_{dx} = x_{df} \times C_j = x_{dx} \times l_j \times T_g$

Other cost (e.g. transportation cost) C_q= rational price of transportation j_y × traffic volume Y

Then, the material consumption cost $x_w W$ can be broken down into three items: $x_{w\_raw} W_{raw}$, $x_{w\_secondary} W_{secondary}$, and $x_{w\_energy} W_{energy}$. The capital occupation cost $x_t T$ can be broken down into fixed capital occupation cost $x_t T_g$ and current capital occupation cost $x_t T_l$. Load all the items into formula 18.143 and we can get:

---

[14] XSB is the abbreviation of the author's name Xu, Shoubo.

[15] [Xu Xu84].

[16] Total social consumption cost here refers to the direct and indirect cost generated by a certain technological scheme. It does not include the direct and indirect cost that are not generated by the technological scheme.

$$Z = (j_{w\text{-}raw} + x_{w\_raw})W_{raw} + \left(j_{w\text{-}secondary} + x_{w\_secondary}\right)W_{secondary} + (j_{w\text{-}energy} + x_{w\_energy})W_{energy} + \left(v + x_{gf}v + x_r\right)R + \left(l_j + x_{dx}l_j + x_t\right)T_g + x_t T_l + (j_y + x_y)Y + (j_d + x_d)D \tag{18.144}$$

Set

$$\begin{aligned}
j_{shadow_raw} &= j_{w\text{-}raw} + x_{w_raw} \\
j_{shadow_secondary} &= j_{w\text{-}secondary} + x_{w_secondary} \\
j_{shadow_energy} &= j_{w\text{-}energy} + x_{w_energy} \\
j_{shadow_labor} &= j_r + x_r = v + x_{gf}v + x_r \\
j_{shadow_fixed_asset} &= l_j + x_{dx}l_j + x_t \\
j_{shadow_current_asset} &= x_t \\
j_{shadow_transportation} &= j_y + x_y \\
j_{shadow_natural_resource} &= j_d + x_d
\end{aligned} \tag{18.145}$$

Load these values into formula 18.144 and we can get:

$$Z = j_{shadow\_raw}W_{raw} + j_{shadow\_secondary}W_{secondary} + j_{shadow\_energy}W_{energy} + j_{shadow\_labor}R\, j_{shadow\_fixed\_asset}T_g + j_{shadow\_current\_asset}T_l + j_{shadow\_transportation}Y + j_{shadow\_land}D \tag{18.146}$$

Summarize formula 18.146, we can get:

$$Z = j_{w\_shadow}W + j_{r\_shadow}R + j_{t\_shadow}T + j_{y\_shadow}Y + j_{d\_shadow}D \tag{18.147}$$

In this formula, j_{w_shadow} is the shadow price of input. j_{r_shadow} is the shadow price of labor. j_{t_shadow} is the shadow price of capital. j_{y_shadow} is the shadow price of transportation. j_{d_shadow} is the shadow price of natural resources.

Compare formulas 18.143 and 18.147 and we can see that the total social consumption cost (social cost) Z is the cost for input. It can be calculated based on the rational prices for inputs and the economic effect coefficients, or based on the shadow prices for inputs. The above formulas show that the shadow price of an input in consumption cost is the sum of its rational price (or cost per unit) and its economic effect coefficient. For instance, the shadow price for material is the sum of the rational price of material (raw material or energy) per unit and the economic effect coefficient of material utilization. The shadow price for labor is the sum of the wage and wage surcharge per unit and the economic effect coefficient of labor utilization. The shadow price for fixed capital is the sum of the depreciation rate of capital per unit (including heavy repair) and the economic effect coefficient of capital utilization. The shadow price for current capital is the economic effect coefficient of capital utilization per unit. The shadow price for transportation capacity is the sum of the rational price of transportation capacity per unit and the economic effect coefficient of transportation capacity utilization. The shadow price for natural resources is the sum of the rational price of natural resources per unit and the economic effect coefficient of natural resources utilization.

According to the theory of total social benefit in the technological economic effect, the total social benefit includes both direct benefit and indirect benefit. Its calculation formula is as following (based on net income evaluation methods).

$$S = S_{direct} + S_{indirect} = j_i G + x_i G \tag{18.148}$$

In this formula, the direct benefit S_{direct} is the result of the rational price j_i of output i multiplied by the amount of output G. The direct benefit S_{direct} considers the supply and demand effect of output i. Generally, it is the economic effect coefficient x_i of output i multiplied by the amount of output G. Set $j_{i\_shadow} = j_i + x_i$. Then formula 18.148 can then change to the following form.

$$\mathrm{S} = j_{i\_shadow} \cdot G \tag{18.149}$$

In this formula, j_{i_shadow} is the shadow price for output i.

Formula 18.149 can be used for calculating the total social benefit with a shadow price. It can be seen that the formula for calculating the shadow price of output is the same as the one for calculating the shadow price of input.

The shadow prices for input and output mentioned above are all based on the rational prices of input and output with the consideration of the supply and demand effect of input and output. Thus, these shadow prices can be called rational prices. But they are general rational prices, not the narrowly defined ones that do not consider the supply and demand effect of input and output. Although the shadow price can reflect indirect costs and benefits, some indirect costs and benefits still cannot be reflected. Other calculation methods are required to reflect them. In addition, the aforementioned methods for calculating the shadow price of input and output are only suitable for the situation when the input and output that are directly connected with foreign markets, namely import and export trade, do not exist. If the input and output directly connected with foreign markets exist, such as direct import, direct export, import replacement, or export replacement, the shadow prices for these inputs and outputs can be calculated by following the calculation methods for international shadow prices (price in international market × reasonable exchange rate), or by following the calculation methods for domestic shadow prices (domestic reasonable price + economic effect coefficient).

Among the six methods for calculating the shadow price, the first five are holistic approaches, while the sixth one is a decomposition approach. The holistic approach calculates shadow price as a whole, whereas the decomposition approach calculates shadow price in two steps. The holistic approach is called linear programming dualization, which can be hard to apply in practice. Therefore, it is a theoretical calculation method for shadow price. Two measurements are available to make the shadow price widely adopted in practice. One is to find the solution based on the holistic approach. The other is to find the solution based on the decomposition approach. It seems that these two measurement s are both valid to find practical calculation methods for shadow price.

Here are the characteristics of the decomposition approach. (1) It is based on the rational domestic prices and it suits China's basic condition. On the one hand, commodities in the domestic market have a rational price ratio. On the other hand, rational prices in domestic market are more stable and are easier to be predicted compared with the prices in the international market. The unstable prices in the international market can be converted into rational domestic prices with a rational exchange rate. It should be noted that a rational exchange rate cannot be achieved without a rational domestic price. In addition, the size of foreign trade is impacted by the price in the international market as well the rational price (generalized) in the domestic market. If the price in the international market is lower than the generalized rational price in the domestic market, it is not economical to export. In contrast, if the price in the international market is higher than the generalized rational price in the domestic market, it is not economical to import. Thus, it is reasonable for the decomposition approach to choose the rational price in the domestic market as the base for calculating the shadow price. (2) The supply and demand effect of input and output in the decomposition is calculated by using economic effect coefficients exclusively. This approach can deal with the supply and demand effect under different conditions, namely the short-term effect, the long-term effect, and the opportunity effect. For different supply and demand effects, the methods for calculating economic effect coefficients vary. However, the traditional theory of shadow pricing can only deal with the opportunity effect, not the short-term effect or the long-term effect. (3) The decomposition approach is simple and practical. It can be used for calculating several rational prices and economic effect coefficients based on the reality. For present irrational prices, two adjustments can be performed to achieve the practical shadow prices. The first adjustment is to change the present prices into rational prices with the formula of rational price. The second adjustment is to calculate the supply and demand effect with the formula of economic effect coefficients. Although these two adjustments are not very accurate, the shadow price can be achieved by combining them. (4) The term shadow price was initiated by western scholars in the late 1950s. The shadow price, as the name suggests, is not the actual price. From the decomposition approach, we can see that the shadow price consists of the actual rational price and the virtual economic effect coefficient. The latter is actually the shadow price or the shadow coefficient. Right now, some people have a very wide understand of shadow price. They call anything that adjusts the present price (e.g. eliminating tax) shadow price. This is not appropriate and it is easy to cause confusion.

18.9.3 Calculating Costs and Benefits with Shadow Price

It can be seen from the above discussion that the costs and benefits of technological schemes can be calculated with the shadow price directly in macro technological economy. In formulas 18.147 and 18.149, the shadow prices for input and output vary based on whether imports and exports exist. Next, we take the input and output of material as an example to explain the calculation methods.

1. **Prices of input products**

The prices of input products must be calculated based on the prices at factory (user price).

(1) Non-foreign trade goods (domestic supply). The input products might be used for diverse purposes, such as increasing production, making savings, competing with other technological schemes, or utilizing surplus materials. Despite these purposes, the domestic shadow price (generalized rational price) will be applied on them. Here is the formula.

$$\begin{aligned}\text{Domestic shadow price } j_{w\_shadow} = & \text{ rational price of materials } j_w \\ & + \text{ economic effect coefficient of material utilization } x_w\end{aligned} \quad (18.150)$$

In this formula, the rational price of materials j_w can be obtained via the rational price formula. Alternatively, adjusting prices according to the requirement of rational price can achieve a practical approximate rational price. The economic effect coefficient of material utilization x_w has four values to choose from, based on the supply and demand situation of a certain input. The first situation does not consider the impact of supply and demand status on price and takes $x_w = 0$. The second situation considers the long term effect and utilizes surplus materials. It takes $x_w = x_{w\_long\_term}$. In the third situation, a balance between supply and demand exists. Increasing production and saving materials can meet market demand. Some people argue that x_w should be zero. In fact, however, x_w should take $x_{w\_opportunity}$ with opportunity effect considered. The reason is that although an overall balance between supply and demand exists, the results generated by the same input vary across sectors, regions, and firms. The same input will generate different results if it is invested in two firms. If the opportunity effect is considered, firms that do not generate good results will abandon the opportunity to use an input. As a result, input goes to firms that generate good results. This process is the appropriate allocation of resources. If the opportunity effect is neglected when a balance exists between supply and demand and x_w is set zero, the appropriate allocation of resources will be groundless. In the fourth situation, supply falls short of demand. Competition exists among technological schemes. The input of other technological schemes need to be attracted. In this case, the short-term effect of input should be taken into consideration. x_w should take $x_{w\_short\_term}$.

(2) Foreign trade goods.

I. Direct imports (foreign supply). To increase import, the lower price between the international shadow price and the domestic shadow rice should be selected.

$$\text{International shadow price } j_{w\_shadow\_international} = \text{CIF } j_{cif} \times \text{ rational exchange rate } l_{exchange} + \text{domestic transportation and trade cost } j_{tranportaion\_trade} \quad (18.151)$$

If importing is more reasonable than choosing domestic supply, the international shadow price should be adopted. If importing is not reasonable, there is no need to import. Domestic supply should be chosen and the domestic shadow price should be adopted.

II. Substitute for import (domestic supply). If an input comes from domestic supply and this input can substitute for an import, the cost of this input should choose import price. If the import price is too expensive and the domestic shadow price is cheap, the cheaper prices should be adopted.

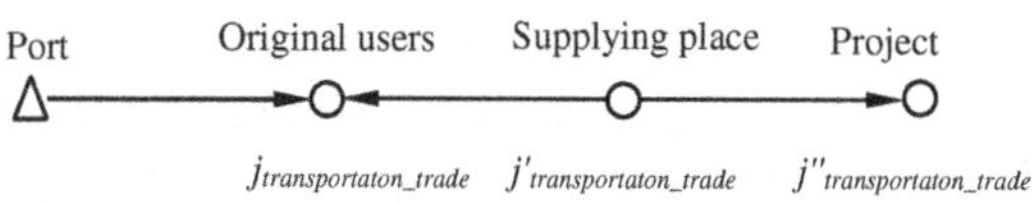

$$\begin{aligned}\text{International shadow price } j_{w\_shadow\_foreign} &= \text{CIF } j_{cif} \times \text{ rational exchange rate } l_{exchange}\\ &+ \text{domestic transportation and trade cost from port to original users } j_{transportaton\_trade}\\ &- \text{transportation and trade cost from supplying place to original users } j''_{transportaton\_trade}\\ &+ \text{transportation and trade cost from supplying place to project } j'_{transportaton\_trade}\end{aligned} \quad (18.152)$$

III. Exportable (domestic supply). The utilized input is from domestic supply. The input is exportable. Thus, it can be calculated with export price. If the export price is lower than the domestic price, it will not be rational to export. In this case, the input should not be exported. Instead, it should be traded in the domestic market. Therefore, the domestic price should be adopted. The price for exportable goods should be chosen from the international shadow price and the domestic shadow price. The shadow price with the larger value should be selected.

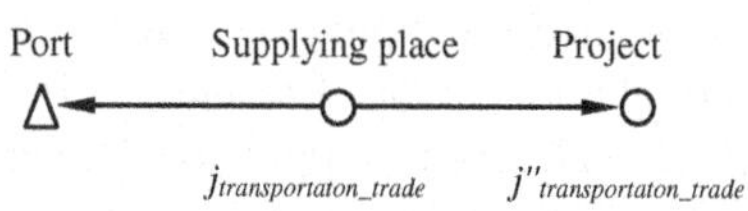

$$\begin{aligned}\text{International shadow price } j_{w\_shadow\_foreign} &= \text{FOB } j_{fob} \times \text{ rational exchange rate } l_{exchange}\\ &- \text{domestic transportation and trade cost from supplying place to port } j_{transportaton\_trade}\\ &+ \text{transportation and trade cost from supplying place to project } j''_{transportaton\_trade}\end{aligned} \quad (18.153)$$

2. **Prices of output products**

Output prices must be calculated with factory price.

(1) Non-foreign trade goods (domestic supply). The output products might be used for diverse purposes, such as competing with other firms, increasing consumption, satisfying demand, avoiding occupying materials of other technological schemes, or increasing surplus. Despite these purposes, the domestic shadow price will be applied to them. The value of x_w varies in different situation. The approaches usedto determine the value of output products are the same as those for input products. For the situation of oversupply, such as increasing surplus and forcing other firms to reduce production, x_w should take $x_{w\_long\_term}$. For the situation when a balance exists between supply and demand, such as increasing material consumption and satisfying demand, the opportunity effect should be considered and x_w should take $x_{w\_opportunity}$. For the situation when supply falls short of demand, x_w should take $x_{w\_short\_term}$. For the purpose of simplification, the impact of supply and demand can be neglected and x_w can take zero.
(2) Foreign trade goods.

I. Direct exports (supply foreign markets). The output products are exported and supply foreign markets. Thus, their prices should be calculated based on international shadow prices. However, if exporting products is not economical, export should be stopped and the domestic shadow price should be applied instead. In other words, prices of products for direct export should choose the higher one between international shadow price and domestic shadow price.

$$\begin{aligned}&\text{International shadow price } j_{w\_shadow\_international} = \text{FOB } j_{fob} \times \text{ rational exchange rate} l_{exchange}\\&-\text{domestic transportation and trade cost from project to port } j_{tranportaion\_trade}\end{aligned} \quad (18.154)$$

If the size of the international market is limited and the export of technological scheme *A* impacts that of technological scheme *B*, the indirect influence should be considered in a national economy evaluation.

II. Exportable (supply domestic market). For those output products that can be exported but actually are in supply in the domestic market, their prices should choose the higher one between the international shadow price and the domestic shadow price. For instance, the output product of a firm is planned to be exported. However, the amount of this product is not enough for exporting. As a result, this product is provided in the domestic market. Now a new project allows the firm to increase the production of this product. Other than supporting the domestic market, the product can now be exported. In this case, the output of the new project can be calculated with international shadow price.

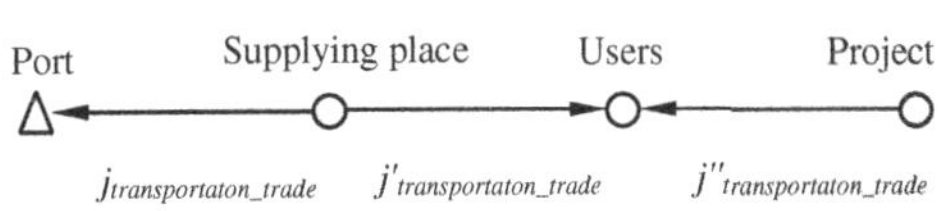

$$\begin{aligned}&\text{International shadow price } j_{w\_shadow\_foreign} = \text{FOB } j_{fob} \times \text{ rational exchange rate } l_{exchange}\\&-\text{domestic transportation and trade cost from supplying place to port } j_{transportaton\_trade}\\&-\text{transportation and trade cost from supplying place to users } j''_{transportaton\_trade}\\&+\text{transportation and trade cost from project to users } j''_{transportaton\_trade}\end{aligned} \tag{18.155}$$

III. Substitute for import (supply domestic market).

For output products that supply the domestic market and can substitute for imported products, their prices should choose the cheaper one between international shadow price and domestic shadow price.

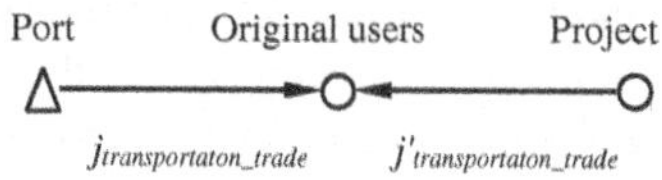

$$\begin{aligned}&\text{International shadow price } j_{w\_shadow\_foreign} = \text{CIF } j_{cif} \times \text{ rational exchange rate } l_{exchange}\\&+\text{transportation and trade cost from port to original users } j_{transportaton\_trade}\\&-\text{transportation and trade cost from project to original users } j'_{transportaton\_trade}\end{aligned} \tag{18.156}$$

The formulas listed above for calculating the international shadow price all consider the cost of transportation and trade. If this cost is not considered, the international shadow price can be calculated by multiplying the price in international market (port price) with the rational exchange rate.

Similarly, the costs and benefits for input and output other than materials can be calculated in the same way.

There are two methods to categorize non-foreign trade goods and foreign trade goods. According to the first method, the goods that are allowed by the foreign trade policy in a country and are tradable are foreign trade goods, whereas untradeable goods are non-foreign trade goods. The second method treats goods that are allowed by the foreign trade policy in a country, are tradable, and have economic rationality as foreign trade goods. Tradable goods that do not have economic rationality and untradeable goods are treated as non-foreign trade goods by the second method. If the first method is chosen, the shadow price for foreign trade goods should be the economic rational one selected between the foreign trade shadow price and the domestic shadow price. This method is relatively flexible and practical. If the second method is chosen, all foreign trade goods regulated by a country must be calculated with the foreign shadow price. However, sometimes, due to the change of domestic shadow price, foreign trade goods might lose their economic rationality, while non-foreign trade goods might gain economic rationality. Accordingly, the foreign trade shadow price based on the second method becomes useless. In this sense, the first method is better than the second one. As such, this book adopts the first method.

18.10 Calculation Methods of Economic Proportion for Comprehensive Utilization Technological Schemes

In a technological economic calculation, there are two types of comprehensive utilization technological schemes. One type is cross-sector comprehensive utilization technological schemes, such as the pivotal water conservancy project, the joint production project for metallurgy and fertilizer, and the joint production project for oil refining and petrochemistry. Several sectors in the national economy are involved in these technological schemes. The other type includes inter-sector comprehensive utilization technological schemes, such as passenger transport and freight schemes for railroad, the comprehensive utilization scheme for public buildings, the joint production project for coke-oven plants, the joint production project for thermoelectric plants, and the production project for petroleum refining plants. Only one sector in the national economy is involved in these technological schemes. In order to evaluate the economic effect of comprehensive utilization technological schemes, to allocate the benefits and costs (including material consumption) to sectors and products, to make plans, and to conduct economic calculation, the economic indices of comprehensive utilization technological schemes need to be split up properly. Next, the economic allocation methods for comprehensive utilization technological schemes are introduced, based on two situations. The first situation is when the products of comprehensive utilization technological schemes can be provided by non-comprehensive utilization technological schemes. The second situation is when the products of comprehensive utilization technological schemes cannot be provided by non-comprehensive utilization technological schemes.

18.10.1 Economic Allocation Methods for Comprehensive Utilization Technological Schemes with Separate Alternatives Available

1. **The first allocation method-deduction method**

Suppose the total economic benefits of a comprehensive utilization technological scheme is S^{Σ}, the total social consumption cost is Z^{Σ}, and there are three separate alternatives, with the economic benefit and social consumption cost S_1, S_2, S_3 and Z_1, Z_2, Z_3, respectively. If the economic effect of a main sector (corresponding to the first alternative) needs to be evaluated, the following allocation method can be applied.

First subtract S_2 and S_3 from S^{Σ}. Next, subtract Z_2 and Z_3 from Z^{Σ}. Then, the proportion that this sector (the first sector in this case) should be allocated in the comprehensive utilization technological scheme S_1^{Σ} and Z_1^{Σ} can be obtained. The economic effect index of this sector can be calculated $E_{al}^{\sum} = \frac{S^{\sum}-S_2-S_3}{Z^{\sum}-Z_2-Z_3} = \frac{S_1^{\sum}}{Z_1^{\sum}}$. In addition, the economic effect index for the corresponding first alternative can be calculated as well $E_{al} = \frac{S_1}{Z_1}$. Finally, we can see which scheme is more economical by comparing the values of E_{al} and $E_{al}^{\sum}$.

This allocation method is relatively simple and convenient and can generate correct results for economic comparison. However, it has drawbacks when it is applied for allocating the benefits and the costs among the sectors and the products in practice. The reason is that this method attributes all of the benefits and troubles of a comprehensive utilization technological scheme to a single sector. Allocation does not happen.

2. **The second allocation method-proportion method**

Suppose the economic effect index of a comprehensive utilization technological scheme is all known, including $T^{\sum}$, $C^{\sum}$, $x_wW^{\sum}$, $x_yY^{\sum}$, $x_rR^{\sum}$, $x_tT^{\sum}$, $x_dD^{\sum}$, and $S^{\sum}$. The economic effect index of the joint technological scheme composed of each separate alternative are $\sum T_i$, $\sum C_i$, $\sum x_wW_i$, $\sum x_yY_i$, $\sum x_rR_i$, $\sum x_tT_i$, $\sum x_dD_i$, and $\sum S_i$. The economic effect index of each separate alternative are T_i, C_i, x_wW_i, x_yY_i, x_rR_i, x_tT_i, x_dD_i, and S_i. Then, each economic effect index can be allocated based on proportion. Here are the steps.

$$T_i^{\sum} = \frac{T^{\sum}}{\sum T_i} T_i \tag{18.157}$$

$$C_i^{\sum} = \frac{C^{\sum}}{\sum C_i} C_i \tag{18.158}$$

$$Z_i^{\sum} = C_i^{\sum} + x_i T_i^{\sum} \tag{18.159}$$

This allocation method is more rational than the first one but, because the costs are allocated based on proportion, this method still has drawbacks.

3. **The third allocation method-two step method**

This method can be carried out in two steps. In the first step, the benefits generated by a comprehensive utilization technological scheme are allocated to all sectors (or all products) based on proportion. What do the benefits mean here? Suppose the investment on a comprehensive utilization technological scheme is $T^{\sum}$, the cost is $C^{\sum}$, the resource occupation is $D^{\sum}$, the labor occupation is $R^{\sum}$, the material consumption is $W^{\sum}$, the transportation capacity occupation is $Y^{\sum}$, and the total production is $S^{\sum}$. In the joint scheme composed of each separate alternative, the investment is $\sum T_i$, the cost is $\sum G_i$, resource occupation is $\sum D_i$, labor occupation is $\sum R_i$, material consumption is $\sum W_i$, transportation capacity occupation is $\sum Y_i$, and the total production is $\sum S_i$. If the total production $S^{\sum}$ of the comprehensive utilization technological scheme is bigger than that of the joint scheme, the increased production $\Delta S = (S^{\sum} - \sum S_i)$ is beneficial. If the cost $C^{\sum}$ of the comprehensive utilization technological scheme is smaller than that of the joint scheme $\sum C_i$, the saved cost $\Delta C = (\sum C_i - {}^{\sum})$ is beneficial as well. By parity of reasoning, the benefit for other economic indices can be calculated too. If it is clear that the saving in cost belongs to the benefit of a comprehensive utilization technological scheme; the decreasing of cost in sector *i* can be calculated with the following formula based on proportion method.

$$\Delta C_i = \frac{C_i}{\sum C_i} \Delta C \tag{18.160}$$

Next, the allocated cost for sector *i* can be calculated with the following formula.

$$C_i \sum = C_i - \Delta C_i = \frac{c^{\sum}}{\sum c_i} C_i \tag{18.161}$$

Suppose the total consumption cost $Z^{\sum}$ of the comprehensive utilization technological scheme saves ΔZ compared with the total consumption cost $\sum Z_i$ of the joint project. The total allocated consumption cost for sector *i* is:

$$Z_i^{\sum} = Z_i - \Delta Z_i = \frac{z^{\sum}}{\sum z_i} Z_i \tag{18.162}$$

The other savings on consumption can be calculated with the above method. To get the allocation of the increment ΔS in the total production of the comprehensive utilization technological scheme, calculate the difference between the total production $S_i^{\sum}$ obtained by each sector after they join the comprehensive utilization and the original total production S_i, namely $\Delta S_i = S^{\sum} - S_i$. For instance, the irrigation benefit $S_{irration}^{\sum}$ in a pivotal water conservancy project is bigger than the irrigation benefit $S_{irration}$ in a separate individual irration scheme. The increased benefit should be allocated to irrigation sectors.

In the second step, the increased consumption cost is allocated to sectors based on the size of the benefit they get. Here are the steps. Suppose the investment $T^{\sum}$ of a comprehensive utilization technological scheme is larger than the investment $\sum T_i$ of a joint project. The extra spending is $\Delta T = T^{\sum} - \sum T_i$. Then the investment $T_i^{\sum}$ on sector *i* is larger than the original investment. The increment is $\Delta T_i^{\sum} = T_i + \Delta T_i$. ΔT_i can be calculated by the following formula.

$$\Delta T_i = \frac{\Delta S_{ci}}{\Delta S_c} \Delta T \tag{18.163}$$

In this formula, ΔS_{ci} is the sum of the benefit allocated to section *i*. ΔS_c is the sum of the increased benefit between the comprehensive utilization technological scheme and the joint project. Similarly, this method can be applied to other indices, including labor, land resources, and resource consumption.

The third allocation method overcomes the drawbacks of the first two methods. It can be used for accurately evaluating the economic effect of each sector participating in a comprehensive utilization technological scheme. In addition, this method is helpful for sectors to fairly bear the cost in the comprehensive utilization technological scheme, and as a result, to motivate them in the comprehensive utilization technological scheme.

18.10.2 Economic Allocation Methods for Comprehensive Utilization Technological Schemes Without Separate Alternatives Available

In practice, it is very hard to find separate alternatives for some comprehensive utilization technological schemes. The benzene, tar, coke, and coal gas produced by coke-oven plant comprehensive utilization schemes are good examples. Several allocation methods are introduced next.

1. **The first allocation method**

This method is very similar to the deduction method introduced earlier. It deducts the benefit and cost of a comprehensive utilization technological scheme one by one. In other words, it subtracts the benefit and the cost of byproducts gradually. The deduction method introduced earlier deducts the benefit and cost based on a separate alternative. In contrast, this method deducts the benefit and cost based on the general expenditure in the market. For instance, when the cost of benzene is deducted from the consumption cost of a coke-oven plant in a comprehensive utilization scheme, the cost of benzene is calculated by subtracting profits from the price of benzene in market. Obviously, this method has drawbacks.

2. **The second allocation method**

Essentially, the method is very close to the proportion method introduced earlier. It allocates benefit and cost based on proportion in production. For example, the production in a comprehensive utilization technological scheme is a direct benefit. The bigger the production, the more cost should be allocated, and vice versa. Therefore, if the investment T^{Σ} and cost C^{Σ} of a comprehensive utilization technological scheme is known, and the production of each product S_i is known as well, the allocated investment T_i^{Σ} and cost C_i^{Σ} for each product should be:

$$T_i^{\Sigma} = \frac{s_i}{s^{\Sigma}} \cdot T^{\Sigma} \tag{18.164}$$

$$C_i^{\Sigma} = \frac{s_i}{s\sum} \cdot C^{\Sigma} \tag{18.165}$$

In the above formulas, S^{Σ} is the sum of each production in a comprehensive utilization technological scheme.

This method is better than the first one, but it still has drawbacks. To use this method, the prices of products must be known. Furthermore, the change of price will impact the allocation.

In order to overcome this drawback, scholars have proposed a fixed-rate method.[17] Here are its steps.

(1) Obtain the allocated value $G_i \cdot j'_{gi}$ of an item in a comprehensive utilization technological scheme by multiplying its specified productive rate with its allocated unit price.[18] (2) Calculate the allocation rate of an item by dividing its allocated value with its total allocated value $y_i = \frac{G_i \cdot j'_{gi}}{\sum G_i \cdot j'_{gi}}$. (3) Calculate the allocated cost for each item by multiplying its allocation rate with the shared cost (e.g. cost, investment), such as $C_i^y = y_i \cdot C^{\Sigma}$ and $T_i^y = y_i \cdot T^{\Sigma}$. (4) Calculate the total cost for each item by adding its allocated cost with its specific cost, such as $C_i^{\Sigma} = C_i^y + C_i^z$ and $T_i^{\Sigma} = T_i^y + T_i^z$. This method chooses the allocated unit price to replace the product price. As a result, the impact caused by price fluctuation can be reduced. In addition, the specific cost for each item is different. If allocation is based on product price, those items having a large specific cost will be allocated more cost. This is not rational. It is more reasonable to calculate this based on the allocated unit price. Accordingly, the fixed-rate method has advantages. Other methods, such as the heat value method, the volume method, and the weight method, are proposed as well. However, these methods work only under certain conditions.

References

[Ca71] Canada, J. R. (1971). Intermediate Economic Analysis for Management and Engineering. Englewood Cliffs, N.J. Prentice-Hall.

[Da72] Dasgupta, P., Sen, A., & Marglin, S. (1972). Guidelines for project evaluation. In UNIDO. Project Formulation and Evaluation (Vol. 2). United Nations. UNIDO.

[Li68] Little, I. M., & Mirrlees, J. A. (1968). Manual of Industrial Project Analysis In Developing Countries: Volume II.

[Sq75] Squire, L., & Van der Tak, H. G. (1975). Economic analysis of projects. World Bank Publications.

[17] Shanghai Coal Gas Company (1963). Calculation methods for the cost of products in joint project of gas manufacturing and coking.

[18] In other literature, allocated unit price j'_{gi} is proportion in product price after tax and specific cost are subtracted. The author argues that allocated unit price is actual income. From the perspective of a country, tax is a type of income. Therefore, tax can be kept in allocated unit price for macro technological economy.

[Sq75] Squire, L., & Van der Tak, H. G. (1975). Economic analysis of projects. World Bank Publications.

[Xu65] Xu, S.B. (1965). *Methodology for Technological Economy*. In Research Report from Comprehensive Investigation Committee of China Academy of Science.

[Xu84] Xu, S.B. (1984). Technological Economics. Volume one and volume two. Chinese Technology Association.

[Zh84] Zhu, X. B. (1984). Theories and methods for effect coefficients of resource utilization. Master thesis in the department of Technological Economy, Graduate School at the Chinese Academy of Social Sciences.

Chapter 19
Methods for Technological Economic Evaluation

19.1 Introduction

As the core of technological economics, methods for technological economic evaluation can be applied for assessing and improving firms' economic benefits and economic efficiency, for evaluating and improving social economic benefits and economic efficiency, for evaluating economic effect of technological economic schemes, and for supporting decision. Thus, methods for technological economic evaluation are closely tied to the fate of technological schemes and the development of the national economy. Incorrect methods can cause huge damages to a country and to its firms. At present, there many available methods for technological economic evaluation. Some are macro, while others are micro. Some are dynamic, while others are static. Some originate in China, while others have been introduced from the Soviet Union, from countries in eastern Europe, or from western countries. These methods have diverse names and signs. They are not systematic, nor are they convenient to use. Accordingly, the author compares and studies the methods for technological economic evaluation in China and those from other countries. He identifies the similarities and differences among these methods and proposes three method systems for macro and micro technological economic evaluation. These method systems are based on the methods that the author proposed for economic evaluation in the early 1960s. They also reference some methods in the fields of foreign departmental economics, engineering economics, and cost-benefit analysis.

Methods for technological economic evaluation discussed in the literatures can have confusing levels and names. For instance, some propose an evaluation method of economy, an evaluation method of operation research, and an evaluation method of determinism. Others propose an evaluation method of economic effect, an evaluation method of comparison, and an evaluation method of intuitive judgment. Actually, the evaluation method of economy and the evaluation method of operation research are not at the same level, nor are the evaluation method of economic effect and

S. Xu, *Technological Economics*,
https://doi.org/10.1007/978-981-15-8582-1_19

the evaluation method of comparison. Methods for technological economic evaluation can be categorized by the economic evaluation standard index or by evaluation approaches (analysis, comparison, optimization, and decision). The evaluation method of economic effect and the evaluation method of the economy are based on an economic evaluation standard index. The evaluation method of comparison and the evaluation method of operation research are based on evaluation approaches. These two categories are not comparable. Methods for technological economic evaluation should be categorized by the economic standard index first, because the economic standard index is at the first level and is the most important. They reflect the economic essential of methods for technological economic evaluation. The 60 methods for technological economic evaluation in the three series discussed in the coming sections are categorized based on the economic standard index. Each method for technological economic evaluation has its own economic meaning. Each technological scheme must adopt the methods for technological economic evaluation at the first level. The methods for technological economic evaluation at the second level are optional. For example, the evaluation method of operation research is optional; its application is not mandatory. In fact, methods at the second levels should not be called methods for technological economic evaluation. They are just some applications, such as the application of operation research and the application of comparison. As such, only methods at the first level are discussed in this chapter. Those at the second level are discussed in Chap. 21.

19.2 Comparison Between Evaluation Methods for Micro and Macro Technological Economy

19.2.1 Characteristics and Effects of Evaluation Methods for Micro and Macro Technological Economy

The evaluation methods for the macro technological economy reveal the laws in the macro technological economy and reflect the overall relation of interests across a society. In contrast, the evaluation methods for the micro technological economy only reflect the relation of interests at the micro and local levels. Analysis and evaluation of the macro technological economy plays a key role in the selection of technological schemes. When the evaluation of macro technological economy is in conflict with the evaluation of the micro technological economy, the latter should yield. Thus, for technological economic issues, an analysis and evaluation of macro technological economy should be conducted first. Only when the result of the evaluation of the macro technological economy is positive is it useful to perform an evaluation of micro technological economy. In practice, however, the evaluation of the micro technological economy is usually conducted first. It is appropriate to follow this order, because micro economic benefits do exist and attention should be paid on them. If only the macro-economic effects are considered and the micro-economic effects are neglected, firms will lose motivation. As a result, any macro-economic effects will be affected. Analysis and evaluation of the micro technological economy can examine micro-economic effects and can further provide suggestions for state-level policy making. In this way, micro-economic benefits can be achieved.

19.2.2 Common Characteristics of Evaluation Methods for Micro and Macro Technological Economy

Evaluation methods for the micro and the macro technological economy are used for calculating economic effects. They share the following common characteristics:

(1) Division and subtraction

Evaluation methods for the micro and the macro technological economy have two formats: division and subtraction.

(2) Total amount and increment

The result calculated with total amount is the absolute economic effect, whereas that calculated with the increment is the relative economic effect. Calculations with the total amount and the increment are useful for evaluating the micro and the macro technological economy.

(3) Static and dynamic

Although static and dynamic approaches can be adopted for evaluating both the micro and the macro technological economy, dynamic approaches with time factors considered are more frequently used. Dynamic calculation can be based on present value and on final value.

(4) Total value and annual value

Total value means the overall account for a calculation period or a service period. Annual value refers to the yearly average account for a calculation period or a service period. Calculations of total value and annual value are useful for evaluating the micro and the macro technological economy, although an annual value calculation is a better approach for comparing several technological schemes with a different service period. Total value calculation requires the same calculation period or service period.

Four common characteristics are listed, along with the main methods for micro and macro technological economy evaluation (see Table 19.1).

Table 19.1 The main methods for technological economy evaluation

No.	Methods for macro technological economy evaluation			
	Methods based on national income (net output value)			
	Name	Symbol	Synonym and symbol	Derived from
1	Social (total) productivity of labor II	E_b	Social excess (total) productivity of labor II	–
2	Social national income	E_d	Social excess national income, net present value of national income (*NNPV*)	–
3	Social additional (total) productivity of labor II	E_{bf}	Social additional excess (total) productivity of labor II, social marginal productivity of labor II	–
4	Social additional national income rate	E_{df}	Social additional excess national income rate, social marginal national income rate	–
5	Annual national income	$S_{g\text{-}static}$	–	E_d
6	Investment-national income ratio	$L_{tg\text{-}static}$	–	E_b, E_d
7	Investment recovery period	$n_{c\text{-}static}$	–	E_b, E_d
8	Additional investment- national income ratio	$L_{ftg\text{-}static}$	Marginal investment- national income ratio	E_{bf}, E_{df}
9	Additional investment recovery period	$n_{fc\text{-}static}$	–	E_{bf}, E_{df}
10	Annual computational costs	$Z_{u\text{-}static}$	–	E_b, E_d
11	(Dynamic) investment- national income ratio	X_{tg}	Dynamic investment net output value ratio (*NIRR*)	E_b, E_d

(continued)

Table 19.1 (continued)

No.	Methods for macro technological economy evaluation			
	Methods based on national income (net output value)			
	Name	Symbol	Synonym and symbol	Derived from
12	(Dynamic) investment excess national-income ratio	L_{tg}	–	E_{df}
13	(Dynamic) investment recovery period	n_c	–	E_b, E_d
14	(Dynamic) additional investment-national income ratio	X_{ftg}	Marginal investment-national income ratio, net increased dynamic investment-national income ratio ($\Delta NIRR$)	E_{bf}, E_{df}
15	(Dynamic) additional investment recovery period	n_{fc}	Marginal investment recovery period	E_{bf}, E_{df}
16	Total consumption costs	$Z_{u\sum}$	–	E_b, E_d
17	Annual consumption costs	Z_u	–	E_b, E_d
18	Domestic competitiveness	$E_{domestic}$	–	E_d
19	International competitiveness	$E_{international}$	Ratio of international competitiveness and present value	E_b etc.
20	Swap rate	L_{swap}	Cost of foreign exchange	E_b
No.	Methods for macro technological economy evaluation			
	Methods based on net income			
	Name	Symbol	Synonym and symbol	Derived from
1	Social (total) productivity of labor I	E_a	Social excess (total) productivity of labor I	E_b
2	Social net income	E_c	Social excess net income, net present value of national investment income (NPV), economic net present value	E_d
3	Social additional (total) productivity of labor I	E_{af}	Social additional (total) productivity of labor I, social marginal productivity of labor I	E_{bf}

(continued)

Table 19.1 (continued)

No.	Methods for macro technological economy evaluation			
	Methods based on national income (net output value)			
	Name	Symbol	Synonym and symbol	Derived from
4	Social additional net income rate	E_{cf}	Social additional excess net income rate, social marginal net income rate	E_{df}
5	Annual net income	$S_{c\text{-}static}$	–	E_c
6	Investment net income ratio	$L_{tc\text{-}static}$	Profit-tax rate of capital, national rate of return on investment	E_a, E_c
7	Investment recovery period	$n_{c\text{-}static}$	–	E_a, E_c
8	Additional investment net income ratio	$L_{ftc\text{-}static}$	Marginal investment net income ratio,national rate of return on investment, net increase national rate of return on investment	E_{af}, E_{cf}
9	Additional investment recovery period	$n_{fc\text{-}static}$	Comparative investment recovery period	E_{af}, E_{cf}
10	Annual computational costs	Z_{static}	–	E_a, E_c
11	(Dynamic) investment net income ratio	X_{tc}	Dynamic national rate of return on investment, economic internal rate of return (*EIRR*)	E_a, E_c
12	(Dynamic) investment excess net income ratio	L_{tc}	Economic net present value (*ENPV*) rate	E_{cf}
13	(Dynamic) investment recovery period	n_c	–	E_a, E_c
14	(Dynamic) additional investment net income ratio	X_{ftc}	Net incremental internal rate of return (ΔIRR)	E_{af}, E_{cf}
15	(Dynamic) additional investment recovery period	n_{fc}	–	E_{af}, E_{cf}
16	Total consumption costs	$Z_{\sum}$	–	E_a, E_c
17	Annual consumption costs	Z	–	E_a, E_c
18	Domestic competitiveness	$E_{domestic}$	–	E_c

(continued)

Table 19.1 (continued)

No.	Methods for macro technological economy evaluation			
	Methods based on national income (net output value)			
	Name	Symbol	Synonym and symbol	Derived from
19	International competitiveness	$E_{international}$	Ratio of international competitiveness and present value	E_c etc.
20	Swap rate	L_{swap}	Cost of foreign exchange	E_c
No.	Methods for micro technological economy evaluation			
	Methods based on profit			
	Name	Symbol	Synonym and symbol	Derived from
1	Enterprise (total) labor productivity	E_c	Enterprise excess (total) labor productivity, benefit-cost ratio	E_a
2	Enterprise profit	E_j	Enterprise excess profit, net present value (*NPV*), financial net present value	E_c
3	Enterprise additional (total) labor productivity	E_{ef}	Enterprise additional excess (total) labor productivity, the ratio of incremental profit to incremental costs, enterprise marginal labor productivity	E_{af}
4	Enterprise additional profit rate	E_{ff}	Enterprise additional excess profit rate, Enterprise marginal profit rate	E_{cf}
5	Annual profit	$S_{c\text{-}static}$	–	E_c
6	Return on investment	$L_{tl\text{-}static}$	–	E_a, E_c
7	Investment recovery period	$n_{c\text{-}static}$	–	E_a, E_c
8	Additional return on investment	$L_{ftl\text{-}static}$	–	E_{af}, E_{cf}
9	Additional investment recovery period	$n_{fc\text{-}static}$	–	E_{af}, E_{cf}
10	Annual computational costs	$Z_{enterprise\_static}$	–	E_a, E_c

(continued)

Table 19.1 (continued)

No.	Methods for micro technological economy evaluation			
	Methods based on profit			
	Name	Symbol	Synonym and symbol	Derived from
11	(Dynamic) return on investment	X_{tl}	Internal rate of return (*IRR*), discount rate, rate of returns, financial internal rate of return	E_a, E_c
12	(Dynamic) excess return on investment	L_{tl}	financial net present value rate, net present value index (*NPVI*)	E_{cf}
13	(Dynamic) investment recovery period	n_c	–	E_a, E_c
14	(Dynamic) additional return on investment	X_{ftl}	Marginal return on investment,internal rate of return of incremental investment	E_{af}, E_{cf}
15	(Dynamic) additional investment recovery period	n_{fc}	Marginal investment recovery period	E_{af}, E_{cf}
16	Total consumption costs	$Z_{\sum\text{-}enterprise}$	Present value comparison method	E_a, E_c
17	Annual consumption costs	$Z_{enterprise}$	Annual cost comparison method, annuity method	E_a, E_c
18	Domestic competitiveness	$E_{domestic}$	–	E_c
19	International competitiveness	$E_{international}$	Ratio of international competitiveness and present value present value rate	E_c etc.
20	Swap rate	L_{swap}	Cost of foreign exchange	E_c

No.	Common characteristics								
	One		Two		Three			Four	
	Division	Subtraction	Gross	Increment	Static	Dynamic		Gross value	Annual value
						Present value	Final value		
1	√	–	√	–	–	√	√	√	√

(continued)

Table 19.1 (continued)

No.	Common characteristics								
	One		Two		Three			Four	
	Division	Subtraction	Gross	Increment	Static	Dynamic		Gross value	Annual value
						Present value	Final value		
2	–	√	√	–	–	√	√	√	√
3	√	–	–	√	–	√	√	√	√
4	√	–	–	√	–	√	√	√	√
5	–	√	√	–	√	–	–	–	√
6	√	–	√	–	√	–	–	–	√
7	√	–	√	–	√	–	–	–	√
8	√	–	–	√	√	–	–	–	√
9	√	–	–	√	√	–	–	–	√
10	√	√	√	–	√	–	–	–	√
11	√	–	√	–	–	√	√	√	–
12	√	–	√	–	–	√	√	√	–
13	√	–	√	–	–	√	√	√	–
14	√	–	–	√	–	√	√	√	–
15	√	–	–	√	–	√	√	√	–
16	√	√	√	–	–	√	√	√	–

(continued)

Table 19.1 (continued)

No.	Common characteristics								
	One		Two		Three			Four	
	Division	Subtraction	Gross	Increment	Static	Dynamic		Gross value	Annual value
						Present value	Final value		
17	✓	✓	✓	–	–	✓	✓	–	✓
18	–	✓	–	✓	✓	✓	✓	✓	✓
19	✓	–	✓	–	–	✓	✓	✓	–
20	✓	–	✓	–	–	✓	✓	✓	–

19.2.3 The Differences Between Evaluation Methods for Macro and Micro Technological Economy

The evaluation methods for the macro and the micro technological economy have the following differences:

1. Different position

Different positions can be taken when evaluating a technological scheme. The evaluation methods for the micro technological economy start from the position of a certain firm or department, and then analyze and calculate the economic benefits generated by a technological scheme. The evaluation methods for the macro technological economy start from the position of a society or a country, and then analyze and calculate the internal and external economic benefits generated by a technological scheme. The former calculates the local economic effects, whereas the latter calculates the total economic effects in a society.

2. Different purpose

The purpose of the macro technical and economic evaluation is to provide scientific basis for decisions regarding technical solutions, but the purpose of the micro technical and economic evaluation is to evaluate the technical solutions in terms of the balance of financial payments according to the current financial systems. The results of the micro technical and economic evaluation can be used to compare with the existing enterprises to judge technical solutions and to provide the basis for the reasonable distribution of interests between the enterprise and the country. If the macro technical and economic evaluation result is beneficial to the state, but the micro technical and economic evaluation result is detrimental to the enterprise, the state should take measures such as price adjustments, tax cuts, and subsidies, so as to allow the enterprise to gain reasonable interests. Macro control is also required for individual economy, although it can make decisions microscopically.

3. Different economic meanings

Both macro and micro technological economy evaluations analyze income and expenditure, benefit and cost, gain and loss, and input and output. In terms of income and expenditure, some items are fixed, while others are flexible. Among the technological economy evaluation methods, sales revenue, current capital collection, and residual collection belong to the category of income. Investment and costs for raw materials, energy, and heavy repair belong to expenditure. However, wage, tax, and basic depreciation expenses can be dealt with differently. Sometimes, they can be treated as income. But sometimes, they are expenditures. From the perspective of a macro technological economy analysis, wages are one kind of personal income Accordingly, wages are a kind of national income. However, wages can be treated as a portion of cost, as well. In this case, wages are net income. Similarly, at the country level, tax is a kind of income. Thus, the macro technological economy evaluation categorizes tax into income. In contrast, the micro technological economy evaluation categorizes tax into expenditure. The basic depreciation expense has the same characteristic; it is expenditure, as well as income. In a technological economy evaluation, the basic depreciation expense belongs to expenditure if the investment cost is not calculated. If the investment cost is calculated, the basic depreciation expense should be removed from costs in order to avoid counting both investment cost and basic depreciation expense. Or, basic depreciation expense can be treated as income. The content of the balance of payment (the statement of cash flow) adopted in the macro and the micro technological economy evaluation methods is listed in Table 19.2.

4. Different calculation scope

Table 19.2 The content of the statement of cash flow adopted in the macro and the micro technological economy evaluation methods

Macro technological economy evaluation	Micro technological economy evaluation	
	Total Capital	Own Fund
Income 1. Income (direct) 2. Income (indirect) 3. Basic depreciation collection[*] 4. Residual collection 5. Current capital collection 6. Wage 7. Subtotal	**Income** 1. Income (includes allowance) 2. Basic depreciation collection[*] 3. Residual collection 4. Current capital collection 5. Subtotal	**Income** 1. Income 2. Basic depreciation collection[*] 3. Residual collection 4. Current capital collection 5. Subtotal
Expenditure 1. Investment (direct) 2. Investment (indirect) 3. Costs (direct) 4. Costs (indirect) 5. Costs of material consumption[**] 6. Costs of transportation capacity occupation[**] 7. Costs of labor occupation[**] 8. Costs of natural resources consumption[**] 9. Subtotal	**Expenditure** 1. Investment 2. Costs 3. Taxes 6. Interests 7. Others 8. Subtotal	**Expenditure** 1. Own fund investment 2. Repayment of loan interest 3. Repayment of loan principal 4. Costs 5. Interests of taxes 6. Others 7. Subtotal
Net income of fund	**Net income of fund**	**Net income of fund**
Accumulated net income of fund	**Accumulated net income of fund**	**Accumulated net income of fund**

Note[*] If the cost in expenditure is changed to operation cost (in other words, if the basic depreciation expense is deducted from cost), this item should not be counted as income

[**] If shadow price is adopted in cost calculation, this cost should not be calculated again

A micro technological economy evaluation only considers the direct economic effect inside a firm generated by technological schemes; the indirect economic effect outside a firm will not be considered. Thus, it is relatively easier, compared with a macro technological economy evaluation, which considers both the direct and the indirect economic effects. Calculations of indirect economic effects are complicated and vary across technological schemes. Whether a macro technological economy evaluation is successful depends on the calculation and on the analysis of indirect economic effects.

5. Different index

A macro technological economy evaluation needs to reflect the rules of the technological economy, whereas a micro technological economy evaluation needs to reflect the facts. Because of this difference, they choose different indices. A micro technological economy analysis and calculation can adopt the present price and allowance, the present tax rate and interest rate, the present exchange rate, and the actual service period. A macro technological economy analysis and calculation should adopt the rational price, the rational tax rate and interest rate (namely five indirect costs), the rational exchange rate, and the calculation service period, or should combine the rational prices with the five indirect costs and then calculate with shadow prices.

The main differences between the macro technological economy evaluation methods and the micro technological economy evaluation methods are listed in Table 19.3.

In practice, micro technological economy calculation is easy and macro technological economy calculation is complicated. Sometimes, macro technological economy calculation can only be conducted approximately and incompletely by changing the profit goal into a net income or national income goal, adjusting irrational prices, or considering several indirect economic effects. Although these approaches can only assess the macro technological economy incompletely, they are still very useful.

19.3 Evaluation Methods for Macro Technological Economy

The two most important indices for assessing the economic effects of technological schemes are net income (profit and tax) and national income (net output value). Accordingly, evaluation methods for the macro technological economy can be categorized into two series: one is net income methods, and the other is national income methods. Each method has four basic means. In additional, 16 approaches can derive from the four means.

Table 19.3 The differences between macro technological economy evaluation methods and micro technological economy evaluation methods

Macro technological economy evaluation methods	Micro technological economy evaluation methods
1. Adopt national income and net income for serving the entire national economy 2. Consider indirect economic effects 3. Calculate the five indirect costs (the costs of capital occupation, the costs of materials occupation, the costs of transport capability occupation, the costs of labor occupation, and the costs of natural resource occupation); Do not calculate present tax rate and interests 4. Adopt rational price and do not consider allowance* 5. Adopt a reasonable interest rate (shadow interest rate) 6. Do not consider loans and repayment (except foreign loans) 7. Consider time factors. Calculate with investment economic effect coefficients (foreign loans are calculated with lending rate) 8. Adopt a calculation period	1. Adopt methods based on profits for serving firms' benefit 2. Do not consider indirect economic effects 3. Do not calculate the five indirect costs; Calculate present tax rate and interest rate 4. Adopt present price and consider allowance 5. Adopt the present interest rate 6. Consider loans and repayment 7. Do not consider time factors, or consider time factors and calculate with present deposit and loan interest rate. 8. Adopt a service period

Note *If shadow prices (the generalized rational prices) are adopted, the five indirect costs do not need to be calculated

19.3.1 Net Income Series Methods

1. Social (total) labor productivity I E_a method[1]

$$E_a = \frac{S_\Sigma(\text{or } X_\Sigma)}{Z_\Sigma} \quad (E_a \geq 1) \tag{19.1}$$

2. Social net income E_c method

$$E_c = S_\Sigma - Z_\Sigma \quad (E_c \geq 0) \tag{19.2}$$

S_Σ and Z_Σ in formulas 19.1 and 19.2 are the total amount in a given period (n_j years). The total amount can be calculated based on the annual amount or by directly adding the investment in each year together. The calculation method based on annual amount is initially proposed by the author in early 1960s. It has two steps. In the first step, all of the occupied inputs are converted into one annual consumption input, namely the annual amount. In the second step, all of the annual amounts are added together.

[1]The word total can be omitted for the convenience of reading and writing.

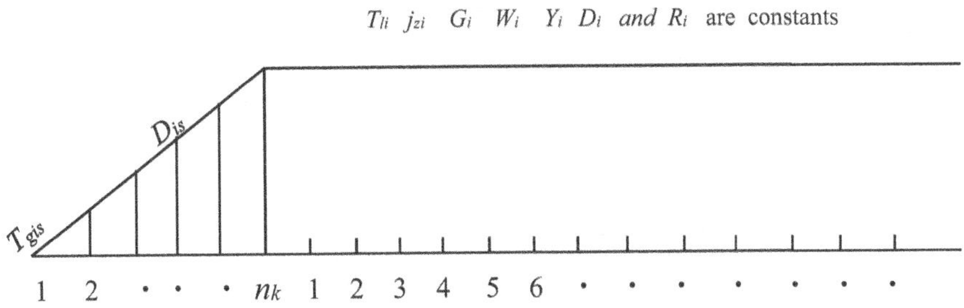

Fig. 19.1 The first situation in technological scheme developing process (the easiest situation)

For example, the annual amount can be calculated by converting occupied input (investment and land) into annual consumption input (the costs of capital occupation and land occupation) and then adding the result with the annual consumption input (cost). This method unifies occupation and consumption as well as investment and cost. It has many advantages in practice. The direct adding method calculates the total amount by adding the input of each year in a given period together. For instance, investment and cost can be added together directly.

(1) **The calculation method based on annual amount**

The method is built on two assumptions. The first assumption is that a technological scheme only produces one product. The other assumption is that the investment occupation (including fixed assets and current assets) of a technological scheme is processed as capital occupation. Labor, material, and resources, in investment, are not treated as the utilization of labor, material, and natural resource. Although this is an approximate approach, it is acceptable in practice.

In order to compare the conditions of product production and quality between technological schemes, four situations with different outputs will be discussed next. Further, in order to compare the condition regarding time, each situation is analyzed based on its four development stages and its four length of services.[2]

I. **Different technological schemes have the same production and quality**. Technological schemes input and occupy all investment T_g and resources D (such as land) in construction period (the year of n_k). When the construction is finished, the designed production level is achieved immediately. In addition, the production G and quality P are the same in all years. The costs C, materials W, natural resources D, occupied transport capacity Y, labor force R, and current capital T_l are the same in all years as well (as shown in Fig. 19.1). In the figure, i represents different technological schemes; s represents different years (i and s have the same meaning in the following figures). This situation is the simplest output and development process.

[2] In order to make this chapter shorter, only the simplest and the most complicated output situations and development process are discussed.

The technological characteristics of technology schemes vary. As a result, the lengths of service for technology schemes are not the same. For those technological schemes with different lengths of service, comparable condidtions about time should be considered. Next, for the purpose of convenience, the lengths of service for each technological scheme should fall into four situations. In situation one, the lengths of service for technological schemes are n_{f1}, n_{f2}, ...n_{fi} respectively. Their values are close to the required calculation length n_j (see Fig. 19.2a). In situation two, the values that are compared are smaller than the calculation length n_j (see Fig. 19.2b). In situation three, some of the values that are compared are larger than the calculation length n_j, while others are smaller (see Fig. 19.2c). In situation four, the values that are compared are largerer than the calculation length n_j (see Fig. 19.2d).

According to the principle of time comparison, the economic effects of technological schemes should be evaluated based on the same period, namely the calculation period, regardless of the lengths of their service. Next, we will discuss the four situations of the length of service for technological schemes in details.

In the first situation (shown in Fig. 19.2a), because the length of service for each technological scheme is very close to or even equal to the calculation period n_j, the evaluation results based on the two periods will be the same. Furthermore, the investment cost (fixed assets) for each technological scheme will be used up in the total n_j years, except for residuals, and the benefits for each technological scheme will be realized in the total n_j years. As such, the total social consumption and total social benefits for each technological scheme can be calculated with the following formulas.

I. Calculation of the total social consumption of technological schemes (or total social cost, total social expenditure, total social spending).

The following formulas and the calculations in the later sections of this chapter follow two rules. First, when time factors are considered, all of the occupation costs are calculated from the beginning of a year and all of the consumption costs are calculated from the next year, with compound interest. Second, the costs caused by the input in a certain year, including the occupation and consumption of capital, materials, natural resources, transportation, and labor, are calculated from that year. Here is the formula for calculating the total social consumption cost $Z_{\sum}$ with the

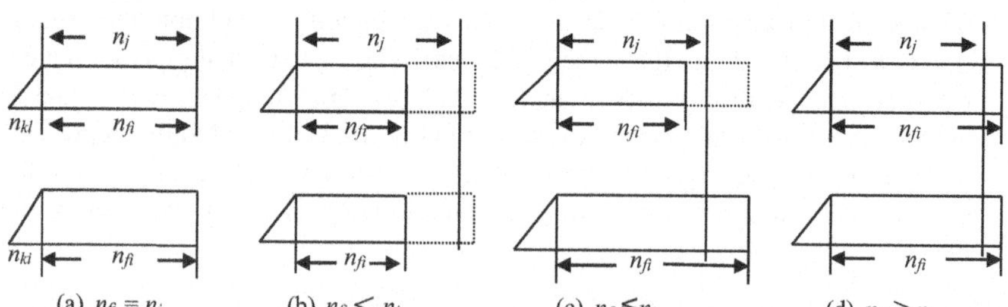

Fig. 19.2 Four situations of the length of service for technological schemes

time factor considered:

$$
\begin{aligned}
Z_{\Sigma} &= \sum_{s=1}^{n_j+n_k} Z_s\theta^{n_j+n_k-s} = \sum_{s=1}^{n_j} Z_{zs}\theta^{n_j-s} = Z_z\frac{\theta^{n_j}-1}{\theta-1} \\
&= \left[(x_tT_{g1}] + x_dD_1)\frac{\theta^{n_j}-1}{\theta-1} + \cdots\cdots + (x_tT_{gnk} + x_dD_{nk})\frac{\theta^{n_j+1}-1}{\theta-1}\right] \\
&+ \left[(C + x_wW + x_yY + x_dD + x_rR + x_tT_l)\frac{\theta^{n_j}-1}{\theta-1}\right] \\
&- \left[x_t\sum_{s=1}^{n_j} C_{js}\frac{\theta^{n_j-s}-1}{\theta-1} - T_c\right] \\
&= C + x_wW + x_yY + x_dD + x_rR + x_tT_z + x_dD_z)\frac{\theta^{n_j}-1}{\theta-1}
\end{aligned} \tag{19.3}
$$

where Z_s is the annual social consumption cost of the technological scheme in the construction period and the calculation period. Z_{zs} is the annual social consumption cost of the technological scheme converted into the calculation period. Z_z is the average annual social consumption cost of the technological scheme converted into the calculation period. T_z is the average annual capital occupation amount of the technological scheme converted into calculation period.

$$
T_z = T_{gz} + T_l - T_j + T_{cz} \tag{19.3.1}
$$

where T_{gz} is the average annual fixed capital occupation amount of the technological scheme converted into the calculation period (in n_j years).

$$
T_{gz} = T_{g1}\frac{\theta^{n_j+n_k}-1}{\theta^n j-1} + \cdots\cdots + T_{gnk}\frac{\theta^{n_j+1}-1}{\theta^n j_{-1}} = \sum_{s=1}^{n_k} T_{gs}\frac{\theta^{n_j+n_k-s+1}-1}{\theta^n j_{-1}} \tag{19.3.2}
$$

T_l is the average annual current capital occupation amount of the technological scheme in the calculation period.

$$
T_l = k_lT_g \tag{19.3.3}
$$

T_j is the average annual basic depreciation deduction of the technological scheme in the calculation period.

$$
T_j = \sum_{s=1}^{n_j} C_{js}\frac{\theta^{n_j-s}-1}{\theta^{n_j-1}} = \frac{c_j}{\theta-1} - \frac{n_jc_j}{\theta^n j-1} \tag{19.3.4}
$$

T_{cz} is the average annual fixed residual of the technological scheme converted into the calculation period.

$$T_{cz} = T_c \frac{1}{\theta^n j - 1} \tag{19.3.5}$$

C_j is the actual annual basic depreciation deduction of the technological scheme in the calculation period.

$$C_j = l_j T_g \tag{19.3.6}$$

D_z is the average annual natural resource occupation of the technological scheme converted into the calculation period.

$$D_z = D_1 \frac{\theta^{n_j+n_k} - 1}{\theta^{n_j} - 1} + \cdots\cdots + D_{nk} \frac{\theta^{n_j+1} - 1}{\theta^{n_j} - 1} = \sum_{s=1}^{n_k} D_s \frac{\theta^{n_j+n_k-s+1} - 1}{\theta^{n_j} - 1} \tag{19.3.7}$$

k_l is the coefficient of the current capital of the technological scheme.

In formula 19.3, *W, Y, D, R*, and *T* have many sub-categories. For example, material W has sub- categories W_{steel}, W_{cement}, and W_{energy}. Natural materials D has sub-categories D_{land}, D_{water}, and D_{air}. Therefore, $\sum x_w W$, $\sum x_y Y$, $\sum x_d D$, $\sum x_r R$, and $\sum x_t T$ should be adopted. But to simplify, the expressions $x_w W$, $x_y Y$, $x_d D$, $x_r R$, and $x_t T$ are chosen in this book.

In the above formulas, fixed assets and current capital are considered separately. The former is usually occupied gradually in construction process, just as with land. Thus, the social consumption costs $x_t T_g$ and $x_d D$, by using fixed assets, occur in the construction period. If the time factor is considered, these costs should be calculated till the end of the n_j year. The total amount should be:

$$x_t T_{g1} \frac{\theta^{n_j+n_k} - 1}{\theta - 1} + \cdots\cdots + x_t T_{gnk} \frac{\theta^{n_j+1} - 1}{\theta - 1} \tag{19.3.8}$$

and

$$x_d D_1 \frac{\theta^{n_j+n_k} - 1}{\theta - 1} + \cdots\cdots + x_d D T_{nk} \frac{\theta^{n_j+1} - 1}{\theta - 1} \tag{19.3.9}$$

These are the important items in formula 19.3. In formula 19.3.8, T_{gl} is the investment in the first year of the construction period. In the first year, the capital occupation cost is $x_t T_{gl,}$ which occurs in each year of the construction period and the production period. With the time coefficient considered, the capital occupation cost in each year can be achieved as $x_t T_{g1} \frac{\theta^{n_j+n_k} - 1}{\theta - 1}$. Similarly, the capital occupation cost generated by the investment in the second year of construction period T_{g2} is $x_t T_{g2}$. When the production period is over, the total cost will be $x_t T_{g2}\frac{\theta^{n_j+n_k-1}-1}{\theta-1}$. The capital occupation cost generated by the investment in the last year of the construction period T_{gnk} is $x_t T_{gnk}$. When the production period is over, the total cost will be $x_t T_{gnk}\frac{\theta^{n_j+1}-1}{\theta-1}$. Add these costs together and the total amount of costs can be achieved as shown in formula 19.3.8. The same method can be applied to calculate the occupation costs of land.

However, the amount of fixed asset occupation will decrease continuously once the production period begins, due to the annual deprecation cost. The amount of decrease in the value of fixed assets is the basic depreciation C_j (excluding the costs of heavy repair C_{dx}). As a result, the social consumption cost caused by the fixed asset occupation of technological schemes will decrease correspondingly. The amount of decrease in n_j years is:

$$x_t \sum_{s=1}^{n_t} C_{js} \frac{\theta^{n_j-s} - 1}{\theta - 1} \tag{19.3.10}$$

This is the second-to-last portion of formula 19.3.

Now, let us discuss how to deal with residuals. In the calculation of the total social consumption cost $Z_{\sum}$ above, it is assumed that all of the expenditures in the calculation period are calculated, and those which are not in the calculation period are not calculated. For instance, the residual of the fixed assets consists of two parts. One is the net residual of fixed assets T_{cl} that is not counted into basic depreciation. This part can be calculated by subtracting the handling fee from the fixed asset residual. The other one is part of the basic depreciation T_{c2} that is not reclaimed completely in the calculation period. It can be calculated by subtracting the reclaimed basic depreciation $n_j C_j$ from the total basic depreciation $n_f C_j$, which is supposed to be reclaimed. These two residuals are the costs that are not spent in the calculation period. Therefore, they are not included in the total social consumption cost $Z_{\sum}$. This can be demonstrated by the following formulas:

Suppose $x_w W, x_y Y, x_r R, x_d D$, and $x_d D_z$ are all zero. Formula 19.3 can be simplified as below:

$$Z_{\Sigma} = (C + x_t T_z)\frac{\theta^{n_j} - 1}{\theta - 1} \tag{19.3.11}$$

Load T_z to the above formula,[3]

$$Z_{\Sigma} = C\frac{\theta^{n_j} - 1}{\theta - 1} + x_t\left(\sum_{s=1}^{n_k} T_{gs}\frac{\theta^{n_j+n_k-s+1} - 1}{\theta^{n_j} - 1} + T_1 - \frac{c_j}{\theta - 1} + \frac{nC_j}{\theta^{n_j} - 1}\right)\frac{\theta^{n_j} - 1}{\theta - 1}$$

[3] T_c, the loss of residual in T_z, is not considered here, or $T_c = 0$.

$$
\begin{aligned}
&= C\frac{\theta^{n_j}-1}{\theta-1}+\sum_{s=1}^{n_k}T_{gs}\theta^{n_j+n_k-s+1}-\sum_{s=1}^{n_k}T_{gs}+T_l\theta^{n_j}-T_l-C_j\frac{\theta^{n_j}-1}{\theta-1}+n_iC_j \\
&= (C-C_j)\frac{\theta^{n_j}-1}{\theta-1}+T_{construction}\cdot\theta^{n_j}-T_{basic}+T_l\theta^{n_j}-T_l+n_jC_j \\
&= (C-C_j)\frac{\theta^{n_j}-1}{\theta-1}+(T_{construction}+T_l)\theta^{n_j}-T_l-\left(T_{basic}-n_iC_j\right)
\end{aligned}
\tag{19.3.12}
$$

$$
\because \quad T_{basic}=n_fC_j+T_{c1} \tag{19.3.13}
$$

$$
\begin{aligned}
\therefore \quad Z_\Sigma &= (C-C_j)\frac{\theta^{n_j}-1}{\theta-1}+(T_{constuction}+T_l)\theta^{n_j}-T_l-\left(n_fC_j+T_{cl}-n_iC_j\right) \\
&= (C-C_j)\frac{\theta^{n_j}-1}{\theta-1}+(T_{constuction}+T_l)\theta^{n_j}-T_l-\left[(nf-n_j)C_j+T_{cl}\right]
\end{aligned}
\tag{19.3.14}
$$

In formula 19.3.14, the last item is the net residual of fixed assets, which is the sum of T_{cl} and T_{c2}. It can be seen that the net residual of fixed assets is deducted from the total social consumption cost in formula 19.3. In other words, the net residual of fixed assets is completely reclaimed. If the net residual of fixed assets is not reclaimed, a cost of residual retirement T_{cO} should be added into the total social consumption cost in the calculation period. This is what the last item in formula 19.3 means. General speaking, the net residual of fixed assets is usually reclaimed. Thus, the last item in formula 19.3, the cost of residual retirement, is zero. If the net residual of fixed assets is not reclaimed at all, the value of T_c can be calculated in this way: $T_c = T_{C1} + T_{c2} = (n_f - n_j)\,C_j + T_{c1}$.

The total amount of the annual cost of technological schemes and materials consumption cost in n_j years (with the time factor considered) is:

$$
C\frac{\theta^{n_j}-1}{\theta-1}+x_wW\frac{\theta^{n_j+1}-1}{\theta-1} \tag{19.3.15}
$$

These are the first items in formula 19.3.

The occupation of current asset, labor, and transportation, and the utilization of natural resources begins when production starts. If the production volume remains the same and other conditions stay unchanged, these occupation and utilization figures will not change in each year of calculation period. They will remain the same until the end of n_j years. Accordingly, the total social consumption cost in the n_j years, with the time factor considered, will be:

$$
x_yY\frac{\theta^{n_j}-1}{\theta-1},\ x_dD\frac{\theta^{n_j}-1}{\theta-1},\ x_rR\frac{\theta^{n_j}-1}{\theta-1},\ x_tT_l\frac{\theta^{n_j}-1}{\theta-1}, \tag{19.3.16}
$$

These are the last four items in formula 19.3.

It can be seen that formula 19.3 calculates the sum of several costs.

II. Calculation of the total social benefits of technological schemes $S_{\sum}$ (or total production, total income).

The following formulas and later calculations in this book are built on the assumption that the production (income) in a certain year is calculated from the next year, with compound interest. With the time factor considered, the total social benefits of the technological schemes can be calculated with the following formula:

$$S_{\Sigma} = \sum_{s=1}^{n_j+n_k} S_s \theta^{n_j+n_k-s} = \sum_{s=1}^{n_j+n_k} S_{zs} \theta^{n_j-s} \tag{19.4}$$

where S_s is the annual social benefit of the technological scheme in the construction period and the calculation period. S_{zs} is the annual social benefit of the technological scheme converted into the calculation period.

Suppose that there are no production and income in construction period and that the value or price of a product j_{zs} remains unchanged. In other words, a fixed price is adopted. In this case,

$$j_{z1} = \cdots\cdots = j_{zn_i} = j_z$$

Meanwhile, the production of each technological scheme is the same in each year,

$$G_1 = \cdots\cdots = G_{ni} = G$$

Thus, formula 19.4 can be converted to:

$$S_{\Sigma} = j_z G \frac{\theta^{n_j} - 1}{\theta - 1} \tag{19.5}$$

Accordingly, the social labor productivity I for each technological scheme can be calculated with the following formula:

$$E_a = \frac{S_{\Sigma}}{Z_{\Sigma}} = \frac{j_z G}{C + x_w W + x_y Y + x_d D + x_r R + x_t T_z + x_d D_z} \tag{19.6}$$

The net social income can be calculated with the following formula:

$$E_c = S_{\Sigma} - Z_{\Sigma} = \left[j_z G - \left(C + x_w W + x_y Y + x_d D + x_r R + x_t T_z + x_d D_z \right) \right] \frac{\theta^{n_j} - 1}{\theta - 1} \tag{19.7}$$

According to the evaluation standards for social labor productivity I and social net income, the economic condition for that specific technological scheme is:

$$E_a \geq 0 \quad or \quad E_c \geq 0 \tag{19.8}$$

The relative economic condition for the technological scheme is:

$$E_a = ZD \quad \text{or} \quad E_c = ZD \tag{19.9}$$

Because the production volume and the quality of each technological scheme are the same, the relative economic condition for technological scheme can be simplified as:

$$Z_z = C + x_w W + x_y Y + x_d D + x_r R + x_t T_z + x_d D_z = ZX \tag{19.10}$$

In the second situation (shown in Fig. 19.2b), because the length of service for each technological scheme is shorter than the calculation period n_j, reconstruction is required for each technological scheme after its service period is over. In this way, these technological schemes can be compared in the n_j years.

The total amount of social benefits for each technological scheme is:

$$S_\Sigma = j_z G \frac{\theta^{n_j} - 1}{\theta - 1} \tag{19.11}$$

The total amount of total social cost for each technological scheme is:

$$\begin{aligned} Z_\Sigma &= \sum_{s=1}^{n_j} Z_z \theta^{n_j - s} \\ &= \left[\left(C + x_w W + x_y Y + x_d D + x_r R + x_t T_z + x_d D_z \right) \frac{\theta^{n_f} - 1}{\theta - 1} \right] \theta^{n_j - n_f} \\ &= \left[C + x_w W + x_y Y + x_d D + x_r R + x_t T_z + x_d D_z \right] \frac{\theta^{n_j - n_f} - 1}{\theta - 1} \\ &= \left(C + x_w W + x_y Y + x_d D + x_r R + x_t T_z + x_d D_z \right) \frac{\theta^{n_j} - 1}{\theta - 1} \end{aligned} \tag{19.12}$$

Based on these two formulas, the social labor productivity I and the net social income for each technological scheme can be calculated as below:

$$E_a = \frac{j_z G}{C + x_w W + x_y Y + x_d D + x_r R + x_t T_z + x_d D_z}$$

Or

$$E_c = \left[j_z G - \left(C + x_w W + x_y Y + x_d D + x_r R + x_t T_z + x_d D_z \right) \right] \frac{\theta^{n_j} - 1}{\theta - 1}$$

These two formulas are the same as (19.6) and (19.7). Therefore, the formulas for calculating the economic condition and the relative economic condition for this specific technological scheme are the same as (19.8) and (19.9). Because the outputs of technological schemes are the same, the relative economic conditions for technological schemes can be simplified as:

$$Z_z = C + x_w W + x_y Y + x_d D + x_r R + x_t T_{\bar{x}} + x_d D_z = ZX \tag{19.13}$$

Obviously, this is the same as (19.10).

In the third situation (shown in Fig. 19.2c), the length of service for each technological scheme might be longer or shorter than the calculation period n_j. In order to compare technological schemes, reinvestment (fixed assets) is required for those technological schemes having a shorter service period after their service periods are over. But no addition investment is needed for those technological schemes which have a longer service period. The calculation methods discussed above can be applied in this situation.

In the fourth situation (shown in Fig. 19.2d), because the length of service for each technological scheme is longer than the calculation period n_j, some portion of its investments on infrastructure T_{c2} have not been reclaimed yet at the end of the n_j year. If the residual of investment is reclaimed completely, T_c is equal to 0. If the residual is not reclaimed, the loss on depreciation T_c should be added. In these two scenarios, formulas 19.8, 19.9, and 19.10 are still applicable.

The above discussion indicates that, regardless of the length of service for technological schemes, the same formulas can be adopted to assess them by converting their length into n_j years. In the derivation of the above formulas, the calculation period n_j does not have a specific value. Accordingly, it can be assigned with different values.

III. **Different technological schemes have different production and different quality**.

Technological schemes have investment and occupied land in a construction period. They might generate a small amount of production. When the construction is finished, the technological schemes continue having investment, occupying land, and generating production. However, the production, the product price, the occupation of labor, transportation, the current assets, and the consumption of material and natural resources vary in each year (shown in Fig. 19.3).

This situation is the most complicated one in the technological scheme development process. Calculation formulas based on this situation have generalization. Next, let us discuss how to calculate social labor productivity I and social net income.

In this situation, the total social benefit of a technological scheme in $n_j + n_k$ years can be calculated as below:

$$S_\Sigma = \sum_{s=1}^{n_j+n_k} j_{zs} G_s \theta^{n_j+n_k-s} \tag{19.14}$$

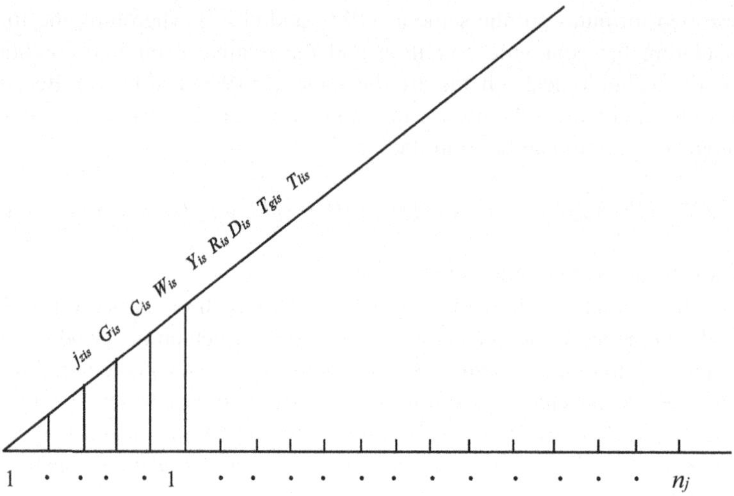

Fig. 19.3 The fourth situation in the technological scheme development process (the most complicated one)

The total social consumption cost of a technological scheme in $n_j + n_k$ years is

$$Z_\Sigma = \sum_{s=1}^{n_j+n_k} Z_s \theta^{n_j+n_k-s}$$
$$= \sum_{s=1}^{n_j+n_k} \left[C_s + x_w W_s + x_y Y_s + x_r R_s + x_r \left(T_{gs} + T_{ls} - \sum_{s=1}^{n_j} c_j (s-1) + T_{cs} \right) \right.$$
$$\left. + x_d D_s \right] \theta^{n_j+n_k-s} \tag{19.15}$$

Accordingly, social labor productivity I and social net income can be calculated as below:

$$E_a = \frac{\sum_{s=1}^{n_j+n_k} j_{zs} G_s \theta^{n_j+n_k-s}}{\sum_{s=1}^{n_j+n_k} z_s \theta^{n_j+n_k-s}} \tag{19.16}$$

$$E_c = \sum_{s=1}^{n_j+n_k} j_{zs} G_s \theta^{n_j+n_k-s} - \sum_{s=1}^{n_j+n_k} Z_s \theta^{n_j+n_k-s} \tag{19.17}$$

The economic condition for that specific technological scheme is:

$$E_a \geq 1 \quad or \quad E_c \geq 0 \tag{19.18}$$

The relative economic condition for the technological scheme is:

$$E_a = ZD \quad or \quad E_c = ZD \tag{19.19}$$

In practice, two conversion approaches are adopted to calculate the benefits and costs in each year together, namely considering the time factor. The first approach converts the benefits and costs in each year with compound interest into the present value in the last year, also called "the time value" or "the final value" of the last year. Time value coefficients can be applied in this approach. The formulas above adopt this approach. The other approach converts benefits and costs in coming years with compound interest into the present value. The discount factor can be applied in this approach. No matter which approach is adopted, the results will be the same. The target of the first approach is the last year of the calculation period, whereas the target of the second one is the beginning of the first year in the calculation period or the construction period. Conversion of E_a and E_c in the simplest and the most complicated situations can be calculated with present value.

A. *The simplest situation*

I. Converting to the beginning of calculation period.

$$Z_\Sigma = \sum_{s=1}^{n_j} Z_{zs} \frac{1}{\theta^s} = \left(C + x_w W + x_y Y + x_d D + x_r R + x_t T_z + x_d D_z\right) \frac{\theta^{n_j - s} - 1}{(\theta - 1)\theta^n j} \tag{19.20}$$

$$S_\Sigma = \sum_{s=1}^{n_j} S_{zs} \frac{1}{\theta^s} = j_z G \frac{\theta^{n_j - s} - 1}{(\theta - 1)\theta^{n_j}} \tag{19.21}$$

$$E_a = \frac{S_\Sigma}{Z_\Sigma}, \quad E_c = S_\Sigma - Z_\Sigma \tag{19.22}$$

II. Converting to the beginning of construction period.

$$Z_\Sigma = \sum_{s=1}^{n_j + n_k} Z_s \frac{1}{\theta^s} = \left(C + x_w W + x_y Y + x_d D + x_r R + x_t T_z + x_d D_z\right) \times \frac{\theta^{n_j} - 1}{\theta - 1} \times \frac{1}{\theta^n j^{+n_k}} \tag{19.23}$$

$$S_\Sigma = \sum_{s=1}^{n_j + n_k} S_s \frac{1}{\theta^s} = j_z G \frac{\theta^{n_j} - 1}{\theta - 1} \times \frac{1}{\theta^n j^{+n_k}} \tag{19.24}$$

$$E_a = \frac{S_\Sigma}{Z_\Sigma}, \quad E_c = S_\Sigma - Z_\Sigma \tag{19.25}$$

B. *The most complicated situation (Converting to the beginning of construction period)*

$$E_a = \frac{\sum_{s=1}^{n_j+n_k} j_{zs} G_s \frac{1}{\theta^s}}{\sum_{s=1}^{n_j+n_k} z_s \frac{1}{\theta^s}} \tag{19.26}$$

$$E_c = \sum_{s=1}^{n_j+n_k} (j_{zs} G_s - Z_s) \frac{1}{\theta^s} \tag{19.27}$$

(2) **The calculation method based on total amount**

As a matter of convenience, $x_w W$, $x_y Y$, $x_r R$, and $x_d D$ are not considered. As such, the social consumption cost in the construction period and the calculation period is:

$$Z_\Sigma = \sum_{s=1}^{n_j+n_k} T_s \theta^{n_j+n_k-s+1} + \sum_{s=1}^{n_j+n_k} C_{jys} \theta^{n_j+n_k-s} - \left(\sum_{s=1}^{n_k} T_{gs} - n_j C_j \right) - T_1 \quad \text{(time value)} \tag{19.28}$$

Or

$$Z_\Sigma = \sum_{s=1}^{n_j+n_k} T_s \frac{1}{\theta^{s-1}} + \sum_{s=1}^{n_j+n_k} C_{jys} \frac{1}{\theta^s} - \left(\sum_{s=1}^{n_k} T_{gs} - n_j C_j \right) \frac{1}{\theta^{n_j+n_k}} - T_1 \frac{1}{\theta^{n_j+n_k}} \quad \text{(present value)} \tag{19.29}$$

$$S_\Sigma = \sum_{s=1}^{n_j+n_k} S_s \theta^{n_j+n_k-s} \quad \text{(time value)} \tag{19.30}$$

Or

$$S_\Sigma = \sum_{s=1}^{n_j+n_k} S_s \frac{1}{\theta^s} \quad \text{(present value)} \tag{19.31}$$

Thus,

$$E_a = \frac{S_\Sigma}{Z_\Sigma}, \quad E_c = S_\Sigma - Z_\Sigma \tag{19.32}$$

The social net income in the construction period and the calculation period is:

$$E_c = \sum_{s=1}^{n_j+n_k} S_s\theta^{n_j+n_k-s} - \sum_{s=1}^{n_j+n_k} T_s\theta^{n_j+n_k-s+1} - \sum_{s=1}^{n_j+n_k} C_{jys}\theta^{n_j+n_k-s} + \left(\sum_{s=1}^{n_k} T_{gs} - n_jC_j\right) + T_1 \quad \text{(time value)} \tag{19.33}$$

Or

$$E_c = \sum_{S=1}^{n_j+n_k} S_S\frac{1}{\theta^s} - \sum_{S=1}^{n_j+n_k} T_S\frac{1}{\theta^{s-1}} - \sum_{S=1}^{n_j+n_k} C_{jys}\frac{1}{\theta^s} + \left(\sum_{s=1}^{n_k} T_{gs} - n_jC_j\right)\frac{1}{\theta^{n_j+n_k}} + T_1\frac{1}{\theta^{n_j+n_k}} \text{ (present value)} \tag{19.34}$$

Suppose that the technological scheme development process is the simplest situation. The above two formulas can be converted as below:

$$E_c = S\frac{\theta^{n_j}-1}{\theta-1} - (T_{constuction} + T_1)\theta^{n_j} - C_{jy}\frac{\theta^{n_j}-1}{\theta-1} + \left(T_{construction} - n_jC_j\right) + T_l \text{ (time value)} \tag{19.35}$$

Or

$$E_c = S\frac{\theta^{n_j}-1}{(\theta-1)\theta^{n_j+n_k}} - T_{constuction}\frac{1}{\theta^{n_k}} - T_1\frac{1}{\theta^{n_k}} - C_{jy}\frac{\theta^{n_j}-1}{(\theta-1)\theta^{n_j+n_k}} + \left(T_{construction} - n_jC_j\right) + T_l\frac{1}{\theta^{n_j+n_k}} \text{ (present value)} \tag{19.36}$$

The calculation method based on the total amount can be derived from the calculation method based on the annual amount. For instance, formula 19.3.11 calculates the total social consumption cost (time value) based on the annual amount. Formula 19.3.12 can be achieved by extending T_z. Load formula 19.3.12 into 19.7 to calculate the social net income as below:

$$\begin{aligned} E_c &= S\frac{\theta^{n_j}-1}{\theta-1} - (C - C_j)S\frac{\theta^{n_j}-1}{\theta-1} + (T_{construction} + T_1)\theta^{n_j} + T_1 + \left(T_{construction} - n_jC_j\right) \\ &= S\frac{\theta^{n_j}-1}{\theta-1} - (T_{construction} + T_1)\theta^{n_j} - C_{jy}\frac{\theta^{n_j}-1}{\theta-1} + \left(T_{construction} - n_jC_j\right) + T_l \quad \text{(time value)} \end{aligned} \tag{19.37}$$

Formulas 19.37 and 19.35 are the same. This proves that the calculation method based on the total amount can be derived from the calculation method based on the annual amount. These two methods will generate the same results.

(3) **Comparison between the calculation method based on annual amount and the calculation method based on total amount**

These two methods have been applied, in practice, for calculating the total amount. However, the calculation method based on the annual amount has two advantages. First, based on the annual amount, this method can be used for generating the annual social net income, the direct cost, and the social cost. Among them, the direct cost is necessary for firms. In contrast, the calculation method based on total amount does not calculate the annual direct cost and the social cost. Second, the calculation method based on the annual amount can be used for setting rational prices or for adjusting prices. For example, the formula for the social consumption cost of a product per unit based on the calculation method based on annual amount is the formula for the rational price or the adjustment price. However, the calculation method based on the total amount does not generate this formula. Therefore, the calculation method based on the annual amount has much clearer economic meanings, as well as practical features.

(4) **Assessing formulas for economic evaluation**

At present, many domestic literatures introduce foreign macro economy evaluation methods, such as the social income net present value method (the national income net present value method) and the net production present value method. Here are their formulas:

Net production present value method

$$NPV_n = \sum_{t=0}^{n} (S_A + MI_A - I_A - R_F + R_E)_{tat} \tag{19.38}$$

Social income present value method

$$NPV_m = \sum_{t=0}^{n} (S_A + MI_A - W - I_A - R_F + R_E)_{tat} \tag{19.39}$$

In the above two formulas, S_A is the annual sales. MI_A is the annual cost of material input. I_A is the cost of investment. R_F is the amount of capital flowing overseas. R_E is the outside income (when the outside cost is negative). W is the wage. a_t is the discount factor.

Convert the symbols in the above formulas into the ones in this book, and one gets the following formulas.

$$E_d = \sum_{s=0}^{n_k+n_j} \left(S - C_u + C_j - T - \Delta Z + \Delta S\right)_s \theta^{-s} \tag{19.40}$$

$$E_c = \sum_{s=0}^{n_k+n_j} \left(S - C_{jy} - T - \Delta Z + \Delta S\right)_s \theta^{-s} \tag{19.41}$$

Let us compare the formulas for calculating the social income net present value and the social net income. It can be seen that the formulas for calculating NPV_n and NPV_m are both based on the total amount. As mentioned earlier, this method does not have the advantages that the method based on annual amount has. In addition, the formulas for calculating the social income net present value and the social net income have drawbacks. First, they consider C_r only, while neglecting C_w, C_r, C_R, and C_D. Second, S_A should not adopt the annual sales because the sale prices of products might not be equal to the amount of necessary labor consumption in a society, namely the rational prices of products in a free competition market. Sales income is suitable for micro economic evaluation. In a macro economic evaluation, only when sale price is the same as rational price can sales income be adopted. Third, current capital is not consumption, but occupation. Current capital is deducted in the two formulas above in the same way as material consumption. This is incorrect, because current capital should be reclaimed. Fourth, other than basic depreciation, fixed assets still have residuals to reclaim. This is not reflected in the formulas above. Fifth, it is easy to generate misunderstandings by calculating total amount from the year t = 0, because technological schemes have no investment, cost, or output in the year t = 0. Therefore, the calculation should begin from the year t = 1. Sixth, R_F is not general, because the evaluation on most technological schemes does not consider international relations. In addition, the meaning of R_E is not clear. Seventh, the two formulas above adopt present value. In fact, time value is both more convenient and more practical. Finally, the social net income method is called "the social excess net income method." The social national income (net production) method is also called the social excess national income (net production) method. These names are more suitable compared with the social income net present value method and the net production present value method.

In summary, the macro technological economic evaluation formulas based on the principle of the standards for evaluating greater, faster, better, and more economic results fit the national situation in China better and are more advanced, especially the calculation method based on annual amount, which is superior to those introduced from overseas.

(5) **Conversion between total amount and annual amount**

All of the formulas above calculate the total social income $S_{\sum}$, the total social consumption cost $Z_{\sum}$, and the total social net income in the period of $n_j + n_k$ years. The total social net income is represented by E_c in the formulas above. In order to be different from the annual average social net income, $E_{c\sum}$ is adopted for representing the total social net income in the following sections. If the average annual total social income in the period of $n_j + n_k$ years is S, the average annual total social consumption cost is Z, and the average annual social net income is E_c, the following conversion formulas can be adopted for evaluating a technological scheme:

First, convert the total time value (final value) at the end of the n year into the annual average in the n years by multiplying the total time value at the end of the n year with the accumulated time value annual average coefficient $\frac{\theta - 1}{\theta^n - 1}$.

For example,

$$S = S_\Sigma \times \frac{\theta - 1}{\theta^{n_j + n_k} - 1} \quad (19.42)$$

$$Z = Z_\Sigma \times \frac{\theta - 1}{\theta^{n_j + n_k} - 1} \quad (19.43)$$

$$E_c = E_{c\Sigma} \times \frac{\theta - 1}{\theta^{n_j + n_k} - 1} \quad (19.44)$$

where S_Σ, E_Σ, and $E_{c\Sigma}$ are the known total time values at the end of n year. S, Z, and E_c are the converted annual average values in n years. In the above formulas, $n = n_j + n_k$.

Second, convert the total present value at the beginning of n years into the annual average in the n years by multiplying the total present value at the beginning of n years with the accumulated present value annual average coefficient $\frac{(\theta - 1)^n}{\theta^n - 1}$.

For example,

$$S = S_\Sigma \times \frac{(\theta - 1)\theta^{n_j + n_k}}{\theta^{n_j + n_k} - 1} \quad (19.45)$$

$$Z = Z_\Sigma \times \frac{(\theta - 1)\theta^{n_j + n_k}}{\theta^{n_j + n_k} - 1} \quad (19.46)$$

$$E_c = E_{c\Sigma} \times \frac{(\theta - 1)\theta^{n_j + n_k}}{\theta^{n_j + n_k} - 1} \quad (19.47)$$

where S_Σ, E_Σ, and $E_{c\Sigma}$ are the known total present values at the beginning of n year. S, Z, and E_c are the converted annual average values in n years. In the above formulas, $n = n_j + n_k$.

Here is a practical example. Suppose there are two technological schemes A and B. The construction period for technological scheme A is three years. The investment in it during the first year is 900,000 Yuan (RMB). There is no investment in the second year or the third year. The construction period for technological scheme B is one year. Its investment is 900,000 Yuan. The two technological schemes begin to produce at the same time. Their production values are both 300,000 Yuan/year (production 10,000 tons/year * rational price 30 Yuan/ton). Technological scheme A occupies current capital 50,000 Yuan. Its annual cost is 150,000 Yuan, in which basic depreciation is 60,000 Yuan. Technological scheme B occupies current capital 100,000 Yuan. Its annual cost is 170,000 Yuan, in which the basic depreciation is 60,000 Yuan. Which technological scheme will generate a better economic effect?

Let us calculate this using the social (total) labor productivity I method first. Set $x_t = 0.15$, $n_j = 15$ years, and x_w, x_y, x_r, and x_d are all equal to zero.

$$S_{\Sigma A} = 300,000 \times \frac{\theta^{15} - 1}{\theta - 1} = 300,000 \times 47.58 = 14,270,000 \text{ Yuan}$$

$$S_{\Sigma B} = 300,000 \times 47.58 = 14,270,000 \text{ Yuan}$$

$$T_{zA} = 900,000 \times \frac{\theta^{18} - 1}{\theta^{15} - 1} + 5 - \frac{6}{\theta - 1} + \frac{15 \times 6}{\theta^{15} - 1} = 1,207,000 \text{ Yuan}$$

$$T_{zB} = 900,000 \times \frac{\theta^{16} - 1}{\theta^{15} - 1} + 10 - \frac{6}{\theta - 1} + \frac{15 \times 6}{\theta^{15} - 1} = 879,000 \text{ Yuan}$$

$$Z_A = C_A + x_t T_{zA} = 15 + 0.15 \times 1,207,000 = 331,000 \text{ Yuan/year}$$

$$Z_B = C_B + x_t T_{zB} = 17 + 0.15 \times 879,000 = 302,000 \text{ Yuan/year}$$

$$Z_{\Sigma A} = Z_A \times \frac{\theta^{15} - 1}{\theta - 1} = 331,000 \times 47.58 = 15,774,000 \text{ Yuan}$$

$$Z_{\Sigma B} = Z_B \times \frac{\theta^{15} - 1}{\theta - 1} = 302,000 \times 47.58 = 14,366,000 \text{ Yuan}$$

$$Z_{aA} = \frac{S_{\Sigma A}}{Z_{\Sigma A}} = \frac{14,270,000}{15,774,000} = 0.906$$

$$Z_{aB} = \frac{S_{\Sigma B}}{Z_{\Sigma B}} = \frac{14,270,000}{14,366,000} = 0.993$$

The social (total) labor productivities of these two technological schemes are both smaller than one. This indicates that their social (total) labor productivities are lower than the average level. Therefore, their economic effects are not good. If the social (total) labor productivity is equal to one, a technological scheme reaches the average level. If the social (total) labor productivity is greater than one, a technological scheme has excess labor productivity. The result also indicates that technological scheme B has better economic effect than technological scheme A.

This example can be calculated with social net income E_c method.

$$E_{cA} = S_{\Sigma A} - Z_{\Sigma A} = 14,270,000 - 15,774,000 = -1,504,000 \text{ Yuan}$$

$$E_{cB} = S_{\Sigma B} - Z_{\Sigma B} = 14,270,000 - 14,366,000 = -96,000 \text{ Yuan}$$

These two formulas adopt final value (time value). Convert final value into time value as below.

$$E_{cA} = \frac{-1,504,000}{\theta^{18}} = -122,000 \text{ Yuan}$$

$$E_{cB} = \frac{-96,000}{\theta^{18}} = -8,100 \text{ Yuan}$$

The social net income of these two technological schemes is, for each, smaller than zero. This indicates that they do not meet the requirement of net income set by the state. If the social net income is equal to zero, a technological scheme meets the requirement of net income set by the state. If greater than zero, a technological scheme has excess net income. The result also indicates that technological scheme *B* has better economic effects than technological scheme *A*.

(3) Social additional (total) labor productivity I E_{af} method.

$$E_{af} = \frac{\Delta S_{\Sigma}(\text{or } \Delta X_{\Sigma})}{\Delta Z_{\Sigma}} \quad \left(E_{af} = ZD \quad E_{af} \geq 1\right) \tag{19.48.1}$$

$$E_{af} = \frac{dS_{\Sigma}(\text{or } dX_{\Sigma})}{dZ_{\Sigma}} \quad \left(E_{af} = ZD \quad E_{af} \geq 1\right) \tag{19.48.2}$$

$$E_{af} = \frac{dS_{\Sigma}(or\ dX_{\Sigma})}{dZ_{\Sigma}} \quad \left(E_{af} = \lambda \quad E_{cf} \geq 0\right) \tag{19.48.3}$$

where Δ and d are the increments achieved by comparing technological schemes.

Load the values in the above practice example into formula 19.48.1 and the result will be:

$$E_{af} = \frac{\Delta S_{\Sigma}}{\Delta Z_{\Sigma}} = \frac{S_{\Sigma A} - S_{\Sigma B}}{Z_{\Sigma A} - Z_{\Sigma B}} = \frac{14,270,000 - 14,270,000}{15,774,000 - 14,366,000} = \frac{0}{1,408,000} = 0$$

Technological scheme *A* invests 1,408,000 Yuan more than technological scheme *B*, but its outputs do not increase. Thus, technological scheme *A* does not have a better economic effect than technological scheme *B*. However, it is not clear whether technological scheme *A* or technological scheme *B* has economic issues.

(4) Social additional net income rate E_{cf} method.

$$E_{cf} = \frac{\Delta E_c}{\Delta T}; \frac{\Delta E_c}{\Delta W}; \frac{\Delta E_c}{\Delta Y}; \frac{\Delta E_c}{\Delta R}; \frac{\Delta E_c}{\Delta D}; \frac{\Delta E_c}{\Delta N}; \quad (E_{cf} = ZD \quad E_{cf} \geq 0) \tag{19.49.1}$$

$$E_{cf} = \frac{\partial E_c}{\partial T}; \frac{\partial E_c}{\partial W}; \frac{\partial E_c}{\partial Y}; \frac{\partial E_c}{\partial R}; \frac{\partial E_c}{\partial D}; \frac{\partial E_c}{\partial N}; \quad \left(E_{cf} = ZD \quad E_{cf} \geq 0\right) \tag{19.49.2}$$

$$E_{cf} = \frac{\partial E_c}{\partial T}; \frac{\partial E_c}{\partial W}; \frac{\partial E_c}{\partial Y}; \frac{\partial E_c}{\partial R}; \frac{\partial E_c}{\partial D}; \frac{\partial E_c}{\partial N}; \quad \left(Ecf = \lambda \quad E_{cf} \geq 0\right) \tag{19.49.3}$$

where the denominators are the increment of input on a certain production element. The nominators are the increment of social excess net income.

Load the values in the above practice example into formula 19.49.1 and the result will be:

$$E_{cf} = \frac{\Delta E_C}{\Delta T} = \frac{E_{CA} - E_{CB}}{T_{\Sigma A} - T_{\Sigma B}} = \frac{-122,000 - (-8,100)}{\left(90 + \frac{5}{\theta^3}\right) - \left(\frac{90}{\theta^2} + \frac{10}{\theta^3}\right)} = \frac{-113,900}{187,000} = -0.61$$

Technological scheme *A* invests 187,000 more Yuan than technological scheme *B*, but its social net income decreases 113,900 Yuan. Thus, technological scheme *A* does not have a better economic effect than technological scheme *B*. Again, this method cannot evaluate the absolute economic effect of technological schemes.

The calculation formulas for the aforementioned E_{cf} and E_{cf} methods have three formats. The first format is fit for the situation that occurs when input varies directly with output (see Fig. 19.4). The second format is fit for the situation that occurs when input and output have a nonlinear increasing relationship (see Fig. 19.5). The

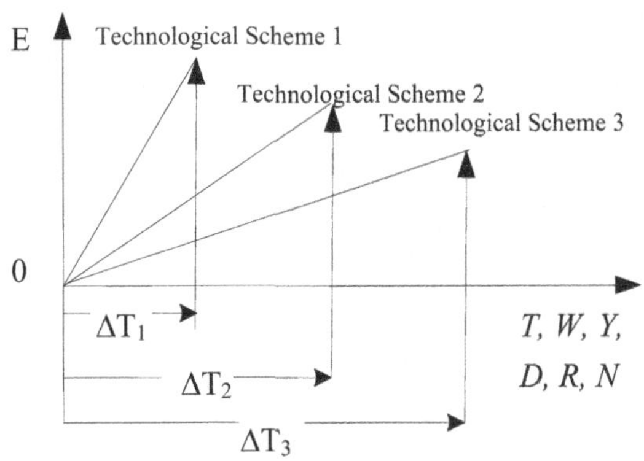

Fig. 19.4 Reasonable utilization and distribution methods for capital, materials, transportation capacity, natural resources, manpower, and time (A)

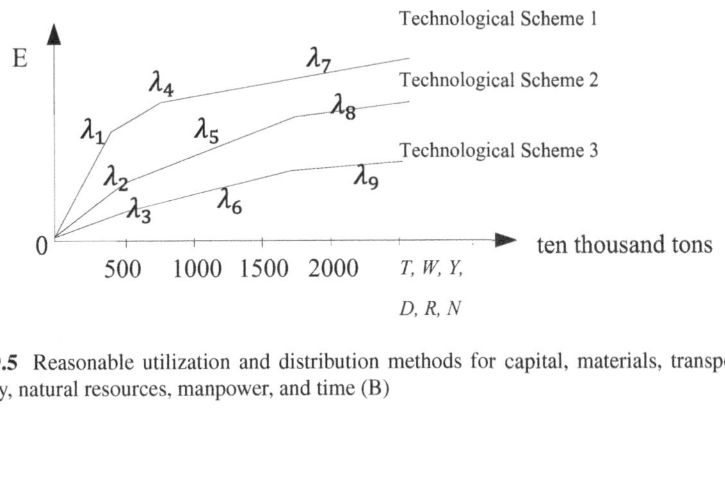

Fig. 19.5 Reasonable utilization and distribution methods for capital, materials, transportation capacity, natural resources, manpower, and time (B)

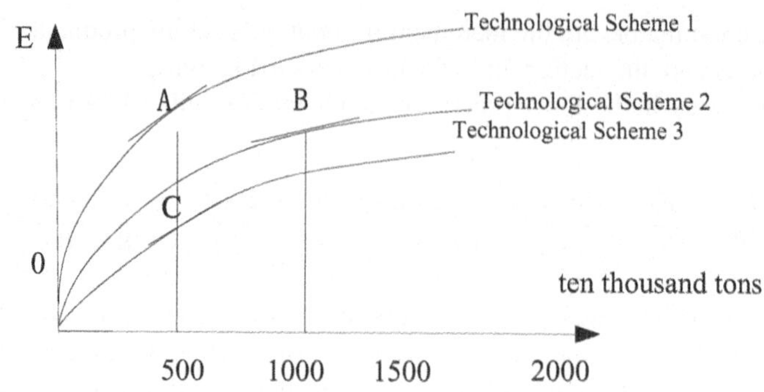

Fig. 19.6 Reasonable utilization and distribution methods for capital, materials, transportation capacity, natural resources, manpower, and time (C)

third format is fit for the situation that occurs when input and output have a curved relationship (see Fig. 19.6).

Example 1 Suppose that there are three schemes for utilizing a sum of capital. The first scheme needs ΔT_1 5,000,000 Yuan. Its economic effect ΔE_{c1} is 1,000,000 Yuan. The second scheme needs ΔT_2 10,000,000 Yuan and generates an economic effect ΔE_{c2} of 1,000,000 Yuan. The third scheme needs ΔT_3 15,000,000 Yuan and generates an economic effect ΔE_{c3} of 750,000 Yuan (see Table 19.4). Calculated with formula 19.49.1, E_{cf1} is 0.2, E_{cf2} is 0.1, and E_{cf3} is 0.05. This indicates that the first scheme is the most rational utilization, that the third scheme is the least rational utilization, and that the second scheme is in the middle. The sum of the capital should be allocated to the first scheme first, then to the second one, and finally to the third one. Suppose that the available capital is 10,000,000 Yuan. Based on the calculation results, the first scheme gets 5,000,000 Yuan, the full amount that it requires. The second scheme gets 5,000,000 Yuan, only half of its requirement. The third scheme will not get any capital. This allocation will generate the greatest economic effect ($5,000,000 \times 0.2 + 5,000,000 \times 0.1 = 1,500,000$ Yuan). Thus, formula 19.49.1 is only applicable to the situation shown in Fig. 19.4, where E_c has proportional relationship with T (W, Y, D, R, N).

Example 2 There are 20,000,000 tons of materials that are needed to be allocated to factories *A*, *B*, and *C*. Each factory has four schemes to utilize these materials. Table 19.5 shows the details of the amount of material utilization and the achieved

Table 19.4 Schemes for capital allocation and utilization Unit: 10,000 Yuan

Scheme	T	E_c
1	500	100
2	1000	100
3	1500	75

Table 19.5 Schemes for material allocation and utilization

Small schemes		1	2	3	4
Factory					
1	W (10,000 t)	0	500	1,000	2,000
	E_c (10,000 Yuans)	0	40,000	45,000	50,000
2	W (10,000 t)	0	500	1,500	2,000
	E_c (10,000 Yuans)	0	20,000	35,000	37,500
3	W (10,000 t)	0	500	1,500	2,000
	E_c (10,000 Yuans)	0	10,000	15,000	15,000

social net income for each scheme. How can we allocate the 20,000,000 tons of materials to generate the greatest economic benefits?

A figure can be drawn based on the data in Table 19.5 (see Fig. 19.5). In this example, output has a nonlinear increasing relationship with input. In this situation, formula 19.49.2 should be adopted. First, calculate the E_{cf} (λ) for each scheme. For factory 1, $E_{cf1} = 0$, $E_{cf2} = 80$ Yuan/ton, $E_{cf3} = 10$ Yuan/ton, and $E_{cf4} = 5$ Yuan/ton. For factory 2, $E_{cf1} = 0$, $E_{cf2} = 40$ Yuan/ton, $E_{cf3} = 15$ Yuan/ton, and $E_{cf4} = 5$ Yuan/ton. For factory 3, $E_{cf1} = 0$, $E_{cf2} = 20$ Yuan/ton, $E_{cf3} = 5$ Yuan/ton, and $E_{cf4} = 0$ Yuan/ton. Second, allocate materials by following the order of small schemes and the value of E_{cf}. The order is: (1) 5 million tons for factory 1 ($\lambda_1 = 80$ Yuan/ton), (2) 5 million tons for factory 2 ($\lambda_2 = 40$ Yuan/ton), (3) 5 million tons for factory 3 ($\lambda_3 = 20$ Yuan/ton), (4) 15 million tons for factory 2 ($\lambda_4 = 15$ Yuan/ton), (5) 10 million tons for factory 1 ($\lambda_5 = 10$ Yuan/ton), (6) 20 million tons for factory 1, 20 million tons for factory 2, and 15 million tons for factory 3 ($\lambda_6 = 5$ Yuan/ton), (7) 20 million tons for factory 3 ($\lambda_7 = 0$Yuan/ton). Based on this order, the 20 million tons of material can be allocated in this way: 5 million tons to factory 1 and 15 million tons to factory 2. The total economic effect E_{cf} is 750 million Yuan. Third, adjust the initial allocation to achieve the greatest economic effects. Because factory 2 changes continuously between 5 million tons and 15 million tons according to Fig. 19.5, 5 million tons can be deducted from factory 2 and allocated to factory 3. As such, the economic effect of factory 2saves 75 million Yuan, whereas that of factory 3 increases by 100 million Yuan. There will be 25 million Yuan net increase. Thus, the final allocation will be 5 million tons for factory 1, 10 million tons for factory 2, and 5 million tons for factory 3. The total economic effect E_{cf} is 775 million Yuan.

Example 3 Because input and output have a curved relationship as shown in Fig. 19.6, some dots on these curves with the same tangent slope can be found. In addition, the amount of capital, materials, transportation capacity, natural materials, labor, and time is enough for each scheme to get some of the needed items. In this situation, the allocation should adopt formula 19.49.3. Let us calculate it with the graphic method. First, draw a tangent for curve 1 at point a. The slope is E_{cf1}. Then, draw two parallel tangents for curve 2 and curve 3, respectively. We will get points B and C with the same slope E_{cf2} and E_{cf3}. If there are 20 million tons of materials needed to be allocated, the abscissa of point A is 5 million tons, the abscissa of point B is 10 million tons, and the abscissa of point C is 5 million tons. This is the best allocation. If the amount of materials is less than 20 million tons, a new allocation should be found by finding three points on these curves with the same tangent slope. In this way, the sum of material consumption for each scheme is equal to the amount they get from the allocation.

The author proposed the four methods discussed above in 1960 s. He later, in 1980, improved them. E_c calculates the economic benefit. E_a, E_{af}, and E_{cf} calculate the economic efficiency. They all measure economic effect. The benefit-cost analysis adopted overseas actually measures the economic effect. The difference between E_c and E_a is that E_c is subtraction, while E_a is division. E_{af} and E_{cf} measure relative economic efficiency, whereas E_a and E_c measue absolute economic efficiency and absolute economic benefit. E_{cf} is actually the rational allocation for each single material, including capital, materials, transportation capacity, labor, natural resources, and time. E_c is actually the rational allocation for multiple resources with linear programming.

The indicators mentioned above, such as social (total) labor productivity I, social net income, social total additional labor productivity I, and social additional net income, all measure excess economic efficiency and excess economic benefit. They are used for measuring normal economic efficiency and normal economic benefit, because the calculation of input cost (Z) for these indicators considers the normal income that the state should receive. When the input and the output of a technological scheme are equal, its excess net income is zero. But because it gets the normal net income, the technological scheme is economically rational in this case. When the output is larger than the input, excess net income exists. The larger the excess net income, the larger the economic effect of a technological scheme. When the output is smaller than the input, excess net income is negative. In this case, the technological scheme does not meet the requirement of net income set by the state. Thus, it is not economical. Accordingly, the standards for accessing the economic effect of technological schemes are $E_a \geq 1$, $E_c \geq 0$, $E_{af} \geq 1$, and $E_{cf} \geq 0$. These standards answer the question of why some technological scheme are economical even though their social net income is zero. Thus, the author argues that it should be more accurate to call social (total) labor productivity I as social excess (total) labor productivity I, social net income as social excess net income, social total additional labor productivity I as social excess total additional labor productivity I, and social additional net income as social excess additional net income.

19.3.2 Derived Methods from Net Income Series Methods

Sixteen methods can be derived from the four basic net income methods discussed above. Due to the lack of space, the mathematical justification for each derived method is skipped.

1. Annual net income $S_{c\text{-}static}$ (static)

$$S_{c\text{-}static} = S - C(S_{c\text{-}static} \geq \text{prescribed value}) \tag{19.50.1}$$

$$S_{c\text{-}static} = S - C_{jy} = S - C + C_j(S_{c\text{-}static} \geq \text{prescribed value}) \tag{19.50.2}$$

$$S_{c\text{-}static} = S - C + C_j - C_W - C_Y - C_R - C_D(S_{c\text{-}static} \geq \text{prescribed value}) \tag{19.50.3}$$

where C_{jy} is the operational cost and C_j is the basic deprecation cost. The other symbols have the same meanings discussed in previous sections.

Among the three formulas, 19.50.1 counts the depreciation cost as cost, while 19.50.2 counts the depreciation cost as income. Thus, the operational cost (exclude depreciation cost) is adopted in formula 19.50.2. In practice, if investment on fixed assets is counted as input, the depreciation cost charged yearly should be counted as income, rather than as cost. If the occupation cost of a fixed asset is counted in input, the depreciation cost should be included in the calculation. In other words, count depreciation cost as cost. Formula 19.50.3 counts depreciation cost as income, and counts material consumption, transportation occupation, labor occupation, and natural resource occupation as cost. The value of $S_{c\text{-}static}$ calculated with the annual net income method should be greater than the prescribed value, which can be gotten by multiplying the prescribed value of investment net income rate with investment occupation. If the depreciation cost is counted as income, the depreciation income should be added to the prescribed value.

Let us work on the example after formula 19.47 again. The prescribed value of the annual net income for scheme A is $0.15 \times 900{,}000 = 142{,}500$ Yuan when the depreciation cost is excluded, and 202,500 Yuan when depreciation cost is included. The prescribed value of annual net income for scheme B is $0.15 \times 1{,}000{,}000 = 150{,}000$ Yuan when depreciation cost is excluded, and 210,000 Yuan when depreciation cost is included. The annual net incomes for schemes A and B total investment on fi:

$$\begin{aligned}
S_{c\text{-}static\text{-}A} &= S_A - C_A = 300,000 - 150,000 = 150,000\ \text{Yuan/year} \geq 142,000\ \text{Yuan/year}\\
S_{c\text{-}static\text{-}B} &= S_B - C_B = 300,000 - 170,000 = 130,000\ \text{Yuan/year} \leq 150,000\ \text{Yuan/year}\\
S_{c\text{-}static\text{-}A} &= S_A - C_A + C_{jA} = 210,000\ \text{Yuan/year} \geq 202,500\ \text{Yuan/year}\\
S_{c\text{-}static\text{-}B} &= S_B - C_B + C_{jB} = 190,000\ \text{Yuan/year} \leq 210,000\ \text{Yuan/year}\\
S_{c\text{-}static\text{-}A} &= 210,000\ \text{Yuan/year} \geq 202,500\ \text{Yuan/year}\\
S_{c\text{-}static\text{-}B} &= 190,000\ \text{Yuan/year} \leq 210,000\ \text{Yuan/year}
\end{aligned}$$

It can be seen that the annual net incomes of scheme A are greater than the prescribed value. Therefore, it is economical. In contrast, the annual net incomes of scheme B are smaller than the prescribed value. Thus, it is not economical.

2. Investment net income rate $L_{tc\text{-}static}$ (static)

$$L_{tc\text{-}static} = \frac{S - C}{T}(L_{tc\text{-}static} \geq \text{prescribed value}) \quad (19.51.1)$$

$$L_{tc\text{-}static} = \frac{s - c + c_j}{T}(L_{tc\text{-}static} \geq \text{prescribed value}) \quad (19.51.2)$$

$$L_{tc\text{-}static} = \frac{s - c + c_j - c_W - c_Y - c_R - c_D}{T}(L_{tc\text{-}static} \geq \text{prescribed value}) \quad (19.51.3)$$

where T is the total investment on fixed assets and current capital.

Let us work on the example after formula 19.47. The prescribed value of the investment net income rate for scheme *A* is 0.15 when depreciation cost is excluded, and 0.21 when depreciation cost is included. The prescribed value of the investment net income rate for scheme *B* is 0.15 when depreciation cost is excluded, and 0.21 when depreciation cost is included. The investment net income rates for scheme *A* and *B* can be calculated as below:

$$L_{tc\text{-}static\text{-}A} = \frac{15}{95} = 0.16\ \text{Yuan/Yuan} \cdot \text{year}$$

$$L_{tc-static-B} = \frac{13}{100} = 0.13\ \text{Yuan/Yuan} \cdot \text{year}$$

$$L_{tc\text{-}static\text{-}A} = \frac{21}{95} = 0.22\ \text{Yuan/Yuan} \cdot \text{year}$$

$$L_{tc-\text{static}-B} = \frac{19}{100} = 0.19\ \text{Yuan/Yuan} \cdot \text{year}$$

$$L_{tc\text{ - static}-A} = \frac{21}{95} = 0.22\ \text{Yuan/Yuan} \cdot \text{year}$$

$$L_{tc\text{-}static\text{-}B} = \frac{19}{100} = 0.19\ \text{Yuan/Yuan} \cdot \text{year}$$

The results show that the investment net income rates of scheme *A* are greater than the prescribed value. Therefore, it is economical. In contrast, the investment net income rates of scheme *B* are smaller than the prescribed value. Thus, it is not economical.

3. Investment recovery period $n_{c\text{-}static}$ (static)

$$n_{c\text{-}static} = \frac{T}{S - C}(n_{c\text{-}static} \leq \text{prescribed value}) \quad (19.52.1)$$

$$n_{c\text{-}static} = \frac{T}{S - C + C_j}(n_{c\text{-}static} \leq \text{prescribed value}) \quad (19.52.2)$$

$$n_{c\text{-}static} = \frac{T}{S - C + C_j - C_W - C_Y - C_R - C_D}(n_{c\text{-}static} \leq \text{prescribed value}) \quad (19.52.3)$$

The investment recovery period is the reciprocal of the investment net income rate. Accordingly, the prescribed value of the investment recovery period is the reciprocal of the prescribed value of investment net income rate.

Again, for the example after formula 19.47, the prescribed value of the investment recovery period for scheme A is 6.7 years when depreciation cost is excluded, and 4.7 years when depreciation cost is included. The prescribed value of the investment recovery period for scheme B is 6.7 years when depreciation cost is excluded, and 4.7 years when depreciation cost is included. The investment recovery periods for schemes A and B can be calculated as below:

$$n_{c\text{-}static-A} = \frac{95}{15} = 6.3\text{ years}$$

$$n_{c\text{-}static-B} = \frac{100}{13} = 7.7\text{ years}$$

$$n_{c\text{-}static-A} = \frac{95}{21} = 4.5\text{ years}$$

$$n_{c\text{-}static\text{-}B} = \frac{100}{19} = 5.3\text{ years}$$

$$n_{c\text{-}static\text{-}A} = \frac{95}{21} = 4.5\text{ years}$$

$$n_{c\text{-}static\text{-}B} = \frac{100}{19} = 5.3\text{ years}$$

The results show that the investment recovery periods of scheme A are shorter than the prescribed value, whereas those of scheme B are longer than the prescribed value. Therefore, scheme A is economical, but scheme B is not economical.

4. Additional investment net income rate $L_{ftc\text{-}static}$ (static)

$$L_{ftc\text{-}static} = \frac{\Delta S - \Delta C}{\Delta T}(L_{ftc\text{-}static} \geq \text{prescribed value}) \quad (19.53.1)$$

$$L_{ftc\text{-}static} = \frac{\Delta S - \Delta C + \Delta C_j}{\Delta T}(L_{ftc\text{-}static} \geq \text{prescribed value}) \quad (19.53.2)$$

$$L_{ftc\text{-}static} = \frac{\Delta S - \Delta C + \Delta C_j - \Delta C_W - \Delta C_Y - \Delta C_R - \Delta C_D}{\Delta T}$$
$$(L_{ftc\text{-}static} \geq \text{prescribed value}) \quad (19.53.3)$$

$$L_{ftc\text{-}static} = \frac{\Delta C - \Delta C_j}{\Delta T}(L_{ftc\text{-}static} \geq \text{prescribed value}) \tag{19.53.4}$$

$$L_{ftc\text{-}static} = \frac{\Delta C}{\Delta T}(L_{ftc\text{-}static} \geq \text{prescribed value}) \tag{19.53.5}$$

In formulas 19.53.1, 19.53.2, and 19.53.3, ΔC represents C_1–C_2 and ΔC_j represents C_{j1}–C_{j2}. But in formulas 19.53.4 and 19.53.5, ΔC represents C_2–C_1 and ΔC_j represents C_{j2}–C_{j1}. Formulas 19.53.4 and 19.53.5 are applicable when two schemes are equal.

Load the values in the example after formula 19.47 into the above formulas, and the additional investment net income rates for scheme *A* and *B* are:

$$L_{ftc\text{-}static} = \frac{17 - 15}{95 - 100} = -\frac{2}{5}$$
$$L_{ftc\text{-}static} = \frac{17 - 15}{95 - 100} = -\frac{2}{5}$$
$$L_{ftc\text{-}static} = \frac{17 - 15}{95 - 100} = -\frac{2}{5}$$
$$L_{ftc\text{-}static} = \frac{17 - 15}{95 - 100} = -\frac{2}{5}$$
$$L_{ftc\text{-}static} = \frac{17 - 15}{95 - 100} = -\frac{2}{5}$$

The prescribed value of the additional investment net income rate and the prescribed value of the investment net income rate are the same. The results show that the investment on scheme *A* is 50,000 Yuan less than that on scheme *B,* but scheme *A* generates 20,000 Yuan more net income. Thus, scheme *A* is economical.

5. Additional investment recovery period $n_{fc\text{-}static}$ (static)

$$n_{fc\text{-}static} = \frac{\Delta T}{\Delta S - \Delta C}(n_{fc\text{-}static} \leq \text{prescribed value}) \tag{19.54.1}$$

$$n_{fc\text{-}static} = \frac{\Delta T}{\Delta S - \Delta C + \Delta C_j}(n_{fc\text{-}static} \leq \text{prescribed value}) \tag{19.54.2}$$

$$n_{fc\text{-}static} = \frac{\Delta T}{\Delta S - \Delta C + \Delta C_j - \Delta C_W - \Delta C_Y - \Delta C_R - \Delta C_D}$$
$$(n_{fc\text{-}static} \leq \text{prescribed value}) \tag{19.54.3}$$

$$n_{fc\text{-}static} = \frac{\Delta T}{\Delta C - \Delta C_j}(n_{fc\text{-}static} \leq \text{prescribed value}) \tag{19.54.4}$$

$$n_{fc\text{-}static} = \frac{\Delta T}{\Delta C}\left(n_{fc\text{-}static} \leq \text{prescribed value}\right) \tag{19.54.5}$$

The additional investment recovery period is the reciprocal of the additional investment net income rate. Formulas 19.54.1, 19.54.2, and 19.54.3 are applicable when the S of two schemes are not equal, while formulas 19.54.4 and 19.54.5 are applicable when the S of two schemes are equal.

An additional investment recovery period is called an additional investment payback period as well, or a marginal investment recovery period. Formula 19.54.5 was introduced into the former Soviet Union from the U.S. in the 1930s and was later was applied widely in practice. This formula is applicable to compare two schemes when one has a larger investment and a smaller cost and the other has a smaller investment and a larger cost. The scheme with the larger investment is economical when the extra investment ΔT can be reclaimed via cost saving in n_{fc_static} years and the recovery period n_{fc_static} is equal to or shorter than the prescribed recovery period set by the state.

The advantage of this method is that it is simple and convenient. The calculation only needs the value of ΔT and ΔC. There is no need for the prescribed value of additional investment recovery period $n_{fc\text{-}static}$, which is required for the final step of scheme comparison. However, this method has the following shortcomings:

First, this method is applicable when comparing two technological schemes. If the number of technological schemes is greater than three, use of this method will cause errors. For instance, in practice, people usually compare technological schemes with a so-called basic scheme, and then choose the one having the shortest additional investment recovery period as the best. The result might be incorrect. Here is an example. Suppose that there are three technological schemes whose investment and annual cost are listed in Table 19.6.

If the first technological scheme is chosen as the basic scheme, the additional investment of the second scheme ($\Delta T_{2-1} = \Delta T_2 - \Delta T_1 = 40{,}000$ Yuan) will be reclaimed in one year, whereas the additional investment of the third scheme ($\Delta T_{3-1} = \Delta T_3 - \Delta T_1 = 200{,}000$ Yuan) will be reclaimed in 2.9 years. This result shows that the second scheme is more economical than the third one; thus, the second one should be chosen. However, if we compare the second and third schemes directly, we find that the additional investment of the third scheme ($\Delta T_{3-2} = \Delta T_3 - \Delta T_2 = 160{,}000$ Yuan) will be reclaimed in over 5 years, which is shorter than the value

Table 19.6 Details of three technological schemes

Technological Schemes	Investment T (Ten thousand Yuan)	Cost C (Ten thousand Yuan)	Additional investment recovery period n_{fc} (Year)	
# 1	20	15	–	–
#2	24	11	1	–
#3	40	8	2.9	5.3

Table 19.7 The investment cost and the annual cost of two technological schemes

Technological Schemes	Investment T (Ten thousand Yuan)	Cost C (Ten thousand Yuan)	Additional investment recovery period n_{fc} (Year)
# 1	100	10.01	–
# 2	101	10.00	100

prescribed by the state $n_{fcb} > 5$). Accordingly, the third scheme is more economical than the second one. Indeed, it is the best one among the three in this example.

Second, this method is applicable when the investment cost and the annual cost of two technological schemes are different. The formula of recovery period is not applicable in other situations.

Third, this method can only resolve relative economic issues among exclusive schemes. It cannot be used for choosing complementary schemes.

Fourth, if the investment cost and the annual cost of two technological schemes are very close, results generated by this method are easily thought to be correct. But in fact they are not. For instance, the investment cost and the annual cost of technological scheme A and B are listed in Table 19.7.

Load the values into formula 19.54.5. The results show that the additional investment of scheme B will be reclaimed completely in 100 years, which is much longer than the prescribed value. Thus, scheme B is not economical. However, these two schemes are almost the same regarding their economic effect, because the values of additional investment and saved annual cost achieved by the calculation are very small. They are in the range where errors are accepted.

Fifth, this method can only measure the relative economic effect of technological schemes. It is not capable of calculating the absolute economic effect of technological schemes.

Sixth, it is very hard to set the length of recovery period. Are there any differences between a recovery period of five years and another recovery period of ten years? A misunderstanding of the economic concept of "recovery period" exists. Some argue that the value of the additional investment recovery period must be shorter than the service period of technological schemes. For example, if the additional investment recovery period of a technological scheme is six years, and the length of service of this technological scheme is three years, this technological scheme is not economical because the total additional investment cannot be reclaimed completely in three years. However, this argument is not reasonable because the additional investment recovery period and the length of service cannot be recovered. The former is a measurement for economic effect. It is meaningful to compare the additional investment recovery period with the prescribed value set by the state. Thus, it is meaningless to compare the additional investment recovery period with the length of service. The additional investment recovery period is indeed an investment effect coefficient. Its value is the reciprocal of the investment effect coefficient (see the annual calculation cost).

Seventh, the method based on the additional investment recovery period is static. It does not consider the comparable factors related to time. Meanwhile, it does not deal well with the comparable conditions regarding production, quality, and consumption cost. In particular, this method only considers investment occupation and cost and neglects the impact of the occupation of labor and transportation capacity, material consumption, and the occupation of natural resource on total social consumption cost.

Eighth, formula 19.54.5 is not as rational as formula 19.54.4 because the former calculates investment in its numerator and calculates depreciation cost again in its denominator. Obviously, the same item is calculated twice.

Usually, the prescribed value of additional investment recovery period is the same as that of the investment recovery period.

Load the values in the example after formula 19.47 into formulas 19.54.1, 19.54.2, 19.54.3, 19.54.4, and 19.54.5, and the additional investment recovery periods are:

$$n_{fc\text{-}static} = \frac{95-100}{17-15} = -\frac{5}{2}$$
$$n_{fc\text{-}static} = -\frac{5}{2}$$
$$n_{fc\text{-}static} = -\frac{5}{2}$$
$$n_{fc\text{-}static} = -\frac{5}{2}$$
$$n_{fc\text{-}static} = -\frac{5}{2}$$

The results indicate that scheme *A* has no additional investment. The investment on it is decreasing. The value of its recovery period is negative. In other words, its recovery period is shorter than the prescribed value. Thus, scheme *A* is economical. In contrast, the investment in scheme *B* is 50,000 Yuan more than that in scheme *A*. However, the net income of scheme *B* is 20,000 Yuan less. Its additional investment will never be reclaimed. Therefore, scheme *B* is not economical.

6. Annual calculation cost Z_{static} (static)

$$Z_{static} = C + X_t T (Z_{static} \text{ with the smallest value is the most economical}) \tag{19.55}$$

This formula is converted from the formula of the additional investment recovery period (19.54.5). It was adopted by the former Soviet Union for quite a long while. It is applicable for use in comparing technological schemes when they meet the same requirement or when they generate the same amount of output. The technological scheme with the smallest annual calculation cost is the most economical. In formula 19.55, $X_t T$ is the cost of capital occupation. This formula does not consider the time factor. It does not consider the fact that the reclaimed depreciation cost decreases the cost of capital occupation by a number of years, either. Furthermore, this formula neglects the material consumption cost, and the costs of labor occupation, transportation capacity occupation, and natural resource utilization.

Load the values in the example after formula 19.47 into formula 19.5, and the annual calculation costs for scheme *A* and scheme *B* are:

$$Z_{static\_A} = C_A + X_t T_A = 17 + 0.17 \times 95 = 292,500 \text{ Yuan/year}$$
$$Z_{static\_B} = C_B + X_t T_B = 17 + 0.17 \times 100 = 320,000 \text{ Yuan/year}$$

The results indicate that scheme A is more economical than scheme B.

7. (dynamic) Investment net income rate X_{tc}[4]

   It is known that

$$E_c = f(X_{tc}). \text{ Set } E_c = 0. \text{ Find the value of } X_{tc} (X_{tc} \geq \text{prescribed value}). \quad (19.56.1)$$

   Or it known that

$$E_a = f(X_{tc}). \text{ Set } E_a = 1. \text{ Find the value of } X_{tc} (X_{tc} \geq \text{prescribed value}). \quad (19.56.2)$$

This method calculates the investment net income of technological schemes with the time factor considered. If the (dynamic) investment net income rate of a technological scheme is equal to or larger than the prescribed value, it is economical. Otherwise, it is not economical. The internal benefit rate method proposed by foreign countries is actually the method of investment net income rate when X_w, X_y, X_r, and X_d are all equal to zero. But the name "internal benefit rate" is not accurate, because it does not indicate the benefit rate clearly. It might be the "cost benefit rate" or the "investment benefit rate."

The dynamic investment net income rate is usually calculated via a trial and error procedure. The static investment net income rate is calculated first, and then the pilot calculation value of X_t can be found in the time coefficient X_{lxp} table.

According to the values in the example after formula 19.47, the pilot calculation value of X_t for scheme A is 0.125. Load this value into formula 19.56.1. The value of E_{c_A} is 50,000 Yuan. Thus, a value that is greater than 0.125 should be chosen for X_t. Select the value of X_t as 0.15. Load it into formula 19.56.1. The value of E_{c_A} is 122,000 Yuan. By applying interpolation, the value of X_t can be achieved as 13.3% when $E_c = 0$. Similarly, the value of X_t for scheme B can be achieved as 14.95%.

$$\therefore X_{tc\_A} = 13.3\%$$
$$X_{tc\_A} = 14.95\%$$

[4]For convenience, dynamic is omitted. If a term has no footnote, the status is dynamic. The same hereinafter.

The dynamic investment net income rates of schemes A and B are both smaller than the prescribed value. Relatively speaking, scheme B is more economical than scheme A.

8. (dynamic) Investment excess net income rate L_{tc}

$$L_{tc} = \frac{E_c}{T_\Sigma}(L_{tc} \geq 0) \tag{19.57}$$

This method is applicable to compare technological schemes when investment is limited. Suppose there are two technological schemes. One has a higher social excess net income but it needs more investment. In this case, when investment is limited, it is not enough to compare only their social excess net income; the amount of net income generated by one Yuan should be compared as well. The greater the dynamic investment excess net income rate, the better. At the least, the dynamic investment excess net income rate should greater than zero. Formula 19.57 can be achieved from the social additional net income rate E_{cf} method by setting ΔE_c as E_c and ΔT as T.

Load the values in the example after formula 19.47 into formula 19.57, and the dynamic investment excess net income rates for scheme A and scheme B are:

$$L_{tc\_A} = \frac{E_{c\_A}}{T_{\Sigma A}} = \frac{-12.2}{90 + \frac{5}{\theta^3}} = \frac{-12.2}{93.3} = -0.17\ \text{Yuan/Yuan}$$

$$L_{tc\_B} = \frac{E_{C\_B}}{T_{\Sigma B}} = \frac{-0.81}{\frac{90}{\theta^2} + \frac{10}{\theta^3}} = \frac{-0.81}{74.6} = -0.01\ \text{Yuan/Yuan}$$

The results show that both technological schemes are not economical because their dynamic investment excess net income rates are smaller than zero. Relatively speaking, scheme B is more economical than scheme A.

9. (dynamic) Investment recovery period n_c

(1) Set $\sum_{s=1}^{n_c} T_s \frac{1}{\theta^{s-1}} - \sum_{s=1}^{n_c} (S_s - C_s + C_{js} - C_{ws} - C_{ys} - C_{rs} - C_{ds}) \frac{1}{\theta^s} = 0.$

Find $n_c (n_c \leq \text{prescribed value})$ (19.58.1)

(2) Set $\sum_{s=1}^{n_c} T_s \frac{1}{\theta^{s-1}} - \sum_{s=1}^{n_c} (S_s - C_s + C_{js}) \frac{1}{\theta^s} = 0$. Find $n_c (n_c \leq$ prescribed value)

(19.58.2)

(3) $n_c = \dfrac{-\log\left(1 - \frac{X_t T}{S - C + C_j}\right)}{\log(1 + X_t)}$ $(n_c \leq \text{prescribed value})$ (19.58.3)

where $T = T_{g1}\theta^{nk} + T_{g2}\theta^{nk-1} + \cdots + T_{gnk}\theta + T_1 = \sum_{s=1}^{n_c} T_{gs}\theta^{nk-s+1} + T_l \cdot T_g$ is the investment on fixed asset. n_k is construction period. T_l is the current capital. $\theta = 1 + X_t$.

Load the values in the example after formula 19.47 into formulas 19.58.1 and 19.58.2, and the dynamic investment recovery period for scheme A can be calculated as below:

$$90 + \frac{5}{\theta^3} - 21\frac{\theta^n - 1}{(\theta - 1)\theta^n\theta^3} = 0$$

$$\therefore \frac{\theta^n - 1}{(\theta - 1)\theta^n} = \left(90 + \frac{5}{\theta^3}\right)\frac{\theta^3}{21} = \frac{90\theta^3 + 5}{21} = \frac{141.9}{21} = 6.76$$

Check the time factor X_{lx} table and n_{c_A} is ∞.

For scheme B,

$$90 + \frac{10}{\theta} - 19\frac{\theta^n - 1}{(\theta - 1)\theta^n\theta} = 0$$

$$\therefore \frac{\theta^n - 1}{(\theta - 1)\theta^n} = \frac{90\theta + 10}{19} = \frac{113.5}{19} = 5.97$$

Check the time factor X_{lx} table and n_{c_B} is 16 years. If n_{c_B} is counted from its construction period, the value of n_{c_B} is 16 + 1=17 years.

The dynamic investment recovery periods for schemes A and B can be achieved by applying (19.58.3).

For scheme A,

$$n_{c\_A} = \frac{-\log\left(1 - \frac{X_t(90\theta^3+5)}{30-9}\right)}{\log(1 + 0.15)} = \infty$$

For scheme B,

$$n_{c\_B} = \frac{-\log\left(1 - \frac{X_t(90\theta+10)}{30-11}\right)}{\log(1 + 0.15)} = 16\,\text{years(counted from the time when production begins)}$$

$$n_{c\_B} = 16 + 1 = 17\,\text{years(counted from the time when construction begins)}$$

The results show that neither scheme A nor scheme B is economical, because their dynamic investment recovery periods are longer than the prescribed value 15 years. Relatively speaking, scheme A is less economical.

10. (dynamic) additional investment net income rate X_{ftc}

It is known that

$$\Delta E_c = f(X_{ftc}).\ \text{Set}\ E_c = E_{c1} - E_{c2} = 0.$$

$$\text{Find the value of } X_{ftc}\left(X_{ftc} \geq \text{prescribed value}\right). \quad (19.59.1)$$

Or it is known that

$$E_{af} = f(X_{tc}). \text{ Set } E_{af} = 1. \text{ Find the value of } X_{ftc}\left(X_{ftc} \geq \text{prescribed value}\right) \quad (19.59.2)$$

Based on the values in the example after formula 19.47, the social net incomes of schemes A and B can be calculated as below:

$$E_{c\_A} = -90\theta^{18} - 5\theta^{15} + 30\frac{\theta^{15}-1}{\theta-1} - 9\frac{\theta^{15}-1}{\theta-1} + 5$$

$$E_{c\_B} = -90\theta^{16} - 10\theta^{15} + 30\frac{\theta^{15}-1}{\theta-1} - 11\frac{\theta^{15}-1}{\theta-1} + 10$$

Set $\Delta E_c = E_{c\_A} - E_{c\_B} = 0$, and then

$$90\theta^{16} - 90\theta^{18} + 5\theta^{15} + 2\frac{\theta^{15}-1}{\theta-1} - 5 = 0$$

X_t in the above equation can be calculated by applying a trial and error procedure. Set $X_t = 0.1$, and the result is -7.4. Then set $X_t = 0.09$, and the result is 4.7. Thus, the value of X_t is between 0.09 and 0.1 when result is equal to zero. By applying interpolation, the value of X_{ftc} can be achieved as below:

$$X_{ftc} = X_t = 9 + \frac{4.7(10-9)}{4.7+7.4} = 9.4(\%)$$

The above calculation is based on formula 19.59.1. The result will be the same if formula 19.59.2 is adopted for the calculation. The dynamic additional investment net income rate of scheme A is smaller than the prescribed value of 15%. Thus, scheme A is not economical. Such a relative economic evaluation method cannot be used for assessing whether scheme A or scheme B, per se, is economical.

11. (dynamic) Additional investment recovery period n_{fc}

$$\text{Set} \sum_{s=1}^{n_{fc}} \Delta T_s \frac{1}{\theta^{s-1}} - \sum_{s=1}^{n_{fc}} \left(\Delta S_s - \Delta C_s + \Delta C_{js} - \Delta C_{ws} - \Delta C_{ys} - \Delta C_{rs} - \Delta C_{ds}\right)\frac{1}{\theta^s} = 0.$$

$$\text{Find } n_{fc}\left(n_{fc} \leq \text{prescribedvalue}\right) \quad (19.60.1)$$

$$\text{Set} \sum_{s=1}^{n_{fc}} \Delta T_s \frac{1}{\theta^{s-1}} - \sum_{s=1}^{n_{fc}} \left(\Delta S_s - \Delta C_s + \Delta C_{js}\right)\frac{1}{\theta^s} = 0. \text{ Find } n_{fc}\left(n_{fc} \leq \text{prescribed value}\right) \quad (19.60.2)$$

Load the values in the example after formula 19.47 into formulas 19.60.1 and 19.60.2, and the dynamic additional investment recovery period for scheme A can be calculated as below:

$$90 + \frac{5}{\theta^3} - \frac{90}{\theta^2} - \frac{10}{\theta^2} - \left(\frac{21}{\theta^3} - \frac{19}{\theta^3}\right)\frac{\theta^n - 1}{(\theta - 1)\theta^n\theta^3} = 0$$

$$\frac{\theta^n - 1}{(\theta - 1)\theta^n} = \frac{18.7}{1.3} = 14.4$$

Check the time factor X_{lx} table. The value of n_{fc} is equal to n or ∞.

The result shows that the additional investment that scheme A generates more than scheme B will never be reclaimed. Thus, scheme A is not economical.

12. Total consumption cost $Z_{\sum}$

$$Z_{\Sigma\_curent} = \sum_{s=1}^{n} Z_s \frac{1}{\theta^s} \quad \left(\text{The smaller } Z_{\Sigma\_curent}, \text{ the better}\right) \tag{19.61.1}$$

or

$$Z_{\Sigma\_final} = \sum_{s=1}^{n} Z_s \theta^{n-s} \quad \left(\text{The smaller } Z_{\Sigma\_final}, \text{ the better}\right) \tag{19.61.2}$$

where $Z_{\sum\_current}$ is the total consumption cost calculated based on present value. $Z_{\sum\_final}$ is the total consumption cost calculated based on final value.

This method is applicable to compare technological schemes with the same benefit and length of service (calculation period).

Load the values in the example after formula 19.47 into formulas 19.61.1 and 19.61.2, and the total consumption costs for scheme A and scheme B can be calculated as below:

$$Z_{\Sigma\_A} = 15,774,000 \text{ (final value)}$$
$$Z_{\Sigma\_B} = 14,366,000 \text{ (final value)}$$
$$Z_{\Sigma\_A} = 1,274,000 \text{ (present value)}$$
$$Z_{\Sigma\_B} = 1,160,000 \text{ (present value)}$$

The results show that the total consumption of scheme A is that of scheme B. Thus, scheme A is not as economical as scheme B.

13. Annual consumption cost Z

$$Z = C + x_t T_z + x_w W + x_y Y + x_r R + x_d D_z = ZX \tag{19.62.1}$$

or

$$Z = Z_{\Sigma\_current} \frac{(\theta - 1)\theta^n}{\theta^2 - 1} \quad \text{(The smaller } Z\text{, the better)} \tag{19.62.2}$$

or

$$Z = Z_{\Sigma\_final} \frac{\theta - 1}{\theta^n - 1} \quad \text{(The smaller } Z\text{, the better)} \tag{19.62.3}$$

This method is applicable to compare technological schemes with same benefit but with different length of service.

Load the values in the example after formula 19.47 into formulas 19.62.1 and 19.62.2, and the annual consumption costs for scheme A and scheme B can be calculated as below:

$$Z_A = 331,000\,\text{Yuan/year(final value)}$$
$$Z_B = 302,000\,\text{Yuan/year(final value)}$$
$$Z_A = 218,000\,\text{Yuan/year(present value)}$$
$$Z_B = 198,000\,\text{Yuan/year(present value)}$$

The results show that the annual consumption cost of scheme A is greater than that of scheme B. Thus, scheme A is not as economical as scheme B.

14. Domestic competition $E_{domestic}$

(1) Static approach

$$E_{domestic\_static} = \Delta X_t T + \Delta X_w W + \Delta X_y Y + \Delta X_r R + \Delta X_d D \quad (E_{domestic\_static} \geq 0) \tag{19.63.1}$$

where

$$\Delta X_t = \frac{1}{K} X_{t\_scheme} - X_t \tag{19.63.1.1}$$

$$\Delta X_w = \frac{1}{K} X_{w\_scheme} - X_w \tag{19.63.1.2}$$

$$\Delta X_y = \frac{1}{K} X_{y\_scheme} - X_y \tag{19.63.1.3}$$

$$\Delta X_r = \frac{1}{K} X_{r\_scheme} - X_r \tag{19.63.1.4}$$

$$\Delta X_d = \frac{1}{K} X_{d\_scheme} - X_d \tag{19.63.1.5}$$

where X_{t_scheme} is the investment on technological schemes. X_{w_scheme} is the material utilized by technological schemes. X_{y_scheme} is the transportation capacity utilized by technological schemes. X_{r_scheme} is the labor utilized by technological schemes. X_{d_scheme} is the economic effect coefficient of natural resource utilization (based on net income).

If $\Delta X_t T$, $\Delta X_w W$, $\Delta X_y Y$, $\Delta X_r R$, and $\Delta X_d D$ are all considered, $K = 5$. If two of them are considered, $K = 2$. T, W, Y, R, and D are the amount of investment, materials, transportation capacity, labor, and natural resources respectively utilized by the technological schemes. X_t, X_w, X_y, X_r, and X_d are the prescribed values of related economic effect coefficients. If these prescribed values adopt the national average value, unallocated values can be applied based on actual situation. If repeated calculation occurs, an allocated value can be adopted. The average allocation method is usually adopted, namely multiplying the prescribed values with $\frac{1}{K}$. If the unallocated prescribed value is X_{t_total}, the allocated prescribed value $X_{t\_allocation}$ is $\frac{1}{K}X_{t\_total}$, and so on.

(2) Dynamic approach

$$E_{domestic\_dynamic} = \sum_{s=1}^{n} \left(\Delta x_{ts} T_s + \Delta x_{ws} W_s + \Delta x_{ys} Y_s + \Delta x_{rs} R_s + \Delta x_{ds} D_s\right)\frac{1}{\theta^s} \quad \left(E_{domestic\_dynamic} \geq 0\right) \tag{19.63.2}$$

This approach is straightforward. If the economic effect coefficients of a technological scheme are greater than the prescribed values, this technological scheme has strong domestic competitiveness. If some economic effect coefficients of a technological scheme are good and others are not good, this approach can be applied to assess the economic effect of a technological scheme, comprehensively. As long as the indicators of domestic competition are equal to zero or greater than zero, a technological scheme has competition.

This approach was proposed by the author recently. It is derived from the serial net income-based methods E_c. They are essentially the same, but they have different formats. Here is the mathematic proving process based on the simplest situation:

It is known that

$$E_c = \left(J - C - x_t T_z - x_w W - x_y Y - x_r R - x_d D_z\right)\frac{\theta^n - 1}{(\theta - 1)\theta^{n+nk}} \tag{19.63.3}$$

Suppose that the economic benefit (net income) of a technological scheme is evenly allocated according to the low size of the amount of production condition K. The economic effect coefficients of each allocation of this technological scheme can be calculated by multiplying the economic effect coefficients of this technological scheme with $\frac{1}{K}$ respectively. Here are the formulas:

$$X_{t\_scheme\_allocation} = \frac{1}{K}\frac{J - C}{T_Z} = \frac{1}{K}X_{t\_scheme} \tag{19.63.3.1}$$

$$X_{w\_scheme\_allocation} = \frac{1}{K}\frac{J-C}{W} = \frac{1}{K}X_{w\_scheme} \tag{19.63.3.2}$$

$$X_{y\_scheme\_allocation} = \frac{1}{K}\frac{J-C}{Y} = \frac{1}{K}X_{y\_scheme} \tag{19.63.3.3}$$

$$X_{r\_scheme\_allocation} = \frac{1}{K}\frac{J-C}{R} = \frac{1}{K}X_{r\_scheme} \tag{19.63.3.4}$$

$$X_{d\_scheme\_allocation} = \frac{1}{K}\frac{J-C}{D} = \frac{1}{K}X_{d\_scheme} \tag{19.63.3.5}$$

Load the above formulas into (19.63.3),

$$\begin{aligned} E_C &= \left[\left(\frac{1}{K}X_{t\_scheme} - X_t\right)T_z + \left(\frac{1}{K}X_{w\_scheme} - X_w\right)W + \left(\frac{1}{K}X_{y\_scheme} - X_y\right)Y \right. \\ &\quad \left. + \left(\frac{1}{K}X_{r\_scheme} - X_r\right)R + \left(\frac{1}{K}X_{d\_scheme} - X_d\right)D_z\right]\frac{\theta^n - 1}{(\theta-1)\theta^{n+nk}} \\ &= \left[\Delta X_t T_z + \Delta X_w W + \Delta X_y Y + \Delta X_r R + \Delta X_d D_z\right]\frac{\theta^n - 1}{(\theta-1)\theta^{n+nk}} \end{aligned} \tag{19.63.4}$$

Load the even allocated values for economic effect coefficients in formula (19.63.4),

$$\begin{aligned} E_c &= \left[\left(\frac{1}{K}X_{t\_scheme} - \frac{1}{K}X_{t\_total}\right)T_z + \left(\frac{1}{K}X_{w\_scheme} - \frac{1}{K}X_{w\_total}\right)W \right. \\ &\quad + \left(\frac{1}{K}X_{y\_scheme} - \frac{1}{K}X_{y\_total}\right)Y + \left(\frac{1}{K}X_{r\_scheme} - \frac{1}{K}X_{r\_total}\right)R \\ &\quad \left. + \left(\frac{1}{K}X_{d\_scheme} - \frac{1}{K}X_{d\_total}\right)D_z\right]\frac{\theta^n - 1}{(\theta-1)\theta^{n+nk}} \\ &= \frac{1}{K}\left[\Delta X_t T_z + \Delta X_w W + \Delta X_y Y + \Delta X_r R + \Delta X_d D_z\right]\frac{\theta^n - 1}{(\theta-1)\theta^{n+nk}} \end{aligned} \tag{19.63.5}$$

where $\Delta X_t = X_{t\_scheme} - X_{t\_total.}$ Formula 19.63.5 is for calculating $E_{domestic}$.

Based on the values in the example after formula 19.47, the index of static domestic competition for scheme A and scheme B can be calculated as below with formulas (19.63.1):

$$E_{domestic\_static\_A} = \Delta X_t T_A = (0.16 - 0.15) \times 95 = 9,500 \text{ Yuan} > 0$$
$$E_{domestic\_static\_B} = \Delta X_t T_B = (0.13 - 0.15) \times 100 = -20,000 \text{ Yuan} < 0$$

The results show that the domestic competition of scheme A is economical, whereas that of scheme B is not.

Based on the same example, the index of dynamic domestic competition for schemes A and B can be calculated as below with formulas (19.63.2):

$$E_{domestic\_dynaic\_A} = \left[\Delta X_t T_{z\_A}\right]\frac{\theta^n - 1}{(\theta - 1)\theta^{n+nk}}$$
$$= (0.124 - 0.15) \times 120.7 \times 47.58 \times 0.081 = -121,000 \text{ Yuan}$$
$$E_{domestic\_dynaic\_B} = \left[\Delta X_t T_{z\_B}\right]\frac{\theta^n - 1}{(\theta - 1)\theta^{n+nk}}$$
$$= \left(\frac{13}{87.9} - 0.15\right) \times 87.9 \times 47.58 \times 0.081 = -7,100 \text{ Yuan}$$

The index of domestic competition for schemes A and B are the indices for their social net income. According to the previous calculation, social net income for scheme A is $-122{,}000$ Yuan and the social net income for the scheme B is -8,100 Yuan. Compared with the values of the domestic competition index for scheme A, -121,000 Yuan and for scheme B is $-7{,}100$ Yuan, errors are found due to the calculation. The results of the calculations should be the same.

The results show that from the perspective of static domestic competition, scheme A is economical, while scheme B is not. Regarding dynamic domestic competition, neither of them is economical. Relative speaking, scheme B is more economical than scheme A.

15. International competition $E_{international}$

This method is used for assessing technological schemes that are involved with international trade. It is actually the application of the aforementioned methods, such as E_a, E_c, E_{af}, and E_{cf}. The total social economic benefit S in the following formula is the net foreign exchange income of export products. The total social consumption cost Z is the total domestic consumption cost of export products. Here is an example for calculating international competition $E_{international}$:

(1) Calculating the foreign exchange effect of foreign trade schemes (or import replacement scheme)

$$E_{foreign\_exhange} = \sum_{s=1}^{n} S_s \frac{1}{\theta^s} = \sum_{s=1}^{n} \left(S_{foreign\_s} - Z_{foreign\_s}\right)\frac{1}{\theta^s}$$

where $S_{foreign}$ is the foreign exchange income of export products, $Z_{foreign}$ is the foreign exchange expenditure of export product.

(2) Calculating international competition $E_{a\_internaitonal}$

$$E_{e\_international} = \frac{\sum_{s=1}^{n} S_S \frac{1}{\theta^s}}{\sum_{s=1}^{n} Z_S \frac{1}{\theta^s}} \left(E_{a\_international} \geq 1\right) \qquad (19.64)$$

where S = (the foreign exchange income of export products-the foreign exchange expenditure of export products) x exchange rate. The total domestic input cost of the export product Z = the domestic input cost for per unit export products x the amount of export products.

16. Exchange rate $L_{exchange}$

This method is called "the economic foreign exchange cost." Actually, it is a derivation of the international competition method $E_{international}$. Here is its formula:

$$L_{exchange} = \frac{\sum_{s=1}^{n} Z_s \frac{1}{\theta^s}}{\sum_{s=1}^{n} S_s \frac{1}{\theta^s}} \left(L_{exchange} \leq \text{rational exchange rate}\right) \tag{19.65}$$

where S is the net foreign exchange income of export products calculated with foreign exchange, and Z is the costs of domestic input for export products calculated with Ren Min Bi.

Table 19.8 lists the calculation results of 18 methods, based on net income. The table shows that the results generated by static methods are the same, namely that scheme A is economical whereas scheme B is not economical. The table also shows that the results generated by dynamic methods are the same, namely that neither scheme A nor scheme B is economical. Relatively speaking, scheme B is more economical. The table shows that the static methods and the dynamic methods generate different calculation results.

19.3.3 National Income Series Methods

The national income series methods are similar to the net income series methods. Just switch the total cost C with the cost excluding wage C_u and switch Z with Z_u in net income series methods. An introduction to the national income series methods is skipped.

19.3.4 Principles for Applying Technological Economy Evaluation Methods

The following are some principles for applying the aforementioned technological economy evaluation methods:

(1) It is more reasonable to adopt dynamic evaluation methods than static ones. When possible, dynamic evaluation methods should be adopted first.

Table 19.8 The comparison of the results calculated by macro technological scheme evaluation methods

No.	Evaluation method	Evaluation Standard	Technological Scheme *A*	Technological Scheme *B*	Result of absolute economic evaluation	Result of relative economic evaluation result
1	E_a	≥1	0.906	0.993	Neither technological scheme is economical	Technological scheme *B* is more economical than technological scheme *A*
2	E_c	≥0	−1.504 million Yuan (final value) −0.122 million Yuan (present value)	−96000 Yuan (final value) −8100 Yuan (present value)	Neither technological scheme is economical	Technological scheme *B* is more economical than technological scheme *A*
3	E_{af}	≥1	0	–	–	–
4	E_{cf}	≥0	−0.61	–	–	Technological scheme *B* is more economical than technological scheme *A*
5	S_{c_static} (1) (2) (3)	≥ prescribed value ≥142,500 Yuan ≥150,000 Yuan ≥202,500 Yuan ≥210,000 Yuan ≥202,500 Yuan ≥210,000 Yuan	15 – 21 – 21 –	– 13 – 19 – 19	Technological scheme *A* is economical Technological scheme *B* is not economical Technological scheme *A* is economical Technological scheme *B* is not economical Technological scheme *A* is economical Technological scheme *B* is not economical	Technological scheme *A* is more economical than technological scheme *B* Technological scheme *A* is more economical than technological scheme *B* Technological scheme *A* is more economical than technological scheme *B*

(continued)

Table 19.8 (continued)

No.	Evaluation method	Evaluation Standard	Technological Scheme *A*	Technological Scheme *B*	Result of absolute economic evaluation	Result of relative economic evaluation result
6	L_{tc_static} (1) (2) (3)	≥ prescribed value ≥0.15 ≥0.15 ≥0.21 ≥0.21 ≥0.21 ≥0.21	0.16 – 0.22 – 0.22 –	– 0.13 – 0.19 – 0.19	Technological scheme *A* is economical Technological scheme *B* is not economical Technological scheme *A* is economical Technological scheme *B* is not economical Technological scheme *A* is economical Technological scheme *B* is not economical	Technological scheme *A* is more economical than technological scheme *B* Technological scheme *A* is more economical than technological scheme *B* Technological scheme *A* is more economical than technological scheme *B*
7	n_{c_static} (1) (2) (3)	≥ prescribed value ≤6.7 years ≤6.7 years ≤4.7 years ≤4.7 years ≤4.7 years ≤4.7 years	6.3 – 4.5 – 4.5 –	– 7.7 – 5.3 – 5.3	Technological scheme *A* is economical Technological scheme *B* is not economical Technological scheme *A* is economical Technological scheme *B* is not economical Technological scheme *A* is economical Technological scheme *B* is not economical	Technological scheme *A* is more economical than technological scheme *B* Technological scheme *A* is more economical than technological scheme *B* Technological scheme *A* is more economical than technological scheme *B*

(continued)

Table 19.8 (continued)

No.	Evaluation method	Evaluation Standard	Technological Scheme *A*	Technological Scheme *B*	Result of absolute economic evaluation	Result of relative economic evaluation result
8	L_{fc_static} (1) (2) (3) (4) (5)	≥ prescribed value ≥0.15 ≥0.15 ≥0.15 ≥0.15 ≥0.15	– 2/-5 2/-5 2/-5 2/-5 2/-5 2/-5	– – – – –	– – – – –	Technological scheme *A* is more economical than technological scheme *B* Technological scheme *A* is more economical than technological scheme *B* Technological scheme *A* is more economical than technological scheme *B* Technological scheme *A* is more economical than technological scheme *B* Technological scheme *A* is more economical than technological scheme *B*

(continued)

Table 19.8 (continued)

No.	Evaluation method	Evaluation Standard	Technological Scheme *A*	Technological Scheme *B*	Result of absolute economic evaluation	Result of relative economic evaluation result
9	n_{fc_static} (1) (2) (3) (4) (5)	≤ prescribed value ≤6.7 years ≤6.7 years ≤6.7 years ≤6.7 years ≤6.7 years	−5/2 −5/2 −5/2 −5/2 −5/2	– – – – –	– – – – –	Technological scheme *A* is more economical than technological scheme *B* Technological scheme *A* is more economical than technological scheme *B* Technological scheme *A* is more economical than technological scheme *B* Technological scheme *A* is more economical than technological scheme *B* Technological scheme *A* is more economical than technological scheme *B*
10	Z_{static}	Minimum	292,500 Yuan/year	320,000 Yuan/year	–	Technological scheme *A* is more economical than technological scheme *B*
11	X_{tc}	≥0.15	0.133	0.1495	Neither technological scheme is economical	Technological scheme *B* is more economical than technological scheme *A*
12	L_{tc}	≥0	−0.13	−0.01	Neither technological scheme is economical	Technological scheme *B* is more economical than technological scheme *A*

(continued)

Table 19.8 (continued)

No.	Evaluation method	Evaluation Standard	Technological Scheme *A*	Technological Scheme *B*	Result of absolute economic evaluation	Result of relative economic evaluation result
13	n_c (1) (2) (3)	≤ prescribed value ≤15 years ≤15 years ≤15 years	∞ ∞ ∞	16 16 16	Neither technological scheme is economical Neither technological scheme is economical Neither technological scheme is economical	Technological scheme *B* is more economical than technological scheme *A* Technological scheme *B* is more economical than technological scheme *A* Technological scheme *B* is more economical than technological scheme *A*
14	X_{ftc}	≥0.15	0.098	–	–	Technological scheme *B* is more economical than technological scheme *A*
15	n_{fc} (1) (2)	≤ prescribed value ≤15 years ≤15 years	∞ ∞	– –	– –	Technological scheme *B* is more economical than technological scheme *A* Technological scheme *B* is more economical than technological scheme *A*
16	$Z_{\sum}$	Minimum	15.774 million Yuan (final value) 1.274 million Yuan (present value)	14.366 million Yuan (final value) 1.16 million Yuan (present value)	–	Technological scheme *B* is more economical than technological scheme *A*
17	Z	Minimum	331,000 Yuan (final value) 218,000 Yuan (present value)	302,000 Yuan (final value) 198,000 Yuan (present value)	–	Technological scheme *B* is more economical than technological scheme *A*

(continued)

Table 19.8 (continued)

No.	Evaluation method	Evaluation Standard	Technological Scheme *A*	Technological Scheme *B*	Result of absolute economic evaluation	Result of relative economic evaluation result
18	$E_{domestic\_static}$ $E_{domestic\_dynamic}$	≥0 ≥0	9,500 Yuan −121,500 Yuan	−20,000 Yuan −7,100 Yuan	Technological scheme *A* is economical, while technological scheme *B* is not Neither technological scheme is economical	Technological scheme *A* is more economical than technological scheme *B* Technological scheme *B* is more economical than technological scheme *A*

(2) Of the aforementioned methods, ten are absolute evaluation methods.
These ten absolute evaluation methods are $E_a(E_b)$, $E_c(E_d)$, $S_{c\_static}(S_{g\_static})$, $L_{tc\_static}(L_{tg\_static})$, n_{c_static}, $X_{tc}(X_{tg})$, $L_{tc}(L_{tg})$, n_c, $E_{domestic}$, and $E_{international}$. These methods can be used for assessing the economic effect of an individual technological scheme. The standards are $E_a(E_b)$, $E_{a\_international}$ $(E_{a\_international}) \geq 1$, $E_c(E_d)$, $E_{domestic} \geq 0$, $S_{c\_static}(S_{g\_static})$, $L_{tc\_static}(L_{tg\_static})$, $X_{tc}(X_{tg})$, $L_{tc}(L_{tg}) \geq$ prescribed value, n_{c_static}, $n_c \leq$ prescribed value. Seven of these methods are dynamic evaluation ones.

(3) Of the aforementioned methods, nine are relative evaluation methods.
These nine relative evaluation methods are $E_{af}(E_{bf})$, $E_{cf}(E_{df})$, $L_{ftc\_static}(L_{ftg\_static})$, n_{fc_static}, $Z_{static}(Z_{u\_static})$, $X_{ftc}(X_{ftg})$, n_{fc}, $Z_{\sum}$ $(Z_{u\sum})$,and $Z(Z_u)$. These methods are not applicable to assess the economic effect of an individual technological scheme. Instead, they can only be used to evaluate the relative economic effect of technological schemes. Their standards are $E_{af}(E_{bf}) \geq 1$, $E_{cf}(E_{df}) \geq 0$, $L_{ftc\_static}(L_{ftg\_static})$, $X_{ftc}(X_{ftg}) \geq$ prescribed value, n_{fc_static}, n_{fc}, $Z_{static}(Z_{u\_static})$, $Z_{\sum}$ $(Z_{u\sum})$, $Z(Z_u) \leq$ prescribed value. Six of these methods are dynamic evaluation ones.

(4) Absolute evaluation methods are applicable to compare multiple technological schemes that are interchangeable.
There are two situations. The first one is when the state only requires the economic effect of technological schemes to reach or to exceed the prescribed value, such as $E_c(E_d) \geq 0$ and $E_a(E_b) \geq 1$). The best technological scheme is the one that most exceeds the prescribed value. The economic impacts of the amount of capital, materials, and resources required by technological schemes are considered for assessing technological schemes. In this situation, $E_a(E_b)$ and $E_c(E_d)$ are applicable. In the other situation, the amount of capital and materials provided by the state for certain departments or areas is limited. Rational allocation is required. In this case, the standard for assessing technological schemes is not the largest valued of $E_a(E_b)$ and $E_c(E_d)$, because the larger $E_c(E_d)$ requires more investment. Accordingly, methods that calculate the economic effect of investment per unit, such as $X_{tc}(X_{tg})$ and $L_{tc}(L_{tg})$, are applicable. However, comparison of multiple technological schemes requires both absolute evaluation methods and relative evaluation methods. These methods should be applied together.

(5) Relative evaluation methods are applicable to compare multiple technological schemes that are interchangeable.
The available relative evaluation methods include E_{af}, E_{bf}, E_{cf}, E_{df}, X_{ftc}, X_{ftg}, and n_{fc}. When investment and materials are limited, $E_{cf}(E_{df})$ and $X_{ftc}(X_{ftg})$ should be adopted to allocate investment and materials to multiple technological schemes. Some relative evaluation methods actually compare the economic effect generated by the difference of investment, materials, and transportation capacity between two technological schemes. They do not compare the economic effect generated by two entire technological schemes. It is recommended that technological schemes be assessed with absolute evaluation methods first, and then with relative evaluation methods. The results of

absolute evaluation methods and relative evaluation methods are usually the same, but sometimes, there are differences between the results.

(6) The annual consumption method is applicable to compare technological schemes with the same annual benefit but with different service lengths.

(7) Absolute evaluation methods and relative evaluation methods must meet the requirements for comparison (meeting demand, consumption cost, price, and time).

For example, the social net income or the social national income, based on a unit of product, should be adopted to compare multiple technological schemes in different sizes.

19.4 Evaluation Methods for Micro Technological Economy

Evaluation methods for the micro technological economy are applicable for assessing the economic effects of technological schemes from the perspective of firms. What firms care most about is profit. Therefore, evaluation methods for the micro technological economy are based on profit. They are derived from evaluation methods for the macro technological economy. The reason is that the net income is the result of subtracting the wages from the national income. Profit is the result of subtracting the tax and loan interest from the net income. If firms have to submit part of their profits, the firm profit is their retained profit, which can be calculated by subtracting the tax and the loan interest, as well as several other costs. Profit series methods can be achieved by subtracting tax from income in net income series methods, or by adding tax and loan interest.

Profit series methods consist of four basic methods, namely the total firm excess labor productivity E_e, the firm excess profit E_f, the total firm additional excess labor productivity E_{ef}, and the firm additional excess profit rate E_{ff}.[5] In addition, sixteen methods can be derived from the basic four methods and they are correspond to those evaluation methods for the macro technological economy (see Table 19.1 for details).

19.4.1 Methods Based on Profits

1. Total firm excess labor productivity E_e

$$E_e = \frac{S_{\Sigma\_firm}}{Z_{\Sigma\_firm}} = \frac{\sum_{s=1}^{n} S_{s\_firm}\frac{1}{\theta^S}}{\sum_{s=1}^{n} Z_{s\_firm}\frac{1}{\theta^s}} \quad (E_e \geq 1) \tag{19.66.1}$$

[5]The word total is omitted for convenience.

$$E_e = \frac{X_{\Sigma\_firm}}{Z_{\Sigma\_firm}} \tag{19.66.2}$$

where $X_{\sum\_firm}$ is the total benefit that firms get (in material form) during a certain time period. $S_{\sum\_firm}$ is the total benefit that firms get during a certain time period in currency format. S_{firm} is the annual benefit of the firms. S_{firm}= annual sales S_{sales} – annual taxes based on income S_{tax} (e.g. production tax). $Z_{\sum\_firm}$ is the total consumption cost of firms during a certain time period. S_{firm} is the firm's annual consumption cost. It can be calculated with two methods. The first method calculates the annual investment T, the cost C, the cost tax C_{tax}, the basic depreciation deduction, the current capital reclaim, and the residual reclaim directly. The second method calculates the average of these items first and then calculates the items S_{firm}, such as X,T_{tax}, C, and C_{tax}.

Let us discuss how to deal with tax in technological scheme calculation. From the perspective of the technological economy, tax can be grouped into two categories. The first category of tax is cost, such as the oil burning special tax and the environment pollution surcharge. The other category of tax is income, such as the production tax and the income tax. Accordingly, tax can be treated as cost in the calculation of cost, or it can be treated as income in the calculation of benefits. For those evaluation methods for the micro technological economy based on subtraction (e.g. E_f), the results will be the same regardless of how tax is treated. However, for those evaluation methods for the micro technological economy based on division (e.g. E_e), the results depend on how tax is treated. Therefore, cost tax should be calculated as cost, whereas income tax should be calculated as total economic benefits.

Here is an example. Suppose there are two technological schemes, A and B. The construction period for technological scheme A is three years. The investment on it in the first year is 900,000 Yuan (RMB). There is no investment in the second year and the third year. The construction period for the technological scheme B is one year. Its investment is 900,000 Yuan. The two technological schemes begin to produce at the same time. Their production values are both 600,000 Yuan/year (production 10,000 tons/year *rational price 60 Yuan/ton). Technological scheme A occupies current capital at 50,000 Yuan. Its annual cost is 150,000 Yuan, in which the basic depreciation is 60,000 Yuan. Technological scheme B occupies current capital at 100,000 Yuan. Its annual cost is 170,000 Yuan, in which the basic depreciation is 60,000 Yuan. After technological schemes A and B go into production, they need to pay the production tax at the rate of 5%, the fixed asset occupation tax at the rate of 9.6%, the current capital loan interest rate of 2.5%, and the income tax at the rate of 55%. In addition, the annual basic depreciation is submitted to the state. Which technological scheme will generate a better economic effect?

Now, let us adopt the firm excess labor productivity method. The prescribed return on investment X_{tl} is 10%. The service length is 15 years. $\theta = 1.1$.

$$\begin{aligned} S_{\Sigma\_firm\_A} &= [60 - 0.05 \times 60 - 0.55(60 - 15 - 3 - 5.6 - 0.13)]\frac{\theta^{15} - 1}{(\theta - 1)\theta^{18}} \\ &= 37 \times 5.72 = 2.116 \text{ million Yuan} \end{aligned}$$

$$Z_{\Sigma\_firm\_A} = \left(15 + 0.1 \times T_i, A^{+}6 + 5.6 + 0.13\right)\frac{\theta^{15} - 1}{(\theta - 1)\theta^{18}}$$
$$= 36.9 \times 5.72 = 2.11 \text{ million Yuan}$$

where

$$T_{z\_A} = 90\frac{\theta^{15} - 1}{(\theta - 1)\theta^{18}} + 5 - \frac{6}{\theta - 1} + \frac{15 \times 6}{\theta^{15} - 1} = 1.025 \text{ million Yuan}$$

The annual average product tax for scheme A

$$S_{product\_tax\_A} = 0.05 \times 60 = 3$$

The annual average fixed asset occupation tax for scheme A

$$C_{fixed\_asset\_tax\_A} = 0.096 \times \left(90 - \frac{6}{\theta - 1} + \frac{15 \times 6}{\theta^{15} - 1}\right) = 5.6$$

The average current capital loan interest for scheme A

$$C_{current\_interest\_A} = 0.025 \times 5 = 0.13$$

The annual average income tax for scheme A

$$\mathrm{S}_{income\_tax\_A} = 0.05(60 - 15 - 3 - 5.6 - 0.13) = 20$$

∴ The firm excess labor productivity for scheme A

$$E_{e\_A} = \frac{S_{\Sigma\_firm\_A}}{Z_{\Sigma\_firm\_A}} = \frac{2.116}{2.11} = 1.003 > 1$$

The result shows that the economic effect of scheme A is economical.

$$S_{\Sigma\_firm\_B} = [60 - 0.05 \times 60 - 0.55(60 - 17 - 3 - 5.6 - 0.25)]\frac{\theta^{15} - 1}{(\theta - 1)\theta^{18}}$$
$$= 38.2 \times 5.72 = 2.185 \text{ million Yuan}$$

$$Z_{\Sigma\_firm\_B} = \left(17 + 0.1 \times T_{z\_B} + 6 + 5.6 + 0.25\right)\frac{\theta^{15} - 1}{(\theta - 1)\theta^{18}}$$
$$= 36.9 \times 5.72 = 2.11 \text{ million Yuan}$$

where

$$T_{z\_B} = 90\frac{\theta^{16} - 1}{\theta^{15} - 1} + 10 - \frac{6}{\theta - 1} + \frac{15 \times 6}{\theta^{15} - 1} = 0.801 \text{ million Yuan}$$

$$\therefore E_{e\_B} = \frac{S_{\Sigma\_firm\_B}}{Z_{\Sigma\_firm\_B}} = \frac{2.185}{2.11} = 1.04 > 1$$

The result shows that the economic effect of scheme B is economical. Scheme B is more economical than scheme A.

2. Firm excess profit E_f

$$E_f = S_{\Sigma\_firm} - Z_{\Sigma\_firm} = \sum_{s=1}^{n} \left(S_{s\_firm} - Z_{s_{firm}}\right)\frac{1}{\theta 6}\left(E_f \geq 0\right) \tag{19.67}$$

This is the net present value method that has been adopted widely in western countries. This method has been introduced by domestic scholars, as well. But few discuss its economic meaning. Some think that net present value is the difference between input present value and output present value. Some think that net present value is firms' profit. Others think that net present value is firms' net income present value. These unclear economic meanings of "net present value" indicate that the name "net present value" is not necessarily appropriate. Present value is a kind of converting with the time factor considered. It does not reflect any economic meaning. Because investment has present value, cost has present value, and tax has present value, the term "net present value" does not specify which present value. Furthermore, final value (time value) is another kind of converting with the time factor considered. The net present value method does not calculate net final value. Thus, the net present value method is not complete. Net present value is not firms' profit and benefits, but firms' excess profit (including income from depreciation). The name "firm excess profit" is more suitable than "net present value", because it reflects the economic meaning more precisely. The term "firm excess profit" minimizes misunderstanding. It can choose either the present value or the final value to complete the conversion.

Apply this method to the example above.

$$E_{f\_A} = S_{\sum\_firm\_A} - Z_{\sum\_firm\_A} = 6{,}000 \text{ Yuan}$$
$$E_{f\_B} = S_{\sum\_firm\_B} - Z_{\sum\_firm\_B} = 75{,}000 \text{ Yuan}$$

The results indicate that schemes A and B both have excess profit. Therefore, they are economical. Scheme B is more economical than scheme A.

3. Firm additional excess (total) labor productivity E_{ef}

$$(1)\ E_{ef} = \frac{\Delta S_{\Sigma_{firm}}\left(\text{or } \Delta X_{\Sigma_{firm}}\right)}{\Delta Z_{\Sigma\_firm}}\left(E_{ef} = \text{ZD},\ E_{ef} \geq 1\right) \tag{19.68.1}$$

$$(2)\ E_{ef} = \frac{dS_{\Sigma_{firm}}\left(\text{or}\, dX_{\Sigma_{firm}}\right)}{dZ_{\Sigma\_firm}}\left(E_{ef} = \text{ZD},\, E_{ef} \geq 1\right) \tag{19.68.2}$$

$$(3)\ E_{ef} = \frac{dS_{\Sigma_{firm}}\left(\text{or}\, dX_{\Sigma_{\text{firm}}}\right)}{dZ_{\Sigma\_firm}}\left(E_{ef} = \lambda\right) \tag{19.68.3}$$

Load the values in the above example into formula 15.68.1.

$$E_{ef} = \frac{S_{\Sigma_{firm\_A}} - S_{\Sigma_{firm\_B}}}{Z_{\Sigma_{firm\_A}} - Z_{\Sigma_{firm\_B}}} = \frac{2.116 - 2.185}{2.11 - 2.11} = \frac{-6.9}{0}$$

The results show that the inputs of scheme A and B are close, but scheme B has a higher income of 69,000 Yuan. Thus, scheme B is more economical.

4. Firm additional excess (total) profit E_{ff}

$$(1)\ E_{ff} = \frac{\Delta E_f}{\Delta T};\frac{\Delta E_f}{\Delta W};\frac{\Delta E_f}{\Delta Y};\frac{\Delta E_f}{\Delta R};\frac{\Delta E_f}{\Delta D};\frac{\Delta E_f}{\Delta N};\quad \left(E_{ff} \geq ZD\quad E_{ff} \geq 0\right) \tag{19.69.1}$$

$$(2)\ E_{ff} = \frac{\partial E_f}{\partial T};\frac{\partial E_f}{\partial W};\frac{\partial E_f}{\partial Y};\frac{\partial E_f}{\partial R};\frac{\partial E_f}{\partial D};\frac{\partial E_f}{\partial N};\quad \left(E_{ff} = \text{ZD},\, E_{ff} \geq 0\right) \tag{19.69.2}$$

$$(3)\ E_{ff} = \frac{\partial E_f}{\partial T};\frac{\partial E_f}{\partial W};\frac{\partial E_f}{\partial Y};\frac{\partial E_f}{\partial R};\frac{\partial E_f}{\partial D};\frac{\partial E_f}{\partial N}\quad \left(E_{ff} = \lambda\right) \tag{19.69.3}$$

where the denominator is the increment of input of a production factor (marginal input). The numerator is the increment of input of firms' excess profit (marginal output).

Load the values in the above example into formula 15.69.1.

$$E_{ff} = \frac{\Delta E_f}{\Delta T} = \frac{0.6 - 7.5}{\left(90 + \frac{5}{\theta}\right) - \left(\frac{90}{\theta^2} + \frac{10}{\theta^3}\right)} = \frac{-6.9}{18.7} = -0.37\ \text{Yuan/Yuan}$$

The results show that scheme A has a higher investment of 187,000 Yuan, while it has a lower excess profit of 69,000 Yuan. Thus, scheme B is more economical.

19.4.2 Derived Methods from Those Based on Profits

1. Firm annual profit S_{l_static} (static)

$$(1)\ S_{l\_static} = \text{Income from sales}\ S_{firm} - \text{cost of sales}\ C - \text{Tax}\ M_{tax}\left(S_{l\_static} \geq \text{prescribed value}\right) \tag{19.70.1}$$

$$\begin{aligned}(2)\ S_{l\_static} &= \text{Income from sales } S_{firm} - \text{cost of sales } C_{jy} \\ &- \text{Tax } M_{tax} = \text{Income from sales } S_{finm} \\ &- (\text{Cost of sales } C - \text{basic depreciation } C_j) \\ &- \text{Tax } M_{tax}\left(S_{l\_static} > \text{prescribed value}\right)\end{aligned} \quad (19.70.2)$$

where M_{tax} includes S_{tax} and C_{tax}. In formula 19.70.2, basic depreciation is mixed with profit as firms' income. In fact, income from depreciation is different from income from profit. Formula 19.70.1 is applicable to the situation in which basic depreciation is reclaimed completely. Formula 19.70.2 is applicable to the situation when basic depreciation is held by firms.

In the above example, basic depreciation is supposed to be reclaimed completely. Thus, formula 19.70.1 should be adopted.

$$S_{l\_static\_A} = 60 - 15 - 3 - 5.6 - 0.13 - 20 = 16.3 \geq 9.5\,(\text{prescribed value})$$
$$S_{l\_static\_B} = 60 - 17 - 3 - 5.6 - 0.25 - 18.8 = 15.4 \geq 10\,(\text{prescribed value})$$

The prescribed values are calculated based on the rated return on investment of 10%. The results indicate that scheme *A* and *B* both are economical. Scheme *A* is more economical than scheme *B*.

2. Return on investment L_{tl_static} (static)

$$(1)\ L_{tl\_\mathrm{static}} = \frac{S_{firm} - C - M_{\mathrm{tax}}}{Z_{\Sigma\_firm}} \quad \left(L_{tl\_static} \geq \text{prescribed value}\right) \quad (19.71.1)$$

$$(2)\ L_{tl\_static} = \frac{S_{firm} - C - M_{\mathrm{tax}} + C_{\mathrm{j}}}{T} \quad \left(L_{tl\_static} \geq \text{prescribed value}\right) \quad (19.71.2)$$

Similarly, formula 19.71.1 is applicable to the situation when basic depreciation is reclaimed completely. Formula 19.70.2 is applicable to the situation when basic depreciation is not submitted.

Because in the above example, basic depreciation is supposed to be reclaimed completely. Thus, formula 19.71.1 should be adopted.

$$L_{tl\_static\_A} = \frac{16.3}{95} = 0.17\,\text{Yuan/Yuan.Year} \geq 0.1\,\text{Yuan/Yuan.Year (prescribed value)}$$
$$L_{tl\_static\_B} = \frac{13}{100} = 0.154\,\text{Yuan/Yuan.Year} \geq 0.1\,\text{Yuan/Yuan.Year (prescribed value)}$$

If basic depreciation is not submitted, formula 19.71.2 should be adopted.

$$L_{tl\_static\_A} = \frac{22.3}{95} = 0.23\,\text{Yuan/Yuan.Year} \geq 0.16\,\text{Yuan/Yuan.Year (prescribed value)}$$

$$L_{tl\_static\_B} = \frac{21.4}{100} = 0.214\,\text{Yuan/Yuan.Year} \geq 0.16\text{Yuan/Yuan.Year (prescribed value)}$$

The results indicate that the return on investment of schemes *A* and *B* are higher than the prescribed values. Scheme *A* is more economical than scheme *B*.

3. Investment recovery period n_{c_static} (static)

$$\text{(1) } n_{c\_static} = \frac{T}{S_{\text{firm}} - C - M_{\text{tax}}} \quad \left(n_{c\_static} \leq \text{ prescribed value }\right) \tag{19.72.1}$$

$$\text{(2) } n_{c\_static} = \frac{T}{S_{firm} - C_{\text{jy}} - M_{\text{tax}}} \quad \left(n_{c\_static} \leq \text{prescribed value}\right) \tag{19.72.2}$$

$$\text{(3) Set } \sum_{s=1}^{n_{c\_static}} \left(S_s - C_{\text{jys}} - M_{tax\_s}\right) = T_2, \text{ find } n_{c\_static}\left(n_{c\_static} \leq \text{prescribed value}\right) \tag{19.72.3}$$

$$\text{(4) Set } \sum_{s=1}^{n_{c\_static}} \left(S_s - C_{\text{jys}} - M_{tax\_s} + C_{\text{fixed\_tax}} - M_{reserve\_s} - C_{\text{j\_reserve\_s}}\right) = T_{construction},$$

$$\text{find } n_{c\_static}\left(n_{c\_static} \leq \text{prescribed value}\right) \tag{19.72.4}$$

where M_{tax} includes commercial and industrial taxes, firms' current capital occupation cost, and fixed asset occupation cost. $M_{reserve}$ is the profit that firms reserve. $C_{j\_reserve}$ is the depreciation that firms reserve. Formula 19.72.1 and 19.72.2 are applicable to the situation when the annual profit is the same. Formula 19.72.3 and 19.72.4 are applicable to the situation when the annual profit is different. Formula 19.72.4 calculates the number of years for reclaiming the investment on infrastructure based on submitted profit and depreciation.

In the above example, the basic depreciation is submitted completely. The annual profit is the same. Thus, formula 19.72.1 should be adopted to calculate the investment recovery period.

$$n_{c\_static\_A} = \frac{95}{16.3} = 5.8\,\text{years} \leq 10\,\text{years (prescribedvalue)}$$

$$n_{c\_static\_B} = \frac{100}{54} = 6.5\,\text{years} \leq 10\,\text{years (prescribed value)}$$

The results show that the investment recovery periods of schemes *A* and *B* are each shorter than the prescribed value. Thus, they are economical. Scheme *A* is more economical than scheme *B*.

4. Additional return on investment L_{ft1_static} (static)

$$\text{(1) } L_{ft1\_static} = \frac{\Delta S_{\text{firm}} - \Delta C + \Delta C_{\text{j}} - \Delta M_{\text{tax}}}{\Delta T} \quad \left(L_{ft1\_static} \geq \text{prescribed value}\right) \tag{19.73.1}$$

(2) $L_{ft1\_static} = \dfrac{\Delta C - \Delta C_{\mathrm{j}} + \Delta M_{\mathrm{tax}}}{\Delta T} \quad (L_{ft1\_static} \geq \text{prescribed value})$ (19.73.2)

(3) $L_{ft1\_static} = \dfrac{\Delta C + \Delta M_{\mathrm{tax}}}{\Delta T} \quad (L_{ft1\_static} \geq \text{prescribed value})$ (19.73.3)

The above evaluation methods for the micro technological economy do not deduct the difference of tax in the numerator. This method deducts the difference. Thus, the numerator represents the difference of profit. If the difference of tax is zero, this method becomes the same as the other evaluation methods for the micro technological economy.

In the above example, the additional return on investment can be calculated with formula 19.73.1.

$$L_{ft1\_static} = \frac{(17-15)+(27.65-28.73)}{95-100} = \frac{0.92}{-5}$$

The result shows that the investment of scheme *A* is 50,000 Yuan less than that of scheme *B*, whereas its profit is 9,200 Yuan higher. Thus, scheme *A* is more economical.

5. Additional investment recovery period n_{fc_static} (static)

(1) $n_{fc\_static} = \dfrac{\Delta T}{\Delta S_{\mathrm{firm}} - \Delta C + \Delta C_{\mathrm{j}} - \Delta M_{\mathrm{tax}}} \quad (n_{fc\_static} \leq \text{prescribedvalue})$ (19.74.1)

(2) $n_{fc\_static} = \dfrac{\Delta T}{\Delta C - \Delta C_{\mathrm{j}} + \Delta M_{\mathrm{tax}}} \quad (n_{fc\_static} \leq \text{prescribed value})$ (19.74.2)

(3) $n_{fc\_static} = \dfrac{\Delta T}{\Delta C + \Delta M_{\mathrm{tax}}} \quad (n_{fc\_static} \leq \text{prescribed value})$ (19.74.3)

Based on the value in the above example, formula 19.74.3 should be adopted to calculate the additional investment recovery period.

$$n_{fc\_static} = \frac{-5}{0.92} = -5.435$$

The result shows that scheme *A* does not have additional investment. Instead, investment on scheme *A* decreases, but its profit increases. Thus, scheme *A* is more economical than scheme *B*.

6. Annual calculation cost Z_{firm_static} (static)

$$Z_{firm\_static} = C + X_{t1}T + M_{tax} \quad \left(Z_{firm\_static} = \text{minimum}\right) \tag{19.75}$$

The annual calculation cost method applied to assess firm economic effect does not usually include tax. This is not reasonable, because tax is a kind of expenditure for firms. More taxes mean more costs for firms. Accordingly, tax should be included in the annual calculation cost. In formula 19.75, X_{tl} is the return on investment prescribed by firms.

Based on the values in the above example,

$$Z_{firm\_static\_A} = 15 + 0.1 \times 95 + 28.73 = 532{,}300\ \text{Yuan/year}$$
$$Z_{firm\_static\_B} = 17 + 0.1 \times 100 + 27.65 = 546{,}500\ \text{Yuan/year}$$

The result indicates that scheme A is more economical than scheme B.

7. (dynamic) Return on investment X_{tl}

It is known that

$$E_f = f(X_{tl}).\ \text{Set}\ E_F = 0.\ \text{Find}\ X_{tl}(X_{tl} \geq \text{prescribed value}). \tag{19.76.1}$$

Or it is known that

$$E_e = f(X_{tl}).\ \text{Set}\ E_E = 1.\ \text{Find}\ X_{tl}(X_{tl} \geq \text{prescribed value}). \tag{19.76.2}$$

Dynamic return on investment considers the time factor. In western countries, it is called the "internal rate of return" or the "discount rate." Usually, it is calculated with a trial-and-error procedure. For simple examples, the dynamic return on investment can be calculated with formulas by finding X_{tl} when $E_f = 0$ or $E_e = 1$. For complicated examples, the tabulation method should be applied (see Table 19.9).

Regarding the example above, E_f can be calculated based on the prescribed return on investment 10%. E_f for scheme A is 6000 Yuan and E_f for scheme B is 75,000 Yuan. E_e for scheme A is 1-003 and E_e for scheme B is 1.04. Therefore, X_{tl} for scheme A is 10% and for scheme B is 11%. Both of them are economical. Scheme B is more economical than scheme A.

8. (dynamic) excess return on investment L_{tl}

$$L_{tl} = \frac{E_f}{T} \quad (L_{tl} \geq 0) \tag{19.77}$$

Dynamic excess return on investment is applicable to assess technological schemes when the investment is limited.

Based on the example, the dynamic excess return on investment can be calculated with formula 19.77.

Table 19.9 Examples for firm excess profit E_f and return on investment X_{tl} (dynamic)-scheme A

Period	Construction period			Production period															
Year	1	2	3	1	2	3	4	5	6	7	8	9	10	11	12	13	14	15	Total
Sales S	0	0	0	60	60	60	60	60	60	60	60	60	60	60	60	60	60	60	–
Depreciation reclaim C_j	0	0	0	6	6	6	6	6	6	6	6	6	6	6	6	6	6	6	–
Residual reclaim T_c	0	0	0	0	0	0	0	0	0	0	0	0	0	0	0	0	0	0	–
Current capital reclaim T_l	0	0	0	0	0	0	0	0	0	0	0	0	0	0	0	0	0	5	–
Production tax $S_{production}$	0	0	0	3	3	3	3	3	3	3	3	3	3	3	3	3	3	3	–
Income tax S_{income}	0	0	0	18.3	18.61	18.92	19.23	19.54	19.85	20.16	20.47	20.78	21.09	21.4	21.71	22.02	22.33	22.64	
Fixed asset Investment T_g	90	0	0	0	0	0	0	0	0	0	0	0	0	0	0	0	0	0	–
Current capital Investment T_l	0	0	0	5	0	0	0	0	0	0	0	0	0	0	0	0	0	0	–
Cost C	0	0	0	15	15	15	15	15	15	15	15	15	15	15	15	15	15	15	–
Fixed asset occupation tax C_{tg}	0	0	0	8.64	8.06	7.49	6.91	6.34	5.76	5.18	4.60	4.03	3.45	2.88	2.3	1.72	1.15	0.57	–

(continued)

Table 19.9 (continued)

Period	Construction period			Production period															
Year	1	2	3	1	2	3	4	5	6	7	8	9	10	11	12	13	14	15	Total
Current capital occupation tax C_{tl}	0	0	0	0.13	0.13	0.13	0.13	0.13	0.13	0.13	0.13	0.13	0.13	0.13	0.13	0.13	0.13	0.13	–
Net capital income	−90	0	0	9.93	15.2	15.45	15.7	15.95	16.2	16.45	16.7	16.95	17.2	17.45	17.7	17.95	18.2	23.45	–
X_{tl}= 10% discount coefficient	1.0	0.909	0.826	0.683	0.621	0.565	0.513	0.466	0.424	0.386	0.350	0.319	0.290	0.263	0.239	0.218	0.198	0.180	–
Net capital income present value	−90	–	–	6.78	9.44	8.73	8.05	7.43	6.87	6.35	5.85	5.41	4.99	4.59	4.23	3.91	3.6	4.22	0.5

Note The table supposes that basic depreciation is reclaimed and submitted to the state. Firms do not keep the basic depreciation. Fixed asset occupation tax is set as 9.6%. Current capital occupation tax is set as 2.5%. Income tax is set as 55%. Production tax is set as 5%. Because the excess profit for scheme A is 0.5 (close to zero), the dynamic return on investment is 10%. There is no need to calculate it using the trial and error procedure

$$L_{tl\_A} = \frac{E_{\mathrm{f\_A}}}{T_{\Sigma\_\mathrm{A}}} = \frac{0.6}{90 + \frac{5}{\theta^3}} = \frac{0.6}{93.3} = 0.006$$

$$L_{tl\_B} = \frac{E_{\mathrm{f\_B}}}{T_{\Sigma\_\mathrm{B}}} = \frac{7.5}{90 + \frac{5}{\theta^2} + \frac{10}{\theta^3}} = \frac{7.5}{74.6} = 0.10$$

The results indicate that the two technological schemes are economical because their dynamic excess return on investment are larger than zero. Relatively speaking, scheme B is more economical than scheme A.

9. (dynamic) investment recovery period n_c

(1) Set $\sum_{s=1}^{n_c} T_s \frac{1}{\theta^{s-1}} - \sum_{s=1}^{n_c} (S_s - C_{jys} - M_{tax\_s}) \frac{1}{\theta^s} = 0$, and find n_c ($n_c \leq$ prescribed value) (19.78.1)

(2) $$n_c = \frac{-\log\left(1 - \frac{x_t T}{s - c_{\mathrm{jy}} - M_{\mathrm{tax}}}\right)}{\log(1 + x_t)} (n_c \leq \text{prescribed value}) \tag{19.78.2}$$

Based on the value in the above example, the dynamic investment recovery periods for schemes A and B can be calculated with formula 19.78.1.

For scheme A,

$$90 + \frac{1}{\theta^3} - [60 - 15 - 3 - 0.13 - 0.55(60 - 15 - 3 - 0.13)]\frac{\theta^n - 1}{(\theta - 1)\theta^2\theta^3}$$
$$+ (1 - 0.55)0.096 \times \left(90 - \frac{6}{\theta - 1} + \frac{6 \times n}{\theta^n - 1}\right)\frac{\theta^n - 1}{(\theta - 1)\theta^n\theta^3} = 0$$

Simplify this equation,

$$\frac{\theta^n - 1}{(\theta - 1)\theta^n} = 7.12 + 0.15\frac{\mathrm{n}}{\theta^n}$$

Then n can be calculated with trial and error procedure. $\theta's$ value can be found in the time factor table X_{1x}. In this case, $\theta = 1.1$. The value of n is 13 years when X_{1x} is 7.12. Because the value of X_{1x} is larger than 7.12, n should be larger than 13 years. Set $n = 15$ years. The value of the right side of the above equation is 7.65. Check the X_{1x} table and the value of n is 15 years. At this point, the trial and error procedure is done. The calculation counts the investment recovery period from the beginning of production. If the investment recovery period is counted from the construction period, n_{c_A} is 18 years.

For simplicity, the dynamic investment recovery period n_{c_A} can be found in in Table 19.9 directly. When the accumulation of the present value of net income of capital is zero, the investment is reclaimed completely. According to Table 19.9, n_{c_A} is 15 years if the investment recovery period is counted from the beginning of production, and n_{c_A} is 18 years if the investment recovery period is counted from construction period.

For scheme B,

$$90 + \frac{10}{\theta} - [60 - 17 - 3 - 0.25 - 0.55(60 - 17 - 3 - 0.25)]\frac{\theta^n - 1}{(\theta - 1)\theta^n\theta}$$
$$+ (1 - 0.55)0.096 \times \left(90 - \frac{6}{\theta - 1} + \frac{6 \times n}{\theta^n - 1}\right)\frac{\theta^n - 1}{(\theta - 1)\theta^n\theta} = 0$$

Simplify this equation,

$$\frac{\theta^n - 1}{(\theta - 1)\theta^n} = 6.57 + 0.17\frac{\mathrm{n}}{\theta^n}$$

Apply the trial and error procedure, and the value of n can be found as 13 years. n_{c_B} is 13 years if the investment recovery period is counted from the beginning of production, and n_{c_B} is 14 years if the investment recovery period is counted from the construction period.

The dynamic investment recovery periods of schemes A and B can be calculated with formula 19.78.2, as well.

For scheme A,

$$n_{c\_A} = \frac{-\log\left(1 - \frac{x_t(90\theta^3 + 5)}{17.54 - \frac{0.26\mathrm{n}}{\theta^2 - 1}}\right)}{\log(1 + x_t)} = \frac{0.63}{0.041} = 15\,\text{years}$$

n_{c_A} can be calculated by following the trial and error procedure as well. First neglect $\frac{0.26\mathrm{n}}{\theta^n - 1}$. The value of n_{c_A} is 13 years. Then set n larger than 13, and load 13 into the above formula to calculate n_{c_A}. If the value of n is equal to n_{c_A}, then n_{c_A} can be achieved. The result of the calculation shows that n_{c_A} is 15 years if the investment recovery period is counted from the beginning of production, and n_{c_A} is 18 years if the investment recovery period is counted from construction period.

For scheme B,

$$n_{c\_B} = \frac{-\log\left(1 - \frac{x_t(90\theta + 10)}{16.6 - \frac{0.26\mathrm{n}}{\theta^n - 1}}\right)}{\log(1 + x_t)} = \frac{0.55}{0.041} = 13\,\text{years}$$

n_{c_B} is 13 years if the investment recovery period is counted from the beginning of production, and n_{c_B} is 14 years if the investment recovery period is counted from the construction period.

Accordingly, the investment recovery periods of scheme A and scheme B are both shorter than the calculation period (service of length) of 15 years. They both are economical. Relatively speaking, scheme B is more economical than scheme A.

5. (dynamic) additional investment net income rate X_{ftl}

$$\text{Set } \Delta E_f = 0, \text{ and find } X_{ftl}\left(X_{ftl} \geq \text{prescribed value}\right) \tag{19.79.1}$$

$$\text{Set } \Delta E_{ef} = 1, \text{ and find } X_{ftl}\left(X_{ftl} \geq \text{prescribed value}\right) \tag{19.79.2}$$

The additional investment net income rate for scheme *A* and scheme *B* are:

$$E_{f\_A} = -90\theta^{18} - 5\theta^{15} + 16.3\frac{\theta^{15}-1}{\theta-1} + 5$$

$$E_{f\_B} = -90\theta^{16} - 10\theta^{15} + 15.4\frac{\theta^{15}-1}{\theta-1} + 10$$

Set $\Delta E_f = E_{f\_A} - E_{f\_B} = 0$. Then

$$90\theta^{16} - 90\theta^{18} + 5\theta^{15} + 0.9\frac{\theta^{15}-1}{\theta-1} - 5 = 0$$

Follow the trial and error procedure. X_{ftl} is 0.06. Accordingly, the dynamic additional investment net income rate for scheme *A* is 6%, which is smaller than the prescribed value 10%. Thus, scheme *A* is not economical. This approach only assesses the technological schemes' relative economic effect. In this case, it does not tell whether scheme *A* (*B*) is economical.

6. (dynamic) additional investment recovery period n_{fc}

$$\text{Set} \sum_{s=1}^{n_{fc}} \Delta T_s \frac{1}{\theta^{s-1}} - \sum_{s=1}^{n_{fc}} \left(\Delta S_s - \Delta C_{jys} - \Delta M_{tax\_s}\right)\frac{1}{\theta^s} = 0,$$
$$\text{and find } n_{fc}\left(n_{fc} \leq \text{prescribed value}\right) \tag{19.80}$$

Based on the data in the above example, the dynamic additional investment recovery period n_{fc} is:

$$90 + \tfrac{5}{\theta^3} - \left(17.54 - \tfrac{0.26n}{\theta^2-1}\right)\tfrac{\theta^n-1}{(\theta-1)\theta^n\theta^3} - \tfrac{90}{\theta^2} - \tfrac{10}{\theta^3} + \left(16.6 - \tfrac{0.26n}{\theta^n-1}\right)\tfrac{\theta^n-1}{(\theta-1)\theta^n\theta^3} = 0$$
$$90\theta^3 + 5 - 90\theta - 10 = 0.94\tfrac{\theta^n-1}{(\theta-1)\theta^n}$$

$$\therefore \quad \frac{\theta^n-1}{(\theta-1)\theta^n} = \frac{15.8}{0.94} = 16.8$$

Check the time factor table and find that when $\theta = 1.1$ and X_{LX} is 16.8, $n = \infty$. Thus, the additional investment of scheme *A*, the portion that is higher than the investment on scheme B, will not be reclaimed. As a result, scheme *B* is more economical than scheme *A*.

7. Total consumption cost $Z_{\sum\_firm}$

$$Z_{\Sigma\_firm} = \sum_{s=1}^{n} \left(C_{jys} + M_{tax\_s}\right)\frac{1}{\theta^s} + \sum_{s=1}^{n} T_s \frac{1}{\theta^{s-1}} - (T_1 + T_c)\frac{1}{\theta^n} (Z_\Sigma \text{ takes the minimal value}) \quad (19.81)$$

This approach is applicable for comparing multiple technological schemes with same benefits and lengths of service. The total consumption $Z_\sum$ includes product tax and income tax.

Based on the data in the previous example, the total consumption costs for scheme A and B can be calculated with formula 19.81.

$$Z_{\sum\_firm\_A} = 3.426 \text{ million Yuan}$$
$$Z_{\sum\_firm\_B} = 3.358 \text{ million Yuan}$$

The results indicate that the total consumption cost of scheme A is larger than that of scheme B. Therefore, scheme B is more economical.

8. Annual consumption cost Z_{firm}

(1) If C_{jy} and M_{tax} in each year are the same, the following formula is applicable.

$$Z_{firm} = C_{jy} + M_{tax} + T\frac{(\theta - 1)\theta^n}{\theta^2 - 1} \quad (Z_{firm} \text{ takes the minimal value}) \quad (19.82.1)$$

(2) If C_{jy} and M_{tax} in each year are different, the total amount of consumption costs of each year $Z_\sum$ should be calculated first, then multiply the result with the annual average coefficient of the accumulated present value.

$$Z_{firm} = Z_{\Sigma\ prescribed}\frac{(\theta - 1)\theta^n}{\theta^n - 1}(Z_{firm}\ takes\ the\ minimal\ value) \quad (19.82.2)$$

This approach is applicable for comparing multiple technological schemes with the same benefits but with different length of service.

Based on the data in the previous example, the annual consumption costs for schemes A and B can be calculated as following.

$$Z_{firm\_A} = 15 + 3 + 5.6 + 0.13 + 20 + \left(90\theta^3 + 5\right)\frac{(\theta-1)\theta^{15}}{\theta^{15}-1} - 5\frac{\theta-1}{\theta^{15}-1} = 0.599 \text{ million Yuan}$$
$$Z_{firm\_B} = 17 + 3 + 5.6 + 0.25 + 18.8 + (90\theta + 10)\frac{(\theta-1)\theta^{15}}{\theta^{15}-1} - 10\frac{\theta-1}{\theta^{15}-1} = 0.586 \text{ million Yuan}$$

The results indicate that the annual consumption cost of scheme *A* is larger than that of scheme *B*. Therefore, scheme *B* is more economical.

9. Domestic competitiveness $E_{domestic}$

(1) Static approach

$$E_{domestic\_static} = \Delta X_t T + \Delta X_w W + \Delta X_y Y + \Delta X_r R + \Delta X_d D \quad (E_{domestic\_static} \geq 0) \tag{19.83.1}$$

where

$$\Delta X_t = \frac{1}{K} X_{t\_firm} - X_{t\_tax} \tag{19.83.1.1}$$

$$\Delta X_w = \frac{1}{K} X_{w\_firm} - X_{w\_tax} \tag{19.83.1.2}$$

$$\Delta X_y = \frac{1}{K} X_{y\_firm} - X_{y\_tax} \tag{19.83.1.3}$$

$$\Delta X_r = \frac{1}{K} X_{r\_firm} - X_{r\_tax} \tag{19.83.1.4}$$

$$\Delta X_d = \frac{1}{K} X_{d\_firm} - X_{d\_tax} \tag{19.83.1.5}$$

X_{t_firm}, X_{w_firm}, X_{y_firm}, X_{r_firm}, and X_{d_firm} are the firms' utilization coefficients of investment, materials, transportation capacity, labor, and natural resources, respectively (calculated based on tax). For example,

$$X_{t\_firm} = \frac{1}{K}\left(\frac{J - C - X_t T}{T}\right)$$

$$X_{t\_firm} = \frac{1}{K}\left(\frac{J - C - X_t T}{W}\right), \text{ and so on.}$$

K is the item number of *T, W, Y, R*, and *D* considered by technological schemes.

T, W, Y, R, and *D* are the amount of investment, materials, transportation capacity, labor, and natural resources used by firms.

X_{t_tax}, X_{w_tax}, X_{y_tax}, X_{r_tax}, and X_{d_tax} are the tax rates paid by firms. (The calculation formulas will be discussed later in this book.)

(2) Dynamic approach

$$E_{domestic\_dynamic} = \sum_{s=1}^{n} \left(\Delta X_{ts} T_s + \Delta X_{ws} W_s + \Delta X_{ys} Y_s + \Delta X_{rs} R_s + \Delta X_{ds} D_s\right) \frac{1}{\theta^s}$$

$$\left(E_{domestic\,dyamic} \geq 0\right) \tag{19.83.2}$$

This approach is a variety of the firm excess profit E_f method. The following is the mathematical justification based on the simple situation.

$$E_f = (J - C - X_t T_z - M_{tax})\frac{\theta^n - 1}{(\theta - 1)\theta^2} \quad \left(E_f \geq 0\right) \tag{19.83.3}$$

Categorize the tax interest M_{tax} in formula 19.83.3 into M_{w_tax}, M_{y_tax}, M_{r_tax}, M_{d_tax}, M_{t_tax}, and other tax interest M_{other_tax}, such as the commercial and industrial taxes, the adjustment tax, the profit delivery, and the interests.

$$M_{tax} = M_{w\_tax} + M_{y\_tax} + M_{r\_tax} + M_{d\_tax} + M_{t\_tax} + M_{other\_tax} \tag{19.83.3.1}$$

Set

$$X_{t\_tax} = \frac{M_{t\_tax} + M_{other\_tax}}{T_Z} \tag{19.83.3.2}$$

$$X_{w\_tax} = \frac{M_{w\_tax}}{W} \tag{19.83.3.3}$$

$$X_{y\_tax} = \frac{M_{y\_tax}}{Y} \tag{19.83.3.4}$$

$$X_{r\_tax} = \frac{M_{r\_tax}}{R} \tag{19.83.3.5}$$

$$X_{d\_tax} = \frac{M_{d\_tax}}{D_z} \tag{19.83.3.6}$$

$$\therefore \quad M_{tax} = X_{t\_tax} T_z + X_{w\_tax} W + X_{y\_tax} Y + X_{r\_tax} R + X_{d\_tax} D_z \tag{19.83.3.7}$$

Allocate the economic benefits $J-C$ in formula 19.83.3 evenly to k items. The economic effect coefficients for a firm after the allocation are:

$$X_{t\_firm\_allocation} = \frac{1}{K}\left(\frac{J - C - X_t T_Z}{T}\right) = \frac{1}{K} X_{t\_firm} \tag{19.83.3.8}$$

$$X_{w\_firm\_allocation} = \frac{1}{K}\left(\frac{J - C - X_t T_Z}{W}\right) = \frac{1}{K} X_{w\_firm} \tag{19.83.3.9}$$

$$X_{y\_firm\_allocation} = \frac{1}{K}\left(\frac{J - C - X_t T_Z}{Y}\right) = \frac{1}{K} X_{y\_firm} \tag{19.83.3.10}$$

$$X_{r\_firm\_allocation} = \frac{1}{K}\left(\frac{J - C - X_t T_Z}{R}\right) = \frac{1}{K} X_{r\_firm} \tag{19.83.3.11}$$

$$X_{d\_firm\_allocation} = \frac{1}{\mathrm{K}}\left(\frac{J - C - X_t T_Z}{D_Z}\right) = \frac{1}{\mathrm{K}} X_{d\_firm} \tag{19.83.3.12}$$

Load formulas 19.83.3.7–19.83.3.12 into formula 19.83.3.

$$E_f = \left(\Delta X_t T_z + \Delta X_w W + \Delta X_y Y + \Delta X_r R + \Delta X_d D_z\right) \frac{\theta^n - 1}{(\theta - 1)\theta^n} \tag{19.83.4}$$

where

$$\Delta X_t = \frac{1}{\mathrm{K}} X_{t\_firm} - X_{t\_tax} \tag{19.83.4.1}$$

$$\Delta X_w = \frac{1}{\mathrm{K}} X_{w\_firm} - X_{w\_tax} \tag{19.83.4.2}$$

$$\Delta X_y = \frac{1}{\mathrm{K}} X_{y\_firm} - X_{y\_tax} \tag{19.83.4.3}$$

$$\Delta X_r = \frac{1}{\mathrm{K}} X_{r\_firm} - X_{r\_tax} \tag{19.83.4.4}$$

$$\Delta X_d = \frac{1}{\mathrm{K}} X_{d\_firm} - X_{d\_tax} \tag{19.83.4.5}$$

Formula 19.83.4 is for domestic competition. Thus, $E_{domestic}$ and E_f are actually the same. However, $E_{domestic}$ is straightforward.

Based on the data in the previous example, the static domestic competitiveness index $E_{domestic\_static}$ can be calculated as following.

$$\begin{aligned} E_{domestic\_static\_A} &= \Delta X_t T = \left(\frac{60 - 15 - 0.1 \times 95}{95} - \frac{3 + 5.6 + 20 + 0.13}{95}\right) \times 95 \\ &= 66{,}500 \text{ Yuan} > 0 \\ E_{domestic\_static\_B} &= \Delta X_t T = \left(\frac{60 - 17 - 0.1 \times 100}{100} - \frac{3 + 5.6 + 18.8 + 0.25}{100}\right) \times 100 \\ &= 54{,}000 \text{ Yuan} > 0 \end{aligned}$$

The results show that the domestic competitiveness indices for schemes *A* and *B* are both larger than zero. Therefore, schemes A and B are both economical. Scheme *A* is more economical than Scheme *B*.

Dynamic domestic competitiveness index $E_{domestic\_dynamic}$ can be calculated as following.

$$\begin{aligned} E_{domestic\_dynamic\_A} &= \left(\frac{60 - 15 - 0.1 \times 102.5}{102.5} - \frac{3 + 20 + 5.6 + 0.13 + 6}{102.5}\right) \times 102.5 \times 5.72 \\ &= 6{,}000 \text{ Yuan} \end{aligned}$$

$$E_{domestic\_dynamic\_B} = \left(\frac{60 - 17 - 0.1 \times 80.1}{80.1} - \frac{3 + 18.8 + 5.6 + 0.25 + 6}{80.1}\right) \times 80.1 \times 5.72$$
$$= 75{,}000 \text{ Yuan}$$

The domestic competitiveness indexes above are the values of the firm excess profit for schemes *A* and *B*, actually. The dynamic domestic competitiveness indices of schemes *A* and *B* both are larger than zero. Thus, they both are economical. Scheme *B* is more economical than Scheme *A*.

15. International competitiveness $E_{international}$

This approach is applicable for assessing technological schemes that are involved with international trade. It is actually the application of the methods discussed above, such as E_e, E_f, E_{ef}, and E_{ff}. Firms' direct economic benefit in the following formula is the net foreign exchange income of export products. Firms' direct cost in the following formula is the domestic input cost of export products. Here is the formula for this approach.

$$E_{e\_international} = \frac{\sum_{s=1}^{n} S_{s\_firm} \frac{1}{\theta^s}}{\sum_{s=1}^{n} Z_{s\_firm} \frac{1}{\theta^s}} \left(E_{e\_international} \geq 1\right) \tag{19.84}$$

where

$$\begin{aligned} S_{firm} = {} & (\text{foreign exchange income of export products} \\ & - \text{foreign exchange expenditure of export products}) \\ & \times \text{exchange rate} \end{aligned} \tag{19.84.1}$$

$$Z_{firm} = \text{input cost of export products(including taxes)} \tag{19.84.2}$$

16. Exchange rate $L_{exchange}$

$$L_{exchange} = \frac{\sum_{s=1}^{n} Z_{s\_firm} \theta^{-s}}{\sum_{s=1}^{n} S_{s\_firm} \theta^{-s}} \left(L_{exchange} \leq \text{current exchange rate}\right) \tag{19.85}$$

where S_{firm} is the firms' net foreign exchange income of export products calculated with the foreign exchange. Z_{firm} is the costs of domestic input for export products calculated with Ren Min Bi (RMB).

For simplicity, the zero superscript for each symbol in the above formula (representing firms) is omitted. In addition, the above dynamic formula is calculated based on the present value. It can be calculated based on the final value, as well.

Results generated by the 18 methods discussed above are listed in Table 19.10 for comparison. The table shows that all static calculation methods generate the same results, namely that scheme *A* is economical and scheme *B* is economical as

Table 19.10 The comparison of the results calculated by micro technological scheme evaluation methods

No.	Evaluation method	Evaluation Standard	Technological Scheme *A*	Technological Scheme *B*	Result of absolute economic evaluation	Result of relative economic evaluation result
1	E_e	≥1	1.003	1.04	Both technological schemes are economical.	Technological scheme *B* is more economical than technological scheme *A*
2	E_r	≥0	5000 Yuan	74,000 Yuan	Both technological schemes are economical.	Technological scheme *B* is more economical than technological scheme *A*
3	E_{ef}	≥1	< 0	–	–	Technological scheme *B* is more economical than technological scheme *A*
4	E_{ff}	≥0	−0.37	–	–	Technological scheme *B* is more economical than technological scheme *A*
5	S_{l_static} (1)	≥ prescribed value ≥9.5 ≥10	16.3 –	– 15.4	Technological scheme *A* is economical. Technological scheme *B* is economical.	Technological scheme *A* is more economical than technological scheme *B*
6	L_{tl_static} (1)	≥ prescribed value ≥0.1	0.17	0.154	Both technological schemes are economical.	Technological scheme *A* is more economical than technological scheme *B*

(continued)

Table 19.10 (continued)

No.	Evaluation method	Evaluation Standard	Technological Scheme *A*	Technological Scheme *B*	Result of absolute economic evaluation	Result of relative economic evaluation result
7	n_{c_static} (1)	≤ prescribed value ≤10 years	5.8 years	6.5 years	Both technological schemes are economical.	Technological scheme *A* is more economical than technological scheme *B*
8	L_{ftl_static} (3)	≥ prescribed value ≥0.1	0.92/-5	–	–	Technological scheme *A* is more economical than technological scheme *B*
9	n_{fc_static} (3)	≤ prescribed value ≤10 years	−5/0.92	–	–	Technological scheme *A* is more economical than technological scheme *B*
10	Z_{static}	minimum	53.23	54.65	–	Technological scheme *A* is more economical than technological scheme *B*
11	X_{tl}	≥ prescribed value 0.1	0.1	0.11	Both technological schemes are economical.	Technological scheme *B* is more economical than technological scheme *A*

(continued)

Table 19.10 (continued)

No.	Evaluation method	Evaluation Standard	Technological Scheme *A*	Technological Scheme *B*	Result of absolute economic evaluation	Result of relative economic evaluation result
12	L_{tl}	≥0	0.006	0.10	Both technological schemes are economical.	Technological scheme *B* is more economical than technological scheme *A*
13	n_c (1), (2)	≤ prescribed value ≤15 years ≤15 years	15 years 15 years	13 years 13 years	Both technological schemes are economical. Both technological schemes are economical.	Technological scheme *B* is more economical than technological scheme *A*
14	X_{ftl}	≥ prescribed value 0.1	0.06	–	–	Technological scheme *B* is more economical than technological scheme *A*
15	n_{fc}	≤ prescribed value 10 years	∞	–	–	Technological scheme *B* is more economical than technological scheme *A*
16	$Z_{\sum\_firm}$	minimum	3.426 million Yuan	3.3358 million Yuan	–	Technological scheme *B* is more economical than technological scheme *A*

(continued)

Table 19.10 (continued)

No.	Evaluation method	Evaluation Standard	Technological Scheme *A*	Technological Scheme *B*	Result of absolute economic evaluation	Result of relative economic evaluation result
17	Z_{firm}	minimum	599,000 Yuan	586,000 Yuan	–	Technological scheme *B* is more economical than technological scheme *A*
18	$E_{domestic\_static}$ $E_{domestic\_dynamic}$	≥0 ≥0	665,000 Yuan 6,000 Yuan	54,000 Yuan 75,000 Yuan	Both technological schemes are economical. Both technological schemes are economical.	Technological scheme *A* is more economical than technological scheme *B*. Technological scheme *B* is more economical than technological scheme *A*

well. Scheme A is more economical than scheme B. In addition, all of the dynamic calculation methods generate the same results, namely that both schemes A and B are economical, whereas scheme B is more economical than scheme A. We should adopt the dynamic calculation methods. In practice, attention should be paid to the following issues.

(1) Dynamic methods are better than static ones. Results generated by dynamic methods should be adopted
(2) Among the aforementioned methods, ten are absolute economic evaluation methods, eight of which are dynamic evaluation ones. These ten methods can be applied to assess the economic effects of technological schemes
(3) Among the aforementioned methods, nine are relative economic evaluation methods, six of which are dynamic evaluation ones. These nine methods cannot be applied to assess the economic effects of technological schemes. Instead, they can only be applied to compare multiple technological schemes
(4) When comparing exchangeable multiple technological schemes, absolute evaluation methods are applicable. There are two situations that need to be considered. First, firms just want technological schemes to reach or to surpass the prescribed economic effect values (e.g. $E_f \geq 0$ and $E_e \geq 1$). The technological scheme with the highest economic effect value is the best, regardless of the required investment, material, and resources. In this case, E_e and E_f are applicable. Second, firms have limited capital and materials. They need to allocate each available resource reasonably. In this case, E_e and E_f are not applicable anymore, because the larger E_e, the larger amount of investment is needed. Therefore, the economic effect value of a certain unit of investment is chosen for the standard, such as $L_{tl,}$ and so on
(5) When comparing exchangeable multiple technological schemes, relative evaluation methods are applicable as well, such as E_{ef}, E_{ff}, x_{ftl}, and n_{fc}. When capital and materials are limited, E_{ff} should be adopted to allocate a certain material to multiple technological schemes

19.5 Complete Technological Economy Evaluation Methods

The eight macro technological economy evaluation methods discussed above, namely the social (total) labor productivity I method and II method, the social net income method, the social net production (national income) method, the social additional (total) labor productivity I method and II method, the social additional net income rate method, and the additional net production (additional national income rate), are not complete in practice. Complete technological economy evaluation methods should meet the following requirements:

(1) The six economic indices of each technological scheme, including the benefit index X_i or S_t, material consumption index W, transportation capacity occupation index Y_t, labor occupation index R_t, investment occupation index T_l, natural resource occupation index D_t, must meet the six conditions of comprehensive balance, namely

$$\begin{aligned} &X_i \text{ or } S_t \geq X\ or\ S(required) \\ &W_t \leq W(possible);\ Y_t \leq Y(possible);\ R_t \leq R(possible); \\ &\ T_t \leq T(possible);\ D_t \leq D(possible) \end{aligned} \tag{19.86}$$

where *X or S (required)* is the economic benefit that technological schemes must meet, required by the state plan or market demand. *W (possible), R (possible), T (possible),* and *D(possible)* are the amount of materials, transportation capacity, labor, investment, and natural resources provided by the state and the market for technological schemes. If a technological scheme cannot meet the requirement of any of the six condition, it is not practical, even with the best economic effect.

(2) If the seven indices of a technological scheme meet the following conditions, namely

$$\begin{aligned} &S_t = ZD;\quad C_t = ZX;\quad W_t = ZX;\quad Y_t = ZX;\quad R_t = ZX; \\ &T_t = ZX;\quad D_t = ZX \end{aligned} \tag{19.87}$$

then the technological scheme is the best and the most economical one. In this case, there is no need to calculate comprehensive economic effect indices.

(3) If the seven indices of compared technological schemes are not consistent, for example if the S_t of scheme A is the largest but if C_t is not the smallest and if C_t of scheme B is the smallest but T_t is not the smallest, the comprehensive economic effect indices of each technological scheme should be calculated, including E_{at}, E_{bt}, E_{ct}, E_{dt}, E_{aft}, E_{bft}, E_{cft}, and E_{dft}. One or two of the methods discussed above can be adopted.

We have discussed a complete series of macro technological economy evaluation methods with the conditions of of input and output considered in this chapter. These methods can be expressed in math, namely the technological economy models, the third category of technological economy equations discussed in Chap. 5 in the first section in this book. The most common one is the linear model. In practice, macro control and condition can be realized by the economic effect coefficients in evaluation formulas. Thus, there is no need to apply technological economy math models all the time. As such, the macro technological economy evaluation methods discussed above are complete.

Technological economy math models are applicable to the micro technological economy as well. The conditions of input and output must be considered in micro technological economy evaluation methods.

19.6 Reviews of Relevant Foreign Methods

Since the 1950s, China has gained experience in assessing the technological economy across departments. In the early 1960s, the technological economy was initially set up in China. This discipline has its own theories and methods. Learning overseas experiences is necessary to develop and improve a technological economy with Chinese characteristics. However, overseas experiences should not be copied directly. Accordingly, foreign methods regarding technological economy evaluation are reviewed in this chapter.

19.6.1 Former Soviet Union's Departmental Economics and Methods for Calculating Investment Economic Effect

The term "technological economy" existed in the former Soviet Union, such as technological economy index and technological economy demonstration; however, the discipline of technological economics was not available. The departmental economics in the former Soviet Union is similar to the departmental economics in China. The difference is that the former deals with some aspects of economy management, such as labor organization, planning, and management. The Soviet Union Engineering Economy College specifically recruited students to major in the departmental engineering economy. The analysis method adopted in the departmental engineering economy is investment effect calculation. In the 1920s, the former Soviet Union proposed to compare technological schemes when making the national electrification plan. In the 1930s, the Soviet Union introduced the method for calculating the payback length of an additional investment from western countries and changed it into a calculation method based on annual cost. In 1960, the former Soviet Union officially launched its first method for calculating the investment effect with the name "the standard method for calculating the economic effects of national economic investment and new technologies in Soviet Union" (the first version). In 1969, the first version was revised and was changed into the standard method for calculating the economic effect of investment in Soviet Union (the second version). In 1977, new methods were released with the name "methods for calculating the economic effect of new technologies, creation, and reasonable suggestions in national economy in Soviet Union" (basic principles). In 1980, the former Soviet Union launched methods for calculating the economic effect of investment (the third version). All of these methods adopt the approaches for calculating the payback length of additional investment and for calculating annual costs. The methods in these versions adopt different investment effect standard coefficients. These methods consider the costs of related departments and the loss of investment in a construction period. They choose present value to convert the costs in each year. Because the former Soviet Union had a planned economy, its methods for calculating the economic effect of investment are similar to the macro technological economy evaluation methods in China. Accordingly, China needs to learn the experiences of the former Soviet Union. However, the methods for calculating the economic effect of investment in the former Soviet Union have many drawbacks. For example, they highlight the factor of investment but they neglect the other factors necessary for production, including material, transportation capacity, natural resource, labor, and time. These factors are not counted in the main formulas of these methods. In addition, these methods assume that the benefits are the same. As a result, they only compare costs. Benefits are not compared in these methods.

19.6.2 Technological Economy Demonstration in the Former Soviet Union and East European Countries

The former Soviet Union and Romania combined the initial design of their engineering projects with the work stage before it as a pre-design stage, also called a technological economy demonstration. This is an important step in the procedure for completing an engineering project.

The task of technological demonstration is to develop reconstruction schemes with technological and economical reasonableness based on the requirements of the long-term economy development of a state and on the allocation of production.

Technological demonstration must focus on national economic benefits. Technological schemes must be comparable and must adopt the standard methods for calculating the effect of investment released by the state.

The technological demonstration of engineering projects usually evaluates original documentation, product demand, production scale, variety, quality, and specialization, raw materials, fuel, semi-finished products, the supply of power and water, firm allocation, factory location selection, production processing, infrastructure, and the economic efficiency of a firm. It also has conclusions and suggestions.

A technological demonstration is usually managed by a planning institute in coordination with the agency that makes the development plan and allocations. Sometimes, the exploration unit needs to be involved for the purpose of collecting the original documentation. Technological demonstration is documented as an instruction. Calculation, tables, and figures are included. When making a technological demonstration, the departments in charge should confirm each decision. For instance, the manufacturing department should verify the possibility of production and should provide the basic parameters, weight, and prices of equipment to the design unit. A technological demonstration should follow the laws and regulations regarding the protection and utilization of key resources. The design guidelines and standards for basic construction should be implemented. Technological demonstration designed by firms in industrial sectors should be verified by the State Planning Commission, the National Construction Committee, and the State Scientific and Technological

Commission, and should be approved by the industrial department in charge. Technological demonstration approved by following prescribed procedures is the foundation for developing a statement of planned tasks for technological design. It is also the basis for testing new materials, studying new technological flow, and conducting industrial tests.

Accordingly, technological demonstration in the former Soviet Union is equivalent to the feasibility study in western countries.

19.6.3 Engineering Economics and Economic Analysis Methods in Western Countries

Engineering Economy or Engineering Economics is a newly developed discipline in western countries. It is about applying economic analysis methods in engineering projects. In 1961, the Department of Defense in the U.S. implemented the economic analysis method, such as annual worth method and present worth method, for government investment.. It required that feasible schemes be submitted for each proposal and that the best one be chosen via comparison. These requirements are similar to the methods in engineering economics, a subject which is offered as a course in U.S. colleges. In 1965, engineering economics was listed as a required course in the universities in Taiwan. Since the 1970s, a number of books on engineering economics have been published overseas. The methods adopted by Engineering Economics, such as the annual worth method (or the net annual worth method), the present worth method (or the net present worth method), and the rate of return method, are based on the western economic theories. Their goals are to produce the maximum surplus value or surplus products with the minimum advanced capital.[6] Actually, the names annual worth method, present worth method, and rate of return method do not explain the terms' real economic meaning. Their meaning is closer to micro technological economy evaluation methods.

The engineering analysis methods in western countries and the methods for calculating the economic effect of investment in the former Soviet Union both have their unique characteristics. The former is based on the market economy and focuses on firms' financial assessment and absolute economic effect with a dynamic time factor considered. The latter is based on the planned economy and focuses on social economy and relative economic effect without considering a dynamic time factor.

[6]Complete Works of Marx and Engels, Volume 26, p. 625.

19.6.4 Cost-Benefit Analysis in Western Countries

Cost-benefit analysis is also called benefit-cost analysis. Cost-effectiveness analysis was first proposed in Operational Research (volume 5 No. 4, 1955). Later, the Department of Defense in the U.S. adopted this method. It was then applied widely in the later 1960s and the early 1970s and gradually evolved as cost-benefit analysis. Cost-benefit analysis does not focus only on firms. It chooses profit as the only assessment standard. It considers indirect benefit and cost. In addition, it assesses technological schemes based on the ratio of their benefit and cost. Cost-benefit analysis is usually applied for assessing governmental investments, such as public facilities and welfare projects. It should be pointed out that the development and application of cost-benefit analysis have limitations. It is similar to macro technological economic evaluation methods.

19.6.5 Feasibility Study in Western Countries

A feasibility study is a kind of comprehensive study on an investment in order to support decision making, used in western countries. It was first implemented for developing the Tennessee Valley, back in the 1930s in the U.S. Feasibility studies were gradually improved after World War II. The book Industrial Feasibility Study Manual, published by the United Nations Industrial Development Organization (UNIDO) is the first book to introduce the feasibility study. According to this book, a feasibility study is a kind of comprehensive study. It is related to technological economics because a feasibility study aims to resolve some issues that are technological economic issues as well. However, they are not the same. A feasibility study includes technological testing, geological exploration, fund collecting, firm management, construction work arrangement, etc. Thus, a feasibility study is not equal to the technological economy. The technological economy has its own theories and methods, whereas a feasibility study has its own unique content. Actually, a feasibility study in western countries is very similar to a construction project study in China. A feasibility study has four stages. Stage one is the opportunity study, which has two steps. The first step analyzes the macro plans of the development and the allocation of national economy, as well as the conditions. Then, it explores which engineering construction projects proposed are necessary and possible and what their economic effects are. Finally, it helps to select the appropriate projects. In the second step, the selected projects are further investigated. The benefits and drawbacks are clearly identified. Some key factors that impact the implementation of the projects are identified as well, to support decision making. If the results of studying a proposed project are good, further actions need to be taken. Studies in this stage are general. All of the economic related values come from surveys and estimation, based on experiences. The accuracy range is −30 to 30%. According to the experiences in western countries, costs spent in this stage are from 0.2% to 1.0%

of the whole investment on a project. It takes about 1–2 months to finish work in this stage. In the second stage, the initial feasibility study further investigates the proposed engineering projects and converts the proposal into a complete plan. The initial feasibility study covers ten aspects, including demand prediction, production scale, allocation and factory site, material, energy and transportation, processing technologies and equipment, institution establishment, labor, scheduling, economic analysis and financial analysis, and comprehensive evaluation. This stage aims to make a judgment about whether an initial plan is feasible. It requires comprehensive and detailed work. The accuracy of economic related values needs to be in the range of −20 to 20%. The cost of this stage is about 0.25–1.5% of the total investment. It takes about six months to finish work in this stage. The third stage is built on the conclusion of the initial feasibility study. Further investigation on the aforementioned ten aspects is conducted. The accuracy of economic related values needs to be in the range of −5 to 5%. The cost of this stage depends on the size of the project. Small projects need 1.0–3.0% and large projects need 0.2–1.0% of the total investment. It takes about 1–2 years to finish work in this stage. The fourth stage assesses the engineering projects comprehensively, in order to provide decision making support regarding whether engineering projects should start and when to start.

The four stages of a feasibility study introduced above have unique characteristics, compared with the construction procedure and requirements in the first five-year plan era and in the current time in China. Time and resources are spent in the pre-investment period on much detailed work. Not all of the engineering projects follow the four stages. Sometimes, the initial feasibility study is omitted. Because many aspects are involved in the feasibility study of engineering project, one or two experts cannot finish the study. Thus, usually a group of experts is needed for feasibility study. For large engineering projects, the expert group for a feasibility study should consist of the following members: one engineering economist (or specialized economist), one demand forecast and marketing analysis expert, several specialized engineers, one mechanical engineer, one civil engineer, and one accountant specialized in industrial management. Other experts, such as soil experts, geology experts, and testing experts, are needed for a short period, as well.

The methods adopted in a feasibility study in western countries are mainly economic analysis methods in the engineering economy, namely micro economic effect evaluation methods. But governmental projects adopt cost-benefit analysis methods.

19.6.6 Value Engineering in Western Countries

Value engineering is called "value analysis" as well. It was developed by Lawrence Miles, an American engineer at General Electric, by summarizing his buying experience after World War II. The core of value engineering is feature and cost analysis. Its formula is value = feature/cost. The goal of value engineering is to realize the necessary features at the lowest cost. Products with more features and a low cost have more value. Value engineering needs to know clearly about the features that users really need, to set the target cost for each feature by comparing similar features, and to realize the target costs and features by applying the available knowledge and documents with creativity. In order to achieve the goals of value engineering, Lawrence Miles provided the following 13 principles:

(1) Avoid general and conceptual analysis. Instead, specific analysis is required to find what features are not practical and what approaches are not feasible. Only in this way can issues be found and fixed.
(2) Collect all available cost-related data. Data should be accurate. Some data are generated when production is not in a normal condition. Some data only reflect the situation under faulty management. Such data should not be adopted.
(3) Use reliable information. Market information, technology information, and economic information should be collected by professionals. The collected information should be verified.
(4) Conduct innovation. No matter how authentic a product is, analysis is needed to determine whether its features are reasonable. Keep this in mind: improvement never stops.
(5) Be original. Originality could be something that nobody has ever done. It can also be a revision of the features of existing products or technics. Usually, the latter is easier to carry out.
(6) Find barriers and overcome them. Barriers can come from technologies, or they can be artificial. The cause of barriers needs to be identified clearly, and then the barriers can be overcome.
(7) Take full advantage of technological experts and expand professional knowledge. Other than experts inside a firm, those experts outside the firm should be utilized as well. Ask them good questions, and usually good answers can be gotten.
(8) Convert important tolerance grades into costs and consider them carefully. All tolerance, accuracy, standards, and purity aim to provide certain features. If no feature is provided, no regulation is needed.
(9) If possible, utilize the ready products manufactured by specialized factories.
(10) Utilize and purchase manufacturing techniques from specialized factories.
(11) Adopt specialized processing techniques.
(12) Adopt appropriate standards.
(13) Always ask whether the money should be spent. People have the following concerns when spending money: (a) The spending has a limitation; (b) Achieving the largest function of use and aesthetic function with the money spent; (c) That the received feature is within the reasonable range; and (d) Among several schemes, choose the best one.

It can be seen that value engineering is a kind of method or technology that balances product features and costs. Its goal is to maximize profits. Its economic formulas and cost-benefit analysis formulas are the same. However, value engineering is used for resolving micro and practical issues, such as a part or a procedure. In contrast, cost-benefit analysis is used for resolving large investment projects. The theories and methods of technological economics can be used for resolving not only large planning and design projects, but also for the practical product technological economic issues that are good for value engineering. The techniques and experiences of value engineering are good references to help firms find solutions for increasing product quality, decreasing cost, and improving products' economic effect.

Chapter 20
Methods for Comprehensive Evaluation

20.1 Introduction

Chapter 19 introduces methods for technological economic evaluation, including evaluation methods for the micro and the macro technological economy. Applications of these methods rely on documents and data about the technological economy. However, other than technological economic evaluation, technological schemes need evaluation from the perspectives of politics, national defense, society, culture, technology, economy, environment, and resources, in practice. The selection of technological schemes depends on the result of a comprehensive technological evaluation. This chapter discusses the political evaluation method, the national defense evaluation method, the social evaluation method, the cultural evaluation method, the technology evaluation method, the economic evaluation method, the environmental evaluation method, the resource evaluation method, and the comprehensive technology evaluation method.

20.2 Evaluation Methods Regarding Politics, National Defense, Society, Culture, Technology, Economy, Environment, and Resources

Contents of the evaluation methods from the perspective of politics, national defense, society, culture, technology, economy, environment, and resources are listed in Table 20.1.

Some contents can be quantified, while others cannot. For example, technological evaluation can refer to national technology standards, which have both quantitative and qualitative requirements. There are quantitative requirements for environmental evaluation. Regarding the content of social and cultural evaluation, some are quantitative (such as the employment rate and expected life), while others are qualitative

S. Xu, *Technological Economics*,
https://doi.org/10.1007/978-981-15-8582-1_20

Table 20.1 Contents of the evaluation methods

First-level content	Second-level content	Thlird-level content
Political evaluation	The four cardinal principles; the party's principles and policies; the government's statutes and regulations; political prestige; international influence	–
National defense evaluation	Territorial integrity; sovereignty and security; war preparation; fighting capability; defense capability; safeguarding world peace	–
Social evaluation	Employment; labor; life; healthcare; education; public safety; the stability of society	Labor (safety, industrial accident, condition improvement), life (improvement of conditions, diversification, larger scope of life), healthcare (health, lifespan), education (increasing knowledge, improving cultivation, personnel training)
Cultural evaluation	Socialist core values system; harmonious culture and civilization; promoting and developing Chinese culture; innovation; developing the cultural industry; enriching the spiritual and cultural life; protecting the historical relics	–
Technical evaluation	Feasibility; reliability; advancement; applicability; scientific significance; academic level; intelligence information	Scientific significance (having universal significance on scientific development and having universal significance on the development of certain discipline, and having significance on the development of sub-discipline), academic level (creativity, filling gaps, international level, domestic advanced level)
Economic evaluation	Do more with less; optimizing resource allocation; combination of macro and micro economic effects; combination of national economic evaluation and financial evaluation; combination of long-term and short-term benefits; economic development pattern; economic development strategy; coordinated development of economy	–

(continued)

Table 20.1 (continued)

First-level content	Second-level content	Thlird-level content
Environmental evaluation	Pollution; ecological balance; natural disasters	–
Resource evaluation	Resource protection; resource utilization; resource exploitation; resource exploration	–

only. It is hard to quantify the contents of national defense evaluation and political evaluation. For instance, the requirement of following the four cardinal principles can only be qualified.

Technological schemes can be evaluated based on the quantitative and qualitative requirements of evaluation methods. The two main methods are the graded approach and the index method.

20.2.1 Graded Approach

1. **Graded approach based on survey and consultation**

This approach grades technological schemes according to the evaluation standards via survey and consultation. It is applicable to perform evaluations that have qualitative requirements but no quantitative requirements, such as political evaluations. Surveys and consultations can be conducted in three formats. The first format is conversation Experts and people with experiences can meet together, discussing and evaluating a certain standard of technological scheme. This format is good for people to enlighten each other and to correct onesidedness. The second format is mail. Materials and requirements are mailed to people, who then provide comments anonymously. The feedback is then sorted and sent to certain people if necessary. At the end, objective opinions can be achieved. This format is good for allowing people to express their opinions freely. The third format is interview. The interviewers take special materials and questions and interview related units and individuals, asking for the interviewees' oral or written opinions. Evaluation can choose a five-grade marking system, a hundred-mark system, or other marking systems. Grading is based on the extent to which the technological schemes meet the standards. Usually, there are five levels: best, good, medium, bad, and worst. One hundred or five can be given to the best level. Twenty or one can be given to the worst level (see Table 20.2). Sometimes, grading is set as only two levels: pass (full scores) and failed (zero). It is also fine to set the extent to which technological schemes meet the standards at four levels or at three levels.

Table 20.2 Graded approach

Satisfaction degree Grading system	Best	Good	Medium	Bad	Worst
Hundred-mark system	100	80	60	40	20
Five-grade marking system	5	4	3	2	1

2. **Graded approach based on Quantitative Calculation**

This approach grades based on the value of the requirements from technological economic evaluation standards and the achieved numerical value. For instance, the value for A_{p_best} is five points and the value for A_{p_worst} is one point. The actual value of A_p can be calculated with interpolation method. Here is the formula.

$$Fp = A_p \cdot \frac{F_{p\_best} - F_{p\_worst}}{A_{p\_best} - A_{p\_worst}} \tag{20.1}$$

Or apply the following formula:

$$Fp = A_p \cdot \frac{A_p}{A_{p\_best}} \quad F_{p\_best} \tag{20.2}$$

The graded approach based on quantitative calculation is more objective and accurate than the one based on survey and consultation, which is subjective and inaccurate, and is only applied when quantitative calculation is not applicable.

20.2.2 Index Method

The index method assesses the ratio between the actual value of $A_p$achieved from the evaluation based on a certain standard and the value A_{p0}set by evaluation standards. It can be a percentage or a score. Here is the formula.

(1)

$$I_p = \frac{A_p}{A_{p0}} \tag{20.3}$$

(2)

$$I_p = \frac{A_p}{A_{p0}} \times 100\% \tag{20.4}$$

(3)

$$I_p = \frac{A_p - A_{p0}}{A_{p0}} \tag{20.5}$$

The result of the evaluation depends on the index value $I_p$of a certain item in the evaluation.

20.3 Technical Comprehensive Evaluation Methods

20.3.1 Economic Evaluation Method for Technical Comprehensive Benefits

Before introducing technical comprehensive evaluation methods, let us discuss the economic evaluation for the comprehensive benefits of technological schemes. In this book, Sect. 2 shows that the economic effect is the comparison between benefits and labor consumption (costs). There are political benefits, national defense benefits, social benefits, cultural benefits, technological benefits, economic benefits, environmental benefits, and resource benefits. The combination of these benefits becomes the comprehensive benefits of technological schemes. According to the division principle, the economic evaluation of technical comprehensive benefits can use the following formulas.

$$E_a = \frac{X_{\sum}}{Z_{\sum}} = \frac{F_{\sum}}{Z_{\sum}} \tag{20.6}$$

$$\text{or} \quad E_b = \frac{X_{\sum}}{Z_{u\sum}} = \frac{F_{\sum}}{Z_{u\sum}} \tag{20.7}$$

$$\text{or} \quad E_c = \frac{X_{\sum}}{Z_{\sum\_firm}} = \frac{F_{\sum}}{Z_{\sum\_firm}} \tag{20.8}$$

where

$$\begin{aligned} X_{\sum} &= X_{ecnomic} + X_{politic} + X_{defense} + X_{social} + X_{cultural} + X_{technical} \\ &\quad + X_{environmental} + X_{resource} \\ F_{\sum} &= F_{ecnomic} + F_{politic} + F_{defense} + F_{ocial} + F_{cultural} + F_{technical} \\ &\quad + F_{environmental} + F_{resource} \end{aligned} \tag{20.9}$$

Formula 20.6 is for the social productivity of labor (Formula I), and Formula 20.7 is for the social productivity of labor (Formula II). Formula 20.8 is for the labor productivity of firms and represents the values of comprehensive evaluation per unit of coss. However, each of these three formulas has flaws. Thus, they are not applied in practice very often. Their flaws are: (1) they grade the economic benefit first and then add this score to the results of evaluation of other benefits. Although these formulas generate total scores, they are not reasonable because the economic benefits are calculated with fuzzy math methods. (2) The results calculated with these formulas cannot be used for telling whether the comprehensive benefit of a technological scheme is good or not. Instead, they can only be used for comparison. (3) If the economic benefits of a technological scheme are the main benefits and vary across technological schemes (whereas the benefits in politics, defense, technology, society, culture, environment, and resources are close among technological schemes), evaluation results can be achieved by applying the methods introduced in Chap. 19. In this case, Formulas 20.6, 20.7, and 20.8 will generate the wrong results.

20.3.2 Technical Comprehensive Evaluation Method

1. **Purpose of comprehensive evaluation method**

Evaluation is applied in daily life for assessing an object, including hard technologies and soft technologies. Many objects are very complicated. Accordingly, it is not appropriate to evaluate them just from one certain perspective. Instead, they should be evaluated from multiple angles. For example, comprehensive evaluation methods should be applied to assess the development of the economy and the society in a country, the performance of a department, a factory's construction plan, the design of a machine, the performance of a worker, or a student's study. A comprehensive evaluation method is applicable for two situations. In the first situation, many evaluation indexes can be summed up into one with practical meaning. For instance, the economic evaluation of a product needs to consider the costs of raw materials, energy, wages, depreciation, and heavy repair. These indices can be combined as the cost index. The evaluation method for achieving greater, faster, better, and more economical results actually adopts this comprehensive evaluation method. In the second situation, many evaluation indexes cannot be summed up into one with practical meaning. For instance, assessing the economic and social development in a country can use some indices, such as national income, lifespan, employment rate, and culture level. Assessing the design of a machine can choose some indices, such as cost, power, self-weight, volume, and reliability. Assessing the economic benefits of a project can choose some indices, such as net income and national income (net production). These indices are quite different in requirements and characteristics. Some are not qualitative. Some have different measuring units. Some are unrelated. And some are inconsistent. Thus, the comprehensive evaluation method is used for evaluating diverse contents and indices and, ultimately, for selecting a scheme with the best comprehensive result.

2. **The comprehensive evaluation method**

The comprehensive evaluation method is a multi-objective decision making method. First, it converts qualitative factors into quantitative ones, and then it converts multiple measurement units and even non-measurement units into one unit. Next, it changes multiple objectives, including multiple standards, multiple indices, and multiple factors into a comprehensive single objective. Finally, it conducts evaluation based on the value of a comprehensive single objective. Essentially, the comprehensive evaluation method assesses the results of calculating (adding, multiplying, mixing addition and multiplication, division, and using the least squares technique) the values achieved by applying the graded approach and the index method to specific targets. This comprehensive single objective is an assumed one, which is an indicated value and does not have any scientific meaning. The calculation methods used for comprehensive evaluation calculate the values of comprehensive single objectives. Here are the calculation methods.

(1) Addition. Get the total value or the average of total value by adding the scores of each objective. The result is passed if the achieved total value or the average of the total value is larger than the prescribed number. Otherwise, the result has failed. The object with the highest total value or the average of total value is the best. The formulas for comprehensive evaluation are:

$$F_{\sum} = \sum_{p=1}^{p} x_p F_p \tag{20.10.1}$$

$$\text{or} \quad F = \frac{1}{P} \sum_{p=1}^{p} x_p F_p \tag{20.10.2}$$

where $F_{\sum}$ is the sum of the evaluation scores for each standard, F is the total average of the scores for all standards, F_p is the score of each standard, x_p is the significance coefficient of each standard, and P is the number of the items that need evaluation. Table 20.3 lists the results of evaluation for four technological schemes. It can be seen that the total score of scheme 1 is the highest. Thus, scheme 1 is the best one.

(2) Multiplication. Multiply the score of each standard. Because the result of the multiplication might be too large or too small, its square root is calculated. The nth root is the number of standards adopted in the evaluation. The result of of the nth root is the average score for each standard. The technological scheme with the highest average score is the best one. Here is the formula:

$$F = \sqrt[p]{x_1 F_1 F_2 x_2 \ldots\ldots x_p F_p} \tag{20.11}$$

Table 20.3 Examples of comprehensive evaluation

Standard	Politics	National defense	Society	Culture	Technology	Economy	Environment	Resources	Total score	Average
Scheme 1	100	100	80	80	80	80	80	80	680	85
Scheme 2	100	100	80	80	60	60	60	60	600	75
Scheme 3	100	80	80	60	60	40	60	80	560	70
Scheme 4	100	80	60	60	60	60	40	60	520	65

Note The significance coefficient for each standard is 1. This means that they are equally significant

Table 20.4 Comparison of the addition approach, multiplication approach, and the mix of addition and multiplication

# of technological schemes			1	2	3	4	5
Score based on Standard A			1	2	3	4	5
Score based on Standard B			5	4	3	2	1
Score gap			4	2	0	2	4
Significance of each standard is same	Add	Average score	3	3	3	3	3
	Multiplication	Average score	2.2	2.8	3	2.8	2.2
	Mix of addition and multiplication		5.2	5.8	6	5.8	5.2
Significance of each standard is different	Significance coefficient of Standard B		2	2	2	2	2
	Add	Average score	5.5	5	4.5	4	3.5
	Multiplication	Average score	3.2	4	4.2	4	3.2
	Mix of addition and multiplication		8.7	9	8.7	8	6.7

Note The mix of addition and multiplication methods adopts the sum of the average calculated by the addition approach and the multiplication approach

Addition and multiplication are both graded approaches, but in different formats. It is easy to apply the addition approach and to calculate the significance coefficient of each standard. However, addition has disadvantages. When the score of a standard is zero, the standard cannot be immediately removed from the formula. Furthermore, neither the total score nor the average score reflects the difference among the scores of all standards. In contrast, the multiplication approach allows the removing a standard with the score of zero. The total average score derived using multiplication approach can reflect the difference among the scores of all standards. The larger the difference, the lower the total average score, and vice versa. Thus, the best technological scheme evaluated by multiplication approach has the highest average score. The difference between the scores of each standard is relatively small. Table 20.4 compares the addition approach, the multiplication approach, and the mix of these two approaches. Suppose that there are five technological schemes which are evaluated based on two standards. The results of the evaluation show that four technological schemes get different scores when the two standards are applied. Technological schemes 1 and 5 have the largest difference, whereas technological scheme 3 has the smallest difference. When the addition approach is applied, all of the technological schemes get the same total average score. Therefore, it is hard to tell which technological scheme is better. But when the multiplication approach is applied, the technological schemes get different total average scores. Technological scheme 3 has the largest total average score. Technological schemes 1 and 5 have the smallest total average scores. Accordingly, technological scheme 3 is the best. This example shows that the multiplication approach is better than the addition approach. However, let us see the other example with the same five technological schemes and the same evaluation standards. Standard *B* has a significance coefficient of 2 and is more important than standard *A*. When the addition approach is adopted, the result shows that technological scheme has the highest total average score and is the best one. When the multiplication approach is adopted, the result is not related with any significance. In this case, technological scheme 3 has the highest total average score and is the best one. As such, the multiplication approach is not as good as the addition approach. Given the advantages and disadvantages of the addition approach and the multiplication approach, the following principles should be applied: (1) when the scores achieved with different standards do not vary but the significance of the standards are different, the addition approach is more applicable; (2) when the scores achieved with different standards vary a lot but the significance of the standards are almost the same, the multiplication approach is more applicable; (3) when there is no large difference among the scores and the significance of the standards, either the addition approach or the multiplication approach is applicable; (4) when the scores vary and the significance of the standards are different, neither the addition approach nor the multiplication approach is applicable.

(3) The mix of the addition approach and the multiplication approach. The addition approach cannot reflect the difference among the scores of each standard. Instead, it can reflect the significance of each standard. In contrast, the multiplication approach cannot reflect the significance of each standard, but it can reflect the difference among the scores of each standard. The mix of the addition approach and the multiplication approach can consider the advantages of these two approaches while overcoming their disadvantages. Basically, it adds the average scores achieved by the addition approach and the multiplication approach. Then, the sum is used for evaluating the technological schemes. This mixed approach can reflect not only the significance of each standard, but also the difference among the scores of each standard. It can be applied to any situation, especially when the difference among the scores of each standard and the significance of each standard are both large. Here is its formula:

$$F(add\,and\,multiplication) = F(add) + F(multiplication) \tag{20.12}$$

where $F(add)$ is the average score of all standards calculated with the addition approach. $F(multiplication)$ is the average score of all standards calculated with the multiplication approach.

Table 20.4 shows that when the significance of each standard is the same, the score of technological scheme 3 is the highest among the values calculated with the mix of the addition approach and the multiplication approach. This result is consistent with those calculated with the addition approach and the multiplication approach. As such, the mix of the addition approach and the multiplication approach can replace the addition approach and the multiplication approach. When the significance of each standard is different, technological scheme 1 is the best, based on the value calculated with the addition approach. However, technological scheme 3 is the best based on the value calculated with the multiplication approach. These results are in conflict. Therefore, it is hard to make a judgement about which technological scheme is the best. If the mixed approach is applied, technological scheme 2 gets the highest value, not technological scheme 1 or technological scheme 3. In other words, the comprehensive effect of technological scheme 2 is better than those of the other technological schemes.

(4) Division. When technological schemes are assessed, sometimes a series of standards are applied. For the values of some standards, such as the economic effect, social employment, national defense and security, the larger the better; whereas for some standards, such as environment pollution, resource consumption rate, the smaller the better. In this case, the division approach should be applied to calculate the comprehensive value for each standard. Here is the formula:

$$F = \frac{\beta_1, \beta_2 \ldots . \beta_m}{\alpha_1, \alpha_2 \ldots \ldots \alpha_n} \times 100 \tag{20.13}$$

where $\alpha_1, \alpha_2 \ldots \ldots \alpha_n$ are the ratios or the percentages of those standards. The smaller the values, the better. $\beta_1, \beta_2 \ldots \ldots \beta_m$ are the ratios or the percentages of those standards. The larger the values, the better.

(5) Least Square Method (Goal Programming Method). When assessing each standard comprehensively, a target value can be set for each standard first. The value can then be compared with the value generated with the calculation. This target value is the highest value. When a standard achieves this value, it will get full scores. In general, standards do not achieve this value; there always is a gap. The technological scheme with the smallest gap is the best one. The comprehensive target value for each technological scheme can be calculated with the following formula:

$$F = \sqrt{\sum\nolimits_{p=1}^{p} x_p \left(\frac{A_p - A_{p0}}{A_{p0}} \right)} \tag{20.14}$$

where A_{p0} is the target value for each evaluation standard, and A_p is the actual value of each evaluation standard.

These aforementioned methods for comprehensive evaluation should be adopted based on the actual condition.

The utility function curve method adopted overseas is also called the utility coefficient method. It gets so-called "utility value" by grading each standard according to the value on the curve of utility function. Then the utility values are weighted, added, or multiplied. The final result is called the "total utility value." The technological scheme with the largest total utility value is the best. This method is actually the same as the addition approach and the multiplication approach. The cost-effectiveness analysis adopted overseas is very similar to the utility function curve method. The cost-effectiveness analysis is a method for economic effect analysis; thus, it is not fit for supporting multiple objectives analysis. It should be pointed out that the comprehensive economic indicators and those economic indicators which are inter-connected and can be calculated should not be treated as independent multi-objectives which cannot be calculated. Thus, the aforementioned methods are not for these indicators. For example, production value, investment, and cost can be calculated based on the indicator of social net income (social net income = production value-cost-the coefficient of capital occupation*investment). Therefore, it is not necessary to calculate these three indicators with the addition approach, the multiplication approach, the mixed approach, division, or the least square method. In practice, these approaches are often applied inappropriately.

3. **Methods for Calculating Satisfied Coefficient and Significance Coefficient**

The comprehensive evaluation methods assess technological schemes from two aspects: the degree to which the technological scheme meets the requirements of each standard, and the relative significance degree of each standard. The satisfied coefficient reflects the degree to which the requirements are met. Its value can be calculated with the survey and consultation method and the index method introduced in the previous section. For example, if the degree to which standard *A* is met is 4 and the degree to which standard *B* is met is 1, their satisfied coefficients are 4 and 1, respectively. In addition, these values can be further converted into percentages. The percentage of satisfied degree for standard *A* is $0.8 = \frac{4}{4+1}$. The percentage of satisfied degree for standard *B* is $0.2 = \frac{1}{4+1}$. Thus, the satisfied coefficients for standard *A* and standard *B* are 0.8 and 0.2, respectively.

The significance coefficient reflects the relative significance degree of each standard. It can be achieved by the coercive grading method or by the non-coercive grading method.

(1) **Coercive Grading Method**

a.**04 Method** This method adopts a one-to-one repeating comparison. When two standards are compared and the difference of their significance is large, the more important one gets 4 points, whereas the less important one gets 0 points. When the difference between the significance of two standards is not large, the more important one gets 3 points, whereas the less important one gets 1 point. When the significance of two standards is the same, they both get 2 points. For instance, if standard *A* is more important than standard *B*, standard *A* has the same importance as standard *C*, and standard *B* is less important than standard *C*, the significance coefficients for these three standards can be calculated with the 04 method. The results are shown in Table 20.5. The significance coefficient for standard *A* is 5 or 0.42. The significance coefficient for standard *B* is 2 or 0.16. The significance coefficient for standard *C* is 5 or 0.42.

b. **01 Method** This method adopts a link relative method. When two standards are compared, the more important one gets 1 point, whereas the less important one gets 0 points. The significance coefficients for standard *A*, standard *B*, and standard *C*, calculated with the 01 method are shown in Table 20.6.

c. 13,579 Method This method adopts a link relative method. When the standards are compared, those with the same significance get 1 point. Those relatively important

Table 20.5 The 04 Method

	Standard A	Standard B	Standard C
	3	1	
	2		2
		1	3
Significance coefficient	5	2	5
Significance coefficient	0.42	0.16	0.42

Table 20.6 The 01 method

	Standard A	Standard B	Standard C
	1	0	
	1		0
		0	1
Significance coefficient	2	0	1
Significance coefficient	0.66	0	0.34

Table 20.7 The 13,579 method

Standard	A	B	C
A	1	3	1
B	1/3	1	1/3
C	1	3	1

standards get 3 points. Those important ones get 5 points. Those very important ones get 7 points. Those with the highest significance get 9 points. The judgment matrix can be adopted to calculate significance coefficients. The results are shown in Table 20.7. This method has two approaches: the square root approach and the sum and product approach. The square root approach first multiplies the elements in each line of a matrix and then gets the extraction of root of this product. For instance, the value of a line in Standard A is $\sqrt[3]{1 \times 3 \times 1} = 1.732$. The value of a line in Standard B is $\sqrt[3]{\frac{1}{3} \times 3 \times \frac{1}{3}} = 0.333$. The value of a line in Standard C is $\sqrt[3]{1 \times 3 \times 1} = 1.732$. The sum of these three values is 3.8 ($1.732 + 0.333 + 1.732$). Finally, the significance coefficient for Standard A is $1.732 \div 3.8 = 0.46$. The significance coefficient for Standard B is $0.333 \div 3.8 = 0.08$. The significance coefficient for Standard C is $1.732 \div 3.8 = 0.46$. The sum and product approach first converts the elements in each row of a matrix into percentages. For instance, the sum of the row for Standard A is $1 + 1/3 + 1 = 2.333$. The percentage of this row for Standard A is $1 \div 2.333 = 0.43$. The percentages of this row for Standard B and Standard C are 0.14 and 0.43, respectively. Similarly, the percentages of the row of Standard B for Standard A, Standard B, and Standard C are 0.43, 0.14, and 0.43, respectively. The percentages of the row of Standard C for Standard A, Standard B, and Standard C are 0.43, 0.14, and 0.43, respectively. Then add the percentages in each row. The total percentages of the line of Standard A is $0.43 + 0.43 + 0.43 = 1.29$. The total percentages of the

Table 20.8 Five-grade marking method

	Standard A	Standard B	Standard C
	5	4	3
Significance coefficient	5	4	3
Significance coefficient	0.42	0.33	0.25

line of Standard *B* is 0.14 + 0.14 + 0.14 = 0.42. The total percentages of the line of Standard *C* is 0.43 + 0.43 + 0.43 = 1.29. Lastly, divide these total percentages by their sum. The significance coefficients for Standard *A*, Standard *B*, and Standard *C* are 0.43, 0.14, and 0.43, respectively.

d. **Five-grade Marking Method** The method gives the most important standard 5 points, the important one 4 points, the somewhat important one 3 points, the non-important one 2 points, and the least important one 1 point. Table 20.8 shows an example. This method generates significance coefficients via grading. Compared with the link relative method, five-grade marking method fits for the situation when the number of the objectives is small.

(2) **Non-Coercive Grading Method**

This method does not have any rubric for grading. Technological schemes can be assessed based on their relative significance levels. If Standard *A* is three times more important than Standard *B*, the significance coefficients for Standard *A* and *B* are 3 and 1, respectively. Alternatively, the significance coefficients can be expressed as percentages 0.75 and 0.25.

4. **Dual-Level Comprehensive Evaluation Method and Multi-Level Comprehensive Evaluation Method**

When the index of objectives is one level, the one-level comprehensive evaluation method is applicable. The aforementioned methods are all one-level comprehensive evaluation methods. In practice, the objectives are always multi-level. The upper levels and the lower ones are usually closely connected and have a causal relationship. In this case, the multi-level comprehensive evaluation method should be adopted. The multi-level comprehensive evaluation method has a bottom-up approach and top-down approach.

(1) **Multi-Level Comprehensive Evaluation Method I (bottom-up)**

Initiated by the author in 1983,[1] this approach evaluates indicators from the bottom to the top. See Sect. 8 in Chap. 23 for the example. In this example, comprehensive evaluation is conducted at four levels. Denoted as *A*, the comprehensive benefit indicator for three coal exploitation schemes is at the top level. Denoted as B_1–B_7, standards for politics, internationality, society, technology, economy, environment

[1] Xu Xu83].

and ecology, and natural resources are at the second top level. Denoted as C_1–C_{16}, attributes of the standards are at the third level. Denoted as D_1–D_3, three coal exploitation schemes are at the bottom level. Figure 20.1 shows the structure of the four levels. This approach first calculates F_{cd}, the satisfied coefficient of the three coal exploitation schemes (D_1–D_3) for the standards at the third level. Then it calculates the significance coefficient x_c of the attributes at the third level corresponding to the standards at the second top level. Next, it calculates the satisfied coefficient $x_c F_{cd}$ for the$_{\text{n}}$three coal exploitation schemes regarding the standards at the second top level. And then it calculates the significance coefficient x_b for the standards at the second top level corresponding to the indicator at the top level. Lastly, it calculates the satisfied coefficients $x_b \bullet x_c \bullet F_{cd}$ of these three schemes corresponding to the indicator at the top level. These three schemes can then be assessed based on the values of their satisfied coefficients. The satisfied coefficients for the national scheme, the region scheme, and the local scheme are 10.05, 10.22, and 10.29, respectively. These values indicate that these three schemes all have good comprehensive benefits.

(2) **Multi-Level Comprehensive Evaluation Method II (top-down)**

Initiated by Saaty (1980),[2] this approach adopts the 13,579 method, also called level analysis method, to assess each level from the top to the bottom. This approach first sets the significance coefficient of the indicator at the top level as 1. Then, it calculates the significance coefficient x_b for the standards at the second top level corresponding to the indicator at the top level with the *A-B* judgement matrix. The standards are ranked by their significance coefficients. Next, it calculates the significance coefficient x_c for the attributes at the third level corresponding to the standards at the second top level with the *B-C* judgement matrix. The attributes are ranked by their significance coefficients. Next, it calculates the significance coefficient x_{cd} for the schemes at the bottom level corresponding to the attributes at the third level with the *C-D* judgement matrix. Lastly, it calculates the significance coefficients $x_b \bullet x_c \bullet x_{cd}$ of these three schemes corresponding to the indicator at the top level. These three schemes can then be assessed based on the values of their significance coefficients. The significance coefficients for the national scheme, the region scheme, and the local scheme are 0.3289, 0.3344, and 0.3367, respectively. These values indicate that the comprehensive benefits of these three schemes are very close. The national scheme is not better than the region scheme or the local scheme.

Here are the characteristics of the aforementioned two methods: (1) The comprehensive evaluation value *A* in the multi-level comprehensive evaluation method I is $x_b \bullet x_c \bullet F_{cd}$, while that in the multi-level comprehensive evaluation method II is $x_b \bullet x_c \bullet x_{cd}$. If the values of F_{cd} and x_{cd} are the same, the values of *A* calculated with these two methods are the same. In this case, the results generated by these two methods are the same. The multi-level comprehensive evaluation method II calculates significance coefficients, not satisfied coefficients. Actually, x_{cd} of the bottom level is not the significance coefficient, but the satisfied coefficients of the schemes at the bottom level. In contrast, the multi-level comprehensive evaluation method I

[2]Saaty [Sa80].

calculates both the significance coefficients and the satisfied coefficients. F_{cd} is the satisfied coefficient. Thus, the concept of this method is clear. It better meets the requirements in practice. (2) x_{cd} in the multi-level comprehensive evaluation method II reflects relative good and bad only. F_{cd} in the multi-level comprehensive evaluation method I reflects not only relative good and bad, but also absolute good and bad. For instance, if the economic indicators of the three schemes all show negative values, F_{cd} is able to reflect this situation, but x_{cd} is not. (3) x_{cd} can be graded by the 13,579 method only. F_{cd} can be calculated by multiple methods and its value can be any number, such as 1.3 or 4.2. (4) The significance coefficients in the multi-level comprehensive evaluation method II can be calculated with the square root approach and the sum and product approach, based on the judgement matrix. Some values needs assessment, including the maximum eigenvalue λ_{max}, the deviating coincident indicator CI, the same order average random index RI, and the random rate CR (CI/RI). When $CR < 0.10$, the judgment matrix has the consistency of satisfaction. Otherwise, the judgement needs adjustment. The significance coefficients in the multi-level comprehensive evaluation method I can be calculated with the 01 method, the 04 method, and the five-grade marking method. The result will have a consistency of satisfaction, as well.

5. **Technology Comprehensive Evaluation Method**

The technology comprehensive evaluation method is the application of comprehensive evaluation methods on technological schemes. In other words, it is a comprehensive evaluation method used in technology assessment.

The evaluation standards for technological schemes have eight aspects, which will generate different results. Some might have good results, whereas others might have bad results. Accordingly, it is hard to make decisions based on these results. A comprehensive approach is required to evaluate technological schemes with all standards considered. By doing this, a best-fit technological scheme can be selected. Comprehensive evaluation aims to examine technological schemes thoroughly, to assess their comprehensive effects, and to select the one with the best comprehensive effect. The result of the comprehensive evaluation will provide support for decision making. It should be pointed out that the comprehensive evaluation methods introduced above are applicable in the following situations: (1) Some evaluation standards are suited for qualitative methods only and cannot be calculated quantitatively. Some evaluation standards can be calculated quantitatively, but with different units which cannot be converted into one single unit; (2) The results of the evaluation standards vary. Some are good, while some are bad. However, these results will be all good, or all bad. If they are all good or all bad, there is no need to apply the multi-objective decision making methods; (3) Each evaluation standard is independent. They do not have any inter-relation. It is not applicable to convert these independent standards into a comprehensive standard for calculation. The comprehensive evaluation of technological schemes based on the eight standards meets these requirements. Thus, it is suitable to apply the comprehensive evaluation methods on technological scheme. Of course, standards should be selected for comprehensive evaluation on technological schemes based on their characteristics and on the practical situation.

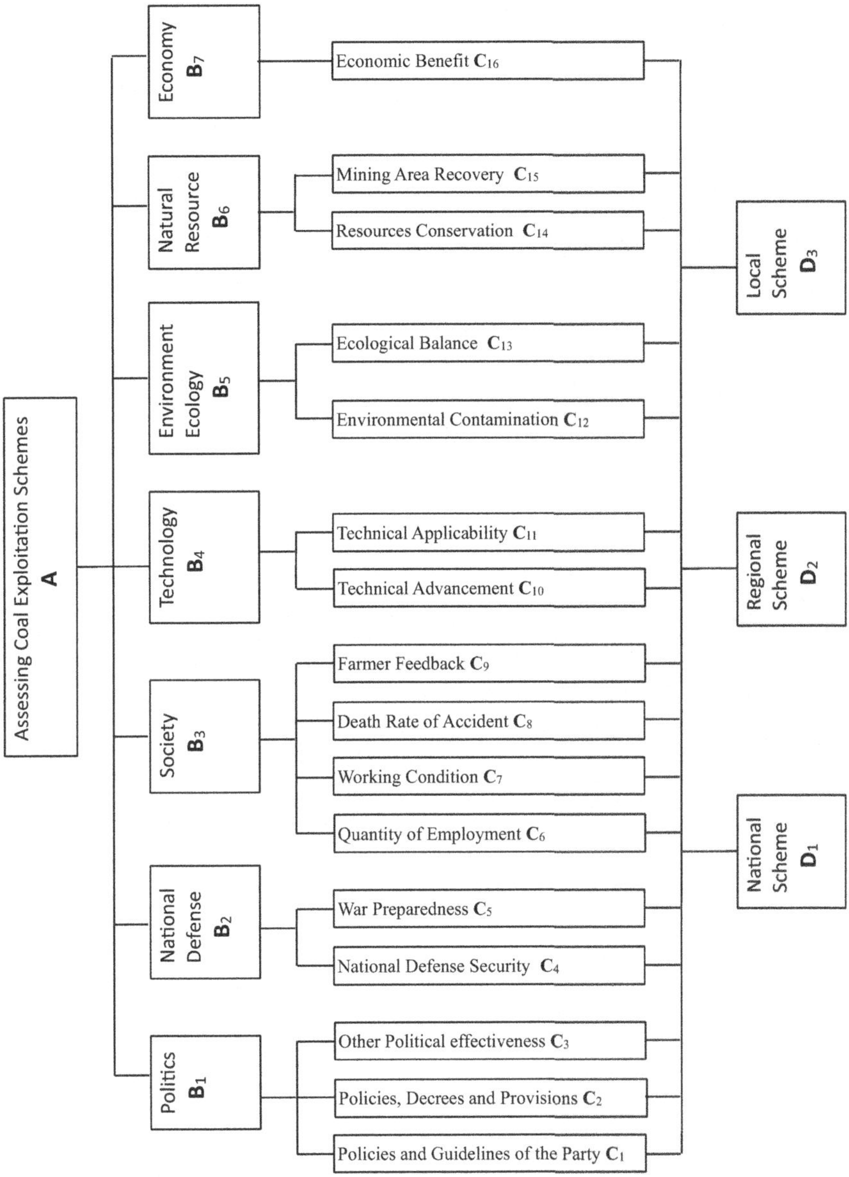

Fig. 20.1 Application of Multi-level synthetic evaluation method I

References

[Sa80] Saaty, T. L. (1980). The Analytic Hierarchy Process, MeGraw Hill, Inc.

[Xu83] Xu, S. (1983). Comprehensive evaluation of the coal exploitation policies in Shanxi Province. Quantitative Technological Economy Study, 6.

Chapter 21
Applications of Various Assessment Methods in the Technological Economy

21.1 Introduction

The previous chapter introduces the evaluation methods for technological schemes at the first level. This chapter introduces the evaluation methods for technological schemes at the second level. The techniques adopted in these methods include comparison, tabulation, figures, analysis, mathematics, computers, and surveying.

21.2 Comparison Method (Scheme Comparison Method) and It Application

Techniques to compare are widely applied in the technological economy. The most common one is the comparison method, which is also called the scheme comparison method. It chooses the best technological schemes by comparing the economic effect and or comprehensive effect of each technological scheme. The comparison method is applicable when the number of technological schemes is small and fixed, when each technological scheme is independent and mutually exclusive, and when the economic effects of the technological schemes are related only with technological economic parameters. If only one technological scheme is available, it can be compared with a situation in which no technological scheme is available. The comparison method is applied widely in practice for economic evaluation and for comprehensive evaluation, such as for engineering management, engineering design and planning, factory site selection, new production manufacturing, technology importing, energy and raw material selection, equipment upgrading and transformation, and farming system selection. Here is an example of the use of economic evaluation for energy computation.

S. Xu, *Technological Economics*,
https://doi.org/10.1007/978-981-15-8582-1_21

Energy computation is underdeveloped, and has been, for quite a long time in China. Total energy computation is only calculated by industrial and mining enterprises, government departments and institutions, and residential houses. A breakdown is not available, and certainly the energy consumption of the smallest unit is not available. For example, the total energy consumption of a factory is available, but the energy consumption of a workshop, not to mention the energy consumption of the devices, is not available. Due to the lack of the energy consumption of the smallest unit, the evaluation of their energy consumption cannot be conducted. This is one main reason for energy waste. Accordingly, energy computation must be conducted, in order to save energy. The implementation of energy computation is actually the evaluation of building more energy computational instruments and metering plants and constructing more energy generating plants. The following example concerns the evaluation of civilian power computation, especially the schemes of building power instrument and meter plants and constructing power plants.

According to some well-known surveys, if civilian power is computed not by household, but by allocating the sum based on the number of households, or without any charge, each household will consume 25–200 watts more power. Each month, a household will consume 3–25 KWHs of power. If a household consumes 80 watts more power and 10 KWHs more power in a month, it will consume 120 KWHs more power in a year. Thus, one meter for one household will save 80 watts and 120 KWHs in one year, on an average. As such, a power meter plant with the annual capacity of 200,000 m will save 16,000 KW and 24,000,000 KWHs a year if these meters are all installed in households. If the saving of the loss in power transmission is taken into consideration, this meter plant will save 18,000 KW and 27,000,000 KWHs a year. In 15 years, 270,000 KW and 3,240,000,000 KWHs will be saved. The fixed capital for the meter plant with the annual capacity of 200,000 m is 1,950,000 Yuan. Current capital is 950,000 Yuan. The cost of a meter is 22 Yuan. Basic depreciation of a meter is 0.5 Yuan. The construction period of a meter plant is three years. The investment for a power plant (including transmission and distribution) is 1000 Yuan per KWH. Current capital is 50 Yuan per KW. The cost for power supply is 0.03 per KWH. The basic depreciation is 0.01 Yuan per KWH. The construction period of a power plant is five years. Next, the schemes of building a power plant and building a power meter plant are evaluated with the comparison method, based on the social productivity method I and on the social net income method. Because the benefits of the two schemes are the same, only the total consumption cost is calculated.

(1) The total consumption cost of a power meter plant

$$\begin{aligned} T_{z1} &= T_{gz1} + T_{l1} + T_{j1} \\ &= \frac{182}{3}\left(\frac{\theta^{18}-1}{\theta^{15}-1} + \frac{\theta^{17}-1}{\theta^{15}-1} + \frac{\theta^{16}-1}{\theta^{15}-1}\right) + 95 - \frac{10}{0.15} + \frac{10\times 15}{8.14-1} \\ &= 255 + 95 - 67 + 21 = 3,040,000\ \text{Yuan} \\ C_1 &= 20\times 22 = 4,400,000\ \text{Yuan} \end{aligned}$$

The total consumption cost of a power meter plant in 15 years $Z_{\sum l}$ is

$$Z_{\sum 1} = (C_1 + x_t\, T_{z1})\frac{\theta^{n_c} - 1}{-1} = (440 + 0.15 \times 304)\frac{1.15^{15} - 1}{1.15 - 1} = 230{,}760{,}000\ \text{Yuan}$$

(2) The total consumption cost of a power plant

$$\begin{aligned} T_{z2} &= T_{gz2} + T_{l2} + T_{j2} \\ &= \frac{1.8 \times 1000}{5}\left(\frac{\theta^{20} - 1}{\theta^{15} - 1} + \frac{\theta^{19} - 1}{\theta^{15} - 1} + \frac{\theta^{18} - 1}{\theta^{15} - 1} + \frac{\theta^{17} - 1}{\theta^{15} - 1} + \frac{\theta^{16} - 1}{\theta^{15} - 1}\right) \\ &\quad + 1.8 \times 50 - \frac{2700 \times 0.01}{0.15} + \frac{2700 \times 0.01 \times 15}{8.14 - 1} = 2{,}8940{,}000\ \text{Yuan} \\ C_2 &= 2700 \times 0.03 = 810,000\ \text{Yuan} \end{aligned}$$

The total consumption cost of a power plant in 15 years $Z_{\sum l}$ is

$$\begin{aligned} Z_{\sum 2} &= (C_2 + x_t\, T_{z2})\sum_{s=1}^{nj}\frac{\theta^{n+1-s_j} - 1}{-1} = (81 + 0.15 \times 2894) \\ &\quad \sum_{s=1}^{nj}\frac{1.15^{16-s} - 1}{1.15 - 1} = 1,364,000,000\ \text{Yuan} \end{aligned}$$

In the calculations above, calculation period n_j is set as 15 years. x_t is set as 0.15. The investments in coal mines and railway are not calculated, because the price of coal in the cost of power generation includes these investments. The results of the calculations show that it is more economical to build a power meter plant than to construct a power plant. A power meter plant with the annual capacity of 200,000 m will save 1,130,000,000 Yuan in the cost of power generation in 15 years. This is an example of the macro technological economy. Some power meter plants have small annual productivity. Due to the lack of scale of economy, these plants operate in the red. This is an example of the micro technological economy. Decision making must be based on the macro technological economy. For those power meter plants that suffer a loss, tax relief can be adopted to let them get some benefits, or to support them to expand production in order to get better economic benefits.

21.3 Tabulation Method and Its Application

The tabulation method uses tables as the tool. Tables are applied widely in the technological economy for displaying indicators and data of technological schemes and for calculating and evaluating the economic benefits of technological schemes. When tables are chosen for evaluating technological schemes, the values of the parameters and variables are set first. Then, these values are loaded into selected economic evaluation formulas. Finally, the indicators of the economic effect are calculated. The calculation process and all values are listed in a table. The evaluation of technological schemes can be conducted by checking the table. The tabulation method and the comparison method are closely related. Thus, they are usually applied together.

Here is an example of assessing energy computation with tabulation method. In this example, social net income is compared for *Scheme A* and *Scheme B*. A table is developed, as shown in Table 21.1. Three approaches are adopted for calculating the annual net income or the national income. The first approach calculates the net income or the national income of a certain year without considering the time factor. The second approach converts the net income or the national income of a certain year into the present value of the prior year with compound interest. The third approach converts the net income or national income of a certain year into the present value with compound interest. The calculation methods and the results are displayed in one table. It can be seen from Table 21.1 that the results achieved with the tabulation method are the same as those gotten with the formula calculation. The tabulation method is ideal for complicated situations. Usually, the economic evaluation of major construction schemes should adopt the tabulation method. Furthermore, another table is developed for calculating the dynamic investment net income rates of schemes (see Table 21.2). The results show that the x_t for *Scheme A* is 13.39% and the x_t for *Scheme B* is 14.95%. Therefore, *Scheme B* is better than *Scheme A*.

21.4 Figure Method and Its Application

Figures are applied in the technological economy for graphic interpretation and illustration. They can be used for displaying the process of technological economic calculation and results. They can also be used to compare technological schemes and to select the best ones. The commonly applied figuring methods in the technological economy include the technological economy optimization figure, the technological economy decision tree, the technological economy network figure, and the technological economy network plan figure.

21.4.1 Technological Economy Optimization Figure

In practice, many technological economy issues have two contradictory aspects. On the one hand, as technological schemes change, certain costs get larger and larger. On the other hand, certain costs get smaller and smaller as technological schemes change. The technological scheme that has the smallest sum of the two aspects of cost is the one with the best economic effect. To find the technological schemes with the best economic effect, one can choose the figure method. Usually, a curve α is drawn to represent the increase of a certain cost Z_1 with the change of technological

Table 21.1 Examples of social net income method

No.	Period		Construction Period			Production Run Period															Total
	Year		1	2	3	1	2	3	4	5	6	7	8	9	10	11	12	13	14	15	–
1	Annual Production S_s (Sales Revenue)	Scheme A	–	–	–	30	30	30	30	30	30	30	30	30	30	30	30	30	30	30	–
		Scheme B	–	–	–	30	30	30	30	30	30	30	30	30	30	30	30	30	30	30	
2	Annual Investment T_s	Scheme A	90	–	–	5	–	–	–	–	–	–	–	–	–	–	–	–	–	–	–
		Scheme B	–	–	–	10	–	–	–	–	–	–	–	–	–	–	–	–	–	–	–
3	Annual Cost C_s	Scheme A	–	–	–	15	15	15	15	15	15	15	15	15	15	15	15	15	15	15	–
		Scheme B	–	–	–	17	17	17	17	17	17	17	17	17	17	17	17	17	17	17	–
4	Annual Basic Depreciation C_{js}	Scheme A	–	–	–	6	6	6	6	6	6	6	6	6	6	6	6	6	6	6	–
		Scheme B	–	–	–	6	6	6	6	6	6	6	6	6	6	6	6	6	6	6	–
5	Actual Annual Ocuupied Investment Tzs	Scheme A	90	90	90	95	89	83	77	71	65	59	53	47	41	35	29	23	17	11	–
		Scheme B	–	–	90	100	94	88	82	76	70	64	58	52	46	40	34	28	22	16	–
6	Annual Occupied Capital $C_{ts}=X_tT_{zs}$	Scheme A	13.5	13.5	13.5	14.25	13.35	12.45	11.55	10.65	9.75	8.85	7.95	7.05	6.15	5.25	4.35	3.45	2.55	1.65	–
		Scheme B	–	–	13.5	15	14.1	13.2	12.3	11.4	10.5	9.6	8.7	7.8	6.9	6	5.1	4.2	3.3	2.4	–
7	Annual Consumption Cost $Z_s = C_s + X_tT_{zs}$	Scheme A	13.5	13.5	13.5	29.25	28.35	27.45	26.55	25.65	24.75	23.85	22.95	22.05	21.15	20.25	19.35	18.45	17.55	16.65	–
		Scheme B	–	–	13.5	32	31.1	30.2	29.3	28.4	27.5	26.6	25.7	24.8	23.9	23	22.1	21.2	20.3	19.4	–
8	Annual Social Net Income (not considering time factors) $E_{cs}=S_s-Z_s$	Scheme A	−13.5	−13.5	−13.5	0.75	1.65	2.55	3.45	4.35	5.25	6.15	7.05	7.95	8.85	9.75	10.65	11.55	12.45	13.35	–
		Scheme B	–	–	−13.5	−2	−1.1	−0.2	−0.7	1.6	2.5	3.4	4.3	5.2	6.1	7.0	7.9	8.8	9.7	10.6	–
9	Annual Total Social Net Income (not considering time factors) $\sum_{s=1}^{n_k+n_j} E_{cs}$	Scheme A	−13.5	−27	−40.5	−39.75	−38.10	−35.5	−32.10	−27.75	−22.5	−16.35	−9.3	−1.35	7.5	17.25	27.9	39.45	51.9	65.25	65.25
		Scheme B	–	–	−13.5	−15.5	−16.6	−16.8	−16.1	−14.5	−12.0	−8.6	−4.3	0.9	7	14	21.9	30.7	40.4	51	51
10	Annual Social Net Income (Convert into the present value of last year) $E_{cs}\theta^{ak+nj-s}$	Scheme A	−145.3	−126.4	−109.9	5.31	10.1	13.6	16.0	17.6	18.5	18.9	18.8	18.4	17.8	17.1	16.2	15.2	14.3	13.4	–
		Scheme B	–	–	−109.9	−14.2	−6.8	−1.1	3.2	6.48	8.8	10.5	11.4	12.0	12.3	12.3	12.0	11.6	11.2	10.6	–
11	Annual Total Social Net Income (Convert into the present value of last year) $\sum_{s=1}^{n_k+n_j} E_{cs}\theta^{ak+nj-s}$	Scheme A	−145.3	−271.7	−381.6	−376.3	−366.2	−352.6	−336.6	−319	−300.5	−218.6	−262.8	−244.4	−226.6	−209.5	−193.3	−178.1	−163.8	−150.4	−150.4
		Scheme B	–	–	−109.9	−124.1	−130.9	−132	−128.8	−122.3	−113.5	−103	−91.6	−79.6	−67.3	−55	−43	−31.4	−20.2	−9.6	−9.6
12	Annual Social Net Income (Convert into present value) $\frac{E_{cs}}{\theta^S}$	Scheme A	−11.7	−10.2	−8.9	0.43	0.82	1.1	1.3	1.41	1.49	1.52	1.52	1.49	1.44	1.38	1.31	1.23	1.16	1.08	–
		Scheme B	–	–	−8.9	−1.14	−0.55	−0.09	0.26	0.25	0.71	0.84	0.92	0.97	0.99	0.99	0.97	0.94	0.90	0.86	–
13	Annual Total Social Net Income (Convert into present value) $\sum_{s=1}^{n_k+n_j}\frac{E_{cs}}{\theta^S}$	Scheme A	−11.7	−21.9	−30.8	−30.4	−29.6	−28.5	−27.2	−25.8	−24.3	−22.8	−21.3	−19.8	−18.4	−17.0	−15.7	−14.4	−13.3	−12.2	−12.2
		Scheme B	–	–	−8.9	−10	−10.6	−10.68	−10.4	−9.9	−9.19	−8.35	−7.43	−6.46	−5.47	−4.48	−3.51	−2.57	−1.67	−0.81	−0.81

Table 21.2. (Dynamic) calculation table for investment net income rate (*Scheme A*)

Period		Construction Period			Production Run Period															16	Total
Year		1	2	3	1	2	3	4	5	6	7	8	9	10	11	12	13	14	15		
Income	Income (direct) S_{direct}	0	0	0	30	30	30	30	30	30	30	30	30	30	30	30	30	30	30	0	
	Income (indirect) $S_{indirect}$	0	0	0	0	0	0	0	0	0	0	0	0	0	0	0	0	0	0	5	
	Depreciation reclaiming C_j	0	0	0	6	6	6	6	6	6	6	6	6	6	6	6	6	6	6		
	Residual of capital assets reclaiming T_I, T_c	0	0	0	0	0	0	0	0	0	0	0	0	0	0	0	0	0	0		
Expenses	Investment (direct) T_{direct}	0	0	0	5	0	0	0	0	0	0	0	0	0	0	0	0	0	0		
	Investment (indirect) $T_{indirect}$	0	0	0	0	0	0	0	0	0	0	0	0	0	0	0	0	0	0		
	Cost (direct) C_{direct}	0	0	0	15	15	15	15	15	15	15	15	15	15	15	15	15	15	15		
	Cost (indirect) $C_{indirect}$	0	0	0	0	0	0	0	0	0	0	0	0	0	0	0	0	0	0		
	Material consumption cost C_W																				
	Transportation occupation cost C_Y																				
	Labor occupation cost C_R																				

(continued)

Table 21.2. (continued)

Period	Construction Period			Production Run Period															16	Total
Year	1	2	3	1	2	3	4	5	6	7	8	9	10	11	12	13	14	15		
Natural resource utilization cost C_D																				
Capital net income	−90	0	0	16	21	21	21	21	21	21	21	21	21	21	21	21	21	21		
Total capital net income	−90	−90	−90	−74	−53	−32	−11	10	31	52	73	94	115	136	157	178	199	220	0.163	
Discount factor of x_t = 10%	1	0.909	0.826	0.683	0.621	0.565	0.513	0.466	0.424	0.386	0.35	0.319	0.29	0.263	0.239	0.218	0.198	0.18	0.82	27.45
Present value of capital net income	−90	0	0	10.93	13.04	11.87	10.77	9.79	8.9	8.11	7.35	6.7	6.09	5.52	5.02	4.6	4.16	3.78	0.138	
Discount factor of x_t = 11%	1	0.9	0.812	0.659	0.593	0.535	0.482	0.434	0.391	0.352	0.317	0.286	0.258	0.232	0.209	0.188	0.17	0.153	0.69	17.82
Present value of capital net income	−90	0	0	10.54	12.45	11.23	10.12	9.11	8.21	7.39	6.66	6.01	5.42	4.87	4.39	3.95	3.57	3.21	0.07	
Discount factor of x_t = 15%	1	0.87	0.756	0.572	0.497	0.432	0.376	0.327	0.284	0.247	0.215	0.187	0.163	0.141	0.123	0.107	0.093	0.081	0.35	−12
Present value of capital net income	−90	0	0	9.15	10.44	9.07	7.9	6.87	5.96	5.19	4.51	3.93	3.42	2.96	2.58	2.25	1.95	1.7		
Dynamic) Investment net income rate x_t (%)	$x_t = 11 + \frac{17.82 \times (15-11)}{17.82+12} = 13.39$																			

Note Investment is the input at the beginning of a year. Cost is calculated at the end of a year. Thus, when calculating the discount factor of an investment, the length of period should remove one year. For example, the discount factor of investment in the sth year should be $\frac{1}{\theta^{s-1}}$.

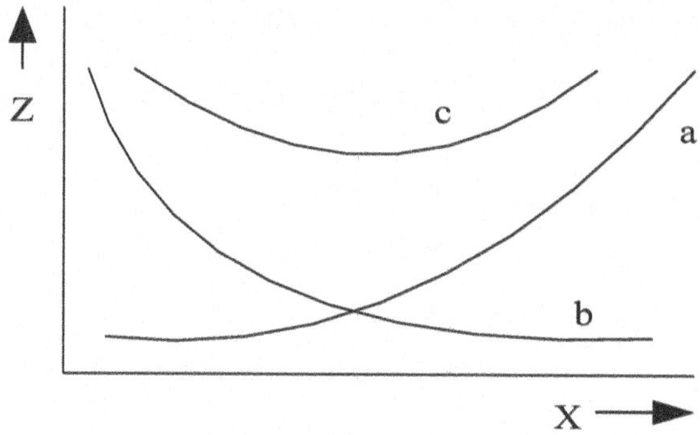

Fig. 21.1 Technological economy optimization figure

scheme X. Another curve β is drawn to represent the decrease of a certain cost Z_2 with the change of technological scheme X. Then, curve c that represents the change of total cost $Z_{\sum}$ with the change of technological scheme X, by merging curve α and curve β. The scheme with the smallest total cost can be found on the curve c (see Fig. 21.1).

21.4.2 Technological Economy Decision Tree and Net Figure

The technological economy decision tree and net figure are good for supporting series decisions in the technological economy.

1. Technological Economy Decision Tree

The technological economy decision tree is adopted for supporting series decisions in uncertain conditions. Here is its procedure: first, draw the shape of the decision tree based on the requirements of the technological economy issues and the collected documents. The shape of the decision tree consists of nodes and branches. There are two types of nodes. Decision nodes are represented by small squares. Branches derived from decision nodes represent technological schemes, which are called scheme branches. Opportunity nodes are represented by small circles. Branches derived from opportunity nodes represent different situations and possibilities, and are called possibility branches. The sum of the possibilities of all branches is 1. Second, the possibilities of all situations are predicted. Third, calculate the expected values of the economic effect indicators in all situations for all schemes from the treetop to the root. Fifth, compare the economic effects of schemes based on the expected values of the economic effect indicators and select the one with the largest expected values of economic effect.

Here is an example. According to available geological data, an area might have oil. Now, a selection needs to make among the following options: (1) dig oil wells immediately or conduct more seismic exploration? (2) If the first oil well is not successful, continue to dig the second one or give up? (3) After seismic exploration,

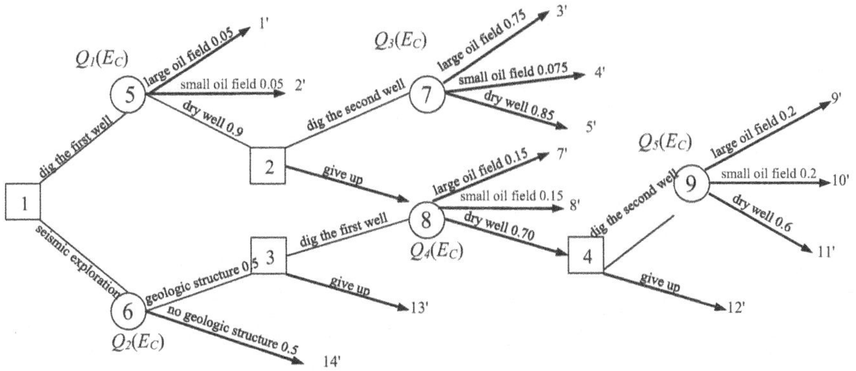

Fig. 21.2 Technological economy decision tree in uncertain conditions

continue to dig the second one or give up? (4) If the first oil well is not successful, continue to dig the second one or give up? The solutions can be found by drawing a technological economy decision tree:

(1) Draw the technological economy decision tree. According to the above four questions, the tree has four decision points, each of which has two schemes available. Each scheme has several results. For example, digging an oil well might have three possible results: finding a large oil field, finding a small oil field, or finding nothing.
(2) Predict the possibilities of the results. The possibility of success on the first oil well is small. The possibility of success on the second oil well is larger. The possibility of success is small if no seismic exploration is conducted. The possibility of success is larger if seismic exploration is conducted. The values of prediction are shown in Fig. 21.2.
(3) Based on the 14 branches in Fig. 21.2, calculate the total social net income of each root. E_{c1} starting from 1 and ending at 1, the social net income is 51,500,000 Yuan in n_j years. E_{c2} starting from 1 and ending at 2, the social net income is 16,500,000 Yuan in n_j years. E_{c3} is 50,000,000 Yuan. E_{c4} is 15,000,000 Yuan. E_{c5} is $-3{,}000{,}000$ Yuan. E_{c6} is $-1{,}500{,}000$ Yuan. E_{c7} is 48,500,000 Yuan. E_{c8} is 13,500,000 Yuan. E_{c9} is 47,000,000 Yuan. E_{c10} is 12,000,000 Yuan. E_{c11} is $-6{,}000{,}000$ Yuan. E_{c12} is $-4{,}500{,}000$ Yuan. E_{c13} is $-3{,}000{,}000$ Yuan. E_{c14} is $-3{,}000{,}000$ Yuan.
(4) Calculate the expected values of social net income for opportunity points 5, 6, 7, 8, 9.

$$Q_1(E_c) = 508.8;\ Q_2(E_c) = 602;\ Q_3(E_c) = 187.5;\ Q_4(E_c) = 1504;\ Q_5(E_c) = 820.$$

(5) Select one scheme for each decision point based on the expected value of social net income. For decision point 1, the seismic exploration scheme is better. For decision point 2, digging a second oil well is better than giving up digging oil wells. For decision point 3, digging the first oil well is better than giving

up digging oil wells. For decision point 4, digging a second oil well is better than giving up digging oil wells. Thus, the best scheme is to conduct seismic exploration first. If the result shows that geologic structure exists, dig a well first. If the well is failed, dig a second well. If geologic structure does not exist, stop digging.

2. Technological Economy Network Figure

This method can be applied by following these steps: First, draw a technological economy network figure based on the requirements of the multiple-level technological economy issues and the collected documents. The figure should include a time variable (also called a phase variable or a level variable) and a status variable. The network figure consists of time, decision points (represented by small squares), and branches. Decision points are status variables. Branches derived from decision points represent technological schemes, namely different statuses (see Fig. 21.3). Second, assess the scheme branches of each decision point from the very last column of the decision points with branches by using the social net income method or the firm excess profit method. For example, if a decision point has two branches, we can calculate the E_c or E_f of each branch and then select the one with the larger value of E_c or E_f as the best scheme. Next, use the value of the selected branch for the calculation of decision points at the level. Third, apply this procedure to the rest of the columns of decision points, stopping at the starting decision point.

Here is an example. The production of coal is 121,000,000 t in 1980 in a certain region. Specifically, state-owned mines produce 55%. Regional mines produce 20.

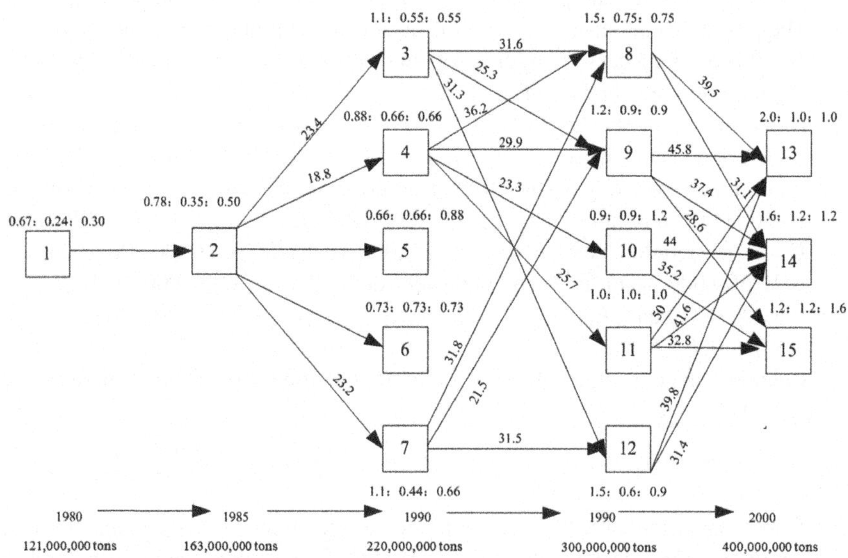

Fig. 21.3 Technological network figure in certain conditions

Local mines produce 25%. It is predicted that the production will reach 400,000,000 t in 2000. Three schemes are proposed: 2:1:1 (50%:25%:25%), 4:3:3 (40%:30%:30%), and 3:3:4 (30%:30%:40%). Which scheme is economically reasonable? What is the best approach to move the structure in 1980 to the best structure in 2000?

Here is solution. (1) Draw the technological economy network figure (see Fig. 21.3). Five stages are set, namely 1980, 1985, 1990, 1995, and 2000. The production of coal at each stage is known. The production structure of 1980 is known. The production structure of 1985 is known as well, according to the Sixth Five-Year Plan. Thus, select the production structures for 1990, 1995, and 2000. Suppose that there are five production schemes for 1990 and 1995, namely 2:1:1, 4:3:3, 3:3:4, 1:1:1, and 5:2:3, and there are three production schemes for 2000, namely 2:1:1, 4:3:3, and 3:3:4. The network figure follows a principle, which supposes that the production of the three types of coal mines keeps increasing, not decreasing, during the five stages. We adopt the social net income method to calculate. In this case, because the price of coal is the same, the social total consumption cost is good for evaluating schemes. The values of the social total consumption costs Z, for the scheme in each branch, are listed in the Fig. (2) Starting from the decision point with branches in 1995, compare and evaluate all of the branches of each decision point. See Table 21.3 for details. (3) Move backwards and evaluate the decision point in 1990. See Table 21.4 for details. Finally, compare and evaluate the schemes of the decision points in 1985. The results are listed in Table 21.5.

The results show that five development modes are available for coal production structure from 1980 to 2000 in a certain region. The economic effects of these five modes are the same:

Table 21.3 Calculation table for coal production structure decision making (not considering time factor)

Decision point / Z value / Decision point	13 (2:1:1)	14 (4:3:3)	15 (3:3:4)	Best structure order	Best structure
8	3,950,000,000 Yuan	3,110,000,000 Yuan	–	14	4:3:3
9	4,580,000,000 Yuan	3,740,000,000 Yuan	2,860,000,000 Yuan	15	3:3:4
10	–	4,400,000,000 Yuan	3,520,000,000 Yuan	15	3:3:4
11	5,000,000,000 Yuan	4,160,000,000 Yuan	3,280,000,000 Yuan	15	3:3:4
12	3,980,000,000 Yuan	3,140,000,000 Yuan	–	14	4:3:3

Table 21.4 Calculation table for coal production structure decision making (not considering time factor)

Decision point Z value Decision point	8 (2:11:1)	9 (4:3:3)	10 (3:3:4)	11 (1:1:1)	12 (5:2:3)	Best structure order	Best structure
3	6,270,000,000 Yuan	5,390,000,000 Yuan	–	–	6,270,000,000 Yuan	9	4:3:3 4:3:3
4	6,730,000,000 Yuan	5,850,000,000 Yuan	5,850,000,000 Yuan	5,850,000,000 Yuan	–	9,10,11	3:3:4 1:1:1
5	–	–	–	–	–	–	–
6	–	–	–	–	–	–	–
7	6,290,000,000 Yuan	5,410,000,000 Yuan	–	–	6,290,000,000 Yuan	9	4:3:3

Table 21.5 Calculation table for coal production structure decision making (not considering time factor)

Decision point / Z value / Decision point	3 (2:1:1)	4 (4:3:3)	7 (5:2:3)	Best structure order	Best structure
2	7,730,000,000 Yuan	7,730,000,000 Yuan	7,730,000,000 Yuan	3,4,7	2:1:1 4:3:3 5:2:3

$$1 \to 2 \to 3 \to 9 \to 15$$
$$1 \to 2 \to 4 \to 9 \to 15$$
$$1 \to 2 \to 4 \to 10 \to 15$$
$$1 \to 2 \to 4 \to 11 \to 15$$
$$1 \to 2 \to 7 \to 9 \to 15$$

If the time factor is considered, the development mode for coal production structure with the best economic effect is $1 \to 2 \to 4 \to 10 \to 15$, or 55%:20%:25% → 48%:22%:30% → 40%:30%:30% → 30%:30%:40% → 30%:30%:40%.

21.4.3 Network Plan Figure

Making a network plan and drawing a network plan figure are adopted to optimize construction time when engineering projects are constructed. There are several schemes in a network plan figure. The goal of a network plan figure is to select the best scheme, namely the feasible work schedule for construction, with the best economic effect. Here are the steps: first, break down the working procedure and develop a procedure list. Second, set the period or the average period for each process in the procedure. Third, assign order numbers for all processes and analyze the logical relationship among the processes. Fourth, make a process list. Fifth, draw an initial network plan figure. Sixth, optimize the network plan figure.

21.5 Analysis Method and Its Application

The analysis method is an approach that corresponds to the comprehensive method. It is widely applied in many disciplines, including in the technological economy. In particular, system analysis is applied in the evaluation methods for the macro technological economy. This section introduces some analysis methods for technological economy evaluation in uncertain conditions, among them technological economy factor analysis, economic critical value analysis, economic safety coefficient analysis, min–max (or max–min) analysis, and max-max (or min-min) analysis.

21.5.1 Technological Economy Factor Analysis

The uncertainty of the parameters in the technological economy causes the uncertainty of the economic effect of technological schemes. Technological economy factor analysis analyzes and calculates the impact of the uncertainty of the parameters in the technological economy on the economic effect and further selects the reasonable economic technological schemes. This method has two approaches: single-factor analysis and multiple-factor analysis. Here are the steps: first, find those uncertain parameters. Second, estimate the range of the values of these parameters. Third, load these values into the economic effect evaluation formula for better and more economical results. Conduct the calculation. Find the value of the impact of the uncertainty of the parameters in the technological economy on economic effect based on the result of calculation. Fourth, select the best-fit technological scheme based on the value of impact. Three approaches can be adopted for estimating the range of the values of uncertain parameters: conservative estimation, high-middle-low estimation, and high-side estimation. In practice, the high-middle-low estimation is applied more frequently than the other two approaches. Technological economy factor analysis can find those factors whose changes affect the economic effect of the technological scheme the most (or those who are the most sensitive to the economic effect of the technological scheme), and those whose changes affect the economic effect of technological scheme the least (or which are the least sensitive to the economic effect of technological scheme). Thus, technological economy factor analysis is also called technological economy sensibility analysis. Technological economy factor analysis is applied widely in practice. Here is an example, in which three technological schemes regarding coal exploitation (state-owned, region-owned, and local-owned coal mines) are evaluated with technological economy factor analysis.

In this example, the coal price, the investment on coal per ton, the cost, and the construction period are four uncertain factors. The range of their value change is between −25 and 25% (see Table 21.6). Calculate the values of the social net income. The values are listed in Table 21.6. According to the values, draw the technological economy factor analysis figure (see Fig. 21.4). Table 21.6 and Fig. 21.4 show that order of the impacts of these factors includes coal price, investment, cost, and construction period. The impact of the construction period on state-owned coal mines is the largest, compared with those on region-owned and local-owned coal mines. Overall, the social net income of state-owned mines is negative, whereas those of region-owned and local-owned coal mines are positive.

Table 21.6 Technological economy factor analysis table

Scheme	Factors	Middle scheme	Coal price		Investment		Cost		Construction period	
			25%	−25%	25%	−25%	25%	−25%	25%	−25%
State-owned coal mines	Coal price (Yuan/ton)	40	50	30	40	40	40	40	40	40
	Investment (Yuan/ton)	100	100	100	125	75	100	100	100	100
	Cost (Yuan/ton)	20	20	20	22	18	25	15	20	20
	Construction period (Year)	8	8	8	8	8	8	8	10	6
	Social net income (Yuan/ton)	−11.7	−1.7	−21.7	−21.6	−5.7	−16.7	−6.7	−18	−6.5
Region-owned coal mines	Coal price (Yuan/ton)	40	50	30	40	40	40	40	40	40
	Investment (Yuan/ton)	40	40	40	50	30	40	40	40	40
	Cost (Yuan/ton)	16	16	16	18	14	20	12	16	16

(continued)

Table 21.6 (continued)

Scheme	Factors	Middle scheme	Coal price		Investment		Cost		Construction period	
			25%	−25%	25%	−25%	25%	−25%	25%	−25%
	Construction period (Year)	3	3	3	3	3	3	3	4	2
	Social net income (Yuan/ton)	16.5	26.5	6.5	12.6	20.4	12.5	20.5	15.8	17.1
Local-owned coal mines	Coal price (Yuan/ton)	40	50	30	40	40	40	40	40	40
	Investment (Yuan/ton)	36	36	36	45	27	36	36	36	36
	Cost (Yuan/ton)	14	14	14	15	13	17.5	11.5	14	14
	Construction period (Year)	2	2	2	2	2	2	2	3	1
	Social net income (Yuan/ton)	19.8	29.8	9.8	17.2	22.4	16.3	22.3	19.2	20.3

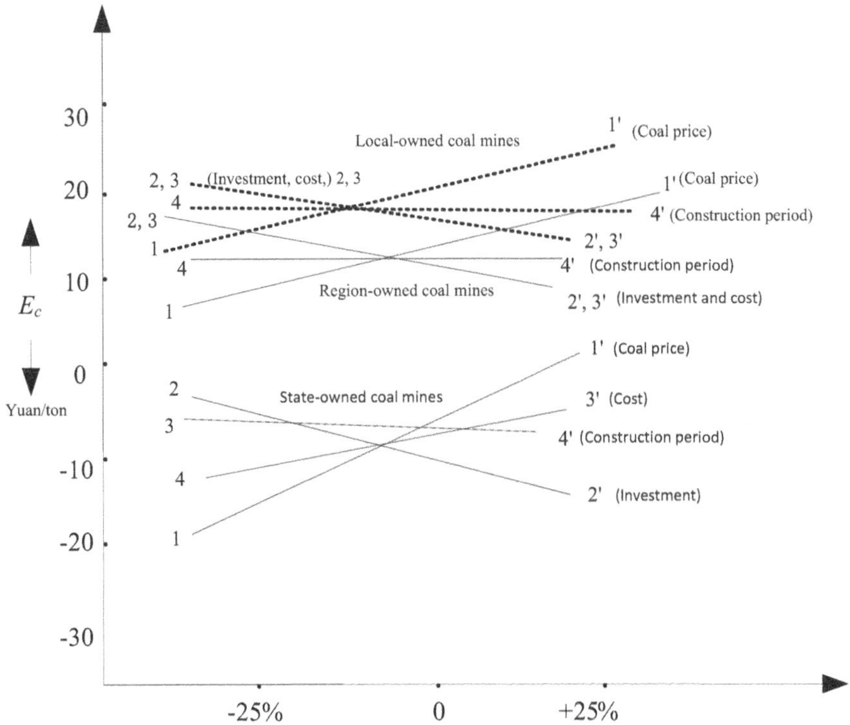

Fig. 21.4 Technological economy factor analysis

21.5.2 Economy Critical Value Analysis

Economy critical value analysis can be used for analyzing the impact of the uncertainty of a certain technological economy parameter on the economic effect of technological schemes. When the cost and the benefit of a technological scheme are equal, the value of a certain technological economy parameter is an economy critical value. This value can be used for analyzing the uncertainty of this parameter on the economic effect of technological schemes. The economy critical value is the cut-off point, which can be used for assessing the economic effect of technological schemes. When the value of a parameter is larger than this point, a technological scheme is not economical. When the value of a parameter is smaller than this point, a technological scheme is economical. Here are the steps for calculating economy critical values:

(1) Analysis of the absolute economic effect of technological schemes

The absolute economic effect of technological schemes is determined by benefit S and cost $Z(Z_u)$. Benefit and cost consist of over 40 technological economic parameters. Each parameter might be an uncertain value. If the benefit S and cost $Z(Z_u)$ of a technological scheme are set with the same value, the critical value of each parameter, such as the critical value of the price of inputs and outputs, the critical value of production, the critical value of cost, the critical value of investment, the critical value of construction period, the critical value of the period of investment recovery, the critical value of economic effect coefficients, the critical value of interest rate, and the critical value of tax, can be calculated. Here are the formulas:

$$S_{\sum} = Z_{\sum};\ S_{\sum} = Z_{u\sum};\ S_{\sum\_firm} = Z_{\sum\_firm}; \tag{21.1}$$

$$\text{or}\quad E_a, E_b, E_e = 1;\ E_c, E_d, E_f = 0 \tag{21.2}$$

Here is an example for calculating the critical value of investment economic coefficient, which is the (dynamic) investment net income rate, the investment national income rate, and the return on investment introduced in Chap. 19. They are the applications of economy critical value analysis in a technological economy evaluation. Next, let us calculate the critical value of X_t for *Scheme A* and *B*, namely (dynamic) investment net income rate, in (19.1).

(a) Find the investment net income rate for *Scheme A*

$$S_{\sum\_scheme\_A} = S_{scheme\_A}\frac{\theta^{n_j}-1}{(\theta-1)\theta^{n_j+n_k}} = f(xt) \tag{21.3}$$

$$Z_{\sum\_scheme\_A} = Z_{scheme\_A}\frac{\theta^{n_j}-1}{(\theta-1)\theta^{n_j+n_k}} = f(xt) \tag{21.4}$$

set $S_{scheme\_A} = Z_{scheme\_A}$, then

$$S_{scheme\_A} = C_{scheme\_A} + x_t T_{z\_scheme\_A} \tag{21.5}$$

$$T_{z\_scheme\_A} = T_{g1}\frac{\theta^{n_j+n_k}-1}{\theta^{n_j}-1} + T_1 - \frac{C_j-1}{\theta-1} + \frac{n_jC_j}{\theta^{n_j}-1} \tag{21.6}$$

Load Formula 21.6 into 21.5,

$$S_{scheme\_A} - C_{scheme\_A} + C_j - \left(x_tT_{g1}\frac{(1+x_t)^{n_j+n_k}-1}{(1+x_t)^{n_j}-1} + x_tT_l + x_t\frac{n_jC_j}{(1+x_t)^{n_j}-1}\right) = 0 \tag{21.7}$$

where x_t is unknown and all other values are known. A trial and error procedure and the graphic method can be applied to find the value of x_t in formula 21.7. Load the known valued into Formula 21.7 first.

$$E_{c\_scheme\_A} = 21 - \left(x_t 90\frac{(1+x_t)^{18}-1}{(1+x_t)^{15}-1} + x_t 5 + x_t\frac{90}{(1+x_t)^{15}-1}\right) = 0 \tag{21.8}$$

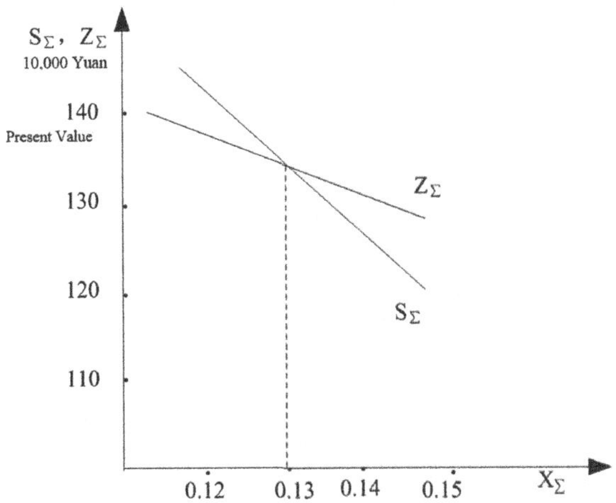

Fig. 21.5 Figure method for finding dynamic investment net income rate

Next, calculate the static investment net income rate $\frac{30-15}{95}$ =0.158. In the investment recovery coefficient table, the number close to 0.158 is 0.15 in the line where the calculation period is 15 years. The corresponding x_t has the value 0.125. Load this value as the first trial value into Formula 21.8 and get the value of $E_{c\_scheme\_A}$ 50,000 Yuan, which is larger than zero. Load x_t again with the value 0.15 and get the value of $E_{c\_scheme\_A}$ −120,000 Yuan, which is smaller than zero. Thus, the value of $x_{t\_scheme\_A,}$ 13.3%, can be got with the interpolation method. Or load the value of x_t into Formulas 21.3 and 21.4 and get $S_\sum$ and $Z_\sum$. Then draw a line for $S_\sum(x_t)$ and a line for $Z_\sum(x_t)$. The $x_t$of the intersection of the two lines is the economy critical value (see Fig. 21.5), namely the investment income rate. According to Fig. 21.5, $x_{t\_scheme\_A}$ is 13.3%. This indicates that the two methods generate the same result. The dynamic investment net income rate for *Scheme A* is 13.3%.

(b) Find the investment net income rate for *Scheme B*

The investment net income rate for *Scheme B* can be calculated with the methods introduced above. The value of $x_{t\_scheme\_B}$ is 14.9%.

The results of this calculation show that *Scheme B* is more economical than *Scheme A*.

The methods introduced above can be applied for calculating the dynamic investment net income rate, the investment national income rate, and the return-on-investment in common conditions. However, in certain conditions, the dynamic investment net income rate, the investment national income rate, and the return-on-investment cannot be calculated or have multiple values. When the static investment net income rate of technological schemes is negative, the lines of $S_\sum$ and $Z_\sum$ will never cross, no matter how x_t changes. Accordingly, the dynamic investment net income rate x_t of technological schemes is not available for calculating (see Fig. 21.6a). In certain conditions, the lines of $S_\sum$ and $Z_\sum$ have two intersections,

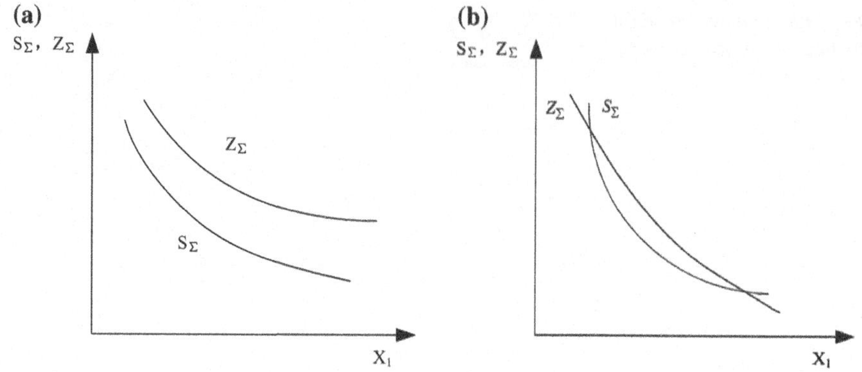

Fig. 21.6 No solution and multiple solutions for x_t

namely two values for x_t (see Fig. 21.6b). These values of x_t should not be adopted because they do not match the fact. The reasons are explained in the following example.

The income and expenditure of a technological scheme in six years are listed in Table 21.7. What is the capital profit rate of this scheme?

Set i as 0.1, 0.15, 0.35, 0.5, 0.65, and 0.8 and find the present value of their profits. According to Table 21.7, when the profit is zero, the values of i are 0.35 and 0.65. Actually, these two values are both on the high side. They do not match the fact. Thus, adjustments need to apply. Here is the procedure. The reason why there are two solutions available for x_t is because the annual total profit change from positive values to negative values more than once. In this case, a positive value changes to a negative one and then changes back to a positive one. Thus, the annual profit needs to be processed with the minimal value of l_b set by the states. The total profit can only change once in one year. Then the value of l when the total profit is zero can be calculated with the time factor considered via converting the present value or time value. In this example, set l_b as 0.15. Convert the profit of the first year with the time value into the profit in the second year $500 \times 1.15 = 5{,}750{,}000$ Yuan. Combine this value with the original profit in the second year −10,000,000 Yuan and get −

Table 21.7 The income and expenditure of a technological scheme in six years

Year	Income (10,000 Yuan)	Expenditure (10,000 Yuan)	Profit (10,000 Yuan)	Total Profit (10,000 Yuan)
1	600	100	+500	+500
2	700	1700	−1000	−500
3	800	800	0	−500
4	1000	750	+250	−250
5	1000	750	+250	0
6	1000	750	+250	+250

4,250,000 Yuan. In this way, the annual total profit changes from positive to negative only once. The capital utilization rate i can be calculated with the present value conversion method and its value is 0.214, which is more accurate than 0.35 and 0.65. The value of i gotten with this adjustment is related to the adopted minimum value of i_b and the values of profits in the years when the adjustment are applied. The smaller the adjusted profit and the closer the adopted value of i_b to the achieved value, the more accurate the achieved value.

Here is another example. The annual economic benefit of a firm is S. The annual consumption cost is Z. S and Z are related to the production and sale volume G. Use economy critical value analysis to analyze the production of this firm. First, set several values for G. Calculate S and Z with the excess profit formula. Draw the lines for the relationship between S and G, as well as between Z and G. The intersection of the two lines is the economy critical value when S equals Z. If the future production and sale volume is larger than the critical value, the operation of this firm is economical. Otherwise, the operation of this firm is not economical (see Fig. 21.7).

(2) Analysis of the relative economic effect of technological schemes

When the social national income, the social net income, and the firm profit of two technological schemes are the same, the difference between their total economic benefits equals the difference between their total costs, and their total economic benefits are the same, or their total costs are the same, the following formula can be applied to calculate the economy critical value of parameters for technological schemes.

$$\Delta S_{\sum} = \Delta Z_{\sum};\ \Delta S_{\sum} = \Delta S_{u\sum};\ \Delta S_{\sum\_firm} = \Delta Z_{\sum\_firm}; \tag{21.9}$$

$$\text{or} \quad E_{af}, E_{bf}, E_{ef} = 1;\ E_{cf}, E_{df}, E_{ff} = 0 \tag{21.10}$$

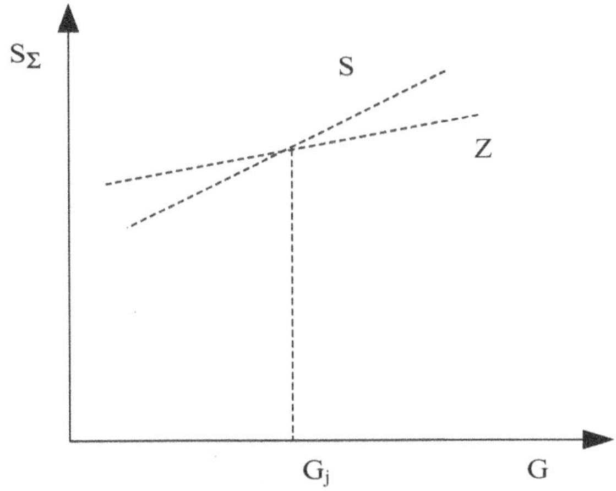

Fig. 21.7 Economy critical value analysis

Fig. 21.8 Maximum investment on energy-saving

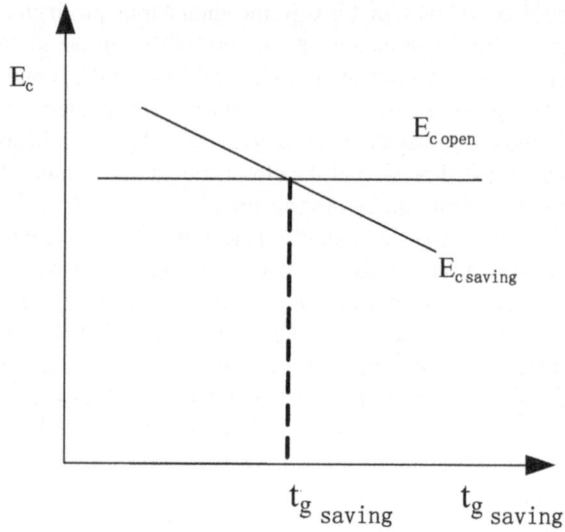

Here is an example. There are two technological schemes. One aims to save energy, whereas the other aims to find more resources. The indicators of the scheme for more resources are known. One uncertain factor for the energy-saving scheme is the investment on energy saving. The question is what is the investment on one ton of coal for energy saving when the energy-saving scheme is economical. Let us apply the economy critical value analysis to find the answer. First, apply the social net income method to calculate the social net incomes for these two schemes $E_{c\_more\_sources}$ and $E_{c\_energy\_saving}$. Set $E_{c\_more\_sources}$ to equal $E_{c\_energy\_saving}$. Then the maximum energy-saving investment on one ton of coal can be calculated. This value is the economy critical value for energy-saving investment. If the actual investment on saving one ton of coal is smaller than the critical value, the energy-saving scheme is economical. Otherwise, the energy-saving scheme is not economical (see Fig. 21.8).

21.5.3 Economic Security Coefficient Analysis

Some technological schemes are risky, such as oil exploration and technology testing. To deal with the risk, the economic security coefficient analysis can be applied. Based on the size of the risk, select the appropriate economic effect security coefficients $k_{security}$ (>1). For instance, the initially set investment net income rate (or investment national income rate) is x_t. With risks considered, the value of x_t should be increased $k_{security}$ times. The larger the risk, the larger $k_{security}$. If the values of social net income E_c or social national income E_d of a technological scheme are larger than zero with risks considered (economic effect security coefficients are adopted), the technological scheme is economical. This method is easy, but the challenge is how to set the values of the economic effect security coefficients according to the size of the risks.

21.5.4 Min-Max (or Max-Min) Analysis and Max-Max (or Min-Min) Analysis

The values of the economic effects of three technological schemes in different conditions are known (see Table 21.8). The probabilities of these economic effects are unknown. In this case, min–max (or max–min) analysis and max-max (or min-min) analysis can be adopted to assess technological schemes.

(1) Min–max (or max–min) analysis. Table 21.8 lists the values of social net income E_c. Each scheme has three values. Min–max analysis chooses the smallest value from the economic effects of the three schemes first (-3, -1, 0 in Table 21.8), and then selects the one with the largest value of economic effect from the rest of the schemes. The result of min–max analysis in this example is *Scheme C*. In contrast, max–min analysis chooses the largest value from the economic effects of the three schemes first, and then selects the one with the smallest value of economic effect from the rest schemes. Essentially, min–max analysis and max–min analysis select the relatively better schemes in the worst situations.
(2) Max-max (or min-min) analysis. Max-max analysis chooses the best from the best technological schemes. In Table 21.8, the largest values are 2, 4, and 3. *Scheme B* is selected because its value is the largest. Min-min analysis chooses the scheme with the smallest social total consumption cost first, and then further selects the scheme with the smallest cost.

21.6 Applications of Mathematics Methods

Mathematics is applied widely and plays a crucial role in the technological economy. Mathematics and calculation methods commonly applied in the technological economy include general mathematics, differentiation, matrices, operational research, probability theory, mathematical statistics, the convergence method, and computers. Because applications of general mathematics (addition, subtraction, subtraction, division, and algebra) in technological economy are easy, this chapter does not discuss them. Instead, this chapter focuses on the applications of other mathematical methods.

Table 21.8 The values of economic effects of three technological schemes

Status Scheme	A	B	C
1	2	0	−3
2	4	−1	2
3	1	3	0

21.6.1 Applications of Optimized Method

Many technological economic issues in production fall into the category of the second format of technological economy formula, such as selecting the best formulation of raw materials, the best technology conditions, and the best technological parameters (temperature, flowrate, pressure, speed, dimension, and intensity). To find the solutions for these issues, several rounds of testing calculations are needed. Then, based on the results, the indicators of economic effect are further calculated. At last, the indicators are compared for selecting the technological scheme with the best economic effect. Optimized methods, such as 0.619 method, the bisection method, the fraction method, and the blind person climbing method, can reduce the number of technological schemes that need testing. Because one can quickly find the technological scheme with the best economic effect using optimized methods, the optimized method is the best approach for working with technological economic issues regarding mass production. It has been promoted by Hua Luogeng, a well-known Chinese mathematician. So far, a number of technological economic issues have been resolved with the help of the optimized method. Thus, the optimized method is well received and has generated a huge economic effect.

21.6.2 Applications of Mathematical Analysis

Differentiation is the main method of mathematical analysis. It is mainly applied to resolve the second format of economic formulas, in which the economic indicators of technological schemes have a mathematical relation with two types of parameters. There is only one parameter that represents a technological scheme. Technological schemes change with the change of this parameter. Differentiation is the method used to select technological schemes with the largest economic effect by finding the solutions for this type of formulas. Here is an example of selecting economic intersecting surface for power lines:

First, according to the construction and operation of power lines, select the annual consumption cost method. Because the change of intersecting surface of power lines does not cause the change of land occupation and labor occupation, the two cost items $x_r R$ and $x_d D$ are not considered. In addition, there is no need to calculate the cost items $x_w W$ and $x_y Y$. Accordingly, the economic indicator that impacts the economic effect of a technological scheme for power line is the total consumption cost Z_l.

$$Z_l = C_l + x_t T_{zl} \tag{21.11}$$

where T_{zl} is the covert investment cost for power line. C_l is the annual cost for power transmission. x_t is the effect coefficient for capital.

The investment in power lines consists of two parts. The first part $t_s \bullet S$ is the portion related with the intersecting surface of power lines. t_s is the investment in one kilometer power line with the intersecting surface of one square millimeter. S is the intersecting surface of the power line. The other part t_l is the portion unrelated with the thickness of power line. t_l is the cost of the insulators and towers required for one kilometer power line. As such, the investment of power lines can be calculated with the following formula:

$$T_{gl} = (t_l + t_s \bullet S)L \tag{21.12}$$

where L is the length of power line.

The investment occupation of power line decreases yearly with the recovery of basic depreciation. Thus, a portion of cost needs to be subtracted from the fixed investment on power line when calculating the economic effect of the occupied investment by power line. This portion of cost can be calculated with the following formula:

$$T_{jl} = C_{jl} \sum_{s=1}^{n_j} \frac{\theta^{n_j - s} - 1}{\theta^{n_j} - 1} \tag{21.13}$$

where $C_{jl} = l_j T_{gl}$.

Set $k_j = \sum_{s=1}^{n_j} \frac{\theta^{n_j - s} - 1}{\theta^{n_j} - 1}$ and load k_j into formula 21.13.

$$T_{jl} = l_j k_j T_{gl} \tag{21.14}$$

If the cost for current capital is not considered in the calculation, the convert investment cost of power line is:

$$T_{jl} = \left(1 - l_j k_j\right)(t_l + t_s S)L \tag{21.15}$$

The annual cost of the power line consists of three portions. The first portion is the depreciation of power line $C_z = l_z T_{gl}$. lz is the comprehensive depreciation rate of power line. The second portion is electricity loss of power line $C_n = j_g \frac{3I^2 r \Upsilon L}{1000S}$. I is the maximum load current of power line. r is the unit resistance of power line. Υ is the number of hours of the maximum loss. j_g is the price of power per unit. The third portion is the other operation costs of power line C_q, including wages and a small repair fee. The annual cost of power line can then be calculated as below.

$$Cl = Cz + Cn + Cq = lz(tl + tsS)L + \frac{3I^2 r \Upsilon L}{1000S} jg + Cq \tag{21.16}$$

Load formula 21.15 and 21.16 into 21.11. The yearly total consumption cost for the power line is:

$$Z_l = C_l + x_t\,T_{zl} = (x_t - x_t l_j k_j + l_z)(t_l + t_s S)L + \frac{3I^2 r \Upsilon L}{1000S} j_g + Cq = f(S) \tag{21.17}$$

In order to get the most economical intersecting surface of power lines, it is necessary to take the derivative on S with formula 21.7. The differential coefficient for S is zero.

$$\frac{dZ_l}{dS} = (x_t - x_t l_j k_j + l_z)t_s L - \frac{3I^2 r \Upsilon L}{1000S^2} j_g = 0$$

Thus, the most economical intersecting surface of power lines is

$$Sj = \sqrt{\frac{3I^2 r \Upsilon j_g}{1000(x_t - x_t l_j k_j + l_z)t_s}} \tag{21.18}$$

Now, it is known that the voltage of a power line is 35,000 V. Its maximum load current I is 100 amperes. Its maximum loss hour Υ is 5,000 h. The power line is made of aluminum. Its unit resistance r is 31.5 ohms/mm^2/km. Its lost power price j_g is 4 cents/KWH. The unit cost of power line t_s is 85 Yuan/mm^2/ km. The comprehensive depreciation rate is 0.026. The basic depreciation rate is 0.02. x_t is 0.15. k_j is 4.56. Load these values into formula 21.18 and learn that the most economical and reasonable intersecting surface for this power line S_j is 116 mm^2.

It can be seen from Formula 21.18 that the value of the intersecting surface of a power line is closely related with loss power price and the maximum loss hour. The value of the intersecting surface of a power line changes with the variance of region, the system loading mode, the loss power price, and the maximum loss hour. Thus, the relationship between the intersecting surface of a power line and the loss power price as well as maximum loss hour.

A matrix is mainly adopted in applications of input and output method in the technological economy. Input and output method is important for studying the connection among the departments of national economy and for developing comprehensive plans with all of the stakeholders considered. In particular, the input and output table can be used for predicting production, consumption, and possible savings, and for calculating standard coefficients for the economic effect.

21.6.3 Applications of Operational Research

Operational research is appropriate for finding the solutions of the third type of economic formulas, which represent technological schemes with multiple parameters. There are several parameters that affect the economic effect of technological schemes. A mathematical function relationship exists between these parameters and the indicators of economic effect. Accordingly, operational research is mainly applied for solving complicated technological economic issues, which can be usually converted into mathematic models.

Several approaches of operational research are adopted in the technological economy, including linear programming, non-linear programming, static programming, and dynamic programming.

Here is an example of programming technological schemes regarding energy balance. The programming of technological schemes for energy balance is very important for a state or a region. The programming is related to the development of the national economy, the utilization of energy, energy users, energy exploitation, production, transportation, and utilization, the condition of energy, the utilization level of energy, the import and export of energy, and the supply of materials and labor. Programming energy balance needs to resolve the following issues: the total need of energy, the need of energy for different usages, the most reasonable energy for each usage, the amount of energy, the allocation of energy between regions and inside each region, the amount of available local energy (including straw), the reasonable outer energy supply, and the amount of external energy. In a region with a lack of energy, such as the eastern area of China, the supply of energy relies on outside resources other than on local production. The balance for power for this region has been studied. Now programming is needed to balance fuel. According to the requirements of the programming, here is the mathematical model:

1. The following conditions are from surveys.

m—This region is divided into m sub-regions ($j - 1, 2, \ldots, m$);

s—The number of users in each sub-region ($k - 1, 2, \ldots, s$);

n—The number of energy categories ($i - 1, 2, \ldots, n$);

i—The number of schemes regarding each user chooses each type of energy ($p - 1, 2, \ldots, i$);

d—The number of energy production sites in a region ($l - 1, 2, \ldots, d$);

e—The number of outer regions that supply this region energy ($r - 1, 2, \ldots, e$);

G_{kj}—The production plan of final products for user k in region j;

w_{ipkj}—Energy i required by scheme p for user k in region j;

W_{il}—The amount of energy i produced by local energy site l;

W_{ir}—The amount of energy i supplied by outer regions;

z_{pkj}—The total consumption cost of scheme p implemented by user k in region j;

z_{il}—The unit energy consumption cost (Yuan/ton) of energy i produced by local energy site l;

z_{ilj}—The unit energy consumption cost (Yuan/ton) of energy i transported from local energy site l to region j;

z_{il}—The unit energy consumption cost (Yuan/ton) of energy i produced by region r;

z_{irj}—The unit energy consumption cost (Yuan/ton) of energy i transported from region$r$ to region j;

2. The unknown values in these issues:

X_{pkj}—The ratio (%) of scheme p implemented by user k in region j;

X_{ikj}—The amount of energy i required by user k in region j;

X_{ikj}—The amount of energy i provided by energy site k and utilized by region j;

X_{irj}—The amount of energy i produced by energy region$r$ and transported to region j;

3. List the constraint conditions based on the known conditions.

(1) The amount of energy transported from outer regions should not exceed that produced by local sites.

$$\sum_{j=1}^{m} X_{irj} \leq W_{ir} \tag{21.19}$$

(2) The amount of utilized energy produced by local sites should not exceed the production capability.

$$\sum_{j=1}^{m} X_{ilj} \leq W_{il} \tag{21.20}$$

(3) The amount of final product of user k in region j must be produced as planned.

$$\sum_{p=1}^{t} G_{pkj} X_{pkj} \leq G_{kj} \tag{21.21}$$

$$\sum_{j=1}^{t} X_{pkj} = 1 \tag{21.22}$$

(4) The amount of energy i required by user k to produce final products.

$$X_{ikj} = \sum_{p=1}^{t} X_{irj} X_{ipkj} \tag{21.23}$$

(5) The amount of energy i required by user k in region j cannot exceed that provided by local sites and suppliers from outer regions.

$$\sum_{l=1}^{d} X_{ilj} + \sum_{r=1}^{e} X_{irj} - \sum_{k=1}^{s} X_{ijk} = 0 \tag{21.24}$$

(6) $X_{pkj} > 0$, $X_{ikj} \geq 0$, $X_{ilj} \geq 0$, $X_{irj} \geq 0$.

4. Because all of the schemes regarding energy balance aim to meet the local requirements, the total consumption cost $Z_{\sum}$ is the target. The target function is:

$$Z_{\sum} = \sum_{j=1}^{m} [\sum_{k=1}^{s} \sum_{p=1}^{t} X_{pkj} zi_{pkj} + \sum_{l=1}^{d} \sum_{l=1}^{n} X_{tlj}(z_{il} + z_{ilj}) + \sum_{r=1}^{e} \sum_{i=1}^{n} X_{irj}(z_{tr} + z_{irj})] = ZX \tag{21.25}$$

where the first portion is the cost of energy utilization. The second portion is the cost of producing and allocating local energy. The third portion is the cost of energy from the outer regions. The best scheme for energy balance is the solution for Formula 21.25, when $Z_{\sum}$ has the minimum value.

The practical issues above can be summarized into this non-linear regression: set$g_i(X) \geq 0$ and $i = 1, 2, \ldots m$. Find the minimum value of $F(X) = F(x_1, x_2, \ldots x_n)$. Because this regression is complicated, a computer is adopted to conduct the calculation. There are many methods for finding the solutions for non-linear regressions,[1] such as using linear regressions approaching non-linear regression, converting non-linear regressions into unconstrained extrema, the network method, random testing, the saddle-point method, the complex method, the feasible direction method, the projected gradient method, and the simple gradient method. For each of these methods, a main programming block diagram needs to be drawn first. Calculation can then be implemented, based on the diagram, with computers. For conciseness, these methods are not introduced here. Please refer to other resources for the details.

21.6.4 Applications of Probability Theory and Mathematical Statistics

In the technological economy, probability theory and mathematical statistics are applied to gather materials and data in certain situations. Particularly, for some technological economic issues that aim for finding reasonable materials and data, probability theory and mathematical statistics should be used. Here are some examples of applications.

[1][Xi78]

The following are methods of probability theory and mathematical statistics applied for technological economic evaluation in uncertain conditions.

(1) The technological economic expected value method. This method applies an expected value for comparing technological schemes. Suppose G is an uncertain parameter in the technological economy. It might have j different values, which are denoted as G_j. The probability of each value is p_j. Because G has different values, the economic indicator E has different values as well. The values are denoted as E_{jk} or E_{kd}. The expected values (or the distribution average) of technological schemes can be calculated with the following formulas:

$$Q(Ec) = \sum_{j=1}^{n} E_{cj} P_j(E_{cj}) \tag{21.26}$$

Or

$$Q(Ed) = \sum_{j=1}^{n} E_{dj} P_j(E_{dj}) \tag{21.27}$$

where

$$\sum_{j=1}^{n} P_j(E_{cj}) = 1.$$

$$\sum_{j=1}^{n} P_j(E_{dj}) = 1.$$

Suppose a technological scheme has two uncertain parameters G and c. The value of G is denoted as G_j with corresponding probability p_j. The value of c is denoted as c_k with corresponding probability p_k. The expected value of this technological scheme is

$$Q(Ec) = \sum_{j=1}^{n} \sum_{k=1}^{m} E_{cjk} P_j(E_{cjk}) P_k(E_{cjk}) \tag{21.28}$$

or

$$Q(Ed) = \sum_{j=1}^{n} \sum_{k=1}^{m} E_{djk} P_j(E_{djk}) P_k(E_{djk}) \tag{21.29}$$

Table 21.9 Two technological schemes with one uncertain parameter

Sales and probability	Good sales (0.6)	Bad sales (0.4)
E_C		
Scheme		
A	50	−10
B	40	20

where

$$\sum_{k=1}^{m} P_k\left(E_{cjk}\right) = 1.$$

$$\sum_{k=1}^{m} P_k\left(E_{djk}\right) = 1.$$

Based on expected values, technological schemes can be compared. The one with the largest expected value is the best technological scheme.

Here is an example. There are two technological schemes which have different economic scales but which produce the same products. Sales of the products are uncertain. The probability of good sales is 0.6, whereas that of bad sales is 0.4. Based on the sales, investment, cost, and price of these two schemes, the social net income E_d and E_d of a unit of product in different sale conditions can be calculated with social net income method (see Table 21.9). Which technological scheme is more economical?

Because the economic scales of these two schemes are different, social net income is chosen as the indicator in this example. The expected values per unit of these two schemes can be calculated with Formula 21.6.

$$\begin{aligned} Q_1(E_c) &= 0.6 \times 50 + 0.4 \times (-10) = 26 \text{ Yuan/t} \\ Q_2(E_c) &= 0.6 \times 40 + 0.4 \times 20 = 32 \text{ Yuan/t} \end{aligned}$$

The expected value of *Scheme B* is larger than that of *Scheme A*. Thus, *Scheme B* is more economical.

Here is another example. In this one, most parameters are the same as those in the above example and sales and cost are uncertain parameters. The probabilities of the uncertain parameters and the net social net income are listed in Table 21.10. Which scheme is more economical?

The expected values of social net income of these two technological schemes can be calculated with Formula 21.8.

$$\begin{aligned} Q_1(E_c) &= 0.6 \times 0.7 \times 50 + 0.4 \times 0.7 \times (-10) + 0.6 \times 0.3 \times 60 + 0.4 \times 0.3 \times 0 = 29 \text{ Yuan/t} \\ Q_2(E_c) &= 0.6 \times 0.7 \times 40 + 0.4 \times 0.7 \times 20 + 0.6 \times 0.3 \times 50 + 0.3 \times 0.4 \times 30 = 35 \text{ Yuan/t} \end{aligned}$$

Table 21.10 Two technological schemes with two uncertain parameters

Scheme and probability	Scheme A		Scheme B	
E_c				
Scheme and probability	Good sales (0.6)	Bad sales(0.4)	Good sales (0.6)	Bad sales (0.4)
High cost (0.7)	50	−10	40	20
Low cost (0.3)	60	0	50	30

Therefore, *Scheme B* is more economical.

Based on the probability of technological economic parameters P_j (E_{cj}) and the expected values $Q(E_{dfd})$, variance and standard deviation can be calculated.

$$\sigma^2 = \sum_{j=1}^{n} (E_{cj})^2 \times P_j E_{cj} - [Q(E_{cj})]^2. \tag{21.30}$$

where σ is variance and σ^2 is standard deviation.

If the values of the economic effects of technological schemes form a normal distribution, the normal distribution curve of the probabilities of economic effects can be drawn based on known expected values and standard deviations. Once expected values, standard deviations, and the probability distribution curve are known, technological schemes can be compared. For example, the expected values of social net income for two technological schemes are known, *Scheme A* 8,000,000 Yuan and *Scheme B* 10,000,000 Yuan. It seems that *Scheme B* is more economical. But if the standard deviation of *Scheme B* is large while that of *Scheme A* is small, it might be better to choose *Scheme A* because the probability loss of *Scheme A* is smaller.

(2) The technological economic simulation method. This method is also called Monte Carlo method. It has three steps: (a) Assign a random number to the probability of each uncertain parameter for technological schemes based on the value of the probability. (b) Select a group of random numbers from the random number table (Table 21.14) or from other resources. The larger the group of random numbers, the better. Take this group of random numbers as the values of economic effect. Calculate the average of this group and get the simulated value of economic effect. (c) Compare technological schemes based on the simulated values. The technological scheme with the largest simulated value is the best one.

Here is an example. There are two technological schemes. Their social net incomes are related with some parameters. Because these parameters are uncertain, their social net incomes are uncertain as well. Their social net incomes and corresponding probabilities are listed in Table 21.11. Compare these two schemes with technological economic simulation method.

Here are the steps of finding the solutions: (a) Assign random numbers to the probabilities of social net income for these two schemes (see Tables 21.12 and 21.13).

Table 21.11 Social net income and the corresponding probability of two technological schemes

Scheme A		Scheme B	
Social net income E_{c1} (Yuan)	Probability $P_1(E_{c1})$	Social net income E_{c2} (Yuan)	Probability $P_2(E_{c2})$
2,00,000	0.1	1,00,000	0.3
3,00,000	0.5	3,00,000	0.4
4,00,000	0.25	5,00,000	0.2
5,00,000	0.15	8,00,000	0.1

Table 21.12 Probability of social net income and the corresponding random number

Scheme A			Scheme B		
E_{c1} (Yuan)	Probability P_1	Random number	E_{c2} (Yuan)	Probability P_2	Random number
2,00,000	0.1	00–09	1,00,000	0.3	00–29
3,00,000	0.5	10–59	3,00,000	0.4	30–69
4,00,000	0.25	60–84	5,00,000	0.2	70–89
5,00,000	0.15	85–99	8,00,000	0.1	90–99

Table 21.13 Random numbers and corresponding values of social net income

Scheme A		Scheme B	
Random number	E_{c1}	Random number	E_{c2}
67	40	73	50
58	30	55	30
10	30	13	10
28	30	28	10
25	30	44	30
2	20	87	50
88	50	29	10
99	50	59	30
55	30	74	50
19	30	81	50

Note The random numbers are selected from Table 21.14

(b) Select two groups of random numbers. Find the values of social net income for the corresponding random number based on the correlated social net income and the random number in Table 21.13. For instance, the random number for *Scheme A* is 67. The corresponding E_{c1} is 400,000 Yuan. The average value for *Scheme A* is 340,000 Yuan and that for *Scheme B* is 320,000 Yuan. (c) According to the values of social net income of these two schemes, it can be seen that *Scheme A is* more economical.

Table 21.14 Random number table

48,867	33,971	29,768	13,151	56,644	49,193	93,469	43,252	14,006	47,173
32,267	69,746	113	51,336	36,551	56,310	85,793	53,453	9744	64,346
27,345	3196	33,877	35,032	98,054	48,358	21,788	98,862	67,491	42,221
55,753	5256	51,557	90,419	40,716	64,589	90,398	37,070	78,318	2918
93,124	50,675	4507	44,001	6365	77,897	84,566	99,600	67,985	49,133
98,658	86,583	97,433	1073	80,495	62,709	61,357	66,903	76,730	79,355
69,216	94,830	41,248	50,712	46,878	87,317	80,545	31,484	3195	14,755
17,901	30,815	78,360	78,260	67,866	42,304	7293	61,290	61,301	4815
88,124	21,868	14,942	25,893	72,695	56,231	18,918	72,534	86,737	77,792
83,464	36,749*	22,336	50,443	83,576	19,238	91,730	39,507	22,717	94,719
91,310	99,003	25,704	55,581	729	22,024	61,319	66,162	20,933	67,713
32,739	38,352	91,256	77,744	75,080	1492	90,984	63,090	53,087	41,301
7751	66,724	3290	56,386	6070	67,150	64,219	48,192	70,478	84,722
55,228	64,156	90,480	97,774	8055	4435	26,999	42,039	16,589	6757
89,013	51,781	81,116	24,383	95,569	97,247	44,437	36,293	29,967	16,088
51,828	81,819	81,038	89,146	39,192	89,470	76,331	56,420	14,527	34,828
59,783	85,454	93,327	6078	64,924	7271	77,563	92,710	42,183	12,380
80,267	47,103	90,556	16,128	41,490	7996	78,454	47,929	81,586	67,024
82,919	44,210	61,607	93,011	26,314	26,865	26,714	43,793	94,937	28,439
77,019	77,417	19,466	14,967	75,521	49,967	74,065	7946	27,881	1070
66,225	61,832	6242	40,093	40,800	76,849	29,929	18,988	10,888	40,344
98,534	12,777	84,601	56,336	34	85,939	32,438	9549	1855	40,550
63,175	70,789	51,345	43,723	6995	11,186	38,615	56,646	54,323	39,632
92,362	7011	9115	78,303	38,901	58,107	95,366	17,226	74,626	78,208
61,832	44,794	65,079	97,130	94,289	73,502	4857	68,855	47,045	6309
42,502	1646	88,493	48,207	1283	16,474	8864	68,322	92,454	19,287
89,733	86,230	4903	55,015	11,811	98,185	32,014	84,761	80,926	14,509
1336	66,633	26,015	66,768	24,846	321	73,118	15,802	13,549	41,335
72,623	56,083	65,799	88,934	87,274	19,417	84,807	90,877	76,472	52,145
74,004	68,388	4090	35,239	94,379	4456	7642	68,642	1026	43,810
9338	54,633	27,684	47,117	67,583	42,496	20,703	68,579	65,883	10,729
51,771	92,019	39,791	60,400	8585	60,680	28,841	9921	520	73,135
69,796	30,304	79,836	20,631	10,743	246	24,979	35,707	75,283	39,211
98,417	33,403	63,448	90,462	91,645	24,919	73,609	26,663	9380	30,515
56,150	18,324	43,011	2660	86,574	86,097	49,339	21,249	90,380	94,375
76,199	75,692	9063	72,999	94,672	69,128	39,046	15,379	98,450	9159
74,978	98,693	21,433	34,676	97,603	48,534	59,205	66,265	3561	83,075

(continued)

Table 21.14 (continued)

85,769	92,530	4407	53,725	96,963	19,395	16,193	51,018	70,333	12,094
63,819	65,669	38,960	74,631	39,650	39,419	93,707	51,365	46,302	26,134
18,892	43,134	19,619	43,200	49,613	50,904	73,502	19,519	11,667	53,294
32,855	17,190	61,587	80,411	22,827	38,852	51,952	47,785	34,952	93,574
29,435	96,277	53,583	92,804	5027	19,736	54,918	66,396	96,547	351
36,211	67,263	82,064	41,624	49,826	17,566	2476	79,368	28,831	2805
73,514	176	41,638	1420	31,850	41,380	11,643	6787	9011	88,924
90,895	93,099	27,850	29,423	98,693	71,762	39,928	35,268	59,359	20,674
69,719	90,656	62,186	50,435	77,015	29,661	94,698	56,057	4388	33,381
94,982	81,453	87,162	28,248	37,921	21,143	62,673	81,224	38,972	92,988
84,136	4211	72,790	4719	34,914	95,609	88,695	60,180	58,790	12,802
58,515	80,581	88,442	65,727	72,121	40,481	6001	13,159	55,324	93,591
20,681	59,164	75,797	8928	68,381	12,616	97,487	84,803	92,457	88,847

Source Engineering Economics, translated by Zhang Guoyang, etc. 1980.

21.7 Applications of Computers

As a modern calculation tool, computers are widely adopted in the technological economy. The main applications are listed below.

21.7.1 Calculation for Technological Economical Evaluation

Calculations in the aforementioned methods for the macro and micro technological economic evaluation can be implemented with computers. A program needs to be developed for each method. Once the program is ready, calculation results can be gotten after loading the data. For instance, the author develops computer programs for social net income method E_c and dynamic investment net income rate X_t. These programs are proven to be efficient and convenient by practice.

21.7.2 Finding Solutions for Technological Economy Models

Complicated technological schemes have many parameters, which consist of complicated technological economy models. In the past, when only manual calculation was available, some of these complicated models could not be resolved, while others cost a huge amount of time and effort. Now, as computers are available, complicated models can be resolved easily. Accordingly, computers will promote the applications of technological economy models, in practice. For example, the author has adopted computers in finding solutions for several technological economy models, such as the planning technological economic model for the energy base of Shanxi, the production balance technological economic model for coal production in Shanxi, and the technological economic model for coal washing in Shanxi.

21.7.3 Technological Economy Forecast

Applications of probability theory, mathematical statistics, and the analysis of input and output are introduced in the previous sections in this chapter. Calculations for these applications are rather complicated. Thus, computers are required to perform calculation for these applications.

21.7.4 Data Processing and Storage for Technological Economy

The technological economy requires huge amount of data. These data need to be processed and stored in databases, which are crucial for technological economy studies.

Computers will be adopted more and more widely in the ongoing technological economy studies.

21.8 Applications of Survey

In the technological economy, a survey is necessary to find problems, to understand problems, to collect data, to test theories, and to summarize experiences. A survey can be categorized into a general survey and a specialized survey. Different from general survey, a specialized survey in the technological economy is performed by experts in order to assess technological schemes from the perspectives of politics, the national defense, society, culture, technology, the environment, and resources, based on the rules. Usually, grading is applied in a specialized survey. Therefore, a specialized survey is called a survey consultation and grading method. The Delphi method is a well-known expert survey approach. Specialized surveys play an important role in the technological economy comprehensive evaluation. The techniques are introduced in the last chapter. Please refer to the corresponding sections for details.

Reference

Xi, S. L. and Zhao, F. Z. (1978). Calculation Methods for Optimization. Oriental Steam Turbine Factory Press.

Part IV
Applications of Technological Economics

Part I, II, and III discuss the overview of technological economics, theories of technological economics, and methods for technological economics, respectively. However, it is important to apply knowledge regarding technological economics in practice.

This part introduces the applications of technological economics. It consists of four parts. Part one presents both ways to find the solutions for technological economics issues and cases based on the theories and methods introduced in previous parts. However, the examples presented in this part are not from studies conducted by the author. Part two introduces studies conducted by the author at various times based on the requirements of the state. The results of these studies have all been adopted by the state or by related sectors and make contributions to the development of the economy and society in China. Some of the results have achieved crucial economic and social benefits. Thus, they have been selected as cases for the application of technological economics theories and methods. On one hand, these cases reflect the role that technological economics plays in the development of national economy. On the other hand, the achievements of the author's studies can be tested by the readers and can be further verified by time. Part three presents ten approaches for improving the economic effect, including the economic effect of firms at the micro-level and the economic effect of society at the macro-level. Part four is the last chapter of this book. In this chapter, the author initially proposes the concept of large management science and the new discipline of large technological economic management.

Chapter 22
Applications of Technological Economics Theories and Methods

22.1 Introduction

This chapter presents the solutions for technological economics issues in different types with different characteristics. The main goal of this chapter is to explain how to apply technological economics in practice. The 21 examples explained in this chapter are not studies conducted by the author.

22.2 Technological Economic Evaluation by Making Full Use of Local Advantages

Local advantages include economic advantages and non-economic advantages, condition advantages and effect advantages, small-scope advantages and large-scope advantages, natural advantages and man-made advantages. From the perspective of the technological economy, making full use of local advantages means giving full scope to local economic advantages, either small-scope or large-scope, natural or man-made. As long as local economic advantages bring good economic effects, they should be used fully. Thus, local advantages need both economic evaluation and comprehensive evaluation. The comprehensive evaluation methods and the methods for greater, faster, better, and more economical results can be adopted. Following is an example of economic evaluation on local advantages regarding the development of chestnut planting in Qianxi county, Hebei province. In this example, the social national income method is applied.

The natural conditions, including the soil, climate, and geographic location of Qianxi county, Hebei province are unique. The main crops produced in Qianxi county are sorghum, corn, and other minor cereals. One local product is chestnut. The quality of chestnut grown in Qianxi county is higher than those grown in Italy and Belgium. Chestnut grown in Qianxi county is mainly exported to Japan. Each year, supply falls short of demand. The research question in this example is whether it is needed

S. Xu, *Technological Economics*,
https://doi.org/10.1007/978-981-15-8582-1_22

to develop planting chestnut in Qianxi county. In other words, is planting chestnut a local advantage for Qianxi county? In order to conduct a technological economics comparison, some conditions need to be set. Suppose that there is a mu of dryland in hilly. The soil is good for crops and chestnut and there is no trees. Here are two schemes:

Scheme one includes planting 16 chestnut trees now and growing crops simultaneously during the formation period. This scheme requires the investment of 120 Yuan on construction to conserve water and soil. The annual non-wage consumption cost is 30 Yuan. Fructification of these chestnut trees begins from the sixth year with a yield of 20 jin per mu. Then the yield per mu increases 15.71% yearly. The annual yield of crops is 500 jin per mu in the first five years. From the sixth year, the annual yield of crops decreases by 3.41% yearly. In the 25th year, the annual yield of crops drops to 200 jin per mu. The calculation period n_j is 25 years. n_k is set as 5 years. The total period of benefit for crops is 25 years. The fructification period of the chestnut trees begins from the 26th year. The economic yield of each chestnut tree is 80 yuan. The total yield of one mu is 12820 yuan. One ton of chestnut can exchange 6.57 tons of wheat via export. In order to compare prices, the price of wheat is set at the domestic reasonable price of j_{wheat} 0.15 yuan/jin. Chestnut loss in processing and transportation is 8%. The operation fee of chestnut is 50 yuan/ton. The distance from Qianxi county to Tianjin is 100 km. The transportation fee is 0.15 yuan/ton kilometer.

Scheme two does not plant trees. Instead, it grows crops only, specifically sorghum, corn, or minor cereals once a year. The annual yield is 400 jin per mu. The price of crops is 0.15/jin. The construction fee invested during the first year is 100 yuan. No construction fee is needed during the following years. The annual consumption cost, other than wages, is 25 yuan. The benefit period is 25 years. x_t is set as 0.15 and θ is set as 1.15.

The following is the calculation with social national income E_d method:

$$\begin{aligned}
E_{d1} = & \sum_{s=1}^{n_k} j_{crops} \cdot G_{crops} \theta^{n_j+n_k-s} + \sum_{s=n_k+1}^{n_j+n_k} j_{crops} \cdot G_{crops} \left(1 - P_{crops}\right)^{s-n_k} \theta^{n_j+n_k-s} \\
& + \sum_{s=1}^{n_k+n_k} j_{chestnut} \cdot \left(1 - \frac{\Delta G_{chestnut}}{G_{chestnut}}\right) G_{chestnut} (1 + P_{chestnut})^{s-n_k-1} \theta^{n_j+n_k-s} \\
& - \sum_{s=1}^{n_j+n_k} (C_{u1} + x_t T_{z1})^{n_j+n_k-s} \\
& \qquad - \sum_{s=n_k+1}^{n_j+n_k} \left(1 - \frac{\Delta G_{chestnut}}{G_{chestnut}}\right) G_{chestnut} (1 + P_{chestnut})^{s-n_k-1} \\
& \left(C_{operation_chestnut} + C_{chestnut_transportation} + C_{crops_transportation}\right) \theta^{n_j+n_k-s} + T_c
\end{aligned} \tag{22.1}$$

where

$G_{crops} = 400$ jin, $j_{chestnut} = 6.57 j_{crops}$, and $j_{crops} = 0.15$/jin.
$\frac{\Delta G_{chestnut}}{G_{chestnut}} = 0.08$, $G_{chestnut} = 20$ jin, and $P_{crops} = 3.41\%$.
$P_{chestnut} = 15.71\%$, $G_{ul} = 30$ yuan/year, and $T_{zl} = 120$ yuan/year.
$C_{operation\_chestnut} = \frac{50\ yuan}{2000\ jin} = C_{trasportation\_crops} = \frac{6.57\times0.15\times100}{2000}$ yuan/jin,
$C_{trasportation\_chestnut} = \frac{0.15\times100}{2000}$ yuan/jin

$T_c = 1280$ yuan/mu, $n_j = 20$ years, $n_k = 5$ years, $\theta = 1.15$.

Load the data above into formula 22.1 and get the social national income of scheme one: 7742 yuan.

$$E_{d2} = \sum_{s=1}^{n_k+n_k} (j_{crops} \cdot G_{crops} - C_{u2} - x_t T_{z2})\theta^{n_j+n_k-s} \tag{22.2}$$

where $C_{u2} = 25$ yuan/year and $T_{z2} = 100$ yuan.

Load the data above into formula 22.2 and get the social national income of scheme two: 4256 yuan.

It can be seen that the social national income of scheme one E_{dl} is 1.82 times of that of scheme two E_{d2}. Based on result of the economic evaluation, Qianxi county has the local advantage to develop chestnut tree planting.

22.3 Technological Economic Issues of Resource Exploration

Resource exploration is a kind of investment with risks. Evaluation of resource exploration cannot be limited to the size of the resource reserve. More importantly, the evaluation should assess the benefits generated by the resource. For example, the evaluation of oil exploration should focus on the economic effect produced by the oil. An example of a technological economy decision tree method regarding oil exploration can be found in Sect. 21.4.2 in Chap. 21.

22.4 Forecast of Market Demands

The purpose of socialist production is to satisfy people's needs and the needs of national economic development. It is important to know clearly what people's needs and the needs of national economic development are and what the volume of the needs is. Questions to enable market forecasting are two: what are the demands and how much are needed? Due to the development of science and technologies, people's needs can be satisfied in different ways. For instance, people have diverse needs for food, clothing, housing, and transportation. When the need for public transportation

Table 22.1 Annual sales from 2001 to 2007. *Unit* Ten thousand pieces

Year	Sales volume y	x (xi -2004)	x^2	xy	y^2	$\widehat{u_i}$	$\widehat{u_i^2}$
2001	3	3	9	9	9	0.23	0.053
2002	4	2	4	8	16	0.68	0.462
2003	2.5	1	1	2.5	6.25	1.375	1.891
2004	5	0	0	0	25	0.57	0.325
2005	4.5	1	1	4.5	20.25	0.48	0.230
2006	5.5	2	4	11	30.25	0.04	0.002
2007	6.5	3	9	19.5	42.25	0.41	0.168
$\sum$	31	0	28	15.5	149	–	3.145

is large, the need of personal transportation (car and motorcycle) is small. When the need for rice is large, the need for flour is small. When the need for chemical fabric is large, the need for cotton cloth is small. When the need for rice is large, the need for flour is small. When the need for coal gas is large, the need for coal is small. Such cross-subsidization among these needs of people's daily life exists among departments in the national economy as well. Accordingly, when performing a market forecast, cross-subsidization must be taken into consideration. The development of science and technologies continuously generates new demands. Thus, it is also important to perform a market forecast on new demands. Methods introduced in Sects. 18.7 and 18.8 in Chap. 18 can be applied to predict market demands. Here is an example: suppose that a factory needs to perform market forecasting for 2008 and 2009, which can direct their raw material purchasing, production, and sales. The forecast can be performed by following the five steps shown in Table 22.1.

Step one: Draw a scatter diagram according to the data in Table 22.1 (The diagram is omitted).

Step two: Get the following linear regression equation based on the trend of sales.

$$y = b_0 + b_{1^x} \tag{22.3}$$

Step three: Estimate parameters b_0 and b_1. Load the data in Table 22.1 into the following formula:

$$\bar{x} = \frac{\sum x_i}{n} = \frac{0}{7} = 0 \quad \bar{y} = \frac{\sum y_i}{n} = \frac{31}{7} = 4.4286$$

$$\sum x_i^2 - \mathrm{n}\bar{x}^2 = 28 - 0 = 28$$

$$\sum x_i y_i - nxy = 15.5 - 0 = 15.5$$

$$\sum y_i^2 - \mathrm{n}\bar{y}^2 = 149 - 7(4.4286)^2 = 11.7$$

$$\therefore\ b_l = \frac{\sum x_i y_i - nxy}{\sum x_i^2 - n\bar{x}^2} = \frac{15.5}{28} = 0.5536$$

$$b_0 = \bar{y} - b_1\bar{x} = 4.4286$$

Thus,

$$\hat{y} = 4.4286 + 0.5536x \tag{22.4}$$

Step four: Calculate the correlation coefficient r and standard deviation S.

$$r = \frac{\sum x_i y_i - nxy}{\sqrt{\left(\sum x_i^2 - n\bar{x}^2\right)\left(\sum y_i^2 - n\bar{y}^2\right)}} = \frac{15.5}{\sqrt{28 \times 11.7}} = 0.8564 \tag{22.5}$$

According to the correlation coeffiecint table,[1] when $n - 2 = 7 - 2 = 5$, $r_{0.05} = 0.754$, $r = 0.8564 > r_{0.05}$.

In order to get the standard deviation, it is necessary to calculate $\widehat{u_l} = y_i - \widehat{y_l}$.

$$\widehat{u_1} = y_1 - \widehat{y_1} = 3 - [4.4286 + 0.5536 \times (-3)] = 0.23$$
$$\widehat{u_2} = y_2 - \widehat{y_2} = 4 - [4.4286 + 0.5536 \times (-2)] = 0.68$$

List the results in Table 22.1 and further calculate $\widehat{u_l}^2$ and $\sum \widehat{u_l}^2$. The standard deviation S can be calculated as shown below:

$$S = \sqrt{\frac{\sum \widehat{u_l}^2}{n}} = \frac{3.145}{7} = 0.67 \tag{22.6}$$

Step five: Conduct the forecasting based on the regression model.

$$\hat{y}_{2008} = 4.4286 + 0.5536 \times 8 = 8.857(\text{ten thousand pieces})$$
$$\hat{y}_{2009} = 4.4286 + 0.5536 \times 9 = 9.411(\text{ten thousand pieces})$$

22.5 Technological Economy Issues of Firm Size

The general large, medium, and small issues are related to firm size. There ia quite a lot of debate about these issues. Some argue that large is the trend, the larger the better regarding firm size, because larger firms have advanced technologies, high labor productivity, and higher quality products. In contrast, others argue that smaller

[1] Statistics Group in Institute of Mathematics of the Chinese Academy of Sciences (1979).

firms are better because they need less investment and their economic effects can be seen more quickly. Furthermore, smaller firms create more jobs. In fact, we must not make sweeping generalizations regarding firm size. A large size is not always good for firms, whereas a small size is not always good for firms, either. From the perspective of the macro level, large firms, medium firms, and small firms all have their places in the market. Relatively speaking, the number of large firms is smaller than that of medium and small firms. In 2008, there were 358,821 firms larger than a certain size in China. Among them, 2,928 were large ones, amounting to 0.8%. The number of medium firms was 32,485, or 9.05%. The standard for categorizing firms based on their sizes is different across countries, at different times. What a firm's size will be. under certain conditions in a certain area, depends on the results of technological economy analyses.

22.5.1 *Factors Impacting Firm Size*

There are eight factors that impact firm size:

1. **Resource condition**

The amount of resources greatly impacts firm size. Particularly in resource exploration industries, firm size relies on resource conditions. Firm size cannot be set arbitrarily.

2. **Transportation condition**

Large firms consume more raw materials and energy. Therefore, they require more advanced transportation conditions. In contrast, small firms have fewer transportation demands.

3. **Technology condition**

Large firms usually adopt advanced technologies, whereas small and medium ones apply medium and traditional technologies.

4. **Capital condition**

Large firms require huge investments, whereas small ones require fewer investments. As a result, large firms are usually operated by the states. Small ones can be operated by a local area, by towns, or by individuals. Firm size is closely related with firm operation and firm ownership.

5. **Time condition**

Large firms require long construction periods; it takes long time for them to achieve full production levels. In contrast, small firms need a much shorter time. In certain conditions when time is limited, small firms are the right option.

6. **Manpower condition**

Large firms have higher labor productivity. They adopt advanced technologies and use less manpower. In contrast, small ones adopt less advanced technologies and require more manpower.

7. **Operation condition**

Large firms are not as flexible as small ones, regarding operation. It is much easier for small firms to adjust their product lines.

8. **Economic effect**

Large firms and small firms can both achieve a good economic effect.

In conclusion, firm size depends on practical conditions. Developed countries have plenty of capital, high-level technologies, expensive labor costs, and good transportation conditions. Thus, it is suitable for them to develop large firms. In undeveloped areas in China, capital is not enough. The number of unemployed workers is large, the technology level is low, and transportation conditions are not good. Therefore, small firms are good option for these areas. When conditions allow, large firms are good options. However, it should be pointed out that, even in developed countries, many small firms exist in addition to large ones.

22.5.2 Economic Evaluation Methods for Firm Size

Firms' economic effects vary with their sizes. Even firms of the same size have different economic effects. In order to set a reasonable firm size, the greater, faster, better, and more economical results method introduced previously can be adopted.

Factors that are related with firm size and that impact firms' economic effect include the construction period, full production period, service period, investment, production cost, transportation cost, and product quality. Their impacts can be reflected in the economic evaluation formulas. Next, let us discuss how these factors impact firms' economic effect.

1. **Construction period**

The construction period impacts firms' economic effect greatly. With the same production volume, it takes more time to build a large firm than to build several small ones. Building some small firms can begin at the same time. Thus, it does not take long to build small firms. However, building a large firm requires a huge amount of resources and lasts a long time. For instance, the construction period for a large coal mine is from 8 to 10 years, or at least 5–6 years. Medium coal mines take 2–4 years. Small coal mines take only 1–2 years. The construction period of large and medium nitrogen fertilizer factories is 7–8 years, whereas that of small nitrogen

Table 22.2 The values of k_g

n_k	0	1	2	3	4	5	6	7	8	9	10
$n_j = 15$ $\theta = 1.1$	1.0	1.13	1.20	1.28	1.36	1.45	1.55	1.65	1.75	1.87	1.99
$n_j = 15$ $\theta = 1.15$	1.0	1.17	1.27	1.38	1.50	1.63	1.77	1.93	2.11	2.31	2.52

fertilizer factories is about 3 years. Firms in other industries share the same requirements for their construction period. Longer construction periods are the disadvantage of large firms. Shorter construction periods are the advantage of small firms.

Suppose t_g is allocated in n_k years. Each year has the same amount of investment $\frac{t_g}{n_k}$, then

$$t_{gz} = \frac{t_g}{n_k}\left(\frac{\theta^{n_j+n_k}-1}{\theta^{n_j}-1}+\cdots+\frac{\theta^{n_j+1}-1}{\theta^{n_j}-1}\right)$$

Set

$$k_g = \frac{1}{n_k}\left(\frac{\theta^{n_j+n_k}-1}{\theta^{n_j}-1}+\cdots+\frac{\theta^{n_j+1}-1}{\theta^{n_j}-1}\right)$$

If n_j and θ and are known, the relation of k_g and n_k can be found in Table 22.2.

The longer the construction period of large firms $n_{k,}$ the larger k_g. As a result, t_{gz} is larger. Accordingly, the annual average capital occupation rate $x_t t_z$ will be larger. For example, there are two firms. One is large and the other is small. They share the same investment per unit t_g. The construction period of the large one is 8 years, whereas that of the small one is 1 year. Then, the annual average capital occupation rate of the large firm is almost twice that of the small one.

2. **Full production period**

The full production period of large firms is usually long because the demand increases annually. In contrast, the full production period of small firms is short. If the production volume cannot reach the level set for the full production period, the social net income will decrease. Thus, a long full production period impacts the economic effect negatively for large firms, but positively for small firms.

3. **Service period**

Large firms have a higher technology level, more advanced equipment, a longer service period, and a smaller depreciation rate. Small firms have a shorter service period and a larger depreciation rate. The depreciation rate impacts the cost of depreciation. Therefore, a longer service period is good for large firms' economic effects. A shorter service period impacts small firms' economic effects.

4. **Investment**

One part of investment varies in direct proportion to a firm's size, whereas the other part is a constant and is not related to a firm's size. When a firm's size become larger, the total investment does not have a corresponding increase. Accordingly, the investment per unit drops. Thus, the investment per unit for large firms is low, but the investment per unit for small firms is high. Investment is related with many factors, such as management system and technology level. Sometimes, investment in large firms is not economical. Instead, investment in small firms is economical. For example, investment in small coal mines in Shanxi province is half of that for large coal mines.

5. **Production cost**

Production cost is a comprehensive index that is related with many factors. In general, large firms have a lower production cost due to advanced technologies, savings on raw materials and energy consumption, lower depreciation costs, and lower labor costs. But this is not always the case; production costs in some small firms are lower than those in large firms.

6. **Transportation cost**

In general, large firms consume more raw materials, have more diversity in their product line, have a longer transportation route, and spend more on transportation. Small firms, however, have a shorter transportation route and spend less on transportation. Sometimes, large firms and smalls firms have the same transportation route, such as the outward transportation of coal from Shanxi province. Large firms have a lower loading cost, due to the centralized production. Small firms can have a higher loading cost because of their scattered locations.

7. **Quality**

Advanced technologies in large firms yield products of high quality. Low level technologies in small firms can yield products of low quality. However, for the mining industry, the qualities of the output of large firms and small firms are the same. Thus, circumstances alter cases.

In short, the setting of firm size needs to consider these factors comprehensively and should be based on the results of comparing technological economics schemes.

22.6 Location of Production and Site Selection

Some scholars point out that location of production has three levels: area position, site position, and factory position. These categories are reasonable, but it is more reasonable to call these three levels area position, local position, and site position.

Area position aims for allocating productivity among economy zones. Local position deals with where to build firms in an economic zone. Site position chooses the right sites for firms. Sometimes, it is very hard to differentiate between area position and local position. Local position might be conducted over a large area. In this case, local position becomes area position. Usually, the scope of a local position is smaller than that of an area position. Economic evaluation and comprehensive evaluation can be adopted to select a location for production. Here is an example of site selection.

Site selection is a basic step in the allocation of a productive force. First, the site must meet the requirements of production, construction, and the workers' living. Second, factories cannot pollute the environment around them, in towns and watersheds. They cannot destroy the views around them, either. Each factory must carefully consider the size of the land the it occupies, along with the terrain, engineering geology, hydrologic geology, the amount and the quality of water resources, the climate, treatment, and discharge of waste water, waste gas, and other wastes, and the power supply, heat supply, transportation, and living conditions. Some factories have been built at sites with bad geological conditions. In order to secure foundations, steel piles are required. Some factories have been built at sites without enough water resources, and have to be relocated in the middle of construction. The views around them are damaged. Some power plants have been built in downtown areas to save building several kilometers of special rail. Thus, extra attention should be paid to the site selection for factories. The results of a site selection must be feasible at the technology level and must be economically reasonable. Other conditions must be taken into consideration, as well. Economic evaluation and comprehensive evaluation are absolutely necessary.

22.7 Selection of Raw Materials

Technological economic issues on the selection of raw materials include the producing and processing of raw materials, alternative selection, savings, allocation, transportation, storage, research, and development. This section mainly covers the technological economics evaluation methods for raw material producing and processing, alternative selection, and saving.

22.7.1 Economic Evaluation Method for Raw Material Producing and Processing

Which raw materials can generate the largest economic benefits? What is the proper process that can generate the largest economic benefits on raw materials? The macro and micro technological economic evaluation methods introduced in Chap. 15 can be applied to find the answers. Next, find an example of the adoption of social net income method E_c (economic net present value method or economic net final value method), a macro technological economics evaluation method.

It is well known that the production and process of raw materials are not the ultimate goals. Raw materials are produced and processed in order to meet the demands of the departments that consume the raw materials. Accordingly, when assessing the economic benefits of producing and processing raw materials, a systematic approach must be adopted. The economic benefits of departments that produce and process raw materials should be considered. Furthermore, the economic benefits of departments that consume raw materials should be considered as well. The economic benefits of all of the departments must be integrated, and the maximum total social economic benefit should be achieved. Here is the formula:

$$E_{ci} = E_{ci\_exploiting} + E_{ci\_producing} + E_{ci\_processing} + E_{ci\_transportation} + E_{ci\_consuming} = \text{Maximum} \tag{22.7}$$

where

$E_{ci\_exploiting}$	is the economic benefits of departments exploiting raw materials.
$E_{ci\_producing}$	is the economic benefits of departments producing raw materials.
$E_{ci\_processing}$	is the economic benefits of departments processing raw materials.
$E_{ci\_transportation}$	is the economic benefits of departments transporting raw materials.
$E_{ci\_consuming}$	is the economic benefits of departments consuming raw materials.
i	represents technological schemes of raw materials.

When comparing the technological schemes of raw material producing and processing, some people choose the production volume of the same raw material as the base. This is not a correct approach, because although the production volume of raw materials is the same, these raw materials might meet different demands. For instance, it is not proper to compare 200,000 cubic meters of aeroconcrete and 200,000 cubic meters of reinforced concrete because, when they are used for wall covering, one square meter of wall surface needs 0.2 cubic meter of aeroconcrete, but it needs 0.28 cubic meter of reinforced concrete. Thus, the economic evaluation should begin with meeting the actual demand. In other words, the comparison should choose the building of the same area of wall surface as the base in this example. For convenience, it is recommended that a unit in Formula 22.7 be chosen as the indicator in order to calculate the maximum value of social net income E_c per unit (one square meter of wall surface in this example). Next, a practical example of aeroconcrete is provided in order to explain the economic evaluation for raw material.

As a new building material, aeroconcrete is made by mixing siliceous materials (such as sand and flyash) with calcareous materials (such as limestone and cement). Next, the foaming agent aluminum powder, and it is agitated, poured, cut, and high pressure steam cured. Two alternatives have been found to conduct an economic evaluation on aeroconcrete. One is common concrete and the other is lightweight aggregate concrete. Similar to aeroconcrete, these two alternatives can be used for building walls, covering surfaces, and making floor slabs. Clay brick is another alternative, but it can only be used for building walls. All together, aeroconcrete has three alternatives. Suppose the $E_{ci\_exploiting}$, $E_{ci\_producing}$, and $E_{ct\_transportation}$ are zero in Formula 22.7. In other words, the price per ton of exploited raw materials is equal to the social consumption cost of exploiting (only x_t is considered. x_w, x_y, x_r, and x_d are all zero). The price per ton of produced raw materials is equal to the social consumption cost of producing. The transportation price per ton of raw materials is equal to the social consumption cost of transportation. Thus, the economic comparison formulas for these four raw materials are:

$$E_{c\_aero} = E_{c\_aero[add]} - E_{c\_aero[use]} = \left(j_{aero} - c_{aero} - x_t t_{z\_aero}\right) w_{aero} + \left(j_{wall\_aero} - c'_{wall\_aero} - x_t t_{z\_wall\_aero} - j_{aero} w_{aero}\right) \quad (22.8)$$

$$E_{c\_com} = E_{c\_com[add]} - E_{c\_com[use]} = \left(j_{com} - c_{com} - x_t t_{z\_com}\right) w_{com} + \left(j_{wall\_com} - c'_{wall\_com} - x_t t_{z\_wall\_com} - j_{com} w_{com}\right) \quad (22.9)$$

$$E_{c\_light} = E_{c\_light[add]} - E_{c\_light[use]} = \left(j_{light} - c_{light} - x_t t_{z\_light}\right) w_{light} + \left(j_{wall\_light} - c'_{wall\_light} - x_t t_{z\_wall\_light} - j_{light} w_{light}\right) \quad (22.10)$$

$$E_{c\_brick} = E_{c\_brick[add]} - E_{c\_brick[use]} = \left(j_{brick} - c_{brick} - x_t t_{z\_brick}\right) w_{brick} + \left(j_{wall\_brick} - c'_{wall\_brick} - x_t t_{z\_wall\_brick} - j_{brick} w_{brick}\right) \quad (22.11)$$

Simplify the above formulas and the following new formulas can be gotten.

$$E_{c\_aero} = j_{wall\_aero} - c'_{wall\_aero} - x_t t_{z\_wall\_aero} - c_{aero} w_{aero} - x_t t_{z\_aero} w_{aero} \quad (22.12)$$

$$E_{c\_com} = j_{wall\_com} - c'_{wall\_com} - x_t t_{z\_wall\_com} - c_{com} w_{com} - x_t t_{z\_com} w_{com} \quad (22.13)$$

$$E_{c\_light} = j_{wall\_light} - c'_{wall\_light} - x_t t_{z\_wall\_light} - c_{light} w_{light} - x_t t_{z\_light} w_{light} \quad (22.14)$$

$$E_{c\_brick} = j_{wall\_brick} - c'_{wall\_brick} - x_t t_{z\_wall\_brick} - c_{brick} w_{brick} - x_t t_{z\_brick} w_{brick} \quad (22.15)$$

where

j_{aero}, j_{com}, j_{light}, and j_{brick} represent the price of aeroconcrete, common concrete, lightweight aggregate concrete, and clay brick, respectively.

j_{wall} represents the price of one square meter of wall surface.

Table 22.3 Economic evaluation of building materials

Materials		Aeroconcrete	Common concrete	Lightweight aggregate concrete	Clay brick
Material processing $j = z = c + x_t t_z$ (yuan/m^3)		50	110	150	40
Material utilization	$c'_{wall} + x_t t_{z\_wall}$ (yuan/m^2)	30	20–40	30	10
	j_w (yuan/m^2)	10	30.8	42	14.4
	w (yuan/m^2)	0.20	0.28	0.28	0.36
Social consumption cost $c'_{wall} + x_t t_{z\_wall} + j_w$ (yuan/m^2)		40	50–70.8	72	24.4

Note One m^3 bricks has 680 pieces

c'_{wall} represents the cost of making one square meter of wall surface.

$x_t t_{z\_wall}$ represents the amount of capital occupied by one square meter of wall surface in one year.

w represents the amount of construction materials needed by making one square meter of wall surface.

c represents the manufacturing cost of construction materials.

t_z represents the amount of capital occupied by construction materials in one year.

Suppose that the prices of wall surfaces made of these four materials are the same. The economic effect of each material will depend on the amount of its social consumption cost. Table 22.3 lists the social consumption costs of these four materials. According to the result in Table 22.3, the economic effect of aeroconcrete is relatively better. Aeroconcrete is a better choice, in this example. But the result is not always the case. The best option depends on the result of the economic effect evaluation in each specific condition. There is no one general solution for all cases.

22.7.2 Economic Evaluation Method for Alternative Raw Materials

In order to increase the economic benefit, users either choose the raw materials that will generate the largest economic benefits among all of the materials with the same features, or they tend to find an alternative at a cheaper price. Accordingly, users need to conduct an economic evaluation on the raw materials. Here is another example using social net income E_c. Different from the example of the economic evaluation on raw material production and processing, this example only compares the social

Table 22.4 Prices of building materials

Materials	Aeroconcrete	Common concrete	Lightweight aggregate concrete
Current price (yuan/m^3)	75	85	123
Construction fee (yuan/m^2)	30	20	30
Need of material (m^3/m^2)	0.20	0.28	0.28

net income generated different raw materials:

$$E_{ct} = E_{ct\_using} = \text{Maximum} \tag{22.16}$$

The calculation of the economic effects must adopt a reasonable price. If the adopted price is not reasonable, errors will occur in the economic evaluation. Here is an example of economic evolution on alternative raw materials:

Suppose a construction company gets a contract to build a house with several stories. There are three raw materials available. The details of these materials are listed in Table 22.4. If tax is not considered, which material should be chosen in order to achieve the largest profit?

Because the sale price per unit of this storied house is the same regardless which material is adopted, the material that has the smallest cost for building the wall surfaces will generate the largest profits. Next, the cost per square meter for each of these three materials is calculated:

Aeroconcrete: $Z_{aero\_firm} = 75 \times 0.2 + 30 = 45$ yuan/m^2
Common concrete: $Z_{com\_firm} = 85 \times 0.28 + 20 = 43.8$ yuan/m^2
Lightweight aggregate concrete: $Z_{light\_firm} = 123 \times 0.28 + 30 = 64.4$ yuan/m^2

It can be seen that the cost, per square meter, of the wall surface made of common concrete is the smallest. Thus, common concrete should be adopted.

This example indicates that if the present prices of construction materials are not reasonable, invisible mistakes will occur in practice. The price of aeroconcrete is cheaper than that of common concrete. However, the result of the calculation shows that common concrete will generate the largest economic benefit. The reason is because an unreasonable price for common concrete is taken in this example. As such, this construction company need to conduct a macro technological economic evaluation, assessing the present prices of construction materials available and further adjusting them into reasonable ones. Here are the steps:

$$E_{c\_aevo} = \text{The reasonable price of wall } j_{wall\_aero} - \text{the social consumption cost of wall } \left(c_{wall\_aero} + x_t t_{z\_wall\_aero}\right)$$

$$= \text{The price of wall } j_{\text{wall aero}} - \text{the construction fee of wall } (c'_{wall\_aero} + x_t t_{z\_wall\_aero}) - \text{cost of materials } j_{aero} w_{aero} \quad (22.17)$$

Set $j_{aero} = z_{aero} = c_{aero} + x_t t_{z\_aero}$, then

$$E_{c\_aero} = j_{wall\_aero} - c'_{wall\_aero} - x_t t_{z\_wall\_aero} - c_{aero} w_{aero} - x_t t_{z\_aero} w_{aero} \quad (22.18)$$

The reasonable prices for the other construction materials can be deduced by analogy.

$$E_{c\_com} = j_{wall\_com} - c'_{wall\_com} - x_t t_{z\_wall\_com} - c_{com} w_{com} - x_t t_{z\_com} w_{com} \quad (22.19)$$

$$E_{c\_light} = j_{wall\_light} - c'_{wall\_light} - x_t t_{z\_wall\_light} - c_{light} w_{light} - x_t t_{z\_light} w_{light} \quad (22.20)$$

$$E_{c\_brick} = j_{wall\_brick} - c'_{wall\_brick} - x_t t_{z\_wall\_brick} - c_{brick} w_{brick} - x_t t_{z\_brick} w_{brick} \quad (22.21)$$

Formulas 22.18 and 22.12 are identical. In other words, the economic evaluation methods for users are the same as those for manufacturers. This calculation will reach the conclusion that aeroconcrete will generate the largest economic benefits.

22.7.3 *Economic Evaluation Method for Saving Raw Materials*

Users need to save raw materials for improving the utilization ratio of raw materials. However, man power, materials, capital, transportation, natural resources, and time are always needed no matter which approach is adopted for saving raw materials. Thus, the approaches for saving raw materials need economic evaluation. The economic evolution methods for saving raw materials are the same as those for selecting alternative raw materials. Only the social net income of one unit of product needs to be examined, after the saving approaches are applied. The calculation must adopt reasonable prices. If a lower price of raw materials is adopted, the result of the approaches for saving raw materials will be impacted negatively.

22.8 Technological Economic Study on Transportation, Post, and Communications

Transportation delivers people and materials, whereas post and telecommunications transfer information. They are each important departments in national economy. Many technological economic issues exist in these departments, such as what the economic effect of transportation, post, and telecommunications will be, how to develop transportation, post, and telecommunications, how to allocate resources for them, and how to compare different approaches in transportation, post, and telecommunications. Other issues include how to conduct comprehensive transportation and reasonable transportation, and how to save turnover volume. The aforementioned economic evaluation and comprehensive evaluation methods are still applicable for finding solutions for these issues. Next, economic evaluation methods for transportation, post, and telecommunications are introduced.

22.8.1 Economic Effect Evaluation for Transportation

1. Methods of economic effects evaluation for transportation

What are the economic effects of transportation? How can they be evaluated? Little research has been done to explore the answers. In China, the road system is underdeveloped. Railways cannot meet the requirements of production and of the people's current life. The investment in transportation from the states is not enough. These issues are related to the question of how to deal with the economic effects of transportation and how to evaluate the economic effects of transportation. In practice, the following formulas are applied to assess the economic effects of transportation:

$$L_{tc} = \frac{net\ income\ of\ transportation\ (S - C)}{investment\ on\ transportation\ T} \quad (22.22)$$

$$L_{tg} = \frac{national\ income\ of\ transportation\ (S - G_u)}{investment\ on\ transportation\ T} \quad (22.23)$$

This method only considers the direct economic effect of the transportation department. Results generated by this method do not reflect the important role of transportation in the economy. Especially in China, the price of transportation is low. Thus, the economic efficiency of the investment in transportation is low. As a result, the rate of return for capital is small. As we know, transportation is good for every aspect in a society. For example, the exploitation of local resources; the development of production; the exchange of commodities; the exchange of science, technology, and culture; people's travel; and national security all rely on transportation. The role that transportation plays in some of these activities cannot be measured directly by its economic effects, while some can be measured by indirect economic effects.

Such economic effects belong to other departments in the economy. They are indirect economic benefits of transportation. How can indirect economic benefits be calculated? Here is an example of transportation for production.

Transportation (circulation) is the bridge between production and consumption. With the support of transportation, production and consumption can be implemented smoothly. The economic effects for production, transportation, and consumption can all be achieved. Without transportation, none of the economic effects for production, transportation, and consumption can be achieved. When transportation is not available, transportation per se does not have any economic effect. There will be overstock because products cannot be sold. No economic effect will be generated in production. On the consumption side, the lack of raw materials and energy will stop production. As a result, the economic benefit of consumption cannot be achieved either. A typical example is the shortage of transportation in Shanxi province. First, the economic benefit of transportation drops. Second, coal is produced but cannot be shipped out; there is huge amount of overstock. Thus, the economic effect of coal production cannot be achieved. Third, other regions, such as Shanghai, cannot get enough coal. Production in these regions cannot continue. At the end, the economic effect of coal consumption is zero. The example of coal transportation in Shanxi province reflects the economic effects of transportation. Tthe indirect economic effect of transportation can be seen particularly clearly. Here is the formula for calculating the economic effect of transportation:

$$\begin{aligned} E_{c\_transportation} &= E_{c\_direct} + E_{c\_indirect} \\ &= E_{c\_transportation\_per\ se} + E_{c\_produciton} + E_{c\_consumption} \\ &= \left(S_{\Sigma transportation\_per\ se} + S_{\Sigma production} + S_{\Sigma consumption}\right) \\ &\quad - \left(Z_{\Sigma transportation\_per\ se} + Z_{\Sigma production} + Z_{\Sigma consumption}\right) \\ &= \left(S_{\Sigma transportation\_per\ se} - Z_{\Sigma transportation\_per\ se}\right) \\ &\quad + \left(S_{\Sigma production} - Z_{\Sigma production}\right) + \left(S_{\Sigma consumption} - Z_{\Sigma consumption}\right) \end{aligned} \tag{22.24}$$

or

$$\begin{aligned} E_{d\_transportation} &= \left(S_{\Sigma transportation\_per\ se} - Z_{\Sigma transportation\_per\ se}\right) \\ &\quad + \left(S_{\Sigma production} - Z_{\Sigma production}\right) + \left(S_{\Sigma consumption} - Z_{\Sigma consumption}\right) \end{aligned} \tag{22.25}$$

Here is example for calculation (see Fig. 22.1). Suppose that the economic benefit for coal production in Shanxi province $S_{production}$ is 5 yuan/ton. The cost $Z_{production}$ is 30 yuan/ton. The social net income for coal production $E_{c\_production}$ is 20 yuan/ton. The economic benefit for coal transportation $S_{trasportation\_per\ se}$ is 60 yuan/ton. The cost $Z_{trasportation\_per\ se}$ is 55 yuan/ton. The social net income for coal transportation $E_{c\_trasportation\_per\ se}$ is 5 yuan/ton. The economic benefit for coal consumption $S_{consumption}$ is 400 yuan/ton. The cost $Z_{consumption}$ is 200 yuan/ton. The social net

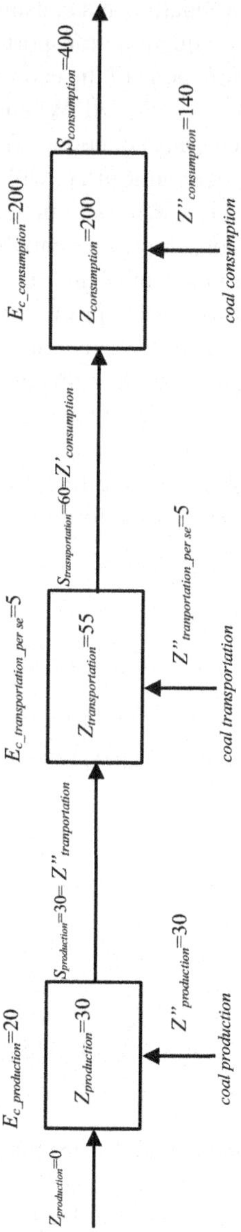

Fig. 22.1 An example of calculating the economic effects of transportation

income for coal consumption $E_{c\_consumption}$ is 200 yuan/ton. If transportation is available, Formula 22.24 is adopted. The total economic benefit of transportation $E_{c\_transportation}$ is 225 yuan/ton. However, transportation capacity is limited, and there are thousands of tons of overstock. The loss is 225 yuan/ton. The loss is caused by the limited transportation capacity.

In practice, coal users want to pay more for transportation in order to get enough coal. Coal producers also want to pay more for transportation in order to decrease overstock. This indicates that the indirect economic effects of transportation do exist. Sometimes, such indirect effects can be many times larger than the direct effects. This example indicates that the transportation price should rise, the investment on transportation should increase, and the development of transportation should be faster. In this way, huge economic benefits will be generated. Some people might argue that it is not reasonable to attribute all economic benefits to transportation. The author thinks that this calculation method is good for evaluating the construction of a road or a railway. When assessing production, consumption, and transportation, the total economic benefits should be allocated reasonably. In other words, the price of transportation should be reasonable so that the investment net income rates of production, transportation, and consumption are close.

The economic effects of transportation are not only dependent upon the economic effects of transportation per se, but they are also related to the categories and the amount of materials that are transported, the economic effects of producing these materials, and the economic effects of consuming these materials. Therefore, if an area has good resources that can be exploited and produced and have good economic effects, and another area needs these products, consuming these products has a good economic effect, and the development of the transportation between the two areas will have large economic benefits. The transportation should be first developed. The evolution method introduced here is good for assessing the economic effects of circulation filed.

2. Calculation methods for economic evaluation of transportation modes

Each transportation mode has its own unique technological characteristics. Railway is good for some regions. Roadways are good for other regions. In some regions, waterways are the best option, whereas in other regions, specific modes, such as pipeline and power line, are the best option. Thus, we should adopt the proper transportation modes, those with the best economic effects, in accordance with actual conditions. Accordingly, it is necessary to calculate, compare, and assess the economic effects of all of the available transportation modes. The comparison needs to consider the speed, damage control, safety, and comfort of each transportation mode. The comparison can adopt the method of greater, faster, better and more economic results. The formulas based on social net income and firm excess profit are.

$$E_c = \sum_{s=1}^{n_j+n_k} (S_\Sigma - Z_\Sigma)\frac{1}{\theta^s} = ZD \tag{22.26}$$

$$E_f = \sum_{s=1}^{n_j+n_k} (S_{\Sigma\_firm} - Z_{\Sigma\_firm}) \frac{1}{\theta^5} = ZD \quad (22.27)$$

Form 22.26 can be simplified as the following format based on social net income.

$$E_c = S - Z = ZD; \quad E_f = S_{firm} - Z_{firm} = ZD \quad (22.28)$$

Given the characteristics of transportation, two more costs should be added when calculating the total consumption cost Z of each transportation mode. One is the capital occupation cost $x_t T_{t\_goods}$ caused by the current capital T_{t_goods} needed by the goods en route. T_{t_goods} can be calculated with the following formula.

$$T_{t\_goods} \frac{j_{z\_average} \Sigma G}{365} \times S_{time}(\text{number of days}) \quad (22.29)$$

where

$j_{z\_average}$ is the average price for good en route (yuan/ton).
$\sum G$ is the annual volume of transport (ton).
S_{time} is the time of goods on the way of transportation (day).

The other is the value C_{goods_damage} that is caused by the loss, damage, and rot in the process of transportation. It can be calculated with the following formula:

$$C_{goods\_danage} = x_{goods\_damage} \times j_{z\_average} \times \sum G \quad (22.30)$$

where

x_{goods_damage} is the coefficient of damage of good en route.

The total consumption cost $Z_{transportation}$ in transportation should be calculated with the following formula:

$$Z_{transportation} = Z_{prepraration} + Z_{collection} \; L_{collection} + Z_{transmit} \; L_{transmit} + Z_{operation} + Z_{unload} + Z_{main\_route} L_{main\_route} + x_t T_{l\_goods} + C_{goods\_damage} \quad (22.31)$$

The total consumption cost in the above formula includes the cost of preparation (strapping, compression, unpacking), the cost of transportation from the collection sites to the main routes, the cost of transportation from the main routes to the final users, the cost of operation at the origin stops to the end stops, the cost of unloading, the cost of transportation on main routes, the current capital occupied by goods en route, and the cost of damages to goods.

When goods are transported via several modes, Formula 22.31 can be applied to compare these modes. Here is the standard for comparison.

$$Z_{transportaion} = ZX \tag{22.32}$$

For convenience, the transport volume per unit (ton, person) or turnover quality (ton/kilometer, person/kilometer) can be applied in the above formulas.

The total cost of each transportation mode consists of two parts. One is unrelated with the distance of transportation. The other is positively related with the distance of transportation.

$$Z_{transportaton\_l} = Z^0_{transportation\_t} + Z^l_{transportation\_l} L'_{transportation\_t} \tag{22.33}$$

When comparing two transportation modes, such as railway and road, the economic critical distance L_j can be calculated as following.

$$L_j = \frac{Z^0_{transportation\_railway} - Z^0_{transportation\_road}}{Z^l_{transportation\_road} - Z^l_{transportation\_railway}} \tag{22.34}$$

If the actual transportation distance is longer than the economic critical distance, railway should be adopted. Otherwise, roadways should be adopted.

22.8.2 Evaluation of Economic Effects for Post and Telecommunications

Post and telecommunications delivery information play an important role in politics, in national defense, in production and construction, and in people's living. It is very hard to assess and to calculate the economic effects for post and telecommunications. Research on this topic is missing now. For a long time, post and telecommunications have been underdeveloped in China. There are many reasons. The two main reasons are lack of understanding and lack of capital. Usually, the following formulas are applied to calculate the economic effects of post and telecommunications:

$$L_{tc} = \frac{\text{the net income of post and telecommunications } (S - C)}{\text{the investment on post and telecommunications } T} \tag{22.35}$$

$$L_{tg} = \frac{\text{the national income of post and telecommunications } (S - C_u)}{\text{the investment on post and telecommunications } T} \tag{22.36}$$

The results gotten from the above formulas are the direct economic benefits of post and telecommunications; the indirect benefits are not considered. Thus, the above evaluation methods cannot reflect the complete economic benefits of post and telecommunications. The prices of post and telecommunications services are particularly low in China. It can even be hard to see the actual economic benefit of post and telecommunications. Next, let us discuss how to calculate the complete economic benefits of post and telecommunications. Unlike transportation, post and telecommunications delivery information is necessary for production and construction. However, without information delivered by post and telecommunications services, production and consumption can still occur, because information can be delivered by the flow of people. Information delivery by people costs in transportation and takes time. The advantage of post and telecommunications is to save the cost of transportation and time required by the flow of people. The savings on costs and time can be easily calculated, but it is hard to tell how much of the increase in economic effect is caused by the saving of time. It is a challenge to calculate the economic effects of time utilization. When calculating the indirect economic effects of post and telecommunications, the economic effects of time must be considered. In some cases, time is life, especially in emergency treatment. Accordingly, the saving of seconds and minutes that is generated by post and telecommunication is valuable. Normally, time is fortune, because all fortune is created by people' work, which requires time. Thus, the economic effects of time do exist. Certain time has a larger economic effect, whereas other time has a smaller economic effect. The economic effects of time vary across regions and among people.

The economic effect of post and telecommunications can be achieved by comparing the information delivery with the flow of people. Here is the formula for calculating the economic effect of post and telecommunications by following the social net income method:

$$\begin{aligned}\Delta E_{c\_post\_telecomm} &= \Delta E_{c\_direct} + \Delta E_{c\_indirect}\\ &= \Delta S_{\Sigma\_post\_telecomm} - \Delta Z_{\Sigma\_post\_telecomm}\\ &= \left(S_{\Sigma\_post\_telecomm\_use} - S_{\Sigma\_transportation\_use}\right)\\ &\quad - \left(Z_{\Sigma\_post\_telecomm\_per\,se} - Z_{\Sigma\_transportation\;per\,se}\right)\\ &= \sum_{s=1}^{n_j+n_k} \left(x_s \Delta S_{time} - \Delta Z_{post\_telecomm} G_s\right)\frac{1}{\theta^s}\end{aligned} \tag{22.37}$$

where

$S_{\sum\_post\_telecomm\_use}$ is the amount of benefit received by the departments that use post and telecommunications services.

$S_{\sum\_transportation\_use}$ is the amount of benefit received by the departments that use the flow of people for information delivery.

$Z_{\sum\_post\_telecomm\_per\,se}$ is the total social consumption cost of information delivery via post and telecommunications.

$Z_{\sum\_transporation\_per\,se}$ is the total social consumption cost of information delivery via the flow of people.

$\Delta\, S_{\sum\_post\_telecomm}$ is the increased amount of benefi generated by post and telecommunications compared with the flow of people.

$\Delta Z_{\sum\_post\_telecomm}$ is the change of the total social consumption cost caused by post and telecommunications compared with the flow of people.
x_s is the the time utilization economic effect coefficient.
ΔS_{time} is the saving of time by post and telecommunications, for example hour/times.
G is the amount of information delivered in one year, for example times/year.

22.9 Economic Evaluation for Production Process

Economic effect varies across production processes. In order to increase the economic benefits, firms should adopt those production processes that are both technologically feasible and economically reasonable. Economic evaluation is required to find the production process with the largest economic effect among many options. Here is an example of the economic evaluation on metal working processes and equipment.

According to the state plan, a mechanical working factory will be built in a site located in southwest China. This factory will produce and process castellated shafts, long shafts, flanged shafts, long bolt shafts, and long tube shafts. Four production process schemes are available for producing and processing these products. The first scheme uses the computerized hydraulic tracing control lathe $C_{720}F_6$. The second scheme uses the one-stroke hydraulic tracing control lathe $C_{712}F_1$. The third scheme uses the common lathe $C_{620\text{-}1}$ and the hydraulic tool rest. The fourth scheme uses the common lathe $C_{620\text{-}1}$ only. The following are the economic evaluation on these four schemes:

1. **Economic benefit index** (s)

Given the fact that all four schemes produce 1000 parts annually with the same quality, the economic benefit indexes for these four schemes are the same. In the calculation of a technological economic comparison, the economic benefit indexes are not considered.

2. **Investment occupancy index** (T_g)

For convenience, the total investment of each scheme is not calculated. Instead, the difference in the investment on a certain part of fixed asset among the four schemes is calculated.[2] These investments include lathes, molds, factory buildings, and dormitory buildings. The calculation methods for these investments are introduced next.

[2]Differences exist among current assets. The differences should be calculated, but due to the lack of documentation, they are neglected here.

Table 22.5 Calculation of the investment on lathes

Indicator	Scheme 1	Scheme 2	Scheme 3	Scheme 4
Time required for making a part t (min)	22.4	26	37.84	43.4
Time required for making 1000 parts in one year $t_{\sum}$ (h)	374	434	631	725
The working hours that one lathe works in one year h (h)	4650	4650	4650	4650
Utilization coefficient of one lathe β (%)	83	65	71.5	82
Effective working hours of a lathe in one year h_O (h)	3860	2980	3250	3720
Required lathes n (set)	0.097	0.146	0.194	0.195
The price of a lathe j_{g_lathe} (including shipping and installation fees) (yuan/set)	70000	49500	12050	8850
The investment on lathes T_{g_lathe} (yuan)	6800	7060	2290	1680

(1) Calculation of the investment on lathes T_{g_lathes}

$$T_{g\_lathe} = n \times j_{g\_lathe}$$

Where n is the number of lathes required to produce 1000 parts in one year, j_{g_lathe} is the price of a lathe. The results of calculation of the investment on lathes are listed in Table 22.5.

(2) Calculation of the investment on mold $T_{g\_explorators}$

$$T_{g\_molds} = A \times j_{g\_molds}$$

where

A is the number of molds required by making 1000 parts in one year.
j_{g_molds} is the price of a mold.

The results of calculation of the investment on molds are listed in Table 22.6.

(3) Calculation of the investment on factory buildings, $T_{g\_factory\ buildings}$

$$T_{g\_factory\ buildings} = n \times F \times j_{g\_factory\ buildings}$$

where

Table 22.6 Calculation of the investment on explorators

Indicator	Scheme 1	Scheme 2	Scheme 3	Scheme 4
A	1	1	1	0
j_{g_molds} (yuan)	30	30	30	30
T_{g_molds} (yuan)	30	30	30	0

n is the number of required lathes,
F is the production area occupied by one lathe,
$j_{g\_factory\ buildings}$ is the cost of one unit of factory building.

The results of calculation of the investment on factory buildings are listed in Table 22.7.

(4) Calculation of the investment on infrastructure related with labor $T_{g\_construction}$

$$T_{g\_construction} = R \times j_{g\_construction}$$

where

R is the number of workers required to produce 1000 parts.
$j_{g\_construction}$ is the investment on construction required by one worker.

The results of calculation of the investment on construction are listed in Table 22.8.

(5) Calculation of the total investment T_g for each scheme

$$T_g = T_{g\_lathe} + T_{g\_molds} + T_{g\_factory\ buildings} + T_{g\_construction}$$

The results of calculation of the total investment are listed in Table 22.9.

The results indicate that the investment in scheme 2 is the highest. The investment in scheme 1 is lower. The investment in scheme 3 is economical. The investment in scheme 4 is the most economical.

Table 22.7 Calculation of the investment on factory buildings

Indicator	Scheme 1	Scheme 2	Scheme 3	Scheme 4
N (set)	0.097	0.146	0.194	0.195
F (m^2)	20	20	18	18
$j_{g\_factory\ buildings}$ (yuan/m^2)	200	200	200	200
$T_{g\_factory\ buildings}$ (yuan)	388	585	698	705

Table 22.8 Calculation of the investment on infrastructure

Indicator	Scheme 1	Scheme 2	Scheme 3	Scheme 4
Labor hours required by producing 1000 parts in one year $t_{\sum}$ (h)	347	434	631	725
The number of labor hours one worker works in one year t_r (h)	2250	2250	2250	2250
The number of workers R (person)	0.166/2[a]	0.193	0.28	0.322
The cost of infrastructure required by one worker $j_{g\_construction}$ (yuan/person)	2000	2000	2000	2000
$T_{g\_construction}$ (yuan)	166	386	560	644

Note [a]One worker operates two lathes

Table 22.9 Calculation of the total investment

Indicator	Scheme 1	Scheme 2	Scheme 3	Scheme 4
T_g (yuan)	7384	8061	3578	3029
T_z (yuan)	5408.4	5975.4	2777.4	2412

Note $T_z = T_g - T_j$, $n_j = 15$ years

3. **Manpower occupancy index (*R*)**

The calculation of investments in the aforementioned four schemes indicates that scheme 1 requires the least amount of manpower: only 0.083 person. Scheme 2 requires 0.193 person. Scheme 3 requires 0.28 person. Scheme 4 requires 0.322 person. In other words, scheme 1 has the highest labor productivity, which is two times of that of scheme 2, three times of that of scheme 3, and four times of that of scheme 4.

4. **Annual operating cost index (*C*)**

(1) Calculation of the cost of energy C_n

$$C_n = \frac{N_b \times \frac{1}{\eta} \times j_{g\_electricity}}{60} \times t \times G + \frac{N_{idle} \times j_{g\_electricity}}{60} \times t_{idle} \times G$$

where

N_b is the power rating of the motor in a lathe.
η is the efficiency of the motor in a lathe.
$j_{g\_electricity}$ is the price of power. It is set as 0.0933 yuan/kwh.
N_{idle} is the power consumption when a lathe is idling.
t is time required to produce one part (minute).
t_{idle} is the idling time required by a lathe to produce one part (minute).

Table 22.10 Calculation of the cost of energy

Indicator	Scheme 1	Scheme 2	Scheme 3	Scheme 4
N_b (kW)	27	15.4	12.5	11.3
η	0.8	0.8	0.75	0.75
N_{idle} (kW)	0.94	0.94	0.72	0.62
t_{idle}	6.74	8.68	12.24	16
C_n (yuan/year)	204	237.3	278.4	276

G is the 1000 parts produced in one year.

The results of the calculation of energy consumed are listed in Table 22.10.

(2) Calculation of wage and the surcharge of wage $C_{g\sum}$

$$C_{g\Sigma} = C_g + C_{gf} = (1 + k_{gf})\left(\frac{t_{operating}}{60} \times \frac{1}{a}\right)G \cdot V_{time} + (1 + k_{gf})\left(\frac{t_{adjustment}}{60} \times \frac{1}{b}\right)G \cdot V'_{time}$$

where

k_{gf} is the additional coefficient of wage. It is set as 0.13.
$t_{operating}$ is the time required to process a part.
$t_{adjustment}$ is the adjustment in time required to process a part.
a is the number of parts simultaneously processed by a worker.
b is the number of parts simultaneously adjusted by a worker.
V_{time} is the hourly wage standard for workers who perform an operation.
V'_{time} is the hourly wage standard for workers who perform an adjustment.

The results of calculation of energy consumed are listed in Table 22.11.

Table 22.11 Calculation of wage and wage surcharge

Indicator	Scheme 1	Scheme 2	Scheme 3	Scheme 4
$t_{operating}$ (min)	19.9	26	37.84	43.4
$t_{adjustment}$ (min)	2.5	4	4	0
a (piece)	2	1	1	1
b (piece)	40	40	40	0
$C_{g\sum}$ (yuan/year)	32.75	89.37	130.07	156

Note Workers performing operations in Scheme 1, Scheme 2, and Scheme 3 are set as level-three, but as level 4 in Scheme 4. Workers performing adjustments in Scheme 1, Scheme 2, Scheme 3, and Scheme 4 are set as level-six. The basic wage for level-three workers is 0.1813 yuan/hour, 0.2146 yuan/hour for level-four workers, and 0.2979 yuan/hour for level-six workers

Table 22.12 Calculation of basic depreciation and overhaul cost

Indicator	Scheme 1	Scheme 2	Scheme 3	Scheme 4
l_z lathe (%)	7.3	7.3	7.3	7.3
l_z explorator (%)	50	50	50	0
l_z factory building (%)	2.2	2.2	2.2	2.2
l_z construction (%)	3.21	3.21	3.21	3.21
c_z lathe (yuan/year)	493	516	166.5	122
c_z explorator (yuan/year)	15	15	15	0
c_z factory building (yuan/year)	8.6	12.9	15.4	15.5
c_z construction (yuan/year)	5.3	12.4	18	20.7
c_z (yuan/year)	521.9	556.3	214.9	158.2

(3) Calculation of basic depreciation and overhaul cost C_z

$$C_Z = C_i + C_{dx} = \sum l_{zi} T_{gi}$$

where

T_{gi} is the ith item of investment on fixed assets.
L_{zi} is the comprehensive depreciation rate of the ith item of investment on fixed assets.

The results of the calculation of basic depreciation and the overhaul costs are listed in Table 22.12:

(4) The other costs C_q include the expenditure of repairing the lathes and the operating cost of the workshops. The expenditure for repairing lathes refers to the costs of checking as well as medium and small repairs. According to the rules, the repair period for lathes is 6 years, in which two medium repairs, six small repairs, and nine checkings must be performed. The repair of lathes consists of machinery repair and electrical repair. The material cost of medium machinery repair is 18 yuan. The labor fee is 13.6 yuan. The material cost of small machinery repair is 7 yuan. The labor fee is 4.5 yuan. The cost of using and operating workshops is 6.5 times the labor fee. The checking fee is 12% of the repair cost. The material cost of a medium electrical repair is 6 yuan. The labor fee is 3.4 yuan. The cost of using and operating workshops is 19.5 yuan. The material cost of small electrical repair is 3 yuan. The labor fee is 0.6 yuan. The cost of using and operating workshops is 3.2 yuan. The checking fee is 12% of repair cost. These costs are all based on a complicated coefficient which varies across lathe models. The complicated coefficients of machinery repair and electrical repair for computerized lathes are both 14. For the $C_{712}F_l$ lathe, the complicated coefficients of machinery repair and electrical repair are 12 and

Table 22.13 The other cost for each scheme

Indicator	Scheme 1	Scheme 2	Scheme 3	Scheme 4
C_q (yuan/year)	159.1	174.6	262.4	247

10, respectively. For the C_{620}-1 hydraulic carriage lathe, the complicated coefficients of machinery repair and electrical repair are 13 and 6, respectively. For *the* C_{620}-1 lathe, the complicated coefficients of machinery repair and electrical repair are 11 and 4.5, respectively. Based on this calculation, the cost of lathe repair for Scheme 1 is 142.5 yuan, for Scheme 2 it is 136 yuan, for Scheme 3 it is 198 yuan, and for Scheme 4 it is 191 yuan.

The cost of using a workshop is calculated based on the number of workers. The annual workshop use cost for one worker is 200 yuan. According to the calculation, the cost of workshop use for Scheme 1 is 16.6 yuan, for Scheme 2 it is 38.6 yuan, for Scheme 3 it is 64.4, and for Scheme 4 it is 56 yuan.

The other costs for each scheme are listed in Table 22.13.

(5) Calculation of the total cost for each scheme

$$C = C_n + C_{g\Sigma} + C_q \text{ yuan/year}$$

According to the calculation results shown above, the total cost is 917.75 yuan/year for Scheme 1, 1058.7 yuan/year for Scheme 2, 885.77 yuan/year for Scheme 3, and 837.2 yuan/year for Scheme 4.

Thus, the cost for Scheme 2 is the highest. Schemes 1 and 3 are in the middle. Scheme 4 is the most economical.

5. **Material consumption index *W* and land occupancy index *D***

The material consumption index and the land occupancy index have small impact on the economic effect comparison. Therefore, they are not calculated.

The economic effect comparison of investment, labor, and cost does not indicate which scheme is the most economical, because these three indicators are conflicting. Thus, the annual consumption cost needs to be calculated. The results are listed in Table 22.14.

The overall economic effect comparison shows that Scheme 4 is the most economical. Schemes 3 and 1 are in the middle. Scheme 2 is the most expensive. Which scheme the factory should adopt depends on the specific circumstances.

Table 22.14 The annual consumption cost for each scheme

Indicator	Scheme 1	Scheme 2	Scheme 3	Scheme 4
Z (yuan/year)	1736.75	1978.7	1341.37	1233.3

Note $Z = C + x_t T_z + x_r R$; $x_t = 0.15$ yuan/year; $x_r = 120$ yuan/year

Schemes 1 and 2 are not economical because their investments in lathes are too high. Accordingly, the investments on lathes in Schemes 1 and 2 must be reduced before they can be adopted widely in practice.

22.10 Economic Evaluation on New Technologies and New Products

When a new technology or a new product is ready, its application in practice depends on the economic effects and the specific circumstances. New technologies and new products with a larger economic benefit are more easily accepted. The amount of economic benefit is decided by the economic evaluation between new technologies or products with old ones.

22.10.1 Economic Evaluation Methods for New Technologies

From the perspective of economic evaluation, new technologies have two categories. One category is those new technologies that are used for producing recurrent consumption materials, such as raw materials, fuel, and energy. The other category is those new technologies that are used for producing fixed assets, such as machinery equipment. The following are the economic evaluation methods for these two types of new technologies.

1. **Economic evaluation for new technologies applied to produce recurrent consumption materials**

Suppose there are two schemes. One is based on a new technology, and the other is based on an existing technology. Each of these two schemes aims to produce G tons of materials in one year. The total annual consumption cost for the new technology scheme is $Z_{new\_produce}$. The total annual consumption cost for the existing technology scheme is $Z_{existing\_produce}$. A survey indicates that the quality of material produced with the new technology is higher than that produced with the existing technology. Thus, the economic effects gotten by users using the two types of material are different. To produce the same amount of final product G_{final}, the total annual consumption cost of the new technology scheme is Z_{new_use}, and the total annual consumption cost of the existing technology scheme is $Z_{existing\_use}$.

When assessing the economic effects of new technologies, the total social labor productivity I method, the total social labor productivity II method, the social net income method, or the social national income method should be applied. The comparison should use the following formulas:

$$Z_{\Sigma\_new} = Z_{new\_produce} + Z_{new\_use} \tag{22.38}$$

$$Z_{\Sigma\_existing} = Z_{exustubg\_produce} + Z_{existing\_use} \tag{22.39}$$

If $Z_{\sum\_new}$ is smaller than $Z_{\sum\_existing}$, the new technology scheme is more economical than the existing technology scheme. In Formulas 22.38 and 22.39, Z_{new_use} and $Z_{existing\_use}$ do not include the cost of raw materials in order to avoid repetitive calculation.

2. **Economic evaluation for new technologies applied to produce fixed assets**

Suppose there are two technological schemes. One is based on new technologies and the other is based on existing technologies. These two schemes produce a type of machine with the amount of G in one year. The annual total consumption cost of the new technology scheme is $Z_{new\_produce}$. The annual total consumption cost of the existing technology scheme is $Z_{existing\_produce}$. The machines produced by each scheme can fit up a mechanical processing factory, which will generate the same amount of final product G_{final} with the same quality and quantity. The annual total consumption cost of machines produced with new technologies is Z_{new_use}. The annual total consumption cost of machines produced with existing technologies is $Z_{existing\_use}$.

The two schemes produce machines, a kind of fixed assets that have a long server period (n_f). For example, in the first year, machines with the amount of G produced with new technologies fit up one mechanical processing factory. Accordingly, the total annual consumption cost of this factory is impacted in the first year. In the service period, the total annual consumption cost of this factory will be impacted continuously. In the second year, machines with the amount of G produced with new technologies fit up another mechanical processing factory. The total annual consumption cost of this factory will be impacted continuously in the service period. By parity of reasoning, machines with the amount of G produced with new technologies will fit up a mechanical processing factory each year. The total annual consumption costs of these factories will all be impacted. This is also the case for machines produced with existing technologies. Thus, Formulas 22.38 and 22.39 cannot be applied directly to evaluate the two schemes.

Instead, the total social labor productivity I method, the total social labor productivity II method, the social net income method, or the social national income method should be applied in the following way:

If $n_f \geq n_j$

$$Z_{\Sigma new} = Z_{new\_produce}\frac{\theta^{n_j}-1}{\theta-1} + Z_{new\_use}\sum_{s=1}^{n_j}\frac{\theta^{n_j-s+1}-1}{\theta-1} \tag{22.40}$$

$$Z_{\Sigma existing} = Z_{existing\_produce}\frac{\theta^{n_j}-1}{\theta-1} + Z_{existing\_use}\sum_{s=1}^{n_j}\frac{\theta^{n_j-s+1}-1}{\theta-1} \tag{22.41}$$

If $n_f \leq n_j$

$$Z_{\Sigma new} = Z_{new\_produce}\frac{\theta^{n_j}-1}{\theta-1} + Z_{new\_use}\left(\sum_{s=1}^{n_j}\frac{\theta^{n_{j-s+1}}-1}{\theta-1} - \sum_{s=1}^{n_j-n_f+1}\frac{\theta^{n_j-s+1-n_f}-1}{\theta-1}\right) \tag{22.42}$$

$$Z_{\Sigma existing} = Z_{existing\_produce}\frac{\theta^{n_j}-1}{\theta-1} + Z_{existing\_use}\left(\sum_{s=1}^{n_j}\frac{\theta^{n_{j-s+1}-1}}{\theta-1} - \sum_{s=1}^{n_j-n_f+1}\frac{\theta^{n_j-s+1-n_f}-1}{\theta-1}\right) \tag{22.43}$$

Z_{new_use} and $Z_{existing\_use}$ in formulas 22.40, 22.41, 22.42, and 22.43 do not include the investment in machines and equipment and the basic depreciation cost, because these costs have been considered. If $Z_{\sum new} < Z_{\sum existing}$, the scheme based on new technologies is more economical.

22.10.2 *Economic Evaluation Method for New Products*

Recurrent consumption materials, such as raw materials and energy, and fixed assets, such as machine, equipment, and buildings, can be evaluated using the same methods that were introduced above for new technologies.

22.11 Technological Economic Evaluation for Technological Transformation and Equipment Replacement

Firms must conduct technological transformation and equipment replacement in order to gain a competitive advantage. Technological transformation and equipment replacement are related, but are not the same. Technological transformation refers to the existing technologies that need to be upgraded. Equipment replacement means that the existing equipment is old and needs replacement. If the existing equipment is not replaced with new equipment based on the existing technology, but is replaced with new equipment based on a new technology, such replacement is a kind of technological transformation. In a word, technological transformation and equipment replacement are both caused by the wear and tear of existing equipment. After several years of use, the existing equipment is aging. It becomes less efficient, poorer in performance, and unsafe. Some equipment serves longer than the service period and needs to be discarded. Meanwhile, new technologies and equipment appear. They are more efficient, more reliable, safer, and more economical. Although some equipment may not have much wear and tear and its service periods do not expire, it still needs to be upgraded. Some technological transformation and equipment replacement is caused by safety concerns, high environmental pollution, or an expired service period. Many other replacements are made to improve economic benefits, increasing production and product variety, improving quality and features, or saving raw material, energy, and natural resources, or saving transportation capacity, labor, the cost of overhaul, and reducing costs. Therefore, it is very important to assess the economic effect of technological transformation and equipment replacement. The following are some methods:

Economic evaluation on technological transformation shares several common characteristics with economic evaluation on equipment replacement: (1) Set the existing technologies and equipment as the benchmark. Set the technological transformation scheme or the equipment replacement scheme as the alternative. (2) Focus on comparing the economic benefits S and total social consumption cost Z of the benchmark and the alternative. Only calculate those items that have difference in S and Z. Skip the items that do not have any difference. (3) Other than the changes in S and Z for a certain firm, the differences in systems should also be considered, including production, circulation, and consumption. In other words, not only the direct economic benefit and direct cost should be considered, but also the indirect economic benefit and indirect cost should be considered. The economic evaluation on technological transformation and equipment replacement can still choose the method with the greater, faster, better and more economic results. For simplicity, the social net income method E_c is adopted in the following example. Here is the formula:

$$\Delta E_c = E_{c\_new} - E_{c\_existing} = \Delta S_\Sigma - \Delta Z_\Sigma \geq 0 \tag{22.44}$$

$$\Delta E_c = \sum_{s=1}^{n_j+n_k} \left[\Delta(j_{zs} G_s) - \Delta Z_s G_s\right] \frac{1}{\theta^s} \geq 0 \tag{22.45}$$

$$\Delta E_c = \sum_{s=1}^{n_j+n_k} \left[\begin{bmatrix} \Delta(j_{zs} G_s) + j_{zos} \Delta G_s - z_s \Delta G_s - c_s \Delta G_s - x_w \Delta w_b G_s - x_y \Delta y_s G_s - x_r \Delta r_s G_s \\ x_d \Delta d_s G_s - x_t \left(\Delta t_{gs} G_s + \Delta t_{ls} G_s - \sum_{s=1}^{n_j} \Delta c_{j[s-1]} G_s + \Delta t_{cs} G_s \right) \end{bmatrix}\right] \frac{1}{\theta^s} \geq 0 \tag{22.46}$$

Or

$$E_{cs} = \sum_{s=1}^{n_j+n_k} \left[\Delta(j_{zis} G_{is}) - \Delta z_{is} G_s\right] \frac{1}{\theta^s} = ZD \tag{22.47}$$

where

$\Delta(j_z G)$ is the change of economic benefit after technological transformation and equipment replacement.

$\Delta j_z = j_z - j_{z0}$ is the change of price (reasonable price based on quality) after technological transformation and equipment replacement.

$\Delta G = G - G_0$ is the change of production (net production) after technological transformation and equipment replacement.

$\Delta z = z - z0 = \frac{z}{G} - \frac{z_0}{G_0}$ is the change in the total social consumption cost of the product in one unit after technological transformation and equipment replacement.

$\Delta C = C - C_0 = \frac{C}{G} - \frac{C_0}{G_0}$ is the change in the cost of product in one unit after technological transformation and equipment replacement.

$\Delta w = w - w_0 = \frac{W}{G} - \frac{W_0}{G_0}$ is the change in the consumption of materials in short supply required by the product in one unit after technological transformation and equipment replacement.

$\Delta y = y - y_0 = \frac{Y}{G} - \frac{Y_0}{G_0}$ is the change in the usage of transportation in short supply required by the product in one unit after technological transformation and equipment replacement.

$\Delta r = r - r_0 = \frac{R}{G} - \frac{R_0}{G_0}$ is the change in the consumption of labor in short supply required by the product in one unit after technological transformation and equipment replacement.

$\Delta d = d - d_0 = \frac{D}{G} - \frac{D_0}{G_0}$ is the change in consumption of natural resources in short supply required by product in one unit after technological transformation and equipment replacement.

$\Delta t_g = t_g - t_{g0} = \frac{T_g}{G} - \frac{T_{g0}}{G_0}$ is the change in the investment in fixed asset occupied by the product in one unit after technological transformation and equipment replacement.

$\Delta t_l = t_l - t_{l0} = \frac{T_l}{G} - \frac{T_{l0}}{G_0}$ is the change in usage of current capital occupied by the product in one unit after technological transformation and equipment replacement.

$\Delta t_c = t_c - t_{c0} = \frac{T_c}{G} - \frac{T_{c0}}{G_0}$ is the change in the residual value of fixed asset for the product in one unit after technological transformation and equipment replacement.

$\Delta c_j = c_j - c_{j0} = \frac{c_j}{G} - \frac{c_{j0}}{G_0}$ is the change in the basic depreciation expense for the product in one unit after technological transformation and equipment replacement.

In the formulas above, the letters with the subscript 0 represent the values before technological transformation and equipment replacement takes place. Letters without the subscript 0 represent the values after technological transformation and equipment replacement takes place. If the result of the calculation of a formula is negative, the new equipment costs more. If the result is positive, the new equipment generates benefits, such as savings in cost.

How to set the service period? The length is determined by two factors. The first one is the internal factor. For instance, after several years of service, a new machine will be less efficient and poorer in performance, due to wear and tear. As a result, its economic benefit and cost will be impacted negatively as time goes on. Although an old machine may still be running and depreciation value and capital occupancy expense will be saved, more money will be spent on maintenance of the old machine. The "service period" is the time when using the existing equipment is economically reasonable. Beyond the service period, using the existing equipment will not be economically reasonable. In this regard, the service period is also called "internal economic service period." The other factor is the external factor. For example, new equipment or a new machine is available on market. It can save energy and raw material and it can reduce cost. In this case, although the existing equipment is still running well without much wear and tear, it does not generate as good an economic benefit as the new one does. As such, the existing equipment needs to be replaced after a certain time, which is called an "external economic service period." Setting the service period needs to consider these two factors: the length of the service period should be shorter than the internal economic service period and the external economic service period. When setting the service period, not only the existing new equipment and new technologies, but also the upcoming new equipment and new technologies need to be considered. In other words, the dynamic impact of technology improvement should be taken into consideration. Sometimes, this kind of consideration might delay technological transformation and equipment replacement or might extend an economic service period.

22.12 Economic Evaluation on Imported Technologies

Imported technologies are technologies introduced from overseas. Importing technologies is different from importing equipment. Importing equipment only from foreign countries is not importing technologies. When technologies are imported, some key equipment, testing instrument, and prototypes will be imported as well. There are many ways to import technologies, such as the technology permit trade, technology service, consulting service, cooperative production, complete set, and project contracting. The buyer should pay the provider for imported technologies.. Some of the payment is investment and some is profit drawing. Economic evaluation on imported technologies can adopt the methods introduced in Chap. 19. In a microeconomic evaluation, the current rate and price are adopted. In a macroeconomic evaluation, the reasonable rate and price are adopted.

22.13 Product Technological Economy-Applications of Value Engineering

Firms produce products or consume products which aim to meet certain demands and gather an economic effect. In order to serve users better and to get more economic effect, firms must study the product technological economy, improving their products, updating their products, and developing new products. Value engineering is a method specifically for studying the product technological economy. It is worth learning. The calculation methods for the macro and micro technological economy introduced in previous chapters can be applied in the product technological economy. Value engineering, which is popular overseas, conducts evaluations with the micro technological economy. It can be called "micro value engineering." Those evaluations using macro technological economy can be called "macro value engineering." In a socialist society, it is macro value engineering, not micro value engineering, that plays a role in product improvement and development. Macro value engineering and micro value engineering use different methods to calculate cost, benefit, and price. However, they share the same practical methods. Next, the product technological economy is discussed, based on micro value engineering. If the economic effect of products is calculated with firm excess labor productivity E_e method in the profit-based approaches, the formulas are:

$$E_e = \frac{S_{\Sigma\_firm}}{Z_{\Sigma\_firm}} = ZD \qquad E_e = \frac{X_{\Sigma\_firm}}{Z_{\Sigma\_firm}} = ZD \tag{22.48}$$

or

$$E_e = \frac{\sum PG}{\sum Z} = ZD \tag{22.49}$$

or

$$E_e = \frac{\sum jG}{\sum Z} = ZD \tag{22.50}$$

where $X_{\sum}$ and $S_{\sum}$ are firms' total economic benefit, which can be physical goods or currency. The total economic benefit X expressed with physical goods is the amount of products G and their quality and feature P. The total economic benefit S expressed with currency is the amount of products G and their price j, because the research target is not the economic effect of a firm, but the economic effect of a certain product. Thus, the above formulas can be changed into the following format:

$$E_{e\_product} = \frac{P}{\sum Z/G} = \frac{P}{z} = ZD \tag{22.51}$$

$$E_{e\_product} = \frac{j}{\sum Z/G} = \frac{j}{z} = ZD \tag{22.52}$$

where P is the quality and feature of a product. j is the price of the product. z is the cost of one product.

Formulas 22.51 and 22.52 are used to calculate product economic effect. They are derived from firm excess labor productivity E_e. They are value formulas in value engineering and value analysis. Actually, value analysis is economic effect analysis. Value is economic effect. Product economic effect formulas indicate that there are three approaches to improve products' economic effect (value). The first approach is to improve products' features or to increase products' prices, and to decrease cost. This is an ideal situation. Sometimes, improving features and increasing prices are conflicted with decreasing cost. Thus, it is necessary to adjust either features or cost reasonably for the purpose of improving the product economic effect.

The second approach is to improve products' features while keeping the same cost. Sometimes, new features raise cost. Thus, it is necessary to consider whether new features increase sales and prices. The third approach is to drop costs while keeping the same features or price. Special attention should be paid to check whether a lower cost decreases features and further impacts sales and prices negatively. In practice, some products have redundant features. Some products are made from materials that do not match their features. Some products are made from expensive raw materials, unnecessarily. The expensive raw materials can be replaced with cheaper ones without any negative impact on features. Some products are not priced properly and do not perform well in sales due to their poor features. In a word, analysis should be conducted to find the proper approach for improving the product economic effect. For similar products, their values can be identified based on the calculation of the product economic effect. Products with high value should be kept, while those with low value should be improved or eliminated. The adoption of an approach depends on the size of products' economic effect. A product usually consists of many parts and raw materials. The economic effect of parts and raw materials affect the final product's economic effect. Thus, it is necessary to study the economic effect of parts and raw material. The methods for assessing the product economic effect are applicable to evaluate both parts and raw material. The following are the methods for evaluating products' features (price), cost, and economic effect:

22.13.1 *Feature* (P, J) *Evaluation*

According to value engineering, what users buy is products' features, not products themselves. Thus, products can be evaluated by evaluating their features. Two approaches can be applied to evaluate products' features. One is feature rating and the other is the feature price (feature cost) approach.

1. **Feature rating**

Products' features (technical features) can be quantified and calculated by rating, so that they can be compared. Products have many features. Some are basic features; others are auxiliary features. For example, the main feature of a thermos bottle is to preserve heat. Its auxiliary features are beauty and convenience for using. Features have several levels, such as the first level feature, the second level feature, and the third level feature. Heat preservation is a first level feature. Heat insulation and sealing are second level features. For a thermos bottle, the second level features serve the first level feature. The evaluation of a feature has two aspects. The first one is the degree of importance of a feature. The other one is how this feature is fulfilled. The importance coefficient $x_{importance\_i}$ represents the level of importance. The fulfillment coefficient $x_{fulfillment\_i}$ represents the degree of fulfillment. These two coefficients can be denoted either with absolute numbers or with relative numbers (percentage). The importance coefficient of a product feature is usually calculated with the survey consultation and rating method, such as the 04 method. A one-on-one recurring comparison is conducted. If there is a huge difference between two features, the more important one gets 4 points, whereas the less important one gets 0 points. If the difference between two features exists but is not very significant, the more important one gets 3 points, whereas the less important one gets 1 point. If there is not much difference between two features, they each get 2 points. Rather than the survey consultation and rating method, the fulfillment coefficient can be calculated with quantity calculation rating method. For instance, a machine gets 5 points if its noise is lower than 65 dB. It gets 1 point if its noise is lower than 75 dB. Then ratio method can be applied to calculate the scores based on the actual noise level. Results gotten with this method are accurate. If possible, this method should be applied in every instance. When the importance coefficient and the fulfillment coefficient of one feature are known, its evaluation coefficient can be calculated with the formula:

$$p_i = x_{importance\_i} \cdot x_{fulfillment\_i}$$

Furthermore, comprehensive evaluation needs to be conducted for each feature. Both the single level and the multiple level comprehensive evaluation methods can then be applied to calculate the comprehensive evaluation value p for one product's total features. Add-multiplication mix method is recommended to calculate comprehensive evaluation value. Once the value of p is known, a product's features can be assessed.

2. **Feature price approach (or feature cost method)**

Features can be calculated in the format of currency, namely price. A product's price can be the price of a similar product, the price that users like to pay, the standard price generated by theoretic calculation, the price calculated with a rating method, or the price gotten by adding the calculated cost based on the rate of cost reduction, profit, and tax. It is well known that price consists of cost, tax, and profit. When price, tax, and profit are given, cost is fixed. Value engineering uses the cost gotten by subtracting tax and profit from the feature price as target cost. The target cost is actually the feature cost, which is one form of feature's value. These calculations are applicable for the micro technological economy. For the macro technological economy, reasonable price and reasonable cost should be adopted.

22.13.2 Expense (Z) Evaluation

"Expense", here, refers to the consumption cost of product (or parts, raw material) in one unit during the calculation period or the service period (lifetime). The items in expense calculation vary between micro technological economic evaluation and macro technologic al economic evaluation. For the micro technological economy, expense includes the cost of production and the cost of users. In particular, it consists of investment, operating cost, tax, and other items. The methods for calculating expense have been introduced in previous chapters. It should be highlighted that expense is usually denoted by the absolute value. But sometimes, expense is denoted by relative value, as well.

22.13.3 Evaluation of Economic Effects

The economic effect of products or parts is the result of feature evaluation and cost evaluation. Based on the analysis of economic effect, measures can be taken to increase economic effect. The size of an economic effect can be used for selecting technological economic schemes as well. In order to increase a product's economic effect, the feature (or raw material) of each part in the product should match the cost of the part (or raw material). Those parts that have main features should be given more weight in the whole cost. Those parts that have secondary features should be given less weight in the whole cost. Here is the formula:

$$E_{ej} = \frac{P_j}{z_j} = \frac{x_{main\_j}}{x_{cost\_j}} \approx 1 \tag{22.53}$$

This formula is used for calculating the value coefficient in value engineering. The feature evaluation value p_j is usually set as the value of the feature importance coefficient x_{main_j}. That is to say, the feature fulfillment coefficient $x_{fulfillment\_j}$ is set as 1. The value of z_j is denoted as x_{cost_j}, the relative value of the cost coefficient. In practice, there are three scenarios: (1) When $E_{ej} = 1$, the actual investment matches with the feature importance coefficient. There is a balance between cost and feature. This is an ideal situation. (2) When $E_{ej} < 1$, the actual investment does not match with the feature importance coefficient. The investment is excessive. Measures should be taken to decrease the cost. (3) When $E_{ej} > 1$, the actual investment does not match with the feature importance coefficient, either. There are two situations. The first one is that the investment is not large enough and users' demands cannot be fulfilled. Thus, more investment must be added to improve the features of parts. The second situation is that although the investment is small, users' demands are fulfilled. This is an ideal situation. This analysis can be used for identifying which parts need improvement. After adjustment, the economic effect coefficient (value coefficient) E_{ej} of each part should be close to 1 or larger than 1. The ultimate goal is to improve the economic effect of the whole product, keeping or increasing the total features while decreasing the expense. When the expense drops to the pre-set level, the target expense (or cost) is achieved.

22.14 Economic Evaluation for Standardization

Each industry has its specific standards, such as the base standard, the method standard, the product standard, the technology standard, and the safety standard. These standards play important roles in people's daily lives. The main advantage of standardization is the achievement of a good economic benefit. The economic benefit of standardization has several levels, such as the benefit of firm standardization, the benefit of department standardization, the benefit of state standardization, and the benefit of international standardization. It is hard to calculate the large scope and the high level of economic benefit. In contrast, it is easy to calculate the economic benefit of firm standardization. Sometimes, it can be very difficult to separate the economic benefit of firm standardization from the economic benefit of other measures. For example, standardization promotes the specialized production of machine parts in Shanghai. Automatic lathes and the non-cutting cold forging process drop the cost from 60 million-170 million yuan to 17 million yuan per ten thousand tons. The cost drops to one quarter or even one tenth of the original one. In this example, standardization drops the cost, together with specialization and new technologies. However, these three measures all generate economic benefit. The economic benefit can be attributed either to new technologies or to specialization. It is very hard to differentiate them. However, if the goal is to determine the necessity of standardization, there is no need to differentiate among these three. Just add the cost of the three measures together and put the total into the standardization scheme. Then, compare this scheme with the scheme in which none of standardization, specialization, or new technologies is adopted. If new technologies and specialization can be applied without standardization and the same good economic effect can be achieved, the economic effect of standardization is zero. If the economic effect of standardization needs to be assessed for other purposes, the economic effect can be allocated according to cost and contribution. The economic effect of some standards does not need allocation. For instance, the cardboard box for packing knitted underwear has more than 450 sizes before standardization. After standardization, the number of sizes drops to 217. Standardization of boxes not only meets the actual requirements, but also makes reuse possible. Each year, over seven thousand tons of cardboard, which is worth of more than three and half million yuan, are saved in China. Standardization has many advantages, especially in raising production, improving quality, saving raw material and energy, saving labor, capital, and transportation. However, the implementation of standardization requires labor, material, capital, transportation capacity, natural forces, and time. Thus, the economic effect of standardization needs to be assessed objectively. The greater, better, faster, and more economical effects method can be adopted to evaluate standardization.

22.15 Economic Evaluation for Environmental Protection

With the rapid development of the economy and society in China, more and more solid wastes, industrial waste water, smoke dust, and sulfur dioxide are generated each year. These contaminants are harmful to the natural environment. Air, water, and land are polluted. Accordingly, human health, all living creatures, the consumption of material, the effects of production, and the ecological balance are affected negatively. Some of the harm caused by environmental pollution can be calculated, but others cannot. Some of environmental pollution improvement has an economic benefit. Others have social benefit. In a word, environmental protection needs to be considered from the perspective of the technological economy. The economic evaluation methods and the comprehensive evaluation methods introduced in the previous chapters can be applied in environmental pollution improvement. The following are some examples.

22.15.1 Economic Effect of Environmental Protection

Environmental protection is usually thought as a kind of expenditure with no economic benefit. However, environmental protection per se does have an economic benefit, which is a decrease in social loss. If no environmental protection measures are taken, pollution will cause economic loss in a variety of aspects, such as a reduction in the output of farming, forestry, animal husbandry, sideline production and fishery, the reduction in the output of special and local product, the erosion of machines, equipment, and buildings, damage in furniture, clothes, and daily appliances, damage in tourist resources, a reduction in tourist income, and a loss of labor. The U.S. estimated the loss caused by air pollution in 1970 is 12.3 billion U.S. dollars, of which 85% is caused by the burning of energy. The amount of energy consumed by the U.S. in 1970 was 2.26 billion tons of standard coal. The average social economic loss caused by the air pollution generated by burning one ton of standard coal is 4.6 dollars. The economic loss caused air pollution in 1980 in China is 4.4 billion dollars (see Table 22.15). The average loss caused by burning one ton of standard coal is 6.2 yuan.[3] Actually, this loss is the usage cost of natural resources for consuming one ton of standard coal (or the tax for environmental resource), namely $x_{d\_air}D_{air}$. The following is the formula for evaluating the economic effect of pollution control on three wastes:

$$E_a = \frac{S_\Sigma}{Z_\Sigma} \geq 1, \quad E_b = \frac{S_\Sigma}{Z_{u\Sigma}} \geq 1 \tag{22.54}$$

$$E_c = S_\Sigma - Z_\Sigma \geq 0, \quad E_d = S_\Sigma - Z_{u\Sigma} \geq 0 \tag{22.55}$$

---

[3] Xu (1986).

Table 22.15 The loss caused by air pollution in 1980 in China

Item	Value (Hundred million yuan)	Percentage (%)
I. Damage of human health	4	9.2
Respiratory disease	3.5	8
Lung cancer	0.42	1
Eye disease	0.08	0.2
II. Loss of residents' living expense	16	36.4
Cleaning and washing clothes	12	27.3
Wearing of clothes	4	9.1
III. Loss in building and equipment	16	36.2
Cleaning	12	27.0
Painting	0.49	1.0
Vehicle washing	0.46	1.0
Paint	1.3	3.0
Corrosion	2.0	4.2
IV. Loss in growth of creature	8	18.2
Grains	5.7	13
Vegetables	1.1	2.5
Livestock	1.2	2.7
Total	44	100

$$\therefore S_\Sigma \geq Z_\Sigma, S_\Sigma \geq Z_{u\Sigma} \tag{22.56}$$

where S_Σ is the reduction of social economic loss and direct economic benefit after the control of environmental pollution. It is calculated based on the annual accumulation in the calculation period.

Z_Σ and $Z_{u\Sigma}$ are the total social consumption cost of environmental pollution control. They are calculated based on the annual accumulation in the calculation period.

If the cost of pollution control on three wastes is smaller or equal to the social economic loss and direct economic benefit, the economic effect of the pollution control is good.

22.15.2 Selection of Measures for Environmental Pollution Control

Some environmental pollution control measures are direct, such as eliminating smoke and dust, as well as treating waste water and waste residue. Some measures are indirect, such as reasonable location of production, reasonable economic structure, and adoption of technologies causing less pollution and saving energy, raw material, water, and other resources. The adoption of environmental pollution control measures depends on the economic evaluation. There are two situations:

1. **The situation without considering economic benefit**

For example, air pollution in some regions already exceeds the set standard. When firms take measures to treat the pollution portion that exceeds the set standard, the direct economic benefit of these measures is not obvious. But they have social benefits, in which social economic benefit (namely indirect economic benefit) exists. However, it is very hard to calculate the social economic benefit. In this case, the following formula should be adopted:

$$E_a = \frac{x}{z} = ZD \quad E_b = \frac{X}{Z_u} = ZD \tag{22.57}$$

or

$$z = ZX \qquad z_u = ZX \tag{22.58}$$

where

X is the physical effect of treatment, such as the reduction of production treatment.

Z and Z_u are the total social consumption costs spent on the treatment of three wastes.

z and z_u are the total social consumption costs spent on the treatment of three wastes in one unit

2. **The situation with economic benefit considered**

After firms take environmental protection measures (especially those measures that use three wastes comprehensively and change harmful wastes into useful things), firms often get a direct effect as well as an indirect effect via protecting the environment. In particular, firms get a direct economic benefit, such as the income from utilizing three wastes. In this case, the following formula should be adopted.

$$E_c = E_{c\_direct} + E_{c\_indirect} = S_\Sigma - Z_\Sigma = S_{\Sigma\_direct} + \Delta S_{\Sigma\_indirect} - Z_\Sigma = ZD \tag{22.59}$$

$$E_d = E_{d\_direct} + E_{d\_indirect} = S_{\Sigma} - Z_{\Sigma u} = S_{\Sigma\_direct} + \Delta S_{\Sigma\_indirect} - Z_{\Sigma u} = ZD \quad (22.60)$$

The environmental protection measure with the largest social net income or social national income has the largest economic effect. When assessing the economic effect, the amount of pollution and the result of pollution treatment should be set at the same standard. For convenience, the calculation in Formulas 22.59 and 22.60 can choose the amount of social net income or social national income achieved by ascertaining the amount, by unit, of waste (polluted air, water, and solids) that has already been treated.

22.15.3 Rational Allocation of Environmental Protection Investment

Regions, departments, and firms have many requests for the implementation of environmental protection projects. However, the limited investment needs to be rationally allocated. The allocation of environmental protection investment can adopt the social accessional net income rate E_{cf} method and the social accessional national income rate E_{df} method.

22.16 Setting the Construction Period

The construction period is usually expected to be short. A shorter construction period has three main advantages. First, production can begin earlier, so that producers and users can receive benefits earlier. Second, the capital occupancy cost can be saved for a longer time. Third, the indirect cost in the construction period, such as construction site administrative expenses, material saving and damage cost, operation cost, and the maintenance cost for unfinished projects, is less. Therefore, the investment in construction is less. The best approaches for reducing the construction period include improving basic construction management, increasing the efficiency of design and construction, and adopting network planning technologies. In order to reduce the construction period, some technological measures can be adopted, such as increasing the amount of equipment and personnel and working overtime. In other words, the direct cost during the construction period should be increased, including labor, energy, ancillary materials, the depreciation and interest of equipment, and investment. In addition, the amount of investment should be increased. Thus, setting the proper length of the construction period is based on analysis and optimization. The optimization of the construction period usually adopts the network planning method, which conducts time optimization, resource-time optimization, and investment-time optimization to plan a production process in a given period and with a certain amount of resources. The setting of the optimized construction period depends on several factors, including the supply of resources, the direct and indirect costs, the amount of expected economic benefit, and the cost of long term capital occupancy. However, the network planning method does not consider the last two factors. Thus, the comprehensive evaluation method with the greater, faster, better and more economical results should be applied to set construction period. The optimization should focus on the input and output, as well as on the total cost and final benefit. This method can be called the "economic benefit-time optimization method."

22.17 Setting up Operation Parameters

Many parameters need to be set up in the process of production, such as the best technical condition, technical parameters (temperature, pressure, flow rate, speed, dimension, and intensity), and the best material blending ratio. The evaluation method with the greater, faster, better and more economical results should be applied to set up the operation parameters by comparing the economic benefit that they generate.

The following is an example of setting up technical parameters for the electrosmelting of steel. After a steel-making electric furnace is built, some parameters need to be set up for it to achieve the largest economic effect, including current intensity, raw material blending ratio, and the amount of material loading. Optimized method can be applied to set up these parameters. Suppose that a firm conducts optimization on the setting of the current intensity, raw material blending ratio, and the amount of material loading. Because the electrosmelting of the steel workshop has been built up, the changes of technical parameters do not affect the investment T, the land occupancy D, or the labor occupancy. Only cost C, material consumption W, and the production volume will be impacted. Accordingly, E_a and E_e formula $\frac{j_g G_l}{Z_l} = ZD$ should be adopted. The optimization process shows that all of the economic indicators of the best scheme are better than those of other schemes, as shown in Table 22.16. Thus, it is not necessary to calculate E_a and E_e. Based on the optimization, current intensity, and raw material blending ratio, the amount of material loading with the largest economic effect are listed below.

1. **Current intensity**
   (1) Melt stage: select a current intensity between 4000–8000 amperes with the 0.618 method. The current intensity, 6500 amperes, has the largest economic effect.
   (2) Oxidation stage: select a current intensity between 4000–8000 amperes with the 0.618 method. The current intensity, 5000 amperes, has the largest economic effect.
   (3) Deoxidization stage: select 650 amperes for the first 10 min when the voltage is 210. Select 5000–5500 amperes for the later stage when the voltage is 120.

Table 22.16 Economic indicators for producing one ton molten steel

Item	Original scheme			Current scheme		
	Unit consumption	Unit price	Cost	Unit consumption	Unit price	Cost
Power (kwh)	1122	0.10 yuan	112.2 yuan	950	0.10 yuan	95 yuan
Fluorite (kg)	35.5	0.19 yuan	6.75 yuan	30	0.19 yuan	5.7 yuan
Lime (kg)	69.3	0.10 yuan	6.93 yuan	60	0.10 yuan	6 yuan
Magnesia (kg)	41.8	0.175 yuan	7.32 yuan	35	0.175 yuan	6.13 yuan
Brine (kg)	11.8	0.10 yuan	1.18 yuan	10	0.10 yuan	1.0 yuan
Electrode (kg)	8.8	1.60 yuan	14.1 yuan	7	1.60 yuan	11.2 yuan
Smelting time[a]	3 h			2 h and 8 min		

[a]A shorter smelting time indicates the increment in production capacity

2. **Raw material blending ration**

   (1) Scrap steel: steel cuttings: pig iron = 280:100:700. The amount of pig iron changes according to the requirements of steel grade.

   (2) Scrap steel lumpiness: Big chunk material (<1.2 m) accounts for 50% and is placed at the bottom of furnace. Medium size material accounts for 30% and is placed in the middle of the furnace. Small size material accounts for 20% and is placed at the top inside the furnace.

3. **The amount of material loading**

   Select 450 kg material with the method of a blind man climbing mountains.

22.18 Setting up Correct Inventory

Setting up the correct inventory is a typical issue in the technological economy. Firms' inventory includes purchased raw materials, energy, parts, and internal products. The correct inventory is actually the economic volume of the production for manufacturing departments in firms. It is the economical ordering amount for purchasing departments. When the annual production volume and the consumption amount are given, the larger production volume can save the expense of preparation and adjustment before production. However, a larger production volume requires a higher holding cost, including the expenses on material receiving, inspection, damage, transport, and depreciation. Accordingly, a reasonable production volume must be set up.

Similarly, a larger purchasing volume can save the expense of ordering and transportation. However, the holding cost increases as well. Thus, a reasonable purchasing volume must be set up. Production volume and purchasing volume are related with inventory. Setting up the correct inventory requires a reasonable production volume and purchasing volume.

The macro and micro annual consumption cost approaches to the evaluation method, with greater, faster, better and more economical results, should be applied to set up correct inventory.

$$Z = Z_{purchaing\_produciton} + Z_{inventory} = ZX \tag{22.61}$$

$$Z_{purchaing\_produciton} = Z_{volume} \times \frac{G}{G_{volume}} \tag{22.62}$$

$$Z_{inventory} = \frac{1}{2} Z_{inventory}\, G_{volume} \tag{22.63}$$

$$\therefore Z = Z_{volume} \times \frac{G}{G_{volume}} + \frac{1}{2} Z_{inventory}\, G_{volume}$$

$$\frac{dZ}{dG_{volume}} = -Z_{volume} \frac{G}{G_{volume}^2} + \frac{Z_{volume}}{2} = 0$$

$$\therefore G_{volume} = \sqrt{\frac{2Z_{volume} G}{Z_{inventory}}} \tag{22.64}$$

where

$Z_{purchasing\_production}$ is the annual expense that firms spend on purchasing and production, such as the transportation cost, order processing cost, and production adjustment fee.

$Z_{inventory}$ is the annual expense that firms spend on inventory, such as the costs of material receiving, inspection, damage, transport, depreciation, and capital occupancy.

G is the required production volume or purchasing volume in one year.

G_{volume} is the amount of production at one time or the amount of purchasing at one time.

$z_{inventory}$ is the expense of purchasing and production at one time.

z_{volume} is the cost of inventory for products in one unit or purchasing in one unit.

22.19 Technological Economy in the Third Industry

The third industry refers to those industries that produce non-material products or services, including commerce, finance, insurance, transportation, service, science, education, healthcare, culture, art, sports, public services, and consulting. The previous chapters introduced examples in transportation and in science research. This chapter mainly introduces applications in other fields. As we know, some of the third industries have direct economic benefits, while others do not. Instead, they have indirect economic benefits. For example, the indirect economic benefit for sports, healthcare, recreation, and travel is the increment in labor productivity and free time. The indirect economic benefit for education is the improvement in management and the increment in labor productivity. The indirect economic benefit for food service is the reduction of waiting time for customers and the decrease in the number of diseases. Overall, the indirect economic benefit in the non-production field includes the saving of time, a higher labor productivity, and a reduction in healthcare spending. These three indirect economic benefit can be calculated by the following formulas:

1. **Calculation of economic benefit generated by time saving**

$$\Delta E_{c\_time} = x_s \cdot \Delta S_{time} \cdot R \tag{22.65}$$

where

x_s is the economic effect coefficient of time utilization.
ΔS_{time} is the amount of labor hour saved by one person in one year.
R is the total amount of people in each year

2. **Calculations of economic benefit generated by improving labor productivity**

$$\Delta E_{c\_labor} = x_r \cdot \Delta\, x_r \cdot R \tag{22.66}$$

where

x_r is the economic effect coefficient of labor utilization.
Δx_r is the increment in percentage, denoted as %

3. **Calculation of economic benefit generated by reduction in healthcare expenses**

$$\Delta E_{c\_time} = j_{healthcare} \cdot \Delta\, r_{frequency} \cdot R_{frequency} \tag{22.67}$$

where

$j_{healthcare}$ is the average expense on one catch of disease.
$\Delta r_{frenquency}$ is the dropping rate of becoming sick. For example, the sick rate might drop 10%,
$\Delta r_{frenquency}$ is 0.10.

$R_{frenquency}$ is the original illness frequency rate with the unit person-time/year

The evaluation methods with greater, faster, better and more economical results can be applied to compare technological schemes in non-production field.

$$E_{c\_nonproduciton} = E_{c\_direct} + E_{c\_indirect} = ZD \tag{22.68}$$

When comparing several schemes that fulfill the same demands, the annual consumption cost method can be applied:

$$Z = ZX \tag{22.69}$$

Sometimes the total social labor productivity method can be applied as well:

$$E_a = \frac{X_\Sigma}{Z_\Sigma} = ZD$$

In this formula, the indirect economic benefit should be deducted from the total social consumption cost Z.

22.20 Economic Evaluation and Comprehensive Evaluation for Scientific Research

22.20.1 Characteristics of Evaluation for Scientific Research

Scientific research has two categories: one is research on natural science, and the other is research on social science. These two types of scientific research can be further categorized into theoretical research, application theory research, and application research (including research and development). Scientific research has its own unique characteristics. Accordingly, economic evaluation and comprehensive evaluation for scientific research should consider these characteristics, including the uncertainty of scientific research effect, the incomplete economy of scientific research effect, the potential effect of scientific research findings, the repeat effect and versatility of scientific research findings, the investment, and the periodicity of scientific research expenditure.

22.20.2 Evaluation Methods for Scientific Research

1. **Evaluation method of scientific research projects**

When selecting research projects, scientific research departments must conduct evaluations. There are two available methods to do the evaluation. One is the economic evaluation, and the other is the comprehensive evaluation. For those research projects with an economic impact, an economic evaluation should be adopted, together with a comprehensive evaluation. For those research projects without a distinct economic impact, a comprehensive evaluation is more applicable. The economic evaluation of scientific research projects should adopt one or more approaches in the evaluation methods of greater, faster, better, and more economic results, as required.

Suppose that there is a scientific research project with a success probability p 0.80. The success of this project will help a department gain an annual social net income of E_c 12.5 million yuan. n_k is 5 years and n_j is 15 years. What will be the maximum of research funding T that might be approved? (The period of scientific research n_{kl} is known to be 5 years and the research funding is evenly allocated to each year with the same amount T during the 5 years).

The E_{cf} method is applied for the calculation:

$$E_{cf} = \frac{PE_c \frac{\theta^n j_{-1}}{\theta - 1} \times \frac{1}{\theta^n k1^{+n} k^{+n} j}}{T \frac{\theta^n k1 - 1}{\theta - 1} \times \frac{1}{\theta^n k1}} = \frac{0.8 \times 1250 \times \frac{\theta^{15} - 1}{\theta - 1} \times \frac{1}{\theta^{25}}}{T \frac{\theta^5 - 1}{\theta - 1} \times \frac{1}{\theta^5}}$$

when $E_{cf} = 1$, the research funding required in each year is $T = 4.3$ million yuan. The maximum research funding in the five years $T_{\sum}$ is $5 \times 4.3 = 21.5$ million yuan.

The comprehensive evaluation on scientific research projects can adopt the standards and methods introduced in Chap. 20.

2. **Evaluation method for scientific research achievements**

The evaluation on scientific research achievements has two purposes: one is to assesss and encourage scientific research, and the other is to commercialize scientific research achievements. Evaluation methods for these two purposes are different.

The evaluation of scientific research achievements can adopt economic evaluation methods and comprehensive evaluation methods. The methods are very similar to those applied for assessing scientific research projects. The differences are: (1) the probability for the success of scientific research should be set as 1; (2) the degree of requirement and success probability to the difficulty and practicability regarding scientific research in comprehensive evaluation should be changed.

Commercialization of scientific research achievements relies on the results of the economic evaluation and the comprehensive evaluation of scientific research achievements.

3. **Evaluation method for science and technology schemes**

Various schemes will be proposed in the scientific research process. The schemes need to be evaluated so that the best one can be selected. The evaluation of science and technology schemes can adopt both economic evaluation methods and comprehensive evaluation methods. They are very similar to those adopted in the evaluation of scientific research project. These methods are not discussed here, in order to avoid repetition.

4. **Reasonable allocation methods for scientific research funding**

The amount of scientific research funding is limited. However, the number of scientific research projects might be large. In order to generate the maximum effect, scientific research funding must be allocated reasonably. A proper ratio should exist among the various funding received by theoretical research, application theoretical research, and application research (including development). These three should support each other. For application research, there might be several projects requiring research. Each project will need a certain amount of research funding. The social accessional net income rate E_{cf} or the social accessional national income rate E_{df} methods can be applied to allocate the research funding reasonably.

5. **Proportion method for the economic effect of scientific research**

Generally, the economic evaluation about whether a user should adopt new scientific research achievements does not need to consider the expenditure spent by research departments and promotion departments, because that expenditure has been spent. In China, such expenditure is paid by the states. Research departments and promotion departments do not calculate economic benefit, nor do they receive economic benefit. As such, the economic benefit of scientific research achievement is received completely by the users. Such a proportion method does not motivate research departments and promotion departments at all. The economic benefit received by users via adopting new scientific research achievements should be allocated among research departments, promotion departments, and users. A reasonable proportion should be set based on the difficulty of research and the size of contribution from research departments, promotion departments, and users, respectively.

22.21 Technological Economy in Daily Life

The technological economy exists in daily life. Examples include what food needs to be bought in the supermarket, going to work by riding a bike or taking a bus, what clothes should be purchased, and whether to buy a refrigerator or a washing machine. The answers to these questions are personal decisions, based on custom, experience, preference, demand, fashion, and the economic condition. Sometimes, calculation is conducted to find the answers. In fact, the technological economy can be applied to find the answers to these questions, as well.

Suppose a family has a savings of 0.5 million yuan. What is a reasonable way to spend this amount of money? There are two options available. One is to keep the money in a bank savings account. The other is to buy a house and to rent it out. If the price of house is 10,000 yuan/m^2, 0.5 million is enough to purchase a house with a usable floor area of 50 m^2. If the monthly house rent is larger than the monthly interest of the savings in the bank account, purchasing and renting out a house is more reasonable than saving the money in a bank account.

22.22 Technological Economy in Construction Projects - Applications of Feasibility Study

A construction project has three stages. Although the stage are given different names across countries, the essentiality does not change (see Table 22.17). According to Table 22.17, the content and requirements of construction projects in China were sketchy and simple compared with those in other countries. Thus, they do not meet the requirements in practice.

Accordingly, more effort is needed in the planning stages of construction projects in China. According to the experiences in foreign countries, the planning stages of construction projects have four phases:

1. **Feasibility Research for projects**

Feasibility research in this phase is equivalent to opportunity research, overseas. Opportunity research reports are actually reports of the concepts of projects. Feasibility research needs to consider the following factors: (1) the increment of the demands in peoples' lives; (2) the demands of other departments and the connection with other departments; (3) the possibility of diversification and alliance; (4) extension; (5) the process of natural resources; (6) the possible alternative for imported products; (7) the demands for export; (8) the experiences of similar countries; (9) the possibilities of manpower, capital, material, and resources; (10) the policies of the states. Tentative plans for construction projects can be categorized into two groups. The first category is the general tentative plan, the outline of which is listed in Table 22.18. The other category is the detail tentative plan. Its outline consists of the following factors: (1) the general economic situation, including the status of national economy development, national principles, policies, and regulations, and the rationality of projects from the perspective of national economy; (2) survey and prediction of product demands; (3) the supply of raw material; (4) location and plant sites; (5) production scale; (6) production methods; (7) personnel and management; (8) the time schedule of project construction; (9) the economic evaluation on firms, including the cost of investment, capital resource, cost and expenditure, and profit rate on funds; (10) the national economy evaluation.

2. **Preliminary study for projects**

A "preliminary study" is equivalent to the "preliminary feasibility study" in foreign countries. The report of the preliminary feasibility study is equivalent to the report of preliminary planning. The outline for the report of preliminary study consists of

Table 22.17 Flow path of construction projects

China				Western Countries		Former Soviet Union	
Proposed improvements		The first-five-year period	Current				
Planning stage	1. Tentative planning phase (feasibility study of project plan) 2. Preliminary planning phase (initial study of project plan) 3. Detail planning phase (detail study of project plan) 4. Development and approval phase (evaluation of project plan)	1. Statement of planned tasks phase (statement of planned tasks, plant site selection)	1. Planning phase (technological economic survey, plant site selection, development of master schedule)	Before invest-ment	1. Tentative planning phase (general opportunity study, specific opportunity study) 2. Preliminary selecting phase (initial feasibility study) 3. Plan development phase (feasibility study) 4. Evaluation and decision phase (evaluation)	Planning stage	1. Planning of national economy development and geographical distribution 2. Technological economic evaluation

(continued)

Table 22.17 (continued)

China				Western Countries		Former Soviet Union	
Construction stage	5. Design phase 6. Construction and installation phase 7. Training phase 8. Preoperation phase	2. Preliminary design phase (developing initial design, technological economic analysis) 3. Construction phase (construction design and annual construction plan, equipment purchase and construction preparation, and construction installation)	2 Design phase (initial design, technical design, construction design, construction preparation) 3. Construction phase (civil construction, equipment installation, personnel training, preoperation)	Investment stage	5. Negotiation and contract signing phase (negotiation and signing contract) 6. Project design phase (concept design, basic design, detailed design) 7. Construction phase (civil construction, equipment installation) 8. Training phase (personnel training) 9. Preoperation phase (preoperation)	Design and construc-tion stage	3. Technical design phase 4. Construction design phase 5. Construction installation phase 6. Preoperation phase
Operation stage	9. Operation phase (production, sales, and maintenance)	4. Completion and commissioning phase (production preparation, completion, inspection, commissioning)	4. Production phase (commissioning)	Production stage	10. Production phase (commissioning)	Production stage	Commissioning

Table 22.18 The outline for general tentative plans

Study based on regions	Study based on departments	Study based on resources
1. Natural conditions in this region	1. The position and role of this department in the industry	1. The characteristics, reserves, and development status of the resource
2. Social and economic conditions in this region	2. The production scale, structure, and growth of this department	2. The role, national and international demand, and utilization of this resource in national economy
3. Export and import in this region	3. The status of products imported by this department	3. Industries based on this resource. Their structure, growth status, technological economy indicators, and development plans
4. Manpower, materials, capital, and resources conditions in this region	4. The prediction of product demand quantity and the possibility of export in this department	4. Main limitations for developing industries based on the resource
5. The development status of industries using local resources	5. Status of gaining local raw materials	5. Predication of the product demand and future of export for the product based on the resource
6. Condition of local infrastructure	6. Condition of local infrastructure	6. Condition of infrastructure
7. The overall list of industries with development potential based on the evaluation of the above items. But the following industries should not be considered: (1) small local demand and high outward transportation expenses; (2) local production conditions are not better than those in other regions; (3) required raw materials are not available locally; (4) export is required but located at inland with poor transportation condition; (5) not consistent with priority in national plans. Then estimate the demands of products and explore the possibility of development based on other available documents	7. Based on the evaluation of the above items, propose tentative plans and explore the possibility of development	7. Based on the evaluation of the above items, propose tentative plans and explore the possibility of development

(continued)

Table 22.18 (continued)

Study based on regions	Study based on departments	Study based on resources
8. Set the optimal production scale for newly built plants and expanded plants	8. Same as left	8. Same as left
9. The estimate ofinvestment expenses, including (1) land, (2) technology, (3) equipment (production equipment, auxiliary equipment, service equipment, spare parts, wearing parts, and tools), (4) civil engineering (cleaning up site, buildings, outdoor engineering), (5) preconstruction expenses (6) current capital	9. Same as left	9. Same as left
10. The estimate of the amount of input, including (1) raw materials, (2) materials, (3) finished products, (4) auxiliary materials, (5) public services (energy and transportation), (6) manpower	10. Same as left	10. Same as left
11. The estimate of cost expense	11. Same as left	11. Same as left
12. The estimate of theannual gain of sales	12. Same as left	12. Same as left
13. Project organization and management	13. Same as left	13. Same as left
14. Project execution schedule	14. Same as left	14. Same as left
15 Investment in departments related to the project (for example, infrastructure)	15. Same as left	15. Same as left
16. Plan of capital source required by the project	16. Same as left	16. Same as left
17. Financial evaluation, including investment recovery period and profit rate of funds	17. Same as left	17. Same as left
18. Economic evaluation	18. Same as left	18. Same as left

the following factors: (1) the main points of the plan, (2) the general situation, (3) the prediction of market demands, (4) the production scale, (5) the geographical distribution and plant site, (6) raw material, energy, and transportation, (7) technical skills and equipment, (8) the establishment of institution, (9) manpower, (10) scheduling, (11) financial evaluation and national economy evaluation on firms, (12) the comprehensive evaluation.

3. **Detailed study for projects**

The "detailed study" is equivalent to "feasibility study" in foreign countries. The report of the feasibility study is the same as the report of the detailed study. The outline for the detailed study is the same as that for the preliminary study.

4. **Evaluation study for projects**

The "evaluation study" for projects is equivalent to the "assessing study" in foreign countries. The report of the assessing study is actually the development and approval of the plan report.

The feasibility study currently adopted in China is actually the plan study for construction projects. It consists of concept development, the preliminary plan study, the detailed plan study, and the plan evaluation. A large amount of technological economic issues exist in the four stages of the plan period. It is very necessary to conduct a firm economic evaluation, a national economic evaluation, and a comprehensive evaluation on construction projects. The following is an example of how micro and macro technological economic evaluation methods can be applied in the feasibility study for construction projects.

This is an example of a feasibility study on the construction project of the outward transport of coal in Shanxi province. In the planning study of making Shanxi province an energy, heavy industry, and chemical engineering base, several schemes are considered to transport coal currently in Shanxi province to outside areas. Railway transport schemes and road transport schemes are among these schemes. The feasibility study of a railway transport scheme and a road transport scheme is conducted using micro technological economic evaluation methods (dynamic return on investment x_{tl} method and firm excess profit E_f method). It is known that the present price for transport via railway is 1 cent per ton kilometer, namely 100 yuan per ten thousand ton kilometer. The investment in one thousand ton kilometer is 950 yuan. The cost including tax, but excluding the basic deprecation fee, is 150 yuan. The present price for transport via road is 0.2 yuan per ton kilometer, namely 2000 yuan per ten thousand ton kilometer. The investment in one thousand ton kilometers is 670 yuan. The cost (including tax but excluding the basic depreciation fee) is 800 yuan. Set the calculation period as 20 years. The lowest return on investment x_{tl} is set as 0.3. The excess profit for firms E_f can be calculated as below:

$$
\begin{aligned}
E_{f\_road} &= \left(j_{road} - C_{jy\_road} - C_{tax\_road}\right)\frac{\theta^n - 1}{(\theta - 1)\theta^n} - t_{road} \\
&= (2000 - 800) \times 3.316 - 670 \\
&= 3309 \text{ yuan/ten thousand ton kilometer} > 0 \quad \text{(present value)} \\
E_{f\_railway} &= (100 - 150) \times 3.316 - 950 \\
&= -1116 \text{ yuan/ten thousand ton kilometer} < 0 \quad \text{(present value)}
\end{aligned}
$$

Next calculate firm return on investment x_{tls}.
Set $E_{f\_road} = 0$, namely

$$(2000 - 800) \times \frac{\theta^n - 1}{(\theta - 1)\theta^n} = 670$$

Suppose the road is useable all the time. Then n = ∞. Therefore,

$$\frac{1 - \frac{1}{\theta^\infty}}{\theta - 1} = \frac{670}{1200}$$

$$x_{tl\_road} = \frac{670}{1200} = 1.79 > 0.3$$

whereas $$x_{tl\_railway} = \frac{-50}{950} = -0.05 < 0.3$$

Thus, the micro economic effect for coal transport via road is better. Coal transport via railway will lose money.

Analysis with the macro technological economic evaluation should consider the following two factors. The evaluation should adopt a systemic approach and should consider the impacts on other departments. Although transporting coal via road has a larger economic effect, the cost of coal users increases 1900 yuan per ten thousand ton kilometer at the end. In addition, the price of transport via railway is not reasonable. It is comparable with the price of the road. For the same amount of goods, the price for railway is 0.01 yuan per ton kilometer, whereas the price for the road is 0.2 yuan per ton kilometer. Next, the social net income E_c method for macro technological economic evaluation is applied to calculate the relative economic effect for transporting coal via railway or road. n_j is set as 20 years. The investment effect coefficient x_t is set as 0.15. The operation cost for road C_{road} excluding tax is 700 yuan per ten thousand ton kilometer. The operation cost for railway $C_{railway}$ excluding tax is 120 yuan per ten thousand ton kilometer.

(1) Considering the impacts on other departments

$$\begin{aligned}E_{c\_road} &= E_{c\_transport} + E_{c\_user}\\ &= (j_{road} - c_{road} + j_{user} - c_{user\_road})\frac{\theta^{n_j} - 1}{(\theta - 1)\theta^{n_j}} - t_{road} - t_{user}\\ E_{c\_railway} &= E_{c\_transport} + E_{c\_user}\\ &= (j_{railway} - c_{railway} + j_{user} - c_{user\_railway})\frac{\theta^{n_j} - 1}{(\theta - 1)\theta^{n_j}} - t_{railway} - t_{user}\\ \Delta E_{c\_railway} &= E_{c\_road} + E_{c\_railway}\\ &= \left[(j_{road} - j_{railway}) - (c_{road} - c_{railway}) + (c_{user\_road} - c_{user\_railway})\right]\\ &\quad \frac{\theta^{n_j} - 1}{(\theta - 1)\theta^{n_j}} - t_{road} - t_{railway}\\ &= [(2000 - 100) - (700 - 120) - (2000 - 100)]\frac{\theta^{n_j} - 1}{(\theta - 1)\theta^{n_j}} - (670 - 950)\\ &= -580 \times 6.26 + 280\\ &= -3350 \text{ yuan/ten thousand ton kilometer}\end{aligned}$$

(2) Adopting a reasonable transporting price

The reasonable transporting price is set as 0.03 yuan per ton kilometer for railway. In order to do the comparison, the transporting price is set as 0.03 yuan per ton kilometer for the road as well. Thus,

$$\begin{aligned}&E_{c\_road} = (300 - 700)]\tfrac{\theta^{n_j} - 1}{(\theta - 1)\theta^{n_j}} - 670 = -3174 \text{ yuan/ten thousand ton kilometer}\\ &E_{c\_railway} = (300 - 120)]\tfrac{\theta^{n_j} - 1}{(\theta - 1)\theta^{n_j}} - 950 = 176 \text{ yuan/ten thousand ton kilometer}\\ &\Delta E_c = -3174 - 176 = -3350 \text{ yuan/ten thousand ton kilometer}\end{aligned}$$

This result indicates that transporting coal via road is far less economical than transporting coal via railway with the total social economic effect considered. The adoption of technological schemes depends on the result of the macro technological economic evaluation. Accordingly, transporting coal via road is not applicable. However, the technological scheme of transporting coal via road was once adopted, based on the result of a micro technological economic evaluation. As a result, the road between Datong and Qinhuangdao benefits from coal transportation, whereas coal users in southern China, mainly Shanghai, Jiangsu, and Zhejiang, suffer from a high cost for coal. Finally, transporting coal via road was abandoned. This example in practice proves that it is not enough to conduct only a micro technological economic evaluation; a macro technological economic evaluation is necessary as well.

References

Statistics Group in Institute of Mathematics of the Chinese Academy of Sciences (1979), Common mathematical statistics methods, Science Press.

Xu, S. B. (1986). The loss caused by air pollution in China. Air pollution and acid rain.

Chapter 23
Applications of Technological Economics

23.1 Introduction

This chapter is the second part of Part IV Application of technological economy. It includes the research results that the author has achieved regarding national demands in different periods. The research results have been adopted by some sections and some government administrations. They have contributed to the social and economic development in China and have generated significant economic and social benefits. This chapter uses some of the research results as cases to explain theoretical methods of technological economics. Particularly, they are 18 cases that the author has worked on in the past 50 years. They are introduced in time order. Thus, they represent the author's research track. These cases not only represent the role of technological economics in national economic development, but also prove the achievements that the author gets in technological economics. The cases in this chapter are real applications in practice. Therefore, formulas and tables are numbered independently for each case. Meanwhile, research background, scientific significance of the achievements, and practical value of each case is explained in details. For the purpose of making each case complete, the contents of some cases are repetitive.

23.2 Design Standard of Heating Systems in China

[Research background, scientific significance of achievements, and practical value] According to the analysis on the meteorological data of China, about 2/3 area in China, particularly northeast, north and northwest regions, need heating systems. The average heating hours are higher than 3000 h in these regions. Houses and buildings in those regions, including urban residential houses, plant workshops, and public buildings need heating systems, namely the equipment for heating. In order provide heat, heating supply devices (boiler rooms and thermal power stations) and heating transmission equipment (heat

S. Xu, *Technological Economics*,
https://doi.org/10.1007/978-981-15-8582-1_23

supply pipelines and network) are needed as well. A complete heating system consists of these elements. For example, there are numerous large and small heating systems in Beijing, including heaters in thousands of square meters of indoor space, several hundred boiler rooms, large thermal power stations, and many kilometers of huge heat supply transmission pipes. The construction of these heating systems cost huge amount of investment and steel. These investment and steel are closely related with heating design standards, especially the standard for outdoor temperature, base on which the indoor heating temperature is calculated. If the standard is lower than that required in practice, the actual heating demand will not be fulfilled. If the standard is higher than that required in practice, investment and steel will be wasted. Therefore, it is very important to set the design standard for calculating outdoor temperature. In the past, the calculation was based on Caipulin empirical formula. In Beijing, the outdoor temperature was set as −13 or −12 °C, which was calculated with the method adopted in Soviet Union construction procedures and widely used in practice. However, the method adopted in foreign countries might not fit for the situation in China. Accordingly, the author proposed a new method for calculating outdoor temperature. Based on the result got from the new method, the outdoor temperature is set as −9 °C instead of −13 or −12 °C for Beijing. The new standard will save huge amount of investment on heating systems. More important, the quality of heating service is easier to maintain. The author's papers on this topic (see Chaps. 1–6 **and** 14 **in the research list at the end of this book) were published and were included in foreign indexes. In specific, the author won the second prize of youth science issued by the Energy Research Institute, Soviet Union Academy of Science in 1959. This is the first award that the author ever received for science research. The author came back to China from Soviet Union in 1960 and presented a paper on the annual conference of Beijing Electric Engineering Society in 1962. The paper was well accepted by experts and later was nominated for the Scientific Invention and Creation Award. The new standard calculated with the proposed method has been adopted in practice and has generated good economic benefits and social benefits.**

The change of outdoor temperature involves complex natural climate factors, including water flow, sun light, and wind. The change is completely out of control of human beings. Therefore, mathematical statistics and probability theory are usually adopted in engineering to study natural phenomena. Accordingly, these methods are applied to study outdoor air temperature in this chapter.

Heat storage capacity, namely heat stability, of buildings varies across construction types. When setting the calculation temperature of outdoor air, we do not choose the instantaneous or hourly temperature of outdoor air. Instead, we choose the mean of temperature of outdoor air during a certain period Z (usually daytime or nighttime). The length of this period Z should be set depending on the heating power inertia indicator ΣD.[1] The larger the value of ΣD, the longer the period Z. In practice, buildings can be categorized into three groups according to their peripheral structure:

(1) Lightweight buildings. The value of ΣD falls between 0 and 4.0. The length of Z should be set as 24 h (one day and one night) for such buildings.
(2) Small buildings. The value of ΣD falls between 4.1 and 7.0. The length of Z should be set as 72 h (three days and three nights) for such buildings.
(3) Heavy buildings. The value of ΣD is higher than 7.1. The length of Z should be set as 120 h (five days and five nights) for such buildings.

Other than climate condition, the heating power inertia indicators should be considered when setting the calculation temperature of outdoor air. Because the structures and materials of buildings are different in northern and southern China, different lengths of Z should be adopted when setting the calculation temperature of outdoor air. For example, in northern China the heat storage capacity of buildings is strong. Thus, a longer Z should be adopted, such as 72–120 h (three days and three nights or five days and five nights). In contrast, in southern China the heat storage capacity of buildings is weak. As a result, a shorter Z should be adopted, such as 24–72 h (one day and one night or three days and three nights). In a word, the length of Z should be set based on the value of ΣD across regions. However, the length of Z was set as five days and five nights in the temporary heating standard issued by the former National Construction Committee. This setting did not consider the differences in the structures and materials of buildings across regions in China. Thus, it is not reasonable. Even in the same region, due to the difference in in the structures and materials of buildings, the length of Z should be different as well.

According to the data of average temperature in daytime and at night retrieved from observation in many years, we can get the average temperature $T_{H(1)}$, $T_{H(3)}$, and $T_{H(5)}$ of one day and one night ($Z = 1$), three days and three nights ($Z = 3$), and five days and five nights ($Z = 5$), respectively, during the continuous coldest time in one year. Then the aggregate method in mathematical statistics is applied to calculate the variation coefficients C_u and C_s. At last, the probability curves and guarantee ratio curves for $T_{H(1)}$, $T_{H(3)}$, and $T_{H(5)}$ can be selected from the Pearson II type theoretical probability curve series (see Fig. 23.1).

Based on the probability curves in the figure, it is easy to find the possibility P of the average temperatures for one day and one night, three days and three nights, and five days and five nights during the continuous coldest time in one year. For instance, the possibility of $T_{H(1)} = -9$ °C (Curve 1) is 85%. In other words, this situation occurs once in more than one year on average. The possibility of $T_{H(3)} = -9$ °C (Curve 2) is 70%. This situation occurs once every 18 months on average. The possibility of $T_{H(5)} = -9$ °C (Curve 3) is 40%. This situation occurs once every 2 and half years on average. The probability of the same outdoor air temperature value is closely related with the length of Z. The longer Z, the smaller possibility.

[1] ΣD is heating power inertia indicator for buildings. $D = R \cdot S$, where R is the thermal resistance of walls in buildings and S is the coefficient of heat absorption for construction materials in buildings.

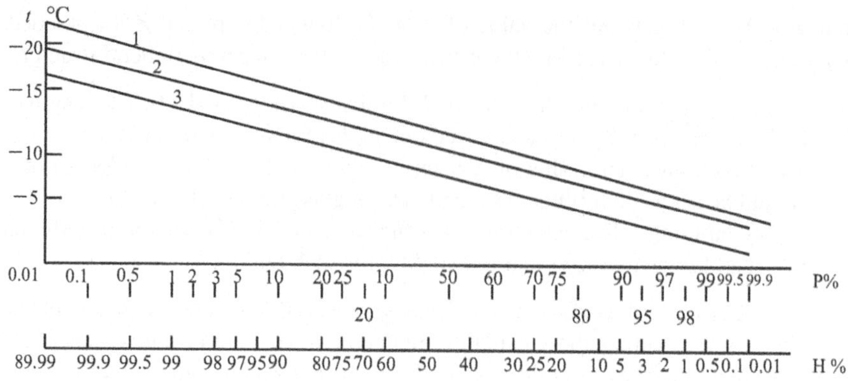

Fig. 23.1 Probability curves and guarantee ratio curves outdoor air temperature (based on the temperature data collected in 29 years in Beijing). Curve 1—$T_{H(1)}$, Curve 2—$T_{H(3)}$, Curve 3—$T_{H(5)}$

If the outdoor air temperature is set as −13 °C, the probability of the situation when the average temperature of one day and one night is −13 °C will be 20%. This situation occurs once roughly every 5 years. For the average temperature of three days and three nights, the probability is 5%. Such situation occurs once roughly every 20 years. For the average temperature of five days and five nights, the probability is 1.3%. Such situation occurs once roughly every 100 years.

This example indicates that it is problematic to set −13 °C as the standard for calculating temperature in heating system design. Whether this standard saves investment and steel is questionable.

When setting temperature of outdoor air, the reliability of accepted heating supply, namely the assurance factor in the calculation for heat supply, must be considered. So far, the number of research on assurance factor in the calculation for heat supply is still small around the world.

Changes of outdoor air temperature do not occur only in one month, one quarter, or one year. Instead, the changes occur across a year. In addition, the changes in different years vary. As such, assurance factor of heat supply is categorized into two groups in this chapter. One group is assurance factor of heat supply in repeat calculation. It is the amount heat required by a heating system for meeting the demands of heating, namely the amount of heat needed for keeping the indoor temperature at 18 °C. If assurance factor of heat supply is set as 100%, a heating system must provide the maximum of heat supply in every year to keep the indoor temperature at 18 °C. The assurance factor of heat supply can be calculated with the following formula:

$$H_r = 100 - P\% \tag{23.1}$$

Figure 23.2 shows the values of the values of assurance factor of heat supply in Beijing. For instance, assurance factor H_r for the situation when $T_{H(5)} = -13$ °C is 98.7%. This indicates that the heat supply will be normal for almost 99 years in a 100-year period.

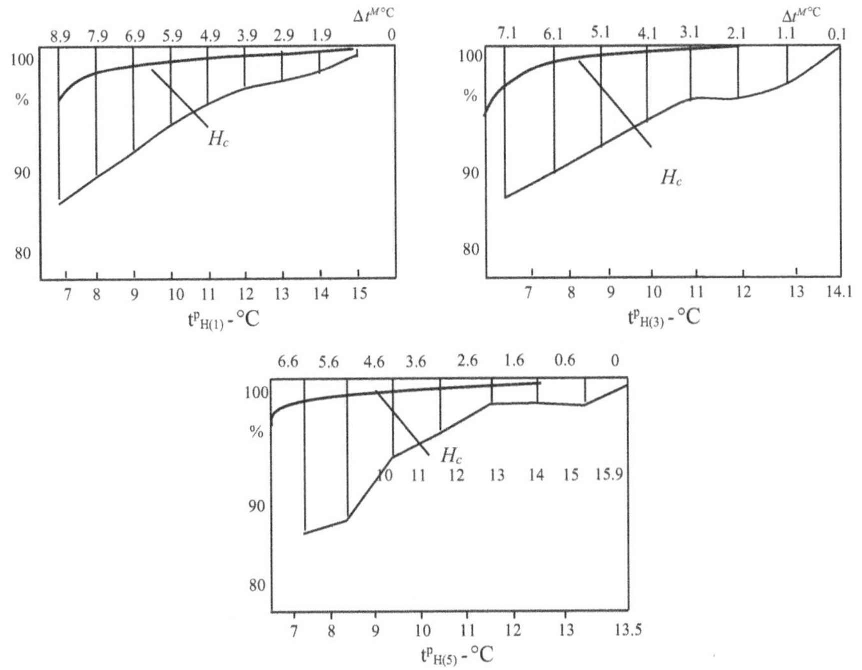

Fig. 23.2 The correlation between the maximum decrease value of indoor temperature Δt^M, assurance factor of heat supply H_c, and the calculation outdoor air temperature (Beijing). *Note* The area within the lines represents the change of assurance factor of heat supply based on the data collected in 29 years in Beijing

The other group is assurance factor of heat supply in extended period, which refers to the length of extended period when a heating system provides the maximum of heating service to keep the indoor temperature at a normal level. Assurance factor of heat supply in repeat calculation can be calculated with the following formula.

$$H_c = 100 - \frac{aZ(1 - H_r)}{n_0} 100\% \tag{23.2}$$

where a is coefficient of average extended period in multiple years when the indoor temperature is not maintained at a normal level.

n_0 is the number of days for the average heating period.

Although assurance factor of heat supply in repeat calculation and assurance factor of heat supply in extended period are both represented with percentage, they are different. For instance, 50% of assurance factor of heat supply in repeat calculation is not equivalent to 50% of assurance factor of heat supply in extended period. Because in the years when 50% of the time period normal heating supply is not available, the length of extended period when normal heating supply is not available might be short whereas the extend in which heating supply is not available might be serve.

Thus, for the same outdoor air temperature, the value of the result calculated with assurance factor of heat supply in extended period is far larger than that calculated with assurance factor of heat supply in repeat calculation. Formula (23.2) reflects this relationship.

According to Formula (23.2), the smaller of the values of a and Z, the larger n_0. As a result, H_0 is larger than H_r.

Therefore, it is more reasonable to calculate outdoor air temperature with assurance factor of heat supply in extended period.

The value of assurance factor of heat supply in extended period, called assurance factor for calculation hereinafter, is connected with many factors, such as standard of residents' living requirement, economic condition in a country, and the supply of steel.

In practice, the higher the value of assurance factor for calculation, the higher quality of heating service received by residence. In other words, the buildings can maintain a normal indoor temperature even in the coldest years, which do not occur very often. As a result, more investment and steel are required for heating systems. Thus, the maximum value of assurance factor for calculation relies on the national investment and the supply of steel. It is not correct to think the higher the value, the better. On the other hand, it is not appropriate to set the value of assurance factor for calculation just from the economic perspective. If we do so, the smaller the value, the better. However, residents' health will be impacted negatively and their living, study, production, and work will be negatively impacted as well. Thus, the bottom line for the value of assurance factor for calculation is to allow people live, study, and work as normal. These two principles must be considered when setting the value of assurance factor for calculation.

Based on experiments, the impact of indoor temperature on human body is listed in the following Table 23.1.

It can be known from the table that when indoor temperature drops to 15–17 °C, people's living, study, and work will not be impacted. As the indoor temperature keeps dropping, the impact on people's health will gradually increase.

Human's feeling is not only impacted by indoor air temperature, but also related with other factors, such as humidity, people's status (sitting, exercising, or working), eating, habits, and clothes. Accordingly, the feeling listed in Table 23.1 is not absolute. Instead, other factors should not be neglected.

According to the rules of design in the Soviet Union Academy of Construction Science, the indoor temperature can only drop 3–5 °C even in the coldest days in winter.

In addition, the drop of assurance factor for calculation is related with other factors, such as the adjustment of heating loads and adding provisional heating devices.

Table 23.1 Effect of indoor temperature on human feeling

T °C	10–12	13–14	15–17	18–20	21–24	25–27
Feeling	Cold	Cool	Comfortable	Most comfortable	Warm	Hot

Adjustment of heating loads can be archived with the following measures: reducing the supply of hot water, reducing heat supply for those buildings where people do not stay very often or where heat emission exists, and reducing ventilation. The measures for increasing heating resources include rising heating load output when electricity loads of thermal power stations drop, and adding electric furnaces and stoves. If necessary, people can wear more clothes. The larger effect that the above measures generate, the smaller value of assurance factor for calculation for heating suppler in a certain area.

In practice, it is reasonable to set assurance factor for calculation as 98–99%. Because the investment and steel are both limited in China, assurance factor for calculation can be set as 97–98% based on specific conditions in certain areas.

Following the aforementioned methods, we set a new value for the calculation of outdoor temperature in Beijing. Specifically, we suggest to adopt the value −9 °C instead of −12 or −13 °C, which is calculated with Soviet Union formulas. Here are the reasons.

(1) According to the results in Fig. 23.2, if the value for the calculation of outdoor temperature is set as −9 °C, the assurance factor for calculation is 98% for the average temperature in three days and three nights. In fact, the assurance factor for calculation changes between 90 and 100%. In this case, the possible drop of room temperature is almost equal to the allowable values (5 °C). Therefore, it is reasonable for calculation outdoor temperature T_H^P to choose −9 °C for protecting people's health and fulfilling their requirements of normal living, study, production, and work. For the average temperature in five days and five nights, the assurance factor for calculation will be larger if the value for the calculation of outdoor temperature is set as −9 °C. The maximum indoor temperature drop will be smaller than the allowable value (smaller than 5 °C). Under the worst conditions, if the average temperature of one day and night is adopted as the calculation temperature in Beijing, the average assurance factor for calculation in multiple years will be 97% if the value for the calculation of outdoor temperature is set as −9 °C. The maximum possible drop value of indoor temperature will be higher than 5 °C (7 °C). However, the time when indoor temperature drops over 5 °C is very rare, only accounting for 0.02–0.07% of the heating period. That is to say, this situation might occur once in decades. Such situation has little impact on the setting of the calculation of outdoor temperature.

If the measures, such as adjustment of heating loads and adding provisional heating devices, are adopted, the actual assurance factor of heat supply can be 100% when T_H^P is set as −9 °C.

According to Fig. 23.2, when the calculation of outdoor temperature is higher than −9 °C, the assurance factor of heat supply drops remarkably (lower than 96%). The actual assurance factor of heat supply will change in a wider range. The maximum possible drop value of indoor temperature Δt^M will be larger than 5 °C.

Therefore, it is reasonable to set a value higher than −9 °C as the calculation outdoor temperature when adjustment of heating loads or adding provisional heating devices is not implemented.

Table 23.2 The range of indoor temperature lower than normal temperature during non-heating-supply period and the duration (Beijing) (non-heating-supply period is based on $T_H = 10$ °C)

Outdoor temperature T_H lower than 15 °C in non-heating-supply period	Possible drop of indoor temperature (°C)	Total time when indoor temperature might drop (average in multiple years) (day and night/year)
14.9–14	0.1–1	22.30
13.9–13	1.1–2	18.20
12.9–12	2.1–3	13.43
11.9–11	3.1–4	8.98
10.9–10	4.1–5	5.58
9.9–9	5.1–6	2.48
8.9–8	6.1–7	1.31
7.9–7	7.1–8	0.73
6.9–6	8.1–9	0.18
5.9–5	9.1–10	0.11
4.9–4	10.1–11	0.07

Note: Heat emission coefficient is set as 3 °C

Usually heating supply begins when outdoor temperature is 10 °C. This valued of temperature is set with the consideration of indoor heat emission. Research shows that heat emission can raise indoor temperature 3–6 °C. During non-heating-supply period, indoor temperature will not keep normal if outdoor temperature drops to 12 or 15 °C. Table 23.2 lists the range of indoor temperature drops during non-heating-supply period and the time when they occur.

Table 23.2 shows that the drop of indoor temperature is obvious and the duration is long in non-heating-supply period. If the drop of indoor temperature and the duration are same in heating-supply period and non-heating-supply period, the calculation outdoor temperature T_H^P will rise to −5 °C in Beijing.

In order to save coal, the temperature when heating supply begins is set as 5 °C in China. Accordingly, indoor temperature drops more and the duration lasts longer in non-heating-supply period. If the existing poor quality of heating supply is continued to be allowed, it is ok to set the calculation temperature as −9 °C or higher. But this is not reasonable to keep people's living, study, work, and production as normal in the long run.

(2) According to Table 23.2, if the calculation outdoor temperature is set as −13 °C (calculated with Soviet Union formula) in Beijing, the assurance factor for heating supply will be close to 100%. However, the range of indoor temperature possible dropping is 0.6–1.1 °C. This will cause huge waste of investment and steel. If the calculation outdoor temperature is set as −9 °C in Beijing, the total heating load will drop 13%. As a result, huge amount of investment will be saved. The estimation on saving only considers the investment on heating supply network and boilers for peak times. The investment on indoor heating devices,

water heating devices, and their running cost are not considered. Therefore, the economic benefit of setting the calculation outdoor temperature as −9 °C will be larger in practice.

(3) The value of T_H^P for Beijing is −13 °C, the result calculated with Caipulin formula of Soviet Union. This value changes to −12 °C if calculated with the method in Soviet Union construction procedures. These two values are too low for China because climate conditions in China and Soviet Union are different. In addition, the calculation methods adopted in Soviet Union have defects.

According to the study conducted by Northern China Power Design Institute of former Water and Electricity Ministry,[2] designs based on −13 or −12 °C generates surplus devices for heating supply. Instead, designs based on −9 °C just meet the requirement of heating supply devices in practice.

23.3 Reasonable Utilization and Allocation of Heavy Oil[3]

[Research background, scientific significance of achievements, and practical value] After the establishment of the People's Republic of China, petroleum was mainly imported. Artificial petroleum was provided by domestic suppliers. Since the establishment of Daqing oil field, gasoline, kerosene, and diesel were self-sufficient in China. However, heavy oil (residual oil) was discarded. Later, the states called all industries for using heavy oil without any charge. Since then, the supply of heavy oil became short. Accordingly, the State Scientific and Technological Commission (SSTCC) called for studies on how to utilize and to allocate heavy oil reasonably. The author conducted a research on heavy oil by interviewing firms who used or produced heavy oil across China. In this study, the author collected huge amount of data and document about technological economy. At the end, the author submitted a report named Rational Utilization and Distribution of Heavy Oil to SSTCC [32]. The results of this study was adopted by China for supporting the development of petrochemical industry in China. Since then, the petrochemical industry in China has developed well. The research shows that it is not reasonable for power plants to burn heavy oil among more than 20 usage of heavy oil. However, coal power plants were called up to use heavy oil in Cultural Revolution. Later, the petroleum reserves were found limited in China. In the task from China Association for Science and Technology (CAST), the author proposed to rationally use 100 million t of oil in 1985 [176]. In this proposal, the author pointed out that power plants should not burn oil. Finally, the power plants changed back to burn coal. What a lesson! The method proposed by the author in this report became a new method for technological economy. This research won the honorable mention issued by

[2] Yan [Ya63].

[3] Xu [Xu65].

Chinese Academy of Sciences (CAS) in 1964. This is the first award that the author ever won in China. The honorable mention is the first award with which China promotes science and technology.

With the rapid development of petroleum industry in China, the yield of heavy oil (residual oil) becomes larger and larger. However, the usages of heavy oil become wider and wider and the demand of heavy oil becomes larger and larger as the development of science and technology. As a result, despite the rise in the production of heavy oil, the demands of heavy oil can still not be fulfilled. In order to utilize heavy oil rationally, the usages of heavy oil must be ranked. The heavy oil should be allocated based on the ranking list. The ranking should fulfil the demands in the society and consider the size of economic effect. If heavy oil is the only option for certain usages, these usages should have priorities to fulfil demands. However, the usages of heavy oil are usually ranked according to their economic effects. Therefore, economic effect of each usage of heavy oil must be calculated and evaluated. In this way, scientific supports can be provided for the states to make energy policies and to developing allocation plans for heavy oil.

The author conducted field study on production and utilization of heavy oil in China. The usages of heavy oil can be categorized into four groups. In the first category, heavy oil is used as fuel for boilers in power plants, civil and industrial boilers, and boilers for boats and trains; for metallurgical furnaces, such as open hearth furnace, reverberatory furnace, and crucible; for tunnel furnace and down draught kiln that produces ceramics and refractory materials; for rotary kiln and vertical kiln that produces cement; for tank furnace and pot furnace that produces glass; for mill furnace and annealing furnace that produce steel; for calcining kiln that produces calcined soda; for steamer that produces sodium hudroxide; for drying furnace; and for diesel engines. In the second category, heavy oil is used as chemical raw material. For example, water gas can be mixed with heave oil to produce synthesis gas (synthetic ammonia and methanol). Heave oil can be used for producing synthetic hydrogen via pressurized gasification or ordinary pressure gasification. In the third category, heavy oil is used for producing clean oil and refinery coke that is required for making electrode, insulation materials, and carbofrax because heavy oil can delay coal carbonization. Mixing heavy oil with coal in pit kiln can produce more coke-oven gas, coke for metallurgy, tar, and benzene. Using heavy oil can produce high thermal-value coal gas, tar, benzene, and naphthalene. Heavy oil can be injected into blast furnaces for reducing coke ratio and increasing the production and thermal value of coal gas. Injecting heavy oil into water gas furnaces can increase the thermal value of coal gas and recover benzene. In the fourth category, heavy oil is used for other purposes, such as the pavement material of secondary roads.

Each utilization of heavy oil can be regarded as a scheme. Accordingly, there are around 20 schemes for heavy oil utilization. Then social additional net income rate method can be applied to evaluate their economic effects.

$$E_{cf} = \frac{\Delta E_c}{\Delta W} = \frac{\Delta Z}{\Delta W}$$

$$= \frac{\Delta C + x_w \Delta W + x_y \Delta Y + x_r \Delta R + x_t \Delta T + x_d \Delta D}{\Delta W_{\text{heavy\_ oil}}}$$

where $\Delta W_{\text{heavy\_oil}}$ represents the amount of heavy oil consumption. ΔE_c represents the amount of additional net income.

For simplicity, the calculation ignores the economic benefit generated by the saving of man power, land, materials and transportation caused by the use of heavy oil. In the words, $x_r \Delta R$, $x_d \Delta D$, $x_w \Delta W$, and $x_y \Delta Y$ all equal to zero.

Based on the information collected in field survey and the above formula, the economic effect of each utilization of heavy oil can be calculated. Next is an example of using heavy oil as the raw material for synthetic hydrogen. Here are the details of calculation. Coke, anthracite, and brown coal are chosen as materials for producing synthetic hydrogen in China. If brown coal is selected for producing synthetic hydrogen, 1 t of synthetic hydrogen costs 3.5 t of coal. The price of coal is 434.1 yuan per t. The investment per unit is 740 yuan per t. If synthetic hydrogen is produced via applying pressurized gasification on heavy oil, 1 t of synthetic hydrogen costs 0.81 t of heavy oil. The price of heavy oil is 230.21 yuan per t. The investment per unit is 700 yuan per t. The economic effect indicator of producing synthetic hydrogen with heavy oil E_{cf} can be calculated as below.

$$\begin{aligned} E_{cf} &= \frac{(434.1 - 230.21) + 0.15(740 - 700)}{0.81} \\ &= \frac{209.9}{0.81} = 259 \text{ yuan/t} \end{aligned}$$

It can be seen that producing 1 t of synthetic hydrogen with pressurized gasification of heavy oil can save 259 yuan compared with using brown coal.

The economic effect of other utilization of heavy oil can be calculated in the same way. The results are listed in Table 23.3.

The results in Table 23.3 show that heavy oil has the highest economic effect when being used as industrial chemicals, material, and high quality fuel. Value saved by 1 t of heavy oil is 150–330 yuan. Heavy oil has the second highest economic effect when being used as industrial chemicals and when being used comprehensively. For this usage, value saved by 1 t of heavy oil is 50–116 yuan. Heavy oil has the third highest economic effect when being used as low thermal value coal gas. For this usage, value saved by 1 t of heavy oil is 32–66 yuan. Heavy oil has the lowest economic effect when being used as fuel to replace coal. For this usage, value saved by 1 t of heavy oil is −9.932–66 yuan. The negative value means that no saving will be generated. Instead, cost rises when heavy oil is used as fuel.

Allocation of heavy oil can be implemented according to the results of economic effect listed in Table 23.3. The order of allocation in Table 23.3 does not consider certain conditions when special requirements are needed. In practice, these conditions must be taken into consideration. In addition, the table does not consider special conditions in certain regions. Actually, the order of allocation must consider usages

Table 23.3 Effect of utilizing heavy oil and the order of allocation for heavy oil in China[a]

Order of allocation	Usages of heavy oil	Effect of utilizing heavy oil (per t)		
		Substitution of fuel	Weight of substitution fuel	Saving (yuan)
I	Heavy oil is used as raw material, material, and high quality fuel	—	—	150–330
	Heavy oil is used for producing synthetic ammonia through pressurized gasification	Brown coal, coke, anthracite	4.3 t —	259 150
	Heavy oil is oxidized for producing asphalt or used directly as pavement material for roads	—	—	330
	Heavy oil is used as the substitution of coke oven gas in steel making (1) Coke oven gas is used as city gas (2) Coke oven gas is used for making synthetic ammonia	— — Coke oven gas Coke oven gas Diesel	— — 2.5–2.9 kilostere 2.5–2.9 kilostere	178 312[b] 212[c] 200
	Heavy oil is used as fuel for diesel engines		0.9–0.95 t	
II	Heavy oil is used as raw materials and is used comprehensively Heavy oil is processed with delayed coking Coking blended with heavy oil Making coal gas with heavy oil Heavy oil is injected into water gas furnace to carbureting Heavy oil is injected into blast furnace Heavy oil is injected into furnace in fluid bed to increase production of synthetic ammonia Heavy oil is used for producing synthetic ammonia through normal pressure gasification	— Crude oil Coking coal Coking coal Coking coal Coking coal Brown coal Brown coal Coke, anthracite	— — — — — 1.3 t 3 kilostere coal gas 3.9 t —	50–116 116.3 78 75.9 78 50 79.5 87 0

(continued)

Table 23.3 (continued)

Order of allocation	Usages of heavy oil	Effect of utilizing heavy oil (per t)		
		Substitution of fuel	Weight of substitution fuel	Saving (yuan)
III	Heavy oil is used as low thermal value coal gas:			32–66
	Heavy oil is burned in reverberatory furnace	—	—	32.2
	Heavy oil is burned in tank furnace	Mixed gas	6.5 kilostere	52.5
	(1) Changed to use heavy oil	—	—	66
	(2) For new construction	Mixed gas	9 kilostere	52.5
	Heavy oil is burned in tunnel furnace	Mixed gas	9 kilostere	66
	(1) Changed to use heavy oil	—	—	
	(2) For new construction	Mixed gas	9 kilostere	
		Mixed gas	9 kilostere	
IV	Heavy oil as fuel to replace coal			−9.9–19.8
	Heavy oil is burned in calcining furnace	—	—	19.8
	Heavy oil is burned in heating furnace	Clean coal	1.9 t	5.31–0.5
	Heavy oil is burned in reverberatory furnace	Clean coal	1.6-1.75 t	4.7
	Heavy oil is burned in boiler	Clean coal	1.58 t standard coal	1.5
	Heavy oil is burned in down draft kiln	Clean coal	1.5 t	−9.9–0.5
	Heavy oil is burned in small and medium mobile boilers	Clean coal	1.2–1.47 t standard coal	9.1
	Heavy oil is burned in small and medium fixed boilers	High quality coal	1.7 t	0.3–16.7
	Heavy oil is burned in boilers for large power plant	High quality coal	1.34–1.9 t	2.1–3.2
		Raw coal, fault coal	1.44-1.47 t	

[a]Some specific usages of heavy oil are not included in this order. They can be treated with propriety
[b]Compared with producing synthetic ammonia with brown coal through gasification
[c]Compared with producing synthetic ammonia with coke through gasification

as well as regions. The reason is that the same usage of heavy oil might generate different economic effect across regions. When other conditions are the same, heavy oil has the highest economic effect in the regions that are close to petroleum refineries and where coal is expensive. Heavy oil has high economic effect in the regions that are close to petroleum refineries and where coal is cheap. Heavy oil has the lowest economic effect in the regions that are far away from petroleum refineries and where coal is cheap. The order of allocation for heavy oil also needs to consider the way how heavy oil is utilized. For the same usage, heavy oil has higher economic effect for building new firms than for transforming exiting firms, because the cost for building fuel supply systems is much lower when building new firms. However, if existing firms can increase production of current equipment by using heavy oil, they have higher economic effect than new firms.

23.4 Rational Utilization of Industrial Secondary Energy in China[4]

[Research background, scientific significance of achievements, and practical value] Secondary energy is also called complementary energy or waste heat. Complementary energy or waste heat is the energy that is not used in energy consuming devices in national economy, especially in industries. It is redundant and discarded energy. In 1973, the author was assigned the task for in charge of the study on rational utilization of secondary energy in China by the Energy Saving Office under State Planning Commission. Led by State Planning Commission, the author first investigated the utilization of waste heat in Tianjin and wrote a report, which was sent out across China. Later, the author conducted surveys in Beijing, Shanghai, and Liaoning. Furthermore, the author developed utilization plans, which saved plenty of energy in practice. This study initiated the new field of the energy study in China. In 1975, the author designed development strategies for rational utilization of energies and comprehensive utilization of scientific technology in China from 1976 to 1985. The strategies were adopted by State Planning Commission. The strategies also won the Significant Scientific Technology Achievement Award issued by Chinese Academy of Sciences and National Science Congress Award.

Complementary energy falls into seven types: surplus heat of high temperature waste gas, surplus heat of cooling medium, surplus heat of waste gas and waste water, surplus heat of high temperature product and slag, surplus heat from chemical reaction, surplus heat of combustible waste gas and wastes, and overpressure of high pressure fluids. The major complementary energy is surplus heat. Surplus heat accounts for about 17–67% of the total amount of fuel consumed in each industry. The recyclable surplus heat is about the 60% of the total amount of surplus heat. These percentages are smaller than the real ones because the data of surplus heat

---

[4]Xu [Xu73].

is not complete. In terms of regions, the usable industrial surplus heat accounts for 10–20% of the total amount of consumed fuel in Beijing and Tianjin. In Shanghai, the percentage is 25%. Compared with Beijing and Tianjin, Shanghai has a higher percentage because (1) it has more metallurgical firms that generate huge amount of surplus heat; (2) surplus heat includes that come from combustible gas, such as waste gas from refineries and coal gas from blast furnaces; (3) the amount of consumed fuel in the survey does not include non-energy fuel, such as coal for coking and for gasification with synthetic ammonia; (4) power generation industry that consumes huge amount of coal but generates few surplus heat is not included in this survey.

Based on the surveys in Beijing, Tianjin, and Shanghai, metallurgical industry generates the largest amount of surplus heat. Chemical industry and machinery industry generate fewer surplus heat. Light textile, construction materials, and other industries generate the fewest surplus heat. Regarding resource, the largest portion of surplus heat comes from high temperature waste gas. Surplus heat of cooling medium and waste gas and waste water rank next. Few surplus heat come from high temperature product and slag, chemical reaction, combustible waste gas and wastes (see Tables 23.4 and 23.5 for details).

1. **Utilization of surplus heat of high temperature gas (mainly flue gas)**

This type of surplus heat accounts for around 50% of the total complementary energy. It is mainly generated by furnaces and gas turbines in industries such as metallurgical, chemical, machinery, construction materials, ceramics, and power. Some civil furnaces generate surplus heat as well. Surplus heat in high temperature gas generated by furnaces in industries accounts for 30–40% the total amount of fuel consumed by these furnaces. Such kind of surplus heat can be used in the following three ways.

The first way is direct utilization. High temperature gas (500–1000 °C) is used for heating objects at low temperature directly. In this way, the heat of the high temperature gas is absorbed by low temperature objects directly.

Table 23.4 Surplus heat generated by industries

Industry	Percentage (%) of the amount of surplus heat in the amount of consumed fuel	Percentage (%) of the amount of recyclable surplus heat in the amount of consumed fuel
Metallurgy	>50	>30
Chemical	>25	>15
Machinery	>25	>15
Glass enamel	>25	>15
Paper making wood	>28	>17
Textile	About 17	About 10
Construction materials (Annular Kiln)	67	40
Miscellaneous	17	10

Table 23.5 Distribution of surplus heat (Beijing, Tianjin, and Shanghai)

Distribution by industry		Distribution by category	
Industry	Percentage (%)	Category	Percentage (%)
Metallurgy	43.5–54.0	High temperature waste gas	48.4–54.6
Chemical	28.0–33.3	Cooling medium	14.9–23.0
Machinery	4.5–12.3	Waste gas and waste water	10.3–16.0
Light textile	6.1–8.1	High temperature product and slag	6.4–13.5
Construction materials	3.2–4.8	Chemical reaction	4.6–8.8
Miscellaneous	5.4–7.0	Combustible waste gas, liquid and materials	8.3
Total	100	Total	100

(1) Preheat feeding air. Air is blown into furnaces for supporting combustion. At the end, the air is exhausted via chimneys as high temperature flue gas. If normal temperature air is blown into furnaces, a lot of heat inside the furnaces are absorbed by the air and then exhausted. If air is preheated by high temperature flue gas first and then is blown into furnaces, the amount of heat inside the furnaces absorbed by the air will drop a lot. For glass tank furnace and open hearth for steeling, if air is preheated to 1000 °C or so, huge amount of fuel will be saved. Such usage of surplus heat becomes common overseas. Air is preheated by high temperature flue gas for heating furnaces, melting furnaces, and cupola furnaces. In China, cupola furnaces are blown into hot air in some areas. Usually, blown hot air can save fuel 15–20% and increase heat efficiency 10–15% compared with cold air.

(2) Preheat fuel. If fuel is heated by high temperature flue gas first and then is injected into furnaces, the total fuel consumption of furnaces will drop. For instance, coal gas is heated to 280 °C by high temperature flue gas exhausted by the heating furnace in Shanghai Heavy Duty Machine Forging Plant.

(3) Preheat materials. Fuel can be saved when cold materials, such as steel ingot and billets, are heated by high temperature flue gas before they are added into furnaces. In addition, the heating time of the furnaces will be shorter. As a result, the productivity of furnaces will increase. For example, the high temperature flue gas exhausted by a furnace for producing zinc oxide in Shanghai Jinhua Chemical Plant is 900 °C. There used to be a heating furnace for preheating and melting zinc ingot. Now zinc ingot is preheated and melt by the high temperature flue gas exhausted by the zinc oxide furnace. In this way, there is no need to use the preheating furnace. In Japan, steel ingots are preheated to 300 °C by surplus heat of high temperature flue gas and then are loaded into heating furnaces.

(4) Drying. Many materials contain moisture. They need to be dried first and then be loaded into furnaces. Since the temperature required for evaluating moisture is low, high temperature flue gas can be used for drying materials (as low as 40 °C).

In this way, heating furnaces are no longer needed. Fuel and power are saved. For example, Tianjin Chemical Plant uses high temperature flue gas exhausted by calcium carbide furnaces to dry coke. This approach drops moisture of coke from 4–5 to 1%. The quality of coke is improved and more than 700 t of coal is saved in one year. More than 1000 working days are saved. Furthermore, the stable temperature for dry coke avoids burning accidents. Safe production has strong protection. The reverberator for producing lead in Shanghai Jinghua Chemical Plant uses high temperature flue gas to dry materials and achieved good results.

(5) Annealing. Annealing is required for metal processing. Because annealing furnace does not require high temperature, high temperature flue gas can be used for annealing. Dalian Locomotive and Rolling Stock Works builds annealing furnaces at the gas duct of room type forge furnaces. Connected with heating furnaces, the annealing furnaces heat general forged pieces and process annealing with high temperature flue gas (about 800 °C) exhausted by heating furnaces. In this way, huge amount of power is saved.

(6) Desalination of sea water. Surplus heat of high temperature flue gas can be used for desalinating sea water.

The second way is indirect utilization. Different from direct utilization, in this usage surplus heat of high temperature flue gas is used for heating medium, such as water and air. Then the heated medium is applied in different ways.

(1) Generate steam. Surplus heat boilers, instead of boilers burning coal, can be installed in high temperature gas duct to generate steam. This is a very common usage. Surplus heat boilers can be installed when the temperature of flue gas is above 500 °C and the flow of flue gas is over 5000 m^3/hr.

(2) Supply hot water. Metal heat exchangers can use high temperature flue gas for heating cold water. The temperature of flue gas cannot be lower than 100–200 °C, because metal will be corroded below dew point. At present, asbestos cement heat exchangers are adopted and the temperature of flue gas can drop to below dew point (100 °C or even 50–60 °C).

(3) Generate hot air. Flue gas at low temperature can be used for generating hot air with air heat exchangers, thermal wheel, and thermal tubes.

The third way is comprehensive utilization. Use surplus heat of high temperature flue gas to preheat air and coal gas that are blown into furnaces. Or use surplus heat of high temperature flue gas to preheat air and coal gas, and to generate steam with boilers. This is the best usage of surplus heat of high temperature flue gas. The effect is better than that of single usage of surplus heat.

2. **Utilization of surplus heat of high temperature products and slag**

The process of heating at high temperature exists widely across industries, such as metal smelting, melting and processing; gasification of coal and coking; petroleum refining; cement producing; brick making; refractory materials making; and ceramics making. The final products and slag generated in these processing are at high temperature, usually at several hundred centigrade, 1000 centigrade, or even higher. These products can be solid, liquid, or gas. Usually they are not usable before their temperature drops to the normal level. Accordingly, huge amount of heat is emitted in the cooling process. According to the surveys conducted in Beijing, Tianjin, and Shanghai, the surplus heat emitted by final products and slag at high temperature accounts for 6–14% of the total surplus heat. The surplus heat also accounts for a large portion of the total consumed fuel. For example, surplus heat of black metallurgical slag accounts for 2–6% of metallurgical fuel consumption; surplus heat of non-ferrous metal metallurgical slag accounts for 10–14% of metallurgical fuel consumption. The temperature of the slag is higher than 1200 °C. Surplus heat of coke accounts for half of the consumption of fuel for coking. This type of surplus heat has be utilized in some industries, including construction materials, petroleum refining, and metallurgy. However, there is still a large portion of this type of surplus heat has not be utilized yet. Utilizations of this type of surplus heat are similar with those of high temperature gas.

The first way is direct utilization.

(1) Preheat feeding air. For instance, the cooling section in tunnel furnaces allows cold air to absorb the surplus heat of products at high temperature. The preheat air is then blown into the burning section. In cement furnaces, air is preheated to 200–350 °C first by the surplus heat of products at high temperature and then is blown for combustion.
(2) Preheat raw materials. Steam, coal, and diesel oil distilled and cracked from refineries are at high temperature. The surplus heat of them is used for preheat raw materials with heat exchangers. Sometimes, slag at high temperature can be mixed directly with raw materials. In Shanghai Bayi Iron and Steel Plant, the melting period is shorten by preheating raw materials with adding steel slag back into the furnaces. The preheat saves around 5 kWh for 1 t of steel. This plant saves 100,000 kWh in one year.
(3) Drying. Surplus heat of slag at high temperature can be used for drying directly. Mixing slag at high temperature with raw materials containing moisture can evaporate water. The ore for making sulphuric acid at Changsha Chemical Plant sometimes contains over 20% moisture. The ore cannot be loaded into furnaces before moisture is evaporated. By mixing the ore with slag at high temperature, this plant does not need a special drying furnace any more.
(4) Annealing. Hot forged pieces need annealing after they are hammered in forge workshops. Usually hot forged pieces are cooled down first and then are annealed in annealing furnaces. The surplus heat of hot forged pieces can be used for annealing without consuming any power or oil. In the forge workshops at Tianjin Tractor Manufacturing Factory, in the several cylinder type of annealing furnaces, refractory bricks are heated to a certain temperature, and then these furnaces are used for annealing forged pieces with their own surplus heat. In this way, one annealing furnace can save power 150 kWh. In addition, the surplus heat of hot forged pieces can be used for recrystallization and annealing. In this

way, the time of heating with electronic furnace is shorter. In every hour, 20 kWh are saved. The labor productivity doubles by this approach.

(5) Continuous casting. In the past, molten iron at high temperature from blast furnaces in the metallurgical industry cools naturally and becomes slabs. Later, cold slabs are melted for casting. In this process, surplus heat of molten iron at high temperature is completely wasted. Now in Shougang Group and Taiyuan Iron and Steel Group Co., Ltd., this surplus heat is used for continuous casting, in which molten iron is directly for making steel ingots. This new technology saves huge amount of coke.

The second way is indirect utilization.

(1) Generating steam. Products at high temperature and slag, which are at hundred centigrade or even higher than 1000 centigrade, are good for generating steam. Surplus furnaces can be installed at the product cooling section in tunnel furnaces, on steel ingot cooling bed, or at the tubes for up-flow gas of coke ovens to generate steam. In Shanghai No. 2 Steel Plant, surplus furnaces are installed on steel ingot cooling bed to generate steam at the speed of 3 t per h. In Shanghai Ceramics Factory, surplus furnaces are installed at the product cooling section in tunnel furnaces. Stream is generated at the spend of 1 t per h. There are two approaches to use slag at high temperature for generating steam. The firs approach puts a bucket that contains hot slag in the furnace of a surplus heat boiler. The inside surface of the furnace is heated by the hot slag and then heats water into stream. The efficiency of this approach is low. The other approach heats air first to over 1000 °C with the heat of hot slag. Hot air is then flown into boilers for generating stream with high pressure. Dry quenching of coke belongs to this approach. It uses incombustible inertia gases for cooling hot coke. The heated inertia gases are then flown into surplus heat boilers for generating stream. Japan introduces the new technology of dry quenching of coke from the former Soviet Union for recycling the heat of hot coke. This approach allows a coke furnace that produces 56 t of coke per h to generate power 6000 kW with stream.

(2) Generating hot water. Slag at high temperature can be used for heating water. In Shougang Group, hot slag is dumped into a water pool, where water is heated to 90 °C. Surplus heat of products at high temperature can be used for heating water as well. In An Gang Iron and Steel Co., Ltd and Ben Gang Iron and Steel Co., Ltd, the temperature of coal gas from coke ovens is high. Water is used for cooling the hot coal gas. At the end, water is heated to 50–60 °C.

(3) Generating hot air. Products and slag at high temperature can be used for generating hot air. In Nanjing Ceramics Factory and Tianjin Xianfeng Brick and Tile Factory, air is used for cooling products at high temperature from annular kilns and tunnel furnaces. Hot air is then used for drying green bricks.

3. **Utilization of surplus heat of cooling medium**

In industries, equipment that consume energy, such as high temperature furnaces and dynamic electric machines, become hotter and hotter when they are running.

In order to protect the equipment and to maintain their service of life, cooling (not cooling product at high temperature) is required. There are two types of cooling. In the first type, there is no cap for ultimate temperature of cooling medium, such as cooling of certain parts in metallurgical furnaces. Temperatures of cooling water can be from 35–45 to 80–90 °C. Vapourization cooling is an option as well. When cooling water flows through the parts that need cooling, it absorbs lots of heat and then evaporates into steam at low pressure or high pressure. It is better to choose hot water as cooling medium than cold water. Because for the same requirement of cooling, when the temperature of cooling water doubles, the volume of cooling water will drop half. Accordingly, the need for power drops as well. Vapourization cooling is better than water cooling. The volume of cooling water required by vapourization cooling is about 0.05% of that required by water cooling. The amount of power required drops a lot as well. In addition, steam has more applications than hot water. Vapourization cooling is widely used at present. It is used more in open hearths and heating furnaces. In An Gang Iron and Steel Co., Ltd., the test of vapourization cooling for blast furnaces has achieved success. In the second type, low temperature cooling is required so the temperature of cooling medium, such as water, air, and oil, cannot be higher than a certain value. For instance, the temperature of cooling water in high vacuum coolers at power plants should not exceed 25–30 °C. The temperature of cooling water or oil for rolling machines, such as engines, hydraulic machines, crew compressors, and diesel engines should not be higher than 50–60 °C.

Surveys in several regions show that the surplus heat of cooling medium accounts for 15–23% of the total amount of surplus heat. The surplus heat of cooling medium in furnaces accounts for 10–25% of their fuel consumption (the percentage for blast furnaces is 2–8%). The surplus heat of cooling water in power plants accounts for about 50% of their total fuel consumption. In Tianjin Metallurgy Trial Plant, water cooling is replaced by vapourization cooling. Their cooling system generates 10 t of stream per h. Their cooling water for steel making electric furnaces is provided for employees to take a shower.

4. **Utilization of surplus heat of waste stream and waste water**

Surplus heat of waste stream and waste water exist in industries that use steam and hot water, including chemical plants, machinery plants, metallurgical plants, light industry factories, and textile mills. Steam and hot water are usually generated by boilers. In China, there are thousands of industrial boilers and civil boilers. Fuel consumed by these boilers accounts for more than 1/4 of the total national fuel consumption. The total fuel excludes those consumed by power plants and locomotive boilers. Some stream and hot water are generated by thermal power stations or by secondary energies. The usage of steam and hot water is huge in China. After they are used in production or people's life, they become waste stream and waste water. Recycling the surplus heat of waste stream and waste water cannot only save huge amount of fuel, but also save a lot of water.

Surveys in different regions show that the surplus heat of waste stream and waste water account for 10–16% of the total amount of surplus heat.

Waste steam and waste water can be categorized into the following groups: (1) Exhaust from steam-driven machines, including steam hammers, steam engines, and compressors. The pressure of this kind of waste stream is about 1.2–1.4 atmospheric pressure. Their surplus heat accounts for 70–80% of the total consumed steam. (2) Secondary steam. It is generated in the processes of evaporation and concentration (including water in solution evaporates by heating) in industries such as chemical, light industry, and food processing. The pressure of this kind of waste stream is close to one atmospheric pressure. (3) steam condensate and blowdown water of boilers. Temperature of this kind of waste water is about 90–100 °C. (4) Other waste hot water, including water discharged from production and daily life, such as textile, foods, washing and dyeing, and bathrooms. The pressure of this kind of waste water is not high (about 30 °C).

Waste steam and waste water can be reused by following the principle of cascade utilization. At present, waste steam and waste water at high temperature are utilized well by factories. However, the economic effect of utilizing waste steam and waste water at low temperature is not good.

5. **Utilization of surplus heat of chemical reaction**

This kind of surplus heat mainly exists in chemical industry. Chemical reactions occur in chemical production process. One type is endothermic reaction, in which heat is absorbed. The other type is exothermic reaction, in which heat is released. Surplus heat of chemical reaction refers to the heat released in chemical reactions. Exothermic reactions here refer to those that do not need fuel. Strictly speaking, fuel combustion and gasification are exothermic reactions. But they are not counted as exothermic reactions in this chapter. In other words, the surplus heat of chemical reaction is not generated with fuel.

The surplus heat of chemical reaction accounts for 5–9% of the total amount of surplus heat. This kind of surplus heat can be used in the following ways.

(1) Used by chemical reactions themselves. In some chemical reactions, raw materials need to be heated before reaction. During the reaction, heat is released. As such, the heat released during reactions can be used for heating raw materials. In this way, fuel can be saved for heating raw materials. In Changsha Chemical Plant, steam is used for heating raw materials in the process of making manganous sulfate. In the new production process, raw materials are heated by the heat released by the chemical reactions. Without the old steam heating process, over 500 t of coal are saved each year. In Tianjin Dagu Chemical Plant, heat released by the reaction of sodium pentachlorophenate in one water tank is used for heating reaction liquid in the other water tank. The heat generated by these two water tanks are used by each other continuously. In this way, heavy oil used for heating reaction liquid is saved. In one year, 320 t of heavy oil are saved. The production is increased 30%. Furthermore, air pollution by the release of sodium pentachlorophenate is avoided.
(2) Generating steam. Some exothermic reactions are at high temperature and release huge amount of heat. For instance, huge amount of surplus heat at high

temperature is released in the process of making sulfur dioxide gas in sulphur burning furnaces and sulfur iron ore fluidized bed furnaces in sulphuric acid plants. Similar surplus heat is also released in nitric acid oxidation furnaces and synthetic ammonia converters. This kind of surplus heat is used for generating steam in boilers in Shanghai Sulphuric Acid Plant, Nanjin Fertilizer Plant, and Tianjin Paint Factory.

(3) Generating hot water and hot air. Some low temperature exothermic reactions need cooling with water or air. The surplus heat in these chemical reactions can be used for generating hot water and hot air.

6. **Utilization of surplus heat of combustible waste gas, waste liquid, and waste materials**

Combustible waste gas, waste liquid, and waste materials are generated in industrial processes, such as the combustible gas generated by petroleum refineries, waste gases generated by iron alloy furnaces, rotary furnaces, and blast furnaces in metallurgical plants, and waste gases generated by calcium carbide furnaces in chemical plants. These waste gases contain combustible contents, such as carbon monoxide, hydrogen, and carbon. In additional, these waste gases are at high temperature. The surveys show that the surplus heat of wasted gases accounts for about 8% of the total amount of surplus heat.

Waste materials also include combustible waste materials from wood processing plants and paper making plants.

The surplus heat of combustible waste gases can be utilized in three ways.

The first way is direct utilization.

(1) As chemical raw materials. Some waste gases contain a lot of carbon monoxide, which can be used as raw materials for making ammonia and methanol. Such kind of direct utilization has good effect. In Shanghai No. 1 Iron and Steel Plant, waste gas from rotary furnace is provided to Woosung Chemical Plant as raw material.
(2) As fuel. Heating value of some waste gases is as high as 10,000–15,000 kcal/m^3 (waste gas from refineries). Heating value of waste gas from rotary furnaces is 1800 kcal/m^3. Heating value of waste gas from blast furnaces is 800–900 kcal/m^3. In Shanghai Refinery, waste gas is used for fuel. In Siping Chemical Integrated Plant, waste gas from calcium carbide furnaces is used for making lime.
(3) Generating power. Waste gas at high pressure from blast furnaces can be used for generating power as turbine. Iron and steel plants at Mizushima in Japan uses waste gas of blast furnaces to drive a 10,000 kW generator units.

The second way is indirect utilization.

(1) Generating steam. Like flue gas at high temperature, some combustible gases are at high temperature as well. They can be used for generating stream. In

Shanghai No. 1 Iron and Steel Plant, waste gas from oxygen blowing rotary furnaces is used for heating boiler to generate stream.

(2) Generating hot water. When water is used for cooling waste gas, cooling water become hot water.

The third way is comprehensive utilization.

Combustible waste gases usually contain chemical latent heat and physical sensible heat. Some even have motivity. Accordingly, comprehensive utilization is the best way to use surplus heat of waste gas. For example, waste gas from rotary furnaces can be first used for generating steam with boilers. Then it can be used for chemical raw material or fuel. High-pressure waste gas from blast furnaces can be used for generating power as turbine. Then it can be used as fuel. In Shanghai Iron and Steel Plant, waste gas is utilized comprehensively.

In a word, there are many ways for utilizing surplus heat. Generally speaking, comprehensive utilization is the best way. Direct utilization is a better way. Indirect utilization (generating stream, hot water, and hot air) is ok. Therefore, comprehensive utilization should be considered first. Then direct utilization should be considered next. When neither comprehensive utilization nor direct utilization can be applied, indirect utilization can then be applied.

Next, let us talk about using surplus heat for generating stream, hot water, and hot air.

(1) Usages of stream generated by surplus heat

The six types of surplus heat introduced above can all be used for generating stream. The stream can be categorized into two groups. The first category is high pressure stream. The pressure is usually larger than 6–7 kg/cm^2. Sometimes, the pressure is as high as 30–40 kg/cm^2. For example, stream generated by flue gas at high temperature, products and slag at high temperature, chemical reactions, and combustible waste gas, and stream generated by high pressure gasification fall into this category. The second category is low pressure stream. Its pressure is 1–4 kg/cm^2. Stream that is emitted, including vents and secondary steam, and steam cooled by low pressure gasification fall into this category.

Usages of high-pressure stream are the same as those generated by coal-burning boilers. The following are some common usages.

(a) For production processes, such as acid cleaning, drying, concentration, distillation, steaming, boiling, slashing, and atomization from heating heavy oil.
(b) For daily life, such as indoor heating, ventilation, showering, and cooking.
(c) As motivity for driving steam hammer, compressor, oxygenator and pump, ventilator, and other machines.
(d) For generating power with condensed steam turbines, extraction condensed steam turbines, and back pressure condensed steam turbines.
(e) Comprehensive utilization. There are three types of comprehensive utilizations. The first type is to use steam in multiple ways for production and daily life. The second type is to use stream as motivity and in production and daily life.

For example, high pressure stream can be used for driving steam hammers or steam compressors, and then the output of low pressure stream can be provided for production and daily life. High pressure stream can also drive back pressure turbines to rotate motive power machine, and then the output low pressure stream can be provided for production and daily life. The third type is utilization for power generation, production, and daily life. For instance, high pressure stream can drive back pressure turbines (or extraction turbines) to generate power first, and then the output low pressure stream can be used for production and daily life.

(f) Sent to heat supply pipe network for steam supply. High pressure stream can be sent to heat supply pipe network for heating allocation. For example, Shanghai No. 2 Iron and Steel Plant builds a pipe network for high pressure stream generated by surplus heat. The network supplies stream to internal users as well as over 20 external users.

Usages of low pressure stream are similar with those of high pressure stream. But there still some differences. Low pressure steam cannot be transmitted for a long distance. Thus, it can only be utilized locally. It cannot be utilized comprehensively either. Instead, it can be used either for motivity or for production and daily life. When low pressure stream is used for generating power, a special low pressure condense turbine generator unit is needed. The efficiency is fair low.

In order to utilize low pressure stream better, thermal transformers are adopted in some cases to increase pressure. The high pressure stream is then supplied for production and daily life.

The rational order for utilizing stream generated by surplus heat is as below.

I. Low pressure stream is used as motivity first and then for heat supply. In this way, low pressure stream can replace coal-burn boilers and electric motors. Spending on equipment, investment, fuel, and power are saved. This is most rational utilization of low pressure stream. All plants that have the necessary conditions should adopt this order of utilization.

II. Low pressure stream is used for generating power first and then for heat supply. In this way, low pressure stream generates a larger benefit than any other single utilization. Fuel can be saved 15% more than low pressure stream is used for heat supply only, and 80% more than low pressure stream is used for power generation only.

III. Low pressure stream is used for production. In this way, low pressure stream can generate a larger economic benefit than it is used for daily life heat supply only. Daily life heat supply varies with seasons. For instance, heating is supplied in winters but is not needed in summers. In contrast, stream is needed for production all the year round.

IV. Low pressure stream is used for daily life heat supply. Due to the change of seasons, this utilization has low efficiency.

The third and fourth utilizations are common at present because the pressure of surplus heat is not high. In the future, high pressure stream (40 atmospheric pressure) generated by surplus heat should be applied more. In this way, the first and the second utilization of low pressure stream can be realized in practice.

V. Low pressure stream is used for power generation condensed by turbines. However, investment and operation costs of small sized power generating equipment with condensed steam turbines are large. The efficiency is low and few fuel is saved. Thus, this utilization is good when stream is only needed insider of a plant.

(2) Usages of hot water generated by surplus heat

Hot water generated by surplus heat can be categorized into two groups. The first category is high temperature hot water, such as steam condensate water, blowdown water of boilers, high temperature slag water, and high temperature cooling water. The temperature of this kind of hot water is over 50–60 °C, and as high as 90 °C. The second category is low temperature hot water, such as low temperature cooling water in power plants. Its temperature is only 20–30 °C.

High temperature hot water can be used as below.

(a) For production processes, such as dissolving salt and raw materials, heating and, agricultural production.
(b) Sending back to boilers for reuse. Hot water can be used for heating feed water for boilers directly and then be loaded together into boilers. Or hot water can be loaded into boilers directly. Or hot water can be used for heating feed water for boilers indirectly.
(c) For daily life, such as indoor heating, ventilation, and showering.
(d) For generating stream to serve production. Hot water can be converted into stream by thermal pumps.
(e) As motivity or for power generation. After processed with expansion method, low boiling point medium, temperature difference, or semiconductors, hot water can be used as motivity or for generating power.

Right now the first three usages are more common in China. The last two usages are still under testing.

Low temperature hot water has limited usages because their temperature is low and because some low temperature hot water is dirty. Their temperature can be increased by thermal pumps, penetrated steam, or lowering vacuum of condensers in power plants. Then high temperature hot water can be supplied for production and daily life.

The rational order for utilizing hot water generated by surplus heat is as below.

I. For production usage all the year around.
II. Sending hot water back to boilers for reusing.
III. For daily life usage.

It is rational to increase the temperature of low temperature hot water for production usage all the year around. Comparison between stream generating, motivity, and power generating is needed to see which usage is more rational.

(3) Usages of hot air generated by surplus heat

Except surplus heat generated by waste gas, waste water, combustible gases, waste liquid, and waste materials, other surplus heats all generate hot air. Hot air can be at high temperature and at low temperature. Hot air can be used as below.

(a) For production processes. For example, hot air from annular kilns can be used for drying rough parts.
(b) For indoor heating. Hot air can be used for heating workshops.
(c) As motivity. Hot air can be condensed first, and then drives air turbines, or air hammers.
(d) Generating power. Hot air can drive air turbines to generate power.

The best usage of hot air is to be supplied for production all the year around. The better usage is for indoor heating. Comparison is needed to tell whether it is rational to use hot air as motivity or for power generation.

23.5 Issues and Opinions About Energy in China[5]

[Research background, scientific significance of achievements, and practical value] Since the founding of the People's Republic of China, energy industry has been developing fast. The author proposed the planning outline of energy science technologies, which was adopted by the government in 1977. For the implementation of the outline, the author pointed out ten issues about energy in China [55], including establishment of a unified national energy management organization, development of nuclear power, and strengthening rational and efficient utilization of energy. This research result was published at the First National Energy Policy Symposia in December 1979 in Hangzhou. The result was thought highly by the leader of State Scientific and Technological Commission. Later, the central government took the advice of author and establish the National Energy Committee. Yu Qiuli was appointed as the director. The energy research office led by the author was reformed as the Energy Research Institute under Chinese Academy of Science, which is the precursor of the Energy Research Institute under National Development and Reform Committee. The author was then appointed as the counselor of National Energy Committee. Later, the author was in charge of the study on construction of energy base in the energy office in the State Department. The author has been conducting research on energy in the Energy Research Institute under State Planning Commission. The author the result of this study can still serves as a reference now.

[5]Xu [Xu79].

1. **Serious shortage of energy supply**

The outbreak of was in the Middle East in late 1973 caused an energy crisis across the world. This crisis was actually an oil crisis, because oil was the main energy in industrial developed countries. Take the year of 1972, one year before the energy crisis broke out, as an example. Oil accounted for the main portion in energy consumption across the world. The percentage was 75.3% in Japan, 68% in France, 53.5% in West Germany, 45.1% in UK, and 43.8% in the United States. In the United States, the imported oil accounted for 27% of its total oil consumption. The percentages in Japan, West Germany, France, and UK were all higher than 94%. Oil was mainly imported from the Middle East. Therefore, after the Arabian countries in the Middle East implemented oil embargo and rose oil price, the supply of oil was restrained. These countries relying on imported oil had large troubles in production and people's daily life. The development of national economy in these countries was affected greatly and negatively. If the energy crisis were not resolved in a timely manner, economic crisis and politic crisis might occur. Accordingly, these countries took a series of emergency measures for recovering oil supply. Finally, the energy crisis was overcome.

When the supply of energy was restricted, the demand of energy could not be fulfilled. The shortage in energy supply caused energy crisis. Many energy experts predicted that the shortage in energy supply will cause the second energy crisis around 1985. Thus, more and more countries paid attention to energy issue. The energy crisis in 1973 showed that the countries relying on imported oil suffered a lot of loss, especially economic loss. Take Japan as an example. The annual speed of national economy development in Japan was about 10% before the energy crisis. Due to the energy crisis, Japan suffered a drop of 2% in its national economy development. Altogether, Japan lose 12% of its gross domestic production, which was about 48.5 billon US dollars. The US, UK, France, an West German suffered the similar loss.

The supply of energy cannot fulfill the demand in China for a long time. Moreover, the shortage is very serious. It is estimated that about 30% of industrial production capacity cannot be achieved due to the lack of energy. In other words, 30% of the gross industrial production was lost. Because industrial production accounts for about 70% of the national industrial and agricultural production, the loss of gross domestic production caused by the shortage of energy in is about 20%, namely 70 billion of US dollars in each year. This loss is much larger than the loss in Japan caused by energy crisis. The supply of energy in China was damaged by Lin Biao and Gang of Four for a long time. In addition, production of energy was limited. Huge demands of energy cannot be fulfilled. The shortage in the supply of energy is serious. This shortage is affected the development of national economy in China negatively. It further caused a serious imbalance in national economy. We must correctly understand and deal with the serious shortage in energy supply.

2. **Energy per capita is not high in China**

Many people think that China has vast territory and rich resources. Energy sources in China are rich. In terms of gross, water reserve in China ranks the first in the world.

Coal reserve in China ranks the third in the world. However, gross is not the only indicator of resources. Similarly, the gross domestic production of China does not reflect the level of the four modernizations. Thus, the amount of resources per capita is a better indicator. Due to the large population, the amount of resources per capita in China is not large at all. At present, fossil energy sources per capita (based on recoverable reserves) is only 139 t of standard coal in China. The number for Soviet Union is 1037 t, 6 times more than that of China. The number for the United States is 740 t, 4 times more than that of China. The numbers for Yugoslavia and West Germany are several more than that of China. The number for UK, which is lack of energy, is close to that of China. The number of China is smaller than the average level of the whole world. If one person consumes 13 t of energy in one year in China, the same rate as that in the US, the fossil energy reserves will be used up in 13 years. In contrast, the fossil energy reserves in the US will be used up in 57 years. Among the fossil energy reserves in the world, coal accounts for 74%. High-quality fuel oil accounts for 15%, and natural gas accounts for 11%. In contrast, high-quality fuel oil and natural gas accounts for only 3% in China, far lower than the average level in the world. Accordingly, regarding the average energy quantity and quality owned by one person, the level in China is below the average level in the world. The energy reserves in China are not rich at all. More efforts are needed for exploration of energy sources, specifically oil and gas.

3. **Hydropower and nuclear power are laggard**

The experience of foreign countries show that hydropower should be developed first. In developed countries, usable hydropower has been fully exploited. In China, water resource is rich. The theoretical water reserve is 580 million kW, among which the usable water reserve is 180 million kW. These water reserve can generate 900 billion kWh power. However, the installed capacity is only 15.76 million kWh now. The electricity generated is only 44.6 billion kW. The installed capacity and the electricity generated only account for 8.8% and 5% of the usable water reserve. Compared with the rates in developed countries, the level of hydropower exploitation in China is fairly low.

Nuclear power develops fast around the world. For now, more than 20 countries have nuclear power plants. The installed capacity is more than 100 million kW. In China, the military nuclear technologies are advanced, whereas the civilian nuclear technologies are laggard. The work of nuclear power plants has been conducted for 20 years. But China still did not have a nuclear power plant. The level of nuclear power exploitation is even lower than that of hydropower exploitation in China. In order to increase the production of energy, China must focus on developing hydropower, coal, and nuclear power based on the existing conditions. Even if some large oil and gas resources might be found in the future, it is still necessary to develop the aforementioned energy. For quite a long time, China will continue to suffer the shortage of energy.

4. **Energy utilization is neither rational nor efficient**

Irrational utilization of energy is very common in China. The focus of energy utilization is not necessarily but availability. Accordingly, energy utilization lacks economic effect. For example, 59% of power plants across China changed their coal required by the initial designs in recent 20 years. Usually, one power plant uses five, six, or ten types of coal simultaneously. Sometimes, the types of coal are as many as 20. It is well known that the types of coal affect the efficiency of boilers. Sometimes, the change of coal might cause trouble in the operation of boilers. Irrational utilization of oil and gas is worse. It is economic for power plants to burn oil or gas. The larger boilers, the less economic for burning oil and gas. Large boilers have high efficiency when burning coal. Burning oil and gas can increase efficiency only 1–3% for boilers in power plants. For glass furnaces, open hearth furnaces, and heating furnaces, changing coal to oil or gas saves fuel over 30%. In chemical industries, choosing oil or gas as raw materials can save fuel 40–50%. For daily life, natural gas save fuel more than 70%. However, China burned over 38 million t of oil in 1978. Among them, 14 million t are crude oil. Boilers burned around 70% of oil. Practically, boilers in power plants burned over 18 million t of oil, which accounts for 47%. It is estimated that one ton of coal is wasted if power plants burn one ton of oil. The value is 50 yuan. Accordingly, as for the oil burned by power plants, 18 million t of coal are wasted. The total loss of value is 0.9 billion yuan. This is a serious issue.

Energy equipment in China is out of date. Many equipment were produced in 1940 and 1950s. They consume a large amount of coal, oil, and power. Their technology level is fairly low. In addition, they are not maintained and managed well. As a result, the effective heat utilization rate of fuel is rather low, only 28% in average. Calculated in the way, the effective heat utilization rate of fuel is 49% in Japan and 52% in the United States. The effective heat utilization rate of fuel in China is only half of that in overseas. This means a huge waste of energy.

In order to utilize energy better, rational utilization must be implemented first. Based on their unique characteristic, each type of energy should be utilized accordingly. High quality energy should be used as low quality energy. Low quality energy should not be utilized. Measures should be taken to use energy rationally and to increase the heat utilization rate of fuel. Specifically, three steps should be taken. First, management of energy should be improved. Second, small reform projects should be implemented. Third, large reform projects are then implemented.

5. **Low level of energy consumption hinders the development of national economy**

Although the total energy consumption of China ranks the third in the world, the energy consumption per capita is fairly low due to the large size of population. The annual energy consumption per capita in China is only 0.59 t of standard coal. Plant energy consumption per capita in China is 0.88 standard coal. The annual energy consumption per capita in the US is 13 t of standard coal. The rates in Europe and Japan are about 6 t of standard coal and 4 t of standard coal, respectively. These rates are about 5–22 times of that in China. The average annual energy consumption per capita across the world is 2.2 t of standard coal. The rate in China is lower than this average rate, excluding plant energy. The low level of energy consumption in China caused the low level of gross domestic product per capita. The annual gross domestic product per capita in China is 290 US dollars. The annual gross domestic product per capita in the US, West Germany, France, and Japan are 8666 US dollars, 8542 US dollars, 7292 US dollars, and 6263 US dollars, respectively. These numbers are about 20–30 times of that in China. When the economy is adjusted in China, low level of energy consumption will hinder the development of national economy.

National economy can still develop at a certain speed when level of energy consumption is low. However, generalized energy saving must be promoted. Particularly, it includes: (1) improving the efficiency of energy utilization; (2) changing economy structure, product direction and layout; (3) saving materials and reducing the amount of transport turnover; (4) improving the quality of products; (5) rationally allocating and using energy; (6) reducing the growth of population. The generalized energy saving has large potential. It is closely related with every industry, every job position, and every individual. Thus, the generalized energy saving must be promoted vigorously and be implemented in every aspect. It is estimated that the generalized energy saving will yield large effect. It can drive the national economy develop at a certain speed in the condition when the consumption of energy does not increase or just increases a little. For example, during the economy adjustment period in 1963, the consumption of energy dropped 6% whereas the gross domestic product increased 9.5% in China. In the long run, the resolve of energy issue relies on the generalized energy saving.

6. **Lack of national energy reserves and environmental pollution is getting serious**

Energy reserves are necessary for a country. However, due to the long-time shortage of energy supply, China does not have energy reserves. The lack of energy reserves affects the development of national economy negatively. Take power generation industry as an example. Generally speaking, power plants must have energy reserves for equipment maintenance, accidents, loading, and national economy development. With the energy reserves, power plants can deal with equipment maintenance and accidents for meeting the requirements of the development of national economy better. Japan increased its fuel reserves at the country level and firm level for handling emergencies. Right now, the oil reserves of Japanese companies can meet their requirement for 80 days. In contrast, there are always shortages in energy plan in China. Energy reserves is not available at all. As a result, emergencies occur very often in energy supply. Production arrange is always in a mess. Economy suffers from huge losses eventually. In this way, rational utilization of energy cannot be achieved. Thus, the shortage of energy supply must be changed by building energy reserves within a certain time period.

Environment pollution is mostly caused by energy consumption, especially coal burning. The usage of oil generates harmful gas, such as SO_2 and NOx. At present, the annual emission of smoke and dust in China is 14 million t. The annual emission of SO_2 is 15 million t. The pollution in cities, such as Beijing, is serious. With the rise of energy consumption, environment pollution will become worse. Thus, measures must be taken to reduce environment pollution. Otherwise, the national economy development will be impacted negatively by environment pollution.

7. **Research on energy science and technology is weak**

Since the energy crisis in 1973, many countries have paid more attention to energy research. The funding on energy research ranks number two in the US, only lower than space research. Japan has Sunlight Project and Moonlight Project for energy research. Although energy research is one of the eight key research fields in China, little effort has been spent on energy research. Particularly, research on oil exploration, development of power system, energy saving technologies, nuclear power, biogas technologies, and energy technological economy are weak. Due to the lack of study, technologies for energy exploration, exploitation, and utilization are out of date in China. Policies, planning, and design of energy do not meet the requirements in practice.

Energy research is a comprehensive research field. More efforts are need from Chinese Academy of Sciences, Chinese Academy of Social Sciences, industries, universities, provinces, and cities. In addition, coordination and cooperation are needed as well. For example, Chinese Academy of Sciences should study more on new technologies for energy and new energies. Chinese Academy of Social Sciences should study more on energy technological economy. Industries should study more on energy exploitation, energy utilization, and technologies for energy saving. Provinces and cities should conduct studies according to the actual conditions and requirements of energy utilization. Universities should study more on energy in corresponding disciplines and improve training of talents.

8. **Lack of specific and correct energy policy**

In the past, due to the damages caused by Lin Biao and the Gang of Four, China does not have energy policy. In the 30 Industrial Items, energy policy is officially proposed. Some items in the energy policy were implementing, such as coupon-based supply and adjustment of coal price. These items in energy policy are principles without specific content and methods. As a result, it is difficulty to implement them. Some items need more research. The lack of specific energy policy causes negative impact on practice. Coal was replaced by oil in the past. Now oil is replaced by coal. But the policy of changing into coal is missing. Nuclear power plants should be developed. How to develop nuclear power plants still need guidelines in practice.

Energy policy is one part of technology policy. It is the principles and approaches for resolving energy issues based on natural laws and economic laws. In other words, energy policy should be developed based on scientific research. It should be rational in terms of science and economy. Energy policy is the guild line for energy exploration, infrastructure, production, transportation, utilization, research, and international trade. Therefore, the resolving energy issue in China requires correct and specific energy policy. Energy policy should take actions that suit local circumstances and there is no one energy policy fits for all. Energy policy should consider the differences among regions. It should be adjusted based on the changes of situation.

9. **No overall energy plans**

There is no overall energy plans in China. The lack of overall plans causes to treat the head when the head aches, and to treat the foot when the foot hurts. More consideration is given to the emergent issues, regular energies, saving in production, and local issues. Consideration to long term issues, new energies, scientific research, education, and global issues is missing. How to plan energy from a global perspective is overlook. Energy plan is the core of national economy plan. As we know, after the victory of the October Revolution in Russia, Lenin personally developed a plan for overall electrification in Russia. This is the first national economy developing plan that focuses on energy. More than 100 experts in Russia was involved in developing this plan. This is a good example for us to follow. In order to realize the Four Modernizations, we need an overall plan for energy. This plan for energy should include a recent planning (1985), a middle term planning (1990), and a long term planning (2000). Energy plan should be integrated with national economy development. The energy plan is helpful for understanding the level of energy utilization at the end of 2000 and the status of the Four Modernizations.

10. **No state agency for managing nationwide energy sources**

Since the energy crisis in 1973, many countries have established agencies for managing energy at the state level. The US first established the Energy Research and Development Bureau, which changed the name to Department of Energy in 1977. Japan established the Natural Resources and Energy Office. Even Malaysia established the Energy Commission in its State Cabinet. However, energy is in charge by many departments. Coordination and cooperation for energy issues are missing. Due to the lack of agency managing energy issue at the state level, the institutes in industries cannot play their roles well. Energy issues are comprehensive ones. Thus, many departments are involved. Agencies at the state level are needed to coordinate the involved departments. For example, managing energy saving not only needs the effort of economy management department, but also needs coordination and cooperation between industries, resource department, planning department, research department, education department, and propaganda department.

In order to manage energy well, the management level must be improved. Standards for energy must be established. Laws for energy must be made. The most important job is to establish a state-level agency with strong power to manage energy comprehensively. This agency should coordinate and organize work on energy in different industries. This agency should also develop and implement the national policies and plans on energy. The goal of this agency is to make the management of energy meet the requirement of energy development. Managing energy well is the key for resolving the energy issue in China.

23.6 National Income and Net Income Should be the Major Goal of Our National Economy Development[6]

[Research background, scientific significance of achievements, and practical value] Led by the famous economist Yu Guangyuan, the author began to take charge of establishing the Institute of Technical Economy in China Academy of Social Sciences in 1979. In 1980 the first technological economy research institute in China was established. The author was the first director. At the same, the Technological Economy Research Center was established by the State Council. The author was the director in charging of energy group. Since the founding of the People's Republic of China, industrial and agricultural product has been used for economic goal. The author thought that industrial and agricultural product was developed by the planning economy in Soviet Union. It does not fit for China in the reform and opening-up era. It neither fits the actual situation nor lacks the support from technological economy. Accordingly, the author proposed to adopt national income and net income as the goals for economy development. The author's proposal was forwarded to the leaders of the State Council by Ma Hong, the director of Technological Economy Research Center and the vice president of China Academy of Social Sciences. Finally, the proposal was accepted by the state [75]. This research result has both scientific meaning and practical meaning. It is still correct at present. The following is the original proposal.

Since the founding of the People's Republic of China, industrial and agricultural product has been used for economic goal. Practices in many years have proven that this economic goal has some serious drawbacks as indicated below.

1. **Industrial and agricultural product is not consistent with the goal of socialist production**

The goal of socialist production is to meet people's material and cultural demands. However, people's demands are not total product. No matter how many product factories produce, people's demands cannot be meet if the consumption in the circulation is high, the loss is large, the final product is limited, or the product is not needed by the market. Thus, choosing industrial and agricultural product as the economic goal will cause results that are not consistent with the goal of socialist production. For example, producing is the only thing cared by factories. Factories only pursue higher production while neglect people's demands.

[6] Xu [Xu81].

2. **Industrial and agricultural product is not consistent with the interests of workers**

In socialist construction, there should be a goal for the economy development in a country. Each worker should have a goal for their own interests. If the two goals are consistent, workers will have the motivation to work. However, industrial and agricultural product is adopted as the economic goal, whereas workers set their interests as their goal. These two goals are not consistent, because the larger industrial and agricultural product does not mean the more interests for workers. As a result, workers do not have the motivation to work when industrial and agricultural product is adopted as the economic goal.

3. **Industrial and agricultural product is not consistent with the goal of increasing labor productivity**

Lenin said: "Labor productivity is the most important factor to ensure the victory of the new social system...... Capitalism can be completely defeated, and will be completely defeated because socialism will generate new and higher labor productivity."[7] Labor productivity Lenin referred here does not mean the amount of products produced by an individual. Because even if an individual produces a large number of products, the value he or she generates might not be large or might be negative when the cost is high and the consumption in the circulation is high. If this is the case, a higher labor productivity means a less amount of value that is produced. Therefore, it is problematic to choose industrial and agricultural product for the indicator of labor productivity.

4. **Industrial and agricultural product is not consistent with increasing economic effect**

As we know, production has two aspects. One aspect is the product and value that is produced. The other aspect is the manpower, material, and capital that are consumed in the production process. Industrial and agricultural product only represents the first aspect, namely the value. It does not represent the cost that is required to generate the value. The economic effect indicator should represent both the value and the cost. Thus, industrial and agricultural product is not an economic effect indicator. It does not represent the status of economic effect. The Iron and Steel Making Movement in 1958 did increase products and value. But the achievement was not worth of the cost. Its economic effect was bad. In recent years, the agricultural product in some areas increased, but farmers' income did not increase. The increase in product did not bring the rise in income. In contrast, some factories made adjustment of their product. They lowered their product but generated more economic effect. Therefore, industrial and agricultural product does not represent economic effect at all. Choosing it as the economic goal in China will cause more troubles.

---

[7] Lenin [Le61].

5. **Industrial and agricultural product is not consistent with the actual economic condition**

Repeat calculation exists in the process of calculating the products of all departments. False product is inevitable. Accordingly, industrial and agricultural product does not reflect the actual economic condition. This is a serious drawback.

6. **Industrial and agricultural product is not consistent with the speed of national economy development**

At present, the speed of national economy development in China is measured with industrial and agricultural product. The speed of development of industrial and agricultural product is set as the speed of national economy development. This causes the inconsistence between national economy development and economic effect. Fast growth in industrial and agricultural product does not always mean good economic effect. Slow growth in industrial and agricultural product does not always mean bad economic effect. The speed of growth in industrial and agricultural product does not represent the speed of growth in national economy development. The real speed of growth in national economy development should be consistent with the speed of growth in economic effect.

Given the six issues caused by industrial and agricultural product, it is not reasonable to choose industrial and agricultural product as the goal of economic development. Many serious mistakes have occurred in Chinese economic development for a long time. The main reason is that something is wrong with the economic development goal. In other words, a wrong goal was selected. There are two goals for socialist economic development. One is national income. The other is net income. The two goals overcome the six drawbacks of industrial and agricultural product. They are consistent with the goal of socialist production, individual's interest, improving labor productivity, improving economic effect, representing economic condition, and representing the speed of growth in national economy development. Thus, choosing these two economic goals can reflect the goal of socialist production correctly, reflect the real economic condition, combine the national goal and individuals' interests, increase workers' motivation, increase labor productivity, increase economic effect, and promote the development of national economy. These two goals fit for the adjustment period in the Sixth Five-Year Plan, because the speed of growth in production and value is not fast in this period. However, if the economic effect is increased, the speed of growth in national income and net income can be fast. For example, the speed of growth in industrial and agricultural product was 7.9% in 1957, whereas the speed of growth in national income was 4.5%. If the Sixth Five-Year Plan achieves a good result with 3–4% of growth in industrial and agricultural product, the speed of growth in national income can still match that in 1957. In other words, the economic effect is at the level achieved with 7.9% of growth in industrial and agricultural product. Accordingly, adoption of national income and net income follows the guideline in the economy adjustment period. Given the advantages of these two indicators, they fit for any economic goals at any time.

As such, the following suggestions are proposed.

(1) Beginning from the Sixth Five-Year Plan, replace industrial and agricultural product with national income and net income as the economic goal.
(2) National income and net income should be adopted as the main indicator by every department across the country.
(3) Other than indicators of production and value, indicators of reducing capital occupation, reducing cost, and increasing labor productivity should be adopted by every department across the country.

These proposals are available in academia for many years. The author agrees with these measures based on his many experiences in study on technological economy. The author thinks that these measures have large theoretical and practical value. It is time to adopt these measures. These measures will play a vital role in the economy development in China. Many mistakes will be avoided. After the implementation of these measures, departments will not keep asking the state for money and they will be willing to change unreasonable prices.

23.7 Technological Economic Evaluation for Scientific and Technological Progress[8]

[Research background, scientific significance of achievements, and practical value] The 12th National Congress of the Communist Party of China proposed the strategy goal for economic development till 2000 in China. The realization of this goal depends on scientific and technological progress. However, it is not clear how much scientific and technological progress drives economic development and how to calculate. Accordingly, the author intimately proposed the methods for calculating the role of scientific and technological progress [126]. With these methods, the author got the result that 51% of increase in economic benefit from 1977 to 1980 in Shanxi province was achieved by scientific and technological progress. This result gave the construction of energy base in Shanxi province a clear direction. The research result [138] has scientific and practical values. It won the award of Outstanding Report in 1985 issued by Chinese Academy of Social Sciences.

There are two approaches to calculate the impact of scientific and technological progress on economy development. The first one is to calculate each item according to the actual economic effect. the other approach is to deduct the part in the growth of national income caused by the increase of fixed asset and labor. These two approaches are explained in details below.

The first approach. The following formula is adopted to represent the relationship between scientific and technological progress and growth in production, net income and national income.

---

[8]Xu [Xu83a].

$$
\begin{aligned}
\text{Growth in production } \Delta S = {} & \text{Growth in production } \Delta S_{\text{natural\_ science}} \\
& \text{caused by progresses in natural science} \\
& + \text{Growth in production } \Delta S_{\text{social\_ science}} \\
& \text{caused by progresses in social science} \\
& + \text{Growth in production } \Delta S_{\text{non\_ science}} \\
& \text{caused by factors other than scientific and technological progress}
\end{aligned} \tag{23.3}
$$

$$
\begin{aligned}
& \text{Growth in net income or national income} \\
& \quad \Delta S_c = \text{Growth in net income or national income} \\
& \quad \quad \Delta S_{c\_\text{ natural\_ science}} \text{ caused by progresses in natural science} \\
& \quad \quad + \text{Growth in net income or national income} \\
& \Delta S_{c\_\text{ social\_ science}} \text{ caused by progresses in social science} \\
& \quad \quad + \text{Growth in net income or national income} \\
& \Delta S_{c\_\text{ non\_ science}} \text{ caused by factors other than scientific and technological progress}
\end{aligned} \tag{23.4}
$$

Accordingly, the following formulas can be used for calculating the growth in production, net income and national income caused by scientific and technological progress.

$$\Delta S_{\text{science}} = \Delta S_{\text{natural\_science}} + \Delta S_{\text{social\_science}} \tag{23.5}$$

$$\Delta S_{\text{science}} = \Delta S - \Delta S_{\text{non\_ science}} \tag{23.6}$$

$$\Delta S_{\text{c\_ science}} = \Delta S_{\text{c\_ natural\_ science}} + \Delta S_{\text{c\_ social\_ science}} \tag{23.7}$$

$$\Delta S_{\text{c\_ science}} = \Delta S_c - \Delta S_{\text{c\_ non\_ science}} \tag{23.8}$$

Symbols in Formulas (23.5)–(23.8) are the same as those appeared in previous chapters. Formulas (23.5) and (23.7) are positive balance method. Formulas (23.6) and (23.8) are counter balance method. These two methods should be adopted based on actual conditions. Here are some examples.

Suppose there is a factory, which spent 250,000 yuan on investment and had a production of 300,000 yuan. It had an extension project in 1980, which adopted the original technologies, equipment, and raw materials. The products were the same as well. The number of workers increased based on the original quota. This extension project cost 250,000 yuan and generated a growth in production of 300,000 yuan. In this case, Formula (23.6) can be applied to calculate the role of scientific and technological progress in the extension project. The result is zero.

Suppose there is another factory, which implemented a technical reform in 1980. This technical reform did not need any investment. Only the existing equipment was reformed. Due to the increase in efficiency, product quality, and product quantity, the production increased 100,000 yuan annually, which was the result of scientific and technological progress. In this case, Formula (23.5) can be applied to calculate the role of scientific and technological progress in the extension project. The result is 100,000 yuan.

These two examples show that the analysis on growth in production has many drawbacks. Usually, scientific and technological progress reduces the cost of production. However, such economic benefit cannot be calculated with the formulas for analyzing growth in production. Here is another situation. One factory adopts new equipment. Its production increases whereas its cost increases as well. The rise in cost is larger than the rise in production. In this case, the economic benefit of this factory drops actually. This situation cannot be reflected by the formulas for analyzing growth in production. Instead, the formulas for analyzing growth in net income can overcome this drawback. Here is another example. With the increase of the skill level of workers, product efficiency rises accordingly. As a result, wages rise as well. Such economic benefit of increase of wages caused by workers' skill level cannot be reflected by the formulas for analyzing growth in production and for analyzing growth in net income. Instead, this economic benefit can be reflected by the formulas for analyzing growth in national income. Therefore, the formulas for analyzing growth in production, growth in net income, and growth in national income have their unique benefit. Among these three formulas, the one for analyzing growth in national income is better, because it can reflect the comprehensive and real economic benefit caused by scientific and technological progress. The following are two examples of applications of the formula for analyzing growth in national income.

Suppose there is a factory, whose net production in 1980 was 200,000 yuan. On one hand, due to the improvement in management, the quality of its products increased, its cost dropped, and workers' wages increased in 1985. On the other hand, its production doubled because of additional investment and extension. The net production of this factory reached 200,000 yuan. What is the net production caused by scientific and technological progress?

In this example, the production doubled due to additional investment. The net production should double as well, namely 400,000 yuan. In other words, growth in net production caused by non-scientific and technological progress was 200,000 yuan. Accordingly, the formula for analyzing growth in net production (23.8) should be chosen for the calculation.

$$\Delta S_{\text{c\_ science}} = \Delta S_c - \Delta S_{\text{c\_ non\_ science}} = 200,000 \text{ yuan}$$

The result of the calculation shows that growth in net production caused by scientific and technological progress accounts for 50% of the total growth in net production. In other words, half of the economic benefit of this factory is achieved by scientific and technological progress.

Here is another example. Suppose there are two factories. In 1980, their capital occupation were 1,000,000 yuan. Their net production was 200,000 yuan. Due to scientific and technological progress, in 1985 capital occupation of factory *A* rose 500,000 yuan. Net production of factory *A* rose to 400,000 yuan. Capital occupation of factory *B* rose 500,000 yuan. Net production of factory *A* rose to 300,000 yuan. What are the economic effect caused by scientific and technological progress in these two factories?

For factory *A*, the original capital occupation was 1000,000 yuan. The net production was 200,000 yuan. Thus, one hundred of capital achieved net production 20 yuan. After technological reform, one hundred of capital achieved net production 26.7 yuan in 1985. The difference of 6.7 yuan is the economic effect caused by scientific and technological progress. It is known that the capital occupation of factory *A* was 1,500,000 yuan. Growth in net production caused by scientific and technological progress was 100,000 yuan. The 100,000 yuan in the growth of net production 200,000 yuan was caused by scientific and technological progress from 1980 to 1985.

For factory *B*, the original capital occupation was 1,000,000 yuan. The net production was 200,000 yuan. Thus, one hundred of capital achieved net production 20 yuan. After technological reform, one hundred of capital still achieved net production 20 yuan in 1985. This means that the economic effect achieved by factory *B* via technological reform was the same as the original economic effect. Thus, scientific and technological progress did not cause any rise in economic effect for factory *B*.

For factory *A* and *B*, they both implemented technological reform, increased investment, and got growth in net production. If general approaches are applied to analyze the growth, it is easy to reach the conclusion that the growth was caused by scientific and technological progress. However, the analysis above shows that scientific and technological progress did not increase net production in factory *B*. Thus, here is a problem of the selection of approaches to calculate economic effect. The author argues that it is feasible to apply the greater, faster, better and more economic result introduced in Chap. 19 for evaluating the economic effect caused by scientific and technological progress.

It is also reasonable to adopt the rise of labor productivity for evaluating the result caused by scientific and technological progress. Given the large labor force and the shortage of capital in China, it is so reasonable to adopt the rise of labor productivity only for evaluating the result caused by scientific and technological progress. It is better to choose investment and national income rate. For instance, one factory has 1,000,000 yuan of capital and 500 employees. Its annual net production is 100,000 yuan. Its investment and national income rate is 0.1. Its labor productivity is 200 yuan/year. Here are two plans. This first one adds 1,000,000 yuan of capital, 100 workers, and increases net production 100,000 yuan. The second one adds 1,000,000 yuan of capital, 1000 workers, and increases net production 200,000 yuan. The increased investment national income rate for the first plan is 0.1. Its labor productivity is 1000 yuan/year. The increased investment national income rate for the second plan is 0.2. Its labor productivity is 200 yuan/year. The result indicates that with the same amount of investment, the second plan generates 100,000 yuan net production more and 900 more worker position than the first one. Therefore, the second plan is better. However, if labor productivity is chosen as the indicator, the second plan is not so good as the first one.

These are the discussion about the role of scientific and technological progress in factories from the perspective of evaluation on technological economic schemes' economic effect.

The second approach. It is too complicated for a country, an area, or an industry to adopt the first approach. Accordingly, western countries apply production function formulas to calculate the role of scientific and technological progress. Although it is much easier than the first one, production function formulas are still complicated. Here is an approach that is easy and fits for the conditions in China.

(1) Calculation based on the economic effect of investment utilization.

$$\begin{aligned}&\text{The role of scientific and technological progress}\\&\quad=[(\text{Total capital national income rate after scientific and technological progress}\\&\qquad-\text{Total capital national income rate before scientific and technological progress})\\&\qquad\times\text{Total capital occupation after scientific and technological progress}]\\&\quad/(\text{Total national income after scientific and technological progress}\\&\qquad-\text{Total national income before scientific and technological progress})\times 100\%\end{aligned}\tag{23.9}$$

(2) Calculation based on the economic effect of labor utilization.

$$\begin{aligned}&\text{The role of scientific and technological progress}\\&\quad=[(\text{Labor productivity after scientific and technological progress}\\&\qquad-\text{Labor productivity before scientific and technological progress})\\&\qquad\times\text{Total labor occupation after scientific and technological progress}]\\&\quad/(\text{Total national income after scientific and technological progress}\\&\qquad-\text{Total national income before scientific and technological progress})\\&\quad\times 100\%\end{aligned}\tag{23.10}$$

Labor productivity in Formula (23.10) is not the commonly used indicator that reflects the amount of production produced by one individual in one year. Instead, it refers to the amount of national income or net income produced by one individual in one year.

(3) Comprehensive calculation.

$$\begin{aligned}&\text{The role of scientific and technological progress}\\&\quad=1/2\ (\text{The role of scientific and technological}\end{aligned}$$

progress calculated based on investment national income rate
$\times$ significance coefficient + The role of scientific and technological
progress calculated based on labor productivity
$\times$ significance coefficient) $\times$ 100% (23.11)

The comprehensive calculation method has typicality. The importance coefficients in it need to be set according to the actual condition. The sum of these two importance coefficients should be 2. Each of them should fall between 0 and 2. When the importance coefficient for investment national income rate is 0, the comprehensive calculation method changes into the calculation method based on the economic effect of labor utilization. When the importance coefficient for labor productivity is 0, the comprehensive calculation method changes into the calculation method based on the economic effect of investment utilization. At present, the same importance coefficient can be adopted for calculating national economy. The value can be set as 1. The comprehensive calculation method can also be applied to industrial departments. However, the calculation method based on the economic effect of labor utilization is better for agricultural departments. Here is the reason. According statistic data, the net production in agriculture grew 2.4% annually from 1953 to 1980. The growth was caused neither by farming land expansion nor completely by increase in labor force. In fact, the total number of farming land was dropping continuously. The annual drop amount was 4.6 millions μ. Meanwhile, the growth rate of net production of agriculture was faster than that of labor in agriculture. Thus, the growth of economic effect of labor utilization in agriculture in China was caused by farmers' hard work, irrigation, mechanization, electrification, and chemicalization in agriculture, as well as promotion of good seeds and improvement of soil. In addition, the growth was the result of the implementation of policies and measures, as contract responsibility system for production, price increases of agricultural products, and motiving farmers. Economic effect of investment on agriculture was dropping all the time because the investment on farm fundamental construction and irrigation projects required large amount of money and because the prices of agricultural products were low all the time. In this condition, it is not suitable to apply the calculation method based on the economic effect of investment utilization. The author argued that labor productivity in agriculture could reflect the role that scientific and technological progress plays in the development of agricultural economy.

Although the above three methods are not accurate, they are easy and convenient to use. Calculation can be conducted as long as historical statistics data or planning data are available. Based on historical statistics data, these three methods are applied to calculate the role of scientific and technological progress in China. The results are listed in Table 23.6. According to the table, about 33% of the total economic benefit (national income) in national economy was generated by scientific and technological progress from 1962 to 1980. In this period, the investment on scientific research, culture, and education accounted for 4% of the total investment in the national economy. About 80% of investment was spent on production in all departments. The economic benefit generated by this part of investment accounted

Table 23.6 The role of scientific and technological progress in the rise of economic benefit

Period	Calculation based on the economic effect of labor utilization			Calculation based on the economic effect of investment utilization			Comprehensive calculation		
	Total national economy	Industry	Agriculture	Total national economy	Industry	Agriculture	Total national economy	Industry	Agriculture
1962–1980	79	63	64	−14	45	—	33	54	64
1977–1980	78	58	81	0	46	—	39	52	81

for 67% of the total economic benefit. Thus, the economic effect of investment on scientific research, culture, and education is about 10 times of the economic effect of investment on production.

23.8 Technological Economic Study of Coal-Developing Policy[9]

[Research background, scientific significance of achievements and practical value] The Central Committee of the Communist Party of China decided to build energy heavy chemical base in Shanxi province. In 1981, the author was assigned as the chief consultant for the project of building energy heavy chemical base in Shanxi province by the Technological Economy Research Center in the State Council. This project involved 1400 experts in dozens of institutes in Shanxi province and across China. It was finished after 2 years. This project consists of 459 special topics and their planning, 150 piece of figures, and 26 mathematic models. It took the longest time to finish the planning for coal production because there was huge disagreement between the Ministry of Coal and Shanxi Province. The ministry of Coal insisted to keep state-owned coal and did not agree to develop coals owned by local authorities. In contrast, Shanxi province insisted to develop coals owned by local authorities. The two sides both had their arguments. Accordingly, the author applied technological economic methods to fix this issue. Based on the first-hand data collected by the author, the author conducted comprehensive analysis and performed systematic calculation. At the end, the author got quantitative comprehensive evaluation result. The result indicted that the coal industry in Shanxi province should implement the policy of three combinations till the year of 2000 or longer, namely combination of large, middle size, and small coal mines; combination of advanced, middle-level, and traditional technologies; and combination of state ownership and local authority ownership. In specific, the guideline of three rapid developments should be implemented, namely rapid development of large open coal mines, large and middle size coal mines invested by the state and with advance and middle-level technologies; rapid development of middle size coal mines invested by local authorities with middle-level technologies; rapid development of middle size and small coal mines invested by township with applicable technologies. On behalf of Chinese Academy of Social Sciences, the author later gave a report on the special meeting of the project regarding building energy heavy chemical base in Shanxi province hosted by the Ministry of Coal, Shanxi province, Chinese Academy of Social Sciences, and Chinese Academy of Sciences. Leaders and experts on this meeting agree with the author's report unanimously. This case was the first time for the author to apply comprehensive evaluation methods to fix practical issues. The scientific and practical value of the result [139–142]

---

[9] Xu [Xu83b].

made the author win the Outstanding Report Award issued by Chinese Academy of Social Sciences in 1985.

In the past, technological policies were usually made from the perspective of technology only. As a result, it was easy to make technological policies only pursuing advanced technologies. In fact, the purpose of developing technologies is to develop economy. Therefore, economic effect must be taken into consideration when making technology policies. Meanwhile, other factors, such as politics, society, environment, and ecology, should be taken into account as well. The reason is that different technology policies will generate different results in diverse aspects. Those technology policies that fit the actual condition will generate good benefits and promote the development of national economy. In contrast, those technology policies that do not fit the actual condition will cause huge damages to national economy. Developing technology policies must compare multiple schemes. Both technological economy comparison (economic evaluation) and comprehensive comparison (comprehensive evaluation) are needed. Several issues regarding technology policy need to be fixed for the construction of coal energy base in Shanxi province. These issues had been discussed in the past several years, namely the scale (large, middle, and small) issue, coal exploitation technologies (advance, middle, and traditional), and management system (state-owned, local-owned, and town-owned).

For coal exploitation in Shanxi province, three scale size, three level of technologies, and three management systems have exits for quite a long time. These issues are correlated with each other. None of them can be separated in the process of finding solutions. For instance, large coal mines need advance technologies. Due to the large amount of investment and long construction period, large coal mines most are owned and run by the state. Small coal mines usually adopt traditional technologies. So they are owned and run by towns. Middle size coal mines usually apply general machines. They are owned and run by local government. As a result, coal mines owned by the state, local government, and towns represent advance technologies, middle level technologies, and traditional technologies respectively. For convenience, the author conducted political, national defense, social, technical, environmental, ecological, natural resources and economic evaluation on state scheme, local scheme, and town scheme individually. Then a comprehensive evaluation is conducted. The evaluation adopts 5-grade marking system. Five is the full score. One is the lowest score. Zero means veto.

1. **From the political point**

From the political point of view, it is necessary to develop the state-owned, local-owned, and town-owned coal mines. Developing the three level coal mines is consistent to the requirements from the CPC that promote the development of coal mines at all levels and balance the interests among the central government, local government, and town government. For Shanxi province, the key is to manage coal mines letting them follow the rules and regulations issued by the government. Sometimes, small coal mines tend to violate the rules and to perform unauthorized mining. This can be avoided if more education of laws is implemented. In addition, because local schemes and town schemes bring local people more benefits, they are as good as state schemes in terms of political effect.

2. **National defense evaluation**

From the national defense point of view, state-owned, local-owned, and town-owned coal mines generate the same result in Shanxi province. Particularly, local-owned and town-owned coal mines scatter wider. Therefore, their locations are good for combat readiness. Meanwhile, given the scattered locations of state-owned coal mines in Shanxi province, they meet the requirement of combat readiness as well.

3. **Social evaluation**

Due to the low level of mechanization, local-owned and town-owned coal mines need more workers. Thus, they generate more jobs. However, because the number of managerial personnel in stated-owned coal mines is large, the number of employees for producing 10,000 t of coal is the same across state-owned, local-owned, and town-owned coal mines. Town-owned coal mines do not have advantages in terms of generating jobs. However, employees in town-owned coal mines do not consume commodity grain. In contrast, employees in state-owned and local-owned coal mines need to consume commodity grain. Accordingly, town-owned coal mines are better. In terms of working condition, town-owned coal mines are the worst. Local-owned coal mines are better. State-owned coal mines are the best. Accident mortality in town-owned coal mines is the highest. In addition, the social effect of local-owned and town-owned coal mines can be assessed with the feedback of farmers.

4. **Technological evaluation**

Technological evaluation can be performed from two aspects. One is the advance of technologies. The other is the applicability of technologies. The mechanization level in state-owned coal mines is high. Usually, advanced technologies are adopted in state-owned coal mines. The mechanization level in local-owned coal mines is lower. Middle-level technologies are adopted in local-owned coal mines. The mechanization level in town-owned coal mines is the lowest. Traditional technologies are adopted in town-owned coal mines. Regarding the applicability of technologies, coal mining combines are applicable to state-owned coal mines that have stable geological condition, abundant capital, and plenty of skilled workers. Neither local-owned nor town-owned coal mines have such advantages. Thus, middle-level technologies and traditional technologies are fit for local-owned and town-owned coal mines. Advanced technologies, middle-level technologies, and traditional technologies are applicable to state-owned, local-owned, and town-owned coal mines, respectively.

5. **Environmental and ecological evaluation**

In terms of environmental evaluation, exploitation of coal will bring negative effect on environment and cause pollutions, such as acid mine water, gangue spontaneous combustion, and acid water, regardless state-owned, local-owned, or town-owned coal mines. In theory, the pollution caused by exploiting one ton of coal is the same across state-owned, local-owned, and town-owned coal mines. However, pollutions caused by state-owned coal mines are large and concentrated, whereas pollutions caused by local-owned and town-owned coal mines are small and scattered. As a result, pollutions caused by state-owned coal mines are more serious. To be conservative, the author assumes that state-owned coal mines get the same scores in environmental evaluation as those got by local-owned and town-owned coal mines. In terms of ecological evaluation, town-owned coal mines play a better role in maintaining ecological balance. Here are the reasons. First, town-owned coal mines provide fuel for farmers. Without coal, each farmer burns 700–800 kg of straw and firewood every year in average, excluding the fuel for heating in winter. If fuel is not enough, farmers will chop trees and cut grass on hills or mountains. This will damage ecological balance. Second, towns will make money from coal mining. Part of the money can be spent on developing forest industry. More forest will generate more oxygen, keep water, adjust climate, and reduce water loss and soil erosion. For instance, Zuoyun County was very poor in the past. Since 1978, this county have opened 44 small coal mines. It invested more than 4 million yuan on agriculture in two years. In addition, it planted more than 200,000 μ of trees. Animal husbandry was promoted as well. As a result, the ecological balance in this county was well maintained. Local-owned coal mines also promote ecological balance maintenance. But the effect is not as notable as that of town-owned coal mines. Although state-owned coal mines play certain roles in ecological balance maintenance, the effect is as good as those of local-owned and town-owned coal mines.

6. **Natural resources evaluation**

Natural resources here refer to coal. There are two aspects for natural resources evaluation. One is the protection of natural resources. The other is the utilization of natural resources. In terms of protecting natural resources, town-owned coal mines usually perform unauthorized mining and damage resources due to the poor management on them caused by their scattered locations. But this is not their intrinsic flaw. Reasonable planning, strengthened management, and strengthened laws will reduce the damages on natural resources caused by town-owned coal mines. Local-owned and state-owned coal mines perform better in natural resources protection. Thus, they seldom conduct unauthorized mining. Regarding of the utilization of coal, the average rates of recovery for state-owned and local-owned coal mines are 70% and 47%, respectively. About 70% of town-owned coal mines exploit coal at old coal mines, edges, faultage, and outcrop. Their rates of recovery are 100% because they exploit coals that cannot be exploited by state-owned and local-owned coal mines or lost by these coal mines. The rest town-owned coal mines exploit regular coal resource, also known as solid coal. These coal mines adopt traditional methods. Their rates of recovery can be as low as 10–15%. The average is about 25%. These town-owned coal mines need technology upgrade. Once they adopt formal methods, their rates of recovery can be increased to the level of large and middle size coal mines.

7. **Economic evaluation**

Economic evaluation adopts 15 technological economic indicators. The values of these indicators are listed in Table 23.7. For all technological economic indicators except reserves consumption, town-owned coal mines have larger values than local-owned ones. Local-owned coal mines have larger values than state-owned ones. Although state-owned coal mines are the best option at the country level. But they are not as good as local-owned and town-owned one at the region level. This is not an accidental phenomena. Instead, it represents the actual situation in Shanxi province and in China.

(1) Investment and capital sources.

For extension and new construction, town-owned coal mines are the most economical from the perspective of investment. Local-owned ones are economical. State-owned ones are the most expensive. The ratios among these three are 1:0.4–0.5:0.3 (new constructions) and 1:0.46–0.57:0.36–0.38 (extension projects). The reasons are as following. First, town-owned coal mines are built locally. They do not need large amount of spending on land acquisition. Second, workers in town-owned coal mines are local farmers. There is no need to build dorms and public facilities. Third, town-owned coal mines are small and have short service period. The standards of some permanent facilities in town-owned coal mines can be lower than those in local-owned and state-owned ones. Forth, simple equipment at low price are fit for town-owned coal mines. Some construction can use local materials at low prices. Fifth, town-owned coal mines do not pay the surcharges of additional workshop service. They also pay a small amount of surcharge for construction management. Regarding the resources of capital, state-owned coal mines rely on the investment from the state. In contrast, state investment is not the main capital resource for local-owned and town-owned coal mines. The state needs to exploit huge amount of coal, but the capital is not enough. Thus, the solution for this issue is to develop local-owned and town-owned coal mines. It is impossible for the state to invest on local-owned and town-owned coal mines. Furthermore, the effect of such investment is not good.

(2) Costs.

The cost of producing one ton of coal is about 15 yuan for state-owned coal mines. This is the cheapest in China. However, this cost is higher than those of local-owned and town-owned coal mines. The cost of producing one ton of coal is about 13 yuan for local-owned coal mines. For town-owned coal mines, the cost is about 10 yuan. Here are the reasons. Town-owned coal mines pay fewer wages, consume

Table 23.7 Economic evaluation

Indicators	State owned coal mines	Local owned coal mines	Town owned coal mines	Relationship among state owned coal mines, local owned coal mines, and town coal mines	Notes	
Consumption indicators	1. Investment (yuan/t) capital source	65–70 (renovation and expansion) 100 (newly built) Mainly state owned	30–40 (renovation and expansion) 40–50 (newly built) Mainly local owned	25 (renovation and expansion) 30 (newly built) Mainly township owned	1:0.50:0.37 1:0.45:0.30	Refers to mine investment, excluding investment for exploration and utilities
	2. Costs (yuan/t)	About 15 yuan	About 13 yuan	8–12 yuan	1:0.87:0.67	
	3. Labor productivity (ton/labor)	1.292 (0.91)	1.292 (1.00)	1.4 (1.3)	1:0.96:1.04 (1:1.1:1.43)	The values in the parentheses refer to full efficiency of coal mines
	4. Technical personnel (person/1 million t)	59.5	33.6	2.5	1:0.56:0.04	Total consumption cost calculated based on newly built mines. The calculated construction period is 5 years for state owned coal mines, 4 years for local owned coal mines, and 2 years for town owned coal mines. The capital and coefficient is 1.15

(continued)

Table 23.7 (continued)

Indicators	State owned coal mines	Local owned coal mines	Town owned coal mines	Relationship among state owned coal mines, local owned coal mines, and town coal mines	Notes	
	5. Mine timber and steel consumption (m^3/10,000 t, t/10,000 t)	85.3 (mine timber) 8.07 (steel)	91.5 (mine timber)	35–40 (mine timber planed to be 70)	1:1.07:0.47 (mine timber)	
	6. Coal reserves consumption (t/t)	1.43	2.13	3.7	1:1.49:2.59	
	7. Water consumption (t/t)	0.6–1.0	0.5	0.4	1:0.83:0.67	
	8. Land utilization (μ/10,000 t)	6.7	4.5	3.5	1:0.67:0.52	
	9. Total consumption expense (yuan/t)	39	24 (31)[a]	15 (22)	1:0.67:0.38 (1:0.79:0.56)	
Economic effect indicators	10. Direct economic benefit (yuan/t)	50	50	50	1:1:1	I, II and III represent 3 scenarios
	11. Indirect economic benefit (yuan/t)	I 143	138.8	129.2	1:0.97:0.90	
	12. Total economic benefits (yuan/t)	II143	171.8	234.2	1:1.20:1.64	
		III.0	171.8	234.2		
		I 193	188.8	179.2	1:0.97:0.90	

(continued)

Table 23.7 (continued)

Indicators	State owned coal mines	Local owned coal mines	Town owned coal mines	Relationship among state owned coal mines, local owned coal mines, and town coal mines	Notes	
		II 193	221.8	284.2	1:1.15:1.47	
		III 0	221.8	284.2		
Time indicator	13. Construction period (year)	5–9	2–4	1–2	1:0.50:0.30	
	14. Full production period (year)	5	2	About 1 year	1:0.40:0.15	
Economic effect indicator	15. Absolute economic effects (yuan/t) (annual averages)	I 154	164.8 (157.8)	164.8 (157.8)	+10.8 (local) +10.2 (town)	
		II 154	197.8 (190.8)	269.2 (269.2)	+43.8 (local) +115.2 (town)	
		III 0	197.8 (190.8)	269.2 (269.2)	+197.8 (local) +269.2 (town)	
	Absolute economic effects E_c (yuan/t) (15 years, taking into account time factor)	I 7337	7480 (7500)	7813 (7480)	+541 (local) +486 (town)	
		II 7327	9411 (9078)	12808 (12475)	+2084 (local) +5481 (town)	
		III 0	9411 (9078)	12808 (12475)	+9411 (local) +12808(town)	
Rating standard	Total scores	3	4	5		

[a]Values in parentheses consider the roads transportation fee

fewer power, have fewer management personnel, use fewer materials (including mine timber, explosives, and detonators), and have smaller depreciation. In the future, town-owned coal mines will pay more wages with the rise of farmers' income. However, state-owned coal mines will spend more on wages as well. The rise of wages in state-owned coal mines will be faster than that in town-owned coal mines.

(3) Labor productivity.

If all employees are counted, including non-production employees, town-owned coal mines have higher labor productivity than state-owned ones. Because there are more non-production employees in state-owned coal mines.

(4) Technical staff.

In 1980, town-owned coal mines need 2.2 technical staff to produce one million ton of coal. The numbers are 60 and 34 for state-owned and local-owned coal mines, respectively. If only state-owned coal mines are developed, huge number of technical staff will be required. Such requirement will not be fulfilled. Currently, the number of technical staff for producing one million of coal in state-owned coal mines in Shanxi province is still smaller than the number across China (83) as well as the number in foreign countries (173 in Portland). More technical staff in state-owned coal mines in Shanxi province are needed. Compared with state-owned coal mines, the requirement of technical staff in town-owned and local-owned ones is more urgent.

(5) Consumption of mine timber and steel.

State-owned coal mines in Shanxi province consume over 80 cubic meters of mine timber and more than 8 t of steel for producing 10,000 t of coal. Town-owned coal mines use coal pillars instead of mine timber due to the short supply of wood. Accordingly, town-owned coal mines consume fewer wood than state-owned ones. Fewer consumption of wood is good for China. However, the supply of wood for town-owned coal mines should be increased in the future.

(6) Consumption of coal reserves.

The recovery rates of local-owned and town-owned coal mines are low. They waste more resources. Town-owned coal mines use 2.3 t of coal reserves more than state-owned ones for producing one ton of coal. Local-owned coal mines use 0.7 t of coal reserves more than state-owned ones for producing one ton of coal. This is the only indicator that local-owned and town-owned coal mines have lower values than state-owned ones. Local-owned and town-owned coal mines are opposed mainly because of this indicator. The impact that the larger consumption of coal reserves by local-owned and town-owned coal mines on the economic development in Shanxi province and in China will be discussed later.

(7) Consumption of water.

The supply of water is short in Shanxi province. Generally, state-owned coal mines use 0.6–1.0 t of water for producing 1 t of coal. Local-owned ones use 0.5 t of water. Town-owned ones only use fewer than 0.5 t of water. The small and scattered demand of water by town-owned coal mines is easy to fulfilled.

(8) Land occupation.

State-owned coal mines occupy about 6.7 μ of land for producing one million of coal. Most of the land is fertile farmland. In contrast, local-owned and town-owned coal mines occupy fewer land. They often use ravines, cemeteries, and wasteland. The other reason is that town-owned coal mines do not need to build residential buildings and public facilities.

(9) Total social consumption.

Total social consumption Z should be calculated with the formulas in social net income method or national income method. For simplicity, it is assumed that material consumption costs, transportation occupation fee, labor costs, and natural resources consumption and occupation costs have small impact on total social consumption Z. The impact is not considered in the calculation. The construction period is considered in the calculation. In the calculation, principal and interest factor are set as 1.15. Calculation period is set as 15 years. The calculation results show that the total social consumptions of town-owned, local-owned, and state-owned coal mines are 15 yuan, 24 yuan, and 39 yuan per ton, respectively. In the calculation, only a small part of the short distance transportation cost for local-owned and town-owned coal mines is considered. If local-owned and town-owned coal mines need to provide coals for clients not in Shanxi province, the short distance transportation cost will increase. In fact, almost half clients for local-owned and town-owned coal mines are in Shanxi province. Their short distance transportation cost is not high. Accordingly, it is reasonable not to calculate short distance transportation cost in economic evaluation. For conservative reasons, it is assumed that the average transportation distance of one ton of coal for local-owned and town-owned coal mines is 35 km. The transportation cost is set as 0.2 yuan/km. One ton of coal needs 7 yuan for transportation. According to Table 2.7, even the transportation cost is considered, the total social consumptions of town-owned and local-owned coal mines are still lower than that of state-owned coal mines.

(10) Direct economic benefits.

Direct economic benefit refers to the profit gained by coal mines after they sell coals. In other words, it is production value. At present, the prices of coal produced by town-owned, local-owned, and state-owned coal mines are all lower than reasonable prices. In economic evaluation, town-owned, local-owned, and state-owned coal mines all adopt the reasonable price of coal, namely 50 yuan per t. This is the ideal situation. If the demand of coal is large and town-owned and local-owned coal mines go into production several years earlier than state-owned coal mines, the direct economic benefits of town-owned and local-owned coal mines are larger than that of state-owned coal mines.

(11) Indirect economic benefits.

Indirect economic benefits include three aspects. The first is the net economic benefit generated by production value based on the sale of coals. In other words, when coal mines have money, they spend their money on those project that need investment. As a result, the whole economy develops. Net economic benefits (net income) increase continuously as well. The increase of net economic benefits is the indirect economic benefits generated by coal mines. Many examples in Shanxi province have proved this indirect economic benefits. The second aspect means the economic benefit per ton of coal when coal mines sell coals to the states. Once the states have the coals, economic loss caused by shortage of energy will be smaller. It is estimated that one ton of coal reduces economic loss of 143 yuan (this is the average loss across China. One ton of standard coal reduce economic loss of 200 yuan). The third aspect is negative. It refers to the economic loss of coal reserves in the process of coal mining. It is very important to evaluate this loss. At present, the shortage of one ton of coal causes a loss of 143 yuan in national economy. Suppose that the utilization rate of energy rise in the year of 2000. The shortage of one ton of coal causes a loss of 286 yuan in national economy then. Now let us do the calculation based on recovery rate. Town-owned coal mines use 2.3 t of resource when producing 1 t of coal. Local-owned coal mines use 0.7 t of resource when producing one ton of coal. The resources used by town-owned coal mines for producing one ton of coal will be worth of 658 yuan in the year of 2000. This number for local-owned coal mines is 200 yuan in the year of 2000. The cost of resource will be paid back in 15 years if one ton of coal is worth of 13.8 yuan in each year. Because the economic benefit of producing one ton of coal by small coal mines is far higher than 13.8 yuan, town-owned and local-owned coal mines should be developed rapidly now and after the year of 2000.

There are three scenarios for indirect economic benefits. In the first scenario, the investment from the states is abundant. In addition, comprehensive balance is well considered and plannings are well made. The long construction period of state owned coal mines is considered. Thus, the construction of state-owned coal mines begins earlier than that of local-owned and town-owned coal mines. The goal is to let state-owned, local-owned, and town-owned coal mines go into production at the same time and produce the same amount of coal in the same time period. In this way, these three schemes have the same amount of the first type and the second type of indirect economic benefits. Obviously, the third type of indirect economic benefits are different. In the second scenario, given energy crisis and the economic loss caused by the shortage of energy, coal mines must be constructed immediately. Assume that the state capital is sufficient and lots of state-owned coal mines can be constructed to meet the demands. In this case, the first indirect economic benefits of local-owned and town-owned coal mines are better than those of state-owned coal mines, because the construction period of local-owned and town-owned coal mines is shorter. They produce coal earlier than state-owned coal mines. Once they gain income, they can make investment. Thus, they achieve net economic benefits. Similarly, the second type of indirect economic benefits of local-owned and town-owned coal mines are better than those of state-owned coal mines. As for the third indirect economic benefits, three schemes generate different results. In the third scenario, the huge demand of coal in China cannot be met by state-owned coal mines only. It is necessary to run local-owned and town-owned coal mines. In this way, the first and second indirect economic effects generated by local-owned and town-owned coal mines are extra wealth for the country. According to the results of calculation, the total indirect economic benefits for state-owned, local-owned, and town-owned coal mines in the first scenario are 143 yuan/t, 139 yuan/t, and 129 yuan/t, respectively. In the second scenario, 143 yuan/t, 172 yuan/t and 234 yuan/t, respectively. In the third scenario, 0.172 and 234 yuan/t. Among these three scenarios, the latter two are more common. The third one is the most common. The indirect economic benefits of state-owned, local-owned, and town-owned coal mines are different. The indirect economic benefits of local-owned and town-owned coal mines are larger than those of state-owned ones.

(12) Total economic benefits.

It is the sum of direct and indirect economic benefits. In the previous calculation of economic benefits, direct economic benefits were neglected. As a result, wrong decisions were easy to make. The comparison of state-owned, local-owned, and town-owned coal mines shows that their direct economic benefits are the same, whereas their indirect economic benefits are different. Therefore, their total economic benefits are different. In the second scenario above, the overall economic benefits of town-owned coal mines are 91 yuan/t higher than those of state-owned ones. The overall economic benefits of local-owned coal mines are 29 yuan/t higher than those of state-owned ones.

(13) Construction period.

The construction period of state-owned coal mines is 5–6 years in average. It is 1–5 years longer than that of local-owned and town-owned coal mines. Local-owned and town-owned coal mines have the advantages of short construction period and fast return. Compared with state-owned coal mines, local-owned ones have a rise of 33 yuan/t in social net income if they go into production one year earlier. The rise is 66 yuan/t if they go into production two years earlier. The rise is 100 yuan/t if they go into production three years earlier. The rises are applied to town-owned coal mines as well. Town-owned coal mines have shorter construction period because of abundant labor in rural areas, local-supplied construction materials, simple and fast construction, and no need to consider land purchase.

(14) Full production period.

This period starts at the time when coal mines go into production and ends at the time when the designed production capacity is reached. Town-owned coal mines need about one year. Local-owned ones need about 2 years. State-owned one need more than 5 years in average. If a state-owned coal mine has a full production period of 5 years, its net economic benefits drops 19% annually. If a local-owned coal mine has a full production period of 2 years, its net economic benefits drops 9% annually. If a state-owned coal mine has a full production period of 1 year, its net economic benefits drops 4% annually. It can be seen that local-owned and town-owned coal mines are more economical than state-owned ones.

(15) Absolute economic effects.

This is a comprehensive index. In the economic evaluation, two indicators are adopted in social net income method. One is the average annual social net income generated by 1 t of coal. The other is the total social net income generated by one ton of coal based on cumulative calculation in 15 years. The calculation shows that town-owned coal mines have the best absolute economic effects. Local-owned ones have the better absolute economic effects. State-owned ones have the smallest absolute economic effects. In the Sixth Five-Year Plan period, suppose the annual coal production of coal mines is 10 million t. In the second scenario, town-owned coal mines generate 1.15 billion yuan of net income for the state more than local-owned ones annually. To the year of 2000, the accumulated net income in 15 years is 54.8 billion yuan. Similarly, town-owned coal mines generate 0.44 billion yuan of net income for the state more than state-owned ones annually. To the year of 2000, the accumulated net income in 15 years is 20.8 billion yuan. In the calculation the maximum possible economic losses caused by waste of resources in town-owned and local-owned coal mines has been considered. But the extra economic benefits resulted from a shorter full production period of town-owned coal mines has not been taken into account. It can be seen from Table 23.7 that other than developing state-owned coal mines, developing town-owned and local-owned coal mines can save a lot of land, water, and other important resources.

Table 23.7 lists the data for economic evaluation and provides the scores of comprehensive evaluation.

8. **Comprehensive evaluation**

The comprehensive evaluation is calculated with the addition and multiplication mixed method. In the calculation, the significance coefficient is set as 3 and the significance coefficients for the other six evaluations is set as 1 because the economic evaluation is very important. The results of the calculation are shown in Table 23.8.

Table 23.8 show that the comprehensive scores of town owned coal mines, local owned coal mines, and state owned coal mines are 10.24–10.34, 10.19–10.25, and 10.03–10.07, respectively. Thus, the comprehensive effects of local owned coal mines and town owned coal mines are better than those of state owned ones. Although

Table 23.8 Comprehensive evaluation

No.	Name of evaluation	Evaluation content	State owned coal mines	Local owned coal mines	Town owned coal mines
1	Political evaluation	(1) Policies of the party	5	5	5
		(2) Laws and regulations	5	5	5
		(3) Other political effects	5	5	5
		Comprehensive rating	5	5	5
2	National defense evaluation	(1) National security	5	5	5
		(2) War preparedness	5	5	5
		Comprehensive rating	5	5	5
3	Social evaluation	(1) Employees who consume commodity grains and who do not consume commodity grains	4	4	5
		(2) Working conditions	4	3	2
		(3) Accident mortality	3.1–2.8	3.3–2.6	2.6–1.1
		(4) Feedback of farmers	4	4.5	5
		Comprehensive rating	3.7–3.8	3.5–3.7	3.3–3.65
4	Technical evaluation	(1) Technical advancement	5	4	3
		(2) Technical application	1.5 × 5	1.5 × 5	1.5 × 5
		Comprehensive rating	6.25	5.75	5.25
5	Environmental and ecological evaluation	(1) Environmental pollution caused by mining	3	3	3
		(2) Impact on ecological balance	3	3	4

(continued)

Table 23.8 (continued)

No.	Name of evaluation	Evaluation content	State owned coal mines	Local owned coal mines	Town owned coal mines
		Comprehensive rating	3	3	3.5
6	Natural resources evaluation	(1) Protection of coal resources	4	4	3
		(2) Recovery rate of coal resources	4.35	2.64	1.14
		Comprehensive rating	4.18	3.32	2.07
7	Economic evaluation	(1) Investment and its sources			
		(2) Costs			
		(3) Labor productivity			
		(4) Technical personnel			
		(5) Consumption of mine timber and steel			
		(6) Consumption of coal reserves			
		(7) Consumption of water resources			
		(8) Land utilization			
		(9) Total consumption expense			
		(10) Direct economic benefits			
		(11) Indirect economic benefits			
		(12) Total economic benefits			
		(13) Construction period			

(continued)

Table 23.8 (continued)

No.	Name of evaluation	Evaluation content	State owned coal mines	Local owned coal mines	Town owned coal mines
		(14) Full production period			
		(15) Absolute economic effects (net social income)			
		Comprehensive rating	3	4	5
Comprehensive evaluation		Addition: total average	5.16–5.18	5.37–5.4	5.59–5.63
		Multiplication: total average	4.87–4.89	4.82–4.85	4.65–4.71
		Mixed method: total average	10.03–10.07	10.19–10.25	10.24–10.34

[a]The significance coefficient is set as 1.5 because technical application is more important than technical advancement; Rating system is built on investigations

local owned coal mines and town owned coal mines have many shortcomings, their economic benefits are superior.

The following conclusions can be reached based on the preliminary findings of the comprehensive evaluation.

(1) State owned coal mines in Shanxi province have many advantages compared with those stated owned coal mines in other places. Their economic efficiency is the best in China.

According to statistics, the investment per ton coal of state owned coal mines in Shanxi province is 35% lower than the national average. The cost is 24% lower than the national average. But the labor productivity is 45% higher than the national average. From the state perspective, it is appropriate to invest large-scale coal bases in Shanxi province.

(2) Due to the lack of energy and capital, it is impossible to achieve the strategic goal in 2000 if only large coal mines are developed in Shanxi province. The best way is to develop local and township owned coal mines, because they need less state capital and produce coal fast.

The development history of coal industry in Shanxi province and the specific conditions of coal fields (about one-third of the land is coalfield) show that it is necessary to develop local owned and town owned coal mines. The comprehensive evaluation results proved that some factors of local owned and town owned coal mines in Shanxi province are better than those of state owned ones. From the economic perspective, if local owned and town owned coal mines produce extra 10 million t during the sixth five year plan period, town owned coal mines will create extra 1.15 billion yuan, and local owned coal mines will create extra 0.44 billion yuan. Of course, this figure is not very accurate. But it shows the relationship. Therefore, it is necessary to develop local owned and town owned coal mines in Shanxi province. Developing small coal mimes is different from developing small iron and steel works, fertilizers plants, cement plants, small power stations and small machinery factories. Here are the reasons. First, coal mines belong to mining industry. Regardless of the size of coal mines and adopted technology, the same quality of coal is produced. Furthermore, investment on coal mining is low, and economic benefits are good. Second, small coal mines can carry out necessary technological renovation and grow into large ones, such as Shi YiJie Coal Mine. Third, the development of small coal mines is related with the characteristics of coal fields in Shanxi province, such as wide distribution, shallow coal seams, good geological conditions, fast mining operation, and large economic benefits. For the same reason, the United States has also developed small coal mines. In 1977 there were more than 6200 coal mines, among which 5000 are small coal ones with annual output <10 t. Thus, developing local and town owned coal mines in Shanxi province conforms to natural rules and economic laws.

To sum up, coal energy development policy to the year of 2000 and later for Shanxi Province should combine the development of large, medium and small coal mines, combine advanced, intermediate and traditional technologies, and combine state owned coal mines, local owned coal mines and town owned coal mines.

More specifically, the three great development policy should be implemented. In particular, large open pits and medium-sized coal mines based on national investment should be developed. Medium coal mines based on self-financing and intermediate technologies should be developed. Town owned coal mines based on self-financing and appropriate technologies should be developed. The author believes that the relationship of three types of coal mines in Shanxi province is practical at present and in the future. However, with the changes of conditions, cross-relations between them exist as well. For example, town owned coal mines will exploit regular coal resources in the future and deepen the mining depth. As a result, the traditional technologies will not be applicable. Intermediate technologies should be adopted, and the scale should be expanded. In addition, small coal mines that are exploiting formal coal resources will grow as medium and large coal mines through technical renovation and expansion. It should be noted that in order to enable town owned coal mines have stronger vitality, their existing strengths will have to be maintained and promoted. This is because small-scaled town owned coal mines have good structures. Their structures should not be arbitrarily changed. If small coal mines have advanced technology and state investment, this will be against the objective natural laws and economic laws. Similarly, it is not appropriate for large scale coal mines having traditional coal mining technologies and owned by towns.

23.9 Study on the Strategic Problems of Chinese Energy Development[10]

[Research background, scientific significance of achievements, and practical value] China's energy development strategy study is a key project of the sixth five-year plan of National Social Science Fund that the author undertook. When taking charge of scientific researches at Energy Source Office under the State Council, the author organized 34 units and 63 experts to study China's energy development strategy, starting in 1984 and ending in 1989. In the 5 years, this study generated 45 results, made 1 general achievement, made 17 subject achievements and 27 regional achievements, and published 1 book. As the leader of this research team, the author took charge of the overall research design and made 11 subject achievements, 4 of which were achieved by cooperating with others. The achievements of this study involves large amount of work, lots of units, and long period of research. They are the major achievements of energy development strategy since the founding of China. The Author has published over 20 articles [160–162, 173–175, 198–199, 202–203, 213–214, 227–229, 234–239, 242–246]. In addition, the author gave reports at the energy development strategy meeting of developing country held in 1988 in the US, as well as the energy development strategy meeting held at West Berlin University, Germany. When performing assessment, Li Zhisheng, chairman of the Committee of Experts noted that the author's research achievements were practical and highly theoretical, and had made great breakthrough in the energy development strategy theory. These achievements were nationally initiative and pioneering internationally. They have great practical value. Therefore, the research conducted by the author won the Second Prize of Scientific and Technological Progress from State Planning Commission in 1991. The author ranks the first in the author list. Moreover, the author worked on part of the energy development strategy in China Energy in 2000, which was awarded National Science and Technology Progress Award in 1988 [173]. The following is the main content of China's energy development strategy [234].

23.9.1 Content of Energy Development Strategy and Principle Preparation

Economic development has vertical and horizontal structures. The national economy consists of various sectors, industries, enterprises, and units. Economic development involves municipalities, provinces and, counties, and regions. Therefore, the economic development strategy has multi-level vertical and horizontal structure. Accordingly, economic development strategies can be categorized into national economic development strategies, regional economic development strategies, section economic development strategies, industry economic development strategies, and

[10] Xu [Xu89].

enterprise economic development strategies. If economic development strategies are at the highest level, strategic issues are at a lower level. Similarly, the energy development strategy has a multi-level vertical and horizontal structure as well. Energy development strategy can be for a country, a region, or a specific sector.

The development of an energy development strategy should follow the rule that energy development conforms to objective laws during a relatively long period. An energy development strategy consists of strategic thinking, strategic objectives, strategic focus, strategic steps, and strategic policies and measures. It is a very important to make an energy development strategy for China. The following four principles should be followed strategy when making a national energy development strategy.

1. **Objective**

Energy development strategy is not isolated. Instead, it is a part of the overall economic development strategy. So energy development strategy must be compatible with economic development strategies. When making an energy development strategy, the relationship between the energy development strategy and the economic development strategy must be considered.

2. **Long-term**

In order to meet the long-term and strategic development requirements of 12th national congress and 13th national congress of CPC, an energy development strategy must consider the long-term characteristics in this century or a longer period. In addition, each development phase and step must be considered as well.

3. **All-sidedness**

Energy development includes steps such as production, transmission, processing, conversion, storage, utilization and saving, import and export, as well as relationship among energy and economy, society, technologies, and education. Among these steps and relationships, some are more important and should be paid more attention. It is not correct to think an energy development strategy as a source energy development strategy.

4. **Rationality**

Making an energy development strategy must be based on the actual conditions in China and follows objective laws. Qualitative analysis and quantitative analysis should be performed on these laws. For example, strategic thinking, objectives, priorities, steps, policies, and measures must comply with China's reality and follow objective laws, including the socialist economic laws and natural laws. Only after these requirements are met, can an energy development strategy be success in a long run.

23.9.2 Strategic Thinking of China's Energy Development

In the past, due to the lack of strategic thinking, long-term development strategy is not considered when making an energy development strategy. Now it is realized that without the guidance of a long-term development strategy, lots of problems cannot be resolved. Although strategic thinking has been missing for a long time, part of it is applied in practice. Energy is important for national economic development. And economic development requires the development of energy. With the growth of economy, more energy is needed. The larger the elasticity coefficient of energy consumption, the better. Because energy production is not sufficient in China, energy reserves should be developed. And the elasticity coefficient of energy consumption must be reduced. The shortage of energy supply in China has existed for many years. Such shortage has restricted the economic development in China. Accordingly, energy production must be increased. The more energy is produced (for domestic consumption), the better. The author believes that this is a tradition of open source strategy thinking in China. Since the founding of New China to the third plenary session of the 11th national congress of CPC, strategic thinking was applied in energy development. Things changed after the energy crisis in 1973. Since then, developed countries can always get oil at a low price regardless how much oil is needed. Some developed countries with small energy production can import large amount of oil at low cost. This causes a phenomena named energy starvation. In China, the consumption of energy continues to grow. However, waste of energy is getting worse. Issues, such as environmental pollution, energy transportation stress, damage of forests and vegetation, over mining of petroleum resources, and overburden of energy investment appear. Therefore, the traditional open-source strategy should stop.

After the Third Plenary Session of the Eleventh CPC Central Committee, strategic thinking in energy development is gradually produced and developed. Since then, energy development holds the idea that economic development is constrained by energy, and that energy development is in turn affected by economy, energy reserves, transportation, and environmental pollution. Energy development and economic development enhance and restrain each other. Under certain circumstances, economic development does not consume a lot of energy. The most important thing is to improve energy efficiency, to reduce energy consumption, and to pay more attention to the economic and social effects of energy development. More energy should be produced to meet the needs of economic development and people's lives. Energy saving should also be emphasized. The key point of strategic thinking in energy development is to improve the efficiency of energy consumption. This is called strategy of improving energy economy efficiency, in short energy economy efficiency strategy.[11] Practices in these years proved that this new energy development strategy is in line with China's national conditions, the objective laws of energy economy, and the

[11]The author called it Generalized Energy Efficiency Strategy before, but call it Comprehensive Energy Efficiency Strategy now.

requirements of the new technological revolution. Compared with the old open-source strategy, strategy of improving energy economy efficiency has the following three characteristics.

(1) It point outs that the economic development is refrained by energy, and that energy development is affected by economic and other factors, such as energy reserves, transportation, environmental pollution, and ecological balance.
(2) It emphasizes that energy saving is a proactive approach instead of an expedient one. Compared with the open source strategy, energy consumption strategy has ten advantages: ① It does not need to mine underground energy resources, but get energy from the mined energy. In this way, energy saving is a type of open source; ② It does not require building coal mines, oil fields, or power plants; ③ Energy saving gets energy locally. It does not need any transportation facilities; ④ Energy saving can get energy very quickly. However, open-source requires a long period, generally 10 years. Therefore, energy saving needs a shorter period and can get energy quicker; ⑤ Energy saving has good economic benefits. If the investment on energy saving does not exceed 400 yuan/t, energy saving is more economical than open source; ⑥ Energy saving has no pollution whereas open source will generate pollution. Energy saving can improve the environment; ⑦ Energy saving can promote technology progress; ⑧ Energy saving can promote management; ⑨ Energy saving has more approaches than open source. Open source has approaches, such as coal production, oil production, power generation, and development of new energy. Energy saving has a wider range of approaches, which involve saving manpower, material, finance, and natural resources and increase of economic benefits; ⑩ Energy saving can use all types of force in a country, whereas open source relies on the strength of several energy industry sectors only. Thus, energy saving should be given priority at all times. When solving energy problems, we should consider energy saving first, and then open source.
(3) Improving energy economy efficiency and social environmental efficiency is the premise for developing energy. Without this premise, more energy is produced, more energy is wasted. As a result, the overall economic benefits and social environmental benefits will be degraded.

The Sixth Five-Year Plan period (1981–1985) is a transition period for China's energy development strategy. In this period, the traditional strategic thinking of open source is still accepted by some people. However, with the development of economy, more and more people begin to accept energy economy efficiency strategy, which will serve for development of China's energy in a long run. This strategy will be applicable in the year of 2000, 2050, or beyond.

23.9.3 Objective of China Energy Development Strategy

The objectives of China's energy development strategy should be compatible with the China's economic development. The 13th CPC National Congress proposed the strategic goal of China's economic development: In the year of 2000 the GNP shall be quadrupled compared with the year 1980. Chinese live a well-off life. By the middle of the 21 century, per capita GNP should reach the level of moderately developed countries. At that time, Chinese live a more affluent life. Modernization should be realized. Based on the goal of economic development and new strategic thinking of energy development, the author proposes that the goal of China's energy development strategy. Particularly, the goal is to ensure the completion of the objective and tasks of economic development, the maximum economic and social benefits should be obtained with minimal energy consumption. The goal reflects that the development of energy resources should meet the requirements of the overall goal of economic development.

There are five main aspects of the goal, namely energy production, energy technical efficiency, energy saving, energy consumption per unit product, and energy consumption per unit output. The author believes that it is not appropriate to use these aspects as the overall goal of national energy development strategy. Because these aspects cannot reflect the overall situation of energy development. For example, people in energy production sector and energy supply sector think that energy production should be used as the strategic goal. An example question is how much coal, oil and hydro electricity will be produced in the year of 2000. This is understandable and reasonable. However, this question only reflects an aspect of production. It does not reflect other aspects of energy development, such as energy saving. Therefore, it is not appropriate to choose energy production as the goal of energy development strategy. It is reproachless for people in energy technology sector to concern about energy efficiency. In addition, the improvement of efficiency of energy technologies is likely to be chosen as the goal for energy technology sector. This is not appropriate because such a goal does not represent the economic effect obtained after energy is consumed. This is only a technical goal and it does not reflect the relation between energy and technology. Other goals, such as energy consumption, energy consumption per unit product, and energy consumption per unit output, do not reflect all aspects either. Thus, they be chosen as the overall goal of national energy development strategy. The author's studies show that a goal indicator system with multiple indicators can properly represent the targets of China's energy development strategy. This indicator system should have a so-called key indicator, which is the key to understand China's energy development strategy. The energy consumption per unit of gross national product (or national income), or the energy consumption per unit GDP (or national income) is the key indicator. These two key indicators reflect the same thing. In fact, they are reciprocals for each other. These two indicators can fully reflect the overall goal of the energy development strategy. In addition, they have many advantages. The following formulas provide more details about these two indicators.

$$\begin{aligned}&\text{Energy consumption per unit of gross}\\&\text{national product (national income)}\\&\quad=\frac{\text{Gross national product (national income)}}{\text{energy consumption}}\end{aligned}\tag{23.12}$$

$$\begin{aligned}&\text{Energy consumption per unit of gross}\\&\quad\text{national product (national income)}\\&\quad=\frac{\text{Gross national product (national income)}}{\text{Energy demand quantity }-\text{ generalized energy saving}}\end{aligned}\tag{23.13}$$

$$\begin{aligned}&\text{Energy consumption per}\\&\quad\text{unit of gross national product (national income)}\\&\quad=\frac{\text{Gross national product (national income)}}{\text{(final effective utilization of energy/efficiency of energy systems)}}\end{aligned}\tag{23.14}$$

$$\begin{aligned}&\text{Energy consumption per}\\&\quad\text{unit of gross national product}\\&\quad\text{(national income)}\\&\quad=\frac{\text{(Output value }-\text{ costs }+\text{ wages }+\text{ depreciation income)}}{\text{(energy production }\pm\text{ energy imports and exports)}}\end{aligned}\tag{23.15}$$

$$\begin{aligned}&\text{Energy consumption per unit}\\&\quad\text{of gross national product}\\&\quad\text{(national income)}\\&\quad=\frac{\text{per capita gross national product (national income)}}{\text{per capita energy consumption}}\end{aligned}\tag{23.16}$$

$$\begin{aligned}&\text{Energy consumption per unit}\\&\quad\text{of gross national product}\\&\quad\text{(national income)}\\&\quad=\frac{\left[\text{gross national product (national income)/yield}\right]}{\text{energy consumption of product}}\end{aligned}\tag{23.17}$$

$$\begin{aligned}&\text{Energy consumption per unit}\\&\quad\text{of gross national product}\\&\quad\text{(national income)}\\&\quad=\frac{\left[\text{gross national product (national income)/output value}\right]}{\text{energy consumption of product}}\end{aligned}\tag{23.18}$$

The above formulas show that the key indicator is connected with 25 indicators. All these indicators form an objective function, whose goal is energy consumption per unit of gross national product (national income) or energy consumption per unit of gross domestic product (national income). In this way, an indictor system for energy development strategy is ready. In this system, energy consumption per unit of gross national product (national income) or energy consumption per unit of gross domestic product (national income) is the key indicator. This system also include 25 other indicators, namely total industrial and agricultural output value and its average annual growth rate, the annual growth rate of GDP (or national income) or the annual growth rate of industrial and agricultural output value, gross national product (or national income) and its average annual growth rate, energy production, energy consumption, and its average annual growth rate, growth (elasticity) coefficient of energy consumption, energy import and export, energy saving, efficiency of energy systems, energy consumption of industrial and agricultural output value, energy consumption of products and services, per capita energy consumption, per capita GDP (or national income), raw material consumption, population, occupancy of capital, utilization of natural resources, production, labor quantity, quality, price, cost, and gross national product (or national income) structure coefficient of the material production sectors, GDP (or national income) structure factor of service sectors, population structure coefficient. These indicators reflect energy production, energy saving, efficiency of energy system, or the economic development strategy. The strategic objective covers all aspects and things reflecting the nature and rules of energy development. This strategic goal indicates that that there are many approaches to solve problems in energy development. For instance, in a certain time period, the energy production is fixed. Therefore, energy consumption should be more efficient. When utilization efficiency of some energy sources cannot be improved, economic efficiency should be improved. When economic benefits cannot grow, utilization efficiency of energy should be improved. Sometimes when it is hard to save energy, energy production should be increased. When energy export drops, energy import should increase. When energy consumption is restricted, energy production, output value, and economic structure should be improved. These strategic objectives are applicable at the country level, the region level, the sector level, and the enterprise level. They are applicable for energy consuming regions and sections as well as energy producing regions and sections, because energy producing regions and sectors themselves have problems about energy consumption and economic effects.

Some people think that growth (elasticity) coefficient of energy consumption is a better key indicator than energy economic effect coefficient and energy consumption per unit GNP (national income). However, based on the author's research, although energy consumption coefficients are very important indicators for energy development, they are not key indicators because elasticity coefficient of energy consumption only reflect the relationship between growth speed of energy consumption and development speed of national economy. It does not reflect the economic effects of energy unitization or the energy consumption per unit GNP (national income). In fact, key indicators truly reflect the overall rule of energy development, because they can reflect energy consumption and the level of economy, technologies, and management. In the comparison between China and foreign countries or between different provinces, energy economy efficiency or energy consumption per unit GNP (national income), not the growth coefficient of energy consumption, should be adopted. In fact, the growth coefficient of energy consumption only changes efficiency of energy economy or unit gross national product (national income). If the energy consumption per unit gross domestic product (national income) is low, it should be increased and the growth coefficient of energy consumption should be set larger than 1. If the energy consumption of unit gross domestic product (national income) is high, it should be decreased and the growth coefficient of energy consumption should be set lower than 1. Therefore, growth coefficient of energy consumption is based on the energy consumption of energy economic efficiency or unit national gross domestic product (national income) of respective countries.

Some people think if energy consumption per unit gross national product (national income) or energy consumption of unit national gross domestic product (national income) is be chosen as the key indicator, those enterprises with high energy consumption will be impacted negatively. In fact, the development of high energy-consuming industries is determined by objective proportion requirement of the national economic development first, and then the economic benefits. Therefore, these two indicators are appropriate for assessing the energy consumption of all sectors and enterprises.

Some people think that improving economic efficiency and reducing unit energy consumption are to praise the backward, lower standards, move backward, and weaken the development of energy sources. In fact, improving economic efficiency and reducing unit energy consumption are the requirement of new technological revolution for reducing energy consumption. They reflect the advanced scientific and technological level. If devices are not upgraded and management is not improved, unit energy consumption will not be reduced. Reducing energy consumption does not mean lower standards. For example, in the past the power consumption could not be measured by electricity meters. The waste of electricity is high, but the standards are not high. After electricity meters were implemented, power consumption reduced. However, this does not mean standards drop. Because power consumption standards were not degraded at all. The other example is about refrigerators. Some refrigerators use more power, while other use less power. Power saving refrigerators do not lower utilization standards. So reducing energy consumption does not mean lower standards. In addition, reducing energy consumption does not mean retrogression either. In the past thirty years (1949–1979) energy consumption per unit national income increases gradually for many reasons. In the future, with the development of science and technology, reducing energy consumption will mean progress given the situation when energy resources are limited and energy production is not sufficient. Reducing energy consumption means the drop of energy consumption of GNP (national income). In China, with the development of economy and the increase of people's living standards, the total energy consumption will increase and energy production will grow as well. Therefore, reducing the energy consumption per unit GNP (national income) does not mean giving up energy development.

23.9.4 Predication of the Overall Goal of China Energy Development Strategy

1. **The estimated national income and GNP in the year of 2000**

The 12th CPC national congress put forward the economic objective, which requires that gross output value of industry and agriculture is quadrupled by the year 2000. Since industrial and agricultural output values are not economic efficiency indicators, they cannot be used to predict the objectives of energy development strategy. Therefore, we need to predict the national income according to the established industrial and agricultural output value that will be quadrupled. The growth rate of national income is generally lower than that of industrial and agricultural output values according to the analysis of historical data. During 1953–1980, the average annual growth rate of industrial and agricultural output value was 8.2%, while the average annual growth rate of national income was 6.1%. The rate between these two is 74%. Given that economic efficiency will be continuous improved in the next 20 years, the rate between the two should increase accordingly. To be conservative, 80–90% is set. It was in fact 88% during the Sixth Five-Year Plan period. The average annual growth rate of industrial and agricultural output value during 1981–2000 is 7.2%. Therefore, average annual growth rate of national income is 5.8–6.5%. According to the economic objective, the total national income will be 1130–1295 billion yuan, and per capita national income will be 942–1080 yuan in the year of 2000. A middle value of national income, 1.2 trillion yuan, is set. Per capita national income will be 1000 yuan. According to the fact in the Six Five-Year Plan period, the average annual growth of industrial and agricultural output is not 7.2%, but 11%. The annual average growth of national income is not 5.8–6.5%, but 9.7%. Therefore, the industrial and agricultural output value before the year 2000 will not be 2.73 trillion yuan. The national income will not be 1.13–1.295 trillion yuan either. The author predicted that they will be 3.07–4.35 trillion and 1.5–1.86 trillion yuan, respectively. The average annual growth is 7.6–9.5% and 7.3–8.4%, respectively. Per capita income will be 1200–1490 yuan with the average annual growth of 6.0–7.1%. The 13th CPC National Congress proposed the economic development objective that by the year of 2000, GNP will be quadrupled, increasing from 419.3 billion yuan in 1980 to 1.67 trillion yuan in 2000 with the average annual growth rate of 7.2%. The average annual growth during the Six Five-Year Plan period is 10%. Therefore, the author predicted that in the year of 2000 the GNP will be 1.9150–2.2950 trillion yuan with the average annual growth of 7.9–8.9%, and that per capita GNP is 1532–1840 yuan with the average annual growth of 6.6–7.6%.

2. **Estimated energy consumption in the year of 2000**

There are two methods for forecasting energy consumption. The first method predicts the possible energy production in the year of 2000 based on the amount of energy reserves and the amount of investment. The available energy for domestic consumption can be got by deducting the amount of net energy export from the predicted value. The second method can get the amount of required energy by deducting the amount of saved energy from the predicted amount of energy. The first method gets the amount of available energy. The second method gets the amount of required energy. They should be equal. When the amount of estimated available energy is not equal to the amount of required energy, measures should be taken to balance them. If supply is larger than demand, production can drop or export can be increased. When demand is larger than supply, production can be increased and export can be reduced. Energy saving should be considered as well. In short, available energy and needed energy should be adjusted. The goal is to make the actual energy consumption as the technically optimal energy consumption, which can balance supply and demand and has the largest economic benefits, i.e. $N_{\text{supply}} = N_{\text{actual}} = N_{\text{demand}}$.

We first estimate the available energy consumption N_{supply}. According to relevant data, the estimated productions of coal, oil, natural gas, hydropower, and nuclear in the year of 2000 are 1.2–1.3 billion t, 0.2–0.25 billion t, 40–50 billion m^3, 250–280 billion kWh, 50–75 billion kWh, respectively. In total, the estimated productions of energy is 1.3–1.48 billion t of standard coal. The productions of coal, oil, natural gas, hydropower, and nuclear in the year of 2000 are estimated as 1.2–1.4 billion t, 0.2 billion t, 20–25 billion m^3, 200 billion kWh, and 15–25 billion kWh, respectively. The estimated productions of energy equal to 1.247–1.4 billion t of standard coal. In 1982, the 12th CPC national congress proposed that the total output of industry and agriculture should be quadrupled by the year of 2000. Some experts in related sectors estimated that the energy production of China in the year of 2000 is 1.06–1.18 billion t of standard coal. A higher estimation is 1.2 billion t of standard coal. If China does not export coal, the available energy available for domestic consumption is 1.2 billion t. In our estimation, the lower value is 1.247 billion t of standard coal. After the amount for export is deducted, the available energy available for domestic consumption is 1.2 billion t of standard coal. The higher value is 1.24 billion t of standard coal. After the amount for export is deducted, the available energy available for domestic consumption is 1.35 billion t of standard coal. Thus, the lower value in our estimation can meet the requirement of double economy size. The higher value in our estimation can meet the requirement of quadruple economy size.

N_{demand} is energy demand. After the 12th CPC Congress proposed that China's industrial and agricultural output will be quadrupled by the year 2000, many experts predict the energy demand of China in the year of 2000. So far, the following five proposals are available.

The first proposal uses energy quota calculation method[12] in the energy consumption coefficient method initiated by the author. The results in this proposal are reasonable generalized energy saving analysis method is applied. Here is the formula.

$$n_{\Sigma d} = (\mathrm{n}_{\Sigma do} M - \Delta N_{\sum d})/M$$

[12] Xu [Xu82].

where $n_{\Sigma do}$ is the energy consumption of national income in 1980. M is the national income of the year 2000. $\Delta N_{\Sigma d}$ is the energy consumption calculated with the generalized energy saving method. The energy consumption of national income $n_{\Sigma d}$ can be calculated first. Then the domestic energy demand in the year of 2000 can be calculated. The energy consumption of national income in 1980 is 16.34 t of standard coal/10,000 yuan. If neither energy saving nor energy waste is considered, the energy consumption of national income in 2000 will be the same. If national income is quadrupled, the energy consumption should be quadrupled as well. This means that the demand of coal is 2.4 billion t of standard coal. Given that the generalized energy-saving penetrance in China is 50–60%, we take 50%. In other words, 1.2 billion t of stand coal will be saved. Among them, 400 million t are direct saved energy, while 800 million t are indirect saved energy. Among the indirect saved energy, 300 million t are obtained from structural changes. 200 million t are obtained from slow population growth. The rest 300 million t are from the rise of productivity and quality and the drop of costs. Accordingly, the energy demand in the year of 2000 is calculated as 1.2 billion t standard coal. Energy consumption per unit national income drops half to 8.2 t of standard coal/10,000 yuan. The elasticity coefficient of energy consumption is 0.5.[13]

The second proposal was proposed by World Bank in January 1984.[14] It uses the sector comprehensive analysis (i.e. the energy consumption coefficient method) to calculate energy demand based on energy-consuming sectors and the output and energy consumption quota of an industry from the perspective of conversion loss. Given that the industrial and agricultural output in the year of 2000 will be quadrupled, the lower energy consumption is estimated as 1.428 billion t of coal. The higher energy consumption is estimated as is 1.9 billion t of standard coal. The increase coefficient of energy consumption (calculated based on industrial and agricultural output) is 0.61 and 0.82.

The third proposal[15] was proposed by the Energy Research Institute under National Economic Commission in December 1984. It adopts the same analysis method applied in the second proposal. It estimates that the energy demand is 1.44–1.46 billion t of standard coal and that the elasticity coefficienEstimation for energy development strategyt of energy consumption is 0.63 in the year of 2000 when the industrial and agricultural output is quadrupled.

The fourth proposal estimates energy consumption with sector analysis in economic structure through dynamic investment output model based on given conditions.[16] It estimates that the energy demand is 1.37–1.56 billion t of standard coal and that the elasticity coefficient of energy consumption is 0.59–0.68 in the year of 2000 when the industrial and agricultural output is quadrupled.

---

[13]Xu [Xu83c].

[14]World Bank (1984). Outlook of Energy Supply and Demand.

[15]Energy Office of China Economy Commission: Forecast of China's Energy Demand in 2000, December of 1984.

[16]Qiu [QI85].

The fifth proposal adopts the method of elasticity coefficient of energy consumption prediction. It sets the elasticity coefficient of energy consumption as 1 first. In other words, energy demand in the year of 2000 is quadrupled as well, namely 2.4 billion t of standard coal. Next, 300 million t standard coal saved by technical energy saving and 400 million t of standard coal saved by structural energy saving are deducted. The result is 1.7 billion t of standard coal. The elasticity coefficient of energy consumption is forecasted to be 0.75.[17]

Which proposal is the most practical? It is too early to evaluate them. When the strategic goals of China's economic development are achieved in late 1990s (very likely earlier than 2000), we will know which one is the most practical and which one deviates largely by comparing their results with the actual energy consumption. If one estimation reaches 80–90% of the actual amount, it is a good one. If one estimation reaches 90% of the actual amount, it is a very good one. The five-year practice in 1981–1985 show that the first proposal is 100% accurate based on the rate of elasticity coefficient value of average annual energy consumption and predicted value. The accurate rate for the second proposal is 54–72% with a deviation of 28–46%. The accurate rate for the third proposal is 70% with a deviation of 30%. The accurate rate for the fourth proposal is 65–75% with a deviation of 25–35%. The accurate rate for the fifth proposal is 59% with a deviation of 41%. If the goals of the seventh five-year plan are achieved, the accurate rates for the five proposals will be similar to those in the sixth five-year plan. No big changes are expected. However, the situation for the next ten years must be assessed based on the actual results in the future. Therefore, in order to fulfill the goal that energy consumption is quadrupled and reaches 1.2 billion t in the year of 2000, the estimated energy demand and the elasticity coefficient of energy consumption is 0.5 should be adopted. In this way, the demand of energy N_{demand} can be equal to the available energy N_{supply}. Because the strategic objectives made by the Central Committee of CPC might be achieved before the year of 2000, the energy production will exceed the objectives before the year of 2000. Following our estimation, the industrial and agricultural output value in the year of 2000 will be 4.34 times and 6.15 times higher than those in 1980. The national income is 4.07 times higher and the gross national product is 4.07 times higher as well. Energy consumption will increase accordingly. We believe that the higher value 13.5 million t of standard coal in the estimation of energy consumption can meet the demand of energy in the year of 2000.

3. **Estimated overall objective energy development strategy in the year of 2000**

According to the previous prediction, in the year of 2000 after the energy for export is deducted, the lowest energy production is 1.247 billion t of standard coal. With the lowest energy production, the economic goals are developed in details. Specifically, the available energy for consumption is 1.2 billion t of standard coal. The industrial and agricultural output will be quadrupled, reaching 2.83 trillion yuan. The national income is 1130–1295 billion yuan. The GNP is quadrupled, reaching 1.67 trillion yuan. Accordingly, the overall goals for national energy development strategy in

[17]China's Energy in 2000, December of 1984.

the year of 2000 with the lowest energy production are developed. Specifically, energy consumption per unit gross national product is 1392 yuan/1 t of standard coal. National income per unit energy consumption is 942–1080 yuan/1 t of standard coal. Meanwhile, the energy production in the year of 2000 is estimated as 1.4 billion t of standard coal as the highest value after the energy for export is deducted. In this case, the available energy for consumption is 1.35 billion t of standard coal. With the highest energy production, in order to overfill the economic goals, national income should be 1500–1860 billion yuan and GNP should be 1915–2295 billion yuan. Therefore, the overall goal for national energy development strategy in the year of 2000 with the highest energy production are developed. In particular, energy consumption per unit gross national product is 1418–1700 yuan/1 t of standard coal. Energy consumption per unit national income is 1111–1378 yuan/1 t of standard coal.

Now we have two goals. One is a defined goal and the other is excess goal. The former aims to reach 1392 yuan/1 t of standard coal (GNP). The latter aims to reach 1418–1700 yuan/1 t of standard coal (GNP). In 1980 the energy consumption per unit gross national product is 696 yuan/1 t of standard coal. If the defined goal is achieved, the efficiency of energy economy will be doubled. If the excess goal is achieved, efficiency of energy economy will be improved more than double. Table 23.9 lists the values of the main indicators in the target system of China's energy development strategy in the year of 2000. These are the goals that we expect to achieve. They are also the goals that we should strive to achieve.

Can the above goals be achieved? What evidences can prove that such goals can be achieved? What evidences can prove that such goals cannot be achieved? What will be done after such goals are achieved? These questions need answers. Debates exist for the answers.

There were two arguments. One argues that the goals can be achieved but the tasks are very arduous. The potential for energy saving is great. As long as the strategy is correct and correct measures are taken, these goals can be achieved. The other argues that these goals cannot be achieved. The author supports the first argument. Here is the reason. The energy potential in China is estimated by the author with comparison method, generalized energy analysis, and generalized energy-saving model. The results of the estimation show that energy saving potential can reach 50–60%. Compared with provinces that lack coal in 1980, such as Hubei province and Zhejiang province, the energy-saving potential is 50%. Compared with India with data in 1978, energy-saving potential is 55%. In addition, energy-saving potential based on generalized energy saving analysis is 60%. In other words, energy consumption per unit national income or energy consumption per unit GNP will drop 50–60% in the year of 2000 compared with 1980. In 1980, energy consumption of average national income is 16.4 t/10,000 yuan. It will drop 50–60% to 6.56–8.2 t/10,000 yuan in the year of 2000. In 1980, energy consumption of average gross national product (GDP) is 14.4 t/10,000 yuan. It will drop 50–60% to 5.76–7.2 t/10,000 yuan in the year of 2000. Thus, if the energy saving potential is utilized, the overall goal of the energy development strategy is very likely to be achieved.

Table 23.9 Estimation for energy development strategy for China in the year of 2000

Indicators	1980	2000	
		Defined goal	Excess goal
Efficiency of energy economy[a]	696 yuan/1 t of standard coal	1392 yuan/t	1418–1700 yuan/t
Energy consumption for GDP	14.4 t/10,000 yuan	7.2 t/10,000 yuan	7.05–5.9 t/10,000 yuan
GDP	419.3 billion yuan	1670 billion yuan	19,150–22,950 billion yuan
GDP per capita	427 yuan/person	1392 yuan/person	1532–1840 yuan/person
Energy production	637 million t of standard coal	1.25 billion t of standard coal	1.4 billion t of standard coal
Energy consumption	603 million t of standard coal	1.2 billion t of standard coal	1.35 billion t of standard coal
Energy consumption per capita	0.613 t/person	1 t/person	1.08 t/person
Annual increase rate of energy consumption	–	3.6%	4.1%
Annual increase rate of GDP	–	7.2%	7.9–8.9%
Increase coefficient of energy consumption	–	0.5	0.46–0.52
Drop rate of energy consumption in GDP	–	50%	51–59%
Annual energy saving rate	–	3.4%	3.5–4.3%

[a]*Note* If the calculation is based on GNP, the defined goal is 942–1080 yuan/1 t of standard coal. The excess goal is 1111–1378 yuan/1 t of standard coal

The argument that thinks the overall goal cannot be achieved for the following reasons:

(1) The above energy-saving potential is too simplistic. The analysis is not rigorous. The energy saving potential is really large. It should be analyzed specifically. Therefore, the right conclusion cannot be reached without comparison.

This argument is somewhat reasonable. But it is not complete and practical. In fact, there are no precise and scientific methods domestically and abroad for predicting energy saving potential. Even some economic forecasts cannot predict precisely. The reason is that the potential is not an obvious force. In addition, what a long-term forecast provides are not what we should do now. Analogy (comparison method) is one of the most common methods for prediction. It is applied for finding the gap. Analysis with comparison method shows that energy saving potential is large. Without using the comparison method, the answers to the questions whether the potential is not the biggest potential, whether it is possible to achieve, and how it can be achieved remain unknown. Some people think that the achievement of the goal depends on precedent, either domestic or abroad. The results of comparative method show that this strategic goal has many domestic and abroad precedents. Among the oversea precedents, some are in industrial countries and others are in the developing countries. Some are in middle-income countries and others are in low-income countries. Some are in countries with the same social system as China and others are in countries with different social systems. Some are in countries in hot areas and others are in countries in cold areas. Some are in countries with little fertilizer and others are in countries with large amount of fertilizer. In short, 113 countries (regions) (4–5 countries excluded) reached the above goal of energy consumption in 1978 or a long time ago. Take India as an example, because India is a country with ordinary conditions. Some people think that India achieved the goal because it use less fertilizers and its climate is hot. However, the gap of energy consumption between China and India is 26% before 1966. The gap grows to 74% after 1976. Obviously, the larger gap is caused by the internal factor of China. In the next 20 years, energy consumption in the aforementioned countries will be improved based on their conditions. Even if China achieves the goal, gaps still exist between China and these countries. Other than oversea precedents, a southern province lacking coal is a domestic precedent. In 1980, some provinces in southern China, such as Zhejiang and Hubei, reached goal set for the year of 2000. Shanghai even reached a higher level. After 20 years, energy consumption in these provinces will continue to drop. It is reasonable for other provinces to achieve the level of energy consumption in these provinces in 1980. Data shows that provinces with high energy prices tend to achieve lower energy consumption. That is to say, it is possible to drop the national average energy consumption per unit national income by adopting appropriate energy pricing policies. This is called competition. An old saying is to compare, learn, pursue, help, and exceed. These examples show that comparison is a useful method. It can be used for estimating energy saving potential and reducing energy consumption. Accordingly, how to use comparison is a subject.

(2) Energy development must be synchronized with the economic development speed or in advance. In other words, the elasticity coefficient of energy consumption should be equal to or >1. The lower the per capita income, the greater the elasticity coefficient.

In the past it was widely accepted that the elasticity coefficient of energy consumption must be >l. However, this statement has basis. Thus, this statement does not fit situations in all of the countries in the world. Especially, it does not fit the situation in China. The elasticity coefficient of energy consumption represents the relationship between energy development and energy saving. The following is the discussion about how to deal with the relationship between energy development and energy saving.

To solve the energy problem, we must deal with the relationship between energy development and energy saving firstly. Energy development and energy saving are two fundamental approaches to solve the energy problem. Energy development is the foundation, whereas energy saving relies on energy development. Without energy development, there would be no energy saving. Therefore, to solve the energy problem, we must rely primarily on energy development. However, attention should be paid to energy development only. Energy saving coexists with energy development. As such, to solve the energy problem we should not only rely on both energy development and energy saving. We must correctly handle the relationship between them. At the end of this century, what is the most appropriate ratio between China's energy development and energy saving? This is a very important issue. The ratio between energy development and energy saving can be denoted approximately by the coefficient of national energy development or the coefficient of energy consumption growth (the coefficients refer to the ratios between the growth rate of energy development or the growth rate of consumption growth and the speed of national economy development. If energy import/export and storage are not considered, the coefficient of national energy development is the same as the coefficient of energy consumption growth). There are three scenarios. In the first scenario, economic development totally relies on energy development. Now, the coefficient of national energy development is 1 or larger than 1. In other words, the unit energy consumption, such as the energy consumption of GDP or national income, does not drop. No saving occurs. This applies for the whole country, not a certain sector, or a certain enterprise. Because some enterprises and departments can totally dependent on energy saving for production. In addition, this scenario is for a certain time period, not for comparison with other time periods. If compared with other time periods, regardless of the values of elasticity coefficient of energy consumption, it means that energy is saved if the coefficient is lower than that in the previous period. However, if the elasticity coefficient of energy consumption does not drop to l or below in a period, the energy consumption does not drop at the country level. Eeconomy development entirely relies on energy development. The only change is that the degree of reliance is higher before. In the second scenario, economy development rely on both energy development and energy saving. Now, the national average energy consumption drops. The elasticity coefficient of energy consumption is <1 but >0. When the elasticity coefficient is larger than 0.5, economy development rely more on energy development. When the elasticity coefficient is smaller than 0.5, economy development rely more on energy saving. When the elasticity coefficient is equal to 0.5, economy development rely on energy development and energy saving equally. In the third scenario, economic development wholly relies on energy saving. Now, the national average energy consumption drops. The elasticity coefficient of national energy consumption is $= 0$ or <0. In order to correctly handle and make reasonable arrangements for the relationship between energy development and energy saving, it is necessary to carefully determine the elasticity coefficient of energy development or energy consumption. The determination of this coefficient should consider the advantages of energy development and energy saving as well as the economical efficiency and practicality.

When looking back the history of the energy development in the world, we can see that for a very long time, especially in the initial stage of industrialization, economy development wholly relies on energy development due to rich energy resources, low cost of energy development, nonbusy transportation, and low environmental pollution. The elasticity coefficient of energy consumption is always >1. For example, the elasticity coefficient of energy consumption during 1880–1920 in the US is 1.65. The elasticity coefficient of energy consumption during 1955–1960 in Japan is 1.27. The elasticity coefficient of energy consumption during the first five year plan period of industrialization in China is 1.63. In recent decades, because of the continuous improvement in the efficiency of energy consumption, the elasticity coefficients of energy consumption in industrial countries dropped. However, they are still close to 1. During 1960–1973, the elasticity coefficients of energy consumption in the US, West Germany, Japan, France, and UK are 1.07, 1.06, 1.00, 0.91, and 0.71, respectively. Thus, the energy issues in economy development still mainly rely on energy development. After the first five-year plan, China also took this approach with an elasticity coefficient of energy consumption higher than 1. With the development of economy in the countries across the world, the amount of energy development and energy consumption becomes larger and larger. A serial of problems appear, such as environmental pollution, busy energy transportation, over-mining of oil, destruction of forest, and energy waste. A few years ago, many thought that the shortage of energy in China was caused by the low level of energy development and the low value of the elasticity coefficient of energy consumption. Therefore, they proposed to accelerate energy development and increase the value of the elasticity coefficient of energy consumption. This proposal reflects the old approach for energy development. The 12th CPC national congress proposed that by the end of this century the industrial and agricultural output in China should be quadrupled. Guided by the old approach, the elasticity coefficient of energy consumption should be equal to 1 at least, and energy production should be quadrupled as well. This means that energy production should rise from 600 million t of standard coal in 1980 to more than 2.4 billion t of standard coal in the year of 2000, with an annual increase of 1 million t of standard coal. This goal cannot be achieved. Even if it is achieved, serious transportation problems and pollution problems will not be resolved. Therefore, the solution for energy issue cannot rely on energy development only. Instead, both energy development and energy saving should be considered. This means that the elasticity coefficient of energy consumption should be set smaller than 1. In addition, the approach of saving energy has 10 advantages compared with the approach of energy development.

The author compared economic effects of coal exploitation (including transportation) with energy saving. The result is that energy saving is cheaper than coal exploitation if the investment on saving one ton of standard coal (refer to primary energy) does not exceed 400 yuan. In this comparison, benefits do not include energy saving and environmental spending generated by coal exploitation. If these benefits are calculated, the allowable investment on energy saving is higher than 400 yuan. In fact, other than large energy-saving measures, a lot of economic measures and technical measures for energy-saving require little money. In general, they cost <400 yuan. Usually, the economic effect of energy-saving is better than that of energy development. Especially large energy development in many countries reduces energy reserves in the long run. As a result, development conditions become worse. Meanwhile, development costs increase gradually and energy prices rise continuously.

Thus, it is reasonable to give priority to energy saving. This is consistent with the trend of using energy wisely. It is obvious that energy saving should be given priority now and in the future. Priority here means that energy saving should be put in the first place and energy development should be put in the second place when dealing with energy issues.

From the perspectives of potential and possibility of energy development and energy saving, China has plenty of energy sources, especially coal and hydro. Energy development in China has great potential. However, the possibility of energy development is very limited. Due to limited capital, energy production will not be more than 1.4 billion t of standard coal by the year of 2000 in China. Now let us discuss the relationship between energy and economic development. Energy is the constraint of economic development. In turn, economy affects energy development. If only the impact of energy on economy is highlighted, no correct conclusion will be reached. The opinion that higher energy development leads to better economic development is not correct. There is an optimal relationship between energy development and economic development. If this relationship is not treated corrected, issues will occur. For example, the lack of energy requires to develop energy. It is estimated that the rise of 600 million t of standard coal requires an investment of 700 billion yuan, including all investment on secondary energy, but excluding investment on transportation and environmental protection. If energy saving is not considered, energy production needs to reach 1.8 billion t of standard coal. The required investment will be 2.1 trillion yuan. If this is the case, all investment in China is not enough for energy development. By the year of 2000, no investment will be available for other industries and departments. Without investment, other industries and departments cannot develop. As a result, economy development will be impacted negatively. Finally, investment available for energy development will drop as well. Neither economy nor energy will develop well at the end. This is a vicious circle. On the contrary, in a virtuous circle, generalized energy saving is the focus. The efficiency of energy economy is improved. More energy is saved. The pressure on energy development is reduced. The efficiency of economy is improved as well. More economic benefits mean more resources for developing energy and for achieving higher energy economic efficiency. In this way, more energy is saved and less pressure on energy development is generated. When economic benefits are increased, more investments are available for developing energy. When the circle continues, more energy is exploited. More energy is saved. Both energy and economy develop. They promote each other. Thus, energy development should be moderate. More energy development does not always mean good. Meanwhile, the economic effects of energy development should be considered. Investment should be saved and costs should be reduced.

If the based on the estimation of the potential of energy saving, if all goals are achieved in the year of 2000, the elasticity coefficient of energy consumption should be 0.4–0.5. This means that only 40–50% of energy consumption can rely on energy development. In contrast, the energy development strategy proposed by the author indicates that the elasticity coefficient of energy consumption is 0.46–0.52. There are two opposite opinions about whether this coefficient can be achieved in the coming 20 years. One opinion argues that the coefficient can be achieved. The other argues that the coefficient cannot be achieved because there is no precedent. The author agrees with the first opinion. This coefficient changes with historical conditions. The first world energy crisis occurring in 1973 is a turning point in world history. In the time before 1973, the whole world wastes and uses cheap oil. The 1960s is a golden period for economy development in capitalist countries. After 1973, the world realizes that oil is not easy to get. War or political reasons make oil harder to get. In addition, it was thought at that time that oil reserves in the world can support the world consumption for only 30 years or so. Thus, the price of oil continued to rise. Since then, the economy development in most countries in the world, excluding some countries, slow down. People began to pay attention to energy saving. Many measures were taken to reduce energy consumption, and to lower the elasticity coefficient of energy consumption. The second world energy crisis occurring in 1979 proves again that the economy of the world must follow the direction of energy saving. Thus, it is necessary to identify these two historical conditions. In order to provide accurate elasticity coefficient of energy consumption, the conditions before 1973 and after 1973 must be clearly identified. Otherwise, wrong conclusions may be reached. Table 23.10 lists the elasticity coefficients of energy consumption in the major industrial countries before 1973 and after 1973 and the annual energy saving rate. Table 23.11 lists the prediction of the elasticity coefficients of energy consumption to the year of 2000. The table shows that the elasticity coefficients of energy consumption drops in most countries after 1973. The elasticity coefficients of energy consumption in Japan and UK dropped to 0.43 and 0.55, respectively. The annual energy saving rates in Japan and UK are 4.1% and 2.1%, respectively.

Table 23.10 Elasticity coefficients of energy consumption in main industrial countries before and after 1973

Country\Time	Before 1973	After 1973		
	Elasticity coefficients of energy consumption (1963–1973)	Elasticity coefficients of energy consumption (1973–1978)	Average annual energy saving rate (%)	Dropping rate of energy consumption per unit GDP (%)
US	1.07	0.69	2.4	14
Canada	0.94	0.58	–	9.3
Japan	1.00	0.43	4.1	19.1
France	1.00	0.4[b]	2.4	11
Germany[a]	1.06	0.96	2.2	14.1
Italy	1.81	1.15	1.5	11
UK	0.71	0.55	2.1	15
Average	0.98	0.76	–	–

Note [a]Here refers to Western Germany
[b]Time period 1973–1981
Sources World coal conference report, 1979; Energy, Japan, 1982; Energy, Japan, 1983

Table 23.11 Estimation of the elasticity coefficients of energy consumption in the world (1977–2000) (Unit: %)

Country	Annual growth rate of energy consumption	Annual GDP growth rate	Elasticity coefficients of energy consumption
US	1.2–2.2	2.8	0.43–0.78
UK	0.7–1.7	2.0–3.0	0.35–0.57
Japan	2.9–3.2	4.1–4.6	0.70–0.71
Germany[a]	1.6–1.9	2.8-3.3	0.57–0.58
France	2.3–3.1	3.0-4.0	0.77–0.78
Italy	2.3–2.4	2.8–3.3	0.73–0.82
Canada	2.4–3.0	3.5	0.69–0.86
Denmark	1.6–2.4	2.4–3.4	0.67–0.7
Fenland	2.0	3.0	0.67
Holland	2.0–2.85	2.2–3.0	0.91–0.95
Sweden	1.0–1.3	2.6	0.38–0.5
Australia	4.1	3.5	1.17
World	–	–	0.6

Note [a]Here refers to Western Germany

According to long-term prediction, the smallest value of the elasticity coefficients of energy consumption is 0.35. Its average is 0.6 across the world. Based on the report presented by Japan in the fifth meeting of Appraisal Group of Asia-Pacific Energy Research Society in 1982, Japan will adopt a value between 0.52 and 0.63 for the elasticity coefficient of energy consumption in 1990. During his visiting to Ministry of Power in France in 1984, the author knew that France adopted 0.5–0.7 for the elasticity coefficient of energy consumption.

In 1988, the author attended the conference of energy development strategy in developing countries and knew that the elasticity coefficient of energy consumption in the US was negative. Efficiency of energy consumption was high, whereas energy consumption was low in these developed countries. However, since the world energy crisis in 1973, the elasticity coefficients of energy consumption and energy consumption in these countries had dropped for several years. It was predicted that the drop would continue in the coming years. In contrast, the energy utilization efficiency is low and energy consumption is high in China. Compared with these developed countries, the energy strategic goal in China is not high. The goal is to achieve energy saving rate at 3.4–4.3% in the condition of high energy consumption. As long as we work hard, the goal can be achieved, because there are many precedents around the world in the past 10 years. The practice in the Sixth Five-Year Plan has proved this.

Analysis and Forecast of Elasticity Coefficient of Energy Consumption in China

The author believes that the analysis should be conducted in two historical periods. Before the third plenary session of 11th CPC national congress in 1978, economy development in China wasted a lot of energy. Economic efficiency was poor. People's living standard increased very slowly. After the third plenary session of 11th CPC national congress, China adjusted its economy policy. Economy development focuses more on high economic efficiency. In the past, the elasticity coefficient of energy consumption and energy consumption in China both were high. The elasticity coefficient of energy consumption in 1953–1978 was 1.65 (per national income). In recent years, the elasticity coefficient of energy consumption in China dropped drastically. Energy consumption dropped accordingly. The experience gained from 1979–1985 proved that it is possible for economy development through continuous low energy consumption with low elasticity coefficient of energy consumption (national income was 0.52). Some people think that such policy is effective only for a short-term, not for a long-term. We believe that conditions changed, so changes of the elasticity coefficient of energy consumption in recent years are not accidental. In fact, such changes reflect regularities in the new historical conditions. In other words, this change represents a new technological revolutionary trend and the objective requirements in the new historical conditions. The sooner people realize this trend and grasp it, the better position they will be in for the future. For example, if we keep the energy consumption of 23 t of standard coal per 10,000 dollars of gross national product in 1985 unchanged, 13.8 billion t of standard coal will be needed in the next century when the per capita GNP reaches $4000 in China. Even if China becomes a middle-level developed country at that time, it will consume much more energy than the current total energy consumption of one hundred countries and regions in the whole world.

We do not discuss the possibility of getting enough resource, capital, and transportation for such as huge amount of energy. The previous section points out that it is impossible to get enough capital. Now, let see if it is possible to consume such a huge amount of energy. We all know that energy consumption generates a lot of side effects, such as environmental pollution. Actually, atmospheric pollution caused by energy consumption accounts for approximately 80% in the total pollution. It is more serious in China, because coal is the main energy. In early 1980s, China consumes about 600 million t of standard coal, among which coal accounts for more than 70%, oil and gas account for 20%, and hydropower only accounts for 5%. Each year, 21 million t of smoke and dust and 18 million t of sulfur dioxide were emitted into the the atmosphere. According to the data in 1981, 75 cities were investigated. A quarter of them were below the minimum line set by the national standards. Pollution is very serious. The annual average level of sulfur dioxide in atmosphere per m^3 is 0.115 mg among the 75 cities. Pollution in northern cities is more serious than that in southern cities. Acid rain appeared in many regions in southern China. At present, there are three acid rain areas: southwest China (Chongqing and Guiyang), east China (Shanghai, Suzhou, Changzhou and Hangzhou), and central south China (Changsha, Guangzhou, Nanning and Guilin). Data of rainfall in Chongqing from 1979 to 1980 shows that the PH value reaches 4.04–5.33, close to the level of 1966 in European. Yangtze River Bridge, surface of buses, and construction machinery in Chongqing rust quickly due to corrosion of acid rain. Stones in concrete of buildings expose after the outer layer of mortar is eroded by acid rain in 3–4 years. In the summer of 1982, acid rain caused rice plants in 20,000 μ to death in Chongqing. In the same year, the frequency of acid rain in Changzhou and Suzhou in Jiangsu Province are 83.3% and 66.7%, respectively. Based on the records, the monthly average of dust fall in 51 cities is 37.7 t per km^2. This value is a double of the the minimum. In particular, the monthly average of dust fall of the 18 cities in south and of the 33 cities in the north are 18.64 t and 52 t, respectively. The situation of dust fall is more serious in northern cities. Here are the details: Taiyuan, 71.8 t per km^2; Datong, 67.4 t per km^2; Yuci, 80.2 t km^2; Qi County, 154 t per km^2. Dust fall levels in these cities are 2.3–6.7 times of the standard. Dust fall level in Shenyang and Beijing are 61 t per km^2 and 25 t per km^2, respectively. Their levels are higher than the standard as well. According to the data of particulate matter (with particle size of 100 microns or less), the levels of 41 cities are higher than the standard among the 51 cities, accounting for 80.4%. Energy consumption cause serious side effects to national economy. According to the survey in 1970 in the US, the social and economic loss caused by one ton of standard coal is $4.5. The damage on people's health is larger. The author's study shows that the economic loss caused by air pollution in China is 4.4 billion yuan. If the elasticity coefficient of energy consumption in the year of 2000 is still set as 1, meaning that coal is still the main energy, environmental pollution will be approximately tripled. Environmental pollution in the year of 2030 will be 13 times of that in 1980. At present, the energy consumption is only more than 600 million t. Serious environmental pollution occurs. If energy consumption increases, people and creatures in many regions will survive under more serious environmental pollution. National economy will suffer serious losses. In addition, the investment in environmental protection will increase quickly. According to abroad data, investment on environmental protection will account for 10–20% of the total investment for engineering projects. For the whole world, greenhouse effect caused by large consumption of coal reaches a status when mankind must take measures to control it.

The author believes that there is a vicious cycle and a virtuous cycle for the relationship among energy consumption, environmental protection and economy development. If economy development replies on pursuing high energy consumption, pollution will increase significantly. Not only economy but also environment will be impacted negatively. Finally the economy and society cannot develop fast due to the vicious cycle of energy-economy-environmental development. If we start from generalized energy saving and choose appropriate elasticity coefficient of energy consumption, pollution caused by energy consumption will not grow fast. Pollution can be prevented and handled. Huge impacts on economic development and human health will not happen. Accordingly, economy and society will grow smoothly. This is how the virtuous circle of energy-economy-environmental development work. Actually, these two cycles are similar with those discussed early in this section. The previous one focuses on energy exploit, whereas this one focuses on energy consumption. We should follow the virtuous cycle of energy-economy-environment development.

In summary, under the new conditions, China cannot choose a high elasticity coefficient of energy consumption and energy consumption. Otherwise serious consequences will occur.

In the energy development strategic goals discussed above, the author focuses on energy consumption of national income and energy consumption of gross national product (GDP). The author did not mention industrial and agricultural output. This is because industrial and agricultural output indicators have many shortcomings. Many economists think that it is more appropriate to take national income as the economy development goal. In fact, the economy development objectives set by the 12th CPC national congress indicate that industrial and agricultural output should be quadrupled with the premise of improved economic effects, which actually includes the goal of national income. Since 1994, Chinese government formally adopted national income as an assessment indicator, which is important to national economy. The 13th CPC National Congress proposed the goal of gross national product. As such, energy development strategic goals have more realistic meanings. From the perspective of the possibility of achieving the goals, the goals set with national income are easier to achieve compared with those set with industrial and agricultural output. In the past, the economy development in China followed the policy of high output, high energy consumption, and low income. Energy consumption of national income rose rapidly with a 3% annually rate from the first five-year plan to 1980. In the same time period, energy consumption of output had an annual growth rate of 1%. During the fifth five-year plan period, energy consumption of output is 9.85 t/10,000 yuan, whereas the energy consumption of national income is 18.8 t/10,000 yuan. Therefore, the potential of reducing the energy consumption of national income in the future is larger than the potential of reducing energy consumption of industrial and agricultural output. The 13th CPC National Congress proposed a goal of GDP. This goal includes the net output of the tertiary industry with low energy consumption. The tertiary industry is proposed to grow faster in the future. Accordingly, the potential of reducing the energy consumption of gross national product (GDP) is greater.

23.9.5 Arrangement of China's Energy Development Strategy

According to the national economic development strategic plan, China's energy development has two phases. During the first ten years, the goal is to lay a solid foundation for energy construction and energy saving in all aspects, in order to overcome the defects caused by the Cultural Revolution. In other words, the goal is to create a new situation in energy construction and to improve the efficiency of the energy economy, based on energy development. When this goal is achieved, experience will have been accumulated. The second ten years is a new period of economic revitalization. The goal is to follow the energy development strategy, developing energy production steadily, implementing energy saving, and meeting the needs of the rapid development of the national economy and of people's living. Two steps are planned, in order to achieve the strategic goal. The first step is to achieve an efficiency of energy economy by 1990 at 1000 yuan/ton. In other words, energy consumption of gross national product per 10,000 yuan should drop to about 10 t of standard coal with an annual energy saving rate of 3.6%. The floating property gained by this energy saving should continue. More efforts should be spent on gaining larger such floating property. The second step is to achieve an energy economy efficiency of 1392 yuan/ton in 2000 (this is the set goal). China should try harder to let the energy consumption of the gross national product per 10,000 yuan drops to 7.2 t of standard coal, in order to achieve an efficiency of energy economy of 1418–1700 yuan/t, in order to drop the energy consumption of the gross national product per 10,000 yuan to 5.9–7.05 t of standard coal (this is the excess goal), with an annual energy saving rate of 3%.

Coal is the main source of energy in China. Soon after the new China was founded, three-quarters of its coal production was from the Northeastern and Northern areas. During the first five-year plan period and the second five-year plan period, coal production in these two areas increased greatly. At that time, much coal from these two areas was transported to Eastern and Southern China. This is the strategy of moving coal from north to south. During the fourth five-year plan period, the goal is to change the situation of moving coal from north to south. A lot of manpower and resources were expended to find coal in the south. However, these resources were wasted because little coal was found. During the sixth five-year plan period, a strategy was proposed to build an energy base with the Shanxi province as the center and covering the western Inner Mongolia, western Henan province, northern Shanxi province, and Ningxia. This is a turning point for coal development and an important step for energy development in China. The energy base is 1.12 million km^2 with five hundred billion t of coal reserves, which accounts for more than 70% of the coal reserves in China. Coal categories in this energy base are complete. The quality of coal is high. The exploitation conditions are good. With the development in China's eastern coastal areas, both the northern coastal areas and the southern coastal areas have an urgent need for coal. They count on the coal transported from the energy base with Shanxi as the center. Therefore, after the strategy of moving coal from north to south, a new strategy of moving coal from west to east appears. The author thinks that, with the development and construction of the energy base, China's coal transportation pattern has changed greatly. Neither moving coal from north to south nor moving coal from west to east can reflect the new situation of coal transportation in China. Here are the reasons. First, north means northeastern China. Right now, coal supply in the northeast China is in a shortage. No coal is transported, at this time, from the north to the south. Instead, coal in Shanxi province is transported to both the northeast area and the southern area. In 1985, about 20 million t of coal was transported to the Northeast from Shanxi province, and more is expected for the future. Thus, the situation of moving coal from north to south has changed. As for moving coal from west to east, it is reasonable to call the energy base as west because the energy base is in the west of the eastern coastal areas. But at the country level, the energy base is in the central area of China. Coal produced by the energy base is transported in every direction, including the east, north, west, and south. In 1985, coal transported from the energy base to 25 provinces in all directions accounted for 88% of the total coal transportation in China. Among them, 12.37 million t were for Beijing, 13.76 million t for Liaoning, 8.79 million t for Tianjin, 23.77 million t for Hebei, 10.03 million t for Shandong, 10.45 million t for

Shanghai, 11.29 million t for Jiangsu, 6.41 million t for Zhejiang, 3.38 million t for Hunan, 2.76 million for Guangdong, 880,000 t for Guangxi, 2.17 million t for Shanxi, and 360,000 t for Qinghai. It is estimated that, by 2000, coal from this energy base will be transported to the northeast, Beijing–Tianjin–Tangshan, Shandong, the economic zone in Shanghai, the coastal areas in Fujian, Guangdong, and Guangxi, Hunan and Hubei, the inland areas of Guangdong and Guangxi, Sichuan, Gansu, and Qinghai. Therefore, moving coal from west to east is not correct. In fact, the coal development arrangement in China has formed a new situation. Neither moving coal from north to south nor moving coal from west to east can reflect the new situation. The author thinks that the new situation should be summarized as moving coal from the center to all directions. The center refers to the coal in the central region of China. All directions include east, south, west, and north. This new situation is expected to continue until the next century. It indicates a new era of China's energy development and deployment.

23.9.6 Key Points of China's Energy Development Strategy

Some people think that China's energy consumption per capita is still very low and that the potential of gaining floating property through energy saving is rather small and difficult. So they argue that economic development should rely on energy exploitation. Other people think that energy exploitation and energy saving are equally important. They argue that energy saving should be the focus for now. The author thinks that energy exploitation and energy saving are equally important and that energy saving (referring to the generalized energy saving, not general energy savings) should be the focus before the year of 2000. This is determined by the energy development strategy. If we still hold the idea that energy exploitation should take the first place and that energy development should be based on energy exploitation, the strategy of energy exploitation will return. Right now, China's energy efficiency and economic efficiency (gross national product generated by each ton of energy) is the lowest among more than one hundred countries around the world. If more attention is not paid to improve the efficiency of the energy economy, energy saving will not be enhanced. The current situation will never change, and energy development will be a dream that will never come true. By the year 2000, the economy is planned to be quadrupled. However, energy consumption cannot be quadrupled. Therefore, generalized energy saving should be the focus. Only this focus can guarantee energy development and can generate benefits. The key point is that the shortage of energy in China was not caused by low production (comparison with the level of economy development), but by wasting energy resources. More specifically, energy saving is the key to solving the energy problem in China. Generalized energy-saving strategy should be the strategic focus. But this does not mean that energy production is not important. Similarly, energy transition and education are strategic focuses in China's economic development strategy. But this does not mean that industry and agriculture are not important.

The focus of energy saving is to reduce the energy consumption in the industrial sectors, because the industrial sectors consume the largest amount of energy as well as financial and material resources. It cannot be denied that the industrial sectors create the largest amount of economic benefit. In 1980, the energy consumption in the industrial sectors accounted for 67.5% of the total energy consumption. National income from industrial sectors accounted for 46.8% of the total income. At the same time, the industrial sectors wasted a huge amount of energy. It is estimated that 55% of the energy saving potential comes from the industrial sectors (with the adjustment of economic structure excluded). The situation is that the industrial sectors waste a large amount of energy, whereas some people do not have enough energy.

The energy-saving focus of each sector should rely on economic energy saving, because economic energy saving can gain floating property. Meanwhile, technical energy saving is very important, as well. Direct energy conservation and indirect energy saving, which are easy and need small investment, should be undertaken first. Difficult energy saving measures that require a larger investment can be taken next. In addition, energy transportation, energy technology, and education should be the focuses of the strategy, as well.

23.9.7 Guidelines, Policies, and Measures for China's Energy Development Strategy

In 1980, China had the energy policy that energy development and energy saving were both important and that energy saving should be the base in the future. This policy fitted China's conditions at that time, without a doubt. However, keeping energy saving as the base now is not appropriate. Thus, the long-term energy policies can be revised: energy development and energy saving are both important; energy saving should be the basis of the policy, strengthening energy development under the premise of continuous improvement of energy efficiency. Here, energy saving as the basis does not mean the absolute investment or the amount of energy development and saving, but means giving priority to generalized energy saving more than to energy development. According to this strategy, the economy will be quadrupled by the year of 2000. The gross national product will rise from 419.3 billion yuan to 1.67 trillion yuan by the year of 2000. The increase is 1.25 trillion yuan. Among the increased gross national products, only one third can be achieved through energy development (600 million t). The other two-thirds must rely on energy saving (1.2 billion t).[18] Thus, energy saving will play a major role in economy development. Energy saving has the priority.

[18]In general, half of the GDP depends on energy development and the other half depends on energy saving. This refers to the total economic development instead of an incremental economic development. Here, 1/3 depends on energy development and 2/3 depends on energy saving, with the consideration of economic growth.

China's energy development should focus on electricity and be based on coal. Oil and gas should also be developed. In addition, renewable energy and new energy are preferred. The supply of electricity in China is far below the demand. This shortage made only about 20% of industrial production capacity unachievable. Electricity is the main energy required in certain economic sectors. Therefore, energy development should focus on electricity. Production of electricity should be increased gradually. China has rich coal resources. Coal accounts for 85% of all of the available energy in China. Right now, coal accounts for about 70% of the energy consumption. This energy pattern will last for a long time. More oil and gas should be exploited. China has abundant hydropower resources, which should be exploited with priority. Nuclear power should be developed carefully. It is expected that nuclear power will not be developed widely in the twentieth century.

China's energy saving strategy should focus on industrial energy efficiency and should be based on generalized energy saving. Industrial energy efficiency has dual tasks. One is that energy consumption of industrial production should drop. The other is that the industrial sectors should produce energy saving products for other sectors, in order to reduce energy consumption. Therefore, industrial energy efficiency is the focus. Once industrial energy efficiency is achieved, energy saving across all of the national economy sectors will be boosted. Energy saving should also be based on generalized energy because generalized energy will cover every aspect. Generalized energy requires excellent direct energy saving as well as indirect energy saving. In addition, generalized energy requires technical energy saving as well as economic energy saving. During 1981–1985, indirect energy saving and economic energy saving played large roles in the whole economy, accounting for 60–70% the total amount of saved energy.

Energy strategy for the urban areas in China should include the active development of gas, heating, and electrification. In 1980, the power consumption per capita in Beijing was 964°, which is twice the national average (306°). By the year of 2000, electricity consumption per capita in Beijing will be over 2400°. In 1985, about 26.46 million people in 317 cities across China used gas. The users only account for 22.4% of the whole population. Only 27.42 million m^2 of buildings are covered by central heating. By the year 2000, the percentage of usage of gas, heating, and electricity in the urban areas will be greatly increased.

The energy strategy for the rural areas in China should be local development and utilization, and rural energy commercialization, developed through gradually changing the situation of relying on non-commercial energy. For a long time, agriculture was the only kind of economy in rural China. The energy supply in the rural areas mainly relies on non-commercial energy (e.g. wheat stalks as firewood). In recent years, rural industry and the tertiary sectors have developed quickly, in the rural areas. Accordingly, commercial energy consumption has increased substantially. With the increase in farmers' income, the energy for daily life in rural areas will be commercial energy. Therefore, commercialization of rural energy is a trend.

As for the measures for China's energy development strategy, the following are the two new approaches for energy development and energy saving.

1. **Increasing energy exploitation**

It is very important to know how to take the right approach for achieving the goal of energy development. During the next two decades, China's energy issues cannot completely rely on energy development. But still about half of its energy development will have to rely on energy development. In other words, at the end of the twentieth century, the production of primary energy should be doubled from over 600 million t in 1980 to 1.25–1.4 billion t, with an annual average growth rate of 3.7–4.2% and an absolute increase of 32.50–40.00 million t. Records show that from the first five-year plan to 1980, the average annual growth rate of China's primary energy was 9.6%, and that the absolute increase was 21 million t. In the 1970s, the average annual growth rate was 30.7% and the absolute increase was 40 million t. Therefore, in the next two decades, the average annual growth rate should be 3.7–4.2%. Although this rate is not set high, it is still hard to achieve. An annual yield of 30 million t of standard coal is equivalent to an annual increase of 42 million t of raw coal. This amount is equal to the yield of two Datong Mining Bureaus. In order to complete this difficult task, we believe that energy development in the future should take a new approach, with Chinese characteristic of finding more available energy. Methods that have proven to be successful in other countries should be learned, such as strengthening coal washing, improving the quality of commercial coal, and developing hydropower. The energy exploitation approach has ten aspects, as shown below.

(1) Develop different energy.

China has a vast territory with a variety of energy resources. Its coal reserve is the largest in the world. Its hydraulic resources rank first in the world. But these two types of resources have not been developed and utilized well, so far. The development and utilization level for coal and for hydraulic resource are only 10–20% and 4.8%, respectively. These two types of resources should be the focus of future development and should receive more investment. Right now, the usage of oil and gas is not high. Stable development and the recovery rate should be achieved by increasing reserve exploration and development, and particularly, by strengthening offshore oil exploration and exploitation. Bio-fuels, including straw and firewood, are the main sources of fuel in the rural areas in China. Bio-fuels should be cultivated, harvested, and utilized reasonably. Due to a lack of necessary conditions, nuclear power plants cannot be developed at this time. Later, nuclear power should be developed in a stable manner, based on the requirements of economic development. Wind power and solar energy should be developed and utilized according to local conditions. Other energy sources, such as oil shale, coal gangue, urban garbage, and organic waste should be developed and utilized rationally. In short, an integrated energy development system and a balanced and diversified energy production structure should be formed. The goal should be to develop and utilize each type of energy rationally. The mistakes of paying little attention to specific conditions in the development and utilization of energy should be avoided.

(2) Energy in respective regions should be developed rationally.

Energy resources and reserves vary in the regions across China, due to complex natural conditions. For example, more than 60% of coal resources are located in Shanxi and in Inner Mongolia. Few coal reserves are found in the East and Central South of China. About 69% of hydroelectric resources are located in the southwest. Few hydroelectric resources are available in north, northeast, and east China. Oil is mainly distributed across three regions: in the east and west of China and in the sea. Liaoning, Jilin, and Guangdong are rich in oil shale. Solar power is abundant in the west. The coastal areas have abundant wind and tidal energy. The rural areas are very rich in bio-fuel resources. In the past, the energy in the eastern coastal areas was well developed. Fewer efforts were spent on exploiting the coal, oil, and hydraulic resources in the west. In the future, the unique energy available in each region should be developed. Energy resources in each region should be developed rationally according to local conditions. With the energy development in the west, high energy-consuming industries will move westward. Mistakes of unstable development in energy should be avoided.

(3) All sizes of energy production should be developed reasonably.

As for existing energy production, there are few large scale energy enterprises. Instead, there are many small and medium-sized energy enterprises. In Shanxi Province, for example, in 1980, there were 2995 coal mines in total, among which 63 were large coal mines, accounting for 55.5% of the total coal production. There were 2900 small and medium-sized coal mines, accounting for 44.5% of the total coal production. Some people think that small and medium-sized coal mines are better than large ones. This is true for energy processing enterprises, such as coal washing plants, power plants, and oil refineries. But this is not correct for primary energy development companies, because the size of the development depends on the size of coal reserves. In view of the energy resources of all sizes in China, large energy processing enterprises are fit for large coal fields, oil fields, and rivers. Small and medium-sized enterprises are not good choices for large coal fields, oil fields, and rivers. Here are two reasons. The first one is that no energy can be used completely. The other is that economic effects are not good. For example, in Shanxi province, there are several shallow coal fields with the largest coal reserves. These coal fields are suitable for large coal mines with an annual production of four million t. Compared with the many medium coal mines with the same amount of annual production, the investment in large coal mines is 20% less for each ton of coal. Working sites required by large coal mines are 42% less. Similarly, some coal fields, oil fields, and rivers are suitable for small and medium sized enterprises; large enterprises are not good options for them. For instance, in Shanxi Province, there is a small amount of coal available close to large coal fields. It is called leftover coal, outcrop coal, or small coal resources at faults and mined areas. This coal is suitable for small and medium coal mines, because little investment and small costs are required. But it can generate profits quickly. In addition, small and medium coal mines can use coal that they have produced in their operation. At present, small and medium coal mines account for about 70% of the total coal mines in Shanxi province. Meanwhile, these small and medium energy enterprises must be developed rationally. Developing large, medium, and small energy enterprises simultaneously must follow objective laws and the process. A previously large energy enterprise might downsize to a medium one today. Many large energy enterprises have grown from small ones. The size of energy enterprises should be based on local energy sources and conditions.

(4) Energy development methods should be used rationally.

Energy development falls into three types: renovation, expansion, and new construction. At present, there are about 20,000 energy enterprises in China. Most of them are newly built. Some of them have undertaken renovation and expansion and they have grown as large-scale coal, oil, natural gas and, electricity production bases. In the future, all of these 20,000 enterprises should firstly undergo technological innovation, renovation, and expansion. If new enterprises are needed, they should be built at an original energy base. In this way, investment can be reduced and more profits and economic benefits will be generated. Practice has proven that renovation and expansion coal mines cost only one third or a half of the investment building new coal mines. However, due to the limited energy reserves in some energy bases, renovation, expansion, and new construction are not applicable. Therefore, it is necessary to build large energy bases in regions with rich resources. In the past, large coal mines do not produce coal during their construction. But now, with new development methods, they can produce coal during their construction. In short, each development method should be rationally utilized based on the actual condition.

(5) Energy technologies for development must be adopted reasonably.

People used to focus on only the most advanced development technologies. However, they neglected whether these advanced technologies were suitable for the actual conditions, and whether they could generate economic benefits while reduce economic losses. For example, integrated coal mining mechanization is a modern mining technology with high efficiency. It can save manpower and increase safety. But they have great limitations as well. They can only be used in large coal fields or in large mines. Not all coal fields or coal mines can afford their high investment and cost. In contrast, although common mechanization and semi-mechanized coal mining technologies are not very advanced, they can be used in many coal mines and generate economic benefits quickly. Thus, they are a good option for small and medium-sized coal mines, which do not have strong financial and technical resources. Wind power is another example. In foreign countries, the advanced technology of wind power has been adopted. In China, wind power is mainly used for drawing water. No advanced technology is needed. The last example is sewage gas, which is a technology for saving energy. It uses the urine of animals for generating energy. Although its use is not advanced, sewage gas is very applicable in rural areas in China. In short, regardless of the level of technology (advanced, intermediate, or backward), it should be suitable for the actual conditions in China. It must also generate economic benefits. All energy technologies must be adapted to local conditions.

(6) The supporting construction of energy development should be carried out rationally.

Energy development is not the ultimate goal. It must go through circulation and consumption, and then form an entire energy system. Therefore, for energy development, supporting construction of the internal and the external synchronization should also be performed. For example, oil field development must have supporting construction for reserve exploration and pipeline delivering. Hydropower development must have supporting construction for high voltage power transmission projects. Coal development must have supporting construction for mining and transportation engineering. In the past, because the internal supporting construction was neglected, the mining ratio and the production ratio were not balanced. Because the external supporting construction was neglected, coal could not be transported outward from the fields. Power plants were short of coal and railways did not have coal to transport. This should be changed. Future energy development and construction must consider the internal and external supporting construction.

(7) Enhance positive development of energy at all levels.

In the past, energy development has mainly depended upon national investment. In recent years, localities and towns have shown more enthusiasm regarding energy development. As a result, a joint venture of energy development appears. In Shanxi province, for example, during the sixth five-year plan period, the production of town-owned coal mines had an annual growth rate of 24.4%. In contrast, the annual growth rate of state-owned coal mines was only 4.83%. Therefore, investment in mining at all levels should be encouraged. This will lift the burden of state investment and will accelerate energy development. In the past, due to low coal prices and irrational economic policies, coal mining had little profit or no profit at all. No one wanted to invest in coal mining. Now, because of economic benefits, more locally-owned and town-owned coal mines appear. Therefore, it is necessary to encourage enthusiasm in energy development at all levels.

(8) Variety and quality of energy development.

For a long time, due to energy shortages, the demand for energy could not be met. Thus, little attention was paid to the type and the quality of energy. Take coal as an example. In the past, there was no screening, washing, or further processing for raw coal. Few types of coal were provided and their quality was poor. The incorrect type of coal and the wrong approaches affected the efficiency of the furnaces. As a result, production was affected. At the same time, the poor quality of the coal generated much waste rock in coal ash. This cost more in waste transportation. In order to improve the efficiency of energy use, coal types and their quality must be highlighted. The economic benefits of the energy production sector cannot be improved unless the energy quality is improved.

(9) Production, supply, and sales of energy should be reasonably improved.

In the past, little attention was paid to energy production, supply, and sales. This caused a negative impact on energy development itself. Coal in Shanxi was once backlogged. This caused huge losses. Power plants and boilers needed special oil but could only get crude oil. The oil industry could not process crude oil. In addition, the types and quality of energy changed frequently on the supply side. In order to develop and use different energies, the maximum economic benefits should be achieved for each kind of energy. The production, supply, and sales for each type of energy should be carried out rationally. The ultimate goals are to achieve a high quality of energy and economic benefits and to satisfy customers.

(10) The economic benefits of energy developments should be reasonably increased.

Energy development requires a lot of money. More capital is needed if the conditions for energy development are not good. Since the founding of the new China, national investment on energy development has reached 140 billion yuan. The conditions in the coal fields, oil fields, and hydraulic power in the eastern coastal regions have been greatly improved. Most of them have been well developed. Therefore, in the future, the focus should move to the west. Because the west is far away from the regions where energy is consumed, the investment and the cost per unit is higher. In this case, economic benefits should be emphasized. The goal is to develop and supply better energy with less cost.

Economic benefits are important for all of the nine aspects discussed above, such as the proportional relationship among energy sources, the proportional relationship among regional energy development, the proportional relationship among large, medium, and small energy enterprises, the proportional relationship among energy development approaches, the proportional relationship among energy development technologies, the proportional relationship among external supporting constructions, the proportional relationship among state-owned, locally-owned, and town-owned energy enterprises, and the proportional relationship between energy types and energy production, supply, and sales. All of these relationships must be based on economic benefits. In short, developing a type of energy must be reasonable. Improvement of the economic benefits might be unreasonable, because the adoption of a development scheme depends on many factors other than economic benefits. For example, the economic benefits for generating some energy are not high, but they can meet the needs of the society. It is not reasonable to focus on the economic benefits of one sector only and neglect the economic benefits of the whole country.

2. New approach to generalized energy

It is very important to create a new situation for energy saving in order to solve energy problems. We know that the solution for energy problems relies partly on energy saving. Energy saving has been adopted in China for several years, but the approaches have not been sufficient. When talking about energy saving, people naturally think of improving energy efficiency and fuel efficiency and saving coal and electricity. In fact, these approaches have been taken by industrialized countries. Energy saving falls into two types: one is narrow energy saving, and the other is generalized energy saving. Improving energy efficiency belongs to narrow energy saving, namely direct energy saving. Generalized energy saving means achieving a common goal in both energy development and energy consumption. It includes direct energy saving and indirect energy saving in manpower, material, financial, natural resources, and other resources achieved by improved economic efficiency. Generalized energy efficiency is a new approach for saving energy. It combines direct energy saving and indirect energy saving. It also combines energy efficiency and economic effects. The purpose of generalized energy saving is to achieve the maximum economic benefits with the minimum amount of energy.

The practice in recent years has proven that generalized energy saving is a new approach for energy consumption in China. It is able to create a new situation of energy saving in China. Generalized energy saving does not mean that it is not important to energy efficiency through direct energy-saving. On the contrary, direct energy saving is the base for indirect energy saving. It is an important part of generalized energy saving. Therefore, we should do everything to promote, to consolidate, and to develop direct energy-efficiency. At the same time, attention should be paid to indirect energy saving as well. As a new approach, generalized energy-saving includes the following ten aspects.

(1) Reasonably improve the efficiency of energy system.

Due to the poor efficiency of energy equipment, the unreasonable utilization of energy, and the low level of management, the efficiency of the energy system in China is very low. The author estimates that the efficiency of the energy system was about 32% in 1978 in China compared with 40–50% in developed countries. If the efficiency of the energy system grows 0.5% annually, 10 million t of standard coal will be saved each year.

(2) Reasonably save ordinary consumables.

About 60% of the energy was used for producing materials in China, whereas about 50% of energy was used for producing consumables. Because of old machinery and equipment and the low level of technical operations and management, the utilization rate of such consumables is only 20–60%. For example, the utilization rate of steel was 65.8% in 1978. If the utilization rate rises to 80%, 2.5 million t of steel would be saved, equivalent to saving 12.5 million t of energy. Here is another example. The utilization rate of chemical fertilizer was only about 30%. If the utilization rate rises to 60%, about 20 million t of fertilizer would be saved, equivalent to saving around 2000 t of energy. These two examples show that the potential of energy saving in steel and fertilizer only can be over 30 million t. The utilization rates of other materials are low, as well. For instance, utilization rates for irrigation water, timber, glass, and monocrystalline silicon are 50%, 35%, 60%, and 20%, respectively. Because of their low utilization rates, a huge amount of raw materials are wasted in China. Thus, the potential for energy saving in China is rather high.

(3) Reasonably reduce unnecessary transportation.

Transportation is a main service sector. It consumes about 7% of the total energy in the national economy. Due to irrational economic layout, unreasonable transportation scheduling, and a high material consumption rate, unnecessary transportation exists in China. In the future, the economic layout should be improved. In this way, unnecessary transportation can be reduced. As a result, energy will be saved as well. For example, lightweight materials such as aerated concrete and gypsum board, instead of heavy materials such as brick and concrete, are chosen for buildings, the amount of transport will drop 10%. Accordingly, 4 million t of energy will be saved.

(4) Rationally save manpower and reduce the population growth rate.

At present, China's civilian commercial energy consumption (for residential) is about 50 million t. The total energy consumption is 0.32 billion t, including non-commercial energy consumption. The average annual energy consumption is 0.3 t. Since the founding of the new China, the highest population growth rate was 2.9%. In recent years, the population growth rate has dropped to 1.4%, due to the one child policy. The drop in population is about 14 million. This change saves about 4 million t of energy. If the indirect energy consumption is considered, the total saving in energy can be more than 12 million t. Thus, reducing the population growth rate can save a lot of energy. Calculation shows that the one child policy will reduce the population by 0.167 billion. Assuming that energy consumption per capita in 2000 is 1.0 t, 167 million t of energy will be saved in one year. This is a very large potential for energy saving.

(5) Rationally save capital.

Enterprises consume energy and raw materials in their production. In addition, they need fixed assets and liquidity. Capital is material, in fact. When enterprises use more capital, they produce more products and they consume more energy. At present, 100 million in investments consumes 160,000 t of standard coal. The management level of enterprises has been low for a long time, due to the destruction of the Gang of Four. The construction cycle for infrastructure is long, as well. Some enterprises were not operated well, so their capital turnover is very slow. As a result, a lot of capital is occupied. The author estimates that state-owned industrial enterprises occupy more capital (140 billion yuan) than ever before in history. Accordingly, they consume 230 million t of extra energy. In order to save energy, we must take measures to accelerate the cash flow and to reduce the amount of capital occupied by enterprises.

(6) Reasonably save energy consumption for national defense and reduce land utilization

Saving in military expense and the drop of land utilization can save energy as well.

(7) Reasonably increase the yield and labor of enterprises (equipment)

We know that the energy consumption of products and labor will decrease with an increase in efficiency, such as the improvement of transportation. For example, Jiefang trucks can save 40% in fuel with full load compared with a half load. There are 1.5 million trucks in total in China. The actual load for trucks at the local transport sector was 66.7%, whereas it was only 40% for trucks in enterprises. It is estimated that the waste of gasoline is 1.2 million t every year. Now, the production of many plants has not reached its best level. A lot of energy is wasted. Therefore, the potential of energy saving in the business and equipment production is rather large.

(8) Reasonably improve the quality of products and services

Due to out of-dated equipment and technology and a low level of management, the quality of many products and services is very poor in China. The products and services in poor quality waste energy. For example, in large and medium glass factories, the rate of first class products is 73%, on average. This rate is lower than 90%, the best level in history. The rate of finished products for flat glass and steel is about 74%. The rate of finished products for cast iron is about 89%. The damage rates of flat glass and bagged cement in transit are 8–12% and 5–10%, respectively. Therefore, a lot of energy can be saved if the high quality product rate and finished product rate are higher and the rate of non-acceptable products and damage rate are lower.

(9) Reasonably reduce costs

The author estimates that, if the cost of national average production achieves the best level in history, energy consumption will drop 10%, and a rise of 24 billion yuan in net income will be achieved. Therefore, the potential in energy saved by cost reduction is great. Cost reduction should be paid more attention. We should not support those enterprises with a higher cost and less income.

(10) Change the economic structure, product direction, and service direction

Energy consumption in heavy industry is higher than that in light industry and agriculture. For generating the same amount of national income, the ratios of energy consumption in heavy industry, light industry, and agriculture are approximately 13:4:1. It is obvious that energy consumption in heavy industry is about triple of that in light industry, and 13 times that in agriculture. Therefore, it is very important to change this ratio. The author estimates that if the ratio is changed to the level in

1966, the first year of Cultural Revolution, 83 million t of energy will be saved in one year. Because the level of energy consumption in commercial, construction, and service industries is similar to the level in light industry, a lot of energy will be saved via developing the commerce, construction, and service industries. In other words, developing tertiary industry will save a great amount of energy. Therefore, we should establish a reasonable energy-saving economic structure.

It can be seen that the potential of generalized energy saving is large. The author estimates that generalized energy saving will save 60% of the energy consumption. Among the savings, direct energy-saving accounts for 1/3, and indirect energy saving accounts for 2/3. Therefore, generalized energy saving will reduce half of the energy consumption by the year of 2000. The generalized energy conservation means to gain extra energy from technology, management, development, and the reform of national economy.

Generalized energy saving should be one direction for technological renovation. Indirect energy saving includes improving raw materials and manpower, reducing costs, and reducing investment. Thus, technical renovation and generalized energy saving has the same goals. To achieve technical renovation, generalized energy saving must be fulfilled. Generalized energy saving should be always considered during technical renovation.

Adjustment of the national economy structure and reform of the economic management system will be helpful for realizing generalized energy saving. A lot of energy can be saved via adjusting the structure of the national economy. In recent years, energy saving mainly depended upon reasonable adjustment to the economic structure. Reasonable reform of the current economic management system will further promote generalized energy saving.

Generalized energy saving is a new method for socialist economic modernization in China. It should be combined with energy development to solve energy problems. Energy management should be strengthened, in order to achieve better energy development and better generalized energy saving. The government must perform systematic management on energy development, transportation, processing, transformation, storage, distribution, and utilization. The government must also manage energy policies, planning, research, prices, and foreign trade. At the same time, all enterprises must implement generalized energy saving. We firmly believe that under the guidance of the Party's correct guidelines, we can resolve the energy problems with energy development and generalized energy saving. The objectives of the socialist economic construction in China will be realized.

23.10 Energy Saving Problem Analysis and Corresponding Policy Proposals Post-evaluation of China's Generalized Energy Efficiency Strategy Project[19]

Research background, scientific significance of research and practical value.

The national economic and social development of China, the ninth five-year plan and vision goals outline for 2010 (the Outline) is a grand program, which provides the guideline and main tasks for the full realization of China's second strategic goal and the beginning of the third-step strategic goal. The Outline proposes China's economic development strategic objectives for the next 15 years. It requires the energy industry to meet the needs of the national economic growth, particularly, saving energy and developing energy simultaneously, as well as giving priority to saving energy. The year 1980 is the basic year for the three-step strategy of economic development. The strategic goal of quadrupling the economy by the year of 2000 in the first step was already achieved in 1995. This goal was achieved five years early, indicating that Chinese people have made remarkable achievements. During the past 15 years, the achievements in the economy were closely related to the achievements of energy development. During the next 15 years, the energy strategy should follow the policy of saving energy and developing energy simultaneously as well as giving priority to saving energy. To this end, it is necessary to review the past by summarizing the efforts made in energy saving during the past 15 years. Improvements can be made, based on the review. Guidelines can be developed for the future as well. These are the goals of this study. The research achievement [344, 346, 350, 352] focuses on China's energy development strategy, decision-making, and implementation of evaluation for the time period after the reform and the opening up. It is designed to summarize the experience in order to guide our practice in the future, to find problems, and to take countermeasures for improving economic development. In recent years, the State Planning Commission for major project feasibility studies has already begun this evaluation and has made progresses. The results of this study are actually post-evaluation of major research projects. Post-evaluation is still rare in domestic and overseas research. Therefore, this study has important scientific significance and practical value.

23.10.1 Review of Energy Saving in China

China's energy saving efforts have two stages. The first stage is the traditional energy-saving period. It occurred before the reform and the opening up. The second stage is the new energy-saving period. It occurred after the reform and the opening up.

[19] Xu [Xu97].

In the traditional energy-saving period, energy saving is narrow energy saving, or direct energy saving. The objects for the energy saving are coal, oil, natural gas, and electricity. The goal is to improve energy efficiency. According to the author's calculation in 1974, the national energy efficiency is 28% (see Table 23.12). About 72% of the energy was wasted in the format of heat. At that time, the energy efficiency of developed countries was 40–50%, which is 1.3–1.6 times the of energy efficiency of China.

Therefore, the State Planning Commission and Economic Commission determined to promote energy saving. The measures taken included (1) upgrading boilers, furnaces, and residential stoves to improve their thermal efficiency and (2) recycling waste heat to turn waste into treasure. Great achievements have been made after four or five years. In only Beijing, Tianjin, Shanghai, and Liaoning, the amount of energy saved by reusing waste heat is equal to 2.39 million t of standard coal per year. The author estimated that the national energy efficiency (coal) was approximately 31% in 1978 (see Table 23.12).

It should be noted that "energy efficiency", here, refers to narrow energy efficiency, namely the efficiency in the use of energy. The efficiency indicators have many defects, because they are not linked with economic development. In other words, the economy and energy are separated in these indicators.

Table 23.12 Energy efficiency in China (traditional energy saving period)

Items	Calculation in 1974 (coal and fuel oil)			Calculation in 1978 (coal)		
	Ratio (%)	Efficiency (%)	Efficient utilization(%)	Ratio (%)	Efficiency (%)	Efficient utilization (%)
Electricity	20.7	26.5	5.5	19.4	26 * 0.9	4.5
Iron and steel	11.6	80 * 0.3	2.8	13	80 * 0.3	3.1
Metallurgical power supply	7.0	25	1.8	3.2	35	1.12
Synthetic ammonia	2.3	100	2.3	5.0	100	5.0
Industrial furnaces	16	20	3.2	9.7	25	2.43
Industrial boilers	24	55 * 0.6	7.9	23.9	60 * 0.6	8.6
Locomotives	5.0	8.0	0.4	3.2	8.0	0.26
Civil boilers	2.4	40 * 0.8	0.8	6.9	40 * 0.8	2.2
Residential heating	3.4	60	2.0	3.4	60	2.04
Cooking	7.6	15	1.1	7.0	15	1.05
Others	\	\	\	3.2	25	0.8
Total			28			31

After the reform and the opening up in 1979, the author proposed a generalized energy-saving approach in the generalized energy-saving projects. This approach consisted of direct and indirect energy saving, technical energy saving, and economic energy saving. Other than energy, the targets of energy saving include those things that can be gained by consuming energy, such as raw materials, natural forces, transportation capability, and manpower. Since then, China's energy-saving has entered a new historical period. In the new period, energy saving becomes generalized energy saving. The targets of energy saving are not narrow energy efficiency, but the generalized energy efficiency, namely reducing the energy consumption per GDP. This efficiency indicator has strong features, because it links economic development and energy. According to the first measurements in 1982, China's generalized energy efficiency (the reciprocal of energy consumption of gross domestic product (GDP)) in 1978 was \$364/1 t of standard coal. This value is 6 times lower than Japan, 4.8 times lower than France, 3.9 times lower than Germany, 2 times lower than the UK, 1.4 times lower than the US, and 1.9 times lower India. This indicated that China's generalized energy efficiency was one of the lowest in the world. In other words, the energy consumption per GDP in China was one of the highest in the world. Thus, the gap between the generalized energy efficiency in China and foreign countries indicates a great potential for energy saving.

In 1984, the author firstly proposed a generalized energy efficiency strategy. Its core is generalized energy saving. He proposed that, by the year of 2000, energy consumption should be doubled and the economy should be quadrupled. In other words, generalized energy efficiency should be doubled and the energy consumption of gross domestic product (GDP) should reduce to half by the year of 2000.

In 1995, this strategic goal was achieved ahead of time. Compared with 1980, the energy consumption in 1994 grew 2.04 times, meaning that the goal of doubling energy consumption by the year 2000 was achieved six years in advance. By 1995, the GDP had increased 4.28 times compared with 1980, meaning that the goal of doubling the GDP by the year 2000 was achieved five years in advance. Generalized energy efficiency was 1476 yuan/one ton of standard coal in 1995, which is 0.97 times higher than that of 1980 (750 yuan/one ton of standard coal). It is estimated that the goal of doubling generalized energy efficiency could be achieved five years in advance (see Table 23.13).

Perhaps the results are hard to believe. First, the goals of GDP and energy consumption planned for the year 2000 were achieved five or six years in advance. Second, these two goals were achieved successively. The time interval was only one year. Third, the goal of doubling generalized energy efficiency and reducing the gross domestic product (GDP) energy consumption to half was achieved by 1995. The achievement of these three goals indicates the scientific, correct, and wise decision-making of the government, the effectiveness of the national macro-economic management, and people's efforts during the past 15 years. The achievement also indicates that the management of economic and energy development is much better than at any other time in history. Therefore, the experience of the success should be summarized, because it is valuable for China as well as for other developing countries.

Table 23.13 Efficiency of China's generalized energy (new energy saving period)

Year	GDP energy consumption (current price) (1 t of standard coal/10,000 yuan)	GDP Energy consumption (comparable price) (1 t of standard coal/10,000 yuan)	Generalized energy efficiency (current price) (1 t of standard coal/10,000 yuan)	Generalized energy efficiency (comparable price) (1 t of standard coal/10,000 yuan)
1978	15.77	14.67	634	682
1979	14.51	13.98	689	715
1980	13.34	13.34	750	750
1981	12.23	12.50	818	800
1982	11.72	11.97	853	835
1983	11.13	11.49	899	870
1984	9.89	10.71	1011	934
1985	8.55	10.21	1169	980
1986	7.92	9.89	1262	1012
1987	7.24	9.49	1381	1053
1988	6.23	9.16	1605	1092
1989	5.73	9.17	1744	1090
1990	5.32	9.00	1879	1112
1991	4.80	8.66	2083	1154
1992	4.10	7.98	2440	1254
1993	3.35	7.47	2986	1339
1994	2.62	7.01	3810	1426
1995	2.24	6.77	4464	1476

23.10.2 Evaluation of China's Generalized Energy Efficiency Strategic Project

1. **How was China's generalized energy efficiency project studied successfully?**

Evaluation of China's generalized energy efficiency strategic project.

The generalized energy efficiency strategic project, also known as energy economy efficiency strategic project, has the following phases: the prophase, the development phase, and the extended development phase. The success of the generalized energy efficiency strategic project depends on the five-year preparation before development, the five-year elaborate efforts for development, and the four-year expansion and deepening after development. It can be said that the development process of the generalized energy efficiency strategic project is the implementation process of the project.

(1) **From 1979 to 1984, the prophase.**

This period has the three main tasks.

First, in 1979, the experience of utilizing waste heat in the 1970s was summarized. Then, improvement of the narrow energy efficiency and generalized energy efficiency was proposed. The new theory of generalized energy-saving projects jumped out of the narrow circle of traditional energy-saving. According to this theory, energy saving not only means saving energy (direct energy saving), but also means saving all kinds of objects which contain energy (indirect energy saving). The focus is to save energy as well as to improve economic efficiency. The theory combines direct energy-saving and indirect energy-saving. It also combines saving energy and improving economic efficiency. The theory highlights ten advantages and ten measures. Here are the ten advantages.

(1) Energy saving is a kind of energy development requiring no extra energy;
(2) Energy saving does not require the construction of coal mines, oil fields, and power plants;
(3) Energy saving can obtain energy locally with no need of constructing energy transmission facilities;
(4) Energy saving is a kind of energy with quick profits;
(5) Energy saving can generate good economic benefits;
(6) Energy saving has no pollution and is good for environmental protection;
(7) Energy saving can promote technological progress;
(8) Energy saving can promote management;
(9) Energy saving can be applied easily. Energy saving can be achieved by saving manpower, material, capital, transportation capacity, natural forces, and time, and by improvement in economic benefits;
(10) Energy saving can motivate all industries, whereas energy development can only rely on energy production sectors.

The ten measures are:

(1) Reasonably improve the narrow energy efficiency;
(2) Reasonably save raw materials;
(3) Reasonably save transportation capacity;
(4) Reasonably save manpower and reduce population growth;
(5) Reasonably save capital;
(6) Reasonably save natural forces;
(7) Reasonably improve the production and service scale;
(8) Reasonably improve the product quality and service quality;
(9) Reasonably reduce costs;
(10) Reasonably change the economic structure.

Second, in September of 1982, the 12th CPC National Congress proposed the strategic goal of quadrupling the economy by the year 2000. The Economic Research Center of the State Council led the discussion of how to make enough energy supply to achieve the goal. The Research Center and people from State Planning Commission, the Ministry of Coal, the Ministry of Petroleum, the Ministry of Power, the Academy of Social Sciences, and other sectors discussed the resources, finance, transport, and environmental protection required for achieving the goal. They concluded that the energy production in the year of 2000 could reach 1.2 billion t of standard coal, twice as many as that in 1980. They then discussed whether the doubled energy production could ensure that economy would be quadrupled. This was a very difficult problem. Before the reform and opening up, energy development was moving ahead of economic development in China. The elasticity coefficient of energy consumption was 1.58, at that time. In contrast, after the reform and the opening up, the elasticity coefficient of energy consumption had to become 0.5 from 1980 to 2000 in order to achieve the economic goal. There was no domestic or overseas precedent. However, the comparison of energy consumption per unit GDP between China and other over 100 countries shows that the generalized energy efficiency in China was one of the lowest in the world, even 1.9 times lower than that in India. In the generalized energy saving projects, calculations indicated that there were 10 aspects of potential generalized energy-saving. Altogether, 1.4 billion t of standard coal would be saved. Therefore, they made the following final recommendation to the Central Committee: National generalized energy-saving projects can fulfill the potential of energy saving. Doubled energy production can ensure that economy would be quadrupled by the year 2000. The Central Committee adopted the recommendation. The approval can be found in an article named Strengthen Energy Development to Save Energy in *People's Daily* on January 21, 1983.

Third, in order to achieve the goal for this energy saving, the central government decided to build the Shanxi energy base. Under the leadership of the Technical and Economic Research Center of the former State Planning Commission and the State Council, thousands of experts, practitioners, and leaders worked on development planning for the Shanxi energy base from 1982 to 1983. During this prophase, the idea of the generalized energy efficiency strategic projects was formed in China.

(2) **From 1984 to 1989, development phase of China's energy development strategic project.**

This period focused on China's energy development strategy projects.

In order to achieve the economic development goal, a corresponding energy development strategy should be developed and should be in line with China's national conditions. Therefore, in 1983, the government issued a key research project called "China's energy development strategy", which was finally completed in 1989.

The Energy Development Strategy project is the core of the energy development project. "Energy development project" refers to all of the research work and planning work in the energy development strategy, energy development planning, the energy development plan, the energy development policy, and energy development principles. It is a major integrated energy project. It is related to the development of energy project construction, the economic and social development, the improvement of people's living quality, energy engineering and technology development, and environmental resources for sustainable development. The energy development project is a complex multi-energy structure of systematic engineering. Such a huge project needs substantial human and financial resources. It will last for a long time and it cannot be completed once and for all. This is because an energy development project requires billions of capital and millions of workers. The period will be 20 years from 1981. The energy development project will directly affect the energy development in the future. A good energy development project can produce good effects and can avoid losses for long time (ten years or several decades). Under the leadership of the State Planning Commission and the former State Council Energy Office, about 70 experts and practitioners spent five years (from 1984 to 1989) on developing the generalized energy efficiency strategic project. There were similar examples in other countries. For example, in the United States, the World Resources Institute in Washington organized scientists from many countries to work on the world's energy development strategy project for five years, beginning in 1983. The World Resources Institute first proposed an end-use energy strategy, which is very similar to generalized energy efficiency strategy, because both of them are based on energy saving and belong to the energy strategy of sustainable development.

The Energy Development Strategy project is a huge project. It is the first time that China has undertaken such a project. When the central government proposed China's economic development strategy, very little literature regarding China's energy development strategy could be found.

The development of the energy development strategic project should meet the requirements of the aims, focus, steps, and measures of the national economic development strategy. It should also be able to guide the development of specialized energy development strategy projects and regional energy development strategic projects. The development uses the following six methods.

(1) Summarize experience. In order to analyze the future prospects of energy development and explore the long-term issues of energy development in China, the development must be based on a profound understanding of the history and current status, energy production, energy storage, energy distribution, energy consumption, energy import and export, energy and environment, and energy transmission, as well as on their statuses and characteristics.
(2) Learn from abroad. The two oil crises in 1973 and 1979 ended the era of cheap oil. Developed countries suffered from losses in foreign exchange and serious economic recession. As a result, developed countries understood how important oil and reduced oil consumption are. They realized that it is necessary to strengthen the development of alternative oil energy, and coal and nuclear power, and to promote energy saving. In this way, a bad thing changed into a good thing. In contrast, China did not suffer the impact of world oil crises. On the contrary, China consumed a large quantity of oil and exported a large amount of oil for foreign exchange. However, due to the shortage of energy, including coal, oil, and the electricity supply, industrial production was affected in China. Power supply for residences could not be guaranteed. This was actually a chronic energy crisis for the economic development in China. Therefore,

those measures taken by developed countries to deal with oil crises are important for China to study.

(3) Identify the law. When reviewing the energy development in China and the approaches taken by foreign countries after energy crises, we should ask: can the old approach for energy development continue? The answer to this question depends on whether we can find laws that govern energy development and economic development. If there are laws, what are they? Domestic and foreign experts realize this issue, but they have not found the answer. The majority of domestic experts believe that energy growth is proportional to economic growth. They think that energy growth should come before energy development by setting the elasticity coefficient >1. They think that this is the case for developing countries. Some foreign experts do not agree with this opinion. They argue that, after the oil crisis, the economies in the US and the UK still grow, but their energy consumption drops. In other words, their elasticity coefficients of energy consumption are <1. Later, based on a large amount of domestic and overseas data, the author found three laws between energy development and economy development. First, the changes in the energy input coefficient (GDP per unit energy consumption) follow the pattern low $\rightarrow$ up $\rightarrow$ down $\rightarrow$ low. In contrast, the changes in generalized energy efficiency follow the pattern high $\rightarrow$ down $\rightarrow$ up $\rightarrow$ high. Second, the changes in the elasticity coefficient of energy follow the pattern 1 $\rightarrow$ >1 $\rightarrow$ <1 $\rightarrow$ close to 1. Third, energy development should come before economic development. These three laws can prove the old approaches and can foresee the new approaches for energy development. Research has proven this, after the energy crises in the developed countries are in the third period, and that after its reform and opening up, China is in the third period as well. In the third period, generalized energy efficiency increases, whereas the GDP per unit of energy consumption decreases. In other words, the elasticity coefficient of energy development is <1. China is in the early stage of this period, whereas developed countries are in the latter stage of this period.

(4) Conform to national conditions. China's energy development cannot take the old approach or the new approach that is applied in developed countries right now. The old approach leads to an inadequate energy supply, which will greatly restrict the growth of economy. The new approach applied in developed countries requires too much capital for environment protection. China cannot afford it right now. In addition, economic development will be very slow if the new approach is adopted. Therefore, we must find a new strategy that does not constrain rapid economic growth or damage environment, but that can ensure energy supply. These are the actual conditions in China. The new energy development strategy project must fit these conditions.

(5) Make a key breakthrough. The project involves all of the aspects of energy development strategy. It aims to resolve a lot of problems. In the design stage, some key problems must be solved. In this way, the strategic project will have a direction. Studies conducted by experts and practitioners from State Planning Commission, the coal industry, the oil industry, the electricity industry, and CASS concluded that the energy supply can reach no more than 1.2 billion t of

standard coal by the year 2000, a doubled production to that in 1980. But the Central Committee had set the national economic goal: to quadruple the GDP by 1980. Thus, there were three options. First, if the energy development strategy project only considered the actual conditions of energy production, the economic goal could not be achieved. Then the goal set by the Central Committee would have to be adjusted. Second, the energy development strategy project must ensure that energy production would be higher than 2 billion t of standard coal. In this way, the economy could be quadrupled. However, given the limited financial resources, transportation capacity, and environmental protection, this goal for the energy supply cannot be achieved by the year 2000. Therefore, these two options cannot guarantee the realization of the goal set by the Central Committee. These two options do not follow the policy that energy should come first, both domestically and overseas. They do not focus on the key factors: the energy consumption of per unit gross domestic product (GDP) and the generalized energy efficiency. After analyzing a large amount of domestic and overseas data, the author found that energy consumption per unit GDP in China is 1.4–6 times higher than that in developed countries and 1.9 times higher than that in India. China is one of the highest energy consumers per unit GDP of more than 100 countries around the world. Therefore, the potential of energy saving is high in China. The third option proposed that the energy consumption per unit GDP drop to half, compared with that of 1980, and that generalized energy efficiency be doubled. In this way, with a doubled energy supply, the economy can be quadrupled by the year 2000. Energy, the economy, and the environment are all developed. This is a new strategy, named the generalized energy efficiency strategy.

(6) Make a comprehensive arrangement. In order to fulfill the energy development strategy project, the large project can be broken down into three small projects. The first project is the overall strategy work, which is the most important work, and it can guide other projects. The second project includes a secondary energy production and development strategy, an energy consumption and development strategy, an energy import and export strategy, an energy transportation strategy, and an environmental strategy. These secondary strategies specialize in developing the strategic project, in detail. The third project is an energy development strategy projects for provinces, municipalities, and autonomous regions. It is also a national development strategy work, which consists of 44 special reports indicating comprehensive requirements.

China's energy development strategy can be completed with the above six methods. It has the following characteristics.

(1) Objectives, priorities and procedures of the generalized energy efficiency strategic project for the year 2000 are based on sufficient research. They have been achieved in advance.
(2) The generalized energy efficiency strategic project is in line with China's conditions, the requirements of energy development and environmental and

economic coordination, and the requirement of the world's sustainable development strategy. It is applicable in the past and also for a long time into the future.

(3) The three aspects of the generalized energy efficiency strategic project, such as energy development, generalized energy, and rational prices are clear targets. They should be implemented.
(4) The proposed generalized energy efficiency strategic project is the result of long-term investment and joint research. The practice has proven that the combination of central and local leaders and experts, the combination of theory and reality, and long-term investment are solid foundations for this project.

(3) **From 1989 to 1992, the extended development phase.**

In order to better implement the generalized energy efficiency strategy, it is necessary to extend the development. The development of the generalized energy efficiency strategic project took five years. It has been successfully developed and applied in practice. However, given the experience of domestic and international energy technology and economic development, it is necessary to track the energy development regularly so that the quality and the efficiency of the development project can be continuously improved. Therefore, in 1989, in order to implement the eighth five-year plan, the State Planning Commission issued the tasks for a comprehensive energy saving strategy, set up a lead group and eight research groups, organized the provincial and municipal government departments, and adopted social forces. Under the leadership of the State Planning Commission, more than 500 experts, engineers, and technicians from various disciplines worked together for four years. They successfully developed a strategy which was later adopted by the Central Government. In essence, the comprehensive energy saving strategy is similar to the generalized energy efficiency strategy, but as an extension of a huge project, it is more specific and practical.

1. **How could large energy saving achievements be made in the past 15 years?**

Evaluation of China's generalized energy efficiency strategic project

(1) **Leadership and decision making**

Since the sixth five-year plan, the central leadership has paid close attention to energy. Deng Xiaoping noted that, without energy, it is impossible to develop key projects. Meanwhile, in order to find the gap of the GDP between China and foreign countries, energy consumption should be compared with developed countries and with India. The 12th CPC National Congress highlighted energy as a strategic focus and proposed (1) to strengthen energy development and (2) to save energy. The central government first set the goal of quadrupling the GDP, and then proposed to double energy production for achieving this economic goal. In order to achieve these goals, the central government decided to construct the Shanxi energy base. During the

1980s, for the purposes of saving energy and protecting the environment, nations across the globe began to give priority to a sustainable development strategy. This means that the central government paid more attention to the generalized energy saving and to implementing a comprehensive energy saving strategy. Emphasis from the government and scientific decision-making became the key for achieving the generalized energy efficiency strategic project five years in advance.

(2) **Correct policy and consistency**

From the sixth five-year plan, the development of China's economy accelerated. But the development of energy could not catch up. Therefore, the central government proposed an energy development policy for the 1980s. This policy pointed out that energy development and energy saving are equally important, and that energy saving should have priority. The policy changed the traditional thinking of energy development held before the reform and the opening up. It clearly pointed out that energy could be gained from energy development and energy saving. Energy saving should not be neglected; it should be thought equally as important as energy development, in the future. The policy fit the situation in China and had clear targets. The practice of the sixth five year plan proved that the policy was correct. Therefore, it continued in the seventh five-year plan and the eighth five-year plan. Correct and consistent policy is the base for achieving the goal of China's generalized energy efficiency strategic project.

(3) **Strong measures and good implementation**

(1) Delegations sent to Japan, the United States, and Europe gained energy-saving experience. Western countries experienced energy crises in 1973 and in 1979, so they paid special attention to energy saving and have made a lot of achievement. Japan, for example, carried out activities, such as holding an energy-saving month, strengthening enterprise energy management, establishing the rational utilization of energy, and developing a sunlight plan and a moonlight plan.

(2) Consider the actual conditions and take a series of measures to strengthen energy saving. For example, the central government established an organization for leading the energy saving effort. The State Planning Commission and Economic (Trade) Commission established energy management agencies. Related ministries had special institutions for managing energy-saving. Major corporations had energy management personnel. Local energy saving technology service centers were opened across China. In addition, an energy-saving month and an energy-saving week were assigned. Movies and newspapers promoted generalized energy saving projects. Regulations for energy-saving were developed. Laws for energy saving were made. Provisions for generalized energy efficiency goals were made in the five-year plan. Energy assessment was added in the project feasibility studies. If the energy assessment was not passed, projects could not be implemented. Favorable loans were provided for investment in

energy and materials. These measures ensured the realization of great achievements in generalized energy saving.

(3) The sixth five-year plan paid special attention to generalized energy saving. In the sixth five-year plan, the average annual energy saving rate was 5.2%. In the seventh five-year plan, the average annual energy saving rate is 2.5%. For the eighth five-year plan, the average annual energy saving rate is expected to drop, because the central government proposed to implement a comprehensive saving strategy. The annual energy saving rate was set at 5.5% for the eighth five-year plan, the highest level in history. In this way, the energy development strategy goals for the year 2000 were achieved five years earlier.

(4) When implementing the generalized energy-saving projects, close attention was paid to the ten measures for energy development and the measures for rational prices. In this way, great results have been achieved. Energy prices have been adjusted. The adjustments in energy prices have greatly promoted energy production and energy saving.

In a word, effective measures and good implementation were the bases for achieving the generalized energy efficiency strategic goals for the year 2000 five years in advance.

3. **What are the results of the implementation of generalized energy saving objectives established 10 years ago?**

Evaluation of China's generalized energy efficiency strategic project goals

Generalized energy efficiency strategic goals were proposed during the discussion for the energy supply in the year 2000 after the 12th CPC National Congress set the economic goal in September 1982. The central government made a decision that the energy supply should be doubled, in order to ensure that the economic goal could be achieved. Later, this goal became the goal of the generalized energy efficiency strategic project. When this goal was proposed, it generated a lot of debate, both domestic and overseas. In 1984, the World Bank thought that if the economy were quadrupled by 2000, the energy consumption would not be 1.2 billion t but 1.43–1.90 billion t.[20] The State Planning Commission thought that the energy consumption should be 1.44–1.46 billion t.[21] The Nuclear Institute at Tsinghua University thought the energy consumption should be 1.37–1.56 billion t.[22] The China Energy Research Society thought the energy consumption would be 1.7 billion t.[23] All of these estimations were larger than 1.2 billion t. It appears that these estimations adopted traditional prediction methods using energy consumption indicators for industrial and agricultural output. We use the generalized energy saving analysis prediction,

[20]World Bank (1984). Outlook of Energy Supply and Demand.

[21]Energy research institute (1984). Prediction of Energy Demand in China in 2000.

[22]Nuclear research institute (1984). Prediction of Energy Demand in China in 2000, Energy in China in 2000.

[23]Energy research society (1984). Energy in China in 2000.

which adopts the energy consumption of the national income and gross domestic product (GDP) indicators. The comparison between the development objectives and the implementation results of the generalized energy efficiency strategy is listed in Table 23.14.

It should be noted that National Bureau of Statistics changed the GDP in 1980 from 419.3 billion yuan to 451.8 billion yuan (see the China Statistical Yearbook, 1996). Therefore, the three indicators from 1980, namely the generalized energy efficiency, the energy consumption of the GDP, and the GDP per capita, were adjusted accordingly. Due to the adjustment of the four basic indicators in 1980, the target figures for 2000 should be adjusted accordingly. In the comparison, the adjusted targets are compared with achieved targets. Table 23.65 shows that the set goals of the original development strategic project were 1392 yuan/one ton of standard coal and 7.2 t of standard coal/10,000 yuan. After the adjustment, they changed to 1500 yuan/t of standard coal and 6.67 t of standard coal/10,000 yuan. The set goals for generalized energy efficiency were doubled. Energy consumption per unit of GDP was reduced to half. The results in 1995 were 1476 yuan/1 t of standard coal and 6.77 t of standard coal/10,000 yuan. The generalized energy efficiency rose 0.97 times. The energy consumption of the GDP dropped 49%. The goals for the year 2000 were achieved five years earlier. In addition, theenergy consumption growth rate, GDP growth, and the average annual energy saving rate during 1981–1995 were higher than the set goals and the excess goals of 1981–2000.

4. **What are the effects of generalized energy saving in China in the past 15 years?**

Evaluation of generalized energy saving for China generalized energy efficiency strategy

Generalized energy efficiency in 1995 rose 0.97 times that of 1980, from 750 yuan/1 t of coal equivalent to 1476 yuan/1 t of standard coal. Energy consumption of the GDP reduced 49%, from 13.34 t of standard coal/10,000 yuan down to 6.77 t of standard coal/10,000 yuan. Therefore, compared with 1980, the generalized energy saving in 1995 was 1.27 trillion t of standard coal, equivalent to 97% of the energy consumption of the same year. This means that for the quadrupling of the economy, half relied on energy production, and the other half relied on generalized energy saving. This fully proved that the prediction that half of the economic development would depend on the production and the other half would depend on scientific and technological progress proposed by the central government in the early 1980s. Compared with 1980, the generalized energy savings in 1995 reached 1.27 trillion t of standard coal. The following are the reasons why the goals were able to be achieved.

(1) Improve efficiency of energy utilization for energy saving. Improvement of energy efficiency has two meanings. One is the efficiency of the energy systems. The other is the efficiency of the energy products. The efficiency of the energy system refers to the amount of energy generated by using one unit of energy. The efficiency of the energy products is the number of useful products produced by using one unit of energy. Table 23.15 shows the efficiency of the energy systems.

Table 23.14 Evaluation of China's energy development strategic goals for 2000

Index	Unit	Statistic in 1980	Set values of strategic goals		1980	Adjusted values of strategic goals		1995
			Set goal	Excessive goal	Adjusted static	Set goal	Excessive goal	Results
GDP	100 million yuan	4193	16,700	19,150–22,950	4518	18,072	20,634–24,729	19,337
GDP per capita	yuan/person	427	1392	1532–1840	460	1499	1650–1982	1596
Generalized energy coefficient	yuan/ton standard coal	696	1392	1418–1700	750	1500	1528–1832	1476
Energy consumption of GDP	ton standard coal/10,000 yuan	14.4	7.2	7.05–5.90	13.34	6.67	6.54–5.46	6.77
Energy production	10,000 t standard coal	63,735	125,000	140,000	63,735	125,000	140,000	129,034
Energy consumption	10,000 t standard coal	60,275	120,000	135,000	60,275	120,000	135,000	131,000
Energy consumption per capita	ton standard coal/person	0.613	1.00	1.08	0.613	1.00	1.08	1.08
Annual average increase of energy consumption	%		3.6	4.1		3.6	4.1	5.31
Annual average increase of GDP	%		7.2	7.9–8.9		7.2	7.9–8.9	10.18
Elasticity coefficient of energy consumption	%		0.50	0.46–0.52		0.50	0.46–0.52	0.52

(continued)

Table 23.14 (continued)

Index	Unit	Statistic in 1980	Set values of strategic goals		1980	Adjusted values of strategic goals		1995
			Set goal	Excessive goal	Adjusted static	Set goal	Excessive goal	Results
Growth rate of generalized energy efficiency	%		100	104–144		100	104–144	97
Decrease rate of GDP	%		50	51–59		50	51–59	49
Annual average energy saving	%		3.4	3.5–4.3		3.4	3.5-4.3	4.4

Table 23.15 Improvement of energy efficiency

Indicator	Unit	1980	1995	1981–1995 improvement rate
1. Energy saving by improved generating efficiency				
Generating efficiency	%	29.75	32.25	8.4
Power supply efficiency	%	27.42	29.75	8.5
Saving energy	10,000 t standard coal	Reference year	2872	
2. Energy saving by improved locomotive efficiency				
Comprehensive locomotive efficiency	%	9.3	19.3	108
Saving energy	10,000 t standard coal	Reference year	826	
3. Energy saving by improved cooking stoves efficiency in urban areas				
Comprehensive efficiency	%	21	43	105
Saving energy	10,000 t standard coal	Reference year	2775	
4. Energy saving by improved central heating efficiency				
Efficiency of heating boilers	%	40	60	50
Saving energy	10,000 t standard coal	Reference year	4585	
5. Energy saving by improved industrial boiler efficiency				
Efficiency of industrial boilers	%	55	65	18
Saving energy	10,000 t standard coal	Reference year	4764	
6. Energy saving by improved industrial furnaces efficiency				
Efficiency of industrial furnaces	%	20	23	15
Saving energy	10,000 t standard coal	Reference year	2751	
7. Energy saving by improved metallurgical furnaces efficiency				
Efficiency of metallurgical furnaces	%	24	27	13
Saving energy	10,000 t standard coal	Reference year	2181	
Total saved energy in 1995	10,000 t standard coal	Reference year	20,754	

(a) Improve the efficiency of power plants. The efficiency of the power plants was 29.75% in 1980. Due to large capacity, high parameters, and joint thermal units, the efficiency increased gradually. The efficiency of the power plants increased 8.4% and reached 32.3% in 1995. Due to the rise in efficiency, power plants saved about 29 million t of standard coal in 1995.

(b) Improve the efficiency of locomotives. In 1980, the overall efficiency of locomotives was about 9.3%. After steam locomotives were replaced by diesel engines and electric locomotives, the comprehensive efficiency of locomotives increased 107% and reached 19.3% in 1995. This is a great achievement. Compared with 1980, locomotives saved approximate 8.5 million t of standard coal in 1995.

(c) Improve the efficiency of cooking stoves in urban areas. In 1980, the average efficiency of cooking stoves in urban areas was about 20.9%. As gas became more common, coal stoves were gradually replaced by gas stoves and by electric stoves. In urban areas, the gasification rate rose from 16.8% in 1980 to 70% in 1995. The average efficiency of cooking stoves increased 107% and reached 43.2%. Compared with 1980, cooking stoves in urban areas saved approximately 28 million t of standard coal in 1995. Improve the efficiency of cooking stoves in urban areas. In 1980, the average efficiency of cooking stoves in urban areas was about 20.9%. As gas became more common, coal stoves were gradually replaced by gas stoves and by electric stoves. In urban areas, the gasification rate rose from 16.8% in 1980 to 70% in 1995. The average efficiency of cooking stoves increased 107% and reached 43.2%. Compared with 1980, cooking stoves in urban areas saved approximately 28 million t of standard coal in 1995.

(d) Improve the efficiency of heating boiler efficiency in urban areas. In 1980, the average efficiency of small civil heating boilers was about 40%. With the development of central heating in urban areas (see Table 23.16), the efficiency of heating boilers continues to increase. It is estimated that the average efficiency of heating boilers in urban areas will increase 50% and will reach 60%. Compared with 1980, heating boilers in urban areas saved approximately 46 million t of standard coal in 1995.

(e) Improve the efficiency of industrial boilers. The national average efficiency of industrial boilers was 55% in 1980. It rose 18% and reached 68% in 1995. Compared with 1980, industrial boilers saved about 47.5 million t of standard coal in 1995.

(f) Improve the efficiency of industrial furnaces. In 1980, the average efficiency of industrial furnaces was estimated to be 20%. It rose 15% and reached 23% in 1995. Compared with 1980, industrial furnace saved 27.5 million t of standard coal in 1995.

(g) Improve the efficiency of metallurgical furnaces. In 1980, the average efficiency of metallurgical furnaces was estimated to be 24%. It rose 13% and reached 37% in 1995. Compared with 1980, metallurgical furnaces saved 22 million t of standard coal in 1995.

Now we analyze the improvement in efficiency for energy products. The efficiency of energy products is more complex than that of energy systems. Other than the impact of the efficiency of energy systems, other factors affect the efficiency of energy products, including product process technology, production scale, quality, and resource conditions. Changes in the efficiency of energy products are shown in Tables 23.17 and 23.18. The table shows that the average annual increase in efficiency for energy products is about 1% in 15 years. Electrical consumption for some

Table 23.16 Development of central heating in urban areas in China

City	Steam (t/year)			Hot water (million kcal/year)		
	1985	1990	1995	1985	1990	1995
Beijing	5,491,000	5,386,196	1,990,764	1,740,000	3,718,924	19,502,743
Tianjin	84,742	2,340,786	23,665,243	3456	513,988	2,661,641
Shijiazhuang	2,546,988	1,820,000	438,100	17,280	83,980	77,810
Qinhuangdao			169,700			1,148,444
Taiyuan			3,106,645	150,125	286,920	3,676,593
Hohhot			17,000		541,006	1,189,658
Shenyang			825,067	344,688	380,520	1,317,883
Dalian		2,202,183	4,262,366		1,902,528	1,511,682
Changchun		1,450,611	2,703,600	150,268	747,794	3,600,104
Harbin		3,831,779	1,968,691		1,125,494	2,221,269
Lianyungang			357,300			36,436
Ningbo			2,758,673			
Hefei			135,000			22,738
Fuzhou						17,449
Jinan		309,600	13,625,630	22,440	46,080	3,032,370
Qingdao			509,197			4340
Yantai			1,291,376			113,761
Weihai			876,622			224,077
Zhengzhou			1,877,606			924,421
Guangzhou		290,297	930,451			
Xi'an		1,094,948	1,755,876			328,895
Lanzhou		4,846,000	4,846,000			1,767,955
Xining				20,736	32,260	91,907
Yinchuan						3,099,615
Urumchi			448,346		155,815	940,973
Total	8,122,730	23,572,400	68,559,253	2,448,993	9,535,309	47,512,763
Growth rate	1.00	2.90	8.44	1.00	3.89	19.40

energy products, such as coal and oil, increased. Overall, the efficiency of energy products was improved due to changes in resource conditions and improvements in mechanization.

Compared with 1980, the energy efficiency of steel rose by 1995 due to the increase in the efficiency of steel production equipment and the decrease in the energy consumption of steel. It is a great achievement that the steel industry saved 22 million t of standard coal in 1995. Because of the improved efficiency of fertilizer production equipment, the energy efficiency of fertilizer production increased. It is estimated that the fertilizer industry saved 43 million t of standard coal in 1995.

Table 23.17 Changes of efficiency for energy products in China (I)

Items	Unit	1980	1985	1990	1994	Annual average increase
I. Coal industry (Monopoly distribution coal mine)						
Raw coal	t/MW h	29	27	23	19	−3.15
II. Oil industry						
Crude oil	ton/ton standard coal		11.0	8.5		−5.06
III. Electricity industry						
Generating electricity	MW h/ton standard coal	2.42	2.51	2.55	2.62	0.58
Power supply	MW h/ton standard coal	2.23	2.32	2.34	2.42	0.57
IV. Iron and Steel industry						
Steel	ton/ton standard coal		0.57	0.62	0.66	1.55
V. Nonferrous Metallurgy						
Copper	ton/ton standard coal		0.16	0.19		3.20
Aluminum	ton/ton standard coal		0.091	0.087		−0.89
Lead	ton/ton standard coal		0.505	0.512		0.27
VI. Petrochemistry						
Ethylene	ton/ton standard coal			0.63		
VII. Chemical industry						
Synthetic ammonia (large)	ton/ton standard coal		0.73	0.74		0.37
Synthetic ammonia (medium)	ton/ton standard coal		0.45	0.46		0.55
Synthetic ammonia (small)	ton/ton standard coal		0.42	0.44		0.91
Sodium carbonate	ton/ton standard coal		1.53	1.61		1.07
Caustic soda	ton/ton standard coal		0.63	0.65		0.70
Calcium carbide	ton/ton standard coal		0.49	0.52		1.12

(continued)

Table 23.17 (continued)

Items	Unit	1980	1985	1990	1994	Annual average increase
Carbon black	ton/ton standard coal		0.30	0.29		−1.11
Yellow phosphorus	ton/ton standard coal		0.12	0.13		1.66
Tyre	ton/ton standard coal		0.34	0.35		0.61
VIII. construction material industry						
Cement	ton/ton standard coal		4.75		5.75	2.14
Plate glass	Weight case/ton standard coal		27.0	28.7		1.27
IX. Engineering industry						
Electric furnace steel	t/MW h		1.22	1.30		1.16

The improvement in the efficiency of cement production equipment reduced energy consumption. It is estimated that the cement industry saved 17 million t of standard coal in 1995. The increased efficiency reduced energy consumption in transportation. It is estimated that transportation saved 13.50 million t of standard coal in 1995. It should be noted that the improvement in the efficiency of energy products includes energy saved by the energy efficiency of the system. Therefore, it should not be included in the calculation.

Given incomplete data, only rough estimates were made. Based on the rough estimates, the national energy saving was about 303.5 million t of standard coal in 1995, accounting for 23.9% of all generalized energy savings.

(2) Improve the energy efficiency of raw materials

  (a) Energy saved by steel consumption. In 1980, steel consumption per 10,000 yuan of GDP was 0.63 t. It was 0.49 t in 1995. In other words, steel consumption per 10,000 yuan GDP dropped 0.14 t. This drop of steel consumption saved 26 million t in 1995, the equivalent of 37 million t of standard coal.
  (b) Energy saving by fertilizer consumption. In 1980, the input coefficient of fertilizer was 0.280 t/10,000 yuan. It dropped to 0.186 t/10,000 yuan in 1995. The drop in fertilizer consumption per 10,000 yuan GDP is 0.094 t. This drop saved 18.4 million t of fertilizer in 1995, the equivalent of 70 million t of standard coal.

The total energy saving was about 107 million t of standard coal, accounting for 8.2% of the total generalized energy savings. Due to incomplete statistics, the above estimates are low. The following are estimates completed with another method.

Table 23.18 Changes of efficiency for energy products in China (II)

Item	Unit	1980	1985	1990	1994	Annual average increase
X. Chemical fiber industry						
Rayon staple	ton/ton standard coal		0.31	0.32		0.35
Adhesive filament	ton/ton standard coal		0.076	0.073		−0.64
Polyester staple fiber	ton/ton standard coal		0.86	0.96		2.31
PFY	ton/ton standard coal		0.45	0.56		4.72
Nylon	ton/ton standard coal		0.24	0.33		7.25
Acrylic fibers	ton/ton standard coal		0.13	0.18		5.79
Vinylon	ton/ton standard coal		0.298	0.297		−0.05
XI. Fabric industry						
Cotton yarn	t/1000 kWh	0.55	0.50	0.47		−0.65
Cotton cloth	100 m/1000 kWh	49	43	40		−0.45
Dyeing cloth	100,000/ton standard coal		0.225	0.228		0.25
VII. Light industry						
Paper and paper mold	ton/ton standard coal			1.15		
Daily ceramics	ton/ton standard coal		0.83	0.76		−1.69
Daily glass	ton/ton standard coal		1.43	1.56		1.81
Beer	ton/ton standard coal		0.005	0.006		2.98
XIII. Transportation						
Steam locomotives	10,000 t km/ton standard coal	13.21	9.43	11.19	10.59	−0.67
Diesel locomotives	10,000 t km/ton standard coal		24.31	28.69	28.93	0.58
Electric locomotives	10,000 t km/ton standard coal		19.10	21.10	21.80	1.09

According to the national freight traffic statistics, the volume of transportation was 5.465 billion t in 1980 and 12.348 billion t in 1995, an increase of 126% and 6.883 billion t. During the same period, the GDP rose from 451.8 billion yuan to 1.9337 trillion yuan, an increase of 328% and 1.4819 trillion yuan. Thus, material of transportation per 10,000 yuan of GDP dropped from 120 t/10,000 yuan to 64 t/10,000 yuan, a decrease of 47%. The decrease in material transportation means a drop in produced materials. In this period, about 60% of the energy was saved for producing materials. Due to the reduction in the production of materials, the energy saving in 1995 was estimated to be 200 million t of standard coal, accounting for 15.7% of the total generalized energy savings.

(3) Energy saving by improvement in transportation efficiency

In the past 15 years, due to the increase in transportation efficiency, transportation input coefficient continues to drop. In 1980, the input coefficient was 26,600 t km/10,000 yuan. In 1995, the coefficient was 18,500 t km/10,000 yuan, a drop of 31%. Transportation saved 1.574 trillion km in 1995, equivalent to 39.2 million t of standard coal, and accounting for 3.1% of the total generalized energy savings.

(4) Energy saving by improvement in manpower efficiency and reduction of population

During the past 15 years, economic growth has been rapid. Meanwhile, due to the implementation of the one-child policy, the population growth rate has decreased year by year. As a result, the proportion of energy consumed for living is declining. In 1980, energy for living accounted for 15.9%, whereas in 1995 it dropped to 12.6%, a decrease of 20%. Energy consumption for living per 10,000 yuan GDP dropped from 2.12 t/10,000 yuan to 0.83 t/10,000 yuan, a decrease of 61%. Compared with 1980, the total energy saving in living in 1995 was 274.2 million t of standard coal, accounting for 21.6% of the total generalized energy savings.

(5) Energy saving by improvement in capital efficiency

During the past 15 years, capital investment coefficient decreased, to some extent, based on comparable prices. The efficiency of capital utilization increased, with an estimated average annual saving rate of 1%. Compared with 1980, the total energy saving in investment in 1995 was 121.2 million t of standard coal, accounting for 9.5% of the total generalized energy savings.

(6) Energy saving by improvement in natural force efficiency

During the past 15 years, the water shortage has become more and more serious. More attention has been paid to saving water. Continuous improvement in the efficiency of water usage, especially in industry and urban life, has made great achievements in saving water. The saving of water resources results in energy savings.

During the past 15 years, the utilization efficiency of land resources has increased greatly. While the amount of rural farmland continuously declines, food production maintains its growth. In cities, more land value has been realized. Therefore, even though no more energy is consumed, land generates more GDP. As a result, energy is saved.

(7) Energy saving by improvement in enterprise scale

During the past 15 years, the enterprise scale has become larger. Economic efficiency has increased, as well. The average scale of enterprises, including steel mills, power plants, automotive plants, oil refineries, petrochemical plants, color TV factories, and refrigerator plants, has increased greatly in 1995 compared with 1980. This change plays a role in energy saving.

(8) Energy saving by improvement in quality

There are two approaches to improving product quality. One relies on improvement in management and upgrades in technologies. As quality improves and more well-known brands appear, energy will be saved. The other relies on fake and shoddy products. Unqualified products are always available, and their number is large. Fake and inferior products seem to consume less energy than qualified products and seem to save energy. But in fact, they waste energy. Compared with 1980, the quality of products is increasing, and economic efficiency has increased accordingly during the past 15 years. Thus, energy consumption has dropped. This is the trend.

Due to lack of data, quantitative estimates cannot be made for the above three aspects of energy saving.

(9) Energy saving by decrease of material consumption

During the past 15 years, costs have increased because of the increase in wages, interest, and the depreciation rate. Many companies have lost money. It seems that they have not reduced costs by saving energy. In fact, "cost", here, means the cost for material consumption. It does not include wages, benefits, depreciation expenses, and loan interests, because they are part of the GDP. However, the proportion of the total output value of the annual material consumption released by the National Bureau of Statistics (but after 1993, this was not available) rose every year, from 42% in 1952 to 56% in 1978, and then from 56.8% in 1980 to 64.5% in 1992. These changes only show that the cost of material consumption increases each year, but no energy saving in material consumption can be seen. However, our research shows that this is only an appearance, because repeat calculations exist in the calculation of total social material consumption. Therefore, this appearance should be neglected.

Due to lack of real statistics on national material consumption, energy-saving estimates in this respect can be difficult. However, it is certain that the cost of material consumption, excluding rising price factors and repeated calculation factors, should decrease annually. From energy saving achieved by the saving of energy consumption, raw material consumption, capacity consumption, consumption of natural resources, as well as transportation in the whole society, the annual material consumption cost should decrease. The relationship among material consumption and other consumptions should be positive. It is estimated that national material consumption declines more than 1% annually. Compared with 1980, national material consumption dropped 20% in 1995, equivalent to saving about 400 million t of standard coal. This saving accounts for 31.5% of the total generalized energy savings.

(10) Energy saving by adjusting the economic structure

The proportion between the first, the second, and the third industries in China was 30.1: 48.5: 21.4% in 1980. The ratio changed to 20.5:48.8:30.7% in 1995. During the past 15 years, the proportion of the first industry dropped 9.6%. The proportion of the secondary industry rose 0.3%. The proportion of the tertiary industry rose 9.3%. The energy consumption of added value for the first industry is the lowest. It is higher for the tertiary industry and highest for secondary industry. Therefore, saving energy by adjusting the economic structure will be negative if the proportion of the first industry decreases while the proportions of the second and the third industries rise. In other words, the increase in energy consumption is an inevitable trend. It is estimated that the energy consumption in 1995 will rise to 239.3 million t of standard coal due to economic structural changes. It should be noted that this estimation is based on the changes of the structural proportion in the first, second, and third industries. The structural changes between the first, second, and third industries exist anywhere. In addition, the internal structure of the three industries, the product structure, the ownership structure, the technological structure, the energy equipment structure, the foreign trade structure, and the capital structure each have certain impacts as well. Some impacts are positive and some are negative. For example, in 1995, the amount of imported fertilizers was nearly 20 million t, saving about 10 million t of standard coal. The amount of foreign investment was $48.1 billion, saving about 96.2 million t of standard coal. These two saved about 106.2 million t of standard coal. The calculation shows that the structural energy saving is negative 133.10 million t of standard coal. However, the positive effect is far greater than the negative effect, in general. Therefore, we cannot think that the economic structural changes of the past 15 years were not good for energy saving. In fact, the energy saving discussed above includes the impact of the economic structural changes. Compared with 1980, the economic structure in 1995 was better for energy saving. If the economic structure remained unchanged, the goals of doubling energy production and quadrupling GDP would not have been achieved. Due to the lack of data about the changes in the economic structure, it is hard to calculate the exact amount of energy saved by changes in the economic structure.

Therefore, we estimate the energy saved by reduced costs and adjusted economic structures together. It is estimated that, compared with 1980, the energy saved by reduced material consumption and adjusted economic structures in 1995 was about 266.9 million t of standard coal, accounting for 21% of the total generalized energy savings.

The generalized energy saved by the above ten aspects is 12.7 billion t of standard coal in total.

Table 23.19 lists the analysis of generalized energy saving in 1995 in China. The

Table 23.19 Analysis of China's generalized energy saving (1981–1995)

Items of generalized energy saving	Energy saving (10,000 t of standard coal)	Percent (%)	Remarks
1. Energy saving by improved energy efficiency	30,350	23.9	
2. Energy saving by improved efficiency of raw materials	20,000	15.7	
3. Energy saving by improved transportation efficiency	3920	3.1	
4. Energy saving by improved human efficiency	27,420	21.6	
5. Energy saving by improved capital efficiency	12,120	9.5	
6. Energy saving by improved natural force efficiency	6500	5.1	Due to lack of data, rough estimates cannot be distinguished
7. Energy saving by improved scale			
8. Energy saving by improved quality			
9. Energy saving by reduced material consumption costs	26,690	21.0	
10. Energy saving by adjustment in economic structure			
Total	127,000	100	

table shows that direct energy accounts for more than 1/5. In other words, the energy saved by improvement in energy utilization accounts for 23.9%. Indirect energy saving accounts for about 4/5. Among this, the energy saved by improvements in material utilization accounts for 15.7%. Energy saved by improvement in transportation accounts for 3.1%. Energy saved by improvement in manpower utilization and decrease in population growth accounts for 21.6%. Energy saved by improvement in capital utilization accounts for 9.5%. Energy saved by reducing material consumption and adjustment in the economic structure accounts for 21%. Energy saved by improvements in natural resource utilization, increasing scale, and improving quality accounts for about 5.1%. Thus, direct energy-saving and indirect energy-saving are both important.

On the other hand, we analyze the generalized energy saving of 1.27 billion t of standard coal in 1995. The energy consumption of the added value of the first industry dropped from 2.55 t standard coal/10,000 yuan to 1.37 t standard coal/10,000 yuan, a decrease of 46%. This drop saved 46.72 million t of standard coal. The energy consumption of the added value of the second and the third industries dropped from 19.15 t standard coal/10,000 yuan to 10.09 t standard coal/10,000 yuan, a decrease of 47%. This drop saved 854.90 million t of standard coal. Particularly, the energy consumption in the third industry dropped from 15.34 t standard coal 10,000 yuan to 5.12 t standard coal/10,000 yuan, a decrease of 67%. This drop saved 607.69 million t of standard coal. Therefore, the energy consumption of all three industries dropped, due to the energy saving of the added value. Altogether, 1.5093 billion t of standard coal was saved. After the energy saved by economic structural adjustment (which is 239.3 million t of standard coal) is deducted, the actual energy saving is 1.27 billion t of standard coal. Thus, the effects of energy-saving on the above ten items are reflected in the decline of energy consumption of added values in the first, the second, and the third industries. The analysis shows that the secondary industry made the largest contribution to the generalized energy efficiency, accounting for 66.5%. The tertiary industry made the second largest contribution to the generalized energy saving, accounting for 26.1%. The first industry made the least contribution to the generalized energy-saving, accounting for 7.4%. The secondary industry and the tertiary industries are the key contributors to energy saving.

Based on data from the Beijing Yanhua generalized energy-saving pilot project, we conducted a detailed analysis of generalized energy. From 1979 to 1988, generalized energy saving efficiency increased 72%. The elasticity coefficient of the energy consumption is 0.15. About 3.23 million t of standard coal were saved in 1988. Table 23.20 lists the items of energy saving in detail. Direct energy saving, namely energy saving by improved narrow energy efficiency, accounts for about 1/5. Indirect energy saving, namely the energy saved by reducing capital, accounts for about 2/5. Among this, 1/5 is by reduced costs and 1/5 is by reducing raw materials.

23.10.3 Comparison of New and Old Energy Development Strategic Projects in China

Before the reform and the opening up, China had not developed any energy development strategy projects. Therefore, the old energy development strategy, namely energy development, was used in China. Before the energy crisis in 1973, many countries also implemented energy development strategies. At that time, the oil supply was sufficient and the price of oil was cheap. Accordingly, developed countries could import much oil and could consume oil at will. This strategy led to energy starvation. In China, energy waste became more and more serious. Serious problems appeared, such as environmental pollution, energy transportation, damage to forests, overmining of oil resources, and too much investment in energy. The direct result of

Table 23.20 Analysis of Beijing Yanhua generalized energy saving project (1979–1988)

Items of generalized energy saving	Energy saving (10,000 t of standard coal)	Percent (%)	Reasons
1. Energy saving by improved energy efficiency	40	12.4	Efficiency of energy system increases from 54.32 to 66.18%
2. Energy saving by improved efficiency of raw materials	78.7	24.3	Consumption of raw materials, such as ethylene, polypropylene, and BR drops. Energy consumption of raw materials drops
3. Energy saving by improved transportation efficiency	−0.4	−0.1	Raw oil source changes a little, and transportation distance increased
4. Energy saving by improved human efficiency	5.28	1.6	Less manpower, and energy consumption of life decreased
5. Energy saving by improved capital efficiency	140.5	43.5	Less capital, energy consumption of capital decreased
6. Energy saving by improved natural force efficiency	4.7	1.5	Consumption of water is less, and ton hydropower decreased
7. Energy saving by improved scale	25.2	7.8	Production scale increases
8. Energy saving by improved quality	0.18	0.06	Improvement of quality, but good quality does not lead to high price. therefore energy saving is not obvious
9. Energy saving by reduced material consumption costs	80.9	25.0	Costs of products, such as propylene, decreased
10. Energy saving by adjustment in economic structure	−51.7	−16.0	Proportion of propylene production increased
Total	323	100	

this strategy is the rise of the GDP and low generalized energy efficiency. Table 23.21 shows that the energy consumption per unit of GDP during the first five-year plan period increased 5.1% annually. In the second five-year plan, energy consumption per unit of GDP increased 14.9% annually. Later, the annual growth rate of energy consumption per unit of GDP in the fourth five-year plan and the fifth five-year plan periods were 0.8% and 3.5%, respectively. Generalized energy efficiency decreased from 1635 yuan/t of standard coal in 1952 to 682 yuan/t of standard coal in 1978,

Table 23.21 Analysis of energy saving in China (1953–1978 Period of China's old energy development strategy)

Year and time	Energy consumption (10,000 standard coal)	GDP (100 million yuan)	GDP Energy consumption (ton standard coal/10,000 yuan)	Efficiency of generalized energy yuan/ton standard coal	Growth rate of energy consumption (%)	Growth rate of GDP (%)	Elasticity coefficient of energy consumption	Energy saving rate (%)	Energy growth rate (%)	Energy saving 10,000 t of standard coal	Comparable prices of energy growth (100 million yuan)
1952	4905	802	6.12	1635	–	22.3	–	–	–	Reference year	Reference year
1953	5411	914	5.92	1689	10.3	14.0	0.7	3.2	3.3	179	29
1954	6234	967	6.45	1551	15.2	5.8	2.6	−8.9	−8.2	−320	−52
1955	6968	1029	6.77	1477	11.8	6.4	1.8	−5.0	−4.8	−675	−110
1956	8800	1173	7.50	1333	26.3	14.0	1.9	−10.8	−9.7	−1626	−266
1957	9644	1227	7.86	1272	9.6	4.6	2.1	−4.8	−4.6	−2140	−350
1958	17,599	1497	11.76	851	82.5	22.0	3.7	−49.6	−33.1	−8443	−1381
1959	23,926	1620	14.77	677	36.0	8.2	4.4	−25.6	−20.4	−14,018	−2292
1960	30,188	1596	18.91	529	26.2	−1.5	-17.7	−28.1	−21.9	−20,427	−3340
1961	20,390	1123	18.16	551	−32.5	−29.6	1.1	4.0	4.2	−13,522	−2211
1962	16,540	1049	15.77	634	−18.9	−6.6	2.9	13.2	15.2	−10,124	−1655
1963	15,567	1162	13.40	746	−5.9	10.8	−0.5	15.0	17.7	−8460	−1383
1964	16,637	1354	12.29	814	6.9	16.5	0.4	8.3	9.0	−8356	−1366
1965	18,901	1584	11.93	838	13.6	17.0	0.8	2.9	3.0	−9213	−1506
1966	20,269	1853	10.94	914	7.2	17.0	0.4	8.3	9.1	−8936	−1461
1967	18,328	1719	10.66	938	−9.6	−7.2	1.3	2.5	2.6	−7815	−1278

(continued)

Table 23.21 (continued)

Year and time	Energy consumption (10,000 standard coal)	GDP (100 million yuan)	GDP Energy consumption (ton standard coal/10,000 yuan)	Efficiency of generalized energy yuan/ton standard coal	Growth rate of energy consumption (%)	Growth rate of GDP (%)	Elasticity coefficient of energy consumption	Energy saving rate (%)	Energy growth rate (%)	Energy saving 10,000 t of standard coal	Comparable prices of energy growth (100 million yuan)
1968	18,405	1607	11.45	873	0.4	−6.5	−0.1	−7.4	−6.9	−8577	−1402
1969	22,730	1918	11.85	844	23.5	19.4	1.2	−3.5	−3.4	−11,000	−1799
1970	29,291	2364	12.39	807	28.9	23.3	1.2	−4.6	−4.4	−14,833	−2425
1971	34,496	2592	13.31	751	17.8	9.6	1.8	−7.4	−6.9	−18,643	−3048
1972	37,273	2603	14.32	698	8.1	0.4	19.0	−7.6	−7.1	−21,353	−3491
1973	39,109	2820	13.87	721	4.9	8.3	0.6	3.1	3.3	−21,862	−3575
1974	40,144	2851	14.08	710	2.6	1.1	2.4	−1.5	−1.5	−22,707	−3713
1975	45,425	3088	14.71	680	13.2	8.3	1.6	−4.5	−4.3	−26,539	−4339
1976	47,831	3004	15.92	628	5.3	−2.7	−1.9	−8.2	−7.6	−29,459	−4817
1977	52,354	3238	16.17	618	9.5	7.8	1.2	−1.5	−1.5	−32,551	−5322
1978	57,144	3895	14.67	682	9.1	11.7	0.8	9.3	10.2	−33,322	−5448
First five-year plan period (1953–1957)					14.5	8.9	1.63	−5.1	−4.9	−4581	−749

(continued)

Table 23.21 (continued)

Year and time	Energy consumption (10,000 standard coal)	GDP (100 million yuan)	GDP Energy consumption (ton standard coal/10,000 yuan)	Efficiency of generalized energy yuan/ton standard coal	Growth rate of energy consumption (%)	Growth rate of GDP (%)	Elasticity coefficient of energy consumption	Energy saving rate (%)	Energy growth rate (%)	Energy saving 10,000 t of standard coal	Comparable prices of energy growth (100 million yuan)
Second five-year plan period (1958–1962)					11.4	−3.1	>>1	−14.9	−13.0	−66,535	−10,879
Economic adjustment period (1963–1965)					4.5	14.7	0.31	8.9	9.7	−26,030	−4256
Third five-year plan period (1966–1970)					9.2	8.3	1.10	−0.8	−0.8	−51,160	−8365
Fourth five-year plan period (1971–1975)					9.2	5.5	1.67	−3.5	−3.4	−111,105	−18,166
1953–1978					9.9	6.3	1.58	−3.4	−3.3	−354,742	−58,003

Note GDP in the table is calculated based on comparable prices of 1980

with an average annual decline rate of 3.3%. During the traditional energy strategy period, China wasted 35.5 million t of standard coal in total. The loss in the GDP was 5.85 trillion yuan (price in 1980). The environment was seriously polluted.

After the reform and the opening up, the central government began to implement the new energy development strategy, namely the generalized energy efficiency strategic project. Guided by Deng Xiaoping's socialist construction theory, the new strategic project was completed. Table 23.22 shows that during the sixth five-year plan period, the average annual energy consumption per unit of GDP and carbon dioxide emission decreased 5.2%. During the seventh five-year plan period, the average annual energy consumption per unit of GDP and carbon dioxide emission decreased 2.5%. During the eighth five-year plan period, the average annual energy consumption per unit of GDP and carbon dioxide emission decreased 5.8%. Generalized energy efficiency increased from 682 yuan in 1978/t of standard coal to 1476 yuan/t of standard coal in 1995, with an average increase rate of 4.7%. From 1981 to 1995, the cumulative energy saving was 7.18 billion t of standard coal. The saved energy created an extra 5.4 trillion yuan of GDP.

Practice has proven that the two strategies generated different results. Table 23.21 lists the energy saving conditions in China before the reform and opening up. Table 23.22 lists the energy saving conditions in China after the reform and the opening up. Compared with the old strategy, the new strategy has the following six features. It is: 1. Good for energy saving; 2. Good for saving resources; 3. Good for environment protection; 4. Good for rapid economic development; 5. Good for improving people's living standards and living quality; 6. Good for energy, resources, environmental, economic, and demographic co-ordination, and sustainable development. Therefore, we recommend that the Central Government continue implementing the new energy development strategy, namely the generalized energy efficiency strategy. This is a huge project that will benefit future generations. Without the support of the central government, it will not be completed.

23.10.4 Development Outlook and Problems for China's Generalized Energy Efficiency Strategic Project

The generalized energy efficiency strategy was implemented at the beginning of the reform and opening up. During the past 10 years, the domestic and international environments have changed. The changes have affected the implementation of the new strategy. The above analysis shows that, regardless of changes in domestic factors or international environments in the past, at present, or in the future, the impacts from them are good for implementation of the new strategy. The 14th CPC National Congress proposed the goal of establishing a socialist market economic system. This goal requires continuous adjustment and liberalization of energy prices, enhancing the enthusiasm of the energy producers, and forcing enterprises (especially high energy consumers) to save energy and to gain benefits from energy saving. The

Table 23.22 Analysis of energy saving in China (1979–1995 period of China's new energy development strategy)

Year and time	Energy consumption quantity (10,000 t standard coal)	GDP in current price (yuan)	GDP in comparable price (100 million yuan)	GDP energy consumption in current price (ton standard coal/10,000 yuan)	GDP energy consumption in comparable price (ton standard coal/10,000 yuan)	Generalized efficiency in current price (yuan/ton standard coal)	Generalized efficiency in comparable price (yuan/ton standard coal)	Energy consumption growth rate (%)	GDP growth rate (%)	Elasticity coefficient of energy consumption	Energy saving rate (%)	Efficiency growth rate (%)	Energy saving (10,000 t standard coal)	Efficiency increase in comparable price (100 million yuan)
1978	57,144	3624	3895	15.77	14.67	634	682	9.15	11.70	0.78	9.3	10.2	–	–
1979	58,588	4038	4191	14.51	13.98	689	715	2.53	7.60	0.33	4.7	4.9	–	–
1980	60,275	4518	4518	13.34	13.34	750	750	2.88	7.81	0.37	4.6	4.8	Basic year	Basic year
1981	59,447	4862	4755	12.23	12.50	818	800	-1.37	5.26	-0.26	6.3	6.7	3998	300
1982	62,067	5295	5184	11.72	11.97	853	835	4.41	9.01	0.49	4.2	4.4	7093	532
1983	66,040	5935	5749	11.13	11.49	899	870	6.40	10.89	0.59	4.1	4.2	10,655	799
1984	70,904	7171	6621	9.89	10.71	1011	934	7.37	15.18	0.49	6.8	7.3	17,430	1306
1985	76,682	8964	7513	8.55	10.21	1169	980	8.15	13.47	0.60	4.7	4.9	23,551	1765
1986	80,850	10,202	8179	7.92	9.89	1262	1012	5.44	8.86	0.61	3.2	3.3	28,269	2119
1987	86,632	11,963	9125	7.24	9.49	1381	1053	7.15	11.57	0.62	4.0	4.1	35,113	2632
1988	92,997	14,928	10,153	6.23	9.16	1605	1092	7.35	11.27	0.65	3.5	3.7	42,466	3183
1989	96,934	16,909	10,566	5.73	9.17	1744	1090	4.23	4.07	1.04	−0.2	−0.2	44,037	3301
1990	98,703	18,548	10,971	5.32	9.00	1879	1112	1.82	3.83	0.48	1.9	2.0	47,672	3573
1991	103,783	21,618	11,980	4.80	8.66	2083	1154	5.15	9.19	0.56	3.7	3.8	56,050	4201
1992	109,170	26,638	13,686	4.10	7.98	2440	1254	5.19	14.24	0.36	7.9	8.6	73,422	5503
1993	115,993	34,634	15,532	3.35	7.47	2986	1339	6.25	13.49	0.46	6.4	6.8	91,228	6838

(continued)

Table 23.22 (continued)

Year and time	Energy consumption quantity (10,000 t standard coal)	GDP in current price (yuan)	GDP in comparable price (100 million yuan)	GDP energy consumption in current price (ton standard coal/10,000 yuan)	GDP energy consumption in comparable price (ton standard coal/10,000 yuan)	Generalized efficiency in current price (yuan/ton standard coal)	Generalized efficiency in comparable price (yuan/ton standard coal)	Energy consumption growth rate (%)	GDP growth rate (%)	Elasticity coefficient of energy consumption	Energy saving rate (%)	Efficiency growth rate (%)	Energy saving (10,000 t standard coal)	Efficiency increase in comparable price (100 million yuan)
1994	122,737	46,759	17,499	2.62	7.01	3810	1426	5.81	12.66	0.46	6.1	6.5	110,725	8299
1995	131,000	58,478	19,337	2.24	6.77	4464	1476	6.73	10.51	0.64	3.4	3.5	126,987	9518
Fifth five-year plan period (1976–1980)								5.82	7.91	0.74	1.9	2.0		
Sixth five-year plan period (1981–1985)								4.93	10.71	0.46	5.2	5.5	62,727	4702
Seventh five-year plan period (1986–1990)								5.18	7.87	0.66	2.5	2.6	197,556	14,807
Eighth five-year plan period (1991–1995)								5.82	12.00	0.49	5.5	5.8	458,412	34,359
1979–1995								5.00	9.88	0.51	4.4	4.7		
1981–1995								5.31	10.18	0.52	4.4	4.6	718,695	53,868

Note GDP in the table is calculated based on comparable price of 1980

fifth Plenary Session of the 14th CPC National Congress proposed two basic shifts for the next 15 years. Specifically, economic growth should be shifted from the extensive mode to the intensive mode. The goal of this shift is to achieve better direct and indirect energy saving effects, as well as higher generalized energy efficiency. Promoted by the international environment protection and sustainable development strategy, China must save energy, reduce carbon dioxide emissions, and protect the environment.

Guided by the ninth five-year plan and the 2010 vision goals for national economic and social development, the Chinese economy will continue to grow rapidly in the future. The average annual economic growth rate is estimated to be 8% (actually closer to 10%). To achieve the economic goal, the energy supply should grow accordingly. But oil production grows slowly. The situation of energy production and supply are more serious than before. Table 23.23 lists the generalized energy efficiency strategic goals for 2000, 2005, 2010, and 2015. Here are some notes.

(1) Technical solutions 1, 2, and 3 in the table adopt the appropriate speed of economic growth. Technical solutions 4, 5, and 6 adopt a higher economic growth rate;
(2) Technical solutions 1 and 4 in the table use synchronous strategies. The elasticity coefficient of energy consumption for them is 1. Technical solutions 2 and 5 use generalized energy efficiency strategies. The elasticity coefficient of the energy consumption for them is 0.45. Technical solutions 3 and 6 use generalized energy efficiency strategies. The elasticity coefficient of energy consumption for them is 0.30.
(3) The GDP in the table is calculated based on the comparable prices of 1980. Studies suggest that, in the next 15 years, the Chinese economy will continue to develop rapidly. If technical solutions 1 and 4 are adopted, energy consumption in the year 2000 will be 2 billion t of standard coal. Energy consumption in the year 2010 will be 4–5 billion t of standard coal. Such a huge amount of energy consumption is impossible. Therefore, we must adopt the generalized energy efficiency strategy. The goals in technical solutions 2 and 5 are what we should achieve. The goals in technical solutions 3 and 6 are what we should try to achieve. According to the generalized energy efficiency strategy, energy consumption in the year 2000 will be about 1.5 billion t of standard coal. Energy consumption in the year of 2010 will be about 2 billion t of standard coal. Table 23.23 shows that, in the next 15 years, the energy consumption growth rate will be about 3–4% only. The elasticity coefficient of energy consumption is only about 0.3–0.4. Therefore, in the next 15 years, the requirements for energy saving will be higher. The energy-saving situation will be more serious. It is impossible to maintain a high economic growth rate without implementing the generalized energy efficiency strategy.

On the other hand, in the past 15 years, China's generalized energy efficiency has doubled. However, the gap between China and developed countries has become larger, because generalized energy efficiency in developed countries has improved more quickly in the past decade. Table 23.24 lists the gap in generalized energy

Table 23.23 Options for China's energy development strategic goals (1996–2010 period of China's new energy development strategy)

Time	Energy consumption quantity (10,000 t of standard coal)	GDP (100 million yuan)	GDP energy consumption (ton standard coal/10,000 yuan)	Generalized energy efficiency (yuan/ton standard coal)	Energy consumption growth rate (%)	GDP growth rate (%)	Elasticity coefficient of energy consumption	Energy saving rate (%)	Efficiency growth rate (%)
1995	131,000	19,337	6.77	1476	6.73	10.51	0.64	3.4	3.5
2000					Ninth five-year plan period (1996–2000)				
Technical solution 1	192,482	28,412	6.77	1476	8.00	8.00	1.00	0.0	0.0
Technical solution 2	156,340	28,412	5.50	1817	3.60	8.00	0.45	4.1	4.2
Technical solution 3	147,493	28,412	5.19	1926	2.40	8.00	0.30	5.2	5.5
Technical solution 4	210,977	31,142	6.77	1476	10.00	10.00	1.00	0.0	0.0
Technical solution 5	163,250	31,142	5.24	1908	4.50	10.00	0.45	5.0	5.3
Technical solution 6	151,865	31,142	4.88	2051	3.00	10.00	0.30	6.4	6.8
2005					Tenth five-year plan period (2001–2005)				
Technical solution 1	276,333	40,790	6.77	1476	7.50	7.50	1.00	0.0	0.0
Technical solution 2	184,609	40,790	4.53	2210	3.38	7.50	0.45	3.8	4.0
Technical solution 3	164,850	40,790	4.04	2474	2.25	7.50	0.30	4.9	5.1

(continued)

Table 23.23 (continued)

Time	Energy consumption quantity (10,000 t of standard coal)	GDP (100 million yuan)	GDP energy consumption (ton standard coal/10,000 yuan)	Generalized energy efficiency (yuan/ton standard coal)	Energy consumption growth rate (%)	GDP growth rate (%)	Elasticity coefficient of energy consumption	Energy saving rate (%)	Efficiency growth rate (%)
Technical solution 4	332,128	49,026	6.77	1476	9.50	9.50	1.00	0.0	0.0
Technical solution 5	201,307	49,026	4.11	2435	4.28	9.50	0.45	4.8	5.0
Technical solution 6	174,775	49,026	3.56	2805	2.85	9.50	0.30	6.1	6.5
2010					Eleventh five-year plan period (2006–2010)				
Technical solution 1	387,571	57,210	6.77	1476	7.00	7.00	1.00	0.0	0.0
Technical solution 2	215,575	57,210	3.77	2654	3.15	7.00	0.45	3.6	3.7
Technical solution 3	182,901	57,210	3.20	3128	2.10	7.00	0.30	4.6	4.8
Technical solution 4	511,020	75,432	6.77	1476	9.00	9.00	1.00	0.0	0.0
Technical solution 5	245,509	75,432	3.25	3072	4.05	9.00	0.45	4.5	4.8
Technical solution 6	199,678	75,432	2.65	3778	2.70	9.00	0.30	5.8	6.1
2010					1996–2010				

(continued)

Table 23.23 (continued)

Time	Energy consumption quantity (10,000 t of standard coal)	GDP (100 million yuan)	GDP energy consumption (ton standard coal/10,000 yuan)	Generalized energy efficiency (yuan/ton standard coal)	Energy consumption growth rate (%)	GDP growth rate (%)	Elasticity coefficient of energy consumption	Energy saving rate (%)	Efficiency growth rate (%)
Technical solution 1	387,613	57,216	6.77	1476	7.50	7.50	1.00	0.0	0.0
Technical solution 2	215,685	57,216	3.77	2653	3.38	7.50	0.45	3.8	4.0
Technical solution 3	182,903	57,216	3.20	3128	2.25	7.50	0.30	4.9	5.1
Technical solution 4	511,073	75,440	6.77	1476	9.50	9.50	1.00	0.0	0.0
Technical solution 5	245,633	75,440	3.26	3071	4.28	9.50	0.45	4.8	5.0
Technical solution 6	199,681	75,440	2.65	3778	2.85	9.50	0.30	6.1	6.5

Table 23.24 The gap of generalized energy efficiency between China and developed countriesenergy efficiency between China and developed countries (new energy saving period)

Country	Unit	1978	1985	1994
Japan	Dollar/ton standard coal	2556 (**5.6**)	2538 (**3.9**)	6622 (**7.0**)
France	Dollar/ton standard coal	2110 (**4.6**)	1818 (**2.8**)	4115 (**4.3**)
Germany	Dollar/ton standard coal	1788 (**3.9**)	1721 (**2.6**)	4219 (**4.4**)
UK	Dollar/ton standard coal	1095(**2.4**)	1642 (**2.5**)	3195 (**3.4**)
US	Dollar/ton standard coal	862(**1.9**)	1605 (**2.5**)	2217 (**2.3**)
India	Dollar/ton standard coal	1048(**2.3**)	940 (**1.4**)	908 (**1**)
Hong Kong	Dollar/ton standard coal	1805 (**4.0**)	3448 (**5.3**)	6579 (**6.9**)
China[a]	Dollar/ton standard coal	364	421	466
China[b]	Dollar/ton standard coal	454 (**1**)	653 (**1**)	950 (**1**)

Note [a]All data in the table are calculated based on the prices and exchange rates of the listing years. Due to the change of prices and exchange rates, the data are not comparable across years
[b]Figures in parentheses are based on the comparable prices and exchange rates of 1980. They are comparable across years

efficiency between China and developed countries. Table 23.24 shows that compared with 1985, the generalized energy efficiency in Japan, France, Germany, the UK, and the US increased 1.6 times, 1.3 times, 1.5 times, 1 time, and 0.4 time, respectively, in 1994. In 1978, the generalized energy efficiency in China was only $364/ton standard coal, six times lower than Japan, 4.8 times lower than France, 3.9 times lower than Germany, 2 times lower than the UK, 1.4 times lower than the US, and even 1.9 times lower than India. In 1994, the generalized energy efficiency in China was $466/t standard coal, 13 times lower than Japan ($6623/t standard coal), 7.8 times lower than France ($4115/t standard coal), 8 times lower than Germany ($4219/ton standard coal), 5.8 times lower than the UK ($3195/t standard coal), and 3.7 times lower than the US ($2217/t standard coal). The gap between China and developed countries doubled in 15 years. However, the gap between China and India dropped to half. It should be noted that prices and the exchange rate had certain impacts on the gap. But based on the comparable prices of 1980, the gap between China and developed countries is still large. More details are provided in the notes for Table 23.24. Numbers in parentheses mean that the gap is based on the comparable prices and comparable exchange rates of 1980.

Table 23.25 lists the generalized energy efficiency in some countries. The energy consumption for their GDP across different years is compared. Just as in 1980, in 1994, China's generalized energy efficiency is still one of the lowest in the world. But the generalized energy efficiency in Hong Kong is $6579/1 t of standard coal in 1994, 0.9 times higher than in 1985. It is the highest in the world. Its experience in energy saving is worth study. Energy waste is a still serious issue in China. Energy waste was mainly caused by systems. Economic structures also waste energy, particularly some overlapped construction and some small projects with redundant features. Out of date technologies, old equipment, and a lack of innovation cause energy waste, as

Table 23.25 Comparison of generalized energy efficiency and GDP energy consumption among countries and regions

Country or region	Generalized energy efficiency (US dollar/ton standard coal)			GDP energy consumption (ton standard coal/10,000 US dollar)		
	1978	1985	1994	1978	1985	1994
Nepal		6623	5714		1.51	1.75
Burundi	12,240	6211	4808	0.82	1.61	2.08
The Central African Republic[a]	6859	5525	6452	1.46	1.81	1.55
Burkina Faso		5263	8000		1.90	1.25
Nigeria[a]	6798	3401	1383	1.47	2.94	7.23
Niger		3650	3236		2.74	3.09
Upper Volta	5914			1.69		
Togo		3436	3690		2.91	2.71
Haiti	5456	3953	3425	1.83	2.53	2.92
Tanzania		5236	2381		1.91	4.20
Chile[a]	5061	1377	2710	1.98	7.26	3.69
Rwanda		4545	1927		2.20	5.19
Ethiopia[a]	4539	4525	2786	2.20	2.21	3.59
Uganda[a]	4591		6494	2.18		1.54
Saudi Arabia[a]	4572	1695	934	2.19	5.90	10.71
Guatemala	4000	4975	4630	2.50	2.01	2.16
The Ivory Coast	3968			2.52		
Cameroon		3906	4762		2.56	2.10
Paraguay	3759	2141	4310	2.66	4.67	2.32
Switzerland	3650	2907	7092	2.74	3.44	1.41
Oman	3605	1754	1623	2.77	5.70	6.16
Malawi	3392	3058	2421	2.95	3.27	4.13
Republic of Yemen		3289			3.04	
Mali[a]	3250	4184	6289	3.08	2.39	1.59
Libya	3185	1650		3.14	6.06	
Bangladesh	3171	2439	2336	3.15	4.10	4.28
Fiji	3059			3.27		
Afghanistan[a]	2899			3.45		
Ivory Coast		2778	1965		3.60	5.09
Madagascar	2898	5076	2755	3.45	1.97	3.63
Ghana[a]	2862	2028		3.49	4.93	
Salvador	2719	3.86	4525	3.68	3.24	2.21

(continued)

Table 23.25 (continued)

Country or region	Generalized energy efficiency (US dollar/ton standard coal)			GDP energy consumption (ton standard coal/10,000 US dollar)		
	1978	1985	1994	1978	1985	1994
Honduras	2683	2506	2364	3.73	3.99	4.23
United Arab Emirates		2639			3.79	
Kenya	2583	1972	1689	3.87	5.07	5.92
Costa Rica	2574	1704	3096	3.89	5.87	3.23
Japan	2556	2538	6623	3.91	3.94	1.51
Angola[a]	2480			4.03		
Sierra Leone[a]	2312	2994	1795	4.33	3.34	5.57
Zaire[a]	2267	1631		4.41	6.13	
Mauritius[a]	2247	2457	5405	4.45	4.07	1.85
The Sudan*	2246	3448		4.45	2.90	
Burma	2187	1799		4.57	5.56	
Brail	2157	1471	3472	4.64	6.80	2.88
Somalia[a]	2149	2387		4.65	4.19	
Papua New Guinea	2112	2024	3759	4.74	4.94	2.66
France	2111	1818	4115	4.74	5.50	2.43
Nicaragua	2071	2083	1259	4.83	4.80	7.94
Gabon	2067		4016	4.84		2.49
Mauritania	2045	2320	3086	4.89	4.31	3.24
Iceland	2038			4.91		
Denmark	2033	1961	4831	4.92	5.10	2.07
Austria	1951	1984	5128	5.13	5.04	1.95
Sweden	1884	1284	2747	5.31	7.79	3.64
Guinea[a]	1878	4219	5587	5.33	2.37	1.79
Bolivia	1878	1250	1706	5.33	8.00	5.86
Barbados	1861			5.37		
Kuwait[a]	1813	2217	1353	5.52	4.51	7.39
Hong Kong	1805	3448	6579	5.54	2.90	1.52
Iraq[a]	1795			5.57		
Spain	1792	1555	3509	5.58	6.43	2.85
Germany	1788	1712	4219	5.59	5.81	2.37
Dominican Republic	1766	1486	2762	5.66	6.73	3.62

(continued)

Table 23.25 (continued)

Country or region	Generalized energy efficiency (US dollar/ton standard coal)			GDP energy consumption (ton standard coal/10,000 US dollar)		
	1978	1985	1994	1978	1985	1994
Tunisia	1749	1524	2083	5.72	6.56	4.80
Malta	1748			5.72		
Malaysia	1728	1695	1443	5.79	5.90	6.93
Israel	1721	1789	3534	5.81	5.59	2.83
Botswana		1548	5025		6.46	1.99
Algeria[a]	1713	1590	1021	5.84	6.29	9.79
Turkey	1669	1063	1550	5.99	9.41	6.45
Uruguay	1665	1548	5435	6.01	6.46	1.84
Greece	1663	1351	2294	6.02	7.40	4.36
Sri Lanka	1647	1912	4065	6.07	5.23	2.46
Portugal	1644	1052	3311	6.08	9.51	3.02
Belgium	1635	1241	3040	6.12	8.06	3.29
Philippines	1616	1590	1805	6.19	6.29	5.54
Norway	1614	1127	3257	6.20	8.87	3.07
Senegal	1611	2358	3175	6.21	4.24	3.15
Holland	1607	1266	3236	6.22	7.90	3.09
Ecuador	1563	1127	1961	6.40	8.87	5.10
Indonesia	1538	1695	1605	6.50	5.90	6.23
Italy	1509	1751	4545	6.63	5.71	2.20
Thailand	1485	1631	2208	6.73	6.13	4.53
Panama	1481	2320	3247	6.75	4.31	3.08
Pakistan	1475	1220	1110	6.78	8.20	9.01
Finland	1430	1664	2222	6.99	6.01	4.50
Cyprus	1356			7.38		
Australia	1312	1484	2475	7.62	6.74	4.04
New Zealand	1290	1284	2299	7.75	7.79	4.35
Ireland	1232	1292	3195	8.12	7.74	3.13
Iran[a]	1222		448	8.18		22.34
Zambia	1174	663	1852	8.52	15.09	5.40
Columbia	1139	1224	2079	8.78	8.17	4.81
Congo[a]	1135	3344	2865	8.81	2.99	3.49

(continued)

Table 23.25 (continued)

Country or region	Generalized energy efficiency (US dollar/ton standard coal)			GDP energy consumption (ton standard coal/10,000 US dollar)		
	1978	1985	1994	1978	1985	1994
Liberia	1104	953		9.06	10.49	
UK	1095	1642	3195	9.14	6.09	3.13
Peru	1079	1300	4219	9.27	7.69	2.37
Jordan	1078	1416	1044	9.28	7.06	9.58
Republic of Korea	1064	1214	1942	9.40	8.24	5.15
India	1048	941	908	9.54	10.63	11.01
Lebanon	1046			9.56		
Venezuela	1018	895	812	9.82	11.17	12.32
Mexico	966	1129	1859	10.35	8.86	5.38
Syria	946	1311		10.57	7.63	
Zimbabwe	935	1115	803	10.70	8.97	12.46
Egypt	932	726	855	10.73	13.77	11.70
USA	862	1605	2217	11.60	6.23	4.51
Argentina[a]	853	1016	4049	11.73	9.84	2.47
Canada	853	1038	1637	11.73	9.63	6.11
Singapore	828	2398	2469	12.07	4.17	4.05
Yugoslavia[b]	828	752		12.08	13.29	
Jamaica		690	1050		14.50	9.52
Trinidad and Tobago	712	1157	623	14.05	8.64	16.05
Luxembourg	665			15.03		
People's Democratic Republic of Yemen		495			20.21	
Hungary[b]	664	459	1130	15.07	21.79	8.85
South Africa	614	644	917	16.28	15.53	10.90
The Republic of Belarus			501			19.98
Poland[b]	524	417	644	19.08	23.96	15.52
Czech[b]	518		614	19.32		16.28
Russian Federation[b]	510		432	19.60		23.13
Bulgaria[b]	477		299	20.98		33.50
China	364	421	466	27.50	23.73	21.44

Note [a]is data of 1975
[b]is data of 1979
1. In the column of 1978
2. Data for 1978, 1983, 1985 and 1994 are based on prices in corresponding years
3. Due to changes of exchange rates, data are not comparable across years

well. In addition, the low level of management has caused energy waste. When firms lose money, investment in energy does not generate benefits. And worse, some waste was caused by thoughts. In certain conditions, no one cared about energy waste. The potential of the ten aspects in generalized energy-saving is still large – even larger than before. Therefore, the prospect of the generalized energy saving is better than before.

23.10.5 Countermeasures and Suggestions

1. **Continue China's generalized energy efficiency strategy and continue the generalized energy saving project**

In the early 1980s, the CPC Central Committee and the State Council proposed an energy development policy based on China's energy situation. In particular, energy development and energy saving should be equally important and energy saving should have priority. Practice in the past decade has proven that this policy fits China's economic development and energy development. Guided by the policy, China is implementing a generalized energy efficiency strategy. Regarding its generalized energy-saving projects, the goals of doubling energy to ensure quadrupling the economy were achieved five years earlier. In 1995, the elasticity coefficient of energy consumption was 0.51. The energy consumption for every 10,000 yuan GDP (in comparable prices of 1980), decreased from 13.34 t of standard coal in 1980 to 6.67 t of standard coal in 1995, with an average annual energy saving rate of 4.4%. In other words, 42 million t of standard coal were saved in each year. The achievement in generalized energy saving is huge. Generalized energy saving plays a vital role in resolving the problems of energy supply and demand in China.

In the ninth five-year plan, energy-saving is still very challenging. The 15th CPC National Congress clarified the economic development strategic goals for the ninth five-year plan. Based on the goals, we estimated that the annual growth rate of energy demand in the coming 15 years in China will be 3.33%. In 2000 and 2010, the total energy demand will be 1.55 and 2.14 billion t of coal, respectively. They are 1.18 and 1.63 times of the energy demand in 1995 (1.31 billion t of standard coal). The elasticity coefficient of energy consumption for the ninth five-year plan and the next 10 years are set as 0.43 and 0.45, respectively. They are lower than the value for the past 15 years (0.51). The elasticity coefficient of energy consumption should be about 0.45. This means that 55% of the growth of GDP in the next 15 years will rely on energy-saving. The average annual energy saving rate is set as 5%. This means that more than 68 million t of standard coal should be saved in each year. This is higher than any period in history. Therefore, in the next 15 years, the generalized energy efficiency strategy must be followed to finish the generalized energy saving project. The new strategy fits the conditions in China. It has the following six characteristics. It is: 1. Good for saving energy; 2. Good for saving resources; 3. Good for environmental protection; 4. Good for rapid economic development; 5.

Good for the improvement of people's level of living and life quality; 6. Good for coordination and sustainable development among energy, resources, environment, the economy, and the population. We propose that the CPC continue follow the new energy development strategy, namely the generalized energy efficiency strategy. It is a very important project that will benefit future generations. It cannot be finished without the support of the central government.

At the beginning of the ninth five-year plan, economic development began well. The growth rate of the GDP was maintained at a high level, 9.6% in 1996, and over 8% in 1997 (higher than the planned rate). Energy production grew steadily as well. In 1996, coal production was 1.375 trillion t with an annual growth rate of 1%. The production of crude oil reached 157.33 million t with an annual growth rate of 4.9% (highest in the past decade). The production of natural gas reached 20.1 billion cubic meters with annual growth rate of 12% (best in the decade after reform and opening up). The installed capacity reached 235 million kW with an annual increase in installed capacity of 10 million kW in nine consecutive years. The generating capacity was 1.0813 trillion kW h with an annual growth rate of 7.3%. The total energy production is 1.31557 trillion t of standard coal with an annual growth rate of 1.96%. And the energy production situation was good in 1997.

However, we should notice that the situation of energy saving has not been good in the recent years. The growth in energy production could not keep up with the growth in energy consumption. Furthermore, the amount of saved energy was lower than the amount required by the goals. In 1996, the total energy consumption reached 13.8811 billion t of standard coal, an increase of 76.35 million t of standard coal, with a growth rate of 5.82% compared to the previous year. However, the total energy production increased only 25.23 million t, with a growth rate of 1.96% compared to the previous year. The energy production growth rate (1.7%) in 1997 was lower than the predicted growth rate of energy consumption growth (3.8%). Regarding energy saving, the energy-saving rate was 3.45% and the amount of saved energy was 49.67 million t of standard coal in 1996. It is estimated that the energy-saving rate and the amount of saved energy will be higher than those in 1996, but still lower than the requirements of the ninth five-year plan: annual average energy saving rate of 4.21%, and an average annual saved energy of 64.65 million t of standard coal. Attention must be paid to this situation. If energy saving cannot meet the requirement of the goals in the final three years of the ninth five-year plan, an energy shortage might appear for China's economic development.

Energy saving is a very difficult task. It requires all industries and the entire Chinese people to conduct comprehensive saving over a long time. Thus, all industry should give energy saving the highest priority. Both economic stability and rapid and healthy economic development rely on energy saving. In practice, generalized energy saving should be highlighted. Energy efficiency should be improved. Raw materials, manpower, population growth, natural resources, transportation, time, and capital should be saved. Equipment utilization and product quality should be improved. Production costs should be reduced. The industrial structure and product structure should be adjusted. Generalized energy requires the continuously reduction of energy consumption per unit of product and an improvement in the added value of products.

2. **Oil saving should have the top priority**

In China's energy supply and demand, the shortage of oil is the most prominent. During the eighth five-year plan period, the average annual growth rate of oil consumption was 6.94%. This means an average annual increase of 9.16 million t. The elasticity coefficient of oil consumption was 0.58, which was higher than the elasticity coefficient of the entire energy consumption (0.49). In contrast, the average annual growth rate of crude oil production was only 1.64%. This means an average annual increase of 2.35 million t. The elasticity coefficient of oil production (0.14) is less than that of the entire energy production (0.37). In 1996, even though the crude oil production has increased significantly, with a growth rate of 4.9% with an increase of 7.28 million t, the supply could not meet the increase in oil consumption (a growth rate of 5.85%, an increase of 9.39 million t). In order to meet the growing needs of oil consumption, we have to reduce oil exports and to increase oil imports. The net amount of imported oil during the last two years was about 10 million t.

Throughout the 15 years from the beginning of the ninth five-year plan until 2010, national economic development and the requirements of adjusting the structure of energy consumption and reducing environmental pollution generated a high speed increase in the demands for oil and natural gas. It is estimated that in order to achieve the economic development goals and to consider energy saving, the oil demand will reach 200–210 million t and 265–285 million t in the years 2000 and 2010, respectively. The average annual increase in the use of oil in the ninth five-year plan and 10 years after the plan will be 787–987 and 650–800 million t, respectively. However, since the seventh five-year plan, the growth rate of crude oil production in China was slow, and this slow growth will last for a while. It is estimated that the average annual increase of crude oil production in the ninth five-year plan and 10 years after the plan will be 2–2.5 million t. Crude oil production in China can reach only 160 million t and 185 million t in 2000 and 2010, respectively. The shortage in the oil supply will be more than 40–50 million t and more than 80–100 million t in 2000 and 2010, respectively.

There are two ways to fix this shortage issue. One is to buy oil directly from the international markets through trade channels, namely, increasing oil (including crude oil and refined oil) imports. The other one is to exploit more oil, to save energy, and to find alternative ways for importing oil. Alternative ways for importing oil include: increasing the domestic production of oil (synthetic oil) and natural gas; investing in overseas oil exploitation; replacing imported oil with domestic coal; adopting hydropower and new energy; and saving oil consumption. Among these approaches, saving oil consumption is the most practical and the most effective strategy. Different from increasing the production of oil and natural gas, this approach focuses on saving energy. The economic efficiency of oil utilization in China is far lower than that in developed countries. In addition, the efficiency of oil equipment in agriculture, industries and transportation is lower than other countries. The potential for saving energy is huge. The investments and costs of saving energy are both lower than those for energy exploitation. The Beijing Yanshan Petrochemical Company took measures to save energy after the reform and the opening up. It did not consume more oil on power, and it even used less oil on power to maintain an annual growth rate of 7.2% for its added value. This is a typical example of developing production through saving oil.

3. **Effective energy management systems and management methods in the past 15 years should continue. In the new situation, it will be necessary to combine a generalized energy-saving and a comprehensive saving strategy, to combine generalized energy-saving and a transformation of economic growth, and to combine generalized energy-saving and environmental protection, as well as sustainable development strategies**

The government should not release its macro-control management on energy saving. Stable institutions should be established for this macro-control management. The author proposed that the State Planning Commission or the Economic and Trade Commission develop assessment indicators for economic growth mode transformation. All industries should be assessed with these indicators. All levels of energy saving management institutions should implement the energy saving laws carefully, should continue to develop energy-saving schemes and plans, and should revise their energy-saving policies and regulations according to the requirements of energy laws. The author also proposed the establishment of a reporting system for managing energy and raw materials and a monitoring system for energy consumption. In addition, the author proposed to add a section of how to using energy rationally into the feasibility study reports of the fixed assets investment projects. The design and construction of the fixed assets investment projects should follow the energy saving standards and energy saving specifications.

Management of energy saving and reducing energy consumption should continue. Enterprises should do more regarding measurement, statistics, and consumption analysis. They should establish a system to monitor the responsibility of managing energy and raw materials. A reward and punishment system regarding energy saving should also be established. In the process of establishing modern enterprise systems, enterprises should gradually establish their energy saving management systems in accordance with the socialist market economic system. Enterprises should perform comprehensive energy saving management, if conditions allow.

Economic policy encouraging comprehensive saving should be made. In the operating mechanism of the socialist market economy, government action and corporate behavior should be separated. They should each have their own focuses. Other than economic benefits, energy saving has social benefits, environmental benefits, and public interests. Therefore, economic measures, such as investment, pricing, taxes, loans, and accelerated depreciation, should be applied to guide and promote energy saving. Policies promoting energy saving and reducing energy consumption should be made. Research and demonstration projects regarding energy saving should get support.

More attention should be paid to educating the people regarding energy saving and to promoting information sharing regarding energy saving. Information about energy saving should be released in a timely manner by all level of information management institutions and research institutions. Weekly activities that support energy saving should be promoted. In addition, regular events should be held to promote energy saving. The concept of comprehensive energy saving should be promoted in the society. Particularly, people should have the idea that there is enough energy in total but that energy per capita is limited, that energy saving is required, and that wasting energy is prohibited. The roles of associations, councils, and social clubs for energy saving should be promoted. Research on energy saving should get support. Trainings on energy saving should be provided at different levels. The idea of energy saving should be embedded in enterprise trainings and in education in primary schools and middle schools.

4. **Establish national and enterprise energy saving funds**

In the socialist market economy, enterprises should plan and implement energy-saving projects. Enterprises should manage energy-saving funds, as well. For a long time, enterprises in China, especially state-owned enterprises, have lacked the capital for implementing energy saving. Implementing the generalized energy efficiency strategy requires a deepening of ecosnomic reform, improvement in the capacity of self-accumulation, self-transformation, and self-development. Enterprises should be motivated to implement energy saving. Otherwise, regardless how large of the scale of energy development is and how rapid the growth in energy production, the demand for energy consumption will never be met.

Energy saving requires funds. Funds have three resources. First, if the national macro-benefits are good but lack micro-benefits, funds for energy saving will mainly come from national policies, such as preferential loans, tax reductions, or exemptions. Second, if the energy saving has both national macro-benefits and micro-benefits, but a huge amount of capital is needed and the payback time is long, the states should provide certain help. Third, energy saving has great micro-benefits and requires a small amount of capital with a short payback time; enterprises should get capital from energy saving funds, which are set by extracting funding from the benefits generated by energy saving. Therefore, the states should establish energy saving funds. State-owned large and medium-size enterprises should establish energy saving funds, as well, for supporting those main energy saving projects.

5. **Increase direct energy-saving investment, improve energy efficiency, and continue to increase direct energy-saving**

Direct energy-saving will be more difficult in the future. Therefore, technology and management should be improved for increasing direct energy-saving. In order to guide the rational use of energy, improve energy efficiency, and promote the economic growth pattern of energy consumption, the State Planning Commission, the State Economic and Trade Commission, and the State Science and Technology Commission created the China Energy Saving Technology Policy Outline in May 1996. This outline combines short-term and long-term energy saving technologies based on the available energy-saving technologies and process equipment before the year 2000. It also considers the medium-and long-term energy-saving technologies as a technical reserve. Based on China's industrial and technological policies, this outline aims to increase technical content in energy saving and to clarify energy-saving technology goals, their levels, and their means. The outline promotes energy-saving technologies that have been proven to be mature, effective, and quick during the previous ten years practice of energy saving. It also limits and eliminates low cost-effective and out-of-date technologies and equipment. In addition, it promotes foreign advanced technologies that are suitable for China's conditions. All industries should follow and implement the outline, based on their specific circumstances. This is the requirement for achieving the goals for energy saving in the ninth five-year plan.

The conditions in China require the effective conversion of coal. Therefore, it is an important energy-saving approach to develop cogeneration in urban areas. It should be noted that, in areas where heating is needed, cogeneration should be promoted and the ratio of heat and electricity should be increased. Increase the heating unit parameters and capacity. Develop high-capacity regional cogeneration. Meanwhile, cogeneration should be developed in the transformation of low-pressure units in small and medium-sized thermal power plants and industrial boilers. Attention should be paid to the adjustment of the structure of thermal power units. Increase the ratio of large and high efficiency units to reduce the consumption of coal. Moreover, transmission line losses should be reduced in order to increase the efficiency in power supply.

China's air pollution is mainly concentrated in urban areas. Thus, urban areas should adopt more electricity, heating, and coal gas. Developing electricity, heating, and coal gas is the main approach to increasing energy efficiency and to improving air quality.

6. **Increase indirect energy saving in materials, transportation, water, and land utilization to form high-tech generalized energy-saving industry and make it a new economic growth point**

The results of generalized energy saving in the past 15 years show that direct energy-saving accounted for a fifth, and indirect energy saving accounted for about four-fifths. The potential for indirect energy saving in materials, transportation, water, and land utilization is large. In the past, little attention was paid to indirect energy saving technologies. Thus, indirect energy saving technologies must be promoted more in the future. The author thinks that some manufacturers need to change the line of production now and in the future. The first option for them can be industries related to energy saving, namely the fifth energy industry. In this way, high technology can be applied in energy saving industries. Thus, energy saving industries can be a new economic growth point. This emerging industry needs supports from the states and all other aspects. It is necessary to encourage and support the development of new generalized energy-saving technologies. Example projects for generalized energy saving should be built. A technological support system should be developed. Markets for energy saving technologies should be cultivated. Policies and guide catalogs for energy saving technologies should be developed. Catalogs for energy saving mechanical and electrical products and out-of-date mechanical and electrical products should be published. Enterprises should be guides for adopting energy saving technologies, processes, equipment, and materials. Out-of-date enterprises, products, processes, and equipment should be upgraded. Products that save energy, material, and water should be produced.

7. **Optimize economic structures, improve economic efficiency of capital, reduce costs and promote economic energy saving**

The generalized energy saving practice in China shows that the improvement in generalized energy efficiency and in the reduction of consumption per unit of GDP largely depends on economic efficiency. In other words, generalized energy saving can be achieved by avoiding overlapping construction, saving investment in infrastructure, having an accelerated cash flow, reducing the occupation of flow assets, reducing cost, adjusting the economic scale of production, improving quality, adjusting the economic structure, and establishing a generalized energy-saving national economic system. Therefore, when technical energy saving is implemented, the potential for economic energy saving should be more deeply considered. From the perspective of a macro-generalized energy analysis, economic energy saving is an important part of the indirect energy saving. It accounts for about 2/5 of the total generalized energy saving. From the perspective of a generalized energy analysis for an enterprise, economic energy saving accounts for about 3/5, in some enterprises. Among them, energy saved by saved capital accounts for about 2/5. Energy saved by reduced costs accounts for about 1/5.

In recent years, the result of the adjustment in the structure of the first, the second, and the third industries in China has not been ideal. The proportion of added value in the first industry with low energy consumption in the GDP continuously dropped. Meanwhile, the proportion of added value in the third industry with low energy consumption in GDP has dropped, as well. In contrast, the proportion of added value of the second industry with high energy consumption in GDP has risen quickly. As a result, energy saved by the economic structure has been negative. In other words, an extra several million t of standard coal was consumed. It should be noted that the adjustment of economic structure has gained large achievement. More attention should be paid to the adjustment of the economic structure, including industrial structure, product structure, and enterprise scale. The Yanhua generalized energy-saving example shows that the potential for energy saving is large. Energy saved by the adjustment of economic structure should be the continuous focus for a long time to come.

23.11 Problems About Economic Growth Speed[24]

Research background, significance of achievements and practical value.

After the reform and opening up, China's economy has developed quickly. Particularly from 1982 to 1988, the economy growth rate has been mostly in the double digits. However, the speed of economic growth declined sharply after 1989, due to social instability. Therefore, people often discuss the economic growth rate. Topics include its high speed, over high speed, medium speed, and ups and downs. Now it is time to develop the eighth five-year plan. A challenge is to set a reasonable and feasible economic growth rate. To this end, the author undertook a research project on the economic growth rate in the eighth five-year plan and in the 10-year plan developed by the State Planning Commission. First, the author defined high-speed economic growth, medium speed economic growth, and low-speed economic growth. Then, the author studied the law of economic development, both in China and in other countries. Finally, the author proposed a proper economic growth rate in accordance with the actual situation in China for the eighth five-year plan and the 10-year plan. This research won the second prize for scientific and technological progress at the State Planning Commission in 1991 because its results [249, 250] have both theoretical innovation and practical value.

In recent years, people have often discussed the economic growth rate. Topics have included its high speed, over high speed, medium speed, and up and downs. However, there are no clear definitions of these topics. Thus, it is not convenient for practical work and for theoretical studies. For example, the high-speed that some people oppose might be the same as the medium speed that others advocate. The author believes that it is necessary to set a quantitative range for the economic growth rate.

Based on 40-year data about the economic growth rates in China and in other countries, as well as on the summary of comments for economic growth rates, the author proposed to set a quantitative limit for the economic growth rate (see Table 23.26). The table shows that a medium speed falls between 5 and 8%, not including 5 or 8%. High speed refers to those speeds that are equal to or larger than 8%. Those larger than 10%, including 10%, are super high speed. Low speed refers to those speeds that are equal to or smaller than 5%. Those lower than 3%, including 3%, are super low speed. Zero means that the speed is zero. Those smaller than zero are negative speed. Here is an example in which the analysis is based on the quantitative range for the economic growth rate.

---

[24]Xu, S. B. (1990). Basic Thinking of Economic Growth Speed During the "Eighth Five-Year Plan", report from Technical and Economic Research Institute Under SDPC, which won the second prize for scientific and technological progress of the State Planning Commission.

Table 23.26 Quantitative ranges for economic growth rate

I	High speed (wide range)	Medium speed		Low speed (wide range)			
	Higher than 8% (including 8%)	5–8%		Lower than 5% (including 5%)			
II	Over high speed	High speed	Medium speed	Low speed	Over low speed	Zero speed	Negative speed
	>10%	8–10%	5–8%	3–5%	0–3%	0%	Lower than 0%
	(including 10%)	(including 8%)		(including 5%)	(including 3%)		
	Positive growth					Zero growth	Negative growth

23.11.1 *Changes of Economic Growth Rate Fluctuates Periodically. The Cycle is 3–6 Years. The Average Gap Between the Highest Speed and Lowest Speed is 5–10% Points*

1. **The frequency for the appearance of the UV period in all countries is nearly 100%**

According to the economic growth rate during the past 40 years in main countries across the world, the interval between two peaks is normally 1–4 years. In other words, once a peak of the economic growth rate appears, the next peak will appear in 1–4 years. If the interval is one year, it is called a short cycle, which changes in the V shape, namely peak-bottom-peak. If the interval is 2–4 years, it is called a medium cycle. If the interval is 4–6 years, it is called a long cycle, which changes in the U shape, namely peak-down-bottom-up-peak, peak-bottom-up-up-peak, or peak-down-down-bottom-peak. The possibility of the occurrence of the U shape and the V shape in countries is close to 100%. This is a rule which China's economic growth rate changes follow. From 1953 to 1988, nine cycles appeared. Except for one cycle, the other eight were all UV-shaped cycles. Based on this rule, the year 1987 is estimated to be a peak in the ninth period with a GDP growth rate of 11%. The GDP growth rate in 1988 will drop to 10.8%. The GDP growth rate in 1989 will see a bottom, with a GDP growth rate of 3.9%. The GDP growth rate in 1990 is estimated to be 5%. A peak is estimated to occur in 1991, with a GDP growth rate higher than 5%. A peak is estimated to appear between 1993 and 1995. There will be 3–4 peaks in the 1990s.

2. **Gap between peak and bottom changes at a range of 5–10 percentage points**

The average gap in countries with a rapid economic growth rate is large, usually around 10%. The average gap in countries with a slow economic growth rate is small, usually around 5%. For instance, the economic growth rates for Brazil, the US, and the UK are 8.3, 4.9, and 4.1, respectively. From 1953 to 1988, the changes in the economic growth rate in China experienced three booms and busts. The first boom and bust was caused by the Great Leap Forward and the three-year difficulty. The range of change was 52%, dropping from 22% in 1958 to −30% in 1961. The second boom and bust was caused by the political impact of the Cultural Revolution. The range of change was 30.5%. The third boom and bust occurred at the end of the Cultural Revolution. The range of change was 15%. Droppings during these three booms and busts were all over 10%. Other than these three booms and busts, the average change of the other six periods was 11.0. It follows the general law. If a change is positive and falls between 5 and 10%, it is normal, not a boom and bust. In addition, a boom and bust in economic growth refers to the growth rate of the GDP, based on fixed price. Thus, the impact of inflation is deducted. Over-high-speed economic growth is likely to cause inflation. However, if prices are strictly controlled strictly, inflation can be controlled. In essence, the rapid growth of the economy and of inflation are not connected the socialist system. In the ten years after the reform and opening up, the change in the economic growth rate in China was in the range of 0–10%. Even the growth rate of the GDP dropped from 11.3 in 1988 to 3.8% in 1990. These changes are normal. The changes in the growth rate of the GDP in 1990 s in China are also expected to be normal.

23.11.2 Economic Growth Rates Fall into the Categories of Middle-High Speed, Middle-Low Speed, and Interim Speed

1. **Economic growth rates vary across countries and development phases**

The economic growth rates of major countries in the world show that economic growth rates vary across countries and across development phases. They fall into the categories of middle-high speed, middle-low speed, and interim speed. Data of the past 40 years show that the US, West Germany, the UK, and France are developed countries, and their economic growth rates are middle-low speed with a range of 92–100%. In the 1950 and 1960s, the economic growth rate of Japan was middle-high speed with a frequency of 90%. In the 1970s, the economic growth rate of Japan changed to middle-low speed with the frequency of 90%. The economic growth rates of developing countries are usually higher than those of developed countries. But the economic growth rates vary across countries and across development phases. The economic growth rate of China is middle-high speed with the frequency of 68%. The economic growth rate of India is middle-low speed with the frequency of 87%. The economic growth rate of Brail is interim speed. Its frequency of middle-high speed is close to its frequency of middle-low speed. Data of the recent ten years show that the frequency of middle-high speed is 82% in China. It is estimated that the economic growth rate in the 1990s in China will maintain a middle-high speed.

2. **Why did the economic growth rates have the trend listed above?**

The author found that the economic growth rate relies on thousands of certain factors and uncertain factors, particularly seven factors, including national and international political factors, the national defense factor, the social factor, the technological factor, the economic factor, the environmental factor, and the natural resource factor. For example, political stability, climate, management level, scientific and technological progress, and the international situation will directly affect the economic growth rate in China. However, these factors are changing. Some rely on the international situation. Some rely on the weather. They are beyond our control. Although some factors can be controlled, they can be hard to control. The economic growth rates cannot remain the same each year; they change periodically. Booms and busts in the economic growth rates rely on the degree of control. Booms and busts in the economic growth rates occurred in China are related to natural disasters and international sanctions. But the main reasons are political instability and policy mistakes. Therefore, if China maintains political stability and policy continuity, the booms and busts of economic growth rates will be avoided. The change will be in the normal range: 5–10%.

The conomic growth rate is related to the economic development level, to social systems, to natural resources, and to other factors. The economic development level in developed countries is high. Their economy bases are large. Thus, their economic growth rate will not be high. In contrast, the economic development level in developing countries is low. Their economic bases are small. Therefore, developing countries need a high economic growth rate. Meanwhile, it is possible for them to achieve a high economic growth rate. In addition, social systems are very important for the economic growth rate. Compared with India, China has maintained a higher economic growth rate for a long time because the advanced socialist system fits the conditions in China.

The above analysis shows that, other than the three booms and busts, the economic growth rates in the other years are normal. The central government proposed sustainable, steady, and coordinated development. According to our understanding, China's economy should follow the proposal. The economic development should not maintain the same growth rate each year. Instead, periodic change in the economic growth rate is necessary. A low growth rate is not acceptable. The author thinks that the booms and busts of the economic growth rates will not occur in the future. Economic growth rates will fluctuate periodically over a period of 3–6 years. The fluctuation range will be 5–10%. In terms of the three-step economic development strategy proposed by CPC Central Committee, the first step and the second step will require an economic growth rate of 7.2%. This is a middle speed strategy and it has extra room for economic growth. Practice has proven that this strategy conforms to development laws. The author predicts that the economic growth rate will be 7–9% during the eighth five-year plan period. The economic growth rate of 6%, set by the CPC Central Committee, reserves large room for economic growth. The author's study shows that China will benefit the most from middle speed and high speed growth, whereas it will suffer the most from low speed growth. Table 23.27 compares the three economic growth speeds.

23.12 Study of Overall Husbandry Strategy, Planning, and Countermeasures in China[25]

Research background, scientific significance of achievements and practical value.

The Energy Office of the State Council was originally under the leadership of the State Planning Commission. In 1989, the energy office was abolished. The author was transferred to the Technological Economic Research Institute of the State Planning Commission to work as the director. Given the success of China's generalized energy efficiency strategy, the author believes that this strategy must continue. But if the name remains unchanged, industries and people will not be motivated. Only those who care about energy saving will pay attention to this strategy. Thus, the author proposes a comprehensive energy saving strategy. This strategy was chosen as the main research topic for the eighth five-year plan and the ten-year plan. It was studied by experts from all of the industries across China. The leader of the State Planning Commission is the head of this research project. The author served as the leader of this research team, organizing more than 500 experts in 25 institutions. It took the research team three years to finish this project, with 37 achievements, one overall achievement and 20 thematic achievements, ten regional results, and six sectional results. In 1993 the research project was finished. The results were adopted. Achievements [254–259, 273–275, 289, 293, 302] show that it won the first place Science and Technology Progress Award issued by the State Planning Commission in 1993 and the third place national Science and Technology Progress Award in 1995. The author was in charge of this project. He finished the overall achievement and two thematic results. He also worked on over 60 mathematical models. He was the second author of the planning and design for the Yanhua generalized energy-saving pilot project.

[25]Xu, S.B., et al. Study of China's Overall Energy Saving Strategy, Planning and Countermeasures. It took 500 experts from 25 institutions three years to complete this project in 1993. This project has 37 results, one overall achievement, 20 subject results, ten regional results, and six sectional results. It won the first place Science and Technology Progress Award issued by State Planning Commission in 1993 and the third place National Science and Technology Progress award in 1995.

Table 23.27 Comparison of different economic growth rates

Growth rate	Advantages	Disadvantages
High speed (higher than 8%, including 8%)	1. Makes full use of existing production capability 2. Many laborers are employed so as to solve employment issue 3. Makes full use of social factors 4. Achieves social development strategic goals and create more social wealth 5. Improves people's living standards 6. Realizes socialist advantages. Motivates people's enthusiasm	1. Insufficient supply in energy and raw materials funds and transportation 2. Easily leads to inflation. But inflation will not occur if macro control works well 3. Structural adjustment is relatively hard, but it can be achieved with good macro control 4. Easy to compete based on equipment. This will occur only when over-high- speed happens
Medium speed (5–8%)	1. Makes relatively full use of existing production capacity 2. Many laborers can be employed 3. Makes relatively good use of social factors 4. Able to achieve economic development strategic goals and create more social wealth 5. Improves people's living standards quickly 6. Achieves socialist advantages and motivates people's enthusiasm 7. Relatively easy to control prices 8. Relatively easy to adjust structures	1. Less social wealth is created compared with high speed 2. Improvement in people's lives is slower than high speed 3. Cannot make full use of social factors 4. Cannot make full use of human resources. The employment issue is serious

(continued)

Table 23.27 (continued)

Growth rate	Advantages	Disadvantages
Low speed (lower than 5%, including 5%)	1. Easy to control prices 2. Easy to adjust structures	1. Large amount of equipment is idled 2. Many workers have no work to do. Jobless rate rises. Society is instable 3. Many products are stockpiled 4. Cannot make full use of social investment 5. Cannot achieve economic development strategic goals. Little social wealth is created 6. People's live scan not be improved quickly 7. Socialist advantages are not achieved. People's enthusiasm cannot be motivated

23.12.1 Guidelines for China's Energy Saving Development Strategy-Comprehensive Saving Strategy

1. **Opinions about saving**

For a long time, there have been many opinions about saving. The first opinion thinks that saving will limit needs, and will further affect production and daily life. The second opinion thinks that saving is the passive measure, whereas production is the active measure. The third opinion thinks that saving is an expedient measure and a short-term policy. The fourth opinion thinks that saving is a soft task that is invisible and untouchable. It is important in talking but unimportant in action. The fifth opinion thinks that saving is about reducing the usage of those items that are short in supply. It is a small amount of people's business. We believe that a correct understanding of saving is most important.

2. **Satisfactory saving is the main direction for saving**

In real life, there are two kinds of saving. One is restricted saving and the other is satisfactory saving. Restricted saving refers to mandatory restrictions and compression for reasonable demands. For example, power shortages lead to the implementation of power cuts in case of an overload. Without power, many companies will have to stop production. Due to the short supply of liquefied petroleum gas, many families have had to use less liquefied petroleum gas. These savings will affect the production and people's lives. They are hard tasks and passive measures. Thus, they are not permanent solutions. From a long-term standpoint, restrictive saving is not the appropriate direction for saving. However, it will exist for a while. In contrast, satisfactory saving refers to saving that occurs under the conditions when reasonable requirements are met. This kind of saving aims to increase efficiency and reduce waste. It does not limit or lower reasonable requirements. Therefore, it is an active measure and a permanent solution that does not affect production and life. For example, in the past, missing meters caused the waste of a lot of electricity. After meters are installed, the consumption of electricity dropoed dramatically. Another example is the civil refrigerator. Some refrigerators are energy saving, while others are not. Energy saving refrigerators do not affect people's lives at all. In production, many measures can be taken to reduce energy consumption, raw material consumption, and capital occupation. Satisfactory saving indicates scientific and technological progress (including soft and hard scientific and technological progress) and an increase in efficiency. It is the direction of the development for saving. We must promote satisfactory saving in the future. The saving we often talk about is satisfactory saving. It has a larger potential than restricted saving. Take grain, as an example. The potential of satisfactory saving for grain is about more than one hundred million t in China, the equivalent to a quarter of the output of all of the arable land in China. Take transportation as another example. The rate of the empty ride of freight trucks is about 50% in China, a waste of six billion yuan. If these empty freight trucks are utilized, a huge amount of transportation capacity will be saved. Compared with the restrictive saving, the satisfactory saving has no side effects and it is equivalent to production. Therefore, satisfactory saving can be used for replacing production, import, and export. In the late seventh five-year plan period, in 1990, the GDP (calculated based on the price of 1980) was 1.0508 trillion yuan. If the GDP energy consumption remained the same as 1980, the energy consumption in 1990 would be 1.42 billion t of standard coal. However, the actual energy consumption in 1990 was 0.99 billion t of standard coal. More than 400 million t of standard coal was saved, in 1990 only. This is equivalent to producing 400 million t of standard coal. The saving actually replaced the production of 400 million t of standard coal. China has imported oil for a long time. If all of the industries take measures to save oil, this saving can replace import. A good example is to reduce the usage of oil for boiler burning. For some exported products, if satisfactory saving can be implemented, export will be replaced.

3. **Ten advantages of saving**

Because satisfactory saving is equivalent to production, it can replace production. Compared with production, satisfactory saving has the following advantages. First, saving is a kind of production without using any resources. The production of any raw material will consume resources. However, saving energy does not require resources. The total mineral resources in China are large, but the per capita amount is small. Here are some per capita amounts for main mineral resources. Iron ore per capita is 44% of the average iron ore per capita in the world. The percentages for bauxite, refractory clay, phosphate, potash, and oil are 10%, 4%, 76%, 4%, and 21%, respectively. Given the shortage of resources in China, mass production of energy and raw materials are limited by the reserves of resource. This problem can be resolved by satisfactory saving, by replacement in production. Second, saving is a kind of production without any process. Most of the materials saved are those products that are processed. For example, if steel is saved, there is no need to build iron ore, steel mills, and rolling mills. Third, saving is a kind of production with no need for transportation. Because saving occurs at the user site, no products are needed to transport from the producers to the users. In this way, a huge amount of transportation capacity is saved. For instance, compared with 1980, in 1990, China saved 400 million t of standard coal. This saved 800 million t of coal reserve and the construction of coal mines that are need to exploit 400 million t of coal. In addition, this saved 400 million t in transportation capacity. The pressure on transportation was considerably released. Fourth, saving is a kind of production with a quick return. Construction of energy and raw material production bases often takes 5–10 years, which is a long period. The cycle of saving is relatively short, however, and the return is quick. To some extent, saving can solve some urgent problems regarding the shortage of energy. Fifth, saving is a kind of production without pollution. Usually, production generates pollution. Measures are required to reduce pollution and to prevent pollution. Saving is a measure that can prevent pollution fundamentally and can further reduce environment pollution. Sixth, saving is a kind of production with technological progress. For example, saving can wholly rely on existing technology and equipment. Any saving means certain technological progress and improvement in efficiency. Saving cannot be achieved without technological progress. Seventh, saving is a kind of production with management improvement. Production can rely on investment only, without any improvement in management. Saving has to rely on a higher level of macro management and micro-management as well as on scientific decision-making. Waste caused by management was serious in China. The issues in management are related to systems, planning, layout, structure, and policies. It should be noted that the process of saving is to improve the management level and the management system process. Eighth, saving is a kind of production with multiple channels. There are several approaches for producing and processing products. For example, there are two approaches in steel production, namely traditional processing technology and advanced processing technology. However, there are many ways to save steel, such as reducing machine weight, reducing corrosion, extending equipment life, adopting less chipping technology, recycling, replacing steel with wood and plastic, and better cropping. Ninth, saving is a kind of social production. For instance, production development is rather professional. Iron and steel production has to rely on the metallurgical industry. For saving, other than the metallurgical industry, every department can make a contribution. The whole society can be motivated to save. Tenth, saving is a kind of production with good economic benefits. The practices show that the economic benefits generated by saving are usually better than those generated by production. Take energy as an example. If the investment in saving one ton of energy in one year is lower than 400 yuan (based on the fixed prices in 1980), saving is more economical than production. In fact, many energy saving measures do not cost much. In the sixth five-year plan period, when a lot of capital was spent on energy saving measures, the investment spent on saving for one ton of energy was lower than 400 yuan. It can be seen that satisfactory savings have many advantages. It is not a passive measure, but a positive energy development measure. This is one of the important guidelines for energy saving in China.

4. **Six overall saving strategies**

The CPC Central Committee and the State Council think highly of saving. Back in 1956, the second Plenary Session of the 8th CPC National Congress proposed the policy of promoting saving and working against waste. In the next year, Chairman Mao discussed saving in his report On Correct Handling of Contradictions among the People. He pointed out that "China was a socialist country and it was lagging in economy. This was a big contradiction……One solution is comprehensive and continuous saving." Guided by this principle, several mass movements for increasing production and saving were conducted in China, but because of the out-dated economic development policy in the old systems, these activities did not achieve good results. During the Great Leap Forward and the Cultural Revolution, this approach was not taken at all. After the Third Plenary Session of the Eleventh CPC National Congress, the party shifted its focus to economic development, aiming to improve economic efficiency. Saving once again became an important item in the agenda of the CPC Central Committee and State Council. Since the reform and opening up, great achievements have been made in saving through the introduction of technology, technological upgrades, improvements in management, more investment in saving, and enhancing awareness of saving. However, many problems still exist. Particularly, saving is not a strategy goal. Attention is still paid to production, whereas saving is neglected. Waste in living is opposed strongly, but waste in production is still well accepted. When the economy is not good, saving is important. But when the economy is good, saving is forgotten. Saving is just an administrative slogan. Little effort was spent on saving. Restrictive saving is more popular than satisfactory saving. In order to implement a saving strategy and promote saving to a higher level, the following strategies must be taken.

(1) Attention should not be paid to production only. Production and saving are equally important. Saving is a short-term goal.
(2) The focus should change from opposing waste in living to opposing waste in production.
(3) Saving should be implemented in the format of a mass movement. It should not be intermittent, either. Saving should be as continuous as production.
(4) Saving should rely on technological progress and improvement in management, not on administrative slogans.Saving should rely on technological progress and improvement in management, not on administrative slogans.
(5) Change single-element saving to all-element saving.
(6) Saving should not be the business of a few departments and of a small number of people. Saving should be implemented by all of the departments, all of the enterprises, and all of the people.
(7) Change local saving to systemic saving.
(8) Change restrictive saving to satisfactory saving.

In the past decade, these strategies were partly implemented. But they have not yet been completely implemented. Compared with foreign countries, waste in China is serious. The potential for saving is large. In order to implement the above strategies more quickly, a comprehensive saving strategy should be promoted in China. This comprehensive strategy comprises six overall strategies, namely all of the factors, all of the satisfaction, all of the time, all of the aspects, all of the processes, and all of the people.

All factor saving. China has rich human resources, but the per capita of other production factors, including energy, raw materials, transportation capacity, capital, land, water, and mineral resources are very limited. Furthermore, high-quality talents are not sufficient, either. According to the input-output economic laws, the saving of one production factor means increasing the input of other production factors. Similarly, the saving of one production factor can result in the saving of other production factors. Therefore, saving cannot rely on one single factor. All factors involved in saving and comprehensive factor saving should be promoted.

All satisfactory saving. Saving that completely meets reasonable demands is true saving. It is equivalent to production development. All satisfactory saving is the direction for saving in China. We should stick to and advocate this kind of saving.

All time saving. As long as there is input, saving is possible. Investment occurs all the time, so saving exists all the time. Saving should not be intermittent; it should be implemented all the time.

All aspects saving. Saving is closely related with regions, sections, industries, enterprises, and families. Therefore, saving should be implemented across all aspects of social life.

All process saving. Saving occurs in the entire process of production, circulation, distribution, and consumption, including resource exploration, scientific research, planning and design, infrastructure construction, production and operation, circulation, and consumption. Saving is a systemic project. All process saving and systemic saving should be advocated.

All people saving. Saving is a social activity. Everyone should pay attention to saving in production and living. All people saving should be advocated.

In the six overall strategies, all factors, all satisfactory, and all time reflect the purpose and requirements of saving. All aspect, all process and all people indicate who will implement the saving. The core of comprehensive saving is all factor, all satisfactory, and all time saving. The comprehensive saving strategy was proposed based on the thoughts of Chairman Mao and the experiences of successes and failures in practice. It conforms to the objective economic laws.

23.12.2 Goals and Plans for China's Comprehensive Energy Strategy

1. **Comprehensive saving strategic goal ABC and indicator system**

A comprehensive saving strategy is an important part in China's economic development strategy. The former serves the latter. Therefore, the goal of the comprehensive saving strategy should be coordinated with China's new economic development strategy. According to the new economic development strategic goals and the thinking regarding overall strategic saving, the author proposes a comprehensive saving strategy with the overall goal as follows: under the premise to meet the strategic goals of economic development, to make the minimal invest to gain the greatest economic and social benefits. The overall goal of this comprehensive saving should meet the requirements of the overall goal of the economic development strategy. The overall goal of the comprehensive saving is not a single goal, but a multiple level one. Some goals can be quantified, whereas some cannot. Here, we will focus on quantitative indicators that can reflect the overall goal of the comprehensive saving. These quantitative indicators can be chosen in different ways. First, technical efficiency, such as energy efficiency, the utilization of steel, and timber utilization, is chosen as the indicator; second, the quantity of saving, such as how many tons of energy has been saved, how many million tons of steel has been saved, and how much capital has been saved, is chosen as the indicator; third, input per unit is chosen as the indicator; fourth, output per unit is chosen as the indicator. The author found that these indicators could not be chosen for the overall goal of the comprehensive strategic saving, because they were not related to the overall goals of the national economic development strategy. In other words, these indicators do not reflect the requirements of the overall goals of the economic development strategy. Technical efficiency indicators reflect the effective use of production factors. High technical efficiency indicates more saving of production factors, but the drawback of this indicator is that it is not connected with the economy. For example, steel utilization efficiency can be improved from 50 to 80% when manufacturing a machine. The amount of steel consumed drops from 1.6 to 1 t, with a saving of 0.6 t of steel. If the profit of making this machine cannot compensate the steel consumed in manufacturing it, the one ton of steel does not contribute to the economic development at all. Instead, it has a negative impact. In addition, machines with poor steel utilization may generate good economic benefits. Thus, technical efficiency does not reflect the actual contribution to the economic development. The quantity of saving reflects the size of saving, but it does not reflect the requirements of the economic development strategic goals. Input per unit reflects the amount of saved materials, and it is useful for assess the saving in all departments, but this indicator is very professional. It can only be applied for comparing the same products; it is not suitable for comparing different products. Furthermore, it is connected with the economic development goals only if a product is produced for some long-term goals with bad economic benefits. Even though input per unit for this product is low, the production of this product wastes resources. Compared with input per unit, output per unit has advantages. It is suitable for comparing industries. For example, the energy consumption per 10,000 yuan in light industry is lower than that in heavy industry. Therefore, increasing the proportion of light industry can save energy. However, output is not an economic efficiency indicator. It does not reflect the requirements of the economic development strategic goals. It is not suitable for indicating a comprehensive saving strategy. These aforementioned four indicators can only reflect parts of the requirements for comprehensive saving. They cannot reflect all of the requirements of comprehensive saving. The author thinks that the indicators for the comprehensive strategic saving should be found based on the relationship between the input of production factors and economic development. The author found that two relationships exist between the input of production factors and economic development. One is the relationship between the quantity of the production factor input and the quantity of economic development. The other is the relationship between the growth rate of production factor input and the economic growth rate.

Two indicators reflect the first relationship.

(1) Input of GDP (or input coefficient, unit energy consumption of GDP), expressed as the following formula:

$$A = \text{input of production factors}/GDP \tag{23.19}$$

(2) Unit input of GDP (or economic efficiency of input), expressed as the following formula:

$$B = \text{GDP/input of production factors} \tag{23.20}$$

Indicator *A* and indicator *B* are reciprocals of each other. The smaller the indicator *A*, the better. The larger the indicator *B*, the better. For example, it is desirable that 10,000 yuan of GDP energy consumption is small and that the GDP per ton of energy is large.

The indicator reflects that the second relationship is input growth coefficient (or elasticity coefficient of input), expressed as the following formula:

$$C = \text{annual growth rate of input/annual growth rate of economy} \tag{23.21}$$

The elasticity coefficient of input is related to the input coefficient and the economic efficiency of input. When the elasticity coefficient of input is >1, the input coefficient increases and the economic efficiency of input decreases. When the elasticity coefficient of input is equal to 1, the input coefficient and the economic efficiency of input remain unchanged. When elasticity coefficient of input is <1, the input coefficient decreases and the economic efficiency of input increases.

The author thinks that indicators *A*, *B*, and *C* essentially reflect the relationship between the production factors of inputs and the economic development strategic goals. It is reasonable and practical to choose them as indicators of the comprehensive saving strategy goals. From the perspective of the overall goal of comprehensive saving strategy, it is desirable that the input coefficient is small, the economic efficiency of input is large, and that elasticity coefficient of input is <1. They should be determined by the actual circumstances.

The author found that there is a quantitative relationship between three indicators *A*, *B*, and *C* and the 27 indicators. This relationship is an indicator system for a comprehensive saving strategy based on indicators *A*, *B*, and *C*. The 27 indicators are: the GDP and its average annual growth rate, the input production, the import and export of input, the input inventory, the input and its average annual growth rate, the saving of input, the annual saving rate and the total rate of saving, the efficiency of the input system, the input of product per unit, the input of production per unit, the input of labor per unit, the input of income per unit, the input per capita, the GDP (GNP) per capita, the rate of product and production, the rate of production and added value, the rate of labor and income, the rate of income and added value, production, the amount of labor, the quality, the price, the cost, the basic depreciation, the structure coefficient of added value in the material production sectors, the structure coefficient of added value in the service sectors, and the population structure coefficient. Therefore, *A*, *B*, and *C* are comprehensive indicators. They can reflect the status of comprehensive saving and economic benefits (efficiency). They are suitable for use by states, regions, departments, and enterprises.

2. **Development laws of ABC indicators in China**

The author found that the development and change of indicators *A*, *B*, and *C* follow certain laws in China and across the world. The laws of development and change of *A*, *B*, and *C* are the same as those of energy *A*, *B*, and *C*.

(1) Changes in the input coefficient A follow the pattern low → up → down → low. Changes in the economic efficiency of input *B* follow the pattern high → down → up → high. Changes in the input coefficient A follow the pattern low → up → down → low. Changes in the economic efficiency of input *B* follow the pattern high → down → up → high.
(2) Changes in the elasticity coefficient of input *C* follow the pattern near 1 → >1 → <1 → near 1.
(3) Trend of input coefficient and elasticity coefficient of input in China. Changes of input coefficient in China have four cases. In the first case, the input coefficient continues to drop for timber, arable land, water, labor, and grain. This is caused by the constraints of natural resources. In the second case, the input coefficient begins to drop for energy, cast iron, and cotton. In the third case, the input coefficient just reaches the summit but does not yet drop for fertilizer, steel, lead, zinc, sulfuric acid, rubber, and cargo turnover. In the fourth case, the input coefficient is at its highest level and continues to keep this level for cement, aluminum, plastic, and chemical fiber.

3. **Comprehensive saving strategic goals planning and analysis**

(1) Process of comprehensive saving goals planning
The planning for comprehensive saving strategic goals is a comprehensive project. It includes five steps.
The first step is to determine the economic growth target. The second step is, based on the potential of saving and increasing efficiency and on the requirements saving and increasing efficiency, to determine the input coefficient *A*, the input economic efficiency *B*, and the elastic coefficient of input *C* first, and then to determine the saving and increasing efficiency indicators, such as saving efficiency, saving, the comprehensive saving rate and growth rate, efficiency, and the comprehensive growth rate. The third step is to determine the demand for input. The fourth step is to determine the possible supply of input. The fifth step is to make plans for balancing supply and demand. Among the five steps, the second one is the most important.
(2) Principle of comprehensive saving and increasing efficiency goals planning

    (1) Three principles are required to be followed when making economic growth goals. First, follow the objective laws of economic growth in China and in different regions. Second, ensure the completion of national and regional economic growth goals. Third, prepare low, medium, and high plans. In other words, the lowest goal should be considered for reserving some room. The highest goal should also be considered for the direction of effort.

Estimations for regions should be based on local economic growth laws and on the growth goal. Avoid the use of one single plan for all of the regions across the country.

(2) Four principles are required to be followed when making comprehensive saving goals. First, design comprehensive saving schemes according to the economic development predication schemes. Second, consider the differences between the domestic situation and the overseas situation and the differences among regions. Consider the actual potential for saving and the potential for increasing efficiency. Refer to the trend and laws of changes in past years regarding input parameters, input economic efficiency, and the elasticity coefficient of input. Generally, the input coefficient should decrease gradually. The input economic efficiency should increase gradually. The elasticity coefficient of input should be <1. Then, set indicators for the saving rate, saving quantity, increased efficiency rate, and increased efficiency according to the values of *A*, *B*, and *C*. Next, calculate the overall saving rate and the overall increased efficiency rate indicators. Third, given the economic benefits, the input coefficients for some emerging industrial raw materials, such as plastics and chemical fibers, are expected to rise. But overall savings exist for these materials, because they replace raw materials that are short or have poor benefits. For example, plastics replace steel and wood. Cement replaces steel and wood. Chemical fiber replaces cotton. Fourth, consider the impact of per capita consumption level and structural changes.

(3) Two principles for determining the demand of major input. First, according to the requirements of saving and increasing efficiency, set the saving quantity, namely the demand, after the saving is deducted. This is not a zero saving demand, which is the demand when the saving rate is zero, based on input coefficient during the reference period. This is not a negative saving demand, which is the demand when the actual coefficient is larger than the input coefficient during the reference period. Special cases are exempted. Second, consider the actual amount of supply.

(4) Three principles for determining the main input supply. First, satisfy the demand as much as possible—but the total input should be considered. Land, water, and labor are constrained by natural and by demographic conditions. Energy and raw material are constrained by production, import, environment, and resources. Unlimited investment is not possible. Only a modest investment is applicable. Second, prediction must be based on possible production growth. This is the most reliable and most important supply. Produce more to meet the demands. Third, prediction must be based on the possible import quantity. Import can only be a supplement supply, because it is constrained by foreign exchanges and by foreign countries.

(5) When developing supply and demand balance schemes, adjust the schemes, economic growth goals, saving and increasing efficiency goals, input demands, input production, import, or export, if unbalance

appears. The goal is to keep a balance among the economy, the saving and increasing efficiency, the demand, and the supply. The following four principles are for determining which of the above measures is the best. ① Adjustment of economic growth goals must be cautious. Usually, a decrease should be avoided. The minimum increase goal must be achieved. If possible, set higher goals. ② Because the economic benefits and the comprehensive benefits of saving are better than those of production development, more measures for saving and for increasing efficiency should be taken. Higher goals should be set. ③ According to the actual demand and the degree of shortage, adjust the input demand. Set lower goals if possible. Certain demands, such as abundant labor, can be set to higher goals. ④ It is better to set lower goals for major input production supply and import. Avoid setting higher goals for them.

(3) Methods for comprehensive saving and increasing efficiency goals planning

(1) Combination of mathematical model predication and empirical prediction. The same data can be predicated through a variety of mathematical models. Different models generate different results. Therefore, the selection of mathematic modes does not depend on the scientificity of the mathematic modes or on their results, but depends on whether or not the results fit the facts. Thus, prediction based on experience is necessary. The prediction of experts based on experience is very important.

(2) The focus of comprehensive saving and increasing the efficiency goal planning is to determine indicators, both for assessing comprehensive saving and for their values. The core of the indicators for assessing comprehensive saving are the three saving efficiency indicators *A*, *B*, and *C* at the first level and six indicators at the second level, including the saving rate, saving quantity, increasing efficiency rate, increasing efficiency quantity, comprehensive saving rate, and comprehensive increasing efficiency. Altogether, this indicator system has nine indicators. According to demand, these indicators can be grouped into two categories. One category includes the input coefficient, the saving rate, saving quantity, the elasticity coefficient of input, and the comprehensive saving rate. The other category includes the input economic efficiency, the increasing efficiency rate, the elasticity coefficient of input, and the comprehensive increasing efficiency. The first category focuses more on saving. It is widely applied, both in the past and at present. The second category focuses more on increasing the economic efficiency, and it is very important in the socialist market economy condition. In fact, these two groups of assessment indicators are interchangeable. Once one group is known, the other group is known, as well. Thus, either group can be applied for assessment based on the requirement. Here is the calculation method for the two groups of assessment indicators.

Group one:

Input coefficient Input/gross domestic product (GDP)

Saving rate annual saving rate: (1 − t target year input coefficient/input coefficient of reference year) × 100%

total saving rate: (1 − target year input coefficient/input coefficient of reference year) × 100%[26]

saving quantity basic comparison method: (input coefficient of reference year-input coefficient of target year) × target year GDP

relative ratio method: (input coefficient of previous year-input coefficient of present year) × present year GDP[27]

elasticity coefficient of input input growth rate/economic growth rate

comprehensive saving rate saving growth rate/economic growth rate.

Group two:

input economic efficiency gross domestic product (GDP)/input

growth efficiency annual growth efficiency: t(economic efficiency of target year input/economic efficiency of reference year − 1) × 100%

total growth efficiency: (economic efficiency of target year input/economic efficiency of reference year − 1) × 100%

growth basic comparison method: (economic efficiency of target year input-economic efficiency of reference year input) × target year GDP

relative ratio method: (economic efficiency of present year input-economic efficiency of previous year input) × present year GDP

elasticity coefficient of input input growth rate/economic growth rate

comprehensive efficiency efficiency growth/economic growth rate.

(4) Result analysis for comprehensive saving goal planning

   (1) Economic growth goals and analysis of the eighth five-year plan period, ten years, and 2010

The prediction for the comprehensive saving goals must be based on the economic growth goals. Economic growth chooses three periods: the eighth five-year plan, ten years, and 2010. Four schemes are developed for each period. The following four schemes are set for the eighth five-year plan period and for ten years. First, the

[26]Average annual saving rate should be adopted in the planning.

[27]Basic comparison method should be adopted in the planning. The relative ratio method should be adopted in the annual review.

average annual economy growth rate for the eighth five-year plan period and for ten years are both set as 7%. This growth rate was set based on the average speed required by the economic development goal proposed by the 12th and the 13th CPC national congress. According to this goal, the GDP in 2000 should be quadruple that of 1980. This is a low-speed scheme. Second, the average annual economy growth rate for the eighth five-year plan period and the ninth five-year plan period are both set at 8%. This speed is the lower limit value of the high speed. It is lower than the growth rate in the sixth five-year plan period, but close to that of the seventh five-year plan period. Third, the average annual economy growth rate for the eighth five-year plan period and the ninth five-year plan period are both set at 9%. This is the middle value of high speed. Fourth, the average annual economy growth rate for the eighth five-year plan period and the ninth five-year plan period are both set at 10%. This is the lower limit value of over high speed. This is a high speed scheme. When studying schemes for the eighth five-year plan three years ago,[28] the author proposed that the economic growth in the eighth five-year plan period should maintain a middle-high speed. At that time, the low scheme was set as 6%. The high scheme was set as 8%. The middle scheme was set as 7%. The author also pointed out that the average annual economy growth rate for the eighth five-year plan period and for the ninth five-year plan period could not be lower than 6 or 7%. Most likely, it should be higher than 7%. The 14th CPC National Congress proposed that the economic development under the socialist market economic system should be accelerated in the 1990s, striving for a rate of 8 or 9%. The author thought that the growth rate of 8 or 9% could be achieved. 10% is a natural economic growth rate in China. It is also a practical scheme. Therefore, the author proposed the aforementioned four schemes. It is estimated that the GNP per capita in 1995 will be over $800. In 2000, the GNP per capita is estimated to be more than $1000. The goals set by Deng Xiaoping can be achieved. Because 1980 was chosen as the benchmark in the economic development strategy proposed at the 12th CPC National Congress, the fixed prices of the fixed exchange rates in 1980 were adopted in the schemes.

As for the year of 2010, the average annual economy growth rate for 1990s was set as 9%. Based on this rate, the average annual economy growth rates for the 10 years from 2000 to 2010 were set as 6–9%, in four schemes. Given that the first 10 years in the twenty-first century is the mature period for the socialist market economy in China, economic growth can still be at high speed, based on requirements. But because the base is larger, the growth rates in these four schemes were set 1% lower than those in 1990s. The author thought that this was feasible.

(2) Comprehensive saving goals and analysis of the eighth five-year plan period, ten years, and 2010 based on the four principles for determining the comprehensive saving goals, combine mathematical prediction and empirical prediction. Then adjust the goals according to the status of supply and demand. The planning repeats the following process: mathematical model prediction → empirical prediction → input coefficient prediction → saving demand prediction →

[28] Xu, S. B. (1990). Thoughts about economic growth rate in the eighth five-year plan period.

production supply prediction → supply and demand prediction and adjustment, until the expected results are achieved.

Three mathematical models are applied: the curve fitting method, the distributed lag method, and the autoregressive moving average method. There are 21 types of production factor inputs, such as materials, transportation capacity, financial resources, manpower, and natural forces. Each input is estimated based on the input coefficients and the saving demand in the four economic growth schemes in each of the three periods. Prediction and adjustment are implemented repeatedly. One typical model and prediction result is selected from each mathematic model. At the end, one model and its result is selected from the three representative models and results. This result is the comprehensive saving goal recommended by this planning. It should be noted that, although the comprehensive savings goals fall into two groups and nine goals, the input coefficient is the key indicator. Once it is available, the other six goals (excluding the comprehensive saving rate and the comprehensive growth rate) can be easily calculated.

(3) Prediction and analysis of input saving demand in the eighth five-year plan period, ten years, and 2010

According to the input coefficient of comprehensive saving and increasing efficiency goals (or economic efficiency of input), it is easy to calculate the input demand (= input coefficient × GDP or GNP ÷ economic efficiency of input). This demand should be the demand with saving and increasing efficiency considered. It is expected to be fulfilled. Thus, it is called the "saving demand." The saving demand depends on the strength of saving. If the saving strength is large, the saving demand can be small. Saving strength depends on the actual conditions. Table 23.28 lists the expected values of the saving demands for 23 inputs across three periods. The expected values of demand estimated based on saving goals are important for planning production.

(4) Prediction and analysis of input supply in the eighth five-year plan period, ten years, and 2010

Input supply relies on production. Inadequate and superfluous parts rely on import and export. Although a production prediction is very important, it is not the focus of this study. In addition, the economic situation has changed quickly, in recent years. Production prediction in the eighth five-year plan period and in the ten-year plan has changed considerably. To this end, the author has implemented a production prediction. Assume that the production growth rate of input in the eighth five-year plan period is the average annual growth rate in the seventh five-year plan period. The production growth rate of sulfuric acid, soda ash, and caustic soda achieves the average annual growth rate of the 10 years from 1980 to 1990. The production growth rate for most products drops from 1995 to 2000 and from 2000 to 2010, excluding plastic and cargo transportation. The prediction is not perfect, so it can only be used as a reference. The results of the prediction are listed in Table 23.28

Table 23.28 Prediction of saving demand and production of 23 inputs for the eighth five-year plan period, ten years, and 2010

Input	Expected saving			Expected production			Expected annual average growth rate (%)			Note
	1995	2000	2010	1995	2000	2010	1990–1995	1995–2000	2000–2010	
I. Materials										
1. Energy (100 million t of standard coal)	12.6	15.2	20.4	12.6	15.3	20.6	4	4	3	
2. Power (100 million kWh)	9015	13,260	24,650	9396	13,800	24,710	8.6	8	6	
3. Materials (100 million t of standard materials)	33,388	40,333	49,060	34,100	42,520	51,950	6.3	4.5	2	
4. Steel (100 million t)	7890	9160	10,490	7190	9180	11,190	6.9	5	2	
5. Cement (10,000 t)	26,960	33,725	41,400	30,100	38,416	44,530	7.5	5	3	
6. Wood (10,000 m^3)	5855	6340	6390	5430	5295	5300	−2.5	−0.5	0	
7. Plastic (10,000 t)	800	1560	4460	418	840	4040	13	15	17	
8. Cast iron (10,000 t)	1710	1978	2260	1969	2510	3370	7.3	5	3	
9. Aluminum (10,000 t)	140	190	249							
10. Rubber (10,000 t)	119	164	270							
11. Sulfuric acid (10,000 t)	1370	1820	2715	1498	1875	2775	4.6	4.6	4	
12. Sodium carbonate (10,000 t)	520	720	1215	580	740	1205	8.9	5	5	
13. Sodium carbonate (10,000 t)	406	540	745	440	564	760	5.7	5	3	
14. Fertilzers (10,000 t)	2976	3608	3960	2670	3750	4140	7.3	7	1	
15. Grain (10,000 t)	47,445	53,074	64,510	49,300	54,430	63,170	2	2	1.5	
16. Chemical fiber (10,000 t)	276	400	675	290	420	684	11.7	8	5	

(continued)

Table 23.28 (continued)

Input	Expected saving			Expected production			Expected annual average growth rate (%)			Note
	1995	2000	2010	1995	2000	2010	1990–1995	1995–2000	2000–2010	
17. Cotton (10,000 t)	540	615	750	490	540	658	1.7	2	2	
II. Transportation capacity										
1. Freight amount (100 million t)	139	196	335	126	177	317	5.4	7	6	
2. Freight turnover (100 million km)	36,210	49,440	90,000	37,890	50,700	90,800	7.7	6	6	
III. Financial resources (100 million yuan)	28,230	43,140	81,800	31,870	46,827	83,860	9	8	6	
IV. Manpower (10,000 persons)	61,890	69,550	72,500	64,500	71,270	78,700	2.6	2	1	
V. Natural forces										
1.Water (100 million t)	6690	7850	10,000							
2. Land (100 million mu)	95.5	101.3	110							

(5) Prediction and analysis of supply and demand for input in the eighth five-year plan period, ten years, and 2010

Supply and demand must be balanced in planning and in actual economic activates. Based on the predictions of saving demand and production supply, it can be seen that most production factors have achieved balance in supply and demand. Some have a slight surplus, and some suffer a slight shortage. The largest shortage of supply has occurred for plastic, cotton, wood, water, and land. Measures such as increasing production, increasing imports, and promoting saving and increasing saving efficiency might be helpful for maintaining the balance between supply and demand for these products.

(5) Analysis of comprehensive saving potential

Comparison is usually applied for estimating a saving potential. There are four objectives for comparison: ① the advanced level in history; ② the advanced level of others; (3) the advanced level that can be achieved through current science and technology; ④ the theoretically advanced level. There is a large gap between the major input coefficients in China and those in other countries. Gaps also exist among industries and enterprises. The energy input coefficient, namely the energy consumption per 10,000 US dollars in GDP, in China is 1–6 times higher than that in foreign countries. Particularly, the gaps are 1–4 times for steel, 1–11 times for cement, and 1–13 times for fertilizers. The author found that the energy input coefficient in China is the highest among more than 100 countries and regions around the world. In addition, the input coefficients of steel, cement, and fertilizer are likely to be the highest as well. Thus, the potential for comprehensive saving in China is large. If the input coefficients are increased to the level of other countries such as India, the input coefficients of energy, steel, cement, and fertilizer in China will drop to half. Among the saving goals mentioned above, the input coefficients of energy and fertilizer in 2000 are set to drop 50% from those in 1980. The achievement of these goals is possible. Considering the actual conditions in China, the input coefficients of steel, cement, the transportation capacity, and financial resources in 2000 are set to drop 34–44%, 11–22%, 32–36%, and 22–24%, respectively, from their levels in 1980. Due to the constraints of natural conditions, the input coefficients for timber, grain, cotton, manpower, water, and land in 2000 are expected to drop more than 2/3 from their levels in 1980. These goals can be achieved via hard work.

How to reduce these input coefficients, or to increase the economic efficiency of input? The author found that input coefficients are related with input technical efficiency and economic efficiency. In order to reduce input coefficients, input technical efficiency and economic efficiency must be increased simultaneously. In other word, saving for input includes both technical saving and economic saving.

(1) Analysis of saving potential by improving economic efficiency

The author found that about two-thirds of the saving potential of input can be achieved by increasing economic efficiency. This two-thirds is the potential for economic efficiency. Increasing the economic efficiency can be achieved by increasing the production and the quality, by saving capital, by reducing cost, and by adjusting the economic structure. Take energy, as an example. The potential for energy saving generated by adjusting the national economic structure, including the industrial structure, the industry structure, and the product structure, accounts for 25%. The potential for energy saving generated by reducing costs accounts for 18%. The potential for energy saving generated by saving capital accounts for 7%. In the Yanhua, the total amount of saved energy, energy saving generated by these three measures, accounts for 52.4%. In the sixth five-year plan period, the energy input coefficient (GDP energy consumption) dropped 21.4%, most of which was generated by increasing the economic efficiency. The achievement of all of our goals in the future relies on increasing our economic efficiency.

(2) Analysis of saving potential through improving technical efficiency

The author found that about one-third of the saving potential of inputs can be achieved by increasing the technical efficiency. This one-third is the potential for technical efficiency. Due to the low level of management, the effective utilization rate of input in China has been low. Particularly, the effective utilization rates of energy, fertilizers, timber, irrigation water, freight trucks, glass, steel, and industrial fixed assets equipment are 32%, 30%, 35%, 40%, 52%, 60%, 65%, and 70–80%, respectively. Practice has proven that the potential for technical saving in China is large. Achievements can be made only by improving management. This is what is called "receiving floating property." Sometimes, only a small technical improvement is needed. At other times, a major technical improvement is needed. Compared with production development, the cost for saving can be smaller, but good comprehensive benefits can be achieved. For example, the investment on saving one ton of energy is 1/3 less than that of production development.

23.12.3 Steps and Key Points of China's Comprehensive Saving Strategy

1. **Steps for implementing comprehensive saving strategy**

According to the requirements for China's economic development strategy from 1980 to the mid-twenty-first century, there are three steps that must be taken in order to achieve this strategy. The first step is to double the GDP in 1990; the Chinese people can be barely feed and clothed. The second step is to double the GDP again in 2000; the Chinese people will have a comfortable level of living. The third step is to achieve a GDP per capita of $4000 (at the price in 1980); the Chinese people's standard of living should reach the level of developed countries in the 1970s. Accordingly, comprehensive saving should also be implemented in three stages. The first stage will occur from 1980 to 1990. The goal for this stage is to lay foundation, especially for water and land. The second stage will occur from 1990 to 2000. This is a comprehensive saving stage. The foundation for comprehensive saving should be ready in 2000. First, the comprehensive saving should have its own operating mechanism. Second, people must consider that comprehensive saving is as important as production. Third, saving should rely on science and technology. The third stage starts at the beginning of the twenty-first century. In this stage, comprehensive saving will develop quickly. The utilization rates of production factors will increase quickly. The gap between China and developed countries will become more narrow. Based on the domestic and overseas experience in energy saving, comprehensive saving should be implemented in three steps. In the first step, improve management to receive floating property. Reduce wastes in manpower, materials, financial resources, transportation capacity, and natural forces. In the second step, a small reform is implemented. With a small amount of investment, upgrade the existing processes and equipment to achieve a better saving result. In the third step, a large reform is implemented. With a large amount of investment, conduct major reforms on existing processes and equipment.

2. **Key points of comprehensive saving strategy**

Considering the potential of saving, comprehensive saving should focus on production. In recent years, waste exists in every aspect of people's life. But the GNP per capita is China is still low. The consumption level per capita is low as well. Thus, waste in living is limited. Due to the large population, the total amount of waste is huge if everyone wastes just a little. Therefore, attention should be paid to saving in living. But the focus of saving is in production, particularly in the usage of intermediate products. Take energy, as an example. The energy consumption in production accounts for about four-fifths. Other production factors, such as steel, wood, cement, fertilizer, machinery and equipment, chemical fiber, and cotton are all considered as consumption in production. Their saving potential is large.

Given the economic benefits of the saving production factors, the focus is the saving of those production factors that are short in supply, such as oil, coal, natural gas, electricity, steel, cement, wood, plastic, chemical fiber, and fertilizer in materials; fixed assets and liquidity in financial resources; roads and railway in transportation capacity; and water, land, and mineral resources in natural forces. Meanwhile, the saving of those production factors that are abundant in supply also needs attention. The method for these production factors is different. The focus is not saving in usage, but complete utilization. For example, full use should be made of surplus manpower. Otherwise, this manpower will be wasted. Attention should also be paid to time saving.

The saving of each production factor falls into two types: economic saving and technical saving. Economical saving refers to achieving saving by measures of improving economic efficiency, such as reducing costs, adjusting the industry and product structure, improving quality, and increasing economic benefits. Technical saving means achieving saving by measures of improving technical efficiency, such as technical renovation, technical development, and the introduction of technology. The author found that in the total saving, economic saving accounts for two-thirds and technical saving accounts for one third. Economic saving takes effect across every production factor, whereas technical saving takes effect on certain production factors only. Thus, attention should be paid to both economic saving and technical saving. However, in a certain period, economic saving will be the focus. But this does not mean that technical saving is not important or that technical saving should be neglected.

23.12.4 Countermeasures and Measures for Comprehensive Saving in China

Compared with foreign countries, the amount of waste in production factors in China is startling. The author found that there are five kinds of waste in China. The first one is consciousness waste, which is caused by lack of saving awareness and efficiency sense. The second is institutional waste, which is caused by the drawbacks of the old traditional planned economy system. The third is structural waste, which is caused by an unreasonable economic structure. The fourth is technical waste, which is caused by out-of-date technologies. The fifth is management waste, which is the result of a low level of management. For the five kinds of wastes, we propose the following countermeasures.

1. **Enhance people's consciousness in saving and efficiency and reduce consciousness waste**

In a sense, consciousness waste is the largest waste. However, regarding the cost of saving, it is the easiest approach to enhancing people's consciousness in saving and efficiency. Therefore, more efforts are need to enhance people's consciousness in saving and efficiency. The goal is to form the atmosphere of valuing saving and pursuing efficiency.

Public opinion regarding saving and increasing economic efficiency should be led via network, radio, television, newspapers, magazines, and textbooks in the elementary and middle schools. People should realize the importance and the urgency of saving and increasing economic efficiency. People should realize that China has a large population but limited resources. Without implementing comprehensive saving and without increasing economic efficiency, it will be impossible for China to achieve economic development. The three-step strategy will not be achieved. Implementing comprehensive saving and increasing economic efficiency are not expedient measures, but long-term strategies. They are the basic national policy for China.

2. **Deepen reform, perform efficiency revolution, and dig the potential of institutional saving**

Due to institutional reasons, the waste in the production factors of production waste in China is huge. In the old traditional planned economy system, even if saving awareness existed, it was hard to implement comprehensive saving. People always report that economic efficiency is low, and that this low economic efficiency is caused by insufficient capital, insufficient per capita resources, poor resource conditions, an irrational industrial structure, out-of-date technology and equipment, poor labor quality, and a low management level. In fact, these are not the main reasons. The primary reason is the traditional socialist planned economic system. In this system, everything is controlled by a plan made by a small group of people. Everyone passively relies on the government and enjoys equal distribution. There is no competition. The initiative, creativity, and enthusiasm of the over 1.3 billion Chinese people do not play their roles. Therefore, everyone is waiting for capital and resources from the government. Nobody wants to change the poor resource conditions. Few people care about the unreasonable industry structure. No one is motivated to upgrade technology and equipment. There is no difference in payment to reflect the difference in labor quality. Administrative staffs have nothing to do with those at the management level. The most serious drawbacks of the traditional planned economic system are the huge wastes in production factors and the low economic efficiency. No piecemeal reform will work; the only solution is to perform an efficiency revolution,[29] abandoning the low-efficiency planned economic system and adopting the high-efficiency socialist market economic system.

Since the reform and opening up, the second revolution led by Comrade Deng Xiaoping actually led China's efficiency revolution. Our research results show that the waste of production factors under the traditional planned economy system was very serious. The comprehensive saving rate was −8.8%. In contrast, after the reform and opening up (1981–1988), the comprehensive saving rate was 58%. The effect of comprehensive saving was significant. Next, by comparing the input and the output before and after the reform and opening up, we get the following results. In the traditional planned economy period (1954–1978), the average annual GDP growth rate was only 5.7%. The average annual growth rate of input (excluding manpower, grain, cotton, timber, land, and water) was twice the average annual GDP growth rate. Inputs included those on energy and raw material resources, fixed capital and liquidity, goods turnover and transportation capacity, labor, and natural forces (water and land). The elasticity coefficient of inputs was about 2. In the early period of the market economy (1981–1988), the average annual growth rate of the GDP was 10%, almost twice of that in the planned economy period. The average annual growth rate of all major inputs was half of the average annual growth rate of the GDP. The elasticity coefficient was about 0.5%. Thus, the economic efficiency in the early period of market economy was four times of that in the planned economy period. In other words, a new comprehensive input will generate 3 times of net output (GDP) in market economy compared with planned economy. For example, during the planned economy period (1954–1978), a 1% increase in GDP required a 1.58% increase in energy input. In the early period of the market economy (1981–1988), a 1% increase in GDP required 0.56% increase in energy input. During the past 14 years (the early period of socialist market economy), the economic efficiency increased dramatically in China. But compared with other market economy countries, China is still low in

[29]Xu, S.B. (1993). Efficiency revolution in China, "China's technical economy".

economic efficiency. The gap is large. For example, in 1990, the labor productivity in the United States, Japan, Germany, France, the United Kingdom are 36.5 times, 40.8 times, 45.9 times, 45.2 times, and 31 times higher, respectively, than China's. The energy economy efficiency in the United States, Japan, Germany, France, the United Kingdom are 3 times, 9.0 times, 6.9 times, 7.9 times, and 5.1 times higher, respectively, than that of China (see Tables 23.9, 23.10, and 23.11). Therefore, the potential for economic efficiency in China is large. The waste of production factors in China is still serious. Comprehensive saving and increasing economic efficiency must be implemented. The potential for institutional saving can be strengthened by deepening reform and by remaining on the road of the socialist market economy. Only in this way can the gap between China and the developed countries be narrowed.

3. **Accelerate structural adjustment and construct energy saving national economy system**

Compared with developed countries, China's industrial structure is extremely unreasonable. As a result, the level of waste in production factors is rather serious. The waste in production factors is related with institutional reasons. Our study suggests that, under the socialist market economic system, the economic structure can be adjusted by establishing the rules of fair competition and survival of the fittest. A saving type of national economy system can be established by following the value law and by generating more output with less input. Practice has proven that an input of the same quantity of production factors in an unreasonable economic structure can generate a small amount of benefits, or even a negative effect. Instead, input of the same quantity of production factors in a reasonable economic structure will generate the largest amount of benefits. A saving type of national economy system is a system that meets people's demand and generates high economic benefits. It consists of the industrial structures, industry structures, enterprise structures, and product structures of the first, second, and third industries.

The third industry is the saving industry. China has the most undeveloped third industry in the world. Therefore, accelerating the development of the third industry is an important measure to implementing comprehensive saving. The Central Committee has developed strategies and long-term plans for accelerating the development of the third industry. The focus of the industry structure adjustment is the second industry. Short-line industries in the second industry should be developed rapidly. Long-line industries in the second industry should be limited. In short, this is an important measure in implementing national industrial policies for reducing structural waste (Table 23.29).

4. **Enhance scientific progress and increase system efficiency of production factors**

Compared with consciousness waste, institutional waste, and structural waste, the quantity of technical waste is not so large. But technical waste is visible and tangible. It easily draws the attention of both the leaders and the ordinary people. After the reform and opening up, a large amount of manpower, materials, and financial

Table 23.29 Economy efficiency comparison between China and foreign countries in 1990

Indicator	China	US	Japan	Germany	France	UK
GDP (100 million domestic currency)	10,508 (17,681)	54,234	4,257,350	24,034	63,939	5439
GDP (in 100 million US dollars)	7006 (11,797)	54,234	31,676	16,130	1264	10,460
Employment (10,000 persons)	55,329	11,734	6128	2774	2176	2668
Energy input (10,000 t of standard coal)	98,703	250,466	49,590	32,947	22,090	28,816
Fertilizer input (10,000 t)	1880	2311	–	339	362	–
Steel input (10,000 t)	6635	8890	11,033	3844	1700	1901
Sulfuric acid input (10,000 t)	1197	3928	689	403	419	–
Cement input (10,000 t)	20,971	7094	8444	3043	2651	1432
Labor productivity (US dollars/person)	1266 (1)	46,220 (36.5)	51,690 (40.8)	58,147 (45.9)	57,279 (45.2)	39,205 (31)
Energy economy efficiency (US dollars/t)	710 (1)	2165 (3.0)	6388 (9.0)	4895 (6.9)	5642 (7.9)	3630 (5.1)
Economic efficiency of fertilizers (US dollars/t)	37,266 (1)	234,678 (6.3)	–	475,811 (12.8)	344,309 (9.2)	–
Economic efficiency of steel (US dollars/t)	10,559 (1)	61,006 (5.8)	28,710 (2.7)	41,961(4.0)	73,318 (6.9)	55,024 (5.2)
Economic efficiency of sulfuric acid (US dollars/t)	58,530 (1)	138,070 (2.4)	459,739 (7.9)	400,248 (6.8)	297,470 (5.1)	–

(continued)

resources was invested in technology introduction, technical renovation, and technical development. Great achievements have been made. Technical waste is being reduced. However, the lagging of technology in China has not changed. The potential for technical saving is huge. In the future, the guideline that technology is the first productive force must be implemented. Technical progress must be taken. Other

Table 23.29 (continued)

Indicator	China	US	Japan	Germany	France	UK
Economic efficiency of cement (US dollars/t)	3340 (1)	76,450 (22.9)	37,513 (11.2)	53,007 (15.9)	47,016 (14.1)	73,045 (21.9)

Note 1. Data of employed persons are in 1989
2. No consumption data for fertilizers, steel, sulfuric acid, and cement. Production is adopted
3. Data of UK, steel, and cement are in 1987
4. For the GDP of China, values in parentheses are current prices. Values outside parentheses are prices for 1980. Conversion to US dollars is based on the exchange rate in 1980. If the exchange rates of the listing years are adopted, all indicators will have lower values

than the energy utilization system rate, the raw material utilization system rate, the transportation utilization system rate, the capital utilization system rate, the natural resource utilization system rate, the manpower utilization system rate, and the time utilization system rate must be improved. Only in this way can technical waste be reduced. To this end, two measures should be taken.

(1) **Perform scientific research in the whole society**

First of all, make good use of existing scientific and technological institutions and forces. Under the leadership of the saving management team, reorganize the technical service centers and set up a technical network. Carry out a coordination of technical saving. Coordinate horizontally and vertically. Strengthen domestic and foreign technical exchanges and the information exchange. Establish a production and research consortium based on research departments, universities, and colleges. Implement saving research activities vigorously.

Secondly, establish a saving research and management department within the national saving management department. This department will take charge of the national saving technology and science. Particularly, this department will make saving plans, determine key projects, organize scientific research, and explore new saving technologies, new processes, and new products. It will also introduce advanced technology from abroad and will facilitate the application of domestic and overseas technologies. In addition, this department should monitor demonstration projects and should promote mature experience.

(2) **Make saving technical policies**

(1) Energy saving: ① Improve coal combustion and utilization technology and geothermal efficiency. The focus is to improve the thermal efficiency of industrial boilers and industrial kilns that consume 65% of total energy. Develop combined heat and power generation; combined heat, power, and cooling technology; central heating; and mobile heating boilers to improve the efficiency of heating systems. Particularly, develop optimization automation technology for large-scale circulating fluidized bed boiler,

high efficiency burners, high-quality fire-resistant insulation materials, and the heating system optimizing automatic control system. ② Improve energy efficiency. The focus is to increase the efficiency of common mechanical and electrical equipment, such as fans, pumps, motors, compressors, and transformers. Improve the energy saving of eight kinds of high energy consuming product process, including electric furnace steel, ferro alloys, electrolytic aluminum, calcium carbide, caustic soda, synthetic ammonia, cement, bricks, and tiles. ③ Develop mature new energy-saving processes, new technology, new equipment, and new materials for all industries, such as continuous casting and rolling, cement wet processes into dry processes, vertical cylinder preheaters, outside kiln decomposition, hollow bricks, stabilization of crude oil, and light hydrocarbon recovery. Focus on the development of combined cycle power generation, new processes, new technology, new equipment, and new materials with less energy consumption for distillery, paper mills, drug alkali, electrolyzing aluminum, and superconducting materials. ④ Take full advantage of the coal resources in China, and improve the ratio of coal used for power generation and coal washing. ⑤ Improve the efficiency of mechanical and electrical products. The focus is to improve the efficiency of 21 common electrical and mechanical equipment such as fans, pumps, motors, transformers, automotives, diesel engines, and waste heat utilization equipment. Gradually make energy-saving products dominant in production. Develop and apply motor speed control devices, new energy-saving instrumentation, energy saving refrigerators, and new electric lights. ⑥ Adopt low energy consuming and high efficiency transport equipment instead of lagging transport equipment. Based on the supply and demand of electric power and oil in China, gradually replace steam locomotives with electric locomotives and diesel locomotives. Replace petrol cars with large and medium-sized diesel vehicles. Promote fuel-saving technology, methanol, and wind sailing. ⑦ Replace oil with coal. Reduce oil usage in power plants, boilers, furnaces burning oil and oil fields, refineries, and oil for petrochemical plants. Develop coal-water slurry and pure coal. Explore the replacement for crude oil and natural gas. ⑧ Energy for urban people's lives. Focus on the development of shaped coal. Develop coal gas at some large and medium cities where conditions allow. Choose central heating in the northern, northwestern, and northeastern areas. Develop urban marsh gas. Focus on shaped coal, bonding agents, and new coal gas stoves. ⑨ With the same unit construction cost or with little increase in unit construction cost, improve the peripheral structure of the wall. Control heating and cooling temperatures. Reduce heating and air conditioning energy consumption. Improve building energy efficiency. ⑩ Develop soft science. Develop application system engineering and computer technology in energy management, energy saving prediction, and planning.

(2) Materials: ① Improve the finished product rate in the metallurgical industry. Increase product types of high efficiency steel. Improve product quality.

Focus on improving the continuous casting rate to accelerate the pace of transformation of small and medium-sized continuous casting process. Promote the development of high efficiency steel that is badly needed. ② Focus on the development of process technologies for blanks, such as casting, forging, and cold extrusion, as well as the processing process with little or no cutting, in the machinery manufacturing industry. Organize lateral joints as well as military and civilian joints. Develop specialized production and give full play to existing equipment potential. ③ Accelerate the development of powder metallurgy. Focus on the development of a powdered metal product for automobiles, agricultural machinery, and household appliances. ④ Combine domestic resources. Accelerate the development of plastics, composites, and new non-metallic materials. ⑤ Make reasonable use of steel in the construction industry. Promote pre-stressed concrete structures. Focus on the development of special equipment for pulling and anchors and prefabricated parts. Develop multi-floored and large span pre-stressing force buildings. ⑥ Develop material protection technologies. Improve the quality of basic parts.

(3) Water saving: ① Regarding water for agriculture, develop an underground pipeline for delivering water. Develop new irrigation technologies, such as plastic pipe irrigation, sprinkler irrigation, drip irrigation, and infiltrating irrigation. Improve the water utilization efficiency. In the dry areas, promote the dry cultivation of rice and develop dry farming agriculture. ② Regarding water for urban life and industry, renovate the water utilization process and achieve the multi-use and recycling of water. Improve the reuse of water. Develop advanced water-saving equipment. ③ Develop sewage treatment technology so as to make industrial wastewater be processed for reuse and for irrigation.

(4) Utilization of renewable metal resources: ① Develop the process equipment and technology for identifying, sorting, and pretreating waste. Develop decomposition devices and crushing equipment. ② Renovate and improve the regeneration process of common metal. ③ Study comprehensive recycling technologies for complex waste. ④ Develop comprehensive recycling technologies for waste. ⑤ Conduct soft science research. For example, establish a standard for the domestic waste of miscellaneous non-ferrous metals. Investigate the location, number, and variety of main non-ferrous metal scraps. Predict future changes and propose solutions.

5. **Promote management level, and reduce management waste**

In a broad sense, consciousness waste, institutional waste, structural waste, and technical waste are related to the low management level in China. In a narrow sense, management impacts comprehensive saving in the condition of the same system, the same economic structure, the same technology and equipment, and the same level of consciousness saving. Therefore, improving the management level is the key measure for implementing comprehensive saving in China.

(1) Under the conditions of the socialist market economy, comprehensive saving is controlled at the macro level by the national government. Its tasks are: (1) Develop policy and guidelines for comprehensive saving; ② Set goals for comprehensive saving. Develop medium and long-term plans and annual plans for comprehensive saving; ③ Implement measures for comprehensive saving. Supervise the implementation; ④ Research new situations and problems in comprehensive saving and solve them through coordinating with related sectors; ⑤ Develop management systems for comprehensive saving. Collaborate with legal departments to formulate laws for comprehensive saving and monitor their implementation; ⑥ Approve the assessment standards for comprehensive saving. Perform management. Evaluate assessment standards regularly. Release results of comprehensive saving achieved by regions, sections, and key enterprises; ⑦ Monitor demonstration projects for comprehensive saving.
(2) Make comprehensive saving planning. Incorporate comprehensive saving planning into national economic and social development plans.
(3) Make macro-economic policies for comprehensive saving.
(4) The principle that development and saving are both important should implemented in all fields across China. Protection and preferential policies should be given to comprehensive saving for a long time.

23.13 China Efficiency Revolution–Several Problems on Chinese Socialist Market Economy[30]

Research background, scientific significance of achievements and practical value.

The 14th CPC National Congress proposed the socialist market economic system in 1992. Before the congress, the State Planning Commission organized a delegation to Germany, headed by leaders of the Economic Research Center under the State Planning Commission. The author was the deputy head. This delegation first attended lectures hosted by German professors, received training in Heidelberg, and then made on-site visits. This delegation intended to learn the development of social market economy in Germany, particularly the difference between social market economy in Germany and free market economy in the United States as well as the difference between the social market economy in Germany and the socialist planned economy in Soviet Union. The author learned that the social market economy in Germany is a very successful market economy model and that Germans created it by themselves. A market economy pursues efficiency while a society needs fairness. Therefore, a social market economy is an economic system that pursues efficiency and fairness. Accordingly, this model fits China well. As a member of this delegation, the author recognized that this visit was a good chance to learn and to investigate. After returning to China, the delegation wrote a report to the CPC Central Committee. Later, the 14th

[30] Xu, S.B. (1993). Energy revolution in China, "China's technical economy".

CPC National Congress formally proposed to establish a socialist market economic system, which the author knows well. The main difference between China's socialist market economy and the social market economy in Germany is that China is under the leadership of the CPC and its goal is realizing socialism and communism. The author published many articles [280–283, 289], introducing the nature of China's socialist market economy and the social market economy in Germany, as well as highlighting their differences.

The result of this study has four parts. Part one proposes five models for fairness and efficiency development in respective countries, as well as the ideal model. It points out that China's socialist market economy is the fifth mode. Part two presents the ten characteristics of China's socialist market economic system, including the five essential requirements of the socialist economy and the ten common features of the market economy. China's socialist market economic system is different from the three market economic systems in the world. It is the fourth market economic model. Part three discusses five functions for Chinese government to use in order to manage the socialist market economy. It makes proposals for the arrangement of national macro-economic management institutions. Part four shows that there are three developmental phases for China's efficiency revolution. The author predicts that the economic growth rate and the efficiency improvement during this period will be the fastest in the history of China.

23.13.1 Comparison of Two Revolutions: Fairness Revolution and Efficiency Revolution

1. **Contradiction between fairness and efficiency has become increasingly prominent**

The first generation of leadership of the Communist Party, with Comrade Mao Zedong, as the core achieved the greatest revolution in China. They seized power by fighting and overthrew the semi-colonial and semi-feudal systems in China. They established a new China with an independent socialist system, in which people are the owners. They set up a socialist planned economy system and an operation mechanism, liberated and developed productive forces, and improved people's living. This is a great leap in the social and economic history of China. However, this revolution could not build a modern China. Practice of thirty years (after the founding of new China and before the third plenary session of 11th CPC National Congress) in China, as well as experience of former Soviet Union and other socialist countries in Eastern Europe, has proven these: the socialist planned economy system and the operation mechanism can mobilize the enthusiasm, effectively organize productive forces, achieve a certain degree of economic efficiency, achieve a more equitable distribution, coordinate the relationship between fairness and efficiency, and enjoy its own vitality only under the conditions of underdeveloped productivity. However, as modernization continues and as socialist production develops, such vitality gradually reduces or even disappears. In a planned economic system, both businesses and individuals rely on the government. The economy is planned by the government. Distribution of commodities is carried out by the government. There is no competition or fairness awareness in a planned economic system. Compared with developed countries, the entire socio-economic efficiency is very low. People's living cannot be improved. The contradictions between fairness and efficiency have become increasingly prominent.

2. **Five models to solve fairness and efficiency problems**

Fairness and efficiency[31] are two common social and economic problems to be treated seriously and to be solved in every country. The problem is whether fairness is first, efficiency is first, or they are equally important. The ideal condition is that they get equal attention. However, due to the actual conditions and history across different countries, different methods will generate different answers for this problem. From a global perspective, there are four answers, or four models.

In the first mode, economic efficiency is very low and social fairness is very poor. A slave society, a feudal society, and other social systems in lagging countries, such as many developing countries, as well as in old China, belong to this model.

In the second model, economic efficiency is very low or relatively low and social fairness is still very poor. Pre-capitalist countries (that is, countries in the early period of capitalist development which have not faced a serious challenge from socialist countries) belong to this model.

In the third model, the economic efficiency is low or relatively low and social fairness is good. Pre-socialist countries, such as China after the liberation, the former Soviet Union, and the socialist countries in Eastern Europe belong to this model.

In the fourth model, the economic efficiency is high and social fairness has been improved. Modern developed capitalist countries absorb some reasonable parts from socialism.

In the ideal model, the economic efficiency is very high and social fairness is very good. This model is the one that all of the people around the world are pursuing. It is the model for communism. To achieve this ideal model, approaches vary across countries and across historical stages in the same country. Those countries still in

[31] Efficiency is the ratio of output and input. Efficiency includes work efficiency, working efficiency, labor efficiency, production efficiency, energy efficiency, economic efficiency, etc. There are many indicators for assessing efficiency. In the economic field, the major assessment indicator is input economic efficiency, such as production efficiency, capital profit efficiency, capital tax efficiency, net output efficiency, added value efficiency, etc. Input coefficient is also adopted, such as energy consumption per 10,000 tax, steel consumption per 10,000 yuan net output value, capital per 10,000 yuan added value, water consumption per 10,000 output, etc. These indicators reflect economic efficiency from a reverse perspective. Input coefficient and input economic efficiency are reciprocal. The larger the input coefficient, the lower the input economic efficiency. The smaller the input coefficient, the higher the input economic efficiency. Input economic efficiency can also be referred to as economic efficiency. Economic efficiency is the core. Other efficiency directly or indirectly influences economic efficiency.

the first model should transform to the second or third model by force or by peaceful means. Those countries in the second model can transform into the fourth model first. Those countries in the third and fourth models should transform into the ideal model directly. However, the focus for each country might be different. The modern capitalist countries should pay more attention to equal allocation, wherein economic efficiency should also be increased. Those countries with planned economies should improve their economic efficiency, while they also should pay attention to equal allocation. At present, all of the countries in the world are in one of the four models or in the transformation process. Eventually, they are in the ideal model. China was in the third model before the Third Plenary Session of the Eleventh CPC National Congress. After the reform and opening up, China moved toward the direction of the ideal model. The 14th CPC National Congress proposed to establish a socialist market economy. After a while, China will be a modern socialist country with high economic efficiency and good social fairness. Then, it will be in the fifth model, a model close to the ideal model (see Table 23.30).

3. **Urgent efficiency problems to be solved in China**

China aims to transform from the third model into the fifth model. First, the low economic efficiency must be improved. Only in this way can China become rich and will fairness be achieved. Otherwise, only poor fairness will be achieved. Poor fairness is not the goal of socialism. If only fairness is stressed, there will be no difference between enterprises. There will be no reasonable income gap between people. As a result, the enthusiasm and creativity of each person will not be motivated. Social and economic efficiency will not be high. The country will not be rich. People will not be rich either. There will be no idealized and absolute egalitarianism type of fairness in the communist world. At present, the most important and urgent problem for China is efficiency. Efficiency can solve the problem of the shortage of social wealth. Fairness can solve the problem of the distribution of created social wealth. Therefore, efficiency is first, and allocation is second. Unequal allocation affects efficiency as well. However, the priority of efficiency and allocation must be fully

Table 23.30 Fairness and efficiency models

Model	I	II	III	IV	V	Target model
Fairness and efficiency	Social fairness is very poor and economic efficiency is very low	Social fairness is very poor and economic efficiency is low	Social fairness is good and economic efficiency is low or relatively low	Social fairness has been approved and economic efficiency is high	Social fairness is good and economic efficiency is high	Social fairness is very good and economic efficiency is very high
Countries or regions	Lagging countries before capitalism	Pre-capitalist countries	Pre-socialist countries	Modern capitalist countries	Modern socialist countries	Communist world

understood. For example, if 10,000 people create 10 million yuan of social wealth and the per capita share is 1000 yuan; the lowest share being 800 yuan and the highest share being 1200 yuan. In another example, 10,000 people create a wealth of 100 million yuan; the per capita share being 10,000 yuan and the lowest share being 2400 yuan and the highest share being 24,000 yuan. In the first example, the social distribution is good but the economic efficiency is too low. In the second example, the economic efficiency is high but the social fairness is not very good. Which example do you think is better? The author prefers the latter instead of the former. The reasons are as follows: first, although in the latter case the maximum is ten times the minimum, the minimum is nearly twice of the maximum in the first case. This difference means a large improvement in living, even though the maximum in the latter case is much larger than the maximum in the first case. However, improvement of allocation will make everyone happy. Second, for a country, the wealth created in the latter case is ten times that in the first case. Improvement of the whole social wealth is good for a country. Third, in order to promote equal social distribution, the gap of income should be narrowed. The prosperity of the whole country should be achieved. Accordingly, the government can formulate a proper personal income tax and social insurance system. The first case reflects the situation in the planned economic system before the reform and opening up, while the latter case reflects the situation after the reform and opening up in China.

4. **What is the way to solve efficiency problem?**

What is the way for China to increase economic efficiency? The low economic efficiency was caused by many reasons in China, such as lagging technology and equipment, poor quality of labor, low management level, irrational industrial structure, lack of funds, insufficient per capita resources, and poor resource conditions. These factors affect economic efficiency. Other than these domestic factors, there are some international factors. However, the author thinks that these factors are secondary factors, not primary factors. The fundamental reason is the traditional socialist planned economic system, which hinders economic efficiency in a variety of aspects. In a planned economic system, everything is planned by a small number of people. Everyone is passively dependent on the government. In addition, there is no competition. The enthusiasm, initiative, and creativity of more than one billion people have not been motivated. Few people are looking to change lagging technology and equipment. All workers get the same wages regardless the quality of their work. Furthermore, administrative personnel pay little attention to management. No one cares about unreasonable industrial structures. In short, the economic efficiency in a traditional socialist planned economic system is very low. The author thinks that low economic efficiency is the most serious drawback of the traditional planned economic system. If the problem of economic efficiency is not resolved, the whole socialist system will be destroyed. Piecemeal reform is not the solution for this problem. History has proven that the former Soviet Union and Eastern European countries could not solve this problem. Therefore, the solution is to change the economic system. The traditional socialist planned economic system should be abandoned. A new high efficiency economic system should be adopted. The new economic system is the socialist market economic system proposed by the 14th CPC National Congress. Although this new economic system was formally proposed by the 14th CPC National Congress, it first appeared in the conversation between Comrade Deng Xiaoping and foreign guests in 1979. Since the Third Plenary Session of the Eleventh CPC National Congress, China has been on the road to *s* market economy. The transformation from the traditional socialist planned economy to a socialist market economic system is indeed a new revolution, because it is not a piecemeal reform but, rather, a fundamental change.

5. **Inspiration from the comparison of two revolutions**

The first revolution in China focused on regime and ownership. It aimed to fundamentally solve the issue of social fairness. To a certain extent, it solved the problems of low economic efficiency. The second revolution aims to fundamentally solve the problem of low socio-economic efficiency caused by the traditional socialist planned economy. Therefore, the goals of the two revolutions are different. The first revolution aims for power and ownership, whereas the second revolution aims for an economic system. The author thinks that the second revolution is the largest fairness revolution in the history of China. Its significance is not lower than that of the first revolution. It is possible to say that without this revolution led by the central collective leadership with Comrade Deng Xiaoping as the core, the results of the first revolution might be lost. Like the first revolution, the second revolution is led by the Communist Party. However, this revolution does not involve force. It does not change the socialist system fundamentally, either. In addition, it does not cause any social unrest. In a word, this revolution is very smooth and successful without paying a high price or undergoing a major sacrifice.

Some interesting figures can be found by comparing the two revaluations. The first revolution started in 1921 (with the birth of the CPC) and ended in 1949 (with the founding of the new China). It lasted for 28 years in total. The 28 years can be divided into two periods, each with 14 years. During the first period (1921–1935), Comrade Mao Zedong did not seize the leadership of CPC. Therefore, the revolution suffered many setbacks. During the second period (1935–1949), Comrade Mao Zedong seized the leadership of the Party from Zunyi Conference, which was held in 1935. In this period, the revolution achieved many victories and succeeded at last in the entire country. The second revolution started from the Third Plenary Session of the Eleventh CPC National Congress in 1978 and was upgraded at the 14th CPC National Congress, which was held in 1992. It lasted for 14 years. At the Third Plenary Session, Comrade Deng Xiaoping was appointed as the leader of the party. At the same time, he proposed the theory of constructing socialism with Chinese characteristics. He highlighted one center and two basic points. At the 14th CPC National Congress, the socialist market economic system was proposed. At the 14th CPC National Congress, the second revolution entered a new era. The socialist market economy times were written into the Party's constitution. These figures reflect a coincidence in history. The author was inspired by these figures and thinks that the second revolution can also be divided into two periods. The first period is 14 years, and it has already passed. The second period also will be about 14 years. Around 2005, China's socialist market economy will be established. At that time, the efficiency revolution will have achieved a complete victory.

Under the leadership of the Communist Party of China, the first revolution (lasting for 28 years) was completed. Then the traditional planned economy lasted 28 years. Next, the first period of the second revolution lasted 14 years, followed by the second period of 14 years. It can be expected that when three courses (each lasting for 28 years) are completed, China will be the most powerful socialist market economy country with Chinese characteristics in the world. At that time, fairness and efficiency will be coordinated at a higher level.

23.13.2 Chinese Socialist Market Economy will be a New Market Economy Model with Strength of Various Economic Models

The 14th CPC National Congress formally proposed that China would no longer adopt the traditional planned economy model, and that Chinese economic model would transform toward the socialist market economic model. What characteristics does China's socialist market economy have? What are the similarities and differences between it and the market economies of capitalist countries? The author believes that research on these questions is important in theory and in practice. The answers can provide clear direction for establishing and improving this model and for avoiding unnecessary detours.

(1) **Internal characteristics of market economy-five advantages and five disadvantages**

In order to study China's socialist market economy, it is necessary to study the inherent characteristics of market economy. The commodity economy appeared a long time ago, in history. However, the development of the market economy just began in the second half of the eighteenth century. At that time, the steam engines caused the industrial revolution. Machine industry and transportation developed quickly. Domestic and international exchange of commodities expanded continuously. Thus, the market economy began to develop.

At the beginning, the market economy appeared in countries with a capitalist system. It was mistakenly believed that a market economy is peculiar to capitalism and that socialism should not have a market economy. In fact, a market economy is a product of industrial production, transportation, and development of domestic and foreign trade. Just as Comrade Deng Xiaoping pointed out, a market economy is neither capitalist nor socialist. This is a major breakthrough for Marxist theory. The market economy has developed for more than 200 years. As an economic system and operational mechanism, it has its own intrinsic positive and passive characteristics. According to preliminary analysis, the author believes that a market economy has five advantages, which are its major aspects. The market economy also has five disadvantages, which areits secondary aspects. These disadvantages can be overcome to a certain extent through the approaches of the non-market economy.

Here are the five inherent basic characteristics of market economy increasing economic efficiency.

First, independent operational mechanism for enterprises. Enterprises are main body of the market. Accordingly, enterprises should decide by themselves about the location where they will produce, the volume of their production, their production process, and the prices of their products. Enterprises should be responsible for their profits and losses, development, and even elimination. With this mechanism, enterprises have vitality, sense of responsibility, pressure, power, and enthusiasm. This is a fundamental characteristic of a market economy.

Second, value determining mechanism. Market economy works in accordance with law of value. The law of value is the guideline for behaviors. The prices of products should be determined by their costs. In general, prices are determined by the average social costs (including interest costs). If the cost of product in an enterprise is lower than the average cost, the enterprise will gain profit. Thus, enterprises will try to reduce the actual costs. Value determining mechanisms are a very important intrinsic characteristic of market economy.

Third, the supply and demand mechanism. Prices of products are determined by the costs as well as by the supply and demand relationship. If a commodity is in short supply, its price will increase. Enterprises will initially take measures to increase the production of this commodity. Thus, the problem of short supply will be solved. If a commodity is in oversupply, its price will drop. Enterprise will initially take measures to reduce the excessive production of this commodity. Accordingly, oversupply will be alleviated.

Fourth, the competition mechanism. In a market economy, performance and profits do not completely depend on enterprises themselves, but on competitors in the market. But in very few circumstances, companies do not have competitors. These are natural monopoly enterprises. Under normal circumstances, enterprises always have competitors. Sometimes, the number of competitors is large. Therefore, enterprises have to survive and develop while facing competition. The competition mechanism is an inherent characteristic to enhance the progress of enterprises. It promotes the best enterprises to survive.

Fifth, distribution mechanism based on efficiency. The author thinks that, in the market economy, the allocation of new created wealth does not depend on the amount of workers' work. Instead, new created wealth is allocated based on the size of enterprises' benefit and on the contribution of each worker or each production factor to the enterprises' benefit. If one enterprise has good benefit, employees in this enterprise can get more income, including wages and bonuses, compared with employees in enterprises that do not have good benefits. If an enterprise has a negative profit, employees in this enterprise will drop, even though employees in this enterprise work as well as those in enterprises with good profits. Some employees make contributions to the production technology. Some employees make contributions to management. Once enterprises' benefit increase, these employees should get rewards. This is consistent with the distribution mechanism based on efficiency. Sometimes a middleman may have a good income. This is thought of, by some people, as conflict with the distribution principle based on work, because it does not take much time or effort for a middleman to conclude a business. However, a middleman makes much more money than an ordinary worker who does hard work. In fact, this is consistent with the distribution principle, based on efficiency. The above examples show that China is gradually adopting the distribution principle based on efficiency and abandoning the distribution principle based on work in the traditional planned economy system. The author believes that the distribution mechanism based on efficiency is the inherent characteristic of market economy. It can motivate people to create more wealth.[32]

Five basic characteristics of market economy that hinder social fairness.

First, profit oriented. The goal of an enterprise is to make more money and more profits. This goal is reasonable for a market economy. Those enterprises that do not make a profit cannot survive. However, if an enterprise makes profits by unreasonable or illegal means, it will harm consumers' interests, including the interests of the state organs, enterprises, and individuals. Social fairness will be negatively impacted. Oriented by profit, enterprises do not produce, sell, and buy those products with little or no profit but with good social benefits. Enterprises do not care about things that are not good for them, but are good for the country or for the overall situation. Profit orientation is the inherent characteristic of a market economy.

Second, blind production. In order to gain more profits, enterprises like to produce high-profit goods. When all of the enterprises produce the same product, overproduction and redundant construction occur. Finally, some enterprises will be eliminated because of bankruptcy.

Third, monopoly. In a market, the strongest enterprises survive. Some enterprises will become stronger with fewer competitors. They will gain more market share. At the end, monopoly appears. Monopoly will impede scientific and technological progress, damage consumers' interests, and result in an income gap between the rich and the poor.

Fourth, short-term behaviors. In order to pursue immediate profits, enterprises will ignore long-term social benefits. For example, industrial production can result in the destruction of forest resources and in environmental pollution. Such problems did not attract attention in the early stages of the development of market economy.

Fifth, polarization. In a market economy, those people with a strong competitive capacity will make more profits and will become rich. Some will gain a lot of wealth. Those people with poor competitive capacity and without competitive capacity, such as the old, women, children, and the sick, will become poor.

---

[32]The above 2, 3, and 4 inherent characteristics were proposed by Gui Shiyong, the famous economist in the article "about establishment of socialist market economy system" in People's Daily (November 6, 1992).

Regarding the aforementioned five advantages of market economy, they have many forms, such as optimal allocation of resources, timely coordination of production and demand, following the law of value, and motivating enthusiasm. In short, these advantages can promote social and economic efficiency. Regarding the five disadvantages of market economy, they are reflected in several aspects, such as greed, blind production, monopoly, short-term behaviors, and polarization. Although some of them impede the increase of economic efficiency, their impacts are not major.

(2) **Three market economy models in the world**

There are three successful market economy models. They are implemented in capitalist countries.

The first one is the free market economy in the US The free market economy emphasizes the free competition between enterprises and individuals. The government formulates laws and policies to ensure free competition. The government does not value macroeconomic regulation and control.

The second is the planned market economy in Japan, France, and South Korea. A planned market economy emphasizes national macroeconomic regulation and control, including regulation and control of medium and long-term plana and the coordination of economic relations. A planned market economy adopts some of the strengths of the planned economy in socialist countries.

The third is social market economy in Germany. After World War II, the US helped West Germany establish a federal state. The US wanted West Germany to adopt US-style free market economy. However, German economists proposed to establish capitalist market economy, as well as social fairness. The combination of the two was named the social market economy. The social market economy adopts some strengths of the socialist system.

Each of the three economic market models has its own characteristics and is suitable for its own national conditions. The author thinks that the social market economy is more suitable for China than a planned market economy. The strengths of the social market economy should be adopted. Meanwhile, the strengths of the free market economy should be adopted, as well.

(3) **China's new socialist market economy model**

The author believes that China's socialist market economy has two components. One is socialism, and the other is the market economy. This can be expressed by the following formula:

$$\text{Socialist market economy} = \text{socialism} + \text{market economy}$$

First, the market economy in China is the same as the market economy in other countries. There is no difference. The market economy does not belong only to capitalism. Socialism has a market economy as well. Therefore, the aforementioned ten inherent basic characteristics of a market economy exist in capitalist countries with private ownership as the majority and public ownership as the minority, as well as in socialist countries with public ownership as the majority and private ownership as the minority. It is necessary for China to learn and adopt overseas experience in order to establish a socialist market economy.

Second, socialism is different from capitalism. The report of the 14th CPC National Congress pointed out five inherent requirements of socialism: liberating productive forces, developing productive forces, eliminating exploitation, eliminating polarization, and achieving common prosperity. Among the five requirements, the first two requirements are the strengths of the market economy. They are easily achieved. The latter three requirements are the weaknesses of the market economy. They are difficult to achieve. Therefore, the latter three requirements need to be achieved through non-market economy methods based on socialist systems. It shall be noted that socialism consists of material civilization and moral and civic education. Other than the socialist economy, socialism has politics and culture. The meaning of the socialist economy is rather broad. The economy is the base. The base of a market economy can affect its superstructure, thoughts, culture, and spiritual civilization. Therefore, it is important to meet the five essential requirements of socialism.

China's socialist market economy is neither a free market economy, nor a planned market economy, nor a social market economy. Actually, it adopts the strengths of the three types of market economy. It is a new market economy that has been developed with efficiency and social fairness, based on the conditions in China.

23.13.3 How does Government Perform Macro Management in the Socialist Economy in China

The success of China's socialist market economy relies on the macro management of the government. If the Chinese government keeps its role and does not change its functions and management, the socialist market economy will not be achieved. If the government does not perform the function of management and lets enterprises and individuals do whatever they would like to do, the socialist market economy will not be achieved.

First, the government must perform macro management in the socialist market economy.

Second, the government can provide good macro-management in the socialist market economy.

Third, here is the strategy to perform macro-management in the socialist market economy: On the one hand, the government should allow the five advantages of the market economy to play their roles. On the other hand, the government should overcome the five disadvantages of the market economy with socialist methods. The five requirements of socialism must be met. Development of a socialist political, cultural, and spiritual civilization should be well implemented.

More specifically, the following are the five jobs needed for the government to play its role in socialist market economy.

1. **Make strategy, plans, and planning**

Plans should be made based on the requirements of the market economy. Plans should not constrain the economic activities of enterprises. Instead, plans should provide macro information and direction for enterprises. The 14th CPC National Congress pointed out that national plans are one approach of macro controls. Plans should reasonably determine the strategic goals of national economy and social development, predict economic development, control the total amount, adjust important structure, design production layout, monitor land utilization, oversee key projects, and use economic lever comprehensively.

2. **Make laws and policies**

The government should make laws and policies for its role of management in socialist market economy.

Those laws and policies that are not suitable for socialist market economy should be amended. New laws and policies should be made for the development of a socialist market economy. Different from plans, laws and policies require observance. The author thinks that the following is the priority for making laws and policies. First, make a fair competition law, which in Germany is called the Against the Unfair Competition Law. In the early stage of its capitalism, Germany had this law. This law has existed for over a hundred years. It encourages and promotes enterprises for competition, protects reasonable competition among enterprises, and opposes unfair conditions of competition. Second, make policies suitable for the fair competition in China based on the actual conditions. The difference between free competition and fair competition should be highlighted. Free competition is not as good as fair competition. Therefore, China's socialist market economy requires the combination of social fairness from fair competition and competition (the core of a market economy). Fair competition, not free competition, should be advocated in a socialist market economy.

It should be noted that the policy of fair competition is a basic and important economic policy in a market economy. But it cannot substitute for other policies; other policies are important as well. The relationship between fair competition and other policies should be thoroughly considered. Next, Germany is chosen as the example to describe the relationship between fair competition and other policies.

The competition policy is the most basic economic policy in the macro-management of the social market economy in Germany, but it is not the only policy. Many other policies exist in the social market economy in Germany. A very important task of government's macro-management is to coordinate competition policy and other policies, such as the social security policy, the employment policy, the industrial policy, a regional economic policy, a fiscal policy, a monetary policy, and a foreign trade policy. According to the experience of Germany, here are the principles that government should use to coordinate the relationship.

(1) When there are contradictions between competition policy and other policies, if other policies can better meet the overall goal of the social market economy, competition policy can be subject to the requirements of other policies. However, the factors of competition policy should be considered all the time.
(2) Competition policy is a fundamental economic policy used to promote economic growth in the social market economy. Other economic policies developed for achieving other purposes can only work during certain periods. Other economic policies should not conflict with the competitive policy for a long time.
(3) It should be noted that sometimes competition policy and other policies are contradictory. However, in essence, their goals are consistent. They all aim to achieve the overall goal of the social market economy.
(4) The best scenario is when there is no contradiction between competition policy and other policies. If this is the case, it is easy to handle.

(1) Relationship between competition policy and social policies

German social market economic system is the combination of a social and a market economy. A competition policy is the basic policy for managing market economy. Social policies, including a social security policy, a labor policy, an employment policy, and an environmental policy, are the policies for managing society. Therefore, the competition policy and social policies both are important in German social market economy. Normally, a competition policy and a social policy, such as a social security policy, complement each other; there is no contradiction between them. However, when there is contrast between the competition policy and the social policy, such as the employment policy, the competition policy should be subject to the social policy. Its social policies aim to ensure social stability and social equity in Germany as well as to protect the German social system. To some extent, social policy is more important than competition policy.

(2) Relationship between competition policy and other economic policies

The competition policy and other economic policies, such as the industrial policy, the agricultural policy, the energy policy, the transport policy, the regional economic policy, the fiscal policy, the monetary policy, and the foreign trade policy, are components of German economic policies.

Here are the four key goals that German economic policies intend to achieve.

① Maintain a relatively high economic growth rate, in order to improve people's living.
② Maintain a relatively low inflation rate to make prices stable.
③ Maintain a relatively low unemployment rate so that laborers can find jobs.
④ Maintain a reasonable international trade scale to promote a balance of international payment.

German competition policy mainly aims for achieving a high economic efficiency and a maintaining high economic growth rate. Financial, monetary, and fiscal policies intend to control the inflation rate and make prices stable. The industrial policy and the regional policy emphasize employment goals. The foreign trade policy aims to balance international payments. Therefore, the German economic policies support each other, and each has its respective functions. In general, there is no contradiction between competition policy and other economic policies. Thus, it is easy to coordinate their relationship. When there is contradiction between other economic policies (such as the industrial policy and the regional economic policy) and the competition policy, the German government will make a reasonable choice.

(3) Examples

① *Dealing with the contradiction between competition policy and employment policy*

In 1990, after the unification of East Germany and West Germany, East Germany became a new federal state in which the social market economy system was implemented. On the one hand, according to the requirements of competition policy, state-owned enterprises implemented shareholding systems and were privatized, in order to improve the competitiveness and the economic efficiency of enterprises in the domestic market. A large number of employees were laid off. On the other hand, required by employment policy, the unemployment rate should not have been too high for eastern workers. To fix this this contradiction, the government required that foreign and domestic companies who buy state-owned enterprises in eastern Germany provide a certain number of positions for eastern Germany workers. Those who provided larger positions for eastern Germany workers would get advantages in bidding, and they tended to win the biddings. This is a typical example of competition policy subject to the employment policy.

② *Dealing with the contradiction of competition policy and employment policies*

Industrial policies include energy policy, high-tech, and agricultural policies. Sometimes, these policies are inconsistent with the requirements of competition policy. The government should deal with the contradiction.

Energy policy intends to ensure safe and reliable supply of energy. It is also good for environmental protection and for energy conservation. It can be learned from the two energy crises in 1973 and in 1979 that the domestic energy supply is the safest and most reliable approach and that imported energy has risks. Therefore, the energy policy should consider the maintenances of domestic coal production and supply. However, a competition policy intends to enable enterprises to offer energy supply that is both cheap and in high quality. In this way, enterprises can get more profits. In Germany, domestic coal is more expensive than imported coal. According to the competition policy, it is more economical to use imported coal. As such, the energy policy conflicts with the competition policy. The German government coordinates these two policies and makes the competition policy subject to the energy policy. The competition principle should be followed when the requirements of the energy policy are met. Competition should be encouraged in the energy industry.

The high-tech policy intends to develop high-tech items, such as integrated circuits, in Germany. This requires the European Community to develop a high-tech protection policy and opposes the dumping done by Japan and South Korea. But the competition policy requires companies in Germany to compete with foreign enterprises. Foreign trade protection is not expected. When dealing with this conflict, the German government considers all aspects and determines that foreign trade protection be implemented.

Protection measures were taken for agriculture.

③ *Dealing with the contradiction of competition policy and regional economic policy*

In Germany, the production level and income level in 30% of the regions are lower than the national average. Therefore, in order to promote regional economic development and to reduce regional disparities, the central government gives subsidies, such as tax relief and low-interest loans, to some enterprises in these regions. However, state-subsidized enterprises will have a dependency. Especially, long-term subsidies hinder competition in the market. To some extent, state subsidies are bad. To eliminate the conflicts, the German government considered all of the aspects and took on a conditional subsidy policy. First, subsidies were provided to enterprises with economic efficiency. Enterprises having a negative profit did not get any subsidy. Second, enterprises must apply for subsidies. Their applications were assessed based on how many jobs they could create and on what contribution they would make for the regions. Third, the government should make it clear that there would be no long-term subsidies. Enterprises must take technical progress measures to gradually reduce their dependence on subsidies.

Ruhr is Germany's largest coal base. The current coal production is 69 million t. Due to increasing mining depth and rising costs, the price of coal in Ruhr is about 260 marks per ton. The price of imported coal is only 100 marks per ton. Therefore, it is not economical to continue the mass production of coal in Ruhr. However, coal production has been the major industry in Ruhr for a long time. If coal production in Ruhr stops, the economy in this region will be severely affected. Nearly 200,000 miners in Ruhr will lose their jobs. Furthermore, unemployment in the coal industry will cause unemployment in other industries. For example, if one worker loses his job in the coal industry, three workers will lose their jobs in related industries. That will be a big social problem. In addition, it is not appropriate to stop coal production in this region, considering the stability of the domestic energy supply. Therefore, Ruhr coal production involves many policies. The requirements of the competition policy are contradictory to the requirements of the regional economic policy, the employment policy, and the energy policy. In this case, the German government determines that competition policy should be subject to the regional economic policy, the employment policy, and the energy policy. The government gives subsidies to coal production in Ruhr with an annual amount of 10 billion marks.

④ *Dealing with the contradiction of competition policy and foreign trade policy*

Foreign trade policy intends to promote and expand international trade, to protect domestic industries, and to achieve a balance of payments for foreign trade. According to foreign trade policy, some products need trade protection. As mentioned above, Germany has taken foreign trade protection policies in coal, electronic chips, and agriculture. Although the protection affected the implementation of a competition policy during a certain period, it was necessary for the European Economic Community and for Germany.

⑤ *Dealing with the contradiction of competition policy and other economic policies*

In principle, the competition policy can temporarily and conditionally be subject to other economic policies. But the competition policy should not be subject to other economic policies unconditionally, all of the time. In Germany, the Competition Policy Division under the Ministry of Economic Affairs is responsible for overseeing the competition policy and for coordinating the relationship between the competition policy and other policies. In addition, the independent Cartel Office under the Ministry of Economic Affairs is responsible for dealing with issues related to anti-competitive policies.

3. **Organize and coordinate various interests**

In a socialist market economy, enterprises can settle internal matters. But they cannot settle external matters, which should be dealt with by the government. External matters include the interest conflicts between different enterprises; between different regions; between different persons; between individuals, enterprises and the whole country; between different countries; and between economic interests, social interests, political interests, environmental interests, and military interests. These interest conflicts are common and dynamic. Therefore, the government should strengthen its function in coordinating various interest conflicts. In this way, social stability and unity and a booming economy can be achieved.

4. **Provide information and various services**

Enterprises need a large amount of information regarding the domestic and international macro-economic environment and society. It is not easy for enterprises to gather and access this information. Therefore, macro-management institutions in the government should provide such information to enterprises in a timely manner. In this way, the economic activities of enterprises can be correctly guided. Meanwhile, the government should provide the necessary consulting and other services.

5. **Inspect and supervise**

The government should inspect and supervise the implementation of laws and policies all the time. Issues found in inspection or reported by people should be investigated carefully. This is an important job which requires a lot of manpower. For example, in order to inspect and supervise the implementation of the German anti-cartel law and the settlement of related cases, the German government set the Cartel Office with several hundred of employees. State governments have their own Cartel Offices.

Management institutions need to be adjusted according to the changes of the economic system and the macroeconomic management functions of the government. In a traditional planned economy system, a set of planned economic management institutions is established. In the central government, the State Planning Commission serves as the highest institution for managing the national macro-economy. Its main function is to make mandatory plans and planning. In the socialist market economy, the highest national institution is still needed for managing macro-economy. Instead of making mandatory plans and planning, its management functions should be enhanced. It has more tasks than before. It should make laws and policies, coordinate various interests, provide information and other services, and inspect and supervise the implementation of laws and policies. In my opinion, the name "the State Planning Commission" should be changed to "the National Economy and Social Development Commission." It is responsible for macroeconomic management and for fulfilling the aforementioned five functions. In this way, the internal institutions under the State Planning Commission should be reformed. New institutions should be established, such as a Planning Division, a Policy Division, a Competition Secretary, a Coordination Division, an Information Division, a Supervision Division, etc.

23.13.4 Germination, Growth, and Maturity Stages of Socialist Market Economy will be the Time with the Highest Growth Rate in China's History

The socialist market economic system cannot be established overnight. The process lasts a relatively long period. This establishment process can be divided into the following three stages.

1. **Germination stage (1978–1992)**

This stage can be divided into five development phases (see Table 23.31). In the first phase, there was no market at all, but rural reform was implemented. Particularly, the household contract was performed. Farmers obtained independent management rights for land. Control of the prices of agricultural products was released. Town-owned enterprises developed quickly. In fact, the market economy began in the rural areas. Facts proved that the development path is correct. Based on the experience gained in the first phase, a new economic system with a planned economy as primary, and market regulation as secondary, was proposed. Accordingly, market regulation appeared for the first time. In the third phase, the traditional belief that a planned economy and a commodity economy is contradictory was broken through. A socialist planned commodity economy system was proposed. A commodity economy is a

Table 23.31 Development of China's socialist market economy

1949–1978 before reform and opening up		Traditional socialist planned economic system
After reform and opening up	Prophase 1978–1992, 14 years in total	**Germination stage** First phase (1978–1982). 4 years in total. Socialist planned economic system with reform and opening up Second phase (1982–1984). 2 years in total. The 12th CPC National Congress in 1982 proposed that socialist economy should be based on planned economy with market regulation as auxiliary Third phase (1984–1987). 3 years in total. The third plenary session of 12th CPC National Congress proposed socialist planned commodity economic system Fourth phase (1987–1989). 2 years in total. The 13th CPC National Congress in 1987 proposed an economic system with the combination of social plans and market Fifth phase (1989–1992). 3 years in total. The fourth plenary session of 13th CPC National Congress proposed the economic system and operational system combining socialist planned economy and market regulation
	Later stage 1992–2005, 14 years in total	Growth stage (transition 1992–1997) The 14th CPC National Congress in 1992 proposed a socialist market economic system Maturity stage (1997–2005)

general concept. A market economy was thought as an advanced stage of commodity economy. It still belongs to commodity economy. Therefore, the essence of the socialist planned commodity economy is a planned socialist market economy. In this phase, planning and the market economy were mentioned together. In the fourth phase, it was clearly proposed that planning and the market were inherently united. Both of them are very important. In the fifth phase, an economic system that integrates socialist planned economy and market regulation was proposed. In this stage, the market economy was not highlighted as it had been in phase three and phase four. Guidance for the market economy is obvious in the germination stage. The germination of socialist market economy appeared in phase three.

2. **Growth stage (transition period 1992–1997)**

The 14th CPC National Congress officially put forward that China should adopt a socialist market economy and abandon its traditional planned economy. However, it is impossible to transform into market economy from the planned economy overnight. It takes time to change people's mind and traditional practices. Thus, this is a transition period. During this transition period, the impact of the planned economy will reduce gradually. The impact of the market economy will increase. In my view, the length of this transition depends on the degree of reform. It is expected to be five years. In some areas, it might be longer.

3. **Maturity stage (1997–2005)**

In 1997, Hong Kong returned to the motherland China. Because the market economy is well developed in Hong Kong, the return of Hong Kong will promote the development of a market economy in other regions of China. The maturity stage is estimated to be about eight years. In this stage, all of the enterprises, all of the mechanisms, and all of the regions will enter a virtuous cycle of market economy. The market economy system and the operational mechanism will be relatively mature.

The germination stage takes about 14 years. The transition stage and the maturity stage will also take about 14 years.

The author found that the germination stage takes about 14 years and the transition stage and maturity stage will take about 14 years. In total, the process lasts 28 years (1978–2005). The efficiency revolution will occur in China during this period. During this period, the growth rate of the economy will be the highest in the history of China. In this high economic efficiency period, input is low and output is high. The contribution of technical progress and comprehensive saving to economic development is the largest. Therefore, Chinese people's living standards will rise quickly in this period. It is a golden era.

Historical facts have proven that the economic efficiency is very low in the traditional planned economic system. Here is a comparison of the national input-output before and after the reform and opening up. In the traditional planned economy period (1954–1978), the average annual GDP growth rate was only 5.7%. The average annual growth rates of the main inputs were twice the growth rate of the GDP, including input on energy and raw material resources, input on fixed capital and liquidity, input on cargo turnover and cargo traffic capacity, input on labor, and input on natural forces, such as water and land, but excluding manpower, grain, cotton, and timber. The elasticity coefficient was about 2. In the germination stage of the market economy, take 1981–1988 as the example, the average annual GDP growth rate was 10%, almost twice that during the planned economy period. The average annual growth rates of all of the major inputs were only half of the average annual growth rate of GDP. The elasticity coefficient was 0.5. Thus, the economic efficiency in the germination stage of market economy was four times that of planned economy period. In other words, the same comprehensive input generated three times more net output in the market economy (GDP). For example, in the planned economy period (1954–1978), if the annual growth rate of GDP is 1%, the annual growth rate of energy input will be 1.74%. In the birth period of market economy (1981–1988), if the annual growth rate of GDP is 1%, the annual growth rate of energy input will be 0.56%. During the past 14 years of the germination stage of the socialist market economy, economic efficiency has been greatly improved. However, it is still very low compared with other market economy countries. The gap is large. Therefore, the potential for China's economic efficiency is large. During the next 14 years, the economic growth rate in China will maintain a high speed at 8–10%. Rapid development depends partially on increasing inputs. More importantly, growth relies on increasing economic efficiency and the role of the socialist market economic system.

23.14 Major Indices for Measuring Chinese Economic Situations and Their Regulation and Control Approaches[33]

Research background, scientific significance of research and practical value.

Since 1992, when Deng Xiaoping made the southern tour speech, China's economy has developed rapidly. But inflation also rises. For a long time, China's socialist planned economy was characterized by stable prices, except in 1951 and 1961. A double-digit inflation rate never appeared. However, after Deng Xiaoping's southern tour speech, the economic growth rate was double-digit. Inflation rosd by a double-digit rate, as well. When questioned by the western media, China should have its own reasons. As such, the author led a team working overtime day and night and developed China's macroeconomic information system [285, 286, 298]. At the end, the author personally reported the system to leaders in the Central Office, the Fiscal Office, and the Electronic Industry Ministry. This system was accepted and received good comments. This major research effectively answered the questions of the Western media. Theory and practice have proven that Deng Xiaoping's southern tour speech was correct. Although the rate of inflation rose at a double-digit rate in China [312], the comprehensive economic situation was very good. In addition, the Chinese people were happy with the high subsidies for deposit interest rates offered by the central government. The research project was also called the Jinhai Project, meaning the golden Zhongnanhai project.

---

[33]Xu, S.B. et al. (1994). Information system for China's macro economy, developed by Research Institute of technical economy under State Planning Commission.

23.14.1 Major Indicators for Measuring and Assessing China's Economic Situation

1. **Economic growth rate (i.e. economic growth speed)**

The economic growth rate is the most comprehensive index used to measure and to judge the economic situation of a country. The economic growth rate must adopt the GDP growth rate as the economic development strategy target indicator determined by the 13th CPC National Congress. Industrial and agricultural output (IAO) growth rate should be abandoned. GDP and IAO are different. GDP growth is the growth of economic benefits, including the profit and tax growth rate and the wages growth rate. IAO growth is not the growth of economic benefits, but the growth of production, including material consumption growth. Therefore, a high IAO growth rate is not always good. If the growth rate of material consumption cost increases too fast and products are unmarketable, a high IAO growth rate is bad. Therefore, IAO growth needs two way controls, since either too high or too low is not good. In contrast, the GDP is the wealth created by the society. The higher the GDP growth rate, the better. The main task for macro-control is to promote GDP growth. In other words, increase the low GDP growth rate. Raise the high GDP growth rate to a higher level. Or maintain a high GDP growth rate. Avoid dropping the GDP growth rate too much.

A high economic growth rate is the goal for all countries. The issues of overheating the economy, too fast a GDP growth rate, and a dropping GDP growth rate do not exist.

Since the reform and opening up, the economic growth rate in China has changed within the range of 4.1–14.7%, with an average of 8.9%. The economic growth rate was the highest from 1984 to 1988, when the Chinese economy leaped forward. The average annual growth rate was 11.5%. The highest rate was 14.7% (see Table 23.32). Last year (1992), inspired by Comrade Xiaoping's southern tour speech and the guideline of the 14th CPC National Congress, the economic growth rate reached 12.8%. This should not be called overheating. Even the rapid growth rate, at more than 10% in 1960 s in Japan, should not be called overheating.

In short, the average natural growth rate of China's economy in the 1990s should be about 10%. If the actual growth is lower, check whether the demand in investment, consumption, and export is inadequate. Also check whether supply for production, import, and inventory is inadequate. If they are inadequate, find out the economic reasons, such as investment, prices, interest rates, and exchange rates. Non-economic reasons should also be checked, such as political, policy, institutional, international, social, and natural disasters. Once reasons are found, perform macro-control to increase the economic growth rate. One percentage rise in the economic growth

Table 23.32 Major indicators for measuring and assessing the economic situation in China and their values (Unit: %)

Year	Economic growth rate	Structural adjustment rate	Import and export rate	Investment rate	Inflation rate	Unemployment rate	Population growth rate	Economic situation indicator	Economic situation
1978	11.7	–	39.5	–	–	5.3	1.200	–	–
1979	7.6	0.8	42.1	28.3	3.8	(5.1)	1.161	2.23	Relative good
1980	7.9	0.6	30.0	26.7	3.9	4.9	1.187	2.02	Relative good
1981	4.4	2.4	15.4	28.2	2.4	3.8	1.455	1.72	Not good
1982	8.8	2.6	−5.5	30.7	0	3.2	1.568	2.26	Relative good
1983	10.4	1.0	4.8	31.7	1.5	2.3	1.329	3.08	Very good
1984	14.7	1.0	22.8	30.8	5.1	1.9	1.308	3.30	Very good
1985	12.8	6.0	30.0	35.8	10.1	1.8	1.426	3.00	Very good
1986	8.1	2.8	6.1	38.4	5.2	2.0	1.557	2.92	Good
1987	10.9	3.0	11.9	35.4	5.6	2.0	1.661	3.40	Very good
1988	11.3	3.8	24.4	37.7	13.2	2.0	1.573	2.96	Good
1989	4.4	8.2	8.6	37.9	9.3	2.6	1.504	2.05	Relative good
1990	4.1	1.4	3.4	35.2	6.5	2.5	1.439	1.62	Not good
1991	7.7	3.8	17.6	33.9	4.5	2.3	1.298	2.44	Good
1992	12.8	4.6	22.0	34.1	7.8	2.3	1.160	2.92	Good
1993	9.6–12.5	4.2–6.2	11.2–14.8	34.4	6.6–11.2	2.2–2.3	1.178–1.186	2.99–3.72	Good–Very good
1994	8.8–10.7	4.5–6.4	10.2–13.2	34.5	2.4–3.0	2.1–2.3	1.265–1.323	3.36–3.79	Very good
1995	8.1–9.7	4.4–5.8	11.8–26.7	34.6	4.5–6.1	2.1–2.3	1.298–1.367	3.21–3.44	Very good
1996	8.2–11	4.5–6.3	13.9–14.3	34.7	6.0–9.9	2.0–2.3	1.268–1.381	3.14–3.77	Very good

(continued)

Table 23.32 (continued)

Year	Economic growth rate	Structural adjustment rate	Import and export rate	Investment rate	Inflation rate	Unemployment rate	Population growth rate	Economic situation indicator	Economic situation
1997	9.9–10.8	4.5–7.0	9.4–14.5	34.8	7.1–11.3	2.0–2.3	1.241–1.385	2.83–3.77	good–very good
1998	7.6–9.3	4.5–7.5	14.2–15.6	34.9	5.4–8.6	2.0–2.3	1.248–1.387	2.79–3.42	Good–very good
1999	8.5–10.4	4.6–6.2	13.0–14.0	34.9	3.8–6.1	2.0–2.3	1.270–1.387	3.29–3.92	Very good
2000	8.0–9.6	4.6–7.7	13.9–14.6	34.9	8.2–8.3	1.9–2.3	1.279–1.387	3.14–3.27	Very good

Note Data for 1993–2000 are predicted data

rate will generate an over 20 billion yuan increase in the country's taxes, corporate profits, and personal income. The increase is a huge amount of wealth.

2. **Structural transformation rate**

The structural transformation rate is not a key indicator for measuring the economic situation in countries with advanced economic structures. However, because the economic structure in China needs adjustment, the structural transformation rate is a key indicator for measuring China's economic situation. Structural transformation falls into two types: transformation in labor structure and transformation in the GDP. The author found that transformation in the GDP can be used as a key indicator for measuring the economic situation in China. Structural transformation in the GDP can be reflected by current price and fixed price. The current price indicator can reflect the current situation. The fixed price indicator can reflect changes. Here is the trend of the changes of industrial structure in China's GDP since the reform and opening up: The proportion of the primary industry is declining. Based on the fixed price in 1980, the proportions of the primary industry were 33.4 and 17% in 1978 and 1992, respectively, with a drop of 16%. The average annual drop rate is 1%. The proportions of the secondary industry were 45.9 and 57.7% in 1978 and 1992, respectively, with a rise of 12%. The proportions of the tertiary industry were 20.7 and 25.3% in 1978 and 1992, respectively, with a rise of 5%. However, the proportions of the secondary industry and the tertiary industry dropped in 1980, 1981, 1982, 1990, 1991, and 1992. This dropping is not normal.

From 1984 to 1988, the Chinese economy made the largest leap. Structural transformation was the best during this period. Other than the correct transformation direction, the transformation rate was large, between 1.0% and 6.0%, with an annual transformation rate of 3.3%. This transformation is reasonable compared with that of foreign countries (see Tables 23.33 and 23.34).

The annual average transformation rate is estimated to be over 2% in 1990s in China.

Here are the main tasks of macroeconomic regulation and control. On the one hand, control and change the economic structure into a pagoda-shape with the primary industry at the top, the secondary industry in the middle, and the third industry at the bottom. The proportion of the primary industry should drop. The proportion of the secondary industry should drop relatively. The proportion of the tertiary industry should rise more quickly. On the other hand, the annual average transformation rate should be kept above 2%. Accordingly, the growth rate of added value of the tertiary industry should be higher than GDP growth rate, or even higher than the growth rate of industrial added value. The growth rate of the secondary should be higher than that of the primary industry. If the above requirements are not met, effective control measures must be taken immediately.

3. **Growth rate of import and export amount**

Since the reform and opening up, foreign trade contribution to the GDP is growing. The growth rate of total imports and exports has become a key indicator for measuring

Table 23.33 Changes of structural transformation rate in China's economy (Unit: %)

Year	GDP		The first industry		The second industry		The tertiary industry		Changes of structural transformation rate	
	Nominal	Actual	Nominal	Actual	Nominal	Actual	Nominal	Actual	Nominal	Actual
1978	100	100	28.4	33.4	48.6	45.9	23.0	20.7	–	–
1979	100	100	31.5	33.0	47.9	46.2	20.6	20.8	6.2	0.8
1980	100	100	30.4	30.4	49.0	49.0	20.6	20.6	2.2	−5.6
1981	100	100	32.3	31.1	47.3	47.8	20.4	21.1	3.8	−2.4
1982	100	100	33.9	32.0	45.9	46.5	20.2	21.5	3.2	−2.6
1983	100	100	33.9	31.5	45.7	46.6	20.4	21.9	0.4	1.0
1984	100	100	33.2	31.0	44.8	46.6	22.0	22.4	3.2	1.0
1985	100	100	29.8	28.0	45.8	48.9	24.9	23.1	6.8	6.0
1986	100	100	28.5	26.6	46.3	49.7	25.2	23.7	2.6	2.8
1987	100	100	28.3	25.1	46.5	50.8	25.2	24.1	0.4	3.4
1988	100	100	27.2	23.2	46.8	52.5	26.0	24.3	2.2	3.8
1989	100	100	26.4	19.1	45.5	54.2	28.1	26.7	4.2	8.2
1990	100	100	28.4	19.6	43.6	53.5	28.0	26.9	4.0	−1.4
1991	100	100	26.6	18.4	46.2	55.4	27.2	26.2	5.2	−3.8
1992	100	100	24.2	17.0	48.1	57.7	27.7	25.3	4.8	−4.6

Note Minus means unreasonable structural transformation

Table 23.34 Comparison of economic structural transformation between China and foreign countries (Unit: %)

Year	South Korea		UK		Japan		France		US		Germany[a]		China	
	GDP	Labor	GDP	Labor	GDP	Labor	GDP	Labor	GDP	Labor	GDP	Labor	GDP	Labor
1953	–	–	2	–	6	–	4	–	2	–	2	–	–	1.2
1954	14	–	4	–	2	–	2	–	2	–	0	–	–	1.2
1955	10	–	2	–	4	–	2	–	0	–	2	–	–	0.4
1956	4	–	2	–	6	–	2	–	2	–	0	–	–	5.4
1957	4	–	2	–	4	–	0	–	0	–	4	–	–	3.4
1958	6	–	1.8	2	0.8	2	3	0	–	6	4.4	1.2	–	46
1959	14	1.6	0	2.8	2	3.4	2	–	4	1.2	2	1.6	–	12
1960	2	–	12	0.8	16	2.0	0	–	4	1.6	2	3.0	–	9.4
1961	6	–	0	0.4	4	2.8	0	–	2	2.6	2	1.8	–	23
1962	6	–	2	1.6	2	2.6	2	2.0	2	1.0	2	2.0	–	9.8
1963	10	–	0	1.4	2	3.6	2	2.0	0	1.4	2	1.2	–	0.8
1964	8	2.6	0	0.6	2	2.6	2	2.0	2	1.2	0	1.2	–	0.6
1965	14	6.4	0	0.4	2	2.6	2	4.4	2	1.0	2	1.0	–	1.2
1966	4	1.6	2	1.0	0	2.6	0	1.4	0	1.6	2	1.0	–	0.4
1967	10	–	0	4.6	2	6.2	2	2.0	4	1.0	4	1.2	–	0.4
1968	6	–	2	1.0	2	2.6	0	2.0	2	0.6	4	1.0	–	0
1969	2	–	2	0.2	4	2.0	2	1.6	0	0.8	2	2.0	–	1.0
1970	6	3.0	2	0.6	4	2.8	20	1.4	6	1.5	10	1.4	–	2.2
1971	2	4.0	2	5.2	4	3.0	0	1.6	0	2.4	4	1.4	–	2.2
1972	2	5.0	2	2.0	2	2.2	0	1.6	0	0.2	2	1.8	–	1.6

(continued)

Table 23.34 (continued)

Year	South Korea		UK		Japan		France		US		Germany[a]		China	
	GDP	Labor	GDP	Labor	GDP	Labor	GDP	Labor	GDP	Labor	GDP	Labor	GDP	Labor
1973	6	3.8	4	0.6	6	2.8	2	1.4	2	0.8	0	0.6	–	0.8
1974	2	4.0	8	0.8	4	1.6	4	3.0	2	1.0	0	1.8	–	1.0
1975	4	4.6	0	3.4	6	2.6	2	2.4	2	4.2	6	6.4	–	2.2
1976	4	5.2	0	1.6	2	1.0	2	2.0	2	0.4	2	1.2	–	2.8
1977	4	5.6	2	1.0	0	1.4	0	3.2	0	6.0	2	3.2	–	2.6
1978	4	6.8	2	0.6	0	1.2	0	2.0	0	0.6	0	1.2	–	7.6
1979	4	5.2	0	1.0	4	1.2	0	1.8	2	0.2	4	1.0	0.8	1.6
1980	6	5.8	4	2.4	4	1.6	4	1.0	0	1.6	0	0.6	5.6	2.0
1981	2	2.4	2	3.8	4	1.0	4	2.2	2	1.0	4	1.6	2.4	1.4
1982	2	4.4	1	2.4	0	1.6	0	2.0	2	3.4	0	1.8	2.6	1.4
1983	2	4.6	1	2.2	0	1.0	0	2.0	4	1.0	0	1.6	1.0	2.2
1984	2	5.2	2	2.0	0	0.8	4	2.2	0	1.0	6	1.0	1.0	6.0
1985	2	4.4	2	1.4	6	0.2	2	2.0	0	1.2	6	0.8	6.0	3.4
1986	4	2.6	12	1.6	2	1.4	0	–	4	0.6	6	0.4	2.8	2.8
1987	2	–	–	–	8	–	4	–	2	–	4	–	3.0	2.0
1988	–	–	–	–	–	–	–	–	–	–	–	–	3.8	1.2
1989	–	–	–	–	–	–	–	–	–	–	–	–	8.2	–
1990	–	–	–	–	–	–	–	–	–	–	–	–	1.4	–
1991	–	–	–	–	–	–	–	–	–	–	–	–	3.8	–
1992	–	–	–	–	–	–	–	–	–	–	–	–	4.6	–

Note [a]Data is from Western German

China's economic situation. The growth rate of total imports and exports has two indicators: the indicator calculated in US dollars and the indicator calculated in RMB. Practice has shown that the growth rate of total imports and exports calculated in dollars is more appropriate, because the value of US dollars is relatively stable. Calculation based on RMB cannot reflect the scale of foreign trade because of the large change of exchange rate for RMB. For example, based on the current price of GDP and the current exchange rate, foreign trade dependence in China was 12.8% in 1980 and 31.4% in 1990, which is almost double that of the US (16.5%) and of Japan (17%). But, based on the current prices in 1980 and constant exchange rate, foreign trade dependence in China was 12.8% in 1980 and 16.3% in 1990. (The depreciation of the US dollar is not considered. If the depreciation is considered, the foreign trade dependence in 1990 is 12.8%). This number is more close to the facts.

Since the reform and opening up, the growth rate of total imports and exports (in dollars, hereinafter the same) has changed in a wide range from −5.5 to 42.1%. The growth rate of total imports and exports reached the highest level from 1984 to 1988, the economic leap period with an annual growth rate of 15.7% (see Table 23.35).

The average annual growth rate of total imports and exports in the 1990s in China is estimated to be higher than 10%.

Here are the tasks of macro-control: Take measures to promote the average annual growth rate of total imports and exports at a speed higher than 10%. The lowest average annual growth rate of total imports and exports should not be smaller than the GDP growth rate. Neither the foreign trade deficit nor the surplus should be too large. Attention should be paid to the economic efficiency of foreign trade. The scale of the foreign trade should depends on the size of the profit.

4. **Investment rate**

Investment rate reflects economic situation from one aspect. It is the ratio of the sum of the fixed asset investment and the current assets in the GDP. A high investment rate means a large part of newly created wealth is used for expanding reproduction, resulting in rapid economic development. The investment rate falls into two types: one calculated with current prices and the other calculated with fixed prices. These two indicators are applied in different cases. Illustrating the current status requires the adoption of the investment rate calculated with current prices. In order to study the variation of investment rate in different calendar years, the investment rate should be forecast. In this case, the investment rate calculated with fixed prices should be adopted. Changes in China's investment rate are listed in Table 23.36. It can be seen that, since the reform and opening up, China's investment rate has fluctuated within the range of 26.7–38.4%. The fixed assets investment rate has fluctuated within the range of 20.6–31.6%. The current assets investment rate has fluctuated within the range of 4.9–11.3%. Compared with foreign countries, China's investment rate is relatively high. Particularly, the current assets investment rates in 1989 and 1991 were about 10%. This is too high and this is not normal. During the rapid economic

Table 23.35 Changes of growth rate of total imports and exports and foreign trade dependence in China

Year	GDP				Total Export						Total Import						Total Amount of Import and Export						Foreign Trade Dependence	
	Fixed price in 1980		Present price		Present price		Fixed price and Fixed exchange rate		Current price		Present price		Fixed price and Fixed exchange rate		Current price		Present price		Fixed price and Fixed exchange rate		Current price		Fixed price and Fixed exchange rate	Current price
	Amount (0.1 billion yuan)	Growth rate (%)	Amount (0.1 billion yuan)	Growth rate (%)	Amount (0.1 billion yuan)	Growth rate (%)	Amount (0.1 billion yuan)	Growth rate (%)	Amount (0.1 billion yuan)	Growth rate (%)	Amount (0.1 billion yuan)	Growth rate (%)	Amount (0.1 billion yuan)	Growth rate (%)	Amount (0.1 billion yuan)	Growth rate (%)	Amount (0.1 billion yuan)	Growth rate (%)	Amount (0.1 billion yuan)	Growth rate (%)	Amount (0.1 billion yuan)	Growth rate (%)		
1978	3853	11.7	3588	–	97.5	28.5	145.9	28.5	167.6	20.0	108.9	51.0	163.0	51.0	187.4	41.1	206.4	39.5	308	39.5	355	30.3	8.8	9.9
1979	4146	7.6	3998	11.4	136.5	40.1	204.5	40.1	211.7	26.3	156.7	43.9	234.5	43.9	242.9	29.6	293.3	42.1	438	42.1	455	28.2	10.6	11.4
1980	4470	7.9	4470	11.8	181.2	32.7	271.2	32.7	271.2	28.1	200.2	27.8	298.8	27.0	298.8	23.0	381.4	30.0	570	30.0	578	25.3	12.8	12.8
1981	4670	4.4	4773	6.8	220.1	21.5	329.4	21.5	367.6	35.5	220.2	10.0	328.6	10.0	367.7	23.1	440.3	15.4	658	15.4	735	28.9	14.1	15.4
1982	5079	8.8	5193	8.8	223.2	1.4	334.1	1.4	413.8	12.6	192.9	–12.4	287.6	–12.4	357.5	–2.8	416.1	–5.5	622	–5.5	771	4.9	12.3	14.8
1983	5607	10.4	5809	11.9	222.3	–0.4	332.7	–0.4	438.3	5.9	213.9	10.9	319.3	10.9	421.8	18.0	436.2	4.8	652	4.8	860	11.5	11.6	14.8
1984	6431	14.7	6962	19.8	261.4	17.6	391.2	17.6	580.5	32.4	274.1	28.1	408.8	28.1	620.5	47.1	535.5	22.8	800	22.8	1201	39.7	12.4	17.3
1985	7252	12.8	8558	23.0	273.5	4.6	409.3	4.6	808.9	39.3	422.2	54.1	630.7	54.1	1257.8	102.7	696.0	30.0	1840	30.0	2067	72.1	14.3	24.2
1986	7841	8.1	9696	13.5	309.4	13.1	463.1	13.1	1082.1	33.8	429.0	1.5	640.9	1.5	1498.2	19.1	738.5	6.1	1184	6.1	2850	37.9	14.1	29.4
1987	8697	10.9	11301	16.7	394.4	27.5	590.3	27.5	1470.0	35.8	432.2	6.7	644.7	0.7	1614.2	7.7	826.5	11.9	1235	11.9	3084	8.2	14.2	27.3
1988	9680	11.3	14068	23.5	475.2	20.5	711.2	20.5	1766.7	20.2	552.8	27.9	824.8	27.9	2055.3	27.3	1827.9	24.4	1536	24.4	3822	23.9	15.9	27.3
1989	10100	4.4	15993	13.7	525.4	10.6	786.4	10.6	1956.0	10.7	591.4	7.0	882.6	7.0	2199.9	7.1	1116.8	8.6	1669	8.6	4156	8.7	16.5	26.1
1990	10508	1.1	17907	12.0	620.9	18.2	929.3	18.2	2985.8	52.6	533.5	–9.8	795.7	–9.8	2574.3	17.0	1154.4	3.1	1725	3.4	5560	33.8	16.4	31.4
1991	11321	7.7	19855	10.9	719.1	15.8	1076.2	15.8	3830.6	28.3	637.9	19.6	684.7	19.6	3398.7	32.0	1357.0	17.6	2028	17.6	7229	30.0	17.9	36.4
1992	12770	12.8	23938	20.6	850.0	18.2	1272.1	18.2	–	–	806.0	26.4	1206.2	26.4	–	–	1656.0	22.0	2475	22.0	–	–	–	–1q

growth period (1984–1988), the investment rate was the highest, with an annual average of 35.6%. The annual average investment rate of fixed assets was 29.3%. The annual average investment rate of current assets was 6.3%. The total investment on fixed assets in 1992 is 758.2 billion yuan. The investment rate calculated in the current price is 31.7%. This is normal.

The average annual investment rate in the 1990s is estimated to be about 35%, with the average annual investment rate of fixed assets at 30% and the average annual investment rate of current assets at 5%.

Here are the tasks for macroeconomic regulation and control. Lower the investment rate of current assets. When it is about 10%, it should be reduced to about 5%. It is normal for an investment rate of fixed assets to reach 30%. No need to lower it.

Table 23.36 Changes in China's investment rate

Indicator\Year	1979	1980	1981	1982	1983	1984	1985	1986	1987	1988	1989	1990	1991	1992
Investment of fixed assets (present price: 100 million yuan)	850	920	990	1230	1430	1833	2543	3020	3641	4497	4138	4449	5509	7582
Investment of current assets (present price: 100 million yuan)	323	272	328	267	296	343	745	748	580	871	1756	1712	1346	(1000)
Total investment (present price: 100 million yuan)	1173	1192	1318	1497	1726	2176	3288	3768	4221	5368	5894	6161	6855	(8582)
Total investment (fixed price: 100 million yuan)	1173	1192	1318	1557	1778	1980	2598	3014	3081	3650	3831	3697	3839	–
GDP (present price: 100 million yuan)	3998	4470	4773	5193	5809	6962	8557	9696	11,301	14,068	15,993	17,695	19,854	23,938
GDP (fixed price: 100 million yuan)	4146	4470	4670	5079	5607	6431	7252	7841	8697	9680	10,100	10,508	11,321	12,770
Investment rate (present price)	29.3	26.7	27.6	28.8	29.7	31.3	38.4	38.9	37.4	38.2	36.9	34.8	34.5	(35.8)
Investment rate for fixed assets	21.3	20.6	20.8	23.7	24.6	26.3	29.7	31.1	32.2	32.0	25.9	25.1	27.7	31.7
Investment rate for current assets	8.0	6.1	6.8	5.1	5.1	5.0	8.7	7.8	5.2	6.2	11.0	9.7	6.8	–

(continued)

Table 23.36 (continued)

Indicator\Year	1979	1980	1981	1982	1983	1984	1985	1986	1987	1988	1989	1990	1991	1992
Investment rate (fixed price)	28.3	26.7	28.2	30.7	31.7	30.8	35.8	38.4	35.4	37.7	37.9	35.2	33.9	–
Investment rate for fixed assets	20.6	20.6	21.3	25.3	26.3	25.9	27.7	30.7	30.5	31.6	26.6	25.4	27.2	31.7
Investment rate for current assets	7.7	6.1	6.9	5.4	5.4	4.9	8.1	7.7	4.9	6.1	11.3	9.8	6.7	–

5. **Inflation rate**

Inflation is a widely recognized important indicator for measuring an economic situation. There are three indicators to measuring inflation: the composite price increase rate, the retail price increase rate, and the consumer price index (CPI). The three indicators are called "inflation rate indicators." But each of them has unique usage. CPI is thought of as the most appropriate inflation rate indicator by researchers. At present, retail price increase rate is close to the CPI in China. Therefore, the retail price increase rate can also be used for measuring inflation. Since the reform and opening up, China's inflation rate has fallen in the range of 0–13.2% with an average of around 6% (see Table 23.32). The economy in China leaped from 1984 to 1988. In this period, the inflation rate was 7.8%. However, the inflation rate from 1985 to 1988 was more than 10%. This high inflation rate was caused by many reasons. Many people think that it was caused by the high GDP growth rate. Actually, this is not entirely the case. In fact, a high GDP growth rate will increase total supply and reduce inflation. In Chinese history, the economic growth rate was very high in some years, but no inflation occurred. In contrast, a low economic growth rate is likely to cause a high inflation rate. Brazil's economic growth rate in the 1980s was <5%. Its inflation rate was higher than 100%. In recent years, the Russian economic growth rate has been negative. Its inflation rate was higher than 2000%. It can be concluded that a high economic growth rate does not necessarily cause inflation and that a low economic growth does not necessarily cause inflation. In other words, there is no connection between economic growth and inflation. Even when high economic growth rate impacts inflation, it is not suggested to drop the economic growth rate artificially in order to curb inflation. Instead, measures such as controlling prices, controlling money in circulation, controlling loan scale, increasing bank interest rates, and increasing the import supply should be adopted to curb inflation. Curbing inflation is not the ultimate goal. For example, in 1988 the inflation rate was 13%. After the inflation rate was deducted, the actual economic growth rate was 11%. At that time, in order to drop the inflation rate, measures were taken to artificially depress economic growth. In 1990, the inflation dropped to half. But the actual economic growth rate fell six or seven%. In other words, more than 80 billion yuan was lost (in profits and wages). If this money has been distributed to people, everyone could have gotten about 80 yuan on the average. People will accept a high inflation rate if they receive some benefit.

The average annual inflation rate is estimated to be 6% in the 1990s.

Here are tasks for macro-control: Take measures to lower the inflation rate to 6–7%. Do not artificially reduce the economic growth rate. When the inflation rate is too high, apply other measures first. If they do not work, drop the growth rate of the GDP. Before dropping the growth rate of GDP, check if it is worthy to do so.

6. **Unemployment rate**

Although the unemployment rate is a social indicator, it can reflect the economic situation. When the economic situation is good, unemployment will be low, and vice versa. Therefore, the unemployment rate is an internationally recognized important indicator for measuring the economic situation. In foreign countries, the unemployment rate is applied to the whole society. This is reasonable. In China, however, the unemployment rate means only the unemployment rate in urban areas. It was adopted temporarily as it is now. In the future, the unemployment rate should be expanded to the whole society.

The unemployment rate in urban areas is important for rural areas. Since the reform and opening up, China's unemployment rate in urban areas changed between 1.8 and 5.3%, with the average about 2.5% (see Table 23.32).

The unemployment rate in urban areas was the lowest during the economic leap period from 1984 to 1988. The average unemployment rate was 1.94%.

The average annual urban unemployment rate in the 1990s is estimated to be 2%.

Here are the tasks for macro-control: Take measures to lower unemployment rate to around 2%. The goal is to keep it below 2%. The CPC Central Committee has decided to focus more on developing the tertiary industry. This is an important measure to reduce the unemployment rate in the 1990s. Economic growth increases employment.

7. **Population growth rate**

The population growth rate is not important for foreign countries. But it is very important for China. Excessive population growth will increase the economic burden for the society and will affect economic development. In addition, excessive population growth affects the economic development strategy in the long run. Furthermore, excessive population growth negatively impacts the growth of GDP per capita.

Since the reform and opening up, China's population growth rate changed in the range of 11.61–16.61‰ with an average of 13‰ (see Table 23.32).

During the economic leap period from 1984 to 1988, the population growth rate was high, with an average population growth rate of 15.1‰. This is a reminder that family planning should catch up with rapid economic growth.

The average annual population growth rate in the 1990s is estimated to be about 12‰.

Here are the tasks for macro-control. Take measures to lower population growth rate to around 12‰. The goal is to keep it below 12‰. The lessons of quick population growth in the economic leap period from 1984 to 1988 should be learned. Economic development and family planning are both important.

8. **Main conclusions**

According to the experience of foreign countries, the number of indicators for measuring economic situation should be small. Indicators should be practical and typical. They should be able to reflect the entire situation. For example, Germany has the famous cube corners, namely the economic growth rate, the inflation rate, the unemployment rate, and total imports and exports. Japan has five indicators, including the nominal GDP growth rate of 7–6%, the actual economic growth of 4% (nominal GDP growth rate minus inflation rate), the retail price increase rate at 3%, the unemployment rate at 2%, and the wholesale price increase rate at 1%. These are the well-known control indicators of 764,321. Many indicators have been proposed and have been studied by departments in China. According to incomplete statistics, the minimal number of recommended indicators is 4. The maximum of recommended indicators is 17 (see Table 23.38). Even so, not all indicators are included. Based on how the economic activities run in the national economy in China, the author proposed seven indicators, namely the economic growth rate, the economic structural transformation rate, the total imports and exports growth rate, the investment rate, the inflation rate, the unemployment rate, and the population growth rate. These seven indicators reflect the economy well. They are the top level indicators and they are practical. Table 23.38 shows that the indicators for measuring and assessing economic situation form a system. Altogether, there are 47 indicators. Among them, seven are the key indicators. Each key indicator has sub-indicators. For example, the economic growth rate has 20 sub-indicators. The economic structure transformation rate has three sub-indicators. The growth rate of total imports and exports has five sub-indicators. The investment rate has nine sub-indicators. The inflation rate has five sub-indicators. The unemployment rate has three sub-indicators. The population growth rate has one sub-indicator. Sub-indicators are local, whereas key indicators are global. The seven key indicators are recommended for use, but sub-indicators can be used as well. It is not appropriate to measure and judge an economic situation with local indicators. For example, the fiscal indicator and the personal income growth rate are included in the economic growth rate. The seven key indicators are practical. Among them, the economic structure transformation rate and the investment rate are widely applied across the world. They are easy to calculate and can reflect the whole picture of economy. In addition, applying them is easy too (Table 23.37).

23.14.2 Comprehensive Assessment for Economic Situation with the Seven Key Indicators

These seven key indicators have quantitative values. In normal circumstances, high values for the four key indicators mean that economic situation is good. These indicators include the economic growth rate, the economic structure transformation rate, total import and export growth, and the investment rate. Low values for three indicators means that economic situation is not good. These indicators include the inflation

Table 23.37 Indicator system for measuring and assessing economic situation

Category	Indicator	Recommendation	Source 1		Source 2			Source 3		Source 4		
			1	2	1	2	3	1	2	1	2	3
I	Economic growth rate	√	√	√	√	√	√	√	√	√	√	√
II	Economic structure transformation rate	√	–	–	–	–	√	–	–	–	–	–
III	Growth rate of total imports and exports	√	√	–	–	–	–	–	–	√	√	
IV	Investment rate	√	–	–	–	–	–	–	–	–	–	–
V	Inflation rate	√	√	√	–	√	√	–	–	–	–	√
VI	Unemployment rate	√	√	√	√	√	–	–	–	–	√	√
VII	Population growth rate	√	–	–	√	√	–	–	–	–	√	–
I	Growth rate of first industry added value	–	–	–	–	–	–	–	–	–	√	–
	Growth rate of agricultural added value	–	–	–	√	–	–	√	√	–	–	–
	Growth rate of second industry added value	–	–	–	–	–	–	–	–	–	–	–
	Growth rate of industrial added value	–	–	–	–	–	–	–	–	–	√	–
	Growth rate of light industry added value	–	–	–	–	–	–	–	–	–	√	–
	Growth rate of heavy industry added value	–	–	–	–	–	–	–	–	–	√	–
	Growth rate of total industrial added value	–	–	–	√	–	–	√	√	–	–	–
	Growth rate of construction industry added value	–	–	–	–	–	–	–	–	–	√	–
	Growth rate of third industry added value	–	–	–	√	–	–	–	–	–	√	–
	Growth rate of GNP per capita	–	–	–	–	–	–	–	–	√	–	–
	Growth rate of national income	–	–	–	–	–	–	√	√	–	–	–
	Growth rate of fiscal revenue	–	–	–	√	√	–	√	√	√	–	–
	Growth rate of fiscal payments	–	–	–	√	√	–	√	√	–	–	–

(continued)

Table 23.37 (continued)

Category	Indicator	Recommendation	Source 1		Source 2			Source 3		Source 4		
			1	2	1	2	3	1	2	1	2	3
	Fiscal deficit	–	–	–	–	√	–	√	√	–	–	–
	Growth rate of funds outside budget	–	–	–	–	–	–	–	–	√	–	–
	Growth rate of CPI	–	–	–	–	–	–	–	√	√	–	√
	Growth rate of rural income per capita	–	–	–	–	–	–	–	√	√	–	√
	Comprehensive saving efficiency	–	–	–	–	–	–	–	–	–	–	–
	Equipment efficiency	–	–	–	–	–	–	–	–	–	–	√
II	Ratio of three industries in GDP	–	–	–	–	–	–	–	–	–	–	–
	Ratio of Industry and agriculture	–	–	–	–	–	–	–	–	–	–	–
	Ratio of Light and heavy industry	–	–	–	–	–	–	–	–	–	–	–
III	Import growth rate	–	–	–	–	–	–	–	–	–	√	√
	Export growth rate	–	–	–	–	–	–	–	–	–	√	√
	Foreign trade dependence	–	–	–	–	–	–	–	–	–	–	–
	International payments	–	–	–	–	√	–	–	–	–	–	√
	Foreign debt scale	–	–	–	–	–	–	–	–	–	–	√
IV	Investment rate of fixed assets	–	–	–	√	√	√	√	√	–	√	–
	Investment rate of current assets	–	–	–	–	–	–	–	–	–	–	–
	Balance between credits and payments	–	–	–	√	√	–	–	–	–	–	–
	Scale of newly added loans	–	–	–	–	–	–	√	√	–	–	–
	Savings deposit growth rate	–	–	–	–	–	–	–	–	√	–	–

(continued)

Table 23.37 (continued)

Category	Indicator	Recommendation	Source 1		Source 2			Source 3		Source 4		
			1	2	1	2	3	1	2	1	2	3
	Growth rate of residential savings	–	–	–	–	–	–	√	√	–	–	–
	Consumption growth	–	–	–	–	√	–	–	–	–	–	–
	Retail commodity growth rate	–	–	–	–	–	–	√	√	–	–	–
	CPI growth rate	–	–	–	√	–	–	–	√	√	–	–
V	Money supply	–	–	–	–	√	–	–	√	–	–	√
	Retail price index growth rate	–	–	√	–	–	–	√	√	–	√	√
	Wholesale price index growth rate	–	–	√	–	–	–	–	–	–	–	–
	Service price index growth rate	–	–	–	–	–	–	–	–	–	√	–
	CPI	–	–	–	–	–	–	–	√	–	√	√
VI	Employment rate	–	–	–	–	√	–	–	–	–	–	–
	Urban unemployment rate	–	–	–	–	–	–	–	–	–	–	–
	Rural unemployment rate	–	–	–	–	–	–	–	–	–	–	–
VII	Labor growth rate	–	–	–	–	–	–	–	–	–	–	–

Note Source 1 is oversea data
Source 2 is State Planning Commission
Source 3 is the Chinese Academy of Social Sciences
Source 4 is State Statistics Bureau

rate, the unemployment rate, and the population growth rate. In the same period, these seven key indicators are not balanced. Some indicators have good values, while some do not have good values. For example, a low inflation rate indicates that the economic situation is good. But this period has a low economic growth rate. In this case, it is not easy to assess the economic situation.

Therefore, the author has proposed an advanced comprehensive evaluation method. Recently, an application software was developed to comprehensively assess the economic situation. This software is simple, easy, and practical. A comprehensive index of the economic situation can be easily generated by China's economic situation assessment software package. Based on this index, assessment can be implemented. The economic situation is categorized into very good, good, relatively good, and bad.

23.14.3 Comprehensive Assessment Results of China's Economic Situation After Reform and Opening Up

With China's economic situation assessment software package, assessment of China's economic situation can be generated. The results match the facts. They are shown in Table 23.32.

1. Since the reform and opening up, the economic situation of China has held the status of very good, good, and relatively good, most of the time. Particularly, 27% of the years were very good. 27% were good. 33% were relatively good. 13% were bad.
2. During the economic leap period from 1984 to 1988, the economic situation was very good or good in each year. If inflation rate had not been over 10% in 1988, the economic situation in this year would have been very good, as well.
3. In 1992, due to the excessive growth of the secondary industry, the growth rate of the tertiary industry is less than GDP growth. The ratio of the tertiary industry in GDP did not rise, but dropped. This keeps the low ratio of the tertiary industry in the GDP in China. Therefore, the economic situation in 1992 is in the upper limit of good status. If there were no such abnormal industrial structure, the economic situation in 1992 would be very good.
4. The economic growth rate is the most important indicator that affects the economic situation deeply. The second most important are the inflation rate and the economic structure transformation rate. The third most important is the unemployment rate. The fourth most important are the growth rate of total imports and exports, the investment rate, and the population growth rate.

Facts have proven that, during the economic leap period from 1984 to 1988, economy grew rapidly. Total imports and exports and the investment rate grew quickly, as well. The unemployment rate was low. Tertiary industry developed quickly. The economic structure transformation rate was the best. Only the inflation rate and the population growth rate were not so good.

23.14.4 Approaches and Means for Macro Control

There are many approaches and means for macro control. This chapter does not introduce them one by one. These approaches fall into five types, namely political approaches, economic approaches, diplomatic approaches, administrative approaches, and legal approaches. The author wants to highlight economic system reform. The socialist market economy proposed by Comrade Deng Xiaoping and the 14th CPC National Congress is an efficiency revolution. It is the fundamental means to ensure and control China's economic situation development in the correct direction. This approach is not available in capitalist countries. Table 23.38 lists goals and approached in China's macro-control in the 1990s.

23.14.5 Several Suggestions

1. Currently, macro control is somewhat dispersed. There is an urgent need for a high level macroeconomic management agency. This agency should combine short term, medium term, and long term assessment and regulation at the state level. For example, the implementation of industry policies will be impossible without the coordination of fiscal and monetary policies. This problem should be solved as soon as possible.
2. Macro control cannot stop at reports. Timely inspection and assessment are required to ensure the implementation of macro control measures. Macro control measures should be authoritative.
3. A specific agency should assess the economic situation with consolidated standards and with China's economic situation assessment software package. The results should be released publicly. Assessing results from other agencies should be provided, as well. Conclusions of assessment should rely on the practice. The software package should be upgraded continuously.
4. At present, too many indicators have been adopted by departments and experts to monitor the economic situation monthly. For example, the economic cyclical variation index (DI index) is adopted in Japan. The composite index was adopted in China. Actually, these two indices reflect the status of the economic operation, not the economic situation. Further research is required to explore the connection between the economic operation and the economic situation. It may be common to misunderstand an overheating economic operation as a bad economic situation. Measures proposed by this study can be applied to measuring the economic situation monthly, quarterly, semiannually, and yearly.

Table 23.38 Macro-control goals and measures in the 1990s in China

Macro control goals	Control goals in the 1990s	Control requirements	Control methods	Control approaches
Economic growth rate	Annual average is about 10%, (the following is the same)	Try to raise the growth rate. Prevent declining	Since reform and opening up, 40% depends on added investment, and 60% depends on technical progress. Continue this method in the future, because many key problems cannot be solved without high efficiency of inputs. Focus on fixing insufficient consumption demand	Political, economic, diplomatic, administrative, and legal
Economic structure transformation rate	Higher than 2%	Growth rate of the secondary industry should be higher than that of the first industry. Growth rate of the third industry should be higher than GDP growth rate and growth rate of the secondary industry	Rely on industry policies. Banks and fiscal policies should keep the direction of investment	
Growth rate of total imports and exports	Higher than 10–15%	Try to raise the growth rate. Keep it higher than GDP growth rate. Keep the reasonable size of foreign trade surplus and deficit	Adjust exchange rates and taxes. Actual foreign trade dependence should not be too low	
Investment rate	About 35%	Lower investment rate of current assets. If it is about 10%, lower it. Keep high investment rate of fixed assets	Adjust bank interests and loan scale	

(continued)

Table 23.38 (continued)

Macro control goals	Control goals in the 1990s	Control requirements	Control methods	Control approaches
Inflation rate	About 6%	Try to lower the rate. Keep it below 10%. Do not artificially decrease economic growth rate	Control prices, money in circulation and M2 money amount	
Unemployment rate	About 2%	Try to lower the rate. Keep it below 2%	Increase employment. Develop the third industry. Shorten working days.	
Population growth rate	About 12‰	Try to lower the rate. Keep it below 12‰	Implement family planning and social insurance	

23.15 Scientific Index for Transition of Economic Growth Modes[34]

Research background, scientific significance of achievements and practical value.

The Fifth Plenary Session of the 14th CPC National Congress in September of 1995 pointed out that the key for achieving the goals in 2000 and 2010 is the implementation of two fundamental transformations. One is the transfer from the traditional planned economic system to the socialist market economic system. The other is the transfer from an extensive economic growth mode to an intensive economic growth mode. In order to effectively implement the Central Government's policy on the transformation of the economic growth mode, there is an urgent need for a scientific indicator system to quantitatively answer the problems of general concern, such as what is extensive economy growth mode? What is the intensive economy growth mode? How can the transformation be performed quickly? What is the fundamental transformation? What are the good results of transformation? However, such an indicator system is not available at the present time. Given the need for this indicator system, the author undertook the research project "Transformation of the Economic Growth Mode" issued by Macroeconomic Research Academy of the State Planning Commission in early 1995. The research aimed to propose an indicator system for measuring the transformation of the economic growth mode. Here are the requirements of this indicator system: First, this indicator system should answer

[34]Xu, S. B., et al. (1996). Study on transition of economic growth models in China, research report of project group of industrial economy and research institute of technical economy under State Planning Commission.

the questions that the leaders of the Party, government officials, enterprises, and general people have. Second, this indicator system should reflect the requirements of the economic growth laws as well as the essence of economic growth activities. It should remove the illusions. Third, this indicator system should be operable so that national government, local governments, respective sectors and enterprises can make calculations according to available statistical tools or information and can obtain quantitative results. Based on the three requirements, the author deepened the study on the project "Study on China's Comprehensive Strategy, Planning and Countermeasures" issued by the State Planning Commission several years ago. In November 1995 and in January 1996, the author presented two articles "Economic Growth Mode Transformation of Large and Medium-Sized State-Owned Enterprises" and "Countermeasures of Enterprises during the Economic Growth Mode Transformation" at the Enterprise Strategy Forum hosted by the China Academy of Management. These two articles initially proposed an indicator system for measuring the economic growth mode transformation. The system was thought highly of by both experts and enterprises. Later, the articles were published in journals edited by the State Planning Commission, the State Economic and Trade Commission, the State Council Research Office, the Policy Research Office of CPC Central Committee, the Ministry of Machinery Industry, the National Bureau of Statistics, and the China Enterprise Management Association. China's central television reported it, as well. The two articles attracted much attention across the whole society. Furthermore, a reporter from Economic Daily did a serial report of the indicator system in Thoughts on Transforming the Economic Growth Mode during the National People's Congress and the Chinese People's Political Consultative Conference in 1996. This indicator system was applied in the Ministry of Coal Industry, at Liaohe Oilfield, and at other sectors and enterprises. In 1997, the author published a book "How to Assess the Economic Growth Mode" [See results of scientific researches 303–310, 318–334, 336, 340–342].

23.15.1 Why Transform Economic Growth Mode

1. **Objective laws require transforming economic growth mode**

Economic growth includes two aspects: economic growth quantity and economic growth quality. In short, economic growth quantity mainly refers to the economic growth rate, whereas economic growth quality mainly refers to the economic growth mode.

The economic growth rate and the economic growth mode follow some objective rules in China, just as in other countries in the world. They cannot be transformed freely.

Here are the laws for economic growth rate: First, the changes of the economic growth rate follow a wave pattern. The changes are periodic, and a cycle lasts 3–6 years in general. When the cycle is three years, the changes follow a V-shape pattern.

When the cycle is six years, the changes follow a U-shaped pattern. The gap between the peaks and the bottoms is 5–10%. This is called the V–U change rule. Second, the speed of the economic growth rate falls into medium and high-speed type, medium and low-speed type, and intermediate type. The speed of the economic growth rate in developing countries is generally higher than that in developed countries. Speeds in economic growth rates can be different in different periods and in different countries.

Here are the laws for economic growth mode: First, the economic growth mode follows this pattern: low intensive economy in agricultural society → improvement of intensive economy → high intensive economy in modern society. Second, the economic growth modes fall into fully extensive economy, extensive and intensive combination economy, and intensive economy. Economic growth modes vary across countries and periods. In the early agricultural society, the economic growth was completely extensive. The level of the intensive economy was very low. In agricultural development, intensive economy is improved continuously. In the early industrialization, new factories were constructed that consumed a lot of money, energy, and raw materials. Intensive economic growth was low. So was the level of intensive economy. In the mid-term of industrialization, the intensive economy was greatly improved. The level of intensive economy was improved accordingly. In modern society, the level of intensive economy is rather high. Intensive economy is maintained at a certain level.

From founding of the new China to the third Plenary Session of the Eleventh CPC National Congress (1978), agricultural economic development was intensive farming due to limited arable land. However, because of industrialization, China's economy was extensive. Thus, the intensive economy level was declining. Since the reform and opening up in 1978, the economic growth mode has begun to change. The extensive economy and the intensive economy were combined. Therefore, the level of intensive economy was improved. Economic development in China follows the objective laws of economic growth mode.

2. **Significance of economic growth mode transformation**

Transformation of the economic growth mode follows its own laws. The economic growth mode should not be changed freely. However, if the transformation completely relies on spontaneous change, it will take a very long time. Sometimes, a negative transformation might occur. This has been proven by facts in China and around the world. Therefore, it is important that people should consciously promote the economic growth modes in accordance with the objective laws in order to achieve the leap from spontaneous change to conscious change. Since the reform and opening up, the CPC Central Committee has always stressed that the purpose of transformation is to increase the economic growth rate and to raise the level of intensive economy. In other words, economic development should follow the objective laws of the economic growth rate and economic growth modes. In this way, the nation and people can soon be rich. Thus, first, the third Plenary Session of the Eleventh CPC National Congress put forward "shifting Party's work focus and people's attention to socialist modernization." This was a change in the party's work focus. Second, the 12th CPC

National Congress proposed "shifting all economic work to the track of improving economic efficiency." This was a change in the economic work focus. Third, the 13th CPC National congress put forward that the economic growth strategic objectives should be changed from agricultural output value into gross domestic product (GDP), and stressed "shifting from extensive operation to intensive operation, and making economic development relied on scientific and technological progress and improved labor quality." This was a change in the economic growth strategy. The fourth change was about the economic system and the economic growth mode. The 14th CPC National Congress proposed to establish a socialist market economic system. The Fifth Plenary Session of the 14th CPC National Congress pointed out that "two fundamental transformations should be achieved." One is the transformation from the traditional planned economic system to a socialist market economic system. The other is the change in the economic growth mode from extensive to intensive.

The first transformation CPC Central Committee proposed is the premise. If the work focus of CPC were not shifted to economic work, the following three transformations would not happen. The 12th CPC National Congress proposed that future economic work should be focused on an improvement of economic efficiency. In essence, the requirements of these transformations are the same as those of the transformation of the economic growth modes. Therefore, 10 years ago, the government proposed to transform the economic growth modes. Practice in the past 10 years has proven that China's economic growth modes have improved a lot since the reform and opening up. However, compared with foreign countries, the level of the intensive economy in China is still too low. Economic growth must be intensive. Rapid economic growth in the future will require speeding up the transformation from the extensive growth mode to the intensive growth mode. Compared with the transformation goals proposed at the 12th CPC National Congress, the transformation goal of economic growth modes proposed at the Fifth Plenary Session of 14th CPC National Congress is more practical, realistic, and historical.

First, the transformation of economic growth mode is the requirement for establishing socialist market economic system. In short, the core of the socialist market economic system is to optimize allocation of resources and to improve economic efficiency. The extensive economic growth mode cannot improve the economic efficiency. Thus, it conflicts with the market economic system. Without transformation of the extensive economic growth mode, a market economic system cannot be established and the transformation of economic system will be impossible. Without the transformation of economic systems, transformation of economic growth modes will be impossible. The two are complementary and are mutually reinforcing.

Second, transformation of the economic growth modes is the requirement for scientific development and technical conversion. Although the input is large and many scientific and technological achievements have been achieved, China's science and technology input is low compared with that of developed countries. The ratio of scientific and technological achievements converted to the productive forces is small, only about 20%. In other words, a large number of scientific and technological achievements have not been applied, in practice. The extensive economic growth mode has no urgent requirements for advanced scientific and technological achievements and the application of advanced scientific and technological achievements. Accordingly, the CPC Central Committee proposed to change the extensive economic growth mode. The proposal requires that advanced scientific and technological achievements be applied and that the conversion of China's science and technology be promoted to a productive force and to enhance science and technology. At the same time, after the economic growth mode is transformed, more input will be applied for science and technology. Thus, science and technology will develop more quickly. Economic growth modes and technological progress are also complementary and are mutually reinforcing.

Third, the transformation of the economic growth mode is the requirement for improving the management of the socialist market economic capacity. Without transformation of the extensive economic growth mode, management thinking, management methods, and management systems, management tools and management models in the traditional planned economic system will not be changed. Transformation of economic growth modes will require changes to low-efficiency management as well as the management not suitable for a socialist market economy. Therefore, the transformation of economic growth modes can contribute to improving national macroeconomic management and enterprise micro-management for the socialist market economy, enhancing management capability, and achieving management objectives. In return, good management can help to change the economic growth mode. Economic growth modes and management are also complementary and are mutually reinforcing.

Fourth, the transformation of economic growth modes is the requirement for adjusting the economic structure. The extensive economic growth mode consumes a large amount of intermediate products, including energy and raw materials. The extensive economic growth mode causes an imbalance between intermediate consumer products and final consumer products, the imbalance between manufacturers of intermediate products and manufacturers of final products, and the imbalance among the primary, the secondary, and the tertiary industries. Extensive economic growth mode generates an energy wasting economic structure with more production input and fewer products. This economic structure cannot meet people's living standards. Transformation of the extensive economic growth mode to the intensive economic growth mode is actually the transition from the energy-wasting economic structure to the energy saving economic structure. Without the transformation of the economic growth mode, an adjustment in the economic structure will be impossible, and vice versa. Economic growth modes and economic structure are also complementary and are mutually reinforcing.

Fifth, transformation of the economic growth mode is the requirement for improving people's living standards. Improvement of People's living standards requires adding consumption, changing the consumer demand structure, and improving the quality of life. The extensive economic growth mode requires a large number of resources in the production processes, resulting in high production costs. When the prices of energy and raw material rise, the extensive economic growth mode cannot solve the problem through reducing consumption, but passes the high prices on to consumers, resulting in inflation, and influencing people's consumption levels. Due to high input and low output, when the economy develops rapidly, the extensive economic growth mode consumes a lot of resources, causing environmental pollution, influencing people's quality of life, and sharpening the contradictions between population, resources, the environment, and the economy. Therefore, a sustainable development strategy cannot be implemented. Transformation of the economic growth mode from extensive to intensive will ensure the improvement of people's living standards as well as their cultural level and labor quality. Without transformation of the economic growth mode, people's living standards will not be improved. On the other hand, the improvement of labor quality is also an important factor in ensuring economic growth mode transformation. Economic growth modes and people's living standards are also complementary and are mutually reinforcing.

In short, the proposal to transform the economic growth modes by CPC Central Committee is very important and is fully in line with the objective law and the actual situation in China. After the Fifth Plenary Session of the 14th CPC National Congress proposed the transformation of the economic growth mode from extensive to intensive, there are three different understandings about extensive economic growth and intensive economic growth.

According to the first understanding, extensive and intensive refer to production and operation methods, namely extensive management and intensive management. They do not refer to the expanded reproduction mode. Based on the second understanding, the original meaning of extensive in English is extension. The original meaning of "intensive" in English is concentrated. Therefore, extensive and intensive refer to an expanded reproduction mode, namely the extension of expanded reproduction and the connotation of expanded reproduction. In fact, the terms extensive and intensive can be translated into extensive expanded reproduction and intensive expanded reproduction. But people are familiar with the denotation and the connotation. According to the third understanding, extensive and intensive refer to production and management, as well as to the expanded reproduction mode, i.e. a combination of these two. Although the first two understandings are reasonable, the third one is most appropriate for the actual meaning of economic growth mode. Economic growth contains two aspects: the economic growth of existing enterprises and new enterprises through production and operation and the economic growth of existing enterprises and new enterprises through expanding production and improving production capacity. Accordingly, the economic growth mode should include two aspects as well, namely the production and operation mode and the expanded reproduction mode. The economic growth mode is closely related with production and operation mode. Good production and operation usually have good economic growth modes, and vice versa. However, economic growth modes are not equal to production and operation modes. Similarly, the economic growth mode largely depends on expanded reproduction modes. Good expanded reproduction modes have good economic growth modes, and vice versa. An expanded reproduction mode is not equal to an economic growth mode, either. The CPC Central Committee proposed the transformation from the extensive economic growth mode to the intensive economic growth mode, referring to the transformation of the production and the operation modes as well as to the expanded reproduction mode. Compared with foreign countries, the production and operation modes are very extensive in China. In addition, the expanded reproduction mode is very extensive in China, as well. Both of them need to be transformed.

23.15.2 Transformation of Economic Growth Mode Requires a Scientific Evaluation Indicator System

1. **What problems need to be solved by the evaluation indicator system for economic growth mode transformation**

After the Fifth Plenary Session of the 14th CPC National Congress proposed the fundamental transformation from an extensive economic growth mode to an intensive economic growth mode, all of the regions, sectors, industries and enterprises paid special attention to the transformation. Here are some important questions for the transformation: What indicators can be used to measure and to assess the transformation of economic growth modes? What is extensive? What is intensive? What is ordinary transformation? What is fundamental transformation? Which transformation is good? So far, there is no quantitative indicator system for answering these questions.

Therefore, the evaluation indicator system for transformation of economic growth mode should provide a quantitative base to answer the following five questions:

(1) Is the economic growth mode of the nation, sectors, and enterprises intensive or extensive? Is the economic growth mode of the nation, sectors, and enterprises intensive or extensive?
(2) What are the direction and the speed of the transformation of the economic growth mode?
(3) To what extent should the transformation of economic growth mode reach?
(4) What effects will the transformation of economic growth mode generate?
(5) What is approach to compare the effects of the transformation of the economic growth mode?

The following is an evaluation indicator system which can answer the above five questions quantitatively.

2. **Evaluation indicator system for the transformation of economic growth mode**

In order to completely evaluate the economic efficiency of enterprises, in 1995, the Ministry of Finance began to adopt a new evaluation indicator system. Meanwhile, in order to completely evaluate completely the basic situation and the dynamic status of large and medium sized enterprises, the State Economic and Trade Commission and the National Bureau of Statistics began to adopt a new indicator system. The former system evaluated the economic efficiency of enterprises from the perspective of corporate investors, creditors, and the states, whereas the latter evaluates the overall economic strength, the input and output capacity, the operating capacity, the profitability, the solvency and development capacity, and the total running status of enterprises. These two systems both adopt static financial assessment indicators and data.

The evaluation indicator system for the transformation of economic growth mode proposed by the author is related to these two evaluation indicator systems, but it is different from them. The fundamental difference is that it adopts dynamic economic assessment indicators and data from economic growth. This evaluation indicator system includes 11 indicators, namely extensiveness, intensiveness, level of intensiveness, input coefficients, input economic efficiency, improvement of the intensiveness level, saving rate, increasing rate of efficiency, effect of the improved intensiveness, amount of saving, and amount of increased efficiency. The following is a detailed introduction of these indicators.

23.15.3 *Indicators for Measuring and Assessing Extensive and Intensive Economic Growth Modes*

1. **Calculation method for extensiveness**

Before transforming the economic growth mode, it is necessary to know clearly about the past economic growth mode, the current economic growth mode, and the future economic growth mode. Economic growth modes can be measured by the indicator of their extensiveness. Extensiveness is the input elasticity coefficient indicator of the production factors. It is a key indicator for measuring and assessing the economic growth modes of nations, regions, sectors, and enterprises. It is the ratio between the input increasing rate of production factors and the economic growth rate. It reflects the proportion of extensive growth in the total economic growth. If the proportion is large, extensiveness is large. If the proportion is small, extensiveness is small.

This is the formula for calculating extensiveness.

$$\text{Extensiveness} = \text{elasticity coefficient of inputs} \tag{23.22}$$

$$\begin{aligned}
&\text{Elasticity coefficient of inputs}\\
&\quad = \text{input growth rate/economic growth rate}\\
&\quad = \big[(1 + \text{economic growth rate}) \times (\text{input coefficient of assessment year}\\
&\qquad /\text{input coefficient of reference year})^{1/t} - 1\big]\\
&\qquad \div \text{ economic growth rate}\\
&\quad = \big[(1 + \text{economic growth rate}) \times (\text{input economic of assessment}\\
&\qquad /\text{input economic efficiency of assessment year})^{1/t} - 1\big]\\
&\qquad \div \text{ economic growth rate}
\end{aligned} \tag{23.23}$$

This indicator can be expressed by integers or percentages.

Extensiveness falls into two types: individual extensiveness and comprehensive extensiveness. Input of each production factor has its own individual input elasticity coefficient. This is individual extensiveness, the ratio between the individual input growth rate and the economic growth rate. Individual extensiveness can be used for assessing whether a single input growth mode is extensive or intensive. If all of the individual extensiveness numbers are small, the extensiveness of the whole economic growth mode is small. However, when a certain individual extensiveness is small, other individual extensiveness are not small. It is hard to assess the extensiveness of the whole economic growth mode. Therefore, comprehensive extensiveness should be applied. Comprehensive extensiveness is the ratio between comprehensive input growth rate and economic growth rate. Here is the formula for calculating comprehensive extensiveness.

$$\begin{aligned}&\text{Comprehensive extensiveness}\\&\quad=\text{comprehensive input elasticity coefficient}\\&\quad=\text{comprehensive input growth rate/economic growth rate}\end{aligned}\tag{23.24}$$

$$\begin{aligned}&\text{Or comprehensive extensiveness}\\&\quad=\text{comprehensive input elasticity coefficient}\\&\quad=\sum i \text{ input weight}\times i\text{ input elasticity coefficient}\end{aligned}\tag{23.25}$$

The input elasticity coefficient has the following applications.

(1) Directly reflect the relationship between supply and saving for a certain production input. For example, if the input elasticity coefficient of steel is equal to or >1, this means that economic growth completely relies on the input of steel. If the input elasticity coefficient of steel is <1 and >0, this means that economic growth depends on the input of the steel supply as well as on the saving of steel. The input elasticity coefficient represents the ratio of steel input. The value 1 is the input elasticity coefficient. It represents the ratio between the input of steel and the saving of steel. For example, the input elasticity coefficient of steel was 0.8 in the ninth five-year plan period. This means that 80% of economic growth relied on the steel supply and 20% of economic growth relied on steel saving. If the input elasticity coefficient of steel is = 0 or <0, this means that economic growth completely relies on steel saving.

(2) The input elasticity coefficient can be used for increasing, lowering, and stabilizing input the economic efficiency and input coefficient. To increase the input economic efficiency and lower input coefficient, set the input elasticity coefficient at <1. To reduce the input economic efficiency and increase the input coefficient, set the input elasticity coefficient at >1. To maintain the input economic efficiency and the input coefficient, set the input elasticity coefficient equal to 1.

(3) If the economic growth rate is known, the input quantity can be estimated with an input elasticity coefficient. If input supply is known, the economic growth rate can be estimated.

The following are the calculation methods for input growth rate and economic growth rate.

(1) *Calculation methods for input growth rate*

The input growth rate refers to the individual input growth rate of material, financial resources, manpower, transportation, natural forces, and time. It can also refer to the comprehensive input growth rate.

The individual input growth rate should be calculated with material inputs. Particularly, it seems that the input growth rate of capital can be calculated with value. But when comparable prices are adopted and the factor of price rising is removed, the input growth rate can be calculated with value reflects the growth rate of materials. Similarly, the other five input growth rates all reflect the growth rate of materials. Here is the formula.

① Individual input growth rate

$$= (\text{material input of assessment year/material input of reference year})^{1/t} \tag{23.26}$$

Asset growth rate should be calculated with comparable prices. Usually, only fixed assets and current assets in current prices are available. They need to be converted into comparable prices with an investment price correction coefficient. Here is the method for conversion.

A. Conversion of total input of fixed assets:

$$\begin{array}{l}\text{Total input of fixed assets}\\ \text{of all years calculated}\\ \text{with comparable prices of}\\ \text{a certain year}\end{array} = \begin{array}{l}\text{Investment stock of fixed}\\ \text{assets calculated through}\\ \text{comparable prices of the}\\ \text{previous year}\end{array} + \begin{array}{l}\text{Fixed assets}\\ \text{investment of}\\ \text{current year}\\ \text{(current price)}\end{array} \times \begin{array}{l}\text{Correction}\\ \text{coefficient of}\\ \text{investment price}\\ \text{of current year}\end{array} \tag{23.27}$$

B. Conversion of total input of current assets:

$$\begin{array}{l}\text{Total input of current}\\ \text{assets of various years}\\ \text{calculated with}\\ \text{comparable prices of a}\\ \text{certain year}\end{array} = \begin{array}{l}\text{Total investment}\\ \text{of current assets}\\ \text{of current year}\\ \text{(current price)}\end{array} \times \begin{array}{l}\text{Correction}\\ \text{coefficient of}\\ \text{investment price}\\ \text{of current year}\end{array} \tag{23.28}$$

C. Investment price index in all years

$$\text{Investment price index in all year} = \frac{\text{GDP in all years calculated with comparable prices} - \text{Consumption in all years calculated with comparable prices}}{\text{GDP in prices of current year} - \text{Consumption in current year}}$$

$$= \frac{\text{GDP in all years calculated with comparable prices} - \text{CPI} \times \text{Consumption rate}}{\text{Investment rate}} \quad (23.29)$$

D. The investment price correction coefficient across all years can be calculated based on an annual investment price index. For example, set the price in 1994 as the base. The investment in 1992 can be converted into the investment based on the price in 1994 by multiplying it with the investment price growth rates of 1994 and 1993. Meanwhile, the price rise in 1992 should be considered, as well. If the investment in 1992 already includes the price rise in 1992, no action is needed. If not, the investment price growth rate in 1992 should be multiplied, as well. Because the price rise and the investment occur in the same year, only half of the price rise rate should be considered, not the full price rise rate. Table 23.39 lists investment price correction coefficients based on comparable prices in 1995.

For enterprises, the investment price correction coefficient can be determined according to theinvestment price growth rate of fixed assets and the price growth rate of liquidity assets.

Table 23.39 Investment price correction coefficient (national)

Year	1995	1994	1993	1992	1991	1990	
Correction coefficient	1.000	1.072	1.195	1.326	1.745	1.906	
Year	1989	1988	1987	1986	1985	1984	
Correction coefficient	2.097	2.160	2.319	2.541	2.541	2.891	
Year	1983	1982	1981	1980	1979	1978	
Correction coefficient	3.272	3.304	3.177	3.177	3.177	3.272	
Year	1977	1976	1975	1974	1973	1972	
Correction coefficient	3.336	3.367	3.336	3.145	3.145	3.145	
Year	1971	1970	1969	1968	1967	1966	
Correction coefficient	3.145	3.177	2.605	1.779	2.224	2.669	
Year	1965	1964	1963	1962	1961	1960	
Correction coefficient	2.224	2.541	2.637	4.670	3.908	3.908	
Year	1959	1958	1957	1956	1955	1954	1953
Correction coefficient	3.399	3.209	2.796	2.510	1.938	2.033	1.620

② *Comprehensive input growth rate*

Two methods can be applied to calculate the comprehensive input growth rate. The first one is the value calculation method. It converts the material consumption expenses or costs of each year (the current prices) into the prices in a certain comparable year with a material consumption price correction coefficient. The second one is the material calculation method. It integrates the material input growth rate related to the consumption expenses or costs into a comprehensive input growth rate.

A. Value calculation method

Here is the formula for computing the comprehensive input growth rate.

$$\begin{aligned}&\text{Comprehensive input growth rate}\\&\quad=[(\text{comprehensive input of the final year/comprehensive input of reference year})^{1/t}-1]\\&\quad\times 100\%\end{aligned}\qquad(23.30)$$

Comprehensive investment is the sum of manpower, materials, financial resources, natural forces (land, mineral resources, etc.), transportation, and time. To facilitate the calculation, indicators, such as total material consumption, total costs, or total consumption costs (total costs + capital costs), are adopted.

Because material consumption costs are closely related to price of production goods, the price index for production goods is adopted to calculate the correction coefficient of material consumption. Then material consumption expenses in various years based on current prices are converted into the comparable prices of a certain year with this correction coefficient (see Table 23.40).

Table 23.40 Correction coefficients of material consumption prices (national)

Year	1995	1994	1993	1992	1991	1990	
Correction coefficient	1.000	1.136	1.326	1.772	1.937	2.092	
Year	1989	1988	1987	1986	1985	1984	
Correction coefficient	2.184	2.597	2.953	3.186	3.307	3.595	
Year	1983	1982	1981	1980	1979	1978	
Correction coefficient	3.645	3.642	3.635	3.642	3.660	3.715	
Year	1977	1976	1975	1974	1973	1972	
Correction coefficient	3.772	3.815	3.802	3.738	3.745	3.753	
Year	1971	1970	1969	1968	1967	1966	
Correction coefficient	3.751	3.783	3.624	3.442	3.499	3.575	
Year	1965	1964	1963	1962	1961	1960	
Correction coefficient	3.418	3.495	3.499	3.412	3.387	3.771	
Year	1959	1958	1957	1956	1955	1954	1953
Correction coefficient	3.818	3.860	3.904	3.843	3.760	3.720	3.709

B. Material calculation method

This is a comprehensive input growth rate achieved by integrating individual material input growth rate. Here is its calculation formula.

$$\text{Comprehensive input growth rate} = \sum i \text{ input weight} \times i \text{ input growth rate} \quad (23.31)$$

where the weight of each input can be determined according to its ratio in the total output value.

(2) *Calculation method of economic growth rate*

Before the 13th CPC National Congress, the goal of China's economic development was measured by the output of industrial and agricultural output. Accordingly, the economic growth rate referred to the growth rate of the output of the industrial and agricultural sectors. The 12th CPC National Congress proposed the goal that, by 2000, the output of the industrial and agricultural sectors should be quadrupled, compared with 1980. To achieve this goal, the average annual economic growth rate should be 7.2%. After the 13th CPC National Congress, the measurement for China's economic development goal changed into GDP (GNP). This was a significant change in the history of economic development in China. Actually, GNP, GDP, and added value all refer to the same thing. They all include national tax revenue, bank interest income, social income (such as all kinds of funds), wages and welfare income, corporate profits, and corporate depreciation. For enterprises, the industrial output value was the indicator for assessment in the past. Now, the indicator changed into industrial added value, because added value is entirely consistent with GDP. Therefore, the economic growth rate now refers to the growth rate of national and local GDP, as well as to the growth rate of the added value of industries and enterprises. It is the actual growth rate of economic efficiency, not the growth rate of only the industrial and agricultural sectors. The economic growth rate should include the tax growth rate, the interest growth rate, the profit growth rate, the wage growth rate, the sponsorship growth rate, and the basic depreciation income growth rate. When economic growth rate is fixed, the amount and growth of the six types of income are closely related to the national distribution policy. For the country, regions, sectors, and enterprises, they should pursue the total amount and growth rate of the GDP, GNP, and added value first. Then, they can deal with reasonable distribution.

There are two methods for calculating the total amount of GDP and GNP and added value: the production method and the distribution method.

① *Production method.*

The total amount of GDP, GNP or added value can be attained by deducting the intermediate material consumption costs from the total output. Here is the formula.

$$\text{GDP (GNP)} = \text{Total output value} - \text{Intermediatematerial consumption costs}$$
$$\text{Added value} = \text{Total output value} - \text{Intermediatematerial consumption costs}$$

There are two types of total output value: the production output value and the sales output value. The sales output value refers to the total value of sales, excluding inventory value. At present, the total production output value is generally chosen for the calculation of GDP and added value.

Other than the cost of energy and raw materials, intermediate material consumption costs include management fees and sales expenses. Wages, welfare, and depreciation expenses in the management fees should not be considered as material consumption costs. Other entertainment expenses, such as a business entertainment expense, labor union funds, staff education expenses, rental fees, consulting fees, legal fees, low value consumables amortization, intangible assets amortization, repairs, and fire fees, audit fees can be treated as intermediate material consumption costs. Except for wages and welfare, the other expenses in sales expenses can be treated as intermediate material consumption costs, including transportation costs, finishing costs, insurance, storage fees, travel costs, inspection fees, and advertising expenses.

② *Distribution method*

From the perspective of distribution, GDP and added value consist of six kinds of income by five subjects, namely country, creditors, society, enterprises, and workers.

Here are the formulas.

$$\begin{aligned}\text{GDP} = {} & \text{national tax revenue} + \text{bank interest income} \\ & + \text{related social income (such as sponsorship)} \\ & + \text{wages and welfare} \\ & + \text{depreciation income of enterprises} \\ & + \text{profit income of enterprises} \\ = {} & \text{sum of added value of industrial sectors}\end{aligned}$$

$$\begin{aligned}\text{Added value} = {} & \text{national tax revenue} + \text{bank interest income} \\ & + \text{related social income (such as sponsorship)} \\ & + \text{wages and welfare} \\ & + \text{depreciation income of enterprises} \\ & + \text{profit income of enterprises} \\ = {} & \text{net output value (material production sectors)} \\ & + \text{depreciation income} \\ = {} & \text{total social contribution of enterprises} \\ & + \text{depreciation income}\end{aligned}$$

Because of the requirement for balancing revenue and expenditure, added value calculated with the two methods should be the same. However, due to the differences in calculation methods and statistical data, errors might occur. Added value calculated with the two methods is not the same. The difference between the two added values should not be too large. The reasons causing the difference should be analyzed in order to improve accuracy of statistics and calculation.

Economic growth rate in t years can be calculated as below.

$$\begin{aligned}
&\text{GDP growth rate} \\
&\quad = [(\text{GDP of assessment year/GDP of reference year})^{1/t} - 1] \\
&\quad \times\ 100\% \\
&\text{Added value growth rate} \\
&\quad = \big[(\text{added value of assessment year} \\
&\qquad /\text{added value of reference year})^{1/t} - 1\big] \times 100\% \\
&\quad = \big[((\text{total output of assessment year} \\
&\qquad - \text{total material consumption of assessment year} \\
&\qquad /(\text{total output of reference year} \\
&\qquad - \text{total material consumption of reference year}))^{1/t} - 1\big] \\
&\quad \times\ 100\%
\end{aligned} \tag{23.32}$$

GDP and added value are generally calculated based on current prices. In order to evaluate the status of the economic growth modes, GDP and added value need to be converted into comparable GDP and added value with the correction coefficients of GDP and added value. Then, the growth rates, based on comparable price for GDP and added value, can be calculated. The correction of added value in current prices should be performed with the price indices of added value for the first, the second, and the third industries in National Statistical Yearbook (see Table 23.41).

2. **Calculation of intensiveness**

Intensiveness is an indicator corresponding to extensiveness. The sum of intensiveness and extensiveness is 1 or 100%. If the value of one indicator is known, the other can be calculated. Here is the calculation formula.

$$\text{Intensiveness} = 1 - \text{extensiveness}$$

or

$$\text{Intensiveness} = 100\% - \text{extensiveness}$$

If extensiveness is known, intensiveness can be calculated, so that the proper economic growth mode can be chosen. Table 23.42 shows the selection of the economic growth mode based on intensiveness and extensiveness.

Table 23.41 Correction coefficients for the prices of added value (national)

Year	1995	1994	1993	1992	1991	1990	
Correction coefficient	1.000	1.145	1.397	1.627	1.774	1.905	
Year	1989	1988	1987	1986	1985	1984	
Correction coefficient	2.017	2.202	2.499	2.640	2.772	3.091	
Year	1983	1982	1981	1980	1979	1978	
Correction coefficient	3.287	3.312	3.345	3.373	3.500	3.645	
Year	1977	1976	1975	1974	1973	1972	
Correction coefficient	3.701	3.743	3.731	3.667	3.675	3.683	
Year	1971	1970	1969	1968	1967	1966	
Correction coefficient	3.681	3.711	3.556	3.377	3.433	3.507	
Year	1965	1964	1963	1962	1961	1960	
Correction coefficient	3.364	3.429	3.433	3.348	3.323	3.700	
Year	1959	1958	1957	1956	1955	1954	1953
Correction coefficient	3.746	3.787	3.830	3.771	3.689	3.650	3.639

Table 23.42 Economic growth modes

Intensiveness	≤0	≥1 (or 100%)	0–1 (or 100%)	<0.5 (or 50%)	>0.5 (or 50%)
Economic growth mode	Completely extensive	Completely intensive	Mixed	Mainly extensive	Mainly intensive
Extensiveness	≥1 (or 100%)	≤0	1–0 (or 100%)	>0.5 (or 50%)	<0.5 (or 50%)
Economic growth mode	Completely extensive	Completely intensive	Mixed	Mainly extensive	Mainly intensive

Intensiveness requires an individual growth rate for funds, manpower, energy, raw materials, transportation, land, and water—or for their comprehensive input growth rate to be smaller than economic growth rate. An individual growth rate or a comprehensive input growth rate cannot be the same as, or faster than, the economic growth rate, because the state and enterprises will be restrained. More loads are not always good. More inputs are not always good, either. If the individual growth rate or the comprehensive input growth rate does not meet this requirement, the transformation of economic growth mode will not occur.

Before the reform and opening up (1954–1978), the intensiveness of the national energy input growth was −0.74 (−74%). The elasticity coefficient of the national energy input was 1.74. The economic growth was completely in an extensive mode. After the reform and opening up (1978–1994), the intensiveness of the national energy input growth was 0.501 (50.1%). The elasticity coefficient of the national energy input was 0.499, and economic growth was mainly in the intensive mode. This was a big shift in the economic growth mode. The intensiveness of the national input growth of steel and the elasticity coefficient of steel input were −0.89 (−89%) and 1.89, respectively, before the reform and opening up. They changed to 0.1 (10%) and 0.9 after the reform and opening up. These changes indicated that the economic growth had shifted from a fully extensive mode to a mixed extensive-intensive mode.

Before the reform and opening up, the intensiveness of the national freight input growth was −0.26. The elasticity coefficient of the freight input was 1.26. Economic growth was completely in an extensive mode. After the reform and opening up, these values changed to 0.42 and 0.58, respectively. Economic growth was in a mixed extensive-intensive mode. Before the reform and opening up, the intensiveness of the national labor input growth was 0.54. The elasticity coefficient of the national labor input was 0.46. After the reform and opening up, these values changed to 0.69 and 0.31. Economic growth was mainly in an intensive mode. Before the reform and opening up, the intensiveness of the national comprehensive input growth was 0.44. The elasticity coefficient of the national input was 1.44. They changed to 0.2 and 0.8, respectively, after the reform and opening up. These changes indicated that the economic growth shifted from a fully extensive mode to a mixed extensive-intensive mode.

Like extensiveness, intensiveness falls into two types: individual intensiveness and comprehensive intensiveness. Each production factor input has its own individual intensiveness, such as energy intensiveness, material intensiveness, steel intensiveness, capital intensiveness, transportation intensiveness, natural force intensiveness, manpower intensiveness, and construction period intensiveness. Individual intensiveness can be used to determine whether the growth of one individual input is in the extensive mode or in the intensive mode. If all of the individual intensiveness numbers are large, then the total economic growth is in intensive mode. However, when one single intensiveness number is large and other individual intensiveness numbers are small, it will be hard to determine the intensiveness of the total economic growth. In this case, the comprehensive intensiveness index should be applied.

The author found that the comprehensive intensiveness is closely related with individual intensiveness. The trend of comprehensive intensiveness is consistent with that of individual intensiveness. In other words, individual intensiveness has a great impact on comprehensive intensiveness. Individual intensiveness is more specific and is easier to control and to operate. Therefore, individual intensiveness is very useful in practice. Comprehensive intensiveness can be used to determine whether economic growth is in the intensive mode or in the extensive mode. Individual intensiveness can be used to determine whether one input growth rate is in the intensive mode or the extensive mode. Individual intensiveness can facilitate the control of each input growth mode. For example, after the reform and opening up, energy-saving policies and measures played an important role in changing the energy input growth modes. The energy input growth modes further played an important role in transforming the overall economic growth mode.

The author found that the contribution of scientific and technological progress to economic growth is comprehensive intensiveness. The indicator that has been currently adopted to reflect the contribution of scientific and technological progress to economic growth has the following drawbacks. First, the calculation of this indicator considers only two of the six production factors (capital and labor); the other four factors are not considered. Second, this indicator only reflects the status of the economic growth mode during a certain period; it cannot reflect the growth status of input and output for each production factor in each year. Third, it only reflects the ratio of extensive economic growth or intensive economic growth in the total economic growth; it cannot reflect the degree of intensiveness achieved by the transformation of economic growth.

Following are three methods for calculating comprehensive intensiveness.

(1) Evaluation method for elasticity coefficient of material comprehensive input

$$\begin{aligned}&\text{Comprehensive intensiveness}\\&\quad= (1 - \text{elasticity coefficient of material comprehensive input})\\&\quad= \left(1 - \frac{\text{growth rate of material comprehensive input}}{\text{growth rate of added value}}\right) \times 100\%\\&\quad= 100\% - \text{comprehensive extensiveness}\end{aligned} \tag{23.33}$$

or

$$\begin{aligned}&\text{comprehensive intensiveness}\\&\quad= \sum i \text{ input weight} \times i \text{ input individual intensiveness}\end{aligned}$$

(2) Evaluation method for elasticity coefficient of value comprehensive input

$$\begin{aligned}&\text{Comprehensive intensiveness}\\&\quad= (1 - \text{elasticity coefficient of material comprehensive input}) \times 100\%\\&\quad= \left(1 - \frac{\text{growth rate of value comprehensive input}}{\text{growth rate of added value}}\right) \times 100\%\\&\quad= 100\% - \text{comprehensive extensiveness}\end{aligned} \tag{23.34}$$

(3) Methods for comprehensive saving evaluation

(1) Comprehensive intensiveness—comprehensive saving rate

The improvement of the economic efficiency of an enterprise (referring to its enterprise added value), i.e. economic growth of the enterprise, is caused by two factors. One is to develop production by increasing input. The other is to increase the economic efficiency of input by saving input. The former is the extensively expanded reproduction mode of economic growth. The latter is the intensively expanded reproduction mode of economic growth. The former is the extensive economic growth mode. The latter is the intensive economic growth mode. The former can completely rely on the original technology without scientific and technological progress; what it needs is more inputs. The latter must rely on scientific and technological progress to improve the economic efficiency of input. The contribution of scientific and technological progress to the economic growth of the enterprise must be improved. These are two completely different economic growth modes. In the early stage of an enterprise, the former economic growth mode should be adopted. When the enterprise matures, both economic growth modes should be adopted, but the latter should be the major one. This is a law of economic growth.

Here is the formula for calculating the comprehensive saving rate.

$$\text{Comprehensive saving rate} = \text{growth rate of saving/growth rate of economy} \times 100\% \qquad (23.35)$$

(2) Growth rate of saving

The "growth rate of saving" refers to an enterprise's reliance on technological progress to optimize resource allocation, to increase economic efficiency, and to obtain an economic growth rate through intensiveness. "Growth rate of saving" means the overall saving rate, not the individual saving growth rate. There are two methods for calculating the growth rate of saving: the production growth rate deduction method and the input growth rate deduction method.

① Production growth rate deduction method

First, the portion of the growth rate of added value for an enterprise generated by the production growth rate is deducted. The deducted portion is the value of the production growth rate. The rest of the portion is the growth rate of saving. For example, the growth rate of added value for an enterprise is 10%. The production growth rate is 8%. The remaining 2% is the growth rate of saving. This portion is the growth rate of the added value generated by saving. Here is the formula.

$$\begin{aligned}
&\text{Growth rate of saving} \\
&\quad = \frac{\text{Comprehensive output growth rate} - \text{Comprehensive input growth rate}}{\text{Total output of reference year/Total input of reference} - 1} \\
&\quad = \text{Coefficient K (Comprehensive output growth rate} \\
&\qquad\qquad - \text{Comprehensive input growth rate)} \times 100\% \qquad (23.36)
\end{aligned}$$

where coefficient K = total input of reference year/(total output of reference year – total input of reference year). The total input here refers to material consumption costs excluding wages and depreciation.

② Input growth rate deduction method

First, the portion of the growth rate of the added value for an enterprise generated by the input growth rate is deducted. The deducted portion is the value of the input growth rate. The rest of the portion is the growth rate of saving. For example, the growth rate of the added value for an enterprise is 10%. The production growth rate is 8%. The input growth rate is 6%. The remaining 4% (10–6%) is the growth rate of saving. Here is the formula.

$$\begin{aligned}&\text{Growth rate of saving}\\&=\frac{\text{Comprehensive output growth rate}-\text{Comprehensive input growth rate}}{1-\text{Total output of reference year/Total input of reference}}\\&=\text{Coefficient K (Comprehensive output growth rate}\\&\qquad-\text{Comprehensive input growth rate)}\times 100\%\end{aligned}\tag{23.37}$$

where coefficient K = total output of reference year/(total output of reference year – total input of reference year). The total input here is material consumption costs.

The above two methods can be applied to calculate the growth rate of saving based on the historical data or on the estimated future production growth rate of the input growth rate. Once the growth rate of saving is known, the growth rate of added value for an enterprise in the future can be estimated. Here are the formulas.

$$\text{economic growth rate}=\text{growth rate of saving}+\text{growth rate of production}\tag{23.38}$$

or

$$\text{economic growth rate}=\text{growth rate of saving}+\text{growth rate of input}\tag{23.39}$$

If the economic growth rate is known, the growth rate of saving can be calculated when the growth rate of production or the growth rate of input is known.

The above calculation methods and formulas are very useful, in practice. For example, once the production growth rate and the input growth rate are estimated for the ninth five-year plan, the growth rate of saving can be calculated with Formulas (23.36) and (23.37). Then, the growth rate of the added value, namely the economic growth rate, can be calculated with Formulas (23.38) and (23.39). In addition, if the growth rate of saving and the growth rate of added value in 2000 reach the preset goals, the reasonable values of the production growth rate and the growth rate of input can be predicted. For example, with the production growth rate deduction method, the growth rate of saving is calculated and gets the value 5%. If growth rate of the added value is 10, the production growth rate should be 5%. If production growth rate is smaller than 5%, the goal for the growth rate of added value (10%) will not be achieved. If the production growth rate is higher than 5%, the goal for the growth rate of added value will be higher than 10%. The growth rate of saving will be smaller than 5%.

Comparing the two methods for calculating the growth rate of saving, the author thinks that the input growth rate deduction method is better than the production growth rate deduction method. Production growth can cause added value growth. But without input, there can be no production, because production growth is achieved through input growth. Therefore, the growth rate of input should be deducted from the growth rate of added value. This means that production growth is caused by growth of input. The growth rate of added value is caused by production growth. If the growth rate of saving is set as 0, the growth rate of input = the production growth rate = the growth rate of added value. If the growth rate of added value is greater than growth rate of input, the excessive portion is the growth rate of saving. If the growth rate of added value is smaller than the growth rate of input, the growth rate of saving will be negative. This indicates that extra input growth does not create wealth, but wastes resources.

③ Comprehensive approach

The comprehensive approach is a traditional method. If the value of the saving growth rate generated with the input growth rate deduction method is too high, the comprehensive approach can be applied. This method calculates the average of the results generated with the input growth rate deduction method and the production growth rate deduction method. Here is the formula.

$$\text{Comprehensive saving rate} = (\text{comprehensive saving rate I} + \text{comprehensive saving rate II}) \div 2 \quad (23.40)$$

23.15.4 *Indicator for Measuring Transformation Direction of Economic Growth Mode and Transformation Speed*

1. **Improvement rate of intensiveness—saving rate**

"Improvement rate of intensiveness" refers to the degree or the speed of material input saving for each material input. It has two indicators: the total savings rate and the yearly saving rate. The total saving rate is the percentage of saving for a certain input during a period. The yearly saving rate is the percentage of average annual saving. Here are formulas.

$$\text{Yearly saving rate} = [1 - (\text{input coefficient of assessment year} / \text{input coefficient of reference year})^{1/t}] \times 100\% \quad (23.41)$$

$$\text{Total saving rate} = \left[1 - (\text{input coefficient of assessment year} / \text{input coefficient of reference year})^{1/t}\right] \times 100\% \quad (23.42)$$

The comprehensive saving rate corresponds to the individual saving rate. It is the sum of the saving rate for all individual inputs. Here is the formula.

$$\text{Comprehensive saving rate} = \left[1 - (\text{comprehensive input coefficient of assessment year} / \text{comprehensive input coefficient of reference year})\right] \times 100\% \quad (23.43)$$

$$\text{Comprehensive saving rate} = \sum i \text{ input weight} \times i \text{ input saving rate} \quad (23.44)$$

2. **Improvement rate of intensiveness—increasing efficiency rate**

The "increasing efficiency rate" refers to the degree or the speed of the increase in economic efficiency for each input. It has two indicators: the total increasing efficiency rate and the annual increasing efficiency rate. The total increasing efficiency rate is the percentage of increased economic efficiency for an input during a certain period. The annual increasing efficiency rate is the percentage of the average annual increased economic efficiency. Here are the formulas.

$$\text{Annual increasing efficiency rate} = \left[(\text{input economic efficiency of assessment year} / \text{input economic efficiency of reference year})^{1/t} - 1\right] \times 100\% \quad (23.45)$$

$$\text{Total increasing efficiency rate} = \left[(\text{input economic efficiency of assessment year} / \text{input economic efficiency of reference year}) - 1\right] \times 100\% \quad (23.46)$$

The "comprehensive increasing efficiency rate" corresponds to the individual increasing efficiency rate. It refers to the sum of the increasing efficiency rate for each input. Here is the formula.

$$\text{Comprehensive increasing efficiency rate} = \left[(\text{comprehensive input economic efficiency of assessment year} / \text{comprehensive input economic efficiency of reference year}) - 1\right] \times 100\% \quad (23.47)$$

$$\text{Comprehensive increasing efficiency rate} = \sum i \text{ input weight} \times i \text{ input efficiency} \quad (23.48)$$

23.15.5 Indicator for Measuring the Transformation of Economic Growth Modes

1. **Level of intensiveness—input coefficient**

The "input coefficient" is the amount of input required by one unit of added value or one unit of material production such as energy consumption per 10,000 yuan of added value, capital occupancy per 10,000 of added value, land occupancy per 10,000 yuan of added value, manpower occupancy per 10,000 yuan of added value, water consumption per 10,000 yuan of added value, or transportation per 10,000 yuan of added value. A larger input coefficient means a lower level of economic efficiency. In this case, the level of intensiveness is low. A smaller input coefficient means a higher level of economic efficiency. In this case, the level of intensiveness is high. Here are the formulas.

$$\text{Input coefficient} = \text{the amount of input/added value} \tag{23.49}$$

$$\text{Input coefficient} = \text{the amount of input/material production} \tag{23.50}$$

Comprehensive input coefficient

$$\text{Comprehensive input coefficient} = \text{comprehensive input/added value} \tag{23.51}$$

$$\text{Comprehensive input coefficient} = \text{comprehensive input/material production} \tag{23.52}$$

2. **Intensiveness level-input economic efficiency**

"Input economic efficiency" means the amount of added value or material production generated by one unit of input. It is the reciprocal of input coefficient. Low input economic efficiency means a low intensiveness level. High input economic efficiency means a high intensiveness level. Here are the formulas.

$$\text{Input economic efficiency} = \text{added value/input} = 1/\text{input coefficient} \tag{23.53}$$

$$\begin{aligned}\text{Input economic efficiency} &= \text{material production/input}\\ &= 1/\text{input coefficient}\end{aligned} \tag{23.54}$$

Comprehensive input economic efficiency

$$\text{Comprehensive input economic efficiency} = \text{added value/comprehensive input} = 1/\text{comprehensive input coefficient} \quad (23.55)$$

$$\begin{aligned}&\text{Comprehensive input economic efficiency}\\&= \text{material production/comprehensive input}\\&= 1/\text{comprehensive input coefficient}\end{aligned} \quad (23.56)$$

23.15.6 Indicator for Measuring the Economic Effects Generated by Transformation of Economic Growth Modes

1. **Effect of intensiveness improvement—saving**

"Saving" refers to the amount of saved input in one year or a certain period. Here are the formulas.

Basis comparison method:

$$\begin{aligned}\text{Saving} = &\ (\text{input coefficient of reference year} - \text{input coefficient of assessment year})\\&\times \text{added value of assessment year}\end{aligned} \quad (23.57)$$

Relative ratio method:

$$\begin{aligned}\text{Saving} = &\ (\text{input coefficient of previous year} - \text{input coefficient of current year})\\&\times \text{added value of current year}\end{aligned} \quad (23.58)$$

The relative ratio method is applied for annual assessment. The basis comparison method is applied for making medium and long-term plans.

2. **Effect of intensiveness improvement—efficiency quantity**

"Efficiency quantity" refers to the quantity of added economic efficiency during one year or during a certain period. Here are the formulas.

Basis comparison method:

$$\begin{aligned}\text{Efficiency quantity} = &\ (\text{input economic efficiency of assessment year}\\&- \text{input economic efficiency of reference year})\\&\times \text{input of assessment year}\end{aligned} \quad (23.59)$$

Relative ratio method:

$$\begin{aligned}\text{Efficiency quantity} = &\ (\text{input economic efficiency of current year} \\ &- \text{input economic efficiency of previous year}) \\ &\times \text{input of current year} \end{aligned} \tag{23.60}$$

3. **Effect of improved intensiveness level—greater, faster, better, and more economical comprehensive allocation of resources (excessive economic benefits)**

   (1) Evaluation standard for greater, faster, better and more economical allocation of resources

The economic growth mode of enterprises can be the extensive-inefficient type or the intensive-high efficiency type. There are two evaluation criteria for measuring the economic growth mode of enterprises: the absolute evaluation standard and the relative evaluation standard. The absolute evaluation standard means that the output must be greater than the input. If this standard is not met, an enterprise has negative profits. Its growth mode is not the intensive-high efficiency type. This standard is a basic requirement. "Relative evaluation standard" means that, compared with other enterprises, if the output of the comprehensive input of an enterprise is larger than that of other enterprises, its growth mode is good. This standard is an advance requirement. The Yanhua ethylene renovation and expansion project is an intensive-high efficiency project. This conclusion was made based on a comparison with other enterprises. Evaluation of enterprise economic growth mode and allocation of resources should not rely on one single standard only; a comprehensive consideration is required. For example, the single requirement of high production, less investment, fast speed, or high construction quality cannot achieve optimal resource allocation because the economic growth modes of enterprises and their economic efficiency does not depend on the allocation of individual resources, but on the comprehensive allocation of resources, as well as on the combination of greater, faster, better and more economical allocation of resources. When some projects are completed and put into production, their production may be large, but they have a large investment, a long construction period, high cost, and poor quality. Thus, their economic growth modes are not good. Compared with similar projects, some projects achieve a greater, faster, better, and more economical allocation of resources. They are ideal projects and achieve optimal resource allocation. In general, one project might be better in one or more aspects than other projects, but the final evaluation standards shall be the results of greater, faster, better, and more economical comprehensive evaluation. This is the essence of greater, faster, better, and more economical comprehensive optimal allocation of resources. The Yanhua ethylene renovation and expansion project has a good economic growth mode. The result is based on a greater, faster, better, and more economical comprehensive quantitative assessment, not on one single indicator.

(2) Evaluation method for greater, faster, better and more economical allocation of resources

Two quantitative evaluation methods are applied: the economic evaluation method and the comprehensive evaluation method.

(1) Economic evaluation method

The enterprise excessive profit evaluation method in the technological economy, namely the economic net present value evaluation method, is applied.

"Greater" means the output of a project. There are two assessment methods: material production and sales income. The amount of material output depends on production equipment capabilities and on production operations. Sales income depends on material output and on market demand. Therefore, first, "great" means full production or over-full production. If the production cannot meet the standard, the yield will be affected. Second, greater also requires more sales income. More production, less sales, and a high inventory cannot improve economic efficiency. In the past, the traditional planned economy only assessed the material output and neglected sales income. This is a major flaw of the old economic growth mode. Now, the socialist market economy requires greater material output and greater sales income. This is an important requirement for transforming the economic growth mode. Here is a wrong idea, which notes that, because in the past assessing only material production was not correct, now assessing only value quantity y is fine. If the material production assessment is completely replaced with the sales income assessment, enterprises will pursue profit via sales income, such as increasing prices. Thus, it is better to stress two greater, instead of one greater. One is that material production reaches its designed output. The other is full production and full sales. In other words, all products should be sold out. Prices should be increased as well. In this way, sales income also increases. Large production and large sales can increase income, save cost for one unit of product, and achieve the time effect of excess economic efficiency, namely profits from the expansion of reproduction.

"Faster" refers to the construction speed and full production speed of a project. High speed means high economic efficiency. A high construction speed can shorten the construction period and can generate economic benefits in four aspects. First, high construction saves investment in infrastructure, including savings in daily costs and infrastructure interest. Second, it saves in a lower investment depreciation cost. Third, early production generates more products and more economic benefits. Fourth, more economic benefits have a time effect. A fast full production and a short full production period can save fixed costs, generate more economic benefits, and have a time effect.

"Better" refers to the quality of a project and the quality of products. Good quality generates long service life, is safe and reliable, and has a high operation rate, low accident rate, low rejection rate, resulting in more products, less production loss, and less scrap loss. Good quality also reduces product cost (including depreciation costs) and sales cost. In addition, good quality requires a higher price and generates more income. Good quality also has a time effect.

"More economical" refers to the material input of five production factors and input of two values. The material input of the five production factors includes the material input of the fixed assets and the current assets; the input of energy and raw material; the input of transportation; the input of land, water and other natural resources; and manpower. Two value inputs are investments (investments in fixed assets and current assets) and costs. The assessment of inputs for a project is similar to the assessment of outputs for the project. The assessment of inputs for a project consists of the assessment of the material input and the value input. In the past, the traditional planned economy assessed only the material consumption quota and neglected the value consumption quota. Furthermore, the input prices of the production factors were not clear. As a result, many production factors were wasted. In contrast, the assessment of value now becomes the only focus. An increase in prices causes the expansion of nominal investment and nominal cost and a serious contradiction between material consumption and value consumption. Some material consumption decreases. However, the value consumption quickly increases. Therefore, this causes trouble in economic assessment. The author believes that more economic assessment should reflect the savings in material input and value input for one unit of product. In a socialist market economy, the value input of the enterprises should be assessed. However, in order to save investment and costs, the material consumption should be saved first. Next, the production factors at reasonable prices should be selected. Saving material investment and value investment can save investment and interests, can reduce fixed assets depreciation costs, can increase capital gains rate, and can have a time effect. Saving material costs and value costs can save current assets, increase excess profits and taxes, improve the capital interest tax rate, and have a time effect.

Two points shall be noted. First, the greater, faster, better, and more economical quantitative calculation method does not allow repeated calculation. For example, the economic benefits of early production can be reflected in greater economic benefits as well as in faster economic benefits. But they should be calculated only once. Second, the greater, faster, better, and more economical quantitative calculation method only takes into account the economic benefits of one enterprise. It does not take into account the impact of one project on other enterprises.

With the greater, faster, better, and more economical quantitative calculation method, it is easy to calculate the amount of total excess profits and taxes generated by the intensive-high efficiency economic growth mode as well as the excess profits and taxes individually generated by greater, faster, better, and more economical calculations in Yanhua ethylene project. Thus, this method can be applied by national authorities to assess and award projects.

4. **Effect of improved intensiveness level—greater, faster, better, and more economical allocation of resources (excessive economic efficiency)**

With the aforementioned method for excess economic benefits, the total excess profits and taxes generated by the intensive-high efficiency economic growth mode, as well as the excess profits and taxes individually generated by greater, faster, better, and more economical method can be calculated. But because the scale of projects and the total excess profits and taxes vary across projects, only projects with the same scale can be compared, using this method. This is the drawback of the method for excess economic benefits. In order to compare projects with different scales, excess economic efficiency is adopted. It is a comprehensive input economic efficiency indicator that reflects the intensiveness level.

5. **Effect of improved intensiveness level—greater, faster, better, and more economical allocation of resources (comprehensive index)**

The indicator for excessive economic efficiency can be applied for comparing the economic growth modes of projects with various scales. However, it does not consider many factors that are not quantitative. Accordingly, the comprehensive index is applied to consider qualitative factors and to quantify them. With this index, the economic growth modes of diverse projects can be better compared. Here are the details of this method.

Five levels are set for measuring the greater standard: excellent, good, qualified, unqualified, and bad. Those projects with an output of 10% (including 10%) higher than the design value are considered to be excellent. Those projects with an output 1–10% higher than the design value are considered to be good. Those projects with an output equal to the design value are qualified. Those projects with an output 10% lower than the design value are unqualified. Those projects with an output over 10% lower than the design standards are bad.

The standard "fast" refers to construction speed and production speed. Five levels are set for measuring the faster standard: excellent, good, qualified, unqualified, and bad. A construction period over 10% (including 10%) shorter than the standard duration is considered to be excellent. A construction period 1–10% shorter than the standard duration is good. A construction period equal to the standard duration is qualified. A construction period 1–10% longer than the standard duration is unqualified. A construction period over 10% (including 10%) longer than the standard duration is bad. A full production period over 10% (including 10%) shorter than the standard duration is excellent. A full production period 1–10% shorter than the standard duration is good. A full production period equal to the standard duration is qualified. A full production period 1–10% longer than the standard duration is unqualified. A full production period over 10% (including 10%) longer than the standard duration is bad. The significance coefficient of construction speed is set as 0.65. The significance coefficient of full production speed is set as 0.35.

Five levels are set for measuring the better standard: excellent, good, qualified, unqualified, and bad. There are two indicators to assess project quality: reliability and advanceness. Commissioning success with one smooth trial is excellent. Commissioning success with one unsmooth trial is good. Commissioning success with two trials is qualified. Commissioning success with three trials is unqualified. Commissioning success with more than three trials is bad. Regarding advanceness, the level of excellent is assigned when advanced technology and equipment are adopted and when construction quality and product quality meet standards. Good is assigned when relatively advanced technology and equipment are adopted and when construction quality and product quality meet standards. Qualified is assigned when general technology and equipment are adopted and when construction quality and product quality meet standards. Unqualified is assigned when out-of-date technology and equipment are adopted and when construction quality and product quality are low. Bad is assigned when out of date technology and equipment are adopted and when construction quality and product quality are low. The significance coefficient of reliability is set as 0.6. The significance coefficient of advanceness is set as 0.4.

The more economical level has two indicators: investment and costs. Investment includes investment in fixed assets and investment in current assets. Material consumption costs include the material consumption quota and the material consumption costs. Investment in one unit of production capacity over 10% (including 10%) lower than the average fixed quota is considered to be excellent. Investment in one unit of production capacity 1–10% lower than the average fixed quota is good. Investment in one unit of production capacity equal to the average fixed quota is qualified. Investment in one unit of production capacity 1–10% higher than the average fixed quota is unqualified. Investment in one unit of production capacity over 10% higher than the average fixed quota is bad. A cost of material consumption for one unit of product over 10% (including 10%) lower than the average level is excellent. A cost of material consumption for one unit of product 1–10% lower than the average level is good. A cost of material consumption for one unit of product equal to the average level is qualified. A cost of material consumption for one unit of product 1–10% higher than the average level is unqualified. A cost of material consumption for one unit of product over 10% higher than the average level is bad. The significance coefficient of investment is set as 0.2. The significance coefficient of cost is set as 0.8.

A comprehensive evaluation adopts the five-grade marking system: 5 for excellent, 4 for good, 3 for qualified, 2 for unqualified, and 1 for bad. A total average score is calculated with addition and multiplication mixed method. Projects with a total average score over or equal to 4.5 and a comprehensive index over or equal to 90 are excellent. Projects with a total average score over or equal to 3.5 and a comprehensive index over or equal to 70 are good. Projects with a total average score over or equal to 2.5 and a comprehensive index over or equal to 50 are qualified. Projects with a total average score over or equal to 1.5 and a comprehensive index over or equal to 30 are unqualified. Projects with a total average score smaller than 1.5 and a comprehensive index smaller than 30 is bad. The significance coefficients of greater, faster, better, and more economical comprehensive evaluation are usually set at the same level. Significance coefficients can be adjusted based on the actual conditions.

Here are the formulas for comprehensive evaluation.

$$\text{Total average score F addition} = 1/4(\text{F1} + \text{F2} + \text{F3} + \text{F4}) \tag{23.61}$$

$$\text{Total average score F multiplication} = (\text{F1} \times \text{F2} \times \text{F3} \times \text{F4})1/4 \tag{23.62}$$

$$\text{Total average score F addition and multiplication} = (\text{F addition} + \text{F multiplication})/2 \quad (23.63)$$

$$\text{Comprehensive index F comprehensive} = \text{F addition and multiplication}/5 \times 100 \quad (23.64)$$

where F1, F2, F3, and F4 are the scores of greater, faster, better, and more economical, respectively.

Based on this method, construction projects can be evaluated and assigned the level of excellent, good, qualified, unqualified, and bad.

23.15.7 Policies and Measures for Transforming Economic Growth Modes

1. **Deepen reform, implement efficiency revolution, and transform extensive-low efficiency systems into intensive- high-efficiency systems**

Waste of production factors and low economic efficiency are the most serious drawbacks of the traditional planned economy system. Therefore, piecemeal reform does not work. The only solution is to implement an efficiency revolution. Since the reform and opening up, Comrade Deng Xiaoping has led China to implement an efficiency revolution, and the efficiency revolution has greatly improved economic efficiency in China.

The 14th CPC National Congress put forward a socialist market economy system. Deepening the reform and completely implementing the socialist market economy can fully release the huge potential of efficiency held by an institution, and can narrow the gap between China and developed countries.

2. **Pay close attention to scientific and technological progress, transform extensive-low efficiency technologies into intensive-high-efficiency technologies, and comprehensively improve the system efficiency of production factors**

Since the reform and opening up, enterprises have invested a large amount of manpower, material, and financial resources into the introduction of technology, technological renovation, technology development, technological innovation. These measures have made great achievements. Extensive technologies are dropping gradually. But overall, the lag in China's enterprise technology has not yet been changed; the potential of technical efficiency is still large.

In the future, enterprises must implement instruction that technology is the primary productive force. They should pay close attention to scientific and technological progress, develop high and new technology, continue to reduce extensive technology, and transform extensive-low efficiency technologies into intensive-high-efficiency technologies. Enterprises should improve the system efficiency of energy, the system efficiency of raw materials, the system efficiency of transportation, the system efficiency of equipment, the system efficiency of natural resources, the system efficiency of manpower, and the system efficiency of time.

3. **Improve management level, transform extensive-inefficient management into intensive-high-efficiency management as soon as possible, and achieve efficiency potential of management**

Enterprises should strengthen management of their economic growth modes, implement the principle that development and saving are both important, strengthen managing comprehensive saving for the long term, encourage transformation of economic growth modes, and provide assessment indicators in planning and plans.

Enterprise leaders shall make scientific decisions, manage scientifically, improve market competitiveness, and improve economic efficiency.

4. **Speed up structural adjustment, transform extensive-low-efficiency structure into intensive-high-efficiency structure, and build a saving production and management system**

In the socialist market economic system, enterprises should follow the rules of fair competition and should adjust economic structures. Large enterprises should develop comprehensively and collectively.

On the whole, the focus of the industrial structure adjustment is to accelerate the development of the tertiary industry. The focus of the industry structure adjustment is to accelerate the development of short-term industry and to limit the development of the long-term industry. The focus of the product structure adjustment is to accelerate the development of high-tech, low consumption, and high value-added products. Enterprises should follow the same product structure adjustment.

5. **Enhance people's efficiency sense, make great efforts to improve labor quality, and strive to transform the extensive-low efficiency of labor quality into the intensive-high efficiency of labor quality**

In short, all transformations have to rely on people. Therefore, labor quality is most important. Any enterprise has two teams: workers and leaders. Transformation of the economic growth modes for an enterprise relies on these two teams, especially on the quality of leaders. It is a long-term solution to improve the quality of workers.

Guide public opinion. Let employees know the importance and the urgency of the transformation of economic growth modes, enforcing comprehensive saving, and improving economic efficiency. Let employees realize that resources per capita are limited in China. If economic efficiency is not improved, the three-step economic strategic goals will never be realized. Improving economic efficiency is not an expedient measure, but China's basic national policy.

Abandon the misunderstanding that bad economic efficiency is caused by price rise and repeated calculation. Establish confidence and consistently implement the

CPCC and the State Council's policies that all economic work should focus on improving economic efficiency.

23.15.8 Application Cases

1. **Evaluation of national economic growth modes**

The author believes that the relationship between the transformation of the economic system and the transformation of economic growth is very close. The transformation of the economic system is the prerequisite. Without a transformation of economic system, there will be no transformation of economic growth modes. In addition, a transformation of economic system will promote the transformation of economic growth modes. Since the reform and opening up, due to the continuous reform of the economic system, the market economy system has continued to be enhanced. The economic growth mode is transforming from extensive to intensive. Table 23.43 lists the comparison of China's economic growth modes before and after the reform and opening up. The table shows that, since the reform and opening up, China's economic growth mode has changed greatly. But the transformation of economic growth modes varies across production factors.

Table 23.43 indicates the following. ① Due to the limitations of land area, the area of arable land continues to drop. However, the economy is growing. The completely intensive mode is the only choice. ② Because of natural resource constraints, the growth mode of wood changes from mainly extensive (21%) to mainly intensive (73%). ③ Due to the control of population growth, the growth rate of the labor force is lower than the economic growth rate. Intensiveness has to be adopted. After the reform and opening up, intensiveness rose from 54 to 69%. ④ Due to the limitation of resources, finance, transport, and the environment, the growth mode of energy is intensive. The transformation of economic growth modes is notable. The economic growth mode of energy transforms from completely extensive to mainly intensive. Intensiveness increases from 0 to 50.1%. ⑤ The economic growth mode of freight transforms from completely extensive to mainly extensive. Intensiveness increases from 0 to 42%. ⑥ The economic growth mode of sulfuric acid transforms from completely extensive to mainly extensive. Intensiveness increases from 0 to 38%. ⑦ The economic growth mode of steel transforms from completely extensive to mainly extensive. Its intensiveness is 10%. ⑧ The economic growth mode of capital does not change. Its economic growth mode remains completely extensive before and after the reform and opening up. ⑨ In short, the national economic growth mode has changed from completely extensive to a mix of extensive and intensive. The intensiveness is 20%.

The author predicted that the economic growth mode in 2000 and 2010 would continue to shift toward the intensiveness direction (see Table 23.44). Table 23.44 shows that intensiveness of all of the inputs is rising. The average annual increase rate for the level of intensiveness is about 3%. Input coefficient continuously drops.

Table 23.43 Comparison of China's economic growth modes before and after reform and opening up

Period	Before reform and opening up (1954–1978)		After reform and opening up (1979–1992)	
	Input elasticity coefficient	Economic growth mode	Input elasticity coefficient	Economic growth mode
Comprehensive production factor	1.44	Completely extensive (intensiveness 0%)	0.80	Mainly intensive (intensiveness 20)
Energy	1.74	Completely extensive (intensiveness 0%)	0.499	Mainly extensive (intensiveness is 50.1%)
Steel	1.89	Completely extensive (intensiveness 0%)	0.90	Mainly extensive (intensiveness is about 10%)
Wood	0.79	Mainly extensive (intensiveness 21%)	0.27	Mainly intensive (intensiveness is 73%)
Sulfuric acid	2.44	Completely extensive (intensiveness is higher than 0%)	0.62	Mainly extensive (intensiveness is about 38%)
Freight	1.26	Completely extensive (intensiveness is higher than 0%)	0.58	Mainly extensive (intensiveness is 42%)
Total labors	0.46	Completely extensive (intensiveness is about 54%)	0.31	Mainly intensive (intensiveness is 69%)
Arable land	−0.06	Completely intensive (intensiveness is 100%)	−0.03	Completely intensive (intensiveness is 100%)
Capital	2.75	Completely extensive (intensiveness is 0%)	1.08	Completely extensive (intensiveness is 0%)

The economic efficiency of inputs increases continuously. However, compared with foreign countries, the gap is still very large. The gap might not be twice or three times, but it is severalfold or several tens of times. For example, in 1990, labor productivities in the US, Japan, Germany, France, the UK were 37 times, 41 times, 46 times, 45 times, and 31 times higher than that in China, respectively. The economic efficiency

Table 23.44 Prediction of transformation of China's economic growth modes in 2000 and 2010

	Economic growth mode (intensiveness %)			Economic growth mode transforming speed (intensiveness rising rate %)			Achieved level (intensiveness level)			
	1980–1990	1990–2000	2000–2010	1980–1990	1990–2000	2000–2010	1980	1990	2000	2010
I. Material										
1. Energy	44	50	57	3.60	4.05	3.74	13.48	9.35	6.19	4.23
2. Materials	15	52	72	1.22	4.20	4.54	2.85	2.52	1.64	1.03
3. Sulfuric acid	49	52	42	4.01	4.00	2.98	0.171	0.114	0.076	0.056
4. Sodium carbonate	0	17	23	−3.54	1.58	1.47	0.024	0.034	0.029	0.025
5. Caustic soda	47	34	53	3.89	2.79	3.50	0.044	0.029	0.022	0.015
6. Chemical fertilizer	18	62	87	1.47	4.98	5.67	0.284	0.245	0.147	0.082
7. Chemical fiber	0	33	23	−0.95	2.68	1.33	0.019	0.021	0.016	0.014
8. Cotton	68	70	71	5.63	5.71	4.36	0.080	0.045	0.025	0.016
II. Transportation										
1. Freight volume	37	17	21	2.81	1.38	1.40	122.3	91.9	80.0	69.5
2. Goods turnover	10	26	11	0.80	2.07	0.70	2.69	2.48	2.01	1.88
III. Financial resources	19	13	6	1.54	1.08	0.36	2.29	1.96	1.76	1.70
IV. Manpower	67	77	94	5.52	6.20	6.15	9.48	5.37	2.83	1.50
V Natural forces										
1. Water	78	50	65	6.4	5.3	4.1	1.07	0.55	0.32	0.21
2. Land	100	100	100	7.8	7.8	7.8	197	87	41	23

Note ① Unit for input coefficient: material (t/10,000 yuan), freight volume (t/10,000 yuan), goods turnover (t km/10,000 yuan), financial force (10,000 yuan/10,000 yuan), manpower (person/10,000 yuan), water (t/10,000 yuan), land (μ/10,000 yuan)
② Intensiveness = (1 − elasticity coefficient of input) × 100%; intensiveness rising rate = saving rate; intensiveness level = input coefficient

of energy in the US, Japan, Germany, France, the UK were 3 times, 8.8 times, 6.8 times, 7.8 times, and 5 times higher than that in China, respectively. Therefore, the task of transforming economic growth mode is still a challenge. It takes a long time to reach a complete transformation. And transformation levels are not the same across all of China. Enterprises in certain areas can transform faster, so that they can achieve a full transformation earlier (Table 23.45).

2. **Enterprise economic growth mode evaluation—Evaluation of Yanhua ethylene renovation and expansion project.**

23.16 Study on Energy Security and Energy Development Problems[35]

Research background, scientific significance of achievements, and practical value.

With the development of the family car market in China, the contradiction between oil supply and demand becomes increasingly prominent. More and more oil is imported. This causes issues of energy security. Required by the states, the Chinese Association of Productivity Science organizes institutions and experts to study security and development issues for energy and food supplies. The author accepted this task. The author made a report about China's Energy Security and Energy Development Issues at the International Forum of Productive Forces Development held on November 16–18, 2005. The report was thought highly of by experts. This report was published by more than 100 websites in China, and it generated a profound impact. The author believes that the core of China's energy security is oil security. Energy security and energy shortage are different in nature. The way to solve the contradiction between oil supply and demand in China is to implement the alternative oil import strategy. The cores of this strategy are: (1) Highlight the oil supply policy: domestic primary and imported secondary; (2) Highlight the oil production policy: equal importance of natural oil and synthetic oil; (3) Highlight the oil utilization policy: coal in place of oil, gas in place of oil, and saving oil; (4) Highlight the oil import policy: proper amount, proper time, and proper location. The solution for the energy shortage in China is to take the coordinated development strategy of energy and the economy. This strategy is a combination of the moderate economic growth strategy and the comprehensive energy efficiency strategy. It is a new strategy that meets the requirements of scientific development perspective [For details, see research results 379–380, 396–398, 415–420, 434].

[35]Xu [Xu05].

Table 23.45 Greater, faster, better, and more economical evaluation results of resource allocation for Yanhua ethlylene renovation and expansion project

Primary indicator	Secondary indicator	Evaluation	Score	
Greater	Production	Annual production of ethylene is set as 150000 t. Hourly production is set as 56.25 t. In July 1995, hourly production is 57 t, 1.30% higher than the set value. Polyethylene and polypropylene can reach full production. The evaluation result is good	4	
Faster	Construction period	A construction period of 36 months is required to build a new project of ethylene with annual production of 115,000 t. The actual construction period is 25 months, 11 months or 31% shorter. The evaluation result is excellent	5	5
	Full production period	Full production period is set as 3 years and in 1996. The actual full production is in 1995, one year in advance and 33% earlier. The evaluation result is excellent	5	
Better	Reliability	Commissioning is successful with one smooth trial. The evaluation result is excellent	5	4.6
	Advanceness	Equipment is relatively advanced. Construction quality and production quality meet standards. The evaluation result is good	4	
More economical	Investment per unit	Investment per unit for a newly built ethylene project with annual production of 150,000 t is 30,000 yuan/t. Actual investment per unit is 18,700 yuan/t, saving 38%. The Evaluation result is excellent	5	5

(continued)

Table 23.45 (continued)

Primary indicator	Secondary indicator	Evaluation	Score
	Cost per unit	Actual cost is 10% lower than preset cost per unit for a newly built 150,000 t of ethylene. The valuation result is excellent	5
Total average (addition): 4.65			
Total average (multiplication): 4.63			
Total average (addition and multiplication mixed method): 4.64			
Comprehensive index: 93			
Comprehensive assessment conclusion: excellent project			

23.16.1 Analysis of Development of Energy Security and Oil Security in China

1. **The core of energy security in China is oil security**

In recent years, people have talked about our energy security and energy shortage. Some articles have mixed energy security and energy shortage. Therefore, it is necessary to study the relationship between them. The study has both theoretical significance and practical significance.

The author believes that the energy security and energy shortage are two distinct problems in nature; there are fundamental differences between them.

Energy security is at the national level, not for a particular industry, an enterprise, or a location. Therefore, the measurements of energy security are whether the energy supply in a nation depends on a foreign energy supply and the degree of that dependence.

The energy shortage involves the relationship between energy supply and energy demand. It means that an insufficient energy supply cannot meet the needs in energy consumption. An energy shortage can be an issue for a country, an industry, or a location. Therefore, the measurements of the energy shortage are whether the energy supply can meet the needs in energy consumption and to what extent the energy supply can meet the needs in energy consumption. For an energy shortage, it does not matter where the energy supply comes from, domestic or overseas. Here are examples of the energy security and the energy shortage in developed countries and in China.

For a very long time before the world energy crisis in late 1973, developed countries didn't suffer energy shortages, because the energy supply in the world could fully meet their needs for energy consumption. However, because the energy supply in these developed countries mainly relies on foreign countries, they had potential and serious problems regarding energy security. But these problems were not realized for a long time. The energy crisis gave these developed countries a heavy blow, caused them huge losses, and affected their national security. Since then, energy security began to draw people's attention. For a long time after the founding of the new China, the production and supply of coal and petroleum could meet the domestic energy consumption demand. In addition, the items were exported. Similarly, the power supply could completely rely on domestic production, without dependence on foreign supplies. However, due to the rapid economic and social development, the supplies of coal and power fell short of the demand. The shortage occurred all the time. Sometimes, the shortage was very serious and caused negative impacts on economic development. This phenomenon was called the "energy shortage."

The above facts show that no energy shortage does not mean no energy security and that no energy security does not mean no energy shortage. Energy security and energy shortage have something in common: inadequate energy supply. However, the author found that the inadequate energy supply caused by energy insecurity is different from the inadequate energy supply caused by an energy shortage. The inadequate energy supply caused by energy insecurity has externality, abruptness, severity, and national security risk. "Externality" means that the energy crisis is caused by foreign factors. "Abruptness" means that the shortage occurs suddenly. "Severity" refers to the serious consequences caused by the shortage. "National security risk" means that the shortage endangers national security. In short, energy security and an energy shortage are two problems that are totally different in nature. They require different measures to resolve. The author thinks that it is very important to distinguish between them, because this will be helpful for analyzing and studying problems, and further taking proper measures. The key point is that the nature of energy security is not the energy supply, but the degree of dependence on foreign supplies.

As we know, compared with coal, oil has good technical and economic characteristics. Accordingly, oil is a kind of energy that offers high quality for national economic development. It is also an important and indispensable strategic material for military. However, oil resources are not renewable. The reservation of oil is limited. Since the last century, some counties have fought each other frequently to obtain oil. And in 1973 and 1979, the world energy crises occurred.

The author thought that the sharp rise of oil price in 2005 across the world was not normal. It was actually a new energy crisis in a new format. It could be called "the third oil crisis in the world." Unlike the last two crises, China was the victim this time. Attention should be paid to this.

From the perspective of national security, oil is different from coal, power, and other energies. Oil is an important material basis for economic development. More importantly, it is a strategic material for the military. Modern wars rely on oil. Therefore, oil security is the most important energy security. Oil security is the core of energy security. The first world energy crisis in late 1973 was indeed an oil crisis, because oil had been the primary energy for the industrial developed countries since the 1960s. Before the energy crisis, in 1972, the proportion of oil (in the total energy consumption) in the developed countries was the largest: 75.3% in Japan, 68% in

France, 53.5% in West Germany, 45.1% in the UK, and 43.8% in the US Furthermore, oil consumption in these developed countries mainly relied on import. For example, in the US, imported oil accounted for 27% of the total oil consumption. In Japan, West Germany, France, and the UK, imported oil accounted for more than 94% of the total oil consumption. Their oil was mainly imported from the Middle East. Therefore, when wars broke out the Middle East, oil-producing countries implemented an oil embargo and raised oil prices. As such, the oil supply for the developed countries was seriously affected. The shortage in the oil supply caused a huge mess in production and affected people's lives in developed countries. Their economic development was affected negatively. If the energy crisis was not resolved in a timely manner, an economic crisis and a political crisis would occur in these developed countries. Thus, since then, the developed countries have been forced to take measures, such as energy saving, replacing oil with coal, developing new energy, diversifying oil import, and establishing oil reserves.

China has suffered an oil shortage for a long time and has relied on imported oil. In 1959, the Daqing Oil Field was discovered. The oil field was put into production in 1963 after four years of hard work. In late 1959, the Chinese government declared to the world that the time was gone when the Chinese people would rely on foreign oil. Since then, the oil supply was sufficient in China. Oil was even exported for foreign exchange. Furthermore, oil even replaced coal as fuel. Thirty years later, in 1993, China began to depend on foreign oil again, when China became a net importer of oil. Since 1993, the import of oil has increased year by year in China. Especially in the recent decade, due to the rapid development of the petrochemical industry and transportation, the oil demand has increased sharply. The increase in domestic oil falls far behind the rise in oil consumption. In 1993, net oil import was <10 million t. In 2000 and 2004, net oil import rose to 70 million t and 149 million t, respectively. Net oil import was estimated to be 178 million t in 2005. From 2001 to 2005, the average annual increase of net oil import was about 20 million t. If the speed continued, net oil import would reach 280 million t in 2010, and 480 million t in 2020. It can be seen that, with the continuous increase of net oil import, the proportion of oil in the entire energy consumption will continue to increase. China's energy supply will rely more and more on imported oil. If this situation continues, China will repeat what the developed countries had suffered in their energy crises. This will definitely endanger China's energy security. In summary, the core of global energy security is oil security. Oil security is a worldwide problem. Similarly, the core of energy security in China is oil security. Oil security is a serious and practical problem in China, right now.

2. **Analysis of development of energy security in China**

The author believes that a country's energy security can be measured by its energy self-sufficiency rate or its dependence on net imported energy. If the energy self-sufficiency rate or the dependence on net imported energy is small, energy safety is large, vice versa. Here are the formulas:

$$\begin{aligned}\text{Energy security} &= \text{energy self} - \text{sufficiency rate}\\ &= 100\% - (\text{net imported energy supply/energy consumption}) \times 100\%\\ &= 100\% - \text{dependence on net imported energy}\end{aligned} \tag{23.65}$$

where

$$\begin{aligned}&\text{Dependence on net imported energy}\\ &\quad = (\text{net imported energy supply/energy consumption})\\ &\quad \times 100\%\end{aligned} \tag{23.66}$$

$$\text{energy self-sufficiency} = (\text{domestic energy supply/energy consumption}) \times 100\% \tag{23.67}$$

Table 23.46 lists the status of energy safety and oil safety in China since 1970. It can be seen from the table that from 1970 to 1996, China's level of energy was completely self-sufficient and energy security was 100%. In addition, oil was exported. In 1985, the net exported energy was the highest, more than 50 million t of standard coal, mainly due to 35.4 million t (physical quantity) of net exported oil. In 1993, the net exported energy was the lowest, only 1.55 million t of standard coal, mainly because of the net imported 9.88 million t (physical quantity) of oil.

Table 23.46 shows that China changed from a net oil exporter into a net oil importer in 1993. Only four years later, China changed from a net energy exporter into a net energy importer. The reason is that net imported oil was increasing dramatically. Therefore, China now has become a net oil importer and a net energy importer. Since 1997, net energy import had been increasing, and so had the ratio of net energy import. As a result, energy security in China declined. From 1997 to 2002, China's energy self-sufficiency rate was in the range of 96.4–99.4%. Energy security in China was still high.

After the 16th CPC National Congress in (2003), national economic and social development were accelerated. Particularly, the level of energy consumption grew rapidly and the net energy import increased rapidly. China's energy self-sufficiency rate or energy security was estimated to drop to 91.6–92.8%. The reason is that net the oil import in the two years increased too fast. The history of net energy import and export in China has proven that energy security in China relies on oil security.

It should be pointed out that, if one day coal import in China repeats the mode of oil import, energy security in China will rely on oil security and coal security. If this is the case, energy security in China will face a large challenge. The national security of China will face huge threats. However, the author found that this terrible situation would not happen for a few decades or even a longer time. Table 23.47 lists the conventional energy reserves and structure in China. The table shows that China has plenty of coal reserves. If the average annual production is two billion t, the amount of economic exploitable coal reserves in China can be exploited for 57 years. The amount of technical exploitable coal reserves in China can be exploited

Table 23.46 Status of energy security and oil security in China from 1970 to 2005

Year	Net imported (exported) energy (10,000 t of standard coal)	Net imported (exported) oil (10,000 t)	Net imported (exported) coal (10,000 t)	Net imported (exported) energy in total energy consumption ratio (%)	Net imported (exported) oil in oil consumption ratio (%)	Oil consumption in energy consumption ratio (%)	Net imported (exported) oil in energy consumption ratio (%)
1970	−256.9	−48.0	−254.0	−0.88	−3.08	14.64	−0.45
1975	−1984.7	−1210.0	−343.0	−4.37	−55.33	21.00	−11.62
1976	−1400.7	−850.0	−252.0	−2.93	−28.29	22.98	−6.50
1977	−1508.7	−911.0	−283.0	−2.88	−23.60	22.59	−5.33
1978	−1867.8	−1131.0	−342.0	−3.27	−25.27	22.71	−5.74
1979	−2274.2	−1340.0	−493.0	−3.88	−26.37	21.77	−5.74
1980	−2797.8	−1723.5	−460.1	−4.64	−29.65	20.72	−6.14
1981	−2941.5	−1813.2	−484.3	−4.95	−27.09	19.95	−5.40
1982	−3110.2	−1932.5	−472.2	−5.01	−25.12	18.88	−4.74
1983	−3146.5	−1957.7	−477.0	−4.76	−23.65	18.35	−4.34
1984	−4292.4	−2756.2	−483.5	−6.05	−30.34	17.51	−5.31
1985	−5481.8	−3540.4	−581.1	−7.15	−39.66	17.06	−6.76
1986	−5015.1	−3111.9	−780.6	−6.20	−35.53	17.15	−6.09
1987	−5130.9	−2970.4	−1220.2	−5.92	−35.76	17.07	−6.11
1988	−4859.4	−2633.9	−1498.2	−5.23	−32.08	17.17	−5.51
1989	−4009.7	−2041.3	−1471.0	−4.14	−24.35	17.05	−4.15
1990	−4582.3	−2354.8	−1658.7	−4.64	−27.21	16.61	−4.52
1991	−3514.8	−1455.3	−1971.2	−3.39	−15.87	17.08	−2.71
1992	−2257.6	−565.0	−1982.0	−2.07	−5.81	17.50	−1.02
1993	−155.0	988.0	−2099.0	−0.13	9.58	18.21	1.75
1994	−1620.0	290.0	−2702.5	−1.32	2.61	17.40	0.45
1995	−1352.3	1005.0	−3584.2	−1.03	8.68	17.49	1.52
1996	−597.9	1395.0	−3350.3	−0.43	12.15	18.00	2.19
1997	1755.2	3384.0	−3930.0	1.27	27.33	20.40	5.57
1998	854.7	2913.0	−4217.0	0.65	21.81	21.47	4.68
1999	2737.3	4381.0	−4571.0	2.10	29.76	23.25	6.92
2000	4705.7	6974.0	−6813.0	3.61	46.63	24.60	11.47
2001	1670.6	6494.0	−10,150.0	1.24	40.42	24.30	9.82
2002	3667.6	7141.0	−8659.0	2.47	40.96	24.00	9.83
2003	6548.8	9741.0	−9784.0	3.90	49.47	22.70	11.23
2004	14142.9	14,900.0	−10,000.0	7.18	46.56	23.00	10.71

(continued)

Table 23.46 (continued)

Year	Net imported (exported) energy (10,000 t of standard coal)	Net imported (exported) oil (10,000 t)	Net imported (exported) coal (10,000 t)	Net imported (exported) energy in total energy consumption ratio (%)	Net imported (exported) oil in oil consumption ratio (%)	Oil consumption in energy consumption ratio (%)	Net imported (exported) oil in energy consumption ratio (%)
2005	18285.7	17,800.0	−10,000.0	8.44	50.86	23.00	11.70

Note ① Minus sign refers to net export. Plus sign refers to net import. Data for 2005 are preliminary estimates of the author
② Energy security = 100% dependence on net imported energy. "Dependence on net imported energy" means the ratio of net imported energy supply in energy consumption
③ Oil security = 100% dependence on net imported oil. "Dependence on net imported oil" means the ratio of net imported oil supply in energy consumption

for 500 years. Unlike coal, if the average annual production is 0.3 billion t, the amount of economic exploitable oil reserves in China can be exploited for 11 years. The amount of technical exploitable oil reserves in China can be exploited for 53 years. Domestic and overseas situations prove that a country's energy resources play a vital role in energy security. Japan has little energy resources. It has invaded other countries to plunder energy. Since World War II, Japan has completely relied on imported energy. The reason for China to take the policy of "coal first" and "self-reliance first" is that coal is abundant in China. China's coal reserve can support its economic development for a long time. This is completely determined by natural resources; it cannot be changed.

3. **Analysis of development status of oil security in China**

The author found that oil security depends on three rates. The first rate is the proportion of net imported oil in the entire oil consumption, namely the net oil import rate. The second rate is the proportion of domestic oil production in the whole oil energy, namely the oil self-sufficiency rate. The third rate is the proportion of oil consumption in the overall energy consumption. Here are the formulas:

$$\begin{aligned}\text{Oil security} &= 100\% - [(\text{net imported oil supply/oil consumption} \\ &\quad \times (\text{oil consumption/energy consumption})]\ 100\% \\ &= 100\% - \text{dependence on net imported oil} \qquad (23.68)\end{aligned}$$

where

$$\begin{aligned}\text{Dependence on net imported oil} &= (\text{net imported oil supply/energy consumption}) \\ &\quad \times 100\% \qquad (23.69)\end{aligned}$$

Table 23.47 Reserves of common energies and their ratio in China

Energy type	Total energy (100 million t of standard coal)	Raw coal (100 million t)	Crude oil (100 million t)	Natural gas (100 million m^3)	Hydropower (100 million kWh)
I. Total reserves	40,466.4	50,592.2	1000.0	381,400.0	59,221.8
Ratio (%)	100.0	89.3	3.5	1.3	5.9
Global total reserves	1,048,809.7	1,195,748.4	51172.8	79330827.1	413095.0
China's ratio (%)	3.9	4.2	2.0	0.5	14.3
II. Explored total reserves (technically exploitable)	8231.0	10077.0	160.0	20606.0	19233.0
Structure (%)	100.0	87.4	2.8	0.3	9.5
Global total reserves	329697.5	352749.6	25674.6	26630075.2	117549.0
China's ratio (%)	2.5	2.9	0.6	0.1	16.4
Ratio of explored reserves (%)	20.3	19.9	16.0	5.4	
Available years for exploit	766.8	1007.7	98.2	74.3	
Production in 2000	10.9	10.0	1.6	277.3	2224.0
Structure (%)	100.0	67.2	21.4	3.4	8.0
III. Remaining recoverable reserves (economic exploitable)	1391.9	1145.0	32.7	13668.9	12600.0
Structure (%)	100.0	58.8	3.4	1.3	36.5
Global total reserves	13832.9	9842.1	1402.8	1493811.0	73053.0
China's ratio (%)	10.1	11.6	2.3	0.9	17.2

(continued)

Table 23.47 (continued)

Energy type	Total energy (100 million t of standard coal)	Raw coal (100 million t)	Crude oil (100 million t)	Natural gas (100 million m^3)	Hydropower (100 million kWh)
Available years for exploit	129.7	114.5	20.1	49.3	

Note The "explored resource rate" is the total explored reserves divided by total resources. "Available years for exploit" is the explored reserves or the remaining recoverable reserves divided by output in 2000. When calculating respective ratios, the coefficient of respective energy in t of standard coal is: coal, 0.7143; oil, 1.4286, natural gas, 13.3; hydropower is calculated as per standard coal consumption of 404 g and 100 years. Data source: 2001 China Energy Development Report, China Metrology Publishing House, December of 2001

$$\text{Net oil import rate} = (\text{net imported oil supply/oil consumption}) \times 100\% \tag{23.70}$$

$$\begin{aligned}\text{Self-sufficiency of oil} &= (\text{domestic oil supply/oil consumption}) \times 100\% \\ &= 100\% - \text{net oil import rate}\end{aligned} \tag{23.71}$$

China's oil security depends on the proportion of net imported oil in the entire energy, namely its dependence on net imported oil. If a country has a small ratio of oil in its entire energy, this country has a high self-sufficiency, a low net oil import rate, a low dependence on imported oil, and high oil security. This was the case in China for 30 years until 1993. If a country has a large ratio of oil in its entire energy, this country has a low self-sufficiency, a high net oil import rate, a high dependence on imported oil, and low oil security. In 1973, when the first world energy crisis occurred, many developed countries were in this status. For example, Japan had an oil self-sufficiency rate of nearly zero. Its net oil import rate was close to 100%.

Its dependence on imported oil was 71%. Energy security in Japan was low. The threat for energy security was high, because 71% of national economy depended on imported oil. Once the foreign oil supply stopped, almost the entire economy in Japan would have difficulty. France came next, after Japan, with a dependence on imported oil of 64%. The dependence on imported oil for West Germany, the UK, and the US were 50%, 43%, and 12%, respectively. The first world energy crisis caused huge damage, especially in the economy, to the countries that depended on imported oil. For example, the annual GDP growth rate in Japan was about 10% before the first world energy crisis. After the crisis, in 1974, its GDP growth rate dropped to 8. Japan lost 12% of its GDP, around 48.5 billion US dollars. France, West Germany, the UK, and the US suffered huge losses as well. Moreover, after the two world energy crises, the GDP growth rates in the developed countries never reached the levels they had before the crises.

Oil is not the main energy in China. The proportion of oil in China's entire energy is <1/4. Even though the proportion of net imported oil accounts for about 50% of the entire oil consumption, China's dependence on imported oil is only 12%. This level is the same as that of the US in 1973. In this case, even if all foreign oil supply stops, the Chinese national economy will not suffer the same losses as those that Japan, France, West Germany, and the UK suffered in the first world energy crisis.

However, if the ratio of oil energy in China's total energy keeps rising and the ratio of net imported oil in the oil consumption keeps rising, China's dependence of net imported oil will increase. China's energy security will drop, and the threat to energy will increase. Particularly in the case when the international oil price rises sharply, the threat will be larger. In the recent two years, the amount of net imported oil has been about 300 million t in China. The skyrocketing oil prices will cause China a tremendous loss in foreign exchange.

Table 23.48 lists China's net oil imports from 1993 to 2020. Table 23.49 shows the oil production in China from 1980 to 2020. Table 23.50 shows China's oil consumption from 1980 to 2020. Tables 23.46 and 23.48 indicate the changes of net imported oil in China since 1993 and the predictions for net imported oil for the next 15 years. In 1993, China became a net importer of oil with a net imported oil of 9.88 million t and a net oil import rate of 6.7%.[36] In 2000, net imported oil reached 75.76 million t. The net oil import rate was 33.8%. In 2005, China's total oil demand was estimated to be 354 million t. The net imported oil was estimated to be 178 million t. The net oil import rate was estimated to be 50.9%. From 1993 to 2005, the annual rise of net imported oil varied. Basically, there were five cases: 10, 20, 30, 40, and 50 million t. Five schemes were developed based on these five cases to estimate the future amount of net imported oil. The predictions show that, if the average annual growth rate of net imported oil is 10 million t, net oil import rate in 2010, 2015, and 2020 will be 54.4%, 57.4%, and 59.7%, respectively. In other words, more than half of China's oil demand will rely on imported oil. If the average annual growth rate of net imported oil is 20, 30, 40 or 50 million t, the net oil import rate will be higher.

The author found that, if a country wants to achieve oil security, its net import oil rate should be smaller than 50%. If the net import oil rate is larger than 50%, oil security cannot be achieved. If the net import oil rate is larger than 50% for a long time, it lead to a very dangerous situation regarding oil security. It is better to keep the net import oil rate smaller than 30%.[37] In other words, the average annual increase of net oil import during the next 15 years should not be more than 10 million t. Even at this rate, the annual net oil import will be 0.2–0.3 billion t. Given the harsh competition for oil at present, it is not easy to import such a huge amount of oil. Thus, the guidance of a scientific development concept should be followed for taking new developing ideas.

---

[36]Net oil import rate = net oil import/oil consumption = (oil import-oil export)/oil consumption. It should be noted that, in this report, "oil" refers to crude oil and refined oil if no special explanation is provided.

[37]Net oil import rate of the US was 27% when the first world energy crisis occurred in 1973.

Table 23.48 Net oil import and prediction in China from 1993 to 2020

Year	Net oil import			Oil consumption (10,000 t)	Net oil import rate (%)
	Quantity (10,000 t)	Annual increase (10,000 t)	Annual increase rate (%)		
1993	988	988	–	14721	6.7
1994	290	−698	−70.6	14956	1.9
1995	1005	715	246.6	16,065	6.3
1996	1395	390	38.8	17,436	8.0
1997	3384	1989	142.6	19,692	17.2
1998	2913	−471	−13.9	19,818	14.7
1999	4381	1468	50.4	21,131	20.7
2000	7576	3195	72.9	22,437	33.8
2001	7072	−505	−6.7	22,948	30.8
2002	8130	1059	15.0	24,901	32.6
2003	9600	1470	18.1	26,663	36.0
2004	14,900	5300	55.2	32,000	46.6
2005	17,800	2900	19.5	35,000	50.9
2010 Scheme 1	22,800	1000	5.1	41,900	54.4
Scheme 2	27,800	2000	9.3	47,900	58.0
Scheme 3	32,800	3000	13.0	55,400	59.2
Scheme 4	37,800	4000	16.3	60,400	62.6
Scheme 5	42,800	5000	19.2	65,400	65.4
2015 Scheme 1	27,800	1000	4.0	48,400	57.4
Scheme 2	37,800	2000	6.3	60,400	62.6
Scheme 3	47,800	3000	7.8	75,400	63.4
Scheme 4	57,800	4000	8.9	85,400	67.7
Scheme 5	67,800	5000	9.6	95,400	71.1
2020 Scheme 1	32,800	1000	3.4	54,900	59.7
Scheme 2	47,800	2000	4.8	72,900	65.6
Scheme 3	62,800	3000	5.6	95,400	65.8
Scheme 4	77,800	4000	6.1	110,400	70.5
Scheme 5	92,800	5000	6.5	125,400	74.0

Note Oil consumption is the sum of net oil import and domestic oil production. Net oil import can be predicted in accordance with five schemes. Oil consumption can be predicted with five schemes, accordingly. In Schemes 1, 2, and 3, domestic oil production takes the data in Schemes 1, 2 and 3 in Table 23.49. Domestic oil production in Schemes 4 and 5 takes the data in Scheme 3 in Table 23.49. In addition, the data for 2005 are preliminary estimates

Table 23.49 Oil production and prediction in China from 1980 to 2020

Period	Year	Oil production			GDP annual growth rate B (%)	Elasticity coefficient of oil production (A/B)
		Total quantity (10,000 t)	Annual increase (10,000 t)	Average annual growth rate A (%)		
Fifth five-year plan period	1980	10,595	–	–	–	–
Sixth five-year plan period	1981–1985	–	379	3.35	10.71	0.31
	1985	12,490	–	–	–	–
Seventh five-year plan period	1986–1990	–	268	2.06	7.87	0.26
	1990	13,831	–	–	–	–
Eighth five-year plan period	1990–1995	–	235	1.64	12	0.14
	1995	15,005	–	–	–	–
Ninth five-year plan period	1996–2000	–	259	1.67	8.27	0.20
	2000	16,300	–	–	–	–
Tenth five-year plan period	2001–2005	–	271	1.61	8.7	0.19
	2005	17,656	–	–	–	–
Eleventh five-year plan period	2006–2010	–	–	–	–	–
	2010 Scheme 1	19,156	300	1.64	8	0.21
	Scheme 2	20,156	500	2.68	8	0.34
	Scheme 3	22,656	1000	5.11	8	0.64
Twelfth five-year plan period	2011–2015	–	–	–	–	–
	2015 Scheme 1	20,656	300	1.52	7.5	0.20
	Scheme 2	22,656	500	2.37	7.5	0.32
	Scheme 3	27,656	1000	4.07	7.5	0.54
Thirteenth five-year plan period	2016–2020	–	–	–	–	–
	2020 Scheme 1	22,156	300	1.41	7	0.20
	Scheme 2	25,156	500	2.12	7	0.30
	Scheme 3	32,656	1000	3.38	7	0.48

Note Data for 2005 are preliminary estimations of the author

Table 23.50 Oil consumption and prediction in China from 1980 to 2020

Period	Year	Oil consumption			GDP annual growth rate B (%)	Elasticity coefficient of oil consumption (A/B)
		Total Quantity (10,000 t)	Annual increase (10,000 t)	Annual growth rate A (%)		
Fifth five-year plan period	1980	8757	–	–	–	–
Sixth five-year plan period	1981–1985	–	81	0.92	10.71	0.09
	1985	9160	–	–	–	–
Seventh five-year plan period	1986–1990	–	465	4.61	7.87	0.59
	1990	11,486	–	–	–	–
Eighth five-year plan period	1990–1995	–	916	6.94	12.00	0.58
	1995	16,065	–	–	–	–
Ninth five-year plan period	1996–2000	–	1016	5.65	8.27	0.68
	2000	21,145	–	–	–	–
Tenth five-year plan period	2001–2005	–	2771	10.6	8.7	1.22
	2005	35,000	–	–	–	–
Eleventh five-year plan period	2006–2010	–	–	–	–	–
	2010 Scheme 1	41,900	1380	3.66	8.0	0.46
	Scheme 2	47,900	2580	6.48	8.0	0.81
	Scheme 3	55,400	4080	9.62	8.0	1.20
Twelfth five-year plan period	2011–2015	–	–	–	–	–
	2015 Scheme 1	48,400	1300	2.93	7.5	0.39
	Scheme 2	60,400	2500	7.59	7.5	1.01
	Scheme 3	75,400	4000	12.47	7.5	1.66
Thirteenth five-year plan period	2016–2020	–	–	–	–	–
	2020 Scheme 1	54,900	1300	2.55	7.0	0.36
	Scheme 2	72,900	2500	3.83	7.0	0.55
	Scheme 3	95,400	4000	4.82	7.0	0.69

Note Data of 2005 are preliminary estimation of the author

23.16.2 Strategy Choice and Measures for Oil Security in China

1. **Strategy choice of oil security in China**

Due to the third high oil price crisis[38] in 2005 and the rise of the demand for oil in China, the net oil import has increased drastically. The threat to oil security has become larger. It is necessary for China to take a correct strategy to improve its oil security.

For more than half a century, China has implemented the energy policy: coal first and self-reliance. This policy has provided energy security and oil security for China. In the future, this policy should be insisted upon, in order to maintain oil security for China. "Coal first" does not mean that there is no need to develop oil production. "Self-reliance" does not mean dependence on domestic energy production only. It does not mean no imported energy. "Domestic energy first and imported energy second" is the guideline for the energy development strategy in China. Meanwhile, the author has suggested that an alternative oil import strategy to deal with the new situation regarding energy should be adopted.

2. Oil security strategy in China—Alternative oil import strategy

Since the reform and opening up, China's economy has developed rapidly and sustainably. From the sixth five-year plan period to the eighth five-year plan period, the average annual growth rate of the GDP has been 10.2%. Meanwhile, the oil demand from petrochemicals, transportation, agricultural machinery, and furnaces has risen dramatically. However, the average annual growth rate of oil production has declined greatly. The drops in the average annual growth rate of oil production in the sixth five-year plan period, the seventh five-year plan period, and the eighth five-year plan period are 3.4%, 2.1%, and 1.5%, respectively. This high and low phenomenon has changed the status of the oil supply and demand in China. The domestic oil supply has changed from oversupply to shortage. China has changed from an oil exporter to an oil importer. Since 1993, China has become a country that relies on foreign oil. To deal with this situation, China should take oil import strategy or alternative oil import strategy.

The author found that the only solution for the contradiction between oil supply and demand in China is the alternative oil import strategy. Here are the contents of this strategy.

(1) *Strengthen the oil supply policy: domestic production first and import second*

In recent years, many people have stressed the use of two resources and two markets. They argue that these two resources and two markets are equally important. The author thinks that the nature of domestic resources and oversea resources are

[38]② This is the author's opinion.

completely different. Similarly, the nature of domestic market and foreign market are also completely different. From the perspective of safety, the safety of domestic resources and the domestic market is large, whereas the safety of foreign resources and foreign markets has uncertainty and risk. Therefore, it is not correct to treat and to emphasize the two resources and two markets equally. The author thinks that the oil supply in China should continue the policy of "domestic first and import second." In other words, domestic oil resources and market should be primary. Foreign resources and market should be secondary.

(2) *Stress the oil production policy that natural oil and artificial oil are equally important*

Over the years, China has implemented the policy that natural oil is primary and artificial oil is secondary. This policy has fit the actual situation in China. With the reduction of natural oil resources, the contradiction of the supply and demand of natural oil has become more prominent. When the oil price in the international market is very high, the importance, necessity, economy, and feasibility of developing artificial oil greatly increases. Due to sanctions, South Africa has been developing artificial oil for a long time. Its experience is worth of learning.

Therefore, the author proposes to implement a new policy that states that natural oil and artificial oil are equally important in China. In recent years, China has begun to pay attention to the artificial oil industry and has done a lot of research, but this is not enough. Facts have proven that artificial petroleum and alternative petroleum made from coal, oil shale, biological organisms, and waste have great prospects, and that their economic benefits will be better for the country.

(3) *Stress the oil consumption policy: coal in place of oil, natural gas in place of oil, and saving oil*

To deal with the unreasonable waste of oil in industries, it is necessary to stress the policy: coal in place of oil, natural gas in place of oil, and saving oil. In this way, the demand for oil will drop from the beginning. This approach has great potential and great development prospects. From the perspective of utilizing resources reasonably, power plants, boilers, and furnaces should use coal instead of oil and natural gas. Oil and gas can be used for producing chemical products, transportation, and urban living, in which alternative fuels are not available or coal is not suitable, so that oil products and natural gas can be used for chemical products and for transportation that cannot consume other fuels in uses in which coal is not suitable.

(4) *Stress oil import policy: proper quantity, proper time. and proper place*

"Proper quantity" does not mean large quantity of imported oil, but oil imported in the proper quantity. The government should control oil imports. "Proper time" means that oil importing should be done in a timely manner. "Proper place" means that oil should be imported from the right region and country. Oil imports should be diversified and decentralized.

Only with the implementation of an alternative oil import strategy and by following the four policies listed above can the contradiction between China's oil supply and its demand be fixed. Eventually, the status of the domestic oil supply will change. As such, the government should take urgent measures to focus on the implementation and deployment of an alternative oil import strategy. Do not rely completely on oil importing. Focus less on overseas oil exploration. Otherwise, China will lose a lot of foreign exchange. Oil security and energy security will be affected negatively. The development of the oil industry, the coal industry, and related industries will be constrained. Unemployment will become more serious. The economy in the midwestern and northeastern old industrial areas will not grow rapidly. In short, the loss would be catastrophic and irreversible. It seems that oil import strategy is a foreign exchange issue. But, in fact, many other serious issues need to be considered in developing an oil import strategy.

3. **Measures and suggestions for oil security in China**

(1) **Guided by the scientific development outlook, continue the energy development approach of two requirements**

For energy development, developed countries have taken the strategy of "oil first and dependence on oil resources in other countries" for a long time. However, energy development in China has had its own path under the leadership of the CPC, which leads China as it undergoes economic development on its own path. The path is "coal first and self-reliance." Here are the reasons for China to take this energy development path. First, China has a large population and a huge energy demand. As in the case of crops, if China cannot achieve self-reliance, no other country can meet the huge demand of energy from China. Thus, self-reliance is an inevitable choice for energy development in China. Second, fossil energy resources are rich in China. These resources can meet China's demand for a certain time. Among the general fossil energy reserves, coal accounts for more than 90%. Oil and natural gas account for <10%. Therefore, "coal first" is an inevitable choice for energy development in China, as well. Third, for a long time, although developed countries have not had rich energy resources, they have had strong economic and comprehensive strength. Therefore, developed countries have been able to rely on oil provided by other countries. But China is a developing country that does not have strong economic and comprehensive strengths. Thus, China cannot follow the path taken by developed countries.

Since the founding of the new China in 1949, the energy industry has developed rapidly under the guidance of two requirements Particularly, after the reform and opening up, China has adopted the strategy that energy development and energy saving are equally important. Accordingly, China has gained great economic achievements. The energy supply has successfully supported the rapid, coordinated, and sustainable development of the economy and of society. Because of the two requirements, the energy security in China has been well maintained. When the two energy crises (oil crises) occurred in 1973 and 1979, developed countries suffered huge losses, but they did not impact China much. Practice has proven that the two continued requirements strategy fits the actual situation in China and meets the requirements for the scientific development outlook. It is the correct strategy for China to develop energy; it provides protection and energy security in China.

(2) **Guided by the scientific development outlook, implement an alternative oil import strategy and treat the transformation of the energy structure properly**

Since the reform and opening up, many people have thought that China's coal-dominated energy structure had to be changed in order to follow the mode of energy structure in developed countries. The author thinks that energy structure in energy development of a country or the world should follow the objective laws of science.

One characteristic for energy development is the interchangeability between different energies, particularly the interchangeability between coal and oil. Coal and oil can both be used as raw material for producing chemical fertilizers and synthetic materials. They can also be used as fuel for power generation and for the heating supply. However, due to the high heating value, good composition, ow level of pollution, and low price of oil, oil production and consumption has risen sharply since the 1950 and 1960s. Oil has become the replacement for coal. The ratio of oil in the energy structure has exceeded coal, reaching 40%. The ratio of coal in the energy structure has dropped to lower than 30%. In the 1960s, the cheap oil supply promoted economic development in the world. The annual economic growth rate across the world was over 4%, close to 4% in the US, over 5% in West Germany, and over 10% in Japan.

However, oil prices rose sharply after the two oil crises in 1973 and 1979. The price of crude oil was as high as $35 a barrel in the early 1980s. Compared with the price of $2 a barrel in 1973, the price rose over 16 times. Then the international oil price dropped. In 1985–1986, the price of crude oil dropped from $27 a barrel to $10 a barrel. Since then, the price has stayed at around $18 a barrel. In recent years, the international oil price has risen continuously. The price of crude oil has soared to more than $60–70 a barrel in 2005. The price was estimated to reach $100 a barrel. The dramatic change in international oil prices was related to the policies in the oil producing countries of the Middle East, such as limiting production to maintain price. The change is also related to manipulations by some speculators and by governments in certain countries. In addition, the change is related to the policy change of oil saving and oil-substitution, energy structure adjustment, and the decline of oil consumption. For example, the proportion of oil consumption in the total energy consumption in the US dropped from 46.9% in 1973 to 43.6% in 1980 and 43.0% in 1985. Compared with that of 1980, the total oil consumption in the US in 1985 dropped 51.8 million t. Meanwhile, the proportion of coal consumption in the total energy consumption increased 22.3% in 1980 and 26.7% in 1985. Compared with 1980, in 1985, total coal consumption increased 72 million t.

China's energy consumption structure is subject to its energy production structure. In return, China's energy production structure is subject to its energy consumption structure. China has abundant coal resources. Its energy structure has been dominated by coal. However, with the development and utilization of oil, the proportion of coal has decreased significantly. In 1952, in China's energy consumption structure, coal accounted for 94.3% and oil accounted for 3.8%; in 1962, coal accounted for 89.2% and oil accounted for 6.6%. After 1963, due to the development of the Daqing oil field and other oil fields in China, oil production developed quickly and promoted oil consumption. Meanwhile, misguided by the wrong policy, China's energy structure changed. The proportion of oil increased. Oil replaced coal improperly. Some power plants and boilers switched from coal to oil. As a result, one third of the oil that could be used for chemical raw materials and high quality fuel was burned as coal. In 1976, in China's energy consumption structure, the proportion of oil rose to 23.0% (the highest in history). The proportion of coal fell to 69.9% (the lowest in history). These are the results of the so-called optimizing energy structure. Unlike the developed countries, China did not suffer the impacts of oil crises. After the reform and opening up, given its limited oil reserves, China adopted the policy switching from oil back to coal. From 1976 to 1996, the ratio of oil consumption in China's total energy consumption dropped from 23.0 to 18.0%. Meanwhile, the proportion of coal consumption in the total energy consumption increased from 69.9 to 74.7%. This is the achievement of a real optimizing energy structure. It can be seen that the adjustment of the energy structure in China took an indirect route.

Coal and oil replaced each other, due to price changes in energy development across the world. The replacement between coal and oil in China was caused by the change in energy policy. The experience and lesson should be paid special attention.

23.16.3 Analysis of Status of the Energy Bottleneck and Coordinated Development Between Energy and the Economy in China

1. **Energy bottleneck is an objective phenomenon in China**

Since the reform and opening up, people often talk about China's "energy bottleneck." The energy bottleneck has attracted people's attention. In theory, the energy bottleneck has been caused by a short supply of energy. The shortage in the energy supply might be caused by resource constraints, production constraints, transportation constraints, reserve constraints, consumption constraints, environmental constraints, price constraints, policy constraints, or international constraints. Any of these constraints will affect the energy supply and will form an energy bottleneck.

After the founding of the new China in 1949, China implemented a socialist planned economy. The planned economy was characterized with shortage. The supply for many things was in a shortage. Quotas were set for supply. The energy supply for production and living was in a shortage as well. The coal supply was limited. Due to a lack of coal and power, factories ran for four days and were stopped for three days in a week. Residential heating did not work well. Power failures occurred frequently. High power-consuming home appliances were limited in use. The phenomenon of the energy bottleneck was commonly seen. After the reform and opening up, China entered the era of the socialist market economy. In order to accelerate the development of the economy, energy demand was large. But the energy reserves were limited and the energy resources per capita were small. Furthermore, it takes many years to construct energy production and transportation projects. Therefore, when the economy grows rapidly, a shortage of energy supply and energy bottleneck can occur. For a long time, due to limited financial resources, China did not establish large energy reserves. Without enough energy reserves, a shortage of energy supply and an energy bottleneck will occur frequently.

The author found that, in essence, the energy shortage and the energy bottleneck in China are objective phenomena that will be inevitable for a long time.

2. **Analysis of the development status of the energy bottleneck in China**

Until now, studies regarding the energy bottleneck in China are still being completed. Scientific judgment and an evaluation of the energy bottleneck are still missing. In general, people usually conduct identification and assessment after a shortage in the energy supply occurs. No prediction of a shortage is available. Without prediction, no measures can be taken to prevent the shortage. As such, it is important to study the energy bottleneck in China. The study has both theoretical and practical meaning.

The author thinks that the energy bottleneck is caused by economic development and energy supply. On one hand, how much energy does economic development need? On the other hand, how much energy can be supplied? If economic development needs a lot of energy, and the energy supply is not enough, energy becomes a bottleneck and restricts economic development. The status of the energy bottleneck depends on economic development and the energy supply. According to the author's research, scientific judgment and evaluation of the energy bottleneck status should be based on the growth of energy consumption, not on economic development. Therefore, energy consumption growth status is set at 5 levels: negative growth (<0%), low-growth (≤5%), medium growth (>5 to <8%), high-growth (≥8–10%) and ultra-high-growth (≥10%). Accordingly, the status of the energy bottleneck can be set at five levels as well: most unobvious constraints, unobvious constraints, mild restriction, serious constraints, and very serious constraints. Table 23.51 lists the evaluation criteria for the energy bottleneck.

With the evaluation criteria, quantitative and qualitative research can be done for the status of the energy bottleneck, according to the growth of energy consumption. As such, evaluation was conducted for the energy bottleneck in all periods after the founding of the new China, based on the yearly data. The evaluation results are

Table 23.51 Evaluation criteria for energy bottleneck

Status of energy consumption growth	Level	Level
Negative growth (<0%)	Most unobvious constraints	A
Low-growth (≤5%)	Unobvious constraints	B
Medium growth (>5 to <8%)	Mild restriction	C
High-growth (≥8–10%)	Serious constraints	D
Ultra-high-growth (≥10%)	Very serious constraints	E

listed in Table 23.52. After founding of the new China, there were ten five-year plans and one three-year plan (economic adjustment), 11 plans in total. Very serious energy bottlenecks occurred in the first five-year plan period, the second five-year plan period, and the tenth five-year plan period, accounting for 27% of the 11 plan periods. Serious energy bottlenecks occurred in the third five-year plan period and the fourth five-year plan period, accounting for 18% of the 11 plan periods. Mild serious energy bottlenecks occurred in the fifth five-year plan period, the seventh five-year plan period, and the eighth five-year plan period, accounting for 27% of the 11 plan periods. Unobvious energy bottlenecks occurred in the three-year economic adjustment period and the sixth five-year plan period, accounting for 18% of the 11 plan periods. The most unobvious energy bottleneck occurred in the ninth five-year plan period, accounting for 9% of the 11 plan periods. Very serious and serious energy bottlenecks occurred in half of the 11 periods. The author believes that the evaluation results based on this standard match the actual situation. For example, in the ninth five-year plan period when the most obvious energy bottleneck occurred, coal was unmarketable. In recent years, a very serious energy bottleneck has occurred yet again. The changes match the results in Table 23.52. Therefore, the aforementioned energy bottleneck evaluation criteria and the analysis of energy bottleneck have practical meaning.

3. **Analysis of coordinated development between energy and economic status in China**

In order to conduct scientific judgment and evaluation for the status of coordinated development between energy and the economy, the author proposed the energy and economic coordinated development evaluation criteria as shown in Table 23.53.

Based on careful study, the author has adopted two dynamic indicators: the elasticity coefficient of energy consumption growth and the GDP growth rate. The elasticity coefficient of energy consumption growth is the ratio between the energy consumption growth rate and the GDP growth rate. It can reflect energy growth modes (intensive or extensive) and the coordinated development between energy and the economy. The GDP growth rate is a core indicator and an important goal of

Table 23.52 Evaluation of energy bottleneck and coordinated development between energy and the economy in China from 1953 to 2005

Period	Year	Energy consumption growth	Energy bottleneck status	GDP growth status	Elasticity coefficient of energy consumption	Coordinated development between energy and economy	
						Status evaluation	Sorting by plan period
First five-year plan period	1953–1957	Ultra-high growth (14.5%)	Very serious constraints	High growth (8.9%)	1.63	Ordinary	**8**
Second five-year plan period	1958–1962	Ultra-high growth (11.4%)	Very serious constraints	Negative growth (−3.1%)	>>1	Worst	**11**
Economic restructuring period	1963–1965	Low growth (4.5%)	Unobvious constraints	Ultra-high growth (14.7%)	0.31	Good	**2**
Third five-year plan period	1966–1970	High growth (9.2%)	Serious constraints	High growth (8.4%)	1.10	Ordinary	**9**
Fourth five-year plan period	1971–1975	High growth (9.2%)	Serious constraints	Medium growth (5.5%)	1.67	Bad	**10**
Fifth five-year plan period	1976–1980	Medium growth (5.8%)	Mild constraints	Medium growth (7.9%)	0.74	Ordinary	**6**
Before reform and opening up	**1953–1978**	**High growth (9.9%)**	**Serious constraints**	**Medium growth (6.0%)**	**1.66**	**Bad**	**Ranks the third in large periods**
Sixth five-year plan period	**1981–1985**	Low growth (4.9%)	Unobvious constraints	Ultra-high growth (10.7%)	0.46	Good	**3**
Seventh five-year plan period	**1986–1990**	Medium growth (5.2%)	Mild constraints	Medium growth (7.9%)	0.66	Ordinary	**5**
Eighth five-year plan period	**1991–1995**	Medium growth (5.9%)	Mild constraints	Ultra-high growth (12.0%)	0.49	Good	**4**

(continued)

Table 23.52 (continued)

Period	Year	Energy consumption growth	Energy bottleneck status	GDP growth status	Elasticity coefficient of energy consumption	Coordinated development between energy and economy	
						Status evaluation	Sorting by plan period
Economy quadrupled in the twentieth century	**1981–1995**	**Medium growth (5.3%)**	**Mild constraints**	**Ultra-high growth (10.2%)**	**0.52**	**Good**	**Ranks the first in large periods**
Ninth five-year plan period, economic adjustment period	1996–2000	Negative growth (−0.1%)	Most unobvious constraints	High growth (8.3%)	-0.02	Best	**1**
Tenth five-year plan period	2001–2005	Ultra-high growth (11.3%)	Very serious constraints	High growth (9.48%)	1.19	Ordinary	**7**
Ten years cross the century	**1996–2005**	**Medium growth (7.0%)**	**Mild constraints**	**High growth (9.5%)**	**0.73**	**Better**	**Ranks the second in large periods**

Note Ultra-high growth (≥10%), high-growth (≥8–10%), medium growth (>5 to <8%), low growth (≤5%), zero growth (= 0%), negative growth (<0%)

Table 23.53 Evaluation criteria of coordinated development of energy and the economy

Elasticity coefficient of energy consumption growth	GDP growth rate	Level	Level
Negative value	Positive value (Medium growth)	Best	AA
<1	Ultra-high growth (≥10%)	Good	A
≤0.5	High growth (≥8–10%)		
≥1	Ultra-high growth (≥10%)	Better	B
>0.5	High growth (≥8–10%)		
≤0.5	Medium growth (>5 to <8%)		
≥1	High growth (≥8–10%)	Ordinary	C
>0.5	Medium growth (>5 to <8%)		
≤0.5	Low growth (≤5%)		
≥1	Medium growth (>5 to <8%)	Bad	D
>0.5	Low growth (≤5%)		
≥1	Low growth (≤5%)	Bad	E
< 1	Negative growth (<0%)		
≥1	Negative growth (<0%)	Worst	EE

economic development. With the same elasticity coefficient of energy consumption, a higher GDP growth rate means a better coordinated development between energy and economy.

According to the relationship between these two dynamic indicators, coordinated development between energy and the economy is set with five +2 standards, namely: the most best, best, better, ordinary, bad, worst, and the most worst.

The ideal and sustainable situation of coordinated development between energy and the economy is the status when the elasticity coefficient of energy consumption growth is very small, but the GDP growth rate is large.

Using the evaluation criteria for the energy bottleneck, the energy and economy-coordinated development evaluation criteria, and historical data, the author evaluated the status of energy and economy-coordinated development for each period. The results are listed in Table 23.52. The best status of energy and economic development occurred during the ninth five-year plan period, a large economic adjustment period. This status accounted for 9% of the 11 plan periods. In this period, energy growth was negative and economic growth was high. Three periods had good status, accounting for 27% of the 11 plan periods. Five periods had ordinary status, accounting for 45% of the 11 plan periods. One period had bad status, accounting for 9% of the 11 plan periods. The second five-year plan period had the worst status, accounting for 9% of the 11 plan periods. In this period, energy growth had a ultra-high rate and economic growth was negative. Here is the ranking of the 11 periods, based on their energy and economy development status: the ninth five-year plan period is #1, three year adjustment period is #2, the sixth five-year plan period is #3, the eighth five-year plan period is #4, the seventh five-year plan period is #5, the fifth five-year plan period is

#6, the tenth five-year plan period is #7, the first five-year plan period is #8, the third five-year plan period is #9, the fourth five-year plan period is #10, and the second five-year plan period is #11. Here is the other ranking by the large period: the period in the twentieth century when the economy was quadrupled (1981–1995) is #1, ten years across the twenty-first century (1996–2005) is #2, and the period before the reform and opening up (1953–1978) is #3.

Here are the conclusions.

(1) It is a long-term and objective phenomenon in China that energy bottlenecks restrict economic development. This is inevitable. However, proper measures and strategies can be taken to achieve coordinated development between energy and the economy.
(2) An energy bottleneck is the most serious during the period when economic development is rapid. Therefore, it is very important to maintain a moderated economic growth rate.
(3) China is heading for the goal of quadrupling its economy by 2020 and achieving moderate prosperity. The energy bottleneck will not recede, but will be more prominent. Therefore, it is a very important and difficult but worthwhile task to break the energy bottleneck.

23.16.4 Strategy and Measures for Breaking the Energy Bottleneck in China

3. **Strategy for breaking the energy bottleneck**

In 2002, the 16th CPC National Congress formally proposed the ambitious goal that moderate prosperity should be achieved in the twenty-first century. This goal requires quadrupling the GDP of 2000 by 2020. This is a very glorious and very difficult task. Since the new century began, although international environment has changed greatly, the domestic situation improved under the guidance of the scientific development outlook. Given the economic and energy development status in the first five years in the twenty-first century, the economic goal can be achieved in advance. According to the requirements of the task, the annual average growth of GDP should have been 7.18%. In fact, from 2001 to 2005, the average annual growth of GDP was 9.5%. If economic development maintains this rate, the task can be achieved 4–5 years in advance.

However, energy consumption grew too quickly from 2001 to 2005. Table 23.52 shows that the average annual growth rate of energy consumption in the tenth five-year plan period was 11.3%. This was the highest rate among the periods after the reform and opening up, including the sixth five-year plan period, the seventh five-year plan period, the eighth five-year plan period, the ninth five-year plan period, and the tenth five-year plan period. This rate is only lower than those in the first five-year plan period and the second five-year plan period. Particularly, energy consumption's annual growth rate was 15.3 and 16.1% in 2003 and 2004, respectively. These two years had the highest energy consumption annual growth rate, among the 28 years after reform and opening up. The high energy consumption growth rate caused a shortage in energy production, supply, and transportation. The energy bottleneck was very serious. Oil imports rose sharply. Oil security and energy security faced great threats. Environmental pollution became a serious challenge. The author thinks that this situation should not continue. Otherwise, the economic goal will not be achieved. Instead, the economy might decrease. The author finds that the sharp rise of energy consumption in the tenth five-year plan is related to the negative growth of energy consumption during the ninth five-year plan period. Scientific laws show that if a negative economic growth appears in a previous period, a higher growth rate will appear in the next period. Thus, the high growth rate is related to recovery. For example, Table 23.52 shows that negative economic growth occurred in the second five-year plan period, and that ultra-high economic growth appeared in the three year economic adjustment period. As such, the author investigated the situation during the ten years across the century, including the ninth give-year plan period and the tenth five-year plan period. The results show that, during these ten years, the growth in energy consumption was at a medium rate, economic growth rate was high, and the status of energy and economic development was good (see Table 23.52). Realistically speaking, the negative growth of energy consumption in the ninth five-year plan period might be related to some uncertain factors, such as inaccurate data. Therefore, the author believes that the abnormal status of energy and economic development in the tenth five-year plan period was caused by other reasons.

The author thinks that the future situation of energy and economy-coordinated development in China is severe. The oil demand increases rapidly. The net oil import grows sharply. As a result, oil security becomes more severe. Energy security is a large challenge in China. In 2005, the high oil price crisis broke out. Economic development is the main goal. The economic growth rate cannot be low. Particularly, the economy in the midwest areas and the old industrial areas in northeast needs development urgently. The economic development goal is a large challenge. What is the solution? The author thinks that the correct strategy must be taken to deal with the relationship between energy and economy-coordinated development.

According to the experience in developed countries and in China, two strategies are available. The first is a low economic growth strategy. In order to lower energy consumption, the economic growth rate is low, and there is no medium growth, no high growth, and no ultra-high growth. The other one is the moderate economic growth strategy.[39] The economic growth rate is maintained at a medium level, sometimes at a high level or an ultra-high level. And energy consumption grows slowly, sometimes at medium rate.

After the two world energy crises, developed countries adopted the low economic growth strategy In contrast, after the reform and opening up, China adopted the moderate economic growth strategy. China is a developing country with lagging

[39]Low growth (≤5%), medium growth (>5 to <8%), high growth (≥8–10%), ultra-high growth (≥10%).

economy development, especially in the midwest areas. The economy gap between China and the developed countries is still large. Thus, it is proper for China to adopt a low economic growth strategy. It should be noted that the goal of quadrupling the GDP in 2020 is a moderate economic growth strategy. One moderate economic growth strategy was implemented successfully in China in the late twentieth century.

Meanwhile, corresponding to the moderate economic growth strategy, the energy development strategy does not fit the situation in China. Instead, the comprehensive energy efficiency strategy is the only correct choice for China.

It should be noted that the moderate economic growth strategy and the comprehensive energy efficiency strategy match each other. They meet the requirements of the scientific development outlook. They can support the coordinated development between energy and the economy. Thus, they can be called the strategy of coordinated development between energy and the economy.

Based on the strategy of coordinated development between energy and the economy, the author predicts the status of the energy bottleneck and the development between energy and the economy for the next 15 years in China. The results are listed in Table 23.54.

In the predicted results, the author compares and assesses four energy schemes for achieving the goal of quadrupling China's GDP in 2020 (see Table 23.55). Schemes 1, 2, and 3 are not good options. The best option is Scheme 4. This Scheme can double the GDP, but quadrupling the GDP is a challenge. In Scheme 4, the total energy consumption is the smallest, only 2.7 billion t of standard coal and double that in 2000. The annual average energy consumption is set to increase 70 million t of standard coal from 2001 to 2020, quadrupling the GDP in 2020. Comprehensive energy efficiency will be doubled, increasing from 2208 yuan/t standard coal in 2000 to 4428 yuan/t standard coal in 2020. GDP energy consumption drops to half. The annual average energy efficiency is 3.54%. The elasticity coefficient of energy consumption is 0.5. In other words, the great economic goal of quadrupling the GDP in 2020 depends on energy development for one half. The other half is generalized energy saving. The status of the development between energy and the economy is good. Scheme 4 is better than the other three schemes. The author believes that it is possible to achieve Scheme 4 with the guidance of the scientific development outlook. At present, the central government has taken actions to support this Scheme, such as setting up an Energy Leading Group and proposing to build a saving society. In addition, the fifth plenary session of the 16th CPC National Congress proposed the major goal of economic development for the eleventh five-year plan period: "by optimizing structure, improving efficiency and reducing energy consumption, achieve the goal of doubling GDP per capita of 2000 in 2010, significantly improving energy consumption efficiency, and reducing GDP energy consumption 20% lower than that in the tenth five-year plan period...." This is strong support for achieving the energy strategy.

Table 23.54 Prediction of energy bottleneck and energy and economy-coordinated development in China

Period	Year	Energy consumption			GDP annual average growth B (%)	Elasticity coefficient of energy consumption (A/B)	Evaluation and prediction of energy bottleneck	Evaluation and prediction of energy and economy coordinated development status
		Total (10,000 t of standard coal)	Annual average growth (10,000 t of standard coal)	Annual average growth rate A (%)				
The eleventh five-year plan period	2006–2010							
	2010 Scheme 1	281,238	11,754	4.8	8	0.6	Unobvious constraints	Ordinary
	Scheme 2	267,428	8992	3.75	7.5	0.5	Unobvious constraints	Ordinary
	Scheme 3	255,407	6588	2.8	7	0.4	Unobvious constraints	Better
	Scheme 4	239,661	3439	1.5	7	0.21	Unobvious constraints	Better
The twelfth five-year plan period	2011–2015							
	2015 Scheme 1	355,533	14,859	4.8	8	0.6	Unobvious constraints	Ordinary
	Scheme 2	321,475	10,809	3.75	7.5	0.5	Unobvious constraints	Ordinary
	Scheme 3	293,223	7563	2.8	7	0.4	Unobvious constraints	Better
	Scheme 4	258,183	3704	1.5	7	0.21	Unobvious constraints	Better
The thirteenth five-year plan period	2016–2020							

(continued)

Table 23.54 (continued)

Period	Year	Energy consumption			GDP annual average growth B (%)	Elasticity coefficient of energy consumption (A/B)	Evaluation and prediction of energy bottleneck	Evaluation and prediction of energy and economy coordinated development status
		Total (10,000 t of standard coal)	Annual average growth (10,000 t of standard coal)	Annual average growth rate A (%)				
	2020 Scheme 1	449,455	18,784	4.8	8	0.6	Unobvious constraints	Ordinary
	Scheme 2	386,445	12,994	3.75	7.5	0.5	Unobvious constraints	Ordinary
	Scheme 3	336,638	8683	2.8	7	0.4	Unobvious constraints	Better
	Scheme 4	278,136	3990	1.5	7	0.21	Unobvious constraints	Better
Period of quadrupling GDP	2001–2020							
	2020 Scheme 1	449,455	15,958	6.4	8.2	0.78	Mild constraints	Ordinary
	Scheme 2	386,445	12,807	5.6	7.8	0.72	Mild constraints	Ordinary
	Scheme 3	336,638	10,317	4.9	7.8	0.63	Unobvious constraints	Ordinary
	Scheme 4	278,136	7392	3.9	7.8	0.50	Unobvious constraints	Better

Table 23.55 Selection of energy schemes for the goal of quadrupling GDP in the twenty-first century

Period	Year	Total energy consumption (10,000 t of standard coal)	GDP annual average growth rate (%)	Elasticity coefficient of energy consumption	Comprehensive energy efficiency in comparable price (yuan/ton standard coal)	Energy efficiency (%)	Evaluation and prediction of energy and economy coordinated development status
Quadrupling GDP in the twentieth century	1981–1995	131,176 (2.18 times)	10.18 (4.28 times)	0.52	1141	4.4	Good
Quadrupling GDP in the twenty-first century	2001–2020						
	Scheme 1	449,455 (3.45 times)	8.2 (4.84 times)	0.78	3179	1.84	Ordinary
	Scheme 2	386,445 (2.97 times)	7.8 (4.49 times)	0.72	3433	2.23	Ordinary
	Scheme 3	336,638 (2.58 times)	7.8 (4.49 times)	0.63	3659	2.56	Ordinary
	Scheme 4	278,136 (2.13 times)	7.8 (4.49 times)	0.50	4428	3.54	Better

Note 1. Total energy consumption refers to the final year when energy is quadrupled
2. For comparison, comparable prices in 1980 are used in the table

2. **Strategy for alleviating the energy bottleneck in China—the comprehensive energy efficiency strategy**

In 1982, the 12th CPC National Congress officially proposed the great strategic goal that the GDP should be quadrupled in 20 years. At that time, many people, including energy experts, doubted and were concerned about whether this goal could be achieved. Energy was a bottleneck which constrained economic development. It was the biggest obstacle for economic development. Therefore, many people thought that energy would be a major issue for the achievement of the economic development goal. The CPC Central Committee paid much attention to the energy bottleneck. The whole party had the consensus that if the energy bottleneck was not broken, the economic development goal would not be achieved. Therefore, following the strategic thinking of scientific energy development, the CPC Central Committee undertook a series of effective policies and measures, including treating saving and energy development equally, putting saving as the primary focus, building a national energy base in Shanxi, establishing a national energy commission, making a national development plan for energy technologies, establishing energy management agencies, implementing an energy saving month, and making energy saving laws. A miracle occurred in 1995. Compared with 1980, the GDP was quadrupled by 1995 with doubled energy consumption. The goal of quadrupling the GDP with double energy consumption was achieved five years in advance. The economy quadrupling period (1981–1995) has the best status of coordinated development between energy and the economy in the history of China. Therefore, its experience in this period is helpful for China and for other developing countries.

The author found that, when facing the problem of what energy should do to support the quadrupling of the GDP in the 1980s, innovation in the energy development strategy was important.

Before the reform and opening up, no one studied the energy development strategy in China. However, strategic thinking regarding energy development did exist. At that time, energy production should have supported economic development. Energy production should have provided the amount of energy that economic development needs. This was called the "energy development strategy." Before the energy crisis in 1973, many countries adopted this strategy. At that time, the oil supply could fully meet oil demand. The price of oil was very low. This strategy generated energy starvation. In China, more energy was wasted. Some problems, such as the transportation shortage, environmental pollution, destruction of forests, over-exploration of oil resources, and over-investment in energy, appeared. The energy development strategy caused the continuous rise of GDP energy consumption and a drop in comprehensive energy efficiency. During the period when the energy development strategy was implemented, the amount of wasted energy was 3.55 billion t of standard coal. The amount of lost GDP was 5.85 trillion yuan (at the price in 1980). The environment was badly polluted. After the reform and opening up, China developed and implemented a new energy development strategy, namely the comprehensive energy efficiency strategy. From 1981 to 1995, cumulative energy saving was 7.18 billion t of standard coal. An extra GDP of 5.4 trillion yuan was created. Environmental pollution was reduced.

Practice has proven that two strategies lead to two results. Compared with the energy development strategy, the comprehensive energy efficiency strategy had five prominent advantages. First, it could mitigate and reduce the constraint of the energy bottleneck on economic development. Second, it could support the economic goal of quadrupling the GDP in the new century. Third, it could reduce dependence on foreign oil, protect oil security and energy security, and avoid oil and energy crisis in China. Fourth, it could promote coordination and sustainable development of energy, resources, the environment, the economy, and the population. Fifth, it could improve comprehensive energy efficiency, narrow the gap between China and foreign countries, and fundamentally change the low efficiency of manpower, material resources, financial capacity, natural resources, and time. The comprehensive energy efficiency strategy fully met the requirements of the scientific development outlook proposed by the CPC Central Committee.

As mentioned before, the comprehensive energy efficiency strategy is the only correct choice for China. The content of this strategy is listed below.

(1) *Stress the generalized energy saving policy*

Before the reform and opening up, China implemented the energy development strategy. In this strategy, the primary goal was to find more energy. Energy saving was not the focus. Although energy saving was promoted, it was narrow energy saving, not generalized energy saving. After the reform and opening up, China implemented the comprehensive energy efficiency strategy. In this strategy, energy development and energy saving were equally important. Energy saving was the primary focus. Energy saving was generalized energy saving, not narrow energy saving.

The objects for narrow energy saving are coal, oil, natural gas, and electricity. The goal of narrow energy saving is to increase the narrow energy efficiency. In 1974, the author estimated that the narrow energy efficiency in China was 28%, and that 72% of the energy was lost in the form of waste heat. The narrow energy efficiency in developed countries was 40–50%, 12–22% higher than that in China. Therefore, the focuses of narrow energy saving set by the former State Planning Commission were the transformation of boilers, furnaces, and residential stoves for improving thermal efficiency and recycling and for reunsing waste heat. After four or five years of hard work, great achievements were made. In Beijing, Tianjin, Shanghai, and Liaoning, 2.39 million t of standard coal were saved by utilizing waste heat. According to the estimate in 1978, the narrow energy efficiency in China was increased to 31%.

In 1979, after the reform and opening up, the author created a new theory for the generalized energy-saving projects. This generalized energy-saving is comprehensive energy saving, including direct energy saving, indirect energy saving, technical energy saving, and economic energy saving. Other than energy, the objects of generalized energy-saving include those gained by consuming energy, such as materials (raw materials), financial (capital), transportation, manpower, and natural forces. The goal of generalized energy-saving is to improve the comprehensive energy efficiency. The comprehensive energy efficiency is an indicator that measures status of development between the economy and energy. In 1982, the author estimated that the comprehensive energy efficiency (the reciprocal of the GDP energy consumption) in China was $364/t standard coal. This comprehensive energy efficiency was 6 times lower than that of Japan, 4.8 times lower than that of France, 3.9 times lower than that of West Germany, 2 times lower than that of the UK, 1.4 times lower than that of the US, and 1.9 times lower than that of India. It was one of the lowest comprehensive energy efficiencies among over 100 countries in the world. In other words, GDP energy consumption in China was one of the highest in the world. This indicated the huge gap of comprehensive energy efficiency between China and foreign countries. The gap of narrow energy efficiency was larger. The gap of generalized energy-saving was the largest.

The author found that generalized energy-saving has ten advantages and ten measures. The ten advantages are: ① Generalized energy-saving has been achieved via many approaches. Saving manpower, material, financial resources, transportation, natural forces, and time can save energy, because they all consume energy. ② Generalized energy saving can motivate all industries and all departments, whereas energy development relies on a small number of energy production sectors only. ③ Generalized energy saving is a kind of energy development with no need for resources. ④ Generalized energy saving does not require the construction of coal mines, oil fields, and power plants. ⑤ Generalized energy-saving can obtain energy locally. It does not need to construct energy transmission facilities. ⑥ Generalized energy-saving can yield faster results. ⑦ Generalized energy-saving has good economic benefits. ⑧ Generalized energy saving is a pollution-free energy. It is good for environmental protection. ⑨ Generalized energy saving can contribute to technological progress. ⑩ Generalized energy saving can promote the management level. The ten measures for energy saving are: ① Reasonably improve energy utilization efficiency (i.e. narrow energy-saving). ② Reasonably improve raw material utilization efficiency. ③ Reasonably improve transportation efficiency. ④ Reasonably improve manpower utilization efficiency, including reducing population growth. ⑤ Reasonably improve capital utilization efficiency. ⑥ Reasonably improve natural forces utilization efficiency. ⑦ Reasonably increase the scales of production and service. ⑧ Reasonably improve product quality and service quality. ⑨ Reasonably reduce material consumption costs. ⑩ Reasonably adjust the economic structure.

In October 1982, under the leadership of the Economic Research Center in the State Council, the author took charge of the study regarding whether the energy supply could support the achievement of the economic goal of quadrupling the GDP in 2020. The author reached the conclusion that energy production could achieve 1.2 billion t of standard coal in 2000, only doubling the production in 1980. The next question was whether the energy production in 2000 could support the economic goal of quadrupling the GDP. The problem is that energy development was too fast before the reform and opening up with an elasticity coefficient of energy consumption 1.66. However, the elasticity coefficient of energy consumption from 1981 to 2000 was only 0.5. There is no such precedent in the world. After checking the comprehensive energy efficiency in more than 100 countries, the author found that the comprehensive energy efficiency in China is one of the lowest, even 1.9 times lower than India. According to the theory of generalized energy saving projects, the author estimated that the potential of the ten aspects of generalized energy-saving would be 1.4 billion t of standard coal in 2000, higher than the energy production in 2000. Thus, the author made the following suggestion to the CPC central committee: the economic goal of quadrupling GDP in 2000 can be achieved by implementing generalized energy-saving projects and by exploiting the energy saving potential. This suggestion was accepted and adopted by the CPC Central Committee.[40]

In 1995, the economic goal of quadrupling the GDP was achieved five years in advance. Compared with 1980, the generalized energy saving reached 1.27 billion t of standard coal in 1995. Table 23.56 lists the results of generalized energy saving in 1995. Table 23.56 shows that direct energy saving only accounts for just over one fifth. In other words, the amount of energy saved by improving energy efficiency (traditional narrow energy-saving) accounted for 23.9%. Indirect energy saving accounts for about four-fifths. Energy saved by improving raw materials efficiency accounts for 15.7%. Energy saved by improving transportation efficiency accounts for 3.1%. Energy saved by improving manpower efficiency and reducing population growth accounts for 21.6%. Energy saved by improving capital efficiency accounts for 9.5%. Energy saved by reducing material consumption and by adjusting the economic structure accounts for about 21%. Energy saved by improving natural resource efficiency and increasing scale and quality accounts for 5.1%. Thus, if attention were paid only to the traditional direct energy saving and narrow energy saving, the economic goal of quadrupling the GDP would not be achieved. Because the potential and effect of direct energy saving was limited. In contrast, the potential and the effect of indirect energy saving was large, more than three times than that of direct energy saving. Paying enough attention to indirect energy saving is the key for generalized energy saving.

(2) *Stress the energy supply policy of developing more energy*

In the period of quadrupling the GDP, the CPC Central Committee stressed the energy production and the supply policy of developing more energy. This policy supported the achievement of the goal for energy production: 1.2 billion t of standard coal. The CPC Central Committee decided to build a Shanxi-based national coal base. It also called for motivating state-owned coal mines, locally-owned coal mines, and town-owned coal mines. It called for developing coal mines of any size to adopt advanced technology, medium technology, and traditional technology. In addition, it called for developing the oil industry, hydropower, nuclear power, and new energy, according to

[40] Strengthen Energy Development and Reduce Energy Consumption [St83].

Table 23.56 Analysis of generalized energy saving from 1981 to 1995 in China

Item	Energy saving (10,000 t of standard coal)	Percent (%)	Remarks
1. Improve energy utilization efficiency for saving energy	30,350	23.9	–
2. Improve raw materials utilization efficiency for saving energy	20,000	15.7	–
3. Improve transportation efficiency for saving energy	3920	3.1	–
4. Improve manpower utilization efficiency for saving energy	27,420	21.6	–
5. Improve capital utilization efficiency for saving energy	12,120	9.5	–
6. Improve natural forces utilization efficiency for saving energy	6500	5.1	Due to lack of data, individual estimation is not available
7. Improve scale for saving energy			
8. Improve quality for energy saving			
9. Reduce material consumption for saving energy	26,690	21.0	–
10. Adjust economic structure for saving energy			
Total	127,000	100	–

local conditions. These are the requirements of the policy developing more energy. In short, all kinds of energy, energies in various regions, energy production at any scale, energy production with diverse technologies, and energy production with various forms of ownership, should be developed rationally. At that time, different opinions about developing more energy existed. However, practice has proven that the energy supply policy of developing more energy proposed by the CPC Central Committee is correct. Without this policy, the economic goal of quadrupling the GDP would not be achieved, not to mention five years in advance. It should be noted that the Shanxi energy base made a great contribution to the achievement of the goal of quadrupling the GDP. The author found that guided by the scientific development outlook, the Shanxi energy base will continue to play an important role in achieving the goal of quadrupling the GDP again in the new century. Meanwhile, the oil and gas industries should be developed. Particularly, artificial petroleum and substitutes for petroleum should be developed. In addition, hydropower, nuclear power, and new energies should be developed, as well. More importantly, foreign energy resources should be utilized carefully and rationally.

(3) *Stress the energy price policy of rationalizing energy prices*

During the planned economy periods, energy prices were set by the government. The prices did not reflect the relationship between the supply and demand or the law of value. Therefore, unreasonable energy prices existed. On one hand, unreasonable energy prices did not motivate energy producers; they did not promote energy production at all. On the other hand, unreasonable energy prices did not motivate users to save energy, either; they actually promoted energy waste. At that time, the government took some measures other than price, such as subsidies. With the establishment of the socialist market economic system, China joined the WTO. Similar to other products, energy prices need to pay more attention to supply and demand as well as to the law of value. In other words, the rationalization of energy prices was rising. This was good for energy producers and energy users. It could promote energy production and reduce energy waste. Rational energy prices will play a very important role in achieving the economic goal of quadrupling the GDP again in the new century.

(4) *Stress the policy of rationalizing energy structure*

For a long time, China maintained the coal-dominated energy structure. The structure generated good results. But some people suggested that this energy structure should be changed and and switched to an oil- and gas-dominated energy structure, which has been adopted in developed countries. They thought that the oil- and gas-dominated energy structure could reduce the emission of CO_2. The author thinks that, given the situation in China, the best way to reduce the emission of CO_2 is to adopt a generalized energy-saving policy and to develop nuclear power and renewable energy. The adjustment of the energy structure in China should start from the actual conditions in China, should be guided by the scientific development outlook, and should follow objective scientific laws. Many facts around the world have proven that, when adjusting the energy structure, the ratio of oil and gas should be proper (not too large nor too small). A proper energy structure should fit the actual conditions in a country. It should also be feasible and economically reasonable. Optimizing the energy structure should not increase the ratio of oil and gas only. Reducing the ratio of oil and gas is a kind of optimizing energy structure, as well. Increasing nuclear energy and renewable energy is definitely an approach for optimizing the energy structure.

(3) **Measures for alleviating the energy bottleneck in China**

(1) Guided by the scientific development outlook, firmly implement the strategy for coordinated development between energy and the economy

In order to achieve the goal of constructing the moderately prosperous society proposed by the 16th CPC National Congress, the GDP by 2020 should be quadrupled, compared with 2000. To break the energy bottleneck and to support the achievement of the economic goal, the strategy for coordinated development between energy and the economy should be firmly implemented. According to the author's prediction for the energy bottleneck and the development status between energy and economy in the next 15 years, the economic goal of quadrupling the GDP by 2020 can be achieved with doubled energy production, as long as the moderate economic growth strategy and the comprehensive energy efficiency strategy, namely the strategy for coordinated development between energy and the economy, is implemented.

(2) Advocate that generalized energy saving is the fundamental way to break the energy bottleneck in China

In the twentieth century, great achievements for generalized energy saving were made in China due to the promotion of the idea of generalized energy saving. Comprehensive energy efficiency was improved significantly. Table 23.57 lists the changes in the gap of comprehensive energy efficiency between China and developed countries. China implemented the strategy of comprehensive energy efficiency in the twentieth century. Therefore, China achieved the economic goal of quadrupling its GDP in the twentieth century. Comprehensive energy efficiency was increased significantly. However, the gap in comprehensive energy efficiency between China and the developed countries was still large. This is because comprehensive energy efficiency in the developed countries was greatly increased in the recent ten years. Table 23.57 shows that in 2000, comprehensive energy efficiency in China was \$829/t standard coal, 6.8 times lower than that (\$6466/t standard coal) of Japan, 3.3 times lower than that (\$3586/t standard coal) of France, 3.7 times lower than that (\$3952/t standard coal) of Germany, 4.4 times lower than that (\$4468/t standard coal) of the UK, 2.6 times lower than that (\$2967/t standard coal) of the US, and 0.2 times lower than that (\$1025/t standard coal) of India. Thus, as in the ranking in early 1980s, comprehensive energy efficiency in China is still one of the lowest in the world.

Energy waste is still very serious in China. The potential of the ten aspects of generalized energy-saving is enormous. Practice has proven that energy waste is not an isolated problem. The causes are complex. In short, there are five reasons: the systems, economic structure, lagging technologies, low management level, and out-of-date thoughts. Therefore, it is necessary and timely for the CPC Central Committee to call for building a saving-oriented society. The author believes that promoting generalized energy saving is the key for building a saving-oriented society, because the generalized energy saving includes the saving of all resources in all aspects. The comprehensive saving strategy and planning proposed by the former State Planning Commission was adopted by the CPC Central Committee and has achieved great successes. The experience for these successes should be considered.

Table 23.57 Gap of comprehensive energy saving between China and developed countries from 1978 to 2000 (after China implemented new energy development strategy)

Year	US	Japan	Germany	France	UK	India	China
	Dollar/ton standard coal	Dollar/ton standard coal	Dollar/ton standard coal	Dollar/ton standard coal	Dollar/ton standard coal	Dollar/ton standard coal	Dollar/ton standard coal
1978	905	2549	1791	2165	1141	1062	386
1979	983	2238	2067	2538	1455	1139	441
1980	1132	2474	2263	2822	1999	1282	470
1981	1302	2789	1969	2596	2009	1260	445
1982	1418	2642	1961	2533	1810	1109	423
1983	1541	2799	1931	2358	1703	1127	430
1984	1646	2720	1774	2293	1618	1068	341
1985	1739	2880	1784	2354	1654	1026	339
1986	1841	4450	2598	3404	1812	1105	314
1987	1724	4402	2204	3010	2251	–	343
1988	1781	5183	2359	3245	2492	–	396
1989	–	–	–	–	–	–	–
1990	2104	4852	–	3767	3246	1140	394
1991	2025	5587	3533	3947	3454	805	358
1992	2120	5730	3614	3804	2948	753	388
1993	–	–	–	–	–	–	–
1994	2275	6864	4062	4209	3424	745	441
1995	2396	6627	5084	4656	3574	866	534
1996	–	–	–	–	–	–	–
1997	2619	5950	4374	4084	4217	1015	652
1998	2748	5493	4488	4112	4450	998	716
1999	2853	6183	4482	4021	4571	1046	762
2000	2967	6466	3952	3586	4468	1025	829

Note Data in the table are calculated with the prices and exchange rates of the current year

23.17 Material Flow Theory and the Strategy for the Rise of Central China[41]

Research background, scientific significance of achievements and practical value.

On March 27, 2006, the CPC Central Committee held a special meeting to discuss the rise of central China and to develop a strategy for the rise of the central region. In order

[41]Xu, S.B. (2006). Large Logistics and Rise of Central Region, academic report at fourth Chinese industrial enterprises logistics forum in 2006, July 26 2006.

to implement the strategy for the rise of the central region, the author believed that the key was to develop a large material flow. At that important moment, the author was invited to participate in the fourth Chinese Industrial Enterprises Logistics Forum and to give an academic report. The author was pleased to accept the invitation. This study was the first logistics research that the author conducted for regional development. During the meeting, the author presented his research on the logistics research that he conducted during the previous ten years at Beijing Jiaotong University [360, 361, 165–368, 372–378, 181–391, 399, 410–413, 421–423, 427, 436–439, 443–445]. The author thinks that the rise of the central area is the key to China's peaceful rise. Developing a large material flow is the key for the rise of the central region. The author's presentation was well accepted.

23.17.1 The Strategy for the Rise of Central China Creates a Historical Opportunity for the Development of Six Provinces in Central China

Since the reform and opening up, great achievements of economic and social development have been made, all across China. With the correct leadership of CPC Central Committee, the strategy for developing the eastern region was implemented first. Then, the strategy for the rise of western region was implemented. Next, the strategy for revitalizing the northeast area was carried out. Recently, the strategy for the rise of the central region was implemented. The four strategies proposed by CPC Central Committee are components of a strategic campaign for developing different regions in China. It is one part of the overall coordinated development strategy system with Chinese characteristics. Practices have proven that the strategy for developing all of the regions is correct. The strategy played an important role in promoting economic and social development in the aforementioned regions.

On March 27, 2006 the central government held a special meeting whose aim was to promote the rise of central region. The meeting pointed out that promoting the rise of the central region was a major decision made by the CPC Central Committee and the State Council. This strategy came about after the strategy for developing the eastern region, the strategy for the rise of the western region, and the strategy for revitalizing the northeast area. It is an import task for implementing the overall campaign of achieving coordinated development among regions. The meeting set the goal of the strategy: developing the central region as an important grain production base, an energy base, a raw materials base, a modern equipment production base, a hi-tech industry base, and a comprehensive transit hub; promoting the rise of the central region by connection the eastern region and the western region; promoting industrial development in the central region; achieving comprehensive, coordinated, sustainable social development; and making a contribution to constructing a moderately prosperous society. The meeting pointed out that the strategy for the rise of the central region should follow five principles.

Table 23.58 Basic conditions of 6 provinces in Central China (2005)

Central region	Area (10,000 km^2)	Population (10,000 people)	Density (person/km^2)	GDP (100 million yuan)	GDP per capita (yuan)
Shanxi	15	3355	224	4121.2	12,284
Henan	16	9380	586	10535.2	11,232
Hubei	18	5710	317	6484.5	11,356
Hunan	21	6326	301	6473.6	10,233
Anhui	13	6120	471	5375.8	8784
Jiangxi	16	4311	269	4056.2	9409
Total	99	35,202	356	37,046.5	10,524
Ratio in the country (%)	10.3	26.9	261.1	20.3	75

Data source China Statistical Abstract 2006, China Statistics Press

First, deepen reform and expand internal and external opening. Promote system innovation. Let the market allocate resources.

Second, rely on scientific progress and innovation. Take the approach of industrialization.

Third, highlight the focus. Let comparative advantage play its role. Support the grain industry, the energy industry, and the manufacturing industry. Facilitate the growth of city groups. Provide more support for development across China.

Fourth, rely on existing conditions. Develop the habit of self-reliance. Provide support for self-development at the state level.

Fifth, focus on people-oriented and integrated development. Create more jobs. Reduce the number of the poor gradually. Increase public service in urban and rural areas. Strengthen ecological construction and environmental protection. Promote coordinated development between urban and rural areas, and the economy and the society, as well as between man and nature.[42]

The strategy for the rise of the central region proposed by the CPC Central Committee provides the direction for the sustainable economic and social coordinated development in six provinces in the central region. This is a historical development opportunity for the six provinces.

Table 23.58 shows the basic conditions of the six provinces in the central region in 2005. It can be seen from the table that, among the six provinces in central region, Hunan is the largest in area. Anhui is the smallest in area. Henan has the largest population. Shanxi has the smallest population. Shanxi has the highest GDP per capita. Anhui has the smallest GDP per capita. Table 23.59 shows the comparison between the central region and adjacent regions. According to Table 23.59, the ranking of GDP per capita in 2005 is: eastern region #1 (23,497 yuan); northeast #2 (15,924 yuan); central region #3 (10,524 yuan); and western region #4 (9206 yuan). The GDP

[42]Xinhua Net (2006). The Political Bureau of the Central Committee of the CPC held a meeting on March 27 to study the rise of central region. 2006-3-28 8:42:00.

Table 23.59 Comparison between central region and adjacent regions (2005)

Region	Area (10,000 km^2)	Population (10,000 people)	Density (person/km^2)	GDP (100 million yuan)	Per capita GDP (yuan)
Central region (6 provinces)	99	35,202	**356 (2)**	37,047	**10,524 (3)**
Ratio in the country (%)	10.3	26.9	**261**	20.3	**75**
Western region (12 provinces and cities)	686.7	36,270	**53 (4)**	33,390	**9206 (4)**
Ratio in the country (%)	71.5	27.7	**39**	18.3	**66**
Northeast region (3 provinces)	79	10,757	**136 (3)**	17,130	**15,924 (2)**
Ratio in the country (%)	8.2	8.2	**100.0**	9.4	**114**
Eastern region (10 provinces and cities)	90.96	46,388	**510 (1)**	108,999	**23,497 (1)**
Ratio in the country (%)	9.5	35.5	**374**	59.8	**168**
Whole country	960	130,756	**136**	182,321	**13,985**

Data source China Statistical Abstract 2006, China Statistics Press
Note Western 12 provinces and cities are Chongqing, Guangxi, Sichuan, Yunnan, Guizhou, Xizang, Inner Mongolia, Shaanxi, Gansu, Ningxia, Qinghai, and Xinjiang. Three northeast provinces are Heilongjiang, Jilin, and Liaoning. Ten eastern provinces are Beijing, Tianjin, Hebei, Shanghai, Jiangsu, Zhejiang, Fujian, Shandong, Guangdong, and Hainan

per capita in the central region and western region are 75 and 66% of the national average, respectively. Compared with the eastern region, the gap is larger. The GDP per capita in the central region is 45% of that in eastern region. The GDP per capita in the western region is only 39% of that in eastern region. Thus, the strategy for the rise of the central region was proposed by CPC Central Committee in a timely manner. The time when the central region implements the strategy will be the period when the social and economic development accelerates.

23.17.2 *Material Flow is the Key for Accelerating Economic and Social Development in Central Region*

After proposing the new concept of logistics in 1985, the author continued to study the theories of logistics and published several works in the academic journal of Beijing Jiaotong University. The author presented research at the International Logistics Conference held by Beijing Jiaotong University in 2004. The research was well accepted by domestic and overseas experts. They saluted all of the achievements of the author's material flow theory. The author was grateful for this honor. Figure 23.3 shows the seven elements of the material flow theory and their relationship.

There are seven components in the material flow theory: material flow, comprehensive material flow, material flow elements, the nature of material flow, large material flow theory, large material flow engineering, and large material flow industry.

1. **Material flow**

Material flow is the most important component in material flow theory. It is the base for material flow theory. Table 23.60 shows the comparison of material flow in China, Japan, and the western countries. The concept, the English translation, the original time, the attributes, the connotation, the characteristics, and the application field of material flow in China are quite different from those in Japan and the western countries. The material flow theory provides a solid theoretical foundation and the correct direction for the development of logistics and related technologies in China. Material flow combines macro material flow and micro material flow. Its English translation is "material flow", not "logistics." Material flow consists of physical distribution and logistics. Physical distribution and logistics are components of material flow. The

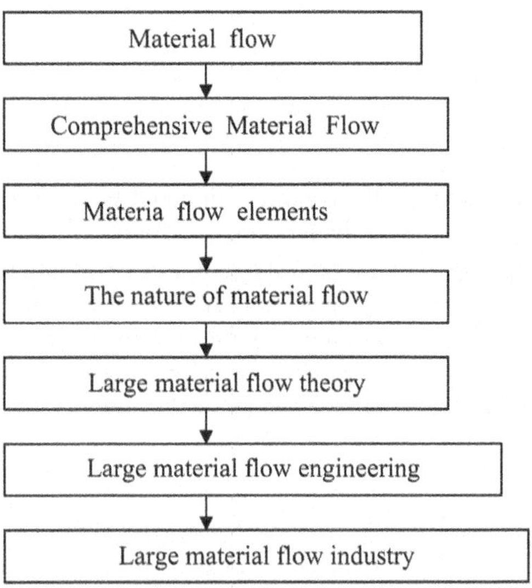

Fig. 23.3 Seven basic theory of material flow and their relationship

Table 23.60 Comparison of the concept of material flow in China, Japan, and western countries

Country	China	Japan	UK	US
Concept (English word)	Material flow (MF)	Physical distribution (PD)	Physical distribution of commodities (PD)	Transfer of military materials, personnel, and equipment (Logistics)
Originating time	1985	1965	1915	1905
Originating attributes	Natural phenomenon, social phenomenon, and economic phenomenon	Economic phenomenon	Economic phenomenon	Military phenomenon
Connotation	Flow of macro materials and micro materials	Physical distribution of materials from suppliers to consumers	Distribution of commodities	Transfer of military materials, personnel, and equipment
Characteristic	All purposeful and unintended behaviors, including management behaviors	Intended economic behavior	Intended economic management behavior	Originally, intended military logistics management behavior. Now a part of supply chain management behaviors
Application field	All fields in economy, society, and nature	Circulation field	Circulation field	Military field and the whole supply chain

concept of material flow had been adopted by American manufacturers previously, but it referred to small material flow, not large material flow.

2. **Comprehensive material flow**

Comprehensive material flow discloses the nature of material flow. A natural material flow existed before human society came into being. Materials exist in nature. They are not commodities or goods. The force of flow comes from nature, not from human beings' economic activities. Because flow is not human beings' activities, it does not have any purpose. Human beings can benefit from material flow in nature, such as hydropower, wind power, and tidal power generation. However, material flow in nature also brings disasters, such as floods, windstorms, landslides, dust storms, polluted air, and polluted water.

Social material flow is the unique characteristic of human society. After individual consumption and agriculture appeared in primitive society, primitive material flow occurred. Material flow in people's daily lives and the flow of wastes are the requirements of human development. They do not serve any economic purpose. They are indispensable in all human societies. Military material flow and disaster relief material flow are social material flow, as well. They are non-profit activities that support human development and social services. They are not economic activities. For social material flow, the materials are those that exist in the nature and those that are exchanged in economic activities. Flow is driven by human beings' social activities. Social material flow is non-profit social activity.

Economic material flow is the important phenomenon that appeared the most recently. In an agricultural society, with the development of production, commodity exchanges and social division appeared. Economic development drove the economic material flow faster and faster. Due to the limitations of the drive for material flow, the scale of material flow was not large. In the early stages of industrial society, because of the development of transportation, economic material flow grew rapidly. In modern society, people began to pay more attention to the so-called third profit source: economic material flow. Economic material flow includes the material flow across regions, industries, and enterprises, the flow of diverse materials, and the flow of attributes. It is the main component of human economic activity. It is enterprises' activity, aiming to create value and surplus value. In economic material flow, materials are commodities. Flow is driven by human beings' economic activities. Economic material flow is for-profit economic activity.

In summary, material flow is an important object and phenomenon. It exists in the economy, society, and nature. It is an economic phenomenon, a social phenomenon, and a natural phenomenon. Thus, material flow consists of economic material flow, social material, and natural material flow; they are connected with each other. The existing material flow is not simple and easy; rather, it is complex. Thus, it is called "comprehensive material flow." The theory of comprehensive material flow is built on comprehensive material flow.

Figure 23.4 shows the details of comprehensive material flow. The figure reflects the relationship among economic material flow, social material flow, and natural material flow. It also reflects various material flows in the economy. Economic material flow, social material flow, and natural material flow are components of large material flow. None of them can represent the entire large material flow. Economic material flow is the core of large material flow. Social material flow and natural material flow are the basis for large material flow.

3. **Material flow elements**

Material flow elements disclose the components of material flow. The author found that material flow consists of six base elements, namely the material, the owner, the region, the time, and information. Natural material flow, social material flow, and economic material flow all comprise these six elements. Among these six elements, material is the most important. It is the core. All materials are moving and flowing. They have owner and region. They need time and information. The core is closely connected with the other five elements. Any material flow must have all of the six

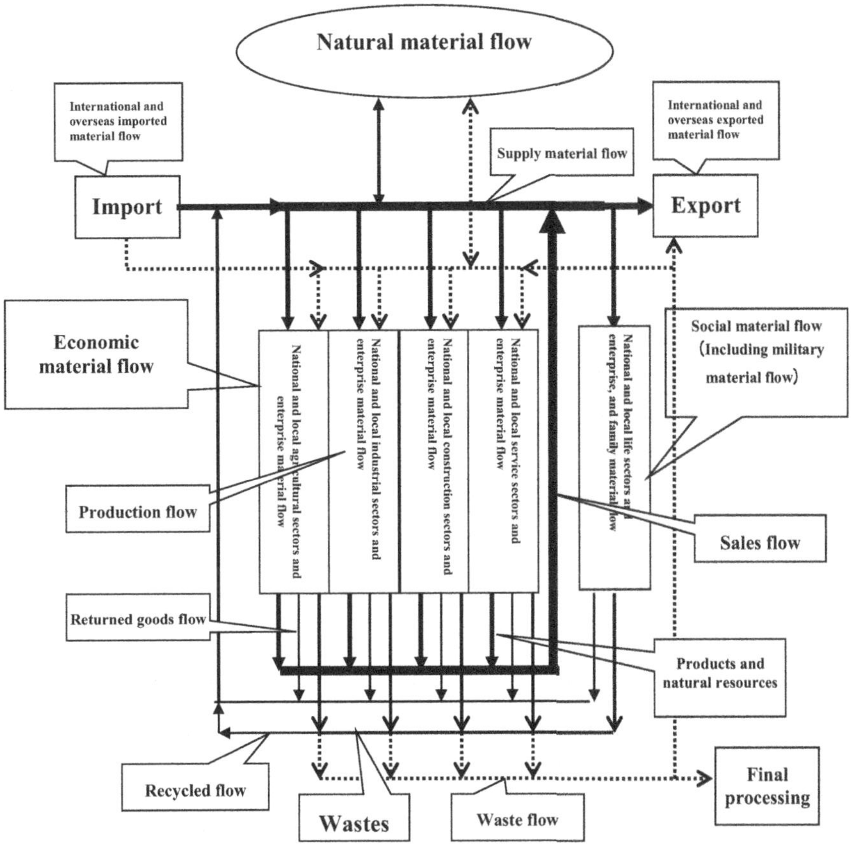

Fig. 23.4 Comprehensive material flow

elements. If any of the six elements is missing, material flow will not exist. This is the six-element theory for material flow (MFORTI). Table 23.61 lists the elements for natural material flow, social material flow, and economic material flow.

4. **The nature of material flow**

Studies suggest that material flow has inherent natures and non-inherent natures. The inherent natures of material flow reflect the nature of the basic elements of material flow. They are the objective characteristics of material flow. Figure 23.5 is the diagram for the nature of material. The figure shows that material flow has six natures: material, flow, subjectivity, region, time, and information. These natures correspond with the six elements in MFORTI.

The non-inherent nature of material flow reflects non-inherent characteristics of non-basic elements. They can be selected at the will of the owner (the Party). Material flow has six non-inherent natures: subjectivity, service, management, technology, economy, and information.

Table 23.61 Elements for natural material flow, social material flow, and economic material flow

Type	Material flow (MF)	Natural matrial flow (NMF)	Serial matrial flow (SMF)	Economic matrial flow (EMF)
M (Material)	Macro substance and micro substance (including living things and non-living things)	Naturally existing materials, not economic commodities	Naturally and socially existing materials and economic commodities	Economic commodities
F (Flow)	Driver of flow comes from nature, social activities and economic activities. Regular movement or irregular movement with carriers or without carriers	Driver of flow comes from nature, not social activities. Regular movement or irregular movement without carriers	Driver of flow comes from social activities. Regular movement with carriers	Driver of flow comes from economic activities. Regular movement with carriers
O (Owner)	Owners in nature, society and economy	Owners in nature	Owners in society	Owners in economy
R (Region)	Regions in nature, society and economy	Regions in nature	Regions in society	Regions in economy
T (Time)	Ancient, modern and contemporary	Ancient, modern and contemporary	Ancient, modern and contemporary	Ancient, modern and contemporary
I (Information)	Material flow information	Material information in nature	Material information in society	Material information in economy

The author believes that material flow has one basic intrinsic property. The nature of the material flow is determined by the nature of material. For example, due to different attributions, the requirements for transportation might be different. The requirements for packaging, processing, and storage might be different, as well. In short, the fundamental characteristic of material flow is the nature of material.

The nature of material includes the characteristics of material M and the characteristics of flow F. All materials have physical entities; they exist objectively. Thus, the characteristic of material M is the fundamental property of material. According to Marxist philosophy, movement is the fundamental property of matter. Movement is the method in which matter exists. Matter and movement are inseparable. "Movement, in a general sense … includes all changes and processes occurring in the universe, from simple positional movement until the thinking."[43] The position

[43]Selected Works of Marx and Engels, Vol, 3, p. 491.

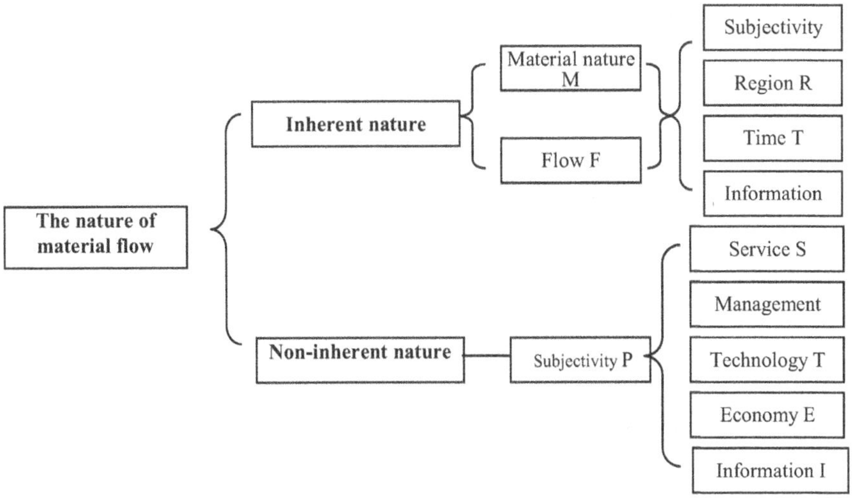

Fig. 23.5 The nature of material flow

movement of matter refers to its material flow. Thus, the characteristic F is a fundamental property of matter, as well. These two fundamental properties are unified and inseparable.

Natural material flow, social material flow, and economic material flow all have subjects. The subject of natural material flow is nature. The subject of social material flow is the society. The subject of economic material flow is the economy. The subjectivity of material flow is determined by subject of the materials. Nature consists of both living and non-living things, such as planets, earth, sand, mountains, mines, rivers, water, sunshine, air, forest, living things, and micro orgasms. Natural substances are the subjects of natural material flow. Subjects of economic material flow include enterprises, industry, organizations, and sectors. Subjects of social material flow include the family, the workplace, and the military. Different subjects have different characteristics. Thus, their material flows are different.

Region is the common property for natural material flow, social material flow, and economic material flow. Each material, either micro material or macro material, has its location. Each flow has its specific flowing area. Region has multi-layers. Region in nature, the society, or the economy has several layers. Take social region and economic region, as an example. The highest level of region includes the five continents and large areas. The next level is country. Each country has a certain number of regions, including province, city, township, and community.

Time is the common property for all materials. Accordingly, time is a common property of natural material flow, social material flow, and economic material flow. In studies of Chinese history, the time before the middle of the nineteenth century is called "the ancient era." The period from mid-nineteenth century to the May Fourth Movement in 1919 is called "the modern era." The period after the May Fourth

Movement is called "the contemporary era." Material flows in these periods have different characteristics.

Information is one of the comprehensive attributes for material flow. According to information theory, information refers to the nature of material and the reflection of the material's movement and mode. Material flow information includes all of the information about physical entity and other information related to the movement of materials. In the information era, the study of information of material flow has important scientific meaning and practical value.

According to the nature of material flow, complicated material flow can be categorized. Figure 23.6 shows the six elements of MFORTI and the way in which they are categorized. Meanwhile, material flow can be categorized based on the non-inherent nature of material flow.

5. **Large material flow theory**

For a long time, it was thought that material flow was the circulation of commodities. It is doing business without the involvement of science and technology. Therefore, technology for material flow has attracted little attention. After the reform and opening up, logistics, a western concept, widely spread in textbooks, magazines, and media. Thus, people think that logistics is material flow and that logistics management is material flow science, so people focus on logistics only, as they cared about

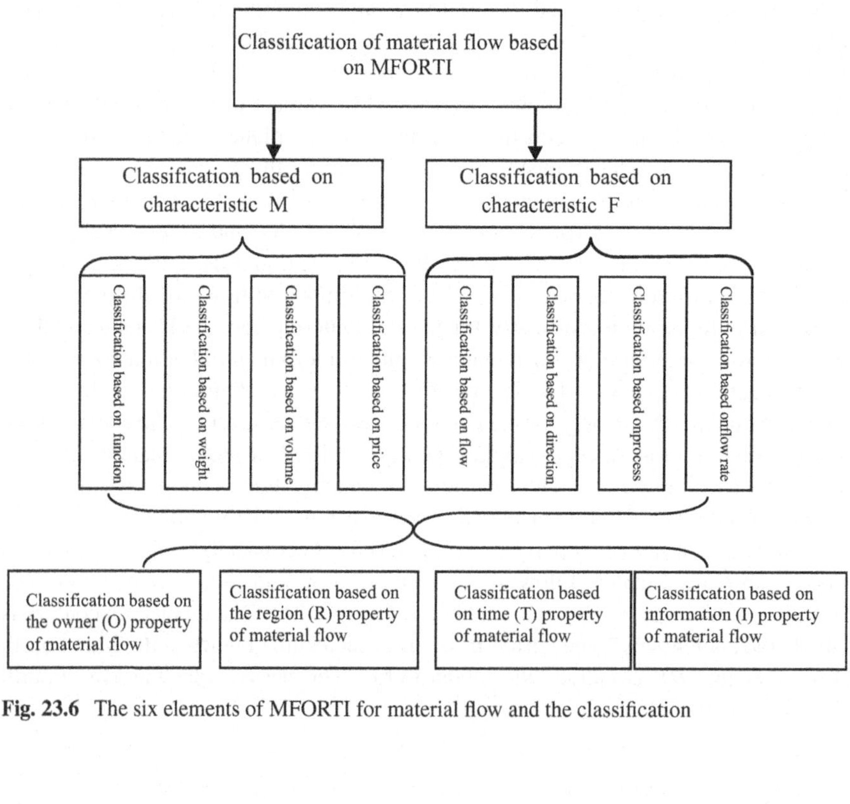

Fig. 23.6 The six elements of MFORTI for material flow and the classification

goods and material before. This misunderstanding hinders the development of the material flow in China. The author thinks that material flow science is a comprehensive science and technology, similar to energy science and technology, environmental science and technology. It involves the natural sciences, the engineering sciences, the humanities, and the social sciences. After the reform and opening up, a new comprehensive science appears, such as energy science and technology, and environmental science and technology. This is the requirement for the development of objects. It is also the requirement of the development of science and technology. Both energy science and technology and environmental science and technology have been developed wel; they are independent disciplines now. However, the development research regarding material flow is slow. Material flow is not an independent discipline, at this time. Directed by the guidelines that (1) science and technology is the first productive force and (2) China should be developed via science education, the author thinks that the study of material flow must take priority. In order to promote the research and development of material flow science, it is necessary to establish an independent material flow discipline. This discipline has four components: the basic disciplines, the engineering disciplines, the scientific theory disciplines, and other disciplines (see Table 23.62 for details).

It should be noted that the disciplines listed in Table 23.62 offer a framework and suggestion only. They need improvement and adjustment based on the actual development of material flow. According to Table 23.62, most disciplines for the material flow are still blank; they need to be explored.

Different from the logistics in western countries, the large material flow science in China is based on the theory for material flow and on the comprehensive theory for material flow. The large material flow science in China is an important component of the large material flow. Logistics in western countries is a sub-discipline of the large material flow.

6. **Large material flow engineering**

The author believes that large material flow engineering consists of the six element of material flow, or the six forces of material flow. It applies material flow science and technologies in the national economy and effectively generates welfare for mankind. Material flow engineering has four characteristics. First, material flow engineering is complex, composed of the six elements of material flow or the six forces of material flow. Second, material flow engineering adopts scientific technologies, including hard scientific technologies and soft scientific technologies. Third, material flow engineering should serve the national economy effectively. Fourth, the goal of material flow engineering is to serve mankind. This is a broad concept for material flow. The commonly mentioned material flow engineering refers to construction projects for logistics. It is a narrow concept.

Here are the six elements for material flow: ① The workers in material flow, referring to all people working in material flow, including management personnel; ②

Table 23.62 Disciplines of material flow science

I Basic disciplines	Distribution engineering
Material flow physics	Loading engineering
Material flow mathematics	Storage engineering
Material flow chemistry	Packaging engineering
Material flow astronomy	Processing engineering
Material flow geography	Information engineering
Material flow geology	Simulation technique
Other disciplines related with material flow basic disciplines	Testing and monitoring technologies
II Engineering discipline	Safety engineering
Comprehensive material flow engineering	**III. Material flow theories**
Economic material flow engineering	Material flow system and network
Regional material flow engineering	Material flow technical economy
Sector material flow engineering	Material flow economy
Circulating material flow engineering	Material flow management
Social material flow engineering	Material flow education
Military material flow engineering	Material flow sociology
Natural material flow engineering	Material flow laws
Material flow infrastructure	Material flow history
Material flow equipment	Other disciplines
Transportation engineering	**IV Other disciplines of material flow**

The objects of material flow, referring to things; ③ The means of labor for material flow, referring to the equipment required by material flow; ④ The working environment for material flow, referring to the natural, social, and political environments related to material flow; ⑤ The working space for material flow, referring to working place related to material flow; ⑥ The working time for material flow, referring to the construction time and the run-time of material flow facilities. Here are the six forces for material flow: ① Manpower, referring to people working for material flow; ② Materials, referring to the energy and raw materials required by material flow; ③ Financial resources, referring to the fixed assets and current assets required by material flow; ④ Transportation, referring to the traffic and transport required by material flow; ⑤ Natural forces, referring to the natural resources, such as water, land, and air, required by material flow; ⑥ The time required by material flow.

Any material flow engineering comprises all of the six elements or six forces. Manufacturing, facilities, services, technology development, planning, and design for material flow rely on the six elements and six forces. This is the Six Element Structure Theory for material flow engineering. The six elements and the six forces are the same, in essence, but they are expressed in different ways. Some elements are completely that same as the corresponding forces, such as the manpower element and manpower force, the time element and time force. Some elements are not the same as the corresponding forces. For example, the "finance force" refers to fixed assets, such as factory buildings, machines, and equipment, which are the means of labor. In addition, finance force includes current assets, which is an object element. Therefore, element and force are not completely the same. The six elements and the six forces are independent. Each element and each force is independent. There is no repeat among them.

Material flow engineering has a six-element structure. The nature, quality, quantity, and ratio of the six elements are different. Thus, the nature of material flow engineering is different. There are transportation material flow engineering, storage material flow engineering, loading material flow engineering, packing material flow engineering, circulation material flow engineering, processing material flow engineering, distribution material flow engineering, information material flow engineering, and management material flow engineering. Material flow engineering can be categorized based on other standards. For example, material flow engineering can be capital intensive, technology-intensive, labor-intensive, physical-intensive, or mental labor-intensive. Material flow engineering can use advanced technology, general technology, or out-of-date technology. Material flow engineering can be intensive or extensive. For instance, automated storage engineering is capital-intensive with advanced technologies. In contrast, general storage engineering is labor intensive and it needs the proper technologies. The six elements are interchangeable to some extent. For example, capital and technology elements can replace manpower and natural forces. With the development of material flow technologies, the portion of technology in the six element structure will increase. This is determined by the six-element theory of material flow.

Material flow engineering can be individual material flow engineering or comprehensive material flow engineering. Individual material flow engineering refers to the material flow engineering for one material, such as coal material flow engineering, oil material flow engineering, electricity material flow engineering, raw materials material flow engineering, machine and equipment material flow engineering, and day-to-day goods material flow engineering. In addition, individual material flow engineering can be used for transportation, distribution, storage, loading, packaging, circulation processing, or information processing. Comprehensive material flow engineering is not the sum of individual material flow engineering; it has its own specific technologies. Technologies for individual material flow engineering are like the technologies for manufacturing car parts. Technologies for comprehensive material flow engineering are like the technologies for designing cars. These two types of technologies cannot replace each other.

This is the theory of large material flow engineering, which is based on generalized material flow engineering. The theory is a major component in the theory of large material flow.

7. **Large material flow industry**

It is well known that the national economy consists of production, circulation, and consumption. The national economy has three forms: the physical form, the value form, and the integrated form (including the physical form and the value form). Thus, production, circulation, and consumption have three forms as well. In fact, the national economy exists in the integrated form. For research purposes, it is necessary to study the national economy in both the physical form and the value form. Marx studied the law of commodity movement from the perspective of value. His study made a great contribution to the development of society and science. The large material flow theory studies the law of commodity movement from the physical perspective.

From the physical perspective, the national economy consists of the production of materials, the movement of materials, and the consumption of materials. In other words, the national economy has three pillars: production, material flow, and consumption. Material flow is not only an industry, but also a group of industries, because material flow involves transportation, distribution, storage, packaging, distribution processing, information, equipment, facilities, technology development, education, services, and management. History has proven that national economic development relies on production and on consumption, as well as on material flow.

For a long time, people have thought that material flow involved only material management and material flow management. Material flow was not thought as an industry. The author believes that material flow is a pillar industry and a pillar industry group. This is the theory of the material flow industry group. This theory is an important part of the large material theory. It is not enough to develop material by considering material flow as an industry; material flow must be thought as an industry group.

The seven basic theories that make up the large material flow theory were introduced. They promote the development of material flow technologies as well as the development of material flow. A well-developed large material flow is the key for achieving fast development of the economy and society in China and for the peaceful rise of China.

Next, let us talk about the relationship between the large material flow theory and the rise of the central region. The author thinks that large material flow will play a key role in the rise of the central region. Here are some suggestions.

(1) **Fully understand the importance of developing the material flow for the rise of central region**. The strategy for the rise of the central region proposed by the CPC Central Committee is to build a national grain production base, an energy and raw material base, a modern equipment manufacturing and high-tech industrial base, and an integrated transport hub. To fulfill this strategy, the material flow for grains, the material flow for energy and raw materials, and the material flow for manufacturing industry and hi-tech products should be developed. Grains, energy, and raw material are important materials for the national economy and for the people's livelihood. After they are produced, they

must be delivered to places across China in a timely and economical manner. Otherwise, crises of production and consumption will occur across the country. The production base will suffer these crises as well. The aftermath of a double crisis is serious. For example, coal in the production base in Shanxi could not be transported to other places. As a result, factories in the south had to stop production due to the lack of coal. Shanxi could not sell its coal and suffered an overstock. Double losses occurred. Thus, the macro benefits of material flow enterprises are far greater than their own benefits. A large material flow is very important to the central area and to the whole country.

(2) **Actively develop modern material flow and traditional material flow**. Material flow is very important for the central region. But the selection of traditional or modern material flow depends on the actual conditions. As for modern equipment manufacturing and hi-tech industries, in order to reduce material flow and to fulfill zero inventory, modern material flow is applicable because products have high technology, high value, small size, and light weight. Grains, energy, and raw materials have low value and large volume. In order to maintain a continuous supply, enough reserves are necessary and zero inventory is rather dangerous. The cost of material flow accounts for a large portion of the total transportation cost. Thus, traditional material flow is appropriate for grains, energy, and raw materials.

(3) **Develop urban material flow as well as rural material flow**. To develop the economy in the central region, the urban economy (including mining cities) and the rural economy should be equally developed. To speed up the development of the urban and the rural economy, the material flow infrastructure should be strengthened, including the construction of comprehensive transport hub. Material flow for the national production base should be developed. The urban material flow and the rural material flow in central China should be greatly developed.

(4) **Develop the economic material flow and the social material flow as well as the natural material flow**. In order to speed up economic development, there is an urgent need to develop the economic material flow for production bases. Meanwhile, in order to accelerate social development, there is a need to develop good social material flow and natural material flow, especially material flow infrastructure in rural areas. It is a social activity instead of an economic activity. Thus, this requires national investment. During the development of the economy, any harmful natural material flow should be reduced.

(5) **Develop third-party material flow, and fourth and fifth-party material flow, as well as X-party material flow**. It is generally believed that the traditional material flow is mostly first and second-party material flow. In fact, the Ministry of Railways, the Ministry of Transportation, the Goods and Materials Department, the Ministry of Commerce, the Ministry of Foreign Trade, and the Ministry of Posts and Telecommunications are the largest third party material flow sectors. These third-party (or even fourth, fifth, and including X party) material flow sectors provide services for the products required by a large number of first-party and second-party sectors. Western countries advocate the development of

third-party material flow, and fourth and fifth party material flow management. The author thinks that they have limitations. The author believes that China's X-party material flow theory better fits the laws of material flow development; different enterprises should choose reasonable X party logistics based on specific circumstances. X can be 1, 2, or 1 +2 +3 ... and so on, but we cannot blindly determine that X = 3 is the best.

23.18 Commodity Material Flow Theory[44]

Research background, scientific significance of achievements, and practical value.

Marx studied the law of the movement of goods in value form. His research made a great contribution to social development and to scientific development. The large material flow theory proposed by the author studied the law of the movement of goods in physical form. The author explored the law of the movement of goods in the modern society, including the movement of commodities, commodity capital, and commodity information. He hopes that this study can make a contribution to social and economic development in the human society. According to the six-element production factor theory[45] and the six-element living factor theory,[46] the six elements for production and living are manpower (labor), financial resources (fixed assets and current assets), materials (raw materials and energy), natural forces (land, water, and minerals), transportation, and time. In a commodity society, these elements are all commodities. They are wealth for human beings, as well. Therefore, commodities and material wealth in the human society can be classified into manpower, financial resources, materials, natural forces, transportation, and time. Commodity material flow is the flow of the six classes of the commodities across and within systems, networks, and chains. The law of commodity material flow is the law of commodity movement.

23.18.1 New Theory of Commodity Material Flow

1. **Any material flow is the flow of material in corresponding systems, networks, and chains—material flow, material flow systems, material flow networks, and material flow chains**

The large material flow includes natural material flow, the social material flow, and the economic material flow. The author thinks that any material flow is the flow

---

[44]Xu [Xu09].

[45]Xu [Xu06].

[46]Xu [Xu07].

of material across and within corresponding systems, networks, and chains. For example, natural material flow is the flow of natural material in natural systems, natural networks, and natural chains. Social material flow is the flow of materials and commodities existing in nature and society in social systems, social networks, and social chains. Economic material flow is the flow of commodities, namely the six production and living elements, in economic systems, economic networks, and economic chains.

Table 23.63 lists natural material flow, social material flow, economic material flow, systems, networks, and chains.

2. **Economic material flow, economic systems, economic networks and economic chains**

Table 23.63 Natural material flow, social material flow, economic material flow, systems, networks, and chains

Nature	Natural material flow	Natural systems	Natural networks	Natural chains
	Flow of natural materials	A natural system refers to an organic integrity consisting of respective natural parts	A natural network refers to a complex natural network of natural members with organic relationship	A natural chain refers to a entity in biological form of respective natural members in natural systems or natural networks
Society	Social material flow	Social systems	Social networks	Social chains
	Flow of materials and commodities in nature and society	A society system refers to an organic integrity consisting of social members	A social network refers to an organic and complex system consisting of social members	A social chain refers to an entity with common interests by respective social members in social systems or social networks through laws or contracts
Economy	Economic material flow	Economic systems	Economic networks	Economic chains
	Flow of six type basic production and living elements (commodities), including commodity material, capital and their information	An economic entity consisting of input party, production party, circulation party and consumption party of six types of production and living elements (commodities)	A complex economic system consisting of input party, production party, circulation party and consumption party of six types of production and living elements (commodities)	An entity with common interests consisting of input party, production party, circulation party and consumption party of six types of production and living elements (commodities)

Table 23.63 provides the following information.

(1) An "economic system" is an organic and economic entity consisting of an input party, a production party, a circulation party and a consumption party from the six types of production and living elements (commodities). Input systems, production systems, circulation systems, and consumption systems are subsystems inside an economic system.
(2) An "economic network" is a complex economic system consisting of an input party, a production party, a circulation party and a consumption party from the six types of production and living elements (commodities). Input networks, production networks, circulation networks, and consumption networks are subnetworks inside an economic network.
(3) An "economic chain" refers to an entity with common interests, consisting of an input party, a production party, a circulation party and a consumption party from the six types of production and living elements (commodities).

Economic chains can be categorized into three groups based on the drivers: the supply economic chain, the demand economic chain, and the demand and supply economic chain. A supply economic chain is also called a supply chain. It is driven by the supply of manufacturers and it is guided by the supply of commodity production. A "supply economy" refers to the form of economy in which production supply enterprises dominate production and supply. In the planned economy period, serious shortage of commodities existed in China, due to its lagging economy. Products were even supplied based on tickets. The supply economy played a dominant role in the national economy. A supply economic chain is fit for sellers' markets, in which the supply of commodities is limited. The demand economic chain is also called the demand chain. It is driven by the demand of consumers' consumption and is guided by meeting consumers' demands. A "demand economy" refers to the form of economy in which production and supply are guided by the demands of consumers. A demand economy is not constrained by production. In developed countries, abundant commodities can meet consumers' diverse demands. A demand economy plays a dominant role in developed countries. A demand economic chain is fit for buyers' markets in which commodities are abundant. After the reform and opening up, a market economy system is under construction in China. China has gradually changed from a seller's market with a limited supply of commodities to a buyer's market with relative abundant commodities. The "demand chain" is developing well in China. The demand and supply economic chain is also called the demand and supply chain. It is driven by manufacturers and consumers together. The demand and supply economy refers to the form of economy in which the demand and supply of commodities are balanced and coordinated. When the demand and supply economy plays a dominant role, neither the guidance of supply nor the guidance of demand is visible. The balance between supply and demand is the main status. However, because there are many kinds of commodities and because new products appear continuously, short supply or oversupply might occur, for certain commodities. Therefore, a small number of supply chains and demand chains do exist in practice.

Based on the above analysis, the author thinks that the demand and supply economy is the normal status for economic development, whereas the supply economy and the demand economy are two extreme cases. The demand and supply chain is a comprehensive economic chain consisting of the supply chain and the demand chain. It is suitable for markets with various commodity supply situations. Thus, normally, the supply and demand of the economic chain should be balanced. Only when the supply and demand of commodities is off balance will the situation in which suppliers dominate or consumers dominate appear.

Based on the domestic and overseas literature, many studies focus on the supply chain, particularly the supply chain of physical commodities, while few studies focus on the supply chains of other properties of commodities. A few studies even focus on the demand and supply chain. The author thinks that the supply chain of physical commodities is only form of the economic chain in a market economy. Based on the nature of commodities, commodity economy chains can be categorized into the commodity physical chain, the commodity value chain, and the commodity information chain. According to the theory of supply and demand for commodities, commodity physical chains can be categorized into the physical supply chain, the physical demand chain, and the physical supply and demand chain. The commodity value chain is the capital chain for commodities. It can be categorized into the capital supply chain, the capital demand chain, and the capital supply and demand chain. The commodity information chain can be categorized into the information supply chain, the information demand chain, and the information supply and demand chain.

According to the six-element production factor theory and the six-element living factor theory, the six types of basic production and living factors are manpower (labor), financial resources (fixed assets and current assets), materials (raw materials and energy), natural forces (land, water, and minerals), transportation, and time. In a commodity economy, these elements are all commodities. They are human beings' wealth. Thus, all of the commodities and wealth in economy can be categorized into manpower, financial resources, material, natural forces, transportation capacity, and time. Table 23.64 lists the classifications of production and living factors based on commodity material flow, commodity system, commodity network, and commodity chain.

According to the law of commodity movement, any economic system, economic network, and economic chain has an input party, a production party, a circulation party, and a consumption party. Table 23.65 shows the four parties in economic system, economic network and economic chain.

According to the theory of commodity nature, any commodity has material form, capital form, and information form. The three flows of commodity refer to the material flow, the capital flow, and the information flow. The three systems of commodity refer to the material system, the capital system, and the information system. The three networks of commodity refer to the commodity material network, the capital network, and the information network. The three chains of commodity refer to the commodity material chain, the capital chain, and the information chain. Table 23.66 shows the three flows, the three systems, the three networks, and three chains of commodities.

Table 23.64 Classifications of production and living factors based on commodity flow material, commodity systems, commodity network, and commodity chain

	Basic production and living factors commodity flow		Basic production and living factors commodity system		Basic production and living factors commodity network		Basic production and living factors commodity chain	
1	Manpower flow	Manpower resource flow	Manpower system	Manpower system	Manpower network	Manpower resource network	Manpower supply and demand chain	Manpower resource supply and demand chain
2	Financial resources flow	Asset resource flow	Financial resource system	Financial resource system	Financial resource network	Financial resource network	Financial resource supply and demand chain	Financial resource supply and demand chain
3	Material flow (note)	Material resource flow	Material system	Material resource system	Material network	material resource network	Material supply and demand chain	Material resource supply and demand chain
4	Natural force flow	Natural resource flow	Natural resource system	Natural resource system	Natural resource network	Natural resource network	Natural resource supply and demand chain	Natural resource supply and demand chain
5	Transportation flow	Transportation resource flow	Transportation system	Transportation resource system	Transportation network	Transportation resource network	Transportation supply and demand chain	Transportation resource supply and demand chain
6	Time flow	Time resource flow	Time system	Time resource system	Time network	Time resource network	Time supply and demand chain	Time resource supply and demand chain

Note Material and material resources here refer to consumable resources, such as energy and raw materials

Table 23.65 Four parties in economic system, economic network, and economic chain

Input party		Production party	
1. Basic production and living factor goods	Manpower resource input party	2. Basic production and living factor goods	Manpower provider
	Financial resource input party		Financial resource production party
	Material resource input party		Material resource production party
	Natural resource input party		Natural resource production party
	Transportation resource input party		Transportation resource production party
	Time resource input party		Time resource provider
Circulation party		**Consumption party**	
3. Basic production and living factor goods	Manpower resource circulation party	4. Basic production and living factor goods	Manpower consumption party
	Financial resource circulation party		Financial resource consumption party
	Material resource circulation party		Material resource consumption party
	Natural resource circulation party		Natural resource consumption party
	Transportation resource circulation party		Transportation resource consumption party
	Time resource circulation party		Time resource consumption party

According to the theory of production factor levels in the technological economy,[47] the social economy consists of diverse production factors. Based on the scope and the level of their role in the social economy, production factors can be grouped into four levels, as shown in Fig. 23.7. The top level is the industrial production factor, and it is followed by the industry production factor, the enterprise production factor, and the basic production factor.

According to the six-element production and living factor theory, any production or living activity must have six basic production and living factors working simultaneously in all human societies. Each of the six basic factors is indispensable. Figure 23.7 shows that the six basic production and living factors comprise both input and output. Input generates output. Thus, no matter what enterprises produce,

[47] Xu and Xu [XuXu06].

Table 23.66 Three flows, three systems, three networks, and three chains of commodities

No	Commodity flow	Commodity flow system	Commodity flow network	Commodity flow chain			
1	Commodity material flow	Commodity material system	Commodity material network	Commodity material chain	Material supply chain	Material demand chain	Material supply and demand chain
2	Commodity capital flow	Commodity capital system	Commodity capital network	Commodity capital chain	Capital supply chain	Capital demand chain	Capital supply and demand chain
3	Commodity information flow	Commodity information system	Commodity information network	Commodity information chain	Information supply chain	Information demand chain	Information supply and demand chain

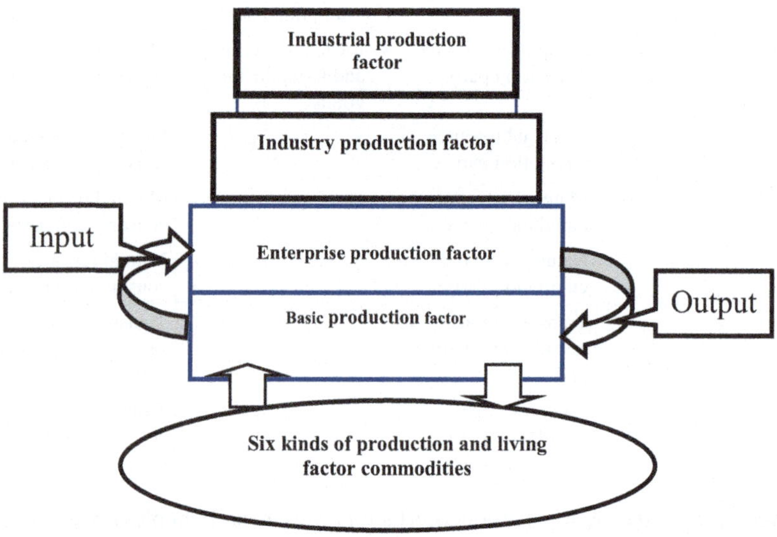

Fig. 23.7 Four-level model of production factors

the output falls into the six basic production and living factors. Input and output are different. Input must have all of the six basic production and living factors. All of these factors are indispensable. Different from input, output can have one of the six basic production and living factors.

According to the theory of the Marxist political economy, a socio-economic system is composed of production, circulation, and consumption. Based on the six-element theory of production and living factors, the author believes that input is a component as well, with the same importance as production. Sometimes, input is

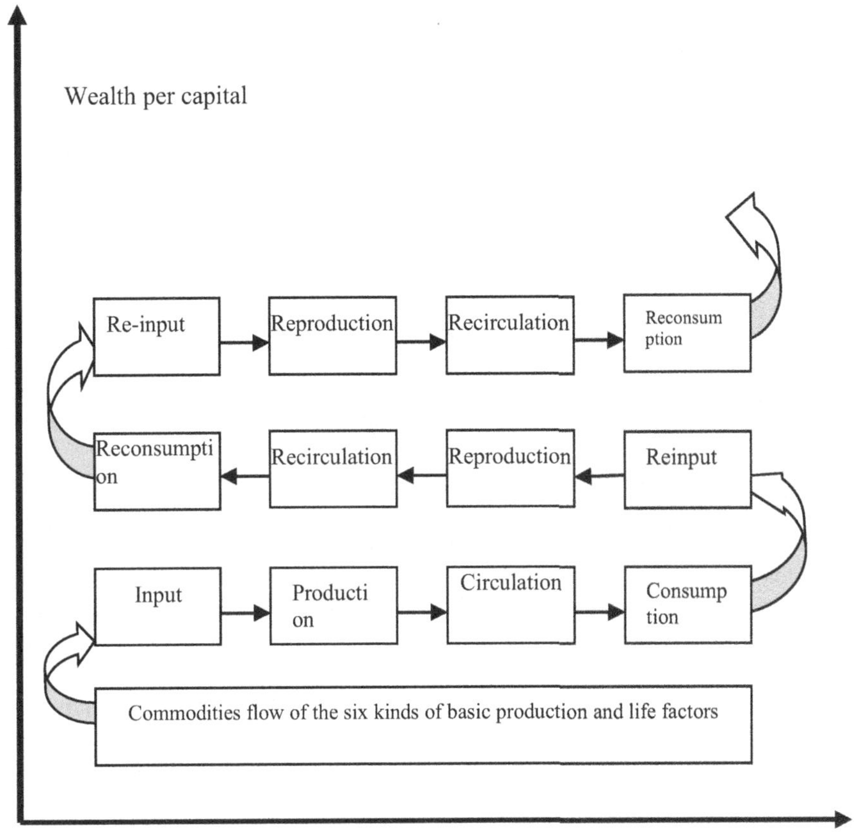

Fig. 23.8 The law of commodity movement during social and economic development

more important than production. Input consists of research, testing, design, construction, financing, procurement of equipment, and so on. It is the base of production. It is also the base of social and economic systems. Therefore, it is necessary to separate input from production and make it an independent component. As a result, a social and economic system consists of four components: input, production, circulation, and consumption (see Fig. 23.8).

It can be seen from the Fig. 23.8 that the input, production, circulation, and consumption of the six basic production and living factor commodities[48] are the economic activities in a society. The input of the six basic production and living factor commodities mainly comes from domestic production and domestic reserve. Foreign investment can be utilized as well. The production of the six basic production and living factor commodities include the production in the primary industry,

[48]In the book, the six inputs, the six basic production and living factors, the six types of basic production and living factors, and the six basic production and living factor commodities all refer to the same meaning.

the secondary industry, and the tertiary industry. The circulation of the six basic production and living factor commodities includes the circulation of products in the primary industry, the secondary industry, and the tertiary industry. The consumption of the six basic production and living factor commodities includes intermediate consumption and final consumption. Final consumption includes domestic accumulation, increasing reserves, and foreign output. The development of the social economy follows the cycle of input, production, distribution, consumption, re-input, re-production, re-circulation, re-consumption, and re-input. Commodities move continuously in this process. As commonalities move, the social economy develops and wealth per capita rises. This is the law of commodity movement in the development of a social economy. Because commodities refer to the six basic production and living factors, the law of commodity movement includes the law of movement about physical commodities, capital, and information.

The three forms of commodities are conflictive and unified.

1. A unified relationship exists among the three forms of commodity material flow. First, the input, production, circulation, and consumption of commodities each have three forms: physical commodities, capital, and information. These three forms are interrelated and interdependent. All are indispensable at any time. If any is missing, a commodity material flow will not exist. Second, these three forms promote each other and develop in tandem. The development of commodity material flow drives the development of commodity capital flow. The development of a commodity capital flow promotes the development of a physical commodity material flow. Similarly, the development of a commodity information flow will promote the development of a physical commodity material flow and a commodity capital flow.
2. The three forms of commodities are conflicting as well. If the physical commodity material flow develops too rapidly and the development of the commodity capital flow cannot keep up with its pace, the development of a physical commodity material flow will be affected. Similarly, if the commodity capital flow develops too fast and the development of the physical commodity material flow cannot keep up with its pace, the development of a commodity capital flow will be affected. Financial crises might occur. If the development of the commodity information flow lags behind, the development of the physical commodity material flow and the development of the commodity capital flow will be greatly affected. Thus, the key to management commodity material flow is to deal well with the contradictory and unified relationship of the commodity material flow. For example, when the commodity capital flow is high and physical commodities are limited, the prices of commodities will rise. Consumers' purchase intentions will be affected. On the contrary, when the amount of physical commodities is too high and the commodity capital flow is low, the prices of commodities will drop. In this case, producers will be affected. The commodity material flow is lagging in undeveloped areas in China. Economic development in these areas is affected

negatively. The contradictory relationship between the three flows is changing. If the contradictory relationship is well dealt with, it can turn into a coordinated one. If the contradictory relationship is not well dealt with, the situation will become more serious. Regional or worldwide financial crises might break out. This is called the contradiction and unification theory of the three commodity flows.

23.18.2 Commerce Theory

1. **Business affairs and business are not the same**

Over the years, people have called economic activities that are based on money with the goal of achieving commodity "circulation commerce" or "business." Commercial affairs refer to affairs[49] related with commerce. Thus, business and business affairs are different. The concept of business is wide; it includes business affairs. However, business affairs do not include business. In the 1990s, the author directed doctoral students to study commercial technical and economic problems with the theories and methods[50] of technological economics. A book, Commercial Technological Economics, was published in 1993.[51] The US proposed building an information highway in the early 1990s. Since then, electronic information technologies have developed rapidly. Meanwhile, economic information and globalization have developed rapidly, as well. Electronic business (e-business) has appeared in western countries. This is called a revolution in business. In the twenty-first century, people now pay more attention to electronic business.

In western literature, electronic business is not called E-business affairs or E-Commerce affairs. In the Chinese translation, electronic business is confused with E-business affairs or E-Commerce affairs.

The author thinks that the translation of electronic business in Chinese should be corrected, for two reasons. First, the existing translation of electronic business in Chinese is not accurate, because electronic business includes electronic business affairs, whereas electronic business affairs do not include electronic business. Second, the correct translation of electronic business can correspond to traditional business. Usually, people call it circulation commerce, not commerce affairs. Compared with traditional business, electronic business is modern business. The name "electronic business affairs" does not correspond to traditional business. The incorrect translation is not helpful for research and practice. Therefore, the author recommends that the correct translation of electronic business be adoptedin Chinese. The correct translation will promote the development of modern business in China.

[49]Powerword (electronic version), Peking University Press, 1988.

[50]Xu [Xu88].

[51]Zhang [Zh93].

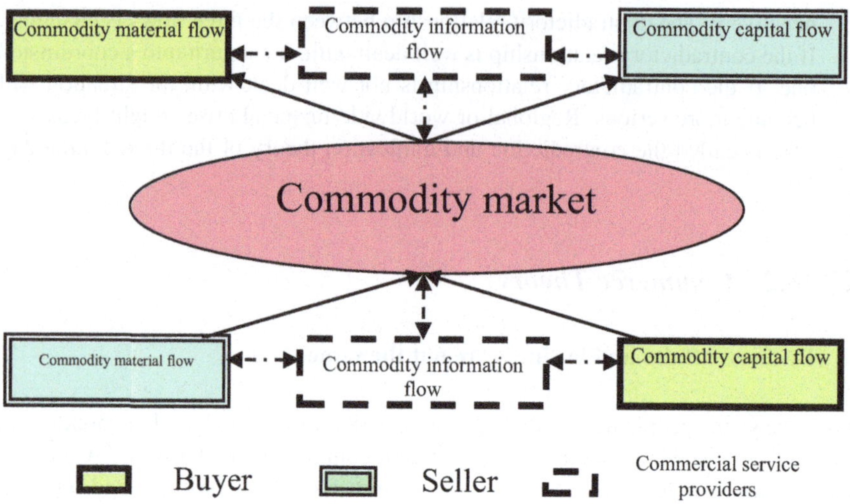

Fig. 23.9 The principle of unification of three flows, integration of three flows, and three flows all-in-one for e-business

2. **Basic principles of commerce**

The author believes that the economic activities in human society are the movement of the physical commodity material flow, the commodity capital flow, and the commodity information flow. Commerce activities are the process of unifying and integrating these three commodity flows (see Fig. 23.9).

Unification of three flows means that commercial transactions must have three flows, namely the physical commodity material flow, the commodity capital flow, and the commodity information flow. Commercial transactions will not be completed if any of the three flows is missing. Even in ancient eras, communication between buyers and sellers was required for commercial transactions. Thus, the three flows depend on each other and they are unified. Unification of three flows is the prerequisite for commercial transactions.

Integration of the three flows means that the three flows merge into one flow when transactions occur. This flow is commercial circulation, also referred to as "business flow." In commercial circulation, the subjects (owners) of physical commodities and capital change. When physical commodities flow from sellers to buyers, capital flows from buyer to sellers. However, the subjects (owners) of physical commodities and capital, per se, do not flow, because the ownership is not physical. Ownership is the common property of commodities and capital. Information of commodities can reflect the ownership of commodities. Thus, in this way, the ownership of commodities and capital can flow with the flow of physical commodities and capital. The flow of ownership can be called "material right flow." But it cannot be separated from the physical commodity material flow and the commodity capital flow. Integration of the physical commodity material flow, the commodity capital flow, and the commodity information flow is the necessary condition for commercial transactions.

In practice, the two parties in commercial transactions conduct transactions based on the information that they gained. Thus, the information flow is the most important among the three flows. It is the key to success in commercial transactions.

Figure 23.9 shows the forms of the commodity material flow and their relationship. Dashed arrows in two opposite directions exist between physical commodity material flow and commodity information flow, as well as between commodity capital flow and commodity information flow. The arrows represent a two directional movement. On one hand, the information of physical commodity and commodity capital flows to enterprises and to markets. On the other hand, the transaction information of physical commodity and commodity capital flows to market. The transaction of physical commodities and capital is completed in the market, according to transaction information. This is the process of commercial activities. It can be seen that the commodity information flow plays a key role in commercial activities, particularly in knowledge economic era. Electronic business is a typical example.

3. **Characteristics of e-business**

The author believes that electronic commodities are the best fit for e-business, and include software, electronic newspapers and magazines, books, electronic goods, product manufacturing design drawings, cultural works, financial products, and equity securities. These electronic commodities have the characteristics of unification of the three flows and integration of the three flows. In addition, they have a new characteristic: three flows all-in-one. Three flows all-in-one has three levels of meaning. First, it means that the three flows are all electronically based. Second, it means that the three flows are in the same information network. Third, it means that the three flows are in a virtual business world.

Figure 23.10 shows the principle of unification of the three flows, integration of three flows, and three flows all-in-one for electronic business. The three flows move before and after people conduct transactions in the e-business market. Buyers and sellers undertake direct transactions. They control their own electronic capital flow and their electronic physical commodity sources flow. E-business service providers control the electronic information flow, providing services for buyers and sellers. After the owners of electronic physical commodity sources and electronic capital take the e-business services, the owners of electronic capital become the owners of electronic physical commodities. The owners of electronic physical commodities become the owners of electronic capital. In this process, the ownership of the capital flow and the physical material flow changed. Then the movement of these two flows controlled by the new owners change. In addition, e-business service providers' activities change accordingly.

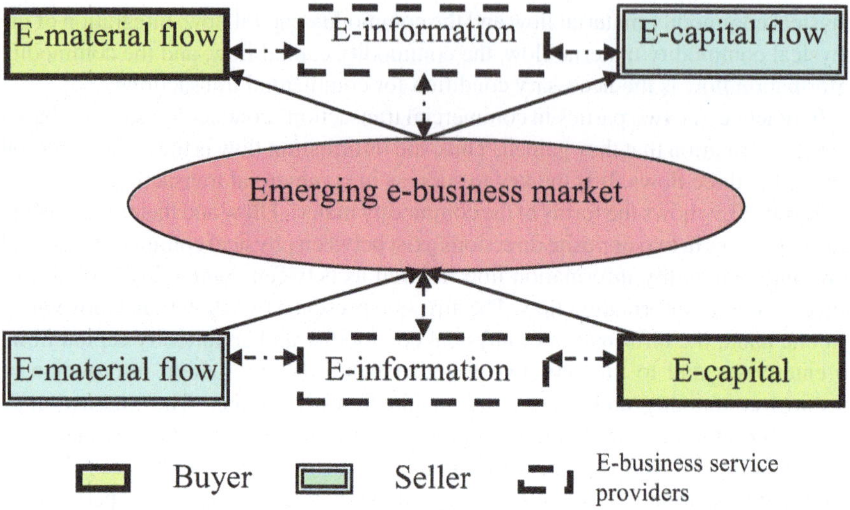

Fig. 23.10 The principle of unification of three flows and the integration of the three flows

23.19 Realization of the Five Modernizations is the New Goal of the Social and Economic Development Strategy in China[52]

Research background, scientific significance of achievements and practical value.

Following Mao Zedong Thought, Premier Zhou Enlai first proposed the concept of the Four Modernizations in the government work report at the First Session of the National People's Congress. In 1975, Premier Zhou Enlai mentioned the Four Modernizations again in the government work report at the Fourth Session of the National People's Congress entrusted by the CPC Central Committee and Chairman Mao Zedong. Since the reform and opening up, the CPC Central Commission has highlighted Four Modernizations. Actually, there are five modernizations, because the modernization of science and technology is at the core of the modernization of services. Impacted by the economic mode of the former Soviet Union, it was thought that only industry and agriculture could create value, while services did not create value as a type of consumption. Thus, the modernization of services was not proposed. The author applied Marxist doctrine and economic theory, as well as the theories of technological economics to explore the laws of the development of human society and the economy. The author initially proposed the concepts of a singular economy era, a dual economy era, a tripartite economy era, and a quadripartite economy era, namely the Theory of Four Economy Eras. The author also initially proposed the concepts of the first age, the second age, the third age…the

[52] Xu [Xu11].

tenth age, namely the Theory of Ten Economic Ages. The quadripartite economy era refers to the period when the service economy, the agricultural economy, the industrial economy, and the knowledge economy integrate. The author found that human society started from service economy (the collecting, hunting, and fishing economy). Later, agricultural economy and industrial economy appeared, and the knowledge economy appeared in modern society. It actually belongs to the service economy. Thus, the development of the modern service economy is very important. The author also found that in the tenth age, knowledge, information, science, and technology in human society reach the highest level. Human beings' wealth also reaches a larger level during the tenth age. According to the Organization for Economic Cooperation and Development (OECD), in 1994, the average ratio in the knowledge economy among the members was 51%. Western Germany, the US, Japan, the UK, Canada, Sweden, the Netherlands, and France began to enter the tenth age when the knowledge economy played a dominant role. In 1996, the knowledge economy played the dominant role in the quadripartite economy in the US, with a ratio of 55.3%.[53] The knowledge economy ranked first. The service economy accounted for 26.7%, ranking second. The industrial economy accounted for 16.4%, ranking third. The agricultural economy accounted for 1.7%, ranking fourth. With the development of the knowledge economy, its ratio will continue to rise. China is at the ninth age. The development of its service economy needs to be accelerated. The over 60 years of economic and social development in China have proven that the five modernizations are the consequentialness of development. The author believes that this study has achieved advanced results, which were submitted to the leaders in the central government.

23.19.1 How were the Four Modernizations Proposed in the Twentieth Century?

The concept of The Four Modernizations was proposed by the first generation of central collective leadership, headed by Mao Zedong, to change the poor and lagging status of old China. It was a goal for economic social development in socialist construction. According to Mao Zedong Thought, in September 1954, Premier Zhou first proposed The Four Modernizations at the government work report in the First Session of the NPC, namely modernizations in industry, agriculture, transportation, and the national defense (see Table 23.67). From late 1959 to early 1960, Mao Zedong said: "socialist construction originally required industrial modernization, agricultural modernization, and scientific and cultural modernization. Now, modernization of the national defense should be added." This is the first time that Chairman Mao fully and clearly presented The Four Modernizations. On December 21, 1964, The Four Modernizations were officially set as the goal of the overall national development strategy. According to the proposal of Chairman Mao, Premier Zhou formally

[53] 46.1% is separated from service and 9.2% is separated from industry.

Table 23.67 How the four modernizations were proposed in the twentieth century

I	Set. 23, 1954 (note 1)	Four modernizations			
		Modern industry	Modern agriculture	Modern transportation	Modern national defense
II	Late 1959 to early 1960 (note 2)	Four modernizations			
		Industrial modernization	Agricultural modernization	Science and technology modernization	National defense modernization
III	Dec 21, 1964 (note 3)	Four modernizations			
		Agricultural modernization	Industrial modernization	National defense modernization	Science and technology modernization
IV	Jan 13, 1975 (note 4)	Four modernizations			
		Agricultural modernization	Industrial modernization	National defense modernization	Science and technology modernization

Note 1. Based on Mao Zedong Thought, Premier Zhou Enlai proposed the concept of four modernizations in the government report at the First Session of the NPC
2. President Mao Zedong first completely and clearly expressed the thought about four modernizations
3. According to the proposal of Mao Zedong, Premier Zhou Enlai officially proposed it in the government work report at third session of NPC
4. Entrusted by CPC Central Committee, Premier Zhou Enlai proposed it again at government work report in the fourth session of NPC
Data source (Xinhua news agency, September 16, Beijing) Presentation of Grand Goal of Four Modernizations [N] Economic Daily, digital version, (4), September 17, 2009

proposed the main task for the future of the national economy in the government work report, "to change China into a socialist strong country with modern agriculture, modern industry, modern national defense, and modern science and technology within a relatively short period, catching up and surpassing the leading level in the world." He also pointed out that The Four Modernizations should be realized in two steps in the twentieth century, namely "the first step is to build an independent and relatively complete industrial system and national economic system; the second step is to achieve the modernization of agriculture, industry, national defense, and science and technology, moving the Chinese economy to the leading position in the world." On January 13, 1975, entrusted by the CPC Central Committee and Mao Zedong, Premier Zhou made a government work report at the Fourth Session of the NPC. He pointed out again, "in the twentieth century, achieve the modernization of agriculture, industry, national defense, and science and technology, moving Chinese economy to the leading position in the world." After the Third Plenary Session of the Eleventh CPC National Congress, under the leadership of the CPC, the task of the Four Modernizations was moved forward. Socialist modernizations with Chinese characteristics have made great achievements in the reform and opening up. The Chinese national economy is leading the world.

23.19.2 Realization of Five Modernizations is the New Goal for Social and Economic Development in the New Century

1. **Necessity of five modernizations in the new century**

Compared with The Four Modernizations, The Five Modernizations offers a new one: service modernization. Before the reform and opening up, China adopted the economic mode of the former Soviet Union. It was thought that only industry and agriculture could create value. Because service mainly is mainly consumption, it was thought not to create value. As such, the assessment of the national economy in China considered industry and agriculture only for a long time. In fact, service creates value too. What service creates is different from what is generated by industry and agriculture in form and value. After the reform and opening up, China adopted the internationally accepted indicators of GDP and GNP to assess its national economy. Beyond industry and agriculture, service is assessed as well. According to the laws of economic development, and with the development of science and technology, more science and technology is required in service. Service plays an important role in promoting the development of the national economy, energy saving, and reducing emissions. Particularly, based on the laws of the development of human society, service becomes more important in the knowledge economy era. Therefore, other than the modernizations of agriculture, industry, the national defense, and science and technology, the modernization of service is indispensable. Facts have proven that the modernization of service has an extensive future. It is particularly good for employment and sustainable development.

2. **Relationship among the five modernizations**

According to the internationally accepted standards for industry classification, science and technology belongs to the tertiary industry (service industry). But science and technology is different from other industries. It is the most active industry, with the most powerful driving force. Just as Comrade Xiaoping said, science and technology is the primary productive force. This statement has been proven by the economic and social development in human society. Particularly, in the twenty-first century, the CPC Central Committee has proposed a science and education strategy of independent innovation. Thus, the modernization of science and technology is most critical. It should be put in a position before the other four modernizations. Modernizations of the first industry, the second industry, and the tertiary

Table 23.68 The order of the five modernizations

Science and technology modernization	Agricultural modernization	Industrial modernization	Service modernization	National defense modernization

industry, namely modernizations of agriculture, industry, and service, provide material based for the modernizations of the national economy and peoples' living. They are important indicators for the development of the human economy and for society. However, the achievement of these modernizations must be guided by the Deng Xiaoping Theory, the theory of the three Representatives, and the theory of scientific development outlook. Therefore, these three modernizations are put after the modernization of science and technology. Historical facts have proven that countries lacking modernization of their national defense will be invaded and enslaved in modern society, and that other modernizations will not be achieved in these countries. Thus, the modernization of the national defense provides protection for science and technology modernization, agricultural modernization, industrial modernization, and service modernization. The order of The Five Modernizations is science and technology modernization, agricultural modernization, industrial modernization, service modernization, and national defense modernization (Table 23.68).

3. **Law of human social and economic development**

From the perspective of technological economics, the first economy in human society is the singular economy (the unitary primitive economy), namely collecting, fishing, and hunting. Based on the classification principle of modern industries, collecting, fishing, and hunting are service industries. They do not produce physical products. Thus, the primitive economy is the service economy, in essence. It belongs to the tertiary industry-service. Thus, the human social economy developed from the service economy. Historical facts have proven that the service economy was the only economy in primitive society, and that the service economy is an indispensable component in all societies. It is becoming even more important. In developed countries, service accounts for the main portion of their economic development. The "dual economy" refers to the integration of service and agriculture. The "tripartite economy" refers to the integration of service, agriculture, and industry. The "quadripartite economy" refers to the integration of service, agriculture, industry, and the knowledge economy. It should be pointed out that the contents of service in these economic eras are different. The service economy began with collecting, fishing, and hunting. With the development of science and technologies, and the social division of labor, agriculture, and industry, the connotation of service changed. At present, the portion of knowledge, information, science, and technologies in service has risen. Services with high technologies are being developed. Human beings enter the quadripartite economy era dominated by the knowledge economy.

Accordingly, human society has gone through four eras, namely the monistic economy era, the dual economy era, the tripartite economy era, and the quadripartite economy era. Other than the singular economy era, each of the other eras has three sub-eras. For example, the dual economy era consists of the post-primitive economy, the transition from the primitive economy to the agricultural economy, and the pre-agricultural era. The tertiary economic era consists of the post-agricultural economy, the transition from the agricultural to the industrial economy, and the pre-industrial economy eras. The quadripartite economy era consists of the post-industrial economy, the transition from the industry to the knowledge economy, and the knowledge economy (see Table 23.69). It can be seen from Table 23.69 that the economy in human society started with 100% service (collecting, fishing, and hunting) in primitive society and ended in a modern society which is dominated by knowledge economy. This process has ten ages. In the tenth age, knowledge, information, science, and technologies reach the highest level in human society. The amount of wealth is large. This age is the ideal status of the development of technological economics. According to the OECD, the average ratio of the knowledge economy among its members in 1994 was 51%. Western Germany, the US, Japan, the UK, Canada, Sweden, Netherlands, and France began to enter the tenth age when the knowledge economy began to play a dominant role. In 1996, the knowledge economy played the dominant role in the quadripartite economy in the US, with a ratio of 55.3%.[54] The knowledge economy ranked the first. The service economy accounted for 26.7% ranking second. The industrial economy accounted for 16.4%, ranking third. The agricultural economy accounted for 1.7%, ranking fourth. With the development of the knowledge economy, its ratio will continue to rise.

According to the Marxism principle that the production relationship and productivity should fit each other, the primitive social system corresponds to the singular economy. Slave social systems and feudal social systems correspond to the dual economy. Capitalist social systems and socialist social systems (pre-communist societies) correspond to the tripartite economy. The post-capitalist social system and the post-socialist social system (communist society) correspond to the quadripartite economy. Table 23.69 lists the mutual relationship among social development forms, their development eras, technical economic development patterns, and their development eras. Primitive society corresponds to the singular economy era. The slavery society and feudal society correspond to the dual economy era. Capitalist society and socialist societies correspond to the tertiary economy era. Post-capitalist, post-socialist societies and communist societies correspond to the quadripartite economy era. Compared with the theories of five forms or six forms in the development of human society from Marx, the tenth age is the ideal era of communist social development mentioned by Marx.

In summary, according to Marxist doctrine and economic theory, the author believes that the classification of human social development process should be based on a single form theory, whereas the classification of human economic development eras should be based on a complex form theory. The author initially proposed the

[54]① 46.1% is from service and 9.2% is from industry.

Table 23.69 Social and economic development classification

Development status of social formation	Development status of technical and economic forms	Singular economy era	Dual economy era		
		First age	Second age	Third age	Fourth age
		Primitive economy era	Post primitive economy-based era	Transition era of primitive agricultural economy	Pre-agricultural economy-based era
Primitive society	Service economy	100%	>50%	~50%	<50%
Slave society	Agricultural economy	0	<50%	~50%	>50%
Feudal society					
Capitalist society	Industrial economy	0	0	0	0
Socialist society					
Capitalist society	Knowledge economy	0	0	0	0
Communist society					

Development status of Social formation	Development status of Technical and economic forms	Tripartite economy era		Quadripartite economy era			
		Fifth age	Sixth age	Seventh age	Eighth age	Ninth age	Tenth age
		Post agricultural economy-based era	Transition era of agriculture-industry	Pre-industry economy based era	Post industry economy based era	Transition era of industry-knowledge economy	Knowledge based era
Primitive society	Service economy	<50%	<50%	<50%	<50%	<50%	<50%
Slave society	Agricultural economy	>50%	~50%	<50%	<50%	<50%	<50%

(continued)

Table 23.69 (continued)

Development status of Social formation	Development status of Technical and economic forms	Tripartite economy era		Quadripartite economy era			
		Fifth age	Sixth age	Seventh age	Eighth age	Ninth age	Tenth age
		Post agricultural economy-based era	Transition era of agriculture-industry	Pre-industry economy based era	Post industry economy based era	Transition era of industry-knowledge economy	Knowledge based era
Feudal society							
Capitalist society Socialist society	Industrial economy	<50%	~50%	>50%	>50%	~50%	<50%
Capitalist society Communist society	Knowledge economy	0	0	0	<50%	~50%	>50%

concepts of the singular economy era, dual economy era, the tripartite economy era, and the quadripartite economy era, namely the Theory of Four Economic Eras. The author also initially proposed the concepts of the first age, the second age, the third age…the tenth age, namely The Theory of Ten Economic Ages. In addition, the author proposed the criteria for assessing each era. The author hopes that these theories will facilitate the study and application of era classification.

References

[LE61] Lenin, V. (1961). Collected Works of Lenin, Vol 29, Page 388. People's Publishing House.

[ST83] Strengthen Energy Development and Reduce Energy Consumption (1983). People's Daily, Jan. 21.

[XU65] Xu, S.B. (1965). Utilization and allocation of heavy oil in China. State Scientific and Technological Commission Publishing House.

[XU79] Xu, S.B. (1979). Issues and opinions about energy in China. Report of comprehensive survey by Chinese Academy of Sciences.

[XU81] Xu, S.B. (1981). National income and net income should be the major goal of economy development. Technological Economy Research.

[XU82] Xu, S.B. (1982). Energy technical economy, Hunan People's publishing House.

[XU83a] Xu, S.B. (1983a). The role of scientific and technological progress in economic construction of Shanxi province. Report of Quantity and Technological Economy Institute in Chinese Academy of Social Sciences.

[XU83b] Xu, S.B. (1983b). Comprehensive evaluation and research on three coal development schemes in Shanxi province. Planning Project of Energy Heavy Chemical Base in Shanxi Province.

[XU88] Xu, S. B. (1988). Technological Economics. Edition 4. Nanjing. Jiangsu People Publishing House.

[XU05] Xu, S.B. (2005). China's energy safety and development problems (China's productivity development international forum collected papers). Compiled by Chinese Association of Productivity Science, Beijing, 113–130.

[XU06] Xu, S.B. (2006). Six-Element Theory of Production Factors, Academic Journal of Beijing Jiaotong University (social science version), 5(3):15–19.

[XU07] Xu, S.B. (2007). Six-Element Theory of Living Factors, Academic Journal of Beijing Jiaotong University (social science version), 6(1):15–18.

[XU09] Xu, S.B. (2009). Study of Commodity Logistics Theory, Management World, P1–9.

[XU11] Xu, S.B. (2011). Five Modernizations Are New Goals of Our Economic and Social Development Strategy, Xinhua weekly financial analysis, 11, 1–3.

[XU73] Xu, S.B. et al. Utilization of industrial secondary energy in China. Report of comprehensive survey by Chinese Academy of Sciences. 1973–1976.

[XU89] Xu, S.B., et al. (1989). Strategically Choice of Energy Development, one achievements of the author. Jiangsu People's Publishing House.

[XU97] Xu, S.B., et al. (1997). Chinese Generalized Energy Efficiency Strategy Engineering, A Report Of SDPC.

[XX06] Xu, B., & Xu, S. B. (2006). Theory of Production Factors. Academic Journal of Beijing Jiaotong University (social science version), 5(4), 15–18.

[YA63] Yan, M.G. (1963). An analysis of changing low-pressure steam to hot water in heating supply systems in cities. A work report of Beijing power design study by Water and Electricity Ministry.

[ZH93] Zhang, H. L. (1993). Commerce Technological Economics [M] China Light Industry Press, Beijing.

[XU83c] Xu, S. B. (1983c). Create a New Situation for Energy Development, Energy Source and Energy Saving.

[QI85] Qiu, D.X. et al. (1985). Predication of China's Energy Demand in 2000, China's Energy in 2000.

Chapter 24
Approaches and Measures for Improving Technological Economic Effect

24.1 Introduction

This chapter is the third part of the applications for technological economics. It focuses on the approaches and measures for improving the technological economic effect from an overall perspective. The ultimate goal for the applications of the technological economy is to improve the technological economic effect. Particularly, this chapter introduces ten approaches to improve the technological economic effect, the factors that impact the economic effect of firms and of society, and the methods for analyzing the economic effect of firms and society.

24.2 Ten Approaches for Improving Economic Effect of Firms and Society

According to the greater, faster, better, and more economical evaluation formula discussed in the previous section, 20 factors in ten aspects impact the economic effect of firms and society (see Fig. 24.1). The following are the ten approaches for improving the economic effect of firms and society.

1. **Enlarge scale and increase types**
   For a firm or a piece of equipment, the amount of economic effect increases with the rise of production and labor quantity. On the contrary, the amount of economic effect decreases when a firm operates under capacity, if its equipment is not fully utilized, and if its production and labor quantity are low.
2. **Improve quality and maintain high quality with low price**
   Quality and feature directly affect the economic effect. Thus, the economic effect can be increased by improving the ratio of finished products and improving the ratio of high-quality products.

S. Xu, *Technological Economics*,
https://doi.org/10.1007/978-981-15-8582-1_24

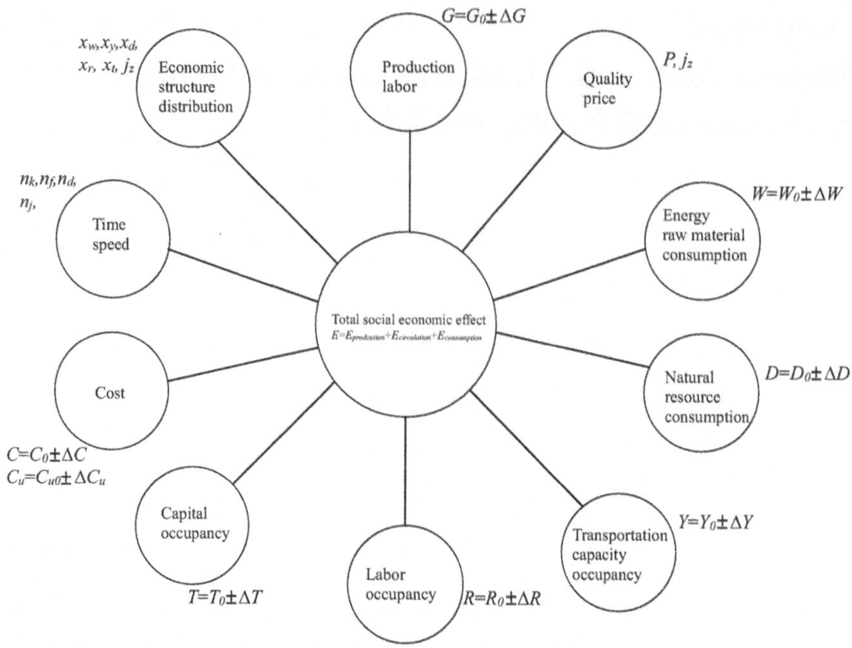

Fig. 24.1 Factors affecting economic effect of firms and society

3. **Improve capital utilization efficiency**
   Saving capital is an important approach for increasing the economic effect and efficiency of firms and of society.
4. **Improve utilization efficiency for energy and raw materials**
   In considering a product's costs, the ratio of energy and raw materials accounts for a large part (50–90%); therefore, saving materials and improving utilization efficiency, especially the utilization efficiency of energy and of raw materials that are short in supply, will play an important role in increasing the economic effect of firms and of society.
5. **Improve utilization efficiency for transportation**
   Improving the utilization efficiency of transportation is one of the main approaches for improving the economic effect of firms and society. Due to unreasonable economic layout, unreasonable transportation schedules, and a higher consumption of materials than the preset quota, a huge amount of waste exists in the amount of transportation labor. Thus, the amount of transportation labor needed can be lessened by improving the economic layout, making reasonable schedules, saving materials, and reducing weight.
6. **Improve utilization efficiency for human capital**
   To improve the economic effect of firms and of society, make full use of human capital by improving the utilization rate of human capital.

7. **Improve utilization efficiency for natural resource**
   Make full use of natural resources, improve utilization efficiency, save natural resources, and make the best use of natural resources. Thus, economic effects of firms and society can be improved for sustainable development.
8. **Improve utilization efficiency for time**
   Time is speed. Thus, time is economic benefits. The economic effects of firms and society can be improved by shortening construction periods, shortening full production periods, and shortening production periods, and by enhancing the speed of capital turnover.
9. **Reduce costs**
   Reducing costs is the most import approach for increasing the economic effect of firms and society.
10. **Adjust economic structure and allocate production factors reasonably**
    Adjusting the economic structure and allocating production factors reasonably is an important approach to use to increase the economic effect of firms and society. Specifically, price is the tool used for economic evaluation and benefit allocation. Unreasonable prices do not objectively reflect the economic effects of enterprises and of society. They do not support reasonable benefit allocation. As a result, stakeholders are negatively affected and negative impacts are generated on the economic effect of firms and society. Therefore, setting reasonable prices is an important approach for increasing the economic effect of firms and society.

24.3 Factors Influencing Economic Effects of Firms and Society

There are many factors that affect the economic effects of firms and society. They fall into three levels (see Fig. 24.2). At the first level are the direct factors, which are the 20 factors in ten aspects shown in Figure 24.1. Based on the analysis results of the first level, ten approaches are proposed to improve the economic effects of firms and society. Factors at the second level are those that affect the ten factors at the first level. Factors at this level high in number and fall into many fields, such as: natural technology, the socio-economy, productivity, production relations, the economic foundation, and the superstructure. They can be summarized into eight aspects, namely: politics, the national defense, society, culture, technology, the economy, the environment, and natural resources. Factors at this level are all domestic ones. In contrast, factors at the third level are international ones. By analyzing the factors at the second and third levels, measures are proposed to improve the economic effects of firms and society. Among them are political measures, which include implementing the policies of the Third Plenary Session of the Eleventh CPC National Congress, further reforming and opening up, reforming the political systems, and promoting cultural and ethical progress. Social measures include developing education and culture and enhancing health. Technical measures include reforming scientific and technical systems and accelerating technical progress. Economic measures include reforming economic

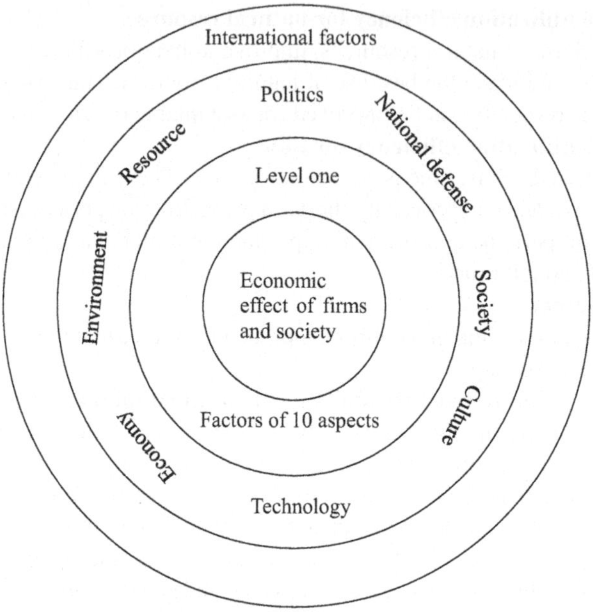

Fig. 24.2 Three levels of factors influencing economic effects of firms and society

structures, increasing production and improving savings, and improving economic management. Accordingly, measures for improving the economic effects of firms and of society should be comprehensive. They must rely on both firms and society and make them engaged. The effect of some measures is obvious, while that of other measures is latent and will not be seen for quite a long time. In this way, socialist modernization in China will be greatly accelerated and people's lives will continue to improve.

24.4 Analytical Methods for Economic Effects of Firms and Society

The previous section discusses some approaches for increasing the economic effect of firms and society. Economic effect can be generated by the following ten approaches: (1) the scale of the economy ΔE_{scale}; (2) the quality of the economic effect $\Delta E_{quality}$; (3) the capital economic effect $\Delta E_{capital}$; (4) the material economic effect $\Delta E_{material}$; (5) the transportation economic effect $\Delta E_{transportation}$; (6) the labor economic effect ΔE_{labor}; (7) the natural resource economic effect $\Delta E_{natural\_resource}$; (8) the time economic effect ΔE_{time}; (9) the cost economic effect ΔE_{cost}; (10) the structure economic effect $\Delta E_{structure}$. The economic effect for firms ΔE_{firm} and the economic effect for society $\Delta E_{society}$ consist of these ten economic effects. Here is the formula:

$$\Delta E_{society}(\Delta E_{firm}) = \Delta E_{scale} + \Delta E_{quality} + \Delta E_{capital} + \Delta E_{material} + \Delta E_{transportation} + \Delta E_{labor} + \Delta E_{natural\_resources} + \Delta E_{time} + \Delta E_{cost} + \Delta E_{strcuture} \quad (24.1)$$

Different technologies generate different economic effects for firms and for society. With the adoption of technologies and various measures, the economic effects of firms and of society will change accordingly. Among these changes, how many are caused by the change in production volume, how many are caused by the change in quality, and how many are caused by the change in structure? The answers rely on a comprehensive analysis of the economic effects of firms and of society. The following is an example of an analysis of the changes in economic effect, based on social net income. For convenience, the simplest development process is adopted. (Capital and land are invested during the construction period and full production begins right after the construction period ends. The benefit and cost in each year are the same.) Suppose the original social economic benefit (the social net income) of a scheme is E_{c0}. Later, efforts from stakeholders increase the social economic benefit to E_c. Thus, the total increment of social net income ΔE_c can be calculated with the following formula:

$$\begin{aligned}\Delta Ec &= Ec - \Delta Ec0 = [(S - Z) - (S_0 - Z_0)]\frac{\theta^n j - 1}{\theta - 1} \\ &= [(jpG - zpG) - (j_0 p_0 G_0 - z_0 p_0 G_0)]\frac{\theta^n j - 1}{\theta - 1} \\ &= \big[(jpG - cpG - x_t t_z pG - x_w wpG - x_y ypG - x_r rpG - x_d dpG - x_d d_z pG) - \\ &\quad \big(j_0 p_0 G_0 - c_0 p_0 G_0 - x_t t_{z0} p_0 G_0 - x_w w_0 p_0 G_0 - x_y y_0 p_0 G_0 - x_r r_0 p_0 G_0 \\ &\quad - x_d d_0 p_0 G_0 - x_d d_z p_0 G_0)\frac{\theta^n j - 1}{\theta - 1}\end{aligned} \quad (24.2)$$

In Formula (24.2), P refers to the certified product rate or the average grade rate. In previous formulas, it is included in production G. In order to ease analysis, it is separated, here. Next, the change of economic benefit in each year, represented in Formula (24.2), is analyzed. In other words, each item in the bracket in Formula (24.2) is explained in detail:

1. **Economic effect analysis for increasing production**

$$\Delta E_{c_s cale} = (j_0 - z_0) p_0 (G - G_0) \quad (24.3)$$

2. **Economic effect analysis for improving quality**
   This includes two parts. One is generated by the improved certified product rate or grade rate. The other is generated by high quality and by reasonable price. Here is the formula:

$$\Delta E_{c_{quality}} = (j_0 - z_0)(p - p_0)G + (j - j_0)pG \quad (24.4)$$

3. **Economic effect analysis for capital**

(1) The situation when the construction period is the same, the annual investment on fixed assets is different, the current assets are different, and the basic depreciation expenses are different.

$$\begin{aligned}\Delta E_{c\_capital} &= x_t(t_{z0} - t_z)pG \\ &= x_t \times \left(t_{gz0} + t_{l0} - t_{j0} - t_{gz} - t_l + t_j\right)pG \\ &= x_t \times \sum_{s=1}^{n_{k0}} (t_{gs0} - t_{gs}) \frac{\theta^n j + nk0^{-s+1} - 1}{\theta^n j - 1} pG \\ &+ x_t \times \sum_{s=1}^{nl} (t_{ls0} - t_{ls}) \frac{\theta^n j^{-s+1} - 1}{\theta^n j - 1} pG \\ &+ x_t \left[\left(\frac{c_{j0}}{\theta - 1} - \frac{n_j c_{j0}}{\theta^n j - 1}\right) - \left(\frac{c_j}{\theta - 1} - \frac{n_j c_{j0}}{\theta^n j - 1}\right)\right] pG\end{aligned} \tag{24.5}$$

(2) The situation when the construction period is zero, the current assets are invested only in the first year of the operating period, and the basic depreciation expense deduction is not considered.

$$\Delta E_{c\_capital} = x_t \times \left(t_{g0} + t_{l0} - t_g - t_l\right)pG = x_t \times (t_0 - t)pG \tag{24.6}$$

(3) When the construction period n_{k0} is different, the economic effect generated by the yearly fixed asset investment cannot be calculated separately. Therefore, it can only be calculated together with the economic benefit generated by changes in the construction period.

4. **Economic effect analysis for material**

$$\Delta E_{c\_material} = x_w(w_0 - w)pG = x_w\left(\frac{1}{lw_0} - \frac{1}{lw}\right)pG \tag{24.7}$$

where $w_0 = \frac{w_0}{G_0}$, $w = \frac{w}{G}$ are the consumption quota for material(raw material and energy), $lw_0 = \frac{-1}{w_0}$, $lw = \frac{-1}{w}$ are the economic effect coefficients of material utilization (represented by production).

5. **Economic effect analysis for transportation**

$$\Delta E_{c\_transportation} = x_y(y_0 - y)pG = x_y\left(\frac{1}{l_{y0}} - \frac{1}{l_y}\right)pG \tag{24.8}$$

Where $y_0 = \frac{y_0}{G_0}$, $y = \frac{y}{G}$ are the consumption quota for transportation. $l_{y0} = \frac{1}{y_0}$, $l_{y0} = \frac{1}{y_0}$ are economic effect coefficients of transportation utilization (represented by production).

6. **Economic effect analysis for manpower**

$$\Delta E_{c\_manpower} = x_r(r_0 - r)pG = x_r\left(\frac{1}{l_{r_0}} - \frac{1}{l_r}\right)pG \tag{24.9}$$

Where $r_0 = \frac{R_0}{G_0}$, $y = \frac{R}{G}$ are the consumption quota for manpower. $l_{r0} = \frac{-1}{r_0}$, $l_r = \frac{-1}{r}$ are the labor productivity (represented by production).

7. **Economic effect analysis for natural resource**

$$\Delta E_{c\_natural\_resource} = \Delta E_{c\_natural\_resource(d)} + \Delta E_{c\_natural\_resource(dz)} \tag{24.10}$$

$$\Delta E_{c\_natural\_resource(d)} = x_d(d_0 - d)pG = x_d\left(\frac{1}{l_{d0}} - \frac{1}{l_d}\right)pG \tag{24.11}$$

where $d_0 = \frac{D_0}{G_0}$, $y = \frac{D}{G}$ are the consumption quotas for natural resources. $l_{d0} = \frac{1}{d_0}$, $l_d = \frac{1}{d}$ are economic effect coefficients of natural resource utilization (represented by production).

$$\Delta E_{c\_natural\ resource(dz)}$$

(1) When the construction period is the same, but the annual investment in land is different

$$\Delta Ec\_material\ resource(dz) = \sum_{s=1}^{n_{k0}} x_d PG(d_{s0} - d_s)\frac{\theta^n j + nk0^{-s+1} - 1}{\theta^n j - 1} \tag{24.12}$$

(2) When construction period is different and the annual investment in land is different
$\Delta E_{c\_natural\ resource(dz)}$ cannot be separate from the economic benefit generated by a shorter construction period. Thus, it is calculated together with the economic benefit generated by a shorter construction period.

8. **Economic effect analysis for time**
When the construction period is shortened but the full production period remains unchanged, the formula below should be adopted:

$$\Delta E_{c\_time} = \Delta E_{c\_time\_construction} = \sum_{s=1}^{n_{ko}} \left(x_t t_{gs0} PG + x_d d_{s0} PG\right)\frac{\theta^n j + n_{k0}^{-s+1} - 1}{\theta^n j - 1}$$

$$-\sum_{s=1}^{nk}\left(x_t t_{gs} PG + x_d d_s PG\right)\frac{\theta^n j + n_{k0}^{-s+1} - 1}{\theta^n j - 1} \tag{24.13}$$

9. **Economic effect analysis for cost**

$$\Delta E_{c\_cost} = pG\Delta c = pG\frac{\Delta c}{c_0}c_0 = pG(c_0 - c) \tag{24.14}$$

10. **Economic effect analysis for structure**
The above formulas do not take into account the product structure. If the product structure is considered, the formula needs to be adjusted. The following is the adjusted formula:

$$\Delta_{Ec\_structure} = \left[\sum_{t=1}^{k}(j_l - z_t)pl\left(\frac{G_t}{G}G - \frac{G_{t0}}{G_0}G\right)\right] \tag{2.15}$$

where i represents product categories.

Chapter 25
The New Discipline System of Management of the Big Technological Economy

25.1 Introduction

This[1] is the fourth of part of the Section: Applications of the Technological Economy, the last chapter of this book. In this chapter, the author initially proposed the concept of big management science, as well as a new discipline system of management of the big technological economy.

25.2 New Concept of Management

What is management? Management is "a process of completing an activity more effectively via working with others or via others' work. The process refers to the activities that managers conduct or in which managers play a role. The roles include planning, organizing, leading and controlling."[2] Management is "one person or several people who coordinate others' activities to achieve goals that cannot be achieved by an individual. The five elements of management are planning, organizing, leading, controlling, and coordinating."[3] These two definitions are basically the same. However, the former highlights effectiveness, whereas the latter does not. The former categorizes leading and coordinating together into the feature of leading. As such, the five elements reduce to four elements. Overall, domestic scholars and overseas scholars share the same concept of management.

Is there any concept of management that is more concise and meaningful? The author initially proposed a definition for management as this: management is actually the process of managing according to reason (M. R.). Managing refers to leading, planning, organizing, and controlling. Reasoning means that the objective laws

---

[1] Xu and Da Xu [XX11].

[2] Robbins [RO96].

[3] Ma and Sun [MS85].

S. Xu, *Technological Economics*,
https://doi.org/10.1007/978-981-15-8582-1_25

that things under management must follow. In other words, management means this: leading, planning, organizing, and controlling. Each of these must follow the objective laws that all things under management must follow.

According to this new concept, management is the combination of control and rules. Control is a verb and rule is a noun. The traditional definition of management consists of controlling and organizing. Both control and organize are verbs.

For simplicity, the difference between the two concepts of management is illustrated by the following formula:

Management (traditional concept) = controlling and organizing (gerunds) = one word
Management (new concept) = controlling (verb) and rules (noun) = composite word

In English, the traditional concept of management adopts manage (verb) and managing (gerund), M for short. For the new concept of management, there is no corresponding word in English. Thus, the author proposes the term "Managing According to Reason", or MR for short.

25.3 New Study Objects

The objects of study for the concept of management are the contradictory relationship between controlling rules and the objective laws of its development and changes.

In his work "On Contradiction", Comrade Mao Zedong pointed out: "scientific studies differ by the unique contradictions possessed by the research objects. The objects in one discipline are studies of the unique contradictions in a certain field. Examples include the positive and negative numbers in mathematics, actions and reactions in mechanics, negative electricity and positive electricity in physics, decomposition and combination in chemistry, productive forces and production relations in he social sciences, struggles between classes, attack and defense in the military, idealism and materialism, and metaphysics and dialectics in philosophy. They have unique contradictions and unique natures, therefore they become objects of study in different disciplines."[4]

Accordingly, management must have its own objects of study, if it is to be treated as an independent discipline like mathematics and physics. The object of the study of management is the unique contradiction possessed by management. If management does not have any unique contradictions, management will not be an independent discipline. Actually, management has a unique contradiction, which is not possessed by other things. It is the contradiction between controlling and rules. The author argues that controlling and rules are a pair of contradictions. Between them, a contradictory and unifying relationship, a development and change relationship, and a general and individual relationship exist. The science that studies the contradictions

[4]Mao [MA66].

and unification and the rules of development and change between controlling and rules is management. In other words, the new concept of management studies the contradictory and unifying relationship between controlling and rules as well as the rules of development and change, regarding the relationship.

First, management is a contradictory entity that consists of controlling and rules. Controlling is the main body of managers. Rules are the laws followed by the objects under management. Supervisors and supervisees are a united entity; they rely on each other. Supervisors cannot exist without supervisees, and vice versa. Good control promotes the development of supervisees. Controlling can drive the development of rules. Rules can promote the improvement of controlling. In a word, controlling and rules unite together and promote each other. Second, controlling and rules are contradictory. For instance, sometimes supervisors enact good measures, but supervisees do not accept them. Sometimes supervisees are easy to manage, but their supervisors are not capable. As such, contradictions exist between controlling and rules. The contradictions will lead to fights. The fighting will improve the skills of supervisors and makes the supervisees easier to manage. In certain conditions, the reverse will happen. Third, the contradiction between control and rules mutually transforms. Sometimes, controlling is the main side of the contradiction and requires the most effort to fix. Sometimes, rules are the main side of the contradiction and require the most effort to fix. Practice has proven that undeveloped controlling can transform into developed controlling, that undeveloped rules can transform into developed rules, that controlling and rules can be improved together, and that controlling and rules can develop together. The goal of management is to extensively study the contradiction between controlling and rules and the laws that the contradiction must following diverse fields, from diverse aspects, and at diverse levels.

25.4 Narrow-Sense Management and Generalized Management

Management can be narrow and/or generalized. Narrow management focuses on studying the behaviors of managers, namely how managers conduct leading, planning, organizing, and controlling.

Generalized management science is not only a discipline, but also a big scientific system, which includes almost all scientific categories and disciplines. In addition to narrow management, generalized management includes all of the science disciplines that study the laws of objects, such as the natural sciences, engineering, philosophy, and the social sciences. Thus, all science disciplines and technologies belong to generalized management.

The ultimate goal for all disciplines is to provide scientific support for management and to serve management. Otherwise, a discipline is useless and will not survive. As mentioned above, Managing According to Reason (MR) notes that management should follow the laws of object development. If management is performed at will and does not conform to reason and to the laws of object development, its goal will not be achieved. In addition, errors will occur. These have been proven by domestic and overseas practices. To perform management, the objects under management must first be fully understood. Then the laws of object development should be studied, understood, and mastered. Finally, management should follow these laws. Such management is true management, via which the ultimate goal can be achieved. This process can be applied to scientific and technological management, to engineering project management, to economic management, to administrative management, and to all other managements in a society.

Management should follow rules that take effect within disciplines. For instance, agricultural management should follow the rules of agriculture and should be supported by agricultural scientific technologies. Industrial management should follow the rules of industries and should be supported by industrial scientific technologies. Government management should follow the rules of government and should be supported by governmental scientific technologies. Management of people should follow the rules regarding people and should be supported by scientific technologies regarding humans. In short, generalized management is a large scientific system that includes all of the science disciplines.

For simplicity, the formula below is developed to show the difference between narrow management and general management:

Narrow management	=	Science of control (leading, planning, organizing, and controlling)
	=	Management
Generalized management	=	Science of control (leading, planning, organizing, and controlling)
	=	Science of rules (natural science, engineering, philosophy, and other social sciences)

25.5 Categories of Management and Disciplines of Management

As a human behavior, management has existed since ancient times. As long as human society consists of people, management has existed, even in primitive society. In our modern society, management has become both more common and more complicated.

At the horizontal level, management exists in each unit, each company, each industry, and each department in national economy, including the primary industry, secondary industry, tertiary industry, agriculture and industry, the construction industry, geological prospecting and water conservancy, transportation, storage, the communications industry, commerce and catering, the financial and insurance industries, real estate and social services, health and sports, social welfare, the education and cultural industry, research and technical services, the Party and government administration, social organizations, military and defense, and resident living. At the vertical level, management exists in the fields of production, in circulation and consumption, and in the stages of production and construction, including tests, survey inspections, planning and design, construction, and production operations. From the perspective of region, management exists in overseas, domestic, society, region, local, rural areas, and urban communities, and includes territorial waters and territorial air space. Management also exists in business, party, government, and guanxi, including between supervisors and supervisees, leaders and the masses, producers and consumers, firms and clients, individual and individual. Therefore, management has a large scope with diverse categories.

According to the targets, management can be categorized by following the four criteria:

1. Based on section, industry, firm, and unit in national economy.
2. Based on the stages in production and construction, including input, production, circulation and consumption, tests, survey inspections, planning and design, construction, the production and operation phase of the design, construction and production operations.
3. Based on the content, including business, party and government administration, and guanxi.
4. Based on overseas, domestic, region, local, and community, including territorial waters and territorial air space.

Correspondingly, the disciplines of management can be categorized according to the target. Because there are thousands of targets, there should be thousands of disciplines of management, as well. The number is far larger than that listed in Chinese national standard disciplines directory.

Thus, generalized management has a promising future. It is the key to the social development and progress of mankind in the 21st century.

25.6 Two Elements of Management-Power and Science

Management and management science are not the same. Management is a kind of human activities and it has existed since ancient times. Management science appears in modern society. Human society, including the primitive society, the slave society, the feudal society, the capitalist society, the socialist society, and the future communist society, develops based on management in diverse fields, diverse aspects, and diverse levels. Therefore, management is powerful and the role of management is immeasurable. It is safe to say that the decisive factor for the development and progress of human society is management.

Management - true management (MR) - can not only let power plays its role, but can also let science and technology release their energy. As we know, science and technology are the first productive forces. That is to say, all science and technology can only play their roles via real management (MR). In this way, they can contribute to the development and progress of human society, serve humankind, serve the realization of the Three Represents, support the implementation of the scientific thought of development, and serve the realization of the ideals of common prosperity and equality in human society. This is what the new concept of management (MR) advocates. This is also the goal of developing a new management science.

The development of human society has proven that management is a kind of power behavior. Therefore, power is the most important factor in management. Without power, management science will not work. Even for the generalized management science, power determines its effect in practice. As we know, management relies on power. No power, no management. Meanwhile, management must follow rules and must rely on science. No science, not rules. Accordingly, management consists of two elements: power and science. Power and science are the indispensable conditions that management must have, simultaneously. Management, power, and science are a triune entity. Management does not work without science and power, and vice versa. Management, power, and science promote each other and develop together.

Management (MR) must rely on power and science. It is the integration of power and science. Power is the guarantee of management (MR), whereas science is the base of advanced management. If science works but power does not exist, management will not continue. As a result, the goal of management will not be achieved. If management only relies on power but does not follow science, it will not succeed. Thus, true Management must rely on both power and science. Neither power nor science can be neglected.

The diagram below shows the relationship between management and management science, management subject and objects, as well as power and science (Fig. 25.1).

It can be seen from the figure that management is just like a giant, whose head is the subject of management. Management science serve the giant directly. One hand represents the target of management, namely human beings. The other hand represents the environment, namely everything other than human beings. The two legs represent the two forces that support the giant. One is power and the other is science, which includes all science and technologies except for management science, such as philosophy, natural science, engineering, and the humanities.

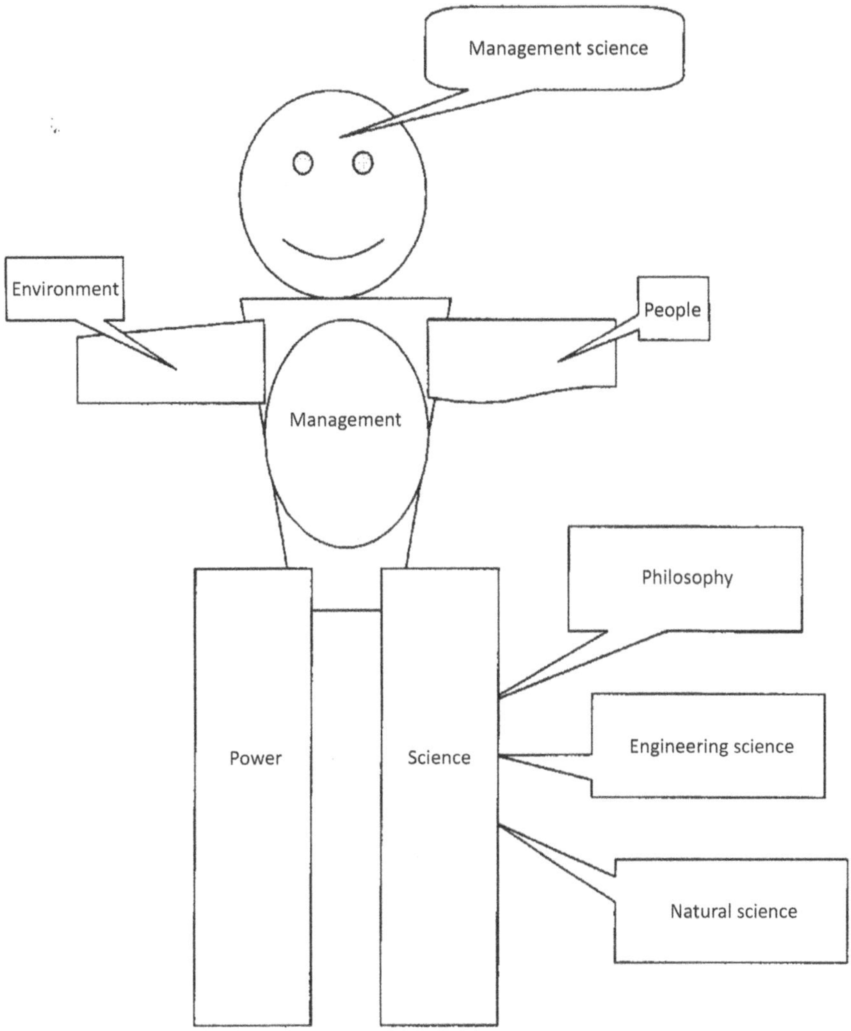

Fig. 25.1 Diagram of Management

25.7 The 21st Century Is a Century of Management (MR)

The 20th century was a great century with great achievements in social development and progress. However, it was also a century when the survival and development of human beings faced huge threats, such as a rapidly growing population, extensive resource development, and serious environmental pollution. In the 21st century, mankind is facing great challenges. Human society needs sustainable development, balanced development, high-level development, and reasonable development. As such, an increase the efficiency of resource utilization, a reduction in resource consumption, the protection of the environment, and the maintenance of the ecological balance are all required. A reduction in the gap between the rich and the poor in regions and countries, constant improvement of the material and cultural living standards of all mankind, constantly reformation and improvement of political and social systems, and a reduction in inequality are all needed. All these issues need real management (MR) and the guidance of the new scientific theory (the science of MR). If all countries, all regions, all peoples, all fields, all aspects, and all levels work hard in applying real management (MR), human society can overcome the above challenges with the existing natural resources, science and technology resources, and human resources.

Management has gone through two stages of development: scientific management and management science. In the 21st century, which is a knowledge economy era, management needs innovation and progress. It is necessary to study real management (MR) deeply and systematically. This is the task of human society, because MR is the force that drives the innovation and development of human society. In a word, there is only one science discipline in human society, namely generalized management science (the science of MR).

25.8 A New Discipline System-Big Technological Economic Management Science

Economics and management science are two different disciplines in the social sciences. According to the National Standard Disciplines Directory, economics has 36 first-level disciplines. Technological Economics is one of them. Management Science has 13 first-level disciplines. Therefore, technological economics and management science are two disciplines. Here are the reasons. First, they are at different discipline levels. Technological economics is a first-level discipline, whereas management science is a category of science. Second, their contents are different. Technological economics studies the contradictory relationship between technology and the economy, whereas management science studies leadership, planning, organization, and control. Based on these two reasons, the author thought it not appropriate to set technological economics and management as a second-level discipline in the Discipline Directory issued by the Ministry of Education. This setting is neither helpful for the development of this discipline nor helpful for the teaching and training of personnel. It is not reasonable to remove the first-level discipline technological economics in the economics category from the National Standard Disciplines Directory. It is not reasonable to put technological economics in the category of management science, either. Even worse, technological economics is set as a second-level discipline in the Discipline Directory issued by the Ministry of Education. In management science, the first-level discipline is Business Administration. Does this mean that other industries do not need technological economics? During China's Ten Years (1963–1972), the Scientific and Technological Development Plan approved by the CPC Central Committee and the State Council in 1963, listed technological economics as one of the seven Science and Technology categories. This setting puts technological economics in a higher position than disciplines. The discipline directory issued by the Ministry of Education does not follow the requirements of building Technological Economics set out by the CPC Central Committee. It even does not match the practical requirements in China. Such a setting does not follow a scientific thought of development. Thus, it will cause problems and needs revision.

According to the new theory of management science, any science, including the natural sciences, engineering, philosophy, the humanities, and the social sciences, needs management. In other words, traditional management science must be integrated with the sciences of objects that are under management. In this way, real management science, or large management science, is developed. Take technological economics as an example. The large category of Technological Economy and Management Science includes at least 30 disciplines, as shown in Table 25.1, including industrial technological economy and management, and agricultural technological economy and management, as well as resource technological economy and management. According to the theories of large management science, it is reasonable for the Ministry of Education to set Technological Economics and Management as a second-level discipline. However, Technological Economics and Management should be put in the Management Science and Economics categories simultaneously. Accordingly, the author proposes that Large Technological Economy and Management Science be an independent discipline.

Thus, new large management scientific theories are important not only for the social and economic development of human society in the 21st century, but also for the development of science and technology.

Table 25.1 Course systems of large technological economy and management science

1. Industrial technological economics	Management science
2. Energy technological economics	
3. Coal technological economics	
4. Oil technological economics	
5. Power technological economics	
6. Chemical technological economics	
7. Metallurgical technological economics	
8. Mechanical technological economics	
9. Constructional material technological economics	
10. Construction technological economics	
11. Light industry technological economics	
12. Textile technological economics	

(continued)

Table 25.1 (continued)

13. Food technological economics	
14. Agricultural technological economics	
15. Farming technological economics	
16. Forestry technological economics	
17. Husbandry technological economics	
18. Fishing technological economics	
19. Transportation technological economics	
20. Postal and Telecommunication technological economics	
21. Commercial technological economics	
22. Business technological economics	
23. Cultural, education and hygiene technological economics	
24. Scientific technological economics	
25. National defense technological economics	
26. Logistics technological economics	
27. Consumption technological economics	
28. Resource technological economics	
29. Environment technological economics	
30. Productive force layout technological economics	

References

[XX11] Xu, S., & Da Xu, L. (2011). Management: a scientific discipline for humanity. Information Technology and Management, 12(2), 51–54.
[RO96] Robbins, S. P. (1996). Management (Edition 4). China Renmin University Press.
[MS85] Ma, H. & Sun. S. Q./(1985). Voluminous Dictionary for Economy and Management. China Social Science Publishing House.
[MA66] Mao, Z. D. (1966). Mao Zedong Anthology. People's Press. Edition one. Page 297.

Appendix A
Terms and Symbols in Technological Economics

Name of index	Chinese pinyin	Symbol	Computer symbol
Economic effects	Jingjixiaoguo	E	E
Effects	Xiaoguo	X	X
Labor consumption	Laodongxiaohaoliang	L	L
Economic performance	Jingjixiaoyi	E−	E1
Economic efficiency	Jingjixiaolv	E+	E2
Income	Xiaoyi (Shouru)	S	S
Expenditure	Feiyong (Zhichu)	Z	Z
Production (labor)	Shengchanliang (Laowuliang)	G	G
Price	Jiage	j_g	JGX
Value	Jiazhi	j_z	JZX
Output value (industrial output value)	Chanzhi	J_g	JG
Labor income	Shouru	S	S
Cost	Chengbenfeiyong (Chengben)	C	C
Material consumption	Wuzixiaohaoliang	W	W
Labor occupation	Laodongli (RenYuan) zhanyongliang	R	R
Amount of transportation capacity employed	Yunlizhanyongliang	Y	Y
Investment expenses	Touzifeiyong (zijinzhanyongliang)	T	T
Amount of natural resources used	Ziranziyuanshiyongliang	D	D
Economic effect coefficient of material utilization	Wuziliyongjingjixiaoguoxishu	x_W	XW

(continued)

S. Xu, *Technological Economics*,
https://doi.org/10.1007/978-981-15-8582-1

(continued)

Name of index	Chinese pinyin	Symbol	Computer symbol
Economic effect coefficient of labor utilization	Laodongliliyongjingjixiaoguoxishu	x_r	XR
Economic effect coefficient of capacity utilization	Yunliliyongjingjixiaoguoxishu	x_y	XY
Economic effect coefficient of investment utilization	Touziliyongjingjixiaoguoxishu	x_t	XT
Economic effect coefficient of natural resource utilization	Ziranziyuanliyongjingjixiaoguoxishu	x_d	XD
Economic effect coefficient of capital utilization	Zijinliyongjingjixiaoguoxishu	x_z	XZ
Calculation period	Jisuanqi	n_j	NJ
Construction period	Jiansheqi	n_k	NK
Period of Service	Fuwuqi	n_f	NF
Ramp up period	Dachanqi	n_d	ND
Interest factor	Benlihexishu	θ	BLH
Social labor productivity I	Shehuilaodongshengchanlv I	E_a	EA
Social labor productivity II	Shehuilaodongshengchanlv II	Eb	EB
Social net income	Shehuichunshouru	E_c	EC
Social national income	Shehuiguominshouru	Ed	ED
Social additional labor productivity I	Shehuifujialaodongshengchanlv I	E_{af}	EAF
Social additional labor productivity II	Shehuifujialaodongshengchanlv II	E_{bf}	EBF
Social additional net income rate	Shehuifujiachunshourulv	E_{cf}	ECF
Added social national income rate	Shehuifujiaguominshourulv	E_{df}	EDF
Enterprise excess labor productivity	Qiyechaoelaodongshengchanlv	E_e	EE
Corporate excess profit	Qiyechaoelirun	E_f	EF
Enterprise additional labor productivity	Qiyefujialaodongshengchanlv	E_{ef}	EEF
Additional profit margin	Qiyefujialirunlv	E_{ff}	EFF
Net income	Chunshouyi	S_c	SC

(continued)

(continued)

Name of index	Chinese pinyin	Symbol	Computer symbol
Additional net income	Fujiachunshouyi	ΔS_c	SCF
Fixed assets	Gudingzichan	T_g	TG
Working capital	Liudongzijin	T_l	TL
Converted investment occupation	Zhesuantouzizhanyong	T_z	TZ
Converted fixed assets	Zhesuangudingzichan	T_{gz}	TGZ
Scrap value of fixed assets	Gudingzichancanzhi	T_c	TC
Converted fixed assets residual	Zhesuangudingzichancanzhi	T_{cz}	TCZ
Basic depreciation deduction for fixed assets	Gudingzichanjibenzhejiukouchu	T_j	TJ
Convert natural resource occupation	Zhesuanziranziyuanzhanyong	D_z	DZ
Raw material cost	Yuancailiaofeiyong	C_{yc}	CYC
Secondary raw materials cost	Fuzhuyuancailiaofeiyong	C_{fy}	CFY
Energy cost	Nengyuanfeiyong	C_n	CN
Labor charge	Gongzifeiyong	C_g	CG
Surcharge on wages	Gongzifujiafeiyong	C_{gf}	CGF
Basic depreciation expense	Jibenzhejiufeiyong	C_j	CJ
Overhaul depreciation expenses	Daxiuzhejiufeiyong	C_{dx}	CDX
Comprehensive depreciation expense	Zonghezhejiufeiyong	C_z	CZ
Basic depreciation rate	Jibenzhejiulv	L_j	LJ
Major repair depreciation rate	Daxiuzhejiulv	L_{dx}	LDX
Comprehensive depreciation rate	Zonghezhejiulv	L_z	LZ
Other expenses	Qitafeiyong	C_q	CQ
Operating expense	Jingyingfeiyong	C_{jy}	CJY
Fees for materials consumption	Wuzixiaohaofei	C_w	CW
Cost of employed transportation capacity	Yunlizhanyongfei	C_y	CY
Fees for use of labor	Laodonglizhanyongfei	C_r	CR
Fund possession cost	Zijinzhanyongfei	C_t	CT

(continued)

(continued)

Name of index	Chinese pinyin	Symbol	Computer symbol
Fees for using natural resources	Ziranziyuanshiyongfei	C_d	CD
Waste loss fee	Feipinsunshifei	C_{fp}	CFP
Production operation expenses	Chejianjingfei	C_{cj}	CCJ
Enterprise administration expense	Qiyeguanlifei	C_{qg}	CQG
Sales expenses	Xiaoshoufei	C_{xs}	CXS
Time value coefficient	Shizhixishu (Zhongzhixishu)	X_s	XS
Discount factor	Zhexianxishu	X_x	XX
Cumulative time value coefficient	Leijishizhixishu	X_{ls}	XLS
Annual mean coefficient of cumulative time value	Leijishizhinianpingjunxishu	X_{lsp}	XL5P
Cumulative discount coefficient	Leijizhexianxishu	X_{lx}	XLX
Annual mean coefficient of cumulative present value	Leijixianzhinianpingjunxishu	X_{lxp}	XLXP
Total cost	Zongxiaohaofeiyong	$Z_{\sum}$	Z∑
Annual cost	Nianxiaohaofeiyong	Z	Z
Additional investment national income rate	Fujiatouziguominshourulv	X_{ftg}	XFTG
Additional investment net income rate	Fujiatouzichunshourulv	X_{ftc}	XFTC
Additional investment profit rate	Fujiatouzilirunlv	X_{ftl}	XFTL
Investment net output rate	Touziguominshourulv	X_{tg}	XTG
Investment net income rate	Touzichunshourulv	X_{tc}	XTC
Return on investment	Touzilirunlv	X_{tl}	XTL
Investment excess national income rate	Touzichaoeguominshuirulv	L_{tg}	LbG
Investment excess tax rate	Touzichaoelishuilv	L_{tc}	LTC
Excess return on investment	Touzichaoelirunlv	L_{tl}	LTL
Additional payback period	Fujiatouzihuishouqi	n_{fc}	NFC

(continued)

(continued)

Name of index	Chinese pinyin	Symbol	Computer symbol
Investment recovery period	Touzihuishouqi	n_c	NC
Domestic competitiveness	Guoneijingzhengli	E_{gn}	EGN
International Competitiveness	Guojijingzhengli	E_{gj}	EGJ
Swap Rate	Huanhuilv	L_{hh}	LHH
Number of scheme numbers	Fanganbianhaoshu	i	I
Number of years	Nianshu	n	N
Maximum	Zuida	ZD	ZD
Minimum	Zuixiao	ZX	ZX

Note 1. Generally, the first letter of Chinese pinyin is used. When the first letter is the same, the most commonly used main indicator name is given priority, and other indicators use symbols that people are accustomed to using as much as possible

2. For the same letter, the uppercase symbol represents the total quantity indicator, and the lowercase symbol represents the unit quantity indicator. For example, the symbol C (upper case) represents the total cost, while c (lower case) represents the unit cost, T represents the total investment expense, and t represents the unit investment expense. Others and so on

3. Use lowercase letters in the footnotes, try to use one letter, preferably the first letter of the Chinese Pinyin, and when there are repetitions, use other symbols that are commonly used

Appendix B
Time Factor Calculator

See Tables B.1, B.2, B.3, B.4, B.5, B.6, B.7, B.8, B.9, B.10, B.11, B.12, B.13, B.14, B.15, B.16, B.17, B.18, B.19, B.20, B.21, B.22, B.23, and B.24.

S. Xu, *Technological Economics*,
https://doi.org/10.1007/978-981-15-8582-1

Table B.1 Time value coefficient x_1

Years n	Time value coefficient $x_1 = \theta^n = (1 + x_2)^n$													
	$x_z =$ 0.01	$x_z =$ 0.02	$x_z =$ 0.03	$x_z =$ 0.04	$x_z =$ 0.05	$x_z =$ 0.06	$x_z =$ 0.07	$x_z =$ 0.08	$x_z =$ 0.09	$x_z = 0.1$	$x_z =$ 0.125	$x_z = 0.15$	$x_z = 0.20$	$x_z = 0.30$
1	1.01	1.02	1.03	1.04	1.05	1.06	1.07	1.08	1.09	1.1	1.125	1.15	1.2	1.3
2	1.02	1.04	1.061	1.082	1.103	1.124	1.145	1.166	1.188	1.21	1.266	1.322	1.44	1.69
3	1.03	1.061	1.093	1.125	1.158	1.191	1.225	1.26	1.295	1.331	1.424	1.521	1.728	2.197
4	1.041	1.082	1.126	1.17	1.216	1.262	1.311	1.36	1.412	1.464	1.602	1.749	2.074	2.856
5	1.051	1.104	1.159	1.217	1.276	1.338	1.403	1.469	1.539	1.611	1.802	2.011	2.488	3.713
6	1.062	1.126	1.194	1.265	1.34	1.419	1.501	1.587	1.677	1.772	2.027	2.313	2.986	4.827
7	1.072	1.149	1.23	1.316	1.407	1.504	1.606	1.714	1.828	1.949	2.281	2.66	3.583	6.275
8	1.083	1.172	1.267	1.369	1.477	1.594	1.718	1.851	1.993	2.144	2.566	3.059	4.3	8.157
9	1.094	1.195	1.305	1.423	1.551	1.689	1.838	1.999	2.172	2.358	2.887	3.518	5.16	10.604
10	1.105	1.219	1.344	1.48	1.629	1.791	1.967	2.159	2.367	2.594	3.247	4.046	6.192	13.786
11	1.116	1.243	1.384	1.539	1.71	1.898	2.105	2.332	2.85	2.853	3.653	4.652	7.43	17.922
12	1.127	1.268	1.426	1.601	1.796	2.012	2.252	2.518	2.813	3.138	4.11	5.35	8.916	23.298
13	1.138	1.294	1.469	1.665	1.886	2.133	2.41	2.72	3.066	3.452	4.624	6.153	10.699	30.288
14	1.149	1.319	1.513	1.732	1.98	2.261	2.579	2.937	3.342	3.797	5.202	7.076	12.839	39.374
15	1.161	1.346	1.558	1.801	2.079	2.397	2.759	3.172	3.642	4.177	5.852	8.137	15.407	51.186
16	1.173	1.373	1.605	1.873	2.183	2.54	2.952	3.426	3.97	4.595	6.853	9.358	18.488	66.542

(continued)

Table B.1 (continued)

Years n	Time value coefficient $x_1 = \theta^n = (1 + x_2)^n$													
	$x_z =$ 0.01	$x_z =$ 0.02	$x_z =$ 0.03	$x_z =$ 0.04	$x_z =$ 0.05	$x_z =$ 0.06	$x_z =$ 0.07	$x_z =$ 0.08	$x_z =$ 0.09	$x_z = 0.1$	$x_z =$ 0.125	$x_z = 0.15$	$x_z = 0.20$	$x_z = 0.30$
17	1.184	1.4	1.653	1.948	2.292	2.693	3.159	3.7	4.328	5.054	7.406	10.761	22.186	86.504
18	1.196	1.428	1.702	2.026	2.407	2.854	3.83	3.996	4.717	5.56	8.332	12.375	26.623	112.455
19	1.208	1.457	1.754	2.107	2.527	3.026	3.617	4.316	5.142	6.116	9.373	14.232	31.948	146.192
20	1.22	1.486	1.806	2.191	2.653	3.207	3.87	4.661	5.604	6.727	10.545	16.367	38.338	190.05
25	1.282	1.641	2.094	2.666	3.386	4.292	5.427	6.848	8.623	10.835	19.003	32.919	95.396	705.641
30	1.348	1.811	2.427	3.243	4.322	5.743	7.612	10.063	13.268	17.449	34.243	66.212	237.376	2619.996
35	1.147	2	2.814	3.946	5.516	7.686	10.677	14.785	20.414	28.102	61.708	133.176	590.668	9727.86
40	1.489	2.208	3.262	4.801	7.04	10.282	14.974	21.725	31.409	45.259	111.199	267.86	1469.772	36118.865
45	1.565	2.438	3.782	5.841	8.985	13.765	21.002	31.92	48.327	72.89	200.384	538.769	3657.262	134106.817
50	1.645	2.692	4.384	7.107	11.467	18.42	29.457	46.902	74.358	117.391	361.099	1083.657	9100.438	497929.223

Table B.2 Discount factor x_2

Year n	Discount factor $x_2 = \frac{1}{\theta^n} = \frac{1}{(1+x_2)^n}$												
	$x_z =$ 0.01	$x_z =$ 0.02	$x_z =$ 0.03	$x_z =$ 0.04	$x_z =$ 0.05	$x_z =$ 0.06	$x_z =$ 0.07	$x_z = 0.08$	$x_z =$ 0.09	$x_z = 0.1$	$x_z =$ 0.125	$x_z =$ 0.15	$x_z =$ 0.20	$x_z = 0.30$
1	0.9901	0.9804	0.9709	0.9615	0.9524	0.9434	0.9346	0.9259	0.9174	0.9091	0.8889	0.8696	0.8333	0.769
2	0.9803	0.9612	0.9426	0.9246	0.907	0.89	0.8734	0.8573	0.8417	0.8264	0.7901	0.7561	0.6944	0.5917
3	0.9706	0.9423	0.9151	0.889	0.8638	0.8396	0.8163	0.7938	0.7722	0.7513	0.7023	0.6575	0.5787	0.4552
4	0.961	0.9238	0.8885	0.8548	0.8227	0.7921	0.7629	0.735	0.7084	0.683	0.6243	0.5718	0.4823	0.3501
5	0.9515	0.9057	0.8626	0.8219	0.7835	0.7473	0.713	0.6806	0.6499	0.6209	0.5549	0.4972	0.4019	0.2693
6	0.942	0.888	0.8375	0.7903	0.7462	0.705	0.6663	0.6302	0.5963	0.5645	0.4933	0.4323	0.3349	0.2072
7	0.9327	0.8706	0.8131	0.7599	0.7107	0.6651	0.6227	0.6302	0.5963	0.5645	0.4933	0.4323	0.3349	0.2072
8	0.9235	0.8535	0.7894	0.7307	0.6768	0.6274	0.582	0.5403	0.5019	0.4665	0.3897	0.3269	0.2326	0.1226
9	0.9143	0.8368	0.7664	0.7026	0.6446	0.5919	0.5439	0.5002	0.4604	0.4241	0.3464	0.2843	0.1938	0.0943
10	0.9053	0.8203	0.7441	0.6756	0.6139	0.5584	0.5083	0.4632	0.4224	0.3855	0.3079	0.2472	0.1615	0.0725
11	0.8963	0.8043	0.7224	0.6496	0.5847	0.5268	0.4751	0.4289	0.3875	0.3505	0.2737	0.2149	0.1346	0.0558
12	0.8874	0.7885	0.7014	0.6246	0.5568	0.497	0.444	0.3971	0.3555	0.3186	0.2433	0.1869	0.1122	0.0429
13	0.8787	0.773	0.681	0.6006	0.5303	0.4688	0.415	0.3677	0.3232	0.2897	0.2163	0.1625	0.0935	0.033
14	0.87	0.7579	0.6611	0.5775	0.5051	0.4423	0.3878	0.3405	0.2992	0.2633	0.1922	0.1413	0.0779	0.0254
15	0.8613	0.743	0.6419	0.5553	0.481	0.4173	0.3624	0.3152	0.2745	0.2394	0.1709	0.1229	0.0649	0.0195
16	0.8528	0.7284	0.6232	0.5339	0.4581	0.3936	0.3387	0.2919	0.2519	0.2176	0.1519	0.1069	0.0541	0.015

(continued)

Table B.2 (continued)

Year n	Discount factor $x_2 = \frac{1}{\theta^n} = \frac{1}{(1+x_2)^n}$													
	$x_z =$ 0.01	$x_z =$ 0.02	$x_z =$ 0.03	$x_z =$ 0.04	$x_z =$ 0.05	$x_z =$ 0.06	$x_z =$ 0.07	$x_z = 0.08$	$x_z =$ 0.09	$x_z = 0.1$	$x_z =$ 0.125	$x_z =$ 0.15	$x_z =$ 0.20	$x_z = 0.30$
17	0.8444	0.7142	0.605	0.5134	0.4363	0.3714	0.3166	0.2703	0.2311	0.1978	1.135	0.0929	0.0451	0.0116
18	0.836	0.7002	0.5874	0.4936	0.4155	0.3503	0.2959	0.2502	0.212	0.1799	0.12	0.0808	0.0376	0.0089
19	0.8277	0.6864	0.5703	0.4746	0.3957	0.3305	0.2765	0.2317	0.1945	0.1635	0.1067	0.0703	0.0313	0.0068
20	0.8195	0.673	0.5537	0.4564	0.3769	0.3118	0.2584	0.21455	0.1784	0.1486	0.0948	0.0611	0.0261	0.0053
25	0.7798	0.6095	0.4776	0.3751	0.2953	0.233	0.1842	0.146	0.116	0.0923	0.0526	0.0304	0.0105	0.0014
30	0.7419	0.5521	0.412	0.3083	0.2314	0.1741	0.1314	0.0994	0.0745	0.0573	0.0292	0.0151	0.0042	0.0004
35	0.7059	0.5	0.3554	0.2534	0.1813	0.1301	0.0937	0.0676	0.049	0.0356	0.0162	0.0075	0.0017	0.0001
40	0.6717	0.4529	0.3066	0.2083	0.042	0.0972	0.0668	0.013	0.0318	0.0221	0.009	0.0037	0.0007	0.000037
45	0.6391	0.4102	0.2644	0.1712	0.1113	0.0727	0.0476	0.0313	0.0207	0.0137	0.005	0.0019	0.0009	0.000007
50	0.608	0.3715	0.2281	0.1407	0.0872	0.0543	0.0339	0.0213	0.0134	0.0085	0.0028	0.0009	0.0001	0.000002

Table B.3 Cumulative time value coefficient x_3

Year n	Cumulative time value coefficient $x_3 = \frac{\theta^n - 1}{\theta - 1}$													
	$x_z =$ 0.01	$x_z =$ 0.02	$x_z =$ 0.03	$x_z =$ 0.04	$x_z =$ 0.05	$x_z =$ 0.06	$x_z =$ 0.07	$x_z =$ 0.08	$x_z =$ 0.09	$x_z = 0.1$	$x_z =$ 0.125	$x_z =$ 0.15	$x_z = 0.20$	$x_z = 0.30$
1	1	1	1	1	1	1	1	1	1	1	1	1	1	1
2	2.01	2.02	2.03	2.04	2.05	2.06	2.07	2.08	2.09	2.1	2.125	2.15	2.2	2.3
3	3.03	3.06	3.031	3.122	3.153	3.184	3.215	3.246	3.278	3.31	3.391	3.472	3.64	3.99
4	4.06	4.122	4.184	4.246	4.31	4.375	4.44	4.506	4.573	4.641	4.814	4.993	5.368	6.187
5	5.101	5.204	5.309	5.416	5.526	5.637	5.751	5.867	5.985	6.105	6.416	6.742	7.442	9.043
6	6.152	6.308	6.468	6.633	6.802	6.975	7.153	7.336	7.523	7.716	8.218	8.754	9.93	12.756
7	7.214	7.434	7.662	7.898	8.142	8.394	8.654	8.923	9.2	9.487	10.246	11.067	12.916	17.583
8	8.286	8.583	8.892	9.214	9.549	9.897	10.26	10.637	11.028	11.436	12.526	13.727	16.499	23.858
9	9.369	9.755	10.159	10.583	11.027	11.491	11.978	12.488	13.021	13.579	15.092	16.786	20.799	32.015
10	10.462	10.95	11.464	12.006	12.578	13.181	13.816	14.487	15.193	15.937	17.979	20.304	25.959	42.619
11	11.567	12.169	12.808	13.486	14.207	14.972	15.784	16.645	17.56	18.531	21.226	24.349	32.15	56.405
12	12.683	13.412	14.192	15.026	15.917	16.87	17.888	18.977	20.141	21.384	24.879	29.002	39.58	74.327
13	13.809	14.68	15.618	16.627	17.713	18.882	20.141	21.495	22.953	24.523	28.989	34.352	48.497	97.625
14	14.947	15.974	17.086	18.292	19.599	21.015	22.55	24.215	26.019	27.975	33.613	40.505	59.196	127.913
15	16.097	17.293	18.599	20.024	21.579	23.276	25.129	27.152	29.361	31.772	38.814	47.58	72.035	167.286
16	17.258	18.639	20.157	21.825	23.657	25.673	27.888	30.324	33.003	35.95	44.666	55.717	87.442	218.472

(continued)

Table B.3 (continued)

Year n	Cumulative time value coefficient $x_3 = \frac{\theta^n - 1}{\theta - 1}$													
	$x_z =$ 0.01	$x_z =$ 0.02	$x_z =$ 0.03	$x_z =$ 0.04	$x_z =$ 0.05	$x_z =$ 0.06	$x_z =$ 0.07	$x_z =$ 0.08	$x_z =$ 0.09	$x_z = 0.1$	$x_z =$ 0.125	$x_z =$ 0.15	$x_z = 0.20$	$x_z = 0.30$
17	18.43	20.012	21.762	23.698	25.84	28.213	30.84	33.75	36.974	40.545	51.249	65.075	105.931	285.014
18	19.615	21.412	23.414	25.645	28.132	30.906	33.999	37.45	41.301	45.599	58.665	75.836	128.117	371.518
19	20.811	22.841	25.117	27.671	30.539	33.76	37.379	41.446	46.018	51.159	66.987	88.212	154.74	483.973
20	22.019	24.297	26.87	29.778	33.066	36.786	40.995	45.762	51.16	57.275	76.361	102.443	186.688	630.165
25	28.243	32.03	36.459	41.646	47.727	54.865	63.249	73.106	84.701	98.347	144.021	212.793	471.981	2348.803
30	34.785	40.568	47.575	56.085	66.439	79.058	94.461	113.283	136.308	164.494	265.946	434.744	1191.881	8729.985
35	41.66	49.994	60.462	73.652	90.32	111.435	138.237	172.317	215.711	271.024	485.66	881.168	2948.339	32422.9
40	48.886	60.402	75.401	95.026	120.8	154.762	199.635	259.057	337.882	442.593	881.592	1779.1	7343.9	120392.9
45	56.481	71.893	92.72	121.029	159.7	212.744	285.749	386.506	525.859	718.905	1595.074	8585.1	18281.3	447019.4
50	64.463	84.579	112.797	152.667	209.348	290.336	406.529	573.77	815.084	1163.909	2880.791	7217.7	45497.1	1,659,760

Table B.4 Annual mean coefficient of cumulative time value x_4

Year n	Annual mean coefficient of cumulative time value $x_4 = \frac{\theta-1}{\theta^n-1}$													
	$x_z =$ 0.01	$x_z =$ 0.02	$x_z =$ 0.03	$x_z =$ 0.04	$x_z =$ 0.05	$x_z =$ 0.06	$x_z =$ 0.07	$x_z =$ 0.08	$x_z =$ 0.09	$x_z = 0.1$	$x_z =$ 0.125	$x_z =$ 0.15	$x_z =$ 0.20	$x_z =$ 0.30
1	1	1	1	1	1	1	1	1	1	1	1	1	1	1
2	0.49751	0.49505	0.49261	0.4902	0.4878	0.48544	0.48309	0.48077	0.47847	0.47619	0.47059	0.46512	0.45455	0.43478
3	0.33002	0.32675	0.32353	0.32035	0.31721	0.31411	0.31105	0.30803	0.30505	0.30211	0.29493	0.28798	0.27473	0.25063
4	0.24628	0.24262	0.23903	0.23549	0.23201	0.22859	0.22523	0.22192	0.21867	0.21547	0.20771	0.20026	0.18629	0.16163
5	0.19604	0.19216	0.18835	0.18463	0.18097	0.1774	0.17389	0.17046	0.16709	0.1638	0.15585	0.14832	0.13438	0.11058
6	0.16255	0.15853	0.1546	0.15076	0.14702	0.14336	0.1398	0.13632	0.13292	0.12961	0.12168	0.11424	0.10071	0.07839
7	0.13863	0.13451	0.13051	0.12661	0.12282	0.11914	0.11555	0.11207	0.10869	0.10541	0.0976	0.09036	0.07742	0.05687
8	0.12069	0.11651	0.11246	0.10853	0.10472	0.10104	0.09747	0.09401	0.09067	0.08744	0.07983	0.07285	0.06061	0.04192
9	0.10674	0.10252	0.09843	0.09449	0.09069	0.08702	0.08349	0.08008	0.0768	0.07364	0.06626	0.05957	0.04808	0.03124
10	0.09558	0.09132	0.08723	0.08329	0.0795	0.07587	0.07238	0.06903	0.06582	0.06275	0.05562	0.04925	0.03852	0.02346
11	0.08645	0.08218	0.07808	0.07415	0.07039	0.06679	0.06336	0.06008	0.05695	0.05396	0.04711	0.04107	0.0311	0.01773
12	0.07885	0.07456	0.07046	0.06655	0.06283	0.05928	0.0559	0.0527	0.04965	0.04676	0.04019	0.03448	0.02526	0.01345
13	0.07241	0.06812	0.06403	0.06014	0.05646	0.05296	0.04965	0.04652	0.04357	0.04087	0.0345	0.02911	0.02062	0.01024
14	0.0669	0.0626	0.05853	0.05467	0.05102	0.04758	0.04434	0.0413	0.03843	0.03575	0.02975	0.02469	0.01689	0.00782
15	0.06212	0.05783	0.05377	0.04994	0.04634	0.04296	0.03979	0.03683	0.03406	0.03147	0.02576	0.02102	0.01388	0.00598
16	0.05794	0.05365	0.04961	0.04582	0.04227	0.03895	0.03586	0.03298	0.0303	0.02782	0.02239	0.01795	0.01144	0.00458

(continued)

Table B.4 (continued)

Year n	Annual mean coefficient of cumulative time value $x_4 = \frac{\theta-1}{\theta^n-1}$													
	$x_z =$ 0.01	$x_z =$ 0.02	$x_z =$ 0.03	$x_z =$ 0.04	$x_z =$ 0.05	$x_z =$ 0.06	$x_z =$ 0.07	$x_z =$ 0.08	$x_z =$ 0.09	$x_z = 0.1$	$x_z =$ 0.125	$x_z =$ 0.15	$x_z =$ 0.20	$x_z =$ 0.30
17	0.05426	0.04997	0.04595	0.0422	0.0387	0.03544	0.03243	0.02963	0.02705	0.02466	0.01951	0.01537	0.00944	0.00351
18	0.05098	0.0467	0.04271	0.03899	0.03555	0.03236	0.02941	0.0267	0.02421	0.02193	0.01705	0.01319	0.00781	0.00269
19	0.04805	0.04378	0.03981	0.03614	0.03275	0.02962	0.02675	0.02413	0.02173	0.01955	0.01493	0.01134	0.00646	0.00209
20	0.04542	0.04116	0.03722	0.03358	0.03024	0.02718	0.02439	0.02185	0.01955	0.01746	0.0131	0.00976	0.00536	0.00157
25	0.03541	0.03122	0.02743	0.02401	0.02095	0.00182	0.01581	0.01368	0.01181	0.01017	0.00694	0.0047	0.00212	0.00043
30	0.02875	0.02465	0.02102	0.01783	0.01505	0.01265	0.01059	0.00883	0.00734	0.00608	0.00376	0.0023	0.00085	0.00011
35	0.024	0.02	0.01654	0.01358	0.01107	0.00897	0.00723	0.0058	0.00464	0.00369	0.00206	0.00113	0.00034	0.00003
40	0.02046	0.01656	0.01326	0.01052	0.00828	0.00646	0.00501	0.00386	0.00296	0.00226	0.00113	0.00056	0.00014	0.00008
45	0.01771	0.01391	0.01079	0.00826	0.00626	0.0047	0.0035	0.00259	0.0019	0.00139	0.00063	0.00028	0.00005	0.00002
50	0.01551	0.01182	0.00887	0.00655	0.00478	0.00344	0.00246	0.00174	0.00123	0.00086	0.00035	0.00014	0.00002	0.00006

Table B.5 Cumulative discount coefficient x_5

Year n	Cumulative discount coefficient $x_5 = \frac{\theta^n - 1}{(\theta - 1)\theta^n}$													
	$x_z =$ 0.01	$x_z =$ 0.02	$x_z =$ 0.03	$x_z =$ 0.04	$x_z =$ 0.05	$x_z =$ 0.06	$x_z =$ 0.07	$x_z =$ 0.08	$x_z =$ 0.09	$x_z = 0.1$	$x_z =$ 0.125	$x_z =$ 0.15	$x_z =$ 0.20	$x_z =$ 0.30
1	0.99	0.98	0.971	0.962	0.952	0.943	0.935	0.926	0.917	0.909	0.889	0.87	0.833	0.769
2	1.97	1.942	1.913	1.886	1.859	1.833	1.808	1.783	1.759	1.679	1.736	1.626	1.528	1.361
3	2.941	2.884	2.829	2.775	2.723	2.673	2.624	2.577	2.531	2.487	2.381	2.283	2.106	1.816
4	3.902	3.808	3.717	3.63	3.546	3.465	3.387	3.312	3.239	3.17	3.005	2.855	2.589	2.166
5	4.853	4.713	4.58	4.452	4.329	4.212	4.1	3.993	3.389	3.791	3.56	3.352	2.991	2.435
6	5.795	5.601	5.417	5.242	5.076	4.917	4.767	4.623	4.486	4.355	4.054	3.784	3.326	2.643
7	6.728	6.472	6.23	6.002	5.786	5.582	5.389	5.206	5.033	4.868	4.492	4.16	3.605	2.802
8	7.652	7.325	7.02	6.733	6.463	6.21	5.971	5.747	5.533	5.335	4.882	4.487	3.837	2.925
9	8.566	8.162	7.786	7.435	7.108	6.802	6.515	6.247	5.995	5.759	5.228	4.772	4.031	3.019
10	9.471	8.983	8.53	8.111	7.722	7.36	7.024	6.71	6.419	6.144	5.537	5.019	4.192	3.091
11	10.368	9.787	9.253	8.76	8.306	7.887	7.499	7.139	6.806	6.495	5.811	5.234	4.327	3.147
12	11.255	10.575	9.954	9.385	8.863	8.384	7.943	7.536	7.16	6.814	6.053	5.421	4.439	3.19
13	12.134	11.348	10.635	9.986	9.394	8.853	8.358	7.904	7.486	7.103	6.269	5.583	4.533	3.223
14	13.004	12.106	11.296	10.563	9.899	9.295	8.745	8.244	7.785	7.367	6.462	5.724	4.611	3.249
15	13.865	12.849	11.938	11.118	10.38	9.712	9.108	8.559	8.062	7.606	6.633	5.847	4.675	3.268
16	14.718	13.578	12.561	11.652	10.838	10.106	9.447	8.851	8.313	7.824	6.785	5.954	4.73	3.283

(continued)

Table B.5 (continued)

Year n	Cumulative discount coefficient $x_5 = \frac{\theta^n - 1}{(\theta-1)\theta^n}$												
	$x_z =$ 0.01	$x_z =$ 0.02	$x_z =$ 0.03	$x_z =$ 0.04	$x_z =$ 0.05	$x_z =$ 0.06	$x_z =$ 0.07	$x_z =$ 0.08	$x_z =$ 0.09	$x_z = 0.1$	$x_z =$ 0.125	$x_z =$ 0.15	$x_z =$ 0.20	$x_z =$ 0.30
17	15.562	14.292	13.166	12.166	11.274	10.477	9.763	9.122	8.543	8.022	6.92	6.047	4.775	3.295
18	16.398	14.992	13.754	12.659	11.69	10.828	10.059	9.372	8.756	8.201	7.04	6.128	4.812	3.304
19	17.226	15.678	14.324	13.134	12.085	11.158	10.336	9.604	8.949	8.365	7.147	6.198	4.844	3.311
20	18.046	16.351	14.877	13.59	12.462	11.47	10.594	9.818	9.129	8.514	7.241	6.259	4.87	3.316
25	22.023	19.523	17.413	15.622	14.094	12.783	11.654	10.675	9.823	9.077	7.579	6.464	4.948	3.329
30	25.808	22.396	19.6	17.292	15.372	13.765	12.409	11.655	10.567	9.644	7.87	6.617	4.992	3.333
35	29.409	24.999	21.487	18.665	16.374	14.498	13.948	11.655	10.567	9.644	7.87	6.617	4.992	3.333
40	32.835	27.355	23.115	19.793	17.159	15.046	13.332	11.925	10.757	9.779	7.928	6.642	4.997	3.333
45	36.095	29.49	24.519	20.72	17.774	15.456	13.606	12.108	10.881	9.863	7.96	6.654	4.999	3.333
50	39.196	31.424	25.73	21.482	18.256	15.762	13.801	12.233	10.962	9.915	7.978	6.661	4.999	3.333

Table B.6 Annual average coefficient of cumulative present value x_6

Year n	Annual average coefficient of cumulative present value $x_6 = \frac{(\theta-1)\theta^n}{\theta^n-1}$													
	$x_z =$ 0.01	$x_z =$ 0.02	$x_z =$ 0.03	$x_z =$ 0.04	$x_z =$ 0.05	$x_z =$ 0.06	$x_z =$ 0.07	$x_z =$ 0.08	$x_z =$ 0.09	$x_z = 0.1$	$x_z =$ 0.125	$x_z =$ 0.15	$x_z =$ 0.20	$x_z =$ 0.30
1	1.01	1.02	1.03	1.04	1.05	1.06	1.07	1.08	1.09	1.1	1.125	1.15	1.2	1.3
2	0.50751	0.51505	0.52261	0.5302	0.5378	0.54544	0.55309	0.56077	0.5685	0.57619	0.59559	0.61512	0.65455	0.73475
3	0.34002	0.34675	0.35353	0.36035	0.36721	0.37411	0.38105	0.38803	0.3951	0.40211	0.41999	0.43798	0.47473	0.55066
4	0.25628	0.26262	0.26903	0.27549	0.28204	0.28859	0.29523	0.30192	0.30874	0.31547	0.33058	0.35027	0.38629	0.46168
5	0.20604	0.21216	0.21835	0.22463	0.23097	0.2374	0.24389	0.25046	0.25714	0.2638	0.2809	0.29832	0.33438	0.41068
6	0.17255	0.17853	0.1846	0.19076	0.19702	0.20336	0.2098	0.21632	0.22292	0.22961	0.24667	0.26424	0.30071	0.37836
7	0.14863	0.15451	0.16051	0.16661	0.17282	0.17914	0.18555	0.19207	0.19869	0.20541	0.22262	0.24036	0.27742	0.35689
8	0.13069	0.13651	0.14246	0.14853	0.15472	0.16104	0.16747	0.17401	0.18073	0.18744	0.20483	0.22285	0.26061	0.34188
9	0.11674	0.12252	0.12843	0.13449	0.14069	0.14702	0.15349	0.16008	0.16681	0.17364	0.19128	0.20657	0.24808	0.33124
10	0.10558	0.11133	0.11723	0.12329	0.1295	0.13587	0.14238	0.14903	0.15579	0.16275	0.1806	0.19925	0.23852	0.32352
11	0.09645	0.10218	0.10808	0.11415	0.12039	0.12679	0.13336	0.14008	0.14693	0.15396	0.17209	0.19107	0.2311	0.31776
12	0.08885	0.09456	0.10046	0.10655	0.11283	0.11928	0.1259	0.1327	0.13966	0.14676	0.16521	0.18448	0.22526	0.31348
13	0.08241	0.08812	0.09403	0.10014	0.10646	0.11296	0.11965	0.12652	0.13358	0.14078	0.15952	0.17911	0.22062	0.31027
14	0.0769	0.0826	0.08853	0.09467	0.10102	0.10758	0.11434	0.1213	0.12845	0.13575	0.15475	0.17469	0.21689	0.30779
15	0.07212	0.07783	0.08377	0.08994	0.09634	0.10296	0.10979	0.11683	0.12404	0.13147	0.15076	0.17102	0.21388	0.306
16	0.06794	0.07365	0.07961	0.08582	0.09227	0.09895	0.10586	0.11298	0.12029	0.12782	0.14738	0.16795	0.21144	0.3046

(continued)

Table B.6 (continued)

Year n	Annual average coefficient of cumulative present value $x_6 = \frac{(\theta-1)\theta^n}{\theta^n-1}$													
	$x_z =$ 0.01	$x_z =$ 0.02	$x_z =$ 0.03	$x_z =$ 0.04	$x_z =$ 0.05	$x_z =$ 0.06	$x_z =$ 0.07	$x_z =$ 0.08	$x_z =$ 0.09	$x_z = 0.1$	$x_z =$ 0.125	$x_z =$ 0.15	$x_z =$ 0.20	$x_z =$ 0.30
17	0.06426	0.06997	0.07595	0.0822	0.0887	0.09544	0.10243	0.10963	0.11705	0.12466	0.14451	0.16537	0.20944	0.30349
18	0.06098	0.0667	0.07271	0.07899	0.08555	0.09236	0.09941	0.1067	0.11421	0.12193	0.14205	0.16319	0.20781	0.30266
19	0.05805	0.06378	0.06981	0.07614	0.08275	0.08962	0.09675	0.10413	0.11174	0.11955	0.13992	0.16134	0.20646	0.30202
20	0.05542	0.06116	0.06722	0.07358	0.08024	0.08718	0.09439	0.10185	0.10954	0.11746	0.1381	0.15976	0.20536	0.30157
25	0.04541	0.05122	0.05743	0.06401	0.07095	0.07823	0.08581	0.09368	0.1018	0.11017	0.13194	0.1547	0.20212	0.30039
30	0.03875	0.04465	0.05102	0.05783	0.06505	0.07265	0.08059	0.08883	0.09734	0.10608	0.12877	0.1523	0.20085	0.30012
35	0.034	0.04	0.04654	0.05358	0.06107	0.06897	0.07723	0.0858	0.09463	0.10369	0.12706	0.15113	0.20034	0.3
40	0.03046	0.03656	0.04326	0.05052	0.05828	0.06646	0.07501	0.08386	0.09296	0.10226	0.12614	0.15056	0.20014	0.3
45	0.02771	0.03391	0.04079	0.04826	0.05626	0.0647	0.0735	0.08259	0.0919	0.10139	0.12563	0.15028	0.20005	0.3
50	0.02551	0.03182	0.03887	0.04655	0.05478	0.06344	0.07246	0.08174	0.09122	0.10086	0.12534	0.15014	0.20002	0.3

Table B.7 Cumulative arithmetic time value coefficient x_7

Year n	Cumulative arithmetic time value coefficient $x_7 = \frac{1}{(\theta-1)}\left(\frac{\theta^n-1}{\theta-1} - n\right)$													
	$x_z =$ 0.01	$x_z =$ 0.02	$x_z =$ 0.03	$x_z =$ 0.04	$x_z =$ 0.05	$x_z =$ 0.06	$x_z =$ 0.07	$x_z =$ 0.08	$x_z =$ 0.09	$x_z = 0.1$	$x_z =$ 0.125	$x_z = 0.15$	$x_z = 0.20$	$x_z = 0.30$
1	0	0	0	0	0	0	0	0	0	0	0	0	0	0
2	1	1	1	1	1	1	1	1	1	1	1	1	1	1
3	3.01	3.02	3.03	3.04	3.05	3.06	3.07	3.08	3.09	3.1	3.125	3.15	3.2	3.3
4	6.04	6.08	6.121	6.162	6.203	6.244	6.285	6.326	6.368	6.41	6.516	6.622	6.84	7.29
5	10.1	10.202	10.305	10.408	10.513	10.619	10.275	10.832	10.941	10.051	11.33	11.615	12.208	13.477
6	15.201	15.406	15.614	15.824	16.039	16.256	16.476	16.699	16.926	17.156	17.746	18.357	19.65	22.52
7	21.353	21.714	22.082	22.457	22.841	23.231	23.629	24.035	24.449	24.872	25.964	27.111	29.58	35.276
8	28.567	29.148	29.744	30.355	30.983	31.625	32.283	32.958	33.649	34.359	36.21	38.178	42.496	52.859
9	36.853	37.731	38.626	39.569	40.532	41.522	42.543	43.595	44.677	45.795	48.736	51.905	58.995	76.717
10	46.222	47.486	48.795	50.152	51.559	53.013	54.521	56.083	57.698	59.374	63.828	68.591	79.794	108.732
11	56.684	58.436	60.259	62.158	64.137	66.194	68.337	70.57	72.891	75.311	81.807	88.995	105.753	151.351
12	68.251	70.605	73.067	75.644	78.344	81.166	84.121	87.215	90.451	93.842	103.033	118.344	137.903	207.756
13	80.934	84.017	87.259	90.67	94.261	98.036	102.009	106.192	110.592	115.226	127.912	142.346	177.483	282.088
14	94.743	98.697	102.877	107.297	111.974	116.918	122.15	127.687	133.545	139.749	156.901	176.698	225.98	379.708
15	109.69	114.671	119.963	125.589	131.573	137.933	144.7	151.902	159.564	167.724	190.514	217.203	285.176	507.621
16	125.787	131.964	138.562	145.613	153.152	161.209	169.829	179.054	188.925	199.496	229.328	264.783	357.211	674.907

(continued)

Table B.7 (continued)

Year n	Cumulative arithmetic time value coefficient $x_7 = \frac{1}{(\theta-1)}\left(\frac{\theta^n-1}{\theta-1} - n\right)$													
	$x_z =$ 0.01	$x_z =$ 0.02	$x_z =$ 0.03	$x_z =$ 0.04	$x_z =$ 0.05	$x_z =$ 0.06	$x_z =$ 0.07	$x_z =$ 0.08	$x_z =$ 0.09	$x_z = 0.1$	$x_z =$ 0.125	$x_z = 0.15$	$x_z = 0.20$	$x_z = 0.30$
17	143.045	150.603	158.719	167.438	176.809	186.882	197.717	209.378	221.908	235.446	273.994	320.5	444.653	893.379
18	161.475	170.615	180.481	191.136	202.649	215.095	228.557	243.128	258.902	275.991	325.243	385.575	550.584	1178.393
19	181.09	192.027	203.895	216.781	230.781	246.001	262.556	280.578	300.203	321.59	383.898	461.411	678.701	1549.911
20	201.901	214.868	209.012	244.452	261.32	279.761	299.935	322.024	346.221	372.749	450.885	549.623	833.441	2033.884
25	324.32	351.514	381.974	416.148	454.542	497.743	546.414	601.324	663.34	733.469	952.166	1251.953	2234.907	7746.01
30	478.489	528.402	585.846	652.123	725.776	817.637	920.867	1041.040	1181.19	1344.939	1887.571	2698.301	5759.409	28999.95
35	666.028	749.722	848.735	966.305	1106.406	1273.914	1474.811	1716.460	2007.89	2360.243	3605.282	5641.134	14566.707	107959.56
40	888.638	1020.096	1180.04	1375.636	1615.994	1912.7	2280.499	2738.206	3309.80	4025.924	6732.735	11593.935	36519.29	401176.28
45	1148.108	1344.632	1590.659	1900.732	2294.002	2795.726	3439.272	4268.820	5342.87	6739.048	12400.588	23600.855	91181.55	1489914.6
50	1446.319	1728.968	2093.225	2566.673	3186.958	4005.599	5093.266	6547.127	8500.89	11139.085	22646.325	47784.773	227235.95	5532369.1

Table B.8 Cumulative arithmetic time value—fund coefficient x_8

Year n	Cumulative arithmetic time value—fund coefficient $x_8 = \frac{Q-1}{\frac{Q^n-1}{Q-1}-n}$													
	$x_z =$ 0.01	$x_z =$ 0.02	$x_z =$ 0.03	$x_z =$ 0.04	$x_z =$ 0.05	$x_z =$ 0.06	$x_z =$ 0.07	$x_z =$ 0.08	$x_z =$ 0.09	$x_z = 0.1$	$x_z =$ 0.125	$x_z =$ 0.15	$x_z =$ 0.20	$x_z =$ 0.30
1	0	0	0	0	0	0	0	0	0	0	0	0	0	0
2	1	1	1	1	1	1	1	1	1	1	1	1	1	1
3	0.3322	0.3311	0.33	0.3289	0.3279	0.3268	0.3257	0.3247	0.3236	0.3226	0.32	0.3175	0.3125	0.303
4	0.1656	0.1645	0.1634	0.1623	0.1612	0.1602	0.1591	0.1581	0.157	0.156	0.1535	0.151	0.1462	0.1372
5	0.099	0.098	0.097	0.0961	0.0951	0.0942	0.0932	0.0923	0.0914	0.0905	0.0883	0.0861	0.0819	0.0742
6	0.0658	0.0649	0.064	0.0632	0.0624	0.0615	0.0607	0.0599	0.0591	0.0583	0.0563	0.0545	0.0509	0.0444
7	0.0468	0.0461	0.0453	0.0445	0.0438	0.043	0.0423	0.0416	0.0409	0.0402	0.0385	0.0369	0.0338	0.0283
8	0.035	0.0343	0.0336	0.0329	0.0323	0.0316	0.031	0.0303	0.0297	0.0291	0.0276	0.0262	0.0235	0.0189
9	0.0271	0.0265	0.0259	0.0253	0.0247	0.0241	0.0235	0.0229	0.0224	0.0218	0.0205	0.0193	0.017	0.013
10	0.0216	0.0211	0.0205	0.0199	0.0194	0.0189	0.0183	0.0178	0.0173	0.0168	0.0157	0.0146	0.0125	0.0092
11	0.0176	0.0171	0.0166	0.0161	0.0156	0.0151	0.0146	0.0142	0.0137	0.0133	0.0122	0.0112	0.0095	0.0066
12	0.0147	0.0142	0.0137	0.0132	0.0128	0.0123	0.0119	0.0115	0.0111	0.0107	0.0097	0.0088	0.0073	0.0048
13	0.0124	0.0119	0.0115	0.011	0.0106	0.0102	0.0098	0.0094	0.009	0.0087	0.0078	0.007	0.0056	0.0035
14	0.0106	0.0101	0.0097	0.0093	0.0089	0.0086	0.0082	0.0078	0.0075	0.0072	0.0064	0.0057	0.0044	0.0026
15	0.0091	0.0087	0.0083	0.008	0.0076	0.0072	0.0069	0.0066	0.0063	0.006	0.0052	0.0046	0.0035	0.002
16	0.0079	0.0076	0.0072	0.0069	0.0065	0.0062	0.0059	0.0056	0.0053	0.005	0.0044	0.0038	0.0028	0.0015

(continued)

Table B.8 (continued)

Year n	Cumulative arithmetic time value—fund coefficient $x_8 = \frac{Q-1}{\frac{Q^n-1}{Q-1}-n}$												
	$x_z =$ 0.01	$x_z =$ 0.02	$x_z =$ 0.03	$x_z =$ 0.04	$x_z =$ 0.05	$x_z =$ 0.06	$x_z =$ 0.07	$x_z =$ 0.08	$x_z =$ 0.09	$x_z = 0.1$	$x_z =$ 0.125	$x_z =$ 0.15	$x_z =$ 0.20	$x_z =$ 0.30
17	0.007	0.0066	0.0063	0.006	0.0057	0.0054	0.0051	0.0048	0.0045	0.0042	0.0036	0.0031	0.0022	0.0011
18	0.0062	0.0059	0.0055	0.0052	0.0049	0.0046	0.0044	0.0041	0.0039	0.0036	0.0031	0.0026	0.0018	0.0008
19	0.0055	0.0052	0.0049	0.0046	0.0043	0.0041	0.0038	0.0036	0.0033	0.0031	0.0026	0.0022	0.0015	0.0006
20	0.005	0.0047	0.0044	0.0041	0.0038	0.0036	0.0033	0.0031	0.0029	0.0027	0.0022	0.0018	0.0012	0.0005
25	0.0031	0.0028	0.0026	0.0024	0.0022	0.002	0.0018	0.0017	0.0015	0.0014	0.0011	0.0008	0.0004	0.0001
30	0.0021	0.0019	0.0017	0.0015	0.0014	0.0012	0.0011	0.001	0.0008	0.0007	0.0005	0.0004	0.0002	0
35	0.0015	0.0013	0.0012	0.001	0.0009	0.0008	0.0007	0.0006	0.0005	0.0004	0.0003	0.0002	0.0001	0
40	0.0011	0.001	0.0008	0.0007	0.0006	0.0005	0.0004	0.0004	0.0003	0.0002	0.0001	0.0001	0	0
45	0.0009	0.0007	0.0006	0.0005	0.0004	0.0004	0.0003	0.0002	0.0002	0.0001	0.0001	0	0	0
50	0.0007	0.0006	0.0005	0.0004	0.0003	0.0002	0.0002	0.0002	0.0001	0.0001	0	0	0	0

Table B.9 Cumulative arithmetic present value coefficient x_9

Year n	Cumulative arithmetic present value coefficient $x_9 = \frac{1}{(\theta-1)\theta^n}\left(\frac{\theta^n-1}{\theta-1}-n\right)$												
	$x_z =$ 0.01	$x_z =$ 0.02	$x_z =$ 0.03	$x_z =$ 0.04	$x_z =$ 0.05	$x_z =$ 0.06	$x_z =$ 0.07	$x_z =$ 0.08	$x_z =$ 0.09	$x_z = 0.1$	$x_z =$ 0.125	$x_z =$ 0.15	$x_z =$ 0.20	$x_z =$ 0.30
1	0	0	0	0	0	0	0	0	0	0	0	0	0	0
2	0.98	0.96	0.94	0.92	0.91	0.89	0.87	0.86	0.84	0.83	0.79	0.76	0.69	0.59
3	2.92	2.85	2.77	2.7	2.63	2.57	2.51	2.45	2.39	2.33	2.19	2.07	1.85	1.5
4	5.8	5.62	5.44	5.27	5.1	4.95	4.79	4.65	4.51	4.38	4.07	3.79	3.3	2.55
5	9.61	9.24	8.89	8.55	8.24	7.93	7.65	7.37	7.11	6.86	6.29	5.78	4.91	3.63
6	14.32	13.68	13.08	12.51	11.97	11.46	10.98	10.52	10.09	9.68	8.75	7.94	6.58	4.67
7	19.92	18.9	17.95	17.07	16.23	15.45	14.71	14.02	13.37	12.76	11.38	10.19	8.26	5.62
8	26.38	24.88	23.48	22.18	20.97	19.84	18.79	17.81	16.89	16.03	14.11	12.48	9.88	6.48
9	33.7	31.57	29.61	27.8	26.13	24.28	23.14	21.81	20.57	19.42	16.88	14.76	11.43	7.23
10	41.84	38.96	36.31	33.88	31.65	29.6	27.72	25.98	24.37	22.89	19.66	16.98	12.89	7.89
11	50.81	47	43.53	40.38	37.5	34.87	32.47	30.27	28.25	26.4	22.39	19.13	14.23	8.45
12	60.57	55.67	51.25	47.25	43.62	40.34	37.35	34.63	32.16	29.9	25.07	21.19	15.47	8.92
13	71.11	64.95	59.42	54.45	49.99	45.96	42.33	39.05	36.07	33.38	27.66	23.14	16.59	9.31
14	82.42	74.8	68.01	61.96	56.55	51.71	47.37	43.47	39.96	36.8	30.16	24.97	17.6	9.64
15	94.48	85.2	77	67.74	63.29	57.55	52.45	47.89	43.81	40.15	32.55	26.69	18.51	9.92
16	107.27	96.13	86.35	77.74	70.16	63.46	57.53	52.26	47.58	43.42	34.84	28.3	19.32	10.14

(continued)

Table B.9 (continued)

Year n	Cumulative arithmetic present value coefficient $x_9 = \frac{1}{(\theta-1)\theta^n}\left(\frac{\theta^n-1}{\theta-1} - n\right)$												
	$x_z =$ 0.01	$x_z =$ 0.02	$x_z =$ 0.03	$x_z =$ 0.04	$x_z =$ 0.05	$x_z =$ 0.06	$x_z =$ 0.07	$x_z =$ 0.08	$x_z =$ 0.09	$x_z = 0.1$	$x_z =$ 0.125	$x_z =$ 0.15	$x_z =$ 0.20	$x_z =$ 0.30
17	120.78	107.56	96.03	85.96	77.14	69.4	62.59	56.59	51.28	46.58	37	29.78	20.04	10.33
18	135	119.46	106.01	94.35	84.2	75.36	67.62	60.84	54.89	49.64	39.04	31.16	20.68	10.48
19	149.9	131.81	116.28	102.89	91.33	51.31	72.6	65.01	58.39	52.58	40.96	32.42	21.24	10.6
20	165.47	144.6	126.8	111.56	98.49	87.23	77.51	69.09	61.78	55.41	42.76	33.58	21.74	10.7
25	252.89	214.26	182.43	156.1	134.23	115.97	100.68	87.8	76.93	67.7	50.11	38.03	23.43	10.98
30	355	291.72	241.36	201.06	168.62	142.36	120.97	103.46	89.03	77.08	55.12	40.75	24.26	11.07
35	470.16	374.88	301.63	244.88	200.58	165.74	138.14	116.09	98.36	83.99	58.43	42.36	24.66	11.1
40	596.86	461.99	361.75	286.53	229.55	185.96	152.29	126.04	105.38	88.95	60.55	43.28	24.85	11.11
45	733.7	551.57	420.63	325.4	255.31	203.11	163.76	133.73	110.56	92.45	61.88	43.51	24.93	11.11
50	879.42	642.36	477.48	361.16	277.91	217.46	172.91	139.59	114.33	94.89	62.71	44.1	24.97	11.11

Table B.10 Cumulative arithmetic present value—fund coefficient x_{10}

Year n	Cumulative arithmetic present value—fund coefficient $x_{10} = \frac{\frac{(\theta-1)\theta^n}{\theta^n-1}}{\theta-1} - n$													
	$x_z =$ 0.01	$x_z =$ 0.02	$x_z =$ 0.03	$x_z =$ 0.04	$x_z =$ 0.05	$x_z =$ 0.06	$x_z =$ 0.07	$x_z =$ 0.08	$x_z = 0.09$	$x_z = 0.1$	$x_z =$ 0.125	$x_z =$ 0.15	$x_z =$ 0.20	$x_z =$ 0.30
1	–	–	–	–	–	–	–	–	–	–	–	–	–	–
2	1.0201	1.0404	1.0609	1.0816	1.1025	1.1236	1.1449	1.1664	1.1881	1.21	1.2656	1.3225	1.44	1.69
3	0.3423	0.3514	0.3606	0.37	0.3796	0.3892	0.399	0.409	0.4191	0.4294	0.4556	0.4828	0.54	0.6658
4	0.1723	0.178	0.1839	0.1899	0.196	0.2022	0.2086	0.215	0.2217	0.2284	0.2458	0.2641	0.3032	0.3918
5	0.1041	0.1082	0.1125	0.1169	0.1214	0.126	0.1308	0.1356	0.1406	0.1457	0.159	0.1732	0.2038	0.2755
6	0.0698	0.0731	0.0765	0.08	0.0836	0.0873	0.0911	0.095	0.0991	0.1033	0.1142	0.126	0.152	0.2143
7	0.0502	0.0529	0.0557	0.0586	0.0616	0.0647	0.068	0.0713	0.0748	0.0784	0.0878	0.0981	0.1211	0.1779
8	0.0379	0.0402	0.0426	0.0451	0.0477	0.0504	0.0532	0.0562	0.0592	0.0624	0.0709	0.0801	0.1012	0.1543
9	0.0297	0.0317	0.0338	0.036	0.0383	0.0407	0.0432	0.0459	0.0486	0.0515	0.0592	0.0678	0.0875	0.1382
10	0.0239	0.0257	0.0275	0.0295	0.0316	0.0338	0.0361	0.0385	0.041	0.0437	0.0509	0.0589	0.0776	0.1268
11	0.0197	0.0213	0.023	0.0248	0.0267	0.0287	0.0308	0.033	0.0354	0.0379	0.0447	0.0523	0.0703	0.1184
12	0.0165	0.018	0.0195	0.0212	0.0229	0.0248	0.0268	0.0289	0.0311	0.0334	0.0399	0.0472	0.0647	0.1121
13	0.0141	0.0154	0.0168	0.0184	0.02	0.0218	0.0236	0.0256	0.0277	0.03	0.0361	0.0432	0.0603	0.1074
14	0.0121	0.0134	0.0147	0.0161	0.0177	0.0193	0.0211	0.023	0.025	0.0272	0.0332	0.04	0.0568	0.1037
15	0.0106	0.0117	0.013	0.0143	0.0158	0.0174	0.0191	0.0209	0.0228	0.0249	0.0307	0.0375	0.054	0.1008
16	0.0093	0.0104	0.0116	0.0129	0.0143	0.0158	0.0174	0.0191	0.021	0.023	0.0287	0.0353	0.0518	0.0986

(continued)

Table B.10 (continued)

Year n	Cumulative arithmetic present value—fund coefficient $x_{10} = \frac{\frac{(\theta-1)\theta^n}{\theta^n-1}}{\theta-1} - n$												
	$x_z =$ 0.01	$x_z =$ 0.02	$x_z =$ 0.03	$x_z =$ 0.04	$x_z =$ 0.05	$x_z =$ 0.06	$x_z =$ 0.07	$x_z =$ 0.08	$x_z = 0.09$	$x_z = 0.1$	$x_z =$ 0.125	$x_z =$ 0.15	$x_z =$ 0.20	$x_z =$ 0.30
17	0.0083	0.0093	0.0104	0.0116	0.013	0.0144	0.016	0.0177	0.0195	0.0215	0.027	0.0336	0.0499	0.0968
18	0.0074	0.0084	0.0094	0.0106	0.0119	0.0133	0.0148	0.0164	0.0182	0.0201	0.0256	0.0321	0.0484	0.0954
19	0.0067	0.0076	0.0086	0.0097	0.0109	0.0123	0.0138	0.0154	0.0171	0.019	0.0244	0.0308	0.0471	0.0943
20	0.006	0.0069	0.0079	0.009	0.0102	0.0115	0.0129	0.0145	0.0162	0.018	0.0234	0.0298	0.046	0.0934
25	0.004	0.0047	0.0055	0.0064	0.0075	0.0086	0.0099	0.0114	0.013	0.0148	0.02	0.0263	0.0427	0.0911
30	0.0028	0.0034	0.0041	0.005	0.0059	0.007	0.0083	0.0097	0.0112	0.013	0.0181	0.0245	0.0412	0.0903
35	0.0021	0.0027	0.0033	0.0041	0.005	0.006	0.0072	0.0086	0.00102	0.0119	0.0171	0.0236	0.0405	0.0901
40	0.0017	0.0022	0.0028	0.0035	0.0044	0.0054	0.0066	0.0079	0.0095	0.0112	0.0165	0.0231	0.0402	0.09
45	0.0014	0.0018	0.0024	0.0031	0.0039	0.0049	0.0061	0.0075	0.009	0.0108	0.0162	0.0228	0.0401	0.09
50	0.0011	0.0016	0.0021	0.0028	0.0036	0.0046	0.0058	0.0072	0.0087	0.0105	0.0159	0.0227	0.04	0.09

Table B.11 Annual mean coefficient of cumulative arithmetic fund x_{11}

Year n	Annual mean coefficient of cumulative arithmetic fund $x_{11} = \frac{1}{\theta-1} - \frac{n}{\theta^n-1}$													
	$x_z =$ 0.01	$x_z =$ 0.02	$x_z =$ 0.03	$x_z =$ 0.04	$x_z =$ 0.05	$x_z =$ 0.06	$x_z =$ 0.07	$x_z =$ 0.08	$x_z =$ 0.09	$x_z = 0.1$	$x_z =$ 0.125	$x_z =$ 0.15	$x_z =$ 0.20	$x_z =$ 0.30
1	0	0	0	0	0	0	0	0	0	0	0	0	0	0
2	0.5	0.5	0.49	0.49	0.49	0.49	0.49	0.48	0.48	0.48	0.48	0.47	0.45	0.43
3	0.99	0.99	0.98	0.97	0.97	0.96	0.96	0.95	0.95	0.94	0.93	0.91	0.88	0.83
4	1.49	1.48	1.47	1.45	1.44	1.43	1.42	1.4	1.39	1.38	1.36	1.33	1.27	1.18
5	1.98	1.96	1.94	1.92	1.9	1.88	1.87	1.85	1.83	1.81	1.77	1.72	1.64	1.49
6	2.47	2.44	2.42	2.39	2.36	2.33	2.31	2.28	2.25	2.22	2.16	2.1	1.98	1.77
7	2.96	2.92	2.88	2.84	2.81	2.77	2.73	2.69	2.65	2.62	2.53	2.45	2.29	2.01
8	3.45	3.4	3.35	3.29	3.25	3.2	3.15	3.1	3.05	3	2.89	2.78	2.58	2.22
9	3.93	3.87	3.81	3.74	3.68	3.61	3.55	3.49	3.43	3.37	3.23	3.09	2.84	2.4
10	4.42	4.34	4.26	4.18	4.1	4.02	3.95	3.87	3.8	3.73	3.56	3.38	3.07	2.55
11	4.9	4.8	4.71	4.61	4.5	4.42	4.33	4.24	4.15	4.06	3.86	3.65	3.29	2.68
12	5.38	5.26	5.15	5.03	4.92	4.81	4.71	4.6	4.5	4.39	4.15	3.91	3.48	2.8
13	5.86	5.72	5.59	5.45	5.32	5.19	5.07	4.94	4.82	4.7	4.42	4.14	3.66	2.89
14	6.34	6.18	6.03	5.87	5.72	5.56	5.42	5.27	5.14	5	4.68	4.36	3.82	2.97
15	6.8	6.63	6.45	6.27	6.1	5.93	5.76	5.59	5.44	5.28	4.92	4.56	3.96	3.03
16	7.29	7.08	6.88	6.67	6.48	6.28	6.09	5.9	5.73	5.55	5.15	4.75	4.09	3.09

(continued)

Table B.11 (continued)

Year n	Annual mean coefficient of cumulative arithmetic fund $x_{11} = \frac{1}{\theta-1} - \frac{n}{\theta^n-1}$													
	$x_z =$ 0.01	$x_z =$ 0.02	$x_z =$ 0.03	$x_z =$ 0.04	$x_z =$ 0.05	$x_z =$ 0.06	$x_z =$ 0.07	$x_z =$ 0.08	$x_z =$ 0.09	$x_z = 0.1$	$x_z =$ 0.125	$x_z =$ 0.15	$x_z =$ 0.20	$x_z =$ 0.30
17	7.76	7.53	7.3	7.07	6.85	6.62	6.41	6.2	6.01	5.81	5.37	4.93	4.2	3.13
18	8.23	7.97	7.71	7.45	7.21	6.96	6.73	6.49	6.27	6.05	5.57	5.08	4.3	3.17
19	8.29	8.41	8.12	7.83	7.56	7.29	7.03	6.77	6.53	6.29	5.76	5.23	4.39	3.2
20	9.17	8.84	8.53	8.21	7.91	7.61	7.33	7.04	6.78	6.51	5.94	5.37	4.46	3.23
25	11.48	10.97	10.48	9.99	9.53	9.07	8.65	8.23	7.85	7.46	6.67	5.88	4.74	3.3
30	13.76	13.02	12.33	11.63	10.99	10.34	9.77	9.19	8.69	8.18	7.2	6.21	4.87	3.32
35	15.98	15	14.06	13.12	12.28	11.43	10.7	9.96	9.34	8.71	7.56	6.4	4.94	3.33
40	18.18	16.89	15.69	14.48	13.42	12.36	11.47	10.57	9.84	9.1	7.81	6.52	4.97	3.33
45	20.33	18.7	17.2	15.7	14.42	13.14	12.09	11.04	10.21	9.37	7.98	6.58	4.99	3.33
50	22.43	20.44	18.63	16.81	15.31	13.8	12.61	11.41	10.49	9.57	8.1	6.62	4.99	3.33

Table B.12 Cumulative arithmetic annual average fund coefficient x_{12}

Year n	Cumulative arithmetic annual average fund coefficient $x_{12} = \frac{1}{\frac{1}{\theta-1} - \frac{n}{\theta^n-1}}$													
	$x_z = 0.01$	$x_z =$ 0.02	$x_z =$ 0.03	$x_z =$ 0.04	$x_z =$ 0.05	$x_z =$ 0.06	$x_z =$ 0.07	$x_z =$ 0.08	$x_z =$ 0.09	$x_z = 0.1$	$x_z =$ 0.125	$x_z =$ 0.15	$x_z =$ 0.20	$x_z =$ 0.30
1	–	–	–	–	–	–	–	–	–	–	–	–	–	–
2	2.01	2.02	2.03	2.04	2.05	2.06	2.07	2.08	2.09	2.1	2.125	2.15	2.2	2.3
3	1.0067	1.0134	1.0201	1.0268	1.0336	1.0404	1.0472	0.054	1.0609	1.0677	1.085	1.1024	1.1375	1.2091
4	0.6722	0.6779	0.6835	0.6892	0.6949	0.7007	0.7064	0.7123	0.7181	0.724	0.7389	0.754	0.7848	0.8487
5	0.505	0.5101	0.5152	0.5204	0.5256	0.5309	0.5362	0.5416	0.547	0.5524	0.5663	0.5804	0.6096	0.671
6	0.4047	0.4095	0.4143	0.4192	0.4241	0.4291	0.4342	0.4393	0.4445	0.4497	0.4631	0.4768	0.5053	0.5664
7	0.3378	0.3424	0.347	0.3517	0.3565	0.3613	0.3662	0.3712	0.3763	0.3814	0.3946	0.4082	0.4367	0.4984
8	0.29	0.2945	0.299	0.3035	0.3082	0.313	0.3178	0.3227	0.3277	0.3328	0.3459	0.3595	0.3883	0.4513
9	0.2542	0.2585	0.2629	0.2674	0.2721	0.2768	0.2816	0.2864	0.2914	0.2965	0.3097	0.3234	0.3526	0.4173
10	0.22263	0.2306	0.2349	0.2394	0.244	0.2486	0.2534	0.2583	0.2633	0.2684	0.2817	0.2956	0.3253	0.392
11	0.2041	0.2082	0.2125	0.217	0.2215	0.2262	0.231	0.2359	0.2409	0.2461	0.2595	0.2736	0.304	0.3727
12	0.1858	0.19	0.1942	0.1986	0.2032	0.2078	0.2127	0.2176	0.2227	0.2279	0.2415	0.2559	0.287	0.3578
13	0.1706	0.1747	0.179	0.1834	0.1879	0.1926	0.1974	0.2024	0.2075	0.2128	0.2266	0.2413	0.2732	0.3461
14	0.1578	0.1619	0.1661	0.1705	0.175	0.1797	0.1846	0.1896	0.1948	0.2002	0.2142	0.2292	0.262	0.3369
15	0.1467	0.1508	0.155	0.1594	0.164	0.1687	0.1737	0.1787	0.184	0.1894	0.2037	0.2191	0.2526	0.3295
16	0.1372	0.1412	0.1455	0.1499	0.1545	0.1593	0.1642	0.1694	0.1747	0.1802	0.1948	0.2104	0.2448	0.3237

(continued)

Table B.12 (continued)

Year n	Cumulative arithmetic annual average fund coefficient $x_{12} = \frac{1}{\frac{1}{\theta-1} - \frac{n}{\theta^n-1}}$												
	$x_z = 0.01$	$x_z = 0.02$	$x_z = 0.03$	$x_z = 0.04$	$x_z = 0.05$	$x_z = 0.06$	$x_z = 0.07$	$x_z = 0.08$	$x_z = 0.09$	$x_z = 0.1$	$x_z = 0.125$	$x_z = 0.15$	$x_z = 0.20$	$x_z = 0.30$
17	0.1288	0.1329	0.1371	0.1415	0.1462	0.151	0.156	0.1612	0.1666	0.1722	0.187	0.203	0.2382	0.319
18	0.1215	0.1255	0.1297	0.1342	0.1388	0.1437	0.1488	0.154	0.1595	0.1652	0.1803	0.1967	0.2327	0.3153
19	0.1149	0.1189	0.1232	0.1276	0.1323	0.1372	0.1424	0.1477	0.1533	0.1591	0.1745	0.1912	0.228	0.3123
20	0.1091	0.1131	0.1173	0.1218	0.1265	0.1315	0.1367	0.1421	0.1478	0.1537	0.1694	0.1864	0.224	0.3098
25	0.0871	0.0911	0.0954	0.1001	0.105	0.1102	0.1158	0.1216	0.1277	0.1341	0.1513	0.17	0.2112	0.3032
30	0.0727	0.0768	0.0812	0.086	0.0912	0.0967	0.1026	0.1088	0.1154	0.1223	0.1409	0.1611	0.2052	0.301
35	0.0626	0.0667	0.0712	0.0762	0.0816	0.0875	0.0937	0.1004	0.1074	0.1148	0.1347	0.1562	0.2024	0.3003
40	0.055	0.0592	0.0639	0.0691	0.0748	0.0809	0.0875	0.0946	0.1021	0.1099	0.1309	0.1535	0.2011	0.3001
45	0.0492	0.0535	0.0583	0.0637	0.0696	0.0761	0.0831	0.0905	0.0984	0.1067	0.1286	0.1519	0.2005	0.3
50	0.0446	0.0489	0.0539	0.0595	0.0657	0.0725	0.0798	0.0876	0.0959	0.1045	0.1272	0.151	0.2002	0.3

Table B.13 Cumulative coefficient of equal time difference x_{13} ($\beta = 1 + x_c,\ \theta = 1 + x_z$)

Year n	$x_c = 0.06$ Cumulative coefficient of equal time difference $x_{13} = \begin{cases} \frac{\theta^n-\beta^n}{\theta-\beta}(\beta \neq \theta) \\ n\theta^{n-1}(\beta = \theta) \end{cases}$					$x_c = 0.08$ Cumulative coefficient of equal time difference $x_{13} = \begin{cases} \frac{\theta^n-\beta^n}{\theta-\beta}(\beta \neq \theta) \\ n\theta^{n-1}(\beta = \theta) \end{cases}$				
	$x_z = 0.04$	$x_z = 0.06$	$x_z = 0.08$	$x_z = 0.10$	$x_z = 0.15$	$x_z = 0.04$	$x_z = 0.06$	$x_z = 0.08$	$x_z = 0.10$	$x_z = 0.15$
1	1	1	1	1	1	1	1	1	1	1
2	2.1	2.12	2.14	2.16	2.21	2.12	2.14	2.16	2.18	2.23
3	3.3076	3.3708	3.4348	3.4996	3.6651	3.3712	3.4348	3.4992	3.5644	3.7309
4	4.6309	4.7641	4.9006	5.0406	5.4059	4.7658	4.9006	5.0388	5.1806	5.5502
5	6.0786	6.3124	6.5551	6.8071	7.4792	6.3168	6.5551	6.8024	7.0591	7.7433
6	7.66	8.0294	8.4178	8.826	9.9394	8.0389	8.4178	8.816	9.2343	10.3741
7	9.3849	9.9296	10.5097	11.1272	12.8488	9.9473	10.5097	11.1081	11.7446	13.5171
8	11.264	12.029	12.8541	13.7435	16.2797	12.059	12.8541	13.1106	14.6329	17.2585
9	13.3084	14.3446	15.4763	16.7117	20.3155	14.3923	15.4763	16.6584	17.9472	21.6982
10	15.5302	16.8948	18.4039	20.0724	25.0523	16.967	18.4039	19.99	21.7409	26.9519
11	17.9422	19.6993	21.667	23.8705	30.601	19.8046	21.667	23.7482	26.0739	33.1536
12	20.5582	22.7796	25.2987	28.1558	37.0895	22.9284	25.2987	27.9797	31.0129	40.4583
13	23.3927	26.1586	29.3348	32.9836	44.6651	26.3638	29.3348	32.7362	36.6924	49.0452
14	26.4614	29.861	33.8145	38.4149	53.4976	30.1379	33.8145	38.0747	43.0152	59.1216
15	29.7807	33.9136	38.7805	44.5172	63.7834	34.2806	38.7805	44.0579	50.254	70.927
16	33.3685	38.3449	44.2795	51.3665	75.7474	38.824	44.2795	50.7547	58.4515	84.7383

(continued)

Table B.13 (continued)

Year n	$x_c = 0.06$ Cumulative coefficient of equal time difference $x_{13} = \begin{cases} \frac{\theta^n - \beta^n}{\theta - \beta} (\beta \neq \theta) \\ n\theta^{n-1} (\beta = \theta) \end{cases}$					$x_c = 0.08$ Cumulative coefficient of equal time difference $x_{13} = \begin{cases} \frac{\theta^n - \beta^n}{\theta - \beta} (\beta \neq \theta) \\ n\theta^{n-1} (\beta = \theta) \end{cases}$				
	$x_z = 0.04$	$x_z = 0.06$	$x_z = 0.08$	$x_z = 0.10$	$x_z = 0.15$	$x_z = 0.04$	$x_z = 0.06$	$x_z = 0.08$	$x_z = 0.10$	$x_z = 0.15$
17	37.2436	43.186	50.3623	59.0424	89.6499	43.8029	50.3623	58.241	67.7226	100.8749
18	41.4261	48.4699	57.084	67.6395	105.7902	49.2551	57.084	66.6003	78.1949	199.7062
19	45.9375	54.2324	64.5051	77.2577	124.513	55.2213	65.5051	75.9244	90.0104	141.6582
20	50.8006	60.512	72.6911	88.0091	146.2156	61.7459	72.6911	86.314	103.3271	167.2226
25	81.3017	101.2234	127.8302	163.5709	318.0787	104.566	127.8302	158.5295	199.3115	372.4354
30	125.0047	162.5516	215.9583	292.6478	671.8698	170.4815	215.9583	279.5182	369.3373	802.1302
35	186.9999	253.7859	354.9629	510.4088	1394.3271	270.9814	354.9629	479.1547	665.8546	1691.2883
40	274.2349	388.1403	571.9402	874.3384	2861.9795	423.0875	571.9402	804.6119	1176.7367	3516.2718
45	396.1718	584.3467	907.7919	1478.1468	5833.3851	651.9818	907.7919	1330.0187	2048.5017	7240.6974
50	565.6735	868.8752	1424.0729	2474.2675	11 835.9699	994.8732	1424.0729	2171.3709	3524.4620	14810.7976

Table B.14 Cumulative coefficient of equal time difference x_{13} ($\beta = 1 + x_c,\ \theta = 1 + x_z$)

Year n	$x_c = 0.10$ Cumulative coefficient of equal time difference $x_{13} = \begin{cases} \frac{\theta^n - \beta^n}{\theta - \beta} (\beta \neq \theta) \\ n\theta^{n-1} (\beta = \theta) \end{cases}$					$x_c = 0.15$ Cumulative coefficient of equal time difference $x_{13} = \begin{cases} \frac{\theta^n - \beta^n}{\theta - \beta} (\beta \neq \theta) \\ n\theta^{n-1} (\beta = \theta) \end{cases}$				
	$x_z = 0.04$	$x_z = 0.06$	$x_z = 0.08$	$x_z = 0.10$	$x_z = 0.15$	$x_z = 0.04$	$x_z = 0.06$	$x_z = 0.08$	$x_z = 0.10$	$x_z = 0.15$
1	1	1	1	1	1	1	1	1	1	1
2	2.14	2.16	2.18	2.2	2.25	2.19	2.21	2.23	2.25	2.3
3	3.4356	3.4996	3.5644	3.63	3.7975	3.6001	3.6651	3.7309	3.7975	3.9675
4	4.904	5.0406	5.1806	5.324	5.6981	5.265	5.4059	5.5502	5.6981	6.0835
5	6.5643	6.8071	7.0591	7.3205	8.0169	7.2246	7.4792	7.7433	8.0169	8.745
6	8.4374	8.826	9.2343	9.6631	10.83	9.5249	9.9394	10.3741	10.83	12.0681
7	10.5464	11.1272	11.7446	12.4009	14.2261	12.219	12.8488	13.5171	14.2261	16.1914
8	12.917	13.7435	14.6329	15.5897	18.3087	15.3678	16.2797	17.2585	18.3087	21.2802
9	15.5773	16.7117	17.9472	19.2923	23.1986	19.0415	20.3155	21.6982	23.1986	27.5312
10	18.5583	20.0724	21.7409	23.5795	29.0363	23.321	25.0523	26.9519	29.0363	35.1788
11	21.8944	23.8705	26.0739	28.5312	35.9855	28.2994	30.601	33.1536	35.9855	44.5011
12	25.6233	28.1558	31.0129	34.2374	44.2364	34.0838	37.0895	40.4583	44.2364	55.8287
13	29.7866	32.9836	36.6324	40.7996	54.0103	40.7974	44.6651	49.0452	54.0103	69.5533
14	34.4304	38.4149	43.0152	48.3318	65.5641	48.5821	53.4978	59.1216	65.5641	86.139
15	39.6051	44.5172	50.254	59.9625	79.1963	57.6011	63.7834	70.927	79.1963	106.1356
16	45.3665	51.3655	58.4515	66.836	95.253	68.0422	75.7474	84.7383	95.253	130.193

(continued)

Table B.14 (continued)

Year n	$x_c = 0.10$ Cumulative coefficient of equal time difference $x_{13} = \begin{cases} \frac{\theta^n - \beta^n}{\theta - \beta} (\beta \neq \theta) \\ n\theta^{n-1} (\beta = \theta) \end{cases}$					$x_c = 0.15$ Cumulative coefficient of equal time difference $x_{13} = \begin{cases} \frac{\theta^n - \beta^n}{\theta - \beta} (\beta \neq \theta) \\ n\theta^{n-1} (\beta = \theta) \end{cases}$				
	$x_z = 0.04$	$x_z = 0.06$	$x_z = 0.08$	$x_z = 0.10$	$x_z = 0.15$	$x_z = 0.04$	$x_z = 0.06$	$x_z = 0.08$	$x_z = 0.10$	$x_z = 0.15$
17	51.7762	59.0424	67.7226	78.1145	114.1359	80.1215	89.6499	100.8749	114.1359	159.0796
18	58.9017	67.6394	78.1949	90.9805	136.3107	94.0876	105.7902	119.7062	136.3107	193.7028
19	66.8177	77.2877	90.0104	105.6384	162.3173	110.2266	124.513	141.6582	162.3173	235.1336
20	75.6063	88.0091	103.3271	112.3182	192.7807	128.8674	146.2156	167.2226	192.7807	284.6354
25	136.1478	163.5709	199.3115	246.2433	441.6849	275.0283	318.0787	372.4354	441.6849	715.6294
30	236.7667	292.6478	369.3373	475.8928	975.2474	572.4398	671.8698	802.1302	975.2474	1727.2636
35	402.6058	510.4088	665.8546	894.1684	2101.4617	1174.8130	1394.3271	1691.2883	201.4617	4053.1681
40	674.3039	874.3384	1176.7367	1645.7911	4452.0858	2391.4775	2861.9758	3516.2718	4452.0858	9316.9929
45	1117.4885	1478.1468	2048.5017	2981.8834	9317.5757	4844.8008	5833.3851	7240.6974	9317.5757	21082.2757
50	1838.0695	2474.2675	3524.4620	5335.9479	19325.3318	9786.8251	11835.9699	14810.7976	19325.3318	47115.5409

Table B.15 Cumulative equal time difference fund coefficient x_{14} ($\beta = 1 + x_c,\ \theta = 1 + x_z$)

Year n	$x_c = 0.06$ Cumulative equal time difference fund coefficient $x_{14} = \begin{cases} \frac{\theta-\beta}{\theta^n-\beta^n} (\beta \neq \theta) \\ \frac{1}{h}\theta^{1-n} (\beta = \theta) \end{cases}$					$x_c = 0.08$ Cumulative equal time difference fund coefficient $x_{14} = \begin{cases} \frac{\theta-\beta}{\theta^n-\beta^n} (\beta \neq \theta) \\ \frac{1}{h}\theta^{1-n} (\beta = \theta) \end{cases}$				
	$x_z = 0.04$	$x_z = 0.06$	$x_z = 0.08$	$x_z = 0.10$	$x_z = 0.15$	$x_z = 0.04$	$x_z = 0.06$	$x_z = 0.08$	$x_z = 0.10$	$x_z = 0.15$
1	1	1	1	1	1	1	1	1	1	1
2	0.4673	0.463	0.4587	0.4545	0.4444	0.4566	0.4525	0.4484	0.4444	0.4348
3	0.2911	0.2857	0.2806	0.2755	0.2633	0.2778	0.2728	0.268	0.2633	0.252
4	0.2039	0.1984	0.193	0.1878	0.1755	0.1899	0.185	0.1802	0.1755	0.1644
5	0.1523	0.1469	0.1417	0.1366	0.1247	0.1384	0.1337	0.1291	0.1247	0.1144
6	0.1185	0.1133	0.1083	0.1035	0.0923	0.105	0.1006	0.0964	0.0923	0.0829
7	0.0948	0.0899	0.0851	0.0806	0.0703	0.0818	0.0778	0.074	0.0703	0.0618
8	0.0774	0.0728	0.0683	0.0641	0.0546	0.0651	0.0614	0.0579	0.0546	0.047
9	0.0642	0.0598	0.0557	0.0518	0.0431	0.0525	0.0492	0.0461	0.0431	0.0363
10	0.0539	0.0498	0.046	0.0424	0.0344	0.0429	0.0399	0.0371	0.0344	0.0284
11	0.0457	0.0419	0.0384	0.035	0.0278	0.0353	0.0327	0.0302	0.0278	0.0225
12	0.039	0.0355	0.0322	0.0292	0.0226	0.0293	0.027	0.0247	0.0226	0.0179
13	0.0336	0.0303	0.0273	0.0245	0.0185	0.0245	0.0224	0.0204	0.0185	0.0144
14	0.029	0.026	0.0232	0.0207	0.0153	0.0206	0.0187	0.0169	0.0153	0.0116
15	0.0252	0.0225	0.0199	0.0176	0.0126	0.0174	0.0157	0.0141	0.0126	0.0094
16	0.022	0.0195	0.0171	0.015	0.0105	0.0147	0.0132	0.0118	0.0105	0.0077

(continued)

Table B.15 (continued)

Year n	$x_c = 0.06$ Cumulative equal time difference fund coefficient $x_{14} = \begin{cases} \frac{\theta-\beta}{\theta^n-\beta^n} (\beta \neq \theta) \\ \frac{1}{h}\theta^{1-n} (\beta = \theta) \end{cases}$					$x_c = 0.08$ Cumulative equal time difference fund coefficient $x_{14} = \begin{cases} \frac{\theta-\beta}{\theta^n-\beta^n} (\beta \neq \theta) \\ \frac{1}{h}\theta^{1-n} (\beta = \theta) \end{cases}$				
	$x_z = 0.04$	$x_z = 0.06$	$x_z = 0.08$	$x_z = 0.10$	$x_z = 0.15$	$x_z = 0.04$	$x_z = 0.06$	$x_z = 0.08$	$x_z = 0.10$	$x_z = 0.15$
17	0.0193	0.0169	0.0148	0.0128	0.0088	0.0125	0.0112	0.0099	0.0088	0.0063
18	0.017	0.0148	0.0128	0.011	0.0073	0.0106	0.0095	0.0084	0.0073	0.0052
19	0.015	0.0129	0.0111	0.0095	0.0062	0.0091	0.008	0.0071	0.0062	0.0043
20	0.0132	0.0114	0.0097	0.0082	0.0052	0.0078	0.0068	0.006	0.0052	0.0035
25	0.0073	0.0061	0.005	0.0041	0.0023	0.0036	0.0031	0.0027	0.0023	0.0014
30	0.0042	0.0034	0.0027	0.0021	0.001	0.0017	0.0015	0.0012	0.001	0.0006
35	0.0025	0.002	0.0015	0.0011	0.0005	0.0009	0.0007	0.0006	0.0005	0.0002
40	0.0015	0.0011	0.0008	0.0006	0.0002	0.0004	0.0003	0.0003	0.0002	0.0001
45	0.0009	0.0007	0.0005	0.0003	0.0001	0.0002	0.0002	0.0001	0.0001	0
50	0.0005	0.0004	0.0003	0.0002	0.0001	0.0001	0.0001	0.0001	0.0001	0

Table B.16 Cumulative equal time difference fund coefficient x_{14} ($\beta = 1 + x_c,\ \theta = 1 + x_z$)

Year n	$x_c = 0.10$ Cumulative equal time difference fund coefficient $x_{14} = \begin{cases} \frac{\theta-\beta}{\theta^n-\beta^n}(\beta \neq \theta) \\ \frac{1}{h}\theta^{1-n}(\beta = \theta) \end{cases}$					$x_c = 0.15$ Cumulative equal time difference fund coefficient $x_{14} = \begin{cases} \frac{\theta-\beta}{\theta^n-\beta^n}(\beta \neq \theta) \\ \frac{1}{h}\theta^{1-n}(\beta = \theta) \end{cases}$				
	$x_z = 0.04$	$x_z = 0.06$	$x_z = 0.08$	$x_z = 0.10$	$x_z = 0.15$	$x_z = 0.04$	$x_z = 0.06$	$x_z = 0.08$	$x_z = 0.10$	$x_z = 0.15$
1	1	1	1	1	1	1	1	1	1	1
2	0.4673	0.463	0.4587	0.4545	0.4444	0.4566	0.4525	0.4484	0.4444	0.4348
3	0.2911	0.2857	0.2806	0.2755	0.2633	0.2778	0.2728	0.268	0.2633	0.252
4	0.2039	0.1984	0.193	0.1878	0.1755	0.1899	0.185	0.1802	0.1755	0.1644
5	0.1523	0.1469	0.1417	0.1366	0.1247	0.1384	0.1337	0.1291	0.1247	0.1144
6	0.1185	0.1133	0.1083	0.1035	0.0923	0.105	0.1006	0.0964	0.0923	0.0829
7	0.0948	0.0899	0.0851	0.0806	0.0703	0.0818	0.0778	0.074	0.0703	0.0618
8	0.0774	0.0728	0.0683	0.0641	0.0546	0.0651	0.0614	0.0579	0.0546	0.047
9	0.0642	0.0598	0.0557	0.0518	0.0431	0.0525	0.0492	0.0461	0.0431	0.0363
10	0.0539	0.0498	0.046	0.0424	0.0344	0.0429	0.0399	0.0371	0.0344	0.0284
11	0.0457	0.0419	0.0384	0.035	0.0278	0.0353	0.0327	0.0302	0.0278	0.0225
12	0.039	0.0355	0.0322	0.0292	0.0226	0.0293	0.027	0.0247	0.0226	0.0179
13	0.0336	0.0303	0.0273	0.0245	0.0185	0.0245	0.0224	0.0204	0.0185	0.0144
14	0.029	0.026	0.0232	0.0207	0.0153	0.0206	0.0187	0.0169	0.0153	0.0116
15	0.0252	0.0225	0.0199	0.0176	0.0126	0.0174	0.0157	0.0141	0.0126	0.0094
16	0.022	0.0195	0.0171	0.015	0.0105	0.0147	0.0132	0.0118	0.0105	0.0077

(continued)

Table B.16 (continued)

Year n	$x_c = 0.10$ Cumulative equal time difference fund coefficient $x_{14} = \begin{cases} \frac{\theta-\beta}{\theta^n-\beta^n} (\beta \neq \theta) \\ \frac{1}{h}\theta^{1-n} (\beta = \theta) \end{cases}$					$x_c = 0.15$ Cumulative equal time difference fund coefficient $x_{14} = \begin{cases} \frac{\theta-\beta}{\theta^n-\beta^n} (\beta \neq \theta) \\ \frac{1}{h}\theta^{1-n} (\beta = \theta) \end{cases}$				
	$x_z = 0.04$	$x_z = 0.06$	$x_z = 0.08$	$x_z = 0.10$	$x_z = 0.15$	$x_z = 0.04$	$x_z = 0.06$	$x_z = 0.08$	$x_z = 0.10$	$x_z = 0.15$
17	0.0193	0.0169	0.0148	0.0128	0.0088	0.0125	0.0112	0.0099	0.0088	0.0063
18	0.017	0.0148	0.0128	0.011	0.0073	0.0106	0.0095	0.0084	0.0073	0.0052
19	0.015	0.0129	0.0111	0.0095	0.0062	0.0091	0.008	0.0071	0.0062	0.0043
20	0.0132	0.0114	0.0097	0.0082	0.0052	0.0078	0.0068	0.006	0.0052	0.0035
25	0.0073	0.0061	0.005	0.0041	0.0023	0.0036	0.0031	0.0027	0.0023	0.0014
30	0.0042	0.0034	0.0027	0.0021	0.001	0.0017	0.0015	0.0012	0.001	0.0006
35	0.0025	0.002	0.0015	0.0011	0.0005	0.0009	0.0007	0.0006	0.0005	0.0002
40	0.0015	0.0011	0.0008	0.0006	0.0002	0.0004	0.0003	0.0003	0.0002	0.0001
45	0.0009	0.0007	0.0005	0.0003	0.0001	0.0002	0.0002	0.0001	0.0001	0
50	0.0005	0.0004	0.0003	0.0002	0.0001	0.0001	0.0001	0.0001	0.0001	0

Table B.17 Cumulative equal—ratio present value coefficient x_{15} ($\beta = 1 + x_c,\ \theta = 1 + x_z$)

Year n	$x_c = 0.06$ Cumulative equal—ratio present value coefficient $x_{15} = \begin{cases} 1 - \beta^n\theta^{-n}(\beta \neq \theta) \\ \frac{n}{\theta}(\beta = \theta) \end{cases}$					$x_c = 0.08$ Cumulative equal—ratio present value coefficient $x_{15} = \begin{cases} 1 - \beta^n\theta^{-n}(\beta \neq \theta) \\ \frac{n}{\theta}(\beta = \theta) \end{cases}$				
	$x_z = 0.04$	$x_z = 0.06$	$x_z = 0.08$	$x_z = 0.10$	$x_z = 0.15$	$x_z = 0.04$	$x_z = 0.06$	$x_z = 0.08$	$x_z = 0.10$	$x_z = 0.15$
1	0.9615	0.9434	0.9259	0.9091	0.8696	0.9615	0.9434	0.9259	0.9091	0.8696
2	1.9416	1.8868	1.8347	1.7851	1.6711	1.9601	1.9046	1.8519	1.8017	1.6862
3	2.9404	2.8302	2.7267	2.6293	2.4099	2.997	2.8839	2.7778	2.678	2.4531
4	3.9585	3.7736	3.6021	3.4428	3.0908	4.0738	3.8817	3.7037	3.5384	3.1734
5	4.9962	4.717	4.4613	4.2267	3.7185	5.192	4.8984	4.6296	4.3831	3.8498
6	6.0538	5.6604	5.3046	4.9821	4.2971	6.3532	5.9343	5.5556	5.2125	4.485
7	7.1318	6.6038	6.1323	5.71	4.8303	7.5591	6.99	6.4815	6.0269	5.0816
8	8.2305	7.5472	6.9447	6.4115	5.3219	8.8114	8.0648	7.4074	6.8264	5.6418
9	9.3503	8.4906	7.742	7.0874	5.7749	10.1119	9.1604	8.3333	7.6113	6.168
10	10.4916	9.0434	8.5246	7.7388	6.1926	11.4623	10.2766	9.2593	8.382	6.6621
11	11.6549	10.3774	9.2926	8.3664	6.5775	12.8647	11.4139	10.1852	9.1387	7.1261
12	12.8406	11.3208	10.0465	8.9713	6.9323	14.321	12.5727	11.1111	9.8817	7.5619
13	14.0491	12.2642	10.7863	9.5542	7.2593	15.8334	13.7533	12.037	10.6111	7.9712
14	15.2808	13.2075	11.5125	10.1158	7.5608	17.4039	14.9562	12.963	11.3273	8.3556
15	16.5362	14.1509	12.2252	10.6571	7.8386	19.0348	16.1818	13.8889	12.0304	8.7165
16	17.8157	15.0943	12.9248	11.1786	8.0947	20.7285	17.4305	14.8148	12.7208	9.0555

(continued)

Table B.17 (continued)

Year n	$x_c = 0.06$ Cumulative equal—ratio present value coefficient $x_{15} = \begin{cases} 1 - \beta^n\theta^{-n}(\beta \neq \theta) \\ \frac{n}{\theta}(\beta = \theta) \end{cases}$					$x_c = 0.08$ Cumulative equal—ratio present value coefficient $x_{15} = \begin{cases} 1 - \beta^n\theta^{-n}(\beta \neq \theta) \\ \frac{n}{\theta}(\beta = \theta) \end{cases}$				
	$x_z = 0.04$	$x_z = 0.06$	$x_z = 0.08$	$x_z = 0.10$	$x_z = 0.15$	$x_z = 0.04$	$x_z = 0.06$	$x_z = 0.08$	$x_z = 0.10$	$x_z = 0.15$
17	19.1199	16.0377	13.6114	11.6812	8.3308	22.4873	18.7028	15.7407	13.3986	9.3739
18	20.4491	16.9811	14.2852	12.1656	8.5484	24.3137	19.999	16.6667	14.064	9.6729
19	21.8039	17.9245	14.9466	12.6323	8.7489	26.2104	21.3198	17.5926	14.7174	9.9537
20	23.1847	18.8679	15.5957	13.082	8.9338	28.18	22.6654	18.5185	15.3589	10.2173
25	30.4976	23.5849	18.6655	15.0969	9.6625	39.2245	29.7843	23.1481	18.3957	11.3137
30	38.5413	28.3019	21.4614	16.7712	10.1473	52.5626	37.6005	27.7778	21.1662	12.1146
35	47.3887	33.0189	24.0078	18.1624	10.4698	68.6709	41.1825	32.4074	23.6938	12.6997
40	57.1201	37.7358	26.3269	19.3184	10.6845	88.1245	55.6053	37.037	25.9999	13.1271
45	67.824	42.4528	28.4392	20.279	10.8272	111.6183	65.9512	41.6667	28.1038	13.4393
50	79.5974	47.1698	30.363	21.0772	10.9222	139.9912	77.3106	46.2963	30.0233	13.6674

Table B.18 Cumulative equal—ratio present value coefficient x_{15} ($\beta = 1 + x_c,\ \theta = 1 + x_z$)

Year n	$x_c = 0.10$ Cumulative equal—ratio present value coefficient $x_{15} = \begin{cases} 1 - \beta^n\theta^{-n}(\beta \neq \theta) \\ \frac{n}{\theta}(\beta = \theta) \end{cases}$					$x_c = 0.15$ Cumulative equal—ratio present value coefficient $x_{15} = \begin{cases} 1 - \beta^n\theta^{-n}(\beta \neq \theta) \\ \frac{n}{\theta}(\beta = \theta) \end{cases}$				
	$x_z = 0.04$	$x_z = 0.06$	$x_z = 0.08$	$x_z = 0.10$	$x_z = 0.15$	$x_z = 0.04$	$x_z = 0.06$	$x_z = 0.08$	$x_z = 0.10$	$x_z = 0.15$
1	0.9615	0.9434	0.9259	0.9091	0.8696	0.9615	0.9434	0.9259	0.9091	0.8696
2	1.9786	1.9224	1.869	1.8182	1.7013	2.0248	1.9669	1.9119	1.8595	1.7391
3	3.0542	2.9383	2.8295	2.7273	2.4969	3.2005	3.0773	2.9617	2.8531	2.6087
4	4.192	3.9926	3.8079	3.6364	3.2579	4.5005	4.282	4.0796	3.8919	3.4783
5	5.3954	5.0867	9.8043	4.5455	3.9858	5.9381	5.589	5.2699	4.9779	4.3478
6	6.6682	6.222	5.8192	5.4545	4.6821	7.5277	7.0069	6.5374	6.1133	5.2174
7	8.0144	7.4002	6.8529	6.3636	5.3481	9.2854	8.5452	7.8871	7.3002	6.087
8	9.4383	8.6228	7.9057	7.2727	5.9851	11.2291	10.2141	9.3242	8.5411	6.9565
9	10.9444	9.8916	8.978	8.1818	6.5945	13.3783	12.0247	10.8545	9.8385	7.8261
10	12.5373	11.2083	10.0702	9.0909	7.1773	15.7549	13.9891	12.4839	11.1948	8.6957
11	14.2222	12.5747	11.1826	10	7.7348	18.3828	16.1202	14.219	12.6127	9.5652
12	16.0042	13.9926	12.3157	10.9091	8.2681	21.2886	18.4323	16.0665	14.0951	10.4348
13	17.8891	15.464	13.4696	11.8182	8.7782	24.5019	20.9407	18.0338	15.6449	11.3043
14	19.8827	16.9909	14.645	12.7273	9.2661	28.0549	23.6621	20.1286	17.2651	12.1739
15	21.9913	18.5755	15.8421	13.6364	9.7328	31.9838	26.6146	22.3592	18.959	13.0435
16	24.2216	20.2199	17.0614	14.5455	10.1792	36.3283	29.8177	24.7343	20.7298	13.913

(continued)

Table B.18 (continued)

Year n	$x_c = 0.10$ Cumulative equal—ratio present value coefficient $x_{15} = \begin{cases} 1 - \beta^n\theta^{-n}(\beta \neq \theta) \\ \frac{n}{\theta}(\beta = \theta) \end{cases}$					$x_c = 0.15$ Cumulative equal—ratio present value coefficient $x_{15} = \begin{cases} 1 - \beta^n\theta^{-n}(\beta \neq \theta) \\ \frac{n}{\theta}(\beta = \theta) \end{cases}$				
	$x_z = 0.04$	$x_z = 0.06$	$x_z = 0.08$	$x_z = 0.10$	$x_z = 0.15$	$x_z = 0.04$	$x_z = 0.06$	$x_z = 0.08$	$x_z = 0.10$	$x_z = 0.15$
17	26.5805	21.9263	18.3033	15.4545	10.6062	41.1322	33.2928	27.2634	22.5812	14.7826
18	29.0755	23.6971	19.5682	16.3636	11.0146	46.4443	37.0629	29.9564	24.5167	15.6522
19	31.7145	25.5347	20.8565	17.2727	11.4053	52.3182	41.1532	32.8239	26.5402	16.5217
20	34.5057	27.4417	22.1687	18.1818	11.779	58.8134	45.5907	35.8773	28.6556	17.3913
25	51.0713	38.1118	29.1031	22.7273	13.4173	103.1677	71.1119	54.3822	40.7658	21.7391
30	72.9996	50.9529	36.7038	27.2727	14.7292	176.4939	116.9793	79.7136	55.89	26.087
35	102.0265	66.4068	45.0348	31.8182	15.7796	297.7158	181.4092	114.3895	74.7786	30.4348
40	140.4501	85.0051	54.1663	36.3636	16.6207	498.1186	278.2476	161.8573	98.3685	34.7826
45	191.3123	107.3875	64.1752	40.9091	17.2942	829.4222	423.7959	226.8357	127.8298	39.1304
50	258.6396	134.3239	75.1459	45.4545	17.8334	1377.1298	642.5554	315.7844	164.6238	43.4783

Table B.19 Cumulative equal—ratio present value fund coefficient x_{16} ($\beta = 1 + x_c,\ \theta = 1 + x_z$)

Year n	$x_c = 0.06$ Cumulative equal—ratio present value fund coefficient $x_{16} = \begin{cases} \frac{\theta-\beta}{1-\beta^n\theta^{-n}} (\beta \neq \theta) \\ \frac{\theta}{n} (\beta = 0) \end{cases}$					$x_c = 0.08$ Cumulative equal—ratio present value fund coefficient $x_{16} = \begin{cases} \frac{\theta-\beta}{1-\beta^n\theta^{-n}} (\beta \neq \theta) \\ \frac{\theta}{n} (\beta = 0) \end{cases}$				
	$x_z = 0.04$	$x_z = 0.06$	$x_z = 0.08$	$x_z = 0.10$	$x_z = 0.15$	$x_z = 0.04$	$x_z = 0.06$	$x_z = 0.08$	$x_z = 0.10$	$x_z = 0.15$
1	1.04	1.06	1.08	1.1	1.12	1.04	1.06	1.08	1.1	1.12
2	0.515	0.53	0.545	0.5602	0.5754	0.5102	0.525	0.54	0.555	0.5702
3	0.3401	0.3533	0.3668	0.3803	0.3941	0.3337	0.3468	0.36	0.3734	0.387
4	0.2526	0.265	0.2776	0.2905	0.3035	0.2455	0.2576	0.27	0.2826	0.2955
5	0.2002	0.212	0.2241	0.2366	0.2493	0.1926	0.2041	0.216	0.2281	0.2406
6	0.1652	0.1767	0.1885	0.2007	0.2133	0.1574	0.1685	0.18	0.1918	0.204
7	0.1402	0.1514	0.1631	0.1751	0.1876	0.1323	0.1431	0.1543	0.1659	0.178
8	0.1215	0.1325	0.144	0.156	0.1684	0.1135	0.124	0.135	0.1465	0.1585
9	0.1069	0.1178	0.1292	0.1411	0.1535	0.0989	0.1092	0.12	0.1314	0.1433
10	0.0953	0.106	0.1173	0.1292	0.1417	0.0872	0.0973	0.108	0.1193	0.1312
11	0.0858	0.0964	0.1076	0.1195	0.1321	0.0777	0.0876	0.0982	0.1094	0.1213
12	0.0779	0.0883	0.0995	0.1115	0.1241	0.0698	0.0795	0.09	0.1012	0.1131
13	0.0712	0.0815	0.0927	0.1047	0.1174	0.0632	0.0727	0.0831	0.0942	0.1062
14	0.0654	0.0757	0.0869	0.0989	0.1117	0.0575	0.0669	0.0771	0.0883	0.1003
15	0.0605	0.0707	0.0818	0.0938	0.1067	0.0525	0.0618	0.072	0.0831	0.0951
16	0.0561	0.0662	0.0774	0.0895	0.1025	0.0482	0.0574	0.0675	0.0788	0.0907

(continued)

Table B.19 (continued)

Year n	$x_c = 0.06$ Cumulative equal—ratio present value fund coefficient $x_{16} = \begin{cases} \frac{\theta-\beta}{1-\beta^n\theta^{-n}} (\beta \neq \theta) \\ \frac{\theta}{n} (\beta = 0) \end{cases}$					$x_c = 0.08$ Cumulative equal—ratio present value fund coefficient $x_{16} = \begin{cases} \frac{\theta-\beta}{1-\beta^n\theta^{-n}} (\beta \neq \theta) \\ \frac{\theta}{n} (\beta = 0) \end{cases}$				
	$x_z = 0.04$	$x_z = 0.06$	$x_z = 0.08$	$x_z = 0.10$	$x_z = 0.15$	$x_z = 0.04$	$x_z = 0.06$	$x_z = 0.08$	$x_z = 0.10$	$x_z = 0.15$
17	0.0523	0.0624	0.0735	0.0856	0.0987	0.0445	0.0535	0.0635	0.0746	0.0867
18	0.0489	0.0589	0.07	0.0822	0.0954	0.0411	0.05	0.06	0.0711	0.0833
19	0.0459	0.0558	0.0669	0.0792	0.0925	0.0382	0.0469	0.0568	0.0679	0.0802
20	0.0431	0.053	0.0641	0.0764	0.0899	0.0355	0.0441	0.054	0.0651	0.0774
25	0.0328	0.0424	0.0536	0.0662	0.0803	0.0255	0.0336	0.0432	0.0544	0.067
30	0.0259	0.0353	0.0466	0.0596	0.0742	0.019	0.0266	0.036	0.0472	0.0602
35	0.0211	0.0303	0.0417	0.0551	0.0702	0.0146	0.0217	0.0309	0.0422	0.0556
40	0.0175	0.0265	0.038	0.0518	0.0675	0.0113	0.018	0.027	0.0385	0.0522
45	0.0147	0.0236	0.0352	0.0493	0.0655	0.009	0.0152	0.024	0.0356	0.0497
50	0.0126	0.0212	0.0329	0.0474	0.0641	0.0071	0.0129	0.0216	0.0333	0.0477

Table B.20 Cumulative equal—ratio present value fund coefficient x_{16} ($\beta = 1 + x_c,\ \theta = 1 + x_z$)

Year n	$x_c = 0.10$ Cumulative equal—ratio present value fund coefficient $x_{16} = \begin{cases} \frac{\theta-\beta}{1-\beta^n\theta^{-n}} (\beta \neq \theta) \\ \frac{\theta}{n} (\beta = 0) \end{cases}$					$x_c = 0.15$ Cumulative equal—ratio present value fund coefficient $x_{16} = \begin{cases} \frac{\theta-\beta}{1-\beta^n\theta^{-n}} (\beta \neq \theta) \\ \frac{\theta}{n} (\beta = 0) \end{cases}$				
	$x_z = 0.04$	$x_z = 0.06$	$x_z = 0.08$	$x_z = 0.10$	$x_z = 0.15$	$x_z = 0.04$	$x_z = 0.06$	$x_z = 0.08$	$x_z = 0.10$	$x_z = 0.15$
1	1.04	1.06	1.08	1.1	1.12	1.04	1.06	1.08	1.1	1.15
2	0.5054	0.5202	0.535	0.55	0.565	0.4939	0.5084	0.523	0.5378	0.575
3	0.3274	0.3403	0.3534	0.3667	0.3801	0.3125	0.325	0.3376	0.3505	0.3833
4	0.2386	0.2505	0.2626	0.275	0.2876	0.2222	0.2335	0.2451	0.2569	0.2875
5	0.1853	0.1966	0.2081	0.22	0.2321	0.1684	0.1789	0.1898	0.2009	0.23
6	0.15	0.1607	0.1718	0.1833	0.1952	0.1328	0.1427	0.153	0.1636	0.1917
7	0.1248	0.1351	0.1459	0.1571	0.1688	0.1077	0.117	0.1268	0.137	0.1643
8	0.106	0.116	0.1265	0.1375	0.149	0.0891	0.0979	0.1072	0.1171	0.1438
9	0.0914	0.1011	0.1114	0.1222	0.1336	0.0747	0.0832	0.0921	0.1016	0.1278
10	0.0798	0.0892	0.0993	0.11	0.1213	0.0635	0.0715	0.0801	0.0893	0.115
11	0.0703	0.0795	0.0894	0.1	0.1112	0.0544	0.062	0.0703	0.0793	0.1045
12	0.0625	0.0715	0.0812	0.0917	0.1029	0.047	0.0543	0.0622	0.0709	0.0958
13	0.0559	0.0647	0.0742	0.0846	0.0958	0.0408	0.0478	0.0555	0.0639	0.0885
14	0.0503	0.0589	0.0683	0.0786	0.0897	0.0356	0.0423	0.0497	0.0579	0.0821
15	0.0455	0.0538	0.0631	0.0733	0.0844	0.0313	0.0376	0.0447	0.0527	0.0767
16	0.0413	0.0495	0.0586	0.0688	0.0799	0.0275	0.0335	0.0404	0.0482	0.0719

(continued)

Table B.20 (continued)

Year n	$x_c = 0.10$ Cumulative equal—ratio present value fund coefficient $x_{16} = \begin{cases} \frac{\theta-\beta}{1-\beta^n\theta^{-n}} (\beta \neq \theta) \\ \frac{\theta}{n} (\beta = 0) \end{cases}$					$x_c = 0.15$ Cumulative equal—ratio present value fund coefficient $x_{16} = \begin{cases} \frac{\theta-\beta}{1-\beta^n\theta^{-n}} (\beta \neq \theta) \\ \frac{\theta}{n} (\beta = 0) \end{cases}$				
	$x_z = 0.04$	$x_z = 0.06$	$x_z = 0.08$	$x_z = 0.10$	$x_z = 0.15$	$x_z = 0.04$	$x_z = 0.06$	$x_z = 0.08$	$x_z = 0.10$	$x_z = 0.15$
17	0.0376	0.0456	0.0546	0.0647	0.0758	0.0243	0.03	0.0367	0.0443	0.0676
18	0.0344	0.0422	0.0511	0.0611	0.0722	0.0215	0.027	0.0334	0.0408	0.0639
19	0.0315	0.0392	0.0479	0.0579	0.069	0.0191	0.0243	0.0305	0.0377	0.0605
20	0.029	0.0364	0.0451	0.055	0.0661	0.017	0.0219	0.0279	0.0349	0.0575
25	0.0196	0.0262	0.0344	0.044	0.0551	0.0097	0.0135	0.0184	0.0245	0.046
30	0.0137	0.0196	0.0272	0.0367	0.0479	0.0057	0.0085	0.0125	0.0179	0.0383
35	0.0098	0.0151	0.0222	0.0314	0.0428	0.0034	0.0055	0.0087	0.0134	0.0329
40	0.0071	0.0118	0.0185	0.0275	0.0389	0.002	0.0036	0.0062	0.0102	0.0287
45	0.0052	0.0093	0.0156	0.0244	0.036	0.0012	0.0024	0.0044	0.0078	0.0256
50	0.0039	0.0074	0.0133	0.022	0.0337	0.0007	0.0016	0.0032	0.0061	0.023

Table B.21 Cumulative equal—ratio fund annual average coefficient x_{17} ($\beta = 1 + x_c,\ \theta = 1 + x_z$)

Year n	$x_c = 0.06$ Cumulative equal—ratio fund annual average coefficient $x_{17} = \begin{cases} \frac{\theta^n-\beta^n}{\theta-\beta}\frac{\theta-1}{\theta^n-1}(\beta \neq \theta) \\ n\theta^{n-1}\frac{\theta-1}{\theta^n-1}(\beta = \theta) \end{cases}$					$x_c = 0.08$ Cumulative equal—ratio fund annual average coefficient $x_{17} = \begin{cases} \frac{\theta^n-\beta^n}{\theta-\beta}\frac{\theta-1}{\theta^n-1}(\beta \neq \theta) \\ n\theta^{n-1}\frac{\theta-1}{\theta^n-1}(\beta = \theta) \end{cases}$				
	$x_z = 0.04$	$x_z = 0.06$	$x_z = 0.08$	$x_z = 0.10$	$x_z = 0.15$	$x_z = 0.04$	$x_z = 0.06$	$x_z = 0.08$	$x_z = 0.10$	$x_z = 0.15$
1	1	1	1	1	1	1	1	1	1	1
2	1.0294	1.0291	1.0288	1.0286	1.0283	1.0392	1.0388	1.0384	1.0381	1.0377
3	1.0596	1.0588	1.058	1.0573	1.0565	1.08	1.0789	1.0778	1.0769	1.0759
4	1.0905	1.089	1.0875	1.0861	1.0847	1.1223	1.1202	1.1182	1.1163	1.1143
5	1.1223	1.1198	1.1174	1.115	1.1127	1.1663	1.1629	1.1595	1.1563	1.1531
6	1.1548	1.1511	1.1475	1.1439	1.1405	1.212	1.2068	1.2018	1.1968	1.1921
7	1.1882	1.183	1.1778	1.1729	1.168	1.2594	1.2521	1.2449	1.238	1.2312
8	1.2225	1.2154	1.2085	1.2018	1.1953	1.3087	1.2987	1.289	1.2796	1.2704
9	1.2575	1.2483	1.2393	1.2307	1.2223	1.36	1.3468	1.334	1.3216	1.3097
10	1.2935	1.2818	1.2704	1.2594	1.2489	1.4132	1.3963	1.3799	1.3641	1.349
11	1.3304	1.3158	1.3017	1.2881	1.2751	1.4685	1.4472	1.4267	1.407	1.3882
12	1.3682	1.3503	1.3331	1.3167	1.301	1.5259	1.4996	1.4744	1.4503	1.4273
13	1.4069	1.3854	1.3647	1.345	1.3263	1.5856	1.5536	1.5229	1.4938	1.4662
14	1.4466	1.4209	1.3964	1.3732	1.3512	1.6476	1.6091	1.5724	1.5376	1.5049
15	1.4873	1.457	1.4283	1.4011	1.3756	1.712	1.6661	1.6226	1.5817	1.5433
16	1.5289	1.4936	1.4602	1.4288	1.3995	1.7789	1.7248	1.6737	1.6259	1.5814

(continued)

Table B.21 (continued)

Year n	$x_c = 0.06$ Cumulative equal—ratio fund annual average coefficient $x_{17} = \begin{cases} \frac{\theta^n-\beta^n}{\theta-\beta}\frac{\theta-1}{\theta^n-1}(\beta \neq \theta) \\ n\theta^{n-1}\frac{\theta-1}{\theta^n-1}(\beta = \theta) \end{cases}$					$x_c = 0.08$ Cumulative equal—ratio fund annual average coefficient $x_{17} = \begin{cases} \frac{\theta^n-\beta^n}{\theta-\beta}\frac{\theta-1}{\theta^n-1}(\beta \neq \theta) \\ n\theta^{n-1}\frac{\theta-1}{\theta^n-1}(\beta = \theta) \end{cases}$				
	$x_z = 0.04$	$x_z = 0.06$	$x_z = 0.08$	$x_z = 0.10$	$x_z = 0.15$	$x_z = 0.04$	$x_z = 0.06$	$x_z = 0.08$	$x_z = 0.10$	$x_z = 0.15$
17	1.5716	1.5307	1.4922	1.4562	1.4229	1.8484	1.7851	1.7256	1.6703	1.6192
18	1.6153	1.5683	1.5243	1.4833	1.4456	1.9206	1.847	1.7784	1.7148	1.6565
19	1.6601	1.6064	1.5564	1.5101	1.4678	1.9956	1.9107	1.8319	1.7594	1.6934
20	1.706	1.645	1.5885	1.5366	1.4895	2.0735	1.9761	1.8862	1.8041	1.7298
25	1.9522	1.845	1.7486	1.6632	1.5885	2.5108	2.3299	2.1685	2.0266	1.9034
30	2.2288	2.0561	1.9064	1.7791	1.6724	3.0397	2.7316	2.4674	2.2453	2.0612
35	2.539	2.2774	2.0599	1.8833	1.7418	3.6792	3.1854	2.7807	2.4568	2.2016
40	2.8859	2.508	2.2078	1.9755	1.7982	4.4524	3.6956	3.1059	2.6587	2.3246
45	3.2733	2.7467	2.3487	2.0561	1.8434	5.387	4.2671	3.4411	2.8495	2.4309
50	3.7053	2.9927	2.482	2.1258	1.879	6.5166	4.9049	3.7844	3.0281	2.5219

Table B.22 Cumulative equal—ratio fund annual average coefficient x_{17} ($\beta = 1 + x_c,\ \theta = 1 + x_z$)

Year n	$x_c = 0.10$ Cumulative equal—ratio fund annual average coefficient $x_{17} = \begin{cases} \frac{\theta^n-\beta^n}{\theta-\beta}\frac{\theta-1}{\theta^n-1}(\beta \neq \theta) \\ n\theta^{n-1}\frac{\theta-1}{\theta^n-1}(\beta = \theta) \end{cases}$					$x_c = 0.15$ Cumulative equal—ratio fund annual average coefficient $x_{17} = \begin{cases} \frac{\theta^n-\beta^n}{\theta-\beta}\frac{\theta-1}{\theta^n-1}(\beta \neq \theta) \\ n\theta^{n-1}\frac{\theta-1}{\theta^n-1}(\beta = \theta) \end{cases}$				
	$x_z = 0.04$	$x_z = 0.06$	$x_z = 0.08$	$x_z = 0.10$	$x_z = 0.15$	$x_z = 0.04$	$x_z = 0.06$	$x_z = 0.08$	$x_z = 0.10$	$x_z = 0.15$
1	1	1	1	1	1	1	1	1	1	1
2	1.049	1.0485	1.0481	1.0476	1.0472	1.0735	1.0728	1.0721	1.0714	1.0698
3	1.1006	1.0993	1.098	1.0967	1.0954	1.1533	1.1512	1.1492	1.1473	1.1425
4	1.1548	1.1522	1.1497	1.1472	1.1447	1.2398	1.2357	1.2317	1.2278	1.2183
5	1.2119	1.2076	1.2033	1.1991	1.195	1.3339	1.3268	1.3199	1.3132	1.297
6	1.272	1.2653	1.2588	1.2524	1.2462	1.436	1.4249	1.4141	1.4036	1.3786
7	1.3353	1.3256	1.3163	1.3071	1.2983	1.547	1.5307	1.5149	1.4995	1.4631
8	1.4019	1.3886	1.3757	1.3632	1.3512	1.6678	1.6448	1.6226	1.601	1.5503
9	1.4719	1.4543	1.4372	1.4207	1.4048	1.7993	1.7679	1.7376	1.7084	1.6401
10	1.5457	1.5228	1.5008	1.4795	1.4591	1.9424	1.9007	1.8605	1.8219	1.7326
11	1.6234	1.5944	1.5664	1.5396	1.514	2.0984	2.0439	1.9917	1.9419	1.8276
12	1.7053	1.669	1.6342	1.6011	1.5695	2.2684	2.1986	2.132	2.0686	1.925
13	1.7915	1.7468	1.7042	1.6637	1.6255	2.4537	2.3655	2.2817	2.2025	2.0247
14	1.8823	1.828	1.7764	1.7277	1.6819	2.6559	2.5457	2.4415	2.3437	2.1266
15	1.9779	1.9126	1.8508	1.7928	1.7386	2.8767	2.7403	2.6122	2.4926	2.2307
16	2.0787	2.0008	1.9275	1.8592	1.7957	3.1177	2.9505	2.7944	2.6496	2.3367

(continued)

Table B.22 (continued)

Year n	$x_c = 0.10$ Cumulative equal—ratio fund annual average coefficient $x_{17} = \begin{cases} \frac{\theta^n-\beta^n}{\theta-\beta}\frac{\theta-1}{\theta^n-1}(\beta \neq \theta) \\ n\theta^{n-1}\frac{\theta-1}{\theta^n-1}(\beta = \theta) \end{cases}$					$x_c = 0.15$ Cumulative equal—ratio fund annual average coefficient $x_{17} = \begin{cases} \frac{\theta^n-\beta^n}{\theta-\beta}\frac{\theta-1}{\theta^n-1}(\beta \neq \theta) \\ n\theta^{n-1}\frac{\theta-1}{\theta^n-1}(\beta = \theta) \end{cases}$				
	$x_z = 0.04$	$x_z = 0.06$	$x_z = 0.08$	$x_z = 0.10$	$x_z = 0.15$	$x_z = 0.04$	$x_z = 0.06$	$x_z = 0.08$	$x_z = 0.10$	$x_z = 0.15$
17	2.1849	2.0927	2.0066	1.9266	1.8529	3.381	3.1776	2.9889	2.8151	2.4446
18	2.2968	2.1886	2.088	1.9952	1.9104	3.6688	3.423	3.1964	2.9893	2.5542
19	2.4147	2.2884	2.1717	2.0649	1.9679	3.9834	3.6882	3.4179	3.1728	2.6656
20	2.539	2.3925	2.2579	2.1356	2.0255	4.3276	3.9748	3.6542	3.3659	2.7785
25	3.2692	2.9814	2.7263	2.5038	2.312	6.604	5.7975	5.0945	4.4911	3.363
30	4.2216	3.7017	3.2603	2.8931	2.592	10.2081	8.4984	7.0808	5.9288	3.973
35	5.4663	4.5803	3.8641	3.299	2.8607	15.9508	12.5125	9.815	7.7538	4.5998
40	7.096	5.6496	4.5424	3.7185	3.1151	25.1667	18.4928	13.5734	10.0591	5.2369
45	9.2332	6.948	5.3001	4.1478	3.3535	40.03	27.4198	18.7338	12.9608	5.8805
50	12.0397	8.5221	6.1427	4.5845	3.5752	64.1057	40.7065	28.8132	16.6039	6.5278

Table B.23 Cumulative equal—ratio annual average fund coefficient x_{18} ($\beta = 1 + x_c,\ \theta = 1 + x_z$)

Year n	$x_c = 0.06$ Cumulative equal—ratio annual average fund coefficient $x_{18} = \begin{cases} \frac{\theta-\beta}{\theta^n-\beta^n}\frac{\theta^n-1}{\theta-1} (\beta \neq \theta) \\ \frac{\theta^{1-n}}{n}\frac{\theta^n-1}{\theta-1} (\beta = \theta) \end{cases}$					$x_c = 0.08$ Cumulative equal—ratio annual average fund coefficient $x_{18} = \begin{cases} \frac{\theta-\beta}{\theta^n-\beta^n}\frac{\theta^n-1}{\theta-1} (\beta \neq \theta) \\ \frac{\theta^{1-n}}{n}\frac{\theta^n-1}{\theta-1} (\beta = \theta) \end{cases}$				
	$x_z = 0.04$	$x_z = 0.06$	$x_z = 0.08$	$x_z = 0.10$	$x_z = 0.15$	$x_z = 0.04$	$x_z = 0.06$	$x_z = 0.08$	$x_z = 0.10$	$x_z = 0.15$
1	1	1	1	1	1	1	1	1	1	1
2	0.9714	0.9717	0.972	0.9722	0.9725	0.9623	0.9626	0.963	0.9633	0.9636
3	0.9438	0.9445	0.9452	0.9458	0.9465	0.926	0.9269	0.9278	0.9286	0.9295
4	0.917	0.9183	0.9195	0.9207	0.9219	0.891	0.8927	0.8943	0.8958	0.8974
5	0.891	0.893	0.895	0.8969	0.8987	0.8574	0.86	0.8624	0.8649	0.8672
6	0.8659	0.8687	0.8715	0.8742	0.8768	0.8251	0.8286	0.8321	0.8355	0.8389
7	0.8416	0.8453	0.849	0.8526	0.8561	0.794	0.7987	0.8033	0.8078	0.8122
8	0.818	0.8228	0.8275	0.8321	0.8366	0.7641	0.77	0.7758	0.7815	0.7871
9	0.7952	0.8011	0.8069	0.8126	0.8181	0.7353	0.7425	0.7496	0.7566	0.7635
10	0.7731	0.7802	0.7871	0.794	0.8007	0.706	0.7162	0.7247	0.7331	0.7413
11	0.7517	0.76	0.7682	0.7763	0.7842	0.681	0.691	0.7009	0.7107	0.7204
12	0.7309	0.7406	0.7501	0.7595	0.7687	0.6553	0.6668	0.6782	0.6895	0.7006
13	0.7108	0.7218	0.7328	0.7435	0.754	0.6307	0.6437	0.6566	0.6694	0.682
14	0.6913	0.7038	0.7161	0.7282	0.7401	0.6069	0.6215	0.636	0.6503	0.6645
15	0.6724	0.6863	0.7001	0.7137	0.7269	0.5841	0.6002	0.6163	0.6322	0.6479
16	0.654	0.6695	0.6848	0.6999	0.7145	0.5621	0.5798	0.5975	0.615	0.6323

(continued)

Table B.23 (continued)

Year n	$x_c = 0.06$ Cumulative equal—ratio annual average fund coefficient $x_{18} = \begin{cases} \frac{\theta-\beta}{\theta^n-\beta^n}\frac{\theta^n-1}{\theta-1}(\beta \neq \theta) \\ \frac{\theta^{1-n}}{n}\frac{\theta^n-1}{\theta-1}(\beta = \theta) \end{cases}$					$x_c = 0.08$ Cumulative equal—ratio annual average fund coefficient $x_{18} = \begin{cases} \frac{\theta-\beta}{\theta^n-\beta^n}\frac{\theta^n-1}{\theta-1}(\beta \neq \theta) \\ \frac{\theta^{1-n}}{n}\frac{\theta^n-1}{\theta-1}(\beta = \theta) \end{cases}$				
	$x_z = 0.04$	$x_z = 0.06$	$x_z = 0.08$	$x_z = 0.10$	$x_z = 0.15$	$x_z = 0.04$	$x_z = 0.06$	$x_z = 0.08$	$x_z = 0.10$	$x_z = 0.15$
17	0.6363	0.6533	0.6701	0.6867	0.7028	0.541	0.5602	0.5795	0.5987	0.6176
18	0.6191	0.6376	0.6561	0.6742	0.6917	0.5207	0.5414	0.5623	0.5831	0.6037
19	0.6024	0.6225	0.6425	0.6622	0.6813	0.5011	0.5234	0.5459	0.5684	0.5905
20	0.5862	0.6079	0.6295	0.6508	0.6714	0.4823	0.5061	0.5302	0.5543	0.5781
25	0.5122	0.542	0.5719	0.6013	0.6295	0.3983	0.4292	0.4612	0.4934	0.5254
30	0.4487	0.4864	0.5246	0.5621	0.5979	0.329	0.3661	0.4053	0.4454	0.4852
35	0.3939	0.4391	0.4855	0.531	0.5741	0.2718	0.3139	0.3596	0.407	0.4542
40	0.3465	0.3987	0.4529	0.5062	0.5561	0.2246	0.276	0.322	0.3761	0.4302
45	0.3055	0.3641	0.4258	0.4864	0.5425	0.1856	0.2344	0.2906	0.3509	0.4114
50	0.2699	0.3342	0.4029	0.4704	0.5322	0.1535	0.2039	0.2642	0.3302	0.3965

Table B.24 Cumulative equal—ratio annual average fund coefficient x_{18} ($\beta = 1 + x_c,\ \theta = 1 + x_z$)

Year n	$x_c = 0.10$ Cumulative equal—ratio annual average fund coefficient $x_{18} = \begin{cases} \frac{\theta-\beta}{\theta^n-\beta^n}\frac{\theta^n-1}{\theta-1} (\beta \neq \theta) \\ \frac{\theta^{1-n}}{n}\frac{\theta^n-1}{\theta-1} (\beta = \theta) \end{cases}$					$x_c = 0.15$ Cumulative equal—ratio annual average fund coefficient $x_{18} = \begin{cases} \frac{\theta-\beta}{\theta^n-\beta^n}\frac{\theta^n-1}{\theta-1} (\beta \neq \theta) \\ \frac{\theta^{1-n}}{n}\frac{\theta^n-1}{\theta-1} (\beta = \theta) \end{cases}$				
	$x_z = 0.04$	$x_z = 0.06$	$x_z = 0.08$	$x_z = 0.10$	$x_z = 0.15$	$x_z = 0.04$	$x_z = 0.06$	$x_z = 0.08$	$x_z = 0.10$	$x_z = 0.15$
1	1	1	1	1	1	1	1	1	1	1
2	0.9533	0.9537	0.9541	0.9545	0.955	0.9315	0.9321	0.9327	0.9333	0.9348
3	0.9086	0.9097	0.9108	0.9118	0.9129	0.8671	0.8686	0.8701	0.8716	0.8752
4	0.8659	0.8679	0.8698	0.8717	0.8736	0.8065	0.8092	0.8119	0.8154	0.8208
5	0.8251	0.8281	0.8311	0.834	0.8368	0.7497	0.7537	0.7576	0.7615	0.771
6	0.7861	0.7903	0.7944	0.7985	0.8024	0.6964	0.7018	0.7071	0.7124	0.7254
7	0.7489	0.7544	0.7597	0.765	0.7703	0.6464	0.6533	0.6601	0.6669	0.6835
8	0.7133	0.7202	0.7269	0.7336	0.7401	0.5996	0.608	0.6163	0.6246	0.6451
9	0.6794	0.6876	0.6958	0.7039	0.7119	0.5558	0.5656	0.5755	0.5854	0.6097
10	0.6469	0.6567	0.6663	0.6759	0.6854	0.5148	0.5261	0.5375	0.5489	0.5772
11	0.616	0.6272	0.6384	0.6495	0.6605	0.4766	0.4893	0.5021	0.515	0.5472
12	0.5864	0.5992	0.6119	0.6246	0.6371	0.4408	0.4548	0.4691	0.4834	0.5195
13	0.5582	0.5725	0.5868	0.6011	0.6152	0.4075	0.4227	0.4383	0.454	0.4939
14	0.5313	0.5471	0.5629	0.5788	0.5946	0.3765	0.3928	0.4096	0.4267	0.4702
15	0.5056	0.5229	0.5403	0.5578	0.5752	0.3476	0.3649	0.3828	0.4012	0.4483
16	0.4811	0.4998	0.5188	0.5379	0.5569	0.3208	0.3389	0.3579	0.3774	0.428

(continued)

Table B.24 (continued)

Year n	$x_c = 0.10$ Cumulative equal—ratio annual average fund coefficient $x_{18} = \begin{cases} \frac{\theta-\beta}{\theta^n-\beta^n}\frac{\theta^n-1}{\theta-1}(\beta \neq \theta) \\ \frac{\theta^{1-n}}{n}\frac{\theta^n-1}{\theta-1}(\beta = \theta) \end{cases}$					$x_c = 0.15$ Cumulative equal—ratio annual average fund coefficient $x_{18} = \begin{cases} \frac{\theta-\beta}{\theta^n-\beta^n}\frac{\theta^n-1}{\theta-1}(\beta \neq \theta) \\ \frac{\theta^{1-n}}{n}\frac{\theta^n-1}{\theta-1}(\beta = \theta) \end{cases}$				
	$x_z = 0.04$	$x_z = 0.06$	$x_z = 0.08$	$x_z = 0.10$	$x_z = 0.15$	$x_z = 0.04$	$x_z = 0.06$	$x_z = 0.08$	$x_z = 0.10$	$x_z = 0.15$
17	0.4577	0.4778	0.4984	0.519	0.5397	0.2958	0.3147	0.3346	0.3552	0.4091
18	0.4354	0.4569	0.4789	0.5012	0.5235	0.2726	0.2921	0.3129	0.3345	0.3915
19	0.4141	0.437	0.4605	0.4843	0.5082	0.251	0.2711	0.2926	0.3152	0.3752
20	0.3939	0.418	0.4429	0.4682	0.4937	0.2311	0.2516	0.2737	0.2971	0.3599
25	0.3059	0.3354	0.3668	0.3994	0.4325	0.1514	0.1725	0.1963	0.2227	0.2974
30	0.2369	0.2701	0.3067	0.3457	0.3858	0.098	0.1177	0.1412	0.1687	0.2517
35	0.1829	0.2183	0.2588	0.3031	0.3496	0.0627	0.0799	0.1019	0.129	0.2174
40	0.1409	0.177	0.2201	0.2689	0.321	0.0397	0.0541	0.0737	0.0994	0.191
45	0.1083	0.1439	0.1887	0.2411	0.2982	0.025	0.0365	0.0534	0.0772	0.1701
50	0.0831	0.1173	0.1628	0.2181	0.2797	0.0156	0.0245	0.0387	0.0602	0.1532

Appendix C
Catalogue of Author's Total Achievement

1959

[1] Shoubo Xu, Некоторые вопросы развития энергетики Китая, 《Общая энергетика》, No. 1 изд. АНСССР, 1959.

[2] Shoubo Xu, Определение максимальных отопительных нагрузок ТЭЦ, Bulletin of the Soviet Academy of Science 《Автоматика и энергетика》.
No. 6, 1959 (won the second prize of youth Science of Energy Institute of Soviet Academy of Sciences in 1959).

1960

[3] Shoubo Xu, Выбор расчетных графиков среднесуточных расходов тепла и воды при проектировании ТЭЦ и ГЭС, 《Общая энергетика》,, No. 3, изд. АНСССР, 1960.

1961

[4] Shoubo Xu, Вопросы энергетического районирования на примере КНР, 《Электричество》, 1960, No. 12.

[5] Shoubo Xu, Некоторые вопросы энерге – тического районирования К. Н. Р. , Associate Doctoral Thesis, Moscow, 1960 (The Lenin Library of the Soviet Union).

[6] Shoubo Xu, Методика выбора оптимальной мощности ТЭЦ в сложных энерго –

системах К. Н. Р. 1960, Read the Symposium.
(Won the second prize of youth Science of Energy Institute of Soviet Academy of Sciences in 1960).

1961

[7] Shoubo Xu, Zhijie Huang. Synthetic Energetic in the Soviet Union. China Daily, August 4, 1961.

S. Xu, *Technological Economics*,
https://doi.org/10.1007/978-981-15-8582-1

1962

[8] Shoubo Xu, The Main Problems of the Future Development of Thermalization in China. Compilation of Papers at Thermalization Academic Conference in 1961. March 1962.

[9] Shoubo Xu, The Developments of Foreign Thermalization. Compilation of Papers at Thermalization Academic Conference in 1961. March 1962.

[10] Shoubo Xu, Zhijie Huang. Some Facts about the Composition of the Fuel Industry. China Daily, May 25, 1962.

[11] Shoubo Xu, Some Information on the Development Speed of the Power Industry, China Daily, August 2, 1962.

[12] Shoubo Xu, Research on the Domestic Development Speed of the Electric Power Industry. Research Report of the Comprehensive Investigation Committee of the Chinese Academy of Sciences, October 1962.

[13] Shoubo Xu, Calculation Method and Principle of Reasonable Water-Heat Ratio of Power System, Annual Conference Paper of Beijing Electrical Engineering Society in 1962.

[14] Shoubo Xu, On The Design Standards of Heating Systems in China, Annual Conference Paper of Beijing Electrical Engineering Society in 1962.
(**Recommended for Scientific Invention and Creation Award in 1962**).

1963

[15] Shoubo Xu, Responsible for drafting the scientific plan outline of "Technology and Economy", Outline of the National Program for Long-Term Scientific and Technological Development from 1963 to 1972, 1963.

[16] Shoubo Xu, Actively carry out technical and economic research, china daily, September 19, 1963.

[17] Shoubo Xu, Technical Economic Methodology Issues (Part 3), Research Report of the Comprehensive Investigation Committee of the Chinese Academy of Sciences, October 1963.

[18] Shoubo Xu, Hydropower and Thermal Power Generation, China Daily, May 6, 1963.

[19] Shoubo Xu, Zhirong Yang. Discussion on Comparable Conditions of Capacity and Electricity in the Comparison of Hydro and Thermal Power Program, Water Conservancy and Hydropower Technology, 1963 (3).

[20] Shoubo Xu, Shiwei Zhu, Some Problems of Rural Electrification in China, Wenhui Daily, April 9, 1963.

[21] Shoubo Xu, On Rural Electrification, Popular Science, 1963 (5).

[22] Shoubo Xu, The Economical Thickness of Thermal Pipelines in China and the Selection of Materials, Annual Conference Paper of Beijing Electrical Engineering Society in 1963.

[23] Lang Wan (Shoubo Xu's pseudonym), Rural Power Network, Popular Science, 1963 (5).

1964

[24] Shoubo Xu, Tasks and Functions of Technical Economic Research, Chemical Technology Data: Chemical Engineering Design, 1964 (1).

[25] Shoubo Xu, Purpose, Task and Method of Technical Economic Research, Chinese Science Bulletin, 1964 (7).

[26] Shoubo Xu, Technical Economic Methodology Issues (Parts 2 and 4), Research Report of the Comprehensive Investigation Committee of the Chinese Academy of Sciences, November 1964.

[27] Shoubo Xu, Reasonable Use of Heavy Oil, China Daily, December 19, 1964.

[28] Shoubo Xu, Several Issues on the Balance of Fuel Kinetic Energy, Chinese Science Bulletin, 1964 (4).

[29] Ligao Chen, Lang Wan (Shoubo Xu's pseudonym). De-icing of Power Lines, Popular Science, 1964 (3).

1965

[30] Shoubo Xu, Technical Economic Methodology Issues (Parts 1 and 5), Research Report of the Comprehensive Investigation Committee of the Chinese Academy of Sciences, June 1965.

[31] Shoubo Xu, Technical Economic Methodology Issues, Research Report of the Comprehensive Investigation Committee of the Chinese Academy of Sciences, June 1965.

[32] Shoubo Xu, etc. Reasonable Utilization and Distribution of Heavy Oil Resources in China. published by National Science and Technology Committee, June 1965.

[33] Shoubo Xu, etc. Research on the Reasonable Utilization of Natural Gas in Sichuan Province, Research Report of the Comprehensive Investigation Committee of the Chinese Academy of Sciences, November 1965.

1973

[34] Shoubo Xu, etc. Investigation Report on Industrial Waste Heat in Tianjin, May 1973, (Planning Commission Document No. 149 of 73).

[35] Shoubo Xu, etc. Investigation Report on Industrial Waste Heat in Shanghai, November 1973.

[36] Shoubo Xu, etc. Heat Energy must be Used and Exhaust Gas must be Recycled (Materials for the National Conservation Conference in 1973), December 1973.

1975

[37] Shoubo Xu, etc. Scientific and Technological Development Plan for Rational and Comprehensive Utilization of Energy Resources in China, 1976-1985 (first draft), August 11, 1975.

1976

[38] Shoubo Xu, etc. Rational Utilization of Industrial Secondary Energy in China, Rational utilization of industrial secondary energy in China, 1973–1976.

(Won the 1978 Major Scientific and Technological Achievement Award of Chinese Academy Sciences, 1978 National Science Conference Award, ranking first).

1977

[39] Shoubo Xu, Utilization Approaches of Industrial Secondary Energy, Energy, 1977 (1).

[40] Shoubo Xu, Main Tasks of Energy Research, Bulletin of the National Natural Science Discipline Planning Conference (162), October 30, 1977.

[41] Shoubo Xu, Responsible for drafting the planning outline of "Energy Science and Technology", the eleventh main task of National Program for Long-Term Scientific and Technological Development, December 1977.

1978

[42] Shoubo Xu, Actively carry out technical and economic research on energy balance issues, Volume of essays of Technical Economy and Management Modernization Issues, Sanlian Bookstore, 1978.

[43] Shoubo Xu, Vigorously Strengthen the Science and Technology Research of Energy Utilization, Energy, 1978 (1).

[44] Shoubo Xu, Discussions on Energy Science and Technology, Scientists' Conversation, China National Radio, May 19, 1978 and August 13, 1978.

[45] Shoubo Xu, Introduction to Energy Science and Technology, Lectures on scientific Knowledge, 1978.

[46] Shoubo Xu, Zhongxin Li, Chengpeng Fu, Minji Yu. Development of Energy Technology Abroad, Energy, 1978 (2).

1979

[47] Shoubo Xu, Principles of Technical Economic Comparison, Collected Papers on Technical Economy and Issues on Management Modernization, China Social Sciences Press, 1979.

[48] Shoubo Xu, Research on Domestic Railway Energy Issues, Research Report of the Comprehensive Investigation Committee of the Chinese Academy of Sciences, manuscript, May 17, 1979.

[49] Shoubo Xu, A Brief Discussion on Energy Problems in China, Energy, 1979 (3).

[50] Shoubo Xu, Energy in Japan, Energy, 1979 (3).

[51] Shoubo Xu, Energy and Agriculture, Scientists' Conversation, China National Radio, August 5, 1979.

[52] Shoubo Xu, Energy Science and Technology, Scientists Talk About Modern Science and Technology, china Popular Science Press, 1979, Beijing Science and Technology Association, Popular Scientific Material, 1979 (9).

[53] Shoubo Xu, Energy Issues in the Development of National Economy, Guangming Daily, November 10, 1979.

[54] Shoubo Xu, The Relationship between Energy and Economic Development. Beijing Daily, November 23, 1979.

[55] Shoubo Xu, Views on the Energy Problem in China, Research Report of the Comprehensive Investigation Committee of the Chinese Academy of Sciences, December 1979.

[56] Shoubo Xu, Research on Rational Utilization of Coke Resources in China, Collection of Research Papers on Rational Utilization of Coke Resources, 1979.

1980

[57] Shoubo Xu, Introduction to Technical Economics, Shanghai Science and Technology Press printed 1–16,000 volumes in 1980, 16,001–30,000 volumes were printed for the second time in May 1981.

[58] Shoubo Xu, On the Science of Technical Economy, Technical Economy and Management Modern Communication, April 10, 1980.

[59] Shoubo Xu, On the Rational Utilization and Preferential Distribution of Materials, Material Management, 1980 (1).

[60] Shoubo Xu, Rational Utilization of Resources. Basic Knowledge of Industrial Economy, Economic Management Press, 1980.

[61] Shoubo Xu, Views on Energy Situation, Technical Economy and Management Science, 1980 (2).

[62] Shoubo Xu, Energy Issues in China's Four Modernizations, Economic Issues, 1980 (1).

[63] Shoubo Xu, Actively carry out scientific research on energy policy, Technical Economy and Management Modern Communication, February 29, 1980.

[64] Shoubo Xu, Recommendations for scientific Research on Energy Policy, China Daily, March 3, 1980.

[65] Shoubo Xu, Prospects of World Energy, China Report, 1980 (1).

[66] Shoubo Xu, Chengchun Hu, Yangfang Tai. We Love Science, 1980 (1).

[67] Shoubo Xu, New Rural Energy in The Future—Biogas, Science Writing, 1980 (4).

[68] Shoubo Xu, Notes on the Investigation of Rural Energy in Mexico, Encyclopedic Knowledge, 1980 (5).

[69] Shoubo Xu, Low Calorific Value Solid Fuels should be focused on Comprehensive Utilization of Building Materials, Technical Economy and Management Modern Communication, 1980.

[70] Shoubo Xu, Energy technology and Economic Issues (1) (2), Tianjin People's Broadcasting Station Lecture, November 5– 9, 1980.

1981

[71] Shoubo Xu, Theories and Methods of Technical Economy, Systematic Lectures on Technical Economics, Department of Popularization of Science and Technology of China Association for Science and Technology, 1981.

[72] Shoubo Xu, Economic Effect Evaluation Method, Lectures on Economic Effects in Beijing (Lecture 15), July 11, 1981.

[73] Shoubo Xu, Basic Principles of Technical Economic Analysis, Research on Financial Issues, 1981 (3).

[74] Shoubo Xu, On the strategic Objectives of China's Social Development, Technical Economic Research, March 31, 1981 (4).

[75] Shoubo Xu, National Income and Net Income should be the Main Goals of Economic Development, Research on Technical Economy, 1981 (8).

[76] Shoubo Xu, etc. Demonstration Opinions on Baosteel's Second Rolling Mill, April 14, April 23, 1981.

[77] Shoubo Xu, Demonstration Opinions on Sino-Japan Cooperative Development of Bohai Oilfield, March 28, 1981.

[78] Shoubo Xu, The Application of Solar Energy in Rural Mexico, new energy, 1981 (3) (cooperation).

[79] Shoubo Xu, etc. Prospects on World Energy (1985–2000), February 1981 (co translation).

[80] Shoubo Xu, Research on Indian Energy Issues, Technical Economic Research, Reference Material, 1981 (18).

[81] Shoubo Xu, Interpretation of "Generalized Energy Saving", Encyclopedic Knowledge, 1981 (11).

[82] Shoubo Xu, On Energy Prices. Technical Economic Research, Reference Material, 1981 (18).

[83] Shoubo Xu, Energy Saving—A Strategic Countermeasure, Outlook, 1981 (7).

[84] Shoubo Xu, On the Energy Conservation Issues of China, Research Report of Institute of Technological Economics, Chinese Academy of Social Sciences, 1981.

[85] Shoubo Xu, Generalized Energy Conservation Theory, Research Report of Institute of Technological Economics, Chinese Academy of Social Sciences, 1981.

[86] Shoubo Xu, Generalized Energy Conservation Theory (1), (2), Energy and Energy Conservation, 1981 (1) (2).

[87] Shoubo Xu, Vigorously Carry Out Energy Saving Work and Improve Energy Economic Effect, Economic Effect Speech, China National Radio, November 10, 1981, Broadcasting Press, 1982.

[88] Shoubo Xu, Comparison Principles and Methods of Technical Economy of Industrial Energy (first volume), (second volume), Power Engineering, 1981 (4) (5).

[89] Shoubo Xu, Calculation and comparison method of economic effect of generalized energy saving, Technical Economic Research, Reference Material, 1981 (14).

[90] Shoubo Xu, Energy and Economic Effects, Lectures on Economic Effects in Beijing (Lecture 12), July 10, 1981.

[91] Shoubo Xu, Technological Economics of Energy, Research Report of Institute of Technological Economics, Chinese Academy of Social Sciences, 1981.

[92] Shoubo Xu, Basic Theories and Methods of Technological Economics of Energy, Research Report of Institute of Technological Economics, Chinese Academy of Social Sciences, 1981.

1982

[93] Shoubo Xu, To make contributions to creating a new situation in the socialist modernization and realizing the grand goal set by the 12th National Congress of the Communist Party of China, Technical Economic Research, Reference Material, 1982 (9).

[94] Shoubo Xu, Technical economic workers should contribute to the realization of the grand strategic goal put forward by the party, Technical Economy and Management Modern Communication, September 10, 1982.

[95] Shoubo Xu, Issues Concerning the Evaluation Theory and Method of Technical Programs— and Comment on Feasibility Studies Abroad, Technical Economics, 1982(3).

[96] Shoubo Xu, Vigorously carry out scientific research on engineering project plan—and Comment on Feasibility Studies Abroad (Part 1), Technical Economic Research, referential material, 1982 (4).

[97] Shoubo Xu, On the evaluation theory and method of engineering project plan—and Comment on Feasibility Studies Abroad (Part 2), Technical Economic Research, 1982 (4), Technical Economic Research, referential material, 1982 (7).

[98] Shoubo Xu, Technical Economic Principles and Methods of National Economic Adjustment, Technical Economic Research, referential material, 1982 (2).

[99] Shoubo Xu, Suggestions on Adopting Unified Symbols in Technical Economy, Technical Economic Research, referential material, 1982 (1).

[100] Shoubo Xu, Evaluation Method of Socialist Economic Effect, China Post and Telecommunications Corporation, Study Reference Materials (27), February 7,1982.

[101] Shoubo Xu, Comparative conditions for economic comparisons of technical programmes. Economic Weekly, July 26, 1982.

[102] Shoubo Xu, On economic effects and economic benefits, Technical and Economic Research reference, no. 5, 1982.

[103] Shoubo Xu, On the question of price in the evaluation of socialist economy, academic seminar on project evaluation, 1982.

[104] Shoubo Xu, Trial method of program evaluation in national economic construction (discussion draft), Quantitative and Technical Economic Communication, No. 9, 1982.

[105] Shoubo Xu, Objective criteria for the selection of technical programmers and methods for comprehensive evaluation, technical and economic research reference material, no. 10, 1982.

[106] Shoubo Xu, On the methodology of comprehensive evaluation—multi-objective decision-making method and its application, Technical economics and management Research, no. 4, 1982.

[107] Shoubo Xu, Economic evaluation, Comprehensive Energy Management Technology, National Economic Commission, 1982.

[108] Shoubo Xu, On the interconnectedness of sciences, Science of Science, no. 1, 1982.

[109] Desheng Yu, Tingsheng Xao, Shoubo Xu, Some policy issues for Industrial research and development in China during the Adjustment period, September 1982.

[110] Shoubo Xu, Economics of Energy Technology, Hunan People's Publishing House, 1982.

[111] Shoubo Xu, On Generalized Energy Conservation, Hunan People's Publishing House, 1982.

[112] Shoubo Xu, Energy issues and Perspectives in China, Technical Economy, no. 1, 1982, reference material, Technical Economy Research, No. 1, 1982.

[113] Shoubo Xu, On energy, Economic Data of Peking University, No. 2, 1982.

[114] Shoubo Xu, On several issues of energy efficiency in Our country, technical and Economic Research reference, no. 3, 1982.

[115] Shoubo Xu, The generalized energy saving is the key to solve the problem of energy, economics weekly on March 15, 1982.

[116] Shoubo Xu, The new way to solve the problem of energy and economics weekly on November 22, 1982.

[117] Shoubo Xu, A Study of China's energy conservation potential from the perspective of energy consumption in the world, Technology and Economics Center of the State Council (36), October 26, 1982.

[118] Shoubo Xu, Some Suggestions on the comprehensive economic planning of Shanxi energy base construction, Coal energy, No. 1, 1982.

[119] Bo Gao, Zonglin Wang, Shoubo Xu, Japan's experience in energy management and conservation, Materials Press, 1982.

[120] Shoubo Xu, Technical and economic theory and method of generalized energy conservation, Chinese Social Science, 1982.

[121] Shoubo Xu, Basic theories and methods of energy technology and economy, Chapter 4 of Energy Management, Energy Press, 1982.

[122] Shoubo Xu, Economic effect calculation and Comparison methods of energy saving, on economic effect, People's Publishing house, 1982.

[123] Shoubo Xu, On technical and economic theory of energy systems, technical and economic Research, ref. No. 6, 1982.

[124] Shoubo Xu, The rational use of resources, Lectures on basic Knowledge of Industrial economy and enterprise management, China Social Sciences Press, 1982.

1983

[125] Shoubo Xu, To strengthen the research of technical economics and to serve for creating a new situation of combining technology and economy, Quantitative and Technical economic Research, 1983, 1.

[126] Shoubo Xu, On the economic evaluation of the role of scientific and technological progress, Technical economics and management Research, 1983, 2.

[127] Shoubo Xu, On the question of price in the national economic evaluation of construction projects, Technical economy, no. 2, 1983.

[128] Shoubo Xu, The role of technology economy in science and technology advisory services, Modern communication of technology economy and management, 25 March 1983.

[129] Shoubo Xu, Time factor calculation table and its application, the quantity and the technical and economic research, no. 4, 1983.

[130] Shoubo Xu, Pilot method of program evaluation in national economic construction (discussion draft), quantitative and technical economic research, No. 5, 1983.

[131] Shoubo Xu, Technical and economic workers should contribute to the realization of the grand strategic objectives proposed by the Party, theory and practice of technical economy, Chinese Society of Technical and economic studies, 1983.

[132] Shoubo Xu, Strengthen energy development and economize energy consumption, People's Daily, January 21, 1983.

[133] Shoubo Xu, Creating a new situation in enterprise energy management, Technical economy and management research, 1983, 1.

[134] Shoubo Xu, Create a new situation of the construction of the energy, the energy and the energy saving 1983, 2.

[135] Shoubo Xu, etc. Research on comprehensive Planning for the construction of Heavy chemical and energy Bases in Shanxi Province, completed in the past two years by 1400 experts from dozens of units in China and Shanxi Province. 459 thematic achievements and their plans, 150 drawings and 26 mathematical models were completed in 1983. As one of the general consultants of planning and research, Xu Shoubo is responsible for the overall design and research of energy base construction project planning. He has personally completed 14 scientific and technological achievements (10 of which are cooperative).

(1985 Excellent Research Report Award of Chinese Academy of Social Sciences, Ranking the First).

[136] Shoubo Xu, Research report on planning technology and economy of Heavy chemical and energy Bases in Shanxi Province, one of the results, Research Group of Planning engineering of heavy chemical and energy Bases in Shanxi Province, 1983.

(1985 Excellent Research Report Award of Chinese Academy of Social Sciences, Ranking the First).

[137] Shoubo Xu, Some Suggestions on the comprehensive planning of energy base construction in Shanxi Province, research group of Shanxi Energy and Heavy chemical industry Base Planning Project, one of the results, 1983.

(1985 Excellent Research Report Award of Chinese Academy of Social Sciences, Ranking the First).

[138] Shoubo Xu, The Effect of Science and Technology Progress of Xu Shoubo In Economic Construction of Shanxi Province, Research report of Institute of Quantitative and Technological Economy, Chinese Academy of Social Sciences (May 1983).

(Awarded Excellent Research Report by Chinese Academy of Social Sciences in 1985).

[139] Shoubo Xu, A comprehensive evaluation of three coal development schemes in Shanxi Province, research group of Shanxi Energy and Heavy chemical Industry Base Planning Project, one of the results, 1983.

(1985 Excellent Research Report Award of Chinese Academy of Social Sciences, Ranking the First).

[140] Shoubo Xu, Comprehensive evaluation and research of the Shanxi coal energy development policy, the quantity and the technical and economic research, 1983, 6.

[141] Shoubo Xu, Comprehensive evaluation of three coal development schemes in Shanxi Province, Energy Policy Research Newsletter, no. 17, 1983.

[142] Shoubo Xu, etc. Comprehensive balance of coal production in Shanxi Province, one of the studies on comprehensive balance engineering, Research group of Shanxi Energy heavy chemical Industry Base Planning Engineering, one of the results, 1983.

(1985 Excellent Research Report Award of Chinese Academy of Social Sciences, Ranking the First).

[143] Shoubo Xu, etc. Comprehensive balance of coal transportation in Shanxi Province, research group of Shanxi Energy and Heavy Chemical Industry Base Planning project, one of the results, 1983.

(1985 Excellent Research Report Award of Chinese Academy of Social Sciences, Ranking the First).

[144] Shoubo Xu, etc. Comprehensive Balance of coal and power transportation in Shanxi Province, part III: Comprehensive Balance Engineering Research Group, Shanxi Energy and Heavy chemical Engineering Base Planning Project, one of the results, 1983.

(1985 Excellent Research Report Award of Chinese Academy of Social Sciences, Ranking the First).

[145] Shoubo Xu, etc. Comprehensive Balance in various sectors of the national economy in Shanxi Province, research group of Comprehensive Balance Engineering, Shanxi Energy and Heavy chemical Industry Base Planning Engineering, one of the results, 1983.

(1985 Excellent Research Report Award of Chinese Academy of Social Sciences, Ranking the First).

[146] Shoubo Xu, etc. Shanxi Province should pay equal attention to coal development and coal saving, research group of Shanxi Energy and Heavy chemical Industry Base Planning Project, one of the achievements, 1983.

(1985 Excellent Research Report Award of Chinese Academy of Social Sciences, Ranking the First).

[147] Shoubo Xu, etc. Energy Model (CTEEMS–S1), research group of Shanxi Energy and Heavy Chemical Base Planning Project, one of the results, 1983.

(1985 Excellent Research Report Award of Chinese Academy of Social Sciences, Ranking the First).

[148] Shoubo Xu,etc. Shanxi coal production balance model—Energy model (CTEEMS–S2), Research group of Shanxi Energy Heavy Chemical Industry Base Planning Project, one of the results, 1983.

(1985 Excellent Research Report Award of Chinese Academy of Social Sciences, Ranking the First).

[149] Shoubo Xu, etc. National Economic Evaluation Model of Shanxi Planned Project—Energy Model (CTEEMS–S3), research group of Shanxi Energy Heavy Chemical Industry Base Planning Engineering, one of the results, 1983.

(1985 Excellent Research Report Award of Chinese Academy of Social Sciences, Ranking the First).

[150] Shoubo Xu, A preliminary study on the technical and economic policy of coal development in Shanxi Province, research group of Shanxi Energy and Heavy chemical Industry Base Planning Project, one of the achievements, 1983.

(1985 Excellent Research Report Award of Chinese Academy of Social Sciences, Ranking the First).

[151] Shoubo Xu, etc. A preliminary study on the management system of shanxi energy and Heavy chemical Industry Base, research group of Shanxi Energy and heavy chemical Industry Base Planning Project, one of the achievements, 1983.

(1985 Excellent Research Report Award of Chinese Academy of Social Sciences, Ranking the First).

[152] Shoubo Xu, Case studies of energy technology and economy, Science of Popular Practical Economic Effects, Science press, 1983.

1984

[153] Shoubo Xu, The technical economics (books 1 and 2), China's science and technology policy research, modern management knowledge branch of China Association for Science and Technology in 1984.

[154] Shoubo Xu, General principles of economic effects, Industrial and technological Economy, No. 1, 2, 1984.

[155] Shoubo Xu, On ways to improve the overall economic effect of society, industrial and technological economy, No. 5, 1984.

[156] Shoubo Xu, Science and technology progress and economic evaluation, textbook compilation of Science and Technology Consulting, China Science and Technology Consulting Service Center, September 1984.

[157] Shoubo Xu, On the Construction of Technical Economics with Chinese Characteristics—The experience of studying Selected Works of Deng Xiaoping, Quantitative and technical economic Studies, Vol. 1, 1984.

[158] Shoubo Xu, Feihong Gong. Technical and economic model of master Planning, Compilation of Mathematical Models of Shanxi comprehensive Planning Economy, 1984.

(Awarded Excellent Research Report by Chinese Academy of Social Sciences in 1985).

[159] Shujin Ji (Pseudonym of Shoubo Xu), Methods of project evaluation, feasibility study and economic evaluation, Shanxi People's Publishing house, 1984.

[160] Shoubo Xu, Talk about energy consumption strategy, Energy and environment, nos. 5 and 6, 1984.

[161] Lang Wan (Pseudonym of Shoubo Xu), Development and prospect of China's energy economy, quantitative and technical economic Research, No. 10, 1984.

[162] Shoubo Xu, On several issues of China's energy development strategy, economic and social development strategy research, 1984.

[163] Shoubo Xu, A comprehensive evaluation of three coal development schemes in Shanxi Province, China energy economics, Energy Press, 1984.

[164] Shoubo Xu, Principles and Methods of technical and economic comparison of industrial energy, plant Energy Saving album, Machinery Industry Press, 1984.

[165] Shoubo Xu, etc. Dynamic programming model of coal production structure, Compilation of Shanxi comprehensive planning Models, one of the results, 1984.

(1985 Excellent Research Report Award of Chinese Academy of Social Sciences, Ranking the First).

[166] Shoubo Xu, etc. Model of project evaluation method, Compilation of Shanxi comprehensive Planning model, one of the results, 1984.

(1985 Excellent Research Report Award of Chinese Academy of Social Sciences, Ranking the First)

[167] Shoubo Xu, On the loss of air pollution in China, Atmospheric environment and acid rain, no. 3, 1984.

[168] Shoubo Xu, Continuation of Necessary for Factory Director, chief Editor of Energy Technology, People's Publishing House, 1984.

1985

[169] Shoubo Xu, General lecture on technical Economics, Quantitative and Technical Economic Research, no. 1–6, 1985.

[170] Shoubo Xu, Technical economics, Science of Science and management of Science and Technology, no. 7, no. 8, 1985.

[171] Shoubo Xu, Technological economy of enterprise scale, Industrial technological economy, no. 1, 1985

[172] Shoubo Xu, Information and economic benefits, Taiyuan Economy, no. 1, 1985.

[173] Shoubo Xu, Energy development strategy in China energy Metallurgy, 2000, February 1, 1985.

(In China in 2000, won the first prize of national Science and Technology Progress in 1988, one of the participants, only the certificate of award, no certificate).

[174] Shoubo Xu, A few questions on China's energy development strategy, quantitative and technical economic research, no. 4, 1985.

[175] Shoubo Xu, A few questions on China's energy development strategy, collection of China's energy development Strategy, 1985.

[176] Shoubo Xu, Suggestions to rational utilization of one hundred million tons of oil, the reasonable use of one hundred million tons of oil symposium proceedings, the People's Republic of China in January 1985.

[177] Shoubo Xu, Some questions on the study of logistics technology and economy, Wu Liu of China. Volume 1, pp. 16–18 (1985).

1986

[178] Shoubo Xu, Technical Economics, 3rd edition, Jiangsu People's Publishing House, 1986.

Shoubo Xu, Research on evaluation methods of technology economy, Industrial technology Economy, nos. 2–5, 1986.

[180] Shoubo Xu, Methods of technical and economic evaluation, Efficiency and management, no. 4, 1986.

[181] Shoubo Xu, On several issues in the economics of environmental technology, Environmental Science in China, no. 1, 1986.

[182] Shoubo Xu, Understanding of some problems in the development of southwest China, Southwest Development, no. 2, 1986.

[183] Shoubo Xu, The road of Economic development in Shanxi Province: integration of coal, electricity, steel and machinery, Shanxi Economic News, November 21, 1986.

[184] Shoubo Xu, Handbook of Modern Engineers, chief Editor of Technology economy and Energy Technology, Beijing Press, 1986.

(National Science and Technology Excellent Book Award in 1986).

[185] Shoubo Xu, China's nuclear power development strategy, Energy Policy Research Newsletter, no. 7, 1986.

[186] Shoubo Xu, etc. Analysis of the international coal market and the possibility and Countermeasures of expanding the foreign exchange of China's coal export Research report of institute of Quantitative and Technical Economics of Chinese Academy of Social Sciences December 1986.

(Won the third prize of excellent Achievement of Institute of Quantitative and Technical Economics, Academy of Social Sciences in 1986).

[187] Shoubo Xu, etc. Analysis of air pollution, Institute of Quantitative and Technical Economics, Chinese Academy of Social Sciences, 1986.

(Awarded the Second Prize of the Outstanding Achievement of Institute of Quantitative and Technical Economics of The Academy of Social Sciences in 1989).

[188] Shoubo Xu, The general situation of Coal logistics in China, Logistics Information, no. 34, 1986.

(Won the Second Prize of China Logistics Research Association in 1987).

1987

[189] Shoubo Xu, Several problems in the development of technical economics in China, Quantitative and technical Economics Research, 1987, No. 1.

[190] Shoubo Xu, The technical principles of economics, modern engineers continue education supplementary notes engineering and technical personnel to continue education ZhuanXiuBan office, in 1987, economic management publishing house in October 1987.

[191] Shoubo Xu, etc. Technical economics problem Solving, office of continuing Education for engineers and Technicians, 1987.

[192] Shoubo Xu, A new index for the comprehensive assessment of the economic benefits of enterprises—the index of domestic competitiveness, Industrial technology economy, no. 3, 1987.

[193] Shoubo Xu, Feng Yan. Time factor calculation method and its application, quantitative economic and technical economic research, 1987, no. 11.

[194] Shoubo Xu, Technological progress and industrial structure change, research report of institute of Quantitative and Technical Economics, Chinese Academy of Social Sciences, July 1987.

[195] Shoubo Xu, An Overview of the regional functions and historical orientation of Shanxi's economic development in the last decade, Shanxi Economic News, October 23, 1987.

[196] Shoubo Xu, New China Quarterly (European Edition), no. 7, 1987.

[197] Shoubo Xu, Capital energy development strategy, research report of institute of Quantitative and Technical Economics, Chinese Academy of Social Sciences, December 1987.

[198] Shoubo Xu, China's nuclear power development strategy, quantitative economic, technological and economic Research, No. 7, 1987.

[199] Shoubo Xu, China's nuclear power development strategy, Energy and Energy Conservation, 1987, no. 1.

[200] Shoubo Xu, Guide to Energy Conservation, trans. Cheng Jigao, Xu Shoubo, Water conservancy and electric Power press, 1987.

[201] Wan Lang (pseudonym of Xu Shoubo), On Energy Forecasting, Beijing Daily, January 27, 1987.

[202] Xu Shoubo. On the development strategy of the energy base economic Zone, World Economic Herald, 27 April 1987.

[203] Xu Shoubo, Fu Jian, Chen Zhongrong. On Energy Base and its Functions, Energy Base Construction, 1987, 1st issue.

[204] Xu Shoubo, Fu Jian, Chen Zhongrong. Function and Development Strategy of China energy Base Economic Zone, Beijing Energy Institute study, August 1987.

[205] Xu Shoubo. China's Environmental Strategy, Research Report of Beijing Energy Society, July 1987.

[206] Xu Shoubo (one of the chief editors), Logistics and Its Application, Economic Science Press, 1987.

[207] Xu Shoubo. Logistics Technology and Economy, Logistics science and Its Application [M]. Economic Sciences Press, 1987, 114–154.

1988

[208] Xu Shoubo. Technical Economics, 4th edition, Jiangsu People's Publishing House, 1988.

(1991 National Philosophy and Social Science Bright Cup Second Prize).

(First Prize of Outstanding Achievement of Institute of Quantitative and Technical Economics, Chinese Academy of Social Sciences).

[209] Xu Shoubo, Ed. English and Chinese Glossary of Technical Economics, Electronic Industry Press, 1988.

[210] Xu Shoubo, Research on Technological Progress and Industrial Structure Change, Quantitative Economy, Technological Economy Research, no. 5, 1988.

[211] Xu Shoubo, He Qian. Leading Industry, Advanced Industry, Antecedent Industry and Emerging Industry, Journal of Technical Economics & Management, Number 1 (1988).

[212] Xu Shoubo. The Development Of Large And Medium-Sized Cities Should Take The Road Of New Consumer Cities, Science and Technology Daily, February 1, 1988.

[213] Shoubo Xu, China's Energy Development Strategy, Conference paper on Energy Development Strategies for Developing Countries, United States, April 1988.

[214] Shoubo Xu, The Environment Development Strategy of China, Conference paper on Energy Development Strategies for Developing Countries, United States, April 1988.

[215] Shoubo Xu, Minhua Peng, Energy Technology, Jiangsu People's Publishing House, 1988.

[216] Shoubo Xu, China's Energy Development Strategy, General Report, One of the Results, Research Report of China's Energy Development Strategy, 1984–1988.
(Won the Second Prize of Scientific and Technological Progress of the State Planning Commission in 1991, Ranking the First).

[217] Shoubo Xu, China's General Strategy for Energy Development, One of the Results, Research Report of China's Energy Development Strategy, 1984–1988.
(Won the Second Prizee of Scientific and Technological Progress of the State Planning Commission in 1991, Ranking the First).

[218] Shoubo Xu, etc. China's Sectoral Energy Development Strategy, One of the Results, Research Report of China's Energy Development Strategy, 1984–1988.
(Won the Second Prize of Scientific and Technological Progress of the State Planning Commission in 1991, Ranking the First).

[219] Shoubo Xu, etc. China's Fuel Development Strategy, One of the Results, Research Report of China's Energy Development Strategy, 1984–1988.
(Won the Second Prize of Scientific and Technological Progress of the State Planning Commission in 1991, Ranking the First).

[220] Shoubo Xu, China's Hydropower Development Strategy, One of the Results, Research Report of China's Energy Development Strategy, 1984–1988.
(Won the Second Prize of Scientific and Technological Progress of the State Planning Commission in 1991, Ranking the First).

[221] Shoubo Xu, China's Nuclear Power Development Strategy, One of the Results, Research Report of China's Energy Development Strategy, 1984–1988.
(Won the Second Prize of Scientific and Technological Progress of the State Planning Commission in 1991, Ranking the First).

[222] Shoubo Xu, China's Energy and Environment Development Strategy, One of the Results, Research Report of China's Energy Development Strategy, 1984–1988.
(Won the Second Prize of Scientific and Technological Progress of the State Planning Commission in 1991, Ranking the First).

[223] Shoubo Xu, China's Energy Import and Export Strategy, One of the Results, Research Report of China's Energy Development Strategy, 1984–1988.
(Won the Second Prize of Scientific and Technological Progress of the State Planning Commission in 1991, Ranking the First).

[224] Shoubo Xu, China's Regional Energy Development Strategy, One of the Results, Research Report of China's Energy Development Strategy, 1984–1988.

(Won the Second Prize of Scientific and Technological Progress of the State Planning Commission in 1991, Ranking the First).

[225] Shoubo Xu, Energy Base Energy Development Strategy, One of the Results, Research Report of China's Energy Development Strategy, 1984–1988.

(Won the Second Prize of Scientific and Technological Progress of the State Planning Commission in 1991, Ranking the First).

[226] Shoubo Xu, Capital Energy Development Strategy, One of the Results, Research Report of China's Energy Development Strategy, 1984–1988.

(Won the Second Prize of Scientific and Technological Progress of the State Planning Commission in 1991, Ranking the First).

[227] Shoubo Xu, On the Objective Law of 2E (Energy, Economy) Development, Academic report of the Technical University of Berlin, West Germany, September 1988 (It is a special research report of China's Energy Development Strategy Research) (Won the second prize of Scientific and Technological Progress of the State Planning Commission in 1991, ranking the first).

[228] Shoubo Xu, On the Capital's Energy Development Strategy, Science and Technology Daily, February 8, 1988.

[229] Shoubo Xu, etc. China's Regional Energy Development Strategy, Energy Base Construction, Number 1 (1988).

1989

[230] Shoubo Xu, Research on Technological Progress and Industrial Structure Change, Chinese Industrial Economy and Technology, Number 6, 1989.

[231] Shoubo Xu, Research and Measurement of Social Discount Rate, Research report of Institute and Economy of State Planning Commission, December 1989.

[232] Shoubo Xu, Chief Editor. Continuing Education of Modern Engineering (Learning Guidance), Workers Press, 1989.

[233] Shoubo Xu, etc. Research on China's Energy Development Strategy, there are 34 units in China, 63 experts. Since 1984, it has taken 5 years to complete, including 45 achievements, 1 total achievement, 17 thematic achievements, 27 regional achievements and 1 monograph, which were all completed in 1989. As the research leader, Shoubo Xu was responsible for the overall design and completed the overall research report and 11 thematic achievements personally. (Four of them are cooperative).

(Won the Second Prize of Scientific and Technological Progress of the State Planning Commission in 1991, Ranking the First).

[234] Shoubo Xu, etc. Strategic Options for Energy Development, One of the Results, Jiangsu People's Publishing House, 1989.

(Won the Second Prize of Scientific and Technological Progress of the State Planning Commission in 1991, Ranking the First).

[235] Shoubo Xu, A New Strategy for World Energy Development—Terminal Energy Utilization Strategy, Technical & Economical Research, Number 13, 1989.

[236] Shoubo Xu, Chinese New Energy Development Strategy—Energy Economy Efficiency Strategy, Technical & Economical Research, Number 13, 1989.

[237] Shoubo Xu, Lagging behind Economic Growth is not the Root cause of Energy Shortage, Technical & Economical Research, Number 13, 1989.

[238] Shoubo Xu, How Much Energy Will It Take for Our Country to Reach $4,000 Per Capita By 2050, Technical & Economical Research, Number 13, 1989.

[239] Shoubo Xu, Chinese Energy Crisis and Its Solutions, Energy Base Construction, Volume 4, 1989.

[240] Shoubo Xu, Capital Energy Development Strategy, Lecture Series on Capital Construction, January 1989.

[241] Shoubo Xu, etc. A Study on the Implementation of Daylight Saving Time in China, Research Report of Beijing Energy Society, 1982–1988.

(Won the Second Prize of Scientific and Technological Progress of Beijing in 1987, ranking the second).

[242] Shoubo Xu, On the Objective Law of Energy Economy Development, Research on Quantitative Economy and Technical Economy, Number 11, 1989.

(Won the First Prize of Excellent Paper in 1989 by the Institute of Technology and Economics of the State Planning Commission).

[243] Shoubo Xu, Look at Our Country's Energy Outlet from The World Two Energy Saving Waves, National Planning Commission Economic Research Center "Reference Materials", Number 18, 1989.

[244] Shoubo Xu, Look at Our Country's Energy Outlet from the World Energy Saving Tide, Economic Daily, October 28, 1989.

(Won the First Prize of Excellent Paper in 1989 by the Institute of Technology and Economics of the State Planning Commission).

[245] Shoubo Xu, The Technological Progress of Enterprises should be Centered on Energy Conservation and Consumption Reduction, Technological Progress of Enterprises, Number 3, 1989.

[246] Shoubo Xu, Chinese Environmental Development Strategy, The Journal of Quantitative & Technical Economics, Number 5, 1989.

[247] Shoubo Xu, etc. Chinese Ecological Crisis, Chines Crisis and Thinking, Tianjin People's Publishing House, 1989.

1990

[248] Shoubo Xu, Raise the People's Awareness of Economic Benefits, Science and Technology Daily, June 28, 1990.

[249] Shoubo Xu, Research on the Speed of Economic Growth, China Technical Economy, Number 1, 1990.

[250] Shoubo Xu, The Basic Idea of the Growth Rate of the Eighth Five-Year Plan Economy, Research report of Institute of Technology and Economy of State Planning Commission, 1990.

(In 1991, he was awarded the second prize of Scientific and Technological Progress by the State Planning Commission, ranking the fifth).

[251] Shoubo Xu, Jianli Gong. Chinese Sectoral Energy Development Strategy, China energy, Number 6,1990.

[252] Shoubo Xu, Reflections on the Problems of Energy Shortage in China, Technological Progress of Enterprises, Number 5 1990.

[253] Shoubo Xu, Energy Conservation is the Real Way to Solve the Energy Problem, Science & Technology Review, Number 4, 1990.

[254] Shoubo Xu, etc. The Basic Idea of the Eighth Five-Year Plan for Overall Economy, Research report of Institute of Technology and Economy of State Planning Commission, 1990.

[255] Shoubo Xu, etc. Research on Chinese Comprehensive Economy Strategy from 1991 to 2000, Research report of Institute of Technology and Economy of State Planning Commission, 1990.

[256] Shoubo Xu, Hanling Zhang. Practice Total Economy, People's Daily, May 7th, 1990.

[257] Shoubo Xu, The Basic Idea of the Eighth Five-Year Plan for Overall Economy, Technological Progress of Enterprises, Number 11, 1990.

[258] Shoubo Xu, The Basic Idea of the Eighth Five-Year Plan for Overall Economy, China's Technological Economy, Number 2, 1990.

[259] Shoubo Xu, etc. Demand Energy from Comprehensive Energy Management, To Create a comprehensive way to save more benefits, the State Planning Commission Institute of Technology and Economy Research Report, 1990.

(Won the second prize of Scientific and Technological Progress of the State Planning Commission in 1991).

1991

[260] Shoubo Xu, We Should Attach Importance to the Overall Technological Progress of Enterprises, Beijing Daily, December 17, 1991.

(Won the second prize in essay competition of Capital Entrepreneur Club and Theory Department of Beijing Daily).

[261] Shoubo Xu, On the Evaluation of Economic Benefit of Our Country in the Past Ten Years-The Contribution of Scientific and Technological Progress in the Past Ten Years, China's Technological Economy, Number 4, 1991; Technological Progress of Enterprises, Number 10,11, 1991.

(Won the first prize of the excellent paper of the Institute of Technology and Economy of the State Planning Commission in 1991).

[262] Shoubo Xu, etc. Application and Theory of Tax Rate and Net Output Value of National Capital-Also Comment on Discount Rate in Western Society, Research report of Institute of Technology and Economy of State Planning Commission, August 1991.

[263] Shoubo Xu, etc. Research on the Comprehensive Development and Utilization Layout of Shenmu Coal in China, Research report of Management World China Enterprise Evaluation Center, July 1991.

[264] Shoubo Xu, Energy Demand and Economic Development, Regional Balance and Countermeasures of Energy Supply and Demand Trend in China, China Materials Publishing House, 1991.

(Won the first prize of science and technology progress of Ministry of Materials in 1992, one of the participants).

[265] Shoubo Xu, etc. A Proposal for the Implementation of Daylight Saving Time in Our Country, 1982–1988.

(Won the first prize of excellent suggestion of Beijing Association for Science and Technology in 1991).

1992

[266] Shoubo Xu, Accelerate the Overall Technological Progress of Enterprises and Improve Economic Efficiency, China's Technological Economy, Number 2, 1992.

[267] Shoubo Xu, China's Economic Growth Rate and Industrial Structure, Institute of Information of State Science and Technology Commission, Technology and Development, Number 4, 1992.

[268] Shoubo Xu, To Have a Positive Growth Rate, China Program Management, Number 8, 1992.

(Won the second prize of Scientific and Technological Progress by the Station Planning Commission, ranking the sixth. The award was entitled: Policy recommendations for the preparation of the two-year rolling plan for 1992 and 1993).

[269] Shoubo Xu, Adopt the Strategy of "Accelerating the Development of Economy" to Strive for a New Stage, China's Technological Economy, Number 3, 1992.

(Won the second prize of Scientific and Technological Progress by the State Planning Commission in 1992, ranking the sixth. The award was entitled: Policy recommendations for the preparation of the two-year rolling plan for 1992 and 1993).

[270] Shoubo Xu, China's Dependence on Foreign Trade is a Big Illusion, China's Technological Economy, Number 5, 1992.

[271] Shoubo Xu, Theory and Practice of Technical Economics in China, My Economic Outlook—A report by one hundred economists in contemporary China, Nanjing: Jiangsu People's Publishing House, 1992, 749–790.

[272] Shoubo Xu, Vigorously Carry Out the Research of Economics of Ideological and Political Work, Political Studies, Number 3, 1992, Tianjin Petrochemical Company Staff Ideological and Political Work Research Society.

[273] Shoubo Xu, A Study on China's Comprehensive Economy Strategy, Reality and Choice—A Report from the Research Center of the State Planning Commission, Shanghai People's Publishing House, October, 1992.

[274] Shoubo Xu, etc. A Study on China's Comprehensive Economy Strategy, One of the results of the research report of China's Comprehensive Economy Strategy, Planning and Countermeasures, 1989–1992.

(Won the first prize of Science and Technology Progress of State Planning Commission in 1993; Won the third prize of National Science and Technology Progress in 1995, ranking the second).

[275] Shoubo Xu, etc. Study on China's Comprehensive Economy Strategy, Planning and Countermeasures (General Report), Study Report of Research Group: A Study of Comprehensive Saving Strategy Planning and Countermeasures in China, December 1992.

(Won the first prize of Science and Technology Progress of State Planning Commission in 1993; Won the third prize of National Science and Technology Progress, ranking the second).

[276] Shoubo Xu, etc. Our National Economy and Energy Develop Harmoniously, Research report of Institute of Technology and Economy of State Planning Commission, December 1992.

[277] Shoubo Xu, etc. During the Three Years of Governance and Rectification, China's Energy Production Growth Rate Dropped Sharply, Why will the Economic Output Steadily Increase? Research report of Beijing Energy Society and Institute of Technology and Economy of State Planning Commission, June 1992.

[278] Shoubo Xu, Professor Xu Shoubo Talks About Increasing the Depreciation Rate of Electric Power Enterprises, China Power News, May 26, 1992.

[279] Shoubo Xu, Runtao Wu etc. Research on the Socialization of Logistics in China, Research report of Logistics Technical and Economic Committee of China Society for the Circulation of Materials, 1992.

1993

[280] Shoubo Xu, Efficiency Revolution-Several Problems of China Socialist Market Economy, Institute of Information, State Science and Technology Commission, Development and Choice, 1993.

[281] Shoubo Xu, China's Efficiency Revolution, China's Technological Economy, Number 1, 1993.

[282] Shoubo Xu, Fairness and Efficiency in Socialist Market Economy, Shanghai Economic Forum, Number 1,1993.

[283] Shoubo Xu, A Few Questions about China's Socialist Market Economy, Tianjin Economy, Number 1, 1993.

[284] Shoubo Xu, etc. Evaluation of Economic and Social Development of the South China Sea Petrochemical Project, Research report of Institute of Technology and Economy of State Planning Commission, December 1993.

[285] Shoubo Xu, To Judge the Main Indicators of China's Economic Situation and Their Ways and Means of Regulation and Control, Management World, Number 4, 1993.

[286] Shoubo Xu, etc. Research on Macro-Control Parameters and Mathematical Models of China's Economic and Social Development, Research report of Institute of Technology and Economy of State Planning Commission, December 1993.

[287] Baohuan Yuan, Shiyong Gui, Zhaomu Lin, Shoubo Xu, Economic Development of the Special Zone Open Area, Jiangsu People's Publishing House, 1993.

[288] Shoubo Xu, etc. The Distributive Theory of Socialist Market Economy—The Theory of Efficiency Distribution, Trends in Economic Theory and Practice, April 15, 1993.

[289] Zhaomu Lin, Shoubo Xu, etc. Competition Policy and Competition Law of Germany, Research recommendations (5), February 26, 1993.

[290] Shoubo Xu, etc. Study on China's Comprehensive Economy Strategy, Planning and Countermeasures, it was completed in 3 years by 500 experts from 25 units across the economy, with a total of 37 achievements, one total achievement, 20 thematic achievements, 10 regional achievements and 6 departmental achievements, all of which were completed in 1993. As the research leaser, Shoubo Xu is responsible for the overall research design, and personally completed the overall results and two thematic results, more than 60 mathematical models, and the overall planning and design of Yanhua Generalized energy conservation comprehensive pilot project.

(First prize of Science and Technology Progress of State Planning Commission in 1993; In 1995, the third prize of National Science and Technology Progress, ranking the second).

[291] Shoubo Xu, China's Energy Efficiency Revolution is the Fundamental Solution to the Energy Bottleneck Problem, China's Technological Economy, Number 5, 1993.

[292] Shoubo Xu, etc. Research on the Development Trend and Countermeasures of Urban and Rural Residents' Use of Large Power Consumption Household Electrical Appliances, Research report of Technical and Economic Research Institute of State Planning Commission and Beijing Institute of Water Conservancy and Electric Power Economics, December 1993.

[293] Shoubo Xu, Total Economy Must Be Elevated to the Status of a Development Strategy, Institute of Information of State Science and Technology Commission, Development and Choice, Science and Technology Literature Press, 1993.

[294] Runtao Wu, Li Wang, Shoubo Xu, etc. Research on Rationalization of Logistics in China, Research report of the Logistics Technical and Economic Committee of the China Society for the Circulation of Materials, December 1993.

1994

[295] Shoubo Xu, Eliminating Waste is the Foundation of Enterprises Management, Chinese and Foreign Management, Number 5, 1994.

[296] Shoubo Xu, Rely on Their Own Strength to Strive for China's Famous Brand, The Consumer Times, July 25, 1994.

[297] Shoubo Xu, How to Evaluate China's Economic Benefits, Guangming Daily, July 8, 1994.

(Won 1994 Excellent Paper Award of the Organizing Committee of China's Economic Efficiency Survey in 1994).

[298] Shoubo Xu, etc. China's Macroeconomic Operation Information System, the State Planning Commission Institute of Technology and Economic Development, October 1994.

[299] Shoubo Xu, etc. Feasibility Study Report of Wenzhou New Urban Area Construction Project, Research report of Institute of Technology and Economy of State Planning Commission, January 1994.

[300] Shoubo Xu, etc. Energy Industry Policy in the 1990s, Research report of Institute of Technology and Economy of State Planning Commission, July 1994.

[301] Shoubo Xu, Economy of Energy, People's Publishing House, 1994.

[302] Shoubo Xu, etc. A Study on the Basic Ideas of China's Comprehensive Economy Planning for 200 and 2010, Research report of Institute of Technology and Economy of State Planning Commission, 1994.

1995

[303] Jianming She, Bingyin Bian, Shoubo Xu, Qingqi Shi. Transforming the Pattern of Economic Growth and Industrial Upgrading, Economic Management Press, August 1995.

[304] Shoubo Xu, etc. Basic Idea on Improving Economic Efficiency in the Nine Five-Year Plan Period, Transforming Economic Growth Mode and Industrial Upgrading, Economic Management Press, 1995.

[305] Shoubo Xu, etc. The Transformation of the Economic Growth Pattern of Large and Medium-Sized State-Owned Enterprises, paper of the Seminar on the Development Strategies of Strategies of Large and Medium-Sized Enterprises in the late 1990s, Institute of Policy Science, Chinese Academy of Management Sciences, 1995. 11.2.

[306] Shoubo Xu, China's Lnad Use and Economic Growth Pattern Change, November 20, 1995.

[307] Shoubo Xu, A SCIENTIFIC Index System is Needed to Measure the Transformation of Economic Growth Mode, International Research Report no.4, Institute of Industrial Economy and Technical Economy, State Planning Commission, November 20, 1995.

[308] Shoubo Xu, The Most Urgent Task for Enterprises-Expanding Reproduction in Connotation, China Enterprise News, State Economic and Trade Commission, 1995. 11. 21.

[309] Shoubo Xu, A Scientific Index System is Needed to Measure the Transformation of Economic Growth Mode. Economic Work Newsletter of the State Economic and Trade Commission, Number 23, 1995.

[310] Shoubo Xu, We need a Scientific System of Indicator to Transform the Pattern of Economic Growth, Economic Work Newsletter of the State Economic and Trade Commission, Number 23, 1995,1995.12.13.

[311] Shoubo Xu, Unlocking the Secrets of Economic Growth, China Market Economy News, February 23, 1995

[312] Shoubo Xu, etc. Inflation in China, China Materials Publishing House, 1995.

[313] Shoubo Xu, The Impact of Macro-Control Policies on Enterprise Development in 1995 and the Ninth Five-Year Plan Period, Paper on Development Strategies of Large and Medium-Sized Enterprises in the Late 1990s, Policy and Development Studies, Vol. 12, 1995, Institute of Policy Science, Chinese Academy of Management Sciences.

[314] Shoubo Xu, Macro-Control: What does it Bring to Enterprises? (Upper and lower parts), Open Daily 1995.4.21, 4 25.

[315] Shoubo Xu, The Impact of Macro-Control Policies on Enterprise Development in this year and the Ninth Five-Year Plan Period, China Electronic News, May 26, 1995.

[316] Shoubo Xu, Study on the System of Resource Utilization Bulletin in Qingdao City, Research Report of Beijing Energy Society, 1994–1995.

[317] Shoubo Xu, etc. Study on the Macro-Economic Evaluation of Liaohe Oilfield in the Ninth Five-Year Plan, research report of Institute of Technology and Economy, State Planning Commission, October 1995.

(Won the third prize of Scientific and Technological Progress of Liaoning Province in 1997, ranking the second).

1996

[318] Shoubo Xu, How to Measure the Economic Growth Mode of Enterprises Scientifically, China Electromechanical Daily, January 9,1996.

[319] Shoubo Xu, Real Transformation of Economic Growth Pattern, China Enterprise Management Association, Enterprise Management, Number 1, 1996.

[320] Shoubo Xu, Five Transformations Must be Realized in the Optimal Allocation of Land. Land in China, National Land Administration, Number 1, 1996.

[321] Shoubo Xu, Measure Economic Growth Pattern to Change to Want a Set of Scientific Index System, Shanxi Economist, Number 1, 1996.

[322] Shoubo Xu, A Scientific Index System is Needed to Measure the Transformation of Economic Growth Pattern, Institute of Industrial Economy and Technical Economy, State Planning Commission, China Technical and Economic Science, Number 1, 1996.

[323] Shoubo Xu, The Transformation Economic Growth Pattern Must Have the Scientific Index System, the State Planning Commission, Science, Technology and Economy Pictorial, Number 2, 1996.

[324] Shoubo Xu, Strategies for Enterprises in the Transformation of Economic Growth Pattern, Institute of Policy Science, Chinese Academy of Management Sciences, Conference Paper of Enterprise Strategy Forum, 1996.1.17.

[325] Shoubo Xu, Problems to be Paid Attention to During the Transformation of Economic Growth Pattern, Internal Research Report of Institute of Industrial Economy and Technical Economy, State Planning Commission, Number 1, 1996.

[326] Shoubo Xu, Economic Growth Pattern Should Pay Attention to the Problems in the Process of Transformation, the National Planning Commission Macroeconomic Research Institute, Reference Materials, Number 9, 1996 1996.3. 15.

[327] Shoubo Xu, Problems to be Noticed in the Transformation of Economic Growth Pattern, Institute of Industrial Economy and Technical Economy, State Planning Commission, China Technical and Economic Science, Number 2, 1996.

[328] Shoubo Xu, etc. Exploration on Transformation of Economic Growth Mode of State-Owned Enterprises, Macroeconomic Management, State Planning Commission, Number 4, 1996.

[329] Shoubo Xu, Problems that should be Paid Attention to During the Transformation of Economic Growth Pattern, Economic Reform and Development, State Planning Commission, Number 5, 1996.

[330] Shoubo Xu, Two Issues that should be Paid Attention to During the Transformation of Economic Growth Patter. National Bureau of Statistics, China's National Conditions, Number 9, 1996.

[331] Shoubo Xu, Problems to be Noticed in the Transformation of the Pattern of Economic Growth, Research Office of the State Council and Policy Research Office of the CPC Central Committee, Number 6, 1996.

[332] Shoubo Xu, On the Transformation Process of Economic Growth Pattern, Shanghai Economic Forecast, Number 26, 1996.

[333] Shoubo Xu, etc. Evaluation Indexes and Problems to be Noticed in Transforming Economic Growth Pattern, Economic Growth Industry Development, Economic Daily Press, 1996.

[334] Shoubo Xu, etc. Research on the Transformation of China's Economic Growth Pattern, Research report of the Institute of Industrial Economy and Technical Economy, State Planning Commission, March 1996.

[335] Shoubo Xu, Science and Technology Handbook for Leading Cadres, chief editor of Technology, Economy, Energy and Environmental Protection, Beijing Press, 1996.

[336] Shoubo Xu, etc. A Model of How to Optimize the Allocation of Resources in a Province—Evaluation of Beijing Yanhua Ethylene Reconstruction ad Expansion Project, Economic Growth Industry Development, Economic Daily Press, 1996.

(Won the third prize of Science and Technology Progress by the State Planning Commission in 1996).

[337] Shoubo Xu Xuchang Xu, China's Energy Technology R&D Selection Criteria, 1996. 9 MIT collaborative research report.

[338] Shoubo Xu, etc. Analysis and Countermeasures of China's Petroleum Problems, Research report of the Institute of Technology and Economy of the State Planning Commission, 1996.

[339] Shoubo Xu, etc. Development Strategy of China's Petroleum Industry in the Coming Century, Research report of China's Energy Development Strategy in the Coming Century, 1996.

[340] Shoubo Xu, etc. Research on the Evaluation Index System of Economic Growth Mode of Key State-Owned Coal Mines, Research Report of Institute of Technology and Economy of State Planning Commission, 1996.

[341] Shoubo Xu, etc. Research on Evaluation Index System of Economic Growth Model of State-Owned of State-Owned Key Coal Mines, On a New Growth Path, Research Report on Coal Industry Transformation of Economic Growth Mode, 1996.

1997

[342] Shoubo Xu, How to Assess the Transformation of Economic Growth Mode, Jiangsu People's Publishing House, 1997.

[343] Shoubo Xu, etc. Study on the Three-Year Rolling Plan of Liaohe Oilfield, Research Group on the Three- Year Rolling Plan of Liaohe Oilfield, October 1997.

[344] Shoubo Xu, etc. Post-Engineering Evaluation of China's Broad Energy Efficiency Strategy, State Planning Commission Research Report, May 1997.

[345] Shoubo Xu, Comprehensive Energy Engineering, 3rd Edition, Jiangsu People's Publishing House, 1997.

[346] Shoubo Xu, etc. China's Energy Development Strategy Across the Country, Research Report of the Research Group of China's Energy Development Strategy Across the Century, November 1997.

[347] Shoubo Xu, etc. Research on the Economic and Rational Development Scale of Liaohe Oilfield, Research Group on the Economic and Rational Development Scale of LIoahe Oilfield, September 1997.

1998

[348] Shoubo Xu, etc. Feasibility Study of Sanchen Audio-Visual and Electronic Chain Lessing Network Project [R], Research Report of Institute of Industrial Economy and Technical Economy, State Planning Commission, June 1998.

[349] Shoubo Xu, etc. Under the New Situation, the Work of Energy Conservation must not be Slack, The National Planning Commission Research Institute, Reference Materials, Number 4, January 19, 1998.

[350] Shoubo Xu, etc. Implementing the Broad Energy Efficiency Strategy, Internal Reference, 1998.

1999

[351] Shoubo Xu, A Study on the Evaluation Index System of Beijing Economic Structure Optimization, Research Report on the Institute of Industrial Economy and Technical Economy, State Planning Commission, December 1999.

[352] Shoubo Xu, etc. Comparison of China's Energy Development Strategies Before and After the Reform and Opening Up, China Economic and Trade Guide, Number 13, 1999.

2000

[353] Shoubo Xu, Research on Evaluation Index System of Material Industry Development in Beijing, Research Report of Institute of Industrial Economy and Technical Economy, State Planning Commission, September 2000.

[354] Xianzhong Mu, Shoubo Xu, Research on Integrated Economy of Natural Gas Industry in Central and Western China, Journal of Chongqing College of Commerce, 2000, No. 3, pp. 55–58.

[355] Shoubo Xu, etc. Policy Recommendation for Improving Energy Efficiency in China, China Economic and Trade Guide, Number 1,2000.

[356] Shoubo Xu, Resources and Development, Resources Information in China, China Environmental Science Press, 2000, pp. 744–778.

2001

[357] Qingchun Shi, Shoubo Xu, Accelerating the Conversion of Household Savings into Effective Investment for New Economic Growth, World Economic Research, Number 2, 2001, pp. 45–47.

[358] Shoubo Xu, The Coordinated Development Strategy of Ecological Environment and Economic Society in China in the New Century, Research Report of the Industrial Development of the State Plannign Commission, March 2001.

2002

[359] Shoubo Xu,Jiacheng Wang. Beijing New Materials Industry Development Technology and Economic Index System, Beijing New Materials Industry Development Technology and Economic Evaluation, Metallurgical Industry Press, 2002, pp. 225–244.

[360] Shoubo Xu, Several Questions about the Theory of Logistics Science, Journal of Beijing Jiaotong University (Social Sciences Edition), 2002, 1(1): 1–4. The first annual academic Conference of China Logistics Association, the First Training Class on Teaching and Curriculum Construction of Logistics Management Major in Colleges and Universities Hosted by Beijing Jiaotong University Entrusted by the Ministry of Education, 2002. Xu, S. Some Issues on MF Theory. Journal of Northern Jiaotong University (Social Sciences Edition). Volume 1, Number 1, pp. 1–4 (2002).

[361] Shoubo Xu, Research on Scientific Classification of MF. Journal of Northern Jiaotong University (Social Sciences Edition), 2002 (2): 21–24. Xu, S. Research on Scientific Classification of MF. Journal of Northern Jiaotong University (Social Sciences Edition). Volume 1, Number 2, pp. 21–24 (2002).

2003

[362] Qingchun Shi, Shoubo Xu, Technical and Economic Analysis of Stock Market Behavior, Journal of Beijing University of Technology (Social Sciences Edition), 2003 Vol. 3 No. 2.

[363] Shoubo Xu, etc. Research on Real Estate Enterprise Management under CRM Model, Research Report of the Research Group of Northern Jiaotong University, August 2003.

[364] Shoubo Xu, Talk about Environmental Protection, Energy and Logistics Issues in Henan Ancai Group Company, Academic Report, 2003. 12. 7.

[365] Shoubo Xu, Research on Several Problems of MF Engineering, Journal of Northern Jiaotong University (Social Sciences Edition), 2003 (1): 21–22. Xu, S. Research on Several Problems of MF Engineering. Journal of Northern Jiaotong University (Social Sciences Edition). Volume 2, Number 1, pp. 21–22 (2003).

[366] Shoubo Xu, Some Issues on MF Theory (Continuation), Some Issues on MF Theory (Continuation), 2003, 2 (3): 25–28. Xu, S. Some Issues on MF Theory (Continuation). Journal of Northern Jiaotong University (Social Sciences Edition). Volume 2, Number 3, pp. 25–28 (2003).

[367] Shoubo Xu, The Establishment and Development of Integrated Logistics Engineering (Thematic Research Report on Medium and Long-term Science and Technology Development Planning in Universities). Research Report of Northern Jiaotong University, 2003.

[368] Shoubo Xu, On the Concept of Logistics in China and its English Terminology, Academic Report on the First Logistics Forum of the National Development Zone held by the China Federation of Things and Qingdao Development Zone, August 30, 2003.

2004

[369] Shoubo Xu, Half by Saving and Half by Open Source, Interview with Academician Xu Shoubo, Journal of Southeast University, October 14, 2004.

[370] Shoubo Xu, Guide of Scientific Development in Economic Revitalization and Resource—Drained City Development in Northeast China, Number 10, 2004.

[371] Shoubo Xu, A Scientific Outlook in Development to Guide the Development of Mining Cities, Journal of Beijing Jiaotong University (Social Science Edition), Number 4, 2004.

[372] Shoubo Xu, A Proposal on the Outline of the Plan for the Development of Logistics Science and Technology, Research Report of Beijing Jiaotong University, Number 5, 2004.

[373] Shoubo Xu, Suggestions on Strengthening Basic Research in Logistics, Research Report of Beijing Jiaotong University, 2004.

[374] Shoubo Xu, Research and Development Frontier of Logistics Science and Technology, IMF/ICL 2004 Thematic Report of International Logistics Conference, Beijing, May 22, 2004.

[375] Shoubo Xu, Prospect of Research and Development on "MF Science and Technology. Journal of Beijing Jiaotong University (Social Sciences Edition), 2004, 3 (3): 1–6.

[376] Shoubo Xu, To Strengthen the Research and Development of Logistics Science and Technology, Research Report of Basic Industry Research Center, Beijing Jiaotong University, 2004.

[377] Proceedings of 2004 International Conference on MF/Logistics [C]. Edited by Shoubo Xu Beijing Jiaotong University press 2004.

[378] Shoubo Xu, Prospect of Research and Development on "MF Science and Technology [A]. Shoubo Xu Proceedings of 2004 International Conference on MF/Logistics [C]. Beijing Jiaotong University Press, 2004, 3–11. Xu, S. Prospect of Research and Development on MF Science and Technology. in Proceedings of 2004 International Conference on MF/Logistic. (Beijing Jiaotong University Press: Beijing, 2004).

2005

[379] Shoubo Xu, China's Energy Security and Development Issues, Proceedings of the International Forum on China's Productivity Development, Edited by the Chinese Productivity Society, Beijing, November 16–18, 2005, pp. 113–130.

[380] Shoubo Xu, An Interview with Xu Shoubo, Academician of Chinese Academy of Engineering, Shanghai News, November 19, 2005.

[381] Shoubo Xu, The Scientific Outlook on Development and the Development of Logistics Science and Technology, China Logistics and Procurement, Number 9, 2005, pp. 58–61.

[382] Shoubo Xu, The Scientific Outlook on Development and the Development of Logistics Science and Technology, Exclusive Pilot, Number 9, 2005, pp. 1–4.

[383] XU Shoubo (Center for Infrastructure Research、Academy of Material Flow, Beijing Jiaotong University, Beijing 100044, P.R. China). The Material Flow. China Business and Market, 2005, 19 (5): 4–7.

[384] Shoubo Xu, The Material Flow, Social Science Research, Number 7, 2005, pp. 99–101 (Won the Excellent Paper Certificate).

[385] Hanping Hou, Shoubo Xu, Structure and Optimization of X Party Material Flow-Based on Fractal of the Material Flow, China Business and Market, 2005, 19(7): 4–7.

[386] HOU Han-ping, XU Shou-bo. Structure and Optimization of X Party Material Flow Company Based on XPMF Fractal Theory [A]. LAN Hua. Proceedings of 2005 International Conference on Management Science & Engineering (12th) (C). Harbin: Harbin University of Technology Press, 2005, 20–21 (ISTP).

[387] Hanping Hou, Shoubo Xu, Operation and Management of X Party Logistics Company Based on Big Logistics Theory [A]. Sustainable Development of Transportation in China—2005 National Doctoral Academic Forum (Transportation) [C] Beijing: China Railway Publishing House, 2005, pp. 749–756, (Won the Excellent Paper Award in 2005 National Doctoral Forum).

[388] Shoubo Xu, The Material Flow [Z]. Xinhua Digest, Number 14, 2005 pp. 49–52.

[389] Shoubo Xu, The Material Flow [Z]. Academic Report of National Network Basic Industry and Policy Seminar, Held by Basic Industry Research Center of Beijing Jiaotong University, October 16, 2005.

[390] Shoubo Xu, The Material Flow [Z]. Academic Report of Cross-Strait Supply Chain and Logistics Forum and Academic Seminar 2005, Held by Southeast University in Nanjing, October 29, 2005.

[391] Xu, S. Scientific Classification on Material Flow (Cont.). Journal of Beijing Jiaotong University (Social Sciences Edition). Volume 4, Number 4, pp. 11–15 (2005).

2006

[392] Shoubo Xu, etc. Feasibility Study Report of Beijing Cultural and Creative Park Construction Project [R], Research Report of Institute Economy and Technical Economy of State Planning Commission, June 2006.

[393] Shoubo Xu, Research on the Theoretical Problems of Basic Industry [R]. Research Report of Basic Industry Research Center, Beijing Jiaotong University, October 2006.

[394] Shoubo Xu, The Theory of Six Elements of Production, Journal of Beijing Jiaotong University (Social Science Edition), Number 3, 2006, pp. 15–19.

[395] Bin Xu, Shoubo Xu, Hierarchical Theory of Factors of Production, Journal of Beijing Jiaotong University (Social Science Edition), Number 4, 2006, pp. 15–18.

[396] Shoubo Xu, etc. Energy Security and Development Research Report, 2005–2006 China Productivity Development Research Report (I), 395–417. China Productivity Society, China Statistics Press, December 2006.

[397] Shoubo Xu, To Attach Great Importance to Energy Security, Interview with Xu Shoubo, Academician of Chinese Academy of Engineering, Enterprise Reform and Management, Number 2, 2006.

[398] Shoubo Xu, Chinese Characteristics of Energy Development under the Guidance of the Scientific Outlook on Development, Modern Artillery Journal, 2006 (12).

[399] Shou Bo Xu (Academy of Material Flow, Beijing Jiaotong University, Beijing, China). A new discipline in the era of knowledge economy: material flow science and technology, Systems Research and Behavioral Science, Volume 23, Issue 2, pp. 251–257, Published Online www.interscience.wiley.com, https://doi.org/10.1002/sres.749, 13 Apr 2006. Copyright©2006 John Wiley & Sons, Ltd. (SSCI).

[400] Hanping Hou, Yaohua Song, Shoubo Xu, On the Transformation Model of Traditional MF to Modern MF, Logistics Technology, 2006, (4): 46–49 (Won the first prize of the Second Excellent Paper of Logistics Technology).

[401] Shoubo Xu, The Theory of Great Logistics and the Strategy of the Rise of Central China, the Academic Report of the 4th China Industrial Enterprise Logistics Forum, July 26, 2006.

[402] Hanping Hou, Shoubo Xu, Research on Synergetic Principle and Control of X Party Material Flow Fractal, Logistics Technology, Number 9, 2006, pp. 5–11.

[403] HOU Han-ping, XU Shou-bo. Study on Nature of Material flow and Transform Model of Material flow Development State [A]. LAN Hua. Proceedings of 2006 International Conference on Management Science & Engineering (13th) [C]. Harbin: Harbin University of Technology Press, 2006, 545–550 (ISTP).

[404] Jingjuan Guo, Shoubo Xu, Study on SC System Dynamics Based on Joint Inventory Control, Logistics Technology, Number 10, 2006, pp. 43–46.

2007

[405] Shoubo Xu, Theory of Six Forces on Essential Factors of Living, Journal of Beijing Jiaotong University (Social Sciences Edition) Number 1, 2007.

[406] Ying Xiong, Jingjuan Guo, Fengping Zhou, Shoubo Xu, Theory of Construction Project Optimization Resources Scheme, Journal of Beijing Jiaotong University (Social Sciences Edition) Number 2, 2007.

[407] Huang Zong-Yuan, Xu Shou-Bo. Study on the Globalization of Industrial Chain and Economic Development Path of Undeveloped Regions on Economic Problems, 2007, 9: 4–9.

[408] Shoubo Xu, Technical Economic Theory of Electronic Commerce (I, II), Research Report of the Institute of Electronic Commerce, Logistics Research Institute, Beijing Jiatong University, October 2007.

[409] Shoubo Xu, The Theory and Practice of Double Protection, Technical Economics and Management Research, 2007, (1): pp. 5–8.

[410] XU Shou-bo (Center for Infrastructure Research, Academy of Material Flow, Beijing Jiaotong University, Beijing 100044, P.R. China). The Material Flow (Cont.). China Business and Market, 2007, 21 (10): 7–10.

[411] Shoubo Xu (School of Economics and Management, Academy of Material Flow, Beijing Jiaotong University, Beijing 100044, P.R. China). The Theory of Material Flow [C], Research and Practical Issues of Enterprise Information Systems II, Volume 1, Edited by Li Xu, AMin Tjoa, Sobail Cbaudhry, IFIP Springer 2007, xxvii–xxxix.

[412] Dong Mu, Lingyun Zhou and Shoubo Xu (School of Economics and Management, Beijing Jiaotong University, Beijing 100044, P.R. China). Research on the

Costing and Data Mining Based on ABC in Logistics Firms [C], Research and Practical Issues of Enterprise Information Systems II, Volume 1, Edited by Li Xu, A Min Tjoa, Sobail Cbaudhry, IFIP Springer 2007, 467–474.

[413] Hanping Hou, Shoubo Xu (School of Economics and Management, Beijing Jiaotong University, Beijing 100044, P.R. China). Emergence and Simulation of Bionic Swarm Intelligence Type X Party Material Flow [C], Research and Practical Issues of Enterprise Information Systems II, Volume 2, Edited by Li Xu, A Min Tjoa, Sobail Cbaudhry, IFIP Springer 2007, 817–821.

2008

[414] Shoubo Xu, Technical Economic Theory of Electronic Commerce (III, IV), Research Report of the Institute of Electronic Commerce, Logistics Research Institute, Beijing Jiaotong University, February 2008.

[415] Shoubo Xu, On the Transformation of China's Energy Development Strategy in the Past 30 Years of Reform and Opening Up, Journal of Beijing Jiaotong University (Social Sciences Edition), Number 3, 2008, pp. 8–14.

[416] Shoubo Xu, On the Transformation of China's Energy Development Strategy in the Past 30 Year of Reform and Opening Up, China Information News, September 1, 2008, p. 1.

[417] Shoubo Xu, On the Transformation of China's Energy Development Strategy in the Past 30 Years of Reform and Opening Up, China National Conditions and Strength, Number 10, pp. 8–12.

[418] Shoubo Xu, New Choice of China's Energy Development Strategy, Merchants Weekly, Number 18, 2008, pp. 32–34 页.

[419] Shoubo Xu, On the Transformation of China's Energy Development Strategy in the Past 30 Years of Reform and Opening Up, The Mayor of Reference, Number 9, 2008 (429), pp. 1–5.

[420] Shoubo Xu, Review of Reformation of China's Energy Development Strategy, Power System and Clean Energy, Number 5, 2008 (112) pp. 1–5.

[421] Yuan Tian, Shoubo Xu, Bohui Song, Shaoosong Huang. Research on the Relations between MF and Economic Development, Journal of Beijing Jiaotong University (Social Sciences Edition), Number 2, 2008, pp. 21–26.

(Won the first prize of the Excellent Paper of China Logistics Association in 2008).

[422] Yuan Tian, S houbo Xu, Bohui Song, Shaosong Huang. Research on the Relations between MF and Economic Development. Journal of Beijing Jiaotong University (Social Sciences Edition), 2008, 7(2): 21–26.

[423] Hanping Hou, Shoubo Xu, A New Mode of Logistics Organization: X Party Logistics Driven by PMF Primitive, China Soft Science. Number 4, 2008, pp. 149–155.

[424] HOU Han-ping, XU Shou-bo. A New Mode of Logistics Organization: X Party Logistics Driven by PMF Primitive, China Soft Science. 2008, 4: 149–155.

[425] Shoubo Xu (School of Economics and Management, Academy of Material Flow, Beijing Jiaotong University, Beijing 100044, China). The concept and theory of material flow. Inf Syst Front (2008) 10: 601–609, Published Online: 5 June 2008. © Springer Science + Business Media. LLC 2008 (SCI).

[426] Shoubo Xu, The Theory of Commodity Material Flow [R]. 2008 IEEE International Conference on Service Operations and Logistics, and Informatics. Beijing. China. October 13, 2008, IEEE/SOLI'2008 Thematic Report of International Conference, 2008. 10. 13 Beijing.

[427] Shoubo Xu, The Theory of Commodity Material Flow, China Business and Market, 2008, 22 (11): 4–7. Shoubo Xu, The Theory of Commodity Material Flow. China Business and Market, 2008, 22 (11): 4–7.

2009

[428] Shoubo Xu, Some Problem about Basic Industrial Theory, Journal of Beijing Jiaotong University (Social Sciences Edition), Number 1, 2009, pp. 1–10.

[429] Bohui Song, Shoubo Xu, Theory of Material Flow Substance, Journal of Beijing Jiaotong University (Social Sciences Edition), Number 1, 2009, pp. 23–27.

[430] Shoubo Xu, Some Problem about Basic Industrial Theory, Industrial Economics, Number 4, 2009, pp. 3–12 (Book and Newspaper Data Center, Renmin University of China).

[431] Shoubo Xu, New Approach to Era-Division Theories of Social and Economic Development, Journal of Beijing Jiaotong University (Social Sciences Edition), Number 2, 2009, pp. 38–41.

[432] Shoubo Xu (School of Economics and Management, Center of China Technological Economics Research, Beijing Jiaotong University, Beijing 100044, China). Theory of Six Forces of Essential Factors of Production. Systems Research and Behavioral Science, Syst. Res. 26, 211–218 (2009), Published online 2 March 2009 in Wiley Inter Science, www.interscience.wiley.com, https://doi.org/10.1002/sres.974 (SSCI).

[433] Ann Oper Res (2009) 168: 1–4. Published online 3 March 2009 Springer Science + Business Media, LLC 2009, https://doi.org/10.1007/s10479-009-0530-7 (SCI.)

[434] Shoubo Xu, Retrospect and Prospect of the Development of "Techno-economic" Science & Technology in the 60 Years of New China, Journal of Beijing Jiaotong University (Social Sciences Edition), Number 4, 2009, pp. 1–6.

[435] Shoubo Xu (School of Economics and Management, Center of China Technological Economics Research, Beijing Jiaotong University, Beijing 100044, China). Doubling Guarantees Quadrupling-Theory and Practice. Systems Research and

Behavioral Science, Syst. Res. 26, 225–234 (2009), Published online 2 March 2009 in Wiley Inter Science, www.interscience.wiley.com, https://doi.org/10.1002/sres.979 (SSCI).

[436] Shoubo Xu, China's Petroleum Development Strategy in the New Century—The Strategy of Replacing Petroleum Import, World Petroleum Industry, Number 3, 2009, pp. 26–29.

[437] Shoubo Xu (School of Economics and Management, Academy of Material Flow, Beijing Jiaotong University, Beijing 100044, China). A Theoretical Study on Commodity Material Flow. Systems Research and Behavioral Science, Syst. Res. 26, 235–249 (2009), Published online 2 March 2009 in Wiley Inter Science, www.interscience.wiley.com, https://doi.org/10.1002/sres.970 (SSCI).

[438] Yuan Tian 1, 2, Shoubo Xu 1, 2, Li Wang3 and Peggy Chaudhry 4* (1 School of Economics and Management, Beijing Jiaotong University, Beijing 100044, China; 2 China Center of Technological Economics Research, Beijing Jiaotong University, Beijing 100044, China; 3 School of Economics and Management, Beihang University, Beijing 100191, China; 4 School of Business, Villanova University, Villanova, PA 19085, USA). On Relationships Between Material Flow and Economic Development in an Economic-material Flow System. Systems Research and Behavioral Science, Syst. Res. 26, 1–9 (2009), Published online 2 March 2009 in Wiley Inter Science, www.interscience.wiley.com, https://doi.org/10.1002/sres.977 (SSCI).

[439] Bohui Song* and Shoubo Xu (School of Economics and Management, Beijing Jiaotong University, Beijing 100044, China). The Theory of Material Flow Substance. Systems Research and Behavioral Science, Syst. Res. 26, 1–8 (2009), Published online 2 March 2009 in Wiley Inter Science, www.interscience.wiley.com, https://doi.org/10.1002/sres.969 (SSCI).

[440] Shoubo Xu, The Frontier Theory of Logistics Industry Development, China Industrial Safety Research Center, Beijing Jiaotong University: Lecture Hall of Beijing Jiaotong University① [C]. Beijing: Beijing Jiaotong University Press, 2009, pp. 28–68.

[441] Shoubo Xu, New Theory of Logistics-Theory of the Material Flow, Compilation of Conference Materials of "China Railway Modern Logistics Development Conference", July 2009, pp. 28–37.

[442] Shoubo Xu, Research on Commodity Logistics Theory, Management World, Number 7, 2009, pp. 1–9.

[443] Shoubo Xu, Research on Commodity Logistics Theory, Logistics Management, 2009 年第 11 期, 第3–12 (Information Center of Books and Newspapers, Renmin University of China).

[444] Shoubo Xu, New Theory of Commodity Logistics, Xinhua Digest, Number 19, 2009, pp. 52–55.

2010

[445] Shoubo Xu, Logistics is the Core of Service Industry, Logistics Technology (Equipment Version), Number 2, 2010, pp. 34–38.

[446] Bohui Song, Shoubo Xu, Discussion on Wuliu Definition, Journal of Beijing Jiaotong University (Social Sciences Edition), September 2010, Number 3, pp. 26–29.

[447] Shoubo Xu, The Material Flow Concept and Theory, Transport Economics and Logistics Review, Volume 1, China Economic Press, July 2010, pp. 1–13.

2011

[448] Shoubo Xu, Study on Comprehensive Appraisement Theory of Technology Program, Journal of Beijing Jiaotong University (Social Sciences Edition), Number 1, 2011, pp. 36–39.

[449] Shoubo Xu, Lida Xu, There are Only One Science in Human Society-Big Management Science, Research Report of Beijing Jiaotong University, March 2011.

[450] Shoubo Xu, LiDa Xu, Management: a scientific discipline for humanity, Published online: 26 March 2011 Springer Science + Business Media, LLC 2011.

[451] Shoubo Xu, The Realization of the Five Modernization is a New Goal of China's Economic and Social Development Strategy, Xinhua Weekly Financial Analysis, Number 11, 2011, pp. 1–3.

The manufacturer's authorised representative in the EU is Springer Nature Customer Service Centre GmbH, Europaplatz 3, 69115 Heidelberg, Germany. If you have any concerns regarding our products, please contact ProductSafety@springernature.com

Printed and bound by CPI Group (UK) Ltd, Croydon, CR0 4YY
30/09/2026
02225334-0001